Thailand

Joe Cummings
Steven Martin

LONELY PLANET PUBLICATIONS
Melbourne • Oakland • London • Paris

THAILAND

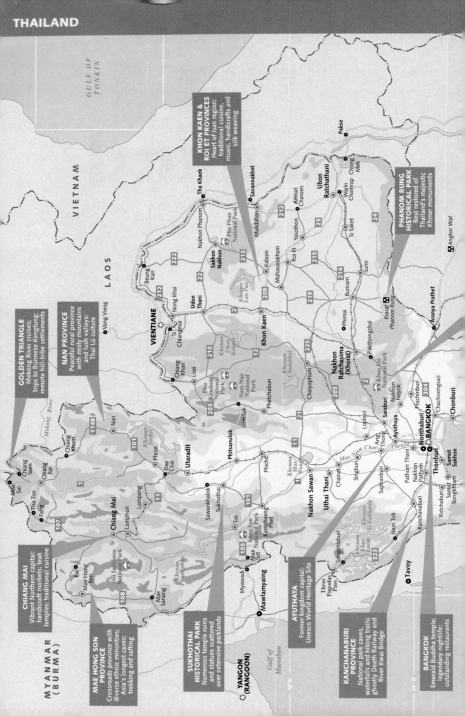

KHON KAEN & ROI ET PROVINCES
Heart of Isan region; traditional cuisine, music, handicrafts and silk weaving

PHANOM RUNG HISTORICAL PARK
Best restored of Thailand's majestic khmer monuments

GOLDEN TRIANGLE
Mekong River cruises; trips to Burmese Kengtung; remote hill-tribe settlements

NAN PROVINCE
Peaceful rural province with misty mountains and lush valleys; Thai Lü culture

CHIANG MAI
Vibrant Northern capital; handicraft markets; teak temples; traditional cuisine

MAE HONG SON PROVINCE
Crossroads province with diverse ethnic minorities; Asia's longest caves; trekking and rafting

SUKHOTHAI HISTORICAL PARK
Numerous temple ruins and statues scattered over extensive parklands

AYUTHAYA
Former kingdom capital; Unesco World Heritage Site

KANCHANABURI PROVINCE
National park caves, waterfalls and hiking trails; ghostly Death Railway and River Kwai Bridge

BANGKOK
Emerald Buddha temple; legendary nightlife; outstanding restaurants

GULF OF TONKIN

VIETNAM

LAOS

MYANMAR (BURMA)

Gulf of Martaban

Angkor Wat

Pakse

Chong Mek

Savannakhet

Tha Khaek

Nakhon Phanom

Mukdahan

Ubon Ratchathani

Warin Chamrap

Si Saket

Amnat Charoen

Yasothon

Sakhon Nakhon

Beung Kan

Nong Khai

Udon Thani

Kalasin

Mahasarakham

Roi Et

Surin

Buriram

Prasat Phanom Rung

Aranya Prathet

Vang Vieng

VIENTIANE

Si Chiangmai

Khon Kaen

Phimai

Pakthongchai

Nakhon Ratchasima (Khorat)

Pakchong

Chaiyaphum

Saraburi

Lopburi

Nakhon Nayok

Ayuthaya

Prachinburi

Chachoengsao

Chonburi

Nonthaburi

BANGKOK

Thonburi

Samut Sakhon

Samut Songkhram

Ratchaburi

Nakhon Pathom

Pathum Thani

Suphanburi

Singburi

Chainat

Nakhon Sawan

Uthai Thani

Phichit

Phitsanulok

Phetchabun

Lom Sak

Loei

Chiang Khan

Den Chai

Phrae

Uttaradit

Sawankhalok

Sukhothai

Kamphaeng Phet

Tak

Lampang

Lamphun

Chiang Mai

Nan

Chiang Kham

Phayao

Chiang Rai

Chiang Saen

Mae Sai

Tha Ton

Fang

Pai

Mae Hong Son

Mae Sariang

Mawlamyaing

Myawadi

Nam Tok

Kanchanaburi

Three Pagodas Pass

Tavoy

YANGON (RANGOON)

Chiang Khong

Long

Ban Phai

Mekong River

Mae Nam Chao Phraya

Khuean Sirikit

Khuean Ubon Ratana

Khuean Lam Pao

Khuean Chulaphorn

Khuean Sri Nakharin

Khuean Khao Laem

Khuean Mae Wong

Phu Phan National Park

Phu Kradung National Park

Nam Nao National Park

Khao Yai National Park

Doi Inthanon National Park

Doi Suthep National Park

Mae Ping National Park

Khun Tan National Park

THAILAND

VIETNAM

HO CHI MINH CITY (SAIGON)

Mekong River

CAMBODIA

Tonle Sap

PHNOM PENH

Sihanoukville

ELEVATION

1000m
500m
200m
100m
0

200km
120mi

100
60

KHAO YAI NATIONAL PARK
Asean National Heritage park; monsoon forests, rich wildlife and hiking trails

Chanthaburi
Trat
B17
Ko Kut
Rayong
Ko Chang
3
Pattaya
Ko Samet
Sattahip

KO CHANG NATIONAL MARINE PARK
Archipelago with secluded coves, rainforest tracts and hilly terrain; coastal walks and diving

SAMUI ARCHIPELAGO
Island resorts; quiet coves and beach bungalows; waterfalls; snorkelling and diving

SOUTHERN TOWNS
Muslim influence; sleepy fishing towns; little-visited Gulf coast beaches

Kota Bharu

MALAYSIA

Narathiwat
Pattani
Yala
Betong
Keroh
Alor Setar
Langkawi
Satun
Sadao
Hat Yai
Songkhla

Ranot
Phatthalung
Trang
Thale Luang

Nakhon Si Thammaraat
408

Ko Pha-Ngan
Ko Samui
Ko Tao
Ang Thong National Marine Park

Surat Thani
Chaiya
41
Krabi
401
Khao Sok National Park
Phang-Nga
Ko Lanta
Ko Yao Yai

Thale Ban National Park
Ko Tao National Marine Park

Hua Hin
Pranburi
Kaeng Krachan National Park
Phetchaburi
Prachuap Khiri Khan
Thap Sakae
Bang Saphan
Chumphon
4
Ranong
Isthmus of Kra
Mergui

GULF OF THAILAND

ANDAMAN SEA

INDIAN OCEAN

SURIN & SIMILAN NATIONAL MARINE PARKS
Extensive coral colonies; excellent snorkelling and diving

Surin Islands
Similan Islands
Phuket

PHUKET PROVINCE
Sophisticated resorts; powdery white beaches; yachting and diving; great seafood

KRABI PROVINCE
Striking limestone outcrops; rock-climbing and sea canoeing; white-sand beaches of Ko Lanta

12°N
10°N
8°N
6°N

98°E
100°E
102°E
104°E
106°E

Thailand
9th edition – July 2001
First published – February 1982

Published by
Lonely Planet Publications Pty Ltd ABN 36 005 607 983
90 Maribyrnong St, Footscray, Victoria 3011, Australia

Lonely Planet Offices
Australia Locked Bag 1, Footscray, Victoria 3011
USA 150 Linden St, Oakland, CA 94607
UK 10a Spring Place, London NW5 3BH
France 1 rue du Dahomey, 75011 Paris

Photographs
Many of the images in this guide are available for licensing from
Lonely Planet Images.
email: lpi@lonelyplanet.com.au

Front cover photograph
Wat Phra Si Sanphet at sunset, Ayuthaya Province (Anders Blomqvist)

ISBN 1 86450 251 7

Contents – Text

ANDAMAN COAST 663

SOUTHERN GULF 758

LANGUAGE 844

GLOSSARY 853

THANKS 857

INDEX 885

METRIC CONVERSION inside back cover

Contents – Maps

ANDAMAN COAST

SOUTHERN GULF

MAP LEGEND

MAP INDEX

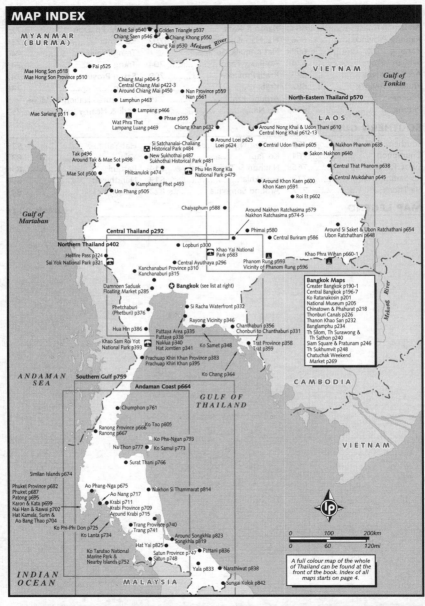

0   100   200km
0   60   120mi

A full colour map of the whole
of Thailand can be found at the
front of the book. Index of all
maps starts on page 4.

The Authors

Joe Cummings

Born in the sub-tropical port of New Orleans, Joe began travelling in South-East Asia shortly after finishing university. Before writing became a full-time job, he played guitar in a succession of bands, volunteered for the Peace Corps, worked as a movie extra, and taught English in Thailand, Malaysia, Taiwan and the US. Along the way he earned an MA degree in Thai language and art history.

For Lonely Planet and other publishers he has written over 30 original guidebooks, phrasebooks and atlases for countries in Asia and North America. For Lonely Planet he has authored the *Thai phrasebook* and the *Lao phrasebook*, the *Bangkok, Thailand's Islands & Beaches, Laos* and *Myanmar* guides, and parts of *South-East Asia on a shoestring*, plus *World Food Thailand*. As a freelance journalist he has written for dozens of periodicals, including *Ambassador, Bangkok Post, International Herald Tribune, Geographical, The Nation, Outside, San Francisco Examiner, South China Morning Post* and *Wall Street Journal*.

Steven Martin

Primed by frequent trips to Tijuana made during a wayward adolescence in San Diego, and inspired by the scenery in Francis Ford Coppola's *Apocalypse Now*, Steven squandered his parents' high school graduation gift of $1000 on a trip to the Philippines. This led to a stint on board a US Navy nuclear-powered attack submarine, and countless hours spent drunk or hungover in various ports of call along the Pacific Rim. Honourably discharged in 1988, Steven stayed in the Philippines until a particularly violent coup attempt convinced him to relocate to Thailand in 1989. Since then Steven has taught English and Spanish, acted in a John Woo film, edited a now-defunct magazine and co-written a guidebook to Laos.

FROM THE AUTHORS

Joe Cummings Thanks to the following people in and out of Thailand who assisted along the way: Lori Ashton, Avia Travel, André Barguirdjian and Mau Travel Service, Richard Barrow, Bulan Boonphan, Nancy and Nima Chandler, Kaneungnit Chotikakul, Thomas Crampton, Nattawud Daoruang, Julian and Pao, Andrew Forbes, EJ Haas, Oliver Hargreave, David Henley, Peter Holmshaw, Brent and Karin Madison, Chris Mendel, Sombat Panarong, Jeff Petry, Simon Robson, Pensri Saenyot, Sapachai, Karen Smith, Ruengsang Sripaoraya, Lada Subhongsang, Theerada Suphaphong, ML Sompongvadee Vikitsreth and Michael Wilson.

The Tourism Authority of Thailand and its employees throughout Thailand, as usual, were of considerable assistance. My partner Lynne Cummings helped out immensely with proofreading, fact-checking, data entry, day-to-day organising, and a hundred other things that made putting this book together an easier and more efficient task.

Thanks also to the hundreds of travellers who have taken time to write, especially letter-writers Dan Goodacre and Deb Smith. Thank you Steven Martin for being so easy to work with.

Steven Martin First and foremost I'd like to thank Thomas Crampton for his boundless generosity and sound advice. Boonpian Sirirat, as usual, provided much insight on Thailand, its people, language and culture. On the road I met and was assisted by Karen Smith in Phuket; Paddy, Misty and Torsten in Ko Pha-Ngan; Bernie Hodges in Songkhla; Attagon Kuachat in Krabi; Khun Pirom in Surin; Apple and Noi in Kanchanaburi; Settasak Akanimart in Ayuthaya; Mickey Maselli in Ko Tao; Mike Wyman in Ko Phi-Phi; Pinyo Bootnoot in Krabi; and Terry Beaton in Kanchanaburi. Last but not least, a heartfelt thanks to Joe and Lynne Cummings for their guidance and friendship throughout this endeavour.

This Book

The first eight editions of Thailand were authored by long-term Thailand resident Joe Cummings. Joe coordinated this 9th edition, sharing the load with Steven Martin, who updated the Central Thailand, Andaman Coast and Southern Gulf chapters, and part of the North-Eastern Thailand chapter. All other chapters were updated by Joe.

From the Publisher

This edition of Thailand was coordinated in Lonely Planet's Melbourne office by Bruce Evans (editing and indexing) and Nicholas Stebbing (mapping and layout). Assisting with editing were Cherry Prior, Julia Taylor and Rachael Antony, while Jane Thompson, Kristin Odijk, Sally O'Brien and Kim Hutchins assisted with proofing. Helping out with maps were Pablo Gastar, Kusnandar and Meredith Mail, and Mark Germanchis assisted with layout. Leonie Mugavin checked travel information and Shahara Ahmed checked health information. Quentin Frayne coordinated the Language chapter, while Bruce Evans helped check Thai script and transliteration throughout. The nifty illustrations, drawn by Martin Harris, Simon Borg, Jenny Bowman and Kate Nolan, were coordinated by Matt King. Glenn Beanland of LPI coordinated the colour photos and the cover was designed by Jenny Jones. Chris Love and Kristin Odijk gave valuable and patient advice along the way.

THANKS
Many thanks to the travellers who used the last edition and wrote to us with helpful hints, advice and interesting anecdotes. Your names appear in the back of this book.

Foreword

ABOUT LONELY PLANET GUIDEBOOKS

The story begins with a classic travel adventure: Tony and Maureen Wheeler's 1972 journey across Europe and Asia to Australia. Useful information about the overland trail did not exist at that time, so Tony and Maureen published the first Lonely Planet guidebook to meet a growing need.

From a kitchen table, then from a tiny office in Melbourne (Australia), Lonely Planet has become the largest independent travel publisher in the world, an international company with offices in Melbourne, Oakland (USA), London (UK) and Paris (France).

Today Lonely Planet guidebooks cover the globe. There is an ever-growing list of books and there's information in a variety of forms and media. Some things haven't changed. The main aim is still to help make it possible for adventurous travellers to get out there – to explore and better understand the world.

At Lonely Planet we believe travellers can make a positive contribution to the countries they visit – if they respect their host communities and spend their money wisely. Since 1986 a percentage of the income from each book has been donated to aid projects and human rights campaigns.

Updates Lonely Planet thoroughly updates each guidebook as often as possible. This usually means there are around two years between editions, although for more unusual or more stable destinations the gap can be longer. Check the imprint page (following the colour map at the beginning of the book) for publication dates.

Between editions up-to-date information is available in two free newsletters – the paper *Planet Talk* and email *Comet* (to subscribe, contact any Lonely Planet office) – and on our Web site at www.lonelyplanet.com. The *Upgrades* section of the Web site covers a number of important and volatile destinations and is regularly updated by Lonely Planet authors. *Scoop* covers news and current affairs relevant to travellers. And, lastly, the *Thorn Tree* bulletin board and *Postcards* section of the site carry unverified, but fascinating, reports from travellers.

Correspondence The process of creating new editions begins with the letters, postcards and emails received from travellers. This correspondence often includes suggestions, criticisms and comments about the current editions. Interesting excerpts are immediately passed on via newsletters and the Web site, and everything goes to our authors to be verified when they're researching on the road. We're keen to get more feedback from organisations or individuals who represent communities visited by travellers.

> Lonely Planet gathers information for everyone who's curious about the planet – and especially for those who explore it first-hand. Through guidebooks, phrasebooks, activity guides, maps, literature, newsletters, image library, TV series and Web site we act as an information exchange for a worldwide community of travellers.

Research Authors aim to gather sufficient practical information to enable travellers to make informed choices and to make the mechanics of a journey run smoothly. They also research historical and cultural background to help enrich the travel experience and allow travellers to understand and respond appropriately to cultural and environmental issues.

Authors don't stay in every hotel because that would mean spending a couple of months in each medium-sized city and, no, they don't eat at every restaurant because that would mean stretching belts beyond capacity. They do visit hotels and restaurants to check standards and prices, but feedback based on readers' direct experiences can be very helpful.

Many of our authors work undercover, others aren't so secretive. None of them accept freebies in exchange for positive write-ups. And none of our guidebooks contain any advertising.

Production Authors submit their raw manuscripts and maps to offices in Australia, USA, UK or France. Editors and cartographers – all experienced travellers themselves – then begin the process of assembling the pieces. When the book finally hits the shops, some things are already out of date, we start getting feedback from readers and the process begins again ...

WARNING & REQUEST

Things change – prices go up, schedules change, good places go bad and bad places go bankrupt – nothing stays the same. So, if you find things better or worse, recently opened or long since closed, please tell us and help make the next edition even more accurate and useful. We genuinely value all the feedback we receive. Julie Young coordinates a well travelled team that reads and acknowledges every letter, postcard and email and ensures that every morsel of information finds its way to the appropriate authors, editors and cartographers for verification.

Everyone who writes to us will find their name in the next edition of the appropriate guidebook. They will also receive the latest issue of *Planet Talk*, our quarterly printed newsletter, or *Comet*, our monthly email newsletter. Subscriptions to both newsletters are free. The very best contributions will be rewarded with a free guidebook.

Excerpts from your correspondence may appear in new editions of Lonely Planet guidebooks, the Lonely Planet Web site, *Planet Talk* or *Comet*, so please let us know if you *don't* want your letter published or your name acknowledged.

Send all correspondence to the Lonely Planet office closest to you:

Australia: Locked Bag 1, Footscray, Victoria 3011
USA: 150 Linden St, Oakland, CA 94607
UK: 10A Spring Place, London NW5 3BH
France: 1 rue du Dahomey, 75011 Paris

Or email us at: talk2us@lonelyplanet.com.au

For news, views and updates see our Web site: www.lonelyplanet.com

HOW TO USE A LONELY PLANET GUIDEBOOK

The best way to use a Lonely Planet guidebook is any way you choose. At Lonely Planet we believe the most memorable travel experiences are often those that are unexpected, and the finest discoveries are those you make yourself. Guidebooks are not intended to be used as if they provide a detailed set of infallible instructions!

Contents All Lonely Planet guidebooks follow roughly the same format. The Facts about the Destination chapters or sections give background information ranging from history to weather. Facts for the Visitor gives practical information on issues like visas and health. Getting There & Away gives a brief starting point for re-searching travel to and from the destination. Getting Around gives an overview of the transport options when you arrive.

The peculiar demands of each destination determine how sub-sequent chapters are broken up, but some things remain constant. We always start with background, then proceed to sights, places to stay, places to eat, entertainment, getting there and away, and getting around information – in that order.

Heading Hierarchy Lonely Planet headings are used in a strict hierarchical structure that can be visualised as a set of Russian dolls. Each heading (and its following text) is encompassed by any preceding heading that is higher on the hierarchical ladder.

Entry Points We do not assume guidebooks will be read from beginning to end, but that people will dip into them. The tradi-tional entry points are the list of contents and the index. In addition, however, some books have a complete list of maps and an index map illustrating map coverage.

There may also be a colour map that shows highlights. These highlights are dealt with in greater detail in the Facts for the Visitor chapter, along with planning questions and suggested itin-eraries. Each chapter covering a geographical region usually begins with a locator map and another list of highlights. Once you find something of interest in a list of highlights, turn to the index.

Maps Maps play a crucial role in Lonely Planet guidebooks and include a huge amount of information. A legend is printed on the back page. We seek to have complete consistency between maps and text, and to have every important place in the text captured on a map. Map key numbers usually start in the top left corner.

Although inclusion in a guidebook usually implies a recommen-dation we cannot list every good place. Exclusion does not necessarily imply criticism. In fact there are a number of reasons why we might exclude a place – sometimes it is simply inappropriate to encourage an influx of travellers.

Introduction

Thailand, or Siam as it was called until 1939, has never been colonised by a foreign power, unlike its South and South-East Asian neighbours. Despite periodic invasions by the Burmese and the Khmers, and brief occupation by the Japanese in WWII, the kingdom has never been externally controlled for long enough to dampen the Thais' individualism.

Although the Thais are often depicted as fun-loving, happy-go-lucky folk (which indeed they often are), they are also proud and strong-minded, and have struggled for centuries to preserve their independence of spirit.

Of course Thailand, like other Asian countries, has been influenced by contact with foreign cultures. But the ever-changing spirit of Thai culture has remained dominant, even in modern city life.

The end result is that Thailand has much to interest the traveller, from trekking in the north's picturesque mountains to chilling out on one of the many exotic islands in the south.

In Bangkok, a city moving to a frenetic pace, travellers can ride long-tail boats along the myriad canals, visit ornate temples, join the crowd at a *muay thai* match or shop in one of the many markets.

Culture enthusiasts will enjoy the lively arts and visiting the ruins of ancient cities, and all travellers will appreciate the tradition of friendliness and hospitality to strangers, as well as one of the world's most exciting cuisines.

Travel in this tropical country is comfortable and down-to-earth. The rail, bus and air travel network is extensive and every place worth visiting is easily accessible. There are many places that warrant a stop, countless sights to see, a multifaceted culture to experience and it is more affordable than ever by today's international travel standards.

Facts about Thailand

HISTORY
Prehistory

The history of the geographical area now known as Thailand reaches far back into hoary antiquity. World-renowned scholar Paul Benedict (author of the book *Austro-Thai Language and Culture*) found that modern linguistic theory (which ties numerous key items in ancient Chinese culture to an early Thai linguistic group), together with recent archaeological finds in Thailand, establishes South-East Asia as a 'focal area in the emergent cultural development of *Homo sapiens*. It now seems likely that the first true agriculturists anywhere, perhaps also the first true metal workers, were Austro-Thai speakers'.

The Mekong River valley and Khorat Plateau areas of what today encompasses significant parts of Laos, Cambodia and Thailand were inhabited as far back as 10,000 years ago. Currently the most reliable sources for archaeological evidence are the Ban Chiang and Ban Prasat areas of North-Eastern Thailand, where rice was cultivated as early as 4000 BC (China by contrast was growing and consuming millet at the time). The Ban Chiang culture began bronze metallurgy before 3000 BC; the Middle East's Bronze Age arrived around 2800 BC, China's a thousand years later.

But were the inhabitants of Ban Chiang 'Thai'? Given the nomadic nature of early Thai culture, and the relative lack of anthropological evidence in these sites, it's so far impossible to say. Exactly where the Thais came from originally continues to be a matter of academic debate. While most scholars favour a region vaguely stretching from Guangxi in southern China to Dien Bien Phu in northern Vietnam, a more radical theory says the Thais descended from an ocean-based civilisation in the western Pacific. The former supposition rests on linguistic theory, particularly the mapping of tones from dialect to dialect, thus establishing migrational directionality. The oceanic proponents trace the development of symbols and myths in Thai art and culture to arrive at their conclusions. Then there are those, like Paul Benedict, who consider the Thais to be indigenous to the area now known as Thailand.

Thai Migration

When trying to trace the origins of the current inhabitants of Thailand, one must consider that their predecessors belonged to a vast, nonunifed zone of Austro-Thai influence that involved periodic migrations along several different geographic lines. The early Thais spread all over South-East Asia, including the islands of Indonesia; and some later settled in southern and South-West China, later to 're-migrate' to Northern Thailand, establishing the first Thai kingdom in the 13th century.

Virtually all of the ethnic groups in these areas, both indigenous and immigrant, belong to the Austro-Thai ethno-linguistic family. In Thailand, historically speaking, these are mostly subgroups identified with the Thai-Kadai and Mon-Khmer language families.

The Thai-Kadai is the most significant ethno-linguistic group in all of South-East Asia, with 72 million speakers in an area extending from the Brahmaputra River in India's Assam state to the Gulf of Tonkin and China's Hainan Island. To the north, there are Thai-Kadai speakers well into the Chinese provinces of Yunnan and Guangxi, and to the south they are found as far as the northern Malaysian state of Kedah. In Thailand and Laos they are the majority populations, and in China, Vietnam and Myanmar (Burma) they are the largest minorities. The major Thai-Kadai groups comprise the Ahom (Assam), the Siamese (Thailand), the Black Thai or Thai Dam (Laos and Thailand), the Thai Yai or Shan (Myanmar and Thailand), the Thai Neua (Laos, Thailand and China), the Thai Lü (Laos, Thailand and China) and the Yuan (Laos and Thailand). All of these groups belong to the Thai half of Thai-Kadai; the Kadai groups are relatively small (less than a million) and include such comparatively obscure languages in southern China as Kelao, Lati, Laha, Laqua and Li.

A linguistic map of southern China, north-eastern India and South-East Asia clearly shows that the preferred zones of occupation by the Thai peoples have been river valleys, from the Red (Hong) River in the south of China and Vietnam to the

Brahmaputra River in Assam, India. At one time there were two terminals for movement into what is now Thailand – the 'northern terminal' in the Yuan Jiang and other river areas in China's modern-day Yunnan and Guangxi provinces, and the 'southern terminal' along Central Thailand's Mae Nam Chao Phraya (Chao Phraya River). The populations remain quite concentrated in these areas today, while areas between the two were intermediate relay points and have always been less populated.

The Mekong River valley between Thailand and Laos was one such intermediate migrational zone, as were river valleys along the Nan, Ping, Kok, Yom and Wang Rivers in Northern Thailand, plus various river areas in Laos and in the Shan State of Myanmar. As far as historians have been able to piece together from scant linguistic and anthropological evidence, significant numbers of Austro-Thai peoples in southern China or northern Vietnam began migrating southward and westward in small groups as early as the 8th century AD, but most certainly by the 10th century. These migrant Thais established local polities along traditional social schemata according to *meuang* (roughly 'principality' or 'city-state'), under the rule of chieftains or sovereigns called *jâo meuang*.

Each meuang was based in a river valley or section of a valley. Some meuang were loosely collected under one jâo meuang or an alliance of several. One of the largest collections of meuang – although not necessarily united – was in southern China and was known as Nan Chao. Yunnan's present-day Xishuangbanna district (called Sipsongpanna in Thailand), a homeland for northern Thai and Thai Lü groups, is often cited as the point of origin for all Thais, but in-depth histories place Thai groups everywhere along the Thai diaspora from Dien Bien Phu in Vietnam to Assam.

In the mid-13th century, the rise to power of the Mongols under Kublai Khan in Song dynasty China caused a more dramatic southward migration of Thai peoples. Wherever Thais met indigenous populations of Tibeto-Burmans and Mon-Khmers in the move south (into what is now Myanmar, Thailand, Laos and Cambodia), they were somehow able to displace, assimilate or coopt them without force. The most probable explanation for this relatively smooth assimilation is that there were already Thai peoples in the area. Such a supposition finds considerable support in current research on the development of Austro-Thai language and culture.

Early Kingdoms

With no written records or chronologies it is difficult to say with certainty what kind of cultures existed among the meuang of Thailand before the middle of the first millennium AD. However, by the 6th century an important network of agricultural communities was thriving as far south as modern-day Pattani and Yala, and as far north and north-east as Lamphun and Muang Fa Daet (near Khon Kaen). Theravada Buddhism was flourishing and may have entered the region during India's Ashoka period, in the 3rd or 2nd century BC, when Indian missionaries are said to have been sent to a land called Suvannabhumi (Land of Gold). Suvannabhumi most likely corresponds to a remarkably fertile area stretching from southern Myanmar, across Central Thailand, to eastern Cambodia. Two different cities in Thailand's central river basin have long been called Suphanburi (City of Gold) and U Thong (Cradle of Gold).

Dvaravati This collection of meuang was given the Sanskrit name Dvaravati (literally 'Place of Gates'), the city of Krishna in the Indian epic poem *Mahabharata*. The French art historian Georges Coedès discovered the name on some coins that were excavated in the Nakhon Pathom area, which seems to have been the centre of Dvaravati culture. The Dvaravati period lasted until the 11th or 12th century AD and produced many works of art, including Buddha images (showing Indian Gupta influence), stucco reliefs on temple walls and in caves, architecture, exquisite terracotta heads, votive tablets and various sculptures.

Dvaravati may have been a cultural relay point for the pre-Angkor cultures of ancient Cambodia and Champa to the east. The Chinese, through the travels of the famous pilgrim Xuan Zang, knew the area as Tuoluobodi, between Sriksetra (Myanmar) and Isanapura (Cambodia).

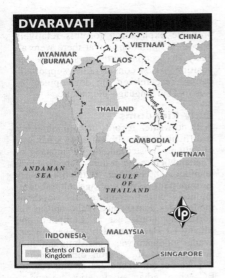

DVARAVATI

Extents of Dvaravati Kingdom

The ethnology of the Dvaravati peoples is a controversial topic, although the standard decree is that they were Mon-Khmer or Mon. The Mon themselves seem to have been descended from a group of Indian immigrants from Kalinga, an area overlapping the boundaries of the modern Indian states of Orissa and Andhra Pradesh. The Dvaravati Mon may have been an ethnic mix of these people and people indigenous to the region (the original Thais).

In any event, the Dvaravati culture quickly declined in the 11th century under the political domination of the invading Khmers, who made their headquarters in Lopburi. The area around Lamphun, then called Hariphunchai, held out against the Khmers until the late 12th or early 13th century, as evidenced by the Dvaravati architecture of Wat Kukut in Lamphun.

Khmer Influence The Khmer conquests from the 7th to 11th centuries introduced Khmer cultural influence in the form of art, language and religion. Some of the Sanskrit terms in Mon-Thai vocabulary entered the language during the Khmer period between the 11th and 13th centuries. Monuments from this period located in Kanchanaburi, Lopburi and many north-eastern towns were constructed in the Khmer style and are comparable to architecture in Angkor.

Elements of Brahmanism, Theravada Buddhism and Mahayana Buddhism were intermixed as Lopburi became a religious centre, and some elements of each Buddhist school – along with Brahmanism – remains to the present day in Thai religious and court ceremonies.

Other Kingdoms While all this was taking place, a distinctly Thai state called Nan Chao (AD 650–1250) was flourishing in what later became Yunnan and Sichuan in China. Nan Chao maintained close relations with imperial China and the two neighbours enjoyed much cultural exchange.

The Mongols, under Kublai Khan, conquered Nan Chao in 1253, but long before this happened the Thai peoples began migrating southward, settling in and around what is today Laos and Northern Thailand.

A number of Thais became mercenaries for the Khmer armies in the early 12th century, as depicted on the walls of Angkor Wat. The Khmers called the Thais 'Syam', possibly from the Sanskrit *shyama* meaning 'golden' or 'swarthy' – at the time the Thais had a deeper skin colour. Whatever the meaning, this was how the Thai kingdom eventually came to be called Syam, or Sayam. In Myanmar and north-western Thailand the pronunciation of Syam became 'Shan'. The English trader James

ANGKOR

Extents of Angkor Kingdom

Coconut mountain, Ko Samui

Lisu hill-tribe girls, Chiang Mai Province

Laid back mahout, Ayuthaya Province

Old learning and new learning in Bangkok

HIGHLIGHTS OF THAILAND'S HISTORY

Timeline: 4500 BC — 500 AD — 1000 AD — 1500 AD — 1700 AD — 1800 AD — 1900 AD — 2000 AD

BAN CHIANG

Rice, pottery and one of the world's first known bronze-metallurgy cultures.

TOM COCKREM

SRIVIJAYA

The Srivijaya kingdom controls much of southern Thailand, with a regional centre at Chaiya in Surat Thani Province.

THAI-KADAI

Thai-kadai peoples begin migrating into the Mekong River Valley from northern Vietnam and southern China.

SUKHOTHAI

Several Thai meuang unite to form what is considered to be the first Thai kingdom. King Ramkhamhaeng presides over a 'Golden Age' of Thai culture.

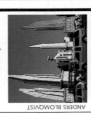

CHERYL CONLAN

BURMESE INVADE AYUTHAYA

Ayuthaya's wealth attracts the attention of the Burmese, who attack in the mid-16th century and again in 1767, reducing the city to a devastated shell.

NICHOLAS REUSS

CONSTITUTIONAL MONARCHY

Following a bloodless coup, Rama VII presides over a change from absolute monarchy to a constitutional monarchy.

ANDERS BLOMQVIST

ECONOMY TODAY

After a decade of energetic economic growth, the Thai economy, fuelled largely by foreign loans, crashes when the national currency suffers precipitous deflation. Prime Minister Chuan Leekpai's government instigates unpopular austerity measures. In 2001 Thaksin Shinawatra is elected Prime Minister on a platform of promises for sweeping economic reforms.

DVARAVATI

Lavo (Lopburi) and other Non-Khmer Buddhist cultures flourish in central and eastern Thailand.

ANDERS BLOMQVIST

KHMER

The spread of the Khmer empire from the 9th to the 13th centuries introduces Khmer influence in art, language and society, and leaves tokens of its architectural brilliance in North-Eastern Thailand.

NICHOLAS REUSS

LANNA KINGDOM

Sukhothai joins Chiang Mai and Phayao to found the kingdom of La Na Thai.

EUROPEANS

The Portuguese establish the first European mission in Ayuthaya.

AYUTHAYA

The 400-year Ayuthaya Kingdom begins to become powerful in the 14th century, eventually conquering Angkor in the 15th century.

PHRAYA TAKSIN

A general from the northern province of Tak, he rallies the Thai forces and drives out the Burmese, appointing himself king at the new capital of Thonburi.

BANGKOK

King Taksin becomes deranged and Chao Phraya Chakri takes over as king, becoming Rama I, the first king of the current Chakri dynasty. He moves the site of the capital across the Chao Phraya River to Bangkok.

DEMOCRACY

Rama VIII dies of a gunshot wound and the present king, Rama IX, succeeds him. Thailand's first democratically elected government comes to power.

THE MILITARY

The army stages a bloodless coup in 1947, setting a pattern of military involvement that is to dog Thai politics for the next four decades. Thai students demonstrate in 1973 and 1976 and are crushed by the military for their efforts. Many of them flee to the forests to join the People's Liberation Army of Thailand (granted amnesty in 1982). Since the 1992 Black May incident, military involvement in Thai politics seems to have had its day.

RICHARD I'ANSON

National Museums

Thailand's Fine Arts Department operates an excellent network of national museums in areas of the country known for historic art and archaeology. The museums typically offer a small exhibit of artefacts from around the country as well as more-extensive displays featuring works of local provenance. At present, visitors have a choice of 35 museums. Most national museums are open from 9 am to 4 pm Wednesday to Sunday; a few are open daily these same hours. Those most worth visiting (in provincial capitals unless otherwise stated) include the following:

provincial capital	museum
Ayuthaya	Chan Kasem Palace
	Chao Sam Phraya National Museum
Bangkok	National Museum
	National Royal Barges Museum
	Wat Benchamabophit National Museum
Chiang Mai	Chiang Mai National Museum
Chiang Rai	Chiang Saen National Museum (in Chiang Saen)
Kamphaeng Phet	Kamphaeng Phet National Museum
Kanchanaburi	Ban Kao Neolithic Museum (in Ban Kao)
Khon Kaen	Khon Kaen National Museum
Lamphun	Lamphun National Museum
Lopburi	Lopburi National Museum
Nakhon Pathom	Phra Pathom Chedi National Museum
Nakhon Ratchasima	Mahawirawong National Museum
	Phimai National Museum (in Phimai)
Nakhon Si Thammarat	Nakhon Si Thammarat National Museum
Nan	Nan National Museum
Phetchaburi	Phra Nakhon Khiri Historical Park
Phitsanulok	Phra Phuttha Chinnarat National Museum
	(at Wat Phra Si Ratana Mahathat)
Songkhla	Matchimawat National Museum
	Songkhla National Museum
Sukhothai	Ramkhamhaeng National Museum
	Sawanworanayok Museum
Suphanburi	U Thong National Museum
Surat Thani	Chaiya National Museum (in Chaiya)
Ubon Ratchathani	Ubon National Museum
Udon Thani	Ban Chiang National Museum (in Ban Chiang)

Lancaster penned the first known English transliteration of the name as 'Siam' in 1592.

Meanwhile southern Thailand – the upper Malay peninsula – was under the control of the Srivijaya empire, the headquarters of which may have been in Palembang, Sumatra, between the 8th and 13th centuries. The regional centre for Srivijaya was Chaiya, near the modern town of Surat Thani. Remains of Srivijaya art can still be seen in Chaiya and its environs.

Sukhothai & Lan Na Thai Periods

Several Thai principalities in the Mekong River valley united in the 13th and 14th centuries, when Thai princes wrested the lower north from the Khmers – whose Angkor government was declining fast – to create Sukhothai (Rising of Happiness). They later took Hariphunchai from the Mon to form Lan Na Thai (literally Million Thai Rice Fields).

In 1238 the Sukhothai kingdom declared its independence under King Si Intharathit and quickly expanded its sphere of influence, taking advantage not only of the declining Khmer power but the weakening Srivijaya domain in the south. Sukhothai is considered by the Thais to be the first true Thai kingdom. It was annexed by Ayuthaya in 1376, by which time a national identity of sorts had been forged.

Many Thais today have a sentimental, romantic view of the Sukhothai period, seeing it as a 'golden age' of Thai politics, religion and culture – an egalitarian, noble period when all the people had enough to eat and the kingdom was unconquerable. A famous passage from Sukhothai's Ramkhamhaeng inscription reads:

This land of Sukhothai is thriving. There is fish in the water and rice in the fields…The King has hung a bell in the opening of the gate over there; if any commoner has a grievance which sickens his belly and grips his heart, he goes and strikes the bell; King Ramkhamhaeng questions the man, examines the case and decides it justly for him.

Among other accomplishments, the third Sukhothai king, Ramkhamhaeng, sponsored a fledgling Thai writing system which became the basis for modern Thai; he also codified the Thai form of Theravada Buddhism, as borrowed from the Singhalese. Under Ramkhamhaeng, the Sukhothai kingdom extended from Nakhon Si Thammarat

LANNA

Extents of Lanna Kingdom

SUKHOTHAI

Extents of Sukhothai Kingdom

in the South to the upper Mekong River valley (Laos), and to Bago (Myanmar). For a short time (1448–86) the Sukhothai capital was moved to Phitsanulok.

Ramkhamhaeng also supported Chao Mangrai (also spelt 'Mengrai') of Chiang Mai, and Chao Khun Ngam Meuang of Phayao, two northern Thai jâo meuang, in the 1296 founding of Lan Na Thai, nowadays often known simply as 'Lanna'. Lanna extended across Northern Thailand to include the meuang of Wiang Chan along the middle reaches of the Mekong River. In the 14th century, Wiang Chan was taken from Lanna by Chao Fa Ngum of Luang Prabang, who made it part of his Lan Xang (Million Elephants) kingdom. Wiang Chan later flourished as an independent kingdom for a short time during the mid-16th century and eventually became the capital of Laos in its royal, French (where it got its more popular international spelling, 'Vientiane') and now socialist incarnations. After a period of dynastic decline, Lanna fell to the Burmese in 1558.

Ayuthaya Period

The Thai kings of Ayuthaya grew very powerful in the 14th and 15th centuries, taking over U Thong and Lopburi, former Khmer strongholds, and moving east in their conquests until Angkor was defeated in 1431. Even though the Khmers were their

AYUTHAYA

Extents of Ayuthaya Kingdom

adversaries in battle, the Ayuthaya kings adopted large portions of Khmer court customs and language. One result of this acculturation was that the Thai monarch gained more absolute authority during the Ayuthaya period and assumed the title *devaraja* (god-king; *thewárâat* in Thai) as opposed to the *dhammaraja* (dharma-king; *thammárâat*) title used in Sukhothai.

Ayuthaya was one of the greatest and wealthiest cities in Asia, a thriving seaport envied not only by the Burmese but by the Europeans, who were in great awe of it. It has been said that London, at the time, was a mere village in comparison. The kingdom sustained an unbroken 400-year monarchical succession through 34 reigns, from King U Thong (1350–69) to King Ekathat (1758–67).

By the early 16th century Ayuthaya was receiving European visitors, and a Portuguese embassy was established in 1511. The Portuguese were followed by the Dutch in 1605, the English in 1612, the Danes in 1621 and the French in 1662. In the mid-16th century Ayuthaya and the independent kingdom of Lanna came under the control of the Burmese, but the Thais regained rule of both by the end of the century. In 1690 Londoner Engelbert Campfer proclaimed 'Among the Asian nations, the Kingdom of Siam is the greatest. The magnificence of the Ayuthaya Court is incomparable'.

An exceptional episode unfolded in Ayuthaya when Constantine Phaulkon, a Greek, became a high official in Siam under King Narai from 1675 to 1688. He kept out the Dutch and the English but allowed the French to station 600 soldiers in the kingdom. Eventually the Thais, fearing a takeover, expelled the French and killed Phaulkon. (The word for a foreigner of European descent in modern Thai is *fàràng,* an abbreviated form of *fàràngsèt,* meaning 'French'.) Siam sealed itself from the West for 150 years following this experience with the fàràng.

The Burmese invaded Ayuthaya again in 1765 and the capital fell after two years of fighting. This time the invaders destroyed everything sacred to the Thais, including manuscripts, temples and religious sculpture. But the Burmese could not maintain a foothold in the kingdom, and Phraya Taksin, a half-Chinese, half-Thai general, made himself king in 1769, ruling from the new capital of Thonburi on the banks of the Mae Nam Chao Phraya, opposite Bangkok. The Thais regained control of the country and further united the provinces to the north with central Siam.

Taksin eventually came to regard himself as the next Buddha; his ministers, who did not approve of his religious fantasies, deposed and then executed. See the 'Phraya Taksin' boxed text for the full story.

THONBURI-RATANAKOSIN

Extents of Thonburi-Ratanakosin Kingdom

Phraya Taksin

Unlike most Thai kings, King Taksin was not born to royalty but into a Chinese merchant family. As a young man, under the patronage of a Thai nobleman, he entered the royal service. In 1764, at the age of 30, he gained the high rank of *phráyaa* and became the governor of the northern province of Tak, assuming the name Phraya Taksin.

During the sacking of Ayuthaya in 1767 Taksin was on his way to the battle with 1000 men, but seeing the capital engulfed in flames he knew the Burmese had won. Instead of going to the gutted capital he headed to the eastern provinces, fighting pockets of Burmese forces as he went.

Taksin gathered around him a steadily growing band of loyal followers, fighters eager to follow his dream of reuniting the country and driving out the Burmese invaders. But it wasn't only the Burmese he had to fight. Thai princes, bandits and strongmen were vying with each other for supremacy. The sacking of Ayuthaya was so complete that the country was left without central government: Ayuthaya's history had gone up in flames with the city's books and even the culture had taken a beating. Without a king, Thailand was foundering and the succession was up for grabs.

Taksin was an intriguing mixture of immense personal power, ruthless authority, exalted philanthropy and impending insanity. After a victory he would mete out punishment for wrongdoers and reward those who had served him well. His anger was fearsome: Once he ordered the execution of a local chief for not coming to see him quickly enough. When a concerned aide tried to talk him out of it, the king's anger was inflamed, and in a burst of fury Taksin drew his own sword and beheaded the lord then and there (leading to a new law against handing the king his sword when he was angry)!

But Taksin was also deeply religious and compassionate. He would hand out provisions and clothes to the poor. In his own words (according to the chronicles), he fought 'only with the well-being and happiness of the people in mind'. After taking Samut Prakan, Taksin entered the enemy's camp and was deeply moved by what he saw:

> ...seeing the bodies of the people killed by disasters, bandits and disease piled up like a mountain, and seeing the people tormented by starvation, looking like hungry ghosts, (the king) was moved to pity, became wearied of his royal status and wanted to return to Chanthaburi, but (the people) pleaded with him to stay. His Majesty, seeing the benefit his staying would have as a factor in his ultimate attainment of supreme enlightenment, accepted their invitation.

The Thai chronicles (*phongsǎawádaan*) are full of references to his amazing powers, subduing wild storms or inducing drought-relieving rains with his 'truth asseverations'. When he arrived at the hostile city of Nakhon Si Thammarat ahead of his army and naval forces, he entered the city with only his elephant and personal aides. The recalcitrant governor, overawed by the presence of the great king, immediately surrendered, and Taksin's army arrived to find their work already done.

Taksin had a sense for drama, too. When he found the governor of Chanthaburi reluctant to join him, and knew he would have to take that city by force, he instructed his army to have their last meal, throw out all remaining food and smash their cooking pots. 'If we can't gain victory and take our breakfast in Chanthaburi', declared the king, 'then let us starve'.

It was Taksin who gathered the scattered Thai forces together and rallied them to fight off the Burmese invaders. It was Taksin who reunited the country and established the new capital of Thonburi. But his bird seems to have flown too high. In the Thai chronicles, the picture emerges of a man who is losing it: He poses in meditation posture and asks his advisers, 'How do I look?'. He begins to punish the just and reward the wicked. He sees insurrection around every corner, and his hand is swift to punish. In the end the country is on the verge of chaos, and his insanity can no longer be accommodated. Taksin is forced to step down. He offers to become a monk and devote himself to meditation, but the new king (once one of Taksin's foremost generals) naturally feels his presence is a danger, and Taksin is wrapped in a sack and beaten to death with clubs of sandalwood – 'done with sandalwood, according to the tradition', as the chronicles would say.

Bruce Evans

Chakri Dynasty

One of Taksin's key generals, Chao Phraya Chakri, came to power and was crowned in 1782 as Phra Yot Fa. He moved the royal capital across the river to Bangkok and ruled as the first king of the Chakri dynasty. In 1809 his son, Loet La, took the throne and reigned until 1824. Both monarchs assumed the task of restoring the culture, which had been severely damaged by the Burmese decades earlier.

The third Chakri king, Phra Nang Klao (reigned 1824–51), went beyond reviving tradition and developed trade with China while increasing domestic agricultural pro- duction. He also established a new royal title system, posthumously conferring 'Rama I' and 'Rama II' upon his two pre- decessors and taking the title 'Rama III' for himself. During Nang Klao's reign, Ameri- can missionary James Low brought the first printing press to Siam and produced the country's first printed document in Thai script. Missionary Dan Bradley published the first Thai newspaper, the monthly *Bangkok Recorder*, from 1844 to 1845.

Rama IV, commonly known as King Mongkut (Phra Chom Klao to the Thais), was a colourful and innovative Chakri king. He originally missed out on the throne in

---

The King and Who?

Many people who watch the musical *The King and I* or the two motion pictures on the same theme, *Anna and the King of Siam* (1946) or *Anna and the King* (1999), may believe they are watching the true story of Anna Leonowens, governess in the court of Siam during the reign of King Mongkut (Rama IV). The semi-comedic portrayals of the king, particularly those starring a shaven-headed Yul Brynner, so insulted the Thai people that the film has been banned from screenings in Thailand be- cause of its historical and cultural distortions.

In reality the author of the original book, *The English Governess at the Siamese Court* (1870), Anna Leon Owens, not only misled the world as to the antics of the king but also as to her impor- tance in the court, where she was employed not as a governess but as an English instructor. She also successfully concealed or distorted many events in her life prior to her five-year stay in Siam.

Fact or Fiction?

What Anna wrote	The Truth
• Her birth name was Anna Crawford and she was born in Wales in 1834.	• Her birth name was Anna Edwards, and she was born in India in 1831.
• Her father was Captain Thomas Crawford, who died during a Sikh uprising in India when Anna was just six years old. Anna and her sis- ter were at school in Wales at the time.	• Her father was Thomas Edwards, a cabinet maker who enlisted in the Bombay infantry. He died three months before Anna was born and her mother remarried to a corporal in the Engi- neers. Anna and her sister were sent to school in England.
• Anna and her sister moved to India on the completion of their education at the age of 14 or 15.	• Anna and her sister returned to India on the completion of their education at the age of 14 or 15.
• In India she eloped, at the age of 17, with an army captain named Thomas Leonowens.	• On her return to India she married, at the age of 18, a clerk called Thomas Leon Owens.
• They lived in London for a while before Thomas Leonowens, now a major, was posted to Singapore. While there, Anna learned that the money that her father had left her had all been lost during the Indian Mutiny.	• Thomas Owens had difficulty in keeping a job and they moved around frequently. They had two children, Louis and Avis.
• Major Thomas Leonowens suffered sunstroke on a tiger hunt and later died, leaving Anna with two small children and no money.	• Thomas Owens died of apoplexy (a stroke) in Penang, Malaya. Anna moved to Singapore.

Courtesy of the students of Sriwittayapaknam School, Samut Prakan

deference to his half-brother, Rama III, and lived as a Buddhist monk for 27 years. During his long monastic term he became adept in Sanskrit, Pali, Latin and English, studied Western sciences and adopted the strict discipline of local Mon monks. He kept an eye on the outside world and, when he took the throne in 1851, immediately courted diplomatic relations with a few European nations, taking care to evade colonisation.

In addition, he attempted to align Buddhist cosmology with modern science, with the aim of demythologising Thai religion (a process yet to be fully accomplished), and founded the Thammayut monastic sect, based on the strict discipline he had followed as a monk. Today, the Thammayut remains a minority, though strongly supported, sect in relation to the Mahanikai, which comprises the largest number of Buddhist monks in Thailand (see the special section 'Religion in Thailand').

King Mongkut loosened Thai trade restrictions and many Western powers signed trade agreements with the monarch. He also sponsored Siam's second printing press and instituted educational reforms, developing a school system along European lines. Although the king courted the West, he did so with caution and warned his subjects: 'Whatever they have invented or done which we should know of and do, we can imitate and learn from them, but do not wholeheartedly believe in them'. Mongkut was the first monarch to show Thai commoners his face in public; he died of malaria in 1868. See the boxed text 'The Wrath of Rahu?' in the Central Thailand chapter.

His son King Chulalongkorn (known to the Thais as Chula Chom Klao or Rama V; reigned 1868–1910) continued Mongkut's tradition of reform, especially in the legal and administrative realms. Educated by European tutors, Chulalongkorn abolished prostration before the king as well as slavery and corvee (state labour). Siam further benefited from relations with European nations and the USA: Railways were built, a civil service was established and the legal code restructured. Although Siam still managed to avoid European colonisation, the king was compelled to concede territory to French Indochina (Laos in 1893 and Cambodia in 1907) and British Burma (three Malayan states in 1909) during his reign.

Chulalongkorn's son, King Vajiravudh (Mongkut Klao or Rama VI; reigned 1910–25), was educated in Britain and during his reign introduced compulsory education and other educational reforms. He further 'Westernised' the nation by making the Thai calendar conform to Western models. His reign was somewhat clouded by a top-down push for Thai nationalism that resulted in strong anti-Chinese sentiment.

Before Vajiravudh's reign, Thai parents gave each of their children a single, original name, with no surname to identify family origins. In 1909 a royal decree required the adoption of Thai surnames for all Thai citizens – a move designed as much to parallel the European system of family surnames as to weed out Chinese names.

In 1912 a group of Thai military officers unsuccessfully attempted to overthrow the monarchy, the first in a series of coup attempts that has continued to the present day. As a show of support for the Allies in WWI, Vajiravudh sent 1300 Thai troops to France in 1918.

Chakri Dynasty

crown title	reign	Westernised name	Thai pronunciation
Rama I	1782–1809	Yot Fa	Phra Phutthayotfa Chulalok
Rama II	1809–1824	Loet La	Phra Phutthaloetla Naphalai
Rama III	1824–1851	Nang Klao	Phra Nang Klao
Rama IV	1851–1868	Mongkut	Phra Chom Klao
Rama V	1868–1910	Chulalongkorn	Phra Chula Chom Klao
Rama VI	1910–1925	Vajiravudh	Phra Mongkut Klao
Rama VII	1925–1935	Prajadhipok	Phra Pokklao
Rama VIII	1935–1946	Ananda Mahidol	Phra Anantha Mahidon
Rama IX	1946–	Bhumibol Adulyadej	Phra Phumiphon Adunyadet

Revolution

While Vajiravudh's brother, King Prajadhipok (Pokklao or Rama VII; reigned 1925–35) ruled, a group of Thai students living in Paris became so enamoured of democratic ideology that in 1932 they mounted a successful coup d'etat against absolute monarchy in Siam. This bloodless revolution led to the development of a constitutional monarchy along British lines, with a mixed military-civilian group in power.

A royalist revolt in 1933 sought to reinstate absolute monarchy, but it failed and left Prajadhipok isolated from the royalist revolutionaries and the constitution-minded ministers. One of the king's last official acts was to outlaw polygamy in 1934, leaving behind the cultural underpinnings for consorts, concubines and minor wives that now support Thai prostitution.

In 1935 the king abdicated without naming a successor and retired to Britain. The cabinet promoted his nephew, 10-year-old Ananda Mahidol, to the throne as Rama VIII, although Ananda didn't return to Thailand from school in Switzerland until 1945. Phibul (Phibun) Songkhram, a key military leader in the 1932 coup, maintained an effective position of power from 1938 until the end of WWII.

Under the influence of Phibul's government, in 1939 the country's name was officially changed from Siam to Thailand – rendered in Thai as *pràthêt thai*. 'Pràthêt' is from the Sanskrit *pradesha* or 'country'. 'Thai' is considered to have the connotation of 'free', although in usage it refers to the Thai, Tai or T'ai peoples, who are found as far east as Tonkin, as far west as Assam, as far north as southern China, and as far south as northern Malaysia.

Ananda Mahidol came back to Thailand in 1945 but was shot dead in his bedroom under mysterious circumstances in 1946. Although there was apparently no physical evidence to suggest assassination, three of Ananda's attendants were arrested two years after his death and executed in 1954. No public charges were ever filed, and the consensus among historians today is that the attendants were 'sacrificed' to settle a karmic debt for allowing the king to die during their watch. His brother, Bhumibol Adulyadej, succeeded him as Rama IX. Nowadays no-one ever speaks or writes publicly about Ananda's death – whether it was a simple gun accident or a regicidal plot remains unclear. Even as recently as 1993 a chapter chronicling the known circumstances surrounding the event in David Wyatt's *A Short History of Thailand* had to be excised before the Thai publisher would print and distribute the title in Thailand.

WWII & Postwar Periods

During the Japanese invasion of South-East Asia in 1941, the Phibul government sided with Japan, and Phibul declared war on the USA and Britain in 1942. But Seni Pramoj, the Thai ambassador in Washington, refused to deliver the declaration. Phibul resigned in 1944 under pressure from the Thai underground resistance (known as Thai Seri), and after V-J Day in 1945, Seni became premier.

In 1946 Seni and his brother Kukrit were unseated in a general election and a democratic civilian group took power under Pridi Phanomyong, a law professor who had been instrumental in the 1932 revolution. Pridi's civilian government, which changed the country's name back to Siam for a short time, only to be overthrown by Phibul, then field marshal, in 1947.

Using the death of Prajadhipok as a pretext, Phibul suspended the constitution and reinstated Thailand as the country's official name in 1949. Phibul's government took an extreme anticommunist stance, refused to recognise the newly declared People's Republic of China and became a loyal supporter of French and US foreign policy in South-East Asia.

In 1951 power was wrested from Phibul by General Sarit Thanarat, who continued the tradition of military dictatorship. However, Phibul somehow retained the actual title of premier until 1957 when Sarit finally had him exiled. Elections that same year forced Sarit to resign and go abroad for 'medical treatment'; he returned in 1958 to launch another coup. This time he abolished the constitution, dissolved the parliament and banned all political parties, maintaining effective power until he died of cirrhosis in 1963. From 1964 to 1973 the Thai nation was ruled by army officers Thanom Kittikachorn and Praphat Charusathien. During this time Thailand allowed the USA to establish several army bases within its borders in support of the US campaign in Vietnam.

Reacting to political repression, 10,000 Thai students publicly demanded a real constitution in June 1973. On 14 October of the same year the military brutally suppressed a large demonstration at Thammasat University in Bangkok, but King Bhumibol and General Krit Sivara, who sympathised with the students, refused to support further bloodshed, forcing Thanom and Praphat to leave Thailand. Oxford-educated Kukrit Pramoj took charge of a 14-party coalition government and steered a leftist agenda past a conservative parliament. Among Kukrit's lasting achievements were a national minimum wage, the repeal of anti-communist laws and the ejection of US military forces from Thailand.

Polarisation & Stabilisation

Kukrit's elected constitutional government ruled until 6 October 1976, when students demonstrated again, this time protesting against Thanom's return to Thailand as a monk. Thammasat University again became a battlefield as border patrol police and right-wing, paramilitary civilian groups (Nawaphon, the Red Guards and the Village Scouts), assaulted a group of 2000 students holding a sit-in. It is estimated that hundreds of students were killed and injured in the fracas, and more than a thousand were arrested. Using public disorder as an excuse, the military stepped in and installed a new right-wing government with Thanin Kraivichien as premier.

This bloody incident disillusioned many Thai students and older intellectuals not directly involved with the demonstrations, the result being that numerous idealists 'dropped out' of Thai society and joined the People's Liberation Army of Thailand (PLAT) – armed communist insurgents based in the hills who had been active in Thailand since the 1930s.

In October 1977 the military replaced Thanin with the more moderate General Kriangsak Chomanand in an effort to conciliate antigovernment factions. When this failed, the military-backed position changed hands again in 1980, leaving Prem Tinsulanonda at the helm. By this time PLAT had reached a peak force numbering around 10,000. A 1981 coup attempt by the 'Young Turks' (a group of army officers who had graduated from the Chulachomklao Royal Military Academy together and styled themselves after a 1908 military movement at the heart of the Ottoman Empire) failed when Prem fled Bangkok for Khorat in the company of the royal family.

Prem served as prime minister through to 1988 and is credited with the political and economic stabilisation of Thailand in the post-Vietnam War years (only one coup attempt in the 1980s!). The major success of the Prem years was a complete dismantling of the Communist Party of Thailand (CPT) and PLAT through an effective combination of amnesty programs (which brought the students back from the forests) and military action. His administration is also considered responsible for a gradual democratisation of Thailand that culminated in the 1988 election of his successor, retired general and businessman Chatichai Choonhavan. Prem continues to serve as a privy councillor and is an elder statesman (rátthàbùrùt) of the country.

It may be difficult for new arrivals to Thailand to appreciate the political distance Thailand covered in the 1980s. Between 1976 and 1981, freedom of speech and the press were rather curtailed in Thailand and a strict curfew was enforced in Bangkok. Anyone caught in the streets after 1 am risked spending the night in one of Bangkok's mosquito-infested 'detention areas'. Under Prem, the curfew was lifted, and dissenting opinions began to be heard again in public.

Traditionally, every leading political figure in Thailand, including Prem, has needed the support of the Thai military, who are generally staunch reactionaries. Considering Thailand's geographic position, it's not difficult to understand, to some extent, the fears of this ultra-conservative group. But as the threat of communist takeover (either from within or from nearby Indochinese states) diminished, the military gradually began loosening its hold on national politics. Under Chatichai, Thailand enjoyed a brief period of unprecedented popular participation in government.

Around 60% of Chatichai's cabinet were former business executives rather than ex-military officers, as compared with 38% in the previous cabinet. Thailand seemed to be entering a new era in which the country's double-digit economic boom ran concurrently with democratisation. Critics praised the political maturation of Thailand, even if they grumbled that corruption seemed as rife as ever. By the end of the 1980s, however, certain high-ranking military officers had become increasingly disappointed, complaining that Thailand was being run by a plutocracy.

February 1991 Coup

On 23 February 1991, in a move that shocked Thailand-observers around the world, the military overthrew the Chatichai administration in a bloodless coup *(pàtìwát)* and handed power to the newly formed National Peace-Keeping Council (NPKC), headed by General Suchinda Kraprayoon. Although it was Thailand's 19th coup attempt and one of 10 successful coups since 1932, it was only the second coup to overthrow a democratically-elected civilian government. Charging Chatichai's civilian government with corruption and vote-buying, the NPKC abolished the 1978 constitution and dissolved the parliament. Rights of public assembly were curtailed but the press was closed down for only one day.

Following the coup, the NPKC appointed a hand-picked civilian prime minister, Anand Panyarachun, former ambassador to the USA, Germany, Canada and the United Nations (UN), to dispel public fears that the junta was planning a return to 100% military rule. Anand claimed to be his own man, but like his predecessors – elected or not – he was allowed the freedom to make his own decisions only in so far as they didn't affect the military. In spite of obvious constraints, many observers felt Anand's temporary premiership and cabinet were the best Thailand had ever had.

In December 1991, Thailand's national assembly passed a new constitution that guaranteed a NPKC-biased parliament – 270 appointed senators in the upper house stacked against 360 elected representatives. Under this constitution, regardless of who was chosen as the next prime minister or which political parties filled the lower house, the government would remain largely in the hands of the military. The new charter included a provisional clause allowing for a 'four-year transitional period' to full democracy, a provision that sounded suspiciously close to the military subterfuge in neighbouring Myanmar.

Elections & Demonstrations

A general election in March 1992 ushered in a five-party coalition government with Narong Wongwan, whose Samakkhitham (Justice Unity) Party received the most votes, as premier. But amid allegations that Narong was involved in Thailand's drug trade, the military exercised its constitutional prerogative and replaced Narong with (surprise, surprise) General Suchinda in April 1992.

In May 1992, several huge demonstrations demanding Suchinda's resignation – led by charismatic Bangkok governor Chamlong Srimuang – rocked Bangkok and larger provincial capitals. Chamlong won the 1992 Magsaysay Award (a humanitarian service award issued by a foundation in the Philippines) for his role in galvanising the public to reject Suchinda. After street confrontations between the protesters and the military near Bangkok's Democracy Monument resulted in nearly 50 deaths and hundreds of injuries, Suchinda resigned, having been premier for less than six weeks. The military-supported government also agreed to institute a constitutional amendment requiring that the prime minister come from the ranks of elected MPs. Anand Panyarachun was reinstated as interim premier, winning praise from several circles for his fair and efficient administration.

The September 1992 elections squeezed in veteran Democrat Party leader Chuan Leekpai with a five-seat majority. Chuan led a coalition government consisting of the Democrat, New Aspiration, Palang Dharma and Solidarity Parties. A food vendor's son and native of Trang Province, the new premier didn't fit the usual Thai prime minister mould since he was not a general, tycoon or academic.

Although well regarded for his honesty and high morals, Chuan accomplished little in the areas of concern to the majority of Thais, most pointedly Bangkok traffic, national infrastructure and the undemocratic NPKC constitution.

By the end of 1993 the opposition was calling for parliamentary dissolution and a royal command appointed a new cabinet for Chuan in December 1994.

Chuan never completed his four-year term and a new general election ushered in a seven-party coalition led by the Chart

Thai (Thai Nationality) Party. At the helm was 63-year-old billionaire Banharn Silapa-archa, whom the press called a 'walking ATM (automated teller machine)'. Two of the largest partners in the coalition, the Palang Dharma and New Aspiration Parties, were former participants of the Chuan coalition government.

Banharn wasn't very popular with the Thai media, which immediately attacked his tendency to appoint from a reservoir of rural politicians known to be heavily involved in money politics. In September 1996 the Banharn government collapsed amid a spate of corruption scandals and a crisis of confidence.

The November national election, marked by electoral violence and accusations of vote buying, saw former deputy prime minister and army commander Chavalit Yongchaiyudh of the New Aspiration Party secure premiership with a dubious mix of coalition partners.

In July 1997, following several months of warning signs that almost everyone in Thailand and in the international community chose to ignore (see Economy later for details), the Thai currency fell into a deflationary tailspin and the national economy crashed and screeched to a virtual halt. In September 1997 Thai parliament voted in a new constitution that guaranteed – at least on paper – more human and civil rights than had hitherto been codified in Thailand. As the first national charter to be prepared under civilian auspices, the 'people's constitution' fostered great hope in a population emotionally battered by the ongoing economic crisis.

Hope faded as Chavalit, living up to everyone's low expectations, failed to deal effectively with the economy and was forced to resign in November 1997. An election brought Chuan Leekpai back into office, where he did a reasonably decent job as an international public relations man for the crisis.

In January 2001, millionaire Thaksin Shinawatra was named prime minister-elect after winning a landslide victory in compulsory nation-wide elections – the first in Thailand to be held under strict guidelines established by the 1997 constitution. Amid accusations of widespread vote-buying and violent protests in 16 provinces, Thailand's Election Commission launched an investigation into election conduct while the constitutionally mandated Counter-Corruption Commission checked into allegations of graft and 'wealth concealment' (tax evasion) in Thaksin's past.

Asean Shifts & Political Reform

Indonesia, the Philippines, Singapore and Thailand founded the Association of South-East Asian Nations (Asean) during a meeting of foreign ministers in Bangkok on 8 August 1967. Spurred by the infamous 1963–66 *konfrontasi* between Indonesia and Malaysia, the organisation was established as an attempt to structure regional relations along more cooperative lines. A 1992 agreement created the Asean Free Trade Area (AFTA), a framework of preferential trade policies that include the lowering and eventual elimination of tariffs on imports and exports among member states. Brunei became the fifth Asean member in 1984, followed by Vietnam in 1995 and both Laos and Myanmar in 1997.

Although Asean's main declared objective is to foster economic cooperation, in reality the organisation's most important accomplishments have been political stabilisation and conflict mediation. In Asean's traditional posture of 'constructive engagement', Asean governments refuse to involve themselves publicly in the internal political affairs of other member countries, while remaining active in the economic sphere. This, it is claimed, is the best way to go about fostering positive political change.

Thailand became the first nation in the grouping to move beyond this 'hear no evil, see no evil' stance, suggesting in 1998 that Asean adopt a new pattern of 'flexible engagement' wherein space is allowed for limited criticism within the group, particularly with regard to human rights. So far only the Philippines and Malaysia have backed Thailand's initiative. The other four member-nations, most vocally Indonesia and Myanmar, have been vehemently opposed to such a change.

Meanwhile many Thai citizens have become fed up with the internal version of 'constructive engagement' with their own government, and in 1999–2000 large-scale demonstrations around the country rocked the Chuan administration. Most demonstrations were asking for government relief from hardships caused by the shrinking economy, while some were demanding that the government dismantle World Bank or Asian Development projects – such as the Kheuan Pak Mun (Pak Mun Dam) – that had been established without their consent. The government has promised land reform to help farmers, but the Kheuan Pak Mun and other issues continue to smoulder, leaving observers to wonder if Thailand isn't heading for a period of unrest similar to that seen in the 1970s.

Despite the economic downturn, Thai cynics will tell you that things *never* change and that the democratic Chatichai, Banharn, Chavalit and Chuan governments may merely be short-lived deviations from the norm of military rule. Hardened cynics might hold the view that Thailand's 20th-century coups and counter-coups were a mere extension of the power plays of early Thai jâo meuang.

Optimists, on the other hand, see Suchinda's hasty resignation as a sign that the military coup, as an instrument of change in Thailand, was only a minor detour on the country's road towards a more responsive and democratic national government.

Corruption remains a problem, and some observers suggest it may have worsened following the 1997 economic crash. Without question, however, Thailand's revised and amended constitution strengthens the nation's future claim to democratic status and political stability, even while the economy remains shaky.

Allegations of vote-buying during the 2000 senate elections prompted the commission overseeing elections to hold five rounds of polls before arriving at a final result. By the final round, the commission was satisfied that elections had been fair, while Thai voters forced to revisit polling booths learned that democracy is *lambàak* (troublesome).

GEOGRAPHY

Thailand has an area of 517,000 sq km, making it slightly smaller than the state of Texas in the USA, or about the size of France. Its shape on the map has been likened to the head of an elephant, with its trunk extending down the Malay peninsula.

The centre of Thailand, Bangkok, is at about 14° north latitude, putting it on a level with Madras, Manila, Guatemala and Khartoum.

The country's longest north-south distance is about 1860km, but its shape makes distances in any other direction 1000km or less. Because the north-south reach spans roughly 16 latitudinal degrees, Thailand has perhaps the most diverse climate in South-East Asia.

The topography varies from high mountains in the north (the southernmost extreme of a series of ranges that extend across northern Myanmar and South-West China to the south-eastern edges of the Tibet Plateau) to limestone-encrusted tropical islands in the South that are part of the Malay Archipelago.

The rivers and tributaries of Northern and Central Thailand drain into the Gulf of Thailand via the Chao Phraya Delta near Bangkok; Mae Nam Mun and other north-eastern waterways exit into the South China Sea via the Mekong River.

These broad geographic characteristics divide the country into four main zones: the fertile central region, dominated by the Mae Nam Chao Phraya; the north-east plateau, the kingdom's poorest region (thanks to 'thin' soil plus occasional droughts and floods), rising some 300m above the central plain; Northern Thailand, a region of mountains and fertile valleys; and the southern peninsula, which extends to the Malaysian border and is predominantly rainforest. The southern peninsular region receives the most annual rainfall and the north-east the least, although the climate in the north is less humid.

Extending from the east coast of the Malay peninsula to Vietnam, the Sunda Shelf separates the Gulf of Thailand from the South China Sea. On the opposite side of the peninsula, the Andaman Sea encompasses the Indian Ocean east of India's Andaman and Nicobar Islands. Thailand's Andaman Sea and Gulf of Thailand coastlines form 2710km of beaches, hard shores and wetlands. Hundreds of oceanic and continental islands lie offshore on both sides – those with tourist facilities constitute only a fraction of the total. Offshore depths in the gulf range from 30m to 80m, while offshore Andaman depths reach over 100m.

CLIMATE
Rainfall

Thailand's climate is ruled by monsoons that produce three seasons in Northern, North-Eastern and Central Thailand, and two seasons in southern Thailand. The three-season zone, which extends roughly from Thailand's northernmost reaches to Phetchaburi Province on the southern peninsula, experiences a 'dry and wet monsoon climate', with the south-west monsoon arriving around July and lasting into November (the 'rainy season'). This is followed by a dry, 'cool' period (the 'cool season') from November till mid-February, followed by much higher relative temperatures (the 'hot season') from March to June.

It rains more and longer in the South, which is subject to the north-east monsoon from November to January, as well as the south-west monsoon. Hence most of southern Thailand has only two seasons, a wet and a dry, with smaller temperature differences between the two.

Although the rains 'officially' begin in July (according to the agricultural calendar), they actually depend on the monsoons in any given year. As a rule of thumb, the dry season is shorter the farther south you go. From Chiang Mai north the dry season may last six months (mid-November to May); in most of Central and North-Eastern Thailand five months (December to May); on the upper peninsula three months (February to May); and below Surat Thani only two months (March and April). Occasional rains in the dry season are known as 'mango showers' (heralding the mango season).

In Central Thailand it rains most during August and September, although there may be floods in October when the ground has reached full saturation. If you are in Bangkok in early October don't be surprised if you find yourself in hip-deep water in certain parts of the city. It rains a little less in the north, August being the wettest. The north-east gets less rain and sometimes has droughts. In Phuket it rains the most in May (an average of 21 out of 30 days) and in October (an average of 22 out of 30 days), as it is hit by both monsoons. Travelling in the rainy season is generally not bad, but unpaved roads may be impassable.

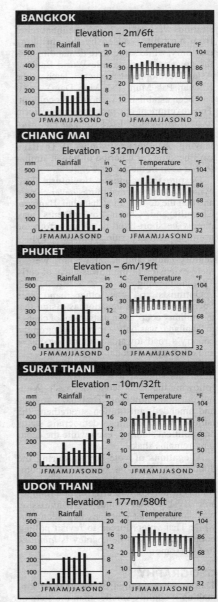

The arrival of the rains brings relief from the hot, dry weather of the preceding months and softens the soil for planting.

Temperature

Most of Thailand – with the mountains in the north and the Khorat Plateau of the North-East notable exceptions – is very humid, with an overall average humidity of 66% to 82%, depending on the season and time of day. The hot part of the dry season reaches its hottest along the north-east plateau, and temperatures easily soar to 39°C in the daytime, dropping only a few degrees at night. The temperature can drop to 13°C at night during the cool season in Chiang Mai and even lower in Mae Hong Son – if you're visiting the North during the cooler months, long-sleeved shirts and pullovers are in order. Because temperatures are more even year-round in the South, when it is 35°C in Bangkok it may be only 32°C in Phuket.

ECOLOGY & ENVIRONMENT
Environmental Policy

Thailand, like all countries with very high population densities, has put enormous pressure on the ecosystems within its borders. Fifty years ago the countryside was around 70% forest; as of 2000 an estimated 20% of the natural forest cover remained. Logging and agriculture are mainly to blame for the decline, and the loss of forest cover has been accompanied by dwindling wildlife resources. Species notably extinct in Thailand include the kouprey (a type of wild cattle), Schomburgk's deer and the Javan rhino, but innumerable smaller species have also fallen by the wayside.

In response to environmental degradation the Thai government has created a large number of protected parks, reserves and sanctuaries since the 1970s, and has enacted legislation to protect specific plant and animal species. The government hopes to raise the total forest cover to 40% by the middle of this century. Thailand has also become a signatory to the UN Convention on International Trade in Endangered Species (CITES).

In 1989 all logging was banned in Thailand following a 1988 disaster in which hundreds of tonnes of cut timber washed down deforested slopes in Surat Thani Province, killing more than 100 people and burying a number of villages. It is now illegal to sell timber felled in the country, and all imported timber is theoretically accounted for before going on the market. The illegal timber trade further diminished with Cambodia's ban on all timber exports, along with the termination of all Thai contracts by the Burmese. Laos is now the number-one source for imported timber in Thailand, both legal and illegal.

These days builders even need government permission to use timber salvaged from old houses. This has helped curb illegal logging operations in the interior, but corruption remains a problem.

Corruption impedes government attempts to shelter 'exotic' species from the illicit global wildlife trade and to preserve Thailand's sensitive coastal areas. The Royal Forest Department is currently under pressure to take immediate action in those areas where preservation laws have gone unenforced, including coastal zones where illegal tourist accommodation has flourished. A crackdown on restaurants serving 'jungle food' (aahǎan pàa), which consists of exotic and often endangered wildlife species like barking deer, bear, pangolin, civet and gaur, has been fairly successful.

The tiger is one of the most endangered of Thailand's large mammals. Although tiger hunting and trapping is illegal, poachers continue to kill the cats for the lucrative overseas Chinese pharmaceutical market; among the Chinese, the ingestion of tiger penis and bone is thought to have curative effects. Taipei, where at least two-thirds of pharmacies deal in tiger parts (in spite of the fact that such trade is forbidden by Taiwanese law), is the world centre for Thai tiger consumption. Around 200 to 300 wild tigers are thought to be hanging on in Khao Yai, Kaeng Krachan, Huay Kha Khaeng/Thung Yai Naresuan, Nam Nao, Thap Lan, Mae Wong and Khao Sok National Parks.

Forestry department efforts are limited by lack of personnel and funds. The average ranger is paid only 75B a day – some aren't paid at all but receive only food and lodging – to take on armed poachers backed by the rich and powerful Chinese godfathers who control illicit timber and wildlife businesses.

Marine resources are also threatened by a lack of long-range conservation goals. The upper portion of the Gulf of Thailand, between Rayong and Prachuap Khiri Khan, was once one of the most fertile marine areas in the world. Now it is virtually dead due to overfishing and the release of mainland pollutants.

Experts say it's not too late to rehabilitate the upper gulf by reducing pollution and the number of trawlers, and by restricting commercial fishing to certain zones. An effective ban on the harvest of *plaa thuu* (mackerel) in the spawning stages has brought stocks of this fish back from the brink of total depletion. The Bangkok Metropolitan Administration (BMA) is currently developing a system of sewage-treatment plants in the Chao Phraya Delta area with the intention of halting all large-scale dumping of sewage into Gulf waters, but similar action needs to be taken along the entire eastern seaboard, which is rapidly becoming Thailand's new industrial centre.

Overdevelopment on Ko Phi Phi is starving the surrounding coral reefs by blocking nutrient-rich run-off from the island's interior, as well as smothering the reefs with pollutants. Ko Samui and Ko Samet also face a similar fate if action isn't taken in the near future.

One encouraging move by the Thai government was the passing of the 1992 Environmental Act, which provides for environmental quality standards and the establishment of national authority to designate conservation and pollution control areas. Pattaya and Phuket immediately became the first locales to be decreed pollution control areas, thus making them eligible for government cleanup funds.

Tourism & the Environment

In some instances tourism has had positive effects on environmental conservation in

Thai Environmentalism

A large number of Thais remain ignorant of the value of taking a pro-environment stance in everyday life or of encouraging ecologically sound tourism. The director of a certain regional Tourism Authority of Thailand (TAT) office once complained to us that ecotourism was *lambàak* (troublesome) for Thai people but there was little she could do about it because 'that's national policy'. Fortunately such attitudes are changing steadily, especially among younger Thais who have grown up in relative affluence but who have begun to perceive the dangers inherent in neglecting environmental conservation.

Even though environmentalism is part of national policy it's obvious that only with strong popular participation can Thailand effect reasonable enforcement of protective laws, which are already plentiful but often ignored. Current examples of 'people power' include the hundreds of forest monasteries that voluntarily protect chunks of forest throughout Thailand. When one such wát was forcibly removed by the military in Buriram Province, thousands of Thais around the country rallied behind the abbot, Phra Prachak, and the wát's protectorship was re-established. On the other side of the coin, wát with less ecologically minded trustees have sold off virgin lands to developers.

Nongovernment organisations play a large role in surveying and designating threatened areas and in educating the public about the environment. In 1983 Wildlife Fund Thailand (WFT) was created, under Queen Sirikit's patronage, as an affiliate of the World Wide Fund for Nature (WWF). The main function of WFT has been to raise public consciousness with regard to the illegal trade in endangered wildlife. Citing the country's free press as a major incentive, the international environmental watchdog organisation Greenpeace is planning to place a regional office in Thailand.

One of the greatest victories by Thai environmentalists was the 1986 defeat of government plans to construct a hydroelectric facility across the Khwae Yai River. The dam was to be placed over a river section in the middle of Thung Yai Naresuan National Park, one of the largest and best preserved monsoon forest areas in South-East Asia. It took four years of organised protest to halt the dam. Since this ground-breaking victory several other power projects have been halted through public protest. On the other hand, there have been some great defeats, one of which was the go-ahead for the construction of the Yadana gas pipeline from Myanmar's Gulf of Mottama to Ratchaburi Province through some of Thailand's most pristine monsoon woodlands (see the boxed text 'The Myanmar-Thailand Pipeline Scam' later in this chapter). Another was the construction of the Kheuan Pak Mun (Pak Mun Dam) in Ubon Ratchathani Province.

Thailand. Conscious that the country's natural beauty is a major tourist attraction for both residents and foreigners, and that tourism is one of Thailand's major revenue earners, the government has stepped up efforts to protect wilderness areas and to add more acreage to the park system. In Khao Yai National Park, for example, all hotel and golf-course facilities were removed in order to reduce human influence on the park environment. As a result of government and private sector pressure on the fishing industry, coral dynamiting has been all but eliminated in the Similan and Surin Islands, to preserve the area for tourist visitation. As described in National Parks of Thailand:

A growing number of conservationists, development experts and government officials believe that boundary markers and even guns do little to halt encroachment. The surrounding communities must somehow be allowed to share in whatever economic benefits a park can offer. Some sanctuaries, like Huay Kha Khaeng, recruit employees from local villages. In Thaleh Noi Wildlife Preserve, local fishermen are hired to take visitors around the lake in their boats to view the rich bird life. Rangers at Laem Son National Park encourage local fishermen to take visitors to outlying islands rather than over-fish the sea. Phu Kradung National Park takes on several hundred locals as porters to carry hikers' gear up the mountain. Some have become so protective of their park that they will report violations of the regulations to the park rangers.

However, tourism has also made negative contributions. Eager to make fistfuls of cash, hotel developers and tour operators have rushed to provide ecologically inappropriate services for visitors in sensitive areas. Concerns about this issue are causing the government to look more closely at Ko Phi Phi and Ko Samet – two national park islands notorious for overdevelopment. Part of the problem is that it's not always clear which lands are protected and which are privately owned.

The Myanmar-Thailand Pipeline Scam

One of the greatest environmental defeats in recent Thai history has been the development of a 700km-long pipeline between natural gas fields in Myanmar's Gulf of Mottama (Martaban) and Ratchaburi Province in Thailand. Roughly 300km of the pipeline extends into Thailand, bisecting some of the most pristine, A-1 classified natural forests in the country. The pipeline cuts through Kanchanaburi Province's Sai Yok National Park, home to more than 300 bird species and nearly 100 mammalian species. Several rare and endemic creatures, including the bumblebee bat (at 2g the world's smallest mammal) and the red-legged royal crab, are expected to suffer direct negative impact. The huge maintenance road cut through the forest alongside the pipeline will also bisect the traditional migration routes of at least two elephant herds in the area, and will provide easy access to the forest for timber and wildlife poachers on both sides of the Thai-Myanmar border.

What makes the pipeline all the more shameful is the way in which the Chavalit government signed agreements for the project in virtual secrecy, without any input from the public until after the bilateral deal was a fait accompli. Even Chavalit's successor, Chuan Leekpai, ordinarily considered an honest official, acted quickly to close public scrutiny of the case. According to Khun Varin Thiemcharas, first vice chairperson of Thailand's Union for Civil Liberty, and Khun Suraphon Duangkhae, deputy secretary general of the Wildlife Fund Thailand, these actions are in direct contravention of Thailand's constitution, which forbids the cutting of A-1 forest for any purpose. These people and many other Thais, including leading intellectual Sulak Sivaraksa, advocate a boycott of PTT (Thailand's state-owned petrol company), Unocal (USA), and Total (France), all of which are in cahoots with Myanmar's generals to develop the pipeline.

It may be too late to stop the pipeline, but it's never too late to let people in Thailand know how you feel about it. For further information, contact:

Union for Civil Liberty (☎ 02-275 4231, 01-921 3852, fax 275 4230) 109 Thanon Suthisamwinichai, Samsennok, Huay Kwang, Bangkok 10320
Wildlife Fund Thailand (☎ 02-521 3435, fax 552 6083) 251/88–90 Thanon Phahonyothin, Bangkhen, Bangkok 10220

Some common problems in marine areas include the anchoring of tour boats on coral reefs and the dumping of rubbish into the sea. Coral and sea shells are also illegally collected and sold in tourist shops. 'Jungle-food' restaurants, featuring menus of endangered species, do a roaring trade near inland national parks. Perhaps the most-visible abuses occur in areas which do not have basic garbage and sewage services, resulting in piles of garbage and open sewage run-off.

The plastic bottles that have been discarded on popular beaches are one of the saddest sights in Thailand. Worse yet are those seen floating in the sea or in rivers, where they are sometimes ingested by marine or river-bank wildlife with fatal results. Many of these bottles started out on beaches, only to be washed into the sea during the monsoon season.

What can the average visitor to Thailand do to minimise the impact of tourism on the environment? Firstly, they can avoid all restaurants serving 'exotic' wildlife species. The main patrons of this type of cuisine are the Thais themselves, along with visiting Chinese from Hong Kong and Taiwan; fortunately such restaurants have become increasingly rare as the Thais educate themselves about the importance of preserving biological diversity.

When you're using hired boats in the vicinity of coral reefs, insist that boat operators not lower anchors onto coral formations. Admittedly, this is becoming less of a problem with established boating outfits, some of whom mark off sensitive areas with blue-flagged buoys, but it is still common among small-time pilots. Likewise, volunteer to collect (and later dispose of) rubbish if it's obvious that the usual mode is to throw everything overboard.

Obviously, it is far more ecologically sensitive to refrain from purchasing coral and items made from coral while in Thailand. Thai law forbids the collection of coral or sea shells anywhere in the country – report any violations in tourist or marine park areas to the Tourism Authority of Thailand (TAT) and the Royal Forest Department, or in other places to the Wildlife Fund Thailand (WFT).

One of the difficulties in dealing with rubbish and sewage problems in tourist areas is that many Thais don't understand why tourists expect different methods of disposal than are used elsewhere in the country. In urban areas and populated rural areas throughout Thailand, piles of rotting rubbish and open sewage lines are frequently the norm – after all, Thailand is still a 'developing' country.

Thais sensitive to Western paternalism are quick to point out that on a global scale the so-called 'developed' countries contribute far more environmental damage than does Thailand (eg, per capita greenhouse emissions for Australia, Canada and the USA average over five tonnes each while Asean countries on average contribute less than 0.5 tonnes per capita).

Hence, in making complaints or suggestions to Thais employed in the tourist industry, it's important to emphasise that you want to work *with* them rather than against them in improving environmental standards.

Whether on land or at sea, refrain from purchasing or accepting drinking water offered in plastic bottles wherever possible. When there's a choice, request glass water bottles, which are recyclable in Thailand. The deposit is refundable when you return the bottle to any vendor who sells drinking water in glass bottles.

For those occasions where only water in plastic bottles is available, you might consider transferring the contents to your own reusable water container, if the vendor or source of the plastic bottle is a more suitable disposal point than your eventual destination. If not, take the bottle with you and dispose of it at a legitimate rubbish collection site.

A few guesthouses are now offering drinking water from large, reusable plastic water containers. This service is available in most areas of Thailand (even relatively remote areas like Ko Chang). Encourage hotel and guesthouse staff to switch from disposable plastic to either glass or reusable plastic.

In outdoor areas where rubbish has accumulated, consider organising an impromptu cleanup crew to collect plastic, styrofoam and other nonbiodegradables for delivery to a regular rubbish pick-up point.

By expressing your desire to use environmentally friendly materials – and by taking direct action to avoid the use and

Small waterfall just outside Chiang Mai

Inhabitants of Wang Suan Phakkat, Bangkok

PHILLIP GAME

Macaque, Khao Chong Krajok, Central Thailand

NICHOLAS REUSS

Cooling lotus blooms add colour to a pond.

PAUL DYMOND

FRANK CARTER

Elephant trekking around Chiang Mai Province

A jungle cascade in Than Bokkharani National Park, Krabi Province

indiscriminate disposal of plastic – you can provide an example of environmental consciousness not only for the Thais but for other international visitors.

Visitors should consider filing letters of complaint regarding any questionable environmental practices with the TAT, WFT and the Royal Forest Department (the addresses for which are following). Municipal markets selling endangered species, such as Bangkok's Chatuchak Market, should also be duly noted – consider enclosing photos to support your complaints. For a list of endangered species in Thailand, contact the WFT.

Write to the following organisations to offer your support for stricter environmental policies or to air specific complaints or suggestions:

Asian Society for Environmental Protection (☎ 02-524 5363) c/o CDG-SEAPO, Asian Institute of Technology, Bangkok 10501
Bird Conservation Society of Thailand 69/12 Ramintra Soi 24, Jarakhe-Bua, Lat Phrao, Bangkok 10230
Friends of Nature 670/437 Thanon Charansanitwong, Bangkok 10700
Magic Eyes 15th floor, Bangkok Bank Bldg, 333 Thanon Silom, Bangkok 10400
Network for Environmentally- & Socially-Sustainable Tourism Thailand (NESSThai; e beartai@bkk.loxinfo.co.th) PO Box 48, Krabi
Office of the National Environment Board 60/1 Soi Prachasamphan 4, Thanon Rama IV, Bangkok 10400
Project for Ecological Recovery 77/3 Soi Nomjit, Thanon Naret, Bangkok 10500
Raindrop Association 105–107 Thanon Ban Pho, Thapthiang, Trang 92000
Royal Forest Department 61 Thanon Phahonyothin, Bangkhen, Bangkok 10900
Siam Environmental Club Chulalongkorn University, Thanon Phayathai, Bangkok 10330
The Siam Society 131 Soi Asoke, Thanon Sukhumvit, Bangkok 10110
Tourism Authority of Thailand (TAT) 202 Thanon Ratchadaphisek, Huay Khwang, Bangkok 10310.
Wildlife Fund Thailand (WFT; ☎ 02-521 3435, fax 552 6083, e pisitnp@mozart .inet.co.th) 251/88–90 Thanon Phahonyothin, Bangkhen, Bangkok 10220
World Wide Fund for Nature (Thailand; ☎ 02-524 6128, e wwfcomms@ait.ac.th) WWF Program Office, Asian Institute of Technology, PO Box 4, Klong Luang, Pathum Thani 12120; Web site: www.wwfthai.ait.ac.th

FLORA & FAUNA

Unique in the region because its north-south axis extends some 1800km from mainland to peninsular South-East Asia, Thailand provides potential habitats for an astounding variety of flora and fauna.

Flora

As in the rest of tropical Asia, most indigenous vegetation in Thailand is associated with two basic types of tropical forest: monsoon forest (with a distinct dry season of three months or more) and rainforest (where rain falls more than nine months per year). Natural forest area – defined as having crowns of trees covering over 20% of the land – covers about 25% of Thailand's land mass. According to the UN World Development Report, Thailand ranks 44th in natural forest cover worldwide (ahead of Cambodia but behind Laos regionally, and tied with Mexico on a global scale).

Forest cover varies by region; according to the forestry department's most recent statistics, Northern Thailand is 43% forested, Central Thailand 23%, eastern Thailand 20%, southern Thailand 17% and North-Eastern Thailand 12%. The most heavily forested province is Chiang Mai, followed by Kanchanaburi.

Monsoon forests amount to about a quarter of all natural forest cover in the country; they are marked by deciduous tree varieties, which shed their leaves during the dry season to conserve water. About half of all forest cover consists of rainforests, which are typically evergreen. Northern, eastern, North-Eastern and Central Thailand contain monsoon forests mainly, while southern Thailand is predominantly a rainforest zone. There is much overlap of the two – some forest zones support a mix of monsoon forest and rainforest vegetation. The remaining quarter of the country's forest cover consists of freshwater swamp forests in the delta regions; forested crags amid the karst topography of both the North and South; mangroves in the South; and pine forests at higher altitudes in the North.

The country's most famous flora includes an incredible array of fruit trees, bamboo (more species than any country outside China), tropical hardwoods and over 27,000 flowering species, including Thailand's national floral symbol, the orchid.

Fauna

As with plant life, variation in the animal kingdom closely affiliates with geographic and climatic differences. Hence, the indigenous fauna of Thailand's northern half is mostly of Indochinese origin while that of the South is generally Sundaic (ie, typical of Peninsular Malaysia, Sumatra, Borneo and Java). The invisible dividing line between the two zoogeographical zones is across the Isthmus of Kra, about halfway down the southern peninsula. The large overlap area between zoogeographical and vegetative zones – from around Prachuap Khiri Khan on the southern peninsula to Uthai Thani in the lower north – means that much of Thailand is a potential habitat for plants and animals from both zones.

Thailand is particularly rich in bird life, with over 1000 recorded resident and migrating species – approximately 10% of the world's bird species. Coastal and inland waterways of the southern peninsula are especially important habitats for South-East Asian waterfowl. Loss of habitat due to human intervention remains the greatest threat to bird survival in Thailand; shrimp farms along the coast are robbing waterfowl of their rich intertidal diets, while in the South the over-harvesting of swiftlet nests for bird's nest soup may threaten the continued survival of the nests' creators.

Indigenous mammals, mostly found in dwindling numbers within Thailand's national parks or wildlife sanctuaries, include tigers, leopards, elephants, Asiatic black bears, Malayan sun bears, gaur (Indian bison), banteng (wild cattle), serow (an Asiatic goat-antelope), sambar deer, barking deer, mouse deer, pangolin, gibbons, macaques, tapir, dolphins and dugongs (sea cows). Forty of Thailand's 300 mammal species, including clouded leopard, Malayan tapir, tiger, Irrawaddy dolphin, goral, jungle cat, dusky langur and pileated gibbon, are on the International Union for Conservation of Nature (IUCN) list of endangered species.

Species of herpetofauna in Thailand number around 313 reptiles and 107 amphibians, and include four sea-turtle species along with numerous snake varieties, of which six are venomous: the common cobra (six subspecies), king cobra (hamadryad), banded krait (three species), Malayan viper, green viper and Russell's pit viper. Although the relatively rare king cobra can reach up to 6m in length, the nation's largest snake is the reticulated python, which can reach a whopping 10m. The country's many lizard species include two commonly seen in homes and older hotels or guesthouses, the *túk-kae* (a large gecko) and the *jîng-jòk* (a smaller house lizard); as well as larger species like the black jungle monitor.

Insect species number some 6000, and the country's rich marine environment counts tens of thousands of species.

National Parks, Reserves & Wildlife Sanctuaries

Despite Thailand's rich diversity of flora and fauna, it has only been in recent years that most of the 80 national parks (only 50 of which receive an annual budget), 122 'nonhunting areas' and wildlife sanctuaries, 57 botanical gardens and arboretums and 1220 forest reserves have been established. Eighteen of the national parks are marine parks that protect coastal, insular and open-sea areas. Together these cover 13% of the country's land and sea area, which is one of the highest ratios of protected to unprotected areas of any nation in the world.

A system of wildlife sanctuaries was first provided for in the Wild Animals Reservation and Protection Act of 1960, followed by the National Parks Act of 1961 which established the kingdom's national park program with the setting up of Khao Yai National Park. The majority of the parks, reserves and sanctuaries are well maintained by the Royal Forest Department, but a few have allowed rampant tourism to threaten the natural environment. Poaching, illegal logging and shifting cultivation have also taken their toll on protected lands, but since 1990 the government has been cracking down with some success.

Most of the national parks are easily accessible, yet only around 5% of the average annual number of visitors is non-Thai. Most parks charge a fee to visit (typically 20B for Thais, 200B for foreigners) and there is usually somewhere to stay for a reasonable cost. For more information on staying in national parks, see Accommodation in the Facts for the Visitor chapter.

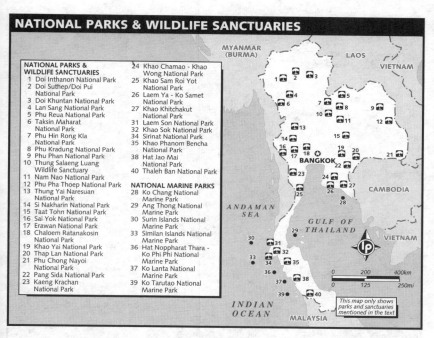

NATIONAL PARKS & WILDLIFE SANCTUARIES

NATIONAL PARKS & WILDLIFE SANCTUARIES
1 Doi Inthanon National Park
2 Doi Suthep/Doi Pui National Park
3 Doi Khuntan National Park
4 Lan Sang National Park
5 Phu Reua National Park
6 Taksin Maharat National Park
7 Phu Hin Rong Kla National Park
8 Phu Kradung National Park
9 Phu Phan National Park
10 Thung Salaeng Luang Wildlife Sanctuary
11 Nam Nao National Park
12 Phu Pha Thoep National Park
13 Thung Yai Naresuan National Park
14 Si Nakharin National Park
15 Taat Tohn National Park
16 Sai Yok National Park
17 Erawan National Park
18 Chaloem Ratanakosin National Park
19 Khao Yai National Park
20 Thap Lan National Park
21 Phu Chong Nayoi National Park
22 Pang Sida National Park
23 Kaeng Krachan National Park

24 Khao Chamao - Khao Wong National Park
25 Khao Sam Roi Yot National Park
26 Laem Ya - Ko Samet National Park
27 Khao Khitchakut National Park
31 Laem Son National Park
32 Khao Sok National Park
34 Sirinat National Park
35 Khao Phanom Bencha National Park
38 Hat Jao Mai National Park
40 Thaleh Ban National Park

NATIONAL MARINE PARKS
28 Ko Chang National Marine Park
29 Ang Thong National Marine Park
30 Surin Islands National Marine Park
33 Similan Islands National Marine Park
36 Hat Nopphrat Thara - Ko Phi Phi National Marine Park
37 Ko Lanta National Marine Park
39 Ko Tarutao National Marine Park

This map only shows parks and sanctuaries mentioned in the text

For a true appreciation of Thailand's geography and natural history, a visit to at least one national park is a must. In Bangkok the reservations office is at the Royal Forest Department's national parks division (☎ 02-561 4292), Thanon Phahonyothin, Bangkhen (north Bangkok). Any bookings from Bangkok must be paid in advance.

GOVERNMENT & POLITICS

Thailand (officially 'Kingdom of Thailand') has been an independent nation since AD 1238, and is the only country in South or South-East Asia never colonised by a foreign power.

Since 1932, the government of Thailand has nominally been a constitutional monarchy inspired by the British model but with a myriad of subtle differences. National polls elect the 500-member lower house (Sapha Phu Thaen Ratsadon or House of Representatives, with four-year terms) and prime minister; until recently the 200 senators of the upper house (Wuthisapha or Senate, six-year terms) were appointed by the prime minister. In Thailand the Senate is not as powerful as the House of Representatives; the latter legislates, while the Senate votes on constitutional changes.

Ten political parties field candidates in national elections, but four receive the bulk of the votes: the Democrat, New Aspiration, National Development and Thai Nation Parties.

The king appoints all judges who sit on Thailand's supreme court (*săan diikaa*).

1997 Constitution

On 27 September 1997, the Thai parliament voted in a new charter, Thailand's 16th such document since 1932 and the first to be decreed by a civilian government. Known as the *rátthammánuun pràchaachon,* or people's constitution, it puts mechanisms in place to monitor the conduct of elected officials and political candidates and to protect civil rights. In many ways the new charter constitutes a bloodless popular revolution, as pro-democracy groups had been fighting for more than 10 years to reform the constitution.

The document makes voting in elections compulsory, allows public access to information from state agencies, provides free

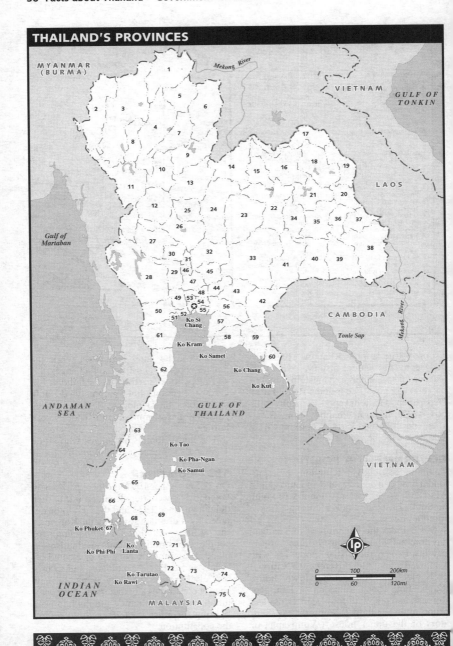

THAILAND'S PROVINCES

THAILAND'S PROVINCES

1	Chiang Rai	27	Uthai Thani	53	Nonthaburi
2	Mae Hong Son	28	Kanchanaburi	54	Bangkok
3	Chiang Mai	29	Suphanburi	55	Samut Prakan
4	Lampang	30	Chai Nat	56	Chachoengsao
5	Phayao	31	Singburi	57	Chonburi
6	Nan	32	Lopburi	58	Rayong
7	Phrae	33	Nakhon Ratchasima	59	Chanthaburi
8	Lamphun	34	Mahasarakham	60	Trat
9	Utaradit	35	Roi Et	61	Phetchaburi
10	Sukhothai	36	Yasothon		(Phetburi)
11	Tak	37	Amnat Charoen	62	Prachuap Khiri Khan
12	Kamphaeng Phet	38	Ubon Ratchathani	63	Chumphon
13	Phitsanulok	39	Si Saket	64	Ranong
14	Loei	40	Surin	65	Surat Thani
15	Nong Bualamphu	41	Buriram	66	Phang-Nga
16	Udon Thani	42	Sa Kaew	67	Phuket
17	Nong Khai	43	Prachinburi	68	Krabi
18	Sakon Nakhon	44	Nakhon Nayok	69	Nakhon Si
19	Nakhon Phanom	45	Saraburi		Thammarat
20	Mukdahan	46	Ang Thong	70	Trang
21	Kalasin	47	Ayuthaya	71	Phattalung
22	Khon Kaen	48	Pathum Thani	72	Satun
23	Chaiyaphum	49	Nakhon Pathom	73	Songkhla
24	Phetchabun	50	Ratchaburi	74	Pattani
25	Phichit	51	Samut Songkhram	75	Yala
26	Nakhon Sawan	52	Samut Sakhon	76	Narathiwat

public education for 12 years, permits communities to manage, maintain, and use local natural resources and forces parliament to consider new laws upon receipt of 50,000 or more signatures in a public referendum. It also establishes several watchdog entities, including the constitution court, administrative court, national anti-corruption commission, national election commission, human rights commission and parliamentary ombudsmen to support the enforcement of the constitution. Other amendments include: Election candidates must hold at least a bachelor's degree, and any legislators who become prime minister or members of the premier's cabinet must relinquish their MP status.

As the pro-democracy newspaper *The Nation* pointed out when the new charter was passed, the document is not a panacea but merely the start of a political reform process. Much depends on the will of Thailand's political legislators to see that the charter guides new legislation and that such legislation is enforced.

Administrative Divisions

For administrative purposes, Thailand is divided into 76 *jangwàt* (provinces). Each province is subdivided further into *amphoe* (districts), which are then subdivided into *kìng-amphoe* (subdistricts), *tambon* (communes or groups of villages), *mùu bâan* (villages), *sùkhǎaphíbaan* (sanitation districts) and *thêtsàbaan* (municipalities). Urban areas with more than 50,000 inhabitants and a population density of over 3000 per sq km are designated *nákhon;* those with populations of 10,000 to 50,000 with not less than 3000 per sq km are *meuang* ('muang' on Roman-script highway signs). The term 'meuang' is also used loosely to mean metropolitan area (as opposed to an area within strict municipal limits).

A provincial capital is an *amphoe meuang*. An amphoe meuang takes the same name as the province of which it is capital, eg, amphoe meuang Chiang Mai (often abbreviated as 'meuang Chiang Mai') means the city of Chiang Mai, capital of Chiang Mai Province.

Except for Krungthep Mahanakhon (Metropolitan Bangkok), provincial governors *(phûu wâa râatchákaan)* are appointed to their four-year terms by the Ministry of the Interior – a system that leaves much potential for corruption. Bangkok's governor and provincial assembly were elected for the first time in November 1985, when Chamlong Srimuang, a strict Buddhist and a former major general, won by a landslide.

The mid-2000 elections saw tough-talking, 10-time former MP Samak Sundaravej take over as Bangkok governor.

District officers *(nai amphoe)* are also appointed by the Ministry of the Interior but are responsible to their provincial governors. The cities are headed by elected mayors *(naayók thêtsàmontrii),* tambon by elected commune heads *(kamnan)* and villages by elected village chiefs *(phûu yài bâan).*

Armed Forces & Police

Thailand spends just 1.3% of its GDP on defence in a typical year. Armed services include the Royal Thai Army (around three million troops), Royal Thai Air Force (40,000) and Royal Thai Navy (45,000) under the Ministry of Defence, as well as the Royal Thai Police (122,000) under the Ministry of the Interior. The latter department is divided into provincial police, metropolitan police, border patrol police and the central investigation bureau. The central bureau includes railway, marine, highway and forestry police along with special branches concerned with trans-provincial crime and national security issues. Police corruption is common; recruits earn just US$150 a month on salary, so many take 'tea money' whenever they can.

Ever since the 1932 revolution, and particularly following WWII, the Thai military has had a substantial influence on the nation's political affairs. Since the constitutional monarchy was established in 1932, generals have commanded the premiership for 46 out of 68 years. Anand Panyarachun, who was the interim premier for two short terms in 1991 and 1992, was able to diminish the military's power considerably when he revoked a 14-year-old ministerial order that gave the supreme commander powers as 'internal peace-keeping director'. At the same time he disbanded the Capital Security Command, an organ that was instrumental in the May 1992 bloodbath. This effectively dissolved all legal and physical structures introduced after the infamous October 1976 coup, including the special command and task forces, which had allowed the use of military forces for internal peace-keeping since that time. Such task forces have not been the military's only source of political ascendancy. High-ranking officers have traditionally held key positions in the shipping, public transport and telecommunications industries as well, thus forming a powerful partnership with big business. Another of Anand's accomplishments was the ousting of military brass from executive posts at the Telephone Organization of Thailand and Thai Airways International.

Following the events of 1991–92, even the generals were admitting that the role of the military had to be reduced. In 1992 General Vimol Wongwanich of the State Railway of Thailand voluntarily resigned his board chairmanship to assume his new position as commander-in-chief – a move that would have been unheard of 20 years before. Vimol claimed he would depoliticise the army and declared the coup d'etat 'obsolete'. One of his first acts was to reshuffle key postings in the Thai armed forces in order to break up the antidemocratic Class 5 clique. Current conditions suggest that military coups are less likely to occur than at any time since 1932.

Monarchy

His Majesty Bhumibol Adulyadej (pronounced 'Phuumiphon Adunyadet') is the ninth king of the Chakri dynasty (founded 1782) and as of 1988 the longest-reigning king in Thai history. Born in the USA in 1927, where his father Prince Mahidol was studying medicine at Harvard University, and schooled in Bangkok and Switzerland, King Bhumibol was a nephew of Rama VII (King Prajadhipok) as well as the younger brother of Rama VIII (King Ananda Mahidol). His full name – including royal title – is Phrabatsomdet Boramintaramahaphumiphonadunyadet.

His Majesty ascended the throne in 1946 following the death of Rama VIII, who had reigned as king for only one year (see History earlier). In 1996 Thailand celebrated the king's 50th year of reign. His Majesty is the world's longest-reigning living monarch.

A jazz composer and saxophonist, King Bhumibol has had jam sessions with the likes of jazz greats Woody Herman and Benny Goodman, and his compositions (sounding like 1940s-style big band with bits of Thai melodic phrasing) are often played on Thai radio. He is fluent in English, French, German and Thai. His royal motorcade is occasionally seen passing along Thanon Ratchadamnoen in Bangkok's

Banglamphu district; the king is usually seated in a yellow vintage Rolls Royce or a 1950s Cadillac.

The king has his own privy council comprising up to 14 royal appointees who assist with the king's formal duties; the president of the privy council serves as interim regent until an heir is throned.

The king and Queen Sirikit have four children: Princess Ubol Ratana (born 1951), Crown Prince Maha Vajiralongkorn (1952), Princess Mahachakri Sirindhorn (1955) and Princess Chulabhorn (1957). A royal decree issued by King Trailok (reigned 1448–88) to standardise succession in a polygamous dynasty makes the king's senior son or full brother his *uparaja (ùpàrâat),* or heir apparent. Thus Prince Maha Vajiralongkorn was officially designated as crown prince and heir when he reached 20 years of age in 1972; if he were to decline the crown or be unable to ascend the throne due to incurable illness or death, the senior princess (Ubol Ratana) would be next in line.

Princess Ubol Ratana married American Peter Jensen in 1972 against palace wishes, thus forfeiting her royal rank, which was reinstated a few years ago. The crown prince has married twice, most recently to an ex-actress. She has fallen from grace and is no longer living in Thailand.

Thailand's political system is officially a constitutional monarchy, but the Thai constitution stipulates that the king be 'enthroned in a position of revered worship' and not be exposed 'to any sort of accusation or action'.

With or without legal writ, the vast majority of Thai citizens regard King Bhumibol as a sort of demigod, partly in deference to tradition but also because of his involvement in impressive public works.

Neither the constitution nor the monarchy's high status prevent Thai people from gossiping about the royal family in private, however. Gathered together, the various whisperings and speculations with regard to royal intrigue would make a fine medieval fable. Many Thais, for example, favour the Princess Sirindhorn for succession to the Thai throne, although none would say this publicly, nor would this popular sentiment appear in the Thai media.

Among the nation's soothsayers, it has long been prophesied that the Chakri dynasty will end with Rama IX; current political conditions, however would suggest the contrary. His Majesty's health has faltered in the last two years, and most Thais are preparing themselves for the transfer of kingship to Prince Maha Vajiralongkorn.

It is often repeated that the Thai king has no political power (by law his position is strictly titular and ceremonial) but in times of national political crisis, Thais have often looked to the king for leadership. Two attempted coups d'etat in the 1980s may have failed because they received tacit royal disapproval. By implication, the successful military coup of 1991 must have had palace approval, whether *post facto* or *a priori.*

The NPKC's 1991 draft constitution was widely condemned until just a few days before its final reading in the national assembly, when the king spoke out during his annual birthday address in favour of leaving the draft unchanged. Out of respect, the assembly passed the constitution in spite of antidemocratic clauses contained therein, even though it would have taken only a few days to revise the draft. This foot-dragging on the part of the government indirectly led to the violence six months later. The unamended constitution continued to be a source of friction between Thailand's political parties for five years. In 1997 the national assembly produced an amended charter reflecting the popular sentiment expressed in 1992; had the king not originally spoken against the amendments they may have been instituted sooner.

Along with nation and religion, the monarchy is very highly regarded in Thai society – negative comment about the king or any member of the royal family is a social as well as legal taboo. See the Society & Conduct section later in this chapter.

ECONOMY
An Almost Dragon

During the 1980s, Thailand maintained a steady GNP growth rate that by 1988 had reached 13% per annum. Thailand in the early and mid-1990s found itself on the threshold of attaining the exclusive rank of NIC (newly industrialised country). Soon, economic experts said, Thailand would be joining Asia's 'little dragons', also known as the Four Dragons or Tigers – Hong Kong, Singapore, South Korea and Taiwan – in becoming a leader in the Pacific Rim economic boom.

The Bubble Bursts

In mid-1997 the 20-year boom went bust throughout South-East and East Asia, with Thailand leading the way. The economies worst affected by the financial turmoil – Thailand, Indonesia, Malaysia, the Philippines and South Korea – displayed certain common pre-crisis characteristics, including wide current account deficits, lack of government transparency, high levels of external debt and relatively low foreign exchange reserves. For the most part the crisis stemmed from investor panic, with the rush to buy dollars to pay off debts creating a self-fulfilling collapse. Between 30 June and 31 October the baht depreciated roughly 40% against the US dollar, and dollar-backed external debt rose to 52.4% of the country's GDP. Such currency problems echoed the European currency crisis of 1992–93, when sudden, unforeseen drops in the pound, lira and other currencies sounded the death knell for a long period of steady growth and economic stability.

By January 1998 the Bank of Thailand stated that worsening economic conditions in the latter half of 1997 resulted in a doubling in the number of bad loans in the banking sector – about 18% of the total. Many banks and finance companies were forced to close in 1998, as the government made valiant efforts to restructure the economy and most especially the financial and property sectors. The International Monetary Fund (IMF) provided a US$17.2 billion rescue package in the form of short-term loans, with the stipulation that Thailand follow IMF's prescriptions for recapitalisation and restructuring.

Following the 1997 recession, the Thai economy shrank 10% in 1998, then grew 4% to 5% in 1999 and 2000. Exports in 1999 increased 13% over the previous year's while manufacturing rose 15%. This growth enabled Thailand to take an 'early exit' from the IMF's loan package in 2000.

By the end of 2000, the economy was healthier than at any time since 1996, according to independent analysts. Despite the IMF bail-out and Thailand's subsequent move out of its recessions, the Thais are living in an era of self-imposed austerity and relatively high unemployment (7.5%). Some observers have concluded that this forced cooling off is the best thing that could have happened to the overheated economy, giving the nation time to focus on infrastructure priorities and offering the Thai citizenry an opportunity to reassess cultural change.

The economic crisis has also precipitated a national discussion about Thailand's role in globalisation. Many Thais with a shallow understanding of the situation fallaciously believe that the IMF somehow forced this situation upon them. Many want to cut all ties with the IMF and World Bank. Some are calling for stronger tariffs on foreign goods. Others acknowledge that the reason Thailand fell into this recession in the first place was because so many middle- and upper-class Thais – not to mention banks – refused to practice any self discipline with regard to credit. As a recent *Bangkok Post* editorial pointed out, 'Developing nations may blame every ill on globalisation, but resistance only seems to widen the gulf between themselves and those who embrace it wholeheartedly.'

What tends to get lost in all the discussions of how bad the Thai economy has been since 1997 is a long-term assessment of the journey the nation has travelled over the last three decades. Along with Malaysia and South Korea, no other country in the world has produced more rapid economic growth or seen such a dramatic reduction in poverty during that period. Per capita income levels in Thailand increased 19-fold in Thailand between 1963 and 1997. Even accounting for the recent baht devaluation, this means most Thais today are economically better off than they were in the 1960s.

See Money in the Facts for the Visitor chapter for an account of the opportunities the baht devaluation has created for many foreign visitors.

The Big Picture

Around 14% of Thailand's exports are agricultural; the country ranks first in the world for rice (followed by the USA and Vietnam) and natural rubber, second in tapioca (after Brazil) and fifth in coconut (following Indonesia, the Philippines, India and Sri Lanka).

Other important agricultural exports include sugar, maize, pineapple, cotton, jute, green beans, soybeans and palm oil. Processed food and beverages – especially canned shrimp, tuna and pineapple – also account for significant export earnings. Thailand's top export markets include the USA, Japan and Singapore.

About 57% of the Thai labour force is engaged in agriculture, 17% in industry (including manufacturing), 15% in services and 11% in commerce. Manufactured goods have become an increasingly important source of foreign exchange revenue and now account for around 40% of Thailand's exports. Textiles, cement, electronics, petrochemical products and car and truck manufacture lead the way.

Thailand boasts the second-largest pick-up truck market in the world after the USA; several international truck manufacturers have established factories in the country – mostly along the eastern seaboard – including Ford, GM, Mazda, Mitsubishi and Toyota. The country also has substantial natural resources, including tin, petroleum and natural gas.

Since 1987, tourism has become a major earner of foreign exchange, occasionally outdistancing even Thailand's largest single export, textiles, with receipts as high as US$6 billion per annum. The Thai government's economic strategy remains focused, however, on export-led growth through the continued development of textiles and other light industries such as electronics, backed by rich reserves of natural resources and a large, inexpensive labour force. Observers predict that such a broad-based economy will continue to make Thailand a major economic competitor in Asia in the long term.

Raw average per capita income by 2000 was US$1949 per year; if measured using the purchasing power parity method (which takes into account the price differences between countries), annually the Thais average US$6020 per capita. With an average net escalation of 11.2% per annum between 1985 and 1995, Thailand ranked highest in Asia in terms of real GDP growth per employee during that decade. At the moment the economy is growing at a rate of 5.2% per annum.

The minimum daily wage in Bangkok and surrounding provinces, 162B (US$4.05), hasn't changed since 1996, although Thai legislators are currently lobbying to raise the figure to 180B. An estimated 20% of Thai citizens control over 60% of the wealth – most of these people are residents of either Bangkok or Phuket.

The incidence of poverty in Thailand (defined by the World Bank in concert with the Ministry of Public Health as falling below the level of income a person needs to buy a basket of food that will satisfy their daily nutritional requirements, along with necessary nonfood items) declined steadily from 30% in 1976 to 6.4% in the 1990s, but rose again after the 1997 economic crash, reaching 12.5% in 2000.

At the end of September 2000 the inflation rate was a low 2% per annum. As in most countries, prices continue to rise.

Regional Economies

Thailand's north-east has the lowest inflation rate and cost of living. This region is poorer than the rest of the country and doesn't get as much tourism; it therefore offers excellent value and is in need of your travel dollar. Hand-woven textiles and farming remain the primary means of livelihood, although Nakhon Ratchasima (Khorat) is an emerging centre for metals and the automotive industry.

In the South the economy is kept fairly stable with fishing, tin mining, palm-oil and rubber production. Tourism gives the South a seasonal boost.

Central Thailand grows fruit (especially pineapples), sugar cane and rice for export, and supports most of Thailand's continually expanding industry (textiles, cement and food processing).

Northern Thailand produces mountain or dry rice (as opposed to water rice, the bulk of the crop produced in Thailand) for domestic use, maize, tea, various fruits and flowers, and is very dependent on tourism. Teak and other lumber were once major products of the North, but since 1989 all logging has been banned in Thailand in order to prevent further deforestation. As in the North-East, many rural areas in the North are quite poor.

Indochina, Asean & Pacific Trade

Aside from its own export-oriented growth, Thailand stands to profit from increased international trade in Laos, Cambodia and Vietnam. At the moment Bangkok is the main launching base for foreign investment in Indochina, and the Thai baht is second only to the US dollar as the currency of choice for regional commerce. In Laos and Cambodia the only foreign banks are Thai; Vientiane and Phnom Penh have even built up portions of their national reserves in baht, thus forming a 'baht bloc'. Thailand continues to profit from the overland transport of international goods to Vietnam through Laos.

The Asean countries (Brunei, Indonesia, Malaysia, Philippines, Singapore, Thailand, Vietnam, Laos and Myanmar) make up the Asean Free Trade Area (AFTA), which is gradually reducing import tariffs and non-tariff barriers among Asean nations until total free trade is reached by 2008. This agreement should prove advantageous for the Thai economy as Thailand has a highly educated, inexpensive labour pool and a large manufacturing sector.

Thailand is also a member of the Asia-Pacific Economic Cooperation (APEC) bloc, which comprises the Asean countries plus Australia, Canada, Chile, China, Hong Kong, Japan, Mexico, New Zealand, Papua New Guinea, South Korea, Taiwan and the USA. APEC meets to discuss trade issues of mutual interest, occasionally agreeing to lower or eliminate trade barriers on specific products.

The kingdom's latest efforts for regional economic influence include plans for a 'southern growth triangle' that would link trade growth in Thailand's five most southern provinces with Malaysia and Indonesia, and a 'northern growth quadrangle' joining Northern Thailand, Yunnan Province in China, northern Laos and north-eastern Myanmar. For the latter plan, the Thai government is offering significant financial assistance for road development between the four countries, beginning with north-south highways connecting Yunnan and Northern Thailand via both Myanmar and Laos. Until the Thai economy gets back on track, however, both growth sectors sit on a back burner.

Tourism

According to statistics put together by the TAT, the country is currently averaging 8.5 million tourist arrivals per year, a nearly 70-fold increase since 1960 – the year the government first began keeping statistics. Historically the country's largest increase in tourism occurred in 1963, a year that saw a 49% increase in visitation over the previous

year, possibly encouraged by the arrival of foreign troops in Vietnam. Ten years later there was another sizable increase (+28% in 1972 and +26% in 1973) as the 'overland trail' from Amsterdam to Australia hit its peak. The country's most recent boom occurred from 1986 to 1990, when tourist arrivals increased by between 10% and 23% per annum.

The recent promotional campaign, called Amazing Thailand 1999/2000, was very well conceived, but the ailing economy truncated plans for a global front as the TAT's promotional budget was slashed in half. Economic trouble in East and South-East Asian countries lowered visitation from Thailand's most important tourist markets. Still, average per-person expenditures increased 8% between 1999 and 2000.

Despite budget cutbacks, the Amazing Thailand campaign has been a clear success, and the stated goal of a cumulative 16 million tourists for the next few years should easily be reached barring unforeseen world or regional events that might cause a reversal of fortune.

The biggest growth in tourism since 1990 has been among the Thais themselves. Spurred by steady economic growth in the 1980s and early 1990s, and by the general lack of funds for international travel in the present economic situation, an estimated 40 million Thais per year are now taking domestic leisure trips. Ten or 15 years ago Western tourists often outnumbered Thais at some of the nation's most famous tourist attractions. Now the opposite is true; except at major international beach destinations like Phuket and Ko Samui, Thai tourists tend to outnumber foreign tourists in most places at a rate of more than five to one.

POPULATION & PEOPLE

The population of Thailand is about 62 million and is currently growing at a rate of 1% to 1.5% per annum (as opposed to 2.5% in 1979), thanks to a vigorous nationwide family-planning campaign.

Over a third of all Thais live in urban areas. Bangkok is by far the largest city in the kingdom, with a population of around seven million (more than 10% of the total population) – too many for the scope of its public services and what little 'city planning' exists. Ranking the nation's other cities by population depends on whether you look at thêtsàbaan (municipal district) limits or at meuang (metropolitan district) limits. By the former measure, the four most-populated cities in descending order (not counting the densely populated 'suburb' provinces of Samut Prakan and Nonthaburi, which rank second and third if considered separately from Bangkok) are Nakhon Ratchasima (Khorat), Chiang Mai, Hat Yai and Khon Kaen. Using the rather misleading meuang measure, the ranking runs Udon Thani, Lopburi, Nakhon Ratchasima (Khorat) and Khon Kaen. Most of the other towns in Thailand have populations below 100,000.

The average life expectancy in Thailand is 69 years, the highest in mainland South-East Asia. Yet only an estimated 59% of all Thais have access to local health services; in this the nation ranks 75th worldwide, behind even countries with lower national incomes, such as Sudan and Guatemala. There is only one doctor per 4166 people, and infant mortality figures are 31 per 1000 births (figures for neighbouring countries vary from 110 per 1000 in Cambodia to 12 in Malaysia). Thailand has a relatively youthful population; only about 12% are older than 50 years and 6% over 65.

On the latest UN Human Development Index, Thailand receives an overall ranking of 69.5, slightly higher than the average (67.5) for 'medium human development' countries.

The Thai Majority

About 75% of citizens are ethnic Thais, who can be divided into the central Thais, or Siamese, of the Chao Phraya Delta (the most densely populated region of the country); the Thai Lao of North-Eastern Thailand; the Thai Pak Tai of southern Thailand; and the northern Thais. Each group speaks its own Thai dialect and to a certain extent practises customs unique to its region. Politically and economically the central Thais are the dominant group, although they barely outnumber the Thai Lao of the North-East.

Small minority groups who speak Thai dialects include the Lao Song (Phetchaburi and Ratchaburi), the Phuan (Chaiyaphum, Phetchaburi, Prachinburi), the Phu Thai

Buddhism has a pervading influence on Thai society. Here a woman offers incense at a *wát* in Bangkok.

(Sakon Nakhon, Nakhon Phanom, Mukdahan), the Shan (Mae Hong Son), the Thai Khorat or Suay (Khorat), the Thai Lü (Nan, Chiang Rai), the Thai-Malay (Satun, Trang, Krabi) and the Yaw (Nakhon Phanom, Sakon Nakhon).

The Chinese

People of Chinese ancestry make up 11% of the population, most of whom are second- or third-generation Hakka, Chao Zhou, Hainanese or Cantonese. In the North there are also a substantial number of Hui – Chinese Muslims who emigrated from Yunnan to Thailand in the late 19th century to avoid religious and ethnic persecution during the Qing dynasty.

Ethnic Chinese probably enjoy better relations with the majority population here than in any other country in South-East Asia, due partly to historical reasons and partly to the traditional Thai tolerance of other cultures – although there was a brief spell of anti-Chinese sentiment during the reign of Rama VI (1910–25). Rama V used Chinese businesspeople to infiltrate European trading houses, a move that helped defeat European colonial designs. Wealthy Chinese also introduced their daughters to the royal court as consorts, developing royal connections and adding a Chinese bloodline that extends to the current king.

Minorities

The second-largest ethnic minority group living in Thailand is the Malays (3.5%), most of whom reside in the provinces of Songkhla, Yala, Pattani and Narathiwat. The remaining 10.5% of the population is divided among smaller non-Thai-speaking groups like the Vietnamese, Khmer, Mon, Semang (Sakai), Moken (*chao leh,* or sea gypsies), Htin, Mabri, Khamu and a variety of hill tribes.

A small number of Europeans and other non-Asians reside in Bangkok and the provinces – their total numbers aren't recorded since very few actually have official Thai immigrant status.

EDUCATION

The literacy rate in Thailand runs at 93.8%, which is one of the highest rates in mainland South-East Asia. In 1993 the government raised compulsory schooling from six to nine years, and in 1997 it decreed that all citizens were entitled to free public schooling for 12 years.

Although high value is placed on education as a way to achieve material success, the system itself tends to favour rote learning over independent thinking at most levels.

Thailand's public school system is organised around six years at the *pràthǒm* (primary) level beginning at age six, followed by six years of *mátháyom* (secondary) education and then the *ùdom* (tertiary) level. In reality less than nine years of formal education is the national norm.

The education statistics don't take into account the teaching provided by Buddhist monks at *wát* (temple-monasteries) in the remote rural areas of Thailand, where monastic schooling may be the only formal education available for the local children.

Private and international schools for the foreign and local elite are found in Bangkok and Chiang Mai, and to a lesser extent in the other large provincial cities. The country boasts 12 public and five private universities, as well as numerous trade schools and technical colleges.

A teaching certificate may be obtained after attending a two year, post-mátháyom program at one of the many teachers colleges scattered throughout the country. Two of Thailand's universities, Thammasat and Chulalongkorn, are considered to be among the top 50 universities in Asia.

ARTS

For information on Thai visual arts see the 'Fire in the Lotus' special section in the Bangkok chapter. Thai music is covered in the 'Music, Theatre & Dance' special section in this chapter.

Literature

Of all classical Thai literature, the *Ramakian* is the most pervasive and influential in Thai culture. The Indian source – the *Ramayana* – came to Thailand with the Khmers 900 years ago, first appearing as stone reliefs on Prasat Hin Phimai and other Angkor temples in the North-East. Eventually, however, the Thais developed their own version of the epic, which was first written down during the reign of Rama I. This version contained 60,000 stanzas and was about 25% longer than the Sanskrit original.

Although the main theme remains the same, the Thais embroidered the *Ramayana* by providing much more biographical detail on arch-villain Ravana (Dasakantha, called Thotsakan, or '10-necked' in the *Ramakian*) and his wife Montho. Hanuman the monkey-god differs substantially in the Thai version in so far as he is very flirtatious with females (in the Hindu version he follows a strict vow of chastity). One of the classic *Ramakian* reliefs at Bangkok's Wat Pho depicts Hanuman clasping a maiden's bared breast as if it were an apple.

Also passed on from Indian tradition are the many *jataka,* or life stories of the Buddha (*chaa-dòk* in Thai). Of the 547 jataka tales in the *Pali Tripitaka* (Buddhist canon) – each one chronicling a different past life – most appear in Thailand almost word-for-word as they were first written down in Sri Lanka.

A group of 50 'extra' stories, based on Thai folk tales of the time, were added by Pali scholars in Chiang Mai 300 to 400 years ago. The most popular jataka in Thailand is one of the Pali originals known as the *Mahajati* or *Mahavessantara (Maha Wetsandon),* the story of the Buddha's penultimate life. Interior murals in the *bòt* (ordination chapels) of Thai *wát* typically depict this jataka and nine others: Temiya, Mahajanaka, Suvannasama, Nemiraja, Mahosatha, Bhuridatta, Candakumara, Narada and Vidhura.

The 30,000-line *Phra Aphaimani,* composed by poet Sunthorn Phu in the late 18th century, is Thailand's most famous classical literary work. Like many of its epic predecessors around the world, it tells the story of an exiled prince who must complete an odyssey of love and war before returning to his kingdom in victory.

Poetry During the Ayuthaya period, Thailand developed a classical poetic tradition based on five types of verse – *chǎn, kàap, khlong, klawn* and *râi.* Each of these forms uses a complex set of strict rules to regulate metre, rhyming patterns and number of syllables. Although all of these poetic systems use the Thai language, chǎn and kàap are derived from Sanskrit verse forms from India, while khlong, klawn and rai are native forms. The Indian forms have all but disappeared from 20th-century use.

During the political upheavals of the 1970s, several Thai newspaper editors, most notably Kukrit Pramoj, composed lightly disguised political commentary in klawn verse. Modern Thai poets seldom use the classical forms, preferring to compose in blank verse or with song-style rhyming.

Modern Literature Thai wunderkind SP Somtow has written and published more titles in English than any other Thai writer. Born in Bangkok, educated at Eton and Cambridge, and now a commuter between two 'cities of angels' – Los Angeles and Bangkok – Somtow's prodigious output includes a string of well-reviewed science fiction/fantasy/horror stories, including *Moon Dance, Darker Angels* and *The Vampire's Beautiful Daughter.* He has also dabbled in avant-garde music (including a royal command ballet), cinema and theatre. The Somtow novel most evocative of Thailand and Thai culture is his 1995 *Jasmine Nights,* which also happens to be one of his most accessible reads. Following a 12-year-old Thai boy's friendship with an African-American boy near Bangkok in the 1960s, this semi-autobiographical work blends Thai, Greek and African myth, American Civil War lore and a dollop of magic realism into a seamless whole. Film rights for *Jasmine Nights* have been picked up by London's Spinfilm.

For a look at rural life in Thailand, the books of Pira Sudham are unparalleled. Sudham was born into a poor family in North-Eastern Thailand and has written *Siamese Drama, Monsoon Country* and *People of Esarn.* These books are not translations – Sudham writes in English in order to reach a worldwide audience. These fiction titles are fairly easy to find in Bangkok but can be difficult to find overseas.

In the Mirror is an excellent collection of translated modern Thai short stories from the 1960s and 1970s. The Siam Society's *Culture & Environment in Thailand* is a collection of scholarly papers by Thai and foreign authors delivered at a 1988 symposium that examined the relationship between Thai culture and the natural world; topics range from the oceanic origins of the Thai race, and nature motifs in Thai art, to attitudes that are evolving in Thailand towards the environment.

Siam in Crisis by Sulak Sivaraksa, one of Thailand's leading intellectuals, analyses modern Thai politics from Sulak's unique Buddhist-nationalist perspective. Sulak has written several other worthwhile titles on Thai culture that have been translated into English. Essays by this contrary and contradictory character posit an ideal that neither Thailand nor any other country will likely ever achieve, and his attempts to use Western-style academic argument to discredit Western thinking can alternately be exasperating and inspiring. Still, as a constant irritant to the Thai government in all things cultural (he refers to Thailand only as 'Siam', for example), he plays a major role in helping to define Thai national identity.

The Lioness in Bloom is an eye-opening collection of 11 short stories written by or about Thai women and translated by Susan Fulop Kepner.

Cinema

In 1922 film director Henry McRay came to Thailand to film the silent *Nang Sao Suwan,* which used Thai actors for all roles and was released in Thailand in 1923. The storyline followed the tribulations of a beautiful young Thai girl with too many suitors. However, no viewable print of this film appears to have survived. Silent films proved to be more popular than talkies right into the 1960s, and as late as 1969 Thai studios were producing up to 130 different silent films a year, all on colour 16mm stock. The usual practice for screening such films was to have live or recorded narrators on hand to accompany the projection.

In the 1970s and 1980s Thai film-production was limited almost entirely to cheap action or romance stories of low quality. The exceptions were a handful of films made for the international festival circuit, films that Thai audiences hardly ever saw or liked, and the occasional period epic of quality, such as *Khunseuk* (Warrior; 1952 and 1976) and *Luk Isan* (Child of the North-East; 1983).

Ironically the post-1997-recession years have seen a substantial leap in the quality of popular Thai cinema. *Fun Bar Karaoke*, a 1997 satire of Bangkok life in which the main characters are an ageing Thai playboy and his daughter, received critical acclaim for its realistic depiction of modern urban living mixed with sage humour. *Nang Nak*, based on a famous Thai ghost story in which a young pregnant woman (named Nak) and her baby die during childbirth, and later come back to haunt her husband, not only featured excellent acting and special effects, but brought out lots of interesting bits on Thai animism. The 1998 film became the largest-grossing film in Thai history, and is now available on video with English subtitles.

The hilarious 2000 film *Satri Lek* (Iron Women), based on the true story of a Lampang volleyball team made up almost entirely of transvestites and transsexuals who won a national (men's) volleyball championship, became Thai cinema's second-largest grossing film thus far. When *Satri Lek* was released in Bangkok, a print with English subtitles was screened at one local cinema, probably a first for any major Thai theatre release. Like *Nang Nak,* the film is available with English subtitles on video.

The next Thai movie likely to garner some international attention is *Queen Suriyothai,* which was scheduled for release at the end of 2000. In the making for nearly two years, this film narrates a well-known episode in Thai history in which a queen in the Ayuthaya court sacrifices her life in a battle against Burma to save her husband's life.

SOCIETY & CONDUCT
Traditional Culture

When outsiders speak of 'Thai culture' they're referring to a complex of behavioural modes rooted in the history of Thai migration throughout South-East Asia, with many commonalities shared by the Lao people of neighbouring Laos, the Shan of north-eastern Myanmar and the numerous tribal Thais found in isolated pockets from Dien Bien Phu (Vietnam), all the way to Assam (India). Nowhere are such norms more generalised than in Thailand, the largest of the Thai homelands.

Practically every ethnicity in Thailand, whether of Thai ancestry or not, has to a greater or lesser degree been assimilated into the Thai mainstream. Although Thailand is the most 'modernised' of the existing Thai (more precisely, Austro-Thai) societies, the cultural underpinnings are evident in virtually every facet of everyday life. Those aspects that might be deemed 'Westernisation' – eg, the wearing of trousers instead of a *phâakhamáa* (wrap-around), the presence of automobiles, cinemas and 7-Eleven stores – show how Thailand has adopted and adapted tools originating from elsewhere.

Such adaptations do not necessarily represent a cultural loss. Ekawit Na Talang, a scholar of Thai culture and head of the Thai government's National Culture Commission, defines culture as 'the system of thought and behaviour of a particular society – something which is dynamic and never static'. Talang and other world culture experts agree that it's paradoxical to try to protect a culture from foreign influences, as cultures cannot exist in a vacuum. Culture evolves naturally as outside influences undergo processes of naturalisation. From this perspective, trying to maintain a 'pure' culture eventually leads to its weakening of the culture. As Talang has theorised, 'Anything obsolete, people will reject and anything that has a relevant role in life, people will adopt and make it part of their culture'.

The Thais themselves don't really have a word that corresponds to the term 'culture'. The nearest equivalent, *wáthánátham,* emphasises fine arts and ceremonies over other aspects usually covered by the concept. So if you ask Thais to define their culture, they'll often talk about architecture, food, dance, festivals and the like. Religion –

obviously a big influence on culture as defined in the Western sense – is considered more or less separate from wáthánátham.

Nevertheless there are certain aspects of Thai society that virtually everyone recognises as 'Thai' cultural markers.

Sànùk

The Thai word sànùk means 'fun'. In Thailand anything worth doing – even work – should have an element of sànùk, otherwise it automatically becomes drudgery. This doesn't mean Thais don't want to work or strive, just that they tend to approach tasks with a sense of playfulness. Nothing condemns an activity more than the description mâi sànùk, 'not fun'. Sit down beside a rice field and watch workers planting, transplanting or harvesting rice some time while you're in Thailand. That it's back-breaking labour is obvious, but participants generally inject the activity with lots of sànùk – flirtation between the sexes, singing, trading insults and cracking jokes. The same goes in an office or a bank, or other white-collar work situation – at least when the office in question is predominantly Thai. (Businesses run by non-Thais don't necessarily exhibit sànùk.) The famous Thai smile comes partially out of this desire to make sànùk.

Face

Thais believe strongly in the concept of saving face, ie, avoiding confrontation and endeavouring not to embarrass yourself or other people (except when it's sànùk to do so). The ideal face-saver doesn't bring up negative topics in conversation, and when they notice stress in another's life, they usually won't say anything unless that person complains or asks for help. Laughing at minor accidents – like when someone trips and falls down – may seem callous to outsiders but it's really just an attempt to save face on behalf of the person undergoing the mishap. This is another source of the Thai smile – it's the best possible face for almost any situation.

Status & Obligation

All relationships in traditional Thai society – and virtually all relationships in the modern Thai milieu as well – are governed by connections between phûu yài ('big person' or senior) and phûu náwy ('little person' or junior). Phûu náwy are supposed to defer to phûu yài following simple lines of social rank defined by age, wealth, status and personal and political power. Examples of 'automatic' phûu yài status include adults (vs children), bosses (vs employees), elder classmates (vs younger classmates), elder siblings (vs younger siblings), teachers (vs pupils), military (vs civilian), Thai (vs non-Thai) and so on.

While this tendency towards social ranking is to some degree shared by many societies around the world, the Thai twist lies in the set of mutual obligations linking phûu yài to phûu náwy. Some sociologists have referred to this phenomenon as the 'patron-client relationship'. Phûu náwy are supposed to show a degree of obedience and respect (together these concepts are covered by the single Thai term kreng jai) towards phûu yài, but in return phûu yài are obligated to care for or 'sponsor' the phûu náwy they have frequent contact with. In such relationships phûu náwy can, for example, ask phûu yài for favours involving money or job access. Phûu yài reaffirm their rank by granting requests when possible; to refuse would be to risk a loss of face and status.

Age is a large determinant where other factors are absent or weak. In such cases the terms phîi (elder sibling) and náwng (younger sibling) apply more than phûu yài and phûu náwy, although the intertwined obligations remain the same. Even people unrelated by blood quickly establish who's phîi and who's náwng; this is why one of the first questions Thais ask new acquaintances is 'How old are you?'.

When dining, touring or entertaining, the phûu yài always picks up the tab; if a group is involved, the person with the most social rank pays the bill for everyone, even if it empties his or her wallet. For a phûu náwy to try and pay would risk loss of face. Money plays a large role in defining phûu yài status in most situations. A person who turned out to be successful in his or her post-school career would never think of allowing an ex-classmate of lesser success – even if they were once on an equal social footing – to pay the bill. Likewise a young, successful executive will pay an older person's way in spite of the age difference.

The implication is that whatever wealth you come into is to be shared – at least partially – with those less fortunate. This doesn't apply to strangers – the average Thai isn't big on charity – but always comes into play with friends and relatives.

Foreigners often feel offended when they encounter such phenomena as two-tiered pricing for hotels or sightseeing attractions – one price for Thais, another for foreigners. But this is just another expression of the traditional patron-client relationship. On the one hand foreigners who can afford to travel to Thailand from abroad are seen to have more wealth than Thai citizens (on average this is self-evident), hence they're expected to help subsidise Thais' enjoyment of these commodities. At the same time, paradoxically, the Thais feel they are due certain special privileges as nationals – what might be termed the 'home-town discount'. Another example: In a post office line, Thais get served first as part of their nature-given national privilege.

Comportment

Personal power (*baará-mii*, sometimes mistranslated as 'charisma') also has a bearing on one's social status, and can be gained by cleaving as close as possible to the ideal 'Thai' behaviour. 'Thai-ness' is first and foremost defined, as might be expected, by the ability to speak Thai. It doesn't matter which dialect, although southern Thai, with its Malay and Yawi influences, is slightly more suspect, mainly due to the South's association with the 'foreign' religion of Islam.

Other hallmarks of the Thai ideal, which has been heavily influenced by Thai Buddhism, include discretion in behaviour towards the opposite sex, modest dress, a neat and clean appearance, and modes of expression and comportment that value the quiet, subtle and indirect rather than the loud, obvious and direct.

The degree to which Thais can conform to these ideals matches the degree of respect they receive from most of their associates. Although high rank – based on age or civil, military or clerical roles – will exempt certain individuals from chastisement by their social 'inferiors', it doesn't exempt them from the way they are perceived by other Thais. This goes for foreigners as well, even though most first-time visitors can hardly be expected to speak idiomatic Thai. But if you do learn some Thai, and you do make an effort to respect Thai social ideals, you'll come closer to enjoying some of the perks awarded for Thai-ness.

Dos & Don'ts

Thais are tolerant of most kinds of behaviour as long as it doesn't insult the two sacred cows of monarchy and religion.

King & Country The monarchy is held in considerable respect in Thailand and visitors should be respectful too – avoid disparaging remarks about anyone in the royal family. One of Thailand's more outspoken intellectuals, Sulak Sivaraksa, was arrested in the early 1980s for lese-majesty because of a passing reference to the king's fondness for yachting (referring to His Majesty as 'the skipper'), and again in 1991 when he referred to the royal family as 'ordinary people'. Although on that occasion he received a royal pardon, later that year Sulak had to flee the country to avoid prosecution for alleged remarks at Thammasat University about the ruling military junta, with reference to the king (Sulak has since returned under a suspended sentence). The penalty for lese-majesty is seven years' imprisonment.

While it's OK to criticise the Thai government and even Thai culture openly, it's considered a grave insult to Thai nationhood as well as to the monarchy not to stand when you hear the national or royal anthems. Radio and TV stations in Thailand broadcast the national anthem daily at 8 am and 6 pm; in towns and villages (even in some Bangkok neighbourhoods) this can be heard over public loudspeakers in the streets. The Thais stop whatever they're doing to stand during the anthem (except in Bangkok where nobody can hear anything above the street noise) and visitors are expected to do likewise. The royal anthem is played just before films are shown in public cinemas; again, the audience always stands until it's over.

Religion Correct behaviour in temples entails several considerations, the most important of which is to dress neatly and to take your shoes off when you enter any building that contains a Buddha image. Buddha images are sacred objects, so don't pose in front of them for pictures and definitely do not clamber upon them.

Continued on page 56

Music, Theatre & Dance

JOHN BORTHWICK

JOE CUMMINGS

TAT

Title Page: Blowing up a storm – *khaen* player at the Phi Ta Khon festival, Loei Province. (Photograph by Joe Cummings)

Top: Fusion of old and new – a hill-tribe rock band, Northern Thailand

Middle: Isan jam session – khaen and hand drum

Bottom: Scene from the *Ramakian* dance drama performed in Phuket Province

MUSIC

JOE CUMMINGS

Throughout Thailand you'll find a wide variety of musical genres and styles, from the serene court music that accompanies classical dance-drama to the chest-thumping house music played at Bangkok's latest discos and dance venues. Even in the Buddhist monasteries throughout Thailand – where music is proscribed by the *vinaya*, or monastic discipline – the chanting of the monks exhibits musical qualities.

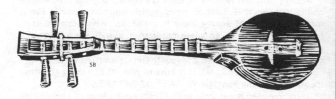

SB

Traditional Music

Classical central Thai music is spicy, like Thai food, and features an incredible array of textures and subtleties, hair-raising tempos and pastoral melodies.

The classical orchestra is called the *pìi-phâat* and can include as few as five players or more than 20. Among the more common instruments is the *pìi*, a woodwind instrument that has a reed mouthpiece; it is heard prominently at Thai boxing matches. The pìi is a relative of a similar Indian instrument, while the *phin*, a stringed instrument plucked like a guitar, is considered native to Thailand. A bowed instrument, similar to ones played in China and Japan, is aptly called the *saw*. The *ránâat èk* is a bamboo-keyed percussion instrument resembling the xylophone, while the *khlùi* is a wooden flute.

One of the more amazing Thai instruments is the *kháwng wong yài*, tuned gongs arranged in a semicircle. There are also several different kinds of drums, some played with the hands, some with sticks. The most important Thai percussion instrument is the *tà-phon* (or *thon*), a double-headed hand-drum that sets the tempo for the ensemble. Prior to a performance, the players make offerings of incense and flowers to the tà-phon, which is considered to be the 'conductor' of the music's spiritual content.

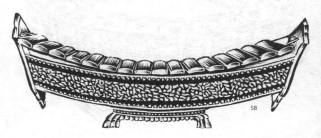

SB

Middle: The *phin* is distinctly Thai but its name has indian origins.

Right: The *ránâat èk*, a type of xylophone with bamboo keys.

The pìi-phâat ensemble was originally developed to accompany classical dance-drama and shadow theatre but can be heard in straight-forward performance these days, at temple fairs as well as concerts. One reason classical Thai music may sound strange to visitors is that it does not use the tempered scale. The standard Thai scale does feature an eight-note octave but it is arranged in seven full-tone intervals, with no semi-tones. Thai scales were first transcribed by Thai-German composer Peter Feit (Phra Chen Duriyanga), who also composed Thailand's national anthem in 1932.

In the North and North-East there are several popular reed instruments with multiple bamboo pipes, which function basically like a mouth-organ. Chief among these is the *khaen,* which originated in Laos; when played by an adept musician it sounds like a rhythmic, churning steam organ. The funky *lûuk thûng* style, which originated in the North-East, has become a favourite throughout Thailand.

If you're interested in learning how to play traditional Thai instruments, contact the Bangkok YMCA (☎ 02-287 1900).

Recommended books include *The Traditional Music of Thailand* by David Morton, and *Thai Music* by Phra Chen Duriyanga (Peter Feit).

Modern Music

Popular Thai music has borrowed much from Western music, particularly its instruments, but still retains a distinct flavour of its own. Although Bangkok bar bands can play fair imitations of everything from Hank Williams to Madonna, there is a growing preference among Thais for a blend of Thai and international styles.

The best example of this is Thailand's famous rock group Carabao. Recording and performing for over 20 years now, Carabao is by far the most popular musical group in Thailand and has even scored hits in Malaysia, Singapore, Indonesia and the Philippines with songs like *Made in Thailand* (the chorus is in English). This band and others have crafted an exciting fusion of Thai classical and lûuk thûng forms with heavy metal. These days almost every other Thai pop group sounds like a Carabao clone, and individual members of the original band are putting out their own albums using the now-classic Carabào sound.

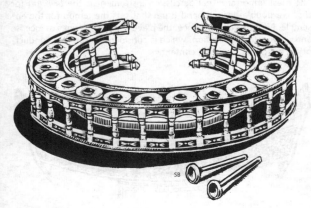

Left: The *kháwng wong yài* consists of tuned gongs arranged in a circular shape.

Another major influence on Thai pop was a 1970s group called Caravan, which created a modern Thai folk style known as *phleng phêua chii-wít* (songs for life). Songs of this nature have political and environmental topics rather than the usual love themes; during the authoritarian dictatorships of the 1970s many of Caravan's songs were officially banned. Though this band dissolved in the early 1980s, they re-form for the occasional live concert. The group's most gifted songwriter, Surachai, continues to record and release solo efforts.

Yet another inspiring movement in modern Thai music is the fusion of international jazz with Thai classical and folk motifs. The leading exponent of this newer genre is the composer and instrumentalist Tewan Sapsanyakorn (also known as Tong Tewan), whose performances use both Western and Thai instruments. The melodies of his compositions are often Thai-based but the improvisations and rhythms are drawn from sources such as Sonny Rollins. Tewan himself plays soprano and alto sax, violin and khlùi with equal virtuosity. When Tewan isn't touring internationally you may catch him and his extremely capable band Tewan Novel Jazz at various Bangkok clubs and occasionally elsewhere in Thailand.

Other groups fusing international jazz and indigenous Thai music include Kangsadarn and Boy Thai; the latter adds Brazilian samba to the mix. Thai instrumentation in world music settings are specialities of Todd Lavelle and Nupap Savantrachas, each of whom scored hits in Thailand during the late 1990s. Fong Nam, a Thai orchestra led by American composer Bruce Gaston, performs an inspiring blend of Western and Thai classical motifs.

Cassette tapes of Thai music are readily available throughout the country from department stores, cassette shops and street vendors. The average price for a Thai music cassette is 90B. Licensed Western music tapes cost 110B to 119B, a bargain by the pricing standards of most Western nations. Cheaper, bootlegged Western tapes cost about 35B each, but the days of pirated tapes in Thailand are numbered now that the US music industry is enforcing international copyright laws.

Music CDs are much more expensive, averaging 400B to 500B per disc for licensed versions, about 100B for pirated ones. Aside from being illegal, bootleg CDs vary highly in quality – some are fine, while some skip or won't play at all. For about 200B you can also buy CDs on which 12 to 15 full CDs have been compressed onto a single disc using MP3 technology. These can only be played on a computer CD drive or on a CD player that accepts MP3.

THEATRE & DANCE

Traditional Thai theatre consists of six dramatic forms: *khŏn*, formal masked dance-drama depicting scenes from the *Ramakian* (the Thai version of India's *Ramayana*) and originally performed only for the royal court; *lákhon*, a general term covering several types of dance-drama (usually for nonroyal occasions) as well as Western theatre; *lí-keh (likay)*, a partly improvised, often bawdy folk play featuring dancing, comedy, melodrama and music; *mánohraa*, the southern Thai equivalent of lí-keh, but based on a 2000-year-old Indian story; *năng*, or shadow plays, limited to southern Thailand; and *lákhon lék* or *hùn lŭang* – puppet theatre.

Naga Books' *Ramakian: The Thai Ramayana* (anonymous author) is a thorough exposition of the Thai version of Indian poet Valmiki's timeless epic.

Monkeys & Demons

Khŏn In all khŏn performances, four types of characters are represented – male humans, female humans, monkeys and demons. Monkey and demon figures are always masked with the elaborate head coverings often seen in tourist promo material. Behind the masks and make-up, all actors are male. Traditional khŏn is a very expensive production – Ravana's retinue alone (Ravana is the *Ramakian's* principal villain) consists of over 100 demons, each with a distinctive mask.

Perhaps because it was once limited to royal venues and hence never gained a popular following, the khŏn or *Ramakian* dance-drama tradition nearly died out in Thailand. Bangkok's National Theatre (☎ 02-224 1342) was once the only place where khŏn was regularly performed for the public; the renovated Chalermkrung Royal Theatre (☎ 02-222 0434) now hosts weekly khŏn performances enhanced by laser graphics and hi-tech audio.

Scenes performed in traditional khŏn (and lákhon performances – see later) come from the 'epic journey' tale of the *Ramayana*, with parallels in the Greek *Odyssey* and the myth of Jason and the Argonauts. The central story revolves around Prince Rama's search for his beloved Princess Sita, who has been abducted by the evil 10-headed demon Ravana and taken to the island of Lanka. Rama is assisted in his search and in the final battle against Ravana by a host of mythical half-animal, half-human characters including the monkey-god Hanuman. See the Literature section for some details on the differences between the Indian *Ramayana* and the Thai *Ramakian*.

Bottom: *Khŏn* performances feature masked figures and elaborately decorated costumes. This character from the *Ramakian* is Hanuman, the powerful and flirtatious monkey king.

SB

Drama Through Dance

Lákhon The more formal *lákhon nai* (inner lákhon, ie, performed inside the palace) was originally performed for lower nobility by all-female ensembles; today it's a dying art, even more so than royal khŏn. In addition to scenes from the *Ramakian*, lákhon nai performances may include traditional Thai folk tales; whatever the story, text is always sung.

Lákhon nâwk (outer lákhon, ie, performed outside the palace) deals exclusively with folk tales and features a mix of sung and spoken text, sometimes with improvisation. Both male and female performers are permitted. Like khŏn and lákhon nai, performances are becoming increasingly rare.

More common these days is the less refined *lákhon chaatrii*, a fast-paced, costumed dance-drama usually performed at upcountry temple festivals or at shrines (commissioned by a shrine devotee whose wish was granted by the shrine deity). Chaatrii stories have been influenced by the older mánohraa theatre of southern Thailand (see later).

A variation on chaatrii that has evolved specifically for shrine worship, *lákhon kâe bon*, involves an ensemble of around 20 members, including musicians. At an important shrine like Bangkok's Lak Meuang, four different kâe bon troupes may alternate performances, each for a week at a time, as each performance lasts from 9 am till 3 pm and there is usually a long list of worshippers waiting to hire them.

In *lákhon phûut* (speaking plays) all dialogue is spoken rather than sung. This is the most modern of Thailand's theatre traditions as well as the most popular in cities and larger towns.

Outrageous Costumes, Melodrama & Slapstick Comedy

Lí-keh In rural and small-town Thailand it is the gaudy and raucous theatre of lí-keh which pulls in the audiences. The art form is thought to have descended from drama-rituals brought to southern Thailand by Arab and Malay traders. The first native public performance in Central Thailand came about when a group of Thai Muslims staged a lí-keh for Rama V in Bangkok during the funeral commemoration of Queen Sunantha. Lí-keh grew very popular under Rama VI and has remained so ever since.

Most often performed at festivals by troupes of travelling performers, lí-keh presents a colourful mixture of folk and classical music, outrageous costumes, melodrama, slapstick comedy, sexual innuendo and up-to-date commentary on Thai politics and society – a bawdy counterpart to the more refined *Ramakian* performances seen in the palaces. *Fàràng* (westerners) – even those who speak fluent Thai – are often left behind by the highly idiomatic, culture-specific language and gestures. Most lí-keh performances begin with the *àwk khàek*, a prelude in which an actor dressed in Malay costume takes the stage to pay homage to the troupe's teacher and to narrate a brief summary of the play to the audience. For true lí-keh aficionados, the coming of a renowned troupe is a bigger occasion than the release of a new James Bond sequel at the local cinema.

Kidnappings & Rescues

Mánohraa Also known simply as *nora*, this is southern Thailand's equivalent to lí-keh and is the oldest surviving Thai dance-drama. The basic story line bears some similarities to the *Ramayana*. In this case the protagonist, Prince Suthon (Sudhana in Pali), sets off to rescue the kidnapped Mánohraa, a *kinnárii*, or woman-bird princess. As in lí-keh, performers add extemporaneous comic rhymed commentary – famed nora masters sometimes compete at local festivals to determine who's the best rapper.

Shadows & Shapes

Năng Shadow-puppet theatre – in which two-dimensional figures are manipulated between a cloth screen and a light source at night-time performances – has been a South-East Asian tradition for perhaps five centuries. Originally brought to the Malay Peninsula by Middle Eastern traders, the technique eventually spread to all parts of mainland and peninsular South-East Asia; in Thailand it is mostly found only in the south. As in Malaysia and Indonesia, shadow puppets in Thailand are carved from dried buffalo or cow hides (known as *năng* in Thai).

Two distinct shadow-play traditions survive in Thailand. The most common, *năng tàlung*, is named after Phattalung Province, where it developed around Malay models. Like their Malay-Indonesian counterparts, Thai shadow puppets represent an array of characters from classical and folk drama, principally the *Ramakian* and *Phra Aphaimani* in Thailand. A single puppetmaster manipulates the cutouts, which are bound to the ends of buffalo-horn handles. Năng tàlung is still occasionally seen at temple fairs in the south, mostly in Songkhla and Nakhon Si Thammarat Provinces. Performances are also held periodically for tour groups or visiting dignitaries from Bangkok.

The second tradition, *năng yài* (literally, big hide), uses much larger cutouts, each bound to two wooden poles held by a puppetmaster; several masters (almost always male) may participate in a single performance. Năng yài is rarely performed nowadays because of the lack of trained năng masters and the expense of the shadow puppets. Most năng yài that are made today are sold to interior designers or tourists; a well-crafted hide puppet may cost as much as 5000B.

In 1994, in order to celebrate the king's 50th year on the throne, the Fine Arts Department initiated a project to restore the original 180-year-old set of năng yài figures used by the Thai royal court. The project required the refurbishing of 352 puppets along with the creation of 100 new ones to complete the royal set, known as Phra Nakhon Wai (City-Shaking) – a tribute to the impact they had on audiences nearly two centuries ago. In addition to the occasional performance in Nakhon Si Thammarat or Bangkok, năng yài can be seen at Wat Khanon in Ratchaburi Province, where năng yài master Khru Chalat is passing the art along to younger men.

Bottom: Shadow puppets are made from cow or buffalo hide.

Royal Marionettes

Lákhon Lék Lákhon lék (little theatre; also known as *hùn lǔang*, or royal puppets), like khǒn, was once reserved for court performances. Metre-high marionettes made of *khòi* paper and wire, wearing elaborate costumes modelled on those of the khǒn, are used to convey similar themes, music and dance movements.

Two puppetmasters are required to manipulate each hùn lǔang – including arms, legs, hands, even fingers and eyes – by means of wires attached to long poles. Stories are drawn from Thai folk tales, particularly *Phra Aphaimani*, and occasionally from the *Ramakian*.

Hùn lǔang is no longer performed, as the performance techniques and puppet-making skills have been lost. The hùn lǔang puppets themselves are highly collectable; the Bangkok National Museum has only one example in its collection. Surviving examples of a smaller, 30cm court version called *hùn lék* (little puppets) are occasionally used in live performances; only one puppeteer is required for each marionette in hùn lék.

Another Thai puppet theatre, *hùn kràbàwk* (cylinder puppets), is based on popular Hainanese puppet shows. It uses 30cm hand puppets that are carved from wood, and they are viewed from the waist up. Hùn kràbàwk marionettes are still being crafted and used in performances to this day.

Continued from page 48

Shorts or sleeveless shirts are considered improper dress for both men and women when visiting temples. Thai citizens wearing either would be turned away by monastic authorities, but except for the most sacred temples in the country (eg, Wat Phra Kaew in Bangkok and Wat Phra That Doi Suthep near Chiang Mai), Thais are often too polite to refuse entry to improperly clad foreigners. Some wát will offer trousers or long sarongs for rent so that tourists dressed in shorts may enter the compound.

Monks are not supposed to touch or be touched by women. If a woman wants to hand something to a monk, the object should be placed within reach of the monk or on the monk's 'receiving cloth', not handed directly to him. When sitting in a religious edifice, keep your feet pointed away from any Buddha images. The usual way to do this is to sit in the 'mermaid' pose in which your legs are folded to the side, with the feet pointing backwards.

Some larger wát in Bangkok charge entry fees. In other temples, a small donation is appropriate. Usually donation boxes are near the entry of the bòt (central sanctuary) or next to the central Buddha image at the rear. In rural wát there may be no donation box available; in these places, it's OK to leave money on the floor next to the central image or even by the doorway, where temple attendants will collect it later.

Social Gestures & Attitudes Traditionally Thais greet each other with a prayer-like palms-together gesture known as a *wâi*. If someone wais you, you should wai back (unless wai-ed by a child or serviceperson). Most urban Thais are familiar with the international-style handshake and will offer the same to a foreigner, although a wai is always appreciated.

Thais are often addressed by their first name with the honorific *khun* or other title preceding it. Other formal terms of address include *nai* (Mr) and *naang* (Miss or Mrs). Friends often use nicknames or kinship terms like *phîi* (elder sibling), *náwng* (younger sibling), *mâe* (mother) or *lung* (uncle), depending on the age differential.

A smile and *sàwàt-dii khráp/khâ* (the all-purpose Thai greeting) goes a long way towards calming the initial trepidation that locals may feel upon seeing a foreigner, whether in the city or the countryside.

When handing things to other people you should use both hands or your right hand only, never the left hand (reserved for toilet ablutions). Books and other written materials are given a special status over other secular objects. Hence you shouldn't slide books or documents across a table or counter-top, and never place them on the floor – use a chair if table space isn't available.

When encounters take a turn for the worse, try to refrain from getting angry – it won't help matters, since losing your temper means a loss of face for everyone present. Remember that this is Asia, where keeping your cool is the paramount rule. Talking loudly is perceived as rude by cultured Thais, whatever the situation. See the earlier sections on Face and Comportment regarding the rewards for 'Thai-ness' – the pushy foreigner often gets served last.

Feet & Head The feet are the lowest part of the body (spiritually as well as physically) so don't point your feet or point at things with your feet. Don't prop your feet on chairs or tables while sitting. Never touch any part of someone else's body with your foot.

In the same context, the head is regarded as the highest part of the body, so don't touch Thais on the head – or ruffle their hair – either. If you touch someone's head accidentally, offer an immediate apology or you'll be perceived as very rude.

Don't sit on pillows meant for sleeping as this represents a variant of the taboo against head-touching. We once watched a young woman on Ko Samet bring a bed pillow from her bungalow to sit on while watching TV; the Thai staff got very upset and she didn't understand why.

Never step over someone, even on a crowded 3rd-class train where people are sitting or lying on the floor. Instead squeeze around them or ask them to move.

In rural areas and at temple fairs food is often eaten while seated on the floor; stepping over the food is a sure way to embarrass and offend your Thai hosts.

Dress & Nudity Shorts (except knee-length walking shorts), sleeveless shirts, tank tops (singlets) and other beach-style attire are not considered appropriate dress for anything other than sporting events. Such dress is especially counterproductive if worn to government offices (eg, when applying for a visa extension). The attitude of 'This is how I dress at home and no-one is going to stop me' gains nothing but contempt or disrespect from the Thais.

Sandals or slip-on shoes are OK for almost any but the most formal occasions. Short-sleeved shirts and blouses with capped sleeves likewise are quite acceptable.

Thais would never dream of going abroad and wearing dirty clothes, so they are often shocked to see westerners travelling around Thailand in clothes that apparently haven't been washed in weeks. If you keep up with your laundry you'll receive much better treatment everywhere you go.

Regardless of what the Thais may or may not have been accustomed to centuries ago, they are quite offended by public nudity today. Bathing nude at beaches in Thailand is illegal. If you are at a truly deserted beach and are sure no Thais may come along, there's nothing stopping you – however, at most beaches travellers should wear suitable attire. Likewise, topless bathing for females is frowned upon in most places except on heavily-touristed islands like Phuket, Samui and Samet. According to Thailand's National Parks Act, any woman who goes topless on a national park beach (eg, Ko Chang, Ko Phi Phi, Ko Samet) is breaking the law. Thais tend to see beach nudity as a sign of disrespect for the locals, rather than as a libertarian symbol or modern custom. Thais are extremely modest in this respect (Patpong-style go-go bars are cultural aberrations, hidden from public view and designed for foreign consumption) and it should not be the visitor's intention to 'reform' them.

Shoes Shoes are not worn inside people's homes, nor in some guesthouses and shops. If you see a pile of shoes at or near the entrance, you should respect the house custom and remove your shoes before entry. Several Thais have confided to us that they can't believe how oblivious some foreigners appear to be of this simple and obvious custom. To them wearing shoes indoors is disgusting and the behaviour of those who ignore the custom is nothing short of boorish.

Visiting Homes Thais can be very hospitable and it's not unusual to be invited home for a meal or a sociable drink. Even if your visit is very brief, you will be offered something to eat or drink, probably both – a glass of water, a cup of tea, a piece of fruit, a shot of rice liquor, or whatever they have on hand. You are expected to partake of whatever is offered, whether you're thirsty or hungry or not; to refuse at least a taste is considered impolite.

Upcountry When travelling in minority villages, try to find out what the local customs and taboos are, either by asking someone or by taking the time to observe local behaviour. Here are several other guidelines for minimising the impact you can have on local communities.

- Many tribes fear photography, so you should always ask permission – through hand gestures if necessary – before pointing your camera at tribespeople and/or their dwellings.
- Show respect for religious symbols and rituals. Avoid touching spirit houses, household altars, village totems and other religious symbols, as this often 'pollutes' them spiritually and may force the villagers to perform purification rituals after you have moved on. Keep your distance from ceremonies being performed unless you've been asked to participate.
- Do not enter a village house without the permission or invitation of its inhabitants.
- Practise restraint in giving things to tribespeople or bartering with them. Food and medicine are not necessarily appropriate gifts if they result in altering traditional dietary and healing practices. The same goes for clothing. If you want to give something to the people you encounter, the best thing is to make a donation to the village school or other community fund.

Treatment of Animals

Thailand is a signatory to the UN Convention on International Trade in Endangered Species (CITES). Educational levels have risen to the point that many international watchdog groups, such as the World Wide Fund for Nature and Wildlife Conservation Society, receive much local support. An illicit trade in endangered and threatened wildlife continues but appears to be much smaller than it was even 12 years ago.

In less developed rural regions of the country, particularly in the North and North-East, and among Thailand's hill tribes, hunting remains a norm for obtaining animal protein. Over-fishing of lakes, rivers and oceans poses a danger to certain fish species.

Harder to understand, at least for some of us, is the taking of monkeys, birds and other animals from the jungle to be kept as pets – usually tied by a rope or chain to a tree, or confined to cages. Several non-government organisations (NGOs), such as the Phuket Gibbon Rehabilitation Centre, are working to educate the public as to the cruelty of such practices, and have initiated wildlife rescue and rehabilitation projects.

In any case wildlife experts agree that the greatest danger faced by Thai fauna is neither hunting nor the illegal wildlife trade but rather habitat loss – as is true for most of the rest of the world. Protect the forests, mangroves, marshes and grasslands, and they will protect the animals.

For further comment on this topic, see the Ecology & Environment section earlier in this chapter.

Prostitution

Thais generally blame 19th-century Chinese immigrants for bringing prostitution to Thailand, but in reality Thailand was fertile ground because of its long-standing concubinary tradition, a legacy inherited from India. The first known literary references to this tradition were recorded by Chinese visitors in the early 1400s. Dutch merchants visiting Pattani in 1604 commented that 'when foreigners come there from other lands to do their business...men come and ask them whether they do not desire a woman' and that in Ayuthaya most of their peers 'had concubines or mistresses, in order (so they said) to avoid the common whores'. Seventeenth-century Ayuthaya, in fact, had an official Thai government office in charge of operating a corps of 600 concubines.

Until 1934 Siam had no laws forbidding polygamy – or even a word for this Judaeo-Christian concept. Most men of wealth counted among their retinue at least one *sŏh phenii* (from the Sanskrit term for a woman trained in the *Kamasutra* and other amorous arts), a word which has come to mean 'prostitute' but which was once better translated as 'courtesan'. In addition, the traditional Thai *mia yài mia nói* (major wife, minor wife) system made it socially permissible for a man to keep several mistresses – all

Thai kings up to Rama IV had *mia nói* (or *sànŏm,* as the royal version was called), as did virtually any Thai male who could afford them until recent times. Even today talk of mia nói hardly raises an eyebrow in Thailand as the tradition lives on among wealthy businessmen, *jâo phâw* (organised crime 'godfathers') and politicians.

The first brothel district in Thailand was established by Chinese immigrants in Bangkok's Sampeng Lane area in the mid-19th century. In the beginning, only Chinese women worked as prostitutes here; when Thai women became involved at the turn of the century, they usually took Chinese names. Prostitution eventually spread from Sampeng's 'green-lantern district' to Chinese neighbourhoods throughout Thailand and is now found in nearly every village, town and city in the kingdom. Ethnic Chinese still control most of the trade, although the prostitutes themselves now come from almost every ethnic background. In the last few years Bangkok has even seen an influx of Russian and Central Asian women – most on Tourist Visas – participating in the sex trade through escort services. Women from nearby countries, particularly Myanmar and China, have also found their way – both willingly and unwillingly – into the trade.

Prostitution wasn't declared illegal until the 1950s, when Field Marshal Phibul bullied his way into the prime minister's seat. The numbers of women working as commercial sex workers (CSWs) increased immediately after prohibition, and the percentage of those aged between 15 and 19 increased from 15% to 25%. In the 1960s and 1970s the Vietnam War brought unprecedented numbers of foreign soldiers to Bangkok and Pattaya on 'rest & recreation' tours, creating a new class of prostitutes who catered to foreigners rather than Thais.

Estimates of the number of Thai residents directly involved in offering sex services vary wildly, depending on the source. Chulalongkorn University's Population Institute, which has carried out intensive studies into the prostitution industry, puts forth a reasoned estimate of 200,000 to 220,000, a figure now widely considered the most realistic. Although often portrayed as Asia's sex capital, according to international human development reports Thailand actually ranks well behind Taiwan, the Philippines and

India (not to mention several Western countries) in per-capita number of sex workers.

Sociologists estimate that as many as 75% of post-puberty single Thai males engage the services of a prostitute at an average of two times a month. In highly urban Bangkok attitudes are changing steadily as non-paid extramarital sex is becoming increasingly common and hence the percentage of Thai clients is significantly lower than elsewhere in the country. Today the highest per-capita concentration of sex workers is found in the North. Brothels are less common in the southern provinces, except in Chinese-dominated Phuket, Hat Yai and Yala, and in Thai-Malaysian border towns, where the clientele is almost exclusively Malay.

Only an estimated 2.5% of all Thai CSWs work in bars and 1.3% in massage parlours. The remaining 96.2% work in 'cafes', barbershops and brothels only rarely patronised by non-Thai clients. In fact, most of the country's sex industry is invisible to the visiting foreigner and it is thought that Thai-to-non-Thai transactions represent less than 5% of the total. Unlike Western prostitution, there are few pimps in Thailand. Instead, a network of procurers/suppliers and brothel owners control the trade, taking a high proportion (or all) of the sex service fees. At its worst, the industry takes girls sold or indentured by their families, sometimes even kidnapped, and forces them to work in conditions of virtual slavery.

In the Patpong-style bar catering to foreigners, on the other hand, most bar girls and go-go dancers are freelance agents; they earn their income from taking a percentage of drinks bought on their behalf and from sex liaisons arranged outside the premises – usually after closing (if they leave during working hours, a customer usually pays a 'bar fine' on their behalf). The average Patpong type bar girl earns 6000B to 7000B per month directly from the bar she works in; fees for extracurricular services are negotiated between customer and prostitute and can run anywhere from 800B to 2000B per assignation – none of which goes to a controller.

Most CSWs are uneducated and come from village areas. Researchers estimate they have a maximum working life of 10 years, although the average is two years or less. Many women return to their villages – some with a nest egg for their families, others with nothing – where surprisingly they are often treated with a measure of respect. The ones that stay in the business long-term appear to suffer the most; if they haven't saved up enough money to retire, they're often unemployable due to mental and physical disabilities acquired during their working lives. Various Thai volunteer groups offer counselling to Thailand's sex workers – helping them to leave the industry or to educate them to the dangers of sexually transmitted infections (STIs), particularly AIDS. Thanks to such efforts, the latest surveys indicate that condom use among sex workers in Thailand averages 94%.

Legal Aspects Commercial sex generates a yearly revenue that amounts to nearly double the annual governmental budget – hence the economics of the industry are quite far-reaching and difficult to regulate. Officially prostitution remains illegal, but the government has been either powerless or unwilling to enforce most laws forbidding the trade ever since it was first outlawed. Largely due to international pressure, prime minister Chuan Leekpai ordered a crackdown on CSWs under 18 years of age in 1993, an act that has had quantifiable results but has by no means banished under-18s from the trade.

Under current Thai law, a jail term of four to 20 years and/or a fine of 200,000B to 400,000B can be imposed on anyone caught having sex with prostitutes under 15 years of age (the age of consent in Thailand). If the child is under 13, the sentence can amount to life imprisonment. Many Western countries have also instituted extra-territorial legislation whereby citizens can be charged for child prostitution offences committed abroad. The Thai government is encouraging people to assist in the eradication of child prostitution by reporting child sexual abuses to the relevant authorities. In this instance, travellers visiting Thailand can contact the tourist police or ECPAT International (☎ 02-215 3388, ℮ ecpatbkk@ksc15.th.com) at 328 Thanon Phayathai, Bangkok 10400.

Facts for the Visitor

SUGGESTED ITINERARIES
See the 'Thailand's Highlights' special section in this chapter for a listing and brief discussion of the country's more outstanding attractions.

With the exception of the upper southern peninsula from Phetchaburi to Surat Thani, Thailand's asymmetric shape doesn't lend itself to simple linear north-south or east-west routes. Depending on your interests and available time you might pick from the following circuits or combine parts of several to create your own travel route.

The standard Tourist Visa is valid for two months, although only a relatively small percentage of visitors stay that long. The 30 days granted to visitors from most countries who arrive without a visa usually suffices and can be extended by simply crossing the border into a neighbouring country and re-entering Thailand sometime the same day.

The following suggested itineraries assume you want to see as much of the country as possible within a given interval. Another approach is to spend more time in a few places rather than less time in many. Depending on your inclinations, you might decide to spend a full two weeks or even more just exploring the North. If you're into Isan (north-eastern) culture, a month spent in the towns and cities along the Mekong River could be very rewarding. And, of course, some people choose to hole up on a beach or island for their entire stay.

Most visitors begin their journey in Bangkok. Depending on how much time you have available, you might want to save your Bangkok explorations until after you've seen other parts of the country. That way Bangkok won't seem quite so overwhelming as on first arrival. You'll also understand more about the Thai character after travelling around the country, and in Bangkok it pays to be a good judge of character – in order to separate the touts from the genuinely friendly.

One Week
Temples & Gulf Beaches For a short Thailand sampler, start with a two-day taste of Bangkok's heavily gilded temples and urban intensity, then flee towards the former royal capital of Ayuthaya to take in the 400-year-old temple and palace ruins, right in the centre of the city. A day in Ayuthaya is enough for most people in a hurry. Transit back through Bangkok and head southeast to Ko Samet, off the eastern Gulf of Thailand coast, for two or three nights on this all-season island before saying farewell to Thailand. Substitute Hat Jomtien near Pattaya for Samet if your tastes run towards international-class hotels rather than simpler beach bungalows.

Floating Markets, River Kwai & Lopburi From Bangkok get an early morning start for one of the floating markets southwest of the city – Damnoen Saduak is the most well known but there are several others in the vicinity. Spend the night in Nakhon Pathom and take in the world's tallest Buddhist monument, Phra Pathom Chedi. Continue on to Kanchanaburi by bus or train to see the world-famous 'Bridge Over the River Kwai' and experience a fairly typical provincial Thai town. Return to Bangkok via Suphanburi and Lopburi, passing through the country's 'rice bowl' and stopping for a night in Lopburi to catch the Khmer and Thai temple ruins there.

Two Weeks
Northern Thailand After completing one of the one-week circuits, take an overnight train (or fly) to Chiang Mai. Shop till you flop at the Chiang Mai Night Bazaar, sample the excellent cuisine of Northern Thailand, and decide whether to move north-west to Mae Hong Son or north-east to Nan. Both areas have mountains and national parks that can be trekked, and hilltribe populations.

North-Eastern Thailand Start with one of the Central Thailand circuits, then take a train to Nakhon Ratchasima (Khorat) and visit the nearby Angkor-period ruins at Phimai. If you want to see more Khmer architectural splendour, make a short journey to the Phanom Rung Historical Park in Buriram Province.

Finish with a travel sector along the Mekong River – from Chiang Khan to Si Chiangmai if you prefer small towns and villages, or from Nakhon Phanom to Ubon Ratchathani if you like cities.

Bangkok to the Malaysian Border After you've had your fill of Bangkok (three or four days does the trick for most people who have two weeks to spend in the country) start your roll down the Malay Peninsula with a two-night, one-day stopover in Phetchaburi, a city of venerable late-Ayuthaya-period temples and a hill-top royal palace.

After Phetchaburi, take your pick of the beaches at Cha-am, Hua Hin or in the vicinity of Prachuap Khiri Khan – places where middle-class Thais vacation; and/or visit Khao Sam Roi Yot National Park, which is good for coastal and hillside hiking.

For serious beach time, zero in on one or more of the three major islands off the coast of Chumphon and Surat Thani provinces – Ko Tao, Ko Pha-Ngan and Ko Samui – depending on your tastes (see Islands & Beaches in the 'Thailand's Highlights' special section for descriptive summaries).

If you're ready for a little culture, sail back to the mainland and visit Chaiya (featuring Srivijaya-era ruins and a world-famous meditation monastery) or Songkhla (featuring Sino-Portuguese architecture and a national museum).

Follow with a night or two in Hat Yai to sample some of Thailand's best Chinese food outside Bangkok and to shop for southern Thai or Malay textiles. For your entry into Malaysia, take the east-coast route via Narathiwat for the best natural scenery, the west coast if you're in a rush to reach Penang or Kuala Lumpur.

One Month
Temples, Trekking & Beaches In a month you can sample many of Thailand's major highlights. Spend a few days in Bangkok (or leave the city for the end) then take a slow ride north with two-night stopovers in Lopburi, Phitsanulok and Sukhothai to take in some of Thailand's most historic temple architecture, ancient as well as modern. From the latter head south-west to Mae Sot, nestled in a zone of Karen and Burmese influence, and explore the less-than-beaten path – with waterfalls,

trekking, rafting, working elephants – stretching from Um Phang to Mae Sariang. Continue north from Mae Sariang along the Mae Hong Son loop to Tha Ton on the Mae Kok (Kok River), and either boat down the Kok to Chiang Rai or take a ride on a *sǎwngthǎew* (pick-up truck) through the mountains on the Myanmar border to the Yunnanese settlement of Mae Salong.

With roughly a week left in your itinerary, choose an island or beach along the upper Gulf of Thailand coast (Pattaya, Ko Samet, Ko Chang or Hua Hin) if you want to get there quickly via Bangkok, or pick from either the Andaman Coast (Phuket, Khao Lak, Krabi, Trang) or lower Gulf coast (Ko Samui, Ko Pha-Ngan, Ko Tao) if you don't mind a longer trip by air, road or rail. If you like your beaches untrammelled it might be worth the extra effort to visit one of the national marine parks off the Andaman Coast – Ko Tarutao, Ko Similan or Ko Surin.

If you have time while in the south, make a side trip to Khao Sok National Park, one of Thailand's most important refuges for tigers and rainforest.

North by North-East If beaches don't matter much to you, go for a major intake of culture and nature by starting with the Lopburi-to–Mae Salong route described earlier. From Mae Salong continue eastward to Nan and Phrae, two of the North's less-travelled provinces, then segue across to Loei Province for the Mekong River loop from Chiang Khan to Ubon.

If there's time at the end of the latter, head into the interior to visit Prasat Hin Phimai and Phanom Rung Historical Parks. The more adventurous can substitute a whirl along the Cambodian border from Ubon to Aranya Prathet via Surin and Si Saket – provinces that are home to a number of smaller and lesser-known Khmer temple sites. Or if you find that temple-trekking has paled by this point, go hiking in Khao Yai National Park, one of Thailand's largest and oldest protected areas.

Two Months
In two months you can combine two or three itineraries to link the best sights of southern, Northern, North-Eastern and Central Thailand.

PLANNING
When to Go
The best overall time vis-a-vis climate for visiting most of Thailand falls between November and March – during these months it rains least and is not so hot. Remember that temperatures are more even in the south, so the south makes a good refuge when the rest of Thailand is miserably hot (April to June). The North is best from mid-November to early December or in February when it begins warming up again. If you're spending time in Bangkok, be prepared to roast in April and do some flood-water wading in October – probably the two worst months, weather-wise, for visiting the capital.

The peak months for tourist visitation are August, November, December, February and March, with secondary peak months in January and July. You should consider travelling during the least crowded months (April, May, June, September and October) if your main objective is to avoid vacationers and to take advantage of discounted rooms and other low-season rates. On the other hand it's not difficult to leave the crowds behind, even during peak months, if you simply avoid some of the most popular destinations (eg, Chiang Mai and all islands and beaches).

Maps
Lonely Planet publishes the 1:1,000,000-scale *Thailand, Vietnam, Laos & Cambodia Road Atlas*. This atlas features over 80 pages of detailed maps, including close-ups of popular destinations and city maps. It has topographic shading, handy trip maps, distance charts and a complete geographic index. It was spot-checked on the ground for accuracy and currency by this author. The atlas is readily available for around US$9 at many Bangkok bookshops as well as overseas.

Periplus Travel Maps publishes a series of five folding sheet maps covering Thailand (one each on Thailand, Bangkok, Chiang Mai, Phuket and Ko Samui), all of which are more reliable than the average commercially available map.

Thailand's Highway Department issues a huge four-map set (although it's not 100% accurate). For around 150B you get very detailed, full-colour road maps of the central,

northern, north-eastern and southern regions. The 1:1,000,000-scale maps include information on 'roads not under control by the Highway Department' – many of the roads you may travel on in the North, for example. Bookshops sometimes sell this set for 250B, including a mailing tube, but the Highway Department, on Thanon Si Ayuthaya in Bangkok, offers the set at a lower price.

The Roads Association of Thailand publishes a good large-format, 48-page, bilingual road atlas called *Thailand Highway Map*. The atlas, which is updated every year, has cut the Highway Department maps to a more manageable size and includes dozens of city maps. It also gives driving distances and lots of travel and sightseeing information. It costs 120B, but beware of inferior knock-offs. A big advantage of the Thailand Highway Maps is that the town and city names are printed in Thai as well as Roman script.

The Lonely Planet atlas or the maps from either the Highway Department or Periplus are more than adequate for most people. Do-it-yourself trekkers, or anyone with a keen interest in geography, may find general survey sheet maps issued by the Thai military to be helpful. These maps are available in several scales, complete with elevations, contour lines, place names (in Thai and Roman script) and roadways. Most trekkers find the 1:250,000-scale maps, of which there are 52 separate sheets costing 60B each, perfectly adequate. Four (Mae Hong Son, Mae Chan, Tavoy and Salavan) of the 52 aren't available to the public because of ongoing border disputes with Myanmar and Laos – the Thai army doesn't want to be accused of propagating incorrect borders.

Even more detailed are the army's 1:50,000 maps (321 sheets at 70B each). The maps can be purchased at the Thai Army Map Department (Krom Phaen Thi Thahan; ☎ 02-222 8844), sometimes referred to as the Royal Survey Department, opposite the Interior Ministry on the western side of Thanon Ratchini in Ko Ratanakosin, very near Wat Ratchabophit. The entrance is on Thanon Kanlayana Maitri.

Continued on page 69

THAILAND'S HIGHLIGHTS

NICHOLAS REUSS

Thailand's travel scene has many faces and exploring all the country has to offer is a lifetime endeavour. Time and money constraints will compel most of us to decide – either in advance or as we go along – which parts we're going to see and which parts will have to be left out. In Thailand it usually pays to be a little under-ambitious with your travel plans; don't try to see too much in too short an interval or your travels may quickly become a chore.

Your recreational and aesthetic inclinations will largely determine the direction you take. The basic threads most visitors are interested in following include islands and beaches, historic temple architecture, trekking, handicrafts and performing arts. These travel aspects are not necessarily mutually exclusive, though it's hard to find one place that has them all! In Songkhla, for example, you'll find handicrafts and beaches, while many places in the North-East offer temple ruins and handicrafts.

One of the highlights of Thailand travel is soaking up the culture. You won't get much of it if you spend most of your time sitting around in guesthouse cafes or on the beach, or trekking with your own kind. At least once during your trip, try going to a small town well off the main tourist circuit, staying at a local hotel and eating in Thai curry shops and noodle stands. It's not as easy as going with the crowd but you'll learn a lot more about Thailand.

Islands & Beaches

Thailand's coastline boasts some of the finest islands and beaches in Asia.

Ko Chang This is an archipelago, with national marine park status in some areas, near the Cambodian border. The main island, Ko Chang, has coastal zones where development is permitted, but so far high-profile development has been kept at bay by its distance from Bangkok and its mountainous geography. It attracts those looking for quiet, economical beach stays and is accessible by boat only.

Ko Samet Only three hours from Bangkok by road and boat on the eastern gulf coast, this small island can be quite overrun on weekends and holidays. The fine white sand and clear blue waters attract a cross-section of expats, Thais and tourists. It is possible to snorkel at the nearby islets. Ko Samet is accessible by boat only.

Pattaya Golf, go-karting, parasailing, wave-running, sailboarding, high-style dining and a notorious nightlife attract those interested in an active, urbanised beach vacation on Thailand's eastern gulf coast. The bay is less than clean – nearby Jomtien is a bit better – though there is fair snorkelling and diving (including shipwrecks) at nearby islands.

Prachuap Khiri Khan This province along the upper Southern Gulf coast offers sandy beaches of medium quality along much of its length, from the well-touristed Hua Hin in the north to little-known Thai resorts near Ao Manao and Bang Saphan. There is not much in the way of diving, but the seafood is superb.

Ko Pha-Ngan Just north of Ko Samui in the gulf, this is the main backpackers' headquarters at the moment as the beach accommodation is the least expensive in the country; some more-upmarket places are emerging, too. There is good snorkelling and diving in some parts of the island, but very little in the way of nightlife except at Hat Rin on the south-eastern tip, which is famous for its full-moon parties. It is accessible by boat only.

Ko Samui Off the coast of Surat Thani, this is Thailand's third-largest island. It was once a haven for backpackers on the Asian trail, but now it's mainly given over to middle-class hotels and guesthouses. The snorkelling and diving is fair and the island is accessible by boat and air.

Ko Tao This small island north of Ko Pha-Ngan has the best diving in the area. Development here has outpaced Ko Pha-Ngan, for the most part due to the diving industry. It is accessible by boat only.

Ko Surin, Ko Similan & Ko Tarutao These Andaman Coast island groups are separate national marine parks that enjoy some of the best protection in Thailand (although not perfect by any means). The islands offer fantastic diving and snorkelling. Accommodation is limited to park bungalows and camping, except for one private island in Tarutao. They are accessible by boat only, and only during the non-monsoon months (November to April).

Phuket Off the Andaman Coast, this is Thailand's largest island and was the first to develop a tourist industry. Nowadays it has become a fairly sophisticated international resort destination, albeit one with the highest number of 'green' hotel developments as well as some highly regarded national parks. There is good diving at nearby islands and reefs and Ao Phang-Nga, and it offers the best Thai cuisine of any of the islands. It is accessible by air and road (via a causeway).

Krabi This province facing Ao Phang-Nga, opposite Phuket on the Andaman Coast, offers a range of beaches and islands ringed with striking limestone formations. Rock-climbing, snorkelling, diving, boating and beach camping are the main activities. It is generally quiet, though accommodation tends to book out from December to February, while it can be nearly deserted during May, June, September and October. The islands, and some beaches, are accessible by boat only.

Trang Trang is a largely undiscovered province on the lower Andaman Coast, though the islands and beaches aren't as pretty as neighbouring Krabi's. There is good diving though you'll need your own gear. The islands are accessible by boat only.

Songkhla, Pattani & Narathiwat These deep-south provinces on the lower Southern Gulf coast near Malaysia are lined with hundreds of kilometres of deserted beach. During the north-east monsoon (November to March) the water tends to be murky due to crosscurrents.

FRANK CARTER

MARK STRICKLAND

ANDERS BLOMQVIST

Top: Beach at Ao Klong Phrao, Ko Chang, Trat Province

Middle: Regal Angelfish, Similan Islands, Phang-Nga Province

Bottom: Sa Phra Nang (Princess Pool) near Phra Nang Beach, Krabi Province

Thailand's Highlights

SIMON BRACKEN

MARY LOU JANSON

PAUL BEINSSEN

Top: Sukhothai Historical Park during the Loi Krathong festival, Sukhothai Province

Middle: A line of Buddha statues at Wat Phra Si Sanphet, Ayuthaya Province

Bottom: Woodcarving at a Bangkok floating market

National Parks

Thailand is rich in national parks, boasting around 80 of them at time of writing. Many more were in the pipeline before the 1997 economic crash brought their development a halt.

Kaeng Krachan National Park Thailand's largest and least-explored park covers almost 3000 sq km of evergreen and mixed deciduous forests along the Myanmar border in Phetchaburi Province. Bisected by the Tenasserim Range, the park serves as a major watershed for upper southern Thailand, feeding the huge Kaeng Krachan Reservoir. For hikers and campers who venture into the interior, wildlife viewing – especially gibbons and hornbills – can be superb. It's best visited November to April.

Doi Inthanon National Park This 482-sq-km park near Chiang Mai surrounds Thailand's tallest peak, Doi Inthanon. The misty upper slopes support a profusion of orchids, lichens, mosses and epiphytes as well as nearly 400 bird varieties – more than any other habitat in Thailand. It can be enjoyed all year round, though the summit is quite cold (by South-East Asian standards) from November to February.

Thung Salaeng Luang Wildlife Sanctuary Formerly a major base for communist insurgents, 1,262-sq-km Thung Salaeng Luang encompasses vast meadows and dipterocarp forests – good hiking territory. The Siamese fireback pheasant is one of its most famous feathered residents. Thung Salaeng Luang has limited facilities and is best visited in the cool season, which is from November to February.

Khao Yai National Park The kingdom's oldest and third-largest national park, in Nakhon Ratchasima Province, is considered one of the best in the world in terms of wildlife variation and scope of protection – it was recently designated as an Asean National Heritage Site. Its 2172-sq-km area encompasses one of the largest intact monsoon forests in South-East Asia, and is home to a sizable herd of wild elephants. Limited accommodation is available and there are hotels and guesthouses in nearby Pak Chong. It is best visited from October to June.

Nam Nao National Park Wide expanses of dry dipterocarp forest, bamboo groves and rolling sandstone hills combine to provide excellent hiking potential in this park, which borders Chaiyaphum Province. There's plenty of wildlife as the park abuts Phu Khiaw Wildlife Sanctuary. Accommodation is very limited, both inside and outside the park. It can be visited all year round, though the forest is most lush from May to November.

Phu Kradung National Park This flat-topped, bell-shaped mountain park in Loei Province is a favourite with Thais for its pine forests and sweeping views. The well-marked 9km ascent offers benches and shelters along the way for hikers; tents can be rented at the summit. Wild elephants are occasionally seen. Phu Kradung is best visited from October to December, as during the rainy season the ascents can become very difficult.

Khao Sok National Park Limestone crags, rainforests and jungle streams provide the perfect environment for some of Thailand's threatened species, including tiger and clouded leopard as well as two species of rafflesia (the world's largest flower), in the western part of Surat Thani Province. Treehouse-style accommodation protects the forest floor and offers visitors an opportunity to experience one of the country's most important ecosystems. The park is best visited from December to February.

Similan Islands National Marine Park Although relatively small, this remote nine-island archipelago off the upper Andaman Coast has become one of Thailand's better-known dive destinations due to its profusion of hard corals growing on huge rock reefs. It is also known for its nesting sea turtles. There are camping and bungalows on one island only. The Similan Islands are best visited from November to April.

Thaleh Ban National Park White meranti forest, waterfalls, limestone formations, a natural lake and varied bird life make up the attractions of this quiet 196-sq-km park, which straddles the Thai-Malaysian border in Satun Province. Camping and bungalows are available. The park is best visited from December to March.

Historic Temple Architecture

The former Thai capitals of Ayuthaya, Lopburi, Kamphaeng Phet, Sukhothai, Si Satchanalai and Chiang Mai offer a range of Buddhist temple architecture, most of it from the 11th to 17th centuries. The Thai government has developed several of these sites into historical parks, complete with on-site museums and impressive temple restorations. For Khmer and Lao temple architecture, head to Isan (isăan; North-Eastern Thailand). Hundreds of Khmer ruins dating from the 8th to 13th centuries – including Angkor-period monuments – dot the Isan countryside.

Ayuthaya Just an hour or two (depending on the traffic) north of Bangkok by road, this former royal capital harbours many 14th- to 18th-century temple ruins on an 'island' created by two rivers and a canal. Although the surrounding urban environment detracts a bit from the World Heritage–designated monuments, the Ayuthaya Historical Park is perfect for those with limited time or a milder interest in Thai temple ruins.

Lopburi Because it features a mix of Khmer and Thai monuments, this central-Thai city is a noteworthy stop. The former palace of King Narai (17th century), whose chief adviser was the Greek adventurer Constantine Phaulkon, is particularly impressive.

Chiang Mai & Lampang These thoroughly northern-Thai cities contain many older wooden temples built in the Shan, Burmese and Lanna styles. Wat Phra That Lampang Luang in Lampang Province, thought to be Thailand's oldest surviving wooden temple, makes an interesting side trip from Chiang Mai.

Sukhothai & Si Satchanalai Both of these former royal cities in lower Northern Thailand have been made into historical parks that feature temple ruins dating back to Thailand's 'Golden Age', the Sukhothai era (13th to 15th centuries). The two World Heritage parks are well maintained; the one at Si Satchanalai is less visited and hence offers more of an off-the-beaten-track atmosphere.

Kamphaeng Phet Another World Heritage site in lower Northern Thailand and featuring Sukhothai-era temple ruins, this is a smaller and well-maintained historical park.

Isan The most impressive sites are those at Prasat Hin Phimai in Nakhon Ratchasima Province and Prasat Hin Khao Phanom Rung (abbreviated to Phanom Rung) in Buriram Province, but don't neglect some of the smaller, out-of-the-way spots if you have the time and inclination. Dozens of famous Lao temples – both ruins and operating wát – can be found along the banks of the Mekong River from Loei and Nong Khai Provinces to Ubon Ratchathani Province.

Museums

Thailand's Fine Arts Department maintains a good national museum system with regional branches throughout the country, and there are also a few idiosyncratic collections sponsored by other organisations, both public and private.

National Museum Housed in a former vice-regal palace in Bangkok, the country's most well-endowed museum contains pottery, sculpture, furniture, clothing and musical instruments from Thailand and many other places in South-East Asia. Phutthaisawan Chapel, a temple building on the grounds, contains some of the country's finest Buddhist mural paintings.

Chao Sam Phraya Museum & Palace Ayuthaya's 500-year history is the source of an extensive display of art and artefacts distributed among two separate national museums.

Nan National Museum This is the best place in Thailand to view art objects from the little-known Nan kingdom in the far north, including pieces of Lao and Thai Lü provenance.

Phimai National Museum This is a relatively new and well-designed museum in the small town of Phimai, containing exhibits of Khmer art from the Angkor period as well as earlier Dvaravati-style art.

Dr Thawi's Folk Museum The nation's best-preserved collection of northern Thai folk utensils, including everything from basketry and ceramics to coconut graters, can be found in this museum in Phitsanulok.

Ko Yo Folklore Museum Near Songkhla, this is a newer museum sponsored by the Institute of Southern Thai Studies, with an impressive array of southern-Thai religious and folk art.

Handicrafts

Thailand's ethnic diversity means that a wide range of handicrafts is available for study or purchase throughout the country.

Chiang Mai As the cultural and business capital of Northern Thailand, Chiang Mai has been the North's main handicrafts centre for over 30 years. Here you'll find virtually every type of craft produced in the region, as well as materials from Myanmar and Laos. Northern specialities include silverware, woodcarving, painted umbrellas, hill-tribe crafts, leather, ceramics and antique furniture.

Nakhon Ratchasima & Surrounds The best selection of handmade cotton and silk textiles is found in the central north-eastern capitals of Nakhon Ratchasima (Khorat), Khon Kaen, Roi Et and Udon Thani. Visit some of these silk-weaving towns to experience Thai weaving techniques first-hand.

Ubon Ratchathani In Thailand's north-eastern corner, this provincial capital offers a good selection of crafts from nearby Cambodia and Laos, plus locally produced silver and ceramics.

Nakhon Si Thammarat This provincial town on the lower Southern Gulf coast is a busy centre for many indigenous handicrafts: nielloware, silverware, shadow-play cutouts and intricate basketry.

Songkhla & Surrounds For cotton prints, sarongs and batik (with Malay-Indonesian design influences), visit the southern provinces of Songkhla, Yala, Pattani and Narathiwat near the Malaysian border.

Continued from page 62

City Maps Lonely Planet's Bangkok city map is printed on durable laminated paper and is a handy reference for getting your bearings in the big city. The tourist brochures that the Tourism Authority of Thailand (TAT) issues for many provinces in Thailand often contain small inset maps of the provincial capital. Except for the TAT's Bangkok map – which is quite good – they're usable but not brilliant. See the individual city sections for information on other city maps.

What to Bring

Bring as little as possible – one medium-sized shoulder bag, duffel bag or backpack should do. Pack lightweight clothes, unless you're going to be in the North in the cool season, in which case you should have a pullover. Natural fibres can be cool and comfortable, except when they get soaked with sweat or rain, in which case they quickly become heavy and block air flow. Some of the lightweight synthetics breathe better than natural fibres, draw sweat away rather than holding it in, and may be more suitable for the beach or mid-rainy season.

Sunglasses can be bought cheaply in Bangkok and most provincial capitals. Slip-on shoes or sandals are highly recommended – besides being cooler than lace-ups, they are easily removed before entering a Thai home or temple. A small torch (flashlight) is a good idea, as it makes it easier to find your way back to your bungalow at night if you are staying at the beach or at a remote guesthouse. A few other handy things include a compass, a plastic lighter for lighting candles and mosquito coils (lighters, candles and 'mossie' coils are available in Thailand) and foam earplugs for noisy nights.

Toothpaste, soap and most other toiletries can be purchased anywhere in Thailand. Sun block and mosquito repellent (except high-percentage DEET – see the Health section later in this chapter) are available, although they can be expensive and the quality of both is generally substandard. If you plan to wash your own clothes, bring along a universal sink plug, a few plastic clothes pegs and 3m of plastic cord (or plastic hangers) for hanging wet clothes out to dry.

If you plan to spend a great deal of time in one or more of Thailand's beach areas, you might want to bring your own snorkel and mask (see Diving & Snorkelling under Activities later in this chapter). This will save you having to rent such gear and will also assure a proper fit. Shoes designed for water sports, eg, Aquasocks, are great for wearing in the water whether you're diving or not. They protect your feet from coral cuts, which easily become infected.

If you plan on bringing a laptop computer along, see Email and Internet Access later in this chapter for information on using computer modem communications in Thailand.

Tampons etc Most Thai women don't use tampons, and thus they can be difficult to find in Thailand. In general only the o.b. brand is available, usually in pharmacies or minimarts that carry toiletries. In Bangkok and Chiang Mai more upscale pharmacies may also carry Tampax brand tampons. Boots stores in Bangkok and Chiang Mai carry their own brand, which are similar to Tampax tampons. If you're coming for a relatively short interval, it's best to bring your own. Sanitary napkins are widely available from minimarts and supermarkets throughout Thailand.

Many women have found that the Keeper Menstrual Cap – a reusable natural rubber device that may be inserted to catch menstrual flow – is a convenient and environmentally friendly alternative to disposable tampons or pads. For information on this product, contact Health Keeper (☎ 800-663 0427, 519-896 8032, fax 896 8031, ⓔ orderinfo@keeper.com), 83 Stonegate Drive, Kitchener, ONT, Canada N2A 2Y8, or check the Web site at www.keeper.com.

Sarong Sense Pick up a *phâakhamáa* (short Thai-style sarong for men) or a *phâasîn* (a longer sarong for women) to wear in your room, on the beach or when bathing outdoors. These can be bought at any local market (different patterns and colours can be found in different parts of the country) and the vendors will show you how to tie them.

The sarong is a very handy item; it can be used to sleep on or as a light bedspread (many Thai guesthouses do not supply top sheets or bedspreads), as a makeshift 'shopping bag', as a turban/scarf to keep off the sun and absorb perspiration, as a towel, as a small hammock and as a device with which to climb coconut palms – to name just a few of its many functions.

An unsewn sarong is not proper street attire. Women can have sarongs sewn into a 'tube' suitable for everyday wear as a skirt. Hooks and eyes may be added to the waistline for ease of keeping the sarong on, or you can learn to tie them in the traditional way.

TOURIST OFFICES

The Tourism Authority of Thailand, a government-operated tourist information and promotion service founded in 1960 and attached to the prime minister's office, maintains 22 offices within the country and 16 overseas.

The quality of the printed information that the TAT produces is second to none among South-East Asian countries, with pamphlets on sightseeing, accommodation and transportation options. The staff is huge; the main office in Bangkok occupies 10 floors of Le Concorde, an office building in the Ratchada area of Huay Khwang.

In addition to the following offices, you'll also find TAT information counters in the international and domestic terminals of Bangkok's Don Muang airport.

Tourist Offices in Thailand

Local TAT offices include:

Ayuthaya (☎ 035-246076/7, fax 246078) Thanon Si Sanphet, Phra Nakhon Si Ayuthaya 13000

Bangkok (☎ 02-694 1222, fax 694 1220/1, ℮ center@tat.or.th) Le Concorde Bldg, 202 Thanon Ratchadaphisek, Huay Khwang, Bangkok 10310;
(☎ 02-282 9773) 4 Thanon Ratchadamnoen Nok, Bangkok 10100

Cha-am (☎ 032-471005, fax 471502, ℮ tatphet@tat.or.th) 500/51 Thang Luang Phetkasem, Amphoe Cha-am, Phetchaburi 76120

Chiang Mai (☎ 053-248604, fax 248605, ℮ tatcnx@samart.co.th) 105/1 Thanon Chiang Mai-Lamphun, Chiang Mai 50000

Chiang Rai (☎ 053-717433, fax 717434, ℮ tatcei@loxinfo.co.th) 448/16 Thanon Singkhlai, Chiang Rai 57000

Hat Yai (☎ 074-243747, 238518, fax 245986, ℮ tathatyai@hatyai.inet.co.th) 1/1 Soi 2, Thanon Niphat Uthit 3, Hat Yai, Songkhla 90110

Kanchanaburi (☎/fax 034-511200) Thanon Saengchuto, Kanchanaburi 71000

Khon Kaen (☎ 043-244498/9, 01-965 9471, fax 244497) 15/5 Thanon Prachasamoson, Khon Kaen 40000

Lopburi (☎ 036-422768, fax 424089) Thanon Wat Phra That, Lopburi 15000

Nakhon Phanom (☎ 042-513490/1, fax 513492, ℮ tat.ne@npu.msu.ac.th) 184/1 Thanon Sonthonvichit, Nakhon Phanom 48000

Nakhon Ratchasima (Khorat; ☎ 044-213666, 01-977 0071, fax 213667) 2102–2104 Thanon Mittaphap, Nakhon Ratchasima 30000

Nakhon Si Thammarat (☎ 075-346515/6, 01-979 1242, fax 346517, ℮ tatnakon@nrt.cscoms.com) Sanam Na Meuang, Thanon Ratchadamnoen Klang, Nakhon Si Thammarat 80000

Narathiwat (☎ 073-516144, 522411, 01-957 5647, fax 522412, ℮ tatnara@cscoms.com) 102/3 Thanon Narathiwat-Tak Bai, Narathiwat 96000;
(☎ 073-612126, fax 615230) Sungai Kolok, next to the immigration post

Pattaya (☎ 038-427667, 01-929 0676, fax 429113, ℮ tatpty@chonburi.ksc.co.th) 609 Mu 10 Thanon Phatamnak, Pattaya 20260

Phitsanulok (☎ 055-252743, 259907, fax 252742, ℮ tatphs@loxinfo.co.th) 209/7–8 Surasi Trade Center, Thanon Borom Trailokanat, Phitsanulok 65000

Phuket (☎ 076-212213, 211036, 01-476 2848, fax 213582, ℮ tathkt@phuket.ksc.co.th) 73–75 Thanon Phuket, Phuket 83000

Rayong (☎/fax 038-655420/1, 01-943 5214, fax 655422, ℮ tatry@infonews.co.th) 153/4 Thanon Sukhumvit, Rayong 21000

Surat Thani (☎/fax 077-288818/9, 01-476 6115, fax 282828, ℮ tatsurat@samart.co.th) 5 Thanon Talat Mai, Ban Don, Surat Thani 84000

Trat (☎/fax 039-597255, ☎ 01-904 4623) 100 Mu 1, Thanon Trat-Laem Ngop, Laem Ngop, Trat 23120

Ubon Ratchathani (☎ 045-243770, 01-967 8581, fax 243771, ℮ tatubon@ubon .a-net.net.th) 264/1 Thanon Kheuan Thani, Ubon Ratchathani 34000

Udon Thani (☎ 042-325406, 01-462 2112, fax 325408) 16/5 Thanon Mukkhamontri, Udon Thani 41000

Tourist Offices Abroad

TAT's international offices include:

Australia
(☎ 02-9247 7549, fax 9251 2465, ℮ info@thailand.net.au) Level 2, 75 Pitt Street, Sydney, NSW 2000

France
(☎ 01-53 53 47 00, fax 45 63 78 88, ℮ tatpar@wanadoo.fr) 90 Avenue des Champs Elysées, 75008 Paris

Germany
(☎ 069-138 1390, ℮ tatfra@t-online.de)
Bethmannstrasse 58, D-60311 Frankfurt/Main

Hong Kong
(☎ 02-2868 0732, fax 2868 4585,
℮ tathkg@hk.super.net) Room 401, Fairmont
House, 8 Cotton Tree Drive, Central

Japan
Osaka: (☎ 06-6543 6654, fax 6543 6660,
℮ tatosa@ca.mbn.or.jp) Technoble Yotsu-
bashi Bldg 3F, 1-6-8 Kitahorie, Nishi-ku,
Osaka 550-0014
Tokyo: (☎ 03-3218 0337, fax 3218 0655)
South Tower 2F, Room 259, Yurakucho Denki
Bldg, 1-7-1 Yurakucho, Chiyoda-ku,
Tokyo 100

Laos
(☎ 21-217157, fax 217158) 79/9 Thanon Lan
Xang, Vientiane, Lao PDR PO Box 12, Nong
Khai 43000

Malaysia
(☎ 603-21623480, fax 21623486,
℮ sawatdi@po.jaring.my) Suite 2201, Level
22, Menara Lion, 165 Jalan Ampang, 50450
Kuala Lumpur

Singapore
(☎ 65-235 7694, fax 733 5653) c/o Royal Thai
embassy, 370 Orchard Rd, 238870

Taiwan
(☎ 02-2502 1600, fax 2502 1603,
℮ tattpe@ms3.hinet.net) 13th floor, Boss
Tower, 111 Sung Chiang Rd

UK
(☎ 020-7499 7679, ℮ info@tat-uk.demon
.co.uk) 49 Albemarle St, London W1X 3 FE

USA
Los Angeles: (☎ 323-461 9814, fax 461 9834,
℮ tatla@ix.netcom.com) 611 North Larch-
mont Blvd, 1st floor, Los Angeles, CA 90004
New York: (☎ 1800-THAILAND, 212-432
0433, fax 912 0920, ℮ tatny@aol.com) 1
World Trade Center, Suite 3729, New York,
NY 10048

VISAS & DOCUMENTS
Passports

Entry into Thailand requires a passport valid
for at least six months from the time of entry.
If you anticipate your passport expiring
while you're in Thailand, you should obtain
a new one before arrival or inquire from your
government whether your embassy in Thailand (if one exists) can issue a new one after
arrival. See Embassies & Consulates later in
this chapter for further information.

Visas

Whichever type of visa you have, be sure to
check your passport immediately after
stamping. Overworked officials sometimes

stamp 30 days on arrival even when you
hold a longer visa; if you point out the error
before you've left the immigration area at
your port of entry, officials will make the
necessary corrections. If you don't notice
this until you've left the port of entry, go to
Bangkok and plead your case at the central
immigration office.

Once a visa is issued, it must be used (ie,
you must enter Thailand) within 90 days.
The Royal Thai embassy in Washington,
DC, maintains one of the best Internet sites
for information about visas for Thailand:
www.thaiembdc.org/consular/visa/visa.htm.

Transit & Tourist Visas The Thai government allows people of 57 different nationalities to enter the country without a
visa for 30 days at no charge. People of 78
other nationalities, such as those from
smaller European countries like Andorra or
Liechtenstein or from West Africa, South
Asia or Latin America, can obtain 15-day
Transit Visas on arrival upon payment of a
300B fee.

A few nationalities (eg, Hungarians)
must obtain a visa in advance of arrival or
they'll be turned back. Check with a Thai
embassy or consulate in advance to be sure
if you plan on arriving without a visa.

Without proof of an onward ticket and
sufficient funds for the projected stay, any
visitor can be denied entry, but in practice
your ticket and funds are rarely checked if
you're dressed neatly for the immigration
check. See Exchange Control in the Money
section later in this chapter for the amount
of funds required per visa type.

Next in length of validity is the Tourist
Visa, which is good for 60 days and costs
US$15. Two passport photos must accom-
pany all applications.

Non-Immigrant Visas The Non-
Immigrant Visa is good for 90 days, must
be applied for in your home country, costs
US$20 and is not difficult to obtain if you
can offer a good reason for your visit. Business, study, retirement and extended family
visits are among the purposes considered
valid. If you want to stay longer than six
months, this is the one to get.

The Non-Immigrant Business Visa (usually abbreviated by Thai immigration officials as 'non-B') allows unlimited entries to

Thailand for one year. The only hitch is that you must leave the country at least once every 90 days to keep the visa valid.

Visa Exceptions Citizens of Brazil, Korea, New Zealand and Peru may enter Thailand without a visa, in accordance with inter-governmental agreements, for a maximum stay of 90 days for purposes of tourism or temporary business only. No extension of stay will be granted, however.

Visa Extensions & Renewals Sixty-day Tourist Visas may be extended by up to 30 days at the discretion of Thai immigration authorities. The Bangkok office (☎ 02-287 3101) is on Soi Suan Phlu, Thanon Sathon Tai, but you can apply at any immigration office in the country – every province that borders a neighbouring country has at least one. The usual fee for extending a Tourist Visa is 500B. Bring along one photo and one copy each of the photo and visa pages of your passport. Normally only one 30-day extension is granted.

The 30-day, no-visa stay can be extended for seven to 10 days (depending on the immigration office) for 500B. You can also leave the country and return immediately to obtain another 30-day stay. There is no limit on the number of times you can do this, nor is there a minimum interval you must spend outside the country.

Extension of the 15-day, on-arrival Transit Visa is only allowed if you hold a passport from a country that has no Thai embassy.

If you overstay your visa, the usual penalty is a fine of 200B each extra day, with a 20,000B limit; fines can be paid at the airport or in advance at the Investigation Unit (☎ 02-287 3101–10), Immigration Bureau, Room 416, 4th floor, Old Building, Soi Suan Phlu, Thanon Sathon Tai, Bangkok.

Extending a Non-Immigrant Visa very much depends on how the officials feel about you – if they like you then they will extend it. Other than the 500B extension fee, money doesn't usually come into it; neat appearance and polite behaviour count for more. Typically, you must collect a number of signatures and go through various interviews, which may result in a 'provisional' extension. You may then have to report to a local immigration office every 10 to 14 days for the next three months until the actual extension comes through.

Becoming a monk doesn't necessarily mean you'll get a longer visa – again, it depends on whom you see and how they feel about you. (See also Tax Clearance later in this entry.)

Retirees 55 years of age or older may extend the 90-day Non-Immigrant Visa by one year at a time. To do this you will need to bring the following documents to the immigration bureau: a copy of your passport, one photo, a 500B extension fee and proof of your financial status or pension. The requirement for the latter is that foreigners aged 60 or older must show proof of an income of not less than 200,000B per year (or 20,000B per month for extensions of less than a year); for those who are aged 55 to 59 the minimum is raised to 500,000/50,000B. According to immigration regulations: 'If the alien is ill, or has weak health and is sensitive to colder climates, or has resided in Thailand for a long period, and is 55 to 59 years of age, special considerations will be granted'.

Foreigners with Non-Immigrant Visas who have resided in Thailand continuously for three years – on one-year extensions – may apply for permanent residency at Section 1, Subdivision 1, Immigration Division 1, Room 301, 3rd floor, Immigration Bureau, Soi Suan Phlu, Thanon Sathon Tai (☎ 02-287 3117); foreigners who receive permanent residence must carry an 'alien identification card' at all times.

The Thai government maintains the One-Stop Visa Centre (☎ 02-693 9333, fax 693 9340), 207 Thanon Ratchadaphisek, Krisda Plaza, where Non-Immigrant Visas for investors, businesspeople and foreign correspondents (only) can be renewed in less than three hours.

Various law offices in Thailand, especially in Bangkok, Chiang Mai and Hat Yai, can assist with visa extensions, renewals and applications – for a fee, of course. Two law offices in Bangkok that have been around awhile are Siam Visa (☎ 02-238 2989, fax 238 2987, @ siamvisa@loxinfo.co.th), on the 7th floor of the Kasemkit Building, Thanon Silom; and Express Visa Service (☎ 02-617 7258 ext 418, fax 272 3764), at Sirida Place, 278 Thanon Viphavadi Rangsit, Soi 3 Yak 10, Latyao, Chatuchak. The preceding mentions do not constitute an endorsement of either agency – be cautious and ask plenty of questions before plunking down your money.

Re-Entry Permits & Multiple-Entry Visas If you need to leave and re-enter the kingdom before your visa expires, say for a return trip to Laos or the like, you may need to apply for a Re-Entry Permit at a Thai immigration office. The cost is 500B; you'll need to supply one passport photo. There is no limit to the number of Re-Entry Permits you can apply for and use during the validity of your visa.

Other than the Non-Immigrant Business Visa, Thailand does not issue multiple-entry visas. If you want a visa that enables you to leave the country and then return, the best you can do is to obtain a visa permitting two entries; this will cost double the single-entry visa. For example, a two-entry, 90-day Non-Immigrant Visa will cost US$40 and will allow you six months in the country, as long as you cross a border with immigration facilities by the end of your first three months. The second half of your visa is validated as soon as you recross the Thai border. All visas acquired in advance of entry are valid for 90 days from the date of issue.

An alternative is to apply for a Re-Entry Permit (or the Multiple Re-Entry Permit, if established as proposed by Thai immigration) after you're already in Thailand, as described previously.

See Non-Immigrant Visas earlier in this section for a description of the multiple-entry Non-Immigrant Business Visa.

Tax Clearance
Anyone who receives income while in Thailand must obtain a tax clearance certificate from the Revenue Department before they'll be permitted to leave the country. The Bangkok office (☎ 02-281 5777, 282 9899) of the Revenue Department is on Thanon Chakkapong, not far from the Democracy Monument. There are also Revenue Department offices in every provincial capital.

Onward Tickets
Thai immigration does not seem very concerned that you arrive with proof of onward travel. Legally speaking, all holders of Tourist Visas or the no-visa 30-day stay permit are *supposed* to carry such proof. In all our years of frequent travel in and out of the kingdom, our onward travel documents haven't been checked a single time.

Travel Insurance
A travel insurance policy to cover theft, loss and medical problems is a good idea. Some policies offer lower and higher medical-expense options; the higher ones are chiefly for countries such as the USA, which have extremely high medical costs. There is a wide variety of policies available, so check the small print.

Some policies specifically exclude 'dangerous activities', which can include scuba diving, motorcycling or even trekking. A locally acquired motorcycle licence is not valid under some policies.

You may prefer a policy which pays doctors or hospitals directly rather than you having to pay on the spot and claim later. If you have to claim later make sure you keep all documentation. Some policies ask you to call back (reverse charges) to a centre in your home country where an immediate assessment of your problem is made.

Check that the policy covers ambulances or an emergency flight home.

Driving Licence & Permits
An International Driving Permit is necessary for any visitor who intends to drive a motorised vehicle while in Thailand. These are usually available from motoring organisations, such as the American Automobile Association (AAA) or the Automobile Association (AA), in your home country. If you'd like to obtain a Thai driving licence, see the Driving Permits section of the Getting Around chapter for details.

Hostel Cards
Hostelling International (HI; formerly known as International Youth Hostel Federation) issues a membership card that allows you to stay at Thailand's member hostels. Without such a card or the purchase of a temporary membership you won't be admitted. See the Accommodation section later in this chapter for more information.

Memberships may be purchased at any member hostel worldwide. For information on Thailand's hostels, check out the Web site at www.tyha.org.

Student Cards

International Student Identity Cards (ISIC) can be used as identification to qualify for the student discount at some museums in Thailand (although these are rare). It's probably not worth getting just for a visit to Thailand, but if you already have one, or plan to use one elsewhere in Asia, then bring it along.

ISIC cards are issued via student-oriented travel agencies with ISIC agreements around the world. Check www.istc.org to find the issuing agency closest to you.

Copies

All important documents (passport data page and visa page, credit cards, travel insurance policy, air/bus/train tickets, driving licence etc) should be photocopied before you leave home. Leave one copy with someone at home and keep another with you, separate from the originals.

You can also store details of your vital travel documents in Lonely Planet's free online Travel Vault. See eKno Communication Service under Post & Communications later in this chapter.

EMBASSIES & CONSULATES
Thai Embassies & Consulates

To apply for a visa, contact the Royal Thai embassy (or consulate) in any of the following countries. In many cases, if you apply in person you may receive a Tourist or Non-Immigrant Visa on the day of application; by mail it generally takes anywhere from two to six weeks.

Australia
Canberra: (☎ 02-6273 1149, 6273 2937) 111 Empire Circuit, Yarralumla, Canberra, ACT 2600
Sydney: (☎ 02-9241 2542) 8th floor, 131 Macquarie St, Sydney, NSW 2000
Canada
Ottawa: (☎ 613-722 4444) 180 Island Park Drive, Ottawa, ON K1Y OA2
Vancouver: (☎ 604-687 1143) 1040 Burrard St, Vancouver, BC V6Z 2R9
China
Beijing: (☎ 010-6532 1903) 40 Guanghua Lu, Beijing 100600
Guangzhou: (☎ 020-8188 6968, ext 3301-03) White Swan Hotel, Southern St, Shamian Island, Guangzhou
Kunming: (☎ 871-316 8916) King World Hotel, 145 Dong Feng Dong Lu, Kunming, Yunnan Province 650051

Shanghai: (☎ 021-6321 9442) 7 Zhongshan Rd, East 1, Shanghai 200002
France
(☎ 01-56 26 50 50) 8 Rue Greuze, 75116 Paris
Germany
(☎ 30-794810) Lepsiusstrasse 64–66, 12162 Berlin
Hong Kong
(☎ 02-2521 6481–5) 8th floor, Fairmont House, 8 Cotton Tree Drive, Central
India
Calcutta: (☎ 033-440 7836, 440 3230/1) 18-B, Mandeville Gardens, Ballygunge, Calcutta 700 019
Mumbai: (☎ 022-363 1404, 369 2543) Malabar View, 4th floor, 33 Marine Drive St, Chowpatty Sea Face, Mumbai 400 007
New Delhi: (☎ 021-6321 9442) 56-N Nyaya Marg, Chanakyapuri, New Delhi, 110021
Indonesia
(☎ 021-390 4052/3/4) Jalan Imam Bonjol 74, Jakarta Pusat 10310
Japan
Osaka: (☎ 06-243 5563, 243 5569) Konoike East Bldg, 4th floor, 3-6-9 Kitakyohoji-machi, Chuo-ku, Osaka 541-0057
Tokyo: (☎ 03-3441 1386/7) 3-14-6 Kami-Osaki, Shinagawa-ku, Tokyo 141
Laos
(☎ 21-214581–3) Thanon Phonkheng, Vientiane Poste 128
Malaysia
Kota Bharu: (☎ 09-744 5266, 748 2545) 4426 Jalan Pengkalan Chepa, 15400 Kota Bharu, Kelantan
Kuala Lumpur: (☎ 03-248 8222, 248 8350) 206 Jalan Ampang, Kuala Lumpur
Penang: (☎ 04-226 8029, 226 9484) No 1 Jalan Tunku Abdul Rahman, 10350 Penang
Myanmar
(Burma; ☎ 01-512017, 512018) 437 Pyay Road, 8 Ward, Kamayut township, Yangon
Nepal
(☎ 01-371410, 371411) Ward No 3, Bansbari, PO Box. 3333, Kathmandu
Netherlands
(☎ 070-345 9703) Laan Copes van Cattenburch 123, 2585 EZ The Hague
New Zealand
(☎ 04-476 8618/9) 2 Cook St, Karori, PO Box 17226, Wellington 5
Philippines
(☎ 02-810 3833, 815 4219) 107B Rada St, Legaspi Village, Makati, Metro Manila
Singapore
(☎ 65-737 2644, 737 2158) 370 Orchard Rd, 238870
UK & Northern Ireland
(☎ 020-7589 0173, 7589 2944) 29–30 Queen's Gate, London SW7 5JB
USA
Chicago: (☎ 312-664 3129) 700 N Rush St, Chicago, Illinois 60611

Los Angeles: (☎ 213-962 9574–77) 611 N Larchmont Blvd, 2nd floor, Los Angeles, CA 90004
New York: (☎ 212-754 1770, 754 2536–8) 351 East 52nd St, New York, NY 10022
Washington DC: (☎ 202-944 3600) 1024 Wisconsin Ave NW, Washington, DC 20007
Vietnam
Hanoi: (☎ 04-823 5092–94) 63–65 Hoang Dieu St, Hanoi
Ho Chi Minh City: (☎ 08-822 2637/8) 77 Tran Quoc Thao St, District 3, Ho Chi Minh City

Embassies & Consulates in Thailand

Bangkok is a good place to collect visas for onward travel, and most countries have diplomatic representation there. The visa sections of most embassies and consulates are open from around 8.30 to 11.30 am weekdays only (call first to be sure, as some are open only two or three days a week).

If you're heading on to India you'll definitely need a visa, and if you're going to Nepal it's highly advisable to have one even though it can be obtained on arrival.

For visits to Myanmar, visas are necessary and available direct from the Myanmar embassy. For Laos, visas can be acquired from the Lao embassy in Bangkok or the Lao consulate in Khon Kaen, on arrival at airports in Vientiane and Luang Prabang, or at the Thai-Lao Friendship Bridge crossing near Nong Khai. Visas are available on arrival in Malaysia, Cambodia and Vietnam.

Countries with diplomatic representation in Bangkok (area code ☎ 02) include:

Australia (☎ 287 2680) 37 Thanon Sathon Tai
Austria (☎ 287 3970–2) 14 Soi Nantha, Thanon Sathon Tai
Bangladesh (☎ 392 9437) 727 Soi 55, Thanon Sukhumvit
Belgium (☎ 236 0150) 44 Soi Phipat, Thanon Silom
Cambodia (☎ 254 6630) 185 Thanon Ratchadamri, Lumphini
Canada (☎ 636 0540) 15th floor, Abdulrahim Bldg, 990 Thanon Phra Ram IV
China (☎ 245 7043) 57 Thanon Ratchadaphisek
Denmark (☎ 213 2021–5) 10 Soi 1, Thanon Sathon Tai
France (☎ 266 8250–6) 35 Soi 36, Thanon Charoen Krung;
(☎ 287 2585–7) consular section (visas) 29 Thanon Sathon Tai
Germany (☎ 287 9000) 9 Thanon Sathon Tai
India (☎ 258 0300–6) 46 Soi Prasanmit (Soi 23), Thanon Sukhumvit

Indonesia (☎ 252 3135) 600–602 Thanon Phetburi
Israel (☎ 260 4854–9) 75 Ocean Tower 2, 25th floor, Soi 19, Thanon Sukhumvit
Japan (☎ 252 6151–9) 1674 Thanon Phetburi Tat Mai
Laos (☎ 539 6667, 539 7341) 520/1–3 Soi 39, Thanon Ramkhamhaeng
Malaysia (☎ 679 2190–/9) 33–35 Thanon Sathon Tai
Myanmar (Burma; ☎ 233 2237, 234 4698) 132 Thanon Sathon Neua
Nepal (☎ 391 7240) 189 Soi Phuengsuk (Soi 71), Thanon Sukhumvit
Netherlands (☎ 254 7701, 252 6103–5) 106 Thanon Withayu
New Zealand (☎ 254 2530–3) 93 Thanon Withayu
Norway (☎ 261 0230–5) 18th floor, UBC II Bldg, 591 Soi 33, Thanon Sukhumvit
Philippines (☎ 259 0139) 760 Thanon Sukhumvit
Singapore (☎ 286 2111, 286 1434) 129 Thanon Sathon Tai
South Africa (☎ 253 8473) 6th floor, Park Place, 231 Soi Sarasin
South Korea (☎ 247 7537) 23 Thanon Thiam-Ruammit, Huay Khwang, Sam Sen Nok
Spain (☎ 252 5132) 701 Diethelm Tower, 7th floor, 93/1 Thanon Withayu
Sri Lanka (☎ 261 1934/5) 13th floor, Ocean Tower II Bldg, 75/6 Soi 19, Thanon Sukhumvit
Sweden (☎ 254 4954/5) 20th floor, Pacific Place, 140 Thanon Sukhumvit
Switzerland (☎ 253 0156–60) 35 Thanon Withayu Neua
UK & Northern Ireland (☎ 253 0191–9) 1031 Thanon Withayu
USA (☎ 205 4000) 120–22 Thanon Withayu
Vietnam (☎ 251 5836–8) 83/1 Thanon Withayu

Your Own Embassy

It's important to realise what your own embassy – the embassy of the country of which you are a citizen – can and can't do to help you if you get into trouble. Generally speaking, it won't be much help in emergencies if the trouble you're in is remotely your own fault. Remember that you are bound by the laws of the country you are in. Your embassy will not be sympathetic if you end up in jail after committing a crime locally, even if such actions are legal in your own country.

In genuine emergencies you might get some assistance, but only if other channels have been exhausted. For example, if you need to get home urgently, a free ticket home is exceedingly unlikely – the embassy would expect you to have insurance. If you have all your money and documents stolen, it might assist with getting a new passport, but a loan for onward travel is out of the question.

CUSTOMS

Like most countries, Thailand prohibits the importation of illegal drugs, firearms and ammunition (unless registered in advance with the Police Department) and pornographic media. A reasonable amount of clothing for personal use, toiletries and professional instruments are allowed in dutyfree, as are one still or one movie/video camera with five rolls of still film or three rolls of movie film or videotape. Up to 200 cigarettes can be brought into the country without paying duty, or other smoking materials to a total of up to 250g. One litre of wine or spirits is allowed in duty-free.

Electronic goods like personal stereos, calculators and computers can be a problem if the customs officials have reason to believe you're bringing them in for resale. As long as you don't carry more than one of each, you should be OK.

For information on currency importation or export, see the Money section later in this chapter.

Antiques & Art

Upon leaving Thailand you must obtain an export licence for any antiques or objects of art you want to take with you. An antique is any 'archaic movable property whether produced by man or by nature, any part of ancient structure, human skeleton or animal carcass, which by its age or characteristic of production or historical evidence is useful in the field of art, history or archaeology'. An object of art is a 'thing produced by craftsmanship and appreciated as being valuable in the field of art'. Obviously these are very sweeping definitions, so if in doubt go to the Fine Arts Department for inspection and licensing.

An application can be made by submitting two front-view photos of the object (no more than five objects to a photo) and a photocopy of your passport, along with the object in question, to one of three locations in Thailand: the Bangkok National Museum, the Chiang Mai National Museum or the Songkhla National Museum. You need to allow three to five days for the application and inspection process to be completed.

Thailand has special regulations for taking a Buddha or other deity image (or any part thereof) out of the country. These require not only a licence from the Fine Arts Department but a permit from the Ministry of Commerce as well. The one exception to this are the small Buddha images (*phrá phim* or *phrá khrêuang*) that are meant to be worn on a chain around the neck; these may be exported without a licence as long as the reported purpose is religious.

Temporary Vehicle Importation

Passenger vehicles (car, van, truck or motorcycle) can be brought into Thailand for tourist purposes for up to six months. Documents needed for the crossing are a valid International Driving Permit, passport, vehicle registration papers (in the case of a borrowed or hired vehicle, authorisation from the owner) and a cash or bank guarantee equal to the value of the vehicle plus 20%. (For entry through Khlong Toey Port or Bangkok International Airport, this means a letter of bank credit; for overland crossings via Malaysia a 'self-guarantee' filled in at the border is sufficient.)

Home Country Customs

Be sure to check the import regulations in your home country before bringing or sending back a large quantity or highvalued Thailand purchases. The limit varies from country to country; the USA, for example, allows US$400 worth of foreign-purchased goods to enter without duty (with no limit on handicrafts and unset gems), while in Australia the total value is limited to A$400.

MONEY
Currency

The basic unit of Thai currency is the *baht* (*bàat*). There are 100 *satang* (*sàtàang*) in one baht; coins include 25-satang and 50-satang pieces and baht in 1B, 5B and 10B coins. Older coins exhibit Thai numerals only, while newer coins have Thai and Arabic numerals. Twenty-five satang equals one *sàlĕung* in colloquial Thai, so if you're quoted a price of six sàlĕung in the market, say, for a banana or a bag of peanuts, this means 1.50B. The term is becoming increasingly rare as ongoing inflation makes purchases of less than 1B or 2B almost obsolete.

Paper currency comes in denominations of 10B (brown), 20B (green), 50B (blue), 100B (red), 500B (purple) and 1000B (beige). A 10,000B bill was on the way when the 1997 cash crunch came, and has been tabled for the moment. Ten-baht bills are being phased out in favour of the 10B coin and have become rather uncommon. Fortunately for newcomers to Thailand, numerals are printed in their Western as well as Thai forms. Notes are also scaled according to the amount; the larger the denomination, the larger the note. Large denominations – 500B and especially 1000B bills – can be hard to change in small towns, but banks will always change them.

Exchange Rates

Exchange rates at the time of writing include:

country	unit		baht
Australia	A$1	=	22.7B
Canada	C$1	=	28.0B
European Union	€1	=	39.0B
France	1FF	=	6.0B
Germany	1DM	=	20.1B
Hong Kong	HK$1	=	5.5B
Japan	¥100	=	36.7B
New Zealand	NZ$1	=	18.6B
Singapore	S$1	=	24.5B
UK	UK£1	=	62.4B
USA	US$1	=	42.7B

Prior to June 1997 the baht was pegged to a basket of currencies heavily weighted towards the US dollar, and for over 20 years its value hardly varied beyond 20B to 26B to US$1. A year after flotation, the baht had slipped approximately 30% against the US dollar. Lately exchange rates seem to have stabilised, but there's always the chance the Thai currency will go for another roller coaster ride. Hence it's a good idea to stay abreast of exchange rates during your stay in Thailand – changing currencies at the right time could extend your budget significantly. Exchange rates are printed in the *Bangkok Post* and *The Nation* every day, or you can walk into any Thai bank and ask to see a daily rate sheet.

Exchanging Money

There is no black-market money exchange for baht, so there's no reason to bring in any Thai currency. The banks or legal money-changers offer the best exchange rates within the country. For buying baht, US dollars are the most readily acceptable currency and travellers cheques get better rates than cash. Since banks charge 23B commission and duty for each travellers cheque cashed, you will save on commissions if you use larger cheque denominations (eg, a US$50 cheque will only cost 23B while five US$10 cheques will cost 115B). British pounds are second to the US dollar in general acceptability.

Note that you can't exchange Malaysian ringgit, Indonesian rupiah, Nepali rupees, Cambodian riel, Lao kip, Vietnamese dong or Myanmar kyat into Thai currency at banks, although some moneychangers along Thanon Charoen Krung and Thanon Silom in Bangkok carry these currencies. The latter can in fact be good places to buy these currencies if you're going to any of these countries. The rates are comparable with black-market rates in countries with discrepancies between the 'official' and free-market currency values.

Visa and MasterCard credit-card holders can get cash advances of up to US$500 (in baht only) per day through some branches of the Thai Farmers Bank, Bangkok Bank and Siam Commercial Bank (and also at the night-time exchange windows in touristy spots like Banglamphu, Chiang Mai, Ko Samui and so on).

American Express (AmEx) card holders can also get advances, but only in travellers cheques. The AmEx agent in Bangkok is SEA Tours (☎ 02-216 5759, 273 0022), Suite 88–92, Payathai Plaza, 8th floor, 128 Thanon Phayathai, Bangkok.

See the Business Hours section later in this chapter for information on bank opening hours.

Exchange Control Legally, any traveller arriving in Thailand must have at least the following amounts of money in cash, travellers cheques, bank draft or letter of credit, according to visa category: Non-Immigrant Visa, US$500 per person or US$1000 per family; Tourist Visa, US$250 per person or US$500 per family; Transit Visa or no visa, US$125 per person or US$250 per family. Your funds may be checked by authorities if you arrive on a one-way ticket or if you look as if you're at 'the end of the road'.

There is no limit to the amount of Thai or foreign currency you may bring into the country. Upon leaving Thailand, you're permitted to take no more than 50,000B per person without special authorisation; exportation of foreign currencies is unrestricted. An exception is made if you're going to Cambodia, Laos, Malaysia, Myanmar or Vietnam, where the limit is 500,000B.

It's legal to open a foreign currency account at any commercial bank in Thailand. As long as the funds originate from abroad, there are no restrictions on their maintenance or withdrawal.

ATM & Credit/Debit Cards An alternative to carrying around large amounts of cash or travellers cheques is to open an account at a Thai bank and request an ATM card. Major banks in Thailand now have automated teller machines (ATMs) in provincial capitals and in many smaller towns as well, open 24 hours. Once you have a card you'll be able to withdraw cash at machines throughout Thailand, whether those machines belong to your bank or another Thai bank. ATM cards issued by Thai Farmers Bank or Bangkok Bank can be used with the ATMs of 14 major banks – there are over 3000 machines throughout the country. A 10B transaction charge is usually deducted for using an ATM belonging to a bank with whom you don't have an account.

Debit cards (also known as cash cards or check cards) issued by a bank in your own country can also be used at several Thai banks to withdraw cash (in Thai baht only) directly from your cheque or savings account back home, thus avoiding all commissions and finance charges. You can use MasterCard debit cards to buy baht at foreign exchange booths or desks at either the Bangkok Bank or Siam Commercial Bank. Visa debit cards can buy cash through the Thai Farmers Bank exchange services.

These cards can also be used at many Thai ATMs, although a surcharge of around US$1 is usually subtracted from your home account each time you complete a machine transaction. Some travellers now use debit or ATM cards in lieu of travellers cheques because they're quicker and more convenient, although it's a good idea to bring along an emergency travellers-cheque fund in case you lose your card. One disadvantage of debit card accounts, as opposed to credit card accounts, is that you can't arrange a 'charge back' for unsatisfactory purchases after the transaction is completed – once the money's drawn from your account it's gone.

Credit cards as well as debit cards can be used for purchases at many shops, hotels and restaurants. The most commonly accepted cards are Visa and MasterCard, followed by AmEx and Japan Card Bureau (JCB). Diner's Club and Carte Blanche are of much more limited use.

Card Problems Occasionally when you try to use a card at upcountry hotels or shops, the staff may try to tell you that only cards issued by Thai Farmers Bank or Siam Commercial Bank are acceptable. With a little patience, you should be able to make them understand that the Thai Farmers Bank will pay the merchant and that your bank will pay the Thai Farmers Bank – and that any Visa or MasterCard issued anywhere in the world is indeed acceptable.

Another problem concerns illegal surcharges on credit-card purchases. It's against Thai law to pass on to the customer the 3% merchant fee charged by banks, but almost all merchants in Thailand do it anyway. Some even ask 4% or 5%! The only exception seems to be hotels (although even a few hotels will hit you with a credit-card surcharge). If you don't agree to the surcharge they'll simply refuse to accept your card. Begging and pleading or pointing out the law doesn't seem to help.

The best way to get around the illegal surcharge is to politely ask that the credit-card receipt be itemised with cost of product or service and the surcharge listed separately. Then when you pay your bill, photocopy all receipts showing the surcharge and request a 'charge back'. Not all banks in all countries will offer such refunds – the banks in the UK, for example, refuse to issue such refunds, while the banks in the USA usually will.

To report a lost or stolen credit/debit card, call the following telephone hotlines in Bangkok: AmEx (☎ 02-273 0022), MasterCard (☎ 02-260 8572), Visa (☎ 02-256 7326), Diners Club (☎ 02-238 3660). See Dangers & Annoyances later in this chapter for important warnings on credit-card theft and fraud.

International Money Transfer If you have a reliable place to take mail in Thailand, one of the safest and cheapest ways to receive money from overseas is to have an international cashier's cheque (or international money order) sent by courier. It usually takes no more than four days for courier mail to reach Thailand from anywhere in the world.

If you have a bank account in Thailand or your home bank has a branch in Bangkok, you can have money wired direct via a telegraphic transfer. This costs a bit more than having a cheque sent; telegraphic transfers take anywhere from two days to a week to arrive. International banks with branches in Bangkok include Bank of America, Bank of Tokyo, Banque Indosuez, Banque Nationale de Paris, Citibank, Deutsche Bank, Hongkong Bank, Chase Manhattan Bank, Merrill Lynch International Bank, Sakura Bank, Standard Chartered Bank, United Malayan Bank and many others.

Western Union (☎ 02-254 9121), justifiably claiming to be 'the fastest way to send money worldwide', has an office in Central department store at 1027 Thanon Ploenchit, as well as in other branches of Central around the city and in Hat Yai and Chiang Mai.

Security

Give some thought in advance to how you're going to carry your financial media – whether travellers cheques, cash, credit and debit cards, or some combination of these. Many travellers favour pouches that can be worn hidden beneath clothing. Hippocket wallets are easy marks for thieves. Pickpockets work markets and crowded buses throughout the country, so it pays to keep your money concealed. See Dangers & Annoyances later in this chapter for more on petty crime.

It's a good idea not to keep all your money in one place; keep an 'emergency' stash well concealed in a piece of luggage separate from other money. Long-term travellers might even consider renting a safety deposit box at a bank in Bangkok or other major cities. Keep your onward tickets, a copy of your passport, a list of all credit card numbers and some money in the box just in case all your belongings are stolen while you're on the road. It's not common, but it does happen.

Costs

Food and accommodation outside Bangkok are generally quite inexpensive and even in Bangkok they are fairly cheap, especially considering the value compared to other countries in South and South-East Asia. Since the baht devaluation, prices have dropped even lower, at least in relation to hard currencies. If measured against the US dollar, for example, the cost of the average hotel room dropped 20% to 25% between June 1997 and June 2000, the price of the average hotel buffet came down 30%, a bowl of rice noodles cost 15% less and the air fare between Bangkok and Phuket fell roughly 25%. With current inflation of baht prices running just 2% per year, these savings will slowly evaporate over the life of this guidebook edition, of course.

Budget-squeezers should be able to get by on 240B per day, outside Bangkok, if they really keep watch on their expenses, especially if they share rooms with other travellers. This estimate includes basic food, guesthouse accommodation, nonalcoholic beverages and local transport, but not film, souvenirs, tours, long-distance transport or vehicle hire. Add another 60B to 85B per day for every large beer (30B to 55B for small bottles) you drink.

Expenses vary, of course, from place to place; where there are high concentrations of budget travellers, for example, food tends to be more expensive and accommodation cheaper. With experience, you can travel in Thailand for even less money if you live like a Thai of modest means and learn to speak the language.

Someone with more money to spend will find that for around 400B to 500B per day, life can be quite comfortable; cleaner and quieter accommodation is easier to find once you pass the 200B-a-night zone in room rates. Of course, a 100B guesthouse room with a mattress on the floor and responsive management is better than a poorly-maintained 500B room with air-con that won't turn off and a noisy all-night card game next door.

In Bangkok there's almost no limit to the amount you *could* spend, but if you avoid the tourist ghettos and ride the public bus system you can get by on slightly more than you would spend in the provinces. Where you stay in Bangkok is of concern, as accommodation is generally more expensive than upcountry. If you can do without air conditioning, accommodation can be found in Bangkok for as little as 75B per person. The noise, heat and pollution in Bangkok may drive many budget travellers to seek more comfort than they might otherwise need in the countryside; 400B per day in Bangkok is the absolute minimum for air-con.

If you can spend 1000B a day for accommodation you'll be able to stay in the best upcountry accommodation Thailand provides, which usually means air-con, hot water, TV and telephone. Those seeking international-class accommodation and food will spend at least 1500B to 2000B a day for a room with all the modern amenities – IDD phone, 24-hour hot water and air-conditioning, carpeting, swimming pool, fitness centre and all-night room service. Such hotels are found only in the major cities and resort areas.

Bangkok is the typical 'primate city' cited by sociologists, meaning that most goods produced by the country as a whole end up in Bangkok, so it's usually as cheap to eat in Bangkok as anywhere else in Thailand. The exception is international food, which Bangkok has more of than anywhere else in the kingdom but charges the most for. International fast-food chains – which Thailand has plenty of – in particular can be real budget-busters. Eat only Thai and Chinese food if you're trying to spend little.

Tipping & Bargaining

Tipping is not normal practice in Thailand, although they're getting used to it in expensive hotels and restaurants. Elsewhere don't bother. The exception is loose change left from a large Thai restaurant bill; for example if a meal costs 288B and you pay with a 500B note, some Thais and foreign residents will leave the 12B coin change on

Sample Prices

item	approximate price
1L petrol	15B
Average metered taxi ride, central Bangkok	75B
Average bus fare, Bangkok	3.50B
Săwngthăew ride, provincial city	10B or 40B to 50B charter
3rd-class train fare, Bangkok–Surat Thani	107B
One day's rental,100cc motorcycle, Hua Hin	200B
Dorm bed, guesthouse or youth hostel	50B to 80B
Guesthouse single, Nong Khai	100B to 150B
Mid-range hotel double, Bangkok	1600B
Budget beach-hotel single, Phuket	500B
Bowl of kŭaytĭaw, Khon Kaen	20B
10 eggs from a market	19B
Can of Campbell's Vegetarian Vegetable soup	42B
Five-dish dinner for three (no booze), ordinary Thai-Chinese khâo tôm restaurant	245B
Substantial lunch for two, average Thai vegetarian restaurant	40B
Small New Orleans BBQ Chicken pizza,Pizza Hut	145B
Large dinner for four (with two large bottles of beer), good non-hotel Thai restaurant	1000B
Dinner for two (with wine), Lord Jim's, Oriental Hotel	3000B
First-run English-language film, Bangkok cinema	90B
Classic French film, Alliance Francaise, Chiang Mai	20B
Copy of the Bangkok Post or The Nation	20B
Monthly rent, modest one-bedroom apartment, Bangkok	10,000B to 15,000B
Monthly rent, economical two-bedroom apartment/house, Chiang Mai	5000B to 10,000B

the change tray. It's not so much a tip as a way of saying 'I'm not so money-grubbing as to grab every last baht'. On the other hand change from a 50B note for a 44B bill will usually not be left behind.

Good bargaining, which takes practice, is another way to cut costs. Anything bought in a market should be bargained for; prices in department stores and most non-tourist shops are fixed. Sometimes accommodation rates can be bargained down. One may need to bargain hard in heavily touristed areas since the one-week, all aircon type of visitor often pays whatever is asked, creating an artificial price zone between the local and tourist market that the budgeter must deal with.

On the other hand the Thais aren't *always* trying to rip you off, so use some discretion when going for the bone on a price. There's a fine line between bargaining and niggling – getting hot under the collar about 5B makes both seller and buyer lose face. Likewise a frown is a poor bargaining tool. Some more-specific suggestions concerning costs can be found in the Accommodation and Shopping sections of this chapter.

The cost of transportation between cities and within them is very reasonable; again, bargaining (when hiring a vehicle) can save you a lot of baht. See the Getting Around chapter for more details on hiring a vehicle.

Value-Added Tax

Thailand has a 7% value-added tax (VAT). The tax applies only to certain goods and services but unfortunately no-one seems to know what's subject to VAT and what's not, so the whole situation can be rather confusing. Legally the tax is supposed to be applied to a retailer's cost for the product. For example, if a merchant's wholesale price is 100B for an item that retails at 200B, the maximum adjusted retail including VAT should be 207B, not 214B. But this rarely stops Thai merchants from adding 'VAT' surcharges to their sales.

Visitors to Thailand who hold valid tourist visas and who depart Thailand by air may apply for a VAT refund on purchases made at certain designated shops and department stores. However the labyrinth of rules and restrictions can seem so complicated that relatively few visitors bother to apply. First of all you must bear a valid tourist visa and not have been in Thailand for more than 180 days in a calendar year. Second, VAT refunds are available only to visitors departing the country by air, and are available only at the departure halls of Thailand's international airports, where you must fill out a VAT refund application and present it to customs officers along with purchased goods and receipts.

Other Consumer Taxes

Tourist hotels will usually add a 10% hotel tax, and sometimes an 8% to 10% service charge as well, to your room bill.

POST & COMMUNICATIONS

Thailand has a very efficient postal service and within the country postage is very cheap.

Bangkok's main post office on Thanon Charoen Krung (New Rd) is open from 8 am to 8 pm weekdays and from 8 am to 1 pm weekends and holidays. A 24-hour international telecommunications service (with telephone, fax, telex and telegram) is located in a separate building to the right and slightly in front of the main post office building.

The AmEx office (☎ 02-216 5757, 273 0022), Suite 88–92, 8th floor, Payathai Plaza, 128 Thanon Phayathai, will also take mail on behalf of AmEx card holders. The hours are 8.30 am to noon and 1 to 4.30 pm weekdays and 8.30 to 11.30 am on Saturday. AmEx won't accept courier packets that require your signature.

Outside Bangkok, the typical provincial main post office is open from 8.30 am to 4.30 pm weekdays and 9 am to noon on Saturday. Larger main post offices in provincial capitals may also be open for a half-day on Sunday.

Postal Rates

Air mail letters weighing 10g or less cost 14B to anywhere in Asia and the Middle East (Zone 1 in Thai postal parlance), 17B to Europe, Africa, Australia and New Zealand (Zone 2), and 19B to the Americas (Zone 3). Each additional 10g costs 5B, 7B and 9B respectively. Aerograms cost 15B regardless of the destination, while postcards are 12B to 15B, depending on size. Printed matter and small packets up to 20g cost 12B, 16B or 18B, depending on the zone.

Letters sent by registered mail cost 25B in addition to the regular air-mail postage.

International express mail service (EMS) fees vary according to 15 zones of destination radiating out from Thailand, ranging from 310B for a document sent to Zone 1 to 2050B for a document sent to Zone 15. EMS packages range from 460B to 2400B. Within Thailand, this service costs only 25B in addition to regular postage.

The rates for parcels shipped by international post vary according to weight (rising in 1kg increments), country of destination and whether they're shipped by surface (takes up to two months) or air (one to two weeks). Sample air rates include: Singapore, 560B for the first kilogram, then 100B for each additional kilogram; UK 990B first kilogram, 400B for each additional kilogram; USA 775B first kilogram and 300B for each additional kilogram.

A service called Economy Air SAL (for Sea, Air, Land) uses a combination of surface and air mail modes with rates beginning at 20B per 50g, plus 7B for each 25g after that. As a comparison, a 2kg parcel sent to the USA by regular air mail would cost 1810B, while the same parcel sent via Economy Air SAL would cost only 888B. There are a few other wrinkles to all this depending on what's in the package. Printed matter, for example, can travel by air more cheaply than other goods.

Parcels sent domestically cost 15B for the first kilogram, plus 10B for each additional kilogram.

Most provincial post offices sell do-it-yourself packing boxes (11 sizes) costing from 7B to 35B; tape and string are provided at no charge. Some of these offices even have packing services, which cost from 4B to 10B per parcel depending on size. Private packing services may also be available in the vicinity of large provincial post offices.

You can insure the contents of a package at the cost of 7B for every US$20 of the value of the goods within, plus an 'operation charge' of 25B.

Receiving Mail

The poste restante service is very reliable. During high tourist months (December to February, July, August) you may have to wait in line at the Bangkok main post office, although the line is much shorter these days with the proliferation of Internet cafes. When you receive mail, you must show ID, sign your name, and write your passport number, the number of the letter and date of delivery in the book provided. There is a fee of 1B for every piece of mail collected, 2B for each parcel. Poste restante is open from 8 am to 8 pm weekdays and 8 am to 1 pm Saturday, Sunday and holidays.

As with many Asian countries, confusion at poste restante offices is most likely to arise over first names and family names. Ask people who are writing to you to print your family name clearly and to underline it. If you're certain a letter should be waiting for you and it cannot be found, it's always wise to check that it hasn't been filed under your first name. Mail can be sent to poste restante at almost any post office in Thailand.

Couriers

Several companies in Thailand offer courier services. The main ones, headquartered in Bangkok, include:

DHL Worldwide (☎ 02-207 0600) 22nd floor, Grand Amarin Tower, Thanon Phetburi Tat Mai

Federal Express (☎ 02-367 3222) 8th floor, Green Tower, Thanon Phra Ram IV

UPS (☎ 02-712 3300) 16/1 Soi 44/1, Thanon Sukhumvit

Telephone

The telephone system in Thailand, operated by the government-subsidised Telephone Organization of Thailand (TOT) under the Communications Authority of Thailand (CAT), is quite efficient and from Bangkok you can usually direct-dial most major centres with little difficulty.

The telephone country code for Thailand is ☎ 66. See the boxed text for Thailand's area codes.

Telephone Office Hours Main post office telephone centres in most provincial capitals are open from 7 am to 11 pm daily; the smaller provincial phone offices may be open from 8 am to either 8 or 10 pm. Bangkok's international CAT phone office (now called the Public Telecommunications Service Center), at the Thanon Charoen Krung main post office, is open 24 hours.

Thai Area Codes

The area codes for Thailand's major cities are presented below. See the relevant destination chapters for the area codes of smaller towns not listed here. Note that zeros aren't needed in area codes when dialling from overseas but they must be included when dialling domestically. To dial a long-distance, domestic phone number (eg to call the THAI office in Bangkok from Chiang Mai) dial ☎ 02-513 0121. The country code for Thailand is ☎ 66. To call Bangkok from overseas, dial ☎ 66-2-513 0121.

Thai cities	codes
Bangkok, Nonthaburi, Pathum Thani, Samut Prakan, Thonburi	☎ 02
Cha-am, Phetchaburi, Prachuap Khiri Khan, Pranburi, Ratchaburi	☎ 032
Kanchanaburi, Nakhon Pathom, Samut Sakhon, Samut Songkhram	☎ 034
Ang Thong, Ayuthaya, Suphanburi	☎ 035
Lopburi, Saraburi, Singburi	☎ 036
Aranya Prathet, Nakhon Nayok, Prachinburi	☎ 037
Chachoengsao, Chonburi, Pattaya, Rayong, Si Racha	☎ 038
Chanthaburi, Trat	☎ 039
Chiang Khan, Loei, Mukdahan, Nakhon Phanom	☎ 042
Nong Khai, Sakon Nakhon, Udon Thani	☎ 042
Kalasin, Khon Kaen, Mahasarakham, Roi Et	☎ 043
Buriram, Chaiyaphum, Nakhon Ratchasima (Khorat)	☎ 044
Si Saket, Surin, Ubon Ratchathani, Yasothon	☎ 045
Chiang Mai, Chiang Rai, Lamphun, Mae Hong Son	☎ 053
Lampang, Nan, Phayao, Phrae	☎ 054
Kamphaeng Phet, Mae Sot, Phitsanulok, Sukhothai, Tak, Utaradit	☎ 055
Nakhon Sawan, Phetchabun, Phichit, Uthai Thani	☎ 056
Narathiwat, Pattani, Sungai Kolok, Yala	☎ 073
Hat Yai, Phattalung, Satun, Songkhla	☎ 074
Krabi, Nakhon Si Thammarat, Trang	☎ 075
Phang-Nga, Phuket	☎ 076
Chaiya, Chumphon, Ko Samui, Ranong, Surat Thani	☎ 077

International Calls To direct-dial an international number (other than those in Malaysia and Laos) from a private phone, simply dial ☎ 001 before the number you're calling. For operator-assisted international calls, dial ☎ 100.

Home Country Direct service is available at Bangkok's main post office, at airports in Bangkok, Chiang Mai, Phuket, Hat Yai and Surat Thani, and at post office CAT centres in Bangkok, Hat Yai, Phuket, Chiang Mai, Surat Thani, Pattaya, Hua Hin and Kanchanaburi. Home Country Direct phones offer easy one-button connection with international operators in some 40 countries around the world. You can also direct-dial Home Country Direct access numbers from any private phone (most hotel phones won't work) in Thailand. For details see the boxed text 'Home Country Direct'.

Hotels generally add surcharges (sometimes as much as 30% over and above the CAT rate) for international long-distance calls; it's always cheaper to call abroad from a CAT telephone office. These offices are almost always attached to a city's main post office, often on the building's 2nd floor, around the side or just behind the main post office. There may also be a TOT office down the road, used only for residential or business service (eg, billing or installation), not public calls; even when public phone services are offered (as at the TOT office on Thanon Ploenchit in Bangkok), TOT offices accept only cash payments – reverse-charge and credit-card calls aren't permitted. Hence the CAT office is generally your best choice.

The procedure for making an international long-distance call *(thorásàp ráwàang pràthêt)*, once you've found the proper office and window, begins with filling out a form with details of the call. Except for reverse-charge calls, you must estimate in advance the time you'll be on the phone and pay a deposit equal to the time/distance rate. There is always a minimum three-minute charge, which is refunded if your call doesn't go through. Usually, only cash or international phone credit cards are acceptable for payment at CAT offices; some provincial CAT offices also accept AmEx and a few take Visa and MasterCard.

If the call doesn't go through you must pay a 30B service charge anyway – unless you're calling reverse charges *(kèp plai thaang)*. For reverse-charge calls it's the opposite, ie, you pay the 30B charge only if the call goes through. Depending on where you're calling, reimbursing someone later for a reverse-charge call to your home country may be less

Home Country Direct

For Home Country Direct service, dial ☎ 001-999 followed by:

country	number
Australia (OTC)	61-1000
Australia (Optus)	61-2000
Canada	15-1000
Canada (AT&T)	15-2000
Denmark	45-1000
Finland	358-1000
France	33-1000
Germany	49-1000
Italy	39-1000
Israel	972-1000
Japan	81-0051
Korea	82-1000
Netherlands	31-1035
New Zealand	64-1066
Norway	47-1000
Singapore	65-0000
Sweden (telephone 1)	46-1000
Sweden (telephone 2)	41-2000
Switzerland	41-1000
UK (BT)	44-1066
UK (MCL)	44-2000
USA (AT&T)	11-1111
USA (MCI)	12001
USA (Sprint)	13877
USA (Hawaii)	14424

expensive than paying CAT/TOT charges – it pays to compare rates at the source and destination. For calls between the USA and Thailand, for example, AT&T collect-rates are less than TOT's direct rates.

Private long-distance telephone offices exist in most towns, but sometimes only for calls within Thailand. Often these offices are just a desk or a couple of booths in the rear of a retail shop. They typically collect a 10B surcharge for long-distance domestic calls and 50B for international calls, and accept cash only.

Whichever type of phone service you use, the least expensive time of day to make calls is from midnight to 5 am (30% discount on standard rates), followed by 9 pm to midnight or 5 to 7 am (20% discount). You pay full price from 7 am to 9 pm (this rate is reduced by 20% on Sunday). Some sample rates for a three-minute call during the daytime include: Africa 55B, Asia 40B, Australia 34B, Europe 46B (UK 42B).

If you're calling from a private phone, you must dial the international access code ☎ 001 before dialling the country code, area code and phone number you wish to reach.

Malaysia & Laos CAT does not offer long-distance service to Laos or Malaysia. To call these countries you must go through TOT. To call Laos you can direct dial ☎ 007 and country code 856, followed by the area code and number you want to reach. For calls to Laos from the ☎ 042 area code in Thailand (including Nong Khai, Loei, Udon Thani and Sakon Nakhon) the rate is 6B per minute; from all other provinces the rate is 18B per minute. Malaysia can be dialled direct by prefixing the code ☎ 09 to the Malaysian number (including area code). If you're dialling from any area code in Thailand that begins with ☎ 07, the rate is 10B to 15B per minute; from all other area codes the rate is 20B to 30B per minute, depending on time of day.

International Phonecards A CAT-issued, prepaid international calling card, called Thai Card, comes in 300B and 500B denominations and allows calls to many countries at standard CAT rates. You can use the Thai Card codes from either end, for example calling the UK from Thailand or calling Thailand from the UK.

Lenso phonecards allow you to make international phone calls from yellow Lenso wall phones. Cards come in two denominations, 250B and 500B, and are sold in various shops. You can also use most major credit cards with Lenso phones and dial AT&T direct-access numbers.

Of course a wide range of other international 'phonecards' – actually calling card access numbers, not true phonecards as you can't insert them in any phone in Thailand – are available outside Thailand.

Internet Phone Of course the cheapest way to call internationally is via the Internet. Some Internet calls – such as from Thailand to the USA – are free, while others are much less costly then regular phone calls. Many Internet cafes in Thailand are set up to allow Internet phone calls. Most charge only the regular per-minute or per-hour fees they charge for any other kind of Internet access if the call itself is a free call, as in the previous example. A few charge extra for Internet phone calls, and of course if the call isn't free you will pay for both Internet time and the call – but this is still often less expensive than using CAT.

Domestic Calls In most destinations there are three kinds of public pay phones in Thailand – 'red', 'blue' and 'green'. The red phones are for local city calls, the blue phones are for both local and long-distance calls (within Thailand) and the green ones are for use with phonecards.

Local calls from pay phones cost 1B for 164 seconds (add more coins for more time). Local calls from private phones cost 3B, with no time limit. Some hotels and guesthouses feature private pay phones that cost 5B per call. Long-distance rates within the country vary from 3B to 12B per minute, depending on the distance.

Card phones are available at most Thai airports as well as major shopping centres and other public areas throughout urban Thailand. Phonecards come in 25B, 50B, 100B, 200B and 240B denominations, all roughly the same size as a credit card; they can be purchased at any TOT office. In airports you can usually buy them at the airport information counter or at one of the gift shops.

Another way to pay for domestic calls is to use the Pin Phone 108 system, which allows you to dial ☎ 108 from any phone – including cellular phones and public pay phones – then enter a PIN code to call any number in Thailand. To use this system, however, you must have your own phone number in Thailand.

Cellular Phones TOT authorises use of private cell phones using two systems, NMT 900MHz (Cellular 900) and GSM, and the older NMT 470MHz. The former system is becoming more common.

It costs 1000B to register a phone and 500B per month for 'number rental' with the 900MHz and GSM, or 300B for 470MHz. Rates are 3B per minute within the same area code, 8B per minute to adjacent area codes and 12B per minute to other area codes. Cell phone users must pay for incoming as well as outgoing calls. Keep this in mind whenever you consider calling a number that begins with the code ☎ 01 – this means you are calling a cell phone number and will therefore be charged accordingly. Please note that you must also dial the zero in '01'.

In Bangkok and Chiang Mai we've seen sidewalk tables where you can make cell phone calls anywhere in Thailand for 3B to 5B per minute. The vendors are able to do this by repeatedly taking advantage of special promotions on new cell phone accounts.

eKno Communication Service

Lonely Planet's eKno global communication service provides low-cost international calls – for local calls you're usually better off with a local phonecard. eKno also offers free messaging services, email, travel information and an online travel vault, where you can securely store all your important documents. You can join online at www.ekno.lonelyplanet.com, where you will find the local-access numbers for the 24-hour customer-service centre. Once you have joined, always check the eKno Web site for the latest access numbers for each country and updates on new features.

Fax, Telex & Telegraph

Telephone offices in main post offices throughout the country offer fax, telegraph and telex services in addition to regular phone services. There's no need to bring your own paper, as the post offices supply their own forms. A few TOT offices also offer fax services. International faxes typically cost 100B to 130B for the first page, and 70B to 100B per page for the remaining pages, depending on the size of the paper and the destination.

Larger hotels with business centres offer the same telecommunication services but always at higher rates.

Email & Internet Access

The Net continues to expand in Thailand, as an increasing number of local Thai-language pages go online and folks get their Net software installed for Thai language. The scene is changing rapidly and nowadays Thailand's better Internet service providers (ISPs) offer upcountry nodes in a dozen or more towns and cities around the country, which means if you are travelling with a laptop you won't necessarily have to pay long-distance charges to Bangkok.

The major limitation in email and Internet access continues to be the CAT, which connects all ISPs via the Thailand Internet Exchange (THIX) at speeds that are relatively low by international standards. The CAT also collects a hefty access charge from local ISPs, which keeps the rates high relative to the local economy.

Nevertheless, Thailand is more advanced in the cybernautic world than any other country in South-East Asia at the moment and rates continue to drop from year to year. Many guesthouses and bars/cafes in Bangkok, Chiang Mai, Ko Samui and Phuket now offer email and Internet log-ons at house terminals. For the visitor who only needs to log on once in a while, these are a less expensive alternative to getting your own account – and it certainly beats lugging around a laptop. The going rate is 1B or 2B per on- and offline minute, although we've seen a few places where slower connections are available at a half-baht per minute. If past experience is any measure, rates will continue to drop.

If you want assurance that you'll find cybercafes in Thailand, check www.netcafeguide.com. However at last pass this site listed only 38 spots in the entire country (several of which haven't existed for over a year) – just a tiny fraction of those up and operating. At any rate you won't need a Web site or a guidebook to find such places in Thailand as they're plentiful in any town with a population over 50,000. For that reason we don't list cybercafes in this guide except for towns where they're a rarity, or where the services offered are especially extensive.

Nowadays most ISPs worldwide offer the option of Web-based email, so if you already have an Internet account at home you can check your email anywhere in Thailand simply by logging onto your ISP's Web site using an Internet browser (such as Microsoft Internet Explorer or Netscape). If you have any doubts about whether your home ISP offers Web-based email, check before you leave home. You may want to register with one of the many free Web-based email services, such as MS Hotmail, Yahoo!, Juno or Lonely Planet's own eKno. You can log onto these services at any cybercafe in Thailand.

Plugging in Your Own Machine In older hotels and guesthouses the phones may still be hard-wired, but in newer hotels RJ11 phone jacks are the standard. For hard-wired phones you'll need to bring an acoustic coupler. Some hotels and guesthouses that feature room phones without RJ11 jacks may have a fax line in the office, and virtually all fax machines in Thailand are connected via RJ11 jacks. Some places will allow guests to use the house fax line for laptop modems, provided online time is kept short.

Longer-term visitors may want to consider opening a monthly Internet account. Local ISPs – of which there were 18 at last count – typically charge around 400B to 500B per month for 20 hours of Net access and 700B to 800B for 40 hours. Low-grade, text-only services are available for as little as 200B a month. With any of these accounts additional per-hour charges are incurred if you exceed your online time.

Temporary Internet accounts are also available from several Thai ISPs. One of the better ones is WebNet, offered by Loxinfo (www.loxinfo.co.th). You can buy a block of 25 hours (500B), or 45 hours (750B), good for up to one year. Purchasers are provided with a user ID, password, Web browser software, local phone access numbers and log-on procedures, all (except the Web browser software) via email. You'll be able to navigate the Internet, check email at your online home address, and access any online services you subscribe to.

INTERNET RESOURCES

A growing number of online entities offer information on Thailand. Many of these Web sites are commercial sites established by tour operators or hotels; the ratio of commercial to noncommercial sites is liable to increase over time if current Internet trends continue. Remember that all URL's (Uniform Resource Locators) mentioned are subject to change without notice. You can use your own Web browser to conduct searches and there's a lot of information out there: A quick search on Yahoo at the time of writing yielded a list of nearly a thousand Web sites devoted to Thailand, plus 479,000 Web pages that mentioned the word 'Thailand'.

Consider starting with the Lonely Planet Web site (www.lonelyplanet.com). Here you'll find succinct summaries on travelling to most places on earth, postcards from other travellers and the Thorn Tree bulletin board, where you can ask questions before you go or dispense advice when you get back. You can also find travel news and updates to this edition, and the subWWWay section links you to the most useful travel resources elsewhere on the Web. Go to www.lonelyplanet.com.au/dest/sea/thai.htm for a direct link to Thailand-related material.

Other useful Web sites include:

Asia Travel Perhaps the best of the many commercial sites with travel-booking capabilities. asiatravel.com/thaiinfo.html

Bangkok Post Contains the entire newspaper (except for ads) daily, and archives of stories for several years.
www.bangkokpost.com

Kidon Media-Link At last check had the best set of Thai newspaper links.
www.kidon.com/media-link/thailand.shtml

Mahidol University Very useful Web site that's searchable by keyword.
www.mahidol.ac.th/Thailand

National Electronics and Computer Technology Center (NECTEC) Contains links on everything from a list of all Thai embassies and consulates abroad and details of visa requirements to weather updates.
www.nectec .or.th

ThaiIndex General information, government office listings, travel listings, a hotel directory and other Web links.
www.thaiindex.com

Thailand.com Looks promising if it can fill its travel section with useful visitor information; its news pages are one of the better examples of on-line Thai news digests.
www.thailand.com

The Nation Another good source of local news with a comprehensive searchable archive. www.nationmultimedia.com

Tourism Authority of Thailand Contains a province guide, up-to-date press releases, tourism statistics, TAT contact information and trip planning hints.
www.tat.or.th or www.tourismthailand.org

Many Web sites with information on Thailand travel earn revenue from hotel bookings and advertising paid for by travel suppliers, hence you should take any recommendations they make with a huge grain of salt. Providing relief from the usual ad-studded pages, students at Sriwittayapaknam School in Samut Prakan Province maintain an intriguing complex of highly informative sites, including the mammoth ThaiStudents.com (www.thaistudents.com), the largest English-language Web site in Thailand.

Aside from the Web, another Internet resource, soc.culture.thai, is a usenet newsgroup. It's very uneven, as it's basically a chat outlet for anyone who thinks they have something to say about Thailand. Still it's not a bad place to start if you have a burning question that you haven't found an answer to elsewhere.

BOOKS
Bookshops

Thailand boasts the largest selection of English-language books and bookshops in South-East Asia. The principal chains are Asia Books and DK Book House; each has branches in half a dozen locations around Bangkok and DK also has branches in larger tourist destinations like Chiang Mai, Ko Samui and Phuket. Some larger tourist hotels also have bookshops with English-language books and periodicals.

See the Bookshop entries under the relevant cities for further details.

The following titles are recommended (publishing details are not always included as they can vary globally).

Lonely Planet

Aside from this guidebook, other Lonely Planet publications of interest to anyone visiting Thailand include the *Thai phrasebook*, the *Hill Tribes phrasebook* and the *Thailand, Vietnam, Laos & Cambodia Road Atlas*. *Thailand's Islands & Beaches* goes into more detail on the kingdom's coastal and marine destinations, while the *Bangkok city guide* presents more-extensive information on Bangkok in a smaller and more portable form. *Diving & Snorkeling Thailand*, hot off the presses, is chock-a-block full of colour photos and essential diving information. Soon to appear is Lonely Planet's *Chiang Mai & Northern Thailand*.

Description & Travel

The earliest Western literature of note on Thailand, Guy Tachard's *A Relation of the Voyage to Siam*, recounts a 1680s French expedition through parts of the country with little literary flair. Shortly after, Simon de la Loubére's 1693 *New Historical Relation of the Kingdom of Siam* chronicled the French mission to the Ayuthaya court in great detail. Maurice Collis novelised this period with a focus on the unusual political relationship between King Narai and his Greek minister, Constantine Phaulkon, in *Siamese White*.

Frank Vincent's *The Land of the White Elephant*, first published in 1873, is a very readable account of an American merchant's travels in Siam. Carl Bock's illustrated *Temples and Elephants* covered similar territory in 1884. Tachard, Loubére, Collis, Vincent and Bock have all been republished by Bangkok publisher White Lotus and are readily available in bookshops in Bangkok, Chiang Mai and Phuket. Other reprints to look for if you're interested in pre-20th century historical detail include *The Kingdom of the Yellow Robe* (1898), by Ernest Young, and the anonymous *An Englishman's Siamese Journals* (1890–93).

Anna Leonowens wrote *The English Governess at the Siamese Court* in 1870. Its largely unauthentic descriptions of Siamese life (see the boxed text 'The King and Who?' in the Facts about Thailand chapter) were later transformed into three Hollywood movies and a Broadway musical.

Joseph Conrad evoked Thailand in several of his pre-WWII novels and short stories, most notably in his 1920s *The Secret Sharer* and *Falk: A Reminiscence*. More detail from the 1920s can be found in *Teak Wallah*, by Reginald Campbell, a Briton who worked as a teak inspector in Northern Thailand.

Pierre Boulle's post-WWII novel *The Bridge on the River Kwai* dramatised the construction and destruction of the Death Railway Bridge in Kanchanaburi Province. In 1957 it was made into an Academy Award–winning motion picture that remains the most internationally famous film having to do with Thailand.

Charles Nicholls' semi-fictional *Borderlines* (1992) takes the reader on a voyage to the Thai-Myanmar border in the company of a colourful group of travellers. Along the way the author weaves cultural insights into the storyline, making the book more than just a beach read.

A beach read is exactly what you can expect from Alex Garland's 1997 novel *The Beach*, a tale of island-hopping backpackers trying to carve out their own private paradise in a national marine park in Thailand. A film based on the novel and starring Leo DiCaprio was released in 2000 and although critical reviews were savaging, cinema earnings topped US$200 million.

Nicholls, Pico Iyer, Robert Anson Hall and several other well-known and not-so-well-known authors have contributed travel essays of varying style to 1994's *Travelers' Tales Thailand*. It was the first title in a now well-known series that assembles travel articles and chapters from various sources into a single anthology devoted to a particular country. Some savvy travel tips are sprinkled throughout the text.

A more serious collection of literature is available in *Traveller's Literary Companion: South-East Asia*, edited by Alastair Dingwall. The Thailand chapter, edited by scholar Thomas John Hudak, is packed with hard-to-find information on the history of literature in Thailand and includes extracts from various works by Thai as well as foreign authors.

A Guide to Khmer Temples in Thailand & Laos, by Michael Freeman, covers 27 Khmer archaeological sites in North-Eastern Thailand, plus two that lie more or less just over the border in Cambodia but are readily accessible from Thailand. It's packed with information, appealing photos and maps.

David Unkovich's *A Motorcycle Guide to the Golden Triangle* (1998, Silkworm Books) is indispensable for anyone wanting to make a motorcycling trip off the beaten track in the mountainous borderlands of Northern Thailand.

Bangkok's own Asia Books has issued several photo-heavy but relatively inexpensive titles on Thailand in its Golden Souvenir series: *Thailand; Chiang Mai & Northern Thailand;* and *The Hill Tribes of Thailand.*

History & Politics

Georges Coedès' classic prewar work on South-East Asian history, *The Indianised States of South-East Asia,* contains ground-breaking historical material on early Thai history, as does WAR Wood's *A History of Siam,* published in the same era. One of the more readable general histories written in the latter half of the 20th century is David Wyatt's *Thailand: A Short History* (Trasvin Publications, Chiang Mai).

At first glance *Siam Mapped: A History of the Geo-Body of a Nation* by Thongchai Winichakul appears to be a simple history of the mapping of Thailand. But a thorough reading will uncover a profound and very well-researched study of Thai notions of identity and sovereignty within the context of South-East Asian history and European involvement in the region.

Concentrating on post-revolutionary Thailand, *The Balancing Act: A History of Modern Thailand* (Asia Books, 1991), by Joseph Wright Jr, starts with the 1932 revolution and ends with the February 1991 coup. Wright's semi-academic chronicle concludes that certain 'natural laws' – endemic to the culture – govern the continuous circulation of elites. Although the book is packed with detail, such deep-structure theorising brings to mind the way Anglo scholars until very recently identified all French political trends as 'Bonapartiste'. Wright's most demonstrable thesis is that, despite the 1932 revolution, democracy has never gained a firm foothold in Thai society.

The best source of information on Thailand's political scene during the turbulent 1960s and 1970s is *Political Conflict in Thailand: Reform, Reaction, Revolution* by David Morrell & Chai-anan Samudavanija.

Thailand's role in the international narcotics trade is covered thoroughly in Alfred McCoy's *The Politics of Heroin in Southeast Asia* and Francis Belanger's *Drugs, the US, and Khun Sa. Chasing the Dragon: Into the Heart of the Golden Triangle,* by Christopher R Cox, contains some decent writing and interesting news titbits as it traces a journalist's path to Khun Sa's former Ho Mong headquarters near the Thai-Myanmar border. Those who have made the trip themselves may find it exaggerates the difficulties inherent in accomplishing a reportorial visit with the Shan warlord, who maintained his own press agent in Chiang Mai.

Although it's fiction, ex-prime minister Kukrit Pramoj's 1961 *Red Bamboo* vividly portrays and predicts the conflict between the Thai communist movement and the establishment during the 1960s and 1970s. His book *Si Phaendin: Four Reigns* (1981), the most widely read novel ever published in Thailand, covers the Ayuthaya era. Both of these novels are available in English-language versions.

Axel Aylwen's novel *The Falcon of Siam* and its sequel *The Falcon Takes Wing* are not up to Kukrit's literary standards but nonetheless capture the feel and historical detail of 17th-century Siam; Aylwen obviously read Collis, Loubére and Tachard closely (see Description & Travel earlier in this section).

Although it's tough to find, *The Devil's Discus* (Cassell & Co, 1964) by Rayne Kruger focuses on the mysterious death of Rama VIII. The book is banned in Thailand for its police-blotter style analysis of a taboo topic.

Natural History

Complete with sketches, photos and maps, *The Mammals of Thailand* (Association for the Conservation of Wildlife, 1988), by Boonsong Lekagul & Jeffrey McNeely, remains the classic on Thai wildlife in spite of a few out-of-date references (it was first published in 1977). Bird lovers should seek out the *Bird Guide of Thailand* (Association for the Conservation of Wildlife, 1972), by Boonsong Lekagul & EW Cronin, for the comprehensive descriptions of Thailand's numerous avian species.

Detailed summaries of Thailand's national parks, along with an objective assessment of current park conditions, are available in *National Parks of Thailand* (Communication Resources, Bangkok) by Gray, Piprell & Graham.

Culture & Society

Naga: Cultural Origins in Siam & the Western Pacific by Sumet Jumsai (Chalermnit Press/DD Books, 1997) is an inspired piece of speculative theory on the supposed oceanic origins of Thai people and culture. With inspiration from the late R Buckminster Fuller, who collaborated with author/architect/Cambridge lecturer Sumet to a limited degree, the book outlines in prose and carefully collected illustrations how the myths, symbols and architecture common to Thailand and other mainland South-East Asian civilisations – in particular the *naga* or sea dragon motif – stem from an earlier phase in Asian-Western Pacific history when most of the peoples of the region inhabited islands and lived largely seafaring lives. The proposed confrontation between 'water-based' Thai culture and 'land-based' Khmer (and later Western) culture is fascinating and of intrinsic value whether or not the oceanic origin theory is accurate.

Culture Shock! Thailand & How to Survive It by Robert & Nanthapa Cooper is an interesting outline on getting along with the Thai way of life, although it's heavily oriented towards Bangkok. *Letters from Thailand* by Botan (translated by Susan Fulop Kepner) and Carol Hollinger's *Mai Pen Rai Means Never Mind* can also be recommended for their insights into traditional Thai culture. *Working with the Thais* by Henry Holmes and Suchada Tangtongtavy covers just about everything you might need to know before entering into a serious work situation in Thailand.

Wondering into Thai Culture, by Mont Redmond, is a collection of newspaper essays that first appeared in *The Nation.* Redmond's ambitious and sincere outings are marred by a convoluted, self-devised transcription of Thai words and a self-important writing style. The book implies that the Thais are children, whose language is deteriorating because of a worldwide 'decline of poetic ability and the rise of commercial prose.' A basic flaw in Redmond's outlook is that he seems reluctant to accept variation and change in either culture or language – processes that are necessary for cultural and linguistic survival. In spite of these criticisms, a book as highly speculative as this is worth reading simply for the dialogue it may stimulate amid old Thailand hands.

Jack Reynolds' 1950s *A Woman of Bangkok* (republished in 1985), a well-written and poignant story of a young Englishman's descent into the world of Thai

brothels, remains the best novel yet published with this theme. Expat writer Christopher G Moore covers the Thai underworld in his 1990s novels *A Killing Smile, Spirit House, A Bewitching Smile* and a raft of others, with an anchor firmly hooked into the go-go bar scene. His description of Bangkok's sleazy Thermae Coffee House (called 'Zeno' in *A Killing Smile*) is the closest literature comes to evoking the perpetual male adolescence to which these places cater.

For a look at Bangkok's infamous Thanon Patpong (Patpong Rd) from a Western female's perspective, read *Patpong Sisters* (1994) by Cleo Odzer, an American who carried out unauthorised anthropological research on the women working in Patpong in the late 1980s. Odzer comes to the unique conclusion that prostitution is empowering work for women who grow up in Thailand with few other employment possibilities. Although such a conclusion flies in the face of statistics (which show that the percentage of women who make up the labour force in Thailand is greater than in either the People's Republic of China or the USA), and generalises from atypical Patpong-style prostitution, the book nonetheless offers many insights into the world of her 'sisters'.

'Hello My Big Big Honey!' Love Letters to Bangkok Bar Girls and Their Revealing Interviews (published in French as *Bonjour Ma Grande Grande Chérie!' Lettres d'Amour aux Filles des Bars de Bangkok et Interviews Révélatrices*), by Richard Ehrlich and Dave Walker, delivers exactly what the title describes. This collection of letters between Thai bar workers and their fàràng (foreigners of European descent) clients – and the verbatim question-and-answer interviews with the women – discloses more about the complex nature of these encounters than 10 academic treatises of a similar size.

For information on books about Buddhism and how it is practised in Thailand, see the 'Religion in Thailand' special section in the Facts for the Visitor chapter.

Hill Tribes

If you're interested in detailed information on hill tribes, seek out the hard-to-find *The Hill Tribes of Northern Thailand* by Gordon Young (Monograph No 1, The Siam Society). Young was born of third-generation

Christian missionaries among the Lahu people, spoke several tribal dialects and was even an honorary Lahu chieftain with the highest Lahu title, the Supreme Hunter. The monograph covers 16 tribes, including descriptions, photographs, tables and maps.

From the Hands of the Hills, by Margaret Campbell, has lots of beautiful pictures. *Peoples of the Golden Triangle,* by Elaine & Paul Lewis, is also very good, very photo-oriented and expensive. Lonely Planet's *Thai Hill Tribes phrasebook* has descriptions of Thailand's major hill tribes, maps and phrases in several hill-tribe languages.

Trekking through Northern Thailand by Ada Guntamala & Kornvika Puapratum (Silkworm Books, Chiang Mai) contains good suggestions for trekking whether you are going out on your own or with a guide. The small book includes route maps and lists of taboos for individual tribes. *The Hill Tribes of Thailand,* published by the Tribal Research Institute at Chiang Mai University, also contains sound advice for trekkers but the hill tribe information is rather skimpy.

Teak House, a Thai publishing house, publishes a series of book-length monographs devoted to individual ethnic groups in South-East Asia, including *The Haw: Traders of the Golden Triangle* (Andrew Forbes & David Henley), *The Akha: Guardians of the Forest* (Jim Goodman) and *The Khon Muang: People & Principalities of North Thailand* (Andrew Forbes & David Henley).

See the Hill Tribes special section in the Northern Thailand chapter for further information on these groups.

Food & Shopping

Lonely Planet's compact *World Food: Thailand,* by Joe Cummings, enables food-conscious visitors to Thailand, as well as residents, to appreciate the full range of Thai cuisine by providing explanations of the cooking methods, extensive menu glossaries and lots of cultural and historical background.

Kasma Loha-unchit's stylish *It Rains Fishes: Legends, Traditions and the Joys of Thai Cooking* brings together Thai culinary lore, cooking techniques and recipes tailored to the American kitchen. Kasma's *Dancing Shrimp* focuses on Thai seafood, with special emphasis on authenticity.

Among the explosion of Thai cookbooks that have appeared in recent years, one of the best remains *Thai Cooking* (formerly *The Original Thai Cookbook*) by Jennifer Brennan. Although *Thailand the Beautiful Cookbook* by Panurat Poladitmontri is expensive and unwieldy, its huge, coffee table–style format contains excellent photography and authentic recipes.

Three small books in the Periplus Nature Guide series, *Tropical Herbs & Spices of Thailand, Tropical Fruits of Thailand* and *Tropical Vegetables of Thailand* make good additions to anyone's library of books on Thai cuisine. For those without access to a complete range of Thai herbs and spices, *Cooking Thai Food in American Kitchens* by Malulee Pinsuvana makes reasonable substitutions.

Shopping in Exotic Thailand (Impact Publications, USA) by Ronald & Caryl Rae Krannich is packed with general shopping tips as well as lists of speciality shops and markets throughout Thailand.

Although it's a bit out of date, John Hoskins' 1988 *Buyer's Guide to Thai Gems & Jewellery* is a must for anyone contemplating a foray into Thailand's gem market. *Arts and Crafts of Thailand* (1994), written by William Warren and photographed by Luca Invernizzi Tettoni, makes a useful primer for delving into the world of Thailand's handicrafts.

FILMS

A number of classic international films have used Thailand either as a subject or as a location – more often the latter. In fact nowadays location shooting in Thailand has become something of a boom industry as Thailand's jungles, rice fields and islands find themselves backdrops for all manner of scripts set in 'exotic' tropical countries. Thailand now maintains a substantial contingent of trained production assistants and casting advisers who work continuously with foreign companies – many of them from Japan, Hong Kong and Singapore – on location shoots.

Jungles & Kingdoms

The first film to come out of Thailand for foreign audiences was *Chang,* a 1927 silent picture shot entirely in Nan Province (then still a semi-independent principality with

Siamese protection). Produced by American film impresarios Copper and Schoedsack – who later produced several major Hollywood hits – *Chang* contains some of the best jungle and wildlife sequences filmed in Asia to date. *Chang* is available on film or video from speciality houses. Around the same time a movie called *I Am from Siam*, produced and narrated by *Bangkok Post* founder Don Gardner and starring none other than King Rama VII, emerged. It's virtually impossible to find this film today outside Thailand's National Film Archives.

Next came *Anna and the King of Siam*, a 1946 American production (filmed on Hollywood sets) starring Rex Harrison and based on the book *The English Governess at the Siamese Court* by Anna Leonowens, who taught English to Rama IV's children in the 19th century. Although the movie opened to very mixed reviews, screenwriter Arthur Miller was honoured with an Academy Award. A 1956 musical remake, *The King and I*, grew from a very successful Broadway stage production starring Yul Brynner (who earned an Oscar for the film). Most recently Jodie Foster starred in *Anna and the King*, which caused quite a stir when the Thai government refused permission to film the movie in Thailand on the grounds that the script contained historical and cultural distortions. Instead the studios used Malaysia as a backdrop (and non-Thai actors speaking Thai badly), and the US$75-million film opened in 1999 to flat reviews. All three films, as well as the musical, are banned in Thailand because they are seen to compromise the dignity of the monarchy.

Probably the most famous movie associated with Thailand is *The Bridge on the River Kwai*, a 1957 Academy Award–winning production stemming from Pierre Boulle's book of the same name and starring Alec Guinness. Although based on WWII events in Thailand, much of the film was shot on location in Sri Lanka (then Ceylon). Another early film of some notoriety was 1962's *The Ugly American*, a Marlon Brando vehicle based on the novel by William J Lederer. In this muddled picture Thailand stands in for the fictional South-East Asian nation of Sarkan. Part-time Thai politician and academic Kukrit Pramoj enjoyed a substantial film role as the fake nation's prime minister. Kukrit went on to become Thailand's prime minister in 1974.

Tarzan Goes to India (1962) was shot not in India but in Thailand.

Bond, Sex, Martial Arts & Vietnam

The Man with the Golden Gun, a pedestrian 1974 James Bond vehicle starring Roger Moore and Christopher Lee, brought the karst islands of Ao Phang-Nga to international attention for the first time. A year later the French soft-porn movie *Emmanuelle* ('Much hazy, soft-focus coupling in downtown Bangkok', wrote *The Illustrated London News*) added to the myth of Thailand as sexual idyll and set an all-time box office record in France. A half-dozen or so Emmanuelle sequels, at least two of which returned to Thailand for script settings, were produced over the next decade.

Virtually every film produced with a Vietnam War theme has been shot either in the Philippines or in Thailand, with the latter ahead by a long shot as the location of choice due to relative logistical ease. The first Vietnam-themed movie to use Thailand as a location was *The Deer Hunter*, which starred Robert DeNiro and relative newcomer Meryl Streep; it won five Oscars in 1978, including Best Picture and Best Director. Christopher Walken played the dramatic Russian-roulette scene in an old neighbourhood on Thanon Charoen Krung, while the Saigon bar scenes were shot in Bangkok's Patpong district. Oliver Stone's *Heaven and Earth* (1993), starring Tommy Lee Jones, is one of the more recent pictures to paint Vietnam on a Thai canvas.

The Killing Fields (1984) skilfully used Thailand as a stand-in for Cambodia in a story about the Khmer Rouge takeover of Phnom Penh. In *Swimming to Cambodia*, a 1987 spin-off of *The Killing Fields*, monologist Spalding Gray recounts numerous behind-the-scenes anecdotes of shooting the film in Thailand.

Jean-Claude Van Damme's *The Kickboxer* brought Thai boxing to the big screen with a bit more class than the average martial arts flick; more than a few foreign pugilists have packed their bags for Bangkok after viewing the movie's exotic mix of ring violence and Thai Buddhist atmospherics. Sly Stallone's 1980s *Rambo* movies (Rambos II & III used Thai locations) did little for Thailand, but the success of *Good Morning Vietnam* (1988), a Robin Williams comedy widely publicised as having been shot in Bangkok and Phuket, helped generate a tourism boom for the country. Also in the 1980s, two very forgettable comedy flicks were filmed in Mae Hong Son: *Volunteers,* a Tom Hanks and John Candy movie about a couple of Peace Corps workers falling afoul of dope peddlers and communists; and *Air America,* with a dashing Mel Gibson falling afoul of more Reds and dope peddlers. In 1988's stylishly grungy, neon-lit *Off Limits* Willem Dafoe sweats a lot as a plain-clothes US military cop; his co-star, Bangkok, once again portrays the streets of Saigon.

In 1994 *Mortal Kombat* leapt from the world of video games to the silver screen with help from Thai locations; other movies of the 1990s have included *Operation Dumbo Drop* and *The Phantom,* both directed by Australian Simon Wincer of *The Man from Snowy River* fame.

James Bond returned to Thailand for the first time since 1974 for the filming of 1997's *Tomorrow Never Dies.* This time 007 was portrayed by Pierce Brosnan, accompanied by action star Michelle Yeoh as he guns a 1200cc BMW motorbike across Bangkok rooftops.

Backpacker Mayhem

Two films released in 1999 and 2000 directly addressed the travel scene in Thailand. Both managed to make Thailand look sinister and dangerous, at least for those who play with drugs. Claire Danes and Kate Beckinsale portray two young Americans imprisoned in Bangkok for trying to smuggle drugs to Hong Kong in *Brokedown Palace* (1999). Based on a true story in which the convicted Australian pair received a relatively light 33-year sentence for a crime that usually warrants execution in Thailand, the movie feeds the same travel paranoia as the 1978 *Midnight Express.* Location filming took place in the Philippines.

Trainspotting's Danny Boyle directed teenage heart-throb Leonardo DiCaprio in a film adaptation of Alex Garland's novel *The Beach* (see Books earlier), which was released in early 2000 to mixed reviews.

Like the novel, the story traces the fate of a small, loose-knit group of world travellers who decide to establish their own beach paradise on an island in Thailand's Ang Thong National Marine Park – right next to a marijuana plantation. Boyle did a better job than Garland in depicting the backpacker scene in Thailand, but he and the producers were later criticised for making alterations to a beach on Ko Phi Phi Leh (the case for lasting damage has yet to be proven). Other Thai locations for *The Beach* included Khao Yai National Park (the waterfall) and the provincial capitals of Phuket (standing in for Thanon Khao San) and Krabi (also Khao San).

NEWSPAPERS

Thailand's 1997 constitution guarantees freedom of the press, although the Royal Police Department reserves the power to suspend publishing licences for national security reasons. Editors nevertheless exercise self-censorship in certain realms, particularly with regard to the monarchy. Monarchical issues aside, Thailand is widely considered to have the freest print media in South-East Asia. In a survey conducted by the Singapore-based Political and Economic Risk Consultancy, 180 expatriate managers in 10 Asian countries ranked Thailand's English-language press the best in Asia. Surprisingly, these expats cited the *Bangkok Post* and *The Nation* more frequently as their source of regional and global news than either the *Asian Wall Street Journal* or the *Far Eastern Economic Review.*

These two English-language newspapers are published daily in Thailand and distributed in most provincial capitals throughout the country – the *Bangkok Post* in the morning and *The Nation* in the afternoon. The *Post,* Thailand's first English daily (established 1946), has a mixed Thai and international staff and tends to feature more objective reporting than *The Nation.* The latter often runs opinion pieces as news and has a habit of scapegoating the West for internal Thai problems. For international news, the *Post* is the better of the two papers and is in fact regarded by many journalists as the best English daily in the region. *The Nation* used to provide the best regional coverage but since the 1997 recession the paper seems to have lost its reporting edge.

The Singapore edition of the *International Herald Tribune* is widely available in Bangkok, Chiang Mai and heavily touristed areas like Pattaya and Phuket.

The most popular Thai-language newspapers are *Thai Rath* and *Daily News,* but they're mostly full of blood-and-guts stories. The best Thai journalism is found in the somewhat less popular *Matichon* and *Siam Rath* dailies. Many Thais read the English-language dailies as they consider them better news sources. The *Bangkok Post* also publishes a Thai-language version of the popular English daily.

MAGAZINES

English-language magazine publishing has faltered with the economic slowdown in Thailand and several mags failed after 1996. Now Thailand's biggest-selling English-language magazine, *Bangkok Metro* injects urban sophistication into the publishing scene with extensive listings on art, culture, cuisine, film and music in Bangkok, along with less extensive Pattaya, Phuket and Chiang Mai pages.

Monthly *Le Gavroche* offers news and feature stories on Thailand for the francophone community.

Many popular magazines from the UK, USA, Australia and Europe – particularly those concerned with computer technology, autos, fashion, music and business – are available in bookshops that specialise in English-language publications (see Bookshops under Books earlier in this chapter).

RADIO

Thailand has more than 400 radio stations, with 41 FM and 35 AM stations in Bangkok alone. Radio station 107 FM, affiliated with Radio Thailand and Channel 9 on Thai public television, broadcasts CNN news coverage of the Asia region almost every hour between 5 pm and 2 am daily, and features some surprisingly good music programs with British, Thai and American DJs. Bilingual DJs at Star FM 102.5 present R&B, pop, rock and alternative music 24 hours a day. Another station with international pop and English-speaking DJs is Radio Bangkok (Gold FMX), 95.5 FM, which plays contemporary hits as well as oldies 24 hours a day.

Looking for Thai music? Station 87.5 FM broadcasts classic Thai pop, including old lûuk thûng styles (see the 'Music, Theatre & Dance' special section) played on accordion.

Chulalongkorn University broadcasts classical music at 101.5 FM from 10.30 pm to 1 am nightly, 'light classical, popular golden oldies and jazz' from 4 to 6.30 pm. A schedule of the evening's programs can be found in the *The Nation* and *Bangkok Post* newspapers.

The BBC World Service, Radio Canada, Radio Japan, Radio New Zealand, Singapore Broadcasting Company and Voice of America (VOA) all have English- and Thai-language broadcasts over short-wave radio. The frequencies and schedules, which change hourly, appear in the *Post* and *The Nation*. BBC and VOA are the most easily received by the average short-wave radio.

Radio France Internationale and Deutsche Welle carry short-wave programs in French and German respectively. Deutsche Welle also broadcasts 50 minutes of English programming three times daily.

TV

Thailand has five VHF TV networks based in Bangkok. Channel 3 is privately owned and offers a wide variety of Thai comedy, dramas, news and movies, mostly in Thai language only; broadcast hours are 5.30 am to midnight.

Channel 5 is a military network and broadcasts from 5 am to 3.05 am. Between 5 and 7 am this network presents a mix of ABC, CNN International and English-subtitled Thai news programs; English-language news at noon also; then CNN headlines again at 12.07 am.

Channel 7 (5.30 am to 12.30 am) is also military owned but the broadcast time is leased to private companies; one of the best features of this channel is the broadcasting of rustic lûuk thûng (see the 'Music, Theatre & Dance' special section in the Facts about Thailand chapter for more information) music videos between 12.15 and 2.10 pm (mixed with news).

Channel 9, the national public television station, broadcasts from 5.30 am until 2 am. An English-language soundtrack is simulcast with Channel 9's evening news program at 7 pm weekdays on radio station FM 107.

Channel 11 is run by the Ministry of Education and features educational programs from 4.40 am to 11 pm, including TV correspondence classes from Ramkham-haeng and Sukhothai Thammathirat open universities. An English-language news simulcast comes over FM 88 at 8 pm.

Upcountry cities generally receive only two networks – Channel 9 and a local private network with restricted hours.

Satellite & Cable TV

As elsewhere in Asia, satellite and cable television services are swiftly multiplying in Thailand, and competition for the largely untapped market is keen. The most successful cable company in Thailand is UBC, available via CaTV, MMDS and DTH systems. Among the many satellite transmissions carried by UBC are six English-language movie channels (including HBO and Cinemax, both censored in Asia for language, nudity and violence), two to four international sports channels, imported TV series, MTV Asia, Channel V (a Hong Kong–based music video telecast), CNN International, CNBC, NHK, BBC World Service Television, the Discovery Channel and all the standard Thai networks. You can access further information on UBC's Web site (www.ubctv.com) or obtain a copy of the free monthly *UBC Magazine* by contacting the company.

Thailand has its own ThaiCom 1 and 2 as uplinks for AsiaSat and as carriers for the standard Thai networks and Thai Sky (TST). The latter includes five channels offering news and documentaries, Thai music videos and Thai variety programs. Other satellites tracked by dishes in Thailand include China's Apstar 1 and Apstar 2. Additional transmissions from these and from Vietnam, Myanmar and Malaysia are available with a satellite dish.

VIDEO SYSTEMS

The predominant VHS video format in Thailand is PAL, a system compatible with that used in most of Europe (France's SECAM format is a notable exception) as well as in Australia. This means if you're bringing video tapes from the USA or Japan (which use the NTSC format) you'll have to bring your own VCR to play them, or else acquire a 'multisystem' VCR with the capacity to play both NTSC and PAL (but not SECAM, except as black-and-white images). Some video shops (especially those

that carry pirated or unlicensed tapes) sell NTSC as well as PAL and SECAM tapes.

Video CD (VCD) is beginning to replace VHS in Thailand and most of the rest of Asia. VCDs can be played on a VCD player or on any computer with a CD-ROM drive. For the latter you'll need to install VCD software, which can be downloaded free from the Internet. Many video shops and street vendors in larger cities sell VCDs of both Thai and international movies.

Digital video discs (DVD) are still relatively rare in Thailand, although they are available at high-end audio shops and some video stores. Many Thai department stores and audio shops sell multiplayers that can play audio CDs, VCDs and DVDs.

PHOTOGRAPHY & VIDEO
Film & Equipment

Print film is fairly inexpensive and widely available throughout Thailand. Japanese print film costs around 100B per 36 exposures, US print film a bit more. Fujichrome Velvia and Provia slide films cost around 265B per roll, Kodak Ektachrome Elite is 230B and Ektachrome 200 about 270B. Slide film, especially Kodachrome, can be hard to find outside Bangkok and Chiang Mai, so be sure to stock up before heading upcountry. VHS video cassettes of all sizes are readily available in the major cities.

Processing

Film processing is generally quite good in the larger cities in Thailand and also quite inexpensive. Dependable E6 processing is available at several labs in Bangkok but is untrustworthy elsewhere. Kodachrome must be sent out of the country for processing, so it can take up to two weeks to get it back.

Pros will find a number of labs in Bangkok that offer same-day pick-up and delivery at no extra cost within the city. IQ Lab (☎ 02-238 4001), at 160 Thanon Silom, opposite the Silom Complex in Bangkok, offers the widest range of services, with all types of processing (except for Kodachrome), slide duping, scanning, digital prints, OutPut slides, photo CDs and custom printing.

Technical Tips

Pack some silica gel with your camera to prevent mould growing on the inside of your lenses. A polarising filter could be useful to cut down on tropical glare at certain times of day. Tripods are a must for shooting interiors in natural light.

For more tips, pick up a copy of *Travel Photography: A Guide to Taking Better Pictures*. Written by internationally renowned travel photographer, Richard I'Anson, it's full colour throughout and designed to take on the road.

Photographing People

Hill tribe people in some of the regularly visited areas expect money if you photograph them, while certain Karen and Akha will not allow you to point a camera at them. Use discretion when photographing villagers anywhere in Thailand as a camera can be a very intimidating instrument. You may feel better leaving your camera behind when visiting certain areas.

Airport Security

The X-ray baggage inspection machines at Thailand's airports are all deemed film safe. Nevertheless if you're travelling with high-speed film (ISO 400 or above) you may want to have your film hand-inspected rather than X-rayed. Security inspectors are usually happy to comply. Packing your film in see-through plastic bags generally speeds up the hand inspection process. Some photographers pack their film in lead-lined bags to ward off potentially harmful rays.

TIME

Thailand's time zone is seven hours ahead of GMT/UTC (London). Thus, noon in Bangkok is 9 pm the previous day in Los Angeles – except during daylight saving time (DST), when it's 10 pm; midnight in New York (DST 1 am); 5 am (the same day) in London; 6 am in Paris; 1 pm in Perth; and 3 pm in Sydney (DST 4 pm).

Thai Calendar

The official year in Thailand is reckoned from 543 BC, the beginning of the Buddhist Era (BE), so that AD 2001 is BE 2544.

ELECTRICITY

Electric current is 220V, 50 cycles. Electrical wall outlets are usually of the round, two-pole type; some outlets also accept flat, two-bladed terminals, and some will accept either flat or round terminals. Any electrical supply shop will carry adaptors for any international plug shape, as well as voltage converters.

WEIGHTS & MEASURES

Dimensions and weight are usually expressed using the metric system in Thailand. The exception is land measure, which is often quoted using the traditional Thai system of *waa, ngaan* and *râi*. Old-timers in the provinces will occasionally use the traditional Thai system of weights and measures in speech, as will boat-builders, carpenters and other craftspeople when talking about their work. Here are some conversions to use for such occasions:

Thai units		metric conversion
1 tàraang waa	=	4 sq m
1 ngaan	=	400 sq m
1 râi	=	1600 sq m
1 bàat	=	15g
1 tàleung or tamleung (4 bàat)	=	60g
1 châng (20 tàleung)	=	1.2kg
1 hàap (50 châng)	=	60kg
1 níu	=	about 2cm (or 1 inch)
1 khêup (12 níu)	=	25cm
1 sàwk (2 khêup)	=	50cm
1 waa (4 sàwk)	=	2m
1 sên (20 waa)	=	40m
1 yôht (400 sên)	=	16km

LAUNDRY

Virtually every hotel in Thailand offers a laundry service. Charges are generally geared to room rates. Cheapest of all are public laundries, where you pay by the kilogram.

Many Thai hotels and guesthouses have laundry areas where you can wash your clothes at no charge; sometimes there's even a hanging area for drying. In accommodation where there is no laundry, do-it-yourselfers can wash their clothes in the sink and hang clothes out to dry in their rooms – see What to Bring earlier in this chapter for useful laundry tools. Laundry detergent is readily available in general mercantile shops and supermarkets.

Laundries that advertise dry-cleaning often don't really dry-clean (they just boil everything!) or they do it badly. Most of the luxury hotels usually have dependable dry cleaning services.

TOILETS

In Thailand, as in many other Asian countries, the 'squat toilet' is the norm except in hotels and guesthouses geared towards tourists and international business travellers. Instead of trying to approximate a chair or stool like a modern sit-down toilet, a traditional Asian toilet sits more-or-less flush with the surface of the floor, with two footpads on either side of the porcelain abyss. For travellers who have never used a squat toilet it takes a bit of getting used to. If you find yourself feeling awkward the first couple of times you use one, you can console yourself with the knowledge that, according to those who study such matters, people who use squat toilets are much less likely to develop haemorrhoids than people who use sit-down toilets.

Next to the typical squat toilet is a bucket or cement reservoir filled with water. A plastic bowl usually floats on the water's surface or sits nearby. This water supply has a two-fold function: Toilet-goers scoop water from the reservoir with the plastic bowl and use it to clean their nether regions while still squatting over the toilet; and since there is usually no mechanical flushing device attached to a squat toilet, a few extra scoops of water must be poured into the toilet basin to flush waste into the septic system.

In larger towns, mechanical flushing systems are becoming more and more common, even with squat toilets. Even more rustic are the toilets in rural areas, which may simply consist of a few planks over a hole in the ground.

Even in places where sit-down toilets are installed, the plumbing may not be designed to take toilet paper. In such cases the usual washing bucket will be standing nearby or there will be a waste basket where you're supposed to place used toilet paper.

Public toilets are common in cinema houses, department stores, bus and train stations, larger hotel lobbies and airports. While on the road between towns and villages it is perfectly acceptable (for both men and women) to go behind a tree or bush or even to use the roadside when nature calls.

BATHING

Some hotels and most guesthouses in the country do not have hot water, although places in the larger cities will usually offer small electric shower heaters in their more expensive rooms. Very few boiler-style water heaters are available outside larger international-style hotels.

Many rural Thais bathe in rivers or streams. Those living in towns or cities may have washrooms where a large jar or cement trough is filled with water for bathing purposes. A plastic or metal bowl is used to sluice the water over the body. Even in homes where showers are installed, heated water is uncommon. Most Thais bathe at least twice a day (a good habit to get into in the tropics), and never use hot water.

If ever you find yourself having to bathe in a public place you should wear a phâakhamáa or phâasîn (the cotton wraparounds); nude bathing is not the norm and most Thais will find it offensive.

HEALTH

Travel health depends on your predeparture preparations, your daily health care while travelling and how you handle any medical problem that does develop. While the potential dangers can seem quite frightening, in reality few travellers experience anything more than an upset stomach.

Predeparture planning

Immunisations Plan ahead for getting your vaccinations: Some of them require more than one injection, and certain vaccinations should not be given together. Note that some vaccinations should not be given during pregnancy or to people with allergies – discuss with your doctor.

Although there is no risk of yellow fever in Thailand, you will need proof of vaccination if you're coming from a yellow fever–infected area (sub-Saharan Africa and parts of South America).

It is recommended you seek medical advice at least six weeks before travel. Be aware that there is often a greater risk of disease with children and during pregnancy.

It's a good idea to carry proof of your vaccinations. If you want immunisations while in Thailand, they are available from a number of sources, including both public hospitals and private clinics. Bangkok is your best bet in terms of finding less-common or more-expensive vaccines. Vaccinations you should consider having for

Medical Kit Check List

Following is a list of items you should consider including in your medical kit – consult your pharmacist for brands available in your country.

- ❑ **Aspirin** or **paracetamol** (acetaminophen in the US) – for pain or fever
- ❑ **Antihistamine*** – for allergies, such as hay fever; to ease the itch from insect bites or stings; and to prevent motion sickness
- ❑ **Antibiotics** – consider including these if you're travelling well off the beaten track; see your doctor, as they must be prescribed, and carry the prescription with you.
- ❑ **Loperamide*** or **diphenoxylate** – which are 'blockers' for diarrhoea; **prochlorperazine** or **metaclopramide** for nausea and vomiting
- ❑ **Rehydration mixture*** – to prevent dehydration, eg due to severe diarrhoea; particularly important when travelling with children
- ❑ **Insect repellent*, sunscreen*, lip balm*** and **eye drops***
- ❑ **Calamine lotion, sting relief spray** or **aloe vera** – to ease irritation from sunburn and insect bites or stings
- ❑ **Antifungal cream** or **powder** – for fungal skin infections and thrush
- ❑ **Antiseptic* (such as povidone-iodine)** – for cuts and grazes
- ❑ **Bandages*, Band-Aids (plasters)*** and other wound dressings
- ❑ **Scissors*, tweezers** and a **thermometer** (note that mercury thermometers are prohibited by airlines)
- ❑ **Cold and flu tablets*, throat lozenges*** and **nasal decongestant**.
- ❑ **Multivitamins*** – consider for long trips, when dietary vitamin intake may be inadequate.

*Easily available in Thailand

Thailand include the following (for more information about the diseases see the individual entries later in this section):

Cholera The current injectable vaccine against cholera gives poor protection and has many side effects, so it is not generally recommended for travellers.

Diphtheria & Tetanus Vaccinations for these two diseases are usually combined and are recommended for everyone. After an initial course of three injections (usually given in childhood), boosters are necessary every 10 years.

Hepatitis A Hepatitis A vaccine (eg, Avaxim, Havrix 1440 or VAQTA) provides long-term immunity (possibly more than 10 years) after an initial injection and a booster at six to 12 months. An injection of gamma globulin can provide short-term protection – two to six months, depending on the dose given. It is reasonably effective and, unlike the vaccine, is protective immediately, but because it is a blood product there are current concerns about its long-term safety.

Hepatitis A vaccine is also available in a combined form, Twinrix, with hepatitis B vaccine. Three injections over six-months are required, the first two providing substantial protection against hepatitis A.

Hepatitis B Travellers who should consider vaccination against hepatitis B include those on a long trip, as well as those visiting countries where there are high levels of hepatitis B infection (of which Thailand is not one), where blood transfusions may not be adequately screened or where sexual contact or needle sharing is a possibility. Vaccination involves three injections, with a booster at 12 months. More rapid courses are available if necessary.

Japanese B Encephalitis Consider vaccination if you're spending a month or longer in rural Northern Thailand, making repeated trips to a risk area or visiting during an epidemic. It involves three injections over 30 days.

Polio Everyone should keep up to date with this vaccination, normally given in childhood. A booster every 10 years maintains immunity.

Rabies Vaccination should be considered if you're spending a month or longer in Thailand, especially if you're cycling, handling animals, caving or travelling to remote areas, and also for children (who may not report a bite). Pretravel rabies vaccination involves three injections over 21 to 28 days. Vaccinated persons who are bitten or scratched by a possibly rabid animal will require two booster injections of vaccine; those not vaccinated require more. Rabies vaccinations are available at nearly every public clinic or hospital in Thailand.

Tuberculosis The risk of TB to travellers in Thailand is usually very low.

Typhoid Vaccination against typhoid may be required if you are travelling for more than a couple of weeks in most parts of Asia. It is now available either as an injection or as capsules to be taken orally. A combined hepatitis A/typhoid vaccine was launched recently but its availability is still limited. Check with your doctor to find out its status in your country.

Malaria Medication Antimalarial drugs do not prevent you from being infected but kill the malaria parasites during a stage in their development and significantly reduce the risk of becoming very ill or dying. Expert advice on medication should be sought, as there are many factors to consider, including the area to be visited, the risk of exposure to malaria-carrying mosquitoes, the side-effects of medication, your medical history and whether you are a child or an adult or pregnant. Travellers to isolated areas in high risk countries may like to carry a treatment dose of medication for use if symptoms occur. See Malaria under Insect-Borne diseases later in this section for information on the prevalence of malaria in Thailand.

Health Insurance Make sure that you have adequate health insurance. See Travel Insurance under Visas & Documents earlier in this chapter for details.

Travel Health Guides If you are planning to be away or travelling in remote areas for a long period of time, you may like to consider taking a more detailed health guide. Lonely Planet's *Healthy Travel Asia & India* is a handy pocket size and packed with useful advice including pretrip planning, emergency first aid, immunisation and disease information and what to do if you get sick on the road. *Travel with Children* from Lonely Planet also includes advice on travel health for younger children.

Guide to Healthy Living in Thailand, published jointly by the Thai Red Cross Society and US embassy, is available in Bangkok from the 'Snake Farm' (Queen Saovabha Memorial Institute; ☎ 02-252 0161) for 100B. This booklet is rich in practical health advice on safe eating, child care, tropical heat, immunisations and local hospitals. It contains wise titbits with a literary flair, including 'Bangkok is a stopping point for many travellers and restless souls. Acute psychiatric emergencies, including alcohol and drug abuse, are, unfortunately, not rare' and 'Bangkok's traffic poses a far greater danger than snakes and tropical diseases combined'.

There are also a number of excellent travel health sites on the Internet. From the Lonely Planet home page there are links at www.lonelyplanet.com/weblinks/wlheal.htm

to the World Health Organization (WHO) and the US Centers for Disease Control and Prevention (CDC).

Other Preparations Make sure you're healthy before you start travelling. If you are going on a long trip make sure your teeth are OK. If you wear glasses take a spare pair and your prescription.

If you require a particular medication take an adequate supply, as it may not be available locally. Take part of the packaging showing the generic name rather than the brand, which will make getting replacements easier. To avoid any problems it's a good idea to have a legible prescription or letter from your doctor to show that you legally use the medication.

Basic Rules

Food Beware of ice cream that is sold in the street or anywhere it might have been melted and refrozen; if there's any doubt (eg, a power cut in the last day or two), steer well clear. Raw or undercooked shellfish such as mussels, oysters and clams should be avoided as well as undercooked meat, particularly in the form of mince.

If a place looks clean and well run and the vendor also looks clean and healthy, then the food is probably safe. In general, places that are packed with travellers or locals will be fine, while empty restaurants are questionable. The food in busy restaurants is cooked and eaten quite quickly with little standing around and is probably not reheated.

Water The number-one rule is be careful of the water and especially ice. If you don't know for certain that the water is safe, assume the worst, although *all* water served in restaurants or to guests in an office or home will be purified. It's not necessary to ask for bottled water unless you prefer it. Reputable brands of Thai bottled water or soft drinks are generally fine, although in some places bottles may be refilled with tap water. Only use water from containers with a serrated seal – not tops or corks. Try to purchase glass water bottles, however, as these are recyclable (unlike the plastic disposable ones).

Fruit juices are made with purified water and are safe to drink. Milk in Thailand is always pasteurised. In rural areas, villagers mostly drink collected rainwater.

Traditional Thai Medicine

International medical practices are mostly restricted to modern hospitals and clinics in Thailand's towns and cities. In villages and rural areas many Thais still practise various forms of traditional healing that were codified in Thailand over 500 years ago. Clinics and healers specialising in traditional Thai medicine can also be found in urban areas; many Thai doctors in fact offer a blend of international medicine and indigenous medical systems.

Traditional Thai medical theory features many parallels with India's Ayurvedic healing tradition as well as Chinese medicine. In practice, however, Thai diagnostic and therapeutic techniques may differ significantly. Obviously influenced to some degree by these traditions, Thai medicine has in turn been the predominant influence on traditional medicine in Cambodia, Laos and Myanmar.

Most Thai medicine as practised today is based on two surviving medical texts from the Ayuthaya era, the *Scripture of Diseases* and the *Pharmacopoeia of King Narai*. Presumably many more texts were available before the Burmese sacked Ayuthaya in 1767 and destroyed the kingdom's national archives. A coexisting oral tradition passed down from healer to healer conforms to the surviving texts; other *materia medica* developed in the Ratanakosin (or old Bangkok) era are founded on both these texts and the oral tradition.

Like medical practitioners elsewhere in the world, traditional Thai physicians perform diagnoses by evaluating the pulse, heartbeat, skin colour/texture, body temperature, abnormal physical symptoms and bodily excretions (eg, blood, urine, faeces) of their patients. Unlike orthodox Western doctors, Thai healers favour a holistic approach that encompasses external, internal and psycho-spiritual conditions. Thus, once diagnosed, patients may be prescribed and issued treatments from among three broad therapeutic categories.

Massage

The most internationally famous type of Thai medical therapy is *ráksǎa thaang nûat* (massage treatment). The extensive and highly refined Thai massage system combines characteristics of massage (stroking and kneading the muscles), chiropractic (manipulating skeletal parts) and acupressure (applying deep, consistent pressure to specific nerves, tendons or ligaments) in order to balance the functions of the four body elements *(thâat tháng sìi)*. These four elements are: earth (*din* – solid parts of the body, including skeleton, muscles, blood vessels, tendons and ligaments); water (*nám* – blood and bodily secretions); fire (*fai* – digestion and metabolism); and air (*lom* – respiration and circulation).

From the Ayuthaya period until the early 20th century, the Thai Ministry of Public Health included an official massage division *(phànàek mǎw nûat)*. Under the influence of international medicine and modern hospital development, responsibility for the national propagation and maintenance of Thai massage was eventually transferred to Wat Pho in Bangkok, where it remains today. Traditional massage therapy has persisted mostly in the provinces, however, and has recently enjoyed a resurgence of popularity throughout the country.

Within the traditional Thai medical context, a massage therapist (*mǎw nûat;* literally, massage doctor) usually applies Thai massage together with pharmacological and/or psycho-spiritual treatments as prescribed for a specific medical problem. Nowadays many Thais also use massage as a tool for

---

Ice is generally produced from purified water under hygienic conditions and is therefore theoretically safe. During transit to the local restaurant, however, conditions are not so hygienic (you may see blocks of ice being dragged along the street), but it's very difficult to resist in the hot season. The rule of thumb is that if it's chipped ice, it probably came from an ice block (which

may not have been handled well) but if it's ice cubes or 'tubes', it was delivered from the ice factory in sealed plastic.

Water Purification In Thailand, virtually no-one bothers with filters, tablets or iodine since bottled water is so cheap and readily available. However, if you are stuck without bottled water, the simplest way of purifying

Traditional Thai Medicine

relaxation and disease prevention, rather than just for specific medical problems. Massage associated with Bangkok's Turkish baths (àap òp nûat) is for the most part performed for recreational or entertainment purposes only (or as an adjunct to prostitution); the techniques used are loosely based on traditional Thai massage.

For problems affecting the nerves rather than the muscular or skeletal structures, many Thais resort to nûat jàp sên (nerve-touch massage), a Chinese-style massage technique that works with the body's nerve meridians, much like acupuncture.

Herbal Medicines

Traditional pharmacological therapy employs prescribed herbs from among 700 plant varieties (plus a limited number of animal sources), which are infused, boiled, powdered or otherwise rendered into a consumable form. Common household medicines (yaa klaang bâan) include the root and stem of bawráphét (Tinospora rumphii, a type of wood climber) for fever reduction; râak cháa-phluu (Piper roots) for stomach ailments; and various yaa hǎwm (fragrant medicines) used as balms for muscle pain or headaches. These medicines are readily available over the counter at traditional medicine shops and, to a lesser extent, in modern Thai pharmacies.

More complex remedies called yaa tamráp lǔang (royally approved/recorded medicine) are prepared and administered only by herbalists skilled in diagnosis, as the mixture and dosage must be adjusted for each patient. One of the most well known yaa tamráp lǔang is chanthá-liilaa, a powerful remedy for respiratory infections and influenza-induced fevers.

As in the Chinese tradition, many Thai herbs find their way into regional cuisine with the intent of enhancing health as well as taste. Phrík thai (black pepper; Piper nigrum), bai kà-phrao (holy basil) and bai maeng lák (a variety of basil) are common curry ingredients that have proven antacid and carminative (antiflatulent) properties. Thais eat soups containing márá (bitter melon) – a known febrifuge – to bring down a fever.

Psycho-Spiritual Healing

A third aspect of traditional Thai medicine called ráksǎa thaang nai (inner healing) or kâe kam kào (literally, old karma repair) includes various types of meditation or visualisation practised by the patient, as well as shamanistic rituals performed by qualified healers. These strategies represent the psycho-spiritual side of Thai medical therapy, and like massage are usually practised in conjunction with other types of treatment. With the increasing acceptance of meditation, hypnosis and biofeedback in international medicine, anthropologists nowadays are less inclined to classify such metaphysical therapy as 'magico-religious', accepting them instead as potentially useful adjunct therapies.

Psycho-spiritual techniques are most commonly reserved for medical conditions with no apparent physical cause or for which other therapies have proved unsuccessful. They are also occasionally used as preventive measures, as in the bai sǐi ceremony of North-Eastern Thailand and Laos. This ceremony, marked by the tying of string loops around a subject's wrists, is intended to bind the 32 khwǎn or personal guardian spirits – each associated with a specific organ – to the individual. The ritual is often performed before a person departs on a major journey.

water is to boil it thoroughly. Vigorous boiling should be satisfactory; however, at high altitude water boils at a lower temperature, so germs are less likely to be killed. Boil it for longer in these environments.

If you plan to do any long back-country camping trips, consider purchasing a water filter. There are two main kinds of filters. Total filters take out all parasites, bacteria and viruses and make water safe to drink. They are often expensive, but they can be more cost effective than buying bottled water. Simple filters (which can even be a nylon mesh bag) take out dirt and larger foreign bodies from the water so that chemical solutions work much more effectively; if water is dirty, chemical solutions may not work at all. It's very important when buying a filter to read the specifications, so that you know exactly what it removes from the water and what it doesn't. Simple filtering will not remove all dangerous organisms, so if you cannot boil water it should be treated chemically. Chlorine tablets will kill many pathogens, but not some parasites like giardia and amoebic cysts. Iodine is more effective in purifying water and is available in tablet form. Follow the directions carefully and remember that too much iodine can be harmful.

Medical Problems & Treatment

Self-diagnosis and treatment can be risky, so you should always seek medical help. Although there are drug dosages in this section, they are for emergency use only. Correct diagnosis is vital. An embassy, consulate or five-star hotel can usually recommend a local doctor or clinic.

In Thailand medicine is generally available over the counter and the price will be much cheaper than in the West. However, be careful when buying drugs, particularly where the expiry date may have passed or correct storage conditions may not have been followed. Bogus drugs are not uncommon and it's possible that drugs that are no longer recommended, or have even been banned, in the West are still being dispensed in Thailand.

Antibiotics should ideally be administered only under medical supervision. Take only the recommended dose at the prescribed intervals and use the whole course, even if the illness seems to be cured earlier. Stop immediately if there are any serious reactions and don't use the antibiotic at all if you are unsure that you have the correct one. Some people are allergic to commonly prescribed antibiotics such as penicillin; carry this information (eg, on a bracelet) when travelling.

Hospitals & Clinics

Thailand's most technically advanced hospitals are in Bangkok. In the North, Chiang Mai has the best medical care; in the North-East it's Udon Thani; and in the south it's Hat Yai and Phuket. Elsewhere in the country, every provincial capital has at least one hospital (of varying quality) as well as several public and private clinics. The best emergency health care can usually be found at military hospitals *(rohng pháyaabaan tháhǎan);* they will usually treat foreigners in an emergency.

See the respective destination chapters for further information on specific hospitals, clinics and other health-care facilities.

Should you need urgent dental care, suggested contacts in Bangkok include:

Benjasiri Dental House (☎ 02-662 2402) 593/6 Thanon Sukhumvit
Dental Polyclinic (☎ 02-314 4397) 2111/2113 Thanon Phetburi Tat Mai
Siam Dental Clinic (☎ 02-252 6660) 412/11–2 Soi 6, Siam Square

For urgent eye care, the best choices are also in Bangkok. Try the Rutnin Eye Hospital (☎ 02-258 0442) at 80/1 Soi Asoke, or the Pirompesuy Eye Hospital (☎ 02-252 4141) at 117/1 Thanon Phayathai.

Counselling Services

Qualified professionals at Community Services of Bangkok (☎ 02-258 4998, ⓔ csb@loxinfo.co.th), 15/1 Soi 33, Thanon Sukhumvit, offer a range of counselling services to foreign residents and newcomers to Thailand.

Members of Alcoholics Anonymous who want to contact the Bangkok group, or anyone needing help with a drinking problem, can call AA at ☎ 02-253 6305 from 6 am to 6 pm or ☎ 02-256 6578 from 6 pm to 6 am for information. There are daily meetings held at the Holy Redeemer Catholic Church, 123/19 Soi Ruamrudee (Ruam Rudi), Bangkok.

Air Ambulance

Medical Wings (☎ 02-535 4736, fax 535 4355, ⓔ ew@bkk.a-net.net.th), in the domestic terminal at Bangkok International Airport, offers aeromedical transportation to or from any of 30 domestic airports in Thailand on a 24-hour basis.

Environmental Hazards

Air Pollution Pollution is something you'll become very aware of in Thailand, especially in Bangkok, where heat, dust and motor fumes combine to form a powerful brew of potentially toxic air. Air pollution can be a health hazard, especially if you suffer from lung diseases such as asthma. It can also aggravate coughs, colds and sinus problems and cause eye irritation or even infections. Consider avoiding badly polluted areas if you think they may jeopardise your health, especially if you have asthma, or invest in an air filter.

Heat Exhaustion Dehydration and salt deficiency can cause heat exhaustion. Take time to acclimatise to high temperatures, drink sufficient liquids and do not do anything too physically demanding.

Salt deficiency is characterised by fatigue, lethargy, headaches, giddiness and muscle cramps; salt tablets may help, but adding extra salt to your food is better.

Anhidrotic heat exhaustion is a rare form of heat exhaustion that is caused by an inability to sweat. It tends to affect people who have been in a hot climate for some time, rather than newcomers. It can progress to heatstroke. Treatment involves removal to a cooler climate.

Heatstroke This serious, occasionally fatal, condition can occur if the body's heat-regulating mechanism breaks down and the body temperature rises to dangerous levels. Long, continuous periods of exposure to high temperatures and insufficient fluids can leave you vulnerable to heatstroke.

The symptoms are feeling unwell, not sweating very much (or at all) and a high body temperature (39° to 41°C, or 102° to 106°F). Where sweating has ceased, the skin becomes flushed and red. Severe, throbbing headaches and lack of coordination will also occur, and the sufferer may be confused or aggressive. Eventually the victim will become delirious or convulse. Hospitalisation is essential, but in the interim get victims out of the sun, remove their clothing, cover them with a wet sheet or towel and then fan continually. Give fluids if they are conscious.

Motion Sickness Eating lightly before and during a trip will reduce the chances of motion sickness. If you are prone to motion sickness try to find a place that minimises movement – near the wing on aircraft, close to midships on boats, near the centre on buses. Fresh air usually helps; reading and cigarette smoke don't. Commercial motion-sickness preparations, which can cause drowsiness, have to be taken before the trip commences. Ginger (available in capsule form) and peppermint (including mint-flavoured sweets) are natural preventatives.

Prickly Heat Prickly heat is an itchy rash caused by excessive perspiration trapped under the skin. It usually strikes people who have just arrived in a hot climate. Keeping cool, bathing often, drying the skin and using a mild talcum or Prickly Heat powder or resorting to air-conditioning may help.

Sunburn In the tropics you can get sunburnt surprisingly quickly, even through cloud cover. Use a sunscreen, a hat, and a barrier cream for your nose and lips. Calamine lotion and aloe vera are good for mild sunburn. Protect your eyes with good-quality sunglasses, particularly if you will be near water or sand.

Infectious Diseases

Diarrhoea Simple things like a change of water, food or climate can all cause a mild bout of diarrhoea, but a few rushed toilet trips with no other symptoms is not indicative of a major problem.

Dehydration is the main danger with any diarrhoea, particularly in children or the elderly, in whom dehydration can occur quite quickly. Under all circumstances *fluid replacement* (at least equal to the volume being lost) is the most important thing to remember. Weak black tea with a little sugar, soda water, or soft drinks allowed to go flat and diluted 50% with clean water are all good.

With severe diarrhoea a rehydrating solution is preferable as it will replace the minerals and salts that have been lost. Commercially available oral rehydration salts (ORS) are very useful; add these salts to boiled or bottled water. In an emergency you can make up a solution of six teaspoons of sugar and a half teaspoon of salt to a litre of boiled or bottled water.

You need to drink at least the same volume of fluid that you are losing in bowel movements and vomiting. Urine is the best guide to the adequacy of replacement – if you have small amounts of concentrated urine, you need to drink more. Keep drinking small amounts often. Stick to a bland diet as you recover.

Gut-paralysing drugs such as loperamide diphenoxylate can be used to bring relief from the symptoms, although they do not actually cure the problem. Only use these drugs if you do not have access to toilets, eg, if you *must* travel. For children under 12 years old these drugs are not recommended. Do not use these drugs if the person has a high fever or is severely dehydrated.

In certain situations antibiotics may be required: diarrhoea with blood or mucus (dysentery), any diarrhoea with fever, profuse watery diarrhoea, persistent diarrhoea not improving after 48 hours and severe diarrhoea. These suggest a more serious cause of diarrhoea and in these situations gut-paralysing drugs should be avoided.

In these situations, a stool test may be necessary to diagnose what bug is causing your diarrhoea, so you should seek medical help urgently. Where this is not possible the recommended drugs for bacterial diarrhoea (the most likely cause of severe diarrhoea in travellers) are norfloxacin 400mg twice daily for three days or ciprofloxacin 500mg twice daily for five days. These are not recommended for children or pregnant women. The drug of choice for children would be co-trimoxazole, with the dosage dependent on the child's weight. A five-day course should be given. Ampicillin or amoxycillin may be given in pregnancy, but medical care is necessary.

Two other causes of persistent diarrhoea in travellers are giardiasis and amoebic dysentery. Giardiasis is caused by a common parasite, *Giardia lamblia.* The symptoms include stomach cramps, nausea, a bloated stomach, watery, foul-smelling diarrhoea and frequent gas (farts). Giardiasis can appear several weeks after you have been exposed to the parasite. The symptoms may disappear for a few days and then return. Unfortunately this can continue for several weeks.

Amoebic dysentery, caused by the protozoan *Entamoeba histolytica,* is characterised by a gradual onset of low-grade diarrhoea, often with blood and mucus. Cramping, abdominal pain and vomiting are less likely than in other types of diarrhoea, and fever may not be present. Amoebic dysentery will persist until treated and can recur and cause other health problems.

You should seek medical advice if you think you have giardiasis or amoebic dysentery, but where this is not possible, tinidazole or metronidazole are the recommended drugs. Treatment is a 2g single dose of tinidazole or 250mg of metronidazole three times daily for five to 10 days.

Fungal Infections Fungal infections occur more commonly in hot weather and are usually found on the scalp, between the toes (athlete's foot) or fingers, in the groin and on the body (ringworm). You get ringworm (which is a fungal infection, not a worm) from infected animals or other people. Moisture encourages these infections.

To prevent fungal infections wear loose, comfortable clothes, avoid artificial fibres, wash frequently and dry yourself carefully. If you do get an infection, wash the infected area at least daily with a disinfectant or medicated soap and water, and rinse and dry well. Apply an antifungal cream or powder like tolnaftate. Try to expose the infected area to air or sunlight as much as possible and wash all towels and underwear in hot water, change them often and let them dry in the sun.

Hepatitis Hepatitis is a general term for inflammation of the liver. It is a common disease worldwide. There are several different viruses that cause hepatitis, and they differ in the way that they are transmitted. The symptoms are similar in all forms of the illness, and include fever, chills, headache, fatigue, feelings of weakness and aches and pains, followed by loss of appetite, nausea, vomiting, abdominal pain, dark urine, light-coloured faeces, jaundiced (yellow) skin and yellowing of the whites of the eyes. People who have had hepatitis should avoid alcohol for some time after the illness, as the liver needs time to recover.

Hepatitis A is transmitted by contaminated food and drinking water. You should seek medical advice, but there is not much you can do apart from resting, drinking lots of fluids, eating lightly and avoiding fatty foods. Hepatitis E is transmitted in the same way as hepatitis A; it can be particularly serious in pregnant women.

There are almost 300 million chronic carriers of Hepatitis B in the world. It is spread through contact with infected blood, blood products or body fluids, for example through sexual contact, unsterilised needles and blood transfusions, or contact with blood via small breaks in the skin. Other risk situations include having a shave, tattoo or body piercing with contaminated equipment. The symptoms of hepatitis B may be more severe than type A and the disease can lead to long-term problems such as chronic liver damage, liver cancer or a long-term carrier state. Hepatitis C and D are spread in the same way as hepatitis B and can also lead to long-term complications.

There are vaccines against hepatitis A and B (see Immunisations earlier in this section), but there are currently no vaccines against the other types of hepatitis. Following the basic rules about food and water (hepatitis A and E) and avoiding risk situations (hepatitis B, C and D) are important preventative measures.

HIV & AIDS Infection with the human immunodeficiency virus (HIV) may lead to acquired immune deficiency syndrome (AIDS), which is a fatal disease. Any exposure to blood, blood products or body fluids may put the individual at risk.

Between 1991 and 1994 Thailand's overall infection rate dropped 77%, an achievement that earned Population Development Agency director Mechai Viravaidya the prestigious Magsaysay Award in 1994. According to the United Nations Human Development Programme, Thailand – like the USA, Australia, and the UK – has belonged to the 'decrease or no growth' category since 1994. The World Health Organisation reports that the infection rate and projected future vulnerability for AIDS in Thailand is now lower than for any other country in South-East Asia. As elsewhere around the globe, however, absolute numbers will only increase with time until or unless a cure is discovered.

In Thailand transmission is predominantly through heterosexual sexual activity (over 80%). The second most common source of HIV infection is intravenous injection by drug users who share needles (about 6%). Apart from abstinence, the most effective preventative is always to practise safe sex using condoms and never share syringes, even those that have been bleached.

The Thai phrase for 'condom' is *thŭng yaang ànaamai*. Since the 1970s, when health educator Mechai Viravaidya initiated a vigorous national program aimed at educating the public about contraception, the most common Thai nickname for 'condom' has been 'Mechai'. Good-quality latex condoms are distributed free by offices of the Ministry of Public Health (MPH) throughout the country – they come in numbered sizes, like shoes! Many Western men find that even the largest size issued by the MPH is too small; one of the better commercial brands available in Thailand is Durex.

HIV/AIDS can also be spread through infected blood transfusions, although this risk is virtually nil in Thailand due to vigorous blood-screening procedures. It can also be spread by dirty needles – tattooing, vaccinations, acupuncture and body piercing can potentially be as dangerous as intravenous drug use if the equipment is not clean.

If you do need an injection, ask to see the syringe unwrapped in front of you, or take a needle and syringe pack with you.

Intestinal Worms These parasites are most common in rural areas. Different worms have different ways of infecting people. Some may be ingested in food such as undercooked meat (eg, tapeworms) and some enter through your skin (eg, hookworms). Infestations may not show up for some time, and although they are generally not serious, if left untreated some can cause severe health problems later. Consider having a stool test when you return home to check for these and determine the appropriate treatment.

Liver Flukes These are tiny worms that are occasionally present in freshwater fish. The main risk comes from eating raw or undercooked fish. Travellers should in particular avoid eating *plaa ráa* (sometimes called *paa daek* in North-Eastern Thailand), an unpasteurised fermented fish used as an accompaniment for rice in the North-East. Plaa ráa is not commonly served in restaurants, but is common in rural areas of the North-East, where it's considered a great delicacy. The Thai government is currently trying to discourage north-easterners from eating plaa ráa and other uncooked fish products. A common roadside billboard in the region these days reads: *ìsǎan mâi kin plaa dìp* (North-Eastern Thailand doesn't eat raw fish).

Liver flukes *(pháyâat bai mái)* are endemic to villages around Sakon Nakhon Province's Nong Han, the largest natural lake in Thailand. Don't swim in this lake! A less common way to contract liver flukes is through swimming in rivers. The only other known contaminated area is in the southern reaches of the Mekong River.

The intensity of symptoms depends very much on how many of the flukes get into your body. At low levels, there are virtually no symptoms at all; at higher levels, an overall fatigue, low-grade fever and swollen or tender liver (or general abdominal pain) are the usual symptoms, along with worms or worm eggs in the faeces. Persons suspected of having liver flukes should have a stool sample analysed by a doctor or clinic. The usual medication is 25mg per kilogram of body weight of praziquantel three times daily after meals for two days.

Schistosomiasis The overall risk of this disease is quite low, but it's highest in the southern reaches of the Mekong River and in the lakes of North-Eastern Thailand – avoid swimming and bathing in these waterways.

Also known as bilharzia, this disease is transmitted by minute worms. They infect certain varieties of freshwater snails found in rivers, streams, lakes and particularly behind dams. The worms multiply and are eventually discharged into the water.

The worm enters through the skin and attaches itself to your intestines or bladder. The first symptom may be a general feeling of being unwell, or a tingling and sometimes a light rash around the area where it entered. Weeks later a high fever may develop. Once the disease is established abdominal pain and blood in the urine are other signs. The infection often causes no symptoms until the disease is well established (several months to years after exposure) and damage to internal organs irreversible.

A blood test is a reliable way to diagnose bilharzia, but the test will not show positive until a number of weeks after exposure.

Sexually Transmitted Infections Gonorrhoea, herpes and syphilis are among these diseases; sores, blisters or rashes around the genitals and discharges or pain when urinating are common symptoms. In some STIs, such as wart virus and chlamydia, symptoms may be less marked or not observed at all, especially in women. Syphilis symptoms eventually disappear completely but the disease continues and can cause severe problems in later years. In Thailand gonorrhoea, nonspecific urethritis (NSU) and syphilis are the most common of these diseases. The treatment of gonorrhoea and syphilis is with antibiotics. Different sexually transmitted infections each require specific antibiotics.

While abstinence from sexual contact is the only 100% effective prevention, using condoms is also effective. A 2000 survey conducted by condom-maker Durex and a senior policy adviser to the WHO found that 82% of Thais between the ages of 16 and 45 always used condoms with casual partners, the highest among the 15 countries surveyed. Canada and Poland scored the lowest, with less than 25%. See HIV & AIDS earlier in this section for information on condom availability in Thailand.

Typhoid Typhoid fever is a dangerous gut infection caused by contaminated water and food. Medical help must be sought.

In its early stages sufferers may feel they have a bad cold or flu on the way, as early symptoms are a headache, body aches and a fever which rises a little each day until it is around 40°C (104°F) or more. The victim's pulse is often slow relative to the degree of fever present – unlike a normal fever where the pulse increases. There may be vomiting, abdominal pain, diarrhoea or constipation.

In the second week the high fever and slow pulse continue and a few pink spots may appear on the body; trembling, delirium, weakness, weight loss and dehydration may occur. Complications such as pneumonia, perforated bowel or meningitis may occur.

Insect-Borne Diseases

Filariasis, Lyme disease, and typhus are all insect-borne diseases, but they do not pose a great risk to travellers. For more information on typhus see Less Common Diseases later in this section.

Malaria This serious and potentially fatal disease is spread by mosquito bites. Malaria risk exists throughout the year in rural Thailand, especially in forested and hilly areas.

Thailand's high-risk areas include northern Kanchanaburi Province (especially Thung Yai Naresuan National Park) and parts of Trat Province along the Cambodian border (including Ko Chang).

According to the CDC and to Thailand's Ministry of Public Health, there is virtually no risk of malaria in urban areas or the main tourist areas (eg, Bangkok, Phuket, Pattaya and Chiang Mai).

If you are travelling in endemic areas it is extremely important to avoid mosquito bites and to take tablets to prevent the onset of this disease. The most recommended malarial preventive for Thailand travel is 100mg of doxycycline taken daily. Western doctors who know the situation in Thailand no longer recommend either chloroquine or mefloquine (Lariam) for Thailand, due to the malaria parasite's near-total resistance to these drugs. Side effects of doxycycline include photosensitivity, ie, your skin will be more easily affected by the sun.

On the other hand the Malaria Division of Thailand's Ministry of Public Health, which is better acquainted with malaria in Thailand than any other health agency in the world, has issued an unequivocal announcement stating 'Malaria chemoprophylaxis is not recommended.' For more information contact the Hospital for Tropical Diseases (☎ 02-246 9000), 420/6 Thanon Ratwithi.

Symptoms of malaria vary widely, ranging from fever, chills and sweating, headache, diarrhoea and abdominal pains to a vague feeling of ill-health, but one of the tell-tale long-term signs is the cyclic nature of the symptoms, coming on every 24 hours or every three days for example. In general if there is fever for two or three days you should seek medical advice for accurate diagnosis, perhaps by taking a blood test. Seek medical help immediately if malaria is suspected. Without treatment, malaria can rapidly become more serious and is sometimes fatal.

Every medical clinic or hospital in Thailand can easily test for malaria and treat the disease. If for some reason medical care is not available, certain malaria tablets can be used for treatment. If you took anti-malaria tablets before contracting malaria, you'll need to use a different malaria tablet for treatment as obviously the first one didn't work.

For Fansidar the treatment dose is three tablets. If cannot obtain Fansidar, then other alternatives are Malarone (atovaquone-proguanil; four tablets once daily for three days), halofantrine (three doses of two 250mg tablets every six hours) or quinine sulphate (600mg every six hours). Be aware also that halofantrine is no longer recommended by the WHO as emergency standby treatment, because of side effects, and should only be used if no other drugs are available.

Travellers are advised to prevent mosquito bites at all times. The main messages are:

- Wear light-coloured clothing.
- Wear long trousers and long-sleeved shirts.
- Use mosquito repellents containing the compound DEET on exposed areas (prolonged overuse of DEET may be harmful, especially to children, but its use is considered preferable to being bitten by disease-transmitting mosquitoes).
- Avoid perfumes or aftershave.
- Use a mosquito net impregnated with mosquito repellent (permethrin) – it may be worth taking your own.
- Impregnate clothes with permethrin, which effectively deters mosquitoes and other insects.

Dengue Fever This viral disease is transmitted by mosquitoes and occurs mainly in tropical and subtropical areas of the world. Generally, there is only a small risk to travellers except during epidemics, which are usually seasonal (during and just after the rainy season).

The *Aedes aegypti* mosquito, which transmits the dengue virus, is most active during the day, unlike the malaria mosquito, and is found mainly in urban areas in and around human dwellings.

Signs and symptoms of dengue fever include a sudden onset of high fever, headache, joint and muscle pains (hence its old name, 'breakbone fever') and nausea and vomiting. A rash of small red spots appears three to four days after the onset of fever. Dengue is commonly mistaken for other infectious diseases, including influenza.

You should seek medical attention if you think you may be infected. Infection can be diagnosed by a blood test. There is no specific treatment for dengue. You should avoid aspirin, as it increases the risk of haemorrhaging.

Recovery may be prolonged, with tiredness lasting for several weeks. Severe complications are rare in travellers but include dengue haemorrhagic fever (DHF), which can be fatal without prompt medical treatment. DHF is thought to be a result of a second infection due to a different strain (there are four major strains) and it usually affects residents of the country rather than travellers.

In 2000 Thailand's Mahidol University announced the development of a vaccine for all serotypes of dengue. The new vaccine began human trials late that year, and if successful the vaccine should be available in 2003 or 2004. As with malaria, the best precaution is to avoid mosquito bites.

Japanese B Encephalitis Mosquitoes transmit this viral infection of the brain. Most cases occur in rural areas as the virus exists in pigs and wading birds. Symptoms include fever, headache and alteration in consciousness. Hospitalisation is needed for correct diagnosis and treatment. There is a high mortality rate among those who have symptoms; of those who survive, many are intellectually disabled.

Cuts, Bites & Stings

Bedbugs & Lice Bedbugs live in various places, but particularly in dirty mattresses and bedding, evidenced by spots of blood on bedclothes or on the wall. Bedbugs leave itchy bites in neat rows. Calamine lotion or a sting-relief spray may help.

All lice cause itching and discomfort. They make themselves at home in your hair (head lice), your clothing (body lice) or in your pubic hair (crabs). You catch lice through direct contact with infected people or by sharing combs, clothing and the like. Powder or shampoo treatment will kill the lice and infected clothing should then be washed in very hot, soapy water and left in the sun to dry.

Bites & Stings Bee and wasp stings are usually painful rather than dangerous. Calamine lotion or a sting-relief spray are good and ice packs will reduce the pain and swelling. However, in people who are allergic to them severe breathing difficulties may occur and require urgent medical care.

There are some spiders with dangerous bites but antivenins are usually available in local hospitals. Scorpions often shelter in shoes or clothing, and their stings are notoriously painful.

There are various fish and other sea creatures that can sting or bite dangerously or that are dangerous to eat – be sure to seek local advice.

Cuts & Scratches Skin punctures can easily become infected in hot climates and may be difficult to heal. Wash well and treat any cut with an antiseptic, such as povidone-iodine. Where possible avoid bandages and Band-Aids, which can keep wounds wet. Coral cuts are notoriously slow to heal and if they are not adequately cleaned, small pieces of coral can become embedded in the wound. Avoid touching and walking on fragile coral in the first place, but if you are near coral reefs, then wear shoes and clean any cut thoroughly.

Leeches & Ticks Leeches may be present in damp rainforest conditions; they attach themselves to your skin to suck your blood. Trekkers often get them on their legs or in their boots. Salt or a lighted cigarette end will make them fall off and an insect repellent may keep them away. Do not pull them off, as the bite is then more likely to become infected. Clean and apply pressure if the point of attachment is bleeding.

You should always check all over your body if you have been walking through a potentially tick-infested area as ticks can cause skin infections and other more serious diseases. If a tick is found attached, press down around the tick's head with tweezers, grab the head and gently pull upwards. Avoid pulling the rear of the body as this may squeeze the tick's gut contents through the attached mouth parts into the skin, increasing the risk of infection and disease. Smearing chemicals on the tick will not make it let go and is not recommended.

Snakes To minimise your chances of being bitten always wear boots, socks and long trousers when walking through undergrowth where snakes may be present. Don't put your hands into holes and crevices, and be careful when collecting firewood.

Snake bites do not cause instantaneous death and antivenins are usually available. Immediately wrap the bitten limb tightly, as you would for a sprained ankle, and then attach a splint to immobilise it. Keep the victim still and seek medical help, if possible with the dead snake for identification. Don't attempt to catch the snake if there is a possibility of being bitten again. Tourniquets and sucking out the poison are now comprehensively discredited.

Snakebite antivenin is available at hospitals throughout Thailand as well as in pharmacies in larger towns and cities.

Women's Health

Gynaecological Problems Antibiotic use, synthetic underwear, sweating and contraceptive pills can lead to fungal vaginal infections, especially when travelling in hot climates. Thrush (yeast infection) or vaginal candidiasis is characterised by a rash, itch and discharge. Nystatin, miconazole or clotrimazole pessaries are the usual treatment, but some people use a more traditional remedy involving vinegar or lemon juice douches, or yoghurt. Maintaining good personal hygiene and wearing loose-fitting clothes and cotton underwear may help prevent these infections.

Sexually transmitted diseases are a major cause of vaginal problems. Symptoms include a smelly discharge, painful intercourse and sometimes a burning sensation when urinating. Medical attention should be sought and male sexual partners must also be treated. For more details see the section on Sexually Transmitted Diseases earlier. Apart from abstinence, the best thing is to practise safer sex using condoms.

Pregnancy It is not advisable to travel to some places while pregnant as some vaccinations normally used to prevent serious diseases (eg, yellow fever) are not advisable during pregnancy. In addition, some diseases (eg, malaria) are much more serious for the mother in pregnancy and may increase the risk of a stillborn child.

Most miscarriages occur during the first three months of pregnancy. Miscarriage is not uncommon and can occasionally lead to severe bleeding. The last three months should also be spent within reasonable distance of good medical care. A baby born as early as 24 weeks stands a chance of survival, but only in a good modern hospital. Pregnant women should avoid all unnecessary medication, although vaccinations and malarial prophylactics should still be taken where needed. Additional care should be taken to prevent illness and particular attention should be paid to diet and nutrition. Alcohol and nicotine, for example, should be avoided.

Less Common Diseases

The following diseases pose a small risk to travellers, and so are only mentioned in passing. Seek medical advice if you think you may have any of these diseases.

Cholera Outbreaks of cholera are very rare in Thailand, and when they do occur they're generally widely reported, so you can avoid such problem areas. *Fluid replacement is the most vital treatment* – the risk of dehydration is severe as you may lose up to 20L a day. If there is a delay in getting to hospital, then begin taking tetracycline. The adult dose is 250mg four times daily. It is not recommended for children under nine years nor for pregnant women. Tetracycline may help shorten the illness, but adequate fluids are required to save lives.

Diphtheria Diphtheria can be a skin infection or a more dangerous throat infection. It is spread by contaminated dust contacting the skin or by the inhalation of infected cough or sneeze droplets. Frequent washing and keeping the skin dry will help prevent skin infection. Treatment needs close medical supervision.

Rabies This fatal viral infection is found in many countries, including Thailand. Many animals (such as dogs, cats, bats and monkeys) can be infected and it is their saliva that is infectious. Any bite, scratch or even lick from an animal should be cleaned promptly and thoroughly. Scrub with soap and running water, and then apply alcohol or iodine solution. It is important that you seek medical help immediately to receive a course of injections.

Tetanus This disease is caused by a germ that lives in soil and in the faeces of horses and other animals. It enters the body via breaks in the skin. The first symptom may be discomfort in swallowing, or stiffening of the jaw and neck; this is followed by painful convulsions of the jaw and whole body. The disease can be fatal but can be prevented by vaccination.

Tuberculosis (TB) There is a world-wide resurgence of TB, and in Thailand it's the seventh leading cause of death. TB is a bacterial infection usually transmitted from person to person by coughing but which may be transmitted through consumption of unpasteurised milk. Milk that has been boiled is safe to drink, and the souring of milk to make yoghurt or cheese also kills the bacilli. Travellers are usually not at great risk as close household contact with the infected person is usually required before the disease is passed on. You may need to have a TB test before you travel as this can help diagnose the disease later if you become ill.

Typhus This disease is spread by ticks, mites or lice. It begins with fever, chills, headache and muscle pains followed a few days later by a body rash. There is often a large painful sore at the site of the bite and nearby lymph nodes are swollen and painful. Typhus can be treated under medical supervision. Seek local advice on areas where ticks pose a danger and always check your skin carefully for ticks after walking in a danger area such as a tropical forest. An insect repellent can help, and walkers in tick-infested areas should consider having their boots and trousers impregnated with benzyl benzoate and dibutylphthalate (see Leeches & Ticks under Cuts, Bites & Stings earlier).

WOMEN TRAVELLERS
Attitudes towards Women
Chinese trader Ma Huan noted in 1433 that among the Thais 'All affairs are managed by their wives, all trading transactions large or small'. In rural areas female family members typically inherit the land and throughout the country they tend to control the family finances.

The most recent United Nations Development Programme (UNDP) Human Development Report noted that on the Gender-related Development Index (GDI) Thailand ranks 40th among 130 countries, thus falling into the 'progressive' category. This ranking is 12 points higher than the overall UN human development index for Thailand, meaning gender-related development in Thailand is further along than the average of all other human development criteria for that country. The organisation also reports that the nation's GDI increase was greater than that of any country in the world between 1975 and 1995. According to the UNDP, Thailand 'has succeeded in building the basic human capabilities of both women and men, without substantial gender imparity'. Noted Thai feminist and Thammasat University professor Dr Chatsumarn Kabilsingh has written that 'In economics, academia and health services, women hold a majority of the administrative positions and manifest a sense of self-confidence in dealing independently with the challenges presented by their careers.'

Thai women constitute 55% of all enrolments in secondary and tertiary schools and about 45% of Thailand's workforce, outranking both China and the USA in both categories. So much for the good news. The bad news is that although women generally fare well in education, the labour force and in rural land inheritance, their cultural standing is a bit further from parity. An oft-repeated Thai saying reminds us that men form the front legs of the elephant, women the hind legs (at least they're pulling equal weight).

On a purely legal level, men enjoy more privilege. Men may divorce their wives for committing adultery, but not vice versa, for example. Men who take a foreign spouse continue to have the right to purchase and own land, while Thai women who marry foreign men lose this right. However, Article 30 of the 1997-ratified Thai constitution states 'Men and women hold equal rights' (few so-called developed countries in the Western world have charters containing such equal rights clauses); we can expect to see a reformation of such discriminatory laws as 'organic' legislation is put in place.

Safety Precautions
According to the latest TAT statistics, around 40% of all foreign visitors to Thailand are women, a ratio higher than the worldwide average and ahead of all other Asian countries (for which the proportion of female visitors runs lower than 35%) with the possible exception of Singapore and Hong Kong. This ratio is growing from year to year and the overall increase for women

visitors has climbed faster than that for men for every year since 1993.

Everyday incidents of sexual harassment are much less common in Thailand than in India, Indonesia or Malaysia and this may lull women who have recently travelled in these countries into thinking that Thailand travel is safer than it is. Over the past decade, several foreign women have been attacked while travelling alone in remote areas, and in August 2000 a British woman was murdered at a guesthouse in Chiang Mai. Such incidents, however, are extremely rare. If you're a woman travelling alone, try to pair up with other travellers when travelling at night or in remote areas. Make sure hotel and guesthouse rooms are secure at night – if they're not, demand another room or move to another hotel or guesthouse.

When in the company of single Thai males, keep an eye on food and drink. In 1999 and 2000 we received a couple of reports from women who alleged they had been drugged and raped by Thai trekking guides in Chiang Mai.

See Dangers & Annoyances for more information and advice.

Jík-Kŏh Small upcountry restaurants are sometimes hang-outs for drunken *jík-kŏh,* an all-purpose Thai term that refers to the teenage playboy-hoodlum-cowboy who gets his kicks by violating Thai cultural norms. These oafs sometimes bother foreign women (and men) who are trying to have a quiet meal ('Are you married?' and 'I love you' are common conversation openers). It's best to ignore them rather than try to make snappy comebacks – they won't understand them and will most likely take these responses as encouragement. If the jík-kŏh persist, leave and go to another restaurant. Unfortunately the restaurant proprietors will rarely involve themselves in such disturbances.

GAY & LESBIAN TRAVELLERS

Thai culture is very tolerant of homosexuality, both male and female. The nation has no laws that discriminate against homosexuals and there is a fairly prominent gay/lesbian scene around the country. Hence there is no 'gay movement' in Thailand as such since there's no antigay establishment to move against. Whether speaking of dress or mannerism, lesbians and gays are generally accepted without comment.

Public displays of affection – whether heterosexual or homosexual – are frowned upon. According to the gay-oriented guide *Thai Scene:*

For many gay travellers, Thailand is a nirvana with a long established gay bar scene, which, whilst often very Thai in culture, is particularly welcoming to tourists. There is little, if any, social approbation towards gay people, providing Thai cultural mores are respected. What people do in bed, whether straight or gay, is not expected to be a topic of general conversation nor bragged about.

The magazine *Pink Ink* writes:

Thai lesbians prefer to call themselves *tom* (for tomboy) or *dee* (for lady), as the term 'lesbian', in Thailand, suggests pornographic videos produced for straight men. Tom and dee, by contrast, are fairly accepted and integrated categories for Thai women, roughly corresponding to the Western terms 'butch' and 'femme'.

Organisations & Publications

Utopia (☎ 02-259 1619, fax 258 3250), at 116/1 Soi 23, Thanon Sukhumvit, Bangkok, is a gay and lesbian multipurpose centre consisting of a guesthouse, bar, cafe, gallery and gift shop. It maintains a well-organised Web site called the Southeast Asia Gay and Lesbian Resources (or Utopia Homo Page) at www.utopia-asia.com as well as an email address (utopia@best com).

Information Thailand has a good Web site on gay and lesbian venues in Bangkok at www.ithailand.com/living/entertainment /bangkok/gay/index.htm.

Monthly *Bangkok Metro* (www.bkkmetro .com) magazine stays abreast of gay and lesbian happenings in the capital, as does the 'Pink Page' of the monthly tourist rag *Guide to Bangkok* (also available at www.geocities .com/WestHollywood/5752/). *Pink Ink* (www.khsnet.com/ pinkink), a Web-only publication by and for Bangkok's English-speaking gay and lesbian community, is another useful resource. Gay Media (www .gay-media.com) contains lots of information on Thailand travel, with special attention to gay venues of all kinds.

Anjaree Group (☎/fax 02-477 1776), PO Box 322, Ratchadamnoen, Bangkok 10200, is Thailand's premier (and only) lesbian society. Anjaree sponsors various group activities and produces a Thai-only newsletter. Bilingual Thai-English Web sites of possible interest to visiting lesbians include www.lesla.com

Gay men may be interested in the services of the Long Yang Club (☎/fax 02-679 7727) at PO Box 1077, Silom Post Office, Bangkok 10504 – a 'multicultural social group for male-oriented men who want to meet outside the gay scene', which has branches in London, Amsterdam, Toronto, Canberra, Ottawa and Vancouver. It has a Web site at www.longyangclub.com.

An in-depth resource for anyone interested in learning more about Thailand's gay and lesbian scene is *Lady Boys, Tom Boys, Rent Boys* by Peter A Jackson.

DISABLED TRAVELLERS

Thailand presents one large, ongoing obstacle course for the mobility-impaired. With its high curbs, uneven sidewalks and nonstop traffic, Bangkok can be particularly difficult – many streets must be crossed via pedestrian bridges flanked with steep stairways, while buses and boats don't stop long enough for even the mildly disabled. Rarely are there any ramps or other access points for wheelchairs.

Hyatt International (Bangkok, Pattaya, Chiang Mai), Novotel (Bangkok, Chiang Mai, Phuket), Sheraton (Bangkok, Phuket), Holiday Inn (Bangkok, Phuket) and Westin (Bangkok and Chiang Mai) are the only hotel chains in the country that make consistent design efforts to provide disabled access for each of their properties. Because of their high employee-to-guest ratios, home-grown luxury hotel chains such as those managed by Dusit, Amari and Royal Garden Resorts are usually very good about making sure that the mobility-impaired are well accommodated in terms of providing staff help where architecture fails. In other accommodation options you're pretty much left to your own resources.

For wheelchair travellers, any trip to Thailand will require a good deal of advance planning; fortunately a growing network of information sources can put you in touch with those who have wheeled through Thailand before. There is no better source of information than someone who's done it. A reader wrote with the following tips:

- The difficulties you mention in your book are all there. However, travel in the streets is still possible, and enjoyable, providing you have a strong, ambulatory companion. Some obstacles may require two carriers; Thais are by nature helpful and could generally be counted on for assistance.
- Don't feel you have to rely on organised tours to see the sights – these often leave early mornings at times inconvenient to disabled people. It is far more convenient (and often cheaper) to take a taxi or hired car. It's also far more enjoyable as there is no feeling of holding others up.
- Many taxis have an LPG tank in the boot (trunk) which may make it impossible to get a wheelchair in and close it. You might do better to hire a private car and driver (this usually costs no more – and sometimes less – than a taxi).
- A túk-túk is far easier to get in and out of and to carry two people and a wheelchair than a taxi. Even the pedicabs can hang a wheelchair on the back of the carriage.
- Be ready to try anything – in spite of my worries, riding an elephant proved quite easy.

Organisations

Three international organisations with information on mobility-impaired travel are:

Access Foundation (☎ 516-887 5798) PO Box 356, Malverne, NY 11565, USA
Mobility International USA (☎ 541-343 1284, ✉ info@miusa.org) PO Box 10767, Eugene, OR 97440, USA;
  Web site: www.miusa.org
Society for the Advancement of Travelers with Handicaps (SATH; ☎ 212-447 7284, ✉ sathtravel@aol.com) 347 Fifth Ave, Suite 610, New York, NY 11242, USA

SATH has a very useful Web site at www.sath.org, full of information for travelling with handicaps of all kinds. It also publishes the magazine *Open Worlds,* following similar themes.

The book *Exotic Destinations for Wheelchair Travelers* by Ed Hansen & Bruce Gordon (Full Data, San Francisco) contains a useful chapter on seven locations in Thailand. Others books of value include *Holidays and Travel Abroad – A Guide for Disabled People* (RADAR, London) and *Able to Travel* (Rough Guides, London, New York).

Accessible Journeys (☎ 610-521 0339), at 35 West Sellers Ave, Ridley Park, Pennsylvania, USA, specialises in organising group travel for the mobility-impaired. Occasionally the agency offers Thailand trips. Its Web site is at www.disabilitytravel.com.

SENIOR TRAVELLERS

Seniors' discounts aren't generally available in Thailand, but the Thais more than make up for this in the respect they show for the elderly. In Thai culture status comes with age; there isn't as heavy an emphasis on youth as in the Western world. Deference for age manifests itself in the way Thais will go out of their way to help older people in and out of taxis or with luggage, and – usually but not always – in waiting on them first in shops and post offices.

Nonetheless, some cultural spheres are for the young. In particular, cross-generational entertainment is less common than in Western countries. There is a strict stratification among discos and nightclubs, for example, according to age group. One place will cater to teenagers, another to people in their early 20s, one for late 20s and 30s, yet another for those in their 40s and 50s, and once you've reached 60 you're considered too old to go clubbing! Exceptions to this rule include the more traditional entertainment venues, such as rural temple fairs and other wát-centred events, where young and old will dance and eat together. For men, massage parlours are another place where old and young mix.

TRAVEL WITH CHILDREN

Like many places in South-East Asia, travelling with children in Thailand can be a lot of fun as long as you come well prepared with the right attitudes, equipment and the usual parental patience. Lonely Planet's *Travel with Children* by Maureen Wheeler contains useful advice on how to cope with kids on the road and what to bring along to make things go more smoothly, with special attention paid to travel in developing countries.

Thais love children and in many instances will shower attention on your offspring, who will find ready playmates among their Thai counterparts and a temporary nanny service at practically every stop.

For the most part parents needn't worry too much about health concerns, although it pays to lay down a few ground rules – such as regular hand-washing – to head off potential medical problems. All the usual health precautions apply (see Health earlier for details); children should especially be warned not to play with animals since rabies is relatively common in Thailand.

DANGERS & ANNOYANCES

Although Thailand is in no way a dangerous country to visit, it's wise to be a little cautious, particularly if you're travelling alone. Solo women travellers should take special care on arrival at Bangkok International Airport, particularly at night. Don't take one of Bangkok's often very unofficial taxis (black-and-white licence plates) by yourself – it's better to take a licensed taxi (yellow-and-black plates) or even the public bus. Both men and women should ensure their rooms are securely locked and bolted at night. Inspect cheap rooms with thin walls for strategic peepholes.

Take caution when leaving valuables in hotel safes. Many travellers have reported unpleasant experiences leaving valuables in Chiang Mai guesthouses while trekking. Make sure you obtain an itemised receipt for property left with hotels or guesthouses – note the exact quantity of travellers cheques and all other valuables.

When you're on the road, keep zippered luggage secured with small locks, especially while travelling on buses and trains. Several readers' letters have recounted tales of thefts from their bags or backpacks during long overnight bus trips, particularly on routes between Bangkok and Chiang Mai or Surat Thani.

Credit Cards

On return to their home countries, some visitors have received huge credit-card bills for purchases (usually jewellery) charged to their cards in Bangkok while the cards had, supposedly, been secure in the hotel or guesthouse safe. It's said that over the two peak months that this first began occurring, credit-card companies lost over US$20 million in Thailand – one major company had 40% of their worldwide losses here! But that was over 10 years ago, and nowadays Thailand's record for credit-card fraud is not that far above average.

You might consider taking your credit cards with you if you go trekking – if the cards are stolen on the trail at least the bandits aren't likely to be able to use them. There are organised gangs in Bangkok specialising in arranging stolen credit-card purchases – and in some cases these gangs pay 'down and out' foreigners to fake the signatures on the credit cards.

Scams

Thais are generally so friendly and laid-back that some visitors are lulled into a false sense of security that makes them particularly vulnerable to scams and con schemes of all kinds. Scammers tend to haunt the areas where first-time tourists go, such as Bangkok's Grand Palace and Wat Pho area. Though you could come across them anywhere in Thailand, the overwhelming majority of scams take place in Bangkok, with Chiang Mai a very distant second.

Most scams begin the same way: A friendly Thai male (or, on rare occasions, a female) approaches a lone visitor – usually newly arrived – and strikes up a seemingly innocuous conversation. Sometimes the con man says he's a university student, other times he may claim to work for the World Bank or a similarly distinguished organisation (some even carry cellular phones). If you're on the way to Wat Pho or Jim Thompson's House, for example, he may tell you it's closed for a holiday. Eventually the conversation works its way around to the subject of the scam – the better con men can actually make it seem like you initiated the topic. That's one of the most bewildering aspects of the con – afterwards victims remember that the whole thing seemed like their idea, not the con artist's.

The scam itself almost always involves either gems or card playing. With gems, the victims find themselves invited to a gem and jewellery shop – your new-found friend is picking up some merchandise for himself and you're just along for the ride. Somewhere along the way he usually claims to have a connection, often a relative, in your home country (what a coincidence!) with whom he has a regular gem export-import business. One way or another, victims are convinced (usually they convince themselves) that they can turn a profit by arranging a gem purchase and reselling the merchandise at home. After all, the jewellery shop just happens to be offering a generous discount today – it's a government or religious holiday, or perhaps it's the shop's 10th anniversary, or maybe they've just taken a liking to you! The latest wrinkle is to say it's a special 'Amazing Thailand' promotion. As one freshly scammed reader recently wrote in: 'Everybody we spoke to mentioned 'Amazing Thailand' before they ripped us off!'

There is a seemingly infinite number of variations on the gem scam, almost all of which end up with the victim making a purchase of small, low-quality sapphires and posting them to their home countries. (If they let you walk out with them, you might return for a refund after realising you've been taken.) Once you return home, of course, the cheap sapphires turn out to be worth much less than you paid for them (perhaps one-tenth to one-half). One jeweller in Perth, Australia, says he sees about 12 people a week who have been conned in Thailand.

Many have invested and lost virtually all their savings; some admit they had been scammed even after reading warnings in this guidebook or those posted by the Tourism Authority of Thailand (TAT) around Bangkok.

Even if you were somehow able to return your purchase to the gem shop in question (one fellow I knew actually intercepted his parcel at the airport before it left Thailand), chances are slim-to-none they'd give a full refund. The con artist who brings the mark into the shop gets a commission of 10% to 50% per sale – the shop takes the rest.

When making credit-card purchases, don't let vendors take your credit card out of your sight to run it through the machine. Unscrupulous merchants have been known to rub off three or four or more receipts with one credit-card purchase; after the customer leaves the shop, they use the one legitimate receipt as a model to forge your signature on the blanks, then fill in astronomical 'purchases'. Sometimes they wait several weeks – even months – between submitting each charge receipt to the bank, so that you can't remember whether you'd been billed at the same vendor more than once.

Drugging

In bars and on trains and buses beware of friendly strangers offering gifts such as cigarettes, drinks, cookies or sweets (candy). Several travellers have reported waking up with a headache sometime later to find that their valuables have disappeared.

Male travellers have also encountered drugged food or drink from friendly Thai

Scams

The Thai police are usually no help whatsoever, believing that merchants are entitled to whatever price they can get. The main victimisers are a handful of shops who get protection from certain high-ranking government officials. These officials put pressure on police not to prosecute or to take as little action as possible. Even TAT's tourist police have never been able to prosecute a Thai jeweller, even in cases of blatant, recurring gem fraud. A Thai police commissioner was recently convicted of fraud in an investigation into a jewellery theft by Thais in Saudi Arabia: He replaced the Saudi gems with fakes! (See the Jewellery entry in the Shopping section of this chapter for information on recent initiatives to protect consumers.)

The card-playing scam starts out much the same: A friendly stranger approaches the lone traveller on the street, strikes up a conversation and then invites them to the house or apartment of his sister (or brother-in-law etc) for a drink or meal. After a bit of socialising a friend or relative of the con arrives on the scene; it just so happens a little high-stakes card game is planned for later that day. Like the gem scam, the card-game scam has many variations, but eventually the victim is shown some cheating tactics to use with help from the 'dealer', some practice sessions take place and finally the game gets under way with several high rollers at the table. The mark is allowed to win a few hands first, then somehow loses a few, gets bankrolled by one of the friendly Thais, and then loses the Thai's money. Suddenly your new-found buddies aren't so friendly any more – they want the money you lost. Sometimes the con pretends to be dismayed by it all. Sooner or later you end up cashing in most or all of your travellers cheques or making a costly visit to an ATM. Again the police won't take any action – in this case because gambling is illegal in Thailand so you've broken the law by playing cards for money.

The common denominator in all scams of this nature is the victims' own greed – the desire for an easy score. Other minor scams involve túk-túk drivers, hotel employees and bar girls who take new arrivals on city tours; these almost always end up in high-pressure sales situations at silk, jewellery or handicraft shops. In this case greed isn't the ruling motivation – it's simply a matter of weak sales resistance.

Follow TAT's number-one suggestion to tourists: Disregard all offers of free shopping or sightseeing help from strangers – they invariably take a commission from your purchases. I would add to this: Beware of deals that seem too good to be true – they're usually neither good nor true. You might also try lying whenever a stranger asks how long you've been in Thailand – if it's only been three days, say three weeks! Or save your Bangkok sightseeing until after you've been upcountry. The con artists rarely prey on anyone except new arrivals.

You should contact the tourist police if you have any problems with consumer fraud. The Tourist Police headquarters (☎ 02-255 2964) is located at 29/1 Soi Lang Suan, Th Ploenchit in Bangkok; you can also contact them through the TAT information office (☎ 02-282 9773, fax 280 1744) on Th Ratchadamnoen Nok near the Ratchadamnoen Boxing Stadium. A police unit (☎ 02-254 1067, 235 4017) that deals specifically with gem swindles is attached. A telephone hotline number ☎ 1155 connects with the tourist police from any phone in Thailand, but only from 8.30 am to 4.30 pm daily.

women in bars and from prostitutes in their own hotel rooms. Female visitors have encountered the same with young Thai men, albeit less frequently. Thais are also occasional victims, especially at the Moh Chit bus terminal and Chatuchak Park, where young girls are drugged and sold to brothels. Conclusion: Don't accept gifts from strangers.

Assault

Robbery of travellers by force is very rare in Thailand, but it does happen. Isolated incidences of armed robbery have tended to occur along the Thai-Myanmar and Thai-Cambodian borders and on remote islands. In February 2000, armed bandits robbed an Australian couple camping illegally in Doi Ang Khang National Park, near the Myanmar border. The couple tried to resist and, during the ensuing scuffle, one of the campers was shot and killed.

The safest practice in remote areas is not to go out alone at night and, if trekking in Northern Thailand, always walk in groups.

Touts

Touting – grabbing newcomers in the street or in train stations, bus terminals or airports to sell them a service – is a longtime tradition in Asia, and while Thailand doesn't have as many touts as, say, India, it has its share. In the popular tourist spots it seems like everyone – young boys waving fliers, túk-túk drivers, săamláw (three-wheeled vehicle) drivers, schoolgirls – is touting something, usually hotels or guesthouses. For the most part they're completely harmless and sometimes they can be very informative. But take anything a tout says with two large grains of salt. Since touts work on commission and get paid just for delivering you to a guesthouse or hotel (whether you check in or not), they'll say anything to get you to the door.

Often the best (most honest and reliable) hotels and guesthouses refuse to pay tout commissions – so the average tout will try to steer you away from such places. Hence don't believe them if they tell you the hotel or guesthouse you're looking for is closed, full, dirty or 'bad'. Sometimes (rarely) they're right but most times it's just a ruse to get you to a place that pays more commission. Always have a careful look yourself before checking into a place recommended by a tout. Túk-túk and săamláw drivers often offer free or low-cost rides to the place they're touting; if you have another place you're interested in, you might agree to go with a driver only if he or she promises to deliver you to your first choice after you've had a look at the place being touted. If drivers refuse, chances are it's because they know your first choice is a better one.

This type of commission work isn't limited to low-budget guesthouses. Taxi drivers and even airline employees at Thailand's major airports – including Bangkok and Chiang Mai – reap commissions from the big hotels as well. At either end of the budget spectrum, the customer ends up paying the commission indirectly through raised room rates. Bangkok International Airport employees are notorious for talking newly arrived tourists into staying at badly located, overpriced hotels.

Bus Touts Watch out for touts wearing (presumably fake) TAT or tourist information badges at Hualamphong train station. They have been known to coerce travellers into buying tickets for private bus rides, saying the train is 'full' or 'takes too long'. Often the promised bus service turns out to be substandard and may take longer than the equivalent train ride due to the frequent changing of vehicles. You may be offered a 24-seat VIP 'sleeper' bus to Penang, for example, and end up stuffed into a minivan all the way. Such touts are 'bounty hunters' who receive a set fee for every tourist they deliver to the bus companies. Avoid the travel agencies (many of which bear 'TAT' or even 'Lonely Planet' signs) just outside the train station for the same reason.

From a reader:

After reading your book's general chapters I was expecting a much worse situation. Compared to travelling in countries like Morocco, Tunisia, Turkey etc I think travelling in Thailand is relatively easy and hassle-free. When people in Thailand tout something usually saying 'No' once – or rarely twice – persuades them that you are not interested. In some countries you have to invest much more energy to get rid of people trying to sell.

Border Areas

A little extra caution should be exercised along Thailand's borders with Cambodia, Myanmar and Malaysia. Along the Thai-Cambodian border, which Cambodia's former Vietnamese-backed regime sealed against the Khmer Rouge with heavy armament, land mines and booby traps, unexploded ordnance (UXO) remains. Most, but not all, of the latter are planted inside Cambodian territory, so it is imperative that you stay away from this border except at Aranya Prathet, which is considered safe from undue UXO risk. It will be at least another 10 years before the mines are cleared in other areas. Armed Khmer bandits are occasionally encountered in the vicinity of Aranya Prathet (but not in Aranya Prathet itself).

The Khao Phra Wihan ruins just inside Cambodia near Ubon Ratchathani were closed to visitors from the Thai side for five years due to heavy skirmishes between Khmer Rouge and Phnom Penh troops. Following Cambodian military victories against the Khmer Rouge, the ruins reopened to the public in August 1998.

The Myanmar border between Um Phang and Mae Sariang occasionally receives shelling from Burmese troops in pursuit of Karen or Mon rebels. Karen rebels are trying to maintain an independent nation called Kawthoolei along the border with Thailand. The situation is complicated by an ongoing split between the Christian and Buddhist Karen insurgents. Between Mae Sot and Tha Song Yang, south of Mae Sariang on the Thai side, are several Karen refugee camps (at last report 12 camps with a total of about 100,000 refugees) populated by civilians who have fled Burmese-Karen armed conflicts, as well as political dissidents from Yangon. The fighting was particularly bad in 1995, when dissident Karen Buddhists, backed by Burmese troops, routed the leading Christian faction; this area continues to be a military hot spot. The risks of catching a piece of shrapnel are substantially lower if you keep several kilometres between yourself and the Thai-Myanmar border in this area – fighting can break out at any time. Mae Sot itself is quite safe these days, although you can still occasionally hear mortar fire in the distance.

In January 2000, 10 gunmen from 'God's Army' – a fringe rebel alliance between Karen independence fighters and Burmese student rebels in Myanmar – crossed into Thailand and took several hundred people hostage at a provincial hospital in Ratchaburi Province. All 10 gunmen were killed when Thai authorities stormed the hospital to end the crisis.

In the Three Pagodas Pass area there is also occasional fighting between Myanmar, Karen and Mon armies, who are competing for control of the smuggling trade between Myanmar and Thailand. Typically, the rebels advance in the rainy season and retreat in the dry; lately this area has been fairly quiet.

The presence of Shan and Wa armies along the Myanmar-Thai border in northern Mae Hong Son makes this area dangerous if you attempt to travel near opium- and amphetamine-trade border crossings – obviously these are not signposted, so take care anywhere along the border in this area.

In early 1996 Khun Sa and 10,000 of his troops surrendered to Yangon, taking most of the punch out of the MTA. However, as many as 8000 MTA fighters, split among four armies, are still active in the area bordering Mae Sai south to Mae Hong Son, so the area is not much safer than when Khun Sa

was around. In March 1998 there was a three-way armed clash between Thai border police, Myanmar forces and the Shan States Army along the Mae Hong Son/Shan State border.

There is also a potential of hostilities breaking out between Myanmar government troops and the Thai army over a disputed Thai-Myanmar border section near Doi Lang, south-west of Mae Sai in Mae Ai district. The territory under dispute amounts to 32 sq km; at the moment the two sides are trying to work things out peaceably according to the 1894 Siam-Britain Treaty, which both countries recognise. The problem is that British mapping of the time made geographical naming errors that unintentionally seem to favour the Burmese side. It is likely that Burmese and Thai troops will remain poised for action on either side of the border until the matter is resolved.

The Thai-Malaysian border is generally safe from insurgent activity these days – although the Pattani United Liberation Organisation supposedly still exists, albeit in small number – but there is still plenty of UXO in rural border areas of Songkhla, Yala and Narathiwat Provinces.

Although Bangkok has generally been safe from terrorist activity, a couple of large truck bombs bound for the Israeli embassy have been intercepted in the city in recent years. The district known as Little Arabia (Soi Nana Neua, off Thanon Sukhumvit) is a known 'hideaway' for Muslim terrorists on the run from other parts of the world.

Drugs

Opium, heroin, amphetamines, hallucinogens and marijuana are widely used in Thailand, but it is illegal to buy, sell or possess these drugs in any quantity. (The possession of opium for consumption, but not sale, among hill tribes is legal.) A lesser-known narcotic, *kràthâwm* (a leaf of the *Mitragyna speciosa* tree), is used by workers and students as a stimulant. A hundred kràthâwm leaves sell for around 200B, and are sold for 5B to 15B each; the leaf is illegal and said to be addictive.

In the south, especially on the rainy Gulf of Thailand islands, mushrooms (*hèt khîi khwai*, 'buffalo-shit mushrooms', or *hèt mao*, 'drunk mushrooms'), which contain the hallucinogen psilocybin, are sometimes sold to or gathered by foreigners. Using or possessing such

Drug Penalties

drug	quantity	penalty
marijuana or hallucinogens		
consumption	any amount	1 year imprisonment and up to 10,000B fine
possession	any amount	up to 5 years imprisonment and up to 50,000B fine
cocaine or morphine		
consumption	any amount	6 months to 10 years imprisonment and up to 5000B fine
possession	less than 100g	5 years imprisonment and 5000B fine
possession	100g +	5 years to life imprisonment and 50,000B to 500,000B fine
heroin		
consumption	any amount	6 months to 10 years imprisonment and 5000B to 10,000B fine
possession	less than 20g	1 to 10 years imprisonment and 10,000B to 100,000B fine
possession	20g + to less than 100g	5 years to life imprisonment and 50,000B to 500,000B fine
possession	100g +	life imprisonment or execution

mushrooms is now illegal and a risky proposition as well, as the dosage is always uncertain: We've heard confirmed stories of a foreigner who swam to his death off Ko Pha-Ngan after a 'special' mushroom omelette, and there have been other confirmed casualties as well. If you must indulge, watch the dosage carefully.

Amphetamine tablets are imported in large quantities from Wa-controlled areas of north-eastern Myanmar and sold inexpensively in Thailand. The quality is low and dosages erratic. This is another illegal drug to be extremely careful of.

Although in certain areas of the country drugs seem to be used with some impunity, enforcement is arbitrary – the only way not to risk getting caught is to avoid the drug scene entirely. Every year perhaps dozens of visiting foreigners are arrested in Thailand for drug use or trafficking and end up doing time in Thai prisons. A smaller, but significant, number die of heroin overdoses. Guesthouses where foreigners hang out are targets of infrequent drug enforcement sweeps.

Ko Pha-Ngan is one of Thailand's leading centres for recreational drug use, and

the Thai police have begun to take notice there as well. Particularly on days leading up to Hat Rin's famous monthly full moon rave, police often set up inspection points on the road between Thong Sala and Hat Rin. Every vehicle, including bicycles and motorcycles, is stopped and the passengers and vehicles thoroughly searched.

The legal penalties for drug offences are stiff: If you're caught using marijuana, mushrooms or LSD, you face a fine of 10,000B plus one year in prison, while for heroin or amphetamines, the penalty for use can be anywhere from six months' to 10 years' imprisonment, plus a fine of 5000B to 10,000B. The going rate for bribing one's way out of a small pot bust is 50,000B.

Drug smuggling – defined as attempting to cross a border with drugs in your possession – carries considerably higher penalties, including execution. Recent arrest records show that citizens of Myanmar, Laos, Malaysia, Cambodia and the UK top the list of those arrested in Thailand for drug trafficking, followed by Australians, Germans, Americans and Italians.

LEGAL MATTERS

In general Thai police don't hassle foreigners, especially tourists. If anything they generally go out of their way not to arrest a foreigner breaking minor traffic laws, rather taking the approach that a friendly warning will suffice.

One major exception is drugs (see Dangers & Annoyances earlier for a general discussion of this topic), which most Thai police view as either a social scourge with regard to which it's their duty to enforce the letter of the law, or an opportunity to make untaxed income via bribes. Which direction they'll go often depends on dope quantities; small-time offenders are sometimes offered the chance to pay their way out of an arrest, while traffickers usually go to jail.

Be extra vigilant about where you dispose of cigarette butts and other refuse when in Bangkok. A strong anti-littering law was passed in Bangkok in 1997, and police won't hesitate to cite foreigners and collect fines of 2000B.

If you are arrested for any offence, the police will allow you the opportunity to make a phone call to your embassy or consulate in Thailand if you have one, or to a friend or relative if not. There's a whole set of legal codes governing the length of time and manner in which you can be detained before being charged or put on trial, but a lot of discretion is left to the police. With foreigners the police are more likely to bend these codes in your favour. However, as with police worldwide, if you don't show respect you will make matters worse.

Thai law does not presume an indicted detainee to be either 'guilty' or 'innocent' but rather a 'suspect' whose guilt or innocence will be decided in court. Trials are usually speedy.

Thailand has its share of attorneys, and if you think you're a high arrest risk for whatever reason, it might be a good idea to get out the Bangkok yellow pages, copy down a few phone numbers and carry them with you.

Tourist Police Hotline

The best way to deal with most serious hassles regarding ripoffs or thefts is to contact the tourist police, who are used to dealing with foreigners, rather than the regular Thai police. The tourist police maintain a hotline – dial ☎ 1155 from any phone in Thailand. Call this number to lodge complaints or to request assistance with regards to personal safety 24 hours a day. You can also call this number between 8.30 am and 4.30 pm daily to request travel information.

The tourist police can also be very helpful in cases of arrest. Although they typically have no jurisdiction over the kinds of cases handled by regular cops, they may be able to help with translation or with contacting your embassy.

Visiting Someone in Prison

If you know someone serving a prison sentence in Bangkok or elsewhere, and would like to visit that person, the normal procedure is to visit the prisoner's Bangkok embassy first. Tell the consular staff the name of the prisoner you would like to visit, and ask to receive a letter from the embassy requesting you be permitted to see that prisoner. The embassy can also provide directions to the prison where the person is being held and let you know what visiting hours are. Ordinarily there are only a couple of days a week when you are permitted to visit. Don't try going directly to the prison without a letter from the prisoner's embassy, as you may be refused entry.

Over the last couple of years – especially since the release of the film *Brokedown Palace,* about two backpackers who receive a long Bangkok prison sentence after getting caught smuggling heroin out of Thailand – visiting imprisoned foreigners in Bangkok has become something of a fad. With the resulting increase in inquiries, both embassy and prison staff are tightening up on the release of prisoner information. The Thai corrections system does not accept the Western notion that anonymous prisoners should receive visitors, although exceptions are sometimes made for missionaries.

For the latest information on visitation policies, contact your embassy in Bangkok.

BUSINESS HOURS

Most government offices are open from 8.30 am to 4.30 pm weekdays, but close from noon to 1 pm for lunch. Regular bank hours in Bangkok are 10 am to 4 pm weekdays, but several banks have special foreign-exchange offices in tourist-oriented areas that are open longer hours (8.30 am to 8 pm) and every day of the week. Note that all government offices and banks are closed on public holidays.

Businesses usually operate between 8.30 am and 5 pm weekdays and sometimes on Saturday morning. Larger shops usually open from 10 am to 6.30 or 7 pm but smaller shops may open earlier and close later. Department stores are usually open between 10 am and 10 pm.

PUBLIC HOLIDAYS & SPECIAL EVENTS

The number and frequency of festivals and fairs in Thailand is incredible – there always seems to be something going on, especially during the cool season between November and February.

The exact dates for festivals may vary from year to year, either because of the lunar calendar, which isn't quite in sync with the solar calendar – or because local authorities have decided to change festival dates. The TAT (see Tourist Offices earlier for contact information) publishes an up-to-date *Major Events & Festivals* calendar each year that is useful for anyone planning to attend a particular event.

January

New Year's Day Public holiday, 1 January. A rather recent public holiday in deference to the Western calendar.

That Phanom Festival An annual week-long homage to the North-East's most sacred Buddhist stupa (Phra That Phanom) in Nakhon Phanom Province. Pilgrims from all over the country, as well as from Laos, attend.

February

Chiang Mai Flower Festival Colourful floats and parades exhibit Chiang Mai's cultivated flora.

Magha Puja (*maakhá buuchaa*) Held on the full moon of the third lunar month to commemorate Buddha preaching to 1250 enlightened monks who came to hear him 'without prior summons'. A public holiday throughout the country, it culminates with a candle-lit walk around the main chapel (*wian tian*) at every wát.

Phra Nakhon Khiri Diamond Festival This is a week-long celebration of Phetchaburi's history and architecture focused on Phra Nakhon Khiri Historical Park (also known as Khao Wang), a hill topped by a former royal palace overlooking the city. It features a sound-and-light show on Khao Wang; the temples are festooned with lights and presentations of Thai classical dance-drama.

Late February–Early March

Chinese New Year Called *trùt jiin* in Thai, Chinese populations all over Thailand celebrate their lunar New Year (the date shifts from year to year) with a week of house-cleaning, lion dances and fireworks. The most impressive festivities take place in the Chinese-dominated province capital of Nakhon Sawan.

March

Asean Barred Ground Dove Festival This is a large dove-singing contest held in the first week of March in Yala that attracts dove-lovers from all over Thailand, Malaysia, Singapore and Indonesia.

Bangkok International Jewellery Fair Held in several large Bangkok hotels, this is Thailand's most important annual gem and jewellery trade show. It runs concurrently with the Department of Export Promotion's Gems & Jewellery Fair.

Phanom Rung Festival A newly established festival to commemorate restoration work in the Phanom Rung Historical Park, an impressive Angkor-style temple complex in Buriram Province. It involves a daytime procession up Phanom Rung Hill and spectacular sound-and-light shows at night. It takes place on the last week of the month – be prepared for very hot weather.

April

Chakri Day This is a public holiday commemorating the founder of the Chakri dynasty, Rama I. It's held on 6 April.

Songkran This is the celebration of the lunar New Year in Thailand. Buddha images are 'bathed', monks and elders receive the respect of younger Thais by the sprinkling of water over their hands, and a lot of water is generously tossed about for fun. Songkran generally gives everyone a chance to release their frustrations and literally cool off during the peak of the hot season. Hide out in your room or expect to be soaked; the latter is a lot more fun. It's held from 13 to 15 April.

May

Coronation Day Public holiday, 5 May. The king and queen preside at a ceremony at Wat Phra Kaew, commemorating their 1950 coronation.

Visakha Puja (*wísǎakhà buuchaa*) A public holiday that falls on the 15th day of the waxing moon in the 6th lunar month, this day commemorates the date of the Buddha's birth, enlightenment and *parinibbana,* or passing away. Activities are centred around the wát, with candle-lit processions, much chanting and sermonising.

Mid-May–Mid-June

Phi Ta Khon Festival One of the wildest in Thailand, this is an animist-Buddhist celebration held in Loei's Dan Sai district (nowadays also in other places around Loei Province) in which revellers dress in garish 'spirit' costumes, wear painted masks and brandish carved wooden phalli. The festival commemorates a Buddhist legend in which a host of spirits (*phĭi*) appeared to greet the Buddha-to-be upon his return to his home town, during his penultimate birth.

Rocket Festival In the North-East, villagers craft large skyrockets of bamboo which they then fire into the sky to bring rain for rice fields. This festival is best celebrated in the town of Yasothon, but is also good in Ubon Ratchathani and Nong Khai. It's known in Thai as Bun Bang Fai.

Royal Ploughing Ceremony To kick off the official rice-planting season, the king participates in this ancient Brahman ritual at Sanam Luang (the large field across from Wat Phra Kaew) in Bangkok. Thousands of Thais gather to watch, and traffic in this part of the city comes to a standstill.

Mid- to late July

Asalha Puja (*àsăanhà buuchaa*) This festival commemorates the Buddha's first sermon.

Candle Festival Khao Phansa (see following) is celebrated in the North-East by parading huge carved candles on floats in the streets. This festival is best celebrated in Ubon Ratchathani.

Khao Phansa (*khâo phansǎa*) A public holiday and the beginning of Buddhist 'lent', this is the traditional time of year for young men to enter the monkhood for the rainy season and for all monks to station themselves in a monastery for the three months. It's a good time to observe a Buddhist ordination.

August

Queen's Birthday This public holiday is celebrated on 12 August. In Bangkok, Thanon Ratchadamnoen Klang and the Grand Palace are festooned with coloured lights.

Mid-September

Thailand International Swan-Boat Races These take place on the Mae Nam Chao Phraya (Chao Phraya River) in Bangkok near Saphan Phra Ram IX (Rama IX Bridge).

Last Week of September

Narathiwat Fair An annual week-long festival celebrating local culture in Narathiwat Province with boat races, dove-singing contests, handicraft displays, traditional southern Thai music and dance. The king and queen almost always attend.

Late September–Early October

Vegetarian Festival A nine-day celebration in Trang and Phuket during which devout Chinese Buddhists eat only vegetarian food. There are various ceremonies at Chinese temples and merit-making processions that bring to mind Hindu Thaipusam in its exhibition of self-mortification. Smaller towns in the south such as Krabi and Phang-Nga also celebrate the vegie fest on a smaller scale.

Mid-October–Mid-November

Kathin (*thâwt kàthǐn*) A month at the end of the Buddhist lent during which new monastic robes and requisites are offered to the Sangha (monastic community). In Nan Province longboat races are held on the Mae Nan (Nan River).

October

Chulalongkorn Day Public holiday, 23 October. This holiday is in commemoration of King Chulalongkorn (Rama V).

November

Loi Krathong On the proper full-moon night, small lotus-shaped baskets or boats made of banana leaves containing flowers, incense, candles and a coin are floated on Thai rivers, lakes and canals. This is a peculiarly Thai festival that probably originated in Sukhothai and is best celebrated in the North. In Chiang Mai, where the festival is called Yi Peng, residents also launch paper hot-air balloons into the sky. At the Sukhothai Historical Park there is an impressive sound-and-light show held at this time.

Surin Annual Elephant Roundup Held on the third weekend of November, Thailand's biggest elephant show is pretty touristy these days. If you have ever had the desire to see a lot of elephants in one place, then here's your chance.

Late November–Early December

River Khwae Bridge Week There are sound-and-light shows every night at the Death Railway Bridge in Kanchanaburi. Events include historical exhibitions and vintage-train rides on the infamous railway.

December

King's Birthday Public holiday, 5 December. This holiday is celebrated with some fervour in Bangkok. As with the queen's birthday, it features lots of lights and other decorations along Thanon Ratchadamnoen Klang. Some people erect temporary shrines to the king outside their homes or businesses.

Constitution Day Public holiday commemorating the establishment of the constitutional monarchy in 1932; 10 December

Considerations for Responsible Diving

The popularity of diving is placing immense pressure on many sites. Please consider the following tips when diving and help preserve the ecology and beauty of reefs:

- Do not use anchors on the reef, and take care not to ground boats on coral. Encourage dive operators and regulatory bodies to establish permanent moorings at popular dive sites.
- Avoid touching living marine organisms with your body or dragging computer consoles and gauges across the reef. Polyps can be damaged by even the gentlest contact. Never stand on corals, even if they look solid and robust. If you must secure yourself to the reef, only hold fast to exposed rock or dead coral.
- Be conscious of your fins. Even without contact the surge from heavy fin strokes near the reef can damage delicate organisms. When treading water in shallow reef areas, take care not to kick up clouds of sand. Settling sand can easily smother the delicate organisms of the reef.
- Practise and maintain proper buoyancy control. Major damage can be done by divers descending too fast and colliding with the reef. Make sure you are correctly weighted and that your weight belt is positioned so that you stay horizontal. If you have not dived for a while, have a practice dive in a pool before taking to the reef. Be aware that buoyancy can change over the period of an extended trip: initially you may breathe harder and need more weighting; a few days later you may breathe more easily and need less weight.
- Take great care in underwater caves. Spend as little time within them as possible as your air bubbles may be caught within the roof and thereby leave previously submerged organisms high and dry. Taking turns to inspect the interior of a small cave will lessen the chances of damaging contact.
- Resist the temptation to collect or buy corals or shells. Aside from the ecological damage, taking home marine souvenirs depletes the beauty of a site and spoils the enjoyment of others.
- The same goes for marine archaeological sites (mainly shipwrecks). Respect their integrity; they may even be protected from looting by law.
- Ensure that you take home all your rubbish, and any litter you may find as well. Plastics in particular are a serious threat to marine life. Turtles will mistake plastic for jellyfish and eat it.
- Resist the temptation to feed fish. You may disturb their normal eating habits, encourage aggressive behaviour or feed them food that is detrimental to their health.
- Minimise your disturbance of marine animals. In particular, do not ride on the backs of turtles as this causes them great anxiety.

ACTIVITIES
Cycling
Details on pedalling your way around Thailand and bicycle hire can be found in the Getting Around chapter.

Trekking
Wilderness walking or trekking is one of Northern Thailand's biggest draws. Typical trekking programs run for four or five days (although it is possible to arrange everything from one- to 10-day treks) and feature daily walks through forested mountain areas coupled with overnight stays in hill-tribe villages to satisfy both ethno- and eco-tourism urges. See the Trekking sections in the Northern Thailand chapter for more detail.

Other trekking opportunities are available in Thailand's larger national parks (including Doi Phu Kha, Kaeng Krachan, Khao Sam Roi Yot, Khao Sok, Khao Yai, Phu Reua and Thap Lan), where park rangers may be hired as guides and cooks for a few days at a time. Rates are reasonable. For more information, see the respective park entries later in this book.

Diving & Snorkelling
Thailand's two coastlines and countless islands are popular among divers for their mild waters and colourful marine life. The biggest diving centre – in terms of the number of participants, but not the number of dive operations – is still Pattaya, simply because it's less than two hours' drive from Bangkok. There are several islands with reefs within a short boat ride from Pattaya and the town is packed with dive shops.

Phuket is the second-biggest jumping-off point – or the biggest if you count dive operations – and has the advantage of offering the largest variety of places to choose from, including small offshore islands less than an hour away; Ao Phang-Nga (a one- to two-hour boat ride), with its unusual rock formations and clear green waters; and the world-famous Similan and Surin Islands in the Andaman Sea (about four hours away by fast boat). Reef dives in the Andaman are particularly rewarding – some 210 hard corals and 108 reef fish have so far been catalogued in this under-studied marine zone, where probably thousands more species of reef organisms live.

In recent years dive operations have multiplied on the palmy islands of Ko Samui, Ko Pha-Ngan and Ko Tao in the Gulf of Thailand off Surat Thani. Chumphon Province, just north of Surat Thani, is another up-and-coming area where there are a dozen or so islands with undisturbed reefs. Newer frontiers include the so-called Burma Banks (northwest of Ko Surin), Khao Lak and islands off the coast of Krabi and Trang Provinces.

All of these places, with the possible exception of the Burma Banks, have areas that are suitable for snorkelling as well as scuba diving, since many reefs are covered by water no deeper than 2m.

Masks, fins and snorkels are readily available for rent not only at dive centres but also through guesthouses in beach areas. If you're particular about the quality and condition of the equipment you use, however, you might be better off bringing your own mask and snorkel – some of the stuff for rent is second-rate. And people with large heads may have difficulty finding masks that fit, since most of the masks are made, or imported, for Thai heads.

Dive Centres Most dive shops rent equipment at reasonable rates and some also offer basic instruction and NAUI or PADI qualification for first-timers – PADI is by far the most prevalent. The average four-day, full-certification course costs around 8000B to 11,000B, including all instruction, equipment and several open-water dives. Shorter, less expensive 'resort' courses are also available.

It's a good idea to shop around the dive companies, not just to compare prices but to suss out the types of instruction, the condition of the equipment and the personalities of the instructors. German and English are the most common languages of instruction, but French and Italian courses are also available. See the relevant destination sections of this book for names and locations of established diving centres.

Dive Seasons Generally speaking, the Gulf of Thailand has a year-round dive season, although tropical storms sometimes blow out the visibility temporarily. On the Andaman Coast the best diving conditions occur between December and April; from May to November monsoon conditions prevail. Whale sharks and manta rays in the offshore Andaman (eg, Similan and Surin Island groups) are a major bonus during planktonic blooms in March and April.

Dive Medicine Due to the overall lack of medical facilities for diving injuries, great caution should be exercised when diving in Thailand. Recompression chambers are located at three permanent facilities:

Apakorn Kiatiwong Naval Hospital (☎ 038-601185) Sattahip, Chonburi, 26km east of Pattaya; urgent care available 24 hours
Somdej Phra Pinklao Naval Hospital (☎ 02-460 0000–19 ext 341, 460 1105) Department of Underwater & Aviation Medicine, Thanon Taksin, Thonburi, Bangkok; open 24 hours
Sub-aquatic Safety Service (SSS; ☎ 076-342518, 01-606 1869, fax 342519) Hat Patong, Phuket

Dive Guidebooks Lonely Planet's richly illustrated *Diving & Snorkeling Thailand* is just out and is full of vital diving information written by resident diving instructors.

Windsurfing

The best combinations of rental facilities and wind conditions are found on Pattaya and Jomtien beaches in Chonburi Province, on Ko Samet, on the west coast of Phuket and on Hat Chaweng on Ko Samui. To a lesser extent you'll also find rental equipment on Hat Khao Lak (north of Phuket), Ko Pha-Ngan, Ko Tao and Ko Chang.

The windsurfing gear rented at Thai resorts is generally not the most complete and up-to-date. For the novice windsurfer this probably won't matter, but hot-doggers may be disappointed in the selection. In Thailand's year-round tropical climate, wetsuits aren't necessary.

If you have your own equipment you can set out anywhere you find a coastal breeze. If you're looking for something undiscovered, you might check out the cape running north from Narathiwat's provincial capital in southern Thailand. In general the windy months on the Gulf of Thailand are mid-February to April. On the Andaman Sea side of the Thai-Malay peninsula winds are strongest from September to December.

Surfing

This sport has never really taken off in Thailand, not least because there doesn't seem to be any sizable, annually dependable breaks (write to us if you find any). Phuket's west coast occasionally kicks up some surfable waves during the south-west monsoon (May to November). We have also seen some fair surf action on the west coast of Ko Chang during the same time of year, and on the east coast of Ko Samet during the dry season (November to February). We'd be willing to bet there's decent surf on Ko Chang's east coast during these months.

Low-quality boards can be rented in Pattaya and on Phuket's Patong Beach (but bigger surf is usually found on Laem Singh and Hat Surin). Coastal areas of Trang Province are historically reputed to receive large waves during the south-west monsoon, but we've never heard of anyone surfing there.

Paddling

Touring the islands and coastal limestone formations around Phuket and Ao Phang-Nga by inflatable canoe has become an increasingly popular activity over the last five years. Typical tours seek out half-submerged caves called *hong* (*hâwng*, Thai for 'room'), timing their excursions so that they can paddle into the caverns at low tide. Several outfits in Phuket and Krabi offer equipment and guides. Fàràng outfitters claim to have 'discovered' the hong, but local fishermen have known about them for hundreds of years. Several islands with partially submerged caves in Ao Phang-Nga have carried the name Ko Hong (Room Island) for at least the last half-century.

You might consider bringing your own craft. Inflatable or folding kayaks are easier to transport, but hardshell kayaks track better. In Thailand's tropical waters an open-top or open-deck kayak – whether hardshell, folding or inflatable – is more comfortable and practical than the closed-deck type with a spray skirt and other sealing paraphernalia, which will only transform your kayak into a floating sauna.

River & Canal Excursions

There are opportunities for boat travel along Thailand's major rivers and canals through the extensive public boat system and aboard a small number of tourist boat services. So far regular leisure boating has been introduced to only the lower Mae Nam Chao Phraya and a few rivers in Northern Thailand. A variety of watercraft are available, from air-conditioned tourist boats along the Mae Nam Chao Phraya around Bangkok to rustic bamboo rafts on the Mae Kok and sturdy whitewater kayaks on the Mae Pai.

The Mekong River, until the late 1980s considered perilous due to regional hostilities, has enormous potential. During the last six years or so short-distance boat trips have been offered in Chiang Rai, Loei and Nong Khai Provinces, and in early 1994 an experimental tour service between Chiang Saen and China was inaugurated (so far the route has yet to be regularised). Central Thailand's vast network of canals, centred on the Chao Phraya Delta and fanning out for hundreds of kilometres in all directions, offers numerous boating opportunities. However, the motorised boat traffic along these waterways has meant that very few foreign visitors have tried canoeing or kayaking this grid. For the adventurous traveller the potential is huge, as by public and chartered long-tail boats you can piece together canal journeys of several days' duration.

For more information on river and canal travel possibilities, see destination chapters later in the book.

COURSES
Language

Several language schools in Bangkok, Chiang Mai and other places where foreigners congregate offer courses in Thai language. Tuition fees average around 250B per hour. Some places will let you trade English lessons for Thai lessons.

It's best to enrol in programs that offer plenty of opportunity for linguistic interaction rather than rote learning or the passe 'natural method'.

Good schools in Bangkok include:

AUA Language Center (☎ 02-252 8170) 179 Thanon Ratchadamri. American University Alumni (AUA) runs one of the largest English-language teaching institutes in the world, so this is a good place to meet Thai students. AUA-produced books are stodgy and outdated, but many teachers make their own – better – instructional materials. Some foreigners who study Thai here complain that there's not enough interaction in class because of an emphasis on the so-called 'natural approach', which focuses on teacher input rather than student practice and has been thoroughly discredited in most Western countries. Others find the approach useful. Paw hòk (6th grade primary-school level, essential for working in the public school system) courses are available.

Chulalongkorn University (☎ 02-218 4888, fax 218 4877, ✉ tkongkar@chula.ac.th) Intensive Thai Office/Faculty of Arts, Chulalongkorn University, Thanon Phayathai. The program here consists of three basic, three intermediate, and three advanced courses, each lasting five weeks. Each course comprises 100 hours of instruction. The instruction fee for each course is 25,000B.

Nisa Thai Language School (☎ 02-286 9323) YMCA Collins House, 27 Thanon Sathon Tai. This school has a fairly good reputation, although teachers may be less qualified than at Union (see later) or AUA language schools. In addition to all the usual levels, Nisa offers a course in preparing for the paw hòk examination. A second location (☎ 02-671 3359) is at 32/14–6 Thanon Yen Akat.

Siri Pattana Thai Language School (☎ 02-213 1206) YWCA, 13 Thanon Sathon Tai. This school offers Thai language lessons as well as preparation for the paw hok exam.

Union Language School (☎ 02-233 4482, 235 4030) Christ Church Thailand Bldg, 109 Thanon Surawong. Generally recognised as the best and most rigorous course (many missionaries study here), this school employs a balance of structure-oriented and communication-oriented methodologies in 80-hour, four-week modules. Private tuition is also available.

AUA also has branches in Chiang Mai, Khon Kaen, Lampang, Mahasarakham, Phitsanulok, Phuket, Songkhla, Ubon and Udon. Most of these branches are housed on Thai college or university campuses. Not all AUAs offer regularly scheduled Thai classes, but study can usually be arranged on an ad hoc basis. Teaching methodologies in upcountry AUAs tend to be more flexible than at the Bangkok unit.

Thai Culture

Chulalongkorn University in Bangkok, the most prestigious university in Thailand, offers a two-week intensive Thai studies course called Perspectives on Thailand. The 60-hour program includes classes in Thai culture, economics, history, politics, religion, art, geography, language, trade and current events. Classes meet six hours a day, five days a week and are offered once a year in July only. Students who have taken the course say they have found the quality of instruction excellent. The cost for this program excluding airfare, meals and lodging is US$950 per person. A fee for optional on-campus accommodation is US$200. For further information contact ☎ 02-218 3393, fax 218 3926, ✉ surapeepan.c@chula.ac.th or write to: Perspectives on Thailand, Continuing Education Center, 5th floor, Vidhyabhathan Bldg, 12 Soi Chulalongkorn, Chulalongkorn University, Bangkok 10330.

Since 1991, Chulalongkorn has offered a two-year master's degree program in Thai Studies in which participants have the opportunity to study and analyse a considerable body of knowledge under the supervision of recognised Thai experts in the field. The language of instruction is English, and tuition and registration fees total 46,000B per semester. Contact Thai Studies Section, Faculty of Arts, Chulalongkorn University, Bangkok 10330, for further information. Non-degree students may enrol in courses offered in the Thai Studies program at a cost of 15,000B, plus a registration fee of 11,000B.

The Oriental Hotel (☎ 02-236 0400 ext 5) offers a lecture series across the river from the hotel as part of a Thai cultural program. Lectures, which are prepared and delivered by professors from some of the country's leading universities, take place from Monday to Friday. The cost is US$40 per person (minimum of three persons in a class), which includes refreshments and trips (where applicable). Lecture subjects include 'Thai Ways', 'Thai Beliefs', 'Thai Dances and Music', 'Thai Art and Architecture' and 'Contemporary Thai Culture'. Reservations are recommended. On request, the following additional courses are available within 24 hours of paid reservation: Thai dance, martial arts and masked dance, Thai music lessons and meditation.

Meditation

Thailand has long been a popular place for Western students of Buddhism, particularly those interested in Buddhist meditation. Two basic systems of meditation are taught, *samatha* and *vipassana*. Samatha aims towards the calming of the mind and development of refined states of concentration, and as such is similar to other traditions of meditation or contemplation found in most of the world's religions.

Unique to Buddhism, particularly Theravada and to a lesser extent Tibetan Buddhism, is a system of meditation known as vipassana (Thai: *wípàtsànaa*) a Pali word that roughly translates as 'insight'.

Foreigners who come to Thailand to study vipassana can choose from dozens of temples and meditation centres *(sămnák wípàtsànaa)* specialising in these teachings. Teaching methods vary but the general emphasis is on observing mind-body processes from moment to moment. Thai language is usually the medium of instruction but several places also provide instruction in English. Some centres and monasteries teach both vipassana and samatha methods, others specialise in one or the other.

Details on some of the more popular meditation-oriented temples and centres are given in destination chapters. Instruction and accommodation are free of charge at temples, although donations are expected.

Short-term students will find that the two-month Tourist Visa is ample for most courses of study. Long-term students may want to consider getting a three- or six-month Non-Immigrant Visa (see Visas & Documents earlier in this chapter). A few Westerners are ordained as monks or nuns in order to take full advantage of the monastic environment. Monks and nuns are generally (but not always) allowed to stay in Thailand as long as they remain in robes.

Places where English-language instruction is usually available include:

Boonkanjanaram Meditation Centre (☎ 038-231865) Hat Jomtien, Pattaya, Chonburi
International Buddhist Meditation Centre (☎ 02-623 6326, afternoons only) Wat Mahathat, Thanon Maharat, Tha Phra Chan, Bangkok
International Buddhist Meditation Centre (☎ 02-240 3700 ext 1480, 511 0439, fax 512 6083) Nakhon Pathom

Sorn-Thawee Meditation Centre Bangkla, Chachoengsao (☎ 038-541405)
Thailand Vipassana Centre (☎ 02-216 4772, fax 215 3408) Pathumwan, Bangkok
Wat Asokaram (☎ 02-395 0003) Bang Na-Trat Highway (32km south of Bangkok), Samut Prakan
Wat Khao Tham Ko Pha-Ngan, Surat Thani
Wat Phra That Chom Thong (☎ 053-362067) 157 Ban Luang Chom Thong, Chiang Mai
Wat Suan Mokkhaphalaram (fax 076-391851 Attn: SMI) Chaiya, Surat Thani
Wat Tapotaram (Wat Ram Poeng; ☎ 053-278620) Chiang Mai
Wiwekasom Vipassana Centre (☎ 038-283766) Ban Suan, Chonburi
World Fellowship of Buddhists (☎ 02-661 1284) Benjasiri Park, next to The Emporium, Soi 24, Thanon Sukhumvit, Bangkok

The International Buddhist Meditation Centre at Wat Mahathat also sponsors weekends at upcountry locations in Pathum Thani, Nakhon Ratchasima and Phetchabun Provinces.

Before visiting one of these centres, it's a good idea to call or write to make sure space and instruction are available. Some places require that lay persons staying overnight wear white clothes. For even a brief visit, wear clean and neat clothing (ie, long trousers or skirt and sleeves that cover the shoulder).

For a detailed look at vipassana study in Thailand, including visa and ordination procedures, read *The Meditation Temples of Thailand: A Guide* published by Silkworm Books (☎ 053-271889), 104/5 Thanon Chiang Mai-Hot, Mu 7, Tambon Suthep, Chiang Mai, or *A Guide to Buddhist Monasteries & Meditation Centres in Thailand* (available from the World Fellowship of Buddhists in Bangkok or online at www.dharmanet.org/thai_94.html).

Useful reading material includes Jack Kornfield's *Living Dharma,* which contains short biographies and descriptions of the teaching methods of 12 well-known Theravada teachers, including six Thais. Serious meditators will want to study *The Path of Purification (Visuddhi Magga),* a classic commentary that reveals every detail of canonical Buddhist practice and includes a Pali-English glossary defining all the tricky terms like *kasina, jhana, nimitta, vipaka* and so on. These books are available at bookshops in Bangkok.

Martial Arts

Many Westerners have trained in Thailand, but few last more than a week or two in a Thai camp – and fewer still have gone on to compete on Thailand's pro circuit.

Muay Thai (Thai Boxing)

Training in *muay thai* takes place at dozens, perhaps as many as a hundred, boxing camps around the country. Most are relatively reluctant to take on foreign trainees, except in special cases where the applicant can prove a willingness to conform *totally* to the training system, the diet and the rustic accommodation, and most of all an ability to learn the Thai language. Rates vary from US$50 to US$200 per week, including food and accommodation. Newcomers interested in training at a traditional muay thai camp can try the Pattaya International Muaythai Training School (☎ 038-410111), at 193/15 Mu 11, Thanon Thepprasit, Pattaya; or Fairtex Muay Thai (☎ 02-385 5148), at 99/2 Mu 3, Soi Buthamanuson, Thanon Thaeparak, Bangpli, Samut Prakan, both of which accept foreign students.

Jitti's Gym Thai Boxing & Homestay (☎ 02-282 3551) at 13 Soi Krasab, Thanon Chakraphong in west Banglamphu, specialises in training foreign students – women as well as men. A one-month stay here costs 10,000B and includes daily training sessions from 7 to 9 am and 3 to 7 pm, plus accommodation and evening meals. If you'd like to try a lesson without making a long-term commitment, you can train during any session for 200B.

A relatively new place that specialises in international training is the Muay Thai Institute (☎ 02-992 0096, e khuna@muaythai.th.net), associated with the respected World Muay Thai Council. The institute is located inside the Rangsit Muay Thai Stadium, north of Bangkok International Airport. The institute offers three main study programs: three basic muay thai courses of 10 days each plus a 90-day 'professional' course; three 15-day courses for muay thai instructors; and three 15-day courses for referees and judges. All text books are available in English, and there is accommodation on site. The fee runs US$160 for 40 hours of instruction (half that for Thais). Most muay thai experts would express scepticism that muay thai could be learned in such relatively short intervals, but the school's credentials are 100% Thai.

Lanna Boxing Camp (☎/fax 053-273133, e muaythai@asiaplus.com) at 64/1 Soi 1 (Soi Chang Kian), Thanon Huay Kaew, Chiang Mai 50300; and Patong Boxing Club (☎ 01-978 9352, fax 076-292189) at 59/4 Mu 4, Thanon Na Nai, Patong Beach, Phuket, specialise in training for foreigners. Be forewarned, however: muay thai training is gruelling and features full-contact sparring, unlike tae kwon do, kenpo, kung fu and other East Asian martial arts.

In Ubon Ratchathani two rustic camps accept foreigners: Phaw Meuang Ubon (☎ 045-242399), 78/1 Thanon Sri Narong; and Sit U-Meuang Ubon (☎ 01-967 3495), Wing 21, Ubon.

In Thailand look for copies of *Muay Thai World,* a biannual periodical published by Bangkok's World Muay Thai Council. Although it's basically a cheap martial arts flick, Jean-Claude Van Damme's *The Kickboxer,* filmed on location in Thailand, gives a more comprehensive, if rather exaggerated, notion of muay thai than most films on the subject.

The Web site www.muaythai.com contains loads of information on muay thai in Thailand, including the addresses of training camps.

Krabi-Krabong

A traditional Thai martial art, *kràbìi-kràbawng* (literally, sword-staff) is taught at several Thai colleges and universities, but the country's best training venue is the Buddhai (Phutthai) Sawan Fencing School of Thailand, at 5/1 Thanon Phetkasem, Thonburi, where Ajaan Samai Mesamarna carries on the tradition as passed down from Wat Phutthaisawan. Several foreigners have trained here, including one American who became the first foreigner to attain *aajaan* (master) status. Pramote Gym also provides krabi-krabong training. See the Spectator Sports section in this chapter for more details.

Thai Massage

Described by some as a 'brutally pleasant experience', this ancient form of healing was first documented in the West by the French liaison to the Thai Royal Court in Ayuthaya in 1690, who wrote: 'When any person is sick in Siam he causes his whole body to be moulded by one who is skilful herein, who gets upon the body of the sick person and tramples him under his feet.'

Unlike in most Western massage methodologies, such as Swedish and Californian techniques, Thai massage does not directly seek to relax the body through a kneading of the body with palms and fingers. Instead a multipronged approach uses the hands, thumbs, fingers, elbows, forearms, knees and feet, and is applied to the traditional pressure points along the various *sên* or meridians (the human body is thought to have 72,000 of these, of which 10 are crucial).

The client's body is also pulled, twisted and manipulated in ways that have been compared to a 'passive yoga'. The objective is to distribute energies evenly throughout the nervous system so as to create a harmony of physical energy flows. The muscular-skeletal system is also manipulated in ways that can be compared to modern physiotherapy and chiropractic.

Thailand offers ample opportunities to study its unique tradition of massage therapy. Wat Pho in Bangkok is considered the master source for all Thai massage pedagogy, although the northern provinces boast a 'softer' version. See the Traditional Massage sections in the Bangkok and Northern Thailand chapters for more information.

Cooking

More and more travellers are coming to Thailand just to learn how to cook. Nowadays many foreign chefs seeking out recipe inspirations for the East-West fusion cuisine are passing through. You, too, can amaze your friends back home after attending a course in Thai cuisine at one of the following places:

The Boathouse (☎ 076-330557, fax 330561; Bangkok ☎ 02-438 1123) Kata Yai Beach, Phuket. The chefs at this outstanding Phuket beach restaurant offer occasional weekend workshops.

Chiang Mai Thai Cookery School (☎ 053-206388, fax 399036, e nabnian@loxinfo.co.th) 1–3 Thanon Moon Muang. This place receives raves for its well-organised courses, which include market and garden visits.

Modern Housewife Centre (☎ 02-279 2834) 45/6–7 Thanon Sethsiri, Bangkok

Oriental Hotel Cooking School (☎ 02-236 0400–39) Soi Oriental, Thanon Charoen Krung, Bangkok. This school features a plush five-day course under the direction of well-known star chef Chali (Charlie) Amatyakul.

Siam Chiang Mai Cookery School (☎ 053-271169, fax 208950) 5/2 Soi 1, Thanon Loi Khraw. There are three different courses and a free cookbook.

Sompet Thai Cookery School (☎/fax 053-280901, e sompet41@chmai.loxinfo.co.th) 100/1 Thanon Chang Khlan. Sompet teaches Thai and vegetarian cooking. Two courses per day are available, and the *Thai and Vegetarian Cookery* book is included in the course fee.

Thai House (☎ 02-280 0740, fax 280 0741) 3677/4 Mu, 8 Tambon Bang Meuang, Amphoe Bang Yai, Nonthaburi. This is a popular residential cooking course about 40 minutes north of Bangkok by boat. The program includes all meals, four nights' accommodation and transfer to and from Bangkok.

UFM Food Centre (☎ 02-259 0620–33) 593/29–39 Soi 33/1, Thanon Sukhumvit, Bangkok. This is the most serious and thorough cooking school in Thailand, with a multilayered curriculum. Most classes are offered in Thai and you will need at least four people for an English-language class.

WORK

Thailand's steady economic growth has provided a variety of work opportunities for foreigners, although in general it's not as easy to find a job as in the more developed countries. The one exception is English teaching; as in the rest of East and South-East Asia, there is a high demand for English speakers to provide instruction. This is not due to a shortage of qualified Thai teachers with a good grasp of English grammar, but rather a desire to have native-speaker models in the classroom.

Teaching English

Those with academic credentials, such as teaching certificates or degrees in English as a second language (ESL) or English as a foreign language (EFL), get first crack at the better-paying jobs at universities and international schools. But there are perhaps hundreds of private language-teaching establishments that hire noncredentialed teachers, by the hour, throughout the country. Private tutoring is also a possibility in the larger cities such as Bangkok, Chiang Mai, Hat Yai, Khon Kaen, Lampang, Phitsanulok, Phuket and Songkhla. International oil companies pay the highest salaries for English instructors but are also quite picky.

Continued on page 135

Religion in Thailand

Religion in Thailand

JERRY ALEXANDER

KAREN TRIST

FRANK CARTER

PAUL DYMOND

PAUL BEINSSEN

LEE FOSTER

Title Page: Reclining Buddha at Wat Pho, Bangkok (Photograph by Juliet Coombe)

Top: Novices and their mentor monk chant a blessing on alms round, Chiang Mai.

Middle: A row of Buddha statues at the Ayuthaya Historical Park

Bottom: Hands of the Buddha at Wat Na Phra Meru, Ayuthaya (top left), and bearing flowers at Sukhothai Historical Park (top right); a small spirit house (bottom right); Buddhist amulets for sale, Banglamphu, Bangkok (bottom left)

BUDDHISM

JULIET COOMBE

Approximately 95% of the Thai citizenry are Theravada Buddhists. Thai scholars occasionally refer to the religion as Lankavamsa (Singhalese lineage) Buddhism because Thailand originally received this form of Buddhism, which differed from the earlier Dvaravati and pre-Dvaravati forms, from Sri Lanka during the Sukhothai period.

Since the Sukhothai period (13th to 15th centuries), Thailand has maintained an unbroken canonical tradition and 'pure' ordination lineage, the only country among the Theravadin countries to have done so. Ironically, when the ordination lineage in Sri Lanka broke down during the 18th century under Dutch persecution, it was Thailand that restored the Sangha (Buddhist monastic community) there. To this day the major sect in Sri Lanka is called Siamopalivamsa (Siam-Upali lineage, Upali being the name of the Siamese monk who led the expedition to Sri Lanka), or simply Siam Nikaya (Siamese sect).

Basically, the Theravada school of Buddhism is an earlier and, according to its followers, less corrupted form of Buddhism than the Mahayana schools found in East Asia or in the Himalayan lands. The Theravada (literally, Teaching of the Elders) school is also called the 'Southern' school since it took a southern route from India, its place of origin, through South-East Asia (Sri Lanka, Myanmar, Thailand, Laos and Cambodia in this case), while the 'Northern' school proceeded north into Nepal, Tibet, China, Korea, Mongolia, Vietnam and Japan.

Theravada doctrine stresses the three principal aspects of existence: *dukkha* (stress, unsatisfactoriness, disease), *anicca* (impermanence, transience of all things) and *anatta* (insubstantiality or nonessentiality of reality – no permanent 'soul'). The truth of anicca reveals that no experience, no state of mind, no physical object lasts; trying to hold onto experience, states of mind and objects that are constantly changing creates dukkha; anatta is the understanding that there is no part of the changing world that we can point to and say 'This is me' or 'This is God' or 'This is the soul'. These three concepts, when 'discovered' by Siddhartha Gautama in the 6th century BC, were in direct contrast to the Hindu belief in an eternal, blissful self *(paramatman)*. Hence Buddhism was originally a 'heresy' against India's Brahmanic religion.

Gautama, an Indian prince-turned-ascetic, subjected himself to many years of severe austerity before he realised that this was not the way to reach the end of suffering. He turned his attention to investigating the arising and passing away of the mind and body in the

Buddha's Words

The Buddha taught his disciples:
When you see, just see.
When you hear, just hear.
When you smell, just smell.
When you touch, just touch.
When you know, just know.

present moment. Seeing that even the most blissful and refined states of mind were subject to decay, he abandoned all desire for what he now saw as unreliable and unsatisfying. He then became known as Buddha, 'the enlightened' or 'the awakened'. Gautama Buddha spoke of four noble truths that had the power to liberate any human being who could realise them. These four noble truths are:

1. The truth of dukkha: 'All forms of existence are subject to dukkha.'
2. The truth of the cause of dukkha: 'Dukkha is caused by *tanha* (grasping).'
3. The truth of the cessation of dukkha: 'Eliminate the cause of dukkha (ie, grasping) and dukkha will cease to arise.'
4. The truth of the path: 'The Eightfold Path is the way to eliminate grasping/extinguish dukkha.'

The Eightfold Path (Atthangika-Magga) leading to the end of dukkha consists of:

1. Right understanding
2. Right mindedness (right thought)
3. Right speech
4. Right bodily conduct
5. Right livelihood
6. Right effort
7. Right attentiveness
8. Right concentration

These eight limbs belong to three different 'pillars' of practice: wisdom or *pañña* (path factors 1 and 2), morality or *sila* (3 to 5) and concentration or *samadhi* (6 to 8). The path is also called the 'Middle Way', since it avoids both the extreme of austerity and the extreme of sensuality. Some Buddhists believe it is to be taken in successive stages, while others say the pillars and/or limbs are interdependent. Another key point is that the word 'right' can also be translated as 'complete' or 'full'.

The ultimate end of Theravada Buddhism is *nibbana* (Sanskrit: *nirvana*), which literally means the 'blowing out' or extinction of all grasping and thus of all suffering (dukkha). Effectively, it is also an end to the cycle of rebirths (both moment-to-moment and life-to-life) that is existence.

In reality, most Thai Buddhists aim for rebirth in a 'better' existence rather than the supramundane goal of nibbana. By feeding monks, giving donations to temples and performing regular worship at the local *wát* (temple) they hope to improve their lot, acquiring enough merit (Pali *puñña;* Thai *bun*) to prevent or at least reduce their number of re-births. Making merit *(tham bun)* is an important social and religious activity in Thailand. The concept of rebirth is almost universally accepted in Thailand, even by non-Buddhists, and the Buddhist theory of karma is well expressed in the Thai proverb *tham dii, dâi dii; tham chûa, dâi chûa* (good actions bring good results; bad actions bring bad results).

The Tiratana (Triple Gems) revered by Thai Buddhists include the Buddha, the Dhamma (the teachings) and the Sangha (the Buddhist community). All are quite visible in Thailand. The Buddha, in his myriad sculptural forms, is found on a high shelf in the lowliest roadside restaurants as well as in the lounges of expensive Bangkok hotels. The Dhamma is chanted morning and evening in every wát and taught to every Thai citizen in primary school. The Sangha is seen everywhere in the presence of orange-robed monks, especially in the early morning hours when they perform their alms-rounds, in what has almost become a travel-guide cliche in motion.

Thai Buddhism has no particular 'Sabbath' or day of the week when Thais are supposed to make temple visits. Nor is there anything corresponding to a liturgy or mass over which a priest presides. Instead, Thai Buddhists visit the wát whenever they feel like it, most often on *wan phrá* (literally, excellent days), which occur every 7th or 8th day depending on

phases of the moon. On such visits typical activities include: the traditional offering of lotus buds, incense and candles at various altars and bone reliquaries around the wát compound; the offering of food to the temple Sangha (monks, nuns and lay residents – monks always eat first); meditating (individually or in groups); listening to monks chanting suttas or Buddhist discourse; and attending a *thêt* or Dhamma talk by the abbot or some other respected teacher. Visitors may also seek counsel from individual monks or nuns regarding new or ongoing life problems.

Monks

Socially, every Thai male is expected to become a monk (Pali *bhikkhu;* Thai *phrá* or *phrá phíksù*) for a short period in his life, optimally between the time he finishes school and the time he starts a career or marries. Men or boys under 20 years of age may enter the Sangha as novices (Pali *samanera;* Thai *nen*) – this is not unusual since a family earns great merit when one of its sons 'takes robe and bowl'. Traditionally, the length of time spent in the wát is three months, during the Buddhist lent *(phansǎa),* which begins in July and coincides with the rainy season. However, nowadays men may spend as little as a week to accrue merit as monks. There are about 32,000 monasteries in Thailand and 460,000 monks; many of these monks are ordained for a lifetime. Of these a large percentage become scholars and teachers, while some specialise in healing and/or folk magic.

The Sangha is divided into two sects: the Mahanikai (Great Society) and the Thammayut (from the Pali *dhammayutika* or 'dharma-adhering'). The latter is a minority sect (the ratio being one Thammayut to 35 Mahanikai) begun by King Mongkut and patterned after an early Mon form of monastic discipline that he had practised as a monk. Members of both sects must adhere to 227 monastic vows or precepts as laid out in the Vinaya Pitaka – Buddhist scriptures dealing with monastic discipline. Overall discipline for Thammayut monks, however, is generally stricter. For example, they eat only once a day – before noon – and must eat only what is in their alms bowl, whereas

Above: An illustration from the 17th-century *Du Royaume De Siam,* by Simon de la Loubère.

most Mahanikais eat twice before noon and may accept side dishes. Thammayut monks are expected to attain proficiency in meditation as well as Buddhist scholarship or scripture study; the Mahanikai monks typically 'specialise' in one or the other. Other factors may supersede sectarian divisions when it comes to disciplinary disparities. Monks who live in the city, for example, usually emphasise study of the Buddhist scriptures while those living in the forest tend to emphasise meditation.

Nuns

At one time the Theravada Buddhist world had a separate Buddhist monastic lineage for females. The female monks were called *bhikkhuni* and observed more vows than monks did – 311 precepts as opposed to the 227 followed by monks. The bhikkhuni sangha travelled from its birthplace in India to Sri Lanka around two centuries after the Buddha's lifetime, taken there by the daughter of King Ashoka, Sanghamitta Theri. However, the tradition died out there following the Hindu Chola invasion in the 13th century. Monks from Siam later travelled to Sri Lanka to restore the male sangha, but because there were no ordained bhikkhunis in Thailand at the time, Sri Lanka's bhikkhuni sangha was never restored.

In Thailand, the modern equivalent is the *mâe chii* (Thai for 'nun,' literally, mother priest) – women who live the monastic life as *atthasila* (eight-precept) nuns. Their total number is estimated to be around 10,000. Thai nuns shave their heads, wear white robes and take vows in an ordination procedure similar to that undergone by monks. Generally speaking, nunhood in Thailand isn't considered as 'prestigious' as monkhood. The average Thai Buddhist makes a great show of offering new robes and household items to the monks at the local wát but pays much less attention to the nuns. This is mainly due to the fact that nuns generally don't perform ceremonies on behalf of lay people, so there is often less incentive for self-interested lay people to make offerings to them. Furthermore, many Thais equate the number of precepts observed with the total merit achieved; hence nunhood is seen as less 'meritorious' than monkhood since mâe chii keep only eight precepts.

This difference in prestige represents social Buddhism, however, and is not how those with a serious interest in Buddhist practice regard the mâe chii. Nuns engage in the same fundamental eremitic activities – meditation and Dhamma study – as monks do, activities that are the core of monastic life. The reality is that wát that draw sizable contingents of mâe chii are highly respected, since women don't choose temples for reasons of clerical status. When more than a few nuns reside at one temple, it's usually a sign that the teachings there are particularly strong. The Institute of Thai Mâe chii, headquartered at Wat Bowonniwet since 1962, publishes a quarterly journal (Thai only) devoted to the activities of Thai Buddhist nuns.

Over the last 20 years or so a small movement to restore the bhikkhuni Sangha in Thailand has arisen. Some women are now ordained in Taiwan or India, where the Mahayana tradition has maintained a bhikkhuni lineage, then return to Thailand to practise as full bhikkhunis. In Nakhon Pathom Province there is one nunnery, called Watra Songtham Kalyani, occupied by such Mahayana-ordained nuns,

Spirit Houses

Many Thai houses or buildings have spirit houses – places for the spirits of the site (phrá phuum) – to live in. Without this vital structure you're likely to have the spirits living in the house with you, which can cause all sorts of trouble. An average spirit house looks rather like a birdhouse-sized Thai temple mounted on a pedestal. A big hotel may have a shrine covering 100 sq metres or more.

How do you ensure that the spirits take up residence in your spirit house rather than in the main house with you? Mainly by making the spirit house a more auspicious place to live in than the main building, through daily offerings of food, flowers, candles and incense. The spirit house should also have a prominent location and should not be shaded by the main house. Thus its position has to be planned from the very beginning and the house installed with due ceremony. If your own house is improved or enlarged, the spirit house should be as well. The local phâw khruu or mâe khruu ('father teacher' or 'mother teacher') usually presides over the initial installation as well as later improvements.

The interior of a spirit house is usually decorated with ceramic or plastic figurines representing the property's guardian spirits. The most important figurine, the jâo thîi (place lord), embodies a phrá phuum who reigns over a specific part of the property. Larger or more elaborate spirit houses may also contain figurines that serve as family, retainers or servants for these resident spirits. Thai believers purchase these figurines – as well as the bowls, dishes and other accoutrements for making daily offerings – at rural temples or, in larger cities, at supermarkets and department stores.

An abandoned or damaged spirit house can't simply be tossed aside like a broken appliance, left to rot or dismantled for firewood. Instead, it should be deposited against the base of a sacred banyan tree or in the corner of a sympathetic wát where benevolent spirits will watch over it.

although the Bangkok clerical establishment doesn't officially recognise the bhikkhunis' high-precept status and the centre can't be called a 'wát' (watra simply means 'practice' in Sanskrit).

An increasing number of foreigners come to Thailand to be ordained as Buddhist monks or nuns, especially to study with the famed meditation masters of the forest wát in North-Eastern Thailand.

Further Information

If you wish to find out more about Buddhism you can contact the World Fellowship of Buddhists (☎ 02-661 1284–89, ⓔ wfb_hq@asianet.co.th), 616 Soi 24, Thanon Sukhumvit, Bangkok. Senior fàràng (Western) monks hold English-language Dhamma/meditation classes here on the first Sunday of each month from 2 to 6 pm; all are welcome.

A Buddhist bookshop across the street from the north entrance to Wat Bowonniwet in Bangkok sells a variety of English-language books on Buddhism. Asia Books and DK Book House also stock Buddhist literature.

For more information on meditation study in Thailand, see the Courses section in this chapter, and also the Meditation Courses section in the Bangkok chapter.

Recommended books about Buddhism include:

Buddhism Explained by Phra Khantipalo
Buddhism, Imperialism, and War by Trevor Ling
Buddhist Dictionary by Mahathera Nyanatiloka
Heartwood from the Bo Tree by Buddhadasa Bhikku
In This Very Life: The Liberation Teachings of the Buddha by Sayadaw
   U Pandita
Living Dharma by Jack Kornfield
The Long View: An Excursion into Buddhist Perspectives by Suratano
   Bhikku (T Magness)
The Mind and the Way by Ajahn Sumedho
Phra Farang: An English Monk in Thailand by Phra Peter Pannapadipo
A Still Forest Pool: the Teaching of Ajahn Chah at Wat Pah Pong com-
   piled by Jack Kornfield & Paul Breiter
Thai Women in Buddhism by Chatsumarn Kabilsingh
Things as They Are by Ajahn Maha Boowa Nyanasampanno
What the Buddha Never Taught by Timothy Ward
What the Buddha Taught by Walpola Rahula
World Conqueror and World Renouncer by Stanley Tambiah
Good, Evil & Beyond: Kamma in the Buddha's Teaching by PA Payutto

Two good sources of publications on Theravada Buddhism are the Bud-
dhist Publication Society, PO Box 6154, Sangharaja Mawatha, Kandy,
Sri Lanka, and the Barre Center for Buddhist Studies, Lockwood Rd,
Barre, MA 01005, USA.

On the Internet, an excellent source is Access to Insight: Readings
in Theravada Buddhism (www.accesstoinsight.org), from which you
can freely download many publications (including many English translations from the Pali canon), all cross-indexed by subject, title, author,
proper names and even Buddhist similes. Two other recommended Internet sites with lots of material on Theravada Buddhism as well as links
to other sites include DharmaNet Electronic Files Archive (www
.dharmanet.org) and Buddha Net (www.buddhanet.net).

OTHER RELIGIONS

A small percentage of Thais and most of the Malays in the south,
amounting to about 4% of the total population, are followers of Islam.
Half a percent of the population – primarily missionised hill tribes and
Vietnamese immigrants – profess Christian beliefs, while the remaining half percent are Confucianists, Taoists, Mahayana Buddhists and
Hindus. Mosques (in the south) and Chinese temples are both common
enough that you will probably come across some in your travels in
Thailand. Before entering any temple, sanctuary or mosque you must
remove your shoes, and in a mosque your head must be covered.

Continued from page 128

If you're interested in looking for teaching work, start with the English-language *Yellow Pages of the Greater Bangkok Metropolitan Telephone Directory*, which contains many upcountry and Bangkok listings. Check all the usual headings – Schools, Universities, Language Schools (over 75 listings in Bangkok alone) and so on. Some organisations, such as Teachers of English to Speakers of Other Languages (TESOL), Suite 300, 1600 Cameron St, Alexandria, Virginia 22314, USA; and International Association of Teachers of English as a Foreign Language, 3 Kingsdown Chamber, Kingsdown Park, Whitstable, Kent CT52DJ, UK, publish newsletters with lists of employment in foreign countries, including Thailand.

A Web site maintained by a fàràng EFL teacher in Bangkok, www.ajarn.com, contains tips on where to find teaching jobs and how to deal with Thai classrooms, as well as current job listings.

Other Jobs & Volunteer Positions

Voluntary and paid positions with organisations that provide charitable services in education, development or public health are available for those with the right educational and/or experiential backgrounds. Contact the usual prospects, such as: Voluntary Service Overseas (VSO; ☎ 020-8780 7200) in London; VSO Canada (☎ 613-234 1364) in Ottawa; Overseas Service Bureau (OSB; ☎ 03-9279 1788) in Melbourne; Volunteer Service Abroad (☎ 04-472 5759) in Wellington, New Zealand; or US Peace Corps (☎ 800-424 8580), in Washington, DC.

The UN supports a number of ongoing projects in the country. In Bangkok interested people can try contacting: United Nations Development Program (☎ 02-282 9619); UN World Food Program (☎ 02-280 0427); World Health Organization (☎ 02-282 9700); Food & Agriculture Organization (☎ 02-281 7844); Unicef (☎ 02-280 5931); or Unesco (☎ 02-391 0577).

Mon, Karen and Burmese refugee camps along the Thailand-Myanmar border can use volunteer help. Since none of the camps is officially sanctioned by the Thai government, few of the big NGOs or multilateral organisations are involved here. This means the level of overall support is low but the need for volunteers is definitely there. If this interests you, travel to the relevant areas (primarily Sangkhlaburi and Mae Sot) and ask around for the 'unofficial' camp locations.

Work Permits

All employment in Thailand requires a Thai work permit. Thai law defines work as 'exerting one's physical energy or employing one's knowledge, whether or not for wages or other benefits', and therefore, theoretically, even volunteer work requires a permit.

A 1979 royal decree closed 39 occupations to foreigners, including architecture, civil engineering and clerical or secretarial services. In 1998 several jobs were reopened to fàràng; you may wish to contact your local Thai embassy or consulate for the latest information on employment in Thailand.

Work permits should be obtained through an employer, who may file for the permit before you enter Thailand. The permit itself is not issued until you enter Thailand on a valid Non-Immigrant Visa.

For information about work permits, contact any Thai embassy abroad or check out the Web site at www.thaiembdc.org/consular/con_info/restpmit/extvisa.html.

ACCOMMODATION

Places to stay in Thailand are abundant, varied and very reasonably priced.

However, a word of warning about touts: Don't believe them if they say a place is closed, full, dirty or crooked. Sometimes they're right but most times it's just a ruse to get you to a place that pays them more commission. (See Dangers & Annoyances earlier for more information about touts.)

Fire

If you're concerned about hotel fire safety, always check the fire exits at Thai hotels to make sure they're open and functioning. In 1997 the 17-storey Royal Jomtien Resort Hotel in Pattaya burned down, taking with it the lives of 80 people. The hotel had no sprinkler system and the fire exits were chained shut. In the wake of the fire, regulations were supposedly tightened up around the country, but we've seen hotels in various locations that also chain or otherwise block off fire exits – to keep guests from skipping the room bill and to block potential thieves.

National Park Camping & Accommodation Facilities

Thailand has 80 national parks and nine historical parks. All but 10 of the national parks have bungalows for rent that sleep as many as 10 people for rates of 500B to 1500B, depending on the park and the size of the bungalow. During the low seasons you can often get a room in one of these park bungalows for 100B per person. A few of the historical parks have bungalows with rates comparable to those in the national parks, mostly for use by visiting archaeologists.

Camping is allowed in all but four of the national parks (Doi Suthep/Doi Pui in Chiang Mai Province, Hat Jao Mai in Trang Province, Nam Tok Phliu in Chanthaburi Province and Thap Lan in Prachinburi Province) for only 5B to 20B per person per night. Some parks have tents for rent at 50B to 100B a night, but always check the condition of the tents before agreeing to rent one. It's a good idea to take your own sleeping bag or mat, and other basic camping gear. You should also take a torch (flashlight), rain gear, insect repellent, a water container and a small medical kit. A few parks also have *reuan thǎew* (longhouses) where rooms are around 150B to 200B for two people.

Advance bookings for accommodation are advisable at the more popular parks, especially on holidays and weekends. Most parks charge an entry fee to visit (20B for Thais, 200B for foreigners, half that for children 14 and under). Be sure to save your receipt for the duration of your stay. You may be asked by a ranger to show proof of having paid.

Temple Lodgings

If you are a Buddhist, or can behave like one, you may be able to stay overnight in some temples for a small donation. Facilities are very basic, however, and early rising is expected. Temple lodgings are usually for men only, unless the wát has a place for lay women to stay. Neat, clean dress and a basic knowledge of Thai etiquette are mandatory. See Meditation under Courses earlier for information on wát in Thailand that will accommodate long-term lay students.

Hostels

There is a Thai branch of Hostelling International (☎ 02-282 0950, fax 628 7416), formerly International Youth Hostel Federation,
at 25/2 Thanon Phitsanulok, Sisao Thewet, Dusit, Bangkok 10300, with member hostels in Bangkok, Ayuthaya, Chiang Mai, Chiang Rai, Lopburi and Phitsanulok. There have been others in Kanchanaburi, Ko Phi Phi and Nan but at the time of writing these were closed. Thai youth hostels range in price from 70B for a dorm bed to 280/350B for air-con single/double room. Since 1992, only HI card holders have been accepted as guests in Thai hostels; membership costs 300B per year or 50B for a one-night membership.

University & School Accommodation

College and university campuses may have inexpensive accommodation during the summer vacation (March to June). There are universities in Chiang Mai, Phitsanulok, Nakhon Pathom, Khon Kaen, Mahasarakham and Songkhla. There are also teachers colleges (*wítháyaalai khruu*) in every provincial capital that may offer summer vacation accommodation. The typical teachers' college dorm room lets for 50B to 80B per night.

Guesthouses

Guesthouses are generally the cheapest accommodation in Thailand and are found in most areas where travellers go in Central, Northern and southern Thailand; they are spreading slowly to the east and North-East as well. Guesthouses vary quite a bit in terms of the facilities on offer, and are particularly popular in Bangkok and Chiang Mai, where stiff competition keeps the rates low. Some are especially good value, while others are mere flophouses. Many serve food, although there tends to be a bland sameness to meals in guesthouses wherever you are in Thailand.

YMCAs & YWCAs

A YMCA or YWCA costs quite a bit more than a guesthouse or hostel, and sometimes more than a local hotel, but they are generally good value. There are Ys in Bangkok, Chiang Mai and Chiang Rai.

Resorts

In most countries 'resort' refers to hotels that offer substantial recreational facilities (eg, tennis, golf, swimming, sailing etc) in addition to accommodation and dining. In Thai hotel lingo, however, the term simply refers to any hotel that isn't located in an urban area. Hence a few thatched beach huts or a cluster of bungalows in a forest may be called a 'resort'. Several places in Thailand fully deserve the resort title under any definition – but it will pay for you to look into the facilities before making a reservation.

Chinese-Thai Hotels

The standard Thai hotels, often run by Chinese-Thai families, are the easiest accommodation to come by and generally have reasonable rates (average 150B for rooms without bath or air-con, 180B to 250B with fan and bath, 250B to 500B with air-con). These may be located on the main street of the town or near bus and train stations.

The most economical hotels are those without air-con; typical rooms are clean and include a double bed and a ceiling fan. Some have attached Thai-style bathrooms (this will cost a little more). Rates may or may not be posted; if not, they may be increased for fàràng, so it is worthwhile bargaining.

It's best to have a look around before agreeing to check in, to make sure the room is clean, that the fan and lights work and so on. If there's a problem, request another room or a discount. If possible, always choose a room off the street and away from the front lounge to cut down on noise.

For a room without air-con, ask for a *hâwng thammádaa* (ordinary room) or *hâwng phát lom* (room with fan). A room with air-con is *hâwng ae*. Sometimes fàràng asking for air-con are automatically offered a 'VIP' room, which usually comes with air-con, hot water, fridge and TV and is about twice the price of a regular air-con room.

Some Chinese-Thai hotels may double as brothels; the perpetual traffic in and out can be a bit noisy but is generally bearable. Unaccompanied males are often asked if they want female companionship when checking into inexpensive hotels. Even certain middle-class (by Thai standards) hotels are reserved for the 'salesman' crowd, meaning travelling Thai businessmen, who frequently expect extra night-time services. Foreign women are usually left alone.

The cheapest hotels may have names posted in Thai and Chinese only, but with experience you will be able to identify them. Many of these hotels have restaurants downstairs; if they don't, there are usually restaurants and noodle shops nearby.

Tourist-Class, Business & Luxury Hotels

These are found only in the main tourist and business destinations: Bangkok, Chiang Mai, Chiang Rai, Hat Yai, Kanchanaburi, Ko Pha-Ngan, Ko Samui, Pattaya, Phuket, Songkhla and a sprinkling of large provincial capitals such as Khon Kaen, Nakhon Ratchasima (Khorat), Phitsanulok, Ubon Ratchathani, Udon Thani and Yala. Prices start at around 600B outside Bangkok and Chiang Mai and proceed to 2000B or more – genuine tourist-class hotels in Bangkok start at 1000B or so and go to 2500B for standard rooms, and up to 5000B or 10,000B for a suite. The Oriental in Bangkok, rated as the number-one hotel in the world by several executive travel publications, starts at US$292 for a standard double or US$444 and up for a suite (tax and service included). These will all have air-con, TV, Western-style showers and baths, toilets, IDD phones and restaurants. Added to room charges will be a 7% government tax (VAT), and most of these hotels will include an additional service charge of 8% to 10%.

In addition to the international hotel chains of the Accor, Hilton, Holiday Inn, Hyatt, Sheraton and Westin, Thailand has several respectable home-grown chains, including Amari, Dusit and Royal Garden.

Discounts Discounts of 30% to 50% for hotels costing 1000B or more per night can easily be obtained through many Thai travel agencies. Several top-end hotels offer discounts of up to 60% for reservations made via the Internet. In the arrival halls of both the international and domestic terminals at Bangkok Airport, the Thai Hotels Association (THA) desk can also arrange discounts. If you are holding Thai International Airways (THAI) tickets, or flew in with THAI, the airlines can arrange substantial discounts.

ENTERTAINMENT
Bars & Member Clubs

Urban Thais are night people and every town has a selection of nightspots. Until five or so years ago they were for the most part male-dominated, but the situation is changing rapidly in the larger cities, where young couples are increasingly seen in bars, discos and other nightspots.

Of the many types of bars, probably the most popular continues to be the 'old-west' style, patterned after Thai fantasies of the 19th-century American West – lots of wood and cowboy paraphernalia. Another style that is a favourite is the 'Thai classic' pub, which is typically decorated with old black-and-white photos of Thai kings Rama VI and Rama VII, along with Thai antiques from Northern and Central Thailand. The old-west and Thai-classic nightspots are generally cosy, friendly and popular with couples as well as singles.

The go-go bars seen in lurid photos published by the Western media are limited to a few areas in Bangkok, Chiang Mai, Pattaya and Phuket's Patong Beach. These are bars in which girls typically wear swimsuits or other scant apparel. In some bars they dance to recorded music on a narrow raised stage. To some visitors it's pathetic, to others an apparent source of entertainment.

'Member clubs' provide a slinky atmosphere of feigned elegance and savoir-faire. A couple of drinks and a chat with the hostesses will typically cost you a minimum of US$50, including membership charges. These clubs are thinly scattered across the Soi Lang Suan and Thanon Sukhumvit areas in Bangkok.

All bars and clubs that don't feature live music or dancing are required to close by 1 am. Many get around the law by bribing the local police.

Coffee Houses

Aside from the Western-style cafe, which is becoming increasingly popular in Bangkok, Chiang Mai and tourist areas, there are two other kinds of cafes or coffee shops in Thailand. One is the traditional Hokkien-style coffee shop (*ráan kaa-fae*) where thick, black, filtered coffee is served in simple, casual surroundings. These coffee shops are common in the Chinese quarters of southern Thai provincial capitals, but less common elsewhere. Frequented mostly by older Thai and Chinese men, they offer a place to read the newspaper, sip coffee and gossip about neighbours and politics.

The other type, called *kaa-feh* (cafe) or 'coffee house', is more akin to a nightclub, where Thai men consort with hostesses. These are the Thai counterparts of *fàràng* go-go bars, except girls wear dresses instead of swimsuits. A variation on this theme is the 'sing-song' cafe in which a succession of female singers take turns fronting a live band. Small groups of men sit at tables ogling the girls while putting away prodigious amounts of whisky. For the price of a few house drinks, the men can invite one of the singers to sit at their table for a while. Some of the singers work double shifts as part-time mistresses; others limit their services to singing and pouring drinks.

Cafes that feature live music are permitted to stay open till 2 am.

Discos

Discos are popular in larger cities; outside Bangkok they're mostly attached to tourist or luxury hotels. The main clientele is Thai, although foreigners are welcome. Some provincial discos retain female staff as professional dance partners for male entertainment, but discos are generally considered fairly respectable nightspots for couples.

Thai law permits discos to stay open till 2 am.

Cinemas

Movie theatres are found in towns and cities throughout the country. Typical cinema programs include US and European shoot-em-ups mixed with Thai comedies and romances. Violent action pictures are always a big draw; as a rule of thumb, the smaller the town, the more violent the film offerings. English-language films are only shown with their original soundtracks in a handful of theatres in Bangkok, Chiang Mai and Hat Yai; elsewhere all foreign films are dubbed in Thai. Ticket prices range from 70B to 100B.

Every film in Thailand begins with a playback of the royal anthem, accompanied by pictures of the royal family projected onto the big screen. All viewers are expected to stand during the royal anthem.

SPECTATOR SPORTS
Muay Thai (Thai Boxing)

Almost anything goes in this martial sport, both in the ring and in the stands. If you don't mind the violence (in the ring), a Thai boxing match is worth attending for the pure spectacle – the wild musical accompaniment, the ceremonial beginning of each match and the frenzied betting throughout the stadium.

Thai boxing is also telecast on Channel 7 from noon to 2 pm every Saturday afternoon, which explains the quiet streets at these times.

History Most of what is known about the early history of Thai boxing comes from Burmese accounts of warfare between Myanmar and Thailand during the 15th and 16th centuries. The earliest reference (AD 1411) mentions a ferocious style of unarmed combat that decided the fate of Thai kings. A later description tells how Nai Khanom Tom, Thailand's first famous boxer and a prisoner of war in Burma, gained his freedom by roundly defeating a dozen Burmese warriors before the Burmese court.

King Naresuan the Great (reigned 1590–1605) was supposed to have been a top-notch boxer himself, and he made muay thai a required part of military training. Later, another Thai king, Phra Chao Seua (the 'Tiger King') further promoted Thai boxing as a national sport by encouraging prize fights and the development of training camps in the early 18th century. There are accounts of massive wagers and bouts to the death during this time. Phra Chao Seua himself is said to have been an incognito participant in many of the matches. Combatants' fists were wrapped in thick horsehide for maximum impact with minimum knuckle damage. They also used cotton soaked in glue and ground glass and, later, hemp. Tree bark and seashells were used to protect the groin from lethal kicks.

No-one trained in any other martial art has been able to defeat a ranking Thai *nák muay* (fighter trained in muay thai) and many martial art aficionados consider the Thai style the ultimate in hand-to-hand fighting. On one famous occasion, Hong Kong's top five kung fu masters were all dispatched by knock-out in less than 6½ minutes. Hong Kong, China, Singapore, Taiwan, Korea, Japan, the USA, Netherlands, Germany and France have all sent their best and none of the challengers has yet beaten a top-ranked Ratchadamnoen/Lumphini Thai boxer (except in nonstadium-sponsored bouts – see International Muay Thai later). American Dale Kvalheim trained in muay thai and won a North-Eastern championship around 25 years ago, becoming the first non-Thai to seize a regional title – but Isan stadiums are a far cry from Bangkok's two muay thai crucibles, Ratchadamnoen and Lumphini.

Modern Muay Thai The high incidence of death and physical injury led the Thai government to institute a ban on muay thai in the 1920s, but in the 1930s it was revived under a set of regulations based on the international Queensberry rules. Bouts were limited to five three-minute rounds separated with two-minute breaks. Contestants had to wear international-style gloves and trunks (always either red or blue) and their feet were taped – to this day no shoes are worn.

There are 16 weight divisions in Thai boxing, ranging from miniflyweight to heavyweight, with the best fighters said to be in the welterweight division. As in international-style boxing, matches take place on a 7.3-sq-metre canvas-covered floor with rope retainers supported by four padded posts, rather in than the traditional dirt circle.

In spite of these concessions to safety, today all surfaces of the body are still considered fair targets and any part of the body, except the head, may be used to strike an opponent. Common blows include high kicks to the neck, elbow thrusts to the face and head, knee hooks to the ribs and low crescent kicks to the calf. A contestant may even grasp an opponent's head between his hands and pull it down to meet an upward knee thrust. Punching is considered the weakest of all blows and kicking merely a way to 'soften up' one's opponent; knee and elbow strikes are decisive in most matches.

A Thai boxer's training and his relationship with his trainer are highly ritualised. When a boxer is considered ready for the ring, he is given a new name, usually with the name of the training camp as his surname. The relationship is perhaps best expressed in the *ram muay* (boxing dance) that precedes every match. The ram muay ceremony usually lasts about five minutes and expresses obeisance to the fighter's guru *(khruu)*, as well as to the guardian spirit of Thai boxing. This is done through a series of gestures and movements performed in rhythm to the ringside musical accompaniment of Thai oboe *(pìi)* and percussion. Each boxer works out his own dance, in conjunction with his trainer and in accordance with the style of his particular camp.

The woven headbands and armbands worn into the ring by fighters are sacred ornaments that bestow blessings and divine protection; the headband is removed after the ram muay ceremony, but the armband, which contains a small Buddha image, is worn throughout the match. After the bout begins, the fighters continue to bob and weave in rhythm until the action begins to heat up. The musicians continue to play throughout the match and the volume and tempo of the music rise and fall along with the events in the ring.

Coloured belts denoting training ranks, such as those issued by karate schools, do not exist in muay thai. As one well-known muay thai trainer has said, 'The only belts Thai boxers are concerned with are the Lumphini Stadium and the Ratchadamnoen Stadium championship belts'. Lumphini and Ratchadamnoen, both in Bangkok, are Thailand's two main muay thai venues.

As Thai boxing has become more popular among Westerners (both spectators and participants) there are increasing numbers of bouts staged for tourists in places like Pattaya, Phuket and Ko Samui. In these, the action may be genuine but amateurish, and the judging way below par. Nonetheless, dozens of authentic matches are held every day of the year at the major Bangkok stadiums and in the provinces (there are about 60,000 full-time boxers in Thailand), and these are easily sought out.

Several Thai nák muay have gone on to win world championships in international-style boxing. Khaosai Galaxy, the greatest Asian boxer of all time, chalked up 19 World Boxing Association (WBA) bantamweight championships in a row before retiring undefeated in December 1991. At any given time Thailand typically claims five concurrent international boxing champions, usually in the bantamweight and flyweight categories.

In some areas of the country a pre-1920s version of muay thai still exists. In North-Eastern Thailand *muay boraan* is a very ritualised form that resembles *taijiquan* (t'ai chi) or classical dance. In pockets of Southern Thailand, fighters practising *muay kàtchii* still bind their hands in hemp, and a more localised southern style in Chaiya known as *muay chaiyaa* uses the elbows and forearms to good advantage. Each year around the lunar New Year (Songkran) in April, near the town of Mae Sot on the Thai-Myanmar border, a top Thai fighter challenges a Burmese fighter of similar class from the other side of the Mae Nam Moei (Moei River) to a no-holds barred, hemp-fisted battle that ends only after one of the opponents wipes blood from his body.

International Muay Thai The World Muay Thai Council (WMTC), a relatively new organisation sanctioned by Thailand's Sports Authority, has begun organising international muay thai bouts in Bangkok stadiums and elsewhere. The WMTC tracks training facilities as well as ranked fighters, and is the first entity to match champions from muay thai camps around the world. So far the largest number of WMTC-affiliated muay thai training facilities are in the USA, followed by Australia, the Netherlands, Canada, Japan, France and the UK.

Although WMTC championship bouts have only been held since 1994, WMTC titles are potentially more prestigious than titles from Bangkok's two main stadiums because all athletes, whether Lumphini or Ratchadamnoen champions (or from elsewhere), can compete. Prior to the establishment of the WMTC it wasn't ordinarily possible for a Ratchadamnoen champ to engage with a Lumphini counterpart.

Most middleweight-and-above WMTC championships are dominated by non-Thais. The Netherlands is now widely considered to produce the world's second-best kickboxers, after Thailand – at the moment 16 champions in the upper WMTC weight divisions are Dutch. Australia is close behind with 10 WMTC champs. In Thailand many muay thai aficionados consider Cameroon's Danny Bille to be the best non-Thai nák muay at the moment. International participation portends a new era for Thai boxing; some observers think it will upgrade the martial art by reconcentrating the focus on fight technique rather than ringside betting.

For complete rankings of champions in all weight divisions at Lumphini, Ratchadamnoen and the WMTC, check www .muaythai.com.

Krabi-Krabong

Another traditional Thai martial art still practised in Thailand is krabi-krabong (kràbìi-kràbawng). This tradition focuses on hand-held weapons techniques, specifically the *kràbìi* (sword), *phlawng* (quarter-staff), *ngáo* (halberd), *dàap săwng meu* (a pair of swords held in each hand) and *mái sun-sàwk* (a pair of clubs). Although for most Thais krabi-krabong is a ritual artefact to be displayed during festivals or at tourist venues, the art is still solemnly taught according to a 400-year-old tradition handed down from Ayuthaya's Wat Phutthaisawan. The king's elite bodyguard are trained in krabi-krabong; many Thai cultural observers perceive it as a 'purer' tradition than muay thai.

Like muay thai of more than 70 years ago, modern krabi-krabong matches are held within a marked circle, beginning with a *wâi khruu* ceremony and accompanied throughout by a musical ensemble. Thai boxing techniques and judo-like throws are employed in conjunction with weapons techniques. Although sharpened weapons are used, the contestants refrain from striking their opponents – the winner is decided on the basis of stamina and the technical skill displayed. Although an injured fighter may surrender, injuries do not automatically stop a match.

For information on muay thai and krabi-krabong training courses in Thailand, see the Martial Arts entry in the Courses section earlier in this chapter.

Takraw

Takraw (*tàkrâw),* sometimes called Siamese football in old English texts, refers to games in which a woven rattan ball about 12cm in diameter is kicked around. The rattan (or sometimes plastic) ball itself is called a *lûuk tàkrâw.* Popular in several neighbouring countries, takraw was introduced to the South-East Asian Games by Thailand, and international championships tend to alternate between the Thais and Malaysians. The traditional way to play takraw in Thailand is for players to stand in a circle (the size depending on the number of players) and simply try to keep the ball airborne by kicking it soccer-style. Points are scored for style, difficulty and variety of kicking manoeuvres.

A popular variation on takraw – and the one used in intramural or international competitions – is played like volleyball, with a net, but with only the feet and head permitted to touch the ball. It's amazing to see the players perform aerial pirouettes, spiking the ball over the net with their feet. Another variation has players kicking the ball into a hoop 4.5m above the ground – basketball with feet, and no backboard!

SHOPPING

Many bargains await you in Thailand if you have the luggage space to carry them back.

Always haggle to get the best price, except in department stores. And don't go shopping in the company of touts, tour guides or friendly strangers as they will inevitably – no matter what they say – take a commission on anything you buy, thus driving prices up.

Textiles

Fabric is possibly the best all-round buy in Thailand. Thai silk is considered the best in the world – the coarse weave and soft texture of the silk means it is more easily dyed than harder, smoother silks, resulting in brighter colours and a unique lustre. Silk can be purchased cheaply in the North and North-East where it is made or, more easily, in Bangkok. Excellent and reasonably priced tailor shops can make your choice of fabric into almost any pattern. A Thai-silk suit should cost around 4500B to 6500B. Chinese silk is available at about half the cost – 'washed' Chinese silk makes inexpensive, comfortable shirts or blouses.

Cottons are also a good deal – common items like the phâakhamáa and the phâasîn (the slightly larger female equivalent) make great tablecloths and curtains. Good ready-made cotton shirts are available, such as the *mâw hâwm* (Thai work shirt) and the *kúay hâeng* (Chinese-style shirt). See the sections on Pasang in the Northern Thailand chapter and Ko Yo in the Southern Gulf chapter for places to see cotton-weaving.

Cotton-weaving has become very popular in the North-East and there are fabulous finds in Nong Khai, Roi Et, Khon Kaen and Mahasarakham. The *mǎwn khwǎan,* a hard, triangle-shaped pillow made in the North-East, makes a good souvenir and comes in many sizes. The North-East is also famous for its *mát-mìi* cloth, thick cotton or silk fabric woven from tie-dyed threads – similar to Indonesia's ikat fabrics.

In the North you can find Lanna-style textiles based on intricate Thai Daeng, Thai Dam and Thai Lü patterns from Nan, Laos and China's Xishuangbanna.

Fairly nice batik (*paa-té)* is available in the South in patterns that are more similar to the batik found in Malaysia than in Indonesia.

Clothing

Tailor-made and ready-made clothes are relatively inexpensive. If you're not particular about style you could pick up an entire wardrobe of travelling clothes at one of Bangkok's many street markets (eg, Pratunam) for what you'd pay for one designer shirt in New York, Paris or Milan.

You're more likely to get a good fit if you resort to a tailor but be wary of the quickie 24-hour tailor shops; the clothing is often made of inferior fabric or the poor tailoring means the arms start falling off after three weeks wear. It's best to ask Thai or longtime foreign residents for a tailor recommendation and then go for two or three fittings.

Shoulder Bags

Thai shoulder bags (yâam) come in many varieties, some woven by hill tribes, others by the northern Thai cottage industry. The best are made by the Lahu hill tribes, whom the Thais call Musoe. The weaving is more skilful and the bags tend to last longer than those made by other tribes. For an extra-large yâam, the Karen-made bag is a good choice, and is easy to find in the Mae Sot and Mae Hong Son areas. These days many hill tribes are copying patterns from tribes other than their own.

Overall, Chiang Mai has the best selection of standard shoulder bags, but Bangkok has the best prices – try the Indian district, Pahurat, for these as well as anything else made of cloth. Roi Et and Mahasarakham in the North-East are also good hunting grounds for locally made shoulder bags. Prices range from 70B for a cheaply made bag to 200B for something special.

Antiques

Real antiques cannot be taken out of Thailand without a permit from the Fine Arts Department. No Buddha image, new or old, may be exported without permission – again, refer to the Fine Arts Department or, in some cases, the Department of Religious Affairs, under the Ministry of Education. Too many private collectors smuggling and hoarding Siamese art (Buddhas in particular) around the world have led to strict controls. See Customs earlier in this chapter for more information on the export of art objects and antiques.

Chinese and Thai antiques are sold in two areas of Bangkok's Chinatown: Wang Burapha (the streets that have Chinese 'gates' over the entrance) and Nakhon Kasem. Some antiques (and many fakes) are sold at the Weekend Market in Chatuchak Park.

Merchandise in the tourist antique shops are, predictably, fantastically overpriced. Recently Northern Thailand has become a good source of Thai antiques – prices are about half what you'd typically pay in Bangkok.

Jewellery

Thailand is the world's largest exporter of gems and ornaments, rivalled only by India and Sri Lanka. The International Colorstones Association (ICA) relocated from Los Angeles to Bangkok's Charn Issara Tower several years ago, and the World Federation of Diamond Bourses (WFDB) has established a Bourse in Bangkok – two events that recognise Thailand as the world trade-and-production centre for precious stones. The biggest importers of Thailand's jewellery are Japan, Switzerland and the USA.

Although rough stone sources in Thailand have decreased dramatically, stones are now imported from Australia, Sri Lanka and other countries to be cut, polished and traded. Native stones, such as sapphires, make up only about 25% of the business. At least 40% of all gem-related exports consist of diamond products, all of which are imported rough and then finished in Thailand by expert Thai gem-cutters, and there are over 30 diamond-cutting houses in Bangkok alone. One of the results of this remarkable growth – in Thailand the gem trade has increased 10% every year for the last two decades – is that the prices are rising rapidly.

If you know what you are doing you can make some really good buys in both unset gems and finished jewellery. Gold ornaments are sold at a good rate as labour costs are low. The best bargains in gems are jade, rubies and sapphires.

Buy from reputable dealers only, preferably members of the Jewel Fest Club, a guarantee program established by the TAT and the Thai Gem and Jewellery Traders Association (TGJTA). When you purchase an item of jewellery from a shop that is identified as a member of the Jewel Fest Club, a certificate detailing your purchase will be issued. This guarantees a refund less 10% if you return the merchandise to the point of sale within 30 days. A refund less 20% is guaranteed if the items are returned after 30 days but within 45 days of purchase. You can obtain a list of members direct from Jewel Fest Club (☎ 02 235 3039, 267 5233–7) or from the TAT.

The biggest centres in Thailand for gem stones native to Thailand, neighbouring Myanmar and Cambodia, are Kanchanaburi, Mae Sot, Mae Sai and Chanthaburi. These are the areas where the Bangkok dealers go to buy their stones.

The Asian Institute of Gemological Sciences (☎ 02-267 4315, fax 267 4320), Jewelry Trade Center, South Tower, 11th floor, 919/1 Thanon Silom, offers month-long and one-day short courses in gemology as well as tours of gem mines. You can bring gems here for inspection but the staff don't assess value, only authenticity and grading.

John Hoskins's book *Buyer's Guide to Thai Gems & Jewellery,* available at Bangkok bookshops, is a useful introduction to Thai gems.

Warning Be wary of special 'deals' that are offered for one day only or that set you up as a 'courier' in which you're promised big money. Many travellers end up losing big. Shop around and *don't be hasty.* Remember: There's no such thing as a 'government sale' or 'factory price' at a gem or jewellery shop; the Thai government does not own or manage any gem or jewellery shops.

See the boxed text 'Scams' in this chapter for detailed warnings on gem fraud.

Hill-Tribe Crafts
Interesting embroidery, clothing, bags (see Shoulder Bags earlier in this section) and jewellery from the northern provinces can be bought in Bangkok at Narayan Phand, Thanon Lan Luang, at branches of the Queen's Hillcrafts Foundation, and at various tourist shops around town.

In Chiang Mai there are shops selling handicrafts all along Thanon Tha Phae and Thanon Loi Khraw, and there is a shop sponsored by missionaries near Prince Royal College. There is a branch of the Queen's Hillcrafts Foundation in Chiang Rai. It's worth shopping around for the best prices and bargaining. The all-round best buys of northern hill-tribe crafts are at the Chiang Mai Night Bazaar – if you know how to bargain and don't mind wading through lots of junk.

Lacquerware
Thailand produces some good lacquerware, a lot of which is made in Myanmar and sold along the northern Myanmar border. Try Mae Sot, Mae Sariang and Mae Sai for the best buys.

Today's styles originated in 11th-century Chiang Mai; in 1558 Myanmar's King Bayinnaung captured a number of Chiang Mai lacquer artisans and brought them to Bago in central Myanmar to establish the tradition of incised lacquerware. Lacquer (not to be confused with *lac,* which comes from an insect), comes from the *Melanorrhea usitata* tree and in its most basic form is mixed with paddy-husk ash to form a light, flexible, waterproof coating over bamboo frames.

To make a lacquerware object, a bamboo frame is first woven. If the item is top-quality, only the frame is bamboo; horse or donkey hairs will be wound round the frame. In lower-quality lacquerware the whole object is made from bamboo. The lacquer is then coated over the framework and allowed to dry. After several days it is sanded down with ash from rice husks, and another coating of lacquer is applied. A high-quality item may have seven layers of lacquer.

The lacquerware is engraved and painted, then polished to remove the paint from everywhere except in the engravings. Multi-coloured lacquerware is produced by repeated applications. From start to finish it can take five or six months to produce a high-quality piece of lacquerware, which may have as many as five colours. Flexibility is one characteristic of good lacquerware: A top-quality bowl can have its rim squeezed together until the sides meet without suffering damage. The quality and precision of the engraving is another thing to look for.

Lacquerware is made into bowls, trays, plates, boxes, containers, cups, vases and many other everyday items. Octagonal folding tables are also popular lacquerware items.

Nielloware
This art came from Europe via Nakhon Si Thammarat and has been cultivated in Thailand for over 700 years. Engraved silver is inlaid with niello – an alloy of lead, silver, copper and sulphur – to form striking black-and-silver jewellery designs. Nielloware is one of Thailand's best buys.

Ceramics
Many kinds of hand-thrown pottery, old and new, are available throughout the kingdom. The best-known ceramics are the greenish

Thai celadon products from the Sukhothai-Si Satchanalai area, and Central Thailand's *benjarong* or 'five-colour' style. The latter is based on Chinese patterns while the former is a Thai original that has been imitated throughout China and South-East Asia. Rough, unglazed pottery from the North and North-East can also be very appealing.

Other Crafts

Under the queen's Supplementary Occupations & Related Techniques (SUPPORT) foundation, a number of regional crafts from around Thailand have been successfully revived. *Málaeng tháp* collages and sculptures are made by the artful cutting and assembling of the metallic, multi-coloured wings and carapaces of female wood-boring beetles (*Sternocera aequisignata*), harvested after they die at the end of their reproductive cycle between July and September. Hailing mostly from the North and North-East, they can nonetheless be found in craft shops all over Thailand.

For 'Damascene ware' *(khraam)*, gold and silver wire is hammered into a cross-hatched steel surface to create exquisitely patterned bowls and boxes. Look for them in more-upmarket Bangkok department stores and craft shops.

Yaan líphao is a type of intricately woven basket made from a hardy grass in southern Thailand. Ever since the queen and other female members of the royal family began carrying delicate yaan líphao purses, they've been a Thai fashion staple. Basketry of this type is most easily found in the southern provincial capitals, or in Bangkok shops that specialise in regional handicrafts.

Furniture

Rattan and hardwood furniture items are often good buys and can be made to order. Bangkok and Chiang Mai have the best selection. With the ongoing success of teak farming and teak recycling, teak furniture has once again become a bargain in Thailand if you find the right places. Asian rosewood is also a good buy.

Fake or Pirated Goods

In Bangkok, Chiang Mai and other tourist centres there is black-market street trade in fake designer goods, particularly Benetton pants and sweaters; Lacoste (crocodile) and Ralph Lauren polo shirts; NBA-franchise T-shirts; Levi's jeans; Reebok sneakers; and Rolex, Dunhill and Cartier watches. Tin-Tin T-shirts are also big. No-one pretends they're the real thing, at least not the vendors. Western companies are applying heavy pressure on Asian governments to get this stuff off the street, but so far have had little success. Members of the International Trademark Association claim that 24% of trademarked goods sold in Thailand are counterfeit or pirated and that they lose 25B for every 100B spent on their products in this country.

In some cases foreign name brands are produced under licence in Thailand and represent good value. A pair of legally produced Levi's 501s, for example, typically costs US$10 from a Thai street vendor, and US$35 to US$45 in the company's home town of San Francisco! Careful examination of the product usually reveals tell-tale characteristics that confirm or deny its authenticity.

Prerecorded cassette tapes are another illegal bargain in Thailand. The tapes are 'pirated', ie, no royalties are paid to the copyright owners. Average prices are from 45B per cassette. In 1991 four of the major tape piraters agreed to stop producing unlicensed tapes, but only on the condition that the police prosecute the myriad smaller companies doing business. As of 1998 it has become difficult to find pirated tapes anywhere in the country except on Bangkok's Thanon Khao San. Licensed tapes, when available, cost 90B to 110B each; Thai music tapes cost the same, which is still quite a bargain. The fidelity of licensed tapes is clearly superior to the pirated equivalents.

Other Goods

Bangkok is famous for its street markets – Pratunam, Chatuchak Park, Khlong Toey, Chinatown, Banglamphu and many more. Even if you don't want to spend any money, they're great places to wander around.

For top-end shopping, the two main areas in Bangkok are around the Oriental Hotel off Thanon Charoen Krung (New Rd), and the River City shopping complex on the river next to the Royal Orchid Sheraton Hotel. At the other end, Thailand's two big department store chains, Robinson and Central, offer reasonably priced clothing, electronics and houseware at several branches throughout Bangkok as well as in other larger cities.

Thai Cuisine

Thai Cuisine

JERRY ALEXANDER

DENNIS JOHNSON

KRAIG LIEB

JULIET COOMBE

JOHN HAY

JERRY ALEXANDER

Title Page: A seafood chef entertains diners at a Patong Beach restaurant. (Photograph by Pau Beinssen)

Top: A food vendor serves up a northern-Thai speciality, *yam phàk kum*

Middle: (Clockwise from top left) grilled chicken feet, baskets of mackerel *(plaa thuu)*, peanuts and mame nuts, chillies

Bottom: Preparing decorative food for a northern-Thai festival

PAUL BEINSSEN

Standing at the crossroads of India, China and Asian Oceania, Thailand has adapted cooking techniques and ingredients from all three of these major spheres of influence as well as from the culinary kits carried by passing traders and empire-builders from the Middle East and southern Europe. Over the centuries, indigenous rudiments fused with imported elements to produce a distinctive native cuisine that is instantly recognisable to any discerning palate. Today Thai cuisine has become so globally appreciated that in a survey polling travel agencies in over 25 countries, Thailand ranked fourth after France, Italy and Hong Kong in the perceived excellence of cuisine.

As with other well-developed world cuisines, it can be categorically divided into several regional variations. You can also distinguish between high and low cuisine – or in Thai terms 'royal' and 'common' cooking – a distinction historically arising from the difference between recipes reserved for court palates and those enjoyed by nonroyals. Nowadays court recipes may mingle with ordinary ones in the same restaurants – such as Bangkok's Thanying, which specialises in the former. However, the overall spirit of the cuisine – and a majority of the ingredients – are shared across all class and regional boundaries.

FOOD

Some people take to the food in Thailand immediately while others don't; Thai dishes can be pungent and spicy – lots of garlic and chillies are used, especially *phrík khîi nǔu* (literally, mouse-shit peppers; these are the small torpedo-shaped devils which can be pushed aside if you are timid about red-hot curries). Almost all Thai food is cooked with fresh ingredients, particularly herbs. Plenty of lime juice, lemon grass and fresh coriander leaf are added to give the food its characteristic tang, and fish sauce (*náam plaa*, generally made from anchovies) or shrimp paste *(kà-pì)* to make it salty.

Other common seasonings include galanga root *(khàa)*, black pepper, three kinds of basil, ground peanuts (more often a condiment), tamarind juice *(náam mákhǎam)*, ginger *(khǐng)* and coconut milk *(kà-thí)*. The Thais eat a lot of what could be called Chinese food (there has always been a large Chinese migrant population), which is generally, but not always, less spicy.

Rice *(khâo)* is eaten with most meals; 'to eat' in Thai is literally 'eat rice' or *kin khâo*. Thais can be very picky about their rice, insisting on the right temperature and cooking times. Ordinary white rice is called *khâo jâo* and there are many varieties and grades. The finest quality Thai rice is known as *khâo hǎwm málí*, or jasmine-scented rice, for its sweet, inviting smell when cooked. In the North and North-East 'sticky' or glutinous rice *(khâo nǐaw)* is common.

Where to Eat

Many smaller restaurants and food stalls do not have menus, so it is worthwhile memorising a standard repertoire of dishes. Most provinces have their own local specialities in addition to the standards and you might try asking for 'whatever is good', allowing the proprietors to choose for you. Of course, you might get stuck with a large bill this way, but with a little practice in Thai social relations you may also get some very pleasing results.

The most economical places to eat – and the most dependable – are noodle shops *(ráan kǔaytǐaw)*, curry-and-rice shops *(ráan khâo kaeng)* and night markets *(tàlàat tôh rûng)*. Most towns and villages have at least one night market and several noodle and/or curry shops. The night markets in Chiang Mai have a slight reputation for overcharging (especially for large parties), but this is usually not the case in Thailand. It helps if you speak Thai as much as possible. Curry shops are generally open for breakfast and lunch only, and are a very cheap source of nutritious food. Another common food venue in larger cities is the *ráan khâo tôm* (literally, boiled rice shop), a type of Chinese-Thai restaurant that offers not just boiled rice soups *(khâo tôm)* but an assortment of *aahǎan taam sàng* (food made to order). In the better places, cooks pride themselves in being able to fix any Thai or Chinese dish you name. One attraction of the ráan khâo tôm is that they tend to stay open late – some are even open 24 hours.

The Right Tool for the Job

If you're not offered chopsticks, don't ask for them. When *fàràng* (westerners) ask for chopsticks to eat Thai food it only puzzles the restaurant proprietors. For white rice, use the fork and spoon provided (fork in the left hand, spoon in the right, or the reverse for left-handers). An even more embarrassing act is trying to eat sticky rice (popular in Northern and North-Eastern Thailand) with chopsticks. Use your right hand instead.

Chopsticks are reserved for eating Chinese-style food (eg, noodles) from bowls or for eating in all-Chinese restaurants. In either case you will be supplied with chopsticks without having to ask. Unlike their counterparts in many Western countries, restaurateurs in Thailand won't assume you don't know how to use them.

Sponsored by the Shell oil company, Thai food critic Thanad Sri bestows upon his favourite dishes at restaurants around Thailand a sign (called Shell Chuan Chim) bearing the outline of a green bowl next to the familiar Shell symbol, which is displayed outside the restaurant. It's not a foolproof guarantee; some restaurants hang onto their signs long after the kitchen has lowered its standards.

What to Eat

Thai food is served with a variety of condiments and sauces, especially fish sauce with sliced chillies (náam plaa phrík) and any number of other dipping sauces (náam jîm) for particular dishes. With noodles you'll also receive jars of ground red peppers (phrík pòn), vinegar with sliced chillies (náam sôm phrík), sugar and possibly ground peanuts (thùa pòn). Egg and oyster dishes come with a spicy orange-red sauce called náam phrík sĩi raachaa (from Si Racha in Chonburi Province, of course). Soy sauce (náam sii-íw) can be requested, though this is normally used as a condiment for Chinese food only.

MSG: Friend or Foe?

Monosodium glutamate (MSG; also known by its Japanese name, ajinomoto, or its Thai name, phŏng chuu rót) is a simple compound of glutamate, water and about two-thirds less sodium by weight than table salt. Glutamate, an amino acid that occurs naturally in virtually every food, is a major component of most natural protein sources such as meat, fish, milk and some vegetables. Like the flavour enhancers salt and sugar, MSG has been in use in Asia for centuries, originally as a distillate of seaweed. Today it's produced through a natural fermentation and evaporation process using molasses made from sugar cane or sugar beets. Despite its white, crystalline appearance, it is not, as many people mistakenly believe, a synthetic substance, nor does it necessarily compound one's intake of sodium. When small quantities of MSG are used in combination with table salt (or with fish sauce or soy sauce) during food preparation, the flavour-enhancing properties of MSG allow for far less salt to be used during and after cooking. Although often presumed to have no flavour of its own, MSG does in fact have a taste identifiable to most Asians and to Westerners who are familiar with its culinary uses – the Japanese call this flavour umami, often translated 'savoury'.

Contrary to popular myth, the human body metabolises glutamate added to food the same way it metabolises glutamate found naturally in food. Although some people report physical reactions to MSG (the so-called 'Chinese restaurant syndrome'), every double-blind, placebo-controlled food research study on humans thus far published has concluded that such reactions can almost always be traced not to MSG but rather to psychological syndromes (a legacy of late 1960s food scares) or to food allergies triggered by ingredients other than MSG. The American College of Allergy and Immunology in 1991 concluded that MSG could not be considered an allergen. If you're one of those few people who insist they have a direct sensitivity to MSG (despite your own everyday ingestion of glutamates naturally present in foods), just say mâi sài phŏng chuu rót (don't add MSG).

Except for 'rice plates' and noodle dishes, Thai meals are usually ordered family-style, ie, two or more people order together, sharing different dishes. Traditionally, the party orders one of each kind of dish, eg, one of chicken, one of fish, one soup etc. One dish is generally large enough for two people. One or two extras may be ordered for a large party. If you come to eat at a Thai restaurant alone and order one of these 'entrees', you had better be hungry or know enough Thai to order a small portion. This latter alternative is not really very acceptable socially; Thais generally consider eating alone in a restaurant unusual – but then as a *fàràng* (westerner) you're an exception anyway.

A cheaper alternative is to order dishes 'over rice' *(râat khâo)*. Curry *(kaeng)* over rice is called *khâo kaeng;* in a standard curry shop khâo kaeng is only 10B to 20B a plate.

Another category of Thai food is called *kàp klâem* – dishes meant to be eaten while drinking alcoholic beverages. On some menus these are translated as 'snacks' or 'appetisers'. Typical kàp klâem include *thùa thâwt* (fried peanuts), *kài sǎam yàang* (literally, three kinds of chicken; a plate of chopped ginger, peanuts, mouse-shit peppers and bits of lime – to be mixed and eaten by hand) and various kinds of *yam*, Thai-style salads made with lots of chillies and lime juice.

Vegetarian Those visitors who wish to avoid eating meat and seafood can be accommodated with some effort. Vegetarian restaurants are increasing in number throughout the country, thanks largely to Bangkok's ex-Governor Chamlong Srimuang, whose strict vegetarianism has inspired a nonprofit chain of vegetarian restaurants *(ráan aahǎan mangsàwírát)* in Bangkok and several provincial capitals. Many of these are sponsored by the Asoke Foundation, an ascetic (some would say heretic) Theravada Buddhist sect that finds justification for vegetarianism in the Buddhist sutras. Look for the green sign out the front of shops (depicting large Thai numerals) – each restaurant is numbered according to the order in which it was established. The food at these restaurants is usually served buffet-style and is very inexpensive – typically 7B to 15B per dish. Most are open only from 7 or 8 am until noon. At an Asoke lecture we attended in Chiang Mai last year, a spokesperson for the foundation said their objective is to *lose* money at these restaurants.

Other easy, though less widespread, venues for vegetarian meals include Indian restaurants, which usually feature a vegetarian section on the menu. Currently these are most prevalent in Bangkok, Chiang Mai, Pattaya and Phuket's Hat Patong. Chinese restaurants are also a good bet since many Chinese Buddhists eat vegetarian food during Buddhist festivals, especially in southern Thailand.

More often than not, however, visiting vegetarians are left to their own devices at the average Thai restaurant. In Thai the magic words are *phǒm kin jeh* (for men) or *dì-chǎn kin jeh* (women). Like other Thai phrases, it's important to get the tones right – the key word, *jeh,* should rhyme with the English 'jay' without the 'y'. Loosely translated this phrase means 'I eat only vegetarian food'. It might also be necessary to follow with the explanation *phǒm/dì-chǎn kin tàe phàk* (I eat only vegetables). Don't worry – this won't be interpreted to mean no rice, herbs or fruit.

In Thai culture, brown or unpolished rice *(khâo klâwng)* was traditionally reserved for prisoners, but nowadays it's occasionally available in vegetarian restaurants.

Those interested in tapping into the Thai vegetarian movement can phone the Vegetarian Society of Bangkok (☎ 02-272 4282) for information on the group's activities. The society usually meets monthly to share a vegetarian feast, swap recipes and discuss the whys and wherefores of vegetarianism. In 1999 the World Vegetarian Congress convened in Chiang Mai.

Food Glossary

The following list gives standard dishes in Thai script with a transliterated pronunciation guide, using the system outlined in the Language chapter at the back of this book.

Soups *(súp)* ซุป
fish-ball soup
  kaeng jèut lûuk chín
แกงจืดลูกชิ้น

mild soup with vegetables and pork
  kaeng jèut
แกงจืด

mild soup with vegetables, pork and bean curd
  kaeng jèut tâo-hûu
แกงจืดเต้าหู้

prawn and lemon-grass soup with mushrooms
  tôm yam kûng
ต้มยำกุ้ง

rice soup with fish/chicken/shrimp
  khâo tôm plaa/kài/kûng
ข้าวต้มปลา/ไก่/กุ้ง

soup with chicken, galanga root and coconut
  tôm khàa kài
ต้มข่าไก่

Egg *(khài)* ไข่
fried egg
  khài dao
ไข่ดาว

hard-boiled egg
  khài tôm
ไข่ต้ม

omelette with vegetables and pork
  khài yát sâi
ไข่ยัดไส้

plain omelette
  khài jiaw
ไข่เจียว

scrambled egg
  khài kuan
ไข่กวน

Noodles *(kǔaytǐaw/bà-mìi)*
ก๋วยเตี๋ยว/บะหมี่

fried noodles with soy sauce
  phàt sii-íw
ผัดซีอิ๊ว

rice noodles with gravy
  râat nâa
ราดหน้า

Mangosteen

MH

rice noodles with vegetables and meat
kŭaytĭaw hâeng
ก๋วยเตี๋ยวแห้ง

rice-noodle soup with vegetables and meat
kŭaytĭaw náam
ก๋วยเตี๋ยวน้ำ

thin rice noodles fried with tofu, vegetables, egg and peanuts
phàt thai
ผัดไทย

wheat noodles in broth with vegetables and meat
bà-mìi náam
บะหมี่น้ำ

wheat noodles with vegetables and meat
bà-mìi hâeng
บะหมี่แห้ง

Rice *(khâo)* ข้าว
boned, sliced Hainan-style chicken with marinated rice
khâo man kài
ข้าวมันไก่

chicken with sauce over rice
khâo nâa kài
ข้าวหน้าไก่

curry over rice
khâo kaeng
ข้าวแกง

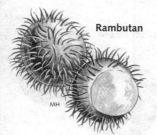

Rambutan

MH

fried rice with pork/chicken/shrimp
khâo phàt mŭu/kài/kûng
ข้าวผัดหมู/ไก่/กุ้ง

'red' pork with rice
khâo mŭu daeng
ข้าวหมูแดง

roast duck over rice
khâo nâa pèt
ข้าวหน้าเป็ด

Curries *(kaeng)* แกง
catfish curry
kaeng plaa dùk
แกงปลาดุก

chicken curry with bamboo shoots
kaeng nàw mái kài
แกงหน่อไม้ไก่

green curry with fish/chicken/beef
kaeng khǐaw-wǎan plaa/kài/néua
แกงเขียวหวานปลา/ไก่/เนื้อ

hot-and-sour fish and vegetable ragout
kaeng sôm
แกงส้ม

hot Thai curry with chicken/beef/pork
kaeng phèt kài/néua/mǔu
แกงเผ็ดไก่/เนื้อ/หมู

mild, Indian-style curry with chicken
kaeng kàrìi kài
แกงกะหรี่ไก่

Muslim-style curry with chicken/beef and potatoes
kaeng mátsàmàn kài/néua
แกงมัสมั่นไก่/เนื้อ

savoury curry with chicken/beef
kaeng phánaeng kài/néua
แกงพะแนงไก่/เนื้อ

Seafood *(aahăan tháleh)*
อาหารทะเล

batter-fried prawns
kûng chúp pâeng thâwt
กุ้งชุบแป้งทอด

catfish
plaa dùk
ปลาดุก

cellophane noodles baked with crab
puu òp wún sên
ปูอบวุ้นเส้น

crisp-fried fish
plaa thâwt
ปลาทอด

eel, freshwater
plaa lăi
ปลาไหล

eel, saltwater
plaa lòt
ปลาหลด

fish
plaa
ปลา

fried prawns
kûng thâwt
กุ้งทอด

green mussel
hăwy málaeng phûu
หอยแมลงภู่

grilled fish
plaa phăo
ปลาเผา

grilled prawns
kûng phăo
กุ้งเผา

oyster
hăwy naang rom
หอยนางรม

oysters fried in egg batter
hăwy thâwt
หอยทอด

roast squid
plaa mèuk yâang
ปลาหมึกย่าง

scallop
hăwy phát
หอยพัด

shark-fin soup
hŭu chàlăam
หูฉลาม

shrimp
kûng
กุ้ง

spicy fried squid
plaa mèuk phàt phèt
ปลาหมึกผัดเผ็ด

spiny lobster
kûng mangkawn
กุ้งมังกร

squid
plaa mèuk
ปลาหมึก

steamed crab
puu nêung
ปูนึ่ง

steamed crab claws
kâam puu nêung
ก้ามปูนึ่ง

steamed fish
plaa nêung
ปลานึ่ง

sweet-and-sour fish
plaa prîaw wăan
ปลาเปรี้ยวหวาน

tilapia (Nile fish)
plaa nin
ปลานิล

whole fish cooked in ginger,
onions and soy sauce
plaa jĩan
ปลาเจี่ยน

Miscellaneous

beef in oyster sauce
néua phàt náam-man hăwy
เนื้อผัดน้ำมันหอย

cellophane noodle salad
yam wún sên
ยำวุ้นเส้น

chicken stir-fried with bean sprouts
kài phàt thùa ngâwk
ไก่ผัดถั่วงอก

chicken stir-fried with cashews
kài phàt mét mámûang
ไก่ผัดเม็ดมะม่วง

chicken stir-fried with chillies
kài phàt phrík
ไก่ผัดพริก

chicken stir-fried with ginger
kài phàt khĭng
ไก่ผัดขิง

chicken stir-fried with holy basil
kài phàt bai kàphrao
ไก่ผัดใบกะเพรา

duck soup
pèt tŭn
เป็ดตุ๋น

fried chicken
kài thâwt
ไก่ทอด

Mango

MH

fried fish cakes with cucumber
sauce
thâwt man plaa
ทอดมันปลา

fried wonton
kíaw kràwp
เกี๊ยวกรอบ

grilled chicken
kài yâang
ไก่ย่าง

hot-and-sour grilled beef salad
yam néua
ยำเนื้อ

morning-glory vine fried in garlic,
chilli and bean sauce
phàk bûng fai daeng
ผักบุ้งไฟแดง

noodles with fish curry
khànŏm jiin náam yaa
ขนมจีนน้ำยา

prawns fried with chillies
kûng phàt phrík phăo
กุ้งผัดพริกเผา

roast duck
pèt yâang
เป็ดย่าง

'satay' or skewers of barbecued
meat
sà-té
สะเต๊ะ

spicy chicken or beef salad
lâap kài/néua
ลาบไก่/เนื้อ

spicy green papaya salad
(north-eastern speciality)
sôm-tam
ส้มตำ

spring rolls
pàw-pía
เปาะเปี๊ยะ

stir-fried mixed vegetables
phàt phàk ruam
ผัดผักรวม

Vegetables *(phàk)* ผัก

bitter melon
márá-jiin
มะระจีน

brinjal (round eggplant)
mákhĕua pràw
มะเขือเปราะ

cabbage
phàk kàlàm (or *kàlàm plii*)
ผักกะหล่ำ
(กะหล่ำปลี)

cauliflower
dàwk kàlàm
ดอกกะหล่ำ

Chinese radish
phàk kàat hŭa
ผักกาดหัว

corn
khâo phôht
ข้าวโพด

cucumber
taeng kwaa
แตงกวา

eggplant
mákhĕua mûang
มะเขือม่วง

garlic
kràthiam
กระเทียม

lettuce
phàk kàat
ผักกาด

long bean
thùa fàk yao
ถั่วฝักยาว

okra (ladyfingers)
kràjíap
กระเจี๊ยบ

onion (bulb)
hŭa hăwm
หัวหอม

onion (green; scallions)
tôn hăwm
ต้นหอม

peanuts (ground nuts)
thùa lísŏng
ถั่วลิสง

potato
man fàràng
มันฝรั่ง

pumpkin
fák thawng
ฟักทอง

taro
phèuak
เผือก

tomato
mákhĕua thêt
มะเขือเทศ

Fruit *(phŏn-lá-mái)* ผลไม้

banana – over 20 varieties
(year-round)
klûay
กล้วย

coconut (year-round)
máphráo
มะพร้าว

Jackfruit

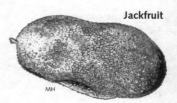

MH

custard-apple
náwy nàa
น้อยหน่า

durian
thúrian
ทุเรียน

grapes
à-ngùn
องุ่น

guava (year-round)
fàràng
ฝรั่ง

jackfruit
khànǔn
ขนุน

lime (year-round)
mánao
มะนาว

longan – similar to rambutan
lamyai
ลำใย

mandarin orange (year-round)
sôm
ส้ม

mango – several varieties
mámûang
มะม่วง

mangosteen
mang-khút
มังคุด

papaya (year-round)
málákaw
มะละกอ

pineapple (year-round)
sàp-pàrót
สับปะรด

pomelo
sôm oh
ส้มโอ

rambeh – small and sour
máfai
มะไฟ

rambutan
ngáw
เงาะ

rose-apple – apple-like texture;
very fragrant (April to July)
chom-phûu
ชมพู่

tamarind – sweet and tart varieties
mákhǎam
มะขาม

sapodilla – sweet and pungent
lámút
ละมุด

watermelon (year-round)
taeng moh
แตงโม

Sweets *(khǎwng wǎan)*
ของหวาน

banana in coconut milk
klûay bùat chii
กล้วยบวชชี

coconut custard
sǎngkhàyǎa máphráo
สังขยามะพร้าว

egg custard
mâw kaeng
หม้อแกง

fried, Indian-style banana
klûay khàek
กล้วยแขก

sticky rice in coconut cream
with ripe mango
khâo nǐaw mámûang
ข้าวเหนียวมะม่วง

sticky rice with coconut cream
khâo nǐaw daeng
ข้าวเหนียวแดง

sweet palm kernels
lûuk taan chêuam
ลูกตาลเชื่อม

sweet shredded egg yolk
fǎwy thawng
ฝอยทอง

Thai custard
sǎngkhàyǎa
สังขยา

Thai jelly with coconut cream
ta-kôh
ตะโก้

Useful Food Words
(For 'I' men use *phǒm*; women use *dì-chǎn*)

I eat only vegetarian food
phǒm/dì-chǎn kin jeh
ผม/ดิฉันกินเจ

I can't eat pork
phǒm/dì-chǎn kin mǔu mâi dâi
ผม/ดิฉันกินหมูไม่ได้

I can't eat beef
phǒm/dì-chǎn kin néua mâi dâi
ผม/ดิฉันกินเนื้อไม่ได้

(I) don't like it hot and spicy
mâi châwp phèt
ไม่ชอบเผ็ด

(I) like it hot and spicy
châwp phèt
ชอบเผ็ด

(I) can eat Thai food
kin aahǎan thai pen
กินอาหารไทยเป็น

What do you have that's special?
mii à-rai phí-sèht?
มีอะไรพิเศษ?

I didn't order this
nîi phǒm/dì-chǎn mâi dâi sàng
นี่ผม/ดิฉันไม่ได้สั่ง

Do you have…?
mii…mǎi?
มี…ไหม?

DRINKS
Non-alcoholic Drinks

Fruit Juices & Shakes The incredible variety of fruits to be found in Thailand means a corresponding availability of nutritious juices and shakes. The all-purpose term for fruit juice is *náam phǒn-lá-mái*. Put *náam* (water or juice) together with the name of any fruit and you can get anything from *náam mánao* (lime juice) to *náam taeng moh* (watermelon juice). When a blender or extractor is used, fruit juices may be called *náam khán,* or squeezed juice (eg, *náam sàp-pàrót khán* – pineapple juice; *náam sôm khán* – orange juice). When mixed in a blender with ice the result is *náam pon* (literally, mixed juice) as in *náam málákaw pon*, a papaya smoothie or shake. Night markets will often have vendors specialising in juices and shakes.

Thais prefer to drink most fruit juices with a little salt mixed in. Unless a vendor is used to serving *fàràng*, your fruit juice or shake will come slightly salted. If you prefer unsalted fruit juices, specify *mâi sài kleua* (without salt).

Sugar cane juice (*náam âwy*) is a Thai favourite and a very refreshing accompaniment to curry-and-rice plates. Many small restaurants or food stalls that don't offer any other juices will have a supply of freshly squeezed náam âwy on hand.

Coffee Over the last 15 years or so, Nescafé and other instant coffees have made deep inroads into the Thai coffee culture at the expense of freshly ground coffee. Typical Thai restaurants, especially those in hotels, guesthouses and other tourist-oriented establishments, will usually serve instant coffee with packets of artificial, non-dairy creamer on the side. Upmarket hotels and coffee shops sometimes also offer filtered and espresso coffees at premium prices.

Traditionally, coffee in Thailand is locally grown (mostly in the hilly areas of Northern and southern Thailand), roasted by wholesalers, ground by vendors and filtered just before serving. Thai-grown coffee may not be as full and rich-tasting as gourmet Sumatran, Jamaican or Kona beans but it's still considerably tastier than Nescafé or other instant products.

Sometimes restaurants or vendors with the proper accoutrements for making traditional filtered coffee will keep a supply of Nescafé just for foreigners (or moneyed Thais, since instant always costs a few baht more per cup than filtered). To get real Thai coffee ask for *kaafae thǔng* (literally, bag coffee) or *kaafae tôm* (boiled coffee), which refers to the traditional method of preparing a cup of coffee by filtering hot water through a bag-shaped cloth filter. Thailand's best coffee of this sort is served in Hokkien-style cafes in the southern provinces. Elsewhere in Thailand, outdoor morning markets are the best places to find kaafae thǔng.

The usual kaafae thǔng is served mixed with sugar and sweetened condensed milk – if you want black coffe, say *kaafae dam* (black coffee); if you don't want sugar, be sure to specify *mâi sài náam-taan* (without sugar).

Tea Both Indian-style (black) and Chinese-style (green or semi-cured) teas are commonly served in restaurants in Thailand. The latter predominates in Chinese restaurants and is also the usual ingredient in *náam chaa*, the weak, often lukewarm tea-water traditionally served in Thai restaurants for free. The aluminium teapots you find on every table in the average restaurant are filled with náam chaa; ask for a plain glass (*kâew plào*) and you can drink as much of this stuff as you like at no charge. For iced náam chaa ask for a glass of ice (usually 1B) and pour your own; for fresh, undiluted Chinese tea, ask for *chaa jiin*.

Black tea, both the imported and Thai-grown kind, is usually available in the same restaurants or food stalls that serve real coffee. An order of *chaa ráwn* (hot tea) almost always results in a cup (or glass) of black tea with sugar and condensed milk. As with coffee you must specify when you order whether you want the tea with or without milk and sugar.

Water Water that has been purified for drinking purposes is simply called *náam dèum* (drinking water), whether boiled or filtered. *All* water offered to customers in restaurants or to guests in an office or home will be purified, so you needn't fret about the safety of taking a sip (see the Health section in the Facts for the Visitor chapter). In restaurants you can ask for *náam plào* (plain water), which is always either boiled or taken from a purified source; it's served by the glass at no charge or you can order by the bottle. A bottle of carbonated water (soda) costs about the same as a bottle of plain purified water but the bottles are smaller.

Drinks Glossary

Beverages *(khrêuang dèum)*
เครื่องดื่ม

bottle
khùat
ขวด

bottled drinking water
náam dèum khùat
น้ำดื่มขวด

coffee, filtered with milk and sugar
kaafae thŭng
(kopíi in the South)
กาแฟถุง/โกพี้

coffee, hot with milk and sugar
kaafae ráwn
กาแฟร้อน

coffee, iced with sugar, no milk
oh-líang
โอเลี้ยง

glass
kâew
แก้ว

ice
náam khăeng
น้ำแข็ง

iced lime juice with sugar (usually with salt too)
náam mánao
น้ำมะนาว

no salt (command)
mâi sài kleua
ไม่ใส่เกลือ

no sugar (command)
mâi sài náam-taan
ไม่ใส่น้ำตาล

orange soda
náam sôm
น้ำส้ม

Ovaltine
oh-wantin
โอวันติน

plain milk
nom jèut
นมจืด

soda water
náam sohdaa
น้ำโซดา

tea, Chinese
chaa jiin
ชาจีน

tea, hot with milk and sugar
chaa ráwn
ชาร้อน

tea, hot with sugar
chaa dam ráwn
ชาดำร้อน

tea, iced with milk and sugar
chaa yen
ชาเย็น

tea, iced with sugar only
chaa dam yen
ชาดำเย็น

tea, weak Chinese
náam chaa
น้ำชา

water, boiled
náam tôm
น้ำต้ม

water, cold
náam yen
น้ำเย็น

water, hot
náam ráwn
น้ำร้อน

water, plain
náam plào
น้ำเปล่า

Alcoholic Drinks

Drinking in Thailand can be quite expensive compared to other consumer activities. The Thai government has placed increasingly heavy taxes on liquor and beer, so that now nearly half the price you pay for a large beer is tax. Whether this is an effort to raise more tax revenue (the result has been a sharp decrease in the consumption of alcoholic beverages and corresponding decrease in revenue) or to discourage consumption, drinking can wreak havoc with your budget. One large bottle (630 mL) of Singha beer costs more than half the minimum daily wage of a Bangkok worker.

According to the UN's Food & Agriculture Organization (FAO), Thailand ranks fifth worldwide in consumption of alcohol, behind South Korea, the Bahamas, Taiwan and Bermuda, and well ahead of Portugal, Ireland and France.

Beer Only a few brands of beer are readily available all over Thailand. Advertised with such slogans as *pràthêht rao, bia rao* (Our Land, Our Beer), the Singha label is considered the quintessential 'Thai' beer by foreigners and locals alike. Pronounced *sĭng*, it claims an enviable 66% of the domestic market. Singha is a strong, hoppy-tasting brew thought by many to be the best beer brewed in Asia. The rated alcohol content is a heady 6%.

Kloster, similarly inspired by German brewing recipes, is a notch smoother and lighter with an alcohol content of 4.7% and generally costs about 5B or 10B more per bottle. Kloster claims only about 5% of Thailand's beer consumption. Like Singha, it's available in cans and bottles.

Boon Rawd Breweries, makers of Singha, also produce a lighter beer called Singha Gold which only comes in small bottles or cans; most people seem to prefer either Kloster or regular Singha to Singha Gold, which is a little on the bland side. Better is Singha's new canned 'draught beer' – if you like cans.

Carlsberg, jointly owned by Danish and Thai interests, waded into the market in the early 1990s and proved to be a strong contender. As elsewhere in South-East Asia, Carlsberg used an aggressive promotion campaign, and when test marketing found the Thais considered it too weak, the company adjusted its recipe to come closer to Singha's 6% alcohol content. In its first two years of business, Carlsberg managed to grab around 25% of the Thai market. Like Kloster, it has a smoother flavour than Singha.

As the beer wars heated up, Singha retaliated with advertisements suggesting that drinking a Danish beer was unpatriotic. Carlsberg responded by creating Beer Chang (Elephant Beer), which matches the hoppy taste of Singha but ratchets the alcohol content up to 7%. Beer Chang has managed to gain an impressive market share mainly because it retails at a significantly lower price than Singha and thus easily offers more bang per baht. Predictably, the next offensive in the war was launched with the marketing of Boon Rawd's new cheaper brand, Leo. Sporting a black and red leopard label, Leo costs only slightly more than Chang but is similarly high in alcohol. To differentiate the new product from the flavour of the competition, Boon Rawd gave Leo a maltier taste.

Dutch giant Heineken, which opened a plant in Nonthaburi in 1995, comes third after Singha and Carlsberg to most national palates, and holds a similar ranking in sales. Other Thailand-produced, European-branded beers you'll find in larger cities include a dark beer called Black Tiger, malty-sweet Mittweida and Amstel lager.

The Thai word for beer is *bia*; draught beer is *bia sòt*.

Spirits Rice whisky is a big favourite in Thailand and somewhat more affordable than beer for the average Thai. It has a sharp, sweet taste not unlike rum, with an alcoholic content of 35%. The most famous brand is Mekong (pronounced *'mâe khǒng'*). In rural areas you'll find several other labels including Kwangthong, Hong Thong, Hong Ngoen, Hong Yok and Hong Tho. Mekong costs around 120B for a large bottle *(klom)* or 60B for the flask-sized bottle *(baen)*. An even smaller bottle, the *kòk,* is occasionally available for 30B to 35B. The Hong brands are less expensive.

More expensive Thai whiskies appealing to the can't-afford-Johnnie-Walker-yet set include Blue Eagle whisky and Spey Royal whisky, each with 40% alcohol content. These come dressed up in shiny boxes, much like the expensive imported whiskies they're imitating.

One company in Thailand produces a true rum, ie, a distilled liquor made from sugar cane, called Sang Som. Alcohol content is 40% and the stock is supposedly aged. Sang Som costs several baht more than the rice whiskies, but for those who find Mekong and the like un-palatable, it is an alternative worth trying.

Other Liquor A cheaper alternative is *lâo khǎo* (white liquor), of which there are two broad categories: legal and bootleg. The legal kind is generally made from sticky rice and is produced for regional con-sumption. Like Mekong and its competitors, it is 35% alcohol, but sells for 50B to 60B per klom, or roughly half the price. The taste is sweet and raw and much more aromatic than the amber stuff – no amount of mixer will disguise the distinctive taste.

The illegal kinds are made from various agricultural products includ-ing sugar palm sap, coconut milk, sugar cane, taro and rice. Alcohol content may vary from as little as 10% or 12% to as much as 95%. Generally this *lâo thèuan* ('jungle liquor') is weaker in the south and stronger in the North and North-East. This is the drink of choice for many Thais who can't afford the heavy government liquor taxes; prices vary but 10B to 15B worth of the stronger concoctions will intoxicate three or four people. These types of home-brew or moonshine are gen-erally taken straight with pure water as a chaser. In smaller towns, almost all garage-type restaurants (except, of course, Muslim restaur-ants) keep some under the counter for sale. Sometimes roots and herbs are added to jungle liquor to enhance flavour and colour.

Herbal liquors are somewhat fashionable throughout the country and can be found at roadside vendors, small pubs and in a few guest-houses. These liquors are made by soaking various herbs, roots, seeds, fruit and bark in *lâo khǎo* to produce a range of concoctions called *lâo yaa dawng.* Many of the *yaa dawng* preparations are purported to have specific health-enhancing qualities. Some of them taste fab-ulous while others are rank.

THAI CUISINE

Wine Thais are becoming increasingly interested in wine-drinking, but still manage only a minuscule average consumption of one glass per capita per year. Wines imported from France, Italy, the USA, Australia, Chile and other countries are available in restaurants and wine shops, but a 340% government tax makes them out of reach for most of us – or at the very least a poor bargain. If the government drops the tax, wine could become very fashionable in Thailand.

Various enterprises have attempted to produce wine in Thailand, most often with disastrous results. However a successful wine was recently produced from a winery called Chateau de Loei, near Phu Reua in Loei Province. Dr Chaiyut, the owner, considerable time and money studying Western wine-making methods; his first vintage, a Chenin Blanc, is quite a drinkable wine. It's available at many of the finer restaurants in Bangkok, Chiang Mai and Phuket.

Getting There & Away

AIR

The per-air-kilometre expense of getting to Bangkok varies quite a bit, depending on your point of departure. However, you can take heart in the fact that Bangkok is one of the cheapest cities in the world to fly out of, due to the Thai government's loose restrictions on air fares and the high level of competition between airlines and travel agencies. The result is that with a little shopping around you can come up with some real bargains. If you can find a cheap one-way ticket to Bangkok, take it, because you are virtually guaranteed to find one of equal or lesser cost for the return trip once you get there.

From most places around the world your best bet will be budget, excursion or promotional fares – when speaking to airlines ask for the various fares in that order. Each carries its own set of restrictions and it's up to you to decide which set works best in your case. Fares fluctuate, but in general they are cheaper from September to April (northern hemisphere) and from March to November (southern hemisphere).

Fares listed in this chapter should serve as a guideline – don't count on them staying this way for long.

Airports & Airlines

Thailand has four international airports, one each in Bangkok, Chiang Mai, Phuket and Hat Yai. Chiang Rai and Sukhothai are both designated as 'international', but at the time of writing they did not actually field any international flights. For a while fledgling Angel Air flew between Chiang Rai and both Kunming in China and Luang Prabang in Laos, but at the time of writing all services had ceased.

A district directly north of Bangkok known as Don Muang has been the main hub for international air traffic in and out of Thailand since 1931. Today it's home to Bangkok International Airport, the busiest airport in South-East Asia in terms of scheduled arrivals and departures.

A second airport, New Bangkok International Airport (NBIA), is intended to replace Don Muang at Nong Ngu Hao, 20km east of Bangkok, in 2004.

Touts

Beware of airport touts – this means anyone trying to steer you away from the public taxi queue outside or asking where you plan to stay while you're in Bangkok. A legion of touts – some in what appear to be airport or airline uniforms – are always waiting in the arrival area, and will begin their badgering as soon as you clear customs. Posing as helpful tourist information agents, their main objective is to get commissions from overpriced taxi rides or hotel rooms. If you're foolish enough to mention the hotel or guesthouse you plan to stay at, chances are they'll tell you it's full and that you must go to another hotel (which will pay them a commission, though they may deny it). Sometimes they'll show you a nice collection of photos; don't get sucked in, as these touted hotels are often substandard and badly located.

The national carrier, Thai Airways International (THAI), dominates inbound and outbound air traffic, but 80 other international airlines also fly in and out of Bangkok. Bangkok Airways flies to Phnom Penh (from Bangkok and Pattaya) and Siem Reap (from Bangkok, Sukhothai and Phuket) in Cambodia, and to Singapore (from Ko Samui).

See the Getting Around chapter for a list of domestic airline offices in Thailand and the Getting There & Away section of the Bangkok chapter for the Bangkok offices of all the international airlines.

For information on arrival and departure procedures in Bangkok, as well as details on getting to and from the international and domestic airports, see the Air section of the Getting Around chapter.

Bangkok International Airport During the last decade, the airport facilities at Bangkok International Airport have undergone a US$200 million redevelopment, including the construction of two new international terminals that are among the most modern and convenient in Asia. Immigration procedures have also been speeded up, although it can still be slow going during peak arrival times (11 pm to midnight). Baggage claim is usually pretty efficient.

The customs area has a green lane for passengers with nothing to declare – just walk through if you're one of these, and hand your customs form to one of the clerks by the exit. Baggage trolleys are free for use inside the terminal.

Currency Exchange The foreign currency booths (Thai Military Bank, Bangkok Bank, Krung Thai Bank) on the ground floor of the arrival hall and in the departure lounge of both terminals give a good rate of exchange, so there's no need to wait till you're in the city centre to change money if you need Thai currency. Each of these banks also operates automated teller machines (ATMs) in the arrival and departure halls.

Post & Communications There is a 24-hour post/telephone office with a Home Country Direct phone service (see the Facts for the Visitor chapter for details of this service) in the departure hall (3rd floor) of Terminal 1. Another 24-hour post office is in the departure lounge; a third one in the arrival hall is open from 9 am to 5 pm weekdays.

The Communications Authority of Thailand (CAT) operates the 24-hour Telecommunications Center on the 2nd floor of Terminal 2, where international phone calls may be arranged in a variety of ways, including by credit card, collect (reverse charges) and Home Country Direct. The telecommunications centre also offers three computer terminals rigged for quick email and Net access. A 300B CATnet card will give you five hours of Internet access on these or any other CAT terminal in Thailand, valid for one year.

On the 4th floor of Terminal 2, Net Center has about seven computer terminals, and charges 75B for the first 15 minutes, 5B per minute thereafter – pretty expensive for Thailand. It accepts credit cards.

Left Luggage & Day Rooms Left-luggage facilities (70B per piece for under 24 hours,

after which the charge is 35B for every 12 hours) are available in the departure hall in both terminals. Both are open 24 hours. In the transit lounge of Terminal 1, clean day rooms with washing and toilet facilities can be rented for US$86 a double per eight hours. Less expensive rooms without bathrooms are available for US$31 per four-hour block.

Hotel Reservations The hotel reservation desks operated by the Thai Hotels Association (THA) at the back of the arrival hall in both terminals offer a selection of accommodation options in the city, but only above the guesthouse price bracket (roughly 900B and above). THA staff can often arrange room rates well below normal walk-in rates.

There have been reports that the THA desks occasionally claim a hotel is full when it isn't, just to move you into a hotel that pays higher commissions. If you protest, the staff may ask you to speak to the 'reservations desk' on the phone – usually an accomplice who confirms the hotel is full. Dial the hotel yourself if you want to be certain.

There are usually one or two other desks in the arrival hall offering similar services, but THA seems to be the most reliable.

Places to Eat On the 4th floor of Terminal 1 is the **Rajthanee Food Mall**, a small 24-hour cafeteria area where you can choose from Thai, Chinese and European dishes at fairly reasonable prices. Next door is the larger **THAI** restaurant with more-expensive fare. On the 2nd floor above the arrival area is a **coffee shop** that is open from 6 am to 11 pm, and there is also a small **snack bar** in the waiting area on the ground floor. The departure lounge has two **snack bars** that serve beer and liquor.

The cheapest place to eat is the no-name **Thai food centre** off the corridor between the international and domestic terminals. As at many other urban food courts in Thailand, you buy refundable coupons from a separate booth to pay for dishes (15B to 35B) ordered at individual booths. It's open from 8 am to 9 pm daily.

Taurus Brewhouse (☎ 02-535 6861), towards the southern end of Terminal 2 on the 4th floor, is a large German-style brew pub. It features brews (95B for 300mL) such as Twister Wheat Beer, Sleepwalker Premium Lager, Mama Bull Pilsner, Head Butt Strong Ale and Naked Killer Ale. The menu of sandwiches, burgers, salads, pastas, soups, pizza and Thai specials is quite good. It's open from 6 pm to midnight daily.

Also on the 4th floor of Terminal 2 is a cluster of fast-food places, including *Swensen's*, *Bill Bentley Pub* (open 24 hours), *Burger King*, *Cafe Select*, *Dairy Queen*, *Baskin-Robbins*, *Mr Donut* and *Pizza Hut*. Opposite these joints is a posh *Chinese restaurant*, and farther south there's a fancy Japanese restaurant called *Nippon Tei*.

At the southern end of Terminal 2, on the departure level, a shop called *Puff and Pie* offers Singaporean-style curry puffs, pastries and other light snacks. On the arrival floor of this terminal there's a *KFC*.

Shopping There are several newsstands and souvenir shops in the arrival and departure areas of both terminals. Duty-free shopping is available in the departure lounge as well.

The domestic terminal has a much better book and magazine selection. If you have enough time to walk across the footbridge from Terminal 1 to the Amari, you'll find an even better bookshop in the hotel's shopping arcade (south of reception).

Facilities Near the Airport If you leave the airport building area and cross the expressway on the pedestrian bridge (just north of the passenger terminal), you'll find yourself in the Don Muang town area, where there are all sorts of shops, a market, lots of small restaurants and food stalls, and even a wát, all within 100m or so of the airport terminal buildings.

The modern and luxurious *Amari Airport Hotel* (☎ 02-566 1020/1) has its own air-con, enclosed footbridge from Terminal 1 and 'special ministay' daytime rates (8 am to 6 pm) for stays of up to a maximum of three hours. For additional information on overnight accommodation in the Don Muang area, see Places to Stay in the Bangkok chapter. The Amari also has a selection of decent *restaurants* serving Italian, Japanese and Thai food.

To/From the Airport See the Bangkok Getting There & Away section for details on transport between Bangkok International Airport and the city.

Other International Airports in Thailand Air travellers heading for southern or Northern Thailand can skip Bangkok altogether by flying directly to these areas. THAI has regular flights to Phuket and Hat Yai from Singapore, to Phuket from Kuala Lumpur and Singapore and to Chiang Mai from Singapore, Kuala Lumpur, Hong Kong, Beijing, Kunming, Yangon, Mandalay and Vientiane.

The Chiang Rai International Airport only services flights to and from Bangkok so far, but THAI hopes to establish international routes to and from other Asian capitals over the next few years.

Bangkok Airways services Sukhothai from Chiang Mai, Bangkok and Siem Reap (Cambodia), and also runs flights between Ko Samui and Singapore.

Buying Tickets

Although other Asian centres are now competitive with Bangkok for buying discounted airline tickets, Bangkok is still a good place for shopping around, especially with the baht trading low against most hard currencies.

Travellers should note, however, that some Bangkok travel agencies have a shocking reputation. Taking money and then delaying or not coming through with the tickets, as well as providing tickets with limited validity periods or severe use restrictions, are all part of the racket. There are a large number of perfectly honest agents, but beware of the rogues.

Booking Problems Booking flights in and out of Bangkok during the high season (December to March) can be difficult. For air travel during these months you should make your bookings as far in advance as possible.

Also, be sure to reconfirm return or ongoing tickets when you arrive in Thailand (THAI claims this isn't necessary with its tickets). Failure to reconfirm can mean losing your reservation.

Departure Tax

All passengers leaving Thailand on international flights are charged an international departure tax (officially called 'airport service charge') of 500B. The tax is not included in the price of air tickets, but is paid at the checkout counter. Only baht is accepted. Be sure to have enough baht left over at the end of your trip to pay this tax – otherwise you'll have to re-visit one of the currency exchange booths.

The USA

The *New York Times, LA Times, Chicago Tribune* and *San Francisco Examiner* all produce weekly travel sections in which you'll find any number of travel agents' ads. Council Travel and STA Travel have offices in major cities nationwide. The magazine *Travel Unlimited* (PO Box 1058, Allston, MA 02134) publishes details of the cheapest air fares and courier possibilities for destinations all over the world from the USA.

It is cheapest to fly to Bangkok via West Coast cities rather than from the East Coast. You can get some great deals through the many bucket shops (who discount tickets by taking a cut in commissions) and consolidators (agencies that buy airline seats in bulk) operating in Los Angeles and San Francisco. Through agencies such as these a return (round-trip) air fare to Bangkok from any of 10 West Coast cities starts at around US$750, with occasional specials (especially in May and September) of just US$525. If you're flying from the East Coast, add US$150 to US$200 to these fares.

One of the most reliable discounters is Avia Travel (☎ 800-950 AVIA, 510-558 2150, fax 558 2158, e avia@avia.com) at Suite E, 1029 Solano Ave, Albany CA 94706. Avia specialises in custom-designed round-the-world fares, eg, San Francisco/Los Angeles-Bangkok-Rome/Paris/London-San Francisco/Los Angeles at US$1135 as well as Circle Pacific fares such as Los Angeles-Tokyo-Taipei-Singapore-Bangkok-Hong Kong-Los Angeles for US$1100. Check Avia's Web site, www.avia.com, for the latest fares. The agency sets aside a portion of its profits for Volunteers in Asia, a nonprofit organisation that sends grassroots volunteers to work in South-East Asia.

Another agency that works hard to get the cheapest deals is Ticket Planet (☎ 800-

799 8888, 415-288 9999, fax 288 9839, e trips@ticketplanet.com), 3rd floor, 59 Grant Ave, San Francisco, CA 94108. One of its Circle Pacific fares, for example, offers a San Francisco-Hong Kong-Bangkok-Kuala Lumpur-Denpasar-San Francisco ticket for around US$1000 plus tax during the low season. You can add Honolulu, Singapore, Jakarta or Yogyakarta to this route for US$50 each stop. It also offers round-the-world air fares for New York-Hong Kong-Bangkok-Bombay/Delhi-Europe-London-NewYork from US$1299. Ticket Planet's Web site, www.ticketplanet.com, will have the most up-to-date fares.

While the airlines themselves can rarely match the prices of the discounters, they are worth checking if only to get benchmark prices to use for comparison. Tickets bought directly from the airlines may also have fewer restrictions and/or less-strict cancellation policies than those bought from discounters.

The airlines that generally offer the lowest fares from the USA include China Airlines, CP Air, EVA Airways, Korean Air and THAI. Each has a budget and/or 'super Apex' fare that costs around US$800 to US$1200 return from Los Angeles, San Francisco or Seattle, depending on the season. Add US$150 to US$200 from the East Coast. Korean Air occasionally runs special fares of just US$550 to US$600 return between San Francisco or Los Angeles and Bangkok. Several of these airlines also fly out of New York, Dallas, Chicago and Atlanta – add another US$150 to US$250 to their lowest fares.

EVA Airways (Taiwan) offers the 'Evergreen Deluxe' class between the USA and Bangkok, via Taipei, which has business-class-sized seats and personal movie screens for about the same cost as regular economy fares on most other airlines.

Canada

Travel CUTS has offices in all major cities. The *Globe & Mail* and the *Vancouver Sun* carry travel agents' ads.

Canadian Pacific flies from Vancouver to Bangkok from around C$950 to C$1100 return for advance-purchase excursion fares. Travellers living in eastern Canada will usually find the best deals out of New York or

San Francisco, adding fares from Toronto or Montreal (see The USA entry earlier).

Australia

Two well-known agents for cheap fares are STA Travel and Flight Centre. STA Travel (☎ 03-9349 2411) has its main office at 224 Faraday St, Carlton, VIC 3053, and offices in all major cities and on many university campuses. Call ☎ 131 776 Australia-wide for the location of the nearest branch or visit the Web site at www.statravel.com.au. Flight Centre (☎ 131 600 Australia wide) has a central office at 82 Elizabeth St, Sydney, and there are dozens of offices throughout Australia. The Web address is www.flightcentre.com.au.

From the east coast of Australia, Thai Airway and Qantas have direct flights to Bangkok starting from around A$995 in the low season to A$1350 in the high season. Garuda Indonesia, Singapore Airlines, Philippine Airlines and Malaysia Airlines also have frequent flights and some good fare deals, with stopovers, to Bangkok.

New Zealand

The *New Zealand Herald* has a travel section in which travel agents advertise fares. Flight Centre (☎ 09-309 6171) has a large central office in Auckland at National Bank Towers (corner of Queen and Darby Sts) and many branches throughout the country. STA Travel (☎ 09-309 0458) has its main office at 10 High St, Auckland, and has other offices in Auckland as well as in Hamilton, Palmerston North, Wellington, Christchurch and Dunedin. The Web address is www.statravel.com.au.

From Auckland, Air New Zealand and THAI have direct flights to Bangkok. Return low-season fares start from around NZ$1247; a return ticket in the high season starts from around NZ$1490. Qantas, Malaysian Airlines and Garuda International also have flights to Bangkok, with stopovers.

The UK & Continental Europe

Discount air travel is big business in London and London-to-Bangkok is arguably the most competitive air route in the world. Typical discounted air fares along this route run from UK£331 to UK£421 return. You may have to call around to get these fares, or better yet check the ads that appear in the travel pages of the weekend broadsheet newspapers, in *Time Out*, the *Evening Standard* or in the free magazine *TNT*.

For students or travellers under 26, popular travel agencies in the UK include STA Travel (☎ 020-7361 6262), at 86 Old Brompton Rd, London SW7; and Usit CAMPUS (☎ 0870-240 1010), at 52 Grosvenor Gardens, London SW1. Both also operate branches throughout the UK and although they cater especially to young people and students they gladly sell tickets to all travellers. STA Travel has a Web site at www.statravel.co.uk, while Usit has one at www.usitcampus.co.uk.

Other recommended travel agencies for all age groups include:

Bridge the World (☎ 020-7734 7447) 4 Regent Place, London W1
   Web site: www.b-t-w.co.uk
Flightbookers (☎ 020-7757 2000) 177–178 Tottenham Court Rd, London W1
   Web site: www.ebookers.com
North-South Travel (☎ 012-45 608 291) Moulsham Mill, Parkway, Chelmsford, Essex CM2 7PX. North-South Travel donates part of its profit to projects in the developing world.
   Web site: www.nstravel.demon.co.uk
Quest Travel (☎ 020-8547 3123) 10 Richmond Rd, Kingston-upon-Thames, Surrey KT2 5HL
   Web site: www.questtravel.co.uk
Trailfinders (☎ 020-7938 3939) 194 Kensington High St, London W8
   Web site: www.trailfinders.co.uk
Travel Bag (☎ 020-7287 5158), 52 Regent St, London W1B 5DX
   Web site: www.travelbag.co.uk

At least two dozen airlines will transport you between the two capitals, although only three of them – British Airways, Qantas Airways and THAI – fly non-stop. If you insist on a non-stop flight, you will probably have to pay between UK£500 and UK£800 return for the privilege (or around UK£100 less if you are a student or under 26). A one-way ticket is usually only slightly cheaper than a return ticket.

One of the cheapest deals going is on Tarom (Romanian Air Transport), which has Brussels-Bangkok-Brussels fares valid for one year. Uzbekistan Airways does a London-Bangkok flight via Tashkent.

Air Travel Glossary

Cancellation Penalties If you have to cancel or change a discounted ticket, there are often heavy penalties involved; insurance can sometimes be taken out against these penalties. Some airlines impose penalties on regular tickets as well, particularly against 'no-show' passengers.

Courier Fares Businesses often need to send urgent documents or freight securely and quickly. Courier companies hire people to accompany the package through customs and, in return, offer a discount ticket which is sometimes a phenomenal bargain. However, you may have to surrender all your baggage allowance and take only carry-on luggage.

Full Fares Airlines traditionally offer 1st class (coded F), business class (coded J) and economy class (coded Y) tickets. These days there are so many promotional and discounted fares available that few passengers pay full economy fare.

Lost Tickets If you lose your airline ticket an airline will usually treat it like a travellers cheque and, after inquiries, issue you with another one. Legally, however, an airline is entitled to treat it like cash and if you lose it then it's gone forever. Take good care of your tickets.

Open-Jaw Tickets These are return tickets where you fly out to one place but return from another. If available, this can save you backtracking to your arrival point.

Overbooking Since every flight has some passengers who fail to show up, airlines often book more passengers than they have seats. Usually excess passengers make up for the no-shows, but occasionally somebody gets 'bumped' onto the next available flight. Guess who it is most likely to be? The passengers who check in late.

Promotional Fares These are officially discounted fares, available from travel agencies or direct from the airline.

Reconfirmation If you don't reconfirm your flight at least 72 hours prior to departure, the airline may delete your name from the passenger list. Ring to find out if your airline requires reconfirmation.

Restrictions Discounted tickets often have various restrictions on them – such as needing to be paid for in advance and incurring a penalty to be altered. Others are restrictions on the minimum and maximum period you must be away.

Round-the-World Tickets RTW tickets give you a limited period (usually a year) in which to circumnavigate the globe. You can go anywhere the carrying airlines go, as long as you don't backtrack. The number of stopovers or total number of separate flights is decided before you set off and they usually cost a bit more than a basic return flight.

Transferred Tickets Airline tickets cannot be transferred from one person to another. Travellers sometimes try to sell the return half of their ticket, but officials can ask you to prove that you are the person named on the ticket. On an international flight tickets are compared with passports.

Travel Periods Ticket prices vary with the time of year. There is a low (off-peak) season and a high (peak) season, and often a low-shoulder season and a high-shoulder season as well. Usually the fare depends on your outward flight – if you depart in the high season and return in the low season, you pay the high-season fare.

Other cheap flights are Lauda Air from London (via Vienna) and Czech Airlines from Prague (via London, Frankfurt and Zurich).

Discount return air fares from other cities in Europe include Amsterdam f999 (on Malev); Munich DM799; Berlin DM896; Paris 2950FF (on Pakistan Airlines); Stockholm 2720kr; Zurich Sfr840 (on Kuwait or Olympic).

Asia
Bangkok There are regular flights to Bangkok International Airport from every major city in Asia and most airlines offer about the same fares for intra-Asia flights. Below is a list of common one-way intra-Asia fares from Bangkok. Return tickets are usually double the one-way fare, although occasionally airlines run special discounts of up to 25% for such tickets.

For fares in the reverse direction, convert to local currency.

from	approx one-way fare
Calcutta	8610B
Colombo	11,980B
Denpasar	15,490B
Ho Chi Minh City	5515B
Hong Kong	8405B
Kathmandu	11,550B
Kuala Lumpur	6475B
Kunming	6210B
Manila	12,230B
Mumbai (Bombay)	13,275B
Osaka	21,910B
Penang	5000B
Phnom Penh	4590B
Seoul	20,870B
Singapore	8005B
Taipei	13,725B
Tokyo	21,910B
Yangon	4225B

Other Places in Asia Thailand's Ministry of Transport allows several regional air carriers to provide regional air services to Myanmar (Burma), Vietnam, Laos and Cambodia. Routes to and from Thailand serviced by foreign carriers include: Yunnan Airlines from Kunming to Bangkok; Silk Air between Singapore and Phuket and between Singapore and Hat Yai; Dragonair between Hong Kong and Phuket; Malaysia Airlines between Kuala Lumpur and Hat Yai; Royal Air Cambodge between Phnom Penh and Bangkok; Lao Aviation between Bangkok and Vientiane; Myanmar Airways International and Biman Bangladesh between Yangon and Bangkok; and Vietnam Airlines between Bangkok and Ho Chi Minh City.

LAND & RIVER
Malaysia

Road You can cross the west-coast border between Malaysia and Thailand by taking a bus to one side and another bus from the other side, the most obvious direct route being between Hat Yai and Alor Setar. This is the route used by taxis and buses but there's a 1km stretch of no-man's land between the Thai border control at Sadao (also known as Dan Nok) and the Malaysian border control at Changlun.

It's much easier to go to Padang Besar, where the train line crosses the border. Here you can get a bus right up to the border, walk across and take another bus or taxi on the other side. On either side you'll most likely be mobbed by taxi and motorcycle drivers wanting to take you to immigration. It's better to walk over the railway bridge into Thailand, and then ignore the touts until you get to 'official' Thai taxis, which will take you all the way to Hat Yai, with a stop at the immigration office (2.5km from the border), for around 50B. The immigration and customs office and bus and train station complex makes the whole transition smoother.

A daily bus runs between Alor Setar, Hat Yai and Kota Bharu.

There's also a border crossing at Keroh (Betong on the Thai side), right in the middle between the east and west coasts. This may be used more now that the Penang–Kota Bharu road is open.

See the Sungai Kolok section in the Southern Gulf chapter for information on crossing the border on the east coast.

Train Riding the rails from Singapore to Bangkok via Butterworth, Malaysia, is a great way to travel to Thailand – as long as you don't count on making a smooth change between the Kereta Api Tanah Melayu (KTM) and State Railway of Thailand (SRT) trains. The Thai train almost always leaves on time; the Malaysian train rarely arrives on time. Unfortunately the Thai train leaves Padang Besar even if the Malaysian railway express from Kuala Lumpur (or the 2nd-class connection from Butterworth) is late. To be on the safe side, purchase the Malaysian and Thai portions of your ticket with departures on consecutive days and plan a Butterworth/Penang stopover.

Bangkok-Butterworth/Penang The daily special express No 35 leaves from Bangkok's Hualamphong station at 2.20 pm, arriving in Hat Yai at 7.05 am the next day and terminating at Padang Besar at 7.50 am. Everyone disembarks at Padang Besar, proceeds through immigration, then boards the 2nd-class KTM train No 99 for a Butterworth arrival at 12.40 pm Malaysian time (one hour ahead of Thai time). The fare to

Padang Besar is 767B for 1st class, 360B for 2nd class, plus an 80B special-express charge and 250B for air-con. There is no 3rd-class seating on this train.

For a sleeping berth in 2nd class add 130B for an upper berth, 200B for a lower. In 1st class it's 520B per person.

Bangkok–Kuala Lumpur & Singapore

For Kuala Lumpur, make the Thai and Malaysian rail connections to Butterworth as described earlier, changing to an express or limited express from Butterworth. There are early-morning, noon and evening services to Kuala Lumpur, and the trip takes from six to seven hours.

There are daily services running between Kuala Lumpur and Singapore – early morning, early afternoon and evening – which take from six to eight hours, depending on what type of train you take.

The information offices at the train terminals in Butterworth (☎ 04-334 7962) and Kuala Lumpur (☎ 03-274 7435) can provide information about schedules, fares and seat availability on the Malaysian and Singaporean services.

Eastern & Oriental Express

In 1991 the State Railway of Thailand (SRT), KTM and Singapore's Eastern & Oriental Express Co (E&O) purchased the rights from Paris' Venice Simplon to operate the new Eastern & Oriental Express between Singapore and Bangkok. The original Orient Express ran between Paris and Constantinople in the 1880s and was considered the grandest train trip in the world; an updated version along the same route was resurrected around 20 years ago and has been very successful. The Singapore-Bangkok version is the first to start and end in the Orient and appears to be even more successful than its historical antecedent. It is also the first rail journey ever to make a direct link between Singapore and Bangkok without a change of trains.

The Eastern & Oriental Express travels at an average speed of 60km/h, completing the 2043km Singapore-to-Bangkok journey in about 40 hours, with a two-hour Butterworth stopover and tour of Georgetown, Penang. As in Europe, this new train offers cruise-ship luxury on rails. Passengers dine, sleep and entertain in 22 train carriages imported from New Zealand and refurbished with lots of brass, teak and old-world tapestry, fitted-out in 1930s style by the same French designer who remodelled the Orient Express in Europe. Aside from the locomotive(s), sleeping coaches, staff coach and luggage cars, the train features two restaurant cars, a saloon car and a bar car, with a combination bar car and open-air observation deck bringing up the rear. All accommodation is in deluxe private cabins with shower, toilet and individually controlled air-con; passengers are attended by round-the-clock cabin stewards (nearly two-thirds of the front-line staff are Thai) in the true pukka tradition.

Tariffs begin at (brace yourself) US$1390 per person for the full route in the bunk-style sleeper and US$2060 in a more spacious state room; half-car presidential suites are available for a mere US$2800. These fares include all table d'hote meals aboard the train and sightseeing tours along the way. Half-routes from Bangkok or Singapore to Butterworth or vice versa are available for a bit more than half-fare, no hotel included. Honeymoon couples comprise a significant part of the clientele.

The Eastern & Oriental Express continues on from Bangkok to Chiang Mai for a separate price of US$900/1150/1650. The train can be booked through E&O in Singapore (☎ 392 3500); Queensland, Australia (☎ 07-3247 6555); or through many travel agents in both cities. Eastern & Oriental Express reservations and information can also be obtained by calling the following numbers: UK (☎ 020-7805 5100); USA (☎ 800-524 2420). Or visit the Web site at www.orient-express.com.

Laos

Road The 1174m Thai-Lao Friendship Bridge (Saphan Mittaphap Thai-Lao) spans a section of the Mekong River between Ban Jommani (near Nong Khai, Thailand) and Tha Na Leng (near Vientiane, Laos) and is the main transportation gateway between the two countries. A parallel rail bridge is planned to extend the Bangkok–Nong Khai railway into Vientiane, although a construction schedule has yet to be announced.

Construction began in early 1996 on a second Mekong bridge to span the river between Thailand's Chiang Khong and Laos'

Huay Xai. Although this bridge was supposed to become operational by 1998, the project was abandoned in 1997 after the drastic drop in the value of the baht. If it ever resumes development, the bridge will link Thailand with China by a road through Bokeo and Luang Nam Thai Provinces in Laos – it is part of an ambitious transport project known as the Chiang Rai to Kunming Road.

Another bridge under discussion would span the Mekong at Mukdahan (opposite Savannakhet) to create a land link between Thailand and Vietnam. The ADB's vaunted title for this development project is 'the Thailand-Lao PDR-Vietnam East-West Corridor'. A similar plan for Nakhon Phanom (opposite Laos' Tha Khaek) is still undergoing a feasibility study.

A land crossing from Pakse (Champasak Province) in Laos to Chong Mek in Thailand's Ubon Ratchathani Province is also open to foreign visitors holding valid visas for Laos. In the opposite direction, from Laos to Thailand, you can receive a visa on arrival, although you will probably have to go to Phibun Mangsahan, near Ubon, to get the visa. See Chong Mek & the Emerald Triangle in the North-Eastern Thailand chapter.

Ferry It's legal for non-Thais to cross the Mekong River by ferry between Thailand and Laos at the following points: Nakhon Phanom (opposite Tha Khaek), Chiang Khong (opposite Huay Xai) and Mukdahan (opposite Savannakhet).

Thais are permitted to cross at all of the above checkpoints plus at least a half-dozen others from Thailand's Loei and Nong Khai Provinces, including Chiang Saen, Ban Khok Phai, Ban Nong Pheu, Ban Pak Huay, Beung Kan, Chiang Khan and Pak Chom. For the most part these checkpoints are only good for day crossings (Thai and Lao only). In the future one or more of these may become available for entry by foreign visitors as well.

Myanmar

Road Several border crossings between Thailand and Myanmar are open to day-trippers or for short excursions in the vicinity. As yet none of these link up with routes to Yangon or Mandalay or other cities of

---

International Border Crossings

These are border points where Thai customs and immigration posts allow foreigners to cross to or from neighbouring countries:

Thailand	Malaysia
Betong	Keroh
Padang Besar	Kaki Bukit
Sadao	Changlun
Sungai Kolok	Rantau Panjang

Thailand	Laos
Chiang Khong	Huay Xai
Chong Mek	Pakse
Mukdahan	Savannakhet
Nakhon Phanom	Tha Khaek
Nong Khai	Vientiane

Thailand	Cambodia
Aranya Prathet	Poi Pet

Thailand	Myanmar
Mae Sai	Tachileik (Thakhilek)
Mae Sot	Myawadi*
Ranong	Kawthoung
Three Pagodas Pass	Payathonzu*

*Entry permitted for day trips only

---

any size. Nor are you permitted to enter Thailand by land from Myanmar.

Mae Sai–Tachileik The infamous bridge, Lo Hsing-han's former 'Golden Triangle' passageway for opium and heroin, spans the Mae Sai (Sai River) between Thailand's northernmost town and the border boomtown of Tachileik (called Thakhilek by the Thai, Shan and Khün peoples). Border permits for up to two weeks may be obtained from the Burmese immigration facility at the border for excursions to Tachileik and beyond as far north as Kengtung and Mengla. You can also use this border as a way to renew your Thai visa if you happen to be in Northern Thailand.

During parts of 1994 and 1995 this border crossing closed for a few months due to fighting between Shan insurgent armies and the Burmese, and it closed again in 1999 during and after the God's Army hostage-taking crisis in Ratchaburi.

Rumour has it that an overland route going all the way to China via Kengtung will soon open here, but so far Mengla is the end of the line. The road continuing west from Kengtung to Taunggyi is in usable condition, although this runs through the opium-poppy harvesting area of the Golden Triangle, a common site for Shan army clashes with the Burmese military, and is definitely off-limits to non-Burmese. It's 163km on from Tachileik to Kengtung, and another 450km from Kengtung to Taunggyi.

Chiang Dao A dirt track turns left 10km north of Chiang Dao in Chiang Mai Province and leads through the small town of Meuang Ngai to Na Ok at the border. This was the most popular opium route from Myanmar 25 or 30 years ago, but the main trading items now are water buffalo and lacquer. It's be wise to be very careful in this area.

Mae Sot–Myawadi This crossing begins a route from Myawadi to Mawlamyaing (Moulmein) via Kawkareik along a rough road that has long been off limits to foreigners due to Mon and Karen insurgent activity in the area. There are regular buses from Tak to Mae Sot in Tak Province. In 1994 the Myanmar government signed an agreement with Thailand to build a bridge across the Mae Moei between Myawadi and Mae Sot (actually 6km from Mae Sot proper). The span was finally completed and opened in 1997, but quickly closed due to international bickering over reclamation of the river banks. In 1998 it was open again for a short time, then closed again, but at the time of writing it was open again.

Foreigners are now permitted to cross from Mae Sot to Myawadi for the day. See the Mae Sot section for details. For now travel is allowed between Myawadi and Mae Sot only – beyond Myawadi is off limits. Myanmar's Yangon junta claims it has plans to open the road from Myawadi all the way to Pa-an in the Kayin State, and Thai groups have managed to receive permission to travel by chartered bus all the way to Yangon.

Just north of Myawadi is Wangkha, and to the south is Phalu (Waley on the Thai side), former Karen and Mon smuggling posts now controlled by Yangon. Foreigners are not permitted to cross here, although some do, via local connections.

Three Pagodas Pass A gateway for various invading armies and an important smuggling route for many centuries, this is one of the most interesting and accessible of the border crossing points.

Now that the Burmese have wrested control from the Mon and Karen armies, there is also legal trading happening at Three Pagodas Pass. The settlement on the Burmese side, called Payathonzu (Three Pagodas), is open on-and-off to foreign tourists for day trips. Travellers have been allowed to go as far as a dozen or so kilometres inside Myanmar from this point, but the roads are so bad that almost no-one makes it even that far. See the Kanchanaburi Province section in the Central Thailand chapter for details.

Prachuap Khiri Khan Not only is there a road over the Mawdaung Pass between Ban Huay Yang and Tanintharyi, there is a major business smuggling timber in from Myanmar. Myanmar's Mon and Karen ethnic groups, rather than the Burmese government, carry on most of this illicit timber trade. The 'toll gate', formerly controlled by Karen guerrillas from the Karen National Union/Karen National Liberation Army, is now once again controlled by Yangon forces. If you can find a local who knows the area well, it's possible to visit near the border crossing point of Dan Singkhon.

Cambodia

Road As of early 1998, there has been a legal border crossing between Cambodia and Thailand at Aranya Prathet, opposite the Cambodian town of Poipet. If you're coming from Cambodia by rail or road, you don't need a Thai visa (or rather you will be granted a free 30-day Tourist Visa on arrival), but in the reverse direction you will need a Cambodian visa. The latter is available from the Cambodian embassy in Bangkok.

The border is open from 8 am to 6 pm daily. You'll have to take a taxi or *moto*

(Cambodian for motorcycle) a further 4km from the crossing to reach Aranya Prathet itself, from whence there are regular buses and trains onward to Bangkok and other points in North-Eastern Thailand. Cambodian officials usually request a US$1 'departure tax' when you arrive at the Cambodian-Thai border. See the Aranya Prathet section for additional details.

Other areas along the border won't be safe for land crossings until mines and booby traps left over from the conflict between the Khmer Rouge and the Vietnamese are removed or detonated.

China

Road The governments of Thailand, Laos, China and Myanmar have agreed to the construction of a four-nation ring road through all four countries. The western half of the loop will proceed from Mae Sai in Thailand to Jinghong in China, via Myanmar's Tachileik, Kengtung and Mengla (near Dalau on the China-Myanmar border); while the eastern half will extend from Chiang Khong in Thailand to Jinghong via Huay Xai in Laos (opposite Chiang Khong), and Boten, Laos (on the Yunnanese border south of Jinghong).

The stretch between Tachileik and Dalau is still very much under construction (some sections towards the Chinese border are complete) but it's possible to arrange one- to three-day trips as far as Kengtung in Myanmar's Shan State (see the Mae Sai section in the Northern Thailand chapter for details). A road between Huay Xai and Boten already exists (built by the Chinese in the 1960s and 1970s) but needs upgrading. Once the roads are built and the visa formalities have been worked out, this loop will provide alternative travel connections between China and South-East Asia, in much the same way as the Karakoram Highway has forged new links between China and South Asia. It's difficult to predict when all the logistical variables will be settled, but progress so far points to a cleared path by 2006.

The eastern half of this loop, from Boten to Huay Xai, Laos, and across to Chiang Khong, Thailand, can be done relatively easily now, although roadways between Boten and Huay Xai are a little rough.

Boat A third way to reach China's Yunnan Province from Thailand is by boat along the Mekong River. Several surveys of the waterway have been completed and a specially constructed express boat made its inaugural run between Sop Ruak, Chiang Rai Province, and China's Yunnan Province in early 1994. For the moment, permission for such travel is restricted to very infrequent private tour groups, but it's reasonable to assume that in the future a scheduled public service may become available. The boat trip takes six hours – considerably quicker than any currently possible road route. However it's only navigable all the way to China during the rainy season and in the period immediately after.

Future Rail Possibilities

At a 1995 summit meeting in Bangkok, representatives of the Association of South-East Asian Nations (Asean) proposed the completion of a regional rail network linking Singapore with China via Malaysia, Thailand, Laos, Cambodia and Vietnam. In all but Laos and Cambodia, railbeds for such a circuit already exist. The plans called for the extension of a rail line across the Mekong River from Thailand to Laos via the existing Thai-Lao Friendship Bridge. If completed this line may some day connect with a proposed north-south line from Vientiane to Savannakhet in Laos and then with a west-east line from Savannakhet to Dong Ha.

A 1998 joint-venture agreement between the Lao government and a company called Lao Railways Transportation purports to establish a railway line along the middle of the Friendship Bridge. After a feasibility study is completed the line, which will reportedly extend to Vientiane and Luang Prabang, is supposed to become operational in four years. Like most other transport projects in Laos, however, it will probably take much longer – if it ever happens at all.

Another rail link undergoing a feasibility study is a spur eastward from Udon Thani, across the Mekong to Tha Khaek, Lao PDR, and across Laos to connect with the Ho Chi Minh City–Hanoi railway in Vietnam.

SEA
Malaysia

There are several ways of travelling between Thailand's southern peninsula and Malaysia by sea. Simplest is to take a long-tail boat between Satun, right down in the south-western corner of Thailand, and Kuala Perlis. The cost is about RM5, or 50B, and boats cross over fairly regularly. You can also take a ferry to the Malaysian island of Langkawi from Satun. There are immigration posts at both ports so you can make the crossing quite officially. From Satun you can take a bus to Hat Yai and then arrange transport to other points in the south. It's possible to bypass Hat Yai altogether by heading directly for Phuket or Krabi via Trang.

You can also take a ferry to Ban Taba on the east coast of Thailand from near Kota Bharu – see the Sungai Kolok section in the Southern Gulf chapter. See Phuket in the Andaman Coast chapter for information on yachts to Penang and other places.

On-again, off-again passenger ferry services also run between Pulau Langkawi and Phuket. Such services never seem to last longer than nine months or so; you can make inquiries through local travel agents.

Myanmar

You can travel by boat between Kawthoung in Myanmar's Tanintharyi Division and the port of Ranong in Thailand via the Gulf of Martaban and Pakchan Estuary. Exiting Myanmar from Kawthaung is now legal, and you don't need a visa to enter Thailand for a stay of 30 days or less. In the reverse direction you won't need a Myanmar visa

for a day trip, but if you plan to stay overnight or to continue farther north, you'll need a valid Myanmar visa.

Cambodia

Travellers can sometimes cross to Cambodia by sea via Hat Lek. See the Trat Province section in the Central Thailand chapter.

Warning

The information in this chapter is particularly vulnerable to change: Prices for international travel are volatile, routes are introduced and cancelled, schedules change, special deals come and go, and rules and visa requirements are amended. Airlines and governments seem to take a perverse pleasure in making price structures and regulations as complicated as possible. You should check directly with the airline or a travel agent to make sure you understand how a fare (and ticket you may buy) works. In addition, the travel industry is highly competitive and there are many lurks and perks.

The upshot of this is that you should get opinions, quotes and advice from as many airlines and travel agents as possible before you part with your hard-earned cash. The details given in this chapter should be regarded as pointers and are not a substitute for your own careful, up-to-date research.

Getting Around

AIR
Domestic Air Services

Three domestic carriers, Thai Airways International (commonly known as THAI), Bangkok Airways and PB Air, operate out of the domestic airports in 28 cities around the country. PB Air only offers domestic flights between Bangkok and Krabi at the moment, along with international services to Medan (Indonesia) and Singapore. A new airline, Air Andaman, is supposed to start business soon with flights out of Phuket.

Most domestic air services are operated by THAI. On certain southern routes, domestic flights through Hat Yai continue on to Kuala Lumpur and Singapore. THAI operates Boeing 737s, ATR-72s and Airbus 300s on its main domestic routes.

The accompanying 'Air Fares & Railways' map shows some of the fares on more popular routes. Note that through fares are generally less than the combination fares – Chiang Rai to Bangkok, for example, is less than the addition of Chiang Rai–Chiang Mai and Chiang Mai–Bangkok fares. This does not always apply to international fares, however.

Domestic Airlines

Bangkok Airways has flights along four main routes: Bangkok-Sukhothai-Chiang Mai; Bangkok-Ko Samui-Phuket; Bangkok-Ranong-Phuket; and U Taphao (Pattaya)-Ko Samui. Bangkok Airways' fares are competitive with THAI's but the company is small and it remains to be seen whether or not it will continue as a serious contender.

The airline's head office (☎ 02-229 3434; reservations ☎ 02-229 3456) is at 60 Queen Sirikit National Convention Centre, Thanon Ratchadaphisek Mai, Khlong Toey, Bangkok 10110. Offices are also in Chiang Mai, Ranong, Sukhothai, Pattaya, Phuket and Ko Samui.

PB Air (☎ 02-261 0220) has an office on the 17th floor of the UBC II Building at 591 Soi 33 Thanon Sukhumvit. The airline is owned by Boon Rawd Brewery of Singha beer fame and uses Fokker F28s on its Bangkok-Krabi route.

A new airline on the scene, Air Andaman, has plans to establish routes from Phuket to Krabi, Chumphon and Surat Thani. Other destinations under discussion include Hua Hin and Yangon.

On the sidelines is Angel Air, a Bangkok-based regional carrier that served several destinations in Thailand and neighbouring countries for a couple of years, then suddenly ceased operations in early 2000 due to financial conditions. The airlines' owners say service will be resurrected in the near future.

THAI Offices Offices for THAI's domestic services can be found throughout Thailand:

Bangkok (head office; ☎ 02-513 0121) 89 Thanon Viphavadi Rangsit;
  (☎ 02-234 3100) 3rd–5th floors, Silom Plaza Bldg, 485 Thanon Silom;
  (☎ 02-280 0110) 6 Thanon Lan Luang;
  (☎ 02-215 2020–4) Asia Hotel, 296 Thanon Phayathai;
  (☎ 02-223 9746–48) 310–311, 3rd floor, Grand China Tower, 215 Thanon Yaowarat;
  (☎ 02-535 2081/2, 523 6121) Bangkok International Airport, Don Muang
Buriram (☎ 044-625066) Phusiam Tours, 24/23 Thanon Romburi
Chiang Mai (☎ 053-210210; reservations ☎ 053-211044, 210210) 240 Thanon Phra Pokklao;
  (☎ 053-277782, 277640) Chiang Mai International Airport
Chiang Rai (☎ 053-711179, 222279) 870 Thanon Phahonyothin;
  (☎ 053-793048–57 ext 162, 163) Chiang Rai International Airport
Hat Yai (☎ 074-230445/6, 244282; reservations ☎ 074-233433) 190/6 Thanon Niphat Uthit;
  (☎ 074-251034) Hat Yai International Airport
Khon Kaen (☎ 043-227701–5) 9/9 Thanon Prachasamoson;
  (☎ 043-246305, 246345) Khon Kaen airport
Lampang (☎ 054-217078, 218199) 314 Thanon Sanambin;
  (☎ 054-225383) Lampang airport
Loei (☎ 042-812344, 812355) 22/15 Thanon Chumsai
Mae Hong Son (☎ 053-611297, 611194) 71 Thanon Singhanat Bamrung;
  (☎ 053-611367) Mae Hong Son airport
Mae Sot (☎ 055-531730, 531440) 76/1 Thanon Prasat Withi

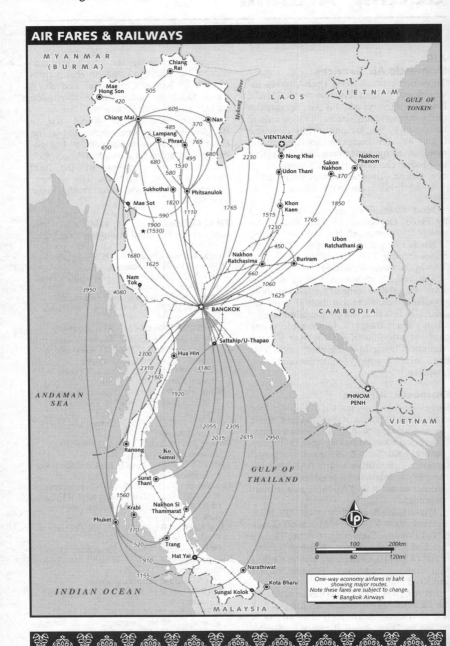

AIR FARES & RAILWAYS

One-way economy airfares in baht
showing major routes.
Note these fares are subject to change.
★ Bangkok Airways

Nakhon Phanom (☎ 042-512940) Bovon Travel Co Ltd, 13 Thanon Ruamjit Thawai; (☎ 042-513357) Nakhon Phanom airport

Nakhon Ratchasima (Khorat; ☎ 044-252114, 257211–3) 40–44 Thanon Suranari

Nakhon Si Thammarat (☎ 075-342491, 343874) 1612 Thanon Ratchadamnoen

Nan (☎ 054-710377, 710498) 34 Thanon Mahaphrom; (☎ 054-771729) Nan airport

Narathiwat (☎ 073-511161, 513090–2) 322–324 Thanon Phuphaphakdi; (☎ 073-511595, 514570) Narathiwat airport

Nong Khai (☎ 042-411530) 102/2 Thanon Chonpratan

Pattani (☎ 073-335939) 9 Thanon Prida

Pattaya (☎ 038-420995–7) Dusit Resort Hotel, Thanon Hat Pattaya Neua

Phitsanulok (☎ 055-258020, 251671) 209/26–28 Thanon Borom Trailokanat

Phrae (☎ 054-511123) 42–44 Thanon Ratsadamnoen

Phuket (☎ 076-258236; reservations ☎ 076-258237) 78/1 Thanon Ranong; (☎ 076-327194) Phuket International Airport

Sakon Nakhon (☎ 042-712259/60) 1446/73 Thanon Yuwaphattana

Songkhla (☎ 074-311012, 314007) 2 Soi 4, Thanon Saiburi

Surat Thani (☎ 077-273710, 273355, 272610) 3/27–28 Thanon Karunarat; (☎ 077-200605, 200611/2) Surat Thani airport

Tak (☎ 055-512164) 485 Thanon Taksin

Trang (☎ 075-218066, 219923) 199/2 Thanon Visetkul; (☎ 075-210804, 215379) Trang airport

Ubon Ratchathani (☎ 045-313340/2, 313344) 364 Thanon Chayangkun; (☎ 045-243037–9, 245612, ext 127) Ubon Ratchathani airport

Udon Thani (☎ 042-246697, 243222) 60 Thanon Mak Khaeng; (☎ 042-246567, 246644) Udon Thani airport

THAI's 24-hour reservation number is ☎ 02-280 0060.

Air Passes

THAI occasionally offers special four-coupon passes – available only outside Thailand for foreign currency purchases – with which you can book any four domestic flights for one fare of around US$199 (50% less for children under 12) as long as you don't repeat the same leg. Additional coupons cost US$49 each, but you may not exceed a total of eight coupons. Unless you plan carefully this isn't much of a saving since it's hard to avoid repeating the same leg in and out of Bangkok. Also, the baht is so low these days it's often cheaper to make domestic flying arrangements in Thailand rather than from abroad.

For more information on the four-coupon deal, known as the 'Amazing Thailand fare', inquire at any THAI office outside Thailand.

Don Muang Domestic Airport

Bangkok's Don Muang airport stands a few hundred metres south of Bangkok International Airport. Facilities include a post and telephone office on the ground floor, a snack bar in the departure lounge and a restaurant on the 2nd floor. THAI operates a free shuttle bus between the international and domestic terminals every 15 minutes between 6 am and 11.20 pm.

See the Bangkok Getting There & Away section for information on transport options to/from the city centre.

BUS
Government Bus

The cheapest and slowest of the Thai buses are the ordinary government-run buses (*rót thammádaa*) that stop in every little town and for every waving hand along the highway. For some destinations – such as smaller towns – these orange-painted buses are your only choice, but at least they leave frequently. The government also runs faster, more comfortable but less frequent air-con buses called *rót ae*, *rót pràp aakàat* or *rót thua;* these are painted with blue markings. If these are available to your destination they are your very best choice since they don't cost that much more than the ordinary stop-in-every-town buses. The government bus company is called Baw Khaw Saw, an abbreviation of *bòrísàt khŏn sòng* (literally, Transportation Company). Every city and town in Thailand linked by bus transportation has a Baw Khaw Saw terminal, even if it's just a patch of dirt by the roadside.

The service on the government air-con buses is usually quite good and includes beverage service and video. On longer routes (eg, Bangkok–Chiang Mai, Bangkok–Nong Khai), the air-con buses even distribute claim checks (receipt dockets) for your baggage. Longer routes may also offer two classes of air-con buses, 2nd class and 1st class; the latter have toilets. 'VIP' buses have fewer seats (30 to 34 instead of 44; some routes have Super VIP, with only 24 seats) so that each seat reclines more. Sometimes these are called *rót nawn* or sleepers. For small to medium-sized people they are more comfortable, but if you're big in girth you may find yourself squashed on the 34-seaters when the person in front of you leans back.

Occasionally you'll get a government aircon bus in which the air-con is broken or the seats are not up to standard, but in general they are more reliable than the private tour buses.

See Getting Around in the Bangkok chapter for information on the main bus terminals in Bangkok.

Private Bus

Private buses are available between major tourist and business destinations all over the country. They can be booked through most hotels or any travel agency, although it's best to book directly through a bus office to be assured that you get what you pay for.

Fares may vary from company to company, but usually not by more than a few baht. However, fare differences between the government and private bus companies can be substantial. Using Bangkok–Surat Thani as an example, state-run buses cost around 180B for the ordinary bus and 346B (1st class) for the air-con, while the private companies charge up to 535B. On the other hand, from Bangkok to Chiang Mai the private buses often cost less than the government buses, although those that charge less offer inferior service. Some private companies' departures are more frequent than for the equivalent Baw Khaw Saw route.

There are also private buses running between major destinations within the various regions, eg, Nakhon Si Thammarat to Hat Yai in the south, and Chiang Mai to Sukhothai in the North. New companies are cropping up all the time. Minibuses are used consistently on hilly or winding routes, eg, Surat to Krabi, and Tak to Mae Sot.

Private air-con buses are usually no more comfortable than the government air-con buses and feature similarly narrow seats and hair-raising rides. The trick the tour companies use to make their buses seem more comfortable is to make you think you're not on a bus by turning up the air-con until your knees knock, handing out pillows and blankets and serving free soft drinks. On overnight journeys the buses usually stop somewhere en route and passengers are awakened to get off the bus for a free meal of fried rice or rice soup. A few companies even treat you to a meal before a long overnight trip.

Like the state-run bus companies, the private companies offer VIP (sleeper) buses on long hauls. In general the private bus companies that deal mostly with Thais are good, while tourist-oriented ones – especially those connected with Thanon Khao San (Khao San Rd) – are awful.

Out of Bangkok, the safest, most reliable private bus services are the ones that operate from the three official Baw Khaw Saw terminals rather than from hotels or guesthouses. Picking up passengers from any points that are not official terminals is actually illegal, and services promised are often not delivered. Although it can be a hassle getting out to the Baw Khaw Saw terminals, you're generally rewarded with safer, more reliable and punctual service.

Service

Although on average the private companies charge more than the government does on the same routes, the service does not always match the higher relative cost. In recent years the service on many private lines has in fact declined, especially on the Bangkok–Chiang Mai, Bangkok–Ko Samui, Surat-Phuket and Surat-Krabi routes.

Sometimes the cheaper lines – especially the ones that are booked on Thanon Khao San in Bangkok – will pull a swifty and switch vehicles at the last moment so that instead of the roomy air-con bus advertised, you're stuck with a cramped van with broken air-con. One traveller recounted how his Thanon Khao San bus stopped for lunch halfway to Chiang Mai and then zoomed off while the passengers were eating – leaving them to finish the journey on their own! To avoid situations like this, it's always better to book bus tickets directly at a bus office – or at the government Baw Khaw Saw station – rather than through a travel agency.

Túk-túk on Bangkok's Thanon Khao San

Express boat on Mae Nam Chao Phraya

Long-tail boat – a great way to get around.

One of Bangkok's new Skytrains

No, not a traffic jam – just another day on Bangkok's streets!

Long-tail boats ferry people between islands along the Andaman Coast.

Northern Thailand is the most mountainous of Thailand's regions.

Another problem with private companies is that they generally spend time cruising the city for passengers before getting under way, meaning that they rarely leave at the advertised departure time.

A reader's letter opined:

Only once did I take a private bus from Thanon Khao San. The service was poor; there was no free food or drink, one-setting air-conditioning and negligible leg room. The bus to Chiang Mai was packed and I was forced to sit right at the front. The ride was terrifying, a roller coaster nightmare journey that saw the driver overtake blindly around sharp corners at speeds of around 100km/h. During the journey the bus was stuck in a traffic jam so the driver decided to take a cross-country short cut; the mud track we were driven along was barely the width of the bus. At one stage we were inconvenienced by a tree blocking our path – no problem. It was chopped down.

Our advice is to take a train or public bus and if this fails then sit at the back of the bus. The public bus journeys we took were far superior; two free meals, plenty of leg room and drivers who had at least a modicum of respect for human life.

Safety

Statistically, private buses meet with more accidents than government air-con buses. Turnovers on tight corners and head-on collisions with trucks are probably due to the inexperience of the drivers on a particular route.

Keep an eye on your bags when riding buses – pilfering by stealth is still the most popular form of robbery in Thailand, though again the risks are not that great – just be aware. Most pilfering seems to take place on the private bus runs between Bangkok and Chiang Mai or Ko Samui, especially on buses booked on Thanon Khao San. Keep zippered bags locked and well secured.

TRAIN

The railway network in Thailand, run by the Thai government through the State Railway of Thailand (SRT) is very well run, on the whole. It isn't possible to take the train everywhere in Thailand, but often it is by far the best public transport. If you travel 3rd class, it is often the cheapest way to cover a long distance; by 2nd class it's about the same as a private tour bus but much safer and more comfortable. Trains take a bit longer than chartered buses on the same journey but are worth the extra travel time, on overnight trips especially.

The trains offer many advantages: There is more space and more room to move and stretch out (even in 3rd class) than there is on even the best buses. The windows are big and usually open, so that there is no glass between you and the scenery (good for taking photos) and more to see. The scenery itself is always better along the train routes than along Thai highways – the trains regularly pass small villages, farmland, old temples etc. The pitch-and-roll of the railway cars is much easier on the bones, muscles and nervous system than the quick stops and starts, the harrowing turns and the pothole jolts endured on buses. The train is safer in terms of both accidents and robberies. Last, but certainly not least, you meet a lot more interesting people on the trains, or so it seems to us.

Rail Routes

Four main rail lines cover 4500km along the northern, southern, north-eastern and eastern routes. There are several side routes, notably between Nakhon Pathom and Nam Tok (stopping in Kanchanaburi) in the western central region, and between Tung Song and Kantang (stopping in Trang) in the south. The southern line splits at Hat Yai, one route going to Sungai Kolok on the Malaysian east-coast border, via Yala; and the other route going to Padang Besar in the west, also on the Malaysian border.

A Bangkok-Pattaya spur has not been as popular as expected but is still running. Within the next few years, a southern spur may well be extended from Khiriratnikhom to Phuket, establishing a rail link between Surat Thani and Phuket. A spur from Den Chai to Chiang Rai in the North has also been under discussion, though nothing concrete has happened yet. The SRT may also renovate the Japanese line between Nam Tok and Sangkhlaburi in Kanchanaburi Province that was built with the forced labour of prisoners of war (POWs) and coolies during WWII.

Closer at hand, the SRT is surveying an unused rail extension between Aranya Prathet in Thailand and Poi Pet in Cambodia, with the intention of resuming rail services between the two countries.

Bangkok Terminals Most long-distance trains originate from Bangkok's Hualamphong station. Before a railway bridge was constructed across the Mae Nam Chao Phraya (Chao Phraya River) in 1932, all southbound trains left from Bangkok Noi, the main station in Thonburi. Today this station services commuter and short-line trains to Kanchanaburi/Nam Tok, Suphanburi, Ratchaburi and Nakhon Pathom (Ratchaburi and Nakhon Pathom can also be reached by train from Hualamphong). Thonburi's Wong Wian Yai station, running services to Samut Songkhram, is rarely used.

A slow night train to Chumphon and Lang Suan, both in southern Thailand, leaves nightly from Thonburi (Bangkok Noi) station but it's rarely used by long-distance travellers – in fact, you won't even see this route listed on the English-language rail schedule, only on the Thai.

Classes

The SRT operates passenger trains in three classes – 1st, 2nd and 3rd – but each class varies considerably depending on whether you're on an ordinary, rapid or express train.

3rd Class A typical 3rd-class car consists of two rows of bench seats divided into facing pairs. Each bench seat is designed to seat two or three passengers, but on a crowded upcountry line nobody seems to care about design considerations. On a rapid train, 3rd-class seats are padded and reasonably comfortable for shorter trips. On ordinary 3rd-class-only trains in the east and North-East, seats are sometimes made of hard wooden slats, and are not recommended for more than a couple of hours at a time. Express trains do not carry 3rd-class cars at all. Commuter trains in the Bangkok area are all 3rd class and the cars resemble modern subway or rapid transit trains, with plastic seats and ceiling hand-straps for standing passengers.

2nd Class In a 2nd-class car, seating arrangements are similar to those on a bus, with pairs of padded seats, usually recliners, all facing towards the front of the train.

In a 2nd-class sleeper, the seats convert into two fold-down berths, one over the other. Curtains provide a modicum of privacy and the berths are fairly comfortable, with fresh linen for every trip. A toilet stall and washbasins are located at one end of the car. Second-class cars are found only on rapid and express trains; some routes offer air-con 2nd class as well as ordinary 2nd class.

1st Class First-class cars provide private cabins. Each has individually controlled air-con (older trains also have an electric fan), a washbasin and mirror, a small table and long bench seats that convert into beds. Drinking water and soap are provided free of charge. First-class cars are available only on rapid, express and special express trains.

Costs

There is a 60B surcharge for express trains (*rót dùan*) and 40B for rapid trains (*rót rehw*). These trains are somewhat faster than the ordinary trains, as they make fewer stops. Some 2nd- and 3rd-class services are air-con, in which case there is a 70B surcharge (note that there are no 3rd-class cars on either rapid or express trains). For the special express trains (*rót dùan phísèt*) that run between Bangkok and Padang Besar and between Bangkok and Chiang Mai there is an 80B surcharge (or 120B if a meal is included).

The charge for 2nd-class sleeping berths is 100B for an upper berth and 150B for a lower berth (or 130B and 200B respectively on a special express). The difference between upper and lower is that there is a window next to the lower berth and a little more head room. The upper berth is still comfortable enough. For 2nd-class sleepers with air-con add 250/320B per upper/lower ticket. No sleepers are available in 3rd class.

Air-con really isn't necessary on night trains, since a steady breeze circulates through the train and cools things down quickly. In fact air-con 2nd class can become uncomfortably cold at night and cannot be regulated by passengers; for this reason we recommend choosing non-air-con.

All 1st-class cabins come with individually controlled air-con. For a two-bed cabin the surcharge is 520B per person. Single 1st-class cabins are no longer available, so if you're travelling alone you may be paired with another rail passenger, although the SRT takes great care not to mix genders.

You can figure on 500km costing around 200B in 2nd class (not including the surcharges for the rapid and express services), roughly twice that in 1st class and less than half in 3rd. Surprisingly, basic fares have changed only slightly over the last decade, although supplementary charges have increased steadily. Currently the government continues to subsidise train travel, particularly 3rd class, to some extent. However there has been some talk of privatising the railway – which would, of course, ring the death knell for the passenger rail system as it has in most other formerly rail-faring countries of the world.

Train Passes The SRT issues a couple of train passes that may save on fares if you plan to ride Thai trains extensively within a relatively short interval. These passes are only available in Thailand, and may be purchased at Hualamphong train station.

The cost for 20 days of unlimited 2nd- or 3rd-class rail travel (blue pass) is 1100B, not including supplementary charges, or 2000B including all supplementary charges; children aged four to 12 pay half the adult fare. Supplementary charges include all extra charges for rapid, express, special express and air-con. Passes must be validated at a local station before boarding the first train. The price of the pass includes seat reservations that, if required, can be made at any SRT ticket office. The pass is valid until midnight on the last day of the pass. However, if the journey is commenced before midnight on the last day of validity, the passenger can use the pass until that train reaches its destination.

Do the passes represent a true saving over buying individual train tickets? The answer is yes only if you can average more than 110km by rail per day for 20 days. If you travel at this pace (or less), then you'll be paying the same amount (or more) as you would if you bought ordinary train tickets directly. On less crowded routes where there are plenty of available 2nd-class seats the passes save time that might otherwise be spent at ticket windows, but for high-demand routes (eg, from Bangkok to Chiang Mai or Hat Yai) you'll still need to make reservations.

Bookings

The disadvantage of travelling by rail, in addition to the time factor mentioned earlier, is that trains can be difficult to book. This is especially true around holiday time, eg, the middle of April approaching the Songkran Festival, since many Thais prefer the train. Trains out of Bangkok should be booked as far in advance as possible – a minimum of a week for popular routes such as the Northern line to Chiang Mai and the southern line to Hat Yai, especially if you want a sleeper. For the North-eastern and eastern lines a few days will suffice. Midweek departures are always easier to book than weekends; during some months of the year you can easily book a sleeper even one day before departure, as long as it's on a Tuesday, Wednesday or Thursday.

Advance bookings may be made one to 60 days before your intended date of departure. If you want to book tickets in advance, go to Hualamphong station in Bangkok, walk through the front of the station house and go straight to the back right-hand corner where a sign says 'Advance Booking' (open from 8.30 am to 4 pm daily). The other ticket windows, lined up in front of the platforms, are for same-day purchases, mostly 3rd class. From 5 to 8.30 am and from 4 to 11 pm, advance bookings can also be made at window Nos 2 to 11.

Reservations are computerised in the Advance Booking office, and you simply take a queue number, wait until your number appears on one of the electronic marquees, report to the desk above which your number appears and make your ticket arrangements. Only cash baht is acceptable here.

Note that buying a return ticket does not necessarily guarantee you a seat on the way back, it only means you do not have to buy a ticket for the return. If you want a guaranteed seat reservation it's best to make that reservation for the return immediately upon arrival at your destination.

Booking trains back to Bangkok is generally not as difficult as booking trains out of Bangkok; however, at some stations it can be quite difficult (eg, buying a ticket from Surat Thani to Bangkok).

Tickets between any station in Thailand can be purchased at Hualamphong station (☎ 02-223 3762, 225 6964, 224 7788, or 225 0300 ext 5200 03). You can also make advance bookings at Don Muang station (across from Bangkok International Airport) and at the Advance Booking offices at train stations in the larger cities. Advance reservations can be made by phone from anywhere in Thailand. Throughout Thailand SRT ticket offices are *generally* open from 8.30 am to 6 pm on weekdays, 8.30 am to noon on weekends and public holidays. Train tickets can also be purchased at certain travel agencies in Bangkok (see the Travel Agencies section in the Bangkok chapter). It is much simpler to book trains through these agencies than to book them at the station; however, they usually add a surcharge of 50B to 100B to the ticket price.

Eating Facilities

Meal service is available in dining cars and at your seat in 2nd- and 1st-class cars. Menus change as frequently as the SRT changes catering services. For a while there were two menus, a 'special food' menu with 'special' prices (generally given to tourists) and a cheaper, more extensive menu. Nowadays all the meals seem a bit overpriced (75B to 200B on average) by Thai standards – if you're concerned with saving baht, bring your own.

Several readers have written to complain about being overcharged by meal servers on the trains. If you do purchase food on board, be sure to check the prices on the menu rather than trusting server quotes. Also check the bill carefully to make sure you haven't been overcharged.

Station Services

Accurate, up-to-date information on train travel is available at the Rail Travel Aids counter in Hualamphong station. There you can pick up timetables, and ask questions about fares and scheduling – one person behind the counter usually speaks a little English. There are two types of timetable available: four condensed English timetables with fares, schedules and routes for rapid, express and special express trains on the four trunk lines; and four Thai timetables for each trunk line, with side lines as well. These latter timetables give fares and schedules for all trains – ordinary, rapid and express. The English timetables only display a couple of the ordinary routes; eg, they don't show the wealth of ordinary trains that go to Ayuthaya and as far North as Phitsanulok.

All train stations in Thailand have baggage storage services (sometimes called the 'cloak room'). The rates and hours of operation vary from station to station. At Hualamphong station the hours are 4 am to 10.30 pm daily and left luggage costs 10B per day per piece for up to five days, after which it goes up to 15B per day. Hualamphong station also has a 10B shower service in the rest rooms.

Hualamphong Station is jammed with modern coffee shops and a coupon-style cafeteria. All stations in the provincial capitals have restaurants or cafeterias as well as various snack vendors. Although Hat Yai station is the only one with a hotel attached, there are usually hotels within walking distance of major stations.

Hualamphong station has a couple of travel agencies where other kinds of transport can be booked, but beware of touts who try and drag you there saying the trains are fully booked when they aren't. Avoid the travel agencies outside the station, which have very poor reputations. Near the front of the station, at one end of the foyer, a Mail Boxes Etc (MBE) provides mailing, courier and packing services from 7.30 am to 7.30 pm Monday to Friday, 9 am to 4 pm Saturday and 9 am to 8 pm Sunday.

CAR & MOTORCYCLE
Roadways

Thailand has over 170,000km of roadways, of which around 16,000km are classified 'national highways' (both two lane and four lane), which means they're generally well maintained. Route numberings are fairly consistent: Some of the major highways have two numbers, one under the national system and another under the optimistic 'Asia Highway' system that indicates highway links with neighbouring countries. Route 105 to Mae Sot on the Myanmar border, for example, is also called 'Asia 1', while Hwy 2 from Bangkok to Nong Khai is 'Asia 12'. For the time being, the only border regularly crossed by non-commercial vehicles is the Thai-Malaysian border.

Kilometre markers are placed at regular intervals along most larger roadways, but place names are usually printed on them in Thai script only. Highway signs in both Thai and Roman script, which show the destinations and the distances, are becoming increasingly common.

Road Distances (km)

	Aranya Prathet	Ayuthaya	Bangkok	Chiang Mai	Chiang Rai	Chumphon	Hat Yai	Hua Hin	Khon Kaen	Mae Hong Son	Mae Sai	Mukdahan	Nakhon Ratchasima	Nakhon Sawan	Nong Khai	Phitsanulok	Phuket	Sungai Kolok	Surat Thani	Tak	Trat	Ubon Ratchathani
Ubon Ratchathani																						...
Trat																					...	729
Tak																				...	727	707
Surat Thani																			...	1072	965	1066
Sungai Kolok																		...	688	1694	1593	1700
Phuket																	...	761	286	1264	1163	1270
Phitsanulok																...	1227	1657	1029	146	690	572
Nong Khai															...	411	1466	1896	1268	557	883	443
Nakhon Sawan														...	546	135	1092	1522	894	172	555	535
Nakhon Ratchasima													...	240	359	347	1107	1357	909	435	524	163
Mukdahan												...	320	547	295	578	1774	2126	1696	608	1119	157
Mae Sai											...	1155	958	692	945	411	1857	2204	1576	547	1397	1237
Mae Hong Son										...	474	1142	1142	604	969	547	1696	2126	1498	441	1397	1106
Khon Kaen									...	829	842	313	193	425	166	295	1300	1730	1102	717	496	277
Hua Hin								...	633	1029	1107	760	440	444	760	560	667	1097	469	597	496	603
Hat Yai							...	810	1443	1917	1917	1570	1250	1235	1570	1370	474	287	401	1407	1306	1413
Chumphon						...	555	269	902	1298	1376	1029	694	694	1068	829	412	842	214	866	765	872
Chiang Rai					...	1308	1849	1039	774	406	68	1087	914	744	890	479	1706	2136	1508	460	1169	1051
Chiang Mai				...	191	1138	1679	869	604	225	259	917	744	444	720	309	1536	1966	1338	280	999	881
Bangkok			...	686	856	531	1072	262	450	924	917	577	257	237	616	377	862	1280	652	414	313	420
Ayuthaya		...	79	607	777	452	993	183	397	845	720	524	204	163	563	298	929	1359	731	335	392	367
Aranya Prathet	...	246	275	844	1014	727	1268	458	432	1013	1082	601	239	409	598	535	1125	1555	927	581	286	444

Road Rules

Thais drive on the left-hand side of the road – most of the time. Other than that just about anything goes, in spite of road signs and speed limits – the Thais are notorious scoff-laws when it comes to driving. Like many places in Asia, every two-lane road has an invisible third lane in the middle that all drivers feel free to use at any time. Passing on hills and curves is common – as long as you've got the proper Buddhist altar on the dashboard, what could happen?

The main rule to be aware of is that right of way belongs to the bigger vehicle; this is not what it says in the Thai traffic law, but it's the reality. Maximum speed limits are 50km/h on urban roads, 100km/h on most highways – but on any given stretch of highway you'll see vehicles travelling as slowly as 30km/h or as fast as 150km/h. Speed traps are common along Hwy 4 in the south and Hwy 2 in the North-East.

Indicators are often used to warn passing drivers about oncoming traffic. A flashing left indicator means it's OK to pass, while a right indicator means that someone's approaching from the other direction.

The principal hazard to driving in Thailand, besides the general disregard for traffic laws, is having to contend with so many different types of vehicles on the same road – bullock carts, 18-wheelers, bicycles, túk-túk and customised racing bikes. This danger is often compounded by the lack of running lights. In village areas the vehicular traffic is lighter but you have to contend with stray chickens, dogs, water buffaloes and goats. Once you get used to the challenge, driving in Thailand is very entertaining.

Checkpoints

Military checkpoints are common along highways throughout Northern and North-Eastern Thailand, especially in border areas. Always slow down for a checkpoint – often the sentries will wave you through without an inspection, but occasionally you will be stopped and briefly questioned. Use common sense and don't act belligerent or you're likely to be detained longer than you'd like.

Rental

Cars, jeeps and vans can be rented in Bangkok, Chiang Mai, Cha-am, Chiang Rai, Mae Hong Son, Pattaya, Phuket, Ko Samui, Hat Yai, Khorat and Udon Thani. A Japanese sedan (eg, Toyota Corolla) typically costs from around 1000B to 1500B per day; minivans (eg, Toyota Hi-Ace, Nissan Urvan) go for around 1800B to 2500B a day. International rental companies tend to charge a bit more; Avis, for example, rents Nissan 1.4 Sentras for 1500B a day (9000B weekly), slightly larger Mitsubishi 1.5 Lancers for 2000B a day (10,200B weekly) and Mitsubishi four-wheel drive (4WD) Pajeros for 2200B per day (13,200B weekly).

The best deals are usually on 4WD Suzuki Caribians or Daihatsu Miras, which can be rented for as low as 800B per day with no per-kilometre fees for long-term rentals and during low seasons. Unless you absolutely want the cheapest vehicle, you might be better off with a larger vehicle (eg, a Mitsubishi 4WD Strada, if you absolutely want a 4WD); Caribians are notoriously hard to handle at speeds above 90km/h and tend to crumple dangerously in collisions. Cars with automatic shift are uncommon. Drivers can usually be hired with a rental for an additional 300B to 400B per day.

Check with travel agencies or large hotels for rental locations. It is advisable always to verify that a vehicle is insured for liability before signing a rental contract; you should also ask to see the dated insurance documents. If you have an accident while driving an uninsured vehicle you're in for some major hassles.

Motorcycles can be rented in major towns and many smaller tourist centres like Krabi, Ko Pha-Ngan, Ko Samui, Mae Sai and Nong Khai. Rental rates vary considerably from one agency to another and from city to city but average around 200B per day. Since there is a glut of motorcycles for rent in Chiang Mai and Phuket these days, they can be rented in these towns for as little as 150B per day (or as low as 100B per day off-season or long-term). A substantial deposit is usually required to rent a car; motorcycle rental usually requires that you leave your passport.

Driving Permits

Foreigners who wish to drive motor vehicles (including motorcycles) in Thailand need an International Driving Permit. If you don't have one, you can apply for a Thai driver's licence at the Police Registration

Division (PRD; ☎ 02-513 0051–5) on Thanon Phahonyothin in Bangkok. Provincial capitals also have PRDs. If you present a valid foreign driver's licence at the PRD you'll probably only have to take a written test; other requirements include a medical certificate and two passport-sized colour photos. The forms are in Thai only, so you may also need an interpreter. Some PRDs request an affidavit of residence, obtainable from your country's embassy in Thailand upon presentation of proof that you reside in Thailand (eg, a utility bill in your name).

Fuel & Oil

Modern petrol (gasoline) stations with electric pumps are in plentiful supply all over Thailand where there are paved roads. In more remote off-road areas petrol (*ben-sin* or *náam-man rót yon*) is usually available at small roadside or village stands – typically just a couple of ancient hand-operated pumps fastened to petrol barrels. The Thai phrase for 'motor oil' is *náam-man khrêuang*.

At the time of writing, regular (*thammá-daa*, usually 91 octane) petrol costs about 14B per litre, while super (*phísèt*, which is 94 to 95 octane) costs a bit more. Diesel (*dii-soen*) fuel is available at most pumps for around 11B per litre. All fuel in Thailand is unleaded.

Motorcycle Touring

Motorcycle travel has become a popular way to get around Thailand, especially in the North. Dozens of places along the guesthouse circuit, including many guesthouses themselves, have set up shop with no more than a couple of motorbikes for rent. It is also possible to buy a new or used motorbike and sell it before you leave the country. A used 125cc bike can be purchased for as low as 20,000B to 25,000B; you'll pay up to 60,000B for a reconditioned Honda MTX or AX-1, and more for the newer and more reliable Honda Degree or Yamaha TTR 250.

Daily rentals range from 150B to 200B a day for a 100cc step-through (eg, Honda Dream, Suzuki Crystal) in low-season months to 500B a day for a good 250cc dirt bike. The motorcycle industry in Thailand has stopped assembling dirt bikes, so many of the rental bikes of this nature are getting on in years. When they're well maintained they're fine; when they're not so well maintained they can leave you stranded, or worse. The latest trend in Thailand is small, heavy racing bikes that couldn't be less suitable for the typical *fàràng* (Western) body.

The legal maximum size for motorcycle manufacture in Thailand is 150cc, though in reality few bikes on the road exceed 125cc. Anything over 150cc must be imported, which means an addition of up to 600% in import duties. The odd rental shop specialises in bigger motorbikes (average 200cc to 500cc) – some were imported by foreign residents and later sold on the local market, but most came into the country as 'parts' and were discreetly assembled, and licensed under the table.

A number of used Japanese dirt bikes are available, especially in Northern Thailand. The 250cc, four-stroke, water-cooled Honda AX-1 and Yamaha TTR combine the qualities of both touring and off-road machines, and feature economical fuel consumption. If you're looking for a more narrowly defined dirt bike, check out the Yamaha Serow.

While motorcycle touring is undoubtedly one of the best ways to see Thailand, it is also undoubtedly one of the easiest ways to cut your travels short, permanently. You can also run up very large repair and/or hospital bills in the blink of an eye. However, with proper safety precautions and driving conduct adapted to local standards, you can see parts of Thailand inaccessible by other modes of transport and still make it home in one piece. Some guidelines to keep in mind:

- If you've never driven a motorcycle before, stick to the smaller 100cc step-through bikes with automatic clutches. If you're an experienced rider but have never done off-the-road driving, take it slowly the first few days.
- Always check a machine over thoroughly before you take it out. Look at the tyres to see if they still have tread, look for oil leaks, test the brakes. You may be held liable for any problems that weren't duly noted before your departure. Newer bikes cost more than clunkers, but are generally safer and more reliable. Street bikes are more comfortable and ride more smoothly on paved roads than dirt bikes; it's silly to rent an expensive dirt bike if most of your riding is going to be along decent roads. A two-stroke bike suitable for off-roading generally uses twice the fuel of a four-stroke bike with the same engine size, thus lowering your cruising range in areas where roadside pumps are scarce.

- Wear protective clothing and a helmet (required by law in 17 provinces – most rental places can provide them). Without a helmet, a minor slide on gravel can leave you with concussion. Long pants, long-sleeved shirts and shoes are highly recommended as protection against sunburn and as a second skin if you fall. If your helmet doesn't have a visor, wear goggles, glasses or sunglasses to keep bugs, dust and other debris out of your eyes. Gloves are also a good idea, to prevent blisters from holding on to the twist-grips for long periods of time. It is practically suicidal to ride on Thailand's highways without taking these minimum precautions for protecting your body.
- For distances of over 100km or so, take along an extra supply of motor oil, and if riding a two-stroke machine carry two-stroke engine oil. On long trips, oil burns fast.
- You should never ride alone in remote areas, especially at night. There have been incidents where fàràng bikers have been shot or harassed while riding alone, mostly in remote rural areas. When riding in pairs or groups, stay spread out so you'll have room to manoeuvre or brake suddenly if necessary.
- Distribute whatever weight you're carrying on the bike as evenly as possible across the frame. Too much weight at the back of the bike makes the front end harder to control and prone to rising up suddenly on bumps and inclines.
- Get insurance with the motorcycle if at all possible. The more reputable motorcycle rental places insure all their bikes; some will do it for an extra charge. Without insurance you're responsible for anything that happens to the bike. If an accident results in a total loss, or if the bike is somehow lost or stolen, you can be out 25,000B plus. To be absolutely clear about your liability, ask for a written estimate of the replacement cost for a similar bike – take photos as a guarantee. Some agencies will only accept the replacement cost of a new bike. Health insurance is also a good idea – get it before you leave home and check the conditions in regard to motorcycle riding.

An excellent Web site for detailed, up-to-date information on motorcycle touring in Thailand can be found at Golden Triangle Rider (www.geocities.com/goldentrianglerider).

BICYCLE

Just about anywhere outside Bangkok, bikes are the ideal form of local transport because they're cheap, nonpolluting and keep you moving slowly enough to see everything. Bicycles can be hired in many locations; guesthouses often have a few for rent at only 30B to 50B per day. Carefully note the condition of the bike before hiring; if it breaks down you are responsible and parts can be very expensive.

Many visitors are bringing their own touring bikes to Thailand these days. For the most part, drivers are courteous and move over for bicycles. Most roads are sealed, with roomy shoulders. Grades in most parts of the country are moderate; exceptions include the far north, especially Mae Hong Son and Nan Provinces, where you'll need iron thighs. There is plenty of opportunity for dirt-road and off-road pedalling, especially in the North, so a sturdy mountain bike would make a good alternative to a touring rig. Favoured touring routes include the two-lane roads along the Mekong River in the North and the North-East – the terrain is mostly flat and the river scenery is inspiring.

One note of caution: Before you leave home, go over your bike with a fine-toothed comb and fill your repair kit with every imaginable spare part. As with cars and motorbikes, you won't necessarily be able to buy that crucial gismo for your machine when it breaks down somewhere in the back of beyond as the sun sets. In addition to bringing a small repair kit with plenty of spare parts, it is advisable to bring a helmet, reflective clothing and plenty of insurance.

No special permits are needed for bringing a bicycle into the country, although bikes may be registered by customs – which means if you don't leave the country with your bike you'll have to pay a huge customs duty. Most larger cities have bike shops – there are several in Bangkok and Chiang Mai – but they often stock only a few Japanese or locally made parts.

You can take bicycles on the train for a little less than the equivalent of one 3rd-class fare. Buses often don't charge (if they do, it will be something nominal); on the ordinary buses they'll place your bike on the roof, and on air-con buses it will be put in the cargo hold.

The 2500-member Thailand Cycling Club, established in 1959, serves as an information clearing house on biking tours and cycle clubs around the country; call ☎ 02-243 5139 or ☎ 241 2023 in Bangkok. One of the best shops for cycling gear in Thailand is the centrally located Probike (☎ 02-253 3384, fax 254 1077), 237/1 Soi Sarasin, opposite Lumphini Park in Bangkok.

HITCHING

Hitching is never entirely safe in any country in the world, and we don't recommend it. Travellers who decide to hitch should understand that there's a small but serious risk. However, many people do choose to hitch, and the advice that follows should help to make the journey as fast and safe as possible.

People have mixed success with hitchhiking in Thailand; sometimes it's great and at other times no one wants to pick you up. It seems easiest in the more touristy areas of the North and south, most difficult in the central and north-eastern regions where fàràng are a relatively rare sight. To stand on a road and try to flag every vehicle that passes by is, to the Thais, something only an uneducated village dweller would do.

If you're prepared to face this perception, the first step is to use the correct gesture used for flagging a ride – the thumb-out gesture isn't recognised by the average Thai. When Thais want a ride they stretch one arm out with the hand open, palm facing down, and move the hand up and down. This is the same gesture used to flag a taxi or bus, which is why some drivers will stop and point to a bus stop if one is nearby.

In general, hitching isn't worth the hassle as ordinary (no air-con) buses are frequent and fares are cheap. There's no need to stand at a bus terminal – all you have to do is stand on any road going in your direction and flag down a passing bus or *săwngthăew* (pick-up truck).

The exception is in areas where there isn't any bus service, though in such places there's not liable to be very much private vehicle traffic either. If you do manage to get a ride it's customary to offer food or cigarettes to the driver if you have any.

BOAT

There is plenty of water in Thailand and you'll probably have opportunities to get out on it sometime during your trip. The true Thai river transport is the long-tail boat *(reua hăang yao),* so-called because the propeller is mounted at the end of a long drive shaft extending from the engine. The engine, which can be anything from a small marine engine to a large car engine, is mounted on gimbals and the whole unit is swivelled to steer the boat. Long-tail boats can travel at a phenomenal speed.

Between the mainland and islands in the Gulf of Thailand or Andaman Sea, all sorts of larger ocean-going craft are used. The standard is an all-purpose wooden boat, eight to 10m long, with a large inboard engine, a wheelhouse and a simple roof to shelter passengers and cargo. Faster, more expensive hovercraft or jetfoils are sometimes available in tourist areas.

LOCAL TRANSPORT

The Getting Around section in the Bangkok chapter has more information on various forms of local transport.

Bus

Bangkok has the most extensive city bus system. A few provincial capitals, such as Phitsanulok and Ubon Ratchathani, also have buses with established routes. Fares average 4B to 8B. For the rest, you must rely on săwngthăew, túk-túk or *săamláw* (three-wheeled pedicabs).

Taxi

Many regional centres have taxi services, but although there may well be meters, they're never used. Establishing the fare before departure is essential. Try to get an idea from a third party as to what the fare should be and be prepared to bargain. In general, fares are reasonably low.

See the relevant destination chapters for more information on taxis.

Săamláw & Túk-Túk

Săamláw means 'three wheels', and that's just what they are – three-wheeled vehicles. There are two types of săamláw, motorised and nonmotorised. You'll find motorised săamláw throughout the country. They're small utility vehicles, powered by a horrendously noisy two-stroke engine (usually LPG-powered) – if the noise and vibration doesn't get you, the fumes will. These săamláw are more commonly known as túk-túk, because of the noise they make. The nonmotorised version, on the other hand, is the bicycle rickshaw, just like you find, in various forms, all over Asia. There are no bicycle săamláw in Bangkok but you will find them elsewhere in the country.

In either form of săamláw the fare must be established, by bargaining if necessary, before departure.

Săwngthăew

A săwngthăew (literally, two rows) is a small pick-up truck with two rows of bench seats down the sides, very similar to an Indonesian *bemo* and akin to a Filipino *jeepney*. Săwngthăew sometimes operate on fixed routes, just like buses, but they may also run a share-taxi type of service or even be booked individually just like a regular taxi. They are often colour-coded, so that red săwngthăew, for example, go to one destination or group of destinations while blue ones go to another.

Motorcycle Taxi

Many cities in Thailand also offer *mawtoe-sai ráp jâang,* 100cc to 125cc motorcycles that can be hired, with driver, for short distances. They're not very suitable if you're carrying more than a backpack or small suitcase, but if you're empty-handed they can't be beat for quick transport over short distances. In addition to the lack of space for luggage, motorcycle taxis also suffer from lack of shelter from rain or sun. Although most drivers around the country drive at safe, sane speeds, the kamikaze drivers of Bangkok are a major exception.

In most cities you'll find motorcycle taxis clustered near street intersections, rather than cruising the streets looking for fares. Fares tend to run 10B to 30B, depending on distance. Some motorcycle taxis specialize in regular, short routes, eg, from one end of a long soi to another. In such cases the fare is usually a fixed 10B, occasionally as low as 5B in small towns.

ORGANISED TOURS

Many operators around the world can arrange guided tours of Thailand. Most of them simply serve as brokers for tour companies based in Thailand; they buy their trips from a wholesaler and resell them under various names in travel markets overseas. Hence, one is much like another and you might as well arrange a tour in Thailand at a lower cost – there are so many available. Two of the largest tour wholesalers in Bangkok are: World Travel Service (☎ 02-233 5900, fax 236-7169) at 1053 Thanon Charoen Krung; and Diethelm Travel

(☎ 02-255 9150, fax 256 0248) at Kian Gwan Building II, 140/1 Thanon Withayu.

Motorcycle tours of Northern Thailand (with extensions into Laos and South-West China) can be organised by Siam Bike Tour (@ davidfl@chmai.loxinfo.co.th).

Bangkok-based Khiri Travel (☎ 02-629 0491, fax 629 0493, @ info@khiri.com) specialises in ecologically oriented tours. It's located opposite the Viengtai Hotel on Soi Rambutri off Thanon Chakrapong.

Overseas Companies

The better overseas tour companies build their own Thailand itineraries from scratch and choose their local suppliers based on which ones best serve these itineraries. Of these, several specialise in adventure and/or ecological tours, including those listed later. Asia Transpacific Journeys, for example, offers trips across a broad spectrum of Thai destinations and activities, from Northern Thailand trekking to sea canoeing in the Phuket Sea, plus tour options that focus exclusively on North-Eastern Thailand. The average trip runs 14 to 17 days.

Ms Kasma Loha-Unchit (☎/fax 510-655 8900) PO Box 21165, Oakland, California 94620, USA, a Thai native living in California, offers highly personalised, 19- to 28-day 'cultural immersion' tours of Thailand. For further information, see her Web site at www.thaifoodandtravel.com.

Asia Transpacific Journeys (☎ 800-642 2742, 303-443 6789, fax 443 7078) 3055 Center Green Dr, Boulder, CO 80301, USA
  Web site: www.southeastasia.com
Club Aventure (☎ 514-527 0999, fax 527 3999, @ info@clubaventure.qc.ca) 759 ave du Mont-Royal Est, Montreal, QUE H2J 1W8, Canada
Exodus (☎ 020-8673 5550, fax 8673 0779) 9 Weir Rd, London SW12 OLT, UK
  Web site: www.exodustravels.co.uk
Intrepid Travel (☎ 03-9473 2626, fax 9419 4426, @ info@intrepidtravel.com.au) 11–13 Spring St, Fitzroy, VIC 3065, Australia
  Web site: www.intrepidtravel.com
Mountain Travel Sobek (☎ 800-227 2384, 510-527 8100, fax 525 7710) 6420 Fairmount Ave, Berkeley, CA 94530, USA
  Web site: www.mtsobek.com

Bangkok

The very epitome of the modern, steamy Asian metropolis, Bangkok (560 sq km, population six million plus) has a wealth of attractions if you can tolerate the traffic, noise, heat (in the hot season), floods (in the rainy season) and polluted air. The city is incredibly urbanised, but beneath its modern veneer lies an unmistakable *khwaam pen thai* ('Thai-ness'). To say that Bangkok is not Thailand is tantamount to saying that New York is not the USA or Paris is not France.

The capital of Thailand was established at Bangkok in 1782 by the first king of the Chakri dynasty, Rama I. The name Bangkok comes from Bang Makok, meaning 'Place of Olive Plums', and refers to the original site, which is only a very small part of what is today called Bangkok by foreigners. The official Thai name is quite a tongue twister:

Krungthep mahanakhon amon ratanakosin mahintara ayuthaya mahadilok popnopparat ratchathani burirom udomratchaniwet mahasathan amonpiman avatansathit sakkathattiya witsanukamprasit

The 1989 album *Fak Thong (Pumpkin)* by rock duo Asanee-Wasan contained the hit 'Krung Thep Mahanakhon', a big-sound raver consisting of Bangkok's full name chanted over a hypnotic rhythm. Roughly translated the name means 'Great City of Angels, Repository of Divine Gems, Great Land Unconquerable, Grand and Prominent Realm, Royal and Delightful Capital City Full of Nine Noble Gems, Highest Royal Dwelling and Grand Palace, Divine Shelter and Living Place of Reincarnated Spirits'.

Fortunately this is shortened to Krung Thep (City of Angels) in everyday usage. Metropolitan Krung Thep includes Thonburi, the older part of the city (and predecessor to Bangkok as the capital). In many ways, it's the most exciting and dynamic city in South-East Asia, with, for example, the region's largest foreign media correspondent base.

Bangkok caters to diverse interests: There are museums, temples and other historic sites for those interested in traditional Thai culture; an endless variety of good restaurants, clubs, international cultural and social events; movies in several languages; discos, heavy-metal pubs, folk cafes; and even modern-art galleries for those people seeking contemporary Krung Thep. As

Highlights

- **Wat Phra Kaew** – exquisite Emerald Buddha, colourful mosaics and glittering spires
- **National Museum** – display of Thailand's sculptural and decorative arts
- **Wat Arun** – views of Bangkok and the Chao Phraya River
- **Vimanmek Teak Mansion** – one of the world's largest golden teak buildings
- **Chalermkrung Royal Theatre** – *khŏn* performances of dance-drama
- **Wat Traimit** – 5½ tonnes of solid gold Buddha hidden away in Chinatown
- **Boat Trip** – along Bangkok's huge canal system
- **Muay Thai** – bouts at Lumphini and Ratchadamnoen stadiums
- **Chinese & Indian market districts** – walking tours of the temples, bazaars, shophouses and alleys
- **Damnoen Saduak & Samut Songkhram** – floating markets and coconut plantations

William Warren, the dean of expat authors in Thailand, has said, 'The gift Bangkok offers me is the assurance I will never be bored'.

Orientation

The eastern side of the Mae Nam Chao Phraya (Chao Phraya River), Bangkok proper, can be divided in two by the main north-south railway. The portion between the river and the railway is old Bangkok (often called Ko Ratanakosin), where most of the older temples and the original palace are located, as well as the Chinese and Indian districts. The part of the city east of the railway, which is many times larger than the old districts, is 'new' Bangkok. It can be divided again into the business and tourist district wedged between Thanon Charoen Krung (New Rd) and Thanon Phra Ram IV, and the sprawling business, residential and tourist district stretching along Thanon Sukhumvit and Thanon Phetburi Tat Mai.

This leaves the hard-to-classify areas below Thanon Sathon Tai (South Sathon Rd, which includes Khlong Toey, Bangkok's main port), and the area above Thanon Phra Ram IV between the railway and Thanon Withayu or Wireless Rd (which comprises an infinite variety of businesses, several movie theatres, civil service offices, the shopping area of Siam Square, Chulalongkorn University and the National Stadium). The areas along the eastern bank of the Mae Nam Chao Phraya are undergoing a surge of redevelopment and many new buildings, particularly condos, are going up.

On the opposite (western) side of the Mae Nam Chao Phraya is Thonburi, which was Thailand's capital for 15 years before Bangkok was founded. Few tourists ever set foot on the Thonburi side except to visit Wat Arun, the Temple of Dawn. *Fàng thon* (Thonburi Bank), as it's often called by Thais, seems an age away from the glittering high-rises on the river's eastern bank, although it is an up-and-coming area for condo development.

Finding Addresses Any city as large and unplanned as Bangkok can be tough to get around. Street names often seem unpronounceable to begin with, compounded by the inconsistency of Romanised Thai spellings. For example, the street often spelt as Rajadamri is pronounced Ratchadamri (with the appropriate tones), or abbreviated as Rat'damri. The 'v' in Sukhumvit should be pronounced like a 'w'. The most popular location for foreign embassies is known both as Wireless Rd and Thanon Withayu (*wítháyú* is Thai for radio).

Many street addresses show a string of numbers divided by slashes and dashes; for example, 48/3–5 Soi 1, Thanon Sukhumvit. This is because undeveloped property in Bangkok was originally bought and sold in lots. The number before the slash refers to the original lot number; the numbers following the slash indicate buildings (or entrances to buildings) constructed within that lot. The pre-slash numbers appear in the order in which they were added to city plans, while the post-slash numbers are arbitrarily assigned by developers. As a result, numbers along a given street don't always run consecutively.

The Thai word *thànŏn* means road, street or avenue. Hence Ratchadamnoen Rd (sometimes referred to as Ratchadamnoen Ave) is always called Thanon Ratchadamnoen in Thai.

A *soi* is a small street or lane that runs off a larger street. In my example, the address referred to as 48/3–5 Soi 1, Thanon Sukhumvit, will be located off Thanon Sukhumvit on Soi 1. Alternative ways of writing the same address include 48/3–5 Thanon Sukhumvit Soi 1, or even just 48/3–5 Sukhumvit 1. Some Bangkok sois have become so large that they can be referred to both as thànŏn and soi, eg, Soi Sarasin/Thanon Sarasin and Soi Asoke/Thanon Asoke.

Smaller than a soi is a *tràwk* (usually spelt *trok*) or alley. Well-known alleys in Bangkok include Chinatown's Trok Itsaranuphap and Banglamphu's Trok Rong Mai.

Maps

A map is essential for finding your way around Bangkok, and there are lots of maps competing for your attention. Apart from Lonely Planet's *Bangkok* city map (see Maps in the Facts for the Visitor chapter), there are more detailed locally produced maps. A bus map is necessary if you intend to spend a lot of time in Bangkok and want to use the fairly economical bus system. One of the most popular, because it clearly shows all the bus routes (and some walking tours), and is cheap, is the *Tour 'n Guide Map to Bangkok Thailand,* often referred to by travellers as the 'blue map' because of its monotonous aqua colour. The map costs 40B and, although it's regularly updated, some bus routes will inevitably be wrong, so take care. The coated paper, which resists stains, is a plus.

Other companies put out similar maps, such as *Bangkok Bus Map* published by Bangkok Guide (it has no coating and doesn't hold up to strenuous wear and tear, but has lots of sightseeing tips) and *Latest Tour's Map to Bangkok & Thailand* (a clone of the 'blue map').

The Tourism Authority of Thailand (TAT) publishes and distributes the free *City Map of Bangkok,* a folded sheet map on coated stock with bus routes, all the major hotels, the latest expressways, sightseeing, hospitals, embassies and more – it's very useful, though a bit hard to read due to the small print. Separate inset maps of Ko Ratanakosin (labelled 'Ratchadamnoen Klang Ave Area'), Thanon Silom, Khlong Saen Saep, Thanon Sukhumvit and Thanon Phra Ram I are very helpful. You can pick it up at the airport TAT desk or at any Bangkok TAT office.

The long-running, oft-imitated and never-equalled *Nancy Chandler's Map of Bangkok* costs 140B and contains a whole host of information on out-of-the-way places, including lots of stuff on where to buy unusual things around the city. The six different water-coloured panels (Greater Bangkok, Chinatown, Thanon Sukhumvit, Chatuchak Weekend Market, Central Shopping Area and Markets of Central Bangkok) are all hand-drawn, hand-lettered and laid out by hand. The 20th edition, published in 2000, includes a handy categorised index booklet.

Another contender on the market, Groovy Map's *Bangkok by Day Map 'n' Guide,* costs 100B and combines an up-to-date bus map, the usual sightseeing features, and a short selection of restaurant and bar reviews, on decent coated stock. It covers a smaller area (only central Bangkok) and lacks street detail – only the main avenues and a handful of *wát*

(temples) are labelled. More successful is Groovy Map's *Bangkok by Night Map 'n' Guide* (100B), which shares the same basic map features as the 'day map', but without any bus routes and many more recommendations for restaurant, bar and night-time entertainment venues.

A detailed map covering a large portion of the city is *Bangkok Map,* a 188-page hardcover street atlas put out by the Agency for Real Estate Affairs, a private company specialising in real-estate surveys of the city. Each page features a colour-coded street grid showing various office and apartment buildings, hotels, restaurants and even many nightclubs. This atlas is available from most bookshops in Bangkok that carry English-language books.

Information

Tourist Offices The Tourism Authority of Thailand (TAT) produces the usual selection of colourful brochures, but is also one of the best tourist offices in Asia for putting out useful hard facts – on plain but quite invaluable duplicated sheets. Many of the staff speak English.

TAT has a desk in the arrivals area of both Terminal 1 (☎ 523 8972) and Terminal 2 (☎ 535 2669) at Bangkok International Airport; both are open 8 am to midnight. The TAT's main office (☎ 694 1222, fax 694 1220, ℮ center@tat.or.th) occupies 10 floors of Le Concorde Building, 202 Thanon Ratchadaphisek, a location in northern Bangkok that's inconvenient for most visitors. TAT says that this is a temporary office – it's hoping to move into a building near Ko Ratanakosin at some point in the future. It's open 8.30 am to 4.30 pm daily.

TAT's information compound (☎ 282 9773, fax 282 9775) on Thanon Ratchadamnoen Nok near the Ratchadamnoen Stadium is more convenient. It's open from 8 am to 4.30 pm daily. TAT also maintains a 24-hour Tourist Assistance Centre (TAC; ☎ 1155) in the compound for matters relating to theft and other mishaps, run by the paramilitary arm of the TAT, the Tourist Police. See the Tourist Police section later in this chapter.

A smaller TAT office (☎ 272 4424) with fewer materials can be found at Chatuchak Market, open 9 am to 4 pm on weekends.

BANGKOK

GREATER BANGKOK

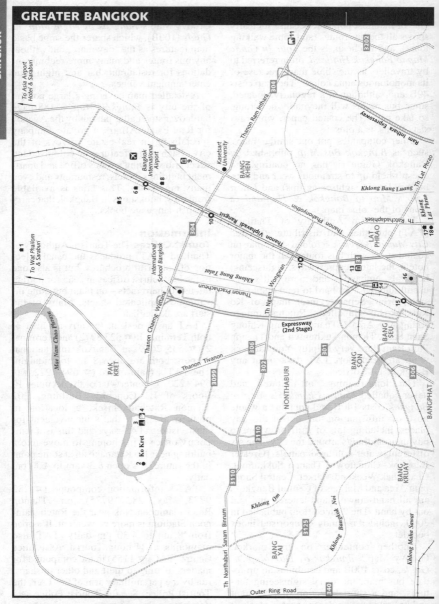

BANGKOK

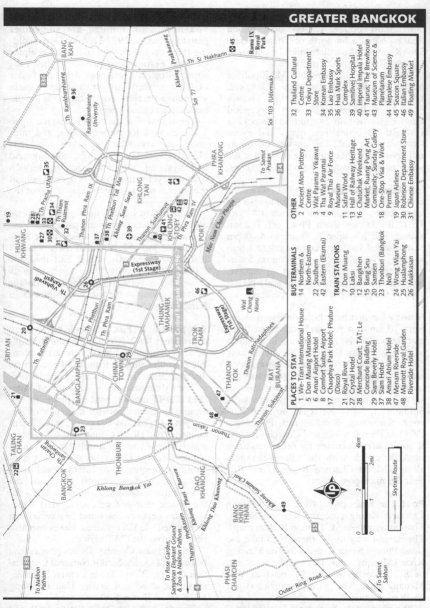

GREATER BANGKOK

PLACES TO STAY
1 We-Train International House
5 Don Muang Mansion
6 Amari Airport Hotel
8 Comfort Suites Airport
17 Chaophya Park Hotel; Phuture (Disco)
21 Royal River
27 Crystal Hotel
28 Merchant Court; TAT; Le Concorde Building
29 Siam Beverly Hotel
37 Siam Hotel
38 Amari Atrium Hotel
47 Menam Riverside
48 Marriott Royal Garden Riverside Hotel

BUS TERMINALS
14 Northern & North-Eastern
22 Southern
42 Eastern (Ekamai)

TRAIN STATIONS
7 Don Muang
10 Laksi
12 Bangkhen
15 Bang Seu
20 Samsen
23 Thonburi (Bangkok Noi)
24 Wong Wian Yai
25 Hualamphong
26 Makkasan

OTHER
2 Ancient Mon Pottery Centre
3 Wat Paramai Yikawat
9 Tha Wat Paramai
9 Royal Thai Air Force Museum
11 Safari World
13 Hall of Railway Heritage
16 Chatuchak Weekend Market; Ruang Pung Art Community; Sunday Gallery
18 One-Stop Visa & Work Permit
19 Japan Airlines
30 Robinson Department Store
31 Chinese Embassy
32 Thailand Cultural Centre
33 Tokyu Department Store
34 Korean Embassy
35 Lao Embassy
36 Hua Mark Sports Complex
39 Samitivej Hospital
40 Imperial Impala Hotel
41 Taurus; The Brewhouse
43 Museum of Science & Planetarium
44 Nepalese Embassy
45 Seacon Square
46 Italian Embassy
49 Floating Market

For Central Bangkok Map p196

Skytrain Route

A tourist information booth at the Chana Songkhram police station on Thanon Chakraphong, a bit north of Thanon Khao San (Khao San Rd), distributes bus maps of the area for a donation of 2B each.

Operated by the Bangkok Metropolitan Authority (BMA), the new Bangkok Tourist Bureau (☎ 225 7612), 17/1 Thanon Phra Athit, Banglamphu, is a very good spot for information. In addition to stocking a wealth of brochures, maps and event schedules, the staff can answer questions and assist with the chartering of boats at the adjacent pier. It's open 9 am to 7 pm daily.

Immigration Department For visa extensions or applications, you'll need to visit the Immigration Department office (☎ 287 3101/10) on Soi Suan Phlu, off Thanon Sathon Tai. It's open 8.30 am to 4.30 pm (with limited staff between noon and 1 pm) weekdays. It's also open till noon on Saturday for re-entry visas only. Most applications or extensions require two photos and a photocopy of the photo page of your passport.

Money Regular bank hours in Bangkok are from 10 am to 4 pm, and automated teller machines (ATMs) are common in all areas of the city. Many Thai banks also have currency exchange offices in tourist-oriented areas, which are open from 8.30 am to 8 pm (some even later) daily. You'll find them in several places along the following roads: Sukhumvit, Nana Neua, Khao San, Patpong, Surawong, Ratchadamri, Phra Ram IV, Phra Ram I, Silom and Charoen Krung. If you're after currency for other countries in Asia, check with the moneychangers along Thanon Charoen Krung (New Rd) near the main post office.

Post The main post office is on Thanon Charoen Krung (see the Thanon Silom, Thanon Surawong & Thanon Sathon map). The easiest way to get there is to take the Chao Phraya River Express to Tha Meuang Khae (Meuang Khae pier) at the river end of Soi Charoen Krung 34, next to Wat Meuang Khae. The main post office is just north of the wát.

The poste-restante counter is open 8 am to 8 pm weekdays, and until 1 pm on weekends and holidays. Each letter you collect costs 1B, and parcels 2B.

The bulging boxes of poste-restante mail you must look through are sometimes daunting, but the 1927 Thai Art Deco building is a treat to hang out in. Italian sculptor Corrado Feroci (also known by his Thai name, Silpa Bhirasri), considered the father of Thai modern art, crafted the garuda sculptures perched atop either side of the building's central tower.

There's also a packaging service open 8.30 am to 4.30 pm weekdays, and until noon Saturday. When the parcel counter is closed (weekday evenings, Sunday and holidays) an informal packing service (using recycled materials) is opened behind the service windows at the centre rear of the building.

Branch post offices throughout the city also offer poste restante and parcel services. In Banglamphu, the post office at the eastern end of Trok Mayom near Sweety Guest House was recently razed and the new Ratchadamnoen post office was built in its place. It's a very convenient location for visitors staying at the many guesthouses in Banglamphu.

Telephone & Fax Bangkok's telephone area code is ☎ 02. If you're ringing from another province, dial ☎ 02 before the number. If you're ringing from another country, dial ☎ 2 after Thailand's area code (☎ 66).

The Communications Authority of Thailand (CAT) international telephone office, around the corner from the main post office, is open 24 hours. At last count, 40 different countries had Home Country Direct service, which means you can simply enter a vacant Home Country Direct booth and get one-button connection to an international operator in any of these countries (see the Post & Communications section in the Facts for the Visitor chapter for a country list). Other countries (except Laos and Malaysia) can be reached via IDD phones. Faxes can also be sent from the CAT office.

Other Home Country Direct phones can be found at Queen Sirikit National Convention Centre, World Trade Centre, Sogo department store and at the Hualamphong MBE (Mail Boxes Etc).

You can also make long-distance calls and send faxes at the Telephone Organization of Thailand (TOT) office on Thanon Ploenchit, but this office only accepts cash and reverse-charge calls are not allowed. Calls to Laos and Malaysia can only be made from the TOT office or from private phones.

Email & Internet Access Internet users can check their email or skim the Net at dozens of Internet cafes, bars and centres throughout the city. Rates are pretty standard throughout the city, at about 1B per minute. Thanon Khao San has the highest concentration of access points in the city (over 30 at last count), so if it's choice you want, head there. Other good areas for Internet centres include Thanon Silom, Thanon Ploenchit and Siam Square. Additionally, many Bangkok guesthouses and hotels nowadays offer Internet access on the premises.

There's not much point in recommending one place over another as they're all struggling to keep up with their competitors, and hence the equipment and functionality changes from month to month. Some places are little more than one terminal set up in the corner of a *ráan cham* (sundries shop), while the better spots offer scanner and printer services for additional charges. A couple of places we recommend include Cyber Cafe (☎ 656 8473), 2nd floor, Ploenchit Center, Thanon Ploenchit, and Bangkok Internet Cafe (☎ 629 3015), next to Prakorp's House & Restaurant on Thanon Khao San.

Internet Resources The Web site www.bangkok.thailandtoday.com posts a solid collection of information on shopping, nightlife, dining and riverside sightseeing with an emphasis on the riverside and Ko Ratanakosin areas.

Travel Agencies Bangkok is packed with travel agencies of every manner and description. Around Thanon Khao San alone there are over a dozen places where you can book bus and air tickets; some are reliable and offer unbelievably low prices, but you should exercise caution because there are always a few bad apples in the bunch. In the past five years at least two agencies on Thanon Khao San closed shop and absconded with payments from dozens of tourists who never received their tickets. The bad agencies change their names frequently, so ask other travellers for advice. Wherever possible, try to see the tickets before you hand over any of your money.

STA Travel maintains reliable offices specialising in discounted yet flexible air tickets at Wall Street Tower (☎ 233 2582), 33/70 Thanon Surawong. Another reliable, long-running agency is Viang Travel (☎ 280 3537), Trang Hotel, 99/8 Thanon Wisut Kasat, in Banglamphu.

Some agencies will book train tickets and pick them up by courier – there's usually a 100B surcharge. Four agencies permitted to arrange direct train bookings (without surcharge) are:

Airland (☎ 255 5432) 866 Thanon Ploenchit
Songserm Travel Center (☎ 982 8100)
  33/11–12 Thanon Chaeng Wattana;
  (☎ 282 8080) 172 Thanon Khao San

If you are heading to Europe and need a Eurail Pass, Dits Travel (☎ 251 8159) at Kian Gwan House, 140 Thanon Withayu, is authorised to issue them.

Guidebooks Lonely Planet's *Bangkok* covers all of the information in this chapter along with extra details concerning business services in the city, as well as excursions to nearby provinces. *Vivre à Bangkok,* published by Une Équipe de Bénévoles Bangkok Accueil for La Commuanutée Francophone en Thaïlande, is a thick spiral-bound book that covers all the usual territory with special attention to French speakers – including, for example, a list of travel agents who speak French. It's available in Bangkok bookshops where foreign-language books are sold, such as Asia Books (see Bookshops in this section).

Magazines & Newspapers Several ad-laden giveaways contain tourist info, but the best source for no-frills information is *Bangkok Metro* magazine, a lifestyle monthly packed with listings on health, entertainment, events, social services, travel tips and consumer-oriented articles. The *Nation* and the *Bangkok Post* also contain useful articles and listings of events.

Bookshops Bangkok has probably the best selection of bookshops in South-East Asia. For new books and magazines the two best bookshop chains are Asia Books and Duang Kamol (DK) Book House. Asia Books lives up to its name by having

Bangkok's best and largest selections of English-language titles on Asia. Its main branch (☎ 252 7277) is at Soi 15, 221 Thanon Sukhumvit. Other large branch shops are at: Landmark Plaza, Soi 3 and Soi 4, Thanon Sukhumvit; 2nd floor, Peninsula Plaza, near the Regent Bangkok on Thanon Ratchadamri; 3rd floor, World Trade Centre, Thanon Ploenchit; Siam Discovery Center, Thanon Phra Ram I; 3rd floor, Thaniya Plaza, Thanon Silom; Times Square, Thanon Sukhumvit; and Emporium complex, Thanon Sukhumvit. Smaller Asia Books stalls can be found in several of the larger hotels and at Thai airports.

DK Book House (☎ 251 6335, 251 1467, 250 1262) has its main branch in Siam Square, 244–246 Soi 2, Thanon Phra Ram I; it's good for textbooks. Additional branches are: on Thanon Sukhumvit across from the Ambassador City complex (excellent for fiction titles); and in the Mahboonkrong shopping centre opposite Siam Square.

There are two other bookshops with English-language books in the Siam Square complex: the Book Chest (Soi 2) and Odeon Store (Soi 1). Kinokuniya in The Emporium shopping centre, Soi 24, Thanon Sukhumvit, is also quite good, not only for Japanese-language materials but for English-language books.

Teck Heng Bookstore (☎ 234 1836), 1326 Thanon Charoen Krung, between the Shangri-La and Oriental Hotels, is one of the better independent bookshops in this neighbourhood and carries quite an up-to-date variety of books on South-East Asia. The owner is very helpful.

Suksit Siam (☎ 225 9531), opposite Wat Ratchabophit at 113–115 Thanon Fuang Nakhon, specialises in books on Thai politics, especially those representing the views of outspoken social critic Sulak Sivaraksa and the progressive Santi Pracha Dhamma Institute (which has offices next door). The shop also has a number of mainstream titles.

Used & Rare Books Shaman Books (☎ 629 0418), 71 Thanon Khao San, carries a good mixture of new and used guidebooks, maps, novels and books on spirituality in several languages. Much smaller, but with an attached outdoor cafe, is Banana Leaf Books & Cafe, off the north-west end of Thanon Khao San. Aporia Books, on the east side of

Thanon Tanao almost opposite the eastern entrance to Thanon Khao San, also offers an extensive selection of new and used books.

Merman Books (☎ 231 3155) is in the Silom Complex, 191 Thanon Silom. Operated by a former Bangkok Post editor, the shop collects all manner of out-of-print and rare books on Asia.

Elite Used Books at Soi 33/1, 593/5 Thanon Sukhumvit (near Villa supermarket) and at 1/12 Soi 3, Thanon Sukhumvit (opposite Nana Inn), carries a decent selection of used foreign-language titles, including English, Chinese, French, German and Swedish. The Chatuchak Weekend Market in Chatuchak Park is also a source of used, often out-of-print books in several languages. On Thanon Khao San in Banglamphu, there are at least three street-side vendors specialising in used paperback novels and guidebooks, including many Lonely Planet titles.

Libraries Besides offering an abundance of reading material, Bangkok's libraries make a peaceful escape from the heat and noise.

In a class all of its own, the Neilson Hays Library (☎ 233 1731), 195 Thanon Surawong, next to the British Club, is a historical monument as well as a good, all-purpose lending library. Built in 1921 by Dr Heyward Hays as a memorial to his wife Jennie Neilson Hays, the classic colonial Asian edifice is operated by the 100-year-old Bangkok Library Association and is the oldest English-language library in Thailand. It has well over 20,000 volumes, including a good selection of children's books and titles on Thailand. The periodical section offers a few Thai magazines, and you can even borrow jigsaw puzzles.

Although the building has only one air-conditioned reading room, the ancient ceiling fans do a good job keeping the other sitting areas cool. The library's Rotunda Gallery hosts monthly art exhibitions and also the occasional art sale. Opening hours are 9.30 am to 4 pm Monday to Saturday and until 2 pm Sunday. Free parking for members is available at the library's small car park near the corner of Thanon Surawong and Thanon Naret.

The National Library (☎ 281 5212) on Thanon Samsen is an impressive institution with a huge collection of Thai material dating back several centuries as well as smaller numbers of foreign-language books. Membership is free. The Siam Society, 131 Soi Asoke, Thanon Sukhumvit, and the National Museum, Thanon Na Phra That, also have collections of English-language materials on the history, art and culture of Thailand.

Although you won't be permitted to borrow books unless you're a Chula student, the library in Chulalongkorn University (south of Siam Square) is a good place to hang out – quiet and air-conditioned.

The Foreign Correspondents Club of Thailand (see the Cultural Centres entry following) has a small selection of books on South-East Asian affairs, as well as current copies of the *International Herald Tribune* and other periodicals. Nonmembers are welcome to browse as long as they buy something at the bar or restaurant.

Cultural Centres Various Thai and foreign associations organise and support cultural events of a wide-ranging nature. They can be good places to meet Bangkok residents and Thais with an international outlook. Some of the more active organisations include:

Alliance Française (☎ 213 2122, 286 3841) 29 Thanon Sathon Tai. French-language courses; translation services; monthly bulletin; French films; a small library and bookshop; French and Thai cafeteria; and music, art and lecture programs.

American University Alumni (AUA; ☎ 252 4021) 179 Thanon Ratchadamri. English and Thai-language courses; newsletter; American films; Test of English as a Foreign Language (TOEFL) preparation; Thai cafeteria; library; and music, art and lecture programs.

British Council (☎ 652 5480, fax 253 5311, e bc.bangkok@britcoun.or.th) Siam Square, 254 Soi Chulalongkorn 64, Thanon Phra Ram I. English-language classes; monthly calendar of events; British films; music, art and drama programs; library and information services; inexpensive Internet services.

Foreign Correspondents Club of Thailand (FCCT; ☎ 652 0580, 254 8165, fax 652 0582, e fcct@asiaaccess.net.th) Penthouse, Maneeya Center Bldg, 518/5 Thanon Ploenchit. Home to wayward journalists and anyone else interested in keeping up with current Thai news, the FCCT appears to be undergoing a renaissance; the club sponsors well-selected films every Monday evening and presents various programs with a news slant several other nights a week; bar and restaurant on the premises.

Goethe-Institut (Thai-German Cultural Centre; ☎ 287 0942) 18/1 Soi Atakanprasit, on Soi Goethe between Thanon Sathon Tai and Soi Ngam Duphli. German-language classes; monthly calendar of events; German restaurant; German films; musical performances; art exhibits.

Thailand Cultural Centre (TCC; ☎ 245 7742) Thanon Ratchadaphisek, Huay Khwang. A variety of local and international cultural events, including musical and theatrical performances, art exhibits, cultural workshops and seminars.

Medical Services Bangkok has three university research hospitals, 12 public and private hospitals, and hundreds of medical clinics. The Australian, US and UK embassies usually keep up-to-date lists of the doctors who can speak English; for doctors who speak other languages, contact the relevant embassy.

Several shop-front clinics in the Thanon Ploenchit area specialise in lab tests for sexually transmitted diseases (STDs). According to *Bangkok Metro* magazine, Bangkok General Hospital has the most sophisticated HIV blood-testing program. Bangkok's better hospitals include:

Bangkok Adventist (Mission) Hospital (☎ 281 1422, 282 1100) 430 Thanon Phitsanulok
Bangkok Christian Hospital (☎ 233 6981–9, 235 1000) 124 Thanon Silom
Bangkok General Hospital (☎ 318 0066, 310 3000) 2 Soi 47, Thanon Phetburi Tat Mai
Bangkok Nursing Home (☎ 233 2610–9) 9 Thanon Convent
Bumrungrad Hospital (☎ 667 1000) 33 Soi 3, Thanon Sukhumvit
Chao Phraya Hospital (☎ 434 0265, 884 7000) 113/44 Thanon Pinklao Nakhon-Chaisi, Bangkok Noi
Mahesak Hospital (☎ 234 2760) 46/7–9 Thanon Mahesak
Phayathai Hospital (☎ 245 2620) 364/1 Thanon Si Ayuthaya
Samitivej Hospital (☎ 381 6728, 381 6831) 133 Soi 49, Thanon Sukhumvit
St Louis Hospital (☎ 212 0033–48) 215 Thanon Sathon Tai

There are plenty of Chinese doctors and herbal dispensaries in Bangkok's Sampeng district, near Thanon Ratchawong, Thanon Charoen Krung, Thanon Yaowarat and Thanon Songwat, including the Art Deco Pow Tai Dispensary at 572–574 Thanon Charoen Krung.

BANGKOK

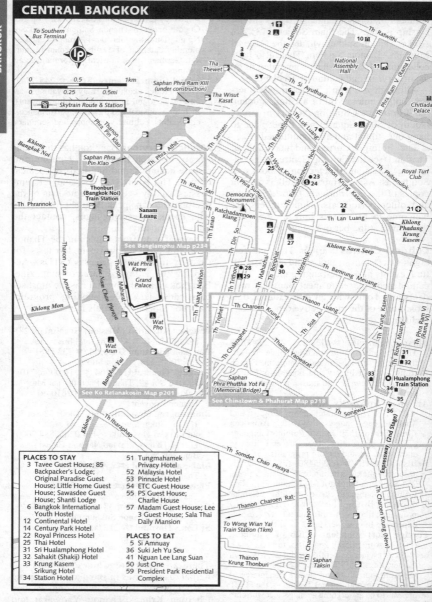

CENTRAL BANGKOK

To Southern
Bus Terminal

0   0.5   1km
0   0.25   0.5mi

Skytrain Route & Station

Khlong
Bangkok Noi

Th Phrannok

Saphan Phra
Pin Klao

Thonburi
(Bangkok Noi)
Train Station

Khlong Mon

Thanon Arun Amarin

Mae Nam Chao Phraya

Thanon Maharat

Bangkok Yai

Khlong

Th Itsaraphap

Tha
Thewet

Saphan Phra Ram XIII
(under construction)

Tha Wisut
Kasat

Th Phra Athit

Thanon
Phra Pin Klao

Th Phra Sumen

Th Khao San

Sanam
Luang

Th Tanao

Wat Phra
Kaew
Grand
Palace

Wat
Pho

Wat
Arun

Th Samsen

Th Pratchadipatai

Th Luk Luang

Th Si Ayuthaya

National
Assembly
Hall

Th Phra Ram V (Rama VI)

Chitlada
Palace

Th Wisut Kasat

Th Ratchadamnoen Nok

Thanon Krung Kasem

Th Phitsanulok

Royal Turf
Club

Democracy
Monument

Th Din So

Th Ratchadamnoen
Klang

See Banglamphu Map p204

Th Fuang Nakhon

Th Tritthong

Th Mahachai

Th Boriphat

Th Worachak

Th Charoen Krung

Th Triphet

Th Chakraphet

Thanon Yaowarat

Saphan
Phra Phuttha Yot Fa
(Memorial Bridge)

See Chinatown & Phahurat Map p218

See Ko Ratanakosin Map p201

Thanon Luang

Th Sua Pa

Th Lan Luang

Khlong
Phadung
Krung
Kasem

Khlong Saen Saep

Th Bamrung Meuang

Th Krung Kasem

Th Rong Muang

Th Phra Ram VI
(Rama VI)

Hualamphong
Train Station

Th Songwat

Th Somdet Chao Phraya

Thanon Charoen Rat

To Wong Wian Yai
Train Station (1km)

Thanon
Krung Thonburi

Thanon Charoen Rat

Th Charoen Nakhon

Th Charoen Krung (New)

Expressway (2nd Stage)

Saphan
Taksin

PLACES TO STAY
3 Tavee Guest House; 85
   Backpacker's Lodge;
   Original Paradise Guest
   House; Little Home Guest
   House; Sawasdee Guest
   House; Shanti Lodge
6 Bangkok International
   Youth Hostel
12 Continental Hotel
14 Century Park Hotel
22 Royal Princess Hotel
25 Thai Hotel
31 Sri Hualamphong Hotel
32 Sahakit (Shakij) Hotel
33 Krung Kasem
   Srikung Hotel
34 Station Hotel

51 Tungmahamek
   Privacy Hotel
52 Malaysia Hotel
53 Pinnacle Hotel
54 ETC Guest House
55 PS Guest House;
   Charlie House
57 Madam Guest House; Lee
   3 Guest House; Sala Thai
   Daily Mansion

PLACES TO EAT
5 Si Amnuay
36 Suki Jeh Yu Seu
41 Nguan Lee Lang Suan
50 Just One
59 President Park Residential
   Complex

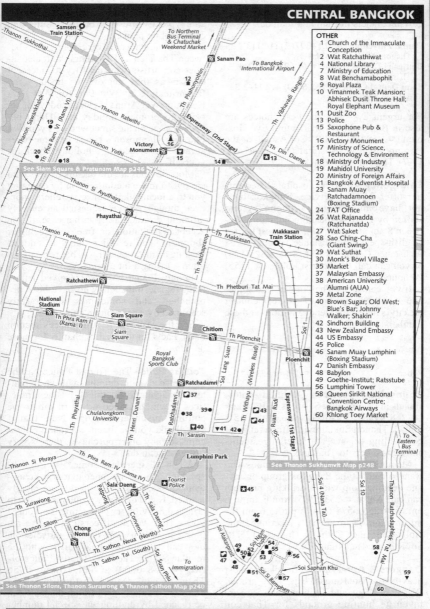

CENTRAL BANGKOK

OTHER
1 Church of the Immaculate Conception
3 Wat Ratchathiwat
4 National Library
7 Ministry of Education
8 Wat Benchamabophit
9 Royal Plaza
10 Vimanmek Teak Mansion; Abhisek Dusit Throne Hall; Royal Elephant Museum
11 Dusit Zoo
13 Police
15 Saxophone Pub & Restaurant
16 Victory Monument
17 Ministry of Science, Technology & Environment
18 Ministry of Industry
19 Mahidol University
20 Ministry of Foreign Affairs
21 Bangkok Adventist Hospital
23 Sanam Muay Ratchadamnoen (Boxing Stadium)
24 TAT Office
26 Wat Rajanadda (Ratchanatda)
27 Wat Saket
28 Sao Ching-Cha (Giant Swing)
29 Wat Suthat
30 Monk's Bowl Village
35 Market
37 Malaysian Embassy
38 American University Alumni (AUA)
39 Metal Zone
40 Brown Sugar; Old West; Blue's Bar; Johnny Walker; Shakin'
42 Sindhorn Building
43 New Zealand Embassy
44 US Embassy
45 Police
46 Sanam Muay Lumphini (Boxing Stadium)
47 Danish Embassy
48 Babylon
49 Goethe-Institut; Ratsstube
56 Lumphini Tower
58 Queen Sirikit National Convention Centre; Bangkok Airways
60 Khlong Toey Market

Should you need urgent dental care, suggested contacts in Bangkok include:

Dental Polyclinic (☎ 314 4397) 2111/2113 Thanon Phetburi Tat Mai
Benjasiri Dental House (☎ 662 2402) 593/6 Thanon Sukhumvit
Siam Dental Clinic (☎ 252 6660) 412/11–2 Soi 6, Siam Square

For urgent eye care, the best choices are also in Bangkok. Try the Rutnin Eye Hospital (☎ 258 0442), 80/1 Soi Asoke, or the Pirompesuy Eye Hospital (☎ 252 4141), 117/1 Thanon Phayathai.

Emergency All of the hospitals listed earlier offer 24-hour service. Bangkok does not have an emergency phone system staffed by English-speaking operators. Between 8 am and midnight, your best bet for English-speaking assistance is the Tourist Assistance Centre (☎ 281 5051, 282 8129) or you can call the Tourist Police (☎ 1155) 24 hours a day.

If you can speak Thai, or can find someone to call on your behalf, you can contact the city's main emergency facilities at these numbers:

Ambulance	☎ 255 1133–6
Fire	☎ 199
Police	☎ 191 or 123

Counselling Services Qualified professionals at Community Services of Bangkok (☎ 258 4998, e csb@loxinfo.co.th), 15/1 Soi 33, Thanon Sukhumvit, offer a range of counselling services to foreign residents and newcomers to Thailand.

Members of Alcoholics Anonymous who want to contact the Bangkok group or anyone needing help with a drinking problem can call AA at ☎ 253 6305 from 6 am to 6 pm or ☎ 256 6578 from 6 pm to 6 am for information. There are daily meetings at the Holy Redeemer Catholic Church, 123/19 Soi Ruamrudee (Ruam Rudi).

Dangers & Annoyances Bangkok's most heavily touristed areas, especially around Wat Phra Kaew and Thanon Khao San, are favourite hunting grounds for Thai con artists of every ilk. They also tend to hang out near Soi Kasem San 1 and Soi Kasem San 2, opposite Mahboonkrong shopping centre and near Jim Thompson's House, and typically dress in business suits and carry mobile phones.

The Chao Phraya River Express piers between Tha Tien and Tha Phra Athit also attract con artists who may try to intercept tourists as they get off the boats – the favourite line is 'Wat Pho (or Wat Phra Kaew, or Wat Arun) is closed today for repairs, government holiday etc'. Don't believe anyone on the street who tells you Wat Pho, Jim Thompson's House or some other attraction is closed for a holiday; check for yourself.

More obvious are the túk-túk drivers who are out to make a commission by dragging you to a local silk, tailor or jewellery shop, even though you've requested an entirely different destination. In either case, if you accept an invitation for 'free' sightseeing or shopping, you're quite likely to end up wasting an afternoon or – as happens all too often – losing a lot of money.

Lonely Planet has also received letters from female travellers who have been approached and sometimes successfully scammed by Thai women con artists.

See the Dangers & Annoyances section in the Facts for the Visitor chapter for more details.

Tourist Police The Tourist Police can be quite effective in dealing with such matters, particularly 'unethical' business practices – which sometimes turn out to be cultural misunderstandings. Note that if you think you've been overcharged for gems (or any other purchase), there's very little they can do.

All in all there are some 500 English-speaking officers stationed in tourist areas – their kiosks, cars and uniforms are clearly marked. If you have any problems related to criminal activity, try contacting the Tourist Police first. When officers can't solve the problem, or if it's out of their jurisdiction, they can act as a bilingual liaison with the regular police. The head Tourist Police office (☎ 678 6800) at TPI Tower, 26/56 Thanon Chan, deals with tourism-related crime, particularly gem fraud; the staff can be reached by dialling the special number ☎ 1155. The Tourist Police also have a branch at the TAT compound on Thanon Ratchadamnoen Nok.

KO RATANAKOSIN AREA
Wat Phra Kaew & Grand Palace
วัดพระแก้ว/พระบรมมหาราชวัง

Also called the Temple of the Emerald Buddha (official name is Wat Phra Si Ratana Satsadaram), this wát adjoins the Grand Palace on common ground that was consecrated in 1782, the first year of Bangkok rule. The 945,000-sq-metre grounds encompass more than 100 buildings that represent 200 years of royal history and architectural experimentation. Most of the architecture, royal or sacred, can be classified Ratanakosin or old Bangkok style, with lots of minor variation.

The wát structures are extremely colourful, comprising gleaming, gilded *chedi* (stupas), polished orange and green roof tiles, mosaic-encrusted pillars and rich marble pediments. Extensive murals depicting scenes from the *Ramakian* (the Thai version of the Indian epic *Ramayana*) line the inside walls of the compound. Originally painted during Rama I's reign (1782–1809), the murals have undergone several restorations, including a major one finished in time for the 1982 Bangkok/Chakri dynasty bicentennial. The murals illustrate the epic in its entirety, beginning at the north gate and moving clockwise around the compound.

Except for an anteroom here and there, the Grand Palace (Phra Borom Maharatchawang) is today used by the king for only certain ceremonial occasions such as Coronation Day (his current residence is Chitlada Palace in the northern part of the city), and is closed to the public. The exteriors of the four buildings are worth a swift perusal for their royal bombast.

Borombhiman Hall (eastern end), a French-inspired structure that served as a residence for Rama VI, is occasionally used to house visiting foreign dignitaries. In April 1981 General San Chitpatima used it as headquarters for an attempted coup. Next west is **Amarindra Hall**, originally a hall of justice but used today for coronation ceremonies.

Largest of the palace buildings is the **Chakri Mahaprasat**, literally 'Great Hall of Chakri' but usually translated as 'Grand Palace Hall'. Built in 1882 by British architects using Thai labour, the exterior shows a peculiar blend of Italian Renaissance and traditional Thai architecture. This is a style often referred to as *fàràng sài chá-daa* (west-

Travels of the Emerald Buddha

The so-called Emerald Buddha, or Phra Kaew Morakot, is not emerald but probably made of jasper quartz or perhaps nephrite jade. It stands 60cm to 75cm high, depending on how it is measured. It's not known for certain where the image originated or who sculpted it, but it first appeared on record in 15th-century Chiang Rai. It is said to have been covered with plaster and gold leaf and placed in Chiang Rai's own Wat Phra Kaew (literally Temple of the Jewel Image). The image supposedly lost its plaster covering in a fall. It next appeared in Lampang where it enjoyed a 32-year stay (again at a Wat Phra Kaew) until it was brought to Wat Chedi Luang in Chiang Mai.

In the mid-16th century Laotian invaders took the image from Chiang Mai to Luang Prabang in Laos. Later it was moved to Wiang Chan (Vientiane). When Thailand's King Taksin waged war against Laos 200 years later, the image was taken back to the Thai capital of Thonburi by General Chakri, who later succeeded Taksin as Rama I, the founder of the Chakri dynasty.

Rama I had the Emerald Buddha moved to the new Thai capital in Bangkok and had two royal robes made for it, one to be worn in the hot season and one for the rainy season. Rama III added another to the wardrobe, to be worn in the cool season. The three robes are still solemnly changed at the beginning of each season by the king himself. The huge *bòt* (central sanctuary) at Wat Phra Kaew in which it is displayed was built expressly for the purpose of housing the diminutive image.

erner in a Thai crown) because each wing is topped by a *mondòp*, a heavily ornamented spire representing a Thai adaptation of the Hindu *mandapa* (shrine). The tallest of the mondòp, in the centre, contains the ashes of Chakri kings; the flanking mondòp enshrine the ashes of Chakri princes. Thai kings traditionally housed their huge harems in the mahaprasat's inner palace area, which was guarded by combat-trained female sentries.

Ratanakosin Temples & River Walking Tour

This walk covers the area of Ko Ratanakosin (Ratanakosin Island), which rests in a bend of the river in the middle of Bangkok and contains some of the city's most historic architecture and prestigious universities. The river bank in this area is dotted with piers and markets, worthwhile attractions in themselves. Despite its name, Ko Ratanakosin is not an island at all, though in the days when Bangkok was known as the 'Venice of the East', Khlong Banglamphu and Khlong Ong Ang – two lengthy adjoining canals that run parallel to the river to the east – were probably large enough for the area to seem like an island.

This circular walk (one to three hours depending on your pace) begins at **Lak Meuang**. At the intersection of Thanon Ratchadamnoen Nai and Thanon Lak Meuang, opposite the southern end of Sanam Luang, the shrine can be reached by taxi, by air-con bus Nos 7 and 39, by ordinary bus Nos 2, 44, 47 and 60 or on foot if you're already in the Royal Hotel area. (If the Chao Phraya River Express is more convenient, you can start this walk from Tha Tien.) By tradition, every city in Thailand must have a foundation stone that embodies the city spirit (*phĭi meuang*) and from which intercity distances are measured. This is Bangkok's most important site of animistic worship; believers throng the area day and night.

From Lak Meuang, walk south across Thanon Lak Meuang and along Thanon Sanamchai with the Grand Palace wall to your right until you come to Thanon Chetuphon on the right (the second street after the palace wall ends, about 500m from Lak Meuang). Turn right onto Thanon Chetuphon and enter **Wat Pho** through the second portico. Officially named Wat Phra Chetuphon, this is Bangkok's oldest temple and is famous for its reclining Buddha and massage school, the oldest in Thailand. Look around, then exit through the same door and turn right onto Thanon Chetuphon, heading towards the river.

Thanon Chetuphon ends at Thanon Maharat after 100m or so; turn right at Maharat and stroll north, passing the **market** area on your left. At the northern end of this block, Thanon Maharat crosses Thanon Thai Wang. On the south-western corner is an older branch of the **Bangkok Bank**; turn left on Thai Wang to glimpse a row of rare Ratanakosin-era shophouses. If you continue along Thanon Thai Wang to the river you'll arrive at **Tha Tien**, one of the pier stops for the Chao Phraya River Express. From an adjacent pier you can catch one of the ferries across the Chao Phraya to **Wat Arun**, which features a striking *prang* – a tall Hindu/Khmer-style pagoda.

Stroll back along Thanon Thai Wang to Thanon Maharat and turn left. On the left along Thanon Maharat are two government buildings serving as headquarters for the departments of internal trade and public welfare. On the right are the Grand Palace walls. Two air-con city buses, Nos 8 and 12, stop along this stretch of Maharat – something to keep in mind when you've had enough walking. About 500m from the Thanon Thai Wang intersection, Thanon Maharat crosses Thanon Na Phra Lan; turn left to reach **Tha Chang**, another express boat stop.

The entrance to the **Grand Palace** and **Wat Phra Kaew** is on the right (southern) side of Thanon Na Phra Lan, less than 100m from Thanon Maharat. The Grand Palace has been supplanted by Chitlada Palace as the primary residence of the royal family, but it is still used for ceremonial occasions. Wat Phra Kaew is a gleaming example of Bangkok temple architecture at its most baroque. You must be suitably attired to enter the palace grounds. Temple staff can provide wraparound sarongs for bare legs.

After wandering around the palace and temple grounds, exit via the same doorway and turn left towards the river again. On the right-hand side you'll pass the entrance to **Silpakorn University**, Thailand's premier university for fine arts studies. Originally founded as the School of Fine Arts by Italian artist Corrado Feroci, the university campus includes part of an old palace built for Rama I. A small bookshop inside the gate to the left offers a number of

English-language books on Thai art. At Thanon Maharat, turn right (past the Siam City Bank on the corner) and almost immediately you'll see vendor tables along the street. Here they're selling cheap amulets representing various Hindu and Buddhist deities. If you're interested in religious amulets, you can get better-quality ones a bit farther north along Thanon Maharat in the large **amulet market** between the road and the river. Opposite the amulet market on Thanon Maharat is **Wat Mahathat**, another of Bangkok's older temples and the headquarters for Thailand's Mahanikai sect, the country's largest monastic sect.

If you're hungry by now, this is an excellent place to eat. Head back along Thanon Maharat from the amulet market just a few metres and turn right at Trok Thawiphon (the Roman-script sign reads 'Thawephọn'). This alley leads to **Tha Maharat**, yet another express-boat stop; on either side of the pier is a riverside restaurant – Maharat to the left and Lan Theh (no Roman-script sign) to the right. Although the food at both is quite adequate, most local residents head past the Lan Theh and into a warren of smaller restaurants and food vendors along the river. The food here is very good and extremely inexpensive – to order, all you'll need is a pointing index finger.

Start walking north again along Maharat past the amulet market and Wat Mahathat to Thanon Phra Chan, around 80m from Trok Thawiphon. Turn left to reach Tha Phra Chan if you want to catch an express boat north or south along the river, or turn right to reach Sanam Luang, the end of the tour. If you take the latter route, you'll pass **Thammasat University** on the left. Thammasat is known for its law and political science faculties; it was also the site of the bloody October 1976 demonstrations, when hundreds of Thai students were killed or wounded by the military.

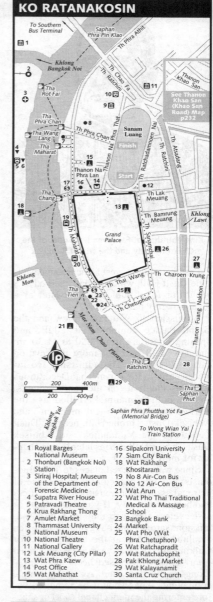

KO RATANAKOSIN

1 Royal Barges National Museum
2 Thonburi (Bangkok Noi) Station
3 Siriraj Hospital; Museum of the Department of Forensic Medicine
4 Supatra River House
5 Patravadi Theatre
6 Krua Rakhang Thong
7 Amulet Market
8 Thammasat University
9 National Museum
10 National Theatre
11 National Gallery
12 Lak Meuang (City Pillar)
13 Wat Phra Kaew
14 Post Office
15 Wat Mahathat
16 Silpakorn University
17 Siam City Bank
18 Wat Rakhang Khositaram
19 No 8 Air-Con Bus
20 No 12 Air-Con Bus
21 Wat Arun
22 Wat Pho Thai Traditional Medical & Massage School
23 Bangkok Bank
24 Market
25 Wat Pho (Wat Phra Chetuphon)
26 Wat Ratchapradit
27 Wat Ratchabophit
28 Pak Khlong Market
29 Wat Kalayanamit
30 Santa Cruz Church

King Phuttha Yot Fa, Rama I, founder of the Chakri dynasty and the city of Bangkok

Last from east to west is the Ratanakosin-style **Dusit Hall**, which initially served as a venue for royal audiences and later as a royal funerary hall.

Admission to Wat Phra Kaew and the Grand Palace compound is 200B, and opening hours are from 8.30 to 11.30 am and 1 to 3.30 pm. For more information call ☎ 224 1833. The admission fee includes entry to the Royal Thai Decorations & Coins Pavilion (on the same grounds) and to both Vimanmek (billed as 'the world's largest golden-teak mansion') and Abhisek Dusit Throne Hall, near the Dusit Zoo. (See the Vimanmek and Abhisek Dusit Throne Hall entries later in this chapter for more details.)

Since wát are sacred places to Thai Buddhists, this one particularly so because of its royal associations, visitors should dress and behave decently. If you wear shorts or a sleeveless shirt you may be refused admission; sarongs and baggy pants are often available on loan at the entry area. For walking in the courtyard areas you must wear shoes with closed heels and toes – thongs aren't permitted. As in any temple compound, shoes should be removed before entering the main chapel *(bòt)* or sanctuaries *(wíhǎan)*.

The most economical way of reaching Wat Phra Kaew and the Grand Palace is by air-con bus No 8 or 12. You can also take the Chao Phraya River Express, disembarking at Tha Chang.

Wat Pho
วัดโพธิ์(วัดพระเชตุพน)

A long list of superlatives for this one: the oldest and largest wát in Bangkok, it features the largest reclining Buddha and the largest collection of Buddha images in Thailand, and was the earliest centre for public education. As a temple site Wat Pho (Wat Phra Chetuphon) dates back to the 16th century, but its current history really begins in 1781 with the complete rebuilding of the original monastery.

The narrow Thanon Chetuphon divides the grounds in two, with each section surrounded by huge whitewashed walls. The most interesting part is the northern compound, which includes a very large bòt enclosed by a gallery of Buddha images and four wíhǎan, four large chedis commemorating the first three Chakri kings (Rama III has two chedis), 91 smaller chedis, an old *Tripitaka* (Buddhist scriptures) library, a sermon hall, a large wíhǎan that houses the reclining Buddha and a school building for classes in Abhidhamma (Buddhist philosophy), plus several less important structures. The temple is currently undergoing renovations.

Wat Pho is the national headquarters for the teaching and preservation of traditional Thai medicine, including Thai massage. A **massage school** convenes in the afternoons at the eastern end of the compound; a massage session costs 200B per hour (300B with herbs), 120B for half an hour. You can also study massage here in seven- to 10-day courses. Other courses include Thai herbal therapy and traditional Thai medicine. A full course of all three takes one to three years to complete; graduation is by exam.

The tremendous **reclining Buddha**, 46m long and 15m high, illustrates the passing of the Buddha into final nirvana (ie, the Buddha's passing away). The figure is modelled out of plaster around a brick core and finished in gold leaf. Mother-of-pearl inlay ornaments the eyes and feet, the feet displaying 108 different auspicious *láksànà* (characteristics of a Buddha). The images on display in the four wíhǎan surrounding the main bòt are interesting. Particularly beautiful are the Phra Chinnarat and Phra Chinnachai Buddhas, in the west and south chapels, both from Sukhothai. The galleries extending between the four chapels feature no less than 394 gilded Buddha images. Rama I's remains are interred in the base of the presiding Buddha image in the bòt.

The temple rubbings for sale at Wat Pho and elsewhere in Thailand come from the 152 *Ramakian* reliefs, carved in marble and obtained from the ruins of Ayuthaya, which line the base of the large bòt. The rubbings are no longer taken directly from the panels but are rubbed from cement casts of the panels made years ago.

You may hire English-, French-, German- or Japanese-speaking guides for 150B for one visitor, 200B for two and 300B for three. Also on the premises are a few astrologers and palmists.

The temple is open to the public from 8 am to 5 pm daily; admission is 20B. Air-con bus Nos 8, 12 and 44 stop near Wat Pho. The nearest Chao Phraya River Express pier is Tha Tien. Call ☎ 221 9911 for more information.

Wat Mahathat
วัดมหาธาตุ

Founded in the 1700s, Wat Mahathat is a national centre for the Mahanikai monastic sect and houses one of Bangkok's two Buddhist universities, Mahathat Rajavidyalaya. The university is the most important place of Buddhist learning in mainland South-East Asia today.

Wat Mahathat and the surrounding area have developed into an informal Thai cultural centre of sorts, though this may not be obvious at first glance. A daily **open-air market** features traditional Thai herbal medicine, and out on the street you'll find a string of shops selling herbal cures and offering Thai massage. On weekends, a large produce market held on the temple grounds brings people from all over Bangkok and beyond. Opposite the main entrance on the other side of Thanon Maharat is a large religious **amulet market**.

The monastery's International Buddhist Meditation Centre offers **meditation instruction** in English on the second Saturday of every month from 2 to 6 pm in the Dhamma Vicaya Hall. Those interested in more intensive instruction should contact the monks in Section 5 of the temple.

The temple complex is officially open to visitors from 9 am to 5 pm daily. Admission is free.

Wat Mahathat is right across the street from Wat Phra Kaew, on the western side of Sanam Luang. Air-con bus Nos 8 and 12 both pass by it, and the nearest Chao Phraya River Express pier is Tha Maharat.

Wat Arun
วัดอรุณฯ

The striking Temple of Dawn, named after the Indian god of dawn, Aruna, appears in all the tourist brochures and is located on the Thonburi side of the Mae Nam Chao Phraya. The present wát was built on the site of 17th-century Wat Jaeng, which served as the palace and royal temple of King Taksin when Thonburi was the Thai capital; hence, it was the last home of the Emerald Buddha before Rama I brought it across the river to Wat Phra Kaew.

The 82m *prang* (Khmer-style tower) was constructed during the first half of the 19th century by Rama II and Rama III. The unique design elongates the typical Khmer prang into a distinctly Thai shape. Its brick core has a plaster covering embedded with a mosaic of broken, multihued Chinese porcelain, a common temple ornamentation in the early Ratanakosin period when Chinese ships calling at Bangkok used tonnes of old porcelain as ballast. Steep stairs reach a lookout point about halfway up the prang from where there are fine views of Thonburi and the river. During certain festivals, hundreds of lights illuminate the outline of the prang at night.

Also worth a look is the interior of the bòt. The main Buddha image is said to have been designed by Rama II himself. The murals date to the reign of Rama V; particularly impressive is one that depicts Prince Siddhartha encountering examples of birth, old age, sickness and death outside his palace walls, an experience that led him to abandon the worldly life. The ashes of Rama II are interred in the base of the bòt's presiding Buddha image.

The temple looks more impressive from the river than it does up close, though the peaceful wát grounds make a very nice retreat from the hustle and bustle of Bangkok. Between the prang and the ferry pier is a huge sacred banyan tree.

Wat Arun is open 8.30 am to 5.30 pm daily; admission is 10B. Call ☎ 466 3167 for more information. To reach Wat Arun from the Bangkok side, catch a cross-river ferry from Tha Tien at Thanon Thai Wang. Crossings are frequent and cost only 2B.

Lak Meuang (City Pillar)
ศาลหลักเมือง

The City Pillar is across the street from the eastern wall of Wat Phra Kaew, at the southern end of Sanam Luang. This shrine encloses a wooden pillar erected by Rama I in 1782 to represent the founding of the new Bangkok capital city, and a shorter companion was added under Rama IV. Rama V built the sheltering pavilion.

The taller pillar originated from a *chaiyápréuk (Cassia laburnum)* or 'tree of victory' cut down in effigy following the Burmese sacking of Ayuthaya in 1767. Through a series of Buddhist-animist rituals, the felling of the tree empowered the Thais to defeat the Burmese in a series of battles. Thus it was considered an especially talismanic choice to mark the founding of the new royal capital. Two metres of the pillar's 4.7m total length are buried in the ground.

The spirit of the pillar – Phra Sayam Thewathirat (Venerable Siam Deity of the State) – is considered the city's guardian deity and receives the daily supplications of countless worshippers, some of whom commission classical Thai dancers to perform *lákhon kâe bon* (propitiatory dances) at the shrine between 11 am and 4 pm daily. The offerings include severed pigs' heads with sticks of incense sprouting from their foreheads.

Sanam Luang
สนามหลวง

Sanam Luang (Royal Field), just north of Wat Phra Kaew, is the traditional site for royal cremations, and for the annual Ploughing Ceremony in which the king officially initiates the rice-growing season. The most recent ceremonial cremation took place here in March 1996, when the king presided over funeral rites for his mother. Before that the most recent Sanam Luang cremations were held, without official sanction, in 1976 for Thai students killed in the demonstrations of that year. A statue of Mae Thorani, the earth goddess (borrowed from Hindu mythology's Dharani), stands in a white pavilion at the northern end of the field. Erected in the late 19th century by King Chulalongkorn, the statue was originally attached to a well that provided drinking water to the public.

Before 1982, Bangkok's famous Weekend Market was regularly held at Sanam Luang (it's now at Chatuchak Park). Nowadays the large field is most popularly used as a picnic and recreational area. A large kite competition is held here during the kite-flying season.

National Museum
พิพิธภัณฑสถานแห่งชาติ

On Thanon Na Phra That, the western side of Sanam Luang, the National Museum is the largest museum in South-East Asia and an excellent place to learn about Thai art. All periods and styles are represented from Dvaravati to Ratanakosin, and English-language literature is available. Room 23 contains a well-maintained collection of traditional musical instruments from Thailand, Laos, Cambodia and Indonesia. Other permanent exhibits include ceramics, clothing and textiles, woodcarving, royal regalia and weaponry.

The museum buildings were built in 1782 as the palace of Rama I's viceroy, Prince Wang Na. Rama V turned it into a museum in 1884.

In addition to the exhibition halls, there is the restored **Buddhaisawan (Phutthaisawan) Chapel.** Inside the chapel (built in 1795) are some well-preserved original murals and one of the country's most revered Buddha images, Phra Phut Sihing. Legend says the image came from Sri Lanka, but art historians attribute it to 13th-century Sukhothai.

Free English-language tours of the museum are given by National Museum volunteers on Wednesday (Buddhism) and Thursday (Thai art, religion and culture), starting from the ticket pavilion at 9.30 am. These guided tours are excellent. The tours are also conducted in German (Thursday), French (Wednesday) and Japanese (Wednesday). For more information on the tours, contact the volunteers at ☎ 215 8173. For general information call ☎ 224 1370. The museum is open 9 am to 4 pm Wednesday to Sunday; admission is 40B.

Royal Barges National Museum
เรือพระที่นั่ง

The royal barges are long, fantastically ornamented boats used in ceremonial processions on the river. The largest is 50m long and requires a rowing crew of 50 men, plus seven umbrella bearers, two helmsmen and two navigators, as well as a flagman, rhythm-keeper and chanter.

The barges are kept in sheds on the Thonburi side of the river. The sheds are next to Khlong Bangkok Noi, near Saphan Phra Pin Klao (Phra Pin Klao Bridge). *Suphannahong,* the king's personal barge, is the most important of the boats. Made from a single piece of timber, it's the largest dugout in the world. The name means 'Golden Swan', and a huge swan head has been carved into the bow of the barge. Lesser barges feature bows carved into other Hindu-Buddhist mythological shapes such as the naga (mythical sea serpent) and the garuda (Vishnu's bird mount).

One of the best times to see the fleet in action on the river is during the royal *kàthǐn* ceremony at the end of *phansǎa* (the Buddhist Rains Retreat, ending with an October or November full moon) when new robes are offered to the monastic contingent.

The barge shed is open 8.30 am to 4.30 pm daily (except 31 December, 1 January and 12 to 14 April). Admission is 50B, but you must pay an additional 100B if you want to take photos. To get there, take bus No 19 or 91 or take a ferry to Tha Rot Fai, then walk down the street parallel to the railway tracks until you come to a bridge over the *khlawng* (canal; also written khlong). Follow the bridge to a labyrinth of concrete walkways that pass through some poor housing areas and eventually lead to the barge sheds. You can also get there by taking a khlawng taxi (5B) up the canal and getting off near the bridge. For further information, call ☎ 424 0004.

CENTRAL BANGKOK AREA
Wat Benchamabophit
วัดเบญจมบพิตร (วัดเบญฯ)

This wát of white Carrara marble (hence its tourist name, 'Marble Temple') was built in the late 19th century under Chulalongkorn (Rama V). The large cruciform bòt is a prime example of modern Thai wát architecture.

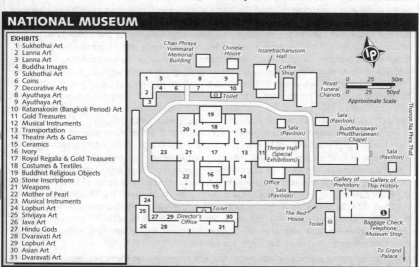

NATIONAL MUSEUM

EXHIBITS
1 Sukhothai Art
2 Lanna Art
3 Lanna Art
4 Buddha Images
5 Sukhothai Art
6 Coins
7 Decorative Arts
8 Ayuthaya Art
9 Ayuthaya Art
10 Ratanakosin (Bangkok Period) Art
11 Gold Treasures
12 Musical Instruments
13 Transportation
14 Theatre Arts & Games
15 Ceramics
16 Ivory
17 Royal Regalia & Gold Treasures
18 Costumes & Textiles
19 Buddhist Religious Objects
20 Stone Inscriptions
21 Weapons
22 Mother of Pearl
23 Musical Instruments
24 Lopburi Art
25 Srivijaya Art
26 Java Art
27 Hindu Gods
28 Dvaravati Art
29 Lopburi Art
30 Asian Art
31 Dvaravati Art

BANGKOK

The base of the central Buddha image, a copy of Phitsanulok's Phra Phuttha Chinnarat, contains the ashes of Rama V. The courtyard behind the bòt exhibits 53 Buddha images (33 originals and 20 copies) representing famous figures and styles from all over Thailand and other Buddhist countries – an education in itself if you are interested in Buddhist iconography.

Wat Ben, as it is called, is on the corner of Thanon Si Ayuthaya and Thanon Phra Ram V, diagonally opposite Chitlada Palace. It's open 8 am to 5.30 pm daily and admission is 20B. Bus Nos 3 (air-con), 5 and 72 stop nearby.

Wat Saket
วัดสระเกศ

Wat Saket is an undistinguished temple except for the Golden Mountain (Phu Khao Thong) on the western side of the grounds, which provides a good view out over Bangkok's rooftops. This artificial hill was

---

Rama V Cult

Since 1991 a new spirit cult has swept the Thai public, involving the veneration of Rama V (reigned 1868–1910; also known as King Chulalongkorn or, to the Thais, Phra Chula Chom Klao). The cult is particularly strong in Bangkok and other large urban centres, as its members tend to be middle-class and nouveau riche Thais with careers in commerce or the professions.

In Bangkok the most visible devotional activities are focused on a bronze statue of Rama V standing in Royal Plaza, opposite the south-eastern corner of the Vimanmek and Abihisek throne hall compound from where the venerated king once ruled the kingdom as absolute monarch. Although originally intended as mere historical commemoration, the statue has quite literally become a religious shrine, where every Tuesday evening thousands of Bangkok residents come to offer candles, flowers (predominantly pink roses), incense and bottles of whisky to the newly ordained demigod. Worship of the statue begins at around 9 pm and continues until early in the morning.

All over Thailand Rama V portraits are selling briskly. Some devotees place the portraits at home altars, while others wear tiny, coloured porcelain likenesses of the king on gold chains around their necks in place of the usual Buddhist amulet. In some social circles Rama V amulets are now more common than any other phrá phim (amulet).

No single event occurred to ignite the Rama V movement; rather, its growth can be traced to a series of events beginning with the 1991 military coup – which caused the intelligentsia to once again lose faith in the constitutional monarchy – on top of the 1990–92 economic recession. Along with the worsening traffic, declining economy and a host of other problems, these events brought about an unfocused, general mistrust of modern politics, technology and affluence among many Thais, who began looking for a new spiritual outlet with some historical relevancy. They seized on Rama V, who without the help of a parliament or the military had brought Thai nationalism to the fore while fending off European colonisation. He is also considered a champion of the common person for his abolition of slavery and corvee (the requirement that every citizen be available for state labour when called).

Ironically few Rama V cultists appear to acknowledge that the much revered Rama V conceded substantial Thai territory to French Indochina and British Malaya during his reign – for a total loss of land greater than any Thai king had allowed since before the Sukhothai era. Rama V also deserves more of the blame for 'Westernisation' than any other single monarch. He was the first king to travel to Europe, which he did in 1897 and again in 1907. After seeing Europeans eating with forks, knives and spoons, he discouraged the Thai tradition of taking food with the hands; he also introduced chairs to the kingdom (before his reign Thais sat on the floor or on floor cushions). Following one European visit he asked his number one concubine to grow her hair long after the European fashion; by custom Thai women had kept their hair cropped short since the Ayuthaya period.

created when a large chedi under construction by Rama III collapsed because the soft soil beneath would not support it. The resulting mud-and-brick hill was left to sprout weeds until Rama IV built a small chedi on its crest.

Frank Vincent, a well-travelled American writer, describes his 1871 ascent in *The Land of the White Elephant:*

From the summit...may be obtained a fine view of the city of Bangkok and its surroundings; though this is hardly a correct statement, for you see very few of the dwelling-houses of the city; here and there a wát, the river with its shipping, the palace of the King, and a waving sea of cocoa-nut and betel-nut palms, is about all that distinctly appears. The general appearance of Bangkok is that of a large, primitive village, situated in and mostly concealed by a virgin forest of almost impenetrable density.

King Chulalongkorn later added to the structure and housed a Buddha relic from India (given to him by the British government) in the chedi.

The concrete walls were added during WWII to prevent the hill from eroding. Every year in November there is a big festival on the grounds of Wat Saket, which includes a candle-lit procession up the Golden Mount.

Admission to Wat Saket is free except for the final approach to the summit of the Golden Mount, which costs 10B. The temple is on Thanon Worachak within walking distance of the Democracy Monument; aircon bus Nos 11 and 12 pass nearby. Opening hours are 8 am to 5 pm. Call ☎ 223 4561 for more information.

Wat Rajanadda
วัดราชนัดดา

Across Thanon Mahachai from Wat Saket, Wat Rajanadda (Ratchanatda) dates from the mid-19th century. It was built under Rama III and is an unusual specimen, possibly influenced by Burmese models.

The wát has a well-known **market** selling Buddhist amulets or magic charms (*phrá phim*) in all sizes, shapes and styles. The amulets not only feature images of the Buddha, but also famous Thai monks and Indian deities. Full Buddha images are also for sale. Wat Rajanadda is an expensive place to purchase a charm, but a good place to look.

Democracy Monument
อนุสาวรีย์ประชาธิปไตย

This large, Art Deco monument – four dismembered, highly stylised angel wings arranged in a circle at the intersection of Thanon Ratchadamnoen, Thanon Din So and Thanon Prachatipatai – was erected in 1932 to commemorate Thailand's momentous transformation from absolute to constitutional monarchy. Italian artist Corrado Feroci designed the monument and buried 75 cannonballs in its base to signify the year BE 2475 (AD 1932). Before immigrating to Thailand to become the nation's 'father of modern art', Feroci designed monuments for Italian dictator Benito Mussolini.

In recent years 'The Demo' has become a favourite spot for public demonstrations, most notably during the anti-military, pro-democratic protests of 1992.

Vimanmek Teak Mansion
พระที่นั่งวิมานเมฆ

Originally constructed on Ko Si Chang in 1868 and moved to the present site in the Chitlada Palace grounds in 1910, this beautiful L-shaped, three-storey mansion contains 81 rooms, halls and anterooms, and is said to be the world's largest golden teak building. The staircases, octagonal rooms and lattice walls are nothing short of magnificent, in spite of which the mansion retains a surprisingly serene and intimate atmosphere.

Vimanmek (Phra Thi Nang Wimanmek) was the first permanent building on the Chitlada Palace grounds. It served as Rama V's residence in the early 1900s, was closed in 1935 and reopened in 1982 for the Ratanakosin bicentennial. The interior of the mansion contains various personal effects of the king, and a treasure trove of early Ratanakosin art objects and antiques.

English-language tours leave every half-hour between 9.30 am and 3 pm. The tours cover around 30 rooms and last an hour. Smaller adjacent buildings display historic photography documenting the Chakri dynasty. Traditional Thai classical and folk dances are performed at 10.30 am and 2 pm in a pavilion off the canal side of the mansion.

Vimanmek is open 9.30 am to 4 pm daily; admission is 50B for adults, 20B for children. It's free if you've already been to the Grand Palace and Wat Phra Kaew and kept the entry ticket for Vimanmek and Abhisek Dusit Throne Hall. As this is royal property, visitors wearing shorts or sleeveless shirts will be refused entry. Call ☎ 628 6300 for further information.

Vimanmek and Abhisek lie towards the northern end of the Chitlada Palace grounds, off Thanon U-Thong Nai (between Thanon Si Ayuthaya and Thanon Ratwithi), across from the western side of the Dusit Zoo. Air-con bus No 3 (Thanon Si Ayuthaya) or air-con bus No 10 (Thanon Ratwithi) will drop you nearby.

Abhisek Dusit Throne Hall
พระที่นั่งอภิเศกดุสิต

This hall is a smaller wood and brick-and-stucco structure completed in 1904 for King Rama V. Typical of the finer architecture of the era, the Victorian-influenced gingerbread and Moorish porticoes blend to create a striking and distinctly Thai exterior. The hall now houses an excellent display of regional handiwork crafted by members of the Promotion of Supplementary Occupations & Related Techniques (SUPPORT) foundation, an organisation sponsored by Queen Sirikit. Among the exhibits are *mát-mìi* cotton and silk, *málaeng tháp* collages (made from metallic, multicoloured beetle wings), damascene and niello ware, and *yaan líphao* basketry.

Abhisek is open from 10 am to 4 pm daily and admission is 50B (or free with a Grand Palace and Wat Phra Kaew ticket). There is a souvenir shop on the premises. As at Wat Phra Kaew and Vimanmek, visitors must be properly dressed. See the Vimanmek Teak Mansion entry for directions to Abhisek Dusit Throne Hall.

Royal Elephant Museum
พิพิธภัณฑ์ช้างต้น

On the same grounds as the Vimanmek Teak Mansion and Abhisek Dusit Throne Hall, two large stables that once housed three 'white' elephants – animals whose auspicious albinism automatically made them crown property – are now a museum.

One of the structures contains photos and artefacts outlining the importance of elephants in Thai history and explaining their various rankings according to physical characteristics. The second stable holds a sculptural representation of a living royal white elephant (now kept at the Chitlada Palace, home to the current Thai king). Draped in royal vestments, the statue is more or less treated as a shrine by the visiting Thai public.

Admission to the Royal Elephant Museum is included in any admission to Vimanmek Teak Mansion and Abhisek Dusit Throne Hall.

Dusit Zoo
สวนสัตว์ดุสิต (เขาดิน)

The collection of animals at Bangkok's 19-hectare Dusit Zoo (Suan Sat Dusit, also called *khǎo din*) includes more than 300 mammals, 200 reptiles and 800 birds, including relatively rare indigenous species such as banteng, gaur, serow and some rhinoceros.

Originally a private botanical garden for Rama V, it was converted to a zoo in 1938 and is now one of the premier zoological facilities in South-East Asia. The shady grounds feature trees labelled in English, Thai and Latin, plus a lake in the centre with paddle boats for hire. There's also a small children's playground.

If nothing else, the zoo is a nice place to get away from the noise of the city and observe how the Thais amuse themselves – mainly by eating. A couple of lakeside restaurants serve a range of good, inexpensive Thai food.

Entry to the zoo is 20B for adults, 5B for children, 10B for those over 60 years; it's open 9 am to 6 pm daily. A small circus performs on weekends and holidays between 11 am and 2 pm. Sunday can be a bit crowded – if you want the zoo mostly to yourself, go on a weekday.

The zoo is in the Dusit district between Chitlada Palace and the National Assembly Hall; the main entrance is off Thanon Ratwithi. Buses that pass the entrance include the ordinary Nos 18 and 28 and the air-con No 10.

Continued on page 215

Over the centuries, traditional Thai artists have taken the principle drama in Theravada Buddhism – the overcoming or taming of human passions via the practice of Buddhism – and made it an integral part of the artistic outcome. Buddhism offers a way to cool the passions through the practice of morality and mental development, an effect that if followed to conclusion will result in the extinguishing of that fire, the defeat of the existential angst produced by the human condition.

In its most simple artistic manifestation, the cooling effect of Buddhism is represented by the lotus, a motif seen throughout Thai Buddhist art, from such obvious examples as the lotus seat upon which Buddha figures sit to the less obvious lotus-bud shapes at the tip of classical Sukhothai chedi.

Less obvious still are the many shapes that combine the lotus bud motif with that of a flame to produce a unitary symbol – a peculiarly Thai innovation that brings human fire into contact with Buddhist cool. You can find this motif everywhere in Thai Buddhist art, and even in much traditional secular art, from the gold-leaf prints dotting lacquered temple walls to the unfurling tails of the *kinnari* (half human, half bird) and other mythical creatures painted into murals or standing in sculpted form on *wíhǎan* porticoes. Even the Buddha's *ùtsànít* – the flame atop the head, representing in this case both the burning out of the passions and enlightenment – in Thai sculpture often features aspects of the lotus bud.

Look closely at some of the most common prints found on traditional cotton *phâasîn,* the sarong once universally worn by Thai women and still worn by some in rural Thailand, and you'll see perhaps dozens of variations on this simple but highly evocative motif.

The juxtaposition and harmonisation of opposites says everything about the human side of Buddhism, the reality in which the coolness of the *padma,* or lotus, is in constant contention with the fire of *raga,* or passion.

Title page: Dazzling detail of the walls of the *bòt* in Wat Phra Kaew, Bangkok (Photograph by Carly Hammond)

Facing page: Phra Phuttha Chinnarat in Phitsanulok, the quintessential Thai Buddha and one of the country's most highly revered Buddhas

Right: The lotus flower inspires many of the forms in Thai art and architecture.

Fire in the Lotus

MANFRED GOTTSCHALK

Architecture: The typically northern-Thai Wat Phra Singh, Chiang Mai

JOE CUMMINGS

Sculpture: Guardian figure relief, Prasat Hin Meuang Tam, Buriram Province

JOHN ELK III

Painting: A scene from the *Ramakian* from the murals at Wat Phra Kaew, Bangkok

Architecture

Considered the highest art form in traditional Thai society, architecture creates and adapts structures within which the people eat, sleep, work and worship. In addition to native Siamese styles of building, within Thailand's borders you'll find splendid examples from historical Khmer, Lao, Mon and northern-Thai traditions. Early texts used by these builders trace the power of all architecture to the Hindu-Buddhist deity Vishvakarman, architect of the universe. Today the power transfers to modern practitioners of the art, who are among the most highly celebrated individuals in Thai society.

Traditional Architecture Traditional home and temple architecture followed relatively strict rules of design that dictated proportion, placement, materials and ornamentation. With the modernisation of Thailand in the 19th and 20th centuries, stylistic codification gave way first to European functionalism and then to stylistic innovation in more recent times.

Traditional Thai residential architecture consists either of single-room wooden houses raised on stilts or more elaborate structures of interlocking rooms with both indoor and shaded outdoor spaces, all supported at least 2m above the ground on stilts. Since originally all Thai settlements were founded along river or canal banks, the use of stilts protected the house and its inhabitants from flooding during the annual monsoon. Even in areas where flooding wasn't common, the Thais continued to raise their houses on stilts until relatively recently, using the space beneath the house as a cooking area, for tethering animals, or for parking their bicycles and motor vehicles. Teak has always been the material of choice for wooden structures, although with the shortage of teak in Thailand nowadays few houses less than 50 years old are constructed of teak.

Rooflines in Central, Northern and Southern Thailand are steeply pitched and often decorated at the corners or along the gables with motifs related to the *naga*, mythical sea serpent, long believed to be a spiritual protector of Thai-speaking cultures throughout Asia. In Southern Thailand bamboo and palm thatch have always been more common building materials than wood, and even today these renewable plant sources remain important construction elements. In certain areas of the South you'll also see thick-walled structures of stuccoed brick, architecture introduced by Chinese, Portuguese, French and British settlements along the Malay Peninsula. In Thailand's four southernmost provinces, it's not unusual to come upon houses of entirely Malay design in which high masonry pediments or foundations, rather than wood stilts, lift the living areas well above the surrounding ground. Roofs of tile or thatch tend to be less steeply pitched, and hipped gables – almost entirely absent in traditional Thai architecture further north – are common in these Malay-influenced buildings.

Temple Architecture Technically speaking, a *wát* (a Thai word, from the Pali-Sanskrit *avasa* or 'dwelling for pupils and ascetics') is a Buddhist compound where men or women can be ordained as monks or nuns. Virtually every village in Thailand has at least one wát, while in towns and cities they're quite numerous. Without an ordination area (designated by *sěmaa,* or stone ordination-precinct markers), a monastic centre where monks or nuns reside is simply a *sămnák sŏng* (Sangha residence). The latter are often established as meditation retreat facilities in forest areas, sometimes in conjunction with larger *wát pàa* (forest monasteries).

The typical wát compound in Thailand will contain at the very least an *uposatha* (*bòt* in central Thai, *sĭm* in northern and north-eastern Thai), a consecrated chapel where monastic ordinations are held, and a *vihara* (*wíhăan* in Thai), where important Buddha images are housed. Classic Thai vihara and uposatha architecture usually involves a steeply pitched roof system tiled in green, gold and red, and often constructed in tiered series of three levels, representing the *tiratana* or triple gems – the Buddha (the Teacher), the Dhamma (Dharma in Sanskrit; the Teaching) and the Sangha (the fellowship of followers of the Teaching). Partial fourth and fifth tiers may also be included to shade porticoes at the front, rear or sides of the building. The front of the wíhăan/bòt, at a minimum, will feature an open veranda; often the veranda will extend around the entire perimeter of the building. Generally speaking wát buildings in North-Eastern Thailand will feature a narrower front profile, while southern Thai temples – perhaps subtly influenced by Malay or Sumatran mosque architecture – will have a broader profile.

Another classic component of temple architecture throughout the country is the presence of one or more *chedi* or *jedi* (from the Pali *cetiya*), also known by the more generic term 'stupa', a solid cone-shaped monument that pays tribute to the enduring stability of Buddhism. Chedi come in a myriad of styles, from simple inverted bowl-shaped designs imported from Sri Lanka to the more elaborate multi-sided chedi of Northern Thailand, heir to the great Thai-Lao kingdoms of Lan Na and Lan Chang (Lan Xang). Many chedi are believed to contain 'relics' (pieces of bone) belonging to the historical Buddha. In North-Eastern Thailand and in Laos such chedi are known as *thâat.* Other structures typically found in wát compounds include one or more *sala* (*săalaa*) or open-sided shelters for community meetings and Dhamma lectures; a number of *kùtì* or monastic quarters; a *hăw trai* or Tripitaka library where Buddhist scriptures are stored; a *hăw klawng* or drum tower (sometimes with a *hăw rákhang* or bell tower); various chedi or stupas (the smaller squarish stupas are *thâat kràdùk* or bone reliquaries, where the ashes of deceased worshippers are interred); plus various ancillary buildings – such as schools or clinics – that differ from wát to wát according to local community needs. Many wát also have a *hăw phĭi wát* or spirit house, for the temple's reigning earth spirit.

A good way to acquaint yourself with these styles is to visit the National Museum in Bangkok, where works from each of the Thai art-style eras (see the boxed text 'Thai Art Styles') are on display. Then, as you travel upcountry and view old monuments and sculpture, you'll know what you're seeing, as well as what to look for.

Historical Parks Since 1981, the Thai government has made the restoration of nine key archaeological sites part of its national economic development plan. As a result, the Fine Arts Department, under the Ministry of Education, has developed nine historical parks *(ùtháyaan pràwàttisàat)*: Ayuthaya Historical Park in Ayuthaya Province, Kamphaeng Phet

Thai Art Styles

The following scheme is the latest one used by Thai art historians to categorise historical styles of Thai art:

Mon Art (formerly Dvaravati, 6th to 11th centuries, and Hariphunchai, 11th to 13th centuries) – Originating in Central, Northern and North-Eastern Thailand, Mon Art is an adaptation of Indian styles, principally Gupta.

Khmer Art (7th to 13th centuries) – Centred in Central and North-Eastern Thailand, this style is characterised by post-classic Khmer styles accompanying the spread of Khmer empires.

Peninsular Art (formerly Srivijaya period) – Centred in Chaiya and Nakhon Si Thammarat, this style exhibits Indian influence in the 3rd to 5th centuries, Mon and local influence in the 5th to 13th centuries and Khmer influence in the 11th to 14th centuries.

Lanna (13th to 15th centuries) – Centred in Chiang Mai, Chiang Rai, Phayao, Lamphun and Lampang, Lanna is influenced by Shan/Burmese and Lao traditions.

Sukhothai (13th to 15th centuries) – Centred in Sukhothai, Kamphaeng Phet and Phitsanulok, this style is unique to Thailand.

Lopburi (10th to 13th centuries) – This central-Thai style is characterised by a mix of Khmer, Pala and local styles.

Suphanburi-Sangkhlaburi (formerly U Thong, 13th to 15th centuries) – This central-Thai style, combining Mon, Khmer and local styles, was a prototype for the later Ayuthaya style.

Ayuthaya A (1350–1488) – This central-Thai style was characterised by Khmer influences which were gradually replaced by revived Sukhothai influences.

Ayuthaya B (1488–1630) – This style had characteristic ornamentation distinctive of the Ayuthaya style, with, for example, crowns and jewels on Buddha images.

Ayuthaya C (1630–1767) – This style is characterised by a baroque stage and then decline.

Ratanakosin (19th century to the present) – This is the Bangkok style which consisted of simpler designs and European influences.

Historical Park in Kamphaeng Phet Province, Muang Singh Historical Park in Kanchanaburi Province, Phanom Rung Historical Park in Buriram Province, Phra Nakhon Khiri Historical Park in Phetchaburi Province, Prasat Hin Phimai Historical Park in Nakhon Ratchasima Province, Si Thep Historical Park in Phetchabun Province, and Sukhothai Historical Park and Si Satchanalai-Chaliang Historical Park in Sukhothai Province.

These parks are administered by the Fine Arts Department to guard against theft and vandalism. The department even managed to get the famous Phra Narai lintel returned to Phanom Rung from the Art Institute of Chicago Museum in 1988. Unesco has declared the ruins at Ayuthaya, Kamphaeng Phet, Si Satchanalai-Chaliang and Sukhothai as World Heritage Sites, which makes them eligible for UN funds and/or expertise in future restoration projects.

Contemporary Architecture Modern Thai architects are among the most daring in South-East Asia, as even a short visit to Bangkok will confirm. Thais began mixing traditional Thai with European forms in the late 19th and early 20th centuries, as exemplified by Bangkok's Vimanmek Teak Mansion, the Author's Wing of the Oriental Hotel, the Chakri Mahaprasat next to Wat Phra Kaew, the Thai-Chinese Chamber of Commerce on Thanon Sathon Tai and any number of older residences and shophouses in Bangkok or provincial capitals throughout Thailand. This style is usually referred to as 'old Bangkok' or 'Ratanakosin'. The recently completed Old Siam Plaza shopping centre, adjacent to Bangkok's Chalermkrung Royal Theatre, is an attempt to revive the old Bangkok school.

In the 1920s and 1930s a simple Thai Deco style emerged, blending European Art Deco with functionalist restraint; surviving examples include the restored Chalermkrung Royal Theatre, the Royal Hotel, Ratchadamnoen Boxing Stadium, Hualamphong station, the main post office building and several buildings along Thanon Ratchadamnoen Klang. According to world Deco expert Carol Rosenstein, Bangkok possesses the richest trove of Art Deco in South-East Asia, surpassing even former colonial capitals such as Hanoi, Jakarta, Kuala Lumpur and Singapore.

Buildings of mixed heritage in the North and North-East exhibit French and English influences, while those in the South typically show Portuguese influence. Shophouses throughout the country, whether 100 years or 100 days old, share the basic Chinese shophouse (hâwng thäew) design where the ground floor is reserved for trading purposes while the upper floors contain offices or residences.

During most of the post-WWII era, the trend in modern Thai architecture – inspired by the European Bauhaus movement – was towards a boring functionalism (the average building looked like a giant egg carton turned on its side). The Thai aesthetic, so vibrant in prewar eras, almost entirely disappeared in this characterless style of architecture.

When Thai architects finally began experimenting again during the building boom of the mid-1980s, the result was hi-tech designs like Sumet Jumsai's famous robot-shaped Bank of Asia on Thanon Sathon Tai in Bangkok. Few people seemed to find the space-age look endearing, but at least it was different. Another trend affixed gaudy Roman and Greek-style columns to rectangular Art Deco boxes in what was almost a parody of Western classical architecture. One of the outcomes of this fashion has been the widespread use of curvilinear balustrade on the balconies of almost every new shophouse, apartment or condominium throughout Thailand, often with visually disruptive results.

More recently, a handful of rebellious architects has begun reincorporating traditional Thai motifs – mixed with updated Western classics – in new buildings. Rangsan Torsuwan, a graduate of MIT (Massachusetts Institute of Technology), introduced the neoclassic (or neo-Thai) style; the best example is the new Grand Hyatt Erawan in Bangkok. Another architect using traditional Thai architecture in modern functions is Pinyo Suwankiri, who has designed a number of government buildings in Bangkok as well as the Cittaphawan Buddhist School in Chonburi.

A good book for those with a general interest in Thai residential design, interior or exterior, is William Warren's *Thai Style* (Asia Books), a coffee-table tome with excellent photography by Luca Invernizzi Tettoni.

Sculpture

On an international scale, Thailand has probably distinguished itself more in sculpture than in any other art form. Although the country hasn't produced any individually world-famous classical or modern sculptors, within the realm of Buddhist art, Thai work is quite well known and well appreciated internationally.

Delicate clay and terracotta engravings found on cave walls and on votive tablets date as far back as the 6th century in Thailand, although if you count the bronze culture of Ban Chiang, sculptural endeavours began at least 4000 years ago.

Historically the most commonly sculpted materials have been wood, stone, ivory, clay and metal. Depending on the material, artisans use a variety of techniques – including carving, modelling, construction and casting – to achieve their designs.

Thailand's most famous sculptural output has been its bronze Buddha images, coveted the world over for their originality and grace. Nowadays historic bronzes have all but disappeared from the art market in Thailand. Most are zealously protected by temples, museums or private collectors.

Painting

As with sculpture, Thai painting traditions were mostly confined to religious art, in which the application of natural pigments to temple walls became the favoured medium. Always instructional in intent, such painted images ranged from the depiction of the *jataka* (stories of the Buddha's past lives) and scenes from the Indian Hindu epic *Ramayana,* to elaborate scenes detailing daily life in Thailand.

Lacking the durability of other art forms, pre-20th century religious painting is limited to very few surviving examples. However the study and application of mural painting techniques have been kept very much alive, and modern mural projects are undertaken practically every day of the year, somewhere within the country. Influenced by international styles, a uniquely Thai movement in secular painting is also flourishing.

Traditional Painting Except for prehistoric and historic cave or rock-wall murals found throughout the country, not much formal painting predating the 18th century exists in Thailand. Presumably there were a great number of temple murals in Ayuthaya that were destroyed by the Burmese invasion of 1767. The earliest surviving temple examples are found at Ayuthaya's Wat Ratburana (1424), Wat Chong Nonsii in Bangkok (1657–1707) and Phetchaburi's Wat Yai Suwannaram (late 17th century).

Nineteenth-century religious painting has fared better; Ratanakosin-style temple art is in fact more highly esteemed for painting than for sculpture or architecture. Typical temple murals feature rich colours and lively detail. Some of the finest are found in Wat Phra Kaew's Wihan Buddhaisawan Chapel in Bangkok and at Wat Suwannaram in Thonburi.

Contemporary Painting The beginnings of Thailand's modern art movement are usually attributed to Italian artist Corrado Feroci, who was first invited to Thailand by Rama VI in 1924. Feroci's design of Bangkok's Democracy Monument was inspired by Italy's fascist art movement of the 1930s. He also created the bronze statue of Rama I that stands at the entry to Memorial Bridge and several monuments around the city. Feroci founded the country's first fine arts institute in 1933, a school that eventually developed into Silpakorn University, Thailand's premier training ground for artists. In gratitude, the Thai government gave Feroci the Thai name Silpa Bhirasri.

Today contemporary Thai painting is exhibited at a number of Bangkok and Chiang Mai venues. One of the most important modern movements in Thai art was an updating of Buddhist themes, begun in the 1970s by painters Pichai Nirand, Thawan Duchanee and Prateung Emjaroen. The movement has grown stronger since their early efforts to combine modern Western schemata and Thai motifs. One Bangkok gallery, the Visual Dhamma Art Gallery, specialises in the display of modern Thai Buddhist art.

Other important venues and sources of support for modern art are Bangkok's luxury hotels. The largest collection of modern Thai painting anywhere in the world is found in the lobbies and public areas of the Grand Hyatt Erawan; the displays are changed regularly.

Continued from page 208

Lumphini Park
สวนลุมพินี

Named after the Buddha's birthplace in Nepal, this is Bangkok's largest and most popular park. It is bordered by Thanon Phra Ram IV to the south, Thanon Sarasin to the north, Thanon Withayu to the east and Thanon Ratchadamri to the west, with entrance gates on all sides. A large artificial lake in the centre is surrounded by broad, well-tended lawns, wooded areas and walking paths – in other words, it's the best outdoor escape from Bangkok without leaving town.

One of the best times to visit the park is in the morning before 7 am when the air is fresh (well, relatively so for Bangkok) and legions of Chinese are practising *taijiquan* (t'ai chi). Also in the morning, vendors set up tables to dispense fresh snake blood and bile, considered health tonics by many Thais and Chinese. Rowing boats and paddle boats can be rented at the lake for 30B per half-hour. A weight lifting area in one section becomes a miniature 'muscle beach' on weekends. Other facilities include a snack bar, an asphalt jogging track, several areas with tables and benches for picnics, and a couple of tables where ladies serve Chinese tea.

During the kite-flying season (mid-February to April), Lumphini becomes a favoured flight zone; kites *(wâo)* can be purchased in the park during these months.

Monk's Bowl Village
บ้านบาตร

This is the only one remaining of three such villages established in Bangkok by Rama I for the purpose of handcrafting monk's bowls *(bàat)*. The black bowls, used by Thai monks to receive alms-food from faithful Buddhists every morning, are still made here in the traditional manner. Due to the expense of purchasing a handmade bowl, the 'village' has been reduced to a single alley in a district known as Ban Baht *(bâan bàat,* Monk's Bowl Village). About half a dozen families still hammer the bowls together from eight separate pieces of steel representing, they say, the eight spokes of the wheel of dharma (which

in turn symbolise Buddhism's Eightfold Path). The joints are fused in a wood fire with bits of copper, and the bowl is polished and coated with several layers of black lacquer. A typical bowl-smith's output is one bowl per day.

To find the village, walk south on Thanon Boriphat south of Thanon Bamrung Meuang, then left on Soi Baan Baht. The artisans who fashion the bowls are not always at work, so it's largely a matter of luck whether you'll see them in action. At any of the houses that make the bowls, you can purchase a fine-quality alms bowl for around 500B to 700B. To see monks' robes and bowls on sale, wander down Thanon Bamrung Meuang near Sao Ching-Cha.

Wat Bowonniwet
วัดบวรนิเวศ

Wat Bowonniwet (also spelt 'Bovornives' and shortened to Wat Bowon), on Thanon Phra Sumen in Banglamphu (Banglamphu map), is the national headquarters for the Thammayut monastic sect, the minority sect in Thai Buddhism. King Mongkut, founder of the Thammayut, began a royal tradition by residing here as a monk – in fact he was the abbot of Wat Bowon for several years. King Bhumibol and Crown Prince Vajiralongkorn, as well as several other males in the royal family, have been temporarily ordained as monks here. The temple was founded in 1826, when it was known as Wat Mai.

Bangkok's second Buddhist university, Mahamakut University, is housed at Wat Bowon. India, Nepal and Sri Lanka all send selected monks to study here. Across the street from the main entrance to the wát are an English-language Buddhist bookshop and a Thai herbal clinic.

Because of its royal status, visitors should be particularly careful to dress properly for admittance to this wát – no shorts or sleeveless shirts

CHINATOWN & PHAHURAT
Chinatown
สำเพ็ง

Bangkok's Chinatown (Sampeng), off Thanon Yaowarat and Thanon Ratchawong, comprises a confusing and crowded array of

Walking Tour – Chinatown & Phahurat

This route meanders through Bangkok's busy Chinese and Indian market districts and is best explored on foot since vehicular traffic in the area is in almost constant gridlock. Depending on your pace and shopping intentions, this lengthy route could take from 1½ to three hours. You can also do this tour in reverse, beginning from the Phahurat fabric market.

Be forewarned that the journey should only be undertaken by those who can withstand extended crowd contact as well as the sometimes unpleasant sights and smells of a traditional fresh market. The reward for tolerating this attack on the senses consists of numerous glimpses into the 'real' day-to-day Bangkok, away from the glittering facade of department stores and office buildings along Bangkok's main avenues – not to mention the opportunity for fabulous bargains. (If you plan to buy anything, you'd better bring along either a phrasebook or an interpreter as very little English is spoken in these areas.)

Start at **Wat Mangkon Kamalawat** (Neng Noi Yee), one of Chinatown's largest and liveliest temples (the name means Dragon Lotus Temple), on Thanon Charoen Krung between Thanon Mangkon and Trok Itsaranuphap. A taxi direct to the temple is recommended over taking a bus, simply because the district is so congested and street names don't always appear in Roman script. If you're determined to go by bus, ordinary bus Nos 25 and 73, air-con bus Nos 1 and 7, and Microbus Nos 5, 14 and 19 pass the temple going east (the temple entrance will be on the left), or you could take ordinary bus No 25, 53 or 73 and get off near the Thanon Mangkon intersection on Thanon Yaowarat, a block south of Thanon Charoen Krung. Yet another alternative is to arrive by Chao Phraya River Express at Tha Ratchawong, then walk four blocks north-east along Thanon Ratchawong to Thanon Charoen Krung, turn right and walk one and a half blocks to the temple.

Whichever approach you choose, to help pinpoint the right area on Thanon Charoen Krung look for neighbouring shops selling fruit, cakes, incense and ritual burning paper for offering at the temple. Inscriptions at the entrance to Wat Mangkon Kamalawat are in Chinese and Tibetan, while the labyrinthine interior features a succession of Buddhist, Taoist and Confucian altars. Virtually at any time of day or night this temple is packed with worshippers lighting incense, filling the ever-burning altar lamps with oil and praying to their ancestors.

Leaving the temple, walk left along Thanon Charoen Krung about 20m to the nearest pedestrian crossing (a policeman is usually directing traffic here), then cross Thanon Charoen Krung and head down the alley on the other side. You're now heading south-west on **Trok Itsaranuphap**, one of Chinatown's main market lanes. This section is lined with vendors purveying ready-to-eat or preserved foodstuffs, including cleaned chickens, duck and fish; though not for the squeamish, it's one of the cleanest-looking fresh markets in Bangkok.

One hundred metres or so down Trok Itsaranuphap you'll cross **Thanon Yaowarat**, a main Chinatown thoroughfare. This section of Thanon Yaowarat is lined with large and small gold shops; for price and selection, this is probably the best place in Thailand to purchase a gold chain (sold by the *bàat*, a unit of weight equal to 15g). From the trok entrance, turn right onto Thanon Yaowarat, walk 50m to the pedestrian crossing and navigate your way across the avenue.

Trok Itsaranuphap continues southward on the other side. Down the lane almost immediately on your left is **Talat Kao** (Old Market) – the entrance is ornamented in Chinese style. This market section off Trok Itsaranuphap has been operating continuously for over 200 years. All manner and size of freshwater and saltwater fin- and shell-fish are displayed here, alive and filleted – or as sometimes is the case, half alive and half filleted.

About 100m farther down Trok Itsaranuphap, past rows of vendors selling mostly dried fish, you'll come to a major Chinatown market crossroads. Running perpendicular to Itsaranuphap in either direction is the famous **Sampeng Lane** (Soi Wanit 1). Turn right onto Sampeng. This is usually the most crowded of Chinatown's market sois – a traffic jam of

Walking Tour – Chinatown & Phahurat

pedestrians, pushcarts and the occasional annoying motorbike twisting through the crowds. Shops along this section of Sampeng sell dry goods, especially shoes, clothing, fabric, toys and kitchenware.

About 25m west, Sampeng Lane crosses Thanon Mangkon. On either side of the intersection are two of Bangkok's oldest commercial buildings, a Bangkok Bank and the venerable **Tang To Kang** gold shop, which are both over 100 years old. The exteriors of the buildings are classic early Ratanakosin (or Bangkok), showing lots of European influence; the interiors are heavy with hardwood panelling. Continue walking another 60m or so to the Thanon Ratchawong crossing (a traffic cop is usually stationed here to part the vehicular Red Sea for pedestrians), cross and re-enter Sampeng Lane on the other side.

At this point, **fabric shops** – many of them operated by Indian (mostly Sikh) merchants – start dominating the selection as the western edge of Chinatown approaches the Indian district of Phahurat. If you're looking for good deals on Thai textiles you're in the right place. But hold off buying until you've had a chance to look through at least a dozen or more shops – they get better the farther you go.

After about 65m is the small Thanon Mahachak crossing and then, after another 50m or so, the larger Thanon Chakrawat (Chakkawat) crossing, where yet another traffic cop assists. Along Thanon Chakrawat in this vicinity, as well as farther ahead along Sampeng Lane on the other side of Thanon Chakrawat, there are many gem and jewellery shops.

If you were to follow Thanon Chakrawat north from Soi Wanit, you could have a look around the Chinese-Thai antique shops of **Nakhon Kasem** (also known as the Thieves Market since at one time stolen goods were commonly sold here) between Thanon Yaowarat and Thanon Charoen Krung. After you re-enter Soi Wanit on the other side of Thanon Chakrawat the jewellery shops are mixed with an eclectic array of house ware and clothing shops until you arrive, after another 50m, at the **Saphan Han** market area, named after a short bridge (*sàphaan*) over Khlong Ong Ang. Clustered along the khlong on either side of the bridge is a bevy of vendors selling noodles and snacks. On the other side of the bridge, Sampeng Lane ends at Thanon Chakraphet, the eastern edge of the Phahurat district.

Thanon Chakraphet is well known for its Indian restaurants and shops selling Indian sweets. One of the best eateries in the area is the Royal India Restaurant, which serves north-Indian cuisine and is justly famous for its tasty selection of Indian breads. To get there, turn left onto Thanon Chakraphet and walk about 70m along the eastern (left) side of the road; look for the Royal India sign pointing down an alley on the left. On the opposite side of Thanon Chakraphet from the Royal India is a Chinese temple. North of this temple, in a back alley on the western side of the road, is a large **Sikh temple** – turn left before the ATM Department Store to find the entrance. Visitors to the temple – reportedly the second-largest Sikh temple outside of India – are welcome but they must remove their shoes. If you arrive on a Sikh festival day you can partake of the *langar* (communal Sikh meal served in the temple).

Several inexpensive Indian food stalls are found in an alley alongside the department store. Behind the store, stretching westward from Thanon Chakraphet to Thanon Triphet, is the **Phahurat Market**, devoted almost exclusively to textiles and clothing. Thanon Phahurat itself runs parallel to, and just north of, the market.

If you're ready to escape the market hustle and bustle, you can catch city buses on Thanon Chakraphet (heading north and then east to the Siam Square and Pratunam areas) or along Thanon Phahurat (heading west and then north along Thanon Tri Thong to the Banglamphu district). Or walk to the river and catch a Chao Phraya River Express boat from Tha Saphan Phut, which is just to the north-west of Phra Phuttha Yot Fa (Memorial) Bridge. If you're doing this route in reverse, you can arrive by Chao Phraya River Express at Tha Saphan Phut.

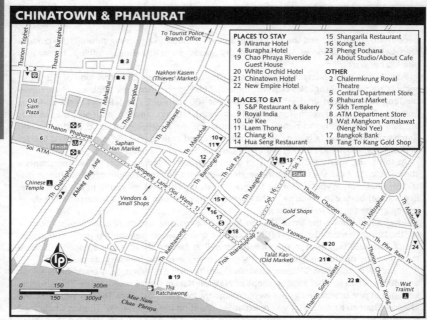

CHINATOWN & PHAHURAT

PLACES TO STAY
3 Miramar Hotel
4 Burapha Hotel
19 Chao Phraya Riverside Guest House
20 White Orchid Hotel
21 Chinatown Hotel
22 New Empire Hotel

PLACES TO EAT
1 S&P Restaurant & Bakery
9 Royal India
10 Lie Kee
11 Laem Thong
12 Chiang Ki
14 Hua Seng Restaurant

15 Shangarila Restaurant
16 Kong Lee
23 Pheng Pochana
24 About Studio/About Cafe

OTHER
2 Chalermkrung Royal Theatre
5 Central Department Store
6 Phahurat Market
7 Sikh Temple
8 ATM Department Store
13 Wat Mangkon Kamalawat (Neng Noi Yee)
17 Bangkok Bank
18 Tang To Kang Gold Shop

jewellery, hardware, wholesale food, automotive and fabric shops, as well as dozens of other small businesses. It's a good place to shop since goods here are cheaper than almost anywhere else in Bangkok and the Chinese proprietors like to bargain, especially along Sampeng Lane (Soi Wanit 1).

Chinese and Thai antiques of varying age and authenticity are available in the so-called Thieves' Market (Nakhon Kasem), but it's better for browsing than buying these days.

During the annual Vegetarian Festival, celebrated fervently by Thai Chinese for the first nine days of the ninth lunar month (September to October), Bangkok's Chinatown becomes a virtual orgy of vegetarian Thai and Chinese food. The festivities are centred around **Wat Mangkon Kamalawat** (Neng Noi Yee), one of Chinatown's largest temples, on Thanon Charoen Krung. All along Thanon Charoen Krung in this vicinity, as well as on Thanon Yaowarat to the south, restaurants offer different vegetarian dishes.

A Chinese population has been living in this area ever since the Chinese were moved

here from Bang Kok (today's Ko Ratanakosin) by the royal government in 1782 to make room for the new capital. A census in the area taken exactly 100 years later found 245 opium dens, 154 pawnshops, 69 gambling establishments and 26 brothels. Pawnshops, along with myriad gold shops, remain a popular Chinatown business, while the other three vices have gone underground; brothels continue to exist under the guise of 'tea halls' *(rohng chaa),* back-street heroin dealers have replaced the opium dens and illicit card games convene in the private upstairs rooms of certain restaurants. Several Chinese-language newspapers are printed and distributed in the district.

At the south-eastern edge of Chinatown stands **Hualamphong station,** built by Dutch architects and engineers just before WWI. One of the city's earliest and best examples of the movement towards Thai Art Deco, the vaulted iron roof and neoclassical portico demonstrate engineering that was state-of-the-art in its time, while the patterned, two-toned skylights exemplify pure de Stijl-style Dutch modernism.

Examples of Thai Deco from the 1920s and 1930s can be found along Chinatown's main streets, particularly Thanon Yaowarat. Vertical towers over the main doorways are often surmounted with Deco-style sculptures – the Eiffel Tower, a lion, an elephant, a Moorish dome. Atop one commercial building on Thanon Songwat near Tha Ratchawong is a rusting model of a WWII vintage Japanese Zero warplane, undoubtedly placed there by the Japanese during their brief 1941 occupation of Bangkok; in style and proportion it fits the surrounding Thai Deco elements.

Phahurat
พาหุรัด

At the edge of Chinatown, around the intersection of Thanon Phahurat and Thanon Chakraphet (Chakkaphet), is a small but thriving Indian district, generally called Phahurat. Here dozens of Indian-owned shops sell all kinds of fabric and clothes. This is the best place in the city to bargain for such items, especially silk. The selection is unbelievable, and Thai shoulder bags (yâam) sold here are the cheapest in Bangkok, perhaps in Thailand.

Behind the more obvious shopfronts along these streets, in the 'bowels' of the blocks, is a seemingly endless Indian bazaar selling not only fabric but household items, food and other necessities. There are some good, reasonably priced Indian restaurants in this area too, and a Sikh temple off Thanon Chakraphet (see the Other Temples section later in this chapter).

Wat Traimit
วัดไตรมิตร

The attraction at Wat Traimit (Temple of the Golden Buddha) is, of course, the impressive 3m-tall, 5.5-tonne, solid-gold Buddha image, which gleams like no other gold artefact we've ever seen.

Sculpted in the graceful Sukhothai style, the image was 'discovered' some 40 years ago beneath a stucco or plaster exterior when it fell from a crane while being moved to a new building within the temple compound. It has been theorised that the covering was added to protect it from 'marauding hordes', either during the late Sukhothai

period or later in the Ayuthaya period when the city was under siege by the Burmese. The temple itself is said to date from the early 13th century.

The golden image can be seen every day from 9 am to 5 pm, and admission is 20B. Nowadays lots of camera-toting tour groups haunt the place (there's even a moneychanger on the premises), so it pays to arrive in the early morning if you want a more traditional feel. Wat Traimit is near the intersection of Thanon Yaowarat and Thanon Charoen Krung, near Hualamphong station. For more information, call ☎ 623 1226.

THANON SILOM, THANON SURAWONG & THANON SATHON AREA
Sri Mariamman Temple
วัดพระศรีมหาอุมาเทวี
(วัดแขกสีลม)

Called Wat Phra Si Maha Umathewi in Thai, this small Hindu temple sits alongside busy Thanon Silom in Bangrak, a district with many Indian residents. The principal temple structure, built in the 1860s by Tamil immigrants, features a 6m facade of intertwined, full-colour Hindu deities, topped by a gold-plated copper dome. The temple's main shrine contains three main deities, Jao Mae Maha Umathewi (Uma Devi, also known as Shakti, Shiva's consort) is at the centre. Her son Phra Khanthakuman (Subramaniam) is on the right.

On the left is Jao Mae Maha Umathewi's other son, the elephant-headed Phra Phikkhanet (Ganesh). Along the left interior wall sit rows of Shivas, Vishnus and other Hindu deities, as well as a few Buddhas, so that just about any non-Muslim, non-Judaeo-Christian Asian can worship here – Thai and Chinese devotees come to pray along with Indians. Bright yellow marigold garlands are sold at the entrance for this purpose.

An interesting ritual takes place in the temple at noon on most days, when a priest brings out a tray carrying an oil lamp, coloured powders and holy water. He sprinkles the water on the hands of worshippers who in turn pass their hands through the lamp flame for purification; then they dip their fingers in the coloured powder and daub prayer marks on their foreheads. On Friday at around 11.30 am, *prasada* (blessed vegetarian food) is offered to devotees.

Thais call this temple Wat Khaek – *khàek* is a Thai colloquial expression for people of Indian descent. The literal translation is 'guest', an obvious euphemism for a group of people you don't particularly want as permanent residents; hence most Indians living permanently in Thailand don't appreciate the term.

Queen Saovabha Memorial Institute (Snake Farm)
สถานเสาวภา

At this Thai Red Cross research institute (☎ 252 0161), formerly known as the Pasteur Institute, venomous snakes (the common cobra, king cobra, banded krait, Malayan pit viper, green pit viper and Russell's viper) are milked daily to make snake-bite antidotes, which are distributed throughout the country.

When the institute was founded in 1923 it was only the second of its kind in the world (the first was in Brazil). The milking sessions – at 11 am and 2.30 pm weekdays, 11 am only on weekends and holidays – have become a major Bangkok tourist attraction. Unlike other 'snake farms' in Bangkok, this is a serious herpetological research facility; a very informative half-hour slide show on snakes is presented before the milking sessions. This will be boring to some, fascinating to others. Feeding time is 3 pm. Admission is 70B. The institute is on Thanon Phra Ram IV (near Thanon Henri Dunant).

A booklet entitled *Guide to Healthy Living in Thailand,* published jointly by the Thai Red Cross and the US embassy, is available here for 100B. You can also get common vaccinations against such diseases as cholera, typhoid, tetanus, polio, encephalitis, meningitis, rabies, small pox and hepatitis A and B. If you are bitten by a strange animal, this is a good place to come for antirabies serum; bring the animal, dead or alive, if possible. The institute is open 8.30 to 11.30 am and 1 to 4 pm weekdays.

There is also an anonymous STD clinic on the grounds of the institute.

SIAM SQUARE & PRATUNAM AREA
Jim Thompson's House
บ้านจิมทอมป์สัน

This is a great spot to visit for authentic Thai residential architecture and South-East Asian art. Located at the end of an undistinguished soi next to Khlong Saen Saep, the premises once belonged to the American silk entrepreneur Jim Thompson, who deserves most of the credit for the current worldwide popularity of Thai silk.

Born in Delaware in 1906, Thompson was a New York architect who briefly served in the Office of Strategic Services (OSS; forerunner of the CIA) in Thailand during WWII. After the war he found New York too tame and moved to Bangkok. Thai silk caught his connoisseur's eye; he sent samples to fashion houses in Milan, London and Paris, gradually building a steady worldwide clientele for a craft that had been in danger of dying out.

A tireless promoter of traditional Thai arts and culture, Thompson collected parts of various derelict Thai homes in Central Thailand and had them reassembled in the current location in 1959. Although for the most part assembled in typical Thai style, one striking departure from tradition is the way each wall has its exterior side facing the house's interior, thus exposing the wall's bracing system.

While out for an afternoon walk in the Cameron Highlands of west Malaysia in 1967, Thompson disappeared under mysterious circumstances and has never been heard from since. That same year his sister was murdered in the USA, fuelling various conspiracy theories to explain the disappearance. Was it communist spies? Business rivals? Or a man-eating tiger? The most recent theory – for which there is apparently some hard evidence – has it that the silk magnate was accidentally run over by a Malaysian truck driver who hid his remains.

The Legendary American – The Remarkable Career & Strange Disappearance of Jim Thompson (Houghton Mifflin, 1970), by William Warren, is an excellent book on Thompson, his career, residence and intriguing disappearance. In Thailand, it has been republished as *Jim Thompson: The*

Legendary American of Thailand (Jim Thompson Thai Silk Co, Bangkok).

On display in the main house are his small but splendid Asian art collection and his personal belongings. The Jim Thompson Foundation has a table at the front where you can buy prints of old Siam maps and Siamese horoscopes in postcard and poster form.

The house, on Soi Kasem San 2, Thanon Phra Ram I, is open 9 am to 4.30 pm daily. Admission is 100B (proceeds go to Bangkok's School for the Blind); children and students under 25 years get in for 50B. Call ☎ 216 7368 or 215 0122 for more information. The khlawng at the end of the soi is one of Bangkok's most lively. Beware of well-dressed touts in the soi who will tell you Thompson's house is closed – it's just a ruse to take you on a buying spree.

Wang Suan Phakkat
วังสวนผักกาด

The Wang Suan Phakkat or Phakkard (also known as Lettuce Farm Palace), once the residence of Princess Chumbon of Nakhon Sawan, is a collection of five traditional wooden Thai houses containing varied displays of art, antiques and furnishings. The landscaped grounds are a peaceful oasis complete with ducks and swans and a semi-enclosed garden.

The diminutive **Lacquer Pavilion** at the back of the complex dates from the Ayuthaya period (the building originally sat in a monastery compound on the Mae Nam Chao Phraya, just south of Ayuthaya) and features gold-leaf *jataka* (Buddha's past life) and *Ramayana* murals as well as scenes from daily Ayuthaya life. Larger residential structures at the front of the complex contain displays of Khmer-style Hindu and Buddhist art, Ban Chiang ceramics and a very interesting collection of historic Buddhas, including a beautiful late U Thong–style image.

The grounds are open from 9 am to 4 pm daily; admission is 100B for foreigners, 50B for Thais (students 20B). It's on Thanon Si Ayuthaya, between Thanon Phayathai and Thanon Ratchaprarop; aircon bus No 3 passes by. Call ☎ 245 4934 for more information.

THANON SUKHUMVIT
Siam Society & Ban Kamthieng
สยามสมาคม/บ้านคำเทียง

At 131 Soi Asoke, Thanon Sukhumvit, the Siam Society is the publisher of the renowned *Journal of the Siam Society* and its members are valiant preservers of traditional Thai culture. A reference library is open to visitors and Siam Society monographs are for sale. Almost anything you'd want to know about Thailand (outside the political sphere, since the society is sponsored by the royal family) can be researched here. An ethnological museum of sorts exhibiting Thai folk art is located on the Siam Society grounds in the Northern-style Ban Kamthieng (Kamthieng House). It was under renovation when we last visited, and as a result the usual 100B entry charge was waived. Ban Kamthieng is open 9 am to 5 pm Tuesday to Saturday. For information call ☎ 661 6470.

GREATER BANGKOK AREA
Rama IX Royal Park
สวนหลวง ร.๙

Opened in 1987 to commemorate King Bhumibol's 60th birthday, Bangkok's newest green area *(sŭan lŭang raw kâo)* covers 81 hectares and includes a water park and botanical gardens. Since its opening, the latter has developed into a significant horticultural research centre. A museum with an exhibition on the life of the king occupies the centre of the park. Call ☎ 328 1385 for more information. Take bus No 2, 23 or 25 to Soi Udomsuk (Soi 103), off Thanon Sukhumvit in Phrakhanong district, then a green minibus to the park. Alternatively, you can take air-con bus No 145 from the Weekend Market, getting off at the first intersection after the two large shopping malls, Seacon Square and Seri Center. Turn left and catch either an orange minibus or *săwngthăew* (also written songthaew) for the remaining 10-minute ride. The park is open 5 am to 6 pm daily and admission is 10B.

Wat Phailom
วัดไผ่ล้อม

Outside Bangkok, on the eastern bank of the Mae Nam Chao Phraya in Pathum Thani Province, this old, wooden Mon wát is noted for the tens of thousands of open-billed storks *(Anastomus oscitans)* that nest in bamboo groves opposite the temple area from December to June. Temple architecture buffs will note the Ayuthaya-style bòt, backed by a Mon chedi.

The temple is 51km from the centre of Bangkok in Pathum Thani's Sam Kok district. Take a Pathum Thani-bound bus (12B) from Bangkok's Northern bus terminal and cross the river by ferry to the wát grounds.

Bus No 33 from Sanam Luang goes all the way to Phailom and back. The Chao Phraya River Express tours from Tha Maharat to Bang Pa-In each Sunday also make a stop at Wat Phailom – see River & Canal Trips later in this chapter.

Ko Kret
เกาะเกร็ด

This island in the middle of the Mae Nam Chao Phraya at Bangkok's northern edge is home to one of Thailand's oldest Mon settlements. The Mon, who between the 6th and 10th centuries AD were the dominant culture in Central Thailand, are skilled potters and Ko Kret remains one of the oldest and largest sources of earthenware in the region. An exhibit of local pottery can be seen at the island's Ancient Mon Pottery Centre; there are also plenty of opportunities to watch the locals craft pottery. A Mon Buddhist temple called **Wat Paramai Yikawat**, also known simply as 'Wat Mon', contains a Mon-style marble Buddha.

To reach Ko Kret, take a Chao Phraya River Express boat to Tha Nonthaburi, then switch to a Chao Phraya Express boat with a green flag (these run from 6.30 to 7.30 am and 4.30 to 6.30 pm daily) and ride to Tha Paramai at Wat Paramai Yikawat on the island. Chao Phraya River Express also offers a cruise to Ko Kret (departs 9 am, returns 3 pm) for 220B (150B for children). The cruise departs from Tha Maharat.

If you have time to kill in Pak Kret town, you can get a good, low-cost massage at the **School for the Blind**, which has a training program in massage therapy.

Every Sunday Chao Phraya River Express runs an excursion boat to Ko Kret from Tha Maharat at 9 am. The tour takes in Wat Paramai, the Ancient Mon Pottery House, Ban Khanom Thai (to watch Thai

sweets being made) and Wat Chaloem Phrakiat. The tour leaves from Wat Chaloem Phrakiat at 2 pm, arriving back at Tha Maharat at 3 pm. Tour prices are 300B per adult, 150B per child.

OTHER TEMPLES

Marked by its enormous, modern-style 32m standing Buddha, **Wat Intharawihan** borders Thanon Wisut Kasat, at the northern edge of Banglamphu. Check out the hollowed-out air-con stupa with a lifelike image of Luang Phaw Toh, a famous monk. Entry to Wat In is by donation.

Wat Suthat, begun by Rama I and completed by Rama II and Rama III, boasts a wíhǎan with gilded bronze Buddha images (including Phra Si Sakyamuni, one of the largest surviving Sukhothai bronzes) and colourful jataka murals depicting scenes from the Buddha's previous lives. Wat Suthat holds a special place in the Thai religion because of its association with Brahman priests who perform important annual ceremonies, such as the Royal Ploughing Ceremony in May. These priests perform rites at two Hindu shrines near the wát – the Thewa Sathaan (Deva Sthan) across the street to the north-west and the smaller Saan Jao Phitsanu (Vishnu Shrine) to the east. The former contains images of Shiva and Ganesh, while the latter is dedicated to Vishnu. The wát holds the rank of Rachavoramahavihan, the highest royal temple grade; the ashes of Rama VIII (Ananda Mahidol, the current king's deceased older brother) are contained in the base of the main Buddha image in Suthat's wíhǎan.

At the nearby **Sao Ching-Cha**, the Giant Swing, a spectacular Brahman festival in honour of the Hindu god Shiva used to take place each year until it was stopped during the reign of Rama VII. Participants would swing in ever-heightening arcs in an effort to reach a bag of gold suspended from a 15m bamboo pole – many died trying. The Giant Swing is a block south of the Democracy Monument.

Wat Chong Nonsi, off Thanon Ratchadaphisek near the Bangkok side of the river, contains notable jataka murals painted between 1657 and 1707. It is the only surviving Ayuthaya-era temple in which both the murals and architecture are of the same period with no renovations. As a single, 'pure' architectural and painting unit, it's considered quite important for the study of late Ayuthaya art; the painting style is similar to that found in the Phetchaburi Province monasteries of Wat Yai Suwannaram and Wat Ko Kaew Sutharam.

There are also numerous temples on the Thonburi side of the river that are less visited. These include **Wat Kalayanamit**, with its towering Buddha statue, and, outside, the biggest bronze bell in Thailand; **Wat Pho Bang-O**, with its carved gables and Rama III-era murals; **Wat Chaloem Phrakiat**, a temple with tiled gables; and **Wat Thawng Nophakhun**, with its Chinese-influenced *uposatha* (bòt). **Wat Yannawa**, on the Bangkok bank of the river near Tha Sathon, was built during Rama II's reign and features a building resembling a Chinese junk.

Just off Thanon Chakraphet in the Phahurat district is a **Sikh Temple** (Sri Gurusingh Sabha) where visitors are welcome to walk around. Basically it's a large hall, somewhat reminiscent of a mosque interior, devoted to the worship of the Guru Granth Sahib, the 16th-century Sikh holy book, which is itself considered to be a 'living' guru and the last of the religion's 10 great teachers. Prasada is distributed among devotees every morning around 9 am.

OTHER SHRINES

On the corner of Thanon Ratchaprarop and Thanon Ploenchit, next to the Grand Hyatt Erawan Hotel, is a large shrine, **San Phra Phrom** (also known as the **Erawan Shrine**), which was originally built to ward off bad luck during the construction of the first Erawan Hotel (torn down to make way for the Grand Hyatt Erawan some years ago). The four-headed deity at the centre of the shrine is Brahma (Phra Phrom in Thai), the Hindu god of creation. Apparently the developers of the original Erawan (named after Airvata, Indra's three-headed elephant mount) first erected a typical Thai spirit house but decided to replace it with the more impressive Brahman shrine after several serious mishaps delayed the hotel construction. Worshippers who have a wish granted may return to the shrine to commission the musicians and dancers who are always on hand for an impromptu performance.

Since the success of the Erawan Shrine, several other flashy Brahman shrines have been erected around the city next to large hotels and office buildings. Next to the World Trade Centre on Thanon Ploenchit is a **large shrine** containing a standing Brahma, a rather unusual posture for Thai Brahmans. Next to Amarin Plaza, near the Chit Lom Skytrain station, is a sizable **Indra Shrine**.

Another hotel shrine worth seeing is the **lingam (phallus) shrine** behind the Hilton International Bangkok in tiny Nai Loet Park off Thanon Withayu. Clusters of carved stone and wooden lingam surround a spirit house and shrine built by millionaire businessman Nai Loet to honour Jao Mae Thapthim, a female deity thought to reside in the old banyan tree on the site. Someone who made an offering shortly thereafter had a baby, and the shrine has received a steady stream of worshippers – mostly women seeking fertility – ever since. Nai Loet Park is fenced off so you must wind your way through the Hilton complex to visit the shrine. Or come via the Khlong Saen Saep canal taxi; ask to get off at Saphan Withayu – look for the TV3 building on the northern side of the canal. At the time of writing, the Hilton International Bangkok announced that it would only allow hotel guests to visit the shrine; this seems preposterous and untenable, given the cultural significance of this shrine to Bangkok Thais.

HISTORIC CHURCHES

Several Catholic churches were founded in Bangkok in the 17th to 19th centuries. Worth seeing is the **Holy Rosary Church** (known in Thai as Wat Kalawan, from the Portuguese 'Calvario') in Talat Noi near the River City shopping complex. Originally built in 1787 by the Portuguese, the Holy Rosary was rebuilt by Vietnamese and Cambodian Catholics in the late 19th century, hence the French inscriptions beneath the stations of the cross. This old church has a splendid set of Romanesque stained-glass windows, gilded ceilings and a Christ statue that is carried through the streets during Easter celebrations. The alley leading to the church is lined with old Bangkok shophouse architecture.

The **Church of the Immaculate Conception** near Saphan Krungthon (north of Saphan Phra Pin Klao) was also founded by the Portuguese and later taken over by Cambodians fleeing civil war. The present building is an 1837 reconstruction on the church's 1674 site. One of the original church buildings survives and is now used as a museum housing holy relics. Another Portuguese-built church is 1913 vintage **Santa Cruz** (Wat Kuti Jin) on the Thonburi side of the Mae Nam Chao Phraya near Saphan Phra Phuttha Yot Fa (Memorial Bridge), usually called Saphan Phut by Thais. The architecture shows Chinese influence, hence the Thai name 'Chinese monastic residence'.

Christ Church, at 11 Thanon Convent next to Bangkok Nursing Home, was established as English Chapel in 1864. The current Gothic-style structure, opened in 1904, features thick walls and a tiled roof braced with teak beams; the carved teak ceiling fans date to 1919.

OTHER MUSEUMS

The **Museum of the Department of Forensic Medicine**, on the ground floor of the Forensic Medicine Building, Siriraj Hospital (Ko Ratanakosin map), on Thanon Phrannok near the Thonburi (Bangkok Noi) train station, is the most famous of 10 medical museums on the hospital premises. Among the grisly displays are the preserved bodies of famous Thai murderers. It's open 9 am to 4 pm weekdays; admission is free.

The **Hall of Railway Heritage**, just north of Chatuchak Park, displays steam locomotives, model trains and other artefacts related to Thai railroad history. It's open 9 am to 5 pm weekdays and 8 am to noon Sunday; admission is free. Call the Thai Railfan Club (☎ 243 2037) for further information.

The **Bangkok Doll Factory & Museum** (☎ 245 3008), 85 Soi Ratchataphan (Soi Mo Leng), off Thanon Ratchaprarop in the Pratunam district, houses a colourful selection of traditional Thai dolls, both new and antique. Dolls are also available for purchase. It's open 8 am to 5 pm Monday to Saturday; admission is free.

Military aircraft aficionados shouldn't miss the **Royal Thai Air Force Museum**, on Thanon Phahonyothin near Wing 6 of the Don Muang airport. Among the world-class collection of historic aircraft is the only existing Japanese Tachikawa trainer, along with a Spitfire and several Nieuports and Breguets. The museum is open 8.30 am to

4.30 pm weekdays and on the first weekend of each month; admission is free.

Bangkok also has a **Museum of Science** and a **planetarium**, which are both on Thanon Sukhumvit between Soi 40 and Soi 42.

ART GALLERIES

Housed in an early Ratanakosin Era building opposite the National Theatre on Thanon Chao Fa, the **National Gallery** (Ko Ratanakosin map; ☎ 282 8525, 281 2224) displays traditional and contemporary art, mostly by artists who receive government support. The general consensus is that it's not Thailand's best, but the gallery is worth a visit for die-hard art fans or if you're in the vicinity. The gallery is closed Monday and Tuesday, and open 9 am to 4 pm on other days. Admission is 30B.

Silpakorn University (near Wat Phra Kaew) is Bangkok's fine arts university and has a gallery of student works. It's open 8 am to 7 pm weekdays; from 8 am to 4 pm weekends and holidays.

Bangkok's latest trend in public art consumption is the 'gallery pub', an effort to place art in a social context rather than leaving it to sterile galleries and museums. **About Studio/About Cafe** (Chinatown & Phahurat map; ☎ 623 1742), 418 Thanon Maitrichit, is the best of the several venues that attempt to combine gallery space with social space. Hours are erratic; despite what may be posted on the front door, figure on finding the place open roughly 7 pm to midnight. You can reach About Studio/About Cafe on bus Nos 4, 25, 73, air-con 23, (or 5, 14 or 19 air-con Microbus). The place that initiated this trend, **Ruang Pung Art Community** (Greater Bangkok map), opposite section 13 in Chatuchak Weekend Market, has been in business for around 12 years. It's open 11 am to 10 pm on weekends only and features rotating exhibits. Also in Chatuchak Market is the very active **Sunday Gallery** (Sunday Plaza), which, contrary to its name, is open 10 am to 5 pm Monday, Wednesday and Friday and 7 am to 7 pm on weekends.

Bangkok's foreign cultural centres hold regular exhibits of foreign and local artists – check the monthly bulletins issued by AUA, Alliance Française, the British Council and the Goethe-Institut (see Cultural Centres under Information earlier in this chapter).

RYAN FOX

Bangkok – a city that never sleeps...

JOHN BORTHWICK

...and never stops...

ANDREW LUBRAN

...unless, perhaps to shop.

View of Mae Nam Chao Phraya from Wat Arun

Bangkok's overpasses – the more they build, the more cars there are!

Several of Bangkok's luxury hotels display top-quality contemporary art in their lobbies and other public areas. The **Grand Hyatt Erawan** (on the corner of Thanon Ratchadamri and Thanon Ploenchit) and the **Landmark Hotel** (Thanon Sukhumvit) have the best collections of contemporary art in the country. The Erawan alone has nearly 2000 works exhibited on a rotating basis.

The **Neilson Hays Library** at 193 Thanon Surawong occasionally hosts small exhibitions in its Rotunda Gallery.

THONBURI CANALS
River & Canal Trips

In 1855 British envoy Sir John Bowring wrote, 'The highways of Bangkok are not streets or roads but the river and the canals. Boats are the universal means of conveyance and communication'. The wheeled motor vehicle has long since become Bangkok's conveyance of choice, but fortunately it hasn't yet become universal. A vast network of canals and river tributaries surrounding Bangkok still carry a motley fleet of watercraft, from paddled canoes to rice barges. In these areas many homes, trading houses and temples remain oriented towards water life and provide a fascinating glimpse into the past, when Thais still considered themselves *jâo náam* (water lords). See also Boat under Getting Around later in this chapter.

Chao Phraya River Express You can observe urban river life from the water for 1½ to three hours for only 10B to 15B by boarding a Chao Phraya River Express boat at Tha Wat Ratchasingkhon, just north of Saphan Krungthep. If you want to ride the entire length of the express route all the way to Nonthaburi, this is where you begin. Ordinary bus Nos 1, 17 and 75 and air-con bus No 4 pass Tha Ratchasingkhon. Or you could board at any other express boat pier in Bangkok for a shorter ride to Nonthaburi; eg, 20 minutes from Tha Phayap (first stop north of Saphan Krungthon), or 30 minutes from Tha Phra Athit (near Saphan Phra Pin Klao). Express boats run about every 15 minutes from 6 am to 6 pm daily.

Khlong Bangkok Noi Taxi Another good boat trip is the Bangkok Noi canal taxi route that leaves from Tha Chang next to Silpakorn University. The farther up the khlawng you go, the better the scenery, with teak houses on stilts, old wát and plenty of greenery.

Stop off at Wat Suwannaram to view 19th-century jataka murals painted by two of early Bangkok's foremost religious muralists. Art historians consider these the best surviving temple paintings in Bangkok. The one-way fare anywhere is 10B to 30B depending on how far you go. The boats run 6.30 am to 11 pm, but are most frequent between 6 and 11 am. Nowadays a tourist boat makes the run for 60B per person; you may find that the regular canal taxis send you to this boat, since they receive a few baht commission from the tourist operators.

Both boats terminate in Bang Yai, a district in Nonthaburi. From a pier at Wat Sao Thong Hin at Bang Yai you can continue by boat taxi down picturesque **Khlong Om** and see durian plantations. Boats leave every 15 minutes between 4 am and 8 pm and the fare is 6B. If you want to make a loop, you can return from Tha Nonthaburi via a Chao Phraya River Express to any pier in central Bangkok (6B to 10B depending on the distance).

Other Canal Taxis From Tha Tien near Wat Pho, get a canal taxi along **Khlong Mon** (leaving every half-hour from 6.30 am to 6 pm, costing 5B) for more typical canal scenery, including orchid farms. A longer excursion could be made by making a loop along Khlongs Bangkok Noi, Chak Phra and Mon, an all-day trip. An outfit called Chao Phraya Chartered Company (☎ 622 7657 ext 111) runs a tour boat to Khlong Mon from Tha River City shopping complex pier each afternoon from 2.30 to 4.30 pm for 420B per person, including refreshments.

Boats to **Khlong Bangkok Yai**, available from either Tha Tien or Tha Ratchini, pass Wat Intharam, where a chedi contains the ashes of Thonburi's King Taksin, who was assassinated in 1782. Fine gold and black lacquerwork adorning the main bòt doors depicts the mythical *naariiphŏn* tree, which bears fruit shaped like beautiful maidens.

It is possible to go as far from Bangkok as Suphanburi and Ratchaburi by boat, though this typically involves many boat connections (see the Central Thailand chapter).

BANGKOK

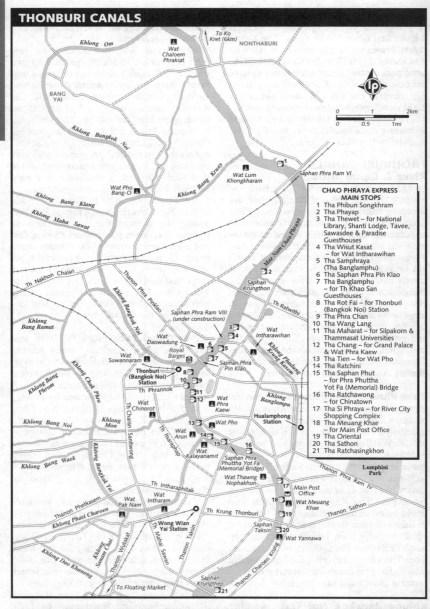

THONBURI CANALS

Khlong Om

To Ko Kret (6km)

NONTHABURI

BANG YAI

Wat Chaloem Prakiat

Khlong Bangkok Noi

Khlong Bang Kruay

Saphan Phra Ram VI

Wat Lum Khongkharam

Wat Pho Bang-O

Khlong Bang Klang

Khlong Maha Sawat

Mae Nam Chao Phraya

Th Nakhon Chaisri

Thanon Phra Pinklao

Khlong Bangkok Noi

Saphan Krungthon

Th Ratwithi

Khlong Bang Ramat

Wat Daowadung

Saphan Phra Ram VIII (under construction)

Wat Intharawihan

Khlong Phadung Krung Kasem

Wat Suwannaram

Royal Barges

Saphan Phra Pin Klao

Thonburi (Bangkok Noi) Station

Th Phrannok

Khlong Bang Phrom

Khlong Chak Phra

Wat Chinorot

Khlong Bang Noi

Th Charan Santiwong

Khlong Mon

Wat Phra Kaew

Khlong Banglampu

Wat Pho

Hualamphong Station

Khlong Bang Wack

Th Itsaraphap

Wat Arun

Wat Kalayanamit

Thanon Phra Ram IV

Lumphini Park

Th Intharaphitak

Saphan Phra Phuttha Yot Fa (Memorial Bridge)

Wat Thawng Nophakhun

Main Post Office

Wat Meuang Khae

Thanon Phetkasem

Wat Pak Nam

Wat Intharam

Th Krung Thonburi

Khlong Phasi Charoen

Wong Wian Yai Station

Thanon Sathon

Saphan Taksin

Th Wutlkat

Th Mahai Sawan

Thanon Taksin

Khlong Dao Khanong

Khlong Sanam Chai

To Floating Market

Saphan Krungthep

Wat Yannawa

Thanon Charoen Krung

CHAO PHRAYA EXPRESS MAIN STOPS

1 Tha Phibun Songkhram
2 Tha Phayap
3 Tha Thewet – for National Library, Shanti Lodge, Tavee, Sawasdee & Paradise Guesthouses
4 Tha Wisut Kasat – for Wat Intharawihan
5 Tha Samphraya (Tha Banglamphu)
6 Tha Saphan Phra Pin Klao
7 Tha Banglamphu – for Th Khao San Guesthouses
8 Tha Rot Fai – for Thonburi (Bangkok Noi) Station
9 Tha Phra Chan
10 Tha Wang Lang
11 Tha Maharat – for Silpakorn & Thammasat Universities
12 Tha Chang – for Grand Palace & Wat Phra Kaew
13 Tha Tien – for Wat Pho
14 Tha Ratchini
15 Tha Saphan Phut – for Phra Phuttha Yot Fa (Memorial) Bridge
16 Tha Ratchawong – for Chinatown
17 Tha Si Phraya – for River City Shopping Complex
18 Tha Meuang Khae – for Main Post Office
19 Tha Oriental
20 Tha Sathon
21 Tha Ratchasingkhon

For details on boat transport on the Bangkok side of the river, where four lengthy canal routes have been revived, see Getting Around later in this chapter. Although they provide quick transport, none of the four right-bank canal routes can be recommended for sightseeing.

Boat Charters If you want to see the Thonburi canals at your own pace, the best thing to do is charter a long-tail boat – it need not be too expensive if you can get a small group together. The usual price is 400B per hour and you can choose from among eight different canals in Thonburi alone. Beware of 'agents' who will try to put you on the boat and rake off an extra commission. Before travelling by boat, establish the price – you can't bargain in the middle of the river.

The piers for hire boats are Tha Chang, Tha Saphan Phut (Memorial Bridge pier) and Tha Si Phraya. Close to the latter, to the rear of the River City shopping complex, is the Tha River City, where the Boat Tour Centre charges the same basic hourly price (400B) and there are no hassles with touts or bargaining. Some boat pilots will discount charter fees to 300B per hour for multi-hour rentals. Of these four piers, Tha Chang usually has the largest selection of boats.

Those interested in seeing Bangkok's deep-water port can hire long-tail boats to Khlong Toey or as far downriver as Pak Nam, which means 'river mouth' in Thai. It's about two hours each way by boat, or a bit quicker if you take a bus or taxi one way.

Dinner Cruises A dozen or more companies in Bangkok run regular cruises along the Chao Phraya for rates ranging from 70B to 1200B per person, depending on how far they go and whether dinner is included with the fare. Most cruises require phone reservations in advance.

The less expensive, more casual boats allow you to order as little or as much as you want from moderately priced menus; a modest charge of 70B per person is added to the bill for the cruise. It's a fine way to dine outdoors when the weather is hot, away from city traffic and cooled by a river breeze. Several of the dinner boats cruise under the well-lit Saphan Phra Ram IX, the

longest single-span cable-suspension bridge in the world. This engineering marvel supports the elevated expressway joining Bangkok's Thanon Tok district with Thonburi's Ratburana district. Those dinner cruises that offer an a la carte menu plus surcharge include:

Khanap Nam Restaurant (☎ 424 8453)
  Saphan Krungthon to Saphan Sathon; twice daily
Riverside Bangkok (☎ 434 0090) Saphan Krungthon to Saphan Phra Ram IX; daily

Loy Nava (☎ 437 4932, 437 7329) offers a more swanky dinner cruise for a set price of 880B for the cruise and dinner, but beer and liquor cost extra. It operates 6 to 8 pm and 8 to 10 pm daily, or by appointment.

The Marriott Royal Garden Riverside Hotel offers a three-hour dinner cruise aboard the *Manohra* for 1200B plus tax and service (about 1413B, excluding drinks).

Sunset Cruises Before its regular three-hour 7.30 pm dinner cruise, the *Manohra* sails at 5 pm from the Marriott Royal Garden Riverside Hotel for an hour-long sunset cocktail cruise. Boarding costs 500B plus tax and service (about 589B altogether), which includes one drink and a light snack. A free river taxi operates between Tha River City and Tha Royal Garden at 4 pm, just in time for the 5 pm cruise departure. Call ☎ 476 0021 for more information.

Longer Cruises All-day and overnight cruises on the river are also available. The Chao Phraya River Express Boat (☎ 222 5330, fax 225 3002/3) does a reasonably priced tour on Sunday only, starting from Tha Maharat at 8 am and returning at 5.30 pm. It includes visits to the Royal Folk Arts & Handicrafts Centre in Bang Sai, Bang Pa-In Palace near Ayuthaya and the bird sanctuary at Wat Phailom in Pathum Thani Province. The price is 330B per adult and 250B for children, excluding lunch, which you arrange on your own in Bang Pa-In. Both Bang Pa-In and Bang Sai charge 50B admission.

Mit Chao Phraya Express Boat Co (☎ 225 6179) operates another moderately priced program through several Thonburi canals, with stops at various historic wát, the Royal Barges and Ko Kret. The tour departs from Tha Chang on Saturday and Sunday at 9.30 am and returns at 4.30 pm. The program costs 200B for adults and 100B for children, excluding admission fees to the aforementioned attractions. It also offers a trip from Tha Chang to Bang Pa-In from 8 am to 5 pm on Sunday. Adults pay 330B, children 250B. Lunch and admission to Bang Pa-In are not included.

The Oriental Hotel's luxurious all air-con *Oriental Queen* (☎ 236 0400) also does a cruise to Bang Pa-In, which leaves at 8 am daily from Tha Oriental and returns by air-con bus at 5 pm. The *Oriental Queen* cruise costs 1900B including lunch and a guided tour. Note that neither of the cruises that visit Bang Pan-In really allow enough time for you to see Ayuthaya properly, so if that's your primary intention, go on your own. On the other hand, we've had letters from history-weary readers who thought 15 to 30 minutes was plenty of time to see the ruins. Two other companies running similar Bang Pa-In and Ayuthaya tours for around 1600B per person are Horizon Cruise (☎ 236 777 ext 1204) from the Shangri-La Hotel, and River Sun Cruise (☎ 266 9316) from the River City shopping centre. The River Sun cruise departs at 8 am and returns at 4.30 pm; lunch is included.

Royal Garden Resorts and the Menam Hotel maintain three restored 50-year-old teak rice barges that have been transformed into four- and 10-cabin cruisers. Decorated with antiques and Persian carpets, these craft represent the ultimate in Mae Nam Chao Phraya luxury, the nautical equivalent of the *Eastern & Oriental Express* train. These barges – two named *Mekhala,* one called *Manohra 2* – typically leave in the afternoon, whether starting out from Bangkok or returning from Ayuthaya. In the evening they anchor at a wát, where a candle-lit dinner is served. The next morning passengers offer food to the monks from the wát, and then the barge moves on to Bang Pa-In. After a tour of the Summer Palace, a long-tail boat takes passengers on a tour of the ruins of Ayuthaya. At present, four Ayuthaya cruises per week are scheduled. The cost for the two-day cruise is variable depending on which barge is used, starting at 6200B to 7370B per person for the *Mekhala* and US$373 to US$426 per

person (plus tax and service) for the superdeluxe, four-cabin *Manohra 2,* and depending on the time of year. Prices include all meals and nonalcoholic beverages, accommodation, guide services, admission fees in Ayuthaya and hotel transfers. Shorter cruises are available by charter. For details contact the Marriott Royal Garden (☎ 476 0021) for the *Manohra 2* or the Menam Hotel (☎ 256 7168) for the *Mekhala.*

THEME & AMUSEMENT PARKS

Just outside Bangkok are a host of artificial tourist attractions that provide either the 'see the whole country in an hour' theme or the standard Western-style amusement park. If these attractions appeal to you, it's often worth booking tickets through travel agencies if the booking includes return transport from your lodgings.

West

Thirty-two kilometres west of Bangkok, on the way to Nakhon Pathom, the **Rose Garden Country Resort** (☎ 253 0295, 295 3261) encompasses a canned Thai 'cultural village' (with demos of handicrafts, dancing, traditional ceremonies and martial arts), swimming pools, tennis courts, a 3-hectare lake, elephant rides and a golf course. Admission to the 24-hectare garden area, which boasts 20,000 rose bushes, is 10B; it's another 220B for the 2.45 pm performances in the cultural village. The resort and rose garden are open 8 am to 6 pm daily, while the cultural village is open 10.30 am to 5 pm. Shuttle buses run between the resort and major Bangkok hotels. There is also a hotel on the premises, should you like the place so much you want to spend the night.

Just 1km north of the Rose Garden, at the 9-hectare **Samphran Elephant Ground & Zoo** (☎ 284 1873), you can see elephant 'roundups' and crocodile shows; a number of other animals can also be observed in zoo-like conditions. Kids generally like this place. It's open daily from 8 am to 5.30 pm, with crocodile wrestling shows at 12.45 and 2.20 pm, elephant shows at 1.45 and 3.30 pm weekdays, a magic show at 1.15 and 3 pm, plus additional shows on weekends and holidays. Admission is 220B for adults, 120B for children.

North-East

In Minburi, 10km north-east of Bangkok, is **Safari World** (Greater Bangkok map; ☎ 518 1000), at 99 Ramindra 1 – a 69-hectare wildlife park said to be the largest 'open zoo' in the world. It's divided into two portions, the drive-through Safari Park and the walk-through Marine Park. The 5km Safari Park drive (aboard air-con coaches or your own vehicle) intersects eight habitats with an assortment of giraffes, lions, zebras, rhinos, monkeys, elephants, orang-utans, and other African and Asian animals (75 mammal species and 300 bird species in all). A Panda House displays rare white pandas, and the Marine Park focuses on trained animal performances by dolphins. Safari World is open 9 am to 5 pm daily; the 'foreigner admission price' is 400B for adults, 300B for children (admission for Thais is 290/185B). It's 45km east of central Bangkok; for public transport catch a No 26 bus from the Victory Monument to Minburi, then a săwngthăew to the park.

South

Two attractions, Ancient City and the Crocodile Farm, in nearby Samut Prakan Province are often included on lists of Bangkok sights. See Samut Prakan Province in the Around Bangkok section later for more details.

SPORTS FACILITIES

The first and grandest of the city's sports facilities is the Royal Bangkok Sports Club (RBSC) between Thanon Henri Dunant and Thanon Ratchadamri (the green oval marked 'Turf' on the Bangkok bus maps). Facilities include a horse track, polo grounds (located elsewhere off Thanon Withayu), a swimming pool, sauna, squash and tennis courts (both hard and grass) and an 18-hole golf course. There's a waiting list for membership, so the only way you're likely to frolic at this prestigious club is to be invited there by a lucky RBSC member.

Membership at the British Club (☎ 234 0247), 189 Thanon Surawong, is open to citizens of Australia, Canada, New Zealand and the UK, or to others by invitation; membership fees are very costly. Among the sports facilities are a pool, golf driving range, and squash and tennis courts.

The least expensive swimming facility in Bangkok is the one operated by the Department of Physical Education (☎ 215 1535) at the National Stadium on Thanon Phra Ram I, next to Mahboonkrong shopping centre. Membership costs just 300B per year plus 25B per hour.

The top-class Clark Hatch Physical Fitness Centres, with weight machines, pool, tennis, squash, aerobics, sauna and massage, can be found at the Hilton International Bangkok, Century Park, Amari Atrium and Amari Watergate Hotels, and in Thaniya Plaza and Charn Issara Tower II; non-hotel guests are welcome.

Sports clubs open to the public include:

Amorn & Sons (☎ 492 8442) 8 Soi Amorn 3, Soi 49, Thanon Sukhumvit; tennis, squash, badminton

Bangna Tennis Court & Swimming Pool (☎ 393 8276) 57/455 Soi Bangna; tennis, swimming

Capitol Club (☎ 661 1210) President Park Residential Complex, Thanon Sukhumvit; aerobics, rock-climbing wall, swimming, tennis, squash, weights, fitness machines

Central Tennis Court (☎ 213 1909) 13/1 Soi Atakanprasit, Thanon Sathon Tai; tennis

Diana Women's Club (☎ 278 1203) 33 Soi 2, Thanon Phahonyothin

Kanpaibun Tennis Court (☎ 391 8784, 392 1832) 10 Soi 40, Thanon Sukhumvit; tennis

Saithip Swimming Pool (☎ 331 2037) 140 Soi 56, Thanon Sukhumvit; tennis, badminton, swimming

Sivalai Club Tennis Court & Swimming Pool (☎ 411 2649) 168 Soi Anantaphum, Thanon Itsaraphap, Thonburi; tennis, swimming

Soi Klang Racquet Club (☎ 391 1194) 8 Soi 49, Thanon Sukhumvit; squash, tennis, racquetball, swimming, aerobics

The Bangkok Gym (☎ 255 2440) 9th floor, Delta Grand Pacific Hotel, 259 Soi 19, Thanon Sukhumvit; weights, sauna, swimming, aerobics

Hash House Harriers

Bangkok has at least five different Hash groups: the regular Bangkok Hash House Harriers; the Harriettes; the Monday HHH; the Siam Sunday HHH; and the Bike Hash. The Bangkok HHH meets at 4.30 pm Saturday (☎ 01-406 8896; men only), while the Bangkok Monday Hash runs at 5.15 pm Monday (☎ 01-925 4344; everyone welcome). The Harriettes meet at 5.30 Wednesday (☎ 01-925 4344; mixed), and the Bike Hash meets monthly on Sunday afternoon for a 20km to 30km mountain-bike ride on the outskirts of Bangkok or overnight trips upcountry.

MEDITATION COURSES

Although at times Bangkok may seem like the most un-Buddhist place on earth, there are several places where foreigners can learn about Theravada Buddhist meditation. (See the Buddhism special section in this chapter for background information on Buddhism in Thailand).

Wat Mahathat

This 18th-century wát opposite Sanam Luang provides meditation instruction from 9 to 10 am, 1 to 2 pm and 8 to 9 pm daily at Section 5, a meditation hall near the monks' residences. Some of the Thai monks here speak English, and there are often Western monks or long-term residents available to interpret. There is also a Saturday session for foreigners at the Dhamma Vicaya Hall. Instruction is based on the Mahasi Sayadaw system of developing the *satipatthana* (foundations of mindfulness). Air-con bus Nos 8 and 12 both pass near the wát; the nearest Chao Phraya River Express pier is Tha Maharat.

Wat Pak Nam

This very large wát, where hundreds of monks and nuns reside during the Buddhist Rains Retreat (*pansăa*), has hosted many foreigners (especially Japanese) over the years. The meditation teacher, Phra Khru Phawana, speaks some English and there are usually people around who can interpret. The emphasis is on developing concentration through *nimitta* (acquired mental images) in order to attain *jhana* (trance absorption states). A small English library is available. Wat Pak Nam is on Thanon Thoet Thai, Phasi Charoen, Thonburi. To get there take bus No 4, 9 or 103. The wát can also be reached by chartered long-tail boat from Tha Chang or Tha Saphan Phut along the river and Thonburi canals.

Wat Rakhang Kositaram

Only a few foreigners have studied at this temple (see Ko Ratanakosin map), but the meditation teacher, Ajahn Mahathawon from Ubon Province in North-Eastern Thailand, has quite a good reputation. The teaching tradition at Wat Rakhang is strongly focussed on Abhidhamma Pitaka, the *pitaka* (one of the three sets of volumes that make up the Theravada Tripitaka, or Buddhist canon) most concerned with Buddhist psychology. Vipassana is considered attainable without strong concentration by means of a dialectic process similar to Krishnamurti's 'choiceless awareness'.

To study here, one ought to be able to speak Thai fairly well; otherwise, an interpreter will have to be arranged. Wat Rakhang is on Thanon Arun Amarin, Thonburi. Cross-river ferries leave frequently from Tha Chang on the opposite bank of the Mae Nam Chao Phraya.

Wat Cholaprathan Rangsarit

The teachers here, Ajahn Pañña (the abbot) and Ajahn Khao, employ a modified version of the Mahasi Sayadaw system of satipatthana. Occasionally there's someone around who can interpret; otherwise it will be necessary to arrange interpretation in advance. This wát also serves as a Bangkok headquarters for monks from Wat Suanmok (see Chaiya in the Southern Thailand chapter). Wat Cholaprathan is in Pak Kret, Nonthaburi Province (although not actually part of Bangkok, Nonthaburi is so connected to Bangkok's urban sprawl you can hardly tell the difference).

World Fellowship of Buddhists

The World Fellowship of Buddhists (WFB; ☎ 661 1284, fax 661 0555), at the back of Benjasiri Park, next to The Emporium, Soi 24, Thanon Sukhumvit, is a clearing house for information on Theravada Buddhism as well as dialogue between various schools of Buddhism. The centre hosts meditation classes (usually led by English-speaking monks from Wat Pa Nanachat, Ubon Ratchathani) from 2 to 6 pm on the first Sunday of every month.

OTHER COURSES

For more information about cooking, language, martial arts and meditation courses in Bangkok, see under Courses in the Facts for the Visitor chapter.

PLACES TO STAY – BUDGET

Bangkok has perhaps the best variety and quality of budget places to stay of any Asian capital, which is one of the reasons why it's such a popular destination for roving world travellers. Because of the wide distribution of places, you might first narrow your choices by deciding which part of the city you want to be in – the tourist shopping ghettos of Thanon Sukhumvit and Thanon Silom-Surawong, the backpackers' ghetto of Banglamphu, the centrally located Siam Square area, boisterous Chinatown or the old travellers' centre around Soi Ngam Duphli, off Thanon Phra Ram IV.

Banglamphu and Chinatown (around Hualamphong station) are the best all-round areas for seeing the real Bangkok, and are the cheapest districts for eating and sleeping. The Siam Square area is also well located, in that it's more or less in the centre of Bangkok and on both Skytrain lines. An extensive selection of city buses pass through the Phra Ram I and Thanon Phayathai intersection near Siam Square.

In Bangkok, budget accommodation is taken to mean places costing 80B to 600B per night.

Banglamphu

If you're on a tight budget head for the Thanon Khao San area, parallel to Thanon Ratchadamnoen Klang – ordinary bus Nos 3, 15, 30, 39, 44, 47, 53, 59 and 79 and aircon bus Nos 11 and 12 will get you there. The Airport Bus (route A-2) also stops nearby. The BTS Skytrain does not extend to Banglamphu, but the new subway under construction will – whenever it's completed. The best way to reach Banglamphu via the Skytrain is to take a Silom line train all the way to its south-western terminus at Saphan Sathon, then take a Chao Phraya River Express boat north along the river and get off at Tha Phra Athit.

This is the main travellers centre and new guesthouses are continually springing up. Rates in Banglamphu are the lowest in Bangkok and, although some of the places are barely adequate (bedbugs are sometimes a problem), a few are excellent value if you can afford just a bit more. At the budget end, rooms are quite small and the dividing walls are thin. Some of these guesthouses have small attached cafes with limited menus. Bathrooms are usually down the hall or out the back somewhere; mattresses may be on the floor.

The least expensive rooms are 80/120B for singles/doubles, though these are hard to

come by due to the hordes of people seeking them out. More common are the 120/160B rooms. Occasionally, triple rooms are available for as low as 180B and dorm beds for 70B. During most of the year, it pays to visit several guesthouses before making a decision, but in the high season (December to February, when Thanon Khao San is bursting with life), you'd better take the first vacant bed you come across. The best time of day to find a vacancy is from 9 to 10 am.

In the early 1980s, when we first stumbled onto Thanon Khao San, there were only two Chinese-Thai hotels on the road, the Nith Jaroen Suk (now called Nith Charoen Hotel) and the Sri Phranakhon (now the Khao San Palace Hotel). Now there are close to 100 guesthouses in the immediate vicinity (hundreds more off Khao San), far too many to list here. If you haven't already arrived with a recommendation in hand, use the Banglamphu and Thanon Khao San area maps and simply pick a place at random for your first night. If you're not satisfied you can stow your gear and explore the area until something better turns up. A tip: the guesthouses along Thanon Khao San tend to be cubicles in modern shophouses, while those in Banglamphu's quieter lanes and alleys are often housed in old homes, some of them with a lot of character. There is also a whole new generation of multistorey hotel-like accommodations, many of them good value.

At the cheaper places it's not worth calling ahead, since the staff usually won't hold a room for you unless you pay in advance. For places that *may* take phone reservations we've included phone numbers. Unless otherwise indicated, the following places are marked on the Thanon Khao San (Khao San Road) map.

Central Banglamphu Many of the places on or just off Thanon Khao San are very similar to one another – small rooms with toilet and shower down the hall. This time around we still liked *Prakorp's House & Restaurant*, which offers 90/180B rooms in a teak house and perhaps the best guesthouse coffee on Khao San. Other OK digs are available at friendly *Bonny Guest House*, the strip's oldest, with single/double rooms for 140B and dorm beds for 60B. *Grand Guest House*, *Lek Guest House* and *Lucky Beer & Guest House*, all in the 100B to 250B range,

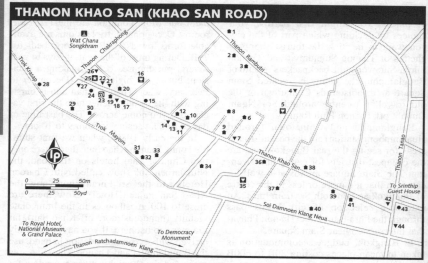

THANON KHAO SAN (KHAO SAN ROAD)

continue to get good reviews. *Chada Guest House* has small but newly renovated rooms for 180/200B single/double. *Chart Guest House* adds air-con for 400B and fan for 100/130B. *Classic Place* has decent single/double rooms with fan for 200/250B and air-con for 390/490B double/triple. *Sitdhi Guest House & Restaurant* is friendly and charges just 100/150B for singles/ doubles with shared facilities. *CH I Guest House* was closed for renovation but the ongoing work indicates it will be a dandy hang-out in the 150B to 300B range when open again.

Moving a little more upmarket, the friendly *Khao San Palace Hotel* (☎ 282 0578), down an alley at 139 Thanon Khao San, is well kept; rooms cost 280B to 390B with fan and private bathroom, 400B to 580B with air-con, TV and hot water. A deluxe room is 730B. Down a parallel alley, the *Nith Charoen Hotel* (☎ 281 9872) has rooms with bathroom and fan for 360B single/double, 700B for air-con. The *Nana Plaza Inn* (☎ 281 6402), near the Siri Guest House towards Thanon Khao San's eastern end, is a large, hotel-like enterprise built around a restaurant; air-con/hot-water rooms go for 500/700B single/double. The similar-looking *D&D Inn* costs 350/500B single/double. Each room has a TV and IDD phone. The four-storey *Siam Oriental* (☎ 620 0312, 190 Thanon Khao San) has decent singles with

fan for 280B and air-con rooms that can accommodate up to four people for up to 650B. There's a large restaurant and a lift.

Parallel to Thanon Khao San but much quieter is Trok Mayom, an alley reserved for mostly pedestrian traffic. *J & Joe* (☎ 281 2949, 281 1198) is a sprawling old teak complex with singles for 90B, doubles for 160B to 180B and triples for 230B, and sitting areas for hanging out; it's often full and a little noisy. There's also *New Joe* (☎ 281 2948, fax 281 5547) on Trok Mayom, a rather modern looking place set off the alley, with an outdoor cafe downstairs. Rooms cost 200/280B single/double with private bathroom, 380B with air-con; email and fax services are available. Up a tiny alley nearby, the relatively new *Barn Thai Guest House* (☎ 281 9041) is very quiet and secure, and offers rooms in an old wooden house or newer wing for 300B to 350B with shared bathroom and 400B for a double with private bathroom. Although priced higher than normal for this neighbourhood, it's kept very clean and the front gate is locked nightly.

Up a narrow soi nearby, *Khao San Privacy Guest House* (Privacy Guest House) offers rooms with fan for 150/200B and with air-con at 380/440B. Farther west, towards Thanon Chana Songkhram, are *Ranee's Guest House* (120/220B with shared bathroom, 350B air-con) and

THANON KHAO SAN (KHAO SAN ROAD)

PLACES TO STAY
1 Viengtai Hotel
2 Au-Thong Restaurant & Guest House
3 Tuptim Bed & Breakfast
6 Nith Charoen Hotel
8 Khao San Palace Hotel
9 Grand Guest House
10 Lucky Beer & Guest House
12 Lek Guest House
13 D&D Inn
17 Chart Guest House
19 Prakorp's House & Restaurant
20 Sitdhi Guest House & Restaurant
29 J & Joe
30 Barn Thai Guest House
31 Ranee's Guest House

32 New Joe Guest House
33 Khao San Privacy Guest House
34 Bonny Guest House
36 Siam Oriental
37 Nana Plaza Inn
38 Classic Place; Central Minimart
39 CH I Guest House
40 7 Holder Guest House
41 Chada Guest House

PLACES TO EAT
4 Chabad House
7 Wally; Orm
11 Center Khao Sarn
14 Royal India Restaurant
18 Hello Restaurant

21 Namastee Indian Cuisine
22 Himalayan Kitchen
26 Chochana; Sarah
27 Gulliver's Traveler's Tavern
42 Arawy Det
44 No. 147 Thai Food

OTHER
5 Susie Pub
15 Shaman Bookstore
16 Hole in the Wall
23 Bangkok Internet Cafe
24 Banana Leaf Books & Cafe
25 Chana Songkhram Police Station
28 Jitti's Gym & Homestay
35 Austin Pub
43 Aporia Books

7 Holder (220B), which seems to cater to Japanese travellers and even has Japanese fonts on its Internet cafe computers.

Walking west along Thanon Rambutri you'll come to two side-by-side guesthouses in old restored wooden buildings with cheery paint jobs. *Au-Thong Restaurant & Guest House* (☎ 629 2172, ✉ au_thong@hotmail .com, 78 Thanon Rambutri) is more of a restaurant that just happens to have a few very simple rooms with shared toilet and shower for 300B. The garden restaurant in front (there's also a small air-con dining room inside the old house) is one of the best eateries in the neighbourhood if you know how to order Thai food. Next door, *Tuptim Bed & Breakfast* (☎ 629 1535, fax 629 1540, ✉ mick@ksc.th.com, 82 Thanon Rambutri) looks similar but the emphasis is on the rooms rather than the food. Tuptim has 19 air-con rooms with shared gender-segregated toilets and hot-water showers for 399/550B, including breakfast. There are also two single rooms with fan for 250B.

West Banglamphu Several long-running guesthouses are on sois between Thanon Chakraphong and the Mae Nam Chao Phraya, putting them within walking distance of Tha Phra Athit where you can catch express boats. This area is also close to the Thonburi (Bangkok Noi) station across the river, the National Museum and the National Theatre. Unless otherwise indicated, the following places are marked on the Banglamphu map.

West of Chakraphong on Soi Rambutri, *Sawasdee House* (☎ 281 8138, fax 629 0994) follows the trend towards hotel-style accommodation in the Thanon Khao San area, with a large restaurant and bar downstairs and small to medium-sized rooms on several floors upstairs. Rooms with fan and shared facilities are 160B to 250B a single and 320B to 360B a double. Rooms with private bathroom and fan cost 400B, while air-con rooms go for 550B.

Right around the bend along Soi Rambutri is the popular *Merry V Guest House* (☎ 282 9267), with rooms from 120B to 350B. The cosy *Green Guest House* (☎ 926 2104) is next door and is slightly less expensive at 100/140B single/double with shared facilities, or 240B with private bathroom. At *My House* on the same soi, the Thai-style downstairs sitting area looks nice, and decent singles/doubles with shared bathroom are 120/200B to 180/300B with private facilities. Air-con is available for 500B.

A rash of new and larger places have opened up towards the south-west end of Soi Rambutri and around the corner to the south on Trok Rong Mai. *Bella Bella House* (☎ 629 3090), just past the soi that leads to New Siam Guest House, is a new five-storey building with a sheltered rooftop area and rooms for 150B single, 220B double. A few doors farther on, *Sawasdee Krungthep Inn* (☎/fax 629 0072) offers rooms in a new four-storey building for 350B a fan double, 400B/450B an air-con single/double, and 500B/600B a triple/quadruple. *Baan Sabai*

BANGKOK

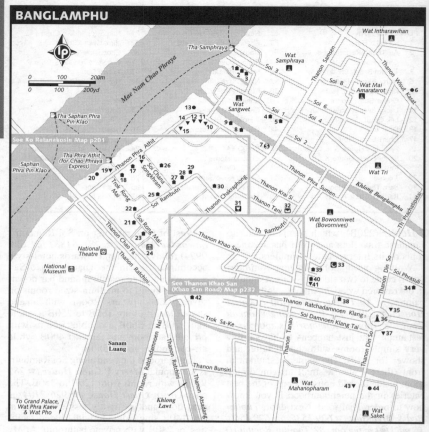

BANGLAMPHU

(☎ 629 1599, fax 629 1595) features a nice large lobby on the ground floor, finished to resemble an old Bangkok-style building. The inn's 64 rooms rent for 170B a fan single, 270B to 320B a fan double and 450B to 480B an air-con double.

Also in this vicinity, off the southern end of Thanon Rambutri, the family run *Chai's House* offers clean rooms for 100/200/300B single/double/triple and 300B single/double with air-con, all with shared bathroom. It's a quiet, security-conscious place with a sitting area out the front. The food must be cheap and good, as it's a favourite gathering spot for local Thai college students on weekends.

Backtracking along Thanon Rambutri and turning left into Soi Chana Songkhram, you'll find the four-storey *New Siam Guest*

House (☎ 282 4554, fax 281 7461), where quiet clean rooms cost 200/250B with shared bathroom, 300B with private bathroom, 495B with air-con; storage lockers are available downstairs. This place seems exceptionally well organised and offers good food in the downstairs cafe; it's almost always full.

Continue towards the river and you'll reach Thanon Phra Athit. On the eastern side of the road, the *Peachy Guest House* (☎ 281 6471) and *New Merry V* are more like small hotels than family-type guesthouses. Peachy has been completely renovated since we last stopped by. Rooms with shared bathroom are 150B single/double, while rooms with air-con and private hot-water bathroom are 350B. Dorm beds cost 55B per person. The New Merry V, north of the Peachy, has

BANGLAMPHU

PLACES TO STAY		
1	Home & Garden Guest House	
2	Clean & Calm Guest House	
3	River House	
4	Villa Guest House	
5	Truly Yours Guest House	
8	Gipsy Guest House	
9	PS Guest House	
17	New Merry V	
18	Peachy Guest House	
21	Baan Sabai	
22	Sawasdee Krungthep Inn	
23	Chai's House	
25	Bella Bella House	
26	New Siam Guest House	
27	Green Guest House	
28	Merry V Guest House	

29	My House	
30	Sawasdee House	
34	Prasuri Guest House	
38	Sweety Guest House	
39	Central Guest House	
40	Srinthip Guest House	
42	Royal Hotel	

PLACES TO EAT		
10	Joy Luck Club	
11	Kuay Tiaw Mae	
12	Roti-Mataba	
14	Khrua Nopparat	
15	108	
16	Raan Kin Deum; Saffron Bakery	
19	Ton Pho	

35	Vijit (VR)	
37	Methavalai Sorn Daeng	
41	Vegetarian Restaurants	
43	Arawy Restaurant	

OTHER		
6	Viang Travel	
7	Siam Commercial Bank	
13	Phra Sumen Fort	
20	UNICEF	
24	National Gallery; National Film Archives	
31	Salvador Dali	
32	Post Office	
33	Mosque	
36	Democracy Monument	
44	City Hall	

comfortable rooms with private hot-water showers for 250B and with shared bathroom for 120B. Air-con rooms are 380B.

East Banglamphu There are several guesthouses clustered in the alleys east of Thanon Tanao. In general, the rooms are bigger and quieter here than at the places around Thanon Khao San. *Central Guest House* (☎ 282 0667) is just off Thanon Tanao on Trok Bowonrangsi – look for the rather inconspicuous signs. Clean, simple singles/doubles go for 80/130B.

Farther south, off Trok Bowonrangsi in an old wooden house, *Srinthip* has singles/doubles from 150B. The entrance is grotty, but the rooms are OK. Around the corner, on a small road parallel to Ratchadamnoen Klang, is the *Sweety Guest House* (☎ 281 6756) with small windowless singles for 80B to 100B, larger doubles for 120B to 200B and air-con rooms for 350B. Sweety has a roof terrace for hanging laundry.

If you follow Trok Mayom straight through, away from Thanon Tanao, you'll reach Thanon Din So. Cross Thanon Din So, walk north from the roundabout and you'll see a sign for *Prasuri Guest House* (☎/fax 280 1428), down Soi Phrasuli on the right; quiet, clean singles/doubles/triples cost 190/220/300B with fan, 330/360/390B with air-con – all rooms have private bathroom.

North Banglamphu The clean, friendly *PS Guest House* (☎ 282 3932) is all the way at the end of Thanon Phra Sumen towards the river, off the south side of Khlong Banglamphu; light and airy rooms go for 130/190/250B single/double/triple (all with shared bathroom). A restaurant is downstairs, and upstairs in the back is a small seating area overlooking the canal. Next door, *Gipsy Guest House* offers a confusing rabbit warren of dark but clean rooms with outside bathroom for 200B streetside, 250B canalside (only the latter have outside windows).

Off Thanon Samsen, north of Khlong Banglamphu, is a small cluster of guesthouses in convenient proximity to the Tha Samphraya river express landing. On Soi 1 Samsen, just off Thanon Samsen, the Thanon Khao San-style *Truly Yours Guest House* (☎ 282 0371) offers 80B to 200B fan rooms over a downstairs restaurant. Farther along Soi 1, *Villa Guest House* (☎ 281 7009) is a quiet, leafy, private old teak house with 10 rooms costing 200B to 450B; it's often full. Up on Soi 3 Samsen (also known as Soi Wat Samphraya), are the *River House* (☎ 280 0876), *Home & Garden Guest House* (☎ 280 1475)* and *Clean & Calm Guest House*, each with small but clean rooms with shared bathroom for 70B to 150B. The latter place is quite popular with West Africans waiting for visas. Note that Soi 3 zigs left, then zags right before reaching these three guesthouses, a good 10-minute walk from Thanon Samsen. River House is the best of the three.

Thewet & National Library Area

The district north of Banglamphu near the National Library is another travellers' enclave. Head north up Thanon Samsen from Thanon Wisut Kasat for 500m or so and cross

BANGKOK

the canal to the place where Thanon Phitsanulok finishes on Thanon Samsen and where Thanon Si Ayuthaya crosses Thanon Samsen. Just beyond this junction is the National Library. Ordinary bus Nos 19 and 53 and air-con bus No 5 pass this intersection, or you can arrive via Chao Phraya River Express boats by getting off at Tha Thewet, at the end of Thanon Si Ayuthaya. If you're coming by taxi, tell the driver 'Wat Thewrat', which is near the pier. The following places are marked on the Central Bangkok map.

Turn on Thanon Si Ayuthaya towards the river (west from Samsen), and on two parallel sois off the northern side of Thanon Si Ayuthaya you'll find four guesthouses run by various members of the same extended family: *Tavee Guest House* (☎ 282 5983), *Sawasdee Guest House* (☎ 282 5349), *85 Backpacker's Lodge* (☎ 282 3231) and *Original Paradise Guest House* (☎ 282 8673). All are well kept, fairly quiet and cost from 150/390B single/double. The Sawasdee also offers dorm beds for just 50B. Standing out from the rest, the nicely decorated and well-run *Shanti Lodge* (☎ 281 2497), on the corner of one of the sois, costs a bit more – 200/230B for rooms with fan, 400/450B with air-con, 100B for a dorm bed. Shanti has the best cafe and sitting area of the lot.

A sixth, independently run place on the same soi as Paradise is *Little Home Guest House* (☎ 281 3412), which is similar to the others in this area except that it has a busy travel agency at the front. Rooms are 150/300B.

Nearby Tha Thewet, a Chao Phraya River Express pier provides good access to the National Library area. From the pier walk east along Thanon Krung Kasem to Thanon Samsen, turn left, cross the canal and take another left onto Thanon Si Ayuthaya. Ordinary bus Nos 3, 16, 30, 31, 32, 33, 53, 64 and 90 and air-con bus Nos 5 and 6 pass Thanon Si Ayuthaya while going up and down Thanon Samsen. Air-con bus No 10 from the airport also passes close to the area along Thanon Ratwithi to the north, before crossing Saphan Krungthon.

East of Thanon Samsen you'll find the *Bangkok International Youth Hostel* (☎ 282 0950, fax 628 7416, ✉ bangkok @tyha.org, 25/2 Thanon Phitsanulok). A bed in the 16-bed fan dorm costs 70B a night, while in the air-con dorm it's 120B. Doubles with fan and private hot-water bathroom cost 250B (no single fan rooms are available), while air-con rooms with private facilities cost 280/350B single/ double. There's a cafeteria downstairs. The hostel no longer accepts nonmembers as guests. Annual Hostelling International (formerly IYHF) membership costs 300B, or you can purchase a temporary membership for 50B. For each temporary membership fee paid, you receive a 'welcome stamp', six of which entitle you to a one-year membership.

Soi Ngam Duphli

This area off Thanon Phra Ram IV is where most budget travellers used to come on their first trip to Bangkok back in the 1970s and early 1980s. With a couple of notable exceptions, most of the places here are not especially cheap and the area has become slightly seedy. Overall, the Banglamphu area has better-value accommodation, although some travellers still prefer Soi Ngam Duphli, which has less of a 'scene' and some good-value places. Several countries maintain embassies on nearby Thanon Sathon, so it's also a convenient location for those with visa/passport business at these embassies. Unless otherwise indicated, the following places are marked on the Central Bangkok map.

The entrance to the soi is on Thanon Phra Ram IV, near the Thanon Sathon Tai intersection, and within walking distance of the verdant Lumphini Park and the Thanon Silom business district. Ordinary bus Nos 13, 14, 74, 109, 115 and 116 and air-con bus No 7 all pass by the entrance to Soi Ngam Duphli along Thanon Phra Ram IV. The nearest Skytrain station is Sala Daeng, on Thanon Silom.

At the northern end of Soi Ngam Duphli near Thanon Phra Ram IV is *ETC Guest House* (☎ 286 9424, 287 1478), an efficiently run, multistorey building with a travel agency downstairs. The rooms are small and uninspiring but clean, and the rates are 140B for singles/doubles with fan and shared bathroom, 180/280B with fan and private bathroom. All room rates include a breakfast of cereal, fruit, toast and coffee or tea.

The *Tungmahamek Privacy Hotel* (☎ 286 2339, 286 8811), across the road and to the south of the mid-range Malaysia Hotel, is fully air-conditioned and costs 370B for a double with private bathroom.

Many 'short-time' residents here give the place a sleazy feel, although it's less of a 'scene' than the Malaysia Hotel.

Turn left (south-east) from Soi Ngam Duphli into Soi Si Bamphen, then turn left at the second soi on the left, then take the first right and you'll end up in a cul-de-sac with guesthouses of varying quality. *Madam Guest House* gets mixed reports for its 160B to 240B rooms with fan. Next door, the *Lee 3 Guest House* is pleasant enough and has large rooms with fan and shared bathroom for 120/160B, 200B for private bathroom. The friendly *Sala Thai Daily Mansion* (☎ 287 1436) is at the end of the alley and has large, clean rooms for 200B to 350B, all with shared bathroom. A sitting area with TV on the 3rd floor makes for a pleasant gathering place, and there is a breezy rooftop terrace. The owner speaks English and her design background is evident in the tasteful furnishings. Many repeat or long-term guests fill the rooms here.

If you continue north along the main soi that passes the previously mentioned guesthouses you'll come to a left turn which deadends at Soi Saphan Khu (parallel to Soi Ngam Duphli). Turn right and you'll come to two rather more upmarket guesthouses on your left, *Charlie House* (☎ 679 8330), with a coffee shop, and *PS Guest House* (formerly Four Brothers Guest House; ☎ 679 8822–4). PS costs 400B per day (6000B per month) for air-con rooms. For information on Charlie House see Places to Stay – Mid-Range.

Chinatown & Hualamphong Station

This area is central and colourful, although rather noisy. There are numerous cheap hotels but it's not a travellers centre like Soi Ngam Duphli or Banglamphu. Watch your pockets and bags around the Hualamphong area, both on the street and on the bus. The cream of the razor artists operate here as train passengers make good pickings. Unless otherwise indicated, the following places are marked on the Chinatown & Phahurat map.

The *New Empire Hotel* (☎ 234 6990–6, fax 234 6997, 572 Thanon Yaowarat) is near the Thanon Charoen Krung intersection, a short walk from Wat Traimit. Aircon singles/doubles with hot water are 450B to 600B, with a few more-expensive rooms for up to 800B – a bit noisy, but a

great location if you like Chinatown. The New Empire is a favourite among Chinese Thais from Thailand's southern regions.

Other Chinatown hotels of this calibre, most without Roman-script signs out the front, can be found along Thanon Yaowarat, Thanon Chakraphet and Thanon Ratchawong. The *Burapha Hotel* (☎ 221 3545–9, fax 226 1723), at the intersection of Thanon Mahachai and Thanon Charoen Krung, on the edge of Chinatown, is a notch better than the Empire and has rooms from 550B.

Straddling the budget and mid-range price range is the *River View Guest House* (Thanon Silom, Thanon Surawong & Thanon Sathon map; ☎ 234 5429, 235 8501, fax 237 5428, @ riverview@mailcity.com, 768 Soi Phanurangsi, Thanon Songwat) in the Talat Noi area south of Chinatown – wedged between Bangrak (Silom) and Chinatown. The building is behind the Jao Seu Kong Chinese shrine, about 400m from the Royal Orchid Sheraton, in a neighbourhood filled with small machine shops. To get there, turn right from the corner of Thanon Si Phraya (facing the River City shopping complex), take the fourth left, then the first right. Large rooms are 490B with fan and private bathroom, 690B with air-con and hot water. As the name suggests, many rooms have a Mae Nam Chao Phraya view; the view from the 8th floor restaurant is superb, even if you have to wake up the staff to get a meal. If you call from the River City complex, someone from the guesthouse will pick you up. It's not far from Tha Ratchawong.

Close to the River View Guest House on Thanon Songwat is the *Chao Phraya Riverside Guest House* (☎ 222 6344, 244 8450, fax 223 1696, 1128 Thanon Songwat), in the heart of a busy area filled with warehouses and trucks loading and unloading all day and, like the River View, hard to find. From Thanon Ratchawong, turn left onto Thanon Songwat, then proceed for 75m and keep an eye out for a Chinese school on the left. Turn right into a soi opposite, and you'll find the guesthouse towards the end of the soi on the left. At the time of writing this place was closed for renovations, but when it reopens this will be another good riverside choice.

Closer to the River City shopping complex, and easier to find, *River City Guest House* (Thanon Silom, Thanon Surawong & Thanon Sathon map; ☎ 235 1429, *fax 237 3127, 11/4–5 Soi 24, Thanon Charoen Krung)* has decent rooms with two twin beds, clean bathroom with tub and hot water, TV, fridge, phone and air-con for 500B a night. There's a Chinese restaurant downstairs, and the management speaks better Mandarin than Thai.

Along the eastern side of Hualamphong station at 445 Thanon Rong Muang, the *Sri Hualamphong Hotel (Central Bangkok map)* is a very long-running and atmospheric spot – if you go in for old Thai-Chinese hotels – with large rooms for 180B with fan. The massive staircase and terrace sitting areas give it a certain charm, although it's probably not the best choice for a woman travelling alone. The *Sahakit Hotel (Shakij; Central Bangkok map)* is a few doors down towards Thanon Phra Ram IV and is quite OK. The rooms cost from 120B, but the staff seem reluctant to take fàràng; if you stay, try to get a 4th-floor room, which has a terrace with a view and the occasional breeze.

Out towards the front of the station, after Thanon Rong Muang makes a sharp curve, is the rather unfriendly *Station Hotel (Central Bangkok map)*, a classic Third-World dive. Recently spruced up a bit, rooms with fan and attached bathroom cost 250B, 400B with air-con.

Costing more but quieter and more secure is the *Krung Kasem Srikung Hotel (Central Bangkok map; ☎ 225 0132, fax 225-4705, 1860 Thanon Krung Kasem)*, south-west of the station. Clean, sizable rooms cost 550B with fan, air-con and hot water. There's a small coffee shop downstairs.

Siam Square

Several good places can be found in this central area, which has the additional advantage of being on the Khlong Saen Saep canal taxi route and both Skytrain lines. In addition, this area has good bookshops, several banks, shopping centres and eight movie theatres within a 10- to 15-minute walk. These places are on the Siam Square & Pratunam map.

There are several upper-end budget places on or near Soi Kasem San 1, off Thanon Phra Ram I near Jim Thompson's House and the National Stadium. The eight-storey *Muangphol Mansion (Muangphon Mansion; ☎ 215 0033, fax 216 8053)*, on the corner of Soi Kasem San 1 and Thanon Phra Ram I, has singles/doubles from 450B. It's

in bad need of remodelling but remains relatively popular. Behind the Muangphol, off this soi, is the apartment-style *Pranee Building (☎ 216 3181, fax 215 0364)*, which has one entrance next to the Muangphol and another on Phra Ram I. Rooms with private bathroom and fan are 300B; air-con rooms with hot water are 450B. The Pranee also offers long-term rental at a 10% discount.

White Lodge (☎ 216 8867, fax 216 8228, 36/8 Soi Kasem San 1) is past the more expensive Reno Hotel (see Places to Stay – Mid-Range later) and on the left. It offers clean if somewhat small rooms at 400B single/ double. There's a pleasant terrace cafe out the front. The next one down on Soi Kasem San 1 is the three-storey *Wendy House (☎ 216 2436, fax 216 8053)*, where small but clean rooms with air-con, hot-water shower and TV go for 350/450B. Rooms with fridges cost 550B. If you're carrying unusually heavy bags, note there's no lift. A small restaurant is on the ground floor.

Next up the soi is the ancient *Star Hotel (☎ 215 0020, 36/1 Soi Kasem San 1)*, a classic mid-1960s Thai no-tell motel, with fairly clean, comfortable, air-con rooms with bathroom and TV for 500B a double (350B without TV).

Opposite the Star is *A-One Inn (☎ 215 3029, fax 216 4771, 25/13–15 Soi Kasem San 1)*, a friendly place that gets a lot of return business. Fair-sized air-con doubles with bathroom, hot water and TV are 450B; spacious triples are 650B (rates may drop 100B in the low season). The similar *Bed & Breakfast Inn (☎ 215 3004)* diagonally opposite has room rates that fluctuate from 380B to 650B depending on room size and demand; the air-con rooms are substantially smaller than those at the A-One Inn, but the rates include a European breakfast.

Thanon Sukhumvit

Staying in this area puts you in the newest part of Bangkok and the farthest from old Bangkok near the river. Taxis take longer to get here because of the one-way street system. On the other hand the Skytrain runs all the way from the start of Sukhumvit at Thanon Ploenchit to well beyond the Eastern Bus Terminal. The majority of hotels in this area are priced in the mid-range, but there are some budget options. These places are on the Thanon Sukhumvit map.

The oldest and most centrally located hotel in the Thanon Sukhumvit area is *The Atlanta* (☎ 252 1650, 252 6069, fax 656 8123, 78 Soi 2, Thanon Sukhumvit). Owned since its construction in the 1950s by Dr Max Henn, a former secretary to the Maharajah of Bikaner and owner of Bangkok's first international pharmacy, the Atlanta is a simple but reliable stand-by with clean, comfortable rooms in several price categories. Rooms with private cold-water shower, fan and one single and/or double bed cost 330/450B single/double. Air-con rooms with hot-water showers go for 450/570/690B single/double/triple. A small air-con suite with two single beds and a small living room costs 500/620/740B, while a large air-con suite with a living room and two bedrooms sleeping up to four persons is 1200B. All rooms have built-in personal safes. Children under 12 can stay with their parents for 60B extra. Monthly stays paid in advance get a 10% discount.

The Atlanta's 1954-vintage swimming pool was the first hotel pool in Thailand; the original 1950s-era hotel lobby is occasionally used as a backdrop for Bangkok fashion shoots. The subdued, simply decorated coffee shop features a heavily annotated menu (itself a crash course in Thai cuisine), a selection of British, German and French newspapers, a sound system playing Thai, classical and jazz (including an hour of King Bhumibol's compositions beginning at noon) and evening video selections that include film classics with Thailand themes (eg, *Chang, Bridge on the River Kwai*). In the lobby area, letter-writing desks, each with its own light and fan, round out the offerings at this Bangkok institution. The Nana Skytrain station is about 15 minutes away on foot.

The L-shaped, aquamarine-coloured *Golden Palace Hotel* (☎ 252 5115, fax 254 1538, 15 Soi 1, Thanon Sukhumvit) has a decent swimming pool, is well situated and costs 490/520B for a room with air-con and bathroom. On the next soi east, the quiet *Best Inn* (☎ 253 0573, 75/5–6 Soi 3, Thanon Sukhumvit) provides smallish rooms with fan for 400B and air-con rooms for 500B.

Moving farther out on Thanon Sukhumvit, the *Miami Hotel* (☎ 253 0369, fax 253 1266, e miamihtl@asiaaccess.net.th, 2 Soi 13, Thanon Sukhumvit) dates back to the 1960s and 1970s Vietnam R&R period. The room and service quality seems to seesaw every

three years or so, but at the moment it's decent value at 400/500B for clean air-con rooms with hot water and TV, plus a small swimming pool and coffee shop; discounts are given for long-term stays.

PLACES TO STAY – MID-RANGE

Bangkok is saturated with small and medium-sized hotels in this category (from roughly 600B to 1800B per night). The clientele are a very mixed bunch of Asian business travellers, Western journalists on slim expense accounts, economy-class tour groups, and a smattering of independent tourists who seem to have chosen their hotels at random. Not quite 'international class', these places often offer guests a better sense of being in Thailand than the luxury hotels.

In the low season (March to November), you may be able to get a low-occupancy discount at these places. Many hotels in this category can also be booked through travel agencies or airport hotel desks for 20% to 40% less than the rates listed here.

Banglamphu

Before Thanon Khao San was 'discovered', the most popular Banglamphu hotel was the *Viengtai Hotel* (Thanon Khao San map; ☎ 280 5434, fax 281 8153, 42 Thanon Rambutri). Over the last decade or so the Viengtai has continually renovated its rooms and raised its prices until it now sits solidly in the mid-price range of Bangkok hotels. Standard singles/doubles/triples in the six-storey old wing are 1225/1575/1750B, while deluxe rooms in the remodelled nine-storey wing are 1575/1750/2275B; breakfast is included. There is a swimming pool on the 3rd floor.

After the Oriental and the Atlanta hotels, the next oldest continually operating hotel in the city is the *Royal Hotel* (Banglamphu map; ☎ 222 9111–26, fax 224 2083), which is still going strong on the corner of Thanon Ratchadamnoen Klang and Thanon Atsadang, about 500m from the Democracy Monument. The Royal's 24-hour coffee shop is a favourite rendezvous and the daily buffet breakfast is quite good; this is one of the few upper mid-range places where there are as many Asian as non-Asian guests. Singles/doubles start at 960/1300B, including tax and service. Most taxi drivers know this hotel as the 'Ratanakosin' (as the Thai sign on top of the building reads), not the Royal.

BANGKOK

THANON SILOM, THANON SURAWONG & THANON SATHON

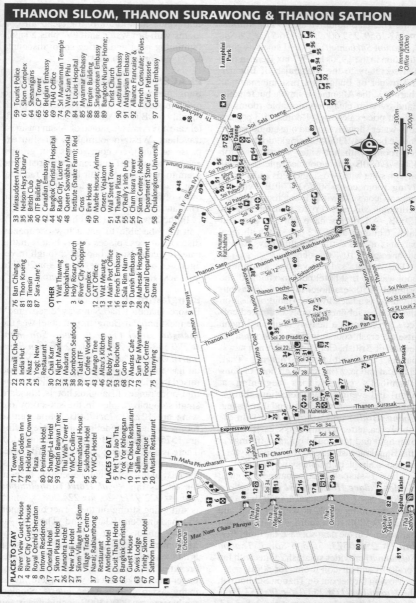

PLACES TO STAY
2 River View Guest House
4 River City Guest House
8 Royal Orchid Sheraton
9 Intown Residence
17 Oriental Hotel
21 Silom Plaza Hotel
26 Manohra Hotel
27 New Fuji Hotel
31 Silom Village Inn; Silom
    Village Trade Centre
37 Narai; Rabianthong
    Restaurant
47 Montien Hotel
60 Dusit Thani Hotel
62 Bangkok Christian
    Guest House
63 Swiss Lodge
67 Trinity Silom Hotel
70 Sathorn Inn
71 Tower Inn
77 Silom Golden Inn
78 Holiday Inn Crowne
    Plaza
80 Peninsula Hotel
82 Shangri-La Hotel
93 Westin Banyan Tree;
    Thai Wah Tower II
94 YMCA Collins
    International House
95 Sukhothai Hotel
96 YWCA Hostel

PLACES TO EAT
5 Pet Tun Jao Tha
7 Yok Yor Khlongsan
10 The Cholas Restaurant
11 Sallim Restaurant
15 Harmonique
20 Muslim Restaurant
22 Himali Cha-Cha
23 India Hut
24 Naaz
25 Yogi; New
    Restaurant
30 Chai Karr
32 Night Market
34 Madura
38 Somboon Seafood
39 Talat ITF
41 Coffee World
43 Mango Tree
46 Mizu's Kitchen
52 Bobby's Arms
53 Le Bouchon
68 Goro
72 Madras Cafe
73 Sun Far Myanmar
    Food Centre
75 Thanying
76 Ban Chiang
81 Thon Krueng
83 Tiensin
87 Sara-Jane's

OTHER
1 Wat Thawng
   Nophakhun
3 Holy Rosary Church
6 River City Shopping
   Complex
12 CAT Office
13 Wat Meuang
14 Main Post Office
16 French Embassy
18 Sala Rim Nam
19 Danish Embassy
28 Mahesak Hospital
29 Central Department
   Store
33 Mirasuddeen Mosque
35 Neilson Hays Library
36 British Club
40 ITF Building
42 Canadian Embassy
44 Bangkok Christian Hospital
45 Radio City; Lucifer
48 Queen Saovabha Memorial
   Institute (Snake Farm); Red
   Cross
49 Eve House
50 Marble House; Arima
   Onsen; Vejakorn
51 Wall Street Tower
54 Thaniya Plaza
55 O'Reilly's Irish Pub
56 Cham Issara Tower
57 Silom Centre; Robinson
   Department Store
58 Chulalongkorn University
59 Tourist Police
61 Silom Complex
64 CP Tower
65 Shenanigans
66 Belgian Embassy
69 THAI Office
74 Sri Mariamman Temple
79 Wat Suan Phlu
84 St Louis Hospital
85 Myanmar Embassy
86 Empire Building
88 Singaporean Embassy
89 Bangkok Nursing Home;
   Christ Church
90 Australian Embassy
91 Malaysian Embassy
92 Alliance Francaise &
   French Consulate; Folies
   Cafe - Patisserie
97 German Embassy

Another mid-range place in this area is the *Thai Hotel* (*Central Bangkok map;* ☎ 282 2831–3, fax 280 1299, 78 Thanon Prachatipatai), which has rooms for 900/1200B.

Chinatown

Mid-range hotels in Chinatown are tough to find. Best bets are the *Chinatown Hotel* (*Chinatown & Phahurat map;* ☎ 225 0230, fax 226 1295, e malaysia@comnet3.ksc .net.th, 526 Thanon Yaowarat), which has rooms for 700B to 1800B, and the *Miramar Hotel* (*Chinatown & Phahurat map;* ☎ 226 3579, fax 225 4994, 777 Thanon Mahachai), where standard singles/doubles cost 600B to 1800B. The *White Orchid Hotel* (*Chinatown & Phahurat map;* ☎ 226 0026, fax 255 6403, 409–421 Thanon Yaowarat), diagonally opposite the Chinatown Hotel, offers nicer accommodation from 900B.

Soi Ngam Duphli & Thanon Sathon

Near the southern end of Soi Ngam Duphli, the *Malaysia Hotel* (*Central Bangkok map;* ☎ 679 7127–36, fax 287 1457, e malaysia@ ksc15.th.com, 54 Soi Ngam Duphli) was once Bangkok's most famous budget travellers' hotel. Nowadays its 120 air-con, hot-water rooms cost 568/648B for a standard single/double, 618/718B with TV and small fridge, and 748/798B with TV, larger fridge and carpet. All rates include tax and service charges. The six-storey Malaysia has a small swimming pool that may be used by nonguests for 50B per day. Since the 1970s, the Malaysia has made a conscious effort to distance itself from the backpackers' market; for a while it seemed to be catering directly to the lonely male hired-sex market. There appear to be fewer prostitutes around the lobby than in the old days – at least before midnight.

Pinnacle Hotel (*Central Bangkok map;* ☎ 287 0111, fax 287 3420, e pinhl@ loxinfo.co.th, 17 Soi Ngam Duphli, Thanon Phra Ram IV) has rooms with published rates of 1800/2200B; however, discounts to 1100/1300B, including breakfast, are readily available. Amenities include a fitness centre with sauna, steam room and outdoor rooftop jacuzzi.

Charlie House (*Central Bangkok map;* ☎ 679 8330, fax 679 7308, 1034/36–37 Soi Saphan Khu), between Lumphini Tower and Soi Ngam Duphli, aims for a slightly more upmarket, security-conscious clientele with carpeted rooms with air-con, phone and TV for 750/900B (discounts up to 40% can be negotiated in low-season months like June and September). There is a coffee shop, and smoking is prohibited throughout the hotel; a sign reads 'Decently dressed ladies, gentlemen and their children are welcome'.

Thanon Silom & Thanon Surawong

This area is packed with upper mid-range places; discounts are often given from April to October. The following places are marked on the Thanon Silom, Thanon Surawong & Thanon Sathon map.

Bangkok's YMCA and YWCA are both in this area. The *YMCA Collins International House* (☎ 287 1900, 287 2727, fax 287 1996, e bkkymca@asiaaccess.net.th, 27 Thanon Sathon Tai) has air-con rooms with TV, fridge, telephone, in-room safe and private bathroom for 1300B to 2300B; suites are 2700B. Credit cards are accepted. Guests may use the Y's massage room, gym, track and swimming pool, and there's a coffee shop on the premises. The recently remodelled *YWCA Hostel* (☎ 286 1936, 13 Thanon Sathon Tai) offers rooms for 700/900B, including breakfast.

On the south side of Thanon Silom, *Sathorn Inn* (☎ 238 1655, fax 237 6668, 37 Soi Suksavitthaya, also known as Soi 9 or Seuksa Withaya, Thanon Silom) offers cosy rooms with air-con, TV and phone for 896B.

Classic mid-range hotels on Thanon Surawong include the *New Fuji* (☎ 234 5364, fax 233 4336) at No 299–310, with rooms from 1124B to 1338B and a 24-hour bar and restaurant.

Close to Thanon Silom shopping, *Silom Village Inn* (☎ 635 6810, fax 635 6817, e silom-village-inn@thai.com, Silom Village Trade Centre, 286 Thanon Silom) charges from 1800B for its rooms. All come with safe-deposit box, air-con, IDD phone, TV and minibar. Discounts of up to 50% are often available.

Tower Inn (☎ 237 8300–4, fax 237 8286, 533 Thanon Silom) is a multistorey hotel with large, comfortable rooms from 1500B. Also on the premises are a pool, gym and restaurant.

The modern five-storey **Silom Golden Inn** (☎ 238 2663, fax 238 2667, 41/4 Soi 19, Thanon Silom) offers 60 modestly furnished air-con rooms with TV, IDD phone, hot-water shower and minibar for 850B single/double and 1300B for a king-size room.

Bangkok Christian Guest House (☎ 233 6303, fax 237 1742, e bcgh@loxinfo.co.th, 123 Sala Daeng Soi 2, Thanon Convent), off Thanon Silom, has very nice air-con rooms for 704B to 2222B (plus 10% service), including breakfast. Lunch and dinner are also available at very low prices.

The friendly **Intown Residence** (☎ 233 3596, fax 236 6886, 1086/6 Thanon Charoen Krung), between Thanon Si Phraya and Soi 30, is a clean, modern, six-storey place with just 20 rooms, each with TV, air-con and phone, for 600B to 700B a single and 700B to 800B a double, including breakfast (subtract 50B per person from all rates if you don't want breakfast). Attached are a respectable coffee shop and a Thai-Chinese restaurant. Monthly rates are also available from 13,000B.

Siam Square, Thanon Ploenchit & Hualamphong

This area tends to offer either upper-end budget or top-end luxury hotels, with little in the middle. The hotels listed here are marked on the Siam Square & Pratunam map.

An old Siam Square stand-by, the **Reno Hotel** (☎ 215 0026, fax 215 3430) on Soi Kasem San 1 is a veteran from the Vietnam War days when a number of hotels opened in Bangkok named after US cities. Standard rooms are 600/720/840B single/double/triple, deluxe rooms are 900/1020B single/double and VIP rooms are 960/1080B. It has a pool.

Jim's Lodge (☎ 255 3100, fax 253 8492), on Soi Ruam Rudi off Thanon Ploenchit, provides clean rooms with TV, fridge, air-con and carpeting in a six-storey building for 930B single/double.

The **Siam Orchid Inn** (☎ 255 3140, fax 255 3144, e siam_orchidinn@ hotmail.com), off Ratchadamri opposite the World Trade Center, offers well-appointed rooms with all the amenities for around 1100B, including breakfast.

Opposite the UK embassy on Thanon Withayu, a little north of Thanon Ploenchit, the **Holiday Mansion Hotel** (☎ 255 0099, fax 253 0130, e hmtel@ksc.th.com, 53 Thanon Withayu) is a simple but well-run mid-range place. It's good-sized rooms come with air-con, IDD phone, stocked minifridge, TV and breakfast for around 1500B single/double. Other amenities include a pool, business centre and 24-hour coffee shop. It's only a three-minute walk from the Ploenchit Skytrain station.

Pratunam

The quiet **Opera Hotel** (Siam Square & Pratunam map; ☎ 252 4031, fax 253 5360, 16 Soi Somprasong 1/Soi 11 Phetburi, Thanon Phetburi) is very near the heart of Pratunam and has air-con doubles with hot water from 590B to 740B. The Opera also has a swimming pool and coffee shop.

A long walk east along the soi opposite the Indra Regent (off Thanon Ratchaprarop) leads eventually to **Borarn House** (Siam Square & Pratunam map; ☎ 253 2252, fax 253 3639, 487/48 Soi Wattanasin), a Thai-style apartment building with rooms for 850/980B with air-con and TV. The old-fashioned **Siam Hotel** (Greater Bangkok map; ☎ 252 5081, fax 254 6609, 1777 Thanon Phetburi Tat Mai) has OK rooms for 750/1200B.

Thanon Sukhumvit

This area has hotels costing 800B to 1500B. Stick to the lower-numbered sois to save crosstown travel time. Many of the Thanon Sukhumvit hotels in this price range were built as R&R hotels for soldiers on leave from Vietnam tours during the Vietnam War era, 1962–74. Some hotels made the transition from the soldiers-on-leave clientele to a traditional tourist base with style and grace, while others continue to have a slightly rough image. All the hotels in this section are marked on the Thanon Sukhumvit map.

A cluster of high-rise hotels on Soi 3 and Soi 4 for the most part cater to male tourists focused on the Nana Entertainment Plaza (NEP) girlie bar scene on Soi 4 (Soi Nana Tai), but they're also conveniently close to the Nana Skytrain station. On Soi 4, just south of NEP, **Nana Hotel** (☎ 255 0121, fax 255 1769) charges 800B to 1500B and has its own women-behind-glass massage parlour for johns who can't manage the 100m walk to NEP. Aside from that, the rooms are just fine. Slightly better and on the same soi farther down is the **Rajah Hotel** (☎ 255 0040, fax 255 7160), with rooms from 500B to 1000B.

The well-run **Parkway Inn**, on Thanon Sukhumvit at Soi 4, near the Landmark Hotel, is good value, if slightly noisy, at 700B to 800B a night.

A block over on Soi 5, but seemingly a world away from the NEP crowd, the older **Fortuna Hotel** (☎ 251 5121, fax 253 6282) offers decent rooms with all the mod cons for 850B to 1400B. Small, friendly **Premier Travellodge** (☎ 253 5078, 253 3201, fax 253 3195, 170–170/1 Soi 8, Thanon Sukhumvit) has rooms with air-con, carpet, safe-deposit box, cable TV and video, refrigerator, phone and fax for a bargain 600B.

The **Federal Hotel** (☎/fax 253 5332, 27 Soi 11, Thanon Sukhumvit) has rooms for 650B to 1600B. The added-on rooms at ground level, which occasionally flood in the rainy season, aren't worth the price, so be sure to get one of the larger, older up-stairs rooms. The small pool and American-style coffee shop are the main attractions. The Asoke Skytrain station is about a 10-minute walk away from these sois.

The **Manhattan** (☎ 255 0166, fax 255 3481, 13 Soi 15, Thanon Sukhumvit) has 203 good-sized and fairly well-kept rooms starting at 1400B. Facing Thanon Sukhumvit near the corner of Soi 15, **Ruamchitt Plaza & Hotel** (☎ 254 0205, fax 253 2406, ℮ ruamjit@ comnet3.ksc.net.th, 199 Thanon Sukhumvit) has rooms starting at 1150/1350B for 84 single/double rooms with air-con, carpet, re-frigerator and TV; amenities include a rooftop pool and attached shopping arcade. In the basement of the arcade is the Thermae Coffee House, an infamous after-hours venue for Thai sex workers. This could have an in-fluence on the clientele at this hotel, although on our visits it has seemed like a perfectly re-spectable place.

Favourites among middle-class business travellers are the two **City Lodges** on Soi 9 (☎ 253 7705, fax 255 4667) and Soi 19 (☎ 254 4783, fax 255 7340). Rooms at ei-ther are 2090B, and include air-con, tele-phone, minibar, TV and video.

Honey Hotel (☎ 253 0646, fax 254 4716, 31 Soi 19, Thanon Sukhumvit) is an older former R&R place with a loyal clientele and rooms costing a reasonable 650B to 800B. Another holdover from the Vietnam War,

the **Rex Hotel** (☎ 259 0106, fax 258 6635, 762/1 Soi 32, Thanon Sukhumvit) has singles/doubles for 1108/1310B.

A few hundred metres down Soi 20 (Soi Nam Phung), the **Premier Inn** (☎ 261 0401, fax 261 0414, 9/1 Soi 20, Thanon Sukhumvit), opposite the Windsor Hotel (see Places to Stay – Top End later), offers rooms and suites with hot water, satellite TV and video for 800B to 1200B, including breakfast. The nearest Skytrain station is Phrom Phong.

Victory Monument Area

Just north of Siam Square, in the Victory Monument area, are several hotels, including the busy, semi-plush **Century Park Hotel** (Central Bangkok map; ☎ 246 7800, fax 246 7197, ℮ century@samart.co.th, 9 Thanon Ratchaprarop). Rooms at this hotel list for 3600B but are readily discounted to half that amount. At the similar **Continental Hotel** (Central Bangkok map; ☎ 278 1385, fax 271 3547, 971/16 Thanon Phahonyothin) singles/doubles cost from 2400B, with dis-counts to 1200B available. The Vietnam War-era **Florida Hotel** (Siam Square & Pratunam map; ☎ 247 0990, fax 247 7419, 43 Phayathai Square, Thanon Phayathai) has air-con singles/doubles for around 800B.

Airport Area

Finding decent, moderately priced accom-modation in the airport area is difficult. Most of the hotels charge nearly twice as much as comparable hotels in the city. Typ-ical is **Don Muang Mansion** (Greater Bangkok map; ☎ 566 3064, 118/7 Thanon Soranakom, Don Muang), which looks classy on the outside but asks 1000B to 1200B for a small air-con room that in Bangkok would cost 500B to 750B. It's possible to negotiate a lower rate of 800B. This is a bargain for the airport area (only one place is cheaper; see We-Train later).

If you can spend more, better value is **Comfort Suites Airport** (Greater Bangkok map; ☎ 552 8921–9, fax 552 8920, ℮ pinap@loxinfo.co.th, 88/117 Viphavadi Rangsit Hwy), which is about five minutes south of the airport by car. Large rooms with all the amenities (satellite TV, air-con, hot-water bathroom and shower) cost 1400B to 1800B if you book through a Bangkok travel agent, 2500B to 2600B for walk-ins. Best of all, the hotel provides a free shuttle to and from the airport every hour. Other facilities at Comfort Suites Airport include a coffee shop, pool, sauna and health club. One negative is that you can hear the planes landing and taking off until around 1 am.

For quite a bit less you could stay at the well-run *We-Train International House* (*Greater Bangkok map;* ☎ 929 2222, 929 2301, fax 929 2300, e *we-train@linethai .co.th, 501/1 Mu 3, Thanon Dechatungkha, Sikan, Don Muang*). Simple but clean rooms with two beds, fan, private hot-water bathroom, fridge and phone cost 180B single/double, 580B with air-con (extra beds cost 150B). You can also get a bed in a dorm with fan for 120B. To these rates add the usual 10% service charge but no tax since it's operated by the nonprofit Association for the Promotion of the Status of Women (but male guests are welcome). Facilities include a pool, Thai massage, laundry service, coffee shop and beauty salon.

One major drawback to We-Train International House is its distance from the airport – you must get a taxi to cross the highway and railway, then go about 3km west along Thanon Dechatungkha to the Thung Sikan school (*rohng rian thûng sĭi-kan*). If you don't have a lot of luggage, walk across the airport pedestrian bridge to reach Don Muang (or the Amari Airport Hotel), then get a taxi – it's much cheaper this way because you avoid the high taxi-desk fees. From the guesthouse there are usually no taxis in the area when you're ready to return to the airport or continue on to Bangkok, but transportation to/from the airport can be arranged on request for 200B one way, or 70B to/from the Amari Airport Hotel.

PLACES TO STAY – TOP END

Bangkok has all sorts of international standard tourist hotels, from the straightforward package places to some of Asia's classic hotels, as well as the two tallest hotels in the world. Several of Bangkok's luxury hotels have made worldwide top 10 or 20 lists in plush travel magazines.

Although there's no single area for top-end hotels, you'll find quite a few around Siam Square, along Thanon Surawong and Thanon Silom, and along the river, while many of the slightly less expensive 'international standard' places are scattered along Thanon Sukhumvit.

Since the 1997 devaluation of the baht, a few top-end places have begun quoting prices in US dollars, while others raised the baht prices to bring exchange levels back in line with 1996 prices.

Even so, you should still be able to negotiate discounts of up to 40% during the low season (anytime except December to March and July to August). Booking through a travel agency almost always means lower rates, or try asking for a hotel's 'corporate' discount. Several top-end hotels offer discounts of up to 60% when you make your reservation via the Internet. THAI can also arrange substantial discounts if you hold a THAI air ticket.

The hotels in this category will add a 10% service charge plus 7% tax to hotel bills.

On the River

The 124-year-old *Oriental Hotel* (*Thanon Silom, Thanon Surawong & Thanon Sathon map;* ☎ 236 0400, 236 0420, fax 236 1937, e *bscorbkk@loxinfo.co.th, 48 Thanon Oriental*), right on the Mae Nam Chao Phraya, is one of the most famous hotels in Asia, right up there with the Raffles in Singapore or the Peninsula in Hong Kong. It's also rated as one of the very best hotels in the world, and is just about the most expensive in Bangkok. The hotel management prides itself on providing highly personalised service through a staff of 1200 (for 35 suites and 361 rooms) – once you've stayed here the staff will remember your name, what you like to eat for breakfast, even what type of flowers you'd prefer in your room.

Nowadays the Oriental Hotel is looking more modern and less classic – the original Author's Wing is dwarfed by the Tower (built in 1958) and River (1976) wings. Authors who have stayed at the Oriental Hotel and had suites named after them include Joseph Conrad, W Somerset Maugham, Noel Coward, Graham Greene, John le Carré, James Michener, Gore Vidal and Barbara Cartland. Room rates start at US$210 and suites are as much as 10 times this price. It's worth wandering in, if only to see the lobby (no shorts, sleeveless shirts or sandals allowed). Apart from the usual luxury recreational facilities, the Oriental also has a Thai Cooking School and a Thai Culture Program.

Another luxury gem along the river is the *Shangri-La Hotel* (Thanon Silom, Thanon Surawong & Thanon Sathon map; ☎ 236 7777, fax 236 8579, e slbk@shangri-la.com, 89 Soi Wat Suan Phlu, Thanon Charoen Krung), with rooms and suites from US$190/210 single/double. Facilities and services include helicopter transport from the airport (at extra cost), pools, full sporting and sauna facilities and nine restaurants (including one of the best Italian eateries in the city). The service is of a very high standard. The capacious lounge areas off the main lobby have a less formal and more relaxed feel than those at the Oriental, and are a favourite rendezvous spot even for non-hotel guests.

On the Thonburi bank of the Mae Nam Chao Phraya, a bit south of central Bangkok, the tastefully appointed *Marriott Royal Garden Riverside Hotel* (Greater Bangkok map; ☎ 476 0021, fax 476 1120, e marriottrgr@minornet.com, 257/1–3 Thanon Charoen Nakhon), near Saphan Krungthep, is highly valued for its serene atmosphere and expansive, airy public areas. The grounds encompass a large swimming pool, lush gardens, two lighted tennis courts and a world-class health club.

Also on the river, the *Royal Orchid Sheraton* (ROS; Thanon Silom, Thanon Surawong & Thanon Sathon map; ☎ 266 0123, fax 236 6656, e rosht@mozart.inet.co.th, 2 Soi Captain Bush, Thanon Si Phraya) has rooms from 10,560B a night. The ROS is known for crisp, efficient service, and the business centre is open 24 hours.

The *Menam Riverside* (Greater Bangkok map; ☎ 688 1000, fax 291 9400, e menamhtl @mozart.inet.co.th), towering over the river at 2074 Thanon Charoen Krung, Yannawa, has rooms from 1500B. The *Royal River* (Greater Bangkok map; ☎ 433 0300, fax 433 5880, 670/805 Thanon Charan Sanitwong, Thonburi) has rooms from 2300B; it receives lots of tour groups.

The *Peninsula Hotel* (Thanon Silom, Thanon Surawong & Thanon Sathon map; ☎ 861 2888, fax 861 1112, e pbk@ peninsula.com, 333 Thanon Charoen Nakhon) is the latest tower hotel to line Mae Nam Chao Phraya. Luxuriously appointed rooms are remarkably well priced at US$119 to US$129 and US$154 for suites, but these rates will most likely increase as the hotel becomes more well known.

Siam Square & Pratunam

People accustomed to heady hotels claim the plush *Regent Bangkok* (☎ 251 6127, fax 251 5390, 155 Thanon Ratchadamri) tops the Oriental Hotel in overall quality for the money. This is particularly true for business travellers because of the Regent's efficient business centre and central location (and local calls are free at the Regent, probably the only luxury hotel in the city to offer this courtesy). The hotel also offers (for around 2000B an hour) an 'office on wheels', a hi-tech, multipassenger van equipped with computers, cell phones, fax machines, TVs and videos, and swivelling leather seats so that small conferences can be held while crossing town. The Regent's rooms start at 9600B.

Another top executive choice is the *Hilton International Bangkok* (☎ 253 0123, fax 253 6509, e bkkhitw@lox2.loxinfo.co.th, 2 Thanon Withayu), where you won't find tour groups milling around in the lobby; its rooms start at 8640B. The expansive grounds are a major plus; only Bangkok's older hotel properties are so fortunate.

Another of this generation, the *Siam Inter-Continental* (☎ 253 0355, fax 254 4388, e bangkok@interconti.com, 967 Thanon Phra Ram I), ensconced in 10.4 hectares (26 acres) of tropical gardens (filled with peacocks, geese, swans and parrots) near Siam Square, takes in a mix of well-heeled, pleasure and business travellers. Standard rooms start at 6000B. Rumour says the Inter-Continental is selling the valuable land it sits on and may be replaced by a shopping centre.

The *Grand Hyatt Erawan* (☎ 254 1234, fax 254 6308), at the intersection of Thanon Ratchadamri and Thanon Ploenchit, was built on the site of the original Erawan Hotel with obvious ambitions to become one of the city's top-ranked hotels. The neo-Thai architecture has been well executed; inside is the largest collection of contemporary Thai art in the world. Adding to the elite atmosphere, the rooms in the rear of the hotel overlook the prestigious Bangkok Royal Sports Club racetrack. For most top-end visitors it vies with the Regent Bangkok or the Novotel Bangkok on Siam Square for having the best location for transport and shopping. Huge rooms start at 11,520B, although a rate of

SIAM SQUARE & PRATUNAM

PLACES TO STAY
1 Siam City Hotel
3 Florida Hotel
6 Indra Regent Hotel
7 Borarn House
9 Amari Watergate Hotel
12 Opera Hotel
14 Asia Hotel
16 A-One Inn
17 Star Hotel; Bed & Breakfast Inn
18 White Lodge; Wendy House
19 Reno Hotel
20 Pranee Building; Muangphol Mansion
32 Siam Inter-Continental
34 Novotel Bangkok on Siam Square
38 Delta Grand Pacific Hotel; Robinson Department Store
39 Siam Orchid Inn
41 Le Meridien President

46 Hilton International Bangkok
49 Holiday Mansion Hotel
50 Golden Palace Hotel
56 Grand Hyatt Erawan
58 Regent Bangkok
67 Jim's Lodge

PLACES TO EAT
21 Thai Sa-Nguan; Watanayon
25 Hard Rock Cafe
29 S&P Restaurant & Bakery
33 Khao Man Kai Siam
52 Fabb Fashion Café; Auberge DAB
59 Whole Earth Restaurant
61 Pan Pan Capri

OTHER
3 Wang Suan Phakkat
4 Post Office

5 Bangkok Doll Factory
8 Pratunam Market
10 Nailert Market
11 Pantip Plaza
15 Indonesian Embassy
15 Tha Ratchathewi (Canal Taxis)
22 Jim Thompson's House
23 National Stadium
24 Mahboonkrong Shopping Centre (MBK)
26 Scala Cinema
27 Siam Center; Siam Discovery Centre
28 Lido Cinema
30 Siam Cinema
31 Post Office
35 Wat Patum
36 World Trade Centre
37 Narayana Phand

40 Gaysorn Plaza; Planet Hollywood
42 TOT Office
43 Central Department Store
44 UK Embassy
45 Norwegian Embassy
47 Post Office
48 Swiss Embassy
51 Bumrungrad Hospital
53 Maneeya Center; FCCT
54 Sogo Department Store
55 Erawan Shrine
57 Peninsula Plaza
60 Israeli Embassy
62 Spanish Embassy
63 Netherlands Embassy
64 US Embassy
65 US Visa Section
66 Vietnamese Embassy

7000/8200B single/double can usually be obtained through a travel agent.

The 34-storey *Amari Watergate* (☎ 653 9000, fax 653 9045, e watergate@amari .com) is right in the centre of Bangkok's busiest district, Pratunam, on Thanon Phetburi. The neoclassical interior design blends Thai and European motifs, guest rooms are large and facilities include a 900-sq-metre Clark Hatch fitness centre, an American-style pub, and highly rated Cantonese and Italian restaurants. The Amari Watergate is on Thanon Phetburi near the Thanon Ratchaprarop intersection. Tour groups check in via a separate floor and lobby. Spacious rooms cost US$184/200; the top three floors contain more luxuriously appointed executive rooms for another US$40 or so.

Other Amari hotels in central Bangkok include the *Amari Atrium* (Greater Bangkok map; ☎ 718 2000, fax 718 2002, e atrium@amari.com) on Thanon Phetburi Tat Mai, east of Soi Asoke, with singles/doubles from US$134/142, and the *Amari Boulevard* (Thanon Sukhumvit map; ☎ 255 2930, fax 255 2950, e boulevard@ amari.com, 2 Soi 5, Thanon Sukhumvit), which has rooms from US$150 a double. Amari also has an airport hotel – see the Airport Area section later in this chapter for details.

Another extremely well-located hotel for business or leisure is the *Novotel Bangkok on Siam Square* (☎ 255 6888, fax 255 1824, e novotel@ksc.th.com) on Soi 6 in Siam Square. Just steps away from one of

Bangkok's most vibrant shopping and entertainment districts, as well as the Siam Skytrain station, the Novotel boasts a full business centre, bakery, pool and various restaurants. The rooms are huge and start at 4961B.

Le Meridien President Hotel & Tower (☎ 656 0444, fax 656 0555, ℮ meridien@ loxinfo.co.th, 135/26 Soi Gaysorn), in the heart of the Thanon Ploenchit shopping area and near the Chit Lom Skytrain station, offers 758 well-appointed rooms and suites from 4200B. Amenities include two pools, a health club, business centre, book shop, tobacco shop, and 10 restaurants and bars.

The *Asia Hotel* (☎ 215 0808, fax 215 4360, ℮ techaru@mozart.inet.co.th, 296 Thanon Phayathai) is a huge place with large rooms starting at 3509B; it's in a good location, but is often full of tour groups and conventioneers. The *Indra Regent* (☎ 208 0033, fax 208 0388, ℮ sales@indrahotel.com, 120/126 Thanon Ratchaprarop), with rooms from 2000B, is similar.

Central Bangkok

Although there are no top-end hotels in the Banglamphu area, a little way east of the district are a couple of highly recommended places. *Royal Princess Hotel (Central Bangkok map;* ☎ 281 3088, fax 280 1314, ℮ larnluang@dusit.com, 269 Thanon Lan Luang) has rooms from 3300B, but discounts down to about half that are often available through travel agents. It's close to the main city THAI office and a short taxi ride from Banglamphu and the river.

Even nicer is the independently owned and operated *Siam City Hotel (Siam Square & Pratunam map;* ☎ 247 0123, fax 247 0165, ℮ siamcity@siamhotels.com, 477 Thanon Si Ayuthaya). Large, well-maintained rooms with all the amenities list for 4272B, but as with the Royal Princess, good discounts are often available through Thai travel agents. The restaurants at the Siam City are highly regarded by Thai businesspeople.

Thanon Silom, Thanon Surawong & Thanon Sathon

Another entry in the luxury market is the *Sukhothai Hotel (*☎ 287 0222; reservations ☎ 285 0303, fax 287 4980, ℮ reservations@ sukhothai.com or info@sukhothai.com, 13/3 Thanon Sathon Tai)*, which features an Asian

minimalist decor, including an inner courtyard with lily ponds; the same architect and interior designer created Phuket's landmark Amanpuri. Superior rooms cost US$220, deluxe rooms US$264; there are also more-expensive suites.

Towering over Thanon Sathon Tai with 216 business suites is the ultra-modern *Westin Banyan Tree (*☎ 679 1200, fax 679 1199, ℮ westinbangkok@westin-bangkok .com)*. The hotel is ensconced on the lower two and top 28 floors of the 60-storey Thai Wah Tower II. The Westin Banyan Tree's huge rooms feature separate work and sleep areas, two-line speaker phones with data ports and two TV sets along with all the other amenities expected of lodgings that start at US$158 a night. The spa and fitness centre – the biggest such hotel facility in Bangkok – spans four floors.

Two top hotels in the district along Thanon Silom and Thanon Surawong are the very Thai *Montien (*☎ 233 7060, fax 236 5218, ℮ montien@ksc15.th.com, 54 Thanon Surawong)*, which has rooms from 4000B, and the great *Dusit Thani (*☎ 236 0450, fax 236 6400, ℮ dusitbkk@dusit.com, 946 Thanon Phra Ram IV)*, which has rooms from US$180/190.

There are many hotels that have similar functional amenities, but are cheaper because of their location or smaller staff-to-guest ratios. In the Thanon Silom and Thanon Surawong areas these include: the *Narai (*☎ 237 0100, fax 236 7161, ℮ narai@narai.com, 222 Thanon Silom)*, with rooms from 3267B, and the *Holiday Inn Crowne Plaza (*☎ 238 4300, fax 238 5289, ℮ admin@hicp-bkk.com, 981 Thanon Silom)*, with rooms from US$149.

With only 57 rooms, the management at the *Swiss Lodge (*☎ 233 5345, fax 236 9425, 3 Thanon Convent)* is able to pay close attention to service details, such as cold towels whenever you enter the lobby from outside. Data-ports and soundproof windows further enhance the attraction for people doing business. Discounted rates start at 2550B for a standard room.

Other top-end hotels in this area include the *Trinity Silom Hotel (*☎ 231 5050 ext 5, fax 231 5417, 150 Soi 5, Thanon Silom)*, a boutique-style place with rooms costing 2300B to 2500B (although substantially discounted rates are available via the Internet).

BANGKOK

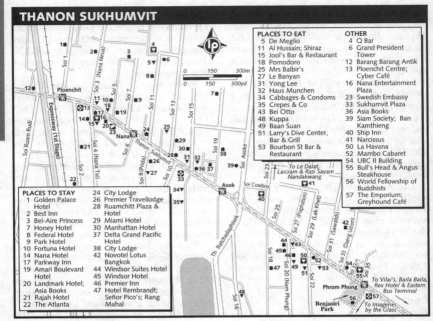

THANON SUKHUMVIT

PLACES TO EAT
- 5 De Meglio
- 11 Al Hussain; Shiraz
- 15 Jool's Bar & Restaurant
- 18 Pomodoro
- 25 Mrs Balbir's
- 27 Le Banyan
- 31 Yong Lee
- 32 Haus Munchen
- 34 Cabbages & Condoms
- 35 Crepes & Co
- 43 Bei Otto
- 48 Kuppa
- 49 Baan Suan
- 51 Larry's Dive Center, Bar & Grill
- 53 Bourbon St Bar & Restaurant

OTHER
- 4 Q Bar
- 6 Grand President Tower
- 12 Barang Barang Antik
- 13 Ploenchit Centre; Cyber Café
- 16 Nana Entertainment Plaza
- 23 Swedish Embassy
- 33 Sukhumvit Plaza
- 36 Asia Books
- 39 Siam Society; Ban Kamthieng
- 40 Ship Inn
- 41 Narcissus
- 50 La Havana
- 52 Mambo Cabaret
- 54 UBC II Building
- 55 Bull's Head & Angus Steakhouse
- 56 World Fellowship of Buddhists
- 57 The Emporium; Greyhound Café

PLACES TO STAY
- 1 Golden Palace Hotel
- 2 Best Inn
- 3 Bel-Aire Princess
- 7 Honey Hotel
- 8 Federal Hotel
- 9 Park Hotel
- 10 Fortuna Hotel
- 14 Nana Hotel
- 17 Parkway Inn
- 19 Amari Boulevard Hotel
- 20 Landmark Hotel; Asia Books
- 21 Rajah Hotel
- 22 The Atlanta
- 24 City Lodge
- 26 Premier Travellodge
- 28 Ruamchitt Plaza & Hotel
- 29 Miami Hotel
- 30 Manhattan Hotel
- 37 Delta Grand Pacific Hotel
- 38 City Lodge
- 42 Novotel Lotus Bangkok
- 44 Windsor Suites Hotel
- 45 Windsor Hotel
- 46 Premier Inn
- 47 Hotel Rembrandt; Señor Pico's; Rang Mahal

Thanon Sukhumvit

The tastefully decorated *Hotel Rembrandt* (☎ 261 7100, fax 261 7017, 19 Soi 18, Thanon Sukhumvit) has 407 large rooms. Starting prices at the time of writing were 2050B, although rack rates were listed at 3950B. Facilities include a swimming pool and the best Mexican restaurant in Bangkok, Señor Pico's of Los Angeles. Another advantage is the proximity to Queen Sirikit National Convention Centre, off Soi 16. The hotel is between the Asoke and Phrom Phong Skytrain stations.

The *Landmark* (☎ 254 0404, fax 253 4259, 138 Thanon Sukhumvit) has 415 well-appointed rooms with discounted rates starting at 2950B. The Landmark's business centre is one of the hotel's strong points; the heavy traffic along this stretch of Thanon Sukhumvit is not.

Delta Grand Pacific Hotel (☎ 651 1000, fax 255 2441, hotel@grandpacifichotel.com, Soi 17–19, Thanon Sukhumvit) offers rooms from US$85. Its Soi 19 location is easy to reach from either Thanon Sukhumvit or Thanon Phetburi, and a nearby pedestrian bridge across Thanon Sukhumvit is an added

bonus. The hotel bears the distinction of containing the highest karaoke lounge in the city, and is attached to Robinson department store.

Windsor Hotel (☎ 258 0160, fax 258 1491, e varaporn@mozart.inet.co.th, 8–10 Soi 20, Thanon Sukhumvit) is a fairly deluxe place with standard rooms for 2000/2400B, and superior rooms 2400/2600B; these rates include a cooked-to-order breakfast. On the premises is a 24-hour coffee shop. Guests of the Windsor have use of all amenities at the *Windsor Suites Hotel* (☎ 262 1234, fax 258 1522, e varaporn@mozart.inet.co.th), which features spacious suites (each with two TVs). Official rates start at 6000B/7000B but are heavily discounted via the Internet. A complimentary buffet breakfast is included. The nearest Skytrain station is Phrom Phong.

Three moderately expensive places in the Thanon Sukhumvit area are roughly similar in size and price: *Bel-Aire Princess* (☎ 253 4300, fax 255 8850, e bela@dusit.com, 16 Soi 5, Thanon Sukhumvit), which has rooms from 2800B; *Park Hotel* (☎ 255 4300, fax 255 4309, 6 Soi 7, Thanon Sukhumvit), which has rooms from 2000B; and the

Imperial Impala Hotel (☎ 259 0053, fax 258 8747, ⓔ taraimpa@asianet.co.th, 9 Soi 24, Thanon Sukhumvit), which has rooms from 3000/3500B.

Accor's well-designed and relatively new *Novotel Lotus Bangkok* (☎ 261 0111, fax 262 1700, 1 Soi 33, Thanon Sukhumvit) contains plush rooms starting at 4100B a night; discounts are often available.

Ratchada

This entertainment and business district in the Huay Khwang neighbourhood of north-eastern Bangkok features several flash hotels along Thanon Ratchadaphisek. The following places are marked on the Greater Bangkok map.

Managed by Singapore's Raffles International, the well-appointed *Merchant Court Hotel* (☎ 694 222, fax 694 2223, ⓔ info@ merchantcourt.th.com, 202 Thanon Ratchadaphisek) occupies one of the two tower blocks of Le Concorde Building. The second tower contains offices, including the TAT headquarters. Rates for superior room are 5000/5500B, deluxe are 6000/6500B, and a studio suite is up to 20,500B a double, excluding tax and service. Rooms on floors set aside for executives offer two phone lines, ergonomically designed writing desk and chair, and optional personal computer and fax/printer. Nonsmoking floors are available. When the subway is finished, there will be a subway station right in front of this hotel.

One of the least expensive places, next to the Le Concorde building and close to several upmarket 'entertainment centres', is the *Siam Beverly Hotel* (☎ 215 4397, fax 215 4049, 188 Thanon Ratchadaphisek), where rates range from 1800B for a superior single to 2200B for a deluxe double, including breakfast. It's not spectacular but the service is friendly and the rooms have all the amenities. The 3rd-floor coffee shop is well priced.

Roughly equivalent in price, the *Chaophya Park Hotel* (☎ 290 0125, fax 290 0167, ⓔ chaopark@asiaaccess.net.th, 247 Thanon Ratchadaphisek) is similar, but a little farther out on the strip. At the lowest end of the scale along the neon-washed Ratchada strip is the *Crystal Hotel* (☎ 274 6441, 274 6020, fax 274 6449, 65 Soi Nathong, Thanon Ratchadaphisek), with rooms from 799B.

Airport Area

The *Amari Airport Hotel* (Greater Bangkok map; ☎ 566 1020, fax 566 1941, ⓔ airport@ amari.com), connected to the airport by an air-conditioned walkway, is obviously the closest hotel to Bangkok International Airport. The Amari offers nonsmoking rooms, a 'ladies' floor, rooms for disabled persons and an executive floor with huge suites and 24-hour butler service. Rates start at US$182 for a standard double; discounts are rarely available since rooms are very much in demand. However, passengers arriving/departing Bangkok by THAI receive a 50% discount when they show their current boarding pass or ticket. Amari also offers 'ministay' rates for stays of up to three hours for US$20, including tax and service, provided the check-in time is between 8 am and 6 pm.

The *Asia Airport Hotel* (Greater Bangkok map; ☎ 992 6999, fax 532 3193) is north of the airport at the 28km marker. Rates for comfortable rooms start at 2000B, but discounts to 1200B or 1500B are often available because the hotel often seems half empty.

PLACES TO EAT

No matter where you go in Bangkok, you're rarely more than 50m away from a restaurant or sidewalk food vendor. The variety of places to eat is simply astounding and defeats all but the most tireless food samplers in their quest to say they've tried everything. As with seeking a place to stay, you can find something in every price range in most districts – with a few obvious exceptions. Chinatown is naturally a good area for Chinese food, while Bangrak and Phahurat (both districts with high concentrations of Indian residents) are good for Indian and Muslim cuisine. Some parts of the city (eg, Siam Square, Thanon Silom, Thanon Surawong and Thanon Sukhumvit) tend to have higher-priced restaurants than others while other areas (eg, Banglamphu and the river area around Tha Maharat) are full of cheap eats.

A meal at the low end of the range should cost 100B or less per person. A restaurant with a little more atmosphere, perhaps air-conditioning, will cost 100B to 200B per person, while even a splurge won't generally cost more than 400B per person. An exception are the restaurants in top-end hotels, which feature prices on a par with, or just below, what you'd expect to pay at any flash hotel in the world.

Of course, there are plenty of vendor stands where you can buy a bowl of noodles or a plate of *râat khâo* (rice with curry poured over it) for 25B to 40B.

As transport can be such a hassle in Bangkok, most visitors choose to eat in a convenient district (rather than seeking out a specific restaurant); this section has therefore been organised by area, rather than cuisine.

Banglamphu & Ko Ratanakosin

This area, near the river and old part of the city, is one of the best for cheap eating establishments. Many of the guesthouses on Thanon Khao San have open-air cafes, which are packed with travellers from November to March and July to August. Unless otherwise indicated, the following places are marked on the Thanon Khao San (Khao San Road) map.

The typical cafe menu has a few Thai and Chinese standards, plus traveller favourites like fruit salads, muesli and yoghurt. None of these stand out, although the side-by-side *Orm* and *Wally* on Thanon Khao San produce fair Thai, international and vegetarian meals at cheap prices. *Hello Restaurant* (open 24 hours, not to be confused with the guesthouse of the same name across the street) and *Center Khao Sarn* on Thanon Khao San are both quite popular, but the food's nothing special. *Arawy Det*, an old Hokkien-style noodle shop on the corner of Thanon Khao San and Thanon Tanao, has somehow managed to stay semi-authentic amid the cosmic swirl. The Roman-script sign reads 'Khao San Seafood Restaurant', and for foreigners the restaurant has a special higher-priced seafood menu. If you want noodles or what the Thais are eating, just point. Opposite the eastern end of Thanon Khao San, on Thanon Tanao, *No 147 Thai Food* is also reasonably authentic.

Up at the intersection of Thanon Khao San and Thanon Chakraphong, the relatively new and air-conditioned *Gulliver's Traveler's Tavern* serves cocktails, shots, beers and an international menu. Meals cost 80B to 100B a dish.

Royal India on the southern side of Thanon Khao San is OK if you don't mind nonstop videos. Two other Indian restaurants on the street are housed over shops towards the north-western end of Thanon Khao San, *Himalayan Kitchen* and *Namastee Indian Cuisine*.

For authentic (and cheap) Thai food check out the several *open-air restaurants* at the western end of Thanon Rambutri.

Chabad House, a Jewish place of worship on Thanon Rambutri, serves Israeli-style kosher food downstairs; it's open noon to 9 pm Sunday to Thursday and until 4.30 pm on Friday. Cheaper falafel and hummus can be found at *Chochana* (another sign reads 'Shoshana'), down a *tràwk* (alley) off Thanon Chakraphong around the corner from Thanon Khao San. Right next door is *Sarah*, also serving Israeli dishes.

A small shop called *Roti-Mataba* (☎ 282 2119), opposite the Phra Sumen Fort on the corner of Thanon Phra Athit and Thanon Phra Sumen near the river, offers delicious *rotii* (fried Indian flatbread), *kaeng mátsàmàn* (Thai Muslim curry), chicken kurma and chicken or vegetable *mátàbà* (a sort of stuffed Indian pancake), and has a bilingual menu; look for a white sign with red letters. An upstairs air-con dining area has recently been added. It's open 7 am to 8 pm, closed Monday. Two doors up from Roti-Mataba, *Kuay Tiaw Mae* serves good *kŭaytĭaw tôm yam* (rice noodles in a spicy lemongrass broth) made with pork, but you can ask for it with tofu instead; real coffee and unique mushroom ice cream are extra attractions.

Along Thanon Phra Athit, north of the New Merry V guesthouse, are several small but up-and-coming Thai places with chic but casual decor and good food at prices local university students can afford. The *Raan Kin Deum* (no Roman-script sign), a few doors down from New Merry V, is a nice two-storey cafe with wooden tables and chairs, traditional Thai food and live folk music nightly; the laid-back atmosphere reaches its acme in the evenings when the place is crowded. Bright and cheery *Saffron Bakery*, opposite the Food & Agriculture Organization on Thanon Phra Athit, has good pastries and fresh coffee, but only a few tables.

Several other places along this strip of Thanon Phra Athit – *Hemlock*, *Suntana*, *Indy*, *To Sit*, *Apostrophe's*, *Dog Days*, *108* and *Joy Luck Club* – create a neighbourhood cafe scene that has been hyperbolically compared with High Street Kensington or

Greenwich Village by the Thai press. The tiny Joy Luck Club has the most interesting interior design – a collection of photos of old American bluesmen, contemporary Thai art and tables containing boxed art under glass. Despite the English names, these cafes see more Thai customers than foreigners, but the staff usually speak a little English. The English-language menus at some Thanon Phra Athit cafes conform to the Thais' worst expectations of what fàràng like to eat; if you can't read Thai, you won't be getting the best dishes on hand. If possible, go with someone who speaks Thai. Most of these places are open in the evenings only.

One of the Thanon Phra Athit places without tuppie (Thai yuppie) pretensions is **Khrua Nopparat** (Banglamphu map; no Roman-script sign), near 108. It's a plainly decorated place with air-con and a good menu of Thai dishes at very reasonable prices. It's popular with neighbourhood residents and is open 10.30 am to 9.30 pm daily. **Ton Pho** (no Roman sign; ☎ 280 0452), next to the Buddhist Association on Thanon Phra Athit, is another great spot for traditional, authentic Thai.

At the Democracy Monument circle on Thanon Ratchadamnoen Klang there are a couple of well-established Thai restaurants, **Vijit** (VR) and the **Methavalai Sorn Daeng**. Both have reasonable prices considering the quality of food and air-con facilities. At lunchtime on weekdays they're crowded with local government office workers. Both stay open until 11 pm or so, another plus.

There's a floating restaurant called **Yok Yor Khlongsan** (☎ 437 1121), opposite River City shopping complex on the Thonburi side of the river. Yok Yor Khlongsan runs inexpensive evening dinner cruises (8 to 10 pm) – you order from the regular menu and pay a nominal 70B charge for the boat service.

Near the National Library and the cluster of guesthouses near Tha Thewet, on the southern side of Thanon Si Ayuthaya almost at the intersection with Thanon Sam Saen, **Si Amnuay** (Central Bangkok map; no Roman-script sign) is a good, clean place for kǔaytǐaw.

If you feel like a genuine splurge and magnificent river views, consider **Supatra River House** (Ko Ratanakosin map; ☎ 411 0305, 266 Soi Wat Rakhang), across the river from Ko Ratanakosin in Thonburi. Housed in an historic former home, the restaurant consists of an elegant indoor dining area as well as a more casual outdoor space on the river. Because of the restaurant's location on a bend in the river, the outdoor section affords unique views of Wat Phra Kaew and Wat Arun on either side of the Chao Phraya, especially at night when both temples are illuminated. Highly recommended is anything in the seafood category, where the kitchen particularly excels. It's open daily. Free ferry service is available from Tha Mahathat to the restaurant, or you can take a pay ferry (2B) to nearby Tha Wang Lang. Certain Chao Phraya River Express boats also stop at Tha Wang Lang, so you could take the Skytrain to the Saphan Taksin station, and the express boat from there. Reservations are recommended.

If Supatra is too rich for the blood, next door is **Krua Rakhang Thong** (Ko Ratanakosin map; the Roman-script sign at the entrance reads 'River View'), a smaller and more casual riverside place with excellent Thai food, including a good selection of vegetarian dishes. Particularly good is the *sôm-tam yâwt má-phráo àwn*, sôm-tam (spicy salad) made with coconut shoots. A small outdoor section upstairs has a few tables, including one or two with the famous dual-temple view. Or budget feast at one of the many food stalls in **Talat Wang Lang**, the market at the back of the pier.

Vegetarian Many of the Thanon Khao San guesthouse cafes offer vegetarian dishes. For all-vegie menus at low prices, check out the string of *vegetarian restaurants* near Srinthip Guest House. To find these out-of-the-way places, turn left on Thanon Tanao at the eastern end of Thanon Khao San, then cross the street and turn right down the first narrow alley, then left at Soi Wat Bowon. A very good Thai vegetarian place is **Arawy** (the Roman-script sign reads 'Alloy'), which is south of Thanon Khao San, across Thanon Ratchadamnoen Klang at 152 Thanon Din So (opposite the Municipal Hall near a 7-Eleven store). This was one of Bangkok's first Thai vegetarian restaurants, inspired by ex-Bangkok Governor Chamlong Srimuang's strict vegetarianism. It's open 7 am to 7 pm daily.

Thanon Silom, Thanon Surawong & Thanon Sathon

This area is at the heart of the financial district so it has a lot of pricey restaurants, along with cheaper ones that attract both office workers and the more flush with cash. Many restaurants are found along the main avenues but there's an even greater number tucked away in sois and alleys. The river end of Thanon Silom and Thanon Surawong towards Thanon Charoen Krung (the Bangrak district) is a good hunting ground for Indian food.

Thai & Other Asian The *Soi Pradit (Soi 20) Night Market*, which assembles each evening off Thanon Silom in front of the municipal market pavilion, is good for cheap eats. During the day there are also a few *food vendors* in this soi, but much better daytime fare can be found amid the mass of food stalls purveying pots of curry and miles of noodles inside *Talat ITF* at the end of Soi 10.

The area to the east of Thanon Silom, off Thanon Convent and Soi Sala Daeng, is a Thai gourmets' enclave. Most of the restaurants tucked away here are very good, but a meal for two will cost 600B to 800B. A great place for traditional Thai and Isan (northeastern Thai) food at moderate prices is *Ban Chiang* (☎ 266 6994, 14 Soi Si Wiang, Thanon Pramuan), a restored wooden house in a verdant setting off Thanon Silom west of Umathewi Temple. Owned by a Thai movie star, *Thanying* (☎ 236 4361, 235 0371, 10 Soi Pramuan, Thanon Silom) has elegant decor and very good, moderately expensive, royal Thai cuisine. It's open 11 am to 11 pm daily; there's a *branch* (☎ 255 9838) at the World Trade Center on Thanon Ploenchit, open 11.30 am to 10.30 pm daily.

Mango Tree (☎ 236 2820), down Soi Than Tawan off Thanon Surawong, offers classic Thai cuisine and live traditional Thai music in a decor of historical photos and antiques. Recommended dishes include *plaa sămlii dàet diaw* (half-dried, half-fried cottonfish with spicy mango salad) and *kài bai toei* (chicken baked in pandanus leaves). Prices are moderate, and it's open daily for lunch and dinner.

A good one-stop eating place with a lot of variety is the Silom Village Trade Centre, an outdoor shopping complex at Soi 24. Although it's basically a tourist spot with higher than average prices, the restaurants are of high quality and plenty of Thais dine here as well. The centrepiece is *Silom Village* (☎ 234 4448), a place with shaded outdoor tables where the emphasis is on fresh Thai seafood, sold by weight. The menu also lists extensive Chinese and Japanese meals. Prices are moderate to high. For a quick and casual meal, the *Silom Coffee Bar* in the trade centre makes a good choice.

Chaii Karr (☎ 233 2549), on Thanon Silom (across from the Holiday Inn and a few shops east of Central department store), is decorated simply with Thai antiques. The medium-price menu is mostly Thai, with a few fàràng dishes, plus 19 varieties of brewed coffee; the Thai mango salad and spicy seafood soup are very good. Thai folk music plays in the background. Chaii Karr is open 10.30 am to 9.30 pm daily.

At the intersection of Thanon Surawong and Thanon Narathiwat Ratchanakharin is famous *Somboon Seafood* (☎ 233 3104), a good, reasonably priced seafood restaurant known for the best crab curry in town. Soy-steamed sea bass *(plaa kràphong nĕung siiíu)* is also a speciality. It's open 4 to 11 pm.

The economic *Maria Bakery & Restaurant (909–911 Thanon Silom)*, opposite Central department store, is well known for its fresh Vietnamese and Thai food, as well as French pastries, pizza and vegetarian food. The restaurant is clean, inexpensive and has air-con.

Mizu's Kitchen on Thanon Patpong 1 has a loyal Japanese and Thai following for its inexpensive but good Japanese food, including Japanese-style steak. Another very good Japanese place, especially for sushi and sashimi, is *Goro (399/1 Soi 7, Thanon Silom)*; prices are reasonable.

The tiny *Harmonique* (☎ 630 6270), on Soi 34 Thanon Charoen Krung, around the corner from the main post office, is a refreshing oasis in this extremely busy, smog-filled section of town. European-managed and unobtrusive, the little shop serves Thai food, plus a variety of teas, fruit shakes and coffee on Hokkien-style marble-topped tables – a pleasant spot to read while quenching your thirst. Dishes are well prepared if pricey (60B to 150B per dish). It's open 11 am to 10 pm daily, closed Sunday.

Sara-Jane's (☎ 676 3338, 55/21 Thanon Narathiwat Ratchanakharin), about a 100m south-east off Thanon Sathon Tai, has the same fantastic Isan and Italian food as the original (see the Siam Square, Thanon Ploenchit & Thanon Withayu section later). This second location has an outdoor eating area and beer garden as well as indoor air-con seating. It's not far from the Chong Nonsi Skytrain station, and thanks to the new pedestrian walkway you can easily cross busy Thanon Sathon.

Indian, Muslim & Burmese Towards the western end of Thanon Silom and Thanon Surawong, in an area known as Bangrak, Indian eateries begin to appear. Unlike most Indian restaurants in Bangkok, the menus in Bangrak tend to steer clear of the usual, boring predilection for north-Indian Moghul-style cuisine.

For authentic south-Indian food (dosa, idli, vada etc), try the *Madras Cafe* (☎ 235 6761, 31/10–11 Trok 13, Thanon Silom) in the Madras Lodge near the Narai Hotel. It is open 9 am to 10 pm daily. *Madura Restaurant* on Soi 22 (Soi Pracheun), between Silom and Surawong, serves south Indian food along with a few Sri Lankan dishes, including enormous *thali* (combination plates). Across the street from the Narai Hotel, near the Sri Mariamman Temple, *street vendors* sometimes sell various Indian snacks.

India Hut (☎ 635 7876), opposite the Manohra Hotel on Thanon Surawong, specialises in Nawabi (Lucknow) cuisine; it's quite good, friendly and has moderate to medium-high in prices (50B to 100B per dish). The vegetarian samosas and fresh prawns cooked with ginger are particularly good. It's three flights of steps off the street, with modern Indian decor.

Himali Cha-Cha (☎ 235 1569, 1229/11 Thanon Charoen Krung) features north Indian cuisine at slightly higher prices. The founder, Cha-Cha, worked as a chef for India's last Viceroy; his son has taken over the kitchen here. It's open for lunch and dinner.

The Cholas, a small air-con place downstairs in the Woodlands Inn off Soi 32 Thanon Charoen Krung, just north of the main post office, serves decent, no-fuss north Indian food for 50B to 80B a dish.

The open-air *Sallim Restaurant*, around the corner from Woodlands on Soi 32 Thanon Charoen Krung, is a cheaper place

with north Indian, Malay and Thai-Muslim dishes – it's usually packed.

Around the corner on Soi 43 (Soi Saphan Yao) is the very popular but basic-looking *Naaz* (pronounced Naat in Thai), often cited as having the richest *khâo mòk kài* (chicken biryani) in the city. The milk tea is also very good, and daily specials include chicken masala and mutton kurma. For dessert, the speciality of the house is *firni*, a Middle Eastern pudding spiced with co-conut, almonds, cardamom and saffron. It's open 7.30 am to 10.30 pm daily.

Yogi, at the western end of Soi Phuttha Osot, is a very simple and inexpensive, all-vegetarian Indian restaurant. The nearby *New Restaurant* (NR Restaurant) is similar but serves non-veg as well as veg. Finding this soi is a little tricky since an expressway bisected the original approach from Thanon Charoen Krung. Now the best way to reach it is by walking north from Thanon Surawong along a soi opposite Thanon Mahesak and the New Fuji Hotel, then turn left at Soi Phuttha Osot and you'll reach Yogi and NR a little way down on the left.

Near the intersection of Thanon Charoen Krung and Thanon Silom, the *Muslim Restaurant* (1356 Thanon Charoen Krung) has been feeding us well for over 20 years. The faded walls and stainless steel tables don't inspire everyone, but it's clean enough and you can fill your stomach with curries and roti for 40B or less. On Soi 20 (Soi Pradit) off Thanon Silom there's a mosque, Masjid (*mátsàyít*) Mirasuddeen, so Muslim *food vendors* are common.

The *Sun Far Myanmar Food Centre* (☎ 266 8787, 107/1 Thanon Pan), between Thanon Silom and Thanon Sathon (near the building that houses the Myanmar embassy), is a cheap place to sample authentic Burmese curries and *thok* (spicy Burmese-style salads). It's open 8 am to 8 pm daily.

The *Rabianthong Restaurant* (☎ 237 0100), in the Narai Hotel on Thanon Silom, offers a very good vegetarian section in its luncheon buffet on *wan phrá* (full, half- and new-moon days) only for 250B.

Tiensin (1345 Thanon Charoen Krung) opposite the entrance of the soi that leads to the Shangri-La Hotel, serves very good Chinese vegetarian cuisine, including many mock meat dishes. It's open 7 am to 9 pm daily.

Other Cuisines If you crave international food, a variety of cuisines are available on and around Thanon Patpong 1 and Patong 2, a short walk from the Sala Daeng Skytrain station.

Probably the best Patpong find is *Le Bouchon* (☎ 234 9109) on Soi Patpong 2, an aircon spot popular with French expats for its decent approximations of Parisian-style bistro fare. *Bobby's Arms*, an Aussie-British pub on the 1st floor of a multistorey car park off Soi Patpong 2, has good fish and chips.

Authentically decorated *O'Reilly's Irish Pub* (☎ 235 1572, 62/1–2 Thanon Silom), at the entrance to Thaniya Plaza (corner of Thanon Silom and Soi Thaniya), opens at 8 am, stays open until 1 or 2 am and features a good menu of reasonably priced pub grub. *Shenanigans* (☎ 266 7160, 1–4 Sivadon Building, Thanon Convent), in the Thanon Silom district, serves a set lunch menu from Monday to Friday, plus other international food daily for lunch and dinner.

Folies Café-Patisserie (☎ 678 4100, 29 Thanon Sathon Tai) at the Alliance Française serves inexpensive to moderately priced French dishes, and is open 8 am to 6 pm Monday to Saturday.

Coffee World, on the northern side of Thanon Silom near the mouth of Soi 10, serves a variety of coffees, teas, Italian sodas, sandwiches and pastries in a large, clean, California-style cafe setting. Foreign magazines and newspapers are on hand for a read.

Siam Square, Thanon Ploenchit & Thanon Withayu

This shopping area is interspersed with several low- and medium-priced restaurants as well as American fast-food franchises. The following places are marked on the Siam Square & Pratunam map.

Can't decide what kind of Asian or fàràng food you're in the mood for? Then head for *S&P Restaurant & Bakery* on Soi 11. The extensive menu features mostly Thai specialities with a few Chinese, Japanese, European and vegetarian dishes, plus a bakery with pies, cakes, pastries and ice cream – all high-quality fare at low to moderate prices (dishes are 45B to 75B, breakfast 35B to 65B).

On the square's Soi 11, the Bangkok branch of London's *Hard Rock Cafe* serves good American and Thai food; prices are about the same as at other Hard Rocks around the world. Look for the túk-túk captioned 'God is my co-pilot' coming out of the building's facade. The Hard Rock stays open until 2 am, which is a bit later than many Siam Square eateries.

On Thanon Phra Ram I, facing Siam Center and in the shadow of the Siam Skytrain station, *Khao Man Kai Siam* serves delicious 35B dishes of *khâo man kài* (chicken rice) in a tiny shop decorated with photos and drawings of Elvis.

On both sides of Thanon Phra Ram I, in Siam Square and Siam Center, you'll find a battery of American fast-food franchises, including *Mister Donut*, *Burger King*, *Pizza Hut*, *Swensen's Ice Cream*, *McDonald's*, *A&W Root Beer* and *KFC*. Prices are close to what you would pay in the USA. Siam Center contains a bevy of good, moderately priced *Thai coffee shops* on its upper floors.

On the 2nd floor of the relatively new Siam Discovery Center (attached to Siam Center by an enclosed walkway), is the sleekly designed *Hartmannsdorfer Brau Haus* (☎ 658 0229), which offers three types of home-brewed German beer and a long menu of German specialities, including house-made sausages. An international buffet of German, Italian and Thai dishes is served 11 am to 3 pm weekdays for 240B, plus tax and service. *Les Artistes Restaurant & Pastry* (☎ 658 0214) on the same floor features various baked goods and a large menu, which includes Italian, Thai and French dishes, served in a fun, modern decor. It's open 7 am to midnight daily.

If you're staying on or nearby Soi Kasem San 1, you don't have to suck motorcycle fumes crossing Thanon Phra Ram I and Thanon Phayathai to find something to eat. Besides the typical hotel coffee shops found on the soi, there are also two very good and inexpensive *curry-and-rice vendors* with tables along the east side of the soi. There is no need to worry about your lack of fluency in Thai, the staff are used to the 'point-and-serve' system.

Right around the corner on Thanon Phra Ram I, next to the liquor dealer with the vintage British and US motorcycles out the front, is *Thai Sa-Nguan* (no Roman-script sign), a fairly clean shop with curry rice dishes and noodles. Next door, the newer and cleaner *Watanayon Restaurant* adds sticky rice and *sôm-tam* to the menu.

Despite its fàràng name, *Sara-Jane's* (☎ 650 9992, *Sindhorn Building, 130–132 Thanon Withayu*) serves very good Isan and Italian food in a casual air-con dining room. The restaurant is inside the Sindhorn Building towards the back. There's a second location on Thanon Narathiwat Ratchanakharin (see the Thanon Silom, Thanon Surawong & Thanon Sathon section).

Fabb Fashion Cafe (☎ 658 2003), Mercury Tower, 540 Thanon Ploenchit), serves good Thai-Italian fusion cuisine for lunch and dinner at moderate to high prices. In the same building, *Auberge DAB* (☎ 658 6222) goes all French with pan-fried French duck liver with raspberry dressing, poached French oysters wrapped in spinach leaves with champagne sauce, roast pigeon and fresh oysters from Brittany among the offerings. The 295B three-course set lunch is your best bet.

Mahboonkrong Shopping Centre Another building studded with restaurants, Mahboonkrong shopping centre (MBK) is diagonally across from Siam Square at the intersection of Thanon Phayathai and Thanon Phra Ram I. A section on the ground floor called Major Plaza contains two cinemas and a good food centre. An older food centre is on the 7th floor; both places have vendors serving tasty dishes from all over Thailand, including vegetarian, at prices averaging 20B to 35B per plate. Hours are from 10 am to 10 pm, but the more popular vendors run out of food as early as 8.30 or 9 pm – come earlier for the best selection. A beer garden on the terrace surrounding two sides of the 7th-floor food centre, with good views of the Bangkok nightscape, is open in the evening.

Scattered around other floors, especially the 3rd and 4th, are a number of popular medium-price places, including *13 Coins* (steak, pizza and pasta), *Kobune Japanese Restaurant*, *Chester's Grilled Chicken*, *Pizza Hut* and many others.

World Trade Centre This relatively new office and shopping complex on the corner of Thanon Ploenchit and Thanon Ratchadamri contains a few upmarket restaurants. On the ground floor of this huge glossy building are *Kroissant House* (coffees, pastries and gelato), *La Fontana* (bistro-style Italian) and the always-satisfying *Vijit* (traditional Thai), a branch of the Democracy Circle restaurant

of the same name. The 6th floor of the centre features *Lai-Lai* and *Chao Sua* (☎ 255 9500), two sumptuous Chinese banquet-style places, plus the elegant traditional Thai *Thanying* (a branch of the original Thanying on Thanon Silom) and the more casual *Narai Pizzeria*. There are also two *food centres* on the 7th floor with standard Thai and Chinese dishes, which are only a little more expensive than the usual Bangkok food centres.

Soi Lang Suan East from Siam Square and off Thanon Ploenchit, Soi Lang Suan offers a number of medium-price eating possibilities. The Italian-owned *Pan Pan Capri* (☎ 252 7104, 45 Soi Lang Suan) is very popular with Western residents for wood-fired pizza (takeaway orders accepted), pastas, salads, gelato (the best in Thailand) and pastries. A low-calorie vegetarian menu is available on request.

The *Whole Earth Restaurant* (☎ 252 5574, 93/3 Soi Lang Suan) is a good Thai vegetarian restaurant (nonvegetarian dishes are also served) with service to match, but it's a bit pricey if you're on a tight budget. The upstairs room features low tables with floor cushions. A second branch (☎ 258 4900, 71 Soi 26, Thanon Sukhumvit) has opened at, and serves both Thai and Indian vegetarian dishes.

Nguan Lee Lang Suan (*Central Bangkok map*), on the corner of Soi Lang Suan and Soi Sarasin, is a semi-outdoor place specialising in Chinese-style seafood and *kài lâo daeng* (chicken steamed in Chinese herbs).

Thanon Sukhumvit

This avenue stretching east all the way to the city limits has hundreds of Thai, Chinese and Western restaurants to choose from. Many restaurants around the major hotels offer mixed Thai, Chinese, European and American menus, but most of these restaurants are of average quality and have above-average prices. Better are the ones dedicated either to Thai or to Western cuisine.

Unless otherwise indicated, the following places are all on the Thanon Sukhumvit map.

Thai & Other Asian Although it's a little grungy, the *Yong Lee Restaurant* at Soi 15, near Asia Books, has excellent Thai and Chinese food at very reasonable prices, and is a long-time favourite among both Thai and fàràng residents alike. There is a second Yong Lee Restaurant between Soi 35 and Soi 37 farther down Thanon Sukhumvit.

This central section of Thanon Sukhumvit is loaded with medium-priced Thai restaurants that have modern decor but real Thai food. *Baan Suan* (☎ 261 6650), next to Bei Otto on Soi 20, is a pleasant garden restaurant with excellent Isan food, including Khon Kaen-style *kài yâang*, chicken grilled over coconut husk coals.

For nouvelle Thai cuisine, you can try *Lemongrass* (☎ 258 8637, 5/1 Soi 24, Thanon Sukhumvit), which has an atmospheric setting in an old Thai house decorated with antiques. The food is exceptional; try the *yam pèt* (Thai-style duck salad). It's open 11 am to 2 pm and 6 to 11 pm daily.

Yet another hidden gem down Thanon Sukhumvit is *Laicram* at Soi 23 (☎ 204 1069). The food is authentic gourmet Thai, but not outrageously priced. One of the house specialities is *hàw mòk hǎwy*, an exquisite thick fish curry steamed with mussels in the shell. Sôm-tam (spicy green papaya salad) is also excellent and is usually served with *khâo man*, rice cooked with coconut milk and *bai toei* (pandanus leaf). It's opening hours are 10 am to 9 pm Monday to Saturday and until 3 pm Sunday.

Le Dalat (☎ 258 4192, 260 1849, 47/1 Soi 23, Thanon Sukhumvit) has the most celebrated Vietnamese cuisine in the city. A house speciality is *nǎem meuang*, grilled meatballs that you place on steamed rice-flour wrappers, then add chunks of garlic, chilli, ginger, starfruit and mango along with a tamarind sauce, and finally wrap the whole thing into a lettuce bundle before popping it into your mouth. It's open 11.30 am to 2.30 pm and 6 to 10 pm daily. There's another branch at 14 Soi 23, Thanon Sukhumvit (☎ 661 7967). The hours are the same.

Also good for a stylish Vietnamese meal is *Pho* (☎ 658 1199), on the 4th floor of Siam Center (Siam Square & Pratunam map). A second branch (☎ 251 8945) can be found in the Alma Link Building at 25 Soi Chitlom, Thanon Ploenchit. About a 50m walk down Sukhumvit Soi 12, *Cabbages & Condoms*, next to the Population & Community Development Association (PDA) headquarters, offers fair Thai food for lunch and dinner in indoor and outdoor dining areas. Instead of after-meal mints, diners get packaged con-

doms; all proceeds go towards sex education/AIDS prevention programs in Thailand. Another 50m down the same soi, *Crepes & Co* serves high-quality crepes of all kinds, European-style breakfasts, and a very nice selection of Mediterranean, Moroccan and Spanish lunch and dinner specialities. It's air-conditioned and prices are moderate.

The Emporium shopping centre, on Thanon Sukhumvit at Soi 24, has several restaurants on its 4th, 5th and 6th floors, as well as the city's trendiest food centre. If you go for the blonde wood and metal LA-cafe-bar-look, try the enormously trendy *Greyhound Cafe* on the 4th floor of The Emporium. The hybrid menu emphasises good, updated Thai supplemented by Italian and Mediterranean cuisine.

Kuppa on Soi 16, Thanon Sukhumvit, is another very fashionable spot among Thais and expats, particularly for late breakfasts.

Hua Lamphong Food Station (☎ 661 3538, 92/1 Soi 34, Thanon Sukhumvit), nowhere near Bangkok's main railway station despite the name, is a large, casual place in a shed-like building with country Thai decor and serves delicious Isan and northern-Thai food.

Indian & Muslim A restaurant with a good variety of moderately priced vegetarian and nonvegetarian Indian food (mostly north Indian) is *Mrs Balbir's* (☎ 651 0498, 155/18 Soi 11/1), behind the Siam Commercial Bank and next to the Swiss Park Hotel. A 150B buffet lunch is served daily. Mrs Balbir has been teaching Indian and Thai cooking for many years and has her own Indian grocery service as well. It's closed on Monday.

A few medium to expensive restaurants serving Pakistani and Middle Eastern food can be found in the 'Little Arabia' area of Soi 3 (Soi Nana Neua). The best value in the whole area is *Al Hussain*, a roofed outdoor cafe (there's also an indoor air-con dining area) on the corner of a lane (Soi 3/5) off the east side of Soi Nana Neua. A steam table holds a range of vegetarian, chicken, mutton and fish curries, along with dahl (curried lentils), *aloo gobi* (spicy potatoes and cauliflower), *nan* and rice. Dishes cost 20B to 40B each. *Shiraz*, on the same soi, is a slightly pricier indoor place that provides hookahs for Middle Eastern gentlemen who while away the afternoon smoking in front of the restaurant. Similar places nearby include *Mehmaan*, *Akbar's*, *Al Hamra*, *Ali* and *Shaharazad*.

The splurge-worthy *Rang Mahal* (☎ 261 7100), an elegant rooftop restaurant in the Hotel Rembrandt on Soi 18, offers very good north- and south-Indian 'royal cuisine' with overly attentive service and cityscape views. Most of the entrees are in the 150B to 230B range. In addition to the regular menu, there are three set menus ranging from 700B to 950B per person. On Sunday the restaurant puts on a sumptuous Indian buffet from 11.30 am to 3 pm. An open-air observation platform on the same floor is reason enough for a visit.

International Cuisine Homesick Brits need look no further than *Jool's Bar & Restaurant* (☎ 252 6413) at Soi 4 (Soi Nana Tai), past Nana Plaza on the left if you're walking from Thanon Sukhumvit. The British-style bar downstairs is a favourite expat hang-out while the dining room upstairs serves decent English food. On the western side of Soi 23, just around the corner from Soi Cowboy, the *Ship Inn* is a small but authentic-looking British pub with food and libation.

Several rather expensive West European restaurants (Swiss, French, German etc) are also found on touristy Thanon Sukhumvit. *Bei Otto* (☎ 262 0892, 1 Soi 20, Thanon Sukhumvit) is one of the most popular German restaurants in town and has a comfortable bar. Attached are a bakery, deli and butcher shop. *Haus München* (☎ 252 5775, 4 Soi 15, Thanon Sukhumvit) serves large portions of good German and Austrian food; prices are reasonable and there are recent German-language newspapers on hand. It's open daily for breakfast, lunch and dinner. Thailand's first microbrewery, *Bräuhaus-Bangkok* (☎ 661 1111, Ground floor, President Park, 99/27 Soi 24, Thanon Sukhumvit) serves German cuisine and fresh brewed beer in a huge air-con dining room or at outdoor tables. An average bill is around 400B.

Nostalgic visitors from the USA, especially those from the South, will appreciate the well-run *Bourbon St Bar & Restaurant* (☎ 259 0328), on Soi 22 (behind the Washington Theatre). The menu emphasises Cajun and Creole cooking, but there are also some Mexican dishes on the menu;

some nights there is also free live music. A large dinner special for two costs 400B. It is also open for breakfast.

Larry's Dive Center, Bar & Grill (☎ 663 4563, e larrybkk@larrysdive.com), a bright-yellow two-storey building on Soi 22, serves American and Tex-Mex fare amid kitschy sand-floor-and-potted-palms decor. The fake newspaper menu ('largest circulation of any newspaper on Soi 22') lists stuffed potato skins, salads, quesadillas, nachos, chili, spicy chicken wings and Larry's food guarantee: 'Served in 30 minutes, or it's cold'. There's an attached dive shop, should you get the urge to go snorkelling in a nearby canal.

One of the top French restaurants in the city, and probably the best that isn't associated with a luxury hotel, is *Le Banyan* (☎ 253 5556, 59 Soi 8, Thanon Sukhumvit) in a charming early Ratanakosin-style house. The kitchen is French-managed and the menu covers the territory from *ragout d'escargot* to *canard maigret avec foie gras*. It has a superb wine list. This is definitely a splurge experience, although the prices are moderate when compared with other elegant French restaurants in the city.

Pomodoro (☎ 254 5282), a place with floor-to-ceiling windows on the ground floor of the Nai Lert Building on Thanon Sukhumvit (between Soi 3 and Soi 5), specialises in Sardinian cuisine. The menu includes more than 25 pasta dishes, and special set lunch menus are available for 180B to 250B.

De Meglio (☎ 651 3838), opposite Grand President Tower on Soi 11, is an elegant but comfortable Italian restaurant with a creative, seasonal menu, including a tasty selection of vegetarian entrees. It's managed by the same company that operates Bräuhaus-Bangkok, so locally brewed German-style beer is available along with imported wines. A cigar lounge is attached.

If you're looking for Mexican food, the city's best can be found at *Señor Pico's of Los Angeles* (☎ 261 7100, 2nd floor, Hotel Rembrandt, Soi 18, Thanon Sukhumvit). This brightly decorated, festive restaurant offers reasonably authentic Tex-Mex cuisine, including fajitas, carnitas, nachos and combination platters. Expect to spend around 500B for two. Live Latin music is the norm most evenings.

Chinatown, Hualamphong & Phahurat

Some of Bangkok's best Chinese and Indian food is found in these adjacent districts, but because few tourists stay in this part of town (for good reason – it's simply too congested) they rarely make any eating forays into the area. A few old Chinese restaurants have moved from Chinatown to locations with less traffic, but many places are still hanging on to their venerable Chinatown addresses, where the atmosphere is still a part of the eating experience.

Most specialise in southern Chinese cuisine, particularly that of coastal Guangdong and Fujian Provinces. This means seafood, rice noodles and dumplings are often the best choices. The large, banquet-style Chinese places are mostly found along Thanon Yaowarat and Thanon Charoen Krung, and include *Laem Thong* (*Chinatown & Phahurat map; 38 Soi Bamrungrat*), just off Thanon Charoen Krung, and *Shangarila Restaurant* (*formerly Yau Wah Yuen; Chinatown & Phahurat map*) near the Thanon Yaowarat and Thanon Ratchawong intersection. Each has an extensive menu, including dim sum before lunchtime. *Lie Kee* (*Chinatown & Phahurat map;* ☎ *224 3587, 360–362 Thanon Charoen Krung*) is an excellent and inexpensive Chinese food court on the 3rd floor of a building on the corner of Thanon Charoen Krung and Thanon Bamrungrat, a block west of Thanon Ratchawong. It's air-conditioned, yet it's difficult to spend more than 50B for lunch.

The best noodle and dumpling shops are hidden away on smaller sois and alleys. At 54 Soi Bamrungrat is the funky *Chiang Ki* (*Chinatown & Phahurat map*), where the 100B *khâo tôm plaa* (rice soup with fish) belies the casual surroundings – no place does it better. *Kong Lee* (*Chinatown & Phahurat map; 137/141 Thanon Ratchawong*) has a very loyal clientele for its *bàmìi hâeng* (dry-fried wheat noodles) – again it's reportedly the best in Bangkok.

Another great noodle place, *Pet Tun Jao Tha* (*Thanon Silom, Thanon Surawong & Thanon Sathon map*), is on the south-eastern edge of Chinatown in the direction of the main post office at 945 Soi Wanit 2, opposite the Harbour Department building. The restaurant's name means 'Harbour Department Stewed Duck' – the speciality is kǔaytǐaw (rice noodles) served with duck or goose, which is either roasted or stewed.

All-night *food hawkers* set up along Thanon Yaowarat at the Thanon Ratchawong intersection, opposite Yaowarat Market and near the Cathay department store; this is the least expensive place to dine out in Chinatown. On weekends parts of these two streets are closed to vehicular traffic, turning the area into a pedestrian mall.

Diagonally opposite About Studio/About Cafe on Thanon Maitrichit, unassuming *Pheng Phochana* serves perhaps the best *kǔaytǐaw khûa kài* (rice noodles stir-fried with egg and chicken) in the city. It's open sunrise to midnight Monday to Saturday.

Suki Jeh Yu Jing (*the English sign reads 'Vegetarian'; Central Bangkok map*), a Chinese vegetarian restaurant just 70m from Hualamphong station down Thanon Phra Ram IV, serves excellent, if a bit pricey, vegetarian food in a clean, air-con atmosphere. The fruit shakes are particularly well made; this is a great place to fortify yourself with food and drink while waiting for a train at Hualamphong. It's open 6 am to 10 pm. Service can be slow, so leave plenty of time to make your train departure.

Over in Phahurat, the Indian fabric district, most places serve north Indian cuisine, which is heavily influenced by Moghul or Persian flavours and spices. For many people, the best north Indian restaurant in town is the *Royal India* (*Chinatown & Phahurat map;* ☎ *221 6565, 392/1 Thanon Chakraphet*) in Phahurat. It can be very crowded at lunchtime, almost exclusively with Indian residents, so it might be better to go there after the standard lunch hour or at night-time. The place has very good curries (vegetarian and nonvegetarian), dhal, Indian breads (including six kinds of *paratha*), *raita, lassis* etc, all at quite reasonable prices. Royal India also has a branch in Thanon Khao San in Banglamphu but it's not as good.

The *ATM department store* (*Chinatown & Phahurat map*) on Thanon Chakraphet near the pedestrian bridge has a food centre on the top floor that features several Indian vendors – the food is cheap and tasty and there's a good selection. Running alongside the ATM building on Soi ATM are several small *teahouses* serving very inexpensive Indian and Nepali food, including lots of fresh chapatis and strong milk tea. At a shop called *Pandey's* you can buy Indian spices and cookware. In the afternoons a Sikh man sets up a *pushcart* on the corner of Soi ATM and Thanon Chakraphet and sells vegetarian samosas, often cited as the best in Bangkok.

Wedged between the western edge of Chinatown and the northern edge of Phahurat, the three-storey *Old Siam Plaza* shopping centre houses a number of Thai, Chinese and Japanese restaurants. The most economical places are on the 3rd floor, where a food centre serves relatively inexpensive Thai and Chinese meals from 10 am to 5 pm. Also found on the 3rd floor are several reasonably priced and comfortable Thai-style coffee shops.

Attached to the adjacent Chalermkrung Royal Theatre is a branch of the highly efficient, moderately priced *S&P Restaurant & Bakery*, where the extensive menu encompasses everything from authentic Thai to well-prepared Japanese, European and vegetarian dishes, along with a selection of pastries and desserts.

Vegetarian During the annual Vegetarian Festival (which is in September/October and is centred around Wat Mangkon Kamalawat on Thanon Charoen Krung), Bangkok's Chinatown becomes a virtual orgy of vegetarian Thai and Chinese cuisine. The restaurants and noodle shops in the area offer hundreds of different dishes. One of the best spreads is at *Hua Seng Restaurant*, which is a few doors west of Wat Mangkon on Thanon Charoen Krung.

Soi Ngam Duphli
Across from the Tungmahamek Privacy Hotel and beside the Malaysia Hotel, an outdoor Thai place called *Just One (Central Bangkok map; ☎ 679 7932, 58 Soi 1, Thanon Sathorn Tai)* is a popular lunch spot.

On the 11th floor of *Lumphini Tower (Central Bangkok map)* on busy Thanon Phra Ram IV is a cafeteria-style food centre open 7 am to 2 pm. Opposite Lumphini Tower on the same road is a warren of *food vendors* with cheap eats.

Another restaurant in the Soi Ngam Duphli area worth mentioning is *Ratsstube (Central Bangkok map; ☎ 287 2822)* in the Thai-German Cultural Centre (Goethe-Institut), on Soi Goethe off Soi Atakanprasit. Home-made sausages and set meals averaging 150B attract a large and steady clientele. The softly lit Euro-Asian decor borders on rococo. It's open 11 am to 2.30 pm and 5.30 to 10 pm weekdays, 11 am to 10 pm Saturday and Sunday.

Dinner Cruises
There are a number of companies that run cruises during which you eat dinner. Prices range from 70B to 1200B per person depending on how far the boats go and whether dinner is included in the fare. For more information, see Dinner Cruises under River & Canal Trips earlier in this chapter.

Hotel Restaurants
For splurge-level food, many of Bangkok's luxury hotels provide memorable – if expensive – eating experiences. With Western cuisine, particularly, the quality usually far exceeds anything found in Bangkok's independent restaurants. Some of the city's best Chinese restaurants are also located in hotels. If you're on a budget, check to see if a lunchtime buffet is available on weekdays; usually these are the best deals, ranging from 150B to 500B per person. Also check the *Bangkok Post* and the *Nation* for weekly specials presented by visiting chefs from far-flung corners of the globe – Morocco, Mexico City, Montreal, no matter how obscure, they've probably done the Bangkok hotel circuit.

The Oriental Hotel has six restaurants, all managed by world-class chefs, and buffet lunches are offered at several. The hotel's *China House (☎ 236 0400 ext 3378)*, set in a charming restored private residence opposite the hotel's main wing, has one of the best Chinese kitchens in Bangkok, with an emphasis on Cantonese cooking. The lunchtime dim sum is superb and is a bargain by luxury hotel standards. Reservations are recommended. The Oriental's *Lord Jim's* is designed to imitate the interior of a 19th-century Asian steamer, with a view of the river; the menu focuses on seafood (lunch buffet available).

Bai Yun (☎ 679 1200), on the 60th floor of the Westin Banyan Tree, specialises in nouvelle Cantonese – an East-West fusion.

Dusit Thani's *Chinatown (☎ 236 0450)* was probably the inspiration for the Oriental's China House, although here the menu focuses on Chao Zhou (Chiu Chau) cuisine as well as Cantonese. Dim sum lunch is available, but it's a bit more expensive than the Oriental's. As at the Oriental, service is impeccable. Dusit also has the highly reputed *Mayflower*, with pricey Cantonese cuisine, and the Vietnamese *Thien Duong*.

For hotel dim sum almost as good as that at the Dusit or Oriental hotels – but at less than a third of the price – try the *Jade Garden* (☎ 233 7060) at the Montien Hotel. Although not quite as fancy in presentation, the food is nonetheless impressive.

For French food, the leading hotel contenders are *Ma Maison* (☎ 253 0123) at the Hilton International, *Le Normandie* (☎ 236 0400 ext 3380) at the Oriental Hotel and *Regent Grill* (☎ 251 6127) at the Regent Bangkok. All are expensive but the meals and service are virtually guaranteed to be of top quality. The Regent Bangkok also offers the slightly less formal *La Brasserie*, specialising in Parisian cuisine.

One of the best Italian dining experiences in the city can be found at the very posh and formal *Grappino Italian Restaurant* (☎ 653 9000) in the Amari Watergate Hotel, on Thanon Phetburi in the busy Pratunam district. All pasta and breads are prepared fresh on the premises daily, and the small but hitech wine cellar is one of Bangkok's best – the grappa selection is unmatched. Grappino is open daily for lunch and dinner; reservations are recommended.

Of a similar quality – or perhaps better – and probably the busiest Italian restaurant in the city, *Biscotti* (☎ 255 5443), in the Regent Bangkok, serves inventive dishes for relatively reasonable prices considering the location and the high quality of the cooking. Reservations are recommended.

The more relaxed *Angelini's* (☎ 236 7777 ext 1766) in the Shangri-La Hotel offers fine Italian cuisine in one of the most impressively chic restaurant decors in Bangkok. Expect to pay 800B to 1000B for dinner for two. An array of upmarket grappas is available at the sleek bar, where a good live pop band is usually playing; open 11 am until late.

The minimalist *Colonnade Restaurant* (☎ 287 0222) at the Sukhothai Hotel lays out a huge 900B brunch, including made-to-order lobster bisque, from 11 am to 3 pm on Sunday. A jazz trio supplies background music. Reservations recommended.

Finally, if eating at one of these exclusive restaurants means spending your life savings, try this middle-class Thai version of dining amid the bright hotel lights of Bangkok. Take a ferry (2B) from the end of the soi in front of the Shangri-La Hotel and cross the river to the wooden pier immediately opposite on the Thonburi shore. Wind through the narrow lanes till you come to a main road (Thanon Charoen Nakhon), then turn left. About 200m down on your left, turn back towards the river till you come to the large and open-air *Thon Krueng* (Ton Khreuang; *Thanon Silom, Thanon Surawong & Thanon Sathon map;* ☎ 437 9671, 723 Thanon Charoen Nakhon). Here you can enjoy a moderately priced Thai seafood meal outdoors with impressive night-time views of the Shangri-La and Oriental hotels opposite. The kitchen has a solid command of the Thai culinary arsenal. The ferry runs till around 2 am.

Other Vegetarian

One of Bangkok's oldest vegetarian restaurants, operated by the Asoke Foundation, is the branch at Chatuchak Weekend Market off Thanon Kamphaeng Phet (near the main local bus stop, a pedestrian bridge and a Chinese shrine – look for a sign reading 'Vegetarian' in green letters). It's open only on weekends from 8 am to noon. Prices are almost ridiculously low – around 7B to 15B per dish. The *cafeteria* at the Bangkok Adventist Hospital at 430 Thanon Phitsanulok also serves inexpensive vegie fare. All the Indian restaurants in town also have vegetarian selections on their menus.

ENTERTAINMENT

In their round-the-clock search for *khwaam sànùk* (fun), Bangkok residents have made their metropolis one that literally never sleeps. To get an idea of what's available, check the entertainment listings in the daily *Bangkok Post* and the *Nation* or the monthly *Bangkok Metro*. The latter maintains a good Web site (www.bkkmetro.com) listing current happenings in the city. Possibilities include classical music performances, rock concerts, videotheque dancing, Asian music and theatre ensembles on tour, art shows and dinner theatre. Boredom should not be a problem in Bangkok, at least not for a short-term visit – but save some energy and money for exploring the rest of the country!

Nightlife

Bangkok's evening entertainment scene goes well beyond its overpublicised naughty nightlife image, a hangover from the days when the City of Angels was an R&R stop for GIs serving in Vietnam in the 1960s and early 1970s.

Today, Bangkok offers a heady assortment of entertainment venues, nightclubs, bars, cafes and discos appealing to every sort of proclivity. Many specialise in live music – rock, country-and-western, Thai pop music and jazz – while you'll find the latest recorded music in the smaller neighbourhood bars and mega-discos. Hotels catering to tourists and businesspeople often contain up-to-date discos as well.

All bars and clubs are supposed to close at 1 or 2 am (the latter closing time is for places with dance floors and/or live music), but in reality only a few obey the law.

Pubs & Bars

Bangkok has long outgrown the days when the only bars around catered to male go-go oglers. Trendy with locals these days are bars that strive for a sophisticated but casual atmosphere, with good service, drinks and music. The Thais often call them pubs but they bear little resemblance to a traditional English pub. Some are 'theme' bars, conceived around a particular aesthetic. All the city's major hotels feature Western-style bars as well.

In Banglamphu *Gulliver's Traveler's Tavern (Thanon Khao San map)*, on the corner of Thanon Khao San and Thanon Chakraphong, is an air-conditioned place with the atmosphere of an American college hang-out. *Salvador Dali (Banglamphu map)*, a block north on Thanon Rambutri (towards the western end) and tucked away amid a row of noodle stands, is a comfortable, two-storey air-con bar with a more intimate feel. The on and off (often closed during slow months) *Hole in the Wall (Thanon Khao San map)* bar on a short, dead-end soi towards the western end of Thanon Khao San is a cheap place to drink and chat with Thanon Khao San denizens.

More happening is the low-key *Susie Pub* in an alley off the northern side of Khao San, and its sister pub down another alley off the southern side of Khao San, *Austin Pub*. Both pack in a heavily Thai clientele. If you want more of the Thai bar scene, head for Thanon Tanao south of Thanon Ratchadamnoen, where you'll find *Window Seat*, *Yellowish*, *Spicy*, *Go 6*, *Song Muai*, *Fifa Pub* and *Zoda*, all of which draw a very young crowd.

Moved from Ho Chi Minh City only recently, *Q Bar (Thanon Sukhumvit map;* ☎ *252 3274)* is tucked away in a curvy building towards the back of Soi 11, Thanon Sukhumvit. Inside there's a choice of full-on DJ sounds on the ground floor, the slightly more subdued upstairs tables or the relatively quiet balcony tables outside. Avoid weekends when it tends to get so crowded it's difficult to move.

Shenanigans (Thanon Silom, Thanon Surawong & Thanon Sathon map; ☎ *266 7160, 1–4 Sivadon Building, Thanon Convent),* in the Thanon Silom district, is one of only two places in Bangkok that serves Guinness on tap. The interior wood panels, glass mirrors and bench seating were all custom-made and imported from Ireland. Bands of varying quality play from Tuesday to Saturday, and the place is often packed from 6 pm till closing. *O'Reilly's Irish Pub* (☎ *632 7515, 62/1-2 Thanon Silom),* at the entrance to Thaniya Plaza (corner of Thanon Silom and Soi Thaniya), draws a slow pint of Guinness or Kilkenny in a comparatively more low-key setting that resembles an old camera shop. Early drinkers will find O'Reilly's open at 11 am. Both pubs feature daily happy hours when their otherwise pricey beers are temporarily discounted.

Three low-key, British-style taverns include *Jool's*, on Soi 4 near Nana Plaza, the *Ship Inn*, just around the corner from Soi Cowboy on the western side of Soi 23, and *Bull's Head & Angus Steakhouse*, on Soi 33/1, Thanon Sukhumvit. Bull's Head tends to get very smoky inside if there's not much of a crowd.

The guitar-shaped bar at Bangkok's *Hard Rock Cafe* (☎ *254 0830)* on Soi 11, Siam Square, features a full line of cocktails and a small assortment of local and imported beers. The crowd is an ever-changing assortment of Thais, expats and tourists. From 10 pm onwards there's also live music.

For slick aerial city views, the place to go is the 93-storey Baiyoke Sky Hotel on Thanon Ratchaprarop in Pratunam. On the 77th floor there's an *observation deck* that's open 24 hours, or you can scope the cityscape while dining in one of the *restaurants* on the 78th and 79th floors. The *Compass Rose*, a bar on the 59th floor of the Westin Banyan Tree on Thanon Sathon Tai, is also sky high; it's open 11.30 am to 1 am.

Brewery Pubs

The Brewhouse (☎ 661 3535, 61/2 Soi 26, Thanon Sukhumvit), associated with the Taurus dance club opposite, features four brews (including the low-alcohol Dynamite Lite and the high-test Naked Killer Ale), in a split-level interior beneath a metallic dome.

In the Siam Discovery Center (attached to the Siam Center by an enclosed walkway), *Hartmannsdorfer Brau Haus (Siam Square & Pratunam map; ☎ 658 0229)* serves fresh beer, sausages, cheeses and other stout German fare in a polished but pleasant atmosphere.

Londoner Brew Pub in the basement of the UBC II Building *(Thanon Sukhumvit map; ☎ 261 0238, Soi 33, Thanon Sukhumvit)* has recently begun serving its own beers and ales, but the ambience is limp.

If you find yourself stuck at Bangkok International Airport, you could do a lot worse than the *Taurus Brewhouse* (☎ 535 6861), towards the southern end of Terminal 2 on the 4th floor, not far from the indoor car park. You'll find the same brews as at its sister establishment, The Brewhouse. The menu of sandwiches, burgers, salads, pastas, soups, pizza and Thai specials is quite good. It's open 6 pm to midnight daily.

Cigar Bars

One half of the lobby in the *Regent Hotel* is devoted to cigar smokers, with Dominican and Cuban brands available from the hotel's humidor; the Regent claims the largest selection of single-malt whiskies in Asia.

La Casa del Habano, in the Oriental Hotel, offers around 25 brands of Cuban cigars from US$3 to US$120 each, with a tiny lounge equipped with a select list of fine cognacs, port and single-malt whiskies. Other hotel cigar lounges include *Cigar Cafe* (Hilton International), *Siam Havana* (Dusit Thani) and *Club 54* (Montien Hotel).

Go-Go Bars

By and large these throwbacks to the 1960s and 1970s are seedy and cater to men only, whether straight or gay. These are concentrated along Thanon Sukhumvit (between Soi 21 and Soi 23), off Thanon Sukhumvit on Soi Nana Tai and in the world-famous Patpong area, between Thanon Silom and Thanon Surawong.

Patpong's neon-lit buildings cover roughly 1.6 hectares (four acres) of land that was once a banana plantation owned by the Bank of Indochina. The bank sold the land to the Hainanese-Thai Patpongphanit family just before WWII for 60,000B (US$2400).

The typical bar measures 4m by 12m deep; the Patpongphanit family collects around 10 million baht (US$250,000) rent per month from Patpong tenants. According to a *Bangkok Metro* interview with the late Patpongphanit patriarch, it wasn't American GIs who originally frequented the Patpong bar business but rather airline staff from some 15 airline offices that established themselves in the area after WWII. Bangkok's first massage parlour, Bangkok Onsen, was established in 1956 to serve Japanese expats and senior Thai police officers. By the 1960s Soi Patpong had a flourishing local nightclub scene that was further boosted by the arrival of US and Australian soldiers in the early 1970s.

Patpong has calmed down a lot over the years and become a world-famous tourist attraction in itself. These days it has developed an open-air market atmosphere as several of the newer bars are literally on the street, and vendors set up shop in the evening hawking everything from roast squid to fake designer watches.

On Patpong's two parallel lanes there are around 35 or 40 go-go bars, plus a sprinkling of restaurants, cocktail bars, discos and live music venues. The downstairs clubs, with names like *King's Castle* and *Pussy Galore*, feature go-go dancing while upstairs the real raunch is kept behind closed doors. Women and couples are welcome. Avoid bars touting 'free' sex shows as there are usually hidden charges and when you try to ditch the outrageous bill the doors are suddenly blocked by muscled bouncers. An exception is *Supergirls*, infamous for its sex-on-a-flying motorcycle show, as covered by *Rolling Stone*. The 1 am closing law is strictly enforced on Soi Patpong 1 and 2.

The gay men's equivalent can be found on nearby Soi Thaniya, Soi Pratuchai and Soi Anuman Ratchathon, where go-go bars feature in-your-face names like *Golden Cock* as well as the cryptic *Super Lex Matsuda*. Along with male go-go dancers and 'bar boys', several bars feature live sex shows, which are generally much better choreographed than the hetero equivalents on Patpong. See Gay & Lesbian Venues in this chapter for other types of venues.

A more direct legacy of the R&R days is *Soi Cowboy*, a single lane strip of 25 to 30 bars off Thanon Sukhumvit, between Soi 21 and Soi 23. By and large it's seedier than Thanon Patpong, and you will see fewer women and couples in the crowd.

Nana Entertainment Plaza, off Soi 4 (Soi Nana Tai), Thanon Sukhumvit, is a three-storey complex with around 20 bars that have surged in popularity among resident and visiting oglers over the last five or more years. NEP comes complete with its own guesthouses in the same complex, used almost exclusively by female bar workers for illicit assignations. The 'female' staff at Casanova consists entirely of Thai transvestites and transsexuals – this is a favourite stop for foreigners visiting Bangkok for sex re-assignment surgery.

Asian tourists – primarily Japanese, Taiwanese and Hong Kong males – flock to the Ratchada entertainment strip (part of Huay Khwang district) along wide Thanon Ratchadaphisek between Thanon Phra Ram IX and Thanon Lat Phrao. Lit up like Las Vegas, this stretch of neon boasts huge male-oriented massage-snooker-and-karaoke and go-go emporiums such as *Caesar's Sauna* and *Emmanuelle* – far grander in scale and more expensive than anything in Patpong.

Discos & Dance Clubs

All the major hotels have international-style discotheques but only a small number – those at the Dusit Thani, the Shangri-La, the Grand Hyatt and the Regent Bangkok – can really be recommended as attractions in themselves. Cover charges are pretty uniform: around 300B on weeknights and around 400B on weekends, including two drinks. Most places don't begin filling up until after 11 pm.

Bangkok is famous for its hi-tech discos that feature mega-watt sound systems, giant-screen video and the latest in light-show technology. The clientele for these dance palaces are mostly young moneyed Thais experimenting with lifestyles of conspicuous affluence, plus the occasional Bangkok celebrity and a sprinkling of bloodshot-eyed expats. Cover charges typically cost 400B to 500B per person and include three drinks on weeknights, two drinks on weekends. The most 'in' disco of this nature continues to be *Phuture* (Greater Bangkok map) on Thanon Ratchadaphisek, attached to the north side of the Chaophya Park Hotel. Another biggie is *Energy Zone* (☎ 433 7147, 14/4 Thanon Arun Amarin) in Thonburi.

Well-heeled Thais and Thai celebrities frequent the more exclusive, hi-tech *Narcissus* (☎ 258 2549, 112 Soi 23, Thanon Sukhumvit). Rivalling Narcissus and perhaps even more popular at the moment, is *Taurus* (☎ 261 3991, Soi 26, Thanon Sukhumvit), which offers a 'classic' pub and gourmet restaurant in addition to the lively disco, spread out over several levels.

A string of small dance clubs on Soi 2 and Soi 4 (Soi Jaruwan), both parallel to Soi Patpong 1 and 2, off Thanon Silom, attracts a more mixed crowd in terms of age, gender, nationality and sexual orientation than either the hotel discos or the mega discos. The norm for recorded music here includes techno, trance, hip-hop and other current dance trends. Main venues – some of which are small and narrow – include *Disco Disco (DD)*, *JJ Park* and *DJ Station* on Soi 2; *Icon*, *Deeper*, *Om Trance*, *Hyper*, *Kool Spot*, *Speed* and *Sphinx* on Soi 4. If you tire of hip-hop and techno, slip into *Que Pasa* for recorded Latin dance sounds. The larger places collect cover charges of around 100B to 300B depending on the night of the week; the smaller ones are free. The clientele at these clubs was once predominantly gay but became more mixed as word got around about the great dance scene. Things don't get started here until relatively late – around midnight; in fact on most nights the Soi 2/Soi 4 dance clubs serve more as 'after hours' hang-outs since they usually stay open past the official 2 am closing time. *Lucifer*, upstairs from Radio City (see Live Music) on Patpong 1, has become one of the most popular techno/rave dance clubs in town and is open midnight to 4 am.

Gay & Lesbian Venues

See the information on Soi 2 and Soi 4 under Discos & Dance Clubs for places that attract mixed gay, straight and bi clientele. In general the Soi 2 clubs are more gay than the Soi 4 bars, although Soi 4's *Telephone* and *The Balcony* are more exclusively gay then other bars on this street. *DJ Station* still boasts Soi 2's hottest gay dance scene, plus *kàthoey* (transvestite) cabaret. *Khrua Silom*, in Silom Alley off Soi 2, attracts a young Thai gay and lesbian crowd; it's a 'kitchen disco', where you stand and dance next to your table. There's a cluster of seedier gay bars around Soi Anuman Ratchathon, off Soi Tantawan, which joins Thanon Surawong opposite the Ramada Hotel – the gay equivalent of Thanon Patpong.

Utopia (☎ 259 9619, 116/1 Soi 23, Thanon Sukhumvit) is a combination bar, gallery, cafe and information clearing house for the local gay and lesbian community – the only such facility in South-East Asia. Friday is the designated women's night, and there are regular film nights as well as Thai lessons. Special events, such as Valentine's Day candle-lit dinners, are held from time to time. It's open noon to 2 am daily. Nearby on Soi 23 are a sprinkling of other gay-oriented bars.

Kitchenette (☎ 381 0861, 1st floor, Dutchess Plaza, 289 Soi 55, Thanon Sukhumvit) is a lesbian and mixed cafe with live music on weekends. Trendy, lesbian-owned *Vega* (☎ 258 8273, 662 6471) on Soi 39, Thanon Sukhumvit, is a casual pub/restaurant that also features live music and dancing, while upstairs there's karaoke. Other lesbian venues include: *By Heart Pub* (☎ 570 1841, 117/697 Soi Sena Nikhom 1, Thanon Phahonyothin, Bang Kapi); *Be My Guest* (mixed crowd) around the corner from Utopia on Soi 31; and *Thumb Up* (mixed), Soi 31, Thanon Sukhumvit.

Number 53 on Soi 53, Thanon Sukhumvit, is a bar-cafe owned by a famous TV make-up artist and favoured by both lesbians and gay males, although as at every other venue mentioned here straights are welcome.

Babylon Bangkok (☎ 213 2108, 50 Soi Atakanprasit, Thanon Sathon Tai) is a four-storey gay sauna that has been described as one of the top 10 gay men's saunas in the world. Facilities include a bar, roof garden, gym, massage room, steam and dry saunas, and spa baths. It's open 5 to 11 pm daily.

Kathoey Cabaret

Transvestite *(kàthoey)* cabarets are big in Bangkok. *Calypso Cabaret* (☎ 261 6355,

216 8937, 296 Thanon Phayathai), in the Asia Hotel, has the largest regularly performing transvestite troupe in town, with nightly shows at 8.15 and 9.45 pm. Tickets cost 700B and include one drink.

On Thanon Sukhumvit just east of Soi 22, a large cinema has been converted for performances by the *Mambo Cabaret* (☎ 259 5128), with shows at 8.30 and 10 pm nightly. Although the audience at both of these cabarets is almost 100% tourists, the shows are very good and include plenty of Thai and Asian themes as well as the usual Broadway camp.

Several of Bangkok's gay bars feature short drag shows during intermissions between dance sets.

Traditional Massage

Massage as a healing art is a centuries-old tradition in Thailand, and it is easy to find a legitimate massage in Bangkok, despite the commercialisation of recent years (see Massage Parlours following). One of the best places to experience a traditional massage, also called 'ancient' massage, is at *Wat Pho*, Bangkok's oldest temple. Massage here costs 200B per hour or 120B for half an hour. For those interested in studying massage, the temple also offers two 30-hour courses – one on general Thai massage, the other on massage therapy – which you can attend for three hours per day for 10 days, or two hours per day for 15 days. Tuition is 7000B (3600B for Thais). A nine-hour foot massage course costs 3600B.

The Wat Pho massage school has moved outside the temple compound to a new location in a nicely restored old Bangkok shophouse on Thanon Sanam Chai, opposite the temple's western wall. For those so inclined there are also longer one- to three-year programs that combine Thai herbal medicine with massage for a full curriculum in Thai traditional medicine. Contact Wat Pho Thai Traditional Medical & Massage School on ☎ 221 2974 or ⓔ watpottm@netscape.net for further information.

Next to Wat Mahathat (towards Thammasat University at the south-eastern corner of Thanon Maharat and Thanon Phra Chan) is a strip of Thai herbal medicine shops offering good massage for a mere 100B an hour.

A more commercial area for Thai massage – still legit – as well as Thai herbal saunas is Thanon Surawong near the infamous Thanon Patpong. Here you'll find *Marble House* (☎ 235 3519, 37/18–19 Soi Surawong Plaza, Thanon Surawong); *Vejakorn* (☎ 237 5576, 37/25 Soi Surawong Plaza, Thanon Surawong); and *Eve House* (☎ 266 3846, 18/1 Thanon Surawong), opposite Soi Thaniya. *Arima Onsen* (☎ 235 2142, 37/10–11 Soi Surawong Plaza) specialises in Japanese-style massage and reflexology. All of these places charge 150B per hour, 250B for 90 minutes and 300B for two hours.

On Thanon Sukhumvit you can find traditional Thai massage at *Buathip Thai Massage* (☎ 255 1045, 4/13 Soi 5, Thanon Sukhumvit) and at *Winwan* (☎ 251 7467) between Soi 1 and Soi 3, Thanon Sukhumvit.

Fees for traditional Thai massage should be no more than 300B per hour, although some places have a 1½ hour minimum. Not every place advertising traditional or ancient massage offers a really good one; sometimes the only thing 'ancient' about the pummelling is the age of the masseuse or masseur. Thai massage aficionados say that the best massages are given by blind masseurs (available at Marble House). Beware of any massage centre that has TVs in the massage rooms, as this often means the massage staff pay more attention to Thai soap operas than to giving a good massage.

Most hotels also provide a legitimate massage service either through their health clubs or as part of room service.

Massage Parlours

It's well known that virtually all of the city's dozens of *àap òp nûat* or 'bathe-steam-massage' (sometimes referred to as 'Turkish bath') parlours also deal in prostitution; less well known is the fact that many (but by no means all) of the women working in the parlours are bonded labour – they are not necessarily there by choice.

All but the most insensitive of males will be saddened by the sight of 50 girls/women behind a glass wall with numbers pinned to their dresses. Often the bank of masseuses is divided into sections according to skill and/or appearance. Most expensive is the 'superstar' section, in which the women try to approximate the look of fashion models or actresses. A smaller section is reserved for women who are actually good at giving massages, and who offer nothing extra. Virtually all massage parlours of this sort insist on condom use if services extend beyond the massage.

Live Music

Bangkok's live music scene has expanded rapidly over the past decade or so, with a multiplicity of new, extremely competent bands and clubs. The three-storey *Saxophone Pub & Restaurant* (Central Bangkok map; ☎ 246 5472, 3/8 Victory Monument, Thanon Phayathai), south-east of the Victory Monument circle, is a Bangkok institution for musicians of several genres. The live music selection changes nightly and features reggae, R&B, jazz or blues from around 9.30 pm to 1.30 am. On Sunday there's an open jam session. The ground floor bar-restaurant serves surprisingly good food. There is no cover charge and you don't need to dress up.

Another very casual spot to hear music is the open-air bar operated by *Ruang Pung Art Community* (Greater Bangkok map; ☎ 513 7225) next to Chatuchak Weekend Market. Thai rock, folk, blues and jam sessions attract an artsy Thai crowd. It's open only 11 am to 10 pm on weekends.

Not to be overlooked is the strip of music bars along Thanon Sarasin (Central Bangkok map), including *Brown Sugar* (mostly jazz) and *Old West* (folk and Thai pop). *Blue's Bar, Johnny Walker* and *Shakin'* usually feature recorded music, with occasional live bands on weekends.

Concept CM2, a multi-themed complex in the basement of the Novotel in Siam Square, hosts a rotation of live Western bands and Thai recording artists – generally focusing on what passes for alternative these days – interspersed with DJ dance music.

The talented house band at *Radio City* (☎ 266 4567), next to the Madrid Restaurant on Soi Patpong 2, performs oldies from the '60s, '70s and '80s. The Thai Elvis and Tom Jones impersonators who perform here occasionally can really get the crowd going.

Dance Fever (☎ 247 4295), a large club at 71 Thanon Ratchadaphisek in the burgeoning 'Ratchada' entertainment district, features a state-of-the-art sound and lighting system, giant video screens, a bar and restaurant. International touring bands like Bush, Blur and others have played there.

The *Metal Zone (Central Bangkok map; ☎ 255 1913)*, around the corner from Thanon Sarasin on Soi Lang Suan, just north of Lumphini Park, offers Thai heavy metal – with plenty of hair throwing and lip-jutting – nightly. Along with the dragons-and-dungeons decor is a regular line-up of bands authentically producing everything from thrash to Gothic to speed metal, Ozzy squeal to Axel rasp, even a few convoluted Helmet tunes. The volume level is perfect – loud enough for chest compression, but not so loud as to extract blood from the ears. *Rock Pub (☎ 208 9664)* on Thanon Phayathai opposite the Asia Hotel is similar to the Metal Zone.

Bangkok's better-than-average *Hard Rock Cafe*, in Siam Square, Soi 11, features live rock music most evenings from around 10 pm to 12.30 am, including some big names (Chris Isaak's incendiary performance in 1994 left boot-nail dents in the bar top).

The spacious *Witch's Tavern (☎ 391 9791, 306/1 Soi 55, Thanon Sukhumvit)* features live pop music nightly.

Imageries By The Glass (2 Soi 24, Thanon Sukhumvit), owned by Thai composer-musician Jirapan Ansvananada, boasts a huge sound board and closed circuit TV for its stage shows, which welcome local as well as foreign bands of all genres.

An eclectic line-up of bands, including touring ones, also play nightly at *The Brewhouse* (see Brewery Pubs earlier in this section).

Many top-end hotels have bars with imported pop bands, of varying talent, who play mostly covers. *Angelini's* in the Shangri-La Hotel usually has one of the better cover bands, as does *Spasso* in the Grand Hyatt Erawan.

Jazz The Oriental's famous *Bamboo Bar* has live jazz nightly in an elegant atmosphere. The Sukhothai Hotel's *Colonnade* offers jazz from Tuesday to Saturday.

Fabb Fashion Cafe (Siam Square & Pratunam map; ☎ 658 2003), 540 Thanon Ploenchit, near the Chit Lom Skytrain station, features jazz piano and saxophone 8 pm to midnight Monday to Saturday.

Latin Clubs featuring all or mostly Latin dance music have exploded in Bangkok over the last couple of years. A Filipino band mixes up the salsa at *Baila Baila (☎ 714 1898)*, off Soi 63 (sub-soi 4), Thanon Sukhumvit, where there are Latin dance lessons nightly.

At the flashier *El Niño (☎ 656 0160)*, in the President Tower Arcade on Thanon Ploenchit, a Colombian band plays nightly Monday to Saturday. Dance lessons are available too. The most serious venue for learning to salsa or cumbia is *The Salsa Club (Siam Square & Pratunam map; ☎ 216 3700)* in the Patumwan Princess Hotel, attached to MBK Centre, Thanon Phra Ram I. *La Havana (Thanon Sukhumvit map; ☎ 204 1166)*, in a small plaza area off Soi 22, Thanon Sukhumvit, features a small Cuban combo nightly that starts playing late, so this is the place to go if the others start to fade early.

Cinema

Dozens of movie theatres around town show Thai, Chinese, Indian and Western movies. The majority of films shown are comedies and shoot-em-ups, with the occasional drama slipping through. These theatres are air-con and quite comfortable, with reasonable rates (70B to 120B). All movies in Thai theatres are preceded by the Thai royal anthem. Everyone in the theatre is expected to stand respectfully for the duration of the anthem.

Movie ads appear daily in both the *Nation* and the *Bangkok Post;* listings in the *Nation* include addresses and program times. *Bangkok Metro* magazine will carries details of film festivals or other special events when they are scheduled.

Foreign films are often altered before distribution by Thailand's board of censors; usually this involves obscuring nude sequences, although gun fights are sometimes also edited from the film.

Film buffs may prefer the weekly or twice weekly offerings at Bangkok's foreign cultural clubs. French and German films screened at the cultural clubs are almost always subtitled in English. Admission is sometimes free, sometimes 30B to 40B. For addresses and phone numbers see the Cultural Centres section earlier in this chapter.

The main theatres showing commercial English-language films in central Bangkok are:

Grand EGV (☎ 658 0458) Siam Discovery Centre
Hollywood Theatre (☎ 208 9194) Hollywood Street Centre, Thanon Phetburi
Indra (☎ 251 6230) Thanon Ratchaprarop
Lido Multiplex (☎ 252 6729) Siam Square, Thanon Phra Ram I
MacKenna (☎ 251 5256) 17/2 Thanon Phayathai
Major Cineplex (☎ 714 2828) Soi 63, Thanon Sukhumvit
Micromack (☎ 252 6215) Ground floor, MacKenna Theatre, Thanon Phayathai
Pantip (☎ 251 2390) Pantip Plaza, Thanon Phetburi Tat Mai
Scala (☎ 251 2161) Siam Square, Soi 1, Thanon Phra Ram I
Seacon 14 (☎ 721 9418) 4th floor, Seacon Square, Thanon Si Nakharin
SF Cinema City (☎ 11 6444) Mahboonkrong shopping centre, Thanon Phra Ram I
Siam (☎ 252 9975) Siam Square, Thanon Phra Ram I
United Artists (☎ 664 8771) 6th floor, The Emporium, Thanon Sukhumvit
United Artists (☎ 673 6060–88) 7th and 8th floors, Central Plaza, Thanon Ratchada-Phra Ram III
Warner (☎ 234 3700–9) 119 Thanon Mahesak
World Trade 1, 2, 3 (☎ 256 9500) 6th floor, World Trade Centre, corner of Thanon Ploenchit and Thanon Ratchadamri
World Trade 4, 5 (☎ 255 9500) basement floor, World Trade Centre, corner of Thanon Ploenchit and Thanon Ratchadamri

Of these cinemas, the most state-of-the-art sound and projection facilities are at Grand EGV and United Artists (both the Central Plaza and Emporium locations).

Video

Video rentals are popular in Bangkok; not only are videos cheaper than regular film admissions, but many films are available on video that aren't approved for theatre distribution by Thailand's board of censors. For those with access to a TV and VCR, the average rental is around 20B to 50B. Thanon Sukhumvit has the highest concentration of video shops; the better ones are found in the residential area between Soi 39 and Soi 55. *Blockbuster* has branches in the city's wealthier areas, especially off Sukhumvit, Ploenchit and Lat Phrao.

Vidéofrance (21/17 Soi 4, Thanon Sukhumvit), near the Hotel Rajah on Soi Nana Tai, has a good selection of French-language videos. Members of the Alliance Française may borrow videos from the AF French video library.

TVs and VCRs (both PAL and NTSC) can be rented at *Silver Bell (☎ 236 2845/2851, 113/1–2 Surawong Centre, Thanon Surawong).*

Theatre & Dance Performance Venues

For more information, see also the Music, Theatre & Dance special section in the Facts about Thailand chapter.

Thai Dance-Drama Thailand's most traditional *lákhon* and *khôn* performances are held at the *National Theatre (☎ 224 1342)* on Thanon Chao Fa near Saphan Phra Pin Klao. The theatre's regular public roster schedules six or seven performances per month, usually on weekends. Admission fees are very reasonable at around 20B to 200B. Seeing a khôn performance (masked dance-drama based on stories from the *Ramakian*) is highly recommended.

Occasionally, classical dance performances are also held at the *Thailand Cultural Centre (☎ 245 7742)* on Thanon Ratchadaphisek and at the *College of Dramatic Arts (☎ 224 1391),* near the National Theatre.

Chalermkrung Royal Theatre The 1993 renovation of the Chalermkrung Royal Theatre (Sala Chaloem Krung), a Thai Deco building at the edge of the city's Chinatown-Phahurat district, provided a striking new venue for khôn performance in Thailand. When originally opened in 1933, the royally funded Chalermkrung was the largest and most modern theatre in Asia, with state-of-the-art motion picture projection technology and the first chilled-water air-con system in the region. Prince Samaichaloem, a former student of the École des Beaux-Arts in Paris, designed the hexagonal building.

The reborn theatre's 80,000-watt audio system, combined with computer-generated laser graphics, enable the 170-member dance troupe to present a technologically enhanced version of traditional khôn. Although the special effects are reasonably impressive, the excellent costuming, set design, dancing and music are reason enough to attend.

When held, the khôn performances last about two hours with intermission. Other

Thai performing arts as well as film festivals may also be scheduled at the theatre. Check Bangkok newspapers for current performance schedules. For ticket reservations, call ☎ 222 0434 or visit the box office in person. The theatre requests that patrons dress respectfully, which means no shorts, tank tops or sandals. Bring a wrap or long-sleeved shirt in case the air-con is running full blast.

The Chalermkrung Royal Theatre is on the corner of Thanon Charoen Krung and Thanon Triphet, adjacent to the Old Siam Plaza complex. Air-con bus Nos 8, 48 and 73 pass the theatre (going west on Thanon Charoen Krung). You can also comfortably walk to the theatre from the western terminus of the Saen Saep canal ferry. Taxi drivers may know the theatre by its original name, Sala Chaloem Krung, which is spelt out in Thai in the lighted sign surmounting the front of the building.

Dinner Theatres Many tourists view performances put on solely for their benefit at one of the Thai classical dance and dinner theatres in the city. The admission prices at these evening venues average 200B to 500B per person and include a 'typical' Thai dinner (often toned down for fàràng palates), a couple of selected dance performances and a martial arts display.

The historic Oriental Hotel has its own dinner theatre, the *Sala Rim Nam (☎ 437 2918, 437 3080)*, on the Thonburi side of the Mae Nam Chao Phraya opposite the hotel. The admission price is well above average but so is the food, the performance and the Thai pavilion decor (teak, marble and bronze); the river ferry between the hotel and restaurant is free. Dinner begins at 7 pm, the dance performance at 8.30 pm.

If you want to focus on the food as much as the dance, and it's a weekend, your best choice is the upmarket *Supatra River House (☎ 411 0305, 266 Soi Wat Rakhang)*, next to Patravadi Theatre in Thonburi. It's opposite Tha Mahathat, from where the restaurant operates its own free ferry nightly. You won't find more authentic Thai food coupled with Thai dance in Bangkok, but note that dance performances – which meander through the restaurant's gardens rather than on a fixed stage – only take place from 8 to 9 pm on Friday and Saturday.

Other dinner theatres include:

Baan Thai Restaurant (☎ 258 5403) 7 Soi 32, Thanon Sukhumvit
Maneeya Lotus Room (☎ 251 0382) 518/5 Thanon Ploenchit
Piman Thai Theatre Restaurant (☎ 258 7866) 46 Soi 49, Thanon Sukhumvit
Suwannahong Restaurant (☎ 245 4448, 245 3747) Thanon Si Ayuthaya

Shrine Dancing

Free performances of traditional *lákhon kâe bon* can be seen daily at the *Lak Meuang* and *Erawan* shrines if you happen to arrive when a performance troupe has been commissioned by a worshipper. Although many of the dance movements are the same as those seen in classical lákhon, these relatively crude performances are specially choreographed for ritual purposes and don't represent true classical dance forms. But the dancing is colourful – the dancers wear full costume and are accompanied by live music – so it's worth stopping to watch.

Muay Thai (Thai Boxing)

Muay thai can be seen at two boxing stadiums, *Sanam Muay Lumphini* (on Thanon Phra Ram IV near Thanon Sathon Tai, near Lumphini Park) and *Sanam Muay Ratchadamnoen* (on Thanon Ratchadamnoen Nok, next to the old TAT office). Admission fees vary according to seating: the cheapest seats in Bangkok are now around 220B for the outer circle or 920B to 1000B ringside (Sunday shows at Ratchadamnoen are 50B to 500B). This is for eight fights of five rounds each. The outer circle seats are quite OK. On Monday, Wednesday, Thursday and Sunday the boxing is at Ratchadamnoen, while on Tuesday, Friday and Saturday it's at Lumphini. The Ratchadamnoen matches begin at 6 pm, except for the Sunday shows, which start at 4 and 8 pm. The Lumphini matches begin at 6.30 pm on Tuesday and Friday, and at 5 and 8.30 pm on Saturday. Aficionados say the best-matched bouts are reserved for Tuesday night at Lumphini and Thursday night at Ratchadamnoen. The restaurants on the northern side of Ratchadamnoen stadium are well known for their delicious *kài yâang* (grilled chicken) and other north-eastern dishes.

Warning At some programs a ticket mafia try to steer every tourist into buying a 500B ringside seat, often claiming all other seats are sold out. It's a pretence; if you walk around the touts you'll find a window selling seats as cheaply as 220B (50B for the Sunday 4pm show at Ratchadamnoen). Ignore the touts and look for windows marked at that price. Don't believe anyone who says seats are sold out, unless you hear it directly from a window ticket vendor.

SHOPPING
Regular visitors to Asia know that, in many ways, Bangkok beats Hong Kong and Singapore for deals on handicrafts, textiles, gems, jewellery, art and antiques – nowhere else will you find the same selection, quality and prices. The difficulty is finding the good spots, as the city's intense urban tangle makes orientation sometimes difficult. *Nancy Chandler's Map of Bangkok* makes a very good buying companion, with annotations on all sorts of small, out-of-the-way shopping venues and markets *(tàlàat)*.

Be sure to read the introductory Shopping section in the Facts for the Visitor chapter before setting out on a buying spree. Amid all the bargains are a number of cleverly disguised rip-off schemes – *caveat emptor*!

Markets
Quite a few different types of markets, in varying sizes, exist in Bangkok.

Weekend Market Also known as Chatuchak Market (Talat Nat Jatujak; Greater Bangkok map), this is the Disneyland of Thai markets; on weekends 8672 stalls cater to an estimated 200,000 visitors a day. Everything is sold here, from live chickens and snakes to opium pipes and herbal remedies. Thai clothing such as the *phâakhamáa* (sarong for men) and the *phâasîn* (sarong for women), *kaang keng jiin* (Chinese pants) and *sêua mâw hâwm* (blue cotton farmer's shirt) are good buys. You'll also find musical instruments, hilltribe crafts, religious amulets, antiques, flowers, clothes imported from India and Nepal, camping gear and military surplus. The best bargains are household goods like pots and pans, dishes, drinking glasses etc.

CHATUCHAK WEEKEND MARKET

1	Buddha Images; Books; Plants	18	Clothing
2	Paintings; Plants	19	Fresh & Dried Food; Ceramic Wares
3	Plants	20	Clothing
4	Plants	21	Clothing
5	Plants; Clothing	22	Miscellaneous
6	Agricultural Products; Clothing	23	Clothing
7	Decorative Rocks; Bonsai	24	Miscellaneous
8	Miscellaneous	25	Miscellaneous
9	Pets; Handicrafts	26	Antiques
10	Miscellaneous		
11	Pets		
12	Clothing		
13	Pets		
14	Clothing		
15	Fresh & Dried Food		
16	Fresh & Dried Food		
17	Fresh & Dried Food		

Note: Key numbers (1-26) also indicate building numbers

If you're moving to Thailand for an extended period, pick up stuff for your kitchen. Don't forget to try out your bargaining skills. There is plenty of interesting and tasty food for sale if you're feeling hungry, and live music in the early evening. And if you need some cash, a couple of banks have ATMs and foreign-exchange booths at the Chatuchak Park offices, near the northern end of the market's Soi 1, Soi 2 and Soi 3. Plan to spend a full day, as there's plenty to see and do.

The main part of the Weekend Market is open from around 8 am to 6 pm on weekends, although some places may stay open as late as 8 pm. There are a few vendors out on weekday mornings and a daily vegetable, plant and flower market opposite the market's southern side. One section of the latter, known as the Aw Taw Kaw Market, sells organically grown (no chemical sprays or fertilisers) fruits and vegetables.

The Weekend Market lies at the southern end of Chatuchak Park, off Thanon Phahonyothin and across from the Northern bus terminal. Air-con bus Nos 2, 3, 9, 10 and 13, and a dozen other ordinary city buses, pass the market – just get off before the Northern bus terminal. Air-con bus No 12 and ordinary bus No 77 conveniently terminate right next to the market. The Skytrain runs direct to Mo Chit station, which stands almost in front of the market.

Nailert Market The Nailert Market (Nai Loet Market; Siam Square & Pratunam map) is a relatively new market complex opposite the Amari Watergate Hotel, on Thanon Phetburi in Pratunam. It was recently opened as a central alternative to Chatuchak Market. The array of goods is similar; it remains to be seen whether the market will succeed, although it's definitely a more convenient location for most visitors.

Flower Markets & Nurseries A good selection of tropical flowers and plants is available at the Thewet Market near Tha Thewet (Thonburi Canals map) on Thanon Krung Kasem, to the north-west of Banglamphu. The city's largest wholesale flower source is the Pak Khlong Market on the right bank of the Mae Nam Chao Phraya at the mouth of Khlong Lawt, between Thanon Atsadang and Saphan Phra Phuttha Yot Fa. Pak Khlong is also a big market for vegetables. The newest and largest plant market is opposite the southern side of Chatuchak Market, near the Northern bus terminal off Thanon Phahonyothin; it's open daily and known as Talat Phahonyothin (Phahonyothin Market).

The best area for nursery plants, including Thailand's famous orchid varieties, is Thonburi's Phasi Charoen district, which is accessible via the Phetkasem Highway north of Khlong Phasi Charoen itself. The latter is linked to the Mae Nam Chao Phraya via Khlong Bangkok Yai. Two places with good selections are Eima Orchid (☎ 454 0366, fax 454 1156), 999/9 Mu 2, Bang Khae, Phasi Charoen, and Botanical Gardens Bangkok (☎ 467 4955), 6871 Kuhasawan, Phasi Charoen. Ordinary bus Nos 7 and 80, plus air-con bus No 9, stop in the Phasi Charoen district.

Other Thai Markets Under the expressway at the intersection of Thanon Phra Ram IV and Thanon Narong in the Khlong Toey district is the Khlong Toey Market, possibly the cheapest all-purpose market in Bangkok (it's best on Wednesday). South of the Khlong Toey Market, closer to the port, is the similar Penang Market, so called because a lot of the goods 'drop off' cargo boats from Penang (and Singapore, Hong Kong etc). Both markets are in danger of being demolished under current urban renewal plans.

Pratunam Market, at the intersection of Thanon Phetburi and Thanon Ratchaprarop, is held daily and is very crowded, but has great deals in new, cheap clothing. You won't see it from the street; you must look for one of the unmarked entrances that lead back behind the main shopfronts. While browsing Pratunam you can easily visit Nailert Market too (see its entry in this section).

The huge Banglamphu Market spreads several blocks over Thanon Chakraphong, Thanon Phra Sumen, Thanon Tanao and Thanon Rambutri, a short walk from the guesthouse area of Thanon Khao San. The Banglamphu Market area is probably the most comprehensive shopping district in the city as it encompasses everything from street vendors to upmarket department stores. Also in the Banglamphu area of Bangkok you'll find the Thewet flower market.

Soi Lalaisap, the 'money-melting street', actually Soi 5, Thanon Silom, has a number of vendors selling all sorts of cheap clothing, watches and household ware during the day.

The Phahurat and Chinatown districts have interconnected markets selling tonnes of well-priced fabrics, clothes and household ware, as well as a few places selling gems and jewellery. The Wong Wian Yai Market in Thonburi, next to the large roundabout directly south-west of Saphan Phra Phuttha Yot Fa, is another all-purpose market – but rarely attracts tourists.

Tourist Markets Thanon Khao San, the main guesthouse strip in Banglamphu, has itself become a shopping bazaar offering cheap audio tapes, used books, jewellery, beads, clothing, Thai 'axe pillows', T-shirts, tattoos, body piercing and just about any other product or service.

At night Patpong Soi 1 and Soi 2 fill up with vendors selling cheap tourist junk, inexpensive clothing, fake watches – you name it. Along both sides of Thanon Sukhumvit between Soi 1 and Soi 5 there are also lots of street vendors selling similar items.

Shopping Centres & Department Stores

The growth of large and small shopping centres has accelerated over the past few years into a virtual boom. Central Department Store is generally regarded as the all-round best of the bunch, for quality and selection, with 12 branches in Bangkok. The flagship store on Thanon Ploenchit near the Chit Lom Skytrain station is probably the best of the bunch; in addition to designer clothes, Western cosmetics, cassette tapes, fabrics, furniture, handicrafts and attached supermarket, the store offers free alteration on all clothing purchases and free delivery to Bangkok hotels. There's also a fix-it area for watch, shoe and clothing repair.

Oriental Plaza (Soi Oriental, Thanon Charoen Krung) and River City shopping complex (near the Royal Orchid Sheraton, off Thanon Charoen Krung and Thanon Si Phraya) are centres for high-end consumer goods. They're expensive but do have some unique merchandise; River City has good-quality art and antique shops on the 3rd and 4th floors.

Along Thanon Ploenchit and Thanon Sukhumvit you'll find many newer department stores and shopping centres, including Sogo, Landmark Plaza and Times Square, but these Tokyo clones tend to be expensive and not that exciting. Peninsula Plaza on Thanon Ratchadamri has a more exclusive selection of shops – many of which have branches at River City and Oriental Plaza – and a good-sized branch of Asia Books. Promenade Decor, in front of the Hilton International Bangkok on Thanon Withayu, is a very posh mall containing jewellery shops, cafes, antiques, furniture showrooms, art galleries and modern Thai art of high quality.

The much smaller Silom Village Trade Centre on Thanon Silom has a few cheaper antique and handicraft shops. Anchored by Central department store, the six-storey Silom Complex nearby remains one of the city's busiest shopping centres. Also on Thanon Silom is the posh Thaniya Plaza, a newer arcade housing clothing boutiques, bookshops, jewellery shops and more.

The eight floors of the World Trade Centre (WTC) near the intersection of Thanon Ploenchit and Thanon Ratchadamri seem to go on and on. The main focus is the Zen department store, which has clothing shops reminiscent of Hong Kong's high-end boutiques. On the 8th floor is Bangkok's premier antidote to the tropics, the World Ice Skating Center. If you're looking for clothing or toys for kids, ABC Babyland on WTC's 2nd floor has just about everything.

Siam Square, on Thanon Phra Ram I near Thanon Phayathai, is a network of some 12 sois lined with shops selling mid-price designer clothes, books, sporting goods and antiques. On the opposite side of Thanon Phra Ram I is Thailand's first shopping centre, built in 1976, the four-storey Siam Center. It features designer and brand-label clothing shops – Benetton, Quicksilver, Chaps, Esprit, Lacoste, Timberland and Guy Laroche to name a few – as well as coffee shops, travel agencies, banks and airline offices. Next to the Siam Center, and connected by an enclosed pedestrian bridge, Siam Discovery Center contains yet more designer stores, such as Calvin Klein, Nine West, Yves Saint Laurent, Armani, plus Asia Books, Habitat and several large restaurants.

One of the most varied and affordable shopping centres is the Mahboonkrong (MBK) shopping centre near Siam Square. It's mostly air-conditioned, but there are many small, inexpensive stalls and shops in addition to the middle-class Tokyu department store. Bargains can be found here if you look. The Travel Mart on MBK's 3rd floor stocks a reasonable supply of travel gear and camping equipment – not the highest quality but useful in a pinch.

North of Siam Square on Thanon Phetburi, Pantip Plaza specialises in computer equipment and software.

Old Siam Plaza, bounded by Thanon Charoen Krung, Thanon Burapha, Thanon Phahurat and Thanon Triphet, is the first new development of any significance in the Chinatown-Phahurat area in over a decade. Along with the renovation and reopening of the adjacent Chalermkrung Royal Theatre, this old Bangkok-style shopping centre represents a minor renaissance for an otherwise shabby and congested district. Most of the shops purvey Thai-style goods or services; one whole side is devoted to gun dealers, another to gem and jewellery shops, the rest to Thai handicrafts, furniture, restaurants and coffee shops.

Antiques & Decorative Items

Real Thai antiques are rare and costly. Most Bangkok antique shops keep a few authentic pieces for collectors, along with lots of pseudo-antiques or traditionally crafted items that look like antiques. The majority of shop operators are quite candid about what's really old and what isn't. Many shops specialise in Thai home decorative items.

Reliable antique shops (using the word 'antique' loosely) include: Elephant House, with branches at Soi Phattana, Thanon Silom (☎ 630 1586) and at 67/12 Soi Phra Phinit (☎ 679 3122), off Soi Suan Phlu; Asian Heritage (☎ 258 4157), 57 Soi 23, Thanon Sukhumvit; and Artisan's (☎ 237 4456) in the Silom Village Trade Centre, Thanon Silom.

River City complex, on the river and attached by a tunnel to the Royal Orchid Sheraton off Thanon Yotha, Si Phaya, contains a number of high-quality art and antique shops on the 3rd and 4th floors. Acala, shop No 312, is a gallery of unusual Tibetan and Chinese artefacts. Old Maps & Prints (☎ 237 0077 ext 432), shop 432, proffers one of the best selections of one-of-a-kind, rare maps and illustrations, with a focus on Asia. The Oriental Plaza shopping complex also has several good, if pricey, antique shops.

Barang-Barang Antik (Thanon Sukhumvit map; ☎ 255 2461), 1047 Thanon Ploenchit, carries a well-curated selection of Indonesian antique and reproduction furniture.

Gaysorn Plaza (Siam Square & Pratunam map), next to Le Meridien President Hotel on Thanon Ploenchit, contains several shops specialising in furniture and home decor accessories, both antique and contemporary Thai. The Thai Craft Museum Shop (☎ 656 1149) on the 2nd and 3rd floors offers craft demonstrations, plus displays of Thai ceramics, textiles, jewellery and more. Triphum (☎ 656 1149), on the 2nd floor, features tasteful South-East Asian art and accessories.

Bronzeware

Thailand has the oldest bronze-working tradition in the world and there are several factories in Bangkok producing bronze sculpture and cutlery. Two factories that sell direct to the public (and where you may also be able to observe the bronze-working process) are Siam Bronze Factory (☎ 234 9436), at 1250 Thanon Charoen Krung between Soi 36 and Soi 38, and Somkij Bronze (☎ 251 0891), at 1194 Thanon Phetburi Tat Mai (New Phetburi). Make sure any items you buy are silicon-coated, otherwise they'll tarnish. To see the casting process for Buddha images, go to the Buddha Casting Foundry next to Wat Wiset Khan on Thanon Phrannok, Thonburi (take a river ferry from Tha Phra Chan or Tha Maharat on the Bangkok side to reach the foot of Thanon Phrannok).

Many vendors at Wat Mahathat's Sunday market sell old and new bronzeware – it is imperative to haggle.

Camera Supplies, Film & Processing

For a wide range of camera models and brands, try one of Sunny Camera's three branches: 1267/1 Thanon Charoen Krung (☎ 235 2123, 233 8378); 144/23 Thanon Silom (☎ 236 8627); and the 3rd floor of the Mahboonkrong shopping centre (☎ 217 9293). Niks (☎ 235 2929), at 166 Thanon Silom on the north-western corner of Soi 12, sells all types of professional equipment, and services Nikon, Mamiya and Rollei. Central Department Store on Thanon Ploenchit has a good camera department with surprisingly reasonable prices.

Film prices in Bangkok are generally lower than anywhere else in Asia, including Hong Kong. Both slide and print films are widely available, although the highest concentration of photo shops can be found along Thanon Silom and Thanon Surawong. In Mahboonkrong shopping centre, FotoFile on the ground floor has the best selection of slide films, including refrigerated pro films.

Quick, professional-quality processing of most film types is available at: Image Quality Lab (IQ Lab; ☎ 238 4001) at 60 Thanon Silom opposite Silom Complex, or (☎ 714 0644) at 9/33 Thana Arcade, Soi 63, Thanon Sukhumvit; and Eastbourne Professional Color Laboratories (☎ 235 5234), 134/4 Thanon Silom.

Gems & Jewellery

Recommending specific shops is tricky, since one coloured stone looks as good as another to the average eye, so the risk of a rip-off is much greater than for most other popular shopping items.

One shop that's been a long-time favourite with Bangkok expats for service and value in

Royal barge procession on Mae Nam Chao Phraya

TOM COCKREM

Roof of a temple *wíhǎan* near the river, Bangkok

DENNIS JOHNSON

Dusit Hall in the Grand Palace complex

RICHARD NEBESKY

CHRIS MELLOR

Palace guard

MARY LOU JANSON

The Shangri-La pool and the Chao Phraya River

TOM COCKREM

Brilliantly lit Wat Pho at night, Bangkok

PAUL BEINSSEN

Food stalls are everywhere in Bangkok – this one's in Chinatown.

JOHN HAY

Drinking roasted-coconut milk

set jewellery is Johnny's Gems (☎ 224 4065) at 199 Thanon Fuang Nakhon (off Thanon Charoen Krung). Another dependable place specialising in unset stones is Lambert Holding (☎ 236 4343) at 807 Thanon Silom.

Handicrafts

Bangkok has excellent buys in Thai handicrafts, although for northern hill-tribe materials you might be able to do better in Chiang Mai. Narayana Phand (Siam Square & Pratunam map; ☎ 252 4670) on Thanon Ratchadamri is a bit on the touristy side but has a large selection and good marked prices – no haggling is necessary. The Central Department Store on Thanon Ploenchit has a large Thai handicrafts section with marked prices.

International School Bangkok (ISB; Greater Bangkok map; ☎ 583 5401) puts on a large charity sale of Thai handicrafts every sixth Saturday or so (except during ISB's summer holiday, June to August). Sometimes you can find pieces here that are practically unavailable elsewhere. At other times it's not very interesting; it all depends on what they're able to collect during the year. Call for the latest sale schedule. ISB is north of the city proper, towards the airport, off Route 304 (Thanon Chaeng Wattana) on the way to Pak Kret, inside the Nichada Thani townhouse complex; the address is 39/7 Soi Nichadathani Samakhi.

Perhaps the most interesting places to shop for handicrafts are the smaller, independent handicraft shops, each with its own style and character. Quality is high at Rasi Sayam (☎ 258 4195), 32 Soi 23, Thanon Sukhumvit. Many of the numerous items sold at Rasi Sayam, including wall-hangings and pottery, are made specifically for this shop.

Another good shop for pottery as well as lacquerware and fabrics (especially the latter) is Vilai's (☎ 391 6106) at 731/1 Soi 55 (Thong Lor), Thanon Sukhumvit.

Nandakwang (☎ 258 1962), 108/3 Soi 23 (Soi Prasanmit), Thanon Sukhumvit, is a branch of a factory shop of the same name in Pasang, Northern Thailand. Nandakwang specialises in high-quality woven cotton clothing and household wares (tablecloths, napkins etc).

Lao Song Handicrafts (☎ 261 6627), 2/56 Soi 41, Thanon Sukhumvit, is a nonprofit place that sells village handicrafts to promote cottage industries.

Khŏn masks of intricately formed wire and papier-mache can be purchased at Padung Cheep on Thanon Chakraphong just south of the Thanon Khao San intersection.

For quality Thai celadon, check Thai Celadon (☎ 229 4383) at 8/6–8 Thanon Ratchadaphisek Tat Mai. Inexpensive places to pick up new Thai pottery of all shapes and sizes at wholesale prices include two places on Soi On Nut, off Soi 77, Thanon Sukhumvit: United Siam Overseas (☎ 721 6320) and Siamese Merchandise (☎ 333 0680). Overseas shipping can be arranged.

Scuba Supplies

Larry's Dive Center, Bar & Grill (see Places to Eat earlier) stocks all manner of diving and snorkelling gear. There's a restaurant and bar attached, so you can eat while you fill your air tanks.

Tailor-Made Clothes

Bangkok abounds in places where you can have shirts, trousers, suits and just about any other article of clothing designed, cut and sewn by hand. Workmanship ranges from shoddy to excellent, so it pays to ask around before committing yourself. Shirts and trousers can be turned around in 48 hours or less with only one fitting. But no matter what a tailor may tell you, it takes more than one or two fittings to create a good suit, and most reputable tailors will ask for two to five sittings. A custom-made suit, no matter what the material is, should cost less than US$250. An all-cashmere suit can be had for as little as US$175 with a little bargaining; bring your own fabric and it will cost even less.

Bangkok tailors can be particularly good at copying your favourite piece of clothing. Designer-made shirts costing upwards of US$100 at home can be knocked off for not much more than a tenth of the designer price. The one area where you need to be most careful is in fabric selection. If possible, bring fabric from home, especially if it's 100% cotton you want. Most of the so-called 'cotton' offered by Bangkok tailors is actually a blend of cotton and a synthetic; more than a few tailors will actually try to pass off full polyester or dacron as cotton. Good-quality silk, on the other hand, is plentiful. Tailor-made silk shirts should cost no more than US$20, depending on the type of silk (Chinese silk is cheaper than Thai).

Virtually every tailor working in Bangkok is of Indian or Chinese descent. Generally speaking the best shops are those found along the outer reaches of Thanon Sukhumvit (out beyond Soi 20 or so) and on or off Thanon Charoen Krung. Thanon Silom also has some good tailors. The worst tailor shops tend to be those in tourist-oriented shopping areas in inner Thanon Sukhumvit, Thanon Khao San, the River City shopping complex and other shopping malls. 'Great deals', like four shirts, two suits, a kimono and a safari suit all in one package, almost always turn out to be of inferior materials and workmanship.

Recommended tailor shops include: Julie at 1279 Thanon Charoen, near Silom Center; Marco Tailor (☎ 252 0689) on Soi 7, Siam Square; and Macway's Exporters (☎ 235 2407) at 715–717 Thanon Silom, opposite the Narai Hotel. In Siam Center on the 3rd floor, Siam Emporium (☎ 251 9617) is also recommended; there's a second branch in the Mandarin Hotel on Thanon Phra Ram IV.

Avoid any tailor shop suggested by a stranger you meet on the street, as these usually pay high commissions to the 'stranger', thus driving the cost of the tailoring far beyond its normal value. Tailoring scams have become almost as notorious as gem scams in Bangkok.

GETTING THERE & AWAY
Air
Bangkok is a major centre for international flights throughout Asia. It is also a major centre for buying discounted airline tickets (see the Getting There & Away chapter), but be warned that the Bangkok travel agency business has a few crooked operators. Domestic flights operated by THAI and Bangkok Airways also fan out from Bangkok (see the Getting Around chapter). Airline offices in Bangkok are:

Aeroflot (☎ 251 1223) Regent House, Thanon Ratchadamri

Air France (☎ 635 1186; reservations ☎ 635 1199) 20th floor, Vorawat Bldg, 849 Thanon Silom

Air India (☎ 235 0557/8) 12th floor, One Pacific Place, 140 Thanon Sukhumvit

Air New Zealand (☎ 254 8440) 14th floor, Sindhorn Bldg, 130–132 Thanon Withayu

Alitalia (☎ 634 1800–9) 3rd floor, SP Tower 3, Unit 15A, 88 Thanon Silom

All Nippon Airways (ANA; ☎ 238 5121) 2nd and 4th floors, CP Tower, 313 Thanon Silom

American Airlines (☎ 254 1270) 518/5 Thanon Ploenchit

Asiana Airlines (☎ 656 8610–7) 18th floor, Ploenchit Center Bldg, Soi 2 Sukhumvit

Bangkok Airways (☎ 229 3434, 253 4014) 60 Queen Sirikit National Convention Centre, Thanon Ratchadaphisek Tat Mai, Khlong Toey

Biman Bangladesh Airlines (☎ 235 7643/4) Chongkolnee Bldg, 56 Thanon Surawong

British Airways (☎ 636 1700) 990 Thanon Phra Ram IV

Canadian Airlines International (☎ 251 4521, 254 8376) Maneeya Center Bldg, 518/5 Thanon Ploenchit

Cathay Pacific Airways (☎ 263 0606) 11th floor, Ploenchit Tower, 898 Thanon Ploenchit

China Airlines (☎ 253 5733; reservations ☎ 253 4242) 4th floor, Peninsula Plaza, 153 Thanon Ratchadamri

China Southwest Airlines (☎ 634 7848–52) Ground floor, Bangkok Union Insurance Bldg, 175–177 Thanon Surawong

Delta Air Lines (☎ 237 6847–9) 7th floor, Patpong Bldg, 1 Thanon Surawong

Druk Air (☎ 235 6326/7) Room 3232, Central Block, Bangkok International Airport

Egypt Air (☎ 231 0504–8) 3rd floor, CP Tower, 313 Thanon Silom

El Al Israel Airlines (☎ 671 6145, 249 8818) 14th floor, Manorom Bldg, 3354/47 Thanon Phra Ram IV

EVA Airways (☎ 367 3388; reservations ☎ 240 0890) 2nd floor, Green Tower, 3656/4–5 Thanon Phra Ram IV

Finnair (☎ 635 1234 ext 102, 103) 6th floor, Vorawat Bldg, 849 Thanon Silom

Garuda Indonesia (☎ 285 6470–3) 27th floor, Lumphini Tower, 1168/77 Thanon Phra Ram IV

Gulf Air (☎ 254 7931–4) 12th floor, Maneeya Center Bldg, 518/5 Thanon Ploenchit

Japan Airlines (JAL; ☎ 692 5185/6; reservations ☎ 692 5151–60) JAL Bldg, 254/1 Thanon Ratchadaphisek

KLM-Royal Dutch Airlines (☎ 679 1100 ext 2) 19th floor, Thai Wah Tower II, 21/133–4 Thanon Sathon Tai

Korean Air (☎ 267 0985/6; reservations ☎ 635 0465–72) 9th floor, Kongboonma Bldg, 699 Thanon Silom

Kuwait Airways (☎ 641 2864–7) 12th floor, RS Tower, 121/50–51 Thanon Ratchadaphisek

Lao Aviation (☎ 236 9822/3) Ground floor, Silom Plaza, 491/17 Thanon Silom

Lauda Air (☎ 267 0873–9) 18th floor, Room 1802, Wall Street Tower, Thanon Surawong

LOT Polish Airlines (☎ 235 2223–7) 485/11–12 Thanon Silom

LTU International Airways (☎ 267 1235–7) 11th floor, Bangkok Gem & Jewelry Tower, 322 Thanon Surawong

Lufthansa Airlines (☎ 264 2484; reservations ☎ 264 2400) 18th floor, Q House, Asoke Bldg, 66 Soi 21, Thanon Sukhumvit

Malaysia Airlines (☎ 263 0520–32; reservations ☎ 263 0565–71) 20th floor, Ploenchit Tower, 898 Thanon Ploenchit

Myanmar Airways International (☎ 630 0334–8) 23rd floor, Jewelry Trade Center Bldg, 919/298 Thanon Silom

Northwest Airlines (☎ 254 0789) 4th floor, Peninsula Plaza, 153 Thanon Ratchadamri

Pakistan International Airlines (PIA; ☎ 234 2961–5, 233 5215/6) 2nd floor, Chongkolnee Bldg, 56 Thanon Surawong

Qantas Airways (☎ 636 1770; reservations ☎ 636 1747) 14th floor, Abdulrahim Place, 990 Thanon Phra Ram IV

Royal Air Cambodge (☎ 653 2261; reservations ☎ 653 2261–6) 17th floor, Pacific Place Bldg, 142 Thanon Sukhumvit

Royal Brunei Airlines (☎ 233 0056) 4th floor, Charn Issara Tower, 942/135 Thanon Phra Ram IV

Royal Jordanian (☎ 638 2960) 4th floor, CP Tower, 313 Thanon Silom

Royal Nepal Airlines (☎ 216 5691–5) 9th floor, Phayathai Plaza Bldg, 128 Thanon Phayathai

Sabena see Swissair

Saudi Arabian Airlines (☎ 266 7393–7) 19th floor, United Center Bldg, 323 Thanon Silom

Scandinavian Airlines (SAS; ☎ 260 0444) 8th floor, Glas Haus Bldg, 1 Soi 25, Thanon Sukhumvit

Singapore Airlines (SIA; ☎ 236 5301; reservations ☎ 236 0440) 12th floor, Silom Center Bldg, 2 Thanon Silom

South African Airways (☎ 635 1413/4) 20th floor, Vorawat Bldg, 849 Thanon Silom

Swissair (☎ 636 2160–6) 21st floor, Abdulrahim Place, 990 Thanon Phra Ram IV

Tarom (☎ 253 1681) 89/12 Bangkok Bazaar, Thanon Ratchadamri

Thai Airways International (THAI; head office ☎ 513 0121; reservations ☎ 280 0060) 89 Thanon Viphavadi Rangsit; (☎ 234 3100–19) 485 Thanon Silom; (☎ 288 0060, 280 0110) 6 Thanon Lan Luang; (☎ 215 2020/1) Asia Hotel, 296 Thanon Phayathai; (☎ 535 2081/2, 523 6121) Bangkok International Airport, Don Muang; (☎ 223 9746–48) 3rd floor, Room 310–311, Grand China Bldg, 215 Thanon Yaowarat

United Airlines (☎ 253 0559; reservations ☎ 253 0558) 14th floor, Sindhorn Bldg, 130–132 Thanon Withayu

Vietnam Airlines (☎ 656 9056–8) 7th floor, Ploenchit Center Bldg, Soi 2 Thanon Sukhumvit

Bus

Bangkok is the centre for bus services that fan out all over the kingdom.

Public Bus There are three main public bus (Baw Khaw Saw) terminals. The Northern and North-Eastern bus terminal (☎ 936 3660 for Northern routes; ☎ 936 0667 for North-Eastern routes) is on Thanon Kamphaeng Phet, just north of Chatuchak Park. It's also commonly called the Moh Chit station (sàthăanii măw chít), or, since it moved to a newer air-con building on the other side of the highway a little farther north, it's sometimes referred to as 'New' Moh Chit (măw chít mài). Buses depart from here for Northern and North-Eastern destinations like Chiang Mai and Nakhon Ratchasima (Khorat), as well as places closer to Bangkok such as Ayuthaya and Lopburi. Buses to Aranya Prathet also go from here, not from the Eastern bus terminal as you might expect. Air-con city bus Nos 4, 10 and 29, along with a dozen or more ordinary city buses, all pass the terminal. The Mo Chit Skytrain station is also within walking distance of the bus terminal.

The Eastern bus terminal (☎ 391 2504), the departure point for buses to Pattaya, Rayong, Chanthaburi and other points east, is a long way out along Thanon Sukhumvit, at Soi 40 (Soi Ekamai) opposite Soi 63. Most folks call it Ekamai station (sàthăanii èkkàmai). Air-con bus Nos 1, 8, 11, 13 and 38 all pass this station, and the Skytrain stops at its own Ekamai station in front of Soi 40.

The Southern bus terminal (☎ 435 1200, 434 7192), for buses south to Phuket, Surat Thani and closer centres to the west like Nakhon Pathom and Kanchanaburi, has one Thonburi location for both ordinary and air-con buses at the intersection of Hwy 338 (Thanon Nakhon Chaisi) and Thanon Phra Pinklao. A convenient way to reach the station is by ordinary city bus Nos 124 and 127.

When travelling on night buses take care of your belongings. Some of the long-distance buses leaving from Bangkok now issue claim checks for luggage stored under the bus, but valuables are still best kept on your person or within reach.

Allow an hour to reach the Northern bus terminal from Banglamphu or anywhere along the river, and more than an hour to reach the Southern bus terminal. The Eastern bus terminal takes 30 to 45 minutes under most traffic conditions. During gridlock, eg, Friday afternoons before a holiday, it can take up to three hours to get across town to the terminals by public transport.

Private Bus The more reputable and licensed private tour buses leave from the public terminals listed previously. Some private bus companies arrange pick-ups at Thanon Khao San and other guesthouse areas – these pick-ups are illegal since it's against municipal law to carry passengers within the city limits except en route to or from an official terminal. This is why the curtains on these buses are sometimes closed when picking up passengers.

Although fares tend to be lower on private buses, the incidence of reported theft is far greater than on the Baw Khaw Saw buses. They are also generally – but not always – less reliable, promising services (such as air-con or VIP seats) that they don't deliver. For safer, more reliable and more punctual service, stick to buses that leave from the official Baw Khaw Saw terminals.

For details on bus fares to/from other towns and cities in Thailand, see the Getting There & Away sections in the relevant destination chapters.

Train

Bangkok is the terminus for the main trunk rail services to the South, North, North-East and East. There are two principal train stations. The big Hualamphong station on Thanon Phra Ram IV handles services to the North, North-East and some of the Southern services. The Thonburi (Bangkok Noi) station handles a few services to the South. If you're heading down to Southern Thailand, make sure you know which station your train departs from. See the Train section in the Getting Around chapter for further details.

GETTING AROUND

Getting around Bangkok may be difficult at first for the uninitiated but once you're familiar with the bus system the whole city is accessible. The main obstacle is the traffic, which moves at a snail's pace during much of the day. This means advance planning is a must when you are attending scheduled events or arranging appointments.

If you can travel by river, canal or Skytrain from one point to another (ie, avoid the roads), it's always the best choice.

To/From the Airport

Bangkok International Airport is in the Don Muang district, approximately 25km north of Bangkok. You have a choice of transport modes from the airport to the city, ranging from 3.50B to 300B.

Airport Bus A 21-seat airport express bus service operates from Bangkok International Airport to four different Bangkok districts for 100B per person. Buses run every 15 minutes from 6 am to midnight. A map showing the designated stops is available at the airport; buses on each route make approximately six stops in each direction. A great boon to travellers on a budget, these buses mean you can avoid hassling with taxi drivers to get a reasonable fare as well as forgo the slow pace of the regular bus routes.

The Airport Bus counter is around 200m to the left (with your back to Terminal 1) of the left-most terminal exit. The routes are:

A-1 To the Silom business district via Pratunam and Thanon Ratchadamri, stopping at big hotels like the Century, Indra, Grand Hyatt Erawan, Regent Bangkok and Dusit Thani.

A-2 To Sanam Luang via Thanon Phayathai, Thanon Lan Luang, Thanon Ratchadamnoen Klang and Thanon Tanao; this is the route you want if you're going to the Victory Monument, Democracy Monument, Siam Square or Banglamphu areas. In Banglamphu, it stops opposite the Food & Agriculture Organization headquarters on Thanon Phra Athit.

A-3 To the Phrakhanong district via Thanon Sukhumvit, including Ekamai bus terminal (for buses east to Pattaya and Trat) and Soi 55 (Soi Thong Lor). Hotel stops include Ambassador and Delta Grand Pacific.

A-4 To Hualamphong train station via Thanon Phra Ram IV and Thanon Phayathai, with stops at Mahboonkrong shopping centre and the Siam Inter-Continental Hotel.

Public Bus Cheapest of all are the public buses to Bangkok, which stop on the highway in front of the airport. There are two non-air-con bus routes and four air-con routes; take note, however, that the non-air-con buses no longer accept passengers carrying luggage.

Air-con bus No 29 costs 16B and plies one of the most useful, all-purpose routes from the airport into the city as it goes to the Siam Square and Hualamphong areas. After entering the city limits via Thanon Phahonyothin (which turns into Thanon Phayathai), the bus passes Thanon Phetburi (where you'll want to get off to change buses for Banglamphu), then Thanon Phra Ram I at the Siam Square and Mahboonkrong intersection (for buses out to Thanon Sukhumvit, or to walk to Soi Kasem San 1 for various lodgings) and finally turns right on Thanon Phra Ram IV to go to the Hualamphong district (where the main train station is located). You'll want to go the opposite way on Thanon Phra Ram IV for the Soi Ngam Duphli lodging area. Bus No 29 runs only from 5.45 am to 8.30 pm, so if you're arriving on a late-night flight you'll miss it.

Air-con bus No 13 also goes to Bangkok from the airport, coming down Thanon Phahonyothin (like No 29), turning left at the Victory Monument to Thanon Ratchaprarop, then south to Thanon Ploenchit, where it travels east along Thanon Sukhumvit all the way to Bang Na. This is definitely the bus to catch if you're heading for the Thanon Sukhumvit area. It costs 16B and operates from 4.30 am to 9 pm.

Air-con bus No 4 costs 16B and operates from 5.45 am to 8 pm. It begins with a route parallel to that of bus No 29 bus – down Thanon Viphavadi Rangsit to Thanon Ratchaprarop and Thanon Ratchadamri (Pratunam district), crossing Thanon Phetburi, Thanon Phra Ram I, Thanon Ploenchit and Thanon Phra Ram IV, then down Thanon Silom and left on Thanon Charoen Krung to Thonburi.

Air-con bus No 10 goes from the airport all the way to the Southern us terminal in Thonburi for 16B and operates from 5.45 am to 8 pm.

Ordinary bus No 59 (no luggage allowed) costs only 3.50B (5B from 10 pm to 6 am) and operates 24 hours – it zigzags through to Banglamphu (the Democracy Monument area) from the airport, a trip that can take up to 1¾ hours or more in traffic. (Air-con No 59 costs 18B and runs from 6 am to 10 pm.)

Ordinary bus No 29 costs 3.50B, or 5B from 11 pm to 5 am, and operates 24 hours. It plies much the same route as air-con bus No 29.

Unless you're really strapped for baht, it's worth the extra 12.50B to 14.50B for the air-con and almost guaranteed seating, especially in the hot season, since the trip to central Bangkok by bus usually takes an hour or more. Even better is the 100B Airport Bus, described earlier.

Terminal Shuttle THAI operates free air-con shuttle buses over two routes between the international and domestic terminals. Both routes go between Terminal 1 and the domestic terminal, so if you're just going between these buildings, you can jump on any bus that comes along. In addition, Route A-1 continues to cargo agent 1 building and the VIP rooms building. This shuttle runs every 20 minutes from 5.20 to 11 pm daily.

Route A-2 adds stops at the customs bureau building, the four-storey car park, cargo agent 4 building and the office of AAT storage division. This shuttle starts at 6 am and runs hourly between 6 am and 5 pm on weekdays.

Train You can also get into Bangkok from the airport by train. After leaving Terminal 1, turn right (north), cross the highway via the pedestrian bridge, turn left and walk about 100m towards Bangkok. Opposite the big Amari Airport Hotel is Don Muang station from where trains depart regularly to Bangkok. The 3rd-class fare from Don Muang is only 5B on the ordinary and commuter trains. Tickets for rapid or express trains cost 45B and 65B respectively.

Trains run frequently between 4.49 am and 8.18 pm and it takes about 45 minutes to reach Hualamphong, the main station in central Bangkok. In the opposite direction trains depart between 7.45 am and 10 pm. From the Hualamphong station you can walk to the bus stop almost opposite Wat Traimit for bus No 53 to Banglamphu.

Some travellers catch trains northward from Don Muang train station to Ayuthaya, Sukhothai, Khorat or other points in the North or North-East, thus avoiding Bangkok altogether.

Taxi The Department of Land Transport has stepped in to police the airport taxi service, and for the moment, at least, there seems to be substantially fewer hassles with airport taxi drivers than in previous years. During the past two years we've had no problems at all getting regular metered taxis.

Metered taxis waiting near the arrival area of the airport are supposed to be airport-regulated. Ignore all the touts waiting in the arrival hall and buy a taxi ticket from the public taxi booth near the kerb outside the hall. Fares differ according to destination and resultant meter reading; most destinations in central Bangkok cost around 200B to 300B.

On top of the metre fare, airport taxis are permitted to collect a 50B airport surcharge. You must also reimburse drivers for any toll charges paid if they take the tollway into the city (20B to 50B) depending on where you get off the tollway. Taking the tollway almost always saves time.

If you end up taking a flat-rate taxi, the driver should pay all toll charges. Two, three, or even four passengers (if they don't have much luggage) can split the fare.

Sometimes unscrupulous drivers will approach you before you reach the taxi booth and try to sell you a ticket for 350B or 400B – ignore them and head for the kerb queue. Touts from the old taxi mafia that used to prowl the arrival area are still around and may approach you with fares of around 200B. Their taxis have white-and-black plates and are not licensed to carry passengers, hence you have less legal recourse in the event of an incident than if you take a licensed taxi (yellow-and-black plates). Robberies have reportedly occurred in these taxis.

A few drivers still try to renegotiate the fare once you're inside a metered cab. The occasional driver will refuse to use his meter and quote a flat rate of 300B to 400B; however, this is more of a rare occurrence than it used to be. Passengers now receive a bilingual Taxi-Meter Information sheet, issued by the Department of Land Transport, which indicates the name of the driver, the cab licence number, the date and the time. A phone number for registering complaints against the driver is listed on this sheet, so if you have a problem you should call and report the driver. The passenger – *not* the driver – is supposed to keep this sheet. The driver may want to glance at the sheet to read your destination, but you should receive it back immediately.

Metered taxis, flagged down on the highway in front of the airport (turn left from the arrival hall), are even cheaper since they don't have to pay the 50B airport surcharge. When the queue at the public taxi desk is particularly long, it's sometimes faster to go upstairs or walk out to the highway and flag one down.

Limousine Three companies maintain counters at the airport offering airport limousine service, which is really just a glorified air-con taxi. THAI Limousine (☎ 535 2801), Airport Associate Limousine (☎ 535 5905, 535 5361) and Prapirab Limousine (☎ 535 1894) all have a starting rate of 650B to destinations in central Bangkok, more than double the usual meter taxi fare. The main advantage is not having to wait in the public taxi queue.

Helicopter The Shangri-La Hotel (☎ 236 7777) can arrange a helicopter service (for hotel guests only) from Bangkok International Airport to the hotel rooftop for around 14,000B per trip; minimum of three persons. An additional three people can fly for 5000B per person. The flight takes around 15 minutes.

Pattaya THAI operates direct air-con buses to Pattaya from the airport thrice daily at 9 am, noon and 7 pm; the fare is 200B one way. Private sedans cost 1500B to 2500B per trip.

Bus

You can save a lot of money in Bangkok by sticking to the Bangkok Metropolitan Transit Authority (BMTA) public buses, which cost 5B for any journey under 10km on the ordinary white-and-blue buses, or 3.50B on the red buses or smaller green buses. Smaller 'baht buses' plying the sois are painted red and maroon, and cost 2B each.

Cream-and-blue air-con buses are available for 6B for the first 8km, and increase by 2B increments up to 16B, depending on the distance travelled. New orange Euro 2 air-con buses cost 12B for any distance, while white-and-pink air-con buses cost 10B. The air-con buses are not only cooler, but are usually less crowded (all bets are off during rush hours).

Most bus lines run from 5 am to 11 pm, except for the all-night cream-and-red ordinary buses, which run from 11 pm to 5 am on some routes and cost 5B. Buddhist monks and novices ride for free.

One air-con service that's never over-crowded is the Microbus – it stops taking passengers once every seat is filled. The fare is a flat rate of 25B – you deposit the money in a box at the front of the bus (exact change only). Until 1998, the buses were painted red and white, but the private company that recently took over the service has announced that the buses will be repainted purple. A couple of useful Microbus lines include: the No 6, which starts on Thanon Si Phraya (near the River City complex) and proceeds to the Siam Square area, then out to Thanon Sukhumvit; and the No 1, which runs between the Victory Monument area and Banglamphu district.

Bus Maps See the Maps section earlier in this chapter for a list of maps of Bangkok, including bus maps.

The best source of all for routes and fares is BMTA's Web site, www.bmta.motc.go.th.

Bus Safety Be careful with your belongings while riding Bangkok buses. The place you are most likely to be 'touched' is on the crowded ordinary buses. Razor artists abound, particularly on buses in the Hualamphong station area. These dexterous thieves specialise in slashing your backpack, shoulder bag or even your trouser pockets with a sharp razor and slipping your valuables out unnoticed. Hold your bag in front of you, under your attention and carry money in a front shirt pocket, preferably (as the Thais do) maintaining a tactile and visual sensitivity to these areas if the bus is packed shoulder to shoulder.

Skytrain

The much-ballyhooed Skytrain elevated rail network finally opened in December 1999 and has proved to be a tremendous boon to those wanting to escape the often horrendous traffic jams on Bangkok's streets. Originally proposed in 1986 and begun in 1994, the result so far is two lines officially known as the Bangkok Mass Transit System (BTS) Skytrain, known to the Thais simply as *rót fai fáa* (sky train).

One line starts from the Mo Chit station in the north, next to the Northern and North-Eastern bus terminal as well as Chatuchak Park, and ends at the On Nut station, near Soi 81, Thanon Sukhumvit. Often referred to as 'the Sukhumvit line', it will reportedly soon be extended 9km farther south-east to Samut Prakan. There is talk of extending this line as far as the new airport under construction in Nong Ngu Hao.

The second line – colloquially known as the 'Silom line' – runs from the National Stadium east to Siam Square and soon after makes an abrupt turn to the south-west, continuing above Thanon Ratchadamri, down Thanon Silom to Thanon Narathiwat Ratchanakharin, then out Thanon Sathon till it terminates next to the foot of Saphan Taksin on the banks of the Mae Nam Chao Phraya. This line will be extended a further 2km over the river and into Thonburi, or so we're told. The extensions are to be completed within three years.

Although the Skytrain has yet to make a sizeable dent in Bangkok traffic, it's estimated that on the average day there are 40,000 fewer cars on the road than before the train's 1999 launch, and that a large number of city residents have switched from BMTA's crowded air-con buses. The latter means that BMTA has lowered the number of buses on the road at any one time, perhaps making a very small contribution to improving city air.

The Skytrain has certainly made a very tangible difference in the lives of many people for whom the Skytrain routes are convenient. In pre-Skytrain Bangkok, if you wanted to take a taxi from Thanon Ploenchit to Chatuchak Weekend Market, for example, the trip might take an hour or more. By Skytrain the same journey is covered in approximately 16 minutes! Getting from Thanon Sukhumvit to Thanon Silom – a nightmare trip by car or taxi during rush hour – can now be accomplished in 15 minutes or less via Skytrain.

Another advantage to the Skytrain is that it offers a pleasant semi-bird's eye view of the city, allowing glimpses of greenery and historic architecture not visible from street level due to high walls.

Riding the Skytrain Trains run frequently from 6 am to midnight along both lines. If you've ever ridden a modern light rail system that used ticket cards with magnetic stripes, you'll have no trouble figuring out the simple Skytrain system. You can change between the two lines at the double-height Siam station (also known as 'Central Station'), in front of Siam Square and Siam Center. Free maps of the system are available at all Skytrain station ticket booths. All trains are air-conditioned, often heavily so.

From your point of departure, fares vary from 10B to 40B depending on which of 23 current stations you plan to disembark from. Ticket machines at each station accept 5B and 10B coins only. You can buy tickets from staffed station ticket booths if you don't have correct change. You can also buy stored-value tickets in 100B increments. These cards can be purchased at all station ticket booths, and at branches of Siam Commercial Bank, Black Canyon Coffee shops and Watsons drug stores. Fares are posted inside every station.

For further information call BTS on ☎ 617 7300 or check www.bts.co.th. Although their English is limited, ticket staff at each station can offer helpful advise about which station to buy a ticket for if you're not sure where you're going.

Subway

Since 1998, the Metropolitan Rapid Transit Authority (MRTA) has been building the city's first-ever subway. The 18-station line is designed to link Hualamphong near the river with Bang Seu in the north via the Queen Sirikit National Convention Centre. Although the line intersects BTS Skytrain routes at two points – near the Asoke Skytrain station and the Mo Chit Skytrain station – engineers have reportedly provided for no pedestrian links between the two services. The estimated launch date for the subway (*rót fai tâi din* or 'underground railway' in Thai) is 2002.

Taxi

Metered taxis (*tháeksii miitôe*) were introduced in Bangkok in 1993, and they now far outnumber the old non-meter taxis. The ones with meters have signs on top reading 'Taxi Meter', the others 'Taxi Thai' or just 'Taxi'. Fares for metered taxis are always lower than for non-metered, the only problem being that they can be a little harder to flag down during peak commuter hours. Demand often outstrips supply from 8 to 9 am and 6 to 7 pm and also late at night when the bars are closing (1 to 2 am). Because

metered-taxi drivers use rented vehicles and must return them at the end of their shifts, they sometimes won't take longer fares as quitting time nears.

Metered taxis charge 35B at flag fall for the first 2km, then 4.50B for the next 10km, 5B for 13km to 20km and 5.50B for any distance over 20km, but only when the cab travels at 6km/h or more; at speeds under 6km/h, a surcharge of 1.25B per minute kicks in. With the rise in fuel prices in late 2000, taxi drivers began petitioning the city to allow them to raise meter fares, so if they get their way these fares will increase. Freeway tolls – 20B to 40B depending where you start – must be paid by the passenger. A 24-hour 'phone-a-cab' service (Siam Taxi; ☎ 377 1771) is available for an extra 20B over the regular metered fare.

For certain routes it can be very difficult to find a taxi driver who's willing to use the meter. One such instance is going from the Southern bus terminal across the river to Bangkok proper – most drivers will ask for a flat 350B but settle for 250B. For those times when you're forced to use a non-metered cab, you'll have to negotiate the fare. Fares to most places within central Bangkok are 60B to 80B and you should add 10B or 20B if it's during rush hour or after midnight. For trips to the airport the non-meter drivers charge 200B to 300B.

You can hire a taxi all day for 1000B to 1500B depending on how much driving is involved.

Bangkok Sightseeing Bus

Bangkok now has a double-decker sightseeing bus that plies a circuit through Ko Ratanakosin and other parts of western Bangkok near the river. The bus service runs between the Grand Palace and Vimanmek mansion, and vice versa. From the Grand Palace, the bus travels along Thanon Ratchadamnoen, past the Democracy Monument and the Loha Prasat at Wat Rajanadda, down Thanon Ratchadamnoen Nok, then right past the Government House. The bus then turns left past Wat Benjamabophit and Chitlada Palace, then back to Vimanmek.

The bus service operates between 9 am and 6 pm daily, and costs 200B per person for foreigners, 100B for Thai tourists. For further information, or for reservations, call ☎ 645 0710 or ☎ 645 0700 ext 116, 117.

Túk-Túk

In heavy traffic, túk-túk are usually faster than taxis since they're able to weave in and out between cars and trucks. On the down side, túk-túk are not air-conditioned, so you have to breathe all that lead-soaked air (at its thickest in the middle of Bangkok's wide avenues), and they're also more dangerous since they easily flip when braking into a fast curve. The typical túk-túk fare nowadays offers no savings over a metered cab – around 40B for a short hop (eg, Siam Square to Soi 2 Sukhumvit).

Túk-túk drivers tend to speak less English than taxi drivers, so many new arrivals have a hard time communicating their destinations. Although some travellers have complained about túk-túk drivers deliberately taking them to the wrong destination (to collect commissions from certain restaurants, gem shops or silk shops), others never seem to have a problem with túk-túk, and swear by them. Beware of túk-túk drivers who offer to take you on a sightseeing tour for 10B or 20B – it's a touting scheme designed to pressure you into purchasing overpriced goods.

Motorcycle Taxi

As passengers become more desperate in their attempts to beat rush-hour gridlocks, motorcycle taxis have moved from the sois to the main avenues. Fares for a motorcycle taxi are about the same as túk-túk except during heavy traffic, when they may cost a bit more.

Riding on the back of a speeding motorcycle taxi is even more hair-raising than riding in a túk-túk. Keep your legs tucked in – the drivers are used to carrying passengers with shorter legs than those of the average fàràng and they pass perilously close to other vehicles while weaving in and out of traffic.

Car & Motorcycle

Cars and motorbikes are easily rented in Bangkok, if you can afford them and have steel nerves. Rates start at around 1500B per day or 9000B per week for a small car, much less for a motorcycle, excluding insurance. For long-term rentals you can usually arrange a discount of up to 35%. An International Driving Permit and passport are required for all rentals.

For long, cross-country trips, you might consider buying a new or used motorcycle and reselling it when you leave – this can end up being cheaper than renting, especially if you buy a good used bike. See the Getting Around chapter for more details.

Here are the names and addresses of a few car-rental companies:

Avis Rent-A-Car (☎ 255 5300–4, fax 253 3734) 2/12 Thanon Withayu;
   (☎ 535 4031/2, 535 4052) Bangkok International Airport;
   (☎ 254 1234) Grand Hyatt Erawan Hotel;
   (☎ 253 0444) Le Meridien President Hotel
Budget Car Rental (☎ 202 0250, fax 203 0249) 19/23 Bldg A, Royal City Avenue, Thanon Phetburi Tat Mai
Grand Car Rent (☎ 248 2991) 233-5 Thanon Asoke-Din Daeng
Highway Car Rent (☎ 266 9393) 1018/5 Thanon Phra Ram IV
Inter Car Rent (☎ 252 9223) 45 Thanon Sukhumvit, near Soi 3
Krung Thai Car Rent (☎ 246 0089, 246 1525) 233–235 Thanon Asoke-Din Daeng
Lumpinee Car Rent (☎ 255 1966, 255 3482) 167/4 Thanon Withayu
National Car Rental (☎ 928 1525) Amari Airport Hotel; (☎ 722 8487) 727 Thanon Si Nakharin
Petchburee Car Rent (☎ 319 7255) 237.1 Thanon Phetburi Tat Mai
SMT Rent-A-Car (see National Car Rental)
Sathorn Car Rent (☎ 633 8888) 6/8–9 Thanon Sathon Neua

There are more rental agencies along Thanon Withayu and Thanon Phetburi Tat Mai. Some also rent motorcycles, but you're better off renting or leasing a bike at a place that specialises in motorcycles. Here are three:

Chusak Yont Shop (☎ 251 9225) 1400 Thanon Phetburi Tat Mai
SSK (☎ 514 1290) 35/33 Thanon Lat Phrao
Visit Laochaiwat (☎ 278 1348) 1 Soi Prommit, Thanon Suthisan

Boat

Bangkok was once called the 'Venice of the East', but much of the original canal system has been filled in for road construction. Larger canals, especially on the Thonburi side, remain important commercial arteries but many of the smaller canals are hopelessly polluted and would probably have been filled in by now if it weren't for their important drainage function. Still there is plenty of transport along and across the Mae Nam Chao Phraya and up adjoining canals. River transport is one of the nicest ways to

Túk-Túk Wars

In 18th-century Bangkok, residents got around on foot, by canal or in human-drawn rickshaws, called *rót chék* or 'Chinese vehicles'. During the early 20th century, the rickshaw gave way to *the* three-wheeled pedicab *(sǎamláw)*, which then added inexpensive Japanese two-stroke engines after WWII to become the onomatopoeic *túk-túk*.

These small three-wheeled taxicabs sound like power saws gone berserk and commonly leave trails of blue smoke whenever they rev up, despite the fact they run on LP gas, a cleaner fuel than diesel or petrol. Objecting Bangkokians have been trying for years to enact a ban on túk-túk. More than a decade ago the city supposedly forbade the further production of any new three-wheeled taxis, but every time we go to Bangkok we see hordes of brand new ones. It's somewhat of a moral dilemma actually, since the túk-túk drivers are usually poor North-Easterners who can't afford to rent the quieter, less polluting Japanese autotaxis. You can buy a túk-túk for around US$1200 from Túk-túk Industry Thailand (☎ 02-437 6983), 463–465 Th Prachathipok, Bangkok.

get around Bangkok as well as, quite often, being much faster than any road-based alternatives. For a start, you get quite a different view of the city; secondly, it's much less of a hassle than tangling with the polluted, noisy and traffic-crowded Bangkok streets.

Along the Mae Nam Chao Phraya the main transport consists of the Chao Phraya River Express (☎ 222 5330, 623 6342), which runs between Tha Wat Ratchasingkhon (Wat Ratchasingkhon pier) in south central Bangkok and Nonthaburi Province from 6 am to 6.40 pm daily. Fares range from 6B to 10B, except for special express boats (denoted by a yellow flag or a red and orange striped flag), which run only between 6 to 9 am and 3 to 7 pm, cost 10B and stop at fewer piers along the way. Bangkok Metropolitan Authority operates four lengthy and useful canal routes: Khlong Saen Saep (Banglamphu to Bang Kapi),

Khlong Phrakhanong (Thanon Sukhumvit to Sinakarin campus), Khlong Bang Luang/ Khlong Lat Phrao (Thanon Phetburi Tat Mai to Saphan Phahonyothin) and Khlong Phasi Charoen in Thonburi (Kaset Bang Khae port to Saphan Phra Ram I). Although the canal boats can be crowded, the service is generally much faster than either a taxi or bus. Along Thanon Sukhumvit, however, the Skytrain is generally preferable.

The Khlong Saen Saep canal service is one of the most useful for most visitors. This one provides a quicker alternative to road transport between the river and eastern Bangkok (ie, outer Sukhumvit and Bang Kapi). The boat from Banglamphu to the Ramkhamhaeng University area, for example, costs 10B and takes only 40 minutes. A bus would take at least an hour under Bangkok's normal traffic conditions. The main detraction from this route is the seriously polluted canal – passengers typically hold newspapers over their clothes and faces to prevent being splashed by the stinking black water. Not the best choice of transport if you're dressed for a formal occasion.

A handy run along this route is by long-tail boat (6B) from the Siam Square area (from Tha Ratchathewi by the bridge next to the Asia Hotel) to Tha Banglamphu near Wat Saket and the Democracy Monument. At its western end, this route intersects a north-south boat route along Khlong Banglamphu and Khlong Phadung Krung Kasem. See the River & Canal Trips section earlier in this chapter for more information on boat travel around Bangkok.

Walking

At first glance, Bangkok doesn't seem like a great town for walking – its main avenues are so choked with traffic that the noise and thick air will probably drive you indoors. However, quiet spots where walks are rewarding do exist, eg, Lumphini Park or neighbourhoods off the main streets. And certain places are much more conveniently seen on foot, particularly the older sections of town along the Mae Nam Chao Phraya where the roads are so narrow and twisting that bus lines don't go there.

For sample walking tours, see the boxed text 'Walking Tour – Chinatown & Phahurat' and 'Ratanakosin Temples & River Walking Tour' earlier in this chapter.

Around Bangkok

If you can negotiate Bangkok's traffic jams, there are a couple of sights not far from the capital which make interesting day trips. The giant stupa at Nakhon Pathom, the floating markets and the Ancient City are all worth seeing, and can all be reached within an hour or so from town.

NAKHON PATHOM
อ.เมืองนครปฐม

postcode 73000 • pop 46,400

Only 56km west of Bangkok, Nakhon Pathom is often referred to by Thais as the oldest city in Thailand – the name in fact is derived from the Pali 'Nagara Pathama', meaning 'First City'. At one time it functioned as the centre of the Dvaravati kingdom, a loose collection of Mon city states that flourished between the 6th and 11th centuries AD in the Mae Nam Chao Phraya valley. Some historians speculate that the area may have been inhabited before India's Asokan period (3rd century BC), as it is theorised that Buddhist missionaries from India visited Nakhon Pathom at that time. Although one could point out that other areas of Thailand were inhabited earlier, Nakhon Pathom may very well be the longest continually inhabited place within Thailand's current borders.

Today's Nakhon Pathom is a typical provincial Thai city whose only visible link to its glorious past is the famous Phra Pathom Chedi.

Phra Pathom Chedi
พระปฐมเจดีย์

The Phra Pathom Chedi, rising to 127m, is the tallest Buddhist monument in the world. The original monument, buried within the massive orange-glazed dome, was erected in the early 6th century by Theravada Buddhists of Dvaravati (possibly at the same time as Myanmar's famous Shwe Dagon stupa), but in the early 11th century the Khmer king, Suriyavarman I of Angkor, conquered the city and built a Brahman prang over the sanctuary. The Burmese of Bagan, under King Anawrahta, sacked the city in 1057 and the prang lay in ruins until

King Mongkut had it restored in 1860. The king built a larger chedi over the remains according to Buddhist tradition, adding four wíhǎan, a bòt, a replica of the original chedi, sǎalaa and assorted prang, and other embellishments. There is even a Chinese temple attached to the outer walls of the chedi, next to which outdoor lí-keh is sometimes performed.

On the eastern side of the monument, in the bòt, is a Dvaravati-style Buddha seated in a European pose similar to the one in Wat Phra Meru in Ayuthaya. It may, in fact, have come from there.

The wát surrounding the chedi enjoys the kingdom's highest temple rank, Ratchavoramahavihan, one of only six temples so honoured in Thailand. King Rama VI's ashes are interred in the base of the Sukhothai-era Phra Ruang Rochanarit, a large standing Buddha image in the wát's northern wíhǎan. Also of interest are the many examples of Chinese sculpture carved from a greenish stone that came to Thailand as ballast in the bottom of 19th-century Chinese junks.

Opposite the bòt is a museum, which contains some interesting Dvaravati sculpture. The museum is open 9 am to 4 pm Wednesday to Sunday; admission is 20B.

Other Attractions

Besides the chedi, the other focuses of the town are **Silpakorn University**, west of the chedi off Phetkasem Hwy, and **Sanam Chan**, adjacent to the university. Sanam Chan, formerly the grounds of Rama VI's palace, is a pleasant park with a canal passing through it. The somewhat run-down palace still stands in the park, but entry to the palace is not permitted.

South-east of the city towards Bangkok, between the districts of Nakhon Chaisi and Sam Phran, stands **Phra Phutthamonthon**. This Sukhothai-style standing Buddha, at 40.7m, is reportedly the world's tallest; it's surrounded by a 2500-râi (400-hectare) landscaped park containing sculptures representing the major stages in the Buddha's life, such as a 6m-high dharma wheel (dhammacakka), carved from a single slab of granite, representing the first sermon. The Buddha statue, which is particularly beautiful, was designed by Corrado Feroci. All Bangkok to Nakhon Pathom buses pass the access road to the park, from there you can walk, hitch or flag one of the frequent săwngthăew into the park itself.

The **Thai Human Imagery Museum** (☎ 034-332607), a bit out of town at the 31km marker on Thanon Pinklao-Nakhon Chaisi (the highway to Bangkok), contains an exhibition of lifelike resin sculptures. A group of Thai artists reportedly spent 10 years studying their subjects and creating the figures, which fall into four categories: famous Buddhist monks of Thailand, former kings of the Chakri dynasty, Thai lifestyles and chess playing. It's open 9 am to 5.30 pm weekdays, 8.30 am to 6 pm weekends; admission for foreigners is 200B (Thais 50B).

Places to Eat

Nakhon Pathom has an excellent *fruit market* along the road between the train station and the Phra Pathom Chedi; the *khâo lăam* (sticky rice and coconut steamed in a bamboo joint) is reputed to be the best in Thailand. There are many good, inexpensive food vendors and restaurants in this area.

An old stand-by on Thanon Thesa, east of the chedi, is the inexpensive Chinese *Tang Ha-Seng* (no Roman-script sign); there are two branches, one at No 71/2–3 and another No 59/1–2.

Song Saeng, on Thanon Ratchadamnoen a few blocks directly west of Phra Pathom Chedi, offers a pleasant Thai săalaa setting with good, medium-priced Thai food.

In the evenings you can get decent Thai food at *Harley Davidson Bong-Pub*, just north of the train station. Although really more of a bar than a restaurant, its menu has a good selection of *kàp klâem* (finger food) and there's live music on Friday and Saturday.

Swensen's and *Pizza Hut* have opened shop on the corner of Thanon Lang Phra and Thanon Phayaphan.

Getting There & Away

Bus Buses for Nakhon Pathom leave the Southern bus terminal in Bangkok every 10 minutes from 5.45 am to 9.10 pm (20B, one hour). Air-con buses (34B) leave about every 20 minutes between 6 am and 10.30 pm. There are two bus routes; be sure to take the *săi mài* (new route) buses as the *săi kào* (old route) buses take a half-hour

longer. In the opposite direction, ordinary (No 83) and air-con (No 997) buses depart for Bangkok from Thanon Phayaphan on the canal side of the road close to the Mitphaisan Hotel.

The location of bus stops in Nakhon Pathom seems to change regularly. At last visit, buses to Kanchanaburi were leaving throughout the day from Thanon Khwa Phra, south-east of Phra Pathom Chedi – get bus No 81. Buses to Damnoen Saduak floating market (bus No 78 – see the Damnoen Saduak Floating Market section following) and to Phetchaburi (bus No 73) leave from the same stop, departing about every 30 minutes.

Train Ordinary trains (3rd class only) leave Thonburi (Bangkok Noi) station for Nakhon Pathom at 7.45 am and 1.30 and 2 pm daily (14B, about 1¼ hours).

There are also rapid (71B 2nd class, 100B 1st class, 1½ hours) and express (91B 2nd class, 120B 1st class, about 1¼ hours) trains to Nakhon Pathom from Hualamphong station roughly hourly between 12.20 and 10.50 pm.

DAMNOEN SADUAK FLOATING MARKET
ตลาดน้ำดำเนินสะดวก

Among the most heavily published photo images of Thailand are those that depict wooden canoes laden with multicoloured fruits and vegetables, paddled by Thai women wearing indigo-hued clothes and wide-brimmed straw hats. Such floating markets *(tàlàat náam)* do exist in various locations throughout the huge canal system that surrounds Bangkok – but if you don't know where to go you may end up at a very unauthentic tourist-show scene.

The lively floating markets on Khlong Damnoen Saduak in Ratchaburi Province, 104km south-west of Bangkok, between Nakhon Pathom and Samut Songkhram, have become well known over the last few years.

Talat Ton Khem is the main, 100-year-old market on Khlong Damnoen Saduak, while **Talat Hia Kui**, just south on the parallel Khlong Hia Kui, gets the most tourists – one area in fact has been set aside especially for tourists, with a large open shop with

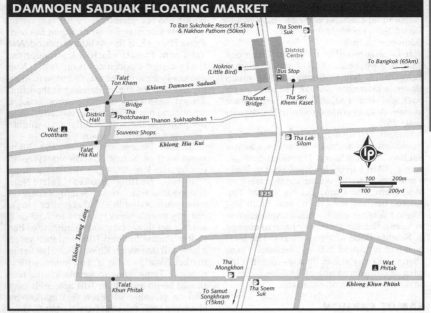

DAMNOEN SADUAK FLOATING MARKET

souvenirs for bus tours as well as souvenir-laden boats. There is a third, less crowded market on a smaller canal, a bit south of Damnoen Saduak, called **Talat Khun Phitak**. To get there, take a water taxi going south from the pier on the eastern side of Khlong Thong Lang, which intersects Damnoen Saduak near the larger floating market; ask for Talat Khun Phitak. You can rent a boat to tour the canals and all three markets (150B per half-hour). Try to arrive by 8 am at the latest – by 9 am the package tours are in full evidence.

Less touristed floating markets can be reached by boating south from Damnoen Saduak to Amphawa district in Samut Songkhram Province. See the following Samut Songkhram section for more information on these markets.

Places to Stay One sure way to beat the tour buses from Bangkok is to spend the night in Damnoen Saduak and get up before the hordes of tourists arrive. There's enough to see to justify spending a night and a day, perhaps longer. Try the clean and quiet *Noknoi (Little Bird; ☎ 032-*

254382), where rooms cost 170B with fan, 300B with air-con. It's about a 15-minute walk from Talat Ton Khem.

Ban Sukchoke Resort (☎ 032-254301) offers comfortable bungalows set over the canal for 450/700B single/double. There is also a small house that sleeps 10 for 1600B. Ban Sukchoke is 1.5km north-west of Damnoen Saduak's market area.

Getting There & Away Bus No 78 goes direct from Bangkok's Southern bus terminal to Damnoen Saduak every 20 minutes, beginning at 6.20 am, but you'll have to get one of the first few buses to arrive in Damnoen Saduak by 8 or 9 am, when the market's at its best. Air-con buses start at 6 am. The trip (35B ordinary, 55B air-con) lasts just short of two hours under normal road conditions.

From the pier nearest the bus station (Tha Seri Khemi Kaset), take a 20B water taxi to the floating market or walk 10 minutes west and south from the terminal along the canal until you come to the Hia Kui market area, where most of the rental boats are found.

Some people spend the night in Nakhon Pathom and catch an early morning bus to Samut Songkhram, asking to be let out at Damnoen Saduak.

It is also possible to get to Damnoen Saduak by bus (8B) from Samut Songkhram. Samut Songkhram is much closer to Damnoen Saduak (20 minutes by bus), and some people find it a better place to stay. A săwngthăew to/from Ratchaburi costs 25B.

One interesting way to return to Bangkok from Damnoen Saduak is by boat via Samut Sakhon. From Khlong Damnoen Saduak, take a 30km trip by long-tail boat to Bang Yang lock, where you can catch a ferry up Mae Nam Tha Chin, getting off at Tha Angton on the river's right bank. From Tha Angton you can catch a bus or săwngthăew to Samut Sakhon (you may have to change in Kratum Baen along the way). The total boat fare is around 25B and includes a boat change halfway at Ban Phaew – worth it for what is considered one of Thailand's most beautiful stretches of waterway.

SAMUT SAKHON
อ.เมืองสมุทรสาคร

postcode 74000 • pop 57,500
Twenty-eight kilometres south-west of Bangkok, Samut Sakhon is popularly known as Mahachai because it straddles the confluence of Mae Nam Tha Chin and Khlong Mahachai. Just a few kilometres from the Gulf of Thailand, this busy port features a lively market area and a pleasant breezy park around the crumbling walls of **Wichian Chodok Fort**. A few rusty cannon pointing towards the river testify to the fort's original purpose of guarding the mouth of Mae Nam Tha Chin from foreign invaders. Before the 17th-century arrival of European traders, the town was known as Tha Jin (Chinese pier) because of the large number of Chinese junks that called here.

Samut Sakhon set a macabre world record in December 1997 when the skeletal remains of 21,347 unclaimed road accident victims (many from Bangkok) were cremated in a specially built electric crematorium at the edge of town. The cremation of the corpses, which had been collected over 11 years by the Paw Tek Teung Foundation (a Chinese benevolent society dedicated to

this purpose), took seven days of constant burning to complete.

A few kilometres west of Samut Sakhon, along Hwy 35, is the Ayuthaya-period **Wat Yai Chom Prasat**, which is known for the finely carved wooden doors on its bòt. You can easily identify the wát from the road by the tall Buddha figure standing at the front. To get here from Samut Sakhon, take a westbound bus (3B) heading towards Samut Songkhram; the wát is only a 10-minute ride from the edge of town.

In Ban Phaew district, around 30km north-west of Samut Sakhon via Hwy 35 (west) and Rte 3079 (north), the Khlong Pho Hak **floating market** (Talat Nam Khlong Pho Hak) convenes daily except on *wan phrá* (Buddhist observance says, roughly once a week) from 4 to 7.30 or 8 am. To get there, take a săwngthăew or bus to Ban Phaew (around 10B) and then catch a long-tail taxi along Khlong Pho Hak to the market 8km away – if you share with a group of Thais going to the market the fare should be no more than 10B apiece. It may also be possible to reach this market by chartered long-tail boat from Samut Sakhon through the canals. The market is also known as Talat Nam Lak Ha (5km-marker floating market).

The Jao Mae Kuan Im Shrine at **Wat Chong Lom** is a 9m-high fountain in the shape of the Mahayana Buddhist Goddess of Mercy and is big with Hong Kong/ Taiwan/Singapore tour groups. The colourful image, which pours a constant stream of water from a vase in her right hand, rests on an artificial hill into which is carved a passageway leading to another Kuan Im shrine.

To get there from the ferry terminal at the harbour end of Thanon Sethakit (Tha Mahachai), take a ferry (1B) to Tha Chalong, and from there take a motorcycle taxi (10B) for the 2km ride to Wat Chong Lom.

Getting There & Away
Bus Ordinary buses to Samut Sakhon (25B, one hour) depart from Bangkok's Southern bus terminal all day. Buses also run between Samut Sakhon and Samut Songkhram (14B, 30 minutes).

Train Samut Sakhon is nearly midway along the 3rd-class, short-line 'Mahachai' train route that runs between Thonburi's

Wong Wian Yai station, located about 1km south of the Phra Phuttha Yot Fa (Memorial) Bridge, and Samut Songkhram. You won't find the Mahachai short line listed on any published State Railway of Thailand (SRT) schedule, whether in English or Thai, as it's strictly a local proposition.

The fare to/from either Thonburi or Samut Songkhram is 10B; there are four departures a day: at 7.30 and 10.10 am and 1.30 and 4.40 pm heading south, and at similar times heading north from Samut Sakhon.

You can continue to Samut Songkhram by train from Samut Sakhon by crossing the river at Ban Laem.

Getting Around

Sǎamláw and motorcycle taxis around town cost 20B to 30B depending on the distance.

SAMUT SONGKHRAM

อ.เมืองสมุทรสงคราม

postcode 75000 • pop 35,000

Wedged between Ratchaburi, Samut Sakhon and Phetchaburi, 416-sq-km Samut Songkhram is Thailand's smallest province. Commonly known as 'Mae Klong', the capital lies along a sharp bend in Mae Nam Mae Klong, 74km south-west of Bangkok and just a few kilometres from the Gulf of Thailand. Due to flat topography and abundant water sources, the area surrounding the capital is well suited for the steady irrigation needed to grow guavas, lychees and grapes. Along the highway from Thonburi, visitors will pass a string of artificial sea lakes used in the production of salt. A profusion of coconut palms makes the area look unusually lush, considering its proximity to Bangkok.

Samut Songkhram would make a good jumping-off point for early morning forays to Damnoen Saduak floating market, 20 minutes away by bus. It does have some decent floating markets of its own, however.

Things to See

Samut Songkhram is a fairly modern city with a large market area between the railway and bus station. The sizable **Wat Phet Samut Worawihan**, in the centre of town near the train station and river, contains a renowned Buddha image called Luang Phaw Wat Ban Laem.

At the mouth of Mae Nam Mae Klong, not far from town, is the province's most famous tourist attraction, a bank of fossilised shells known as **Don Hoi Lot**. The type of shells embedded in the bank come from *hǎwy làwt* (clams with a tube-like shell). The shell bank is best seen late in the dry season (typically April and May) when the river has receded to its lowest level. Many seafood restaurants have been built at the edge of Don Hoi Lot, encroaching on a crab-eating macaque habitat. About 200 remaining simians are threatened by the development. To get to Don Hoi Lot you can hop on a sǎwngthǎew in front of Somdet Phra Phuttalertla Hospital at the intersection of Thanon Prasitwatthana and Thanon Thamnimit; the trip takes about 15 minutes. Or you can charter a boat from Tha Talat Mae Klong, a scenic journey that takes about 45 minutes.

Wat Satthatham, 500m along the road to Don Hoi Lot, is notable for its bòt constructed of golden teak and decorated with 60 million baht worth of mother-of-pearl inlay. The inlay covers the temple's interior and depicts scenes from jataka (stories of the Buddha's past lives) above the windows and the *Ramakian* (the Thai version of the Indian classic, *Ramayana*) below.

King Buddhalertla Naphalai Memorial Park, a 10-minute walk from Talat Nam Amphawa, is a **museum** housed in traditional central-Thai houses set on two hectares. Dedicated to King Rama II, a native of Amphawa district, the museum contains a library of rare Thai books, antiques from early 19th-century Siam and an exhibition of dolls depicting four of Rama II's theatrical works (*Inao, Mani Phichai,* a version of the *Ramakian* and *Sang Thong*). Behind the houses is a lush botanic garden and beyond that is a dramatic-arts training hall. To get there from Talat Nam Amphawa, walk over the bridge and follow the road through the gardens of Wat Amphawan Chetiyaram. The park is open 9 am to 6 pm daily, while the museum is open 9 am to 4 pm Wednesday to Sunday; admission is 10B.

Ban Benjarong (☎ 034-751322) is a small factory in a modern house that produces top-quality benjarong, the traditional five-coloured Thai ceramics. Here you can watch craftsmen painting the intricate arabesques and ornate floral patterns for which benjarong is known. This isn't the glossy stuff you see at Chatuchak Market in Bangkok, but rather the real thing; prices start at about 1000B. A showroom, open 8 am to 10.30 pm daily, displays the many styles produced here. Ban Benjarong is only about 1km from Phuttha Loet La, but it's better to take a 10B motorcycle taxi from there as it's easy to get lost.

Another local attraction is the **Orchid Farm**, which is 4km north of Samut Songkhram on the road to Damnoen Saduak. Despite its commercial and tourism functions, it is really quite impressive for the colour of its orchids. A bus (5B, 10 minutes) goes to the farm.

Some of the most picturesque countryside this close to Bangkok lies along Rte 325 between Damnoen Saduak and Samut Songkhram. Coconut plantations interspersed with small wooden houses line the road and add to the tropical-pastoral atmosphere.

Floating Markets Samut Songkhram Province is crisscrossed with canals intersecting the lazy bends of Mae Nam Mae Klong, creating the perfect environment for traditional Thai floating markets. Three of the better ones are held in Amphawa district, about 7km north-west of Samut Songkhram city via Mae Nam Mae Klong. **Talat Nam Amphawa** convenes in front of Wat Amphawan from 6 to 8 am daily, but is best on weekends. The other two meet only on weekends and on six days a month following the traditional lunar calendar: **Bang Noi floating market** takes place in nearby Bang Noi from 6 to 11 am on the third, eighth and 13th days of both the waxing and waning moons, while the **Tha Kha floating market** meets on the second, seventh and 12th days of the waxing and waning moons. The latter convenes along an open, breezy khlawng lined with greenery and older wooden houses – well worth seeking out.

For most travellers it's easiest to visit on the weekends, but if you want to try to catch the floating market on one of the traditional lunar dates (and thus avoid the tourist crowds), it's not as difficult as you might imagine. Any common Thai calendar, available for a few baht in a homewares market, will show you which days of the solar month coincide with this lunar schedule. These floating markets can be visited by chartered long-tail boat from Ta Talat Mae Klong – figure on 150B to 200B per hour, 300B for all morning.

Getting There & Away

Bus Buses and taxis park at the intersection of Thanon Ratchayat Raksa and Thanon Prasitphatthana. Buses from Bangkok's Southern bus terminal to Damnoen Saduak also stop here, but some buses from Bangkok may drop you off on the main highway, from where you can either walk or take a săamláw or a săwngthăew (5B). Buses to Bangkok (35B ordinary, 55B aircon, 1½ hours) leave from the Damnoen Tour office next to Bangkok Bank. There are also many daily buses to Samut Sakhon (14B, one hour).

Train Samut Songkhram is the southernmost terminus of a 70km railway that originates at Wong Wian Yai station (Thonburi). The all-3rd-class train to/from Bangkok (20B, one hour) departs four times per day (see the Samut Sakhon Getting There & Away section for Bangkok departure times). From Samut Songkhram trains depart at 6.20, 9 and 11.30 am and 3.30 pm. The train station is a five-minute walk from the bus station, where Thanon Kasem Sukhum terminates at Thanon Prasitphatthana, near the river.

SAMUT PRAKAN
อ.เมืองสมุทรปราการ

postcode 10270 • pop 73,600
This small province lies at the mouth of Mae Nam Chao Phraya where it empties into the Gulf of Thailand just 30km south of Bangkok. The city's name means 'Ocean Wall', a reference to the 1893-vintage **Phra Chula Jawm Klao Fort**, 7km south of the provincial hall. Today it's one of Thailand's most densely populated provincial capitals, with over 70,000 people packed into 7.3 sq km.

The province's two major attractions, Ancient City and the Crocodile Farm, are popular day trips from Bangkok. In fact, Samut Prakan is best visited as a day trip – overnight it differs little from spending the night in Bangkok.

Ancient City
เมืองโบราณ

Billed as the largest open-air museum in the world, the Ancient City (Muang Boran) covers more than 80 hectares and presents 109 scaled-down facsimiles of many of the kingdom's most famous monuments. The grounds have been shaped to replicate Thailand's general geographical outline, with the monuments placed accordingly. The main entrance places visitors at the country's southern tip, from where you work your way to the 'northernmost' monuments. A sculpture garden focusing on episodes from the *Ramakian* can also be seen on the premises. For students of Thai architecture or those who won't be able to tour the real thing, it's worth a day's visit (it takes an entire day to cover the area). It's also a good place for long, undistracted walks, as it's usually quiet and never crowded. Fans of *jàk-jàk wong-wong,* the camp, made-for-TV renditions of classical Thai legends that air alongside the cartoons on Saturday morning, will recognise the monuments of Ancient City as they're frequently used as a backdrop for filming. A new zone, occupying almost half as much space as the older zone, contains nine new sites, including replicas of Bangkok's Sao Ching-Cha (Giant Swing), Phra Sumen Mount and a canal with a stationary display of the Royal Barge procession, plus lots of open space for picnics. You can buy noodles and other snacks from boat vendors paddling along the canal.

The Ancient City Co (☎ 226 1936, fax 226 1227) also publishes a lavish bilingual periodical devoted to Thai art and architecture called *Muang Boran.* The journal is edited by some of Thailand's leading art historians.

Ancient City (☎ 323 9253) is 33km from Bangkok along the Old Sukhumvit Hwy. Opening hours are from 8 am to 5 pm; admission to the site is 50B for adults and 25B for children. Public bus No 25 (3.50B) or air-con bus Nos 7, 8 and 11 (12B to 16B) to the Samut Prakan station can take up to two hours depending on traffic; from the station take minibus No 36 (5B), which passes the entrance to Ancient City. Transport can also be arranged through the Bangkok office (☎ 224 1057), 78/1 Democracy Monument Circle, Thanon Ratchadamnoen Klang.

Samut Prakan Crocodile Farm & Zoo
ฟาร์มจระเข้สมุทรปราการ

In the same area as the Ancient City is Samut Prakan Crocodile Farm & Zoo (☎ 387 0020), where you can even see crocodile wrestling! There are over 30,000 crocs here (including the largest known Siamese croc, a boy named Yai who's 6m long and weighs 1114kg), as well as elephants, monkeys and snakes. Many crocs escaped during tempestuous floods in 1995.

The farm is open from 7 am to 6 pm daily with trained-animal shows – including croc wrestling – every hour between 9 and 11 am and 1 and 4 pm daily. Elephant shows take place at 9.30 and 11.30 am, while the reptiles usually get their dinner between 4 and 5 pm. Admission is a steep 300B for adults and 200B for children (50/30B for Thais).

Convention on International Trade in Endangered Species (CITES) certified items – handbags, belts, shoes – made from crocodile hide are available from the farm's gift shop. You can reach the crocodile farm via air-con bus Nos 7, 8 and 11, changing to sǎwngthǎew Nos S1 to S80.

Other Attractions
The Ayuthaya-era **Phra Samut Chedi**, popularly known as Phra Chedi Klang Nam (Chedi in the Middle of the River) for its original location on an island in Mae Nam Chao Phraya, now sits on the river bank in front of the Provincial Hall. Beginning on the fifth day of the waning moon in the 11th lunar month each year (usually in October), the chedi is the site of a nine-day festival with lots of food, music and lights.

The port area of the city, **Pak Nam**, is worth a visit for those interested in international ports. Samut Prakan as a whole is commonly referred to as Meuang Pak Nam.

Places to Eat
The *Pak Nam market* is a good place for cheap food all- day long. At 19/17–18 Thanon Naraiprapsuk, *Wall's* ice-cream restaurant has decent Thai food.

Bang Pu Seaside Resort, a landscaped garden restaurant in nearby Bang Pu Mai district (10km south-east of Samut Prakan via Hwy 3), is a local favourite for long, leisurely meals.

Getting There & Away

Ordinary bus No 25 (3.50B) and air-con bus Nos 7, 8 and 11 (16B) ply regular routes between central Bangkok and Pak Nam. The trip can take up to two hours depending on traffic.

Getting Around

The bus station is located on Thanon Srisamut in front of the harbour and the market. Săwngthăew depart from the market area to Ancient City and the Crocodile Farm for 5B each. To get from the Crocodile Farm to Ancient City, turn right from the farm and walk 10 minutes to Thanon Sukhumvit, or catch a săwngthăew or a motorcycle taxi. On Thanon Sukhumvit, hail a săwngthăew or a minibus (5B); it should take about 10 minutes to get to Ancient City.

Central Thailand

Twenty-four provinces make up Central Thailand, stretching north to Lopburi, south to Prachuap Khiri Khan, west to Kanchanaburi and east to Trat. The rain-fed network of rivers and canals in the central region makes this the most fertile part of Thailand, supporting vast fields of rice, sugar cane, pineapples and other fruit, and cassava.

The people of Central Thailand share a common dialect that is considered 'standard' Thai simply because Bangkok, the seat of power, happens to be in the middle of the region. High concentrations of Chinese are found throughout the central provinces since this is where a large number of Chinese immigrants started out as farmers and merchants. Significant numbers of Mon and Burmese live to the west, and Lao and Khmer to the east due to immigration from bordering lands over hundreds of years.

Ayuthaya Province

AYUTHAYA
พระนครศรีอยุธยา

postcode 13000 • pop 62,100
Approximately 86km north of Bangkok, Ayuthaya served as the Siamese royal capital from 1350 to 1767 and by all accounts it was a splendid city. Prior to 1350, when the capital moved here from U Thong, it was a Khmer outpost. The city was named after Ayodhya (Sanskrit for 'unassailable' or 'undefeatable'), the home of Rama in the Indian epic *Ramayana*. Its full Thai name is Phra Nakhon Si Ayuthaya (Sacred City of Ayodhya).

Although the Sukhothai period is often referred to as Thailand's 'golden age', in many ways the Ayuthaya era was the kingdom's true historical apex – at least in terms of sovereignty, which extended well into present-day Laos, Cambodia and Myanmar (Burma), dynastic endurance (over 400 years) and world recognition. Thirty-three kings of various Siamese dynasties reigned in Ayuthaya until it was conquered by the Burmese. During its heyday, Thai culture

| **Highlights** |

- Ayuthaya Historical Park – World Heritage–listed ruins of a former royal capital
- Ko Samet, Pattaya, Cha-am & Hua Hin – popular beach resorts close to Bangkok
- Kanchanaburi – forests, waterfalls, national parks and the WWII monuments at the River Kwai bridge and Hellfire Pass
- Ko Chang National Marine Park – remote islands offering rainforest tracts, waterfalls, coastal walks, diving and coral reefs
- Three Pagodas Pass – frontier outpost town
- Trat & Aranya Prathet – gem trading on the Cambodian border

and international commerce flourished in the kingdom and Ayuthaya was courted by Dutch, Portuguese, French, English, Chinese and Japanese merchants. By the end of the 17th century Ayuthaya's population had reached one million – virtually all foreign visitors claimed it to be the most illustrious city they had ever seen.

Nowadays Ayuthaya makes a pleasant and convenient escape from Bangkok, especially during the Loi Krathong festival, held

CENTRAL THAILAND

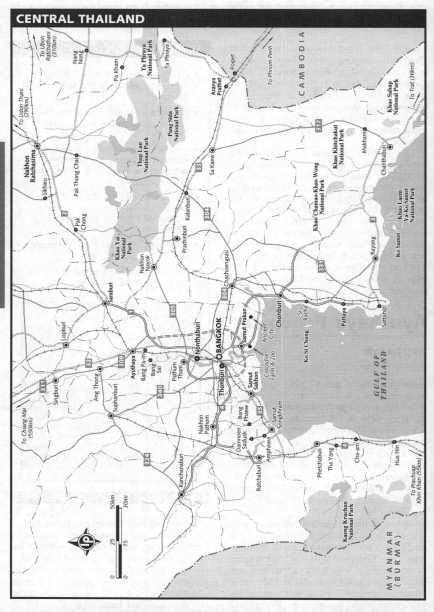

on the full moon of the 12th lunar month. Although celebrations are held at several places around town, the largest spectacle takes place at Beung Phra Ram, the large lake in the centre of the city between Wat Phra Ram and Wat Phra Mahathat. Thousands of Thais, many of them from Bangkok, flock to the event. Several outdoor stages offer a variety of entertainment, from Thai pop bands to *lí-keh* (folk dance-drama). Fireworks are also a big part of the show. A more low-key and traditional celebration takes place at Tha Chan Kasem pier, where families gather to launch their *kràthong* (small lotus-shaped floats topped with incense, flowers and candles) onto the river.

For information about visiting ancient Ayuthaya's significant sites, see the Ayuthaya Historical Park special section later in this chapter.

Orientation & Information

The present-day city is located at the confluence of three rivers *(mâe náam)*: Mae Nam Chao Phraya, Mae Nam Pa Sak and the smaller Mae Nam Lopburi. A wide canal joins them and makes a complete circle around the town. Long-tail boats *(reua hǎang yao)* can be rented from the boat landing across from Chan Kasem Palace for a tour around the river; several of the old *wát* (temple) ruins (Wat Phanan Choeng, Wat Phutthaisawan, Wat Kasatthirat and Wat Chai Wattanaram) may be glimpsed from the canal, along with picturesque views of river life.

Tourist Offices The Tourist Authority of Thailand (TAT; ☎ 035-246076, 01-239 8616) has an office next to the tourist police office (☎ 035-241446, 1155) on Thanon Si Sanphet (Si Sanphet Rd). It's open from 8 am to 4.30 pm daily.

Post & Communications The post office is open from 8.30 am to 4.30 pm weekdays and 9 am to noon Saturday. An international-cardphone and overseas-phone service upstairs in the post office is open from 8 am to 8 pm daily.

National Museums

There are two museums; the main one is the **Chao Sam Phraya National Museum**, which is near the intersection of Thanon Rotchana (the city centre's main street, connecting with the highway to Bangkok) and Thanon Si Sanphet, near the centre of town. It features a basic roundup of Thai Buddhist sculpture with an emphasis on Ayuthaya pieces. A selection of books on Thai art and archaeology are on sale at the ticket kiosk. The museum is open 9 am to 4 pm Wednesday to Sunday; the admission cost is 30B.

The second museum building, **Chantharakasem National Museum** (Chan Kasem Palace or Phra Ratchawang Chan Kasem), is a museum piece in itself, built by the 17th king of Ayuthaya, Maha Thammaracha, for his son Prince Naresuan, who later became one of Ayuthaya's greatest kings. Among the exhibits is a collection of gold treasures from Wat Phra Mahathat and Wat Ratburana. Chan Kasem Palace is in the north-east corner of town, near the river. Hours are 9 am to noon and 1 to 4 pm Wednesday to Sunday; entry here is also 30B.

Ayuthaya Historical Study Centre
ศูนย์ศึกษาประวัติศาสตร์อยุธยา

Funded by the Japanese government, the US$6.8 million Ayuthaya Historical Study Centre (☎ 035-245124) is near the Chao Sam Phraya National Museum. There are actually two buildings, the main one on Thanon Rotchana and an annexe just south of Wat Phanan Choeng on the south bank of the Mae Nam Pa Sak and Mae Nam Chao Phraya junction, in a district that housed a Japanese community during Ayuthaya's heyday. The hi-tech exhibit area in the main building covers five aspects of Ayuthaya's history: city development, port, administration, lifestyles and traditions. The annexe contains an exhibit on foreign relations with Ayuthaya.

The centre is open 9 am to 4.30 pm weekdays, 9 am to 5 pm weekends. Admission to both costs 100B, 50B for students.

Elephant Kraal
เพนียดคล้องช้าง

This is a restored version of the wooden stockade once used for the annual roundup of wild elephants. A huge fence of teak logs planted in the ground at 45-degree angles kept the elephants in; the king had a special raised pavilion from which to observe the thrilling event.

Places to Stay – Budget

Hostels & Guesthouses For budgeters, there are several guesthouses and one hostel in Ayuthaya to choose from. All rent out bicycles for around 50B per day. Several are on or off Thanon Naresuan, not far from the bus station. As elsewhere in Thailand, *săamláw* (three-wheeled pedicab; also written samlor) and *túk-túk* (motorised săamláw) drivers will tell you anything to steer you towards guesthouses that pay commissions (up to 35B per head in this city).

PU Guest House (☎ 035-251213, *20/1 Soi Thaw Kaw Saw*) is a relatively new place with two floors of clean rooms for 140B. Shared bathrooms are outside in a separate building. The friendly owner speaks English and Japanese. Cheap food and drink is available and there are bicycles/motorbikes for rent for 50/250B per day.

Just around the corner, the *TMT Guest House* (☎ 035-251474) has small but clean singles/doubles for 100/140B. The place also has a small restaurant and is popular with Japanese travellers.

Almost directly across the river from the train station in an 80-year-old teak house is the *Reuan Doem* (☎ 035-241978, *48/2 Thanon U Thong*), formerly known as Ayuthaya Youth Hostel. Rustic and atmospheric rooms with ceiling fans and shared bathroom cost 250B. A very good floating restaurant extends from the river side of the house; it is open from 10 am to 11 pm. If you can put up with some ambient noise from the restaurant, it's not a bad choice.

Phaesri Thong Guest House (☎ 035-246010, *8/1 Thanon U Thong*), near Wat Suwan Dararam on the river, is a spotless place with a common balcony sitting area on every level. The top floor has a huge room with dorm beds for 200B per night, while the 1st and 2nd floors offer spacious private rooms with air-con, TV and private bathroom for 500B to 600B. The breezy indoor/outdoor restaurant that overlooks the river offers Thai and *fàràng* (Western) food. Owner Noi speaks English, and the guesthouse has a boat that can be chartered for tours around Ayuthaya for 150B per person.

Near the end of a *soi* (lane) off Thanon Naresuan (not far from the Ayuthaya Hotel; see Places to Stay – Mid-Range later), *Ayuthaya Guest House* (☎ 035-232658) charges 120/160B for singles/doubles in a

house. Next door is *Toto Guest House* (☎ 035-251468), which offers similar fan rooms for 100B to 140B, 500B for air-con and TV. Next to that, a branch of the same family runs the *BJ1 Guest House* (☎ 035-251526), at 100/140B for fan rooms. All three offer minimal food service.

Another BJ relative operates the *New BJ Guest House* (☎ 035-244046, *19/29 Thanon Naresuan*). Fan rooms cost 120/150B, dorm beds 60B. There's a simple dining area out front. One drawback is the traffic noise, as it's right on Thanon Naresuan.

On a back road parallel to Thanon Naresuan and off Thanon Chee Kun, is the hospitable *PS Guest House*, in a two-storey house. Fan and air-con rooms (with shared bathroom) cost 150B and 250B. Home-cooked meals, including vegetarian food, are served on request. Students of the former teacher who operates the guesthouse perform classical Thai dance on Friday evening. At full-moon, boat trips to view the ruins by moonlight are offered for 100B per person.

Hotels Two standard Thai-Chinese–style hotels at the junction of Mae Nam Lopburi and Mae Nam Pa Sak have been accommodating Ayuthaya visitors for over two decades now, and it shows. Both places are pretty run-down. The *U-Thong Hotel* (☎ 035-251136), on Thanon U Thong near Hua Raw Night Market and Chan Kasem Palace, has adequate singles/doubles with fan for 300/370B and with air-con, TV and hot-water shower for 380/450B. A little southeast of the U Thong Hotel, the *Cathay Hotel* (☎ 035-251562, *36/5–6 Thanon U Thong*) charges 150/270B for rather dirty one/two-bed rooms with fan, 300B for a single/double with air-con. Both hotels back up to the river. The U-Thong is the better choice.

Places to Stay – Mid-Range & Top End

The *Wieng Fa Hotel* (☎ 035-241353, *1/8 Thanon Rotchana*) is a friendly, cosy, two-storey place with clean, relatively quiet rooms around a garden courtyard for 450B to 500B. All rooms come with TV, fridge and air-con; English is spoken.

Suan Luang Hotel (Royal Garden; ☎*/fax 035-245537)* is a five-storey hotel beside the Ayuthaya Historical Study Centre. Decent air-con rooms with fridge and TV cost

The Ruins Revival

When Settasak Akanimart moved to Ayuthaya as a child of three, the historic city was undergoing rapid change. The Thai Fine Arts Department had begun restoring temples of brick and stucco that had laid half hidden for over two centuries. Ruins that had long been choked with vines or buried under layers of soil were being cleared and excavated.

'I came to Ayuthaya from Roi Et with my parents, both of whom were civil servants', said Mr Settasak, who now lives in Bangkok and works for the United Nations High Commissioner for Refugees. 'Ayuthaya was much quieter back then and life was slower'.

When restoration work was first initiated, local attitudes towards the ruins were varied. 'Most people didn't think much about the ruins. You saw them every day and they were just another part of the landscape. Other people avoided the ruins – maybe they were afraid that the spirits of people killed when the old city was destroyed still haunted those areas'.

With the economic boom that came in the '80s, the process of restoration was accelerated. Guidelines and support from United Nations Educational, Scientific and Cultural Organization (Unesco) helped to ensure that historic areas were preserved without being commercialised. For the first time since before it was sacked by marauding Burmese, visitors are again looking upon old Ayuthaya with admiration. Still, for some westerners with preconceived ideas of what South-East Asia's past should look like, the restored version might lack romance: Far from being lost cities in the jungle, Thailand's ancient ruins now resemble parks with well-tended lawns and convenient walkways.

Yet if it weren't for the work of the Fine Arts Department, much of what has been preserved might have been lost forever. Before restoration work began, treasure hunters were drawn to old *chedi* (stupas) in search of small Buddha images and other relics of gold and silver said to be cached within. Sometimes this activity would reduce the old stupas to rubble. 'Thieves would dig into the chedi at night and if they found anything of value, it was sold to dealers. Nowadays the ruins are guarded and there is no way thieves can dig without being noticed'.

Of course this has not put a stop to the illicit antiquities trade. The same kind of thing still goes on, only now the dealers are trading in antiquities from Cambodia or Burma – where efforts at restoration and preservation are hampered by corruption and a lack of funds.

While Mr Settasak is not a native of Ayuthaya in the strictest sense, some locals believe that having grown up there is proof of a link to the city's past. 'The old people like to say that anyone who lived in Ayuthaya in a past life will always make their way back to Ayuthaya during successive lives – even if they are born far away from the sacred city'.

a moderate 500B; a couple of six-bed aircon rooms are available for 600B. All rooms have cold-water showers and TV.

My House (☎ 035-335493, fax 335494), on Thanon Rotchana out towards Ratchathani Hospital, has decent rooms with fan for 420B; the isolated location is a definite drawback.

The *Ayothaya Hotel* (☎ 035-232855, fax 251018, 12 Soi 2, Thanon Thetsaban), formerly the Sri Smai Hotel and just off Thanon Naresuan, is a more upmarket place that charges 900B for singles/doubles with air-con, bathroom, fridge and cable TV. There is also a swimming pool.

Moving towards the top end, the *U-Thong Inn* (☎ 035-242236, fax 242235) offers comfortable air-con rooms in the old wing for 1200B, while in the newer wing rooms with separate sitting areas go for 1400B. The new wing is better value. Facilities include a pool, sauna and massage room. Discounts of up to 45% are given in the low season. It's out on Thanon Rotchana past the turn-off for the train station. The six-storey *Ayuthaya Grand Hotel* (☎ 035-335483, fax 335492, 55/5 Thanon Rotchana), out beyond U-Thong Inn, features rooms with all the mod cons for 1200B to 1500B (900B to 1200B during the low season).

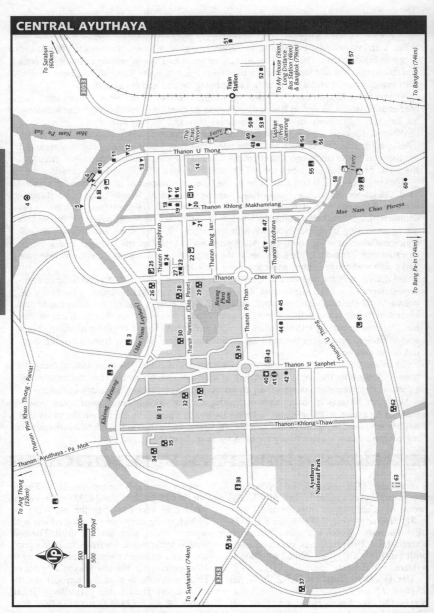

CENTRAL AYUTHAYA

CENTRAL AYUTHAYA

PLACES TO STAY
10 U-Thong Hotel
11 Cathay Hotel
16 Ayothaya Hotel
18 Ayuthaya Guest House; Toto
   Guest House; BJ1 Guest
   House; PU Guest House
19 TMT Guest House; Good
   Luck Restaurant
23 New BJ Guest House
24 PS Guest House
44 Suan Luang (Royal Garden)
   Hotel
47 Wieng Fa Hotel
48 Reuan Doem
50 Tevaraj Tanrin Hotel
51 Ayuthaya Grand Hotel
52 U-Thong Inn
53 Krungsri River Hotel
54 Phaesri Thong Guest House

PLACES TO EAT
5 Hua Raw Night Market
7 Night Market
12 Chainam
13 Rodeo

14 Chao Phrom Market
17 Moon Cafe; Sun Cafe
20 Duangporn
21 Vegetarian Restaurant
27 Malakor
46 Moradok-Thai
49 Floating Restaurants
56 Phae Krung Kao

OTHER
1 Phu Khao Thong Temple
   (Golden Mount Chedi)
2 Wat Phra Meru
3 Wat Kuti Thong
4 Elephant Kraal
6 Pier (Boat Landing)
8 Chan Kasem Palace
9 Main Post Office
15 Bus Station
22 Air-Con Minivans
   to Bangkok
25 Chinese Shrine
26 Wat Suwannawat
28 Wat Ratburana
29 Wat Phra Mahathat
30 Wat Thammikarat

31 Wat Mongkhon Bophit
32 Wat Phra Si Sanphet
33 Royal Palace
34 Wat Chetharam
35 Wat Lokaya Sutha
36 Wat Kasatthirat
37 Wat Chai Wattanaram
38 Queen Suriyothai Memorial
   Pagoda
39 Wat Phra Ram
40 Tourist Police
41 TAT Office
42 City Hall
43 Chao Sam Phraya National
   Museum
45 Ayuthaya Historical Study
   Centre
55 Wat Suwan Dararam
57 Wat Yai Chai Mongkhon
58 Phom Phet Fortress
59 Wat Phanan Choeng
60 Ayuthaya Historical Study
   Centre (Annexe)
61 Mosque
62 Wat Phutthaisawan
63 St Joseph's Cathedral

Ayuthaya's flashiest digs are the nine-storey *Krungsri River Hotel* (☎ 035-244333, fax 243777, 27/2 Thanon Rotchana), where decked-out rooms cost 1650B to 2000B, suites 5000B to 10,000B. Facilities include a pub/coffee house, Chinese restaurant, beer garden, fitness centre, pool, bowling alley and snooker club.

Next door to the Krungsri, the 102-room *Tevaraj Tanrin Hotel* (☎ 035-234873, fax 244139) has similar singles/doubles with river views starting at 1200B, including breakfast. It has a floating restaurant and beer garden.

Places to Eat

The most dependable and least expensive places to eat are the *Hua Raw Night Market*, on the river near Chan Kasem Palace, and the *Chao Phrom Market*, opposite the ferry piers along the eastern side of the island. The *Chainam,* a restaurant near Chan Kasem Palace and next to the U-Thong Hotel, has tables on the river, a bilingual menu and friendly service; it's also open for breakfast.

The *Malakor*, on Thanon Chee Kun opposite Wat Ratburana, is located in a two-storey wooden house with a charming view of the temple and has good, cheap Thai dishes in the 35B to 50B range, plus an excellent selection of coffees.

Next to the TMT Guest House is *Good Luck*, an open-air restaurant under some shady mango trees. Prices range from 40B to 60B per dish for Thai and fàràng food and the portions are generous.

The *Moon Cafe* and *Sun Cafe*, tiny spots on the same soi, serve Thai and fàràng snacks for 60B to 80B per dish. *Duangporn,* on Thanon Naresuan near the main bus station, is an indoor air-con place with Thai and Chinese food for 70B to 180B. A better choice is the *vegetarian restaurant* around the corner from the Duangporn on the opposite side of the canal.

Quite a few restaurants can be found on Thanon Rotchana including *Moradok-Thai*, a Thai food establishment that is very popular with Thai tourists. Dishes cost 60B to 120B and there is a selection of wines. It's a good place to soak up the air-con after touring the ruins.

There are four *floating restaurants* on Mae Nam Pa Sak, three on either side of Saphan Pridi Damrong (Pridi Damrong Bridge) on the west bank, and one on the east bank north of the bridge. Of these, the *Phae Krung Kao* – on the southern side of the bridge on the west bank – has the better reputation; it opens from 10 am to 2 am. North of the bridge on the west bank, *Ruenpae* is similar. The floating *Reuan Doem*, on the river behind the guesthouse of the same name, is also quite good and has the most intimate atmosphere of the riverside places.

In the evenings a very choice *night market* comes to life near the pier *(thâa)* opposite Chan Kasem Palace. Quite a few of the vendors sell Thai-Muslim dishes – look for the green crescent and star on the signs.

For entertainment with your food, try the air-con *Rodeo* on Thanon U Thong. Despite the name and old-west decor, the food is mostly Thai cocktail snacks (an English menu is available); it's only open at night, when a small band plays Thai and international folk music.

Getting There & Away

Bus Ordinary buses run between the Northern and North-Eastern bus station in Bangkok and Ayuthaya's main station on Thanon Naresuan (34B, two hours) every 20 minutes between 5 am and 7 pm. Air-con buses operate along the same route every 20 minutes from 5.40 am to 7.20 pm (47B); the trip takes 1½ hours when traffic north of Bangkok is light, two hours otherwise. Across the street from the New BJ Guest House is a minivan service to Bangkok that runs every 20 minutes from 4 am to 5 pm for 40B.

If you're arriving by bus from some place other than Bangkok or cities nearby, you may be dropped off at the long-distance bus station, 5km east of Saphan Pridi Damrong at the Hwy 32 junction.

Sǎwngthǎew (pick-up trucks used as buses or taxis; also written *songthaew*) to/from Bang Pa-In leave from the bus station on Thanon Naresuan and cost 10B; Bang Pa-In is about 45 minutes away.

Train Trains to Ayuthaya leave Hualamphong station every hour or so between 4.20 am and 10.10 pm. The 3rd-class fare is 15B for the 1½-hour trip; it's hardly worth taking a more expensive class for this short trip. Train schedules are available from the information booth at Hualamphong station.

From Ayuthaya's train station, the quickest way to reach the old city is to walk west to the river, where you can take a short ferry ride across for 1B.

Upon arrival at Bangkok International Airport, savvy repeat visitors to Thailand sometimes choose to board a northbound train direct to Ayuthaya rather than head south into the Bangkok maelstrom. This only works if you arrive by air during the day or early evening, as the last train to Ayuthaya leaves Bangkok's Hualamphong train station at 10.10 pm. There are frequent 3rd-class trains throughout the day between Don Muang station (opposite Bangkok International Airport) and Ayuthaya.

Boat There are no scheduled or chartered boat services between Bangkok and Ayuthaya.

Several companies in Bangkok operate luxury cruises to Bang Pa-In with side trips by bus to Ayuthaya for around 1600B to 1900B per person, including a lavish luncheon. Longer two-day trips in converted rice barges start at 6200B. See River & Canal Trips in the Bangkok chapter for more details.

Getting Around

Sǎwngthǎew and shared túk-túk ply the main city roads for 5B to 10B per person depending on distance. A túk-túk from the train station to any point in old Ayuthaya should cost around 30B; on the island itself figure no more than 20B per trip.

For touring the ruins, your most economical and ecological option is to rent a bicycle from one of the guesthouses (about 50B a day) or walk. You can hire a sǎamláw, túk-túk or sǎwngthǎew by the hour or by the day to explore the ruins, but the prices are quite high by Thai standards (200B per hour for anything with a motor in it, 500B all day when things are slow). Many drivers ask upwards of 700B for a day's worth of sightseeing – it would be much less expensive simply to take separate rides from site to site.

It's also interesting to hire a boat from Tha Chan Kasem to do a semicircular tour of the island and see some of the less accessible ruins. A long-tail boat that will take up to eight people can be hired for 400B for a two- to three-hour trip with stops at Wat Phutthaisawan, Wat Phanan Choeng and Wat Chai Wattanaram. Or, if you happen to be in town during the full moon, check out the ruins by moonlight on boat tours arranged by PS Guest House.

AROUND AYUTHAYA
Bang Pa-In
บางปะอิน

Twenty kilometres south of Ayuthaya is Bang Pa-In, which has a curious collection of **palace buildings** in a wide variety of architectural styles. It's a nice boat trip from Bangkok if you're taking one of the cruise tours, although in itself it's not particularly noteworthy. The palace is open from 8.30 am to 3.30 pm daily. Admission is 50B.

The postcard stereotype here is a pretty little **Thai pavilion** in the centre of a small lake by the palace entrance. Inside the palace grounds, the Chinese-style **Wehat Chamrun Palace** and the **Withun Thatsana** building, which looks like a lighthouse with balconies, are the only buildings open to visitors. The latter was built to give a fine view over gardens and lakes. There are various other buildings, towers and memorials in the grounds plus an interesting topiary garden where the bushes have been trimmed into the shape of a small herd of elephants.

Wat Niwet Thamaprawat, across the river and south from the palace grounds, is an unusual wát that looks much more like a Gothic Christian church than anything from Thailand. Like Bang Pa-In, it was built by Rama V (Chulalongkorn). You get to the wát by crossing the river in a small trolley-like cable car. The crossing is free.

Getting There & Away Bang Pa-In can be reached by minibus (it's really a large săwngthăew; 10B, 45 minutes), which departs around the corner from Ayuthaya's Chao Phrom Market on Thanon Naresuan. From Bangkok there are buses every half-hour or so from the Northern and North-Eastern bus terminal (23B ordinary, 34B air-con). You can also reach Bang Pa-In by train from Bangkok (12B 3rd class).

The Chao Phraya River Express Boat Co does a tour every Sunday from Tha Maharat in Bangkok. The tour goes to Wat Phailom in Pathum Thani province as well as Bang Pa-In and Bang Sai's Royal Folk Arts & Crafts Centre. It leaves Bangkok at 8 am and returns at 5.30 pm. The price is 300B not including lunch, which you arrange in Bang Pa-In. For more expensive river cruises to Bang Pa-In, which include tours of old Ayuthaya, see River & Canal Trips in the Bangkok chapter.

Bang Sai Royal Folk Arts & Crafts Centre
ศูนย์ศิลปาชีพบางไทร

This 115-hectare facility in Beung Yai, Bang Sai district, is an important training centre for artisans. Under the auspices of Queen Sirikit's Promotion of Supplementary Occupations & Related Techniques (SUPPORT) foundation, handicraft experts teach craft techniques to novices while at the same time demonstrating them for visitors.

The centre is open 8.30 am to 5 pm weekdays, to 7 pm weekends (craft demonstrations daily except Monday); admission is 50B. Call ☎ 035-366092 for information.

The Loi Krathong festival here is considered one of the more traditional versions in Central Thailand and some years there is also a festival during Songkran.

Lopburi Province

LOPBURI
อ.เมืองลพบุรี

postcode 15000 • pop 41,200

The town of Lopburi, 154km north of Bangkok, has been inhabited since at least the Dvaravati period (6th to 11th centuries AD), when it was called Lavo. Nearly all traces of Lavo culture were erased by Khmer and Thai inhabitants following the 10th century, but the Lopburi National Museum has many Dvaravati artefacts. Ruins and statuary in Lopburi span a remarkable 12 centuries.

The Angkor empire was extended to include Lavo in the 10th century, when the Prang Khaek (Hindu Shrine), San Phra Kan (Kala Shrine) and Prang Sam Yot (Three Spired Shrine) were built, as well as the impressive *prang* (Khmer-style tower or temple) at Wat Phra Si Ratana Mahathat.

Power over Lopburi was wrested from the Khmers in the 13th century as the Sukhothai kingdom to the north grew stronger, but the Khmer cultural influence remained to some extent throughout the Ayuthaya period. King Narai fortified Lopburi in the mid-17th century to serve as a second capital when the kingdom of Ayuthaya was threatened by a Dutch naval blockade. His palace in Lopburi was built in 1665 and he died there in 1688.

CENTRAL THAILAND

LOPBURI

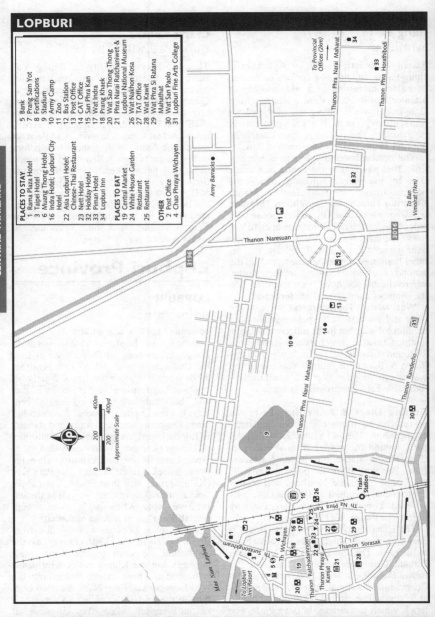

PLACES TO STAY
1 Rama Plaza Hotel
3 Taipei Hotel
6 Muang Thong Hotel
16 Indra Hotel; Lopburi City Hotel
22 Asia Lopburi Hotel; Chinese-Thai Restaurant
23 Nett Hotel
32 Holiday Hotel
33 Piman Hotel
34 Lopburi Inn

PLACES TO EAT
19 Central Market
24 White House Garden Restaurant
25 Restaurant

OTHER
2 Post Office
4 Chao Phraya Wichayen
5 Bank
7 Prang Sam Yot
8 Fortifications
9 Stadium
10 Army Camp
11 Zoo
12 Bus Station
13 Post Office
14 CAT Office
15 San Phra Kan
17 Wat Indra
18 Prang Khaek
20 Wat Sao Thong Thong
21 Phra Narai Ratchaniwet & Lopburi National Museum
26 Wat Nakhon Kosa
27 TAT Office
28 Wat Kawit
29 Wat Phra Si Ratana Mahathat
30 Wat San Paolo
31 Lopburi Fine Arts College

CENTRAL THAILAND

Orientation & Information

The new town of Lopburi dates to around 1940. It is some distance east of the old fortified town and is centred on two large roundabouts. There is really nothing of interest in the new section, so try to stay at a hotel in the old town if you're interested in the palace and temple ruins. All the historical sites in Lopburi can be visited on foot in a day or two.

Tourist Offices There's a TAT office (☎ 036-422768/9, 01-456 4151) on Thanon Phraya Kamjat opposite the White House Garden Restaurant. The staff distribute the usual brochures and can be helpful with advice about your visit.

Post & Communications The Communications Authority of Thailand (CAT) office is located next to the post office on Thanon Phra Narai Maharat, towards the new city, and is open from 8 am to 6 pm. The office has a Home Country Direct phone.

Phra Narai Ratchaniwet
พระนารายณ์ราชนิเวศน์

King Narai's palace is probably the best place to begin a tour of Lopburi. After King Narai's death in 1688, the palace was used only by King Phetracha (Narai's successor) for his coronation ceremony and was then abandoned until King Mongkut ordered restoration in the mid-19th century.

The palace took 12 years to build (1665–77) and French architects contributed to the design. Khmer influence was still strong in Central Thailand at that time so it's not surprising that the palace exhibits an unusual blend of Khmer and European styles.

The main gate into the palace, **Pratu Phayakkha**, is off Thanon Sorasak, opposite the Asia Lopburi Hotel. The grounds are well kept, planted with trees and shrubbery, and serve as a kind of town park for local children and young lovers.

Immediately on the left as you enter are the remains of the king's elephant stables, with the palace reservoir in the foreground. In the quadrangle to the left is the royal reception hall and the **Phra Chao Hao**, which probably served as a *wíhǎan* (hall) for a valued Buddha image. Passing through more stables, you come to the south-west quadrangle with the **Suttha Sawan** pavilion in the

centre. The north-west quadrangle contains many ruins, including what were once an audience hall, various *sǎalaa* (open-sided covered meeting halls or resting places) and residential quarters for the king's harem. The palace is open 7.30 am to 5.30 pm daily.

The **Lopburi National Museum** is located here in three separate buildings. Two of the them house an excellent collection of Lopburi-period sculpture and an assortment of Khmer, Dvaravati, U Thong and Ayuthaya art. The third building features traditional farm implements and dioramas of farm life. *A Guide to Ancient Monuments in Lopburi* by MC Subhadradis Diskul, Thailand's leading art historian, may be available from the counter on the 2nd floor of the museum. Entry is 30B; the museum is open 8.30 am to noon and 1 to 4 pm Wednesday to Sunday.

In mid-February the Phra Narai Ratchaniwet is the focus of the three-day King Narai Festival, which includes the exhibition and sale of locally woven textiles, and *lákhon ling* (traditional drama performed by monkeys).

Wat Phra Si Ratana Mahathat
วัดพระศรีรัตนมหาธาตุ

Directly across from the train station, this large 12th-century Khmer *wát* has been restored by the Fine Arts Department. A tall laterite prang still stands and features a few intact lintels and some ornate stucco. There is also a large *wíhǎan* added by King Narai. Several *chedi* (stupas) and smaller prang dot the grounds – some almost completely restored, some a little tatty; entry is 30B.

Wat Nakhon Kosa
วัดนครโกษา

This *wát* is just north of the train station, near San Phra Kan. It was built by the Khmers in the 12th century and may originally have been a Hindu shrine. U Thong and Lopburi images found at the temple and now in the Lopburi National Museum are thought to have been added later. There's not much left of this *wát*, although the foliage growing on the brick ruins is an interesting sight. However, half-hearted attempts to restore it with modern materials and motifs detract from the overall effect. A recent excavation has uncovered a larger base below the monument.

Monkey Trouble

More than any other place in Thailand, Lopburi is a city besieged by monkeys. The city's original troop of monkeys (actually a type of macaque) inhabits the San Phra Kan during the day and then crosses the street in the evening to roost in the halls of Prang Sam Yot. At some time in the recent past, the band split into two factions. The splinter troop, lead by a half-blind dominant male, gave up the sanctity of the shrine for the temptations of the city. These renegades can be seen making nuisances of themselves by swinging from shop fronts and smearing excrement on the windshields of parked cars. Many human residents of the old city have been forced to attach special monkey foils to their television antennas, lest simian antics spoil TV reception. Some locals even swear that the city-dwelling monkeys have been known to board trains for other provinces, returning to Lopburi once their wanderlust is spent.

Like Thailand's legions of stray dogs, Lopburi's monkey population survives in part due to Buddhist discouragement of killing animals. Moreover, many locals say that Lopburi's monkeys are the 'children' of the Hindu god Kala, and that to harm one would bring on misfortune. For the most part however, the inhabitants of Lopburi seem to agree that the monkeys' delinquent behaviour is outweighed by the tourist dollars that they bring in. In late November, Lopburi holds a feast for the monkeys at Prang Sam Yot to thank them for their contribution to the prosperity of Lopburi. Buffet tables are meticulously laid out with peanuts, cabbage, watermelon, bananas, pumpkin, pineapple, boiled eggs and cucumbers; the latter two items are monkey favourites, causing plenty of spats. Thousands of Thais turn out to watch the spectacle.

While monkeys frolicking on stone temples make for great photo opportunities, visitors to Lopburi should keep in mind that these are wild animals whose natural fear of humans has diminished over time. Monkeys have been known to attack humans, especially would-be photographers who use food to lure monkeys into the range of their camera lenses.

Wat Indra & Wat Racha
วัดอินทราและวัดราชา

Wat Indra stands on Thanon Ratchadamnoen near the corner of Thanon Na Phra Kan. Practically nothing is known of its history and it's now merely a pile of brick rubble. Wat Racha, off Thanon Phraya Kamjat, is another pile of bricks with little-known history.

Wat San Paolo
วัดสันเปาโล

A partial brick and stucco tower off Thanon Ramdecho east of the train station is all that's left of a Jesuit church founded by the Portuguese during King Narai's reign.

Wat Sao Thong Thong
วัดเสาธงทอง

This wát is north-west of the palace centre, behind the central market. The buildings here are in pretty poor shape. The wíhǎan and large seated Buddha are from the Ayuthaya period; King Narai restored the

wíhǎan (changing its windows to an incongruous but intriguing Gothic style) so it could be used as a Christian chapel. Niches along the inside walls contain Lopburi-style Buddhas with *naga* (serpent) protectors.

Chao Phraya Wichayen House
บ้านวิชชาเยนทร์

King Narai built this Thai-European palace as a residence for foreign ambassadors, of whom the Greek Constantine Phaulkon was the most famous. Phaulkon became one of King Narai's advisers and was eventually a royal minister. In 1688, as Narai lay dying, Phaulkon was assassinated by Luang Sorasak, who wanted power for himself. The palace is across the street and north-east of Wat Sao Thong Thong; admission is 30B.

San Phra Kan
ศาลพระกาฬ

To the north of Wat Nakhon Kosa, near the train tracks, is the unimpressive San Phra Kan (Kala Shrine), which contains a crude gold-leaf–laden image of Kala, the Hindu god of time and death. A virtual sea of monkeys surrounds the shrine, falling out of the tamarind trees and scurrying along the steps leading to the sanctuary. They are getting fat on hand-outs, and can be nasty with visitors. A reader wrote to say he was bitten by a monkey and had to receive rabies injections. The shrine is open 5 am to 7 pm daily.

Prang Sam Yot
ปรางค์สามยอด

Opposite the San Phra Kan, near the Muang Thong Hotel, this shrine represents classic Khmer-Lopburi style and is another Hindu-turned-Buddhist temple. Originally, the three prang symbolised the Hindu Trimurti of Shiva, Vishnu and Brahma. Now two of them contain ruined Lopburi-style Buddha images. Some Khmer lintels can still be made out, and some appear unfinished.

A rather uninteresting U Thong–Ayuthaya imitation Buddha image sits in the brick sanctuary in front of the linked prang. At the back, facing the Muang Thong Hotel, are a couple of crudely restored images, probably once Lopburi style. The grounds allotted to Prang Sam Yot are rather small and are virtually surrounded by modern buildings. The best view of the monument would probably be from one of the upper floors of the Muang Thong. The monument is lit up at night. It's open 8 am to 6 pm daily; entry is 30B.

Places to Stay

Old Lopburi Lopburi can be visited as a day trip en route to the north, but if you want to stay overnight there are a number of hotels in the older part of the city you can try. *Asia Lopburi Hotel* (☎/fax 036-411892), on the corner of Thanon Sorasak and Thanon Phraya Kamjat and overlooking Phra Narai Ratchaniwet, is clean and comfortable with good service. It has two Chinese restaurants. Singles/doubles with fan and bathroom cost 140/200B and with air-con up to 250/350B. Ask for a room off the street if traffic noise is bothersome.

The *Nett Hotel* (☎ 036-411738, 17/1–2 Thanon Ratchadamnoen) is on a soi between Thanon Ratchadamnoen and Thanon Phraya Kamjat, parallel to Thanon Sorasak. Clean and quiet rooms with fan and bathroom cost 150/220B, 250/350B with air-con.

Muang Thong Hotel (☎ 036-411036), across from Prang Sam Yot, has noisy and not-so-clean rooms for 120B with fan and bathroom.

Better is the *Taipei Hotel* (☎ 036-411524, 24/6–7 Thanon Surasongkhram), north of the palace area. Clean rooms with private bathroom cost 140B; air-con rooms with TV are available for 290/350B.

The *Rama Plaza Hotel* (☎ 036-411663, fax 411484), farther north on Thanon Surasongkhram, offers clean medium-price rooms with fan and bathroom for 270/320B, 320/400B with air-con. Popular with business travellers, it's often full.

The *Indra Hotel* (☎ 036-411261), on Thanon Na Phra Kan across from Wat Nakhon Kosa, costs 140/180B for clean, spacious rooms with fan and bathroom, and from 250B with air-con. Next door, *Lopburi City Hotel* (☎ 036-411245) is a modern building with smallish air-con rooms for 250/300B.

New Lopburi If you get stuck in the new part of town for some reason, you can choose from *Piman Hotel* (☎ 036-412507), on Soi Ekathot, Thanon Phra Horathibodi, *Holiday Hotel* (☎ 036-411343, Soi Suriyothai 2, Thanon Phra Narai Maharat), or *Lopburi Inn* (☎ 036-412300, fax 411917, 28/8 Thanon Phra Narai Maharat). The first two are mostly middle-class short-time places with rates around 250B to 480B a night. The Lopburi Inn features very nice rooms with all the amenities from 600B.

Ban Vimolrat (Lopburi Youth Hostel; ☎ 036-613390, 5/19 Mu 3, Thanon Naresuan), a 10B motorcycle taxi ride south along Thanon Naresuan (Rte 3016) from new Lopburi's western traffic circle, is a relatively new hostel with dorm rooms for 100B per person with fan and shared bathroom, 150B with air-con. Large furnished double rooms with a TV, fridge, desk and a small balcony cost 350B. The Lopburi train station and Phra Narai Ratchaniwet and Prang Sam Yot ruins will cost 60B in a túk-túk from the youth hostel.

At the top end is the *Lopburi Inn Resort* (☎ 036-420777, fax 412010, 144 Tambon Tha Sala), where rooms with all the modern amenities – including a fitness centre and swimming pool – cost 2200/2400B.

Places to Eat

Several *Chinese restaurants* operate along Thanon Na Phra Kan, parallel to the railway, especially near the Indra Hotel. The food is good but a bit overpriced.

Restaurants on the side streets of Thanon Ratchadamnoen and Thanon Phraya Kamjat can be better value. The *Chinese-Thai restaurant* next to the Asia Lopburi Hotel on Thanon Sorasak, across from the main gate to Phra Narai Ratchaniwet, is a good stand-by.

There are also plenty of cheap *curry vendors* down the alleys and along the smaller streets in old Lopburi.

White House Garden Restaurant, a couple of blocks east of the Asia Lopburi Hotel, is one of the more pleasant spots for a Thai meal in the old city.

The *central market*, off Thanon Ratchadamnoen and Thanon Surasongkhram (just north of the palace), is a great place to pick up *kài thâwt* or *kài yâang* (fried or roast chicken) with sticky rice, *hàw mòk* (fish and coconut curry steamed in banana leaves), *klûay khàek* (Indian-style fried bananas), a wide selection of fruit, satay, *khâo krìap* (crispy rice cakes), *thâwt man plaa* (fried fish cakes) and other delights.

In the heart of the market is a *Sala Mangsawirat* (Vegetarian Pavilion) with inexpensive – but in this case not very appetising – Thai vegie food; like most Thai vegetarian restaurants, it's only open from around 9 am to 2 pm.

A number of milk bars do Thai versions of a Western breakfast (hot dogs substituting for sausages etc). The no-name restaurant on the corner of Thanon Ratchadamnoen and Thanon Na Phra Kan makes up for taking culinary liberties by serving up real coffee from Chiang Mai. In the evenings a night market sets up along Thanon Na Phra Kan.

Getting There & Away

Bus Buses leave for Lopburi every 10 minutes from Ayuthaya or, if you're coming from Bangkok, about every 20 minutes (from 5.30 am to 8.30 pm) from the Northern and North-Eastern bus terminal. From Bangkok it's a three-hour ride that costs 54B ordinary, 72B for air-con; it's about half that price from Ayuthaya.

Lopburi can also be reached from the west via Kanchanaburi or Suphanburi. If you're coming from Kanchanaburi, take bus No 411 to Suphanburi (34B, 2½ hours); there's great scenery all the way. In Suphanburi, get off the bus in the town's main street, Thanon Malaimaen, signed in English, at the intersection that has an English sign pointing to Sri Prachan. From here you can catch a direct bus (No 464) to Lopburi (34B, three hours).

If you happen to miss the direct bus, you can also hopscotch to Lopburi by catching a bus first to Singburi or Ang Thong, across the river from Lopburi. The scenery is even better on the Suphanburi to Singburi leg (28B, 2½ hours) – you'll pass many old, traditional Thai wooden houses (late Ayuthaya style), countless cool rice paddies and small wát of all descriptions. Finally, at the Singburi bus station, catch one of the frequent buses to Lopburi (14B, 45 minutes). The Singburi bus makes a stop in front of Prang Sam Yot in old Lopburi – if you get off here, you won't have to backtrack from the new city. An alternative to the Suphanburi to Singburi route is to take a bus to Ang Thong (12B) and then a share taxi (22B) or bus (18B) to Lopburi. This is a little faster but not quite as scenic.

From the North-East, Lopburi can be reached via Khorat (Nakhon Ratchasima) aboard air-con buses for 69B.

Train Ordinary trains depart Bangkok's Hualamphong station, heading north, at 7.05 and 8.30 am, and take only 20 to 30 minutes longer to reach Lopburi than the rapid or express. These ordinary trains are 3rd class only. Rapid trains leave Bangkok at 7.45 am and 3, 6.10, 8 and 10 pm (2½ hours). Only one express train (No 9) stops in Lopburi, leaving Bangkok at 8.40 am (2nd-class seats only). Fares are 64B in 2nd class and 28B in 3rd class, not including surcharges for rapid or express trains.

There are also regular trains from Ayuthaya to Lopburi (13B in 3rd class, one hour).

Getting Around

Săwngthăew run along Thanon Wichayen and Thanon Phra Narai Maharat between the old and new towns for 5B per passenger; there is also a system of city buses (4B). Săamláw will go anywhere in the old town for 30B.

Ayuthaya Historical Park

Ayuthaya Historical Park

GLENN BEANLAND

PAUL DYMOND

KRAIG LIEB

Title Page: A Khmer-style *prang* flanked by very Thai *garudas*, at Wat Ratburana (Photograph by Glenn Beanland)

Left: One-armed Buddha at Wat Phra Si Sanphet

Bottom Left: A *garuda*, mount of Vishnu, at Wat Ratburana

Bottom Right: Buddha head wrapped in banyan roots at Wat Phra Mahathat

GLENN BEANLAND

A Unesco World Heritage Site, Ayuthaya's historic temples are scattered throughout this once magnificent city, Thailand's former capital, and along the encircling rivers. Several of the more central ruins – Wat Phra Si Sanphet, Wat Mongkhon Bophit, Wat Na Phra Meru, Wat Thammikarat, Wat Ratburana and Wat Phra Mahathat – can easily be visited on foot, although you would be wise to avoid the hottest part of the day (11 am to 4 pm). Or you could add more temples and ruins to your itinerary by touring the city on rented bicycle. An ideal transport combination for visitors who want to see everything would be to hire a bicycle for the central temples and charter a long-tail boat to take a tour of the outlying ruins along the river. See under Getting Around in the Ayuthaya section in this chapter for details on modes and rates of transport. At many of the ruins a 20B to 30B admission fee is collected from 8 am to 6.30 pm.

Wat Phra Si Sanphet

วัดพระศรีสรรเพชญ์

This was the largest temple in Ayuthaya in its time, and it was used as the royal temple/palace for several Ayuthaya kings. Built in the 14th century, the compound once contained a 16m-high standing Buddha covered with 250kg of gold, which was melted down by the Burmese conquerors. It is mainly known for the line of three large *chedi* (stupas) erected in the quintessential Ayuthaya style, which has come to be identified with Thai art more than any other single style. Admission is 30B.

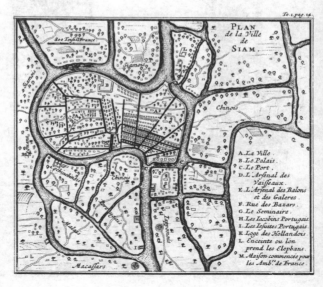

Right: This map of Ayuthaya was published in 1691 in *Du Royaume De Siam*, which recounts the experiences of French envoy Simon de La Loubère. Ayuthaya began receiving European visitors in the early 16th century.

Wat Mongkhon Bophit

วัดมงคลบพิตร

This monastery, near Wat Phra Si Sanphet, contains one of Thailand's largest Buddha images, a 15th-century bronze casting. The present *wíhǎan* (Buddhist image sanctuary) was built in 1956.

Wat Phra Mahathat

วัดพระมหาธาตุ

This wát, on the corner of Thanon Chee Kun and Thanon Naresuan (Chao Phrom), dates back to the 14th century and was built during the reign of King Ramesuan. Despite extensive damage – not much was left standing after the Burmese hordes had finished – the *prang* (Khmer-style tower) is still impressive. It was one of the first prang built in the capital. One of the most photographed sites in Ayuthaya is a Buddha head around which tree roots have grown. Admission is 30B.

Wat Ratburana

วัดราชบูรณะ

The Ratburana ruins are the counterpart to Wat Phra Mahathat across the road; the chedi, however, contain murals of the early Ayuthaya period and are not quite as dilapidated. Admission is 30B.

Left: The french naturalist and explorer Henri Mouhot visited Ayuthaya in the mid-1800s, about a century after the sacking of the city by the Burmese. This etching, published in his *Travels in Siam, Cambodia and Laos 1858–60*, shows a Buddha image decaying among the ruins

Wat Thammikarat

วัดธรรมิกราช

To the east of the old palace grounds, inside the river loop, Wat Thammikarat features overgrown chedi ruins and lion sculptures.

Wat Phanan Choeng

วัดพนัญเชิง

South-east of town on Mae Nam Chao Phraya, this wát was built before Ayuthaya became a Siamese capital. It's not known who built the temple, but it appears to have been constructed in the early 14th century so it's possibly Khmer. The main wíhǎan contains a highly revered 19m-high sitting Buddha image from which the wát derives its name.

The easiest way to get to Wat Phanan Choeng is by ferry from the pier near Phom Phet fortress, inside the south-east corner of the city centre. For a few extra baht you can take a bicycle with you on the boat.

Right: This etching, also from *Travels in Siam, Cambodia and Laos 1858–60*, shows an abandoned temple being engulfed by vegetation.

Wat Na Phra Meru (Phra Mehn)

วัดหน้าพระเมรุ

Across from the old royal palace grounds is a bridge that can be crossed to arrive at Wat Phra Meru. This temple is notable because it escaped destruction from the Burmese in 1767, though it has required restoration over the years. The main *bòt* (central sanctuary) was built in 1546 and features fortress-like walls and pillars. During the Burmese invasion, Myanmar's Chao Along Phaya chose this site from which to fire a cannon at the palace; the cannon exploded and the king was fatally injured, thus ending the sacking of Ayuthaya.

The bòt interior contains an impressive carved wooden ceiling and a splendid Ayuthaya-era, crowned sitting Buddha, 6m high. Inside a smaller wíhǎan behind the bòt is a green-stone Buddha from Sri Lanka in a European pose (sitting in a chair). It is said to be 1300 years old. The walls of the wíhǎan show traces of 18th- or 19th-century murals. Admission to Wat Na Phra Meru is 20B.

Wat Yai Chai Mongkhon

วัดใหญ่ชัยมงคล

Wat Yai, as the locals call it, is south-east of the town proper, but can be reached by minibus for 3B to 4B. It's a quiet, old place that was once a famous meditation wát, built in 1357 by King U Thong. The compound contains a very large chedi from which the wát takes its popular name (*yài* means 'big'), and a large reclining Buddha. There are monks and a community of Buddhist nuns residing here. Admission is 20B.

Other Temples

Just north of Wat Ratburana, to the west of a colourful Chinese shrine, are the smaller ruins of **Wat Suwannawat**. The 400-year-old brick remains of eight chedi, a bòt and a wíhǎan are arranged in a circle – a typical early Ayuthaya layout.

The ruined Ayuthaya-style prang and chedi of **Wat Chai Wattanaram** (admission 20B), on the western bank of Mae Nam Chao Phraya south-west of the city centre, have been restored. These ruins can be reached by boat or by bicycle via a nearby bridge. If you go by road, you'll pass **Wat Kasatthirat** on the way. Admission to Wat Chai Wattanaram costs 20B.

A short boat ride north along Mae Nam Lopburi will bring you to modern **Wat Pa Doh**. In front of the bòt, a unique Sukhothai-style walking Buddha image strides over a narrow arch, symbolising the crossing from samsara to nirvana.

Kanchanaburi Province

The town of Kanchanaburi was originally established by Rama I as a first line of defence against the Burmese, who might use the old invasion route through the Three Pagodas Pass on the Thailand-Myanmar border. It's still a popular smuggling route into Myanmar today.

During WWII, the Japanese used Allied prisoners of war (POWs) to build the infamous Death Railway along this same invasion route, from Mae Nam Khwae Noi to the pass. Thousands of prisoners died as a result of brutal treatment by their captors, their experiences chronicled by Pierre Boulle in his book *The Bridge On the River Kwai* and popularised by the movie of the same name. The bridge is still there (still in use, in fact) and so are the graves of the Allied soldiers.

West and north-west of Kanchanaburi city are several of Thailand's largest waterfalls and most extensive wildlife sanctuaries. Most of the province, in fact, remains sparsely populated and wild.

KANCHANABURI
อ.เมืองกาญจนบุรี

postcode 71000 • pop 38,100
Kanchanaburi lies 130km west of Bangkok in the slightly elevated valley of Mae Nam Mae Klong amid hills and sugar-cane plantations. The weather here is slightly cooler than in Bangkok and the evenings can be especially pleasant by contrast. Meuang Kan, or just Kan (as the locals call it; also Kan'buri), receives enough tourists to warrant its own tourist office, but as a proportion of total visitation, not that many Western visitors make it here. Most tourists are Thai, Japanese, or Hong Kong and Singapore Chinese, who blaze through on air-con buses, hitting the Death Railway Bridge, the cemetery on Thanon Saengchuto and the war museum, and then hurry off to the nearby sapphire mines or one of the big waterfalls before heading north to Chiang Mai or back to Bangkok.

Mae Nam Mae Klong is a focus for much weekend and holiday activity among the Thais. In recent years the city has given the

waterfront area a face-lift, planting casuarina trees and moving most of the floating restaurants offshore. A new bridge spanning the river, another bridge on the way and a new highway bypass north-east of town signify that development has arrived in what was previously a provincial backwater.

You may notice the fish-shaped street signs in Meuang Kan – they represent *plaa yîisòk,* the most common food fish in Mae Nam Mae Klong and its tributaries.

Information
Tourist Offices The TAT office (☎ 034-511200, 01-239 0767) is on Thanon Saengchuto, on the right before the police station as you enter town from Bangkok. A free map of the town and province is available, as well as comprehensive information on accommodation and transport. Hours are 8.30 am to 4.30 pm daily. The tourist police (☎ 034-512795, 516797, 1155) have an office at the northern end of Thanon Saengchuto – any problems with criminal occurrences should be reported to both the tourist police and the regular police.

Money The major Thai banks are represented and offer foreign-exchange services and ATMs (automated teller machines). The highest concentration of banks is found on and off Thanon Saengchuto near the market and bus station.

Punnee Cafe & Bar (☎/fax 034-513503) on Thanon Ban Neua has a money-changing service that's useful on weekends and holidays, although the rate is not as good as at the banks.

Post & Communications The main post office on Thanon Saengchuto is open 8.30 am to 4.30 pm weekdays and 9 am to 2 pm Saturday; international telephone service is available from 7 am to 10 pm daily and a Home Country Direct phone is located outside the post office, available 24 hours a day. There is also a small post office on Thanon Lak Meuang towards the river, close to the Lak Meuang shrine.

Death Railway Bridge
สะพานข้ามแม่น้ำแคว

The so-called Bridge On the River Kwai, or Saphan Mae Nam Khwae, may be of interest

CENTRAL THAILAND

to war historians but really looks quite ordinary. It spans Mae Nam Khwae Yai, a tributary (Khwae Yai literally translates as 'large tributary') of Mae Nam Mae Klong, 3km from Kanchanaburi's Lak Meuang shrine (*làk meuang;* town pillar/phallus), and it is the story behind the bridge that is dramatic. The materials for the bridge were brought from Java by the Imperial Japanese Army during its occupation of Thailand. In 1945 the bridge was bombed several times and was only rebuilt after the war – the curved portions of the bridge are original. The first version of the bridge, completed in February 1943, was all wood. In April of the same year a second bridge of steel was constructed.

It is estimated that 16,000 Prisoners of War (POWs) died while building the Death

Railway to Myanmar, of which the bridge was only a small part. The strategic objective of the railway was to secure an alternative supply route for the Japanese conquest of Myanmar and other Asian countries to the west. Construction of the railway began on 16 September 1942 at existing stations in Thanbyuzayat, Myanmar, and Nong Pladuk, Thailand. Japanese engineers at the time estimated that it would take five years to link Thailand and Myanmar by rail, but the Japanese army forced the POWs to complete the 415km, 1m-gauge railway (of which roughly two-thirds ran through Thailand) in 16 months. Much of the railway was built in difficult terrain that required high bridges and deep mountain cuttings. The rails were finally joined 37km south of Three Pagodas

Pass; a Japanese brothel train inaugurated the line. The Death Railway Bridge was in use for 20 months before the Allies bombed it in 1945. Only one POW is known to have escaped, a Briton who took refuge among pro-British Karen guerrillas.

Although the number of POWs who died during the Japanese occupation is horrifying, the figures for the labourers, many from Thailand, Myanmar, Malaysia and Indonesia, are even worse. It is thought that 90,000 to 100,000 coolies died in the area.

Today little remains of the original railway. West of Nam Tok, Karen and Mon carried off most of the track to use in the construction of local buildings and bridges.

Train enthusiasts may enjoy the **railway museum** in front of the bridge, with engines used during WWII on display. Every year during the first week of December there is a nightly sound-and-light show at the bridge, commemorating the Allied attack on the Death Railway in 1945. It's a big scene, with the sounds of bombers and explosions, fantastic bursts of light, and more. The town gets a lot of Thai tourists during this week, so book early if you want to witness this spectacle.

Getting There & Away The best way to get to the bridge from town is to catch a săwngthăew along Thanon Pak Phraek (parallel to Thanon Saengchuto towards the river) heading north. Regular săwngthăew are 5B and stop at the bridge. You can also take a train from the train station to the bridge for 2B.

Allied War Cemeteries
สุสานทหารสงครามโลกครั้งที่ ๒

There are two cemeteries containing the remains of Allied POWs who died in captivity during WWII; one is in the north of town off Thanon Saengchuto, just before the train station, and the other is across Mae Nam Mae Klong in the west of town and a couple of kilometres down Mae Nam Khwae Noi (Little Tributary River).

The **Kanchanaburi Allied War Cemetery**, better cared for with green lawns and healthy flowers, is usually a cool spot on a hot Kanchanaburi day. It's only a 15-minute walk from the River Kwai Hotel or you can catch a săwngthăew or orange

minibus (No 2) anywhere along Thanon Saengchuto going north – the fare is 5B. Jump off at the English sign in front of the cemetery on the left, or ask to be let off at the *sŭsăan* (cemetery). Just before the cemetery on the same side of the road is a very colourful Chinese cemetery with burial mounds and inscribed tombstones.

To get to the **Chung Kai Allied War Cemetery**, take a 5B ferry from the pier at the western end of Thanon Lak Meuang across Mae Nam Mae Klong, then follow the curving road through picturesque corn and sugar-cane fields until you reach the cemetery on your left. This is a fairly long walk, but the scenery along the way is very pleasant. You can also easily take a bicycle over the new bridge here. Like the more visited cemetery north of town, the Chung Kai burial plaques carry names, military insignia and short epitaphs for Dutch, British, French and Australian soldiers. This cemetery sees less tourists than the Kanchanaburi Allied War Cemetery.

About 1km south-west of the Chung Kai cemetery is a dirt path that leads to **Wat Tham Khao Pun**, one of Kanchanaburi's many cave temples. The path passes through thick forest with a few wooden houses along the way. This wát became notorious in late 1995 when a drug-addicted monk living at the wát murdered a British tourist and disposed of her corpse in a nearby sinkhole. Kan residents – like the rest of Thailand – were absolutely mortified by the crime and many now refer to the cave as 'Johanne's Cave' in memory of the victim. The monk was defrocked and sentenced to death (commuted to life imprisonment without parole by the king in 1996).

Jeath War Museum
พิพิธภัณฑ์สงคราม

This odd museum next to Wat Chaichumphon (Wat Tai) is worth visiting just to sit on the cool banks of Mae Nam Mae Klong. Phra Maha Tomson Tongproh, a Thai monk who devotes much energy to promoting the museum, speaks some English and can answer questions about the exhibits, as well as supply information about what to see around Kanchanaburi and how best to get there. The museum is a replica of the bamboo-*atap* huts used to house Allied

POWs during the occupation. The long huts contain various photographs taken during the war, drawings and paintings by POWs, maps, weapons and other war memorabilia. The acronym Jeath represents the meeting of Japan, England, Australia/America, Thailand and Holland at Kanchanaburi during WWII.

The war museum is at the end of Thanon Wisuttharangsi (Visutrangsi), near the TAT office. The common Thai name for this museum is *phíphítháphan sŏngkhraam wát tâi*. It's open 8.30 am to 6 pm daily; admission is 30B.

WWII Museum
พิพิธภัณฑ์สงครามโลกครั้งที่ ๒

Also called Art Gallery & War Museum, this relatively new, somewhat garish structure just south of the famous Death Railway Bridge looks like a Chinese temple on the outside. The larger, more lavishly built of the two buildings has nothing to do with WWII and little to do with art unless you include the garish murals throughout. The bottom floor contains Burmese-style alabaster Buddhas and a *phrá khrêuang* (sacred amulets) display. Upper floors exhibit Thai weaponry from the Ayuthaya period and a fair collection of historic and modern ceramics. Brightly painted portraits of all the kings in Thai history fill the 4th floor. Finally, on the 5th and uppermost floor – above the royal portraits (flirting with lese-majesty) – is the history of the Chinese family who built the museum, complete with a huge portrait of the family's original patriarch in China.

A smaller building opposite contains WWII relics, including photos and sketches made during the POW period and a display of Japanese and Allied weapons. Along the front of this building stand life-size sculptures of historical figures associated with the war, including Churchill, MacArthur, Hitler, Einstein, de Gaulle and Hirohito. The English captions are sometimes unintentionally amusing or disturbing – a reference to the atomic bomb dropped on Hiroshima, for example, reads 'Almost the entire city was destroyed in a jiffy'. Inside, a glass case contains 106 skeletons unearthed in a mass grave of Asian labourers. The gossip around town says these remains were stolen from a municipal excavation. The museum is open from 9 am to 6 pm daily; entry is 30B.

Lak Meuang (City Pillar)
ศาลหลักเมือง

Like many other older Thai cities, Kanchanaburi has a làk meuang enclosed in a shrine at what was originally the town centre. Kanchanaburi's Lak Meuang shrine is appropriately located on Thanon Lak Meuang, which intersects with Thanon Saengchuto two blocks north of the TAT office.

The bulbous-tipped pillar is covered with gold leaf and is much worshipped. Unlike Bangkok's Lak Meuang you can get as close to this pillar as you like – no curtain.

Within sight of the pillar, towards the river, stands Kanchanaburi's original **city gate**.

Wat Tham Mangkon Thong
วัดถ้ำมังกรทอง

The Cave Temple of the Golden Dragon is well known because of the 'floating nun' – a *mâe chii* (Thai Buddhist nun) who meditates while floating on her back in a pool of water. If you are lucky you might see her, but she seems to be doing this less frequently nowadays (try a Sunday). A nun now in her early 80s began the floating tradition and has passed it on to a younger disciple. Thais come from all over Thailand to see the younger nun float and to receive her blessings. A sizable contingent of young Thai nuns stay here under the old nun's tutelage.

A long and steep series of steps with dragon-sculpted handrails lead up the craggy mountainside behind the main bòt to a complex of limestone caves. Follow the string of light bulbs through the front cave and you'll come out above the wát with a view of the valley and mountains below. One section of the cave requires crawling or duck-walking, so wear appropriate clothing. Bats squeak away above your head and the smell of guano permeates the air.

Another cave wát is off this same road about 1km to 2km from Wat Tham Mangkon Thong towards the pier. It can be seen on a limestone outcrop back from the road some 500m or so. The name is **Wat Tham Khao Laem**. The cave is less impressive than that at Wat Tham Mangkon Thong, but there are some interesting old temple buildings on the grounds.

Getting There & Away Heading south-east down Thanon Saengchuto from the TAT office, turn right on Thanon Chukkadon (marked in English, and past the post office and hospital), or take a săwngthăew (5B) from the town centre to the end of Thanon Chukkadon. A bridge has replaced the river ferry that used to cross here; wait for any săwngthăew crossing the bridge and you can be dropped off in front of the temple for 5B.

The road to the wát passes sugar-cane fields, cattle, karst formations, wooden houses and rock quarries. Alternatively you could ride a bicycle from town – the road can be dusty in the dry season but at least it's flat.

Wat Tham Seua & Wat Tham Khao Noi
วัดถ้ำเสือและวัดถ้ำเขาน้อย

These large hill-top monasteries about 15km south-east of Kanchanaburi are important local pilgrimage spots, especially for Chinese Buddhists. Wat Tham Khao Noi (Little Hill Cave Monastery) is a Chinese temple monastery similar in size and style to Penang's Kek Lok Si. Adjacent is the half-Thai, half-Chinese-style Wat Tham Seua (Tiger Cave Monastery). Both are built on a ridge over a series of small caves. Wat Tham Khao Noi isn't much of a climb, since it's on the side of the slope. Seeing Wat Tham Seua means climbing either a steep set of naga stairs or a meandering set of steps past the cave entrance.

A climb to the top is rewarded with views of Mae Nam Khwae on one side, rice fields on the other. Wat Tham Seua features a huge sitting Buddha facing the river, with a conveyor belt that carries money offerings to a huge alms bowl in the image's lap. The easier set of steps to the right of the temple's naga stairs leads to a cave and passes an aviary with peacocks and other exotic birds. The cave has the usual assortment of Buddha images.

Getting There & Away By public transport, you can take a bus (5B) to Tha Meuang (12km south-east of Kanchanaburi), then a motorcycle taxi (30B) from near Tha Meuang Hospital directly to the temples.

If you're travelling by motorcycle or bicycle, take the right fork of the highway when you reach Tha Meuang, turn right past the hospital onto a road along the canal and then across the Kheuan Meuang (City Dam). From here to Wat Tham Seua and Wat Khao Noi is another 4km. Once you cross the dam, turn right down the other side of the river and follow this unpaved road 1.4km, then turn left towards the pagodas, which can be seen easily from here. The network of roads leading to the base of the hill offers several route possibilities – just keep an eye on the pagodas and you'll be able to make the appropriate turns.

By bicycle, you can avoid taking the highway by using back roads along the river. Follow Thanon Pak Phraek in Kanchanaburi south-east and cross the bridge towards Wat Tham Mangkon Thong, then turn left on the other side and follow the gravel road parallel to the river. Eventually (after about 14km) you'll see the Kheuan Meuang up ahead – at this point you should start looking for the hill-top pagodas on your right. This makes a good day trip by bicycle – the road is flat all the way and avoids the high-speed traffic on the highway. You can break your journey at Ban Tham, a village along the way with its own minor cave wát.

Boat Trips
Rafts Several small-time enterprises offer raft trips up and down Mae Nam Mae Klong and its various tributaries. The typical raft is a large affair with a two-storey shelter that will carry 15 to 20 people. The average rental cost per raft is 1500B for half a day and 3500B for an overnight trip, divided among as many people as you can fit on the boat. Such a trip would include stops at Hat Tha Aw (Tha Aw Beach), Wat Tham Mangkon Thong, Tham Khao Pun and the Chung Kai Allied War Cemetery, plus all meals and one night's accommodation on the raft. Alcoholic beverages are usually extra. Bargaining can be fruitful as there are said to be over 500 rafts available in the city.

Inquire at any guesthouse, the TAT office or at the main pier at the end of Thanon Lak Meuang about raft trips. Perhaps the best are those arranged by groups of travellers who get together and plan their own raft excursions with one of the raft operators.

Long-tail Boats One way to see the same river sights at a lower cost is to hire a long-tail boat instead of a raft. Long-tail boats cost around 400B per hour and can take up to six passengers. For 800B a group could take a two-hour long-tail boat trip to the Jeath War Museum, Wat Tham Khao Pun, Chung Kai Allied War Cemetery and the Death Railway Bridge. Boats can be hired from the boat pier off Thanon Song Khwae or at the Jeath War Museum.

Trekking

Several companies in town offer treks into Kanchanaburi's hinterland. One-day or overnight treks to Karen villages often include elephant rides and a journey down the river on a bamboo raft. Trips to caves, waterfalls and the province's other sights can also be arranged. AS Mixed Travel (☎ 034-512017), next to Apple Guest House, is locally owned and reliable. Prices are a bit more than at other agencies but the quality of the treks is high. Prices per person range from 450B to 850B for a day trip to 1650B to 1890B for two days and one night. The same company has just inaugurated one- and two-day cycling tours and three-day combination cycling/trekking programs. Bicycles and helmets are provided and a support vehicle is always on hand in case of emergencies.

Places to Stay – Budget

Kanchanaburi has numerous places to stay in every price range but especially in the guesthouse category. Those along the river can be a little noisy on weekends and holidays due to the floating disco traffic (although they now stop by 11 pm), so choose your accommodation carefully. Inevitably, there are even karaoke rafts now! A local commission of guesthouse owners is attempting to enact a ban on the floating discos, so perhaps they will soon disappear.

The popularity of floating accommodation has seen a profusion of 'raft rooms' added to the choice of accommodation at riverfront guesthouses. These are essentially rooms constructed on a platform that rests on steel pontoons. Some guesthouses try to cut their expenses by pumping river water into the bathrooms – not a healthy situation if you consider that waste water and sewage are dumped directly into the river. A few guesthouses have gone to great trouble to

hide their elicit plumbing from guests; at other establishments the set up is in plain view. If you are in doubt, before agreeing to take a room simply fill the bathroom sink with water. It will be readily apparent if the water came from the river or not.

Săamláw drivers get a 50B to 100B commission for each foreign traveller they bring to guesthouses from the bus or train station (on top of what they charge you for the ride), so don't believe everything they say with regard to 'full', 'dirty' or 'closed' – see for yourself. Most guesthouses will provide free transport from the bus or train station if you call.

On the River At the junction of Mae Nam Khwae and Mae Nam Khwae Noi is *Nita Raft House* (☎ 034-514521, 27/1 Thanon Pak Phraek), where older singles/doubles with mosquito nets cost 60B and doubles with fan cost 100B or 150B with private shower. It's basic but quite well run, although you should heed the warning about floating discos on weekends and holidays. The manager of Nita Raft House speaks English and can provide good information on the local sights and activities.

Near some floating restaurants is *Sam's Place* (☎ 034-513971, fax 512023, 7/3 Thanon Song Khwae). Singles/doubles with fan and private bathroom cost 150B; air-con rooms cost 300B. The raft has a small coffee shop. A drawback to Sam's is that it's within range of the floating discos.

Next to Sam's Place is *Supakornchai Raft* (☎ 034-512055, 7/4 Thanon Song Khwae), which is similar but not quite as nice. Raft rooms with fan and bathroom cost 150B to 200B for a large bed and 300B to 400B for two large beds.

Two places a little closer to the city centre are the *River Guest House* (☎ 034-512491, 42 Soi Rong Hip Oi 2, Thanon Mae Nam Khwae) and the nearby *J Guest House* (☎ 034-620307). Both are located in a hyacinth-choked lagoon and have raft singles/doubles with shared bathroom for 40B to 80/120B to 150B. Just upriver is the *VN Guest House* (☎ 034-514082, 44 Soi Rong Hip Oi 2, Thanon Mae Nam Khwae), where small, basic raft rooms cost 50B to 70B, 150B with bathroom and 300B with air-con. All are close to the train station and tend to get booked out in the high season.

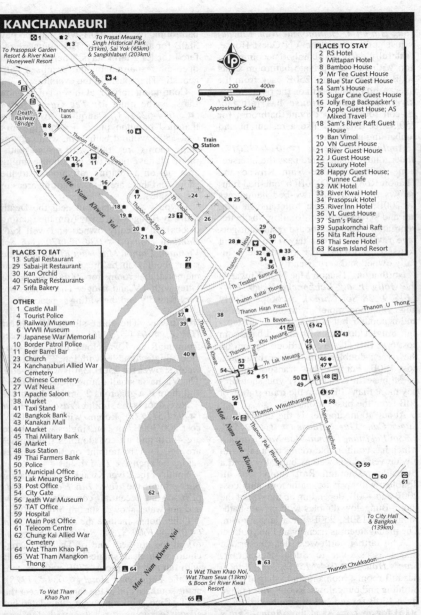

KANCHANABURI

To Prasopsuk Garden
Resort & River Kwai
Honeywell Resort

To Prasat Meuang
Singh Historical Park
(31km), Sai Yok (45km)
& Sangkhlaburi (203km)

Thanon Saengchuto

Thanon Laos

Death Railway Bridge

Thanon Mae Nam Khwae

Train Station

0   200   400m
0   200   400yd
Approximate Scale

Mae Nam Khwae Yai

Thanon Rong Hip Oi

Th Chaokunen

Thanon Ban Neua

Th Tesaban Bamrung

Thanon Kratai Thong

Thanon Hiran Prasat

Th Bovon

Th Khu Meuang

Thanon Song Khwae

Thanon Prasit

Th Lak Meuang

Thanon U Thong

Mae Nam Mae Klong

Thanon Wisuttharangsi

Thanon Pak Phraek

Thanon Saengchuto

Mae Nam Khwae Noi

To City Hall
& Bangkok
(139km)

To Wat Tham Khao Noi,
Wat Tham Seua (13km)
& Boon Sri River Kwai
Resort

To Wat Tham
Khao Pun

Thanon Chukkadon

PLACES TO STAY
2 RS Hotel
3 Mittapan Hotel
8 Bamboo House
9 Mr Tee Guest House
12 Blue Star Guest House
14 Sam's House
15 Sugar Cane Guest House
16 Jolly Frog Backpacker's
17 Apple Guest House; AS
     Mixed Travel
18 Sam's River Raft Guest
     House
19 Ban Vimol
20 VN Guest House
21 River Guest House
22 J Guest House
25 Luxury Hotel
28 Happy Guest House;
     Punnee Cafe
32 MK Hotel
33 River Kwai Hotel
34 Prasopsuk Hotel
35 River Inn Hotel
36 VL Guest House
37 Sam's Place
39 Supakornchai Raft
55 Nita Raft House
58 Thai Seree Hotel
63 Kasem Island Resort

PLACES TO EAT
13 Sutjai Restaurant
29 Sabai-jit Restaurant
30 Kan Orchid
40 Floating Restaurants
47 Srifa Bakery

OTHER
1 Castle Mall
4 Tourist Police
5 Railway Museum
6 WWII Museum
7 Japanese War Memorial
10 Border Patrol Police
11 Beer Barrel Bar
23 Church
24 Kanchanaburi Allied War
     Cemetery
26 Chinese Cemetery
27 Wat Neua
31 Apache Saloon
38 Market
41 Taxi Stand
42 Bangkok Bank
43 Kanakan Mall
44 Market
45 Thai Military Bank
46 Market
48 Bus Station
49 Thai Farmers Bank
50 Police
51 Municipal Office
52 Lak Meuang Shrine
53 Post Office
54 City Gate
56 Jeath War Museum
57 TAT Office
59 Hospital
60 Main Post Office
61 Telecom Centre
62 Chung Kai Allied War
     Cemetery
64 Wat Tham Khao Pun
65 Wat Tham Mangkon
     Thong

Ban Vimol (☎ *034-514831, 48/5 Soi Rong Hip Oi 2, Thanon Mae Nam Khwae)* is just upriver from the VN Guest House. Tastefully decorated bamboo accommodation with fan and private bathroom costs 300B on the river and 250B back from the river. A bit farther north on the river, ***Sam's River Raft Guest House*** has raft fan/air-con rooms with private bathroom for 250/350B. There is also a restaurant and sunbathing platform.

Apple Guest House (☎ *034-512017),* under a huge mango tree near the intersection of Thanon Mae Nam Khwae and Thanon Rong Hip Oi, offers one-bed bungalows for 150B and two-bed bungalows for 200B. All have clean toilet and shower, fan and screened doors to allow for better ventilation. The guesthouse restaurant gets rave reviews and one-day Thai cooking courses are offered. The guesthouse is locally owned and very friendly.

North along Thanon Mae Nam Khwae is the ***Jolly Frog Backpacker's*** (☎ *034-514579, 28 Soi China),* a comparatively huge 'bamboo motel' with good security and a popular but nothing-special restaurant. Singles/doubles with shared bathroom cost 60/110B (120B for a double room on the river); doubles with private bathroom cost 150B. For săamláw transport to any guesthouse in this vicinity, you shouldn't pay more than 20B from the train station or 30B from the bus station.

About 100m upriver is the newly built ***Sugar Cane Guest House*** (☎ *034-624520, 22 Soi Pakistan, Thanon Mae Nam Khwae),* which has comfortable rooms on a raft with a wide veranda as well as bungalows and a riverside restaurant. Raft rooms are all doubles with private bathroom and cost 200B and 400B, depending on the size of the room. Bungalow doubles with private bathroom cost 150B, 250B for a larger room. The management is friendly and helpful.

A bit farther north-west, near the bridge that crosses over to Sutjai Restaurant, ***Sam's House*** (☎ *034-515956, fax 512023)* has raft rooms, rooms in an L-shaped stone building and bungalows. Room prices range from 150B for fan and private bathroom to 300B for air-con. As at the original Sam's Place, there is a terrace restaurant.

Nearby is the new ***Blue Star Guest House*** (☎ *034-512161),* which has A-frame single/double bungalows, all with private bathroom, for 150/300B with fan, or pay 380B for air-con singles. Discounts are offered for long-term stays. There is also an open-air restaurant on the premises with acoustic Thai music in the evenings.

Continuing upriver, at the end of Thanon Laos, is the quiet ***Mr Tee Guest House*** (☎ *034-625103),* another two-storey thatched bamboo place. Rooms upstairs cost 150B without bathroom, while downstairs rooms are 200B with private bathroom; all have fans. The guesthouse dining area sits on a floating raft moored to the shore, and there are pleasant sitting areas in the grounds.

If you want to stay out near the Death Railway Bridge (and away from the floating discos), the locally owned and well kept ***Bamboo House*** (☎ *034-624470, 3–5 Soi Vietnam, Thanon Mae Nam Khwae),* on the river about 1km before the Japanese war memorial, has rooms for 200B to 800B, the latter with TV and fridge. The owners are very friendly and the setting is peaceful.

In Town   The three-storey ***VL Guest House*** (☎ *034-513546),* across the street from the River Kwai Hotel, has clean, spacious singles/doubles with fan, TV and hot-water shower for 250B, 350B with air-con. The VL has a small dining area downstairs and there is a generous 2 pm checkout.

Next door is the similar ***Prasopsuk Hotel*** (☎ *034-511777).* Rooms with fan and TV cost 200/300B, air-con singles with phone are 400B and air-con doubles (no phone) are 550B. A restaurant on the premises serves inexpensive Thai dishes.

South of the River Kwai Hotel on Thanon Saengchuto, the ***River Inn Hotel*** (☎ *034-621056)* has decent air-con rooms with TV and hot-water shower starting from 360B.

Other hotels include the ***Sri Muang Kan*** (☎ *034-511609, 313/1–3 Thanon Saengchuto),* at the northern end of Thanon Saengchuto, with clean singles/doubles for 200B with fan and bathroom, 370B with air-con; and the ***Thai Seree Hotel*** (☎ *034-511128),* at the southern end of the same road near the TAT office, with somewhat dilapidated but adequate rooms for 150B with fan and singles/doubles with air-con for 250/350B.

The bungalow-style ***Luxury Hotel*** (☎ *034-511168, 284/1–5 Thanon Saengchuto)* is a couple of blocks north of the River Kwai Hotel and not as centrally located. All rooms have air-con and cost 350B to 800B.

Places to Stay – Top End
On the River The *Kasem Island Resort* (☎ *034-513359; in Bangkok* ☎ *02-255 3604)* sits on an island in the middle of Mae Nam Mae Klong about 200m from Thanon Chukkadon. The tastefully designed thatched cottages and house rafts are cool, clean, quiet and go for 750B to 1300B. There are facilities for swimming, fishing and rafting as well as an outdoor bar and restaurant. The resort has an office near Thanon Chukkadon, where you can arrange for a free shuttle boat to the island; shuttle service stops at 10 pm.

North of the Death Railway Bridge are several river resorts of varying quality, most featuring standard wooden bungalows for about 800B. About 2km before the turn-off for Rte 323 is the 50-room *Prasopsuk Garden Resort* (☎ *034-513215)*, with air-con townhouse doubles for 600B, air-con bungalows with two bedrooms for 1200B and large bungalows for 10 people for 4000B per night. The *River Kwai Honey-well Resort* (☎ *034-515413; in Bangkok* ☎ *02-221 5472)* offers 20 bungalows with private bathroom on the river bank for 600B to 800B.

On the river, opposite Wat Tham Mangkon Thong to the south, the *Boon Sri River Kwai Resort* (☎ *034-515143; in Bangkok* ☎ *02-415 5875, 420 8518)* offers more of the same for 350B to 800B a night.

The luxurious *Felix River Kwai Kan-chanaburi* (☎ *034-515061, fax 515095; in Bangkok* ☎ *02-255 3410, fax 255 5767)* sits on the western bank of the river, about 2km north of the new one-lane bridge. The very nicely landscaped grounds include two swimming pools. Spacious rooms and suites with IDD phones, cable TV, fridge and personal safe cost 3000B to 20,000B. Nonguests may use the pool for 50B.

In Town Kanchanaburi's original 1st-class hotel, the *River Kwai Hotel* (☎ *034-513348, fax 511269, 284/3–16 Thanon Saengchuto)* offers semideluxe rooms with air-con, hot-water shower, fridge, telephone and TV from 960B. Facilities include a coffee shop, karaoke bar, disco and swimming pool.

Next door is the huge River Paradise massage parlour, bearing a sign on the door that reads 'No women allowed' (working masseuses are exempted of course).

Opposite the River Kwai Hotel, the relatively new, multistorey, 52-room *MK Hotel* (☎ *034-621143/4)*, on Thanon Saengchuto, has two-bed air-con rooms for 250B. For 50B more you can add either TV or hot-water shower. Rooms with all the amenities are available for 400B (500B with breakfast).

Farther north along Thanon Saengchuto, past the train station, is the four-storey *Mittapan Hotel* (☎ *034-515904, fax 514499)*. Standard rooms with all the amenities cost from 650B to 5000B. A large massage parlour and snooker club are next door.

Next comes the nicer *RS Hotel* (☎ *034-625128, fax 514499, 264 Thanon Saengchuto)*, which charges 700B to 6000B and has a swimming pool.

Places to Eat
There are a couple of large outdoor restaurants near the bridge, on the river, but these are for tour groups that arrive en masse throughout the day. If you're hungry, you can save money by eating with the tour bus and săwngthăew drivers in the little noodle places at the northern end of Thanon Pak Phraek.

The greatest proliferation of inexpensive restaurants in Kanchanaburi is along the northern end of Thanon Saengchuto near the River Kwai Hotel. From here south, to where Thanon U Thong crosses Thanon Saengchuto, are many good Chinese, Thai and Isan-style restaurants. As elsewhere in Thailand, the best are generally the most crowded.

The air-conditioned *Kan Orchid*, next to the River Kwai Hotel on Thanon Saengchuto, has a good selection of Thai food and also offers reasonably priced sandwiches, baked goods and ice cream. It's a good place to escape the midday heat.

The restaurant at *Apple Guest House* (see Places to Stay, earlier) goes way above and beyond normal guesthouse fare. Both the *kaeng mátsàmàn* (Muslim-style curry) and *phàt thai* (fried noodles) are highly recommended. Apple also does what is perhaps the best banana pancake in Thailand.

Good, cheap eating places can be found in the *markets* along Thanon Prasit and between Thanon U Thong and Thanon Lak Meuang east of Thanon Saengchuto. In the evenings, a sizable *night market* convenes along Thanon Saengchuto near the Thanon Lak Meuang intersection.

The *Sabai-jit Restaurant*, north of the River Kwai Hotel on Thanon Saengchuto, has an English menu. Beer and Mekong whisky are sold here at quite competitive prices and the food is consistently good. Other Thai and Chinese dishes are served apart from those listed on the English menu. If you see something not listed that you'd like, point.

Punnee Cafe & Bar (☎ 034-513503), on Thanon Ban Neua, serves Thai and European food according to expat tastes and advertises the coldest beer in town. Lots of information on Kanchanaburi is available here; there are also used paperback books for sale or trade. If you're in the mood for Western junk food and air-con ambience, there are branches of *KFC* at both Kanakan Mall near the bus station and Castle Mall on Thanon Saengchuto, on the northern outskirts of town.

Down on the river there are several large floating restaurants where the quality of the food varies but it's hard not to enjoy the atmosphere. Most of them cater to Thais out for a night of drinking and snacking, so if you go, don't expect Western food or large portions – but if you know what to order, you could have a very nice meal here. Recommended is the *Mae Nam*. Across from the floating restaurants, along the road, are several restaurants that are just as good but less expensive; the best on this row is *Jukkru* (no Roman-script sign – look for blue tables and chairs). Although it's a little out of the way, one of the better riverside restaurants in town is *Sutjai*, a garden-style place on the western bank of the river next to the one-lane bridge.

There are also *food vendors* on both sides of Thanon Song Khwae along the river near the new park, where you can buy inexpensive takeaway and picnic on mats along the riverbank. This is a festive and prosperous town and people seem to eat out a lot.

One bakery handles most of the pastry and bread business in Kan. Modern *Srifa Bakery* on the northern side of the bus station has everything from Singapore-style curry puffs to French-style pastries.

Entertainment

If the floating discos and karaoke bars on the river or the disco at the River Kwai Hotel don't appeal to you, try the *Apache Saloon* opposite the Sabai-jit Restaurant on Thanon Saengchuto. This large, old west–style bar/restaurant offers live folk-rock music nightly. *The Raft*, in front of the River Kwai Hotel, also features live Thai bands.

The *Beer Barrel Bar*, 100m north of Sugar Cane Guest House on Thanon Mae Nam Khwae, is a nicely done outdoor beer garden with good prices. Between Mr Tee's and Bamboo House on the corner of Thanon India and Thanon Mae Nam Khwae is another beer garden called *Brew House*.

Getting There & Away

Bus Ordinary buses leave Bangkok for Kanchanaburi from the Southern bus station in Thonburi every 20 minutes from 5 am to 10 pm daily (41B, three hours). Buses back to Bangkok leave Kanchanaburi between the same hours. Air-con (2nd class) buses cost 55B and leave at similar intervals.

First-class air-con buses leave Bangkok's Southern bus station every 15 minutes from 5.30 am to 10.30 pm (68B). These same buses depart Kanchanaburi for Bangkok from opposite the police station on Thanon Saengchuto, not from the bus station. Air-con buses only take about two hours to reach Bangkok. The first bus out is at 4 am; the last one to Bangkok leaves at 7 pm.

Buses to Kanchanaburi leave frequently throughout the day from nearby Nakhon Pathom (25B, 1½ hours). For travellers heading south, Nakhon Pathom makes a good connecting point – this way you avoid having to go back to Bangkok. Other frequent direct bus services are available to/from Ratchaburi (No 461, 31B, 2½ hours) and Suphanburi (No 411, 34B, 2½ to three hours).

Train Ordinary trains leave Thonburi (Bangkok Noi) station at 7.45 am and 1.45 pm, arriving at 10.55 am and 4.35 pm. Only 3rd-class seats are available (25B). Trains return to Bangkok (Bangkok Noi station, Thonburi) from Kanchanaburi at 7.27 am and 2.50 pm, arriving at 10.35 am and 6.10 pm. Ordinary train tickets to Kanchanaburi can be booked on the day of departure only.

Three trains daily depart Kanchanaburi station for the Death Railway Bridge (see under Getting Around in the Kanchanaburi section). The same trains go on to the end of the line at Nam Tok (two hours), which is near Nam Tok Sai Yok (Sai Yok Falls). You can catch the train in Kanchanaburi as mentioned earlier, or at the bridge at 6.18 and 11.08 am and 4.44 pm; the fare is the same (17B). Nam Tok is 8km from Nam Tok Khao Pang and 18km from Hellfire Pass and the Mae Nam Khwae village. Coming back from Nam Tok, there are trains at 5.25 am and 1 and 3.15 pm. The 6.11 am trains between Kanchanaburi and Nam Tok do not run on weekends and holidays.

Tourist Train The SRT runs a special tourist train from Bangkok's Hualamphong station at around 6.30 am, returning at 7.55 pm, on weekends and holidays. The one-way/return fare is 250B for adults, 120B for children. It includes an hour-long stop in Nakhon Pathom to see the Phra Pathom Chedi, an hour at the Death Railway Bridge, a minibus to Prasat Meuang Singh Historical Park (see Around Kanchanaburi later in this chapter for details) for a short tour, a walk along an elevated 'Death Railway' bridge (no longer in use), a three-hour stop at the river for lunch and a bat cave visit, before returning to Bangkok with a one-hour stopover at one of the war cemeteries.

Also on weekends and holidays there's a direct steam train between Kanchanaburi and (10.25 am departure, 2 pm return, with a 90-minute stopover at the waterfall) for 100B one way, 150B return. These tickets should be booked in advance, although it's worth trying on the day even if you're told it's full. The SRT changes the tour itinerary and price from time to time. Call ☎ 034-561052 for further information or check out the SRT Web site at www.srt.motc.go.th.

Share Taxi & Minivan You can also take a share taxi from Thanon Saengchuto to Bangkok for 60B per person. Taxis leave throughout the day whenever five passengers accumulate at the taxi stand. These taxis will make drops at Thanon Khao San or in the Phahurat district. Kanchanaburi guesthouses also arrange daily minivans to Bangkok for 100B per person. Passengers are dropped at Thanon Khao San.

Getting Around

Don't even consider letting a săamláw driver show you around, as they'll want big money. The town is not large, so getting around on foot or bicycle is easy. A săamláw or motorcycle taxi from the bus or train stations to the river area and most guesthouses should cost from 20B to 30B. Săwngthăew run up and down Thanon Saengchuto and Thanon Pak Phraek for 5B per passenger.

Bicycles and motorcycles can be rented at some guesthouses, at the Suzuki dealer near the bus station, at the Punnee Cafe & Bar and at the motorcycle repair shop near Sam's Place. Expect to pay from 150B to 250B per day for a motorbike (more for a dirt bike) and 50B a day for bicycles. Punnee Cafe & Bar also rents out mountain bikes for 80B per 24 hours.

You can take the train from the Kanchanaburi station out to the Death Railway Bridge, a three-minute ride (2B). There are three trains per day at 6.11 am (No 485), 11.01 am (No 257) and 4.37 pm (No 259).

The river ferry across Mae Nam Mae Klong costs 5B per person. Sometimes there's an extra few baht charge for bikes (motor or push) taken on the ferry, although usually it's included in the 5B fare.

AROUND KANCHANABURI

Most of the interesting places around Kanchanaburi are to the north and west of the capital, heading towards Three Pagodas Pass. Many guesthouses and tour agencies in the provincial capital can arrange two-day trips to Three Pagodas Pass, with stops at Hellfire Pass, various waterfalls and hot springs, and a night in Sangkhlaburi.

Kanchanaburi Province has seven major waterfalls, all north-west of Kanchanaburi. They are Erawan, Pha Lan, Trai Trang, Khao Pang, Sai Yok, Pha That and Huay Khamin. Of these, the three most worth visiting – if you're looking for grandeur and swimming potential – are Erawan, Sai Yok and Huay Khamin. Nam Tok Erawan is the easiest to get to from Kanchanaburi, while Sai Yok and Huay Khamin are best visited only if you are able to spend the night near the falls.

Any of these waterfalls could be visited by motorcycle. Many of the guesthouses in town will rent out bikes – offer 150B per day for an 80cc to 100cc bike, more for a dirt bike.

CENTRAL THAILAND

Erawan National Park
อุทยานแห่งชาติเอราวัณ

This 550-sq-km park is the most visited national park in Thailand and one of the most beautiful.

Once in the park, you'll have to walk 2km from the trail entrance to the end of seven levels of waterfalls (the first level is reached 700m from the visitors centre), which feed into Mae Nam Khwae Yai. The trails weave in and out of the numerous pools and falls, sometimes running alongside the water, sometimes leading across footbridges. Wear good walking shoes or sneakers. Also, bring a bathing suit as several of the pools beneath the waterfalls are great for swimming. The uppermost fall is said to resemble Airvata (Erawan in Thai), the three-headed elephant of Hindu mythology.

The waterfalls here, as elsewhere in Kanchanaburi, are best visited during the rainy season or in the first two months of the cool season, when the pools are full and the waterfalls most impressive. The peak crowds at Erawan come in mid-April around the time of the Songkran festival (when there's not much water); weekends can also be crowded. The park is open from 6 am to 6 pm; standard national park admission fees are collected (about 20B for Thais, 200B for foreigners).

Two limestone caves in the park worth visiting are **Tham Phra That** (12km northwest of the visitors centre via a rough road) and **Tham Wang Badan** (west). Thung Na Dam appears 28km before Erawan.

Places to Stay & Eat Official park *bungalows* that sleep up to 15 people cost from 250B to 1000B per night. The park staff can also make arrangements for you to sleep in unofficial housing from 50B to 100B per person, or you can pitch a tent for 5B. Call ☎ 02-579 7223 in Bangkok for more information. *Erawan Resort Guest House* (☎ 01-9078210), off the highway before the park entrance, has small, solid bungalows with attached bathroom on the river for 200B to 1000B. Farther towards Kanchanaburi along the same road, near the 46km marker, *Pha Daeng Resort* (☎ 034-513909) has a variety of air-con rooms and bungalows costing 500B to 2700B a night.

There are *food stalls* near the park entrance and at the bus station, outside the park. To cut down on rubbish, food is not allowed beyond the second level of the falls.

Getting There & Away The first bus to Erawan leaves the Kanchanaburi bus station at 8 am (25B, two hours). Ask for *rót thammádaa pai náam tòk eh-raawan* (ordinary bus going to Nam Tok Erawan). Take this first bus, as you need a full day to appreciate Erawan. The last bus back to Kanchanaburi leaves Erawan at 4 pm. During the high season (November to January), minibuses stop along the river guesthouses in Kanchanaburi around 9 am daily to take visitors to the falls (60B, one hour). The return trip leaves at 4.30 pm.

Nam Tok Huay Khamin
น้ำตกห้วยขมิ้น

Part of little-visited **Si Nakharin National Park**, Huay Khamin (Turmeric Stream) has what are probably Kanchanaburi Province's most powerful waterfalls. The pools under the waterfalls are large and deep and this is an excellent place for swimming. Explorations farther afield in the park can be rewarding for self-contained campers. Elephants and other wildlife are not uncommon.

Getting There & Away Getting to Huay Khamin can be difficult. The 45km road from the Erawan falls is in bad condition and takes at least two hours by motorcycle or rugged 4WD (you must bring your own transport). The falls can also be reached by a similarly rugged – and much longer – dirt road from Rte 323 north of Thong Pha Phum.

An alternative is to charter a boat at Tha Reua Khun Phaen, a pier on the south-eastern shore of Kheuan Si Nakharin (Si Nakharin Reservoir) in the village of Mongkrathae. The price varies – according to your bargaining skills and the mood of the boat pilots – from 1200B to 3500B; this need not be as expensive as it sounds if you bring a group, since the boats can hold up to 20 people. A good price for a long-tail boat with five to 10 people would be 1500B return. If you can afford it, boat is a much better option than road.

Infrequent Si Sawat buses from Kanchanaburi pass Mongkrathae.

Sai Yok National Park
อุทยานแห่งชาติไทรโยค

About 100km north-west of Kanchanaburi, scenic **Nam Tok Sai Yok Yai** and **Nam Tok Sai Yok Noi** are part of 500-sq-km Sai Yok National Park. In addition to the park's water-falls, other attractions include the limestone **caves** of Tham Sai Yok, Tham Kaew and Tham Phra, the remains of a **Death Railway bridge** and Japanese cooking stoves (actually little more than piles of brick), and a network of clear streams that bubble up from springs in the park. There are established footpaths and trails between the falls, caves, railway bridge and the bat cave.

It was at Sai Yok National Park that the famous Russian-roulette scenes in the 1978 movie *The Deer Hunter* were filmed. The area is well known for overnight raft trips that leave from here along Mae Nam Khwae Noi; the waterfalls empty directly into the river. The trips are not cheap, but those who have gone say they're worth the money.

Nam Tok Sai Yok Noi is higher than Nam Tok Sai Yok Yai, but the volume of falling water is greater at the latter. Sai Yok

Yai is more set up for visitors and hence gets bus loads of Thai tourists. Sai Yok Noi is much less visited and the setting is more relaxing.

The eight-room **Tham Daowadung**, one of Thailand's prettiest limestone caves, is farther north in the park while **Tham Lawa** is in the park's far south-eastern corner; both are best visited by taking boat trips to an access point along Mae Nam Khwae Noi, then hiking in. **Hin Dat Hot Springs** is 40 minutes north of Tham Daowadung by boat. The *bàw náam ráwn* (hot springs) are looked after by a Buddhist monastery, so only men are permitted to bathe there.

Notable wildlife in the park includes Kitti's hog-nosed bats (the world's smallest mammal), regal crabs, barking deer, blue pittas, wreathed hornbills, gibbons, Malayan porcupines, slow loris and serow. There are also wild elephants that occasionally cross over from Myanmar. Admission fees are 20B for Thais, 200B for foreigners.

Places to Stay & Eat Forestry department *bungalows* are available at Sai Yok National Park for 500B to 1000B per night; they sleep up to six people. On the river near the suspension bridge, *Saiyok View Raft* (☎ 034-514194) rents tidy rooms on floating rafts with private bathroom for 400B to 600B. During the week you may be able to get these rooms for as low as 300B. There are a couple of other *raft houses* on the river in the park for 350B to 500B a night.

There is a row of permanent *food stalls* next to the parking lot near the visitors centre. Food vendors here can arrange *rooms* for 100B per person.

Getting There & Away If you are going specifically to see the waterfalls, be sure to tell the driver whether you're going to Sai Yok Yai or Sai Yok Noi, as the falls are some 30km apart. The falls can be reached by boarding a bus bound for Thong Pha Phum or Sangkhlaburi. Buses to Sai Yok Yai (35B, almost two hours) leave every 30 minutes between 6 am and 6.30 pm. The last bus back to Kanchanaburi passes at about 4.30 pm. The trip to Sai Yok Noi takes just over an hour (23B). The last bus back to Kanchanaburi passes at about 5 pm. You can also get to Sai Yok Noi by taking the train to Nam Tok and then hiring a

CENTRAL THAILAND

SAI YOK NATIONAL PARK

săwngthăew for half a day to take you to Sai Yok Noi and back to the Nam Tok station. This should cost no more than 400B.

Kheuan Si Nakharin & Si Sawat
เขื่อนศรีนครินทร์และอ.ศรีสวัสดิ์

Route 3199 passes Erawan National Park and continues on to Si Sawat (106km from Kanchanaburi), a town largely inhabited by north-eastern Thais who came to work on the Si Nakharin dam years ago. On the south-eastern bank of the huge Kheuan Si Nakharin is a string of rustic lakeside resorts where individual thatched bungalows cost from 800B to 1000B. Long-tail boats can be hired at the village of Mongkrathae for tours around the lake or across to Nam Tok Huay Khamin.

Prasat Meuang Singh Historical Park
อุทยานประวัติศาสตร์ปราสาท
เมืองสิงห์

Approximately 43km from Kanchanaburi are the remains of an important 13th-century Khmer outpost of the Angkor empire called Meuang Singh. Located on a bend in Mae Nam Khwae Noi, the recently restored city ruins cover 460 *râi* (73.6 hectares) and were declared a historical park under the administration of the Fine Arts Department in 1987. Originally this location may have been chosen by the Khmers as a relay point for trade along Mae Nam Khwae Noi.

All the Meuang Singh shrines are constructed of laterite bricks and are situated in a huge grassy compound surrounded by layers of laterite ramparts. Sections of the ramparts show seven additional layers of earthen walls, suggesting cosmological symbolism in the city plan. Evidence of a sophisticated water system has also been discovered amid the ramparts and moats.

The town encompasses four groups of ruins, although only two groups have been excavated and are visible. In the centre of the complex is the principal shrine, Prasat Meuang Singh, which faces east (towards Angkor). Walls surrounding the shrine have gates in each of the cardinal directions. A reproduction of a sculpture of Avalokiteshvara stands on the inside of the northern wall and establishes Meuang Singh as a Mahayana Buddhist centre. The original is in the National Museum in Bangkok. Inside the main prang is a reproduction of a sculpture of Prajnaparamita, another Mahayana Buddhist deity.

To the north-east of the main *prasat* are the remains of a smaller shrine whose original contents and purpose are unknown. Near the main entrance to the complex at the north gate is a small museum, which contains various sculptures of Mahayana Buddhist deities and stucco decorations, most of which are reproductions.

Clear evidence that this area was inhabited before the arrival of the Khmers can be seen in another small museum to the south of the complex next to the river. The roof shelters two human skeletons arranged in a prehistoric burial site and a detailed explanation of the findings, which included an ornate bronze spoon. A more complete exhibit of local Neolithic remains is at the Ban Kao Neolithic Museum. Entry to the historical park is 40B and it's open 8 am to 5 pm daily.

Ban Kao Neolithic Museum During the construction of the Death Railway along Mae Nam Khwae Noi, a Dutch POW named Van Heekeren uncovered Neolithic remains in the village of Ban Kao (Old Town), about 7km south-east of Meuang Singh. After WWII, a Thai-Danish team retraced Van Heekeren's discovery, concluding that Ban Kao is a major Neolithic burial site. Archaeological evidence suggests it may have been inhabited 10,000 years ago.

A small but well-designed museum, displaying 3000- to 4000-year-old artefacts from the excavation of Ban Kao, has been established near the site. Objects are labelled and include a good variety of early pottery and other utensils, as well as human skeletons. Hours are from 8 am to 4.30 pm Wednesday to Sunday; admission is 30B.

Places to Stay & Eat Guest bungalows were once available for rent near the south gate of the historical park for 500B, but of late it seems they're reserved for visiting archaeologists. If you have your own gear, you could probably *camp* safely by the river. There are a couple of small *restaurants* at the north gate to the park.

The **Ban Rai Rim Kwai** (☎ 034-654077, 333 Mu 2) is 3.5km from the Ban Kao (Tha Kilen) train station. Bungalows and raft houses here cost 1500B to 2500B.

Getting There & Away Ban Kao and Meuang Singh are best reached by train from Kanchanaburi via Ban Kao (Tha Kilen) station, which is only 1km south of Meuang Singh. Walk west towards the river and follow the signs to Meuang Singh. Trains leave Kanchanaburi for Tha Kilen (10B, one hour) at 6.11 and 10.45 am and 4.37 pm daily.

To get to Ban Kao, you may have to walk or hitch 6km south along the road that follows Mae Nam Khwae Noi, although the occasional săwngthăew passes along this road too. Motorcycle taxis are sometimes available at Tha Kilen station for around 25B for the journey to either Ban Kao or Prasat Meuang Singh.

It's possible to get from Kanchanaburi to Meuang Singh and back in one day by catching the 6.11 or 10.45 am train there and the 4.30 pm train back.

If you have your own transport, Ban Kao and/or Meuang Singh would make convenient rest stops on the way to Hellfire Pass or Sangkhlaburi.

Coming from the Erawan National Park area, there's no need to backtrack all the way to Kanchanaburi before heading north on Rte 323. A paved road heads west from Rte 3199 at the 25km marker, then proceeds 16km to meet Rte 323 between the 37km and 38km markers – thus cutting half a day's travel from the old loop. This winding, scenic, lightly trafficked short cut is tremendous for cycling.

Chaloem Ratanakosin National Park (Tham Than Lot)
อุทยานแห่งชาติเฉลิมรัตนโกสินทร์ (ถ้ำธารลอด)

Chaloem Ratanakosin National Park (Tham Than Lot), a 59-sq-km park 97km north of Kanchanaburi, is of interest to speleologists because of two caves, **Tham Than Lot Yai** and **Tham Than Lot Noi**, and to naturalists for its waterfalls and natural forests. Three waterfalls – **Trai Trang**, **Than Ngun** and **Than Thong** – are within easy hiking distance of the bungalows and camp ground. Bungalows

cost from 500B to 1000B per night and sleep 10 to 12 people. Pitch your own tent for 5B per person. Standard national park admission fees apply (see under Sai Yok National Park earlier in this chapter).

Getting There & Away Take a bus from Kanchanaburi to Ban Nong Preu (28B, two to three hours) and then catch a săwngthăew to the park. Most visitors arrive by car, jeep or motorcycle.

Hellfire Pass
ช่องเขาขาด

The Australian-Thai Chamber of Commerce completed the Hellfire Pass Memorial project in 1998. The purpose of the project is to honour the Allied POWs and Asian conscripts who died while constructing some of the most difficult stretches of the Burma-Thailand Death Railway, 80km north-west of Kanchanaburi. 'Hellfire Pass' was the name the POWs gave to the largest of a 1000m series of mountain cuttings through soil and solid rock, which were accomplished with minimal equipment (3.5kg hammers, picks, shovels, steel tap drills, cane baskets for removing dirt and rock, and dynamite for blasting).

The original crew of 400 Australian POWs was later augmented with 600 additional Australian and British prisoners, who worked round the clock in 16- to 18-hour shifts for 12 weeks. The prisoners called it Hellfire Pass because of the way the largest cutting at Konyu looked at night by torch light. By the time the cuttings were finished 70% of the POW crew had died and were buried in the nearby Konyu Cemetery.

The memorial consists of a marked trail that follows the railway remains through the 110m Konyu cutting, then winds up and around the pass and continues through the jungle as far as Compressor cutting (about a three-hour walk). At the far end of Konyu cutting is a memorial plaque fastened to solid stone, commemorating the deaths of the Allied prisoners. There are actually seven cuttings spread over 3.5km – four smaller cuttings and three larger ones.

The Australian-Thai Chamber of Commerce has also cleared a path to the Hin Tok trestle bridge, south-east of the Konyu cutting. This bridge was called the 'Pack of

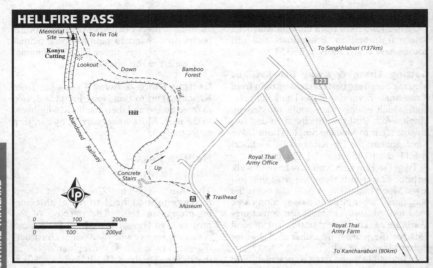

HELLFIRE PASS

Memorial Site
To Hin Tok
Konyu Cutting
Lookout
Down
Bamboo Forest
Trail
Hill
Abandoned Railway
Concrete Stairs
Up
Museum
Trailhead
To Sangkhlaburi (137km)
323
Royal Thai Army Office
Royal Thai Army Farm
To Kanchanaburi (80km)

0   100   200m
0   100   200yd

Cards' by the prisoners because it collapsed three times during construction. Eventually some of the track may be restored to exhibit rolling stock from the WWII era. A museum at the Hellfire Pass trailhead contains artefacts from the era and a short documentary film featuring reminiscences of survivors, which is screened continuously. The memorial and museum is managed by retired Australian lieutenant colonel Terry Beaton and his wife Sheila, and they request that visitors who were POWs in the area (or their descendants) contact them directly so that personalised tours can be given. The museum charges no admission but donations are greatly appreciated.

Getting There & Away Access to Hellfire Pass is via the Royal Thai Army (RTA) farm on Rte 323, between Kanchanaburi and Thong Pha Phum. Proceeding northwest along Rte 323, the farm is 80km from Kanchanaburi, 18km from the Nam Tok train terminus. The entrance to the memorial is well marked.

Once you arrive at the museum, follow the ramp from its entrance down to the trailhead. A fork in the trail gives hikers the option of taking a 500m trail through a bamboo forest or down a concrete stairway directly to the railway. If you can spare the time (about one hour), taking the 'bamboo

trail' is more rewarding as it affords an initial view of the cutting from a lookout point above it. From Konyu cutting, follow the railway south to the concrete stairway that leads back up to the museum, or continue along the railway in a north-westerly direction through four cuttings and over six trestle bridges. This latter hike is only recommended if you arrive early and are up to walking for a few hours. After returning to the museum, you can cool off while watching the documentary short.

Any bus from Kanchanaburi to Thong Pha Phum or Sangkhlaburi will pass the RTA farm, but you'll have to let the bus crew know where you want to get off – tell them *châwng khǎo khàat* (Hellfire Pass). If you're driving, look for the English signs announcing Hellfire Pass on Rte 323.

KANCHANABURI TO THREE PAGODAS PASS

Three Pagodas Pass (Phra Chedi Sam Ong) was one of the terminals of the Death Railway in WWII, and for centuries has been a major relay point for Thai-Burmese trade. Until 1989, when the Myanmar government took control of the Myanmar side of the border from insurgent armies, it was a place that the TAT and the Thai government would rather you'd forget about (much like Mae Salong in the north some years ago), but since then it's been promoted as a tourist destination. There's really not much to see at the pass – the attraction lies in the journey itself and the impressive scenery along the way.

It's an all-day journey and will require you to spend at least one night in Sangkhlaburi, which is a somewhat interesting off-the-track destination in itself. The distance between Kanchanaburi and Sangkhlaburi alone is about 200km, so if you take a motorcycle it is imperative that you fill up before you leave Kanchanaburi and stop for petrol again in Thong Pha Phum, the last town before Sangkhlaburi. By bicycle this would be a very challenging route, but it has been done.

The paved highway used to end in Thong Pha Phum, but now the roads from Thong Pha Phum to Sangkhlaburi and from Sangkhlaburi to Three Pagodas Pass are also paved. The best time to go is in the cooler January and February. During the rainy season nearly the whole of Sangkhlaburi district is under water, making travel difficult.

The road between Kanchanaburi and Thong Pha Phum passes through mostly flat terrain interrupted by the odd limestone outcrop. This is sugar-cane country, and if you're travelling by bicycle or motorcycle during harvest you'll have to contend with huge cane trucks, which strew pieces of cane and dust in their wake – take extra care. Cassava is also cultivated but the cassava trucks aren't such a nuisance.

The road between Thong Pha Phum and Sangkhlaburi is one of the most beautiful in Thailand. It winds through mountains of limestone and along the huge lake created by the Kheuan Khao Laem, a hydroelectric dam near Thong Pha Phum. North of Thong Pha Phum is a major teak reforestation project. In spite of the fact that the road surface is in good condition during the dry season, steep grades and sharp curves make this a fairly dangerous journey, especially the last 25km or so before Sangkhlaburi.

For several years there has been talk of rebuilding the train connection between Nam Tok and Sangkhlaburi, using the old Japanese rail bed. If it ever happens, this will be a spectacular train trip.

Another pipe dream is the construction of a road between Sangkhlaburi and Um Phang in Tak Province, approximately 120km to the north. A very bad dirt road exists now, but it crosses the Thailand-Myanmar border in a couple of places and passes through Karen rebel territory, so it's not really legal. At the moment it's used mostly by trucks carrying ore from Korean-owned antimony mines near the border on the Thai side. During the rainy season it's often impassable due to deep streams that cross the road.

Thong Pha Phum
ทองผาภูมิ

Surrounded by scenic karst topography, the area around the small town of Thong Pha Phum is slowly changing from a simple way station along Rte 323 to a destination in itself. Many of its inhabitants – mainly Mon or Burmese – originally congregated here to work on the construction of the Kheuan Khao Laem.

Mae Nam Khwae Noi runs along the east side of town, and it's possible to raft down river as far as Sai Yok or even all the way to Kanchanaburi. There are some interesting walks and day trips in the area. You can, for example, ford the river over a footbridge close to town to climb a prominent limestone cliff topped by a wát.

Farther afield are **Nam Tok Dai Chong Thong** (35km north via Rte 323), **Nam Tok Kroeng Krawia** (33km north), **Nam Tok Pha That** (30km south at the 105km marker) and **Hin Dat Hot Springs** (32km south at the 107km marker). All are easily accessible from the highway.

More difficult to find, discovered in 1995 by a forest monk, is **Tung Nang Khruan**, a nine-level cascade about 15km north of Thong Pha Phum and about 5km off the road to Sangkhlaburi. You'll need a guide from nearby Ban Tung Nang Khruan and sturdy legs to find it. Eventually a signposted road to the falls will probably be constructed; ask in Thong Pha Phum if you're interested in checking it out.

Places to Stay & Eat The *Som Jainuk Bungalow* (☎ 034-599067, 29/10 Mu 1), on the left-hand side of the town's main street off the highway, has basic but clean rooms with fan and bathroom around a shaded courtyard for 120B. A newer, all air-con building offers large, comfortable rooms

CENTRAL THAILAND

with hot-water showers for 800B. *Si Thong Pha Phum Bungalows* (☎ *034-599058, 78/7 Mu 1*) has large private bungalows for 100B with fan and 250B with air-con, but it's next to a noisy primary school. Better is *Sa Boonyong Bungalows* (☎ *034-599049*), which has 120B rooms with fan similar to those at Som Jainuk, plus air-con rooms for 300B. Since it's a bit farther off the street it tends to be quieter.

Out on the highway the *Ban Chaidaen Phuphaphum Hotel* (☎ *034-599035, fax 599088*) has upmarket rooms with satellite TV, fridge and other amenities for 700B to 1000B.

Green World Hot Spring Resort & Golf Club (☎ *034-599210; in Bangkok ☎ 02-539 4613*), 33km south of town near the 108km marker, is a huge resort with posh rooms costing 600B to 7000B. The nearby *Thong Pha Phum Valley* (☎ *034-542333*) has 12 bungalows for 600B to 2500B. Just beyond the dam west of town are nine rustic lakeside resorts, including *Bangkok Flower*, *Ban Suan Taweechaiphaphum*, *Wang Phai Chalet*, *Khao Laem Resort*, *Phae Rim Kheuan* and *Weekend Garden*. It's mostly a Thai scene, with thatched bungalows in the 500B to 2000B range.

In typical Mon style, several shops and vendors along the main street proffer curry in long rows of pots; instead of two or three curry choices more typical of Thai vendors, the Mon vendors lay out eight or more – all delicious. The best variety is at a shop called *Roi Maw* (Hundred Pots); a branch of the same shop can be found in a relatively new shophouse on the highway just south of town.

A small *night market* convenes near the centre of town each evening with the usual rice and noodle dishes. A riverside restaurant near the highway bridge, *Saep-i-li*, serves good Isan food but it's more set up for drinking and snacking.

Getting There & Away Ordinary buses (No 8203) leave the Kanchanaburi bus station for Thong Pha Phum every half-hour from 6 am until 6.30 pm (50B, about three hours). Air-con buses and minivans to Sangkhlaburi also stop in Thong Pha Phum for about half the regular fare – see the Sangkhlaburi Getting There & Away section for details.

Sangkhlaburi
สังขละบุรี

postcode 71240 • pop 10,300

This small but important Kanchanaburi outpost is inhabited by a mixture of Burmese, Karen, Mon and Thai people, but is mostly Karen and Mon. You'll find very little English spoken out this way – in fact, you may hear as much Burmese, Karen and Mon as Thai.

Hundreds of former residents of Myanmar have moved to the Sangkhlaburi area during the last decade because of fighting in the Three Pagodas Pass area between the Karen and Mon insurgent armies and between Myanmar government forces and the Karen. These groups are also escaping being pressganged as porters for the Myanmar army.

The distance between Kanchanaburi and Sangkhlaburi is about 227km. From Thong Pha Phum to Sangkhlaburi it's 74km.

Information A Siam Commercial Bank in the city centre near the market and Phornphalin Hotel offer foreign-exchange services from 8.30 am to 3.30 pm.

Things to See & Do Sangkhlaburi sits at the edge of the huge lake formed by Kheuan Khao Laem. The town was in fact created after the dam flooded out an older village near the confluence of the three rivers that now feed the reservoir. There's not much to do in town except explore the small **markets** for Burmese handicrafts such as checked cotton blankets, *longyi* (Burmese sarongs) and cheroots. The town comes alive on Mon National Day, celebrated during the last week of July.

Thailand's longest wooden bridge leads over a section of the lake near town to a friendly **Mon settlement** of thatched huts and dirt paths. A market in the village purveys goods smuggled from Myanmar, China and India; there are also a few food vendors with pots of rich Mon curry. The village can be reached in five or 10 minutes by boat (see Boat Trips later in the Sangkhlaburi section) or by walking or cycling over the bridge.

Wat Wang Wiwekaram Also called Wat Mon since most of the monks here are Mon, this monastery is about 3km north of the town on the edge of the reservoir. A tall and revered stupa, Chedi Luang Phaw Uttama, is the centrepiece of the wát. Constructed in the style of the Mahabodhi stupa in Bodhgaya, India, the chedi is topped by 400 *bàat* (about 6kg) of gold. An earlier chedi is located some distance behind the tall one and is 300 to 400 years old. From the edge of the monastery grounds is a view of the tremendous lake and the three rivers that feed into it.

A new section of the Mon temple built across the road features a flashy, multi-roofed wíhǎan with stainless-steel-plated pillars, heavy carved wooden doors and marble banisters. It's surrounded by a carp-filled moat. Local rumour has it that it was built from profits made selling weapons and other supplies to the Mon and Karen armies; the wildest stories even claim that a huge weapons cache is stashed beneath the wíhǎan. A more likely source of support for the wát is the black-market tax collected by the Mon rebel soldiers on all goods smuggled through their territory.

A Burmese handicrafts market convenes at the wát daily from mid-morning until sunset. The selection of wares is as good if not better than what's on offer at Three Pagodas Pass.

Kheuan Khao Laem
เขื่อนเขาแหลม

This huge lake was formed when a dam was constructed across Mae Nam Khwae Noi near Thong Pha Phum in 1983. The lake submerged an entire village at the confluence of the Khwae Noi, Ranti and Sangkhalia Rivers. The spires of the village's **Wat Sam Prasop** (Three Junction Temple) can be seen protruding from the lake in the dry season.

Canoes can be rented for exploring the lake, or for longer trips you can hire a long-tail boat and pilot. Lake boating is a tranquil pastime, best early in the morning with mist and bird life; early evening is also good for bird-watching. At one time a sprawling Mon refugee camp was accessible from the lake but it was recently moved inland. Since relations between Thailand and Myanmar became strained after a series of hostage-taking incidents in late 1999/early 2000, the district's Mon refugee camps have been off limits to visitors.

A branch meditation centre of Kanchanaburi's Sunyataram Forest Monastery is found on the lake's **Ko Kaew Sunyataram** (Sunyataram Jewel Isle). Permission to visit must be obtained from the Sunyataram Forest Monastery, 42km before Sangkhlaburi.

Boat Trips

Burmese Inn and P Guest House & Country Resort (see Places to Stay later) can arrange bamboo-raft or long-tail boat trips on the lake (one of the most popular is a journey by raft along Mae Nam Sangkhalia, taking in a Mon resettlement camp along the way), elephant riding and jungle trekking for 750B to 800B.

Day trips to nearby waterfalls are also a possibility. The rates depend on how many people are on the trip, but they tend to be very reasonable.

Places to Stay

Sangkhlaburi has one hotel, the *Phornphalin Hotel* (☎ 034-595039), which is on the southern edge of town near an army camp and the central market. Rooms cost 200B with fan and bathroom and 350B with air-con; there are also a couple of 'VIP' rooms with TV, fridge and hot-water showers for 700B. The rooms are fairly clean and comfortable.

Down on the lake behind the town is the *P Guest House & Country Resort* (☎ 034-595061, fax 595139). It has bungalows with verandas that have been placed along a slope overlooking the lake; all rooms have a fan and shared bathing facilities and cost 150B. On the downside, you may have to ask the staff to change the bed sheets before you check in. There is a large dining area with a sunset view of the lake but service is very lackadaisical. The guesthouse is about 1.2km from the bus stop in town.

The newer and more friendly *Burmese Inn* (☎/fax 034-595146) is perched in a lagoon with views of the wooden bridge that crosses to the Mon village, about 800m south from the Sangkhlaburi bus station. Run by an Austrian-Thai couple, it offers wooden, thatched-roof bungalows for 80B with shared bathroom and 120B with private bathroom and fan, and larger rooms for 250B to 500B, including one with a TV. Trips to local waterfalls and to Thung Yai Naresuan National Park can be arranged –

there is a good, hand-drawn wall map of the area in the dining area. A motorcycle taxi from the bus stop in Sangkhlaburi to either guesthouse costs 10B.

Above the lake near the bridge to the Mon village is **Samprasop Bungalows** (☎ 034-595050), where single/double air-con rooms with private bathroom in A-frame bungalows cost 600/800B.

Next to P Guest House, the 15-room **Ponnatee Resort** (☎ 034-595134, fax 595270) is a slightly upmarket place with the familiar hillside layout. Plain rooms with fan are overpriced at 800B single/double, 1200B triple. Nearby **Forget Me Not House** (☎ 034-595015, fax 595013) has nicer chalet-style accommodation, although dark inside, with private bathroom for 400B with fan, 700B with air-con. More places are sprouting up on hillsides along the lake. These resorts are oriented towards Thai tourists more than westerners. For now, Sangkhlaburi remains very peaceful – one hopes that local entrepreneurs won't turn it into another Kanchanaburi river scene with all-night floating discos.

Places to Eat
The **Phornphalin Hotel** has a decent restaurant downstairs featuring an extensive English menu. The **Rung Arun** restaurant, opposite the Phornphalin, has a large menu and is also good, and there are three or four other places to eat down the street. The day market in the centre of town sometimes has a couple of vendor **stalls** offering Indian nan and curry. Both **Burmese Inn** and **P Guest House** offer food service.

Shopping
Visitors interested in acquiring some Karen weaving should visit the gift shop operated by Ban Unarak, a home for abandoned children and destitute mothers. The gift shop is located on the road that runs between Burmese Inn and P Guest House.

Getting There & Away
Ordinary bus No 8203 leaves the Kanchanaburi bus station for Sangkhlaburi (80B) at 6, 8.40 and 10.20 am and noon and takes five to six hours, depending on how many mishaps occur on the Thong Pha Phum–Sangkhlaburi road. An air-con bus (121B) leaves at 9.30 am and 1.30 and 3.30 pm and takes four to five hours.

A *rót tûu* (minivan) service from Kanchanaburi to Sangkhlaburi (105B, three hours) leaves seven times daily, from 7.30 am to 4.30 pm, across from the motorcycle taxi stand, stopping at Thong Pha Phum (70B, or 50B from Thong Pha Phum to Sangkhlaburi). The van driver can drop you off at either of the guesthouses or the Phornphalin Hotel on request. In Sangkhlaburi the vans depart from near the market. From either end it's usually best to reserve your seat a day in advance.

If you go by motorcycle or car, you can count on about three hours to cover the 217km from Kanchanaburi to Sangkhlaburi, including three or four short rest stops. Alternatively, you can make it an all-day trip and stop off in Ban Kao, Meuang Singh and Hellfire Pass. Be warned, however, that this is not a trip for an inexperienced motorcycle rider. The Thong Pha Phum to Sangkhlaburi section of the journey (74km) requires sharp reflexes and previous experience on mountain roads. This is also not a motorcycle trip to do alone as stretches of the highway are practically deserted – it's tough to get help if you need it and easy to attract the attention of would-be bandits.

Three Pagodas Pass/Payathonzu
ด่านเจดีย์สามองค์

The pagodas themselves are rather small, but it is the remote nature of this former black-market outpost that draws a trickle of visitors. Control of the Myanmar side of the border once vacillated between the Karen National Union and the Mon Liberation Front, since Three Pagodas (Chedi Sam Ong) was one of several 'toll gates' along the Thailand-Myanmar border where insurgent armies collected a 5% tax on all merchandise that passed. These ethnic groups used the funds to finance armed resistance against the Myanmar government. Now the border crossing and the town on the Myanmar side, Payathonzu, are controlled by the Myanmar government, although much of the long border between the two countries is not under government control.

The Karen people conduct a huge multi-million-dollar business in illegal mining and logging, the products of which are smuggled into Thailand by the truckload under cover of night – not without the palms-up cooperation of the Thai police, of course. Pressure for control of these border points has increased since the Thai government enacted a ban on all logging in Thailand in 1989, which has of course led to an increase in teak smuggling.

In late 1988 heavy fighting broke out between the Karen and the Mon for control of the 'toll gate' here. Since this is the only geographical location for hundreds of kilometres in either direction where a border crossing is convenient, this is where the Mon army (which has traditionally controlled this area) had customarily collected the 5% tax on smuggling. The Karen insurgents do the same at other points north along the Thailand-Myanmar border. Myanmar government pressure on the Karen farther north led to a conflict between the Karen and the Mon over Three Pagodas trade and the village on the Myanmar side was virtually burnt to the ground.

The Myanmar government wrested control of the town in 1989 from both the Karen and Mon. The Burmese seem firmly established at the border for the time being and have renamed the town Payathonzu (Three Pagodas) and filled it with shops catering to an odd mix of occupation troops and tourists.

Foreigners are now allowed to cross the border for day trips but you must complete the necessary paperwork in Sangkhlaburi before coming to the border. Apply for a border pass by visiting the Sangkhlaburi immigration office (around the corner from the Phornphalin Hotel) and providing two passport-sized photos and one copy each of the photo- and visa-pages of your passport. Once your pass is in order, proceed to the border and pay US$10 on the Myanmar side. The crossing is open from 8.30 am to 6 pm. Payathonzu lies 470km by road from Yangon but is considered '75% safe' by the Myanmar military. Apparently insurgent Mon and Karen forces are still in the area and there are occasional firefights.

A true frontier town, Payathonzu has around a half dozen Burmese teahouses (a couple of them with *nam-bya* – the Burmese equivalent to Indian nan bread), one cinema, several mercantile shops with Burmese longyi, cheroots, jade and clothes, and a few general souvenir shops with Mon-Karen-Burmese handicrafts. It is necessary to bargain and traders speak some English and also some Thai. In general the goods are well priced. A Buddhist temple, **Wat Suwankhiri**, can be seen on a bluff near the town.

Nam Tok Kloeng Thaw, 12km from the border in Myanmar, takes a couple of hours by motorcycle to reach from Payathonzu. The road to the falls is open only in the dry season – reportedly the Karen control the waterfall area during the rainy season. Even in good weather, the two-rut track is very rugged and not recommended for motorcycle novices.

A Myanmar military checkpoint at the edge of town usually bars all visitors from leaving the town limits. The border crossing is open from 6 am to 6 pm daily.

Songkran Festival Three Pagodas Pass hosts a large Songkran Festival in April, complete with hemp-fisted Thai-Burmese kick boxing, cockfights, and Karen, Thai, Burmese and Mon folk dancing.

Places to Stay The only place to stay here is at *Three Pagodas Pass Resort* (☎ 034-595316; in Bangkok ☎ 02-412 4159), where large wooden bungalows cost 600B to 1200B (but may be available for half these rates). However, most visitors stay in nearby Sangkhlaburi.

Getting There & Away The 19km paved road to Three Pagodas Pass begins 4km before you reach Sangkhlaburi off Rte 323. At this intersection is a Thai police checkpoint where you may have to stop for minor interrogation, depending on recent events in the Three Pagodas Pass area. Along the way you'll pass a couple of villages inhabited by Mon or Karen people; at one time there was a branch of the All Burma Students Democratic Front here, where self-exiled Yangon students had set up an opposition movement with the intention of ousting the Ne Win government from Myanmar. The students have since moved north to Tak Province.

If you don't have your own wheels, săwngthăew to Three Pagodas Pass (30B) leave about every hour between 6 am and 6.40 pm from a lot near Sangkhlaburi's central market. The last săwngthăew back to Sangkhlaburi leaves Three Pagodas Pass at around 5 or 6 pm.

CENTRAL THAILAND

The border is only a short walk from the săwngthăew stop in Three Pagodas Pass.

THUNG YAI NARESUAN & KHAO LAEM NATIONAL PARKS
อุทยานแห่งชาติทุ่งใหญ่นเรศวร/ อุทยานแห่งชาติเขาแหลม

Approximately 34km south of Sangkhlaburi between the 39km and 40km markers, you'll find a turn-off on the east side of the highway for the 3200-sq-km Thung Yai Naresuan National Park, Thailand's largest protected land parcel. This rough dirt road leads to **Nam Tok Takien Thong**, where pools are suitable for swimming nearly year-round. There are at least two other tracks off the highway into the sanctuary, but to find anything of interest you really should go with a guide – check with the Burmese Inn or P Guest House & Country Resort in Sangkhlaburi. Thung Yai Naresuan is one of the last natural habitats in Thailand for the tiger, whose total numbers nationwide are estimated to be less than 500, perhaps no more than 250.

On the opposite side of the highway near the Thung Yai Naresuan turn-off is a paved road into the recently established Khao Laem National Park. As yet there are no facilities to speak of, but presumably the park was created to protect the riverine habitats near the lake. Standard national park admission fees apply (see under Sai Yok National Park earlier in this chapter).

Tham Sukho is a large limestone cave shrine just off the highway at the 42km marker.

Chonburi Province

SI RACHA
ศรีราชา

postcode 20110 • pop 23,700
About 105km from Bangkok on the eastern coast of the Gulf of Thailand is the small town of Si Racha, home of the famous spicy sauce *náam phrík sĭi raachaa*. Some of Thailand's best seafood, especially the local oysters, is served here accompanied by helpings of this sauce.

On **Ko Loi**, a small rocky island connected to the mainland by a long jetty,

stands a Thai-Chinese Buddhist temple. Farther offshore lies larger Ko Si Chang, flanked by two smaller islands – Ko Kham Yai to the north and Ko Khang Kao to the south. As this grouping of islands provides a natural shelter from the wind and sea, it is used as a harbour by large incoming freighters. Smaller boats transport goods to the Chao Phraya delta some 50km away.

The motorised săamláw in this fishing town and on Ko Si Chang are unlike anywhere else in Thailand – huge motorcycles powered by auto engines, with the plush passenger seating at the rear.

Si Racha Tiger Farm
ฟาร์มเสือศรีราชา

The Si Racha Tiger Farm is an attraction covering 250 râi (40 hectares) off Rte 3241 about 9km south-east of town. The zoo combines a world-famous tiger-breeding facility with a crocodile farm, 'herbivores zone', scorpion farm and circus-like performances.

The tiger farm – said to be the largest and most successful such facility in the world – contains over 130 Bengal tigers. At the unusual 'kinship to the different families complex' you'll see tiger cubs, pigs and dogs living together; don't be too surprised to see sows nursing tiger cubs. The complex is very popular with Asian package tourists who pay to be photographed posing with tiger cubs, iguanas, etc.

The park is open 8 am to 6 pm daily; admission is 250B for adults, 150B for children (60B and 30B respectively for Thais). Animal shows on offer include a crocodile-wrestling show, chimpanzee show and even a 'Scorpion Queen' show. These take place throughout the day and cost 30/20B extra for adults/ kids. For further information call ☎ 038-296571.

Places to Stay

For most people Si Racha is more of a transit point than an overnight stop. The best places to stay in Si Racha are the rambling wooden hotels built on piers over the waterfront.

The *Siriwatana Hotel* (☎ 038-311037, *35 Thanon Jermjompol)*, across from Thanon Tessaban 1 and the Bangkok Bank is the cleanest of the lot and has the best

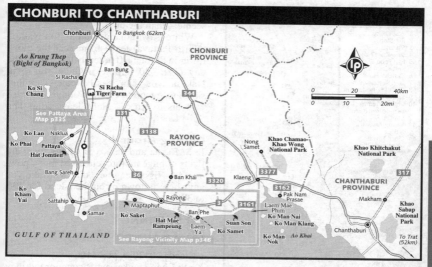

CHONBURI TO CHANTHABURI

service. There are rustic sitting areas with tables outside the rooms along the piers. Basic rooms with fan and shower cost 160B to 180B (up to 280B for a room that sleeps up to five). Simple, inexpensive meals can be prepared on request or you're free to bring your own food and use the tables provided. The *Siwichai*, next to the Siriwatana, has similar rooms for 200B, plus its own pier restaurant. The *Samchai*, on Soi 10, across from Thanon Surasakdi 1, has reasonable rooms for 180B and some air-con rooms (350B) as well. All three are open and breezy, with outdoor tables where you can bring food in the evening from nearby markets.

There are several top-end hotels in town, including the 20-storey *Laemthong Residence Hotel* (☎/fax 038-322886) in the centre of town, just off Thanon Sukhumvit (Hwy 3). Comfortable doubles with all the amenities cost from 963B, including breakfast; facilities on the premises include a swimming pool and tennis courts.

The classy *City Hotel* (☎ 038-322700, fax 322739, 6/126 Thanon Sukhumvit) offers capacious rooms from 2300B, but discounts of up to 30% are sometimes available. An escalator leads from the pavement to the 2nd-floor reception; facilities include a pub, coffee shop, fitness centre and business centre.

Places to Eat

There is plenty of good seafood in Si Racha, but you have to watch the prices. Best known is the Chinese owned *Chua Lee* on Thanon Jermjompol (Joemjomphon), across from the Krung Thai Bank. The seafood is great but probably the most expensive in town.

Next door and across the street are several seafood places with similar fare at much more reasonable prices, such as the *Fast Food Seafood Restaurant* just south of Thanon Tessaban 1.

Jarin, on Tha Soi 14, has very good one-plate seafood dishes, especially *khâo hàw mòk thá-leh* (steamed seafood curry with rice) and *kŭaytĭaw phàt thai kûng sòt* (Thai-style rice noodles with fresh shrimp). It's a great restaurant in which to kill time while waiting for the next boat to Ko Si Chang; prices are low to moderate.

At the end of the pier at Soi 18 is the large *Seaside Restaurant* – now just about the best all-round seafood place in town for atmosphere, service and value. The full-colour bilingual menu includes a tasty grilled-seafood platter stacked with squid, mussels, shrimp and cockles. All these dishes plus generous servings of Haagen-Dazs ice cream.

The cheapest place to eat is in the *market* near the clock tower at the southern end

SI RACHA WATERFRONT

1 Post Office
2 Bus Stop
3 Siwichai
4 Siriwatana Hotel
5 Fast Food Seafood Restaurant
6 Samchai Hotel
7 Jarin Restaurant
8 Chua Lee Restaurant
9 Krung Thai Bank
10 Chinese Temple
11 Seaside Restaurant
12 Market
13 Sawngthaew to Naklua
14 Clock Tower
15 Municipal Office

of town. In the evenings the market offers everything from noodles to fresh seafood, while in the daytime it's a food and clothing market with some noodle and snack stands.

Outside town, off Thanon Sukhumvit (Hwy 3) on the way to Pattaya, there are a couple of good fresh-seafood places. At Ao Udom, a small fishing bay close to town in the same direction, you'll also find several open-air seafood eateries.

Getting There & Away
Buses to Si Racha leave the Eastern bus station in Bangkok every 30 minutes or so from 5 am to 7 pm (35B ordinary, 81B aircon, about 1¾ hours). Ordinary direct buses stop near the pier for Ko Si Chang, but through buses and air-con buses stop on Thanon Sukhumvit (Hwy 3), near the Laemthong Department Store, from where there are túk-túk to the pier.

You can also reach Si Racha by 3rd-class train (28B), although not many people come by this method. Train No 239 leaves Bangkok's Hualamphong station at 6.55 am and arrives at Si Racha at 10.15 am (about

an hour slower – but a good deal more scenic – than the bus).

White săwngthăew bound for Naklua (North Pattaya) leave from near the clock tower in Si Racha frequently throughout the day (12B, 30 minutes). Once you're in Naklua you can easily catch another săwngthăew on to central Pattaya.

Boats to Ko Si Chang leave from Tha Soi 14.

Getting Around
In Si Racha and on Ko Si Chang there are fleets of huge motorcycle taxis, many powered by Nissan engines, that will take you anywhere in town or on the island for 20B to 30B.

KO SI CHANG
เกาะสีชัง

postcode 20120 • pop 4100
Ko Si Chang makes a nifty one- or two-day getaway from Bangkok. There is only one town on the island, facing the mainland; the rest of the tiny island has some history and is fun to explore. The small population is made up of fisherfolk, retired and working mariners and government workers who are stationed with the customs office or with one of the aquaculture projects on the island.

Information
A branch of Thai Farmer's Bank in town – on the main road to the right as you walk up from the pier – does foreign exchange on weekdays.

Things to See & Do
A meditation hermitage, **Yai Phrik Vipassana Centre**, is ensconced in limestone caves and palm huts along the island's centre ridge. The hermit caves make an interesting visit but should be approached with respect – monks and mâe chii (nuns) from all over Thailand come here to take advantage of the peaceful environment for meditation. Be careful that you don't fall down a limestone shaft; some are almost completely covered with vines.

On the opposite side of the island, facing out to sea, are some beaches with decent swimming – take care with the tide and the sea urchins though. Don't come here looking for perfect white sand and turquoise waters, as the island's proximity to shipping lanes and fishing grounds means its shores are less than tidy. Depending on sea currents and time of year, the shoreline can be relatively clean or cluttered with flotsam. For beaches you're better off heading farther south-east to Ko Samet.

Secluded **Hat Tham** (also called Hat Sai) can be reached by following a branch of the ring road on foot to the back of the island. During low tide there's a strip of sand here. A partially submerged cave can be visited at the eastern end of the little bay. There is also a more public – and generally less clean – beach at the western end of the island (about 2km from the pier), near the grounds of the old palace, called **Hat Tha Wang**. Thai residents and visitors from the mainland come here for picnics.

The **palace** was once used by King Chulalongkorn (Rama V) over the summer months, but was abandoned when the French briefly occupied the island in 1893. The main throne hall – a magnificent golden teak structure called Vimanmek – was moved to Bangkok in 1910. Recently the Fine Arts Department began restoring the remaining palace buildings, which were named after the king's consorts, Pongsri, Wattana and Apirom. The palace gardens have also been renovated and you can easily spend a couple of hours strolling here. Keep an eye out for Ko Si Chang's protected species of white squirrel, which is making a steady comeback after being hunted to endangered status.

On the crest of the hill overlooking Hat Tha Wang is a large white chedi that contains **Wat Atsadangnimit**, a small consecrated chamber where King Chulalongkorn used to meditate. The unique Buddha image inside was fashioned 50 years ago by a local monk who now lives in the cave hermitage. Nearby you'll come to a stone outcrop wrapped in holy cloth. The locals call it 'Bell Rock' because if struck with a rock or heavy stick it rings like a bell.

Not far from Wat Atsadangnimit is a large limestone cave called **Tham Sao-wapha**, which appears to plunge deep into the island. If you have a torch, the cave might be worth exploring.

To the east of town, high on a hill overlooking the sea, is a large Chinese temple called **San Jao Phaw Khao Yai**. During Chinese New Year in February, the island is overrun with Chinese visitors from the mainland. This is one of Thailand's most interesting Chinese temples, with shrine caves, several different temple levels and a good view of Si Chang and the ocean. It's a long and steep climb from the road below.

Like most islands along Thailand's eastern seaboard, Ko Si Chang is best visited on weekdays; on weekends and holidays the island can get crowded.

Places to Stay

The cheapest place is the rather characterless **Tiewpai Guest House** (Thiu Phai; ☎ 038-216084) in town, not far from the main piers. Tiewpai has singles/doubles with shared facilities for 150/250B, and nicer rooms with private shower, air-con and TV for 500/600B. Perhaps because Tiewpai has the lowest prices on the island and sends touts to the pier to meet visitors the place is often full, but the staff can be rather cold.

Out near the gate to Hat Tha Wang, **Benz Bungalow** (☎ 038-216091) offers clean rooms facing the sea in a basic hotel-style building or in one of its unique stone bungalows for 500B with fan and bathroom and 800B with air-con.

Near Hat Tham at the back of the island is **Si Phitsanu Bungalow** (☎ 038-216034). Rooms in a row house cost from 600B per night; you can also get a one-bedroom bungalow overlooking the small bay for 800B or a two-bedroom bungalow for 1200B to 1500B. To reach this area from town, take the first right past the Tiewpai Guest House, then follow the road past the Yai Phrik Vipassana Centre. A motorcycle săamláw costs 30B.

Near the Chinese temple is the **Sichang View Resort** (☎ 038-216210), with 10 tidy apartment-style bungalows on nicely landscaped grounds for 800B to 1100B (as low as 500B in low-season months such as June and September).

Sichang Palace (☎ 038-216276) is a three-storey hotel in the middle of town on Thanon Atsadang. Clean, comfortable singles/doubles facing the swimming pool cost 805B, while those with sea views cost 905B. There is also a larger 'suite' for 1400B. During weekends the staff may add 100B to 200B to these prices.

Places to Eat

The town has several small restaurants, but nothing special, with all the Thai and Chinese standard dishes. Along the road that leads to the public beach (Hat Tha Wang) are a couple of rustic *seafood places*.

Sichang Palace and *Sichang View Resort* each have their own restaurants serving good seafood at medium-high prices. *Tiewpai Guest House* offers reasonably priced Thai and Western food.

Getting There & Away

Boats to Ko Si Chang leave hourly from the pier in Si Racha at the end of Soi 14, Thanon Jermjompol. The fare is 30B each way; the first boat leaves at about 6 am and the last at 6 pm. The last boat back to Si Racha from Si Chang is at 5 pm. As you approach Ko Si Chang by boat, check out the dozens of barges anchored in the island's lee. Their numbers have multiplied from year to year as shipping demands by Thailand's booming import and export business have increased.

Getting Around

There are fleets of huge motorcycle taxis that will take you anywhere on the island for 20B to 30B. You can also get a complete tour of the island for 150B per hour. Asking prices for any ride tend to be outrageous; the supply of taxis is plentiful, however, and you can usually get the local price after talking to several drivers.

PATTAYA
พัทยา

postcode 20260 • pop 56,700

Pattaya, 147km south-east of Bangkok, is Thailand's busiest beach resort, with over 12,000 rooms available in hotels, bungalows and guesthouses spread along Hat Pattaya and adjoining Naklua and Jomtien beaches. Hat Pattaya is the most active of the three beaches, a crowded crescent of sand where jet skis and powerboats slice the surf and parasails billow over the palms all day long. Sunburned visitors jam the beachfront road in rented jeeps and motorbikes.

According to TAT statistics, an average one-third of foreign tourists to Thailand visit Pattaya; in a typical November to March season Pattaya receives around a million visitors. Most of them are package tourists from Europe, Russia and the Middle East. Depending on their tastes, some visitors will find Pattaya lacking in culture as well as good taste, since much of the place seems designed to attract tourists interested in a prefabricated, Western-style beach vacation with almost no 'Thai' ingredients.

Hat Pattaya is also not that great (although it must have been at one time) and the town's biggest businesses – water sports and street sex – have driven prices for food and accommodation beyond Bangkok levels. And compared with many other Thai resort areas, it's more money-oriented and less friendly.

Pattaya still continues to attract a loyal following of Bangkok oil-company expats, convention goers and package tourists. Local authorities and travel suppliers have been trying to upgrade Pattaya's image as well as clean the place up in general. Lately it has begun attracting family groups again, as the South Pattaya sex industry has been diminishing slightly.

Pattaya got its start as a resort when US GIs from a base in Nakhon Ratchasima began visiting the one-time fishing village in 1959. US navy men from nearby Sattahip added to the military influx during the Vietnam War years. Nowadays there are still plenty of sailors around, but of many nationalities. National and international convention-goers make up another large segment of the current market, along with Asian golfers seeking out the 12 local golf courses, including courses designed by names such as Robert Trent Jones and Jack Nicklaus.

Pattaya is acclaimed for its seafood, although it's generally way overpriced by national (but not international) standards. Pattaya's lingering notoriety for sex tourism revolves around a collection of discos, outdoor bars and transvestite cabarets comprising Pattaya's red-light district at the southern end of the beach. That part of South Pattaya known as 'the village' attracts a large number of *kàthoey* (transvestites), who pose as female hookers and ply their trade among the droves of sex tourists as well as a prominent gay scene.

The one thing the Pattaya area has going for it is diving centres. There are over a dozen nice islands off Pattaya's shore, although they can be expensive (compared with the rest of Thailand) to reach. If you're a snorkelling or scuba enthusiast, equipment can be booked at any of the several diving shops or diving schools at Hat Pattaya. Ko Lan, the most popular of the islands, even has places to stay.

Information

Tourist Offices The TAT office (☎ 038-427667, ⓔ tatpty@chonburi.ksc.co.th), in a new office at the north-western edge of King Rama IX Park, keeps an up-to-date list of accommodation in the Pattaya area and is very helpful. Hours are from 8.30 am to 7.30 pm. The tourist police office (☎ 038-429371, 1155) is on Thanon Pattaya 2.

Immigration The Pattaya immigration office on Thanon Pattaya Klang is open 8.30 am to 4.30 pm weekdays.

Money The Krung Thai Bank on Soi 15 (Soi Post Office) is open from 10 am to 9 pm. Nearly every bank in Pattaya has an ATM.

Post & Communications The main post office is in South Pattaya on Soi 15. It's open 8.30 am to 4.30 pm weekdays and 9 am to noon on holidays.

The CAT office is located near the corner of Thanon Pattaya Tai and Thanon Pattaya 3. There are also several private long-distance phone offices in town: the best one is the Overseas Cafe, near the intersection of Thanon Hat Pattaya and Thanon Pattaya Tai. Rates are among the lowest in town, and it's open from 9 am to 1 am, allowing you to take advantage of night-time discounts.

Radio Pattaya has a radio station with English-language broadcasts at FM 107.7 MHz. US and British announcers offer a mix of local news and music.

Newspapers & Magazines *Explore Pattaya*, a free monthly magazine distributed round town, contains information on current events, sightseeing and advertisements for hotel and restaurant specials. *What's On Pattaya* is a similar publication. *Pattaya Mail*, a weekly newspaper, publishes articles on political, economic and environmental developments in the area as well as the usual ads.

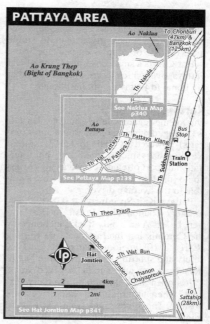

Medical Services Pattaya Memorial Hospital (☎ 038-429422–4, 422741) on Thanon Pattaya Klang offers 24-hour service.

Apakorn Kiatiwong Naval Hospital (☎ 038-601185), 26km south-east of Pattaya in Sattahip, has a fully operative recompression chamber; urgent care is available 24 hours.

Beaches

Curving around Ao Pattaya (Pattaya Bay), **Hat Pattaya** is a relatively scenic crescent of sand backed by a narrow thread of palms and a very dense layer of hotels, restaurants, diving shops, car- and motorbike-rental agencies and other tourist-oriented commercial establishments.

A better beach in the immediate Pattaya area is 6km-long **Hat Jomtien** (Jawmthian), about 2km south of Pattaya. Here the water is cleaner and you're well away from the noisy Pattaya bar scene. The hotels and restaurants are more spread out here as well, so there's a better sense of space and relaxation.

Hat Naklua, a smaller beach north of Pattaya, is also quiet and fairly tastefully

CENTRAL THAILAND

developed. Jomtien and Naklua are where families tend to stay, as Pattaya/South Pattaya is pretty much given over to single male tourists or couples on package tours.

Hat Cliff is a small cove just south of Hat Pattaya, over which looms a set of cliffs that are home to Pattaya's glitziest hotels.

Karting

One of the legacies left behind by US GIs is karting, the racing of miniature autos (go-karts) powered by 5HP to 15HP engines. Karting has since turned into an international sport often described as the closest approximation to Formula One racing available to the average driver.

Pattaya Kart Speedway (☎ 038-422044), at 248/2 Thanon Thep Prasit, in Hat Jomtien, boasts Asia's only track sanctioned by the Commission Internationale de Karting (CIK), a 1080m loop that meets all CIK safety and sporting standards, plus a beginners' track and an off-road (unpaved) track.

It's open 9.30 am to 6.30 pm daily (except when international kart races are hosted). The prices range from 150B for 10 minutes of racing 5HP karts, which are oriented towards children, to 250B for a 10HP to 15HP kart.

Water Sports

Pattaya and Jomtien have some of the best water-sports facilities in Thailand. Water-skiing costs around 1000B per hour including equipment, boat and driver. Parasailing is 200B to 300B a shot (about 10 to 15 minutes) and windsurfing 500B an hour. Game-fishing is also a possibility; rental rates for boats, fishing guides and tackle are quite reasonable.

Hat Jomtien is the best spot for wind-surfing, not least because you're a little less likely to run into parasailors or jet skiers. Surf House International Hotel on Thanon Hat Jomtien rents out equipment and offers instruction.

Scuba Diving Pattaya is the most convenient diving location to Bangkok, but it is far from the best Thailand has to offer. In recent years the fish population has dwindled considerably and visibility is often poor due to heavy boat traffic. Although nearby Ko Lan, Ko Sak and Ko Krok are fine for beginners, accomplished divers may prefer the 'outer islands' of Ko Man Wichai and Ko Rin, which have more visibility. In most places expect 3m to 9m of visibility under good conditions, or in more remote sites 5m to 12m. Farther south-east, shipwrecks *Petchburi Bremen* and *Hardeep* off Sattahip and Samae have created artificial reefs and are interesting dive sites.

Diving costs are quite reasonable: a two-dive excursion averages from 1300B to 1800B for boat, equipment, underwater guide and lunch. Snorkellers may join such day trips for 500B to 800B. For shipwrecks, the price goes up to 2500B to 2900B (depending on the season), and for an overnight trip with five to seven dives, figure up to 6000B per person. Full National Association of Underwater Instructors (NAUI) or Professional Association of Dive Instructors (PADI) certification, which takes three to four days, costs 9000B to 12,000B for all instruction and equipment.

Some shops do half-day group trips to nearby islands for as low as 500B to 800B per person, and to islands a bit farther out from 650B; these prices include lunch, beverages, transport and dive master but no equipment rental beyond mask, fins and snorkel.

Average rental rates per day are: mask fins and snorkel 200B to 250B; regulator w/SPG 300B to 400B; buoyancy compensation device 250B to 400B; weight-belt 150B; tank 150B; wetsuit 300B; or full scuba outfit 1500B. Airfills typically cost 100B to 150B. To protect themselves from steep baht fluctuations, some diving operators quote only in US dollars – a reasonable strategy considering virtually all equipment must be imported.

Pattaya shops advertise trips, and several Pattaya hotels also arrange excursions and equipment, including:

Aquanauts Diving (☎ 038-361724, 710727) Thanon Hat Pattaya

Dave's Diver Den (☎ 038-420411, fax 360095) 190/11 Mu 9, Thanon Pattaya Klang

Larry's Dive (☎ 038-710999) Thanon Pattaya Tai, South Pattaya
Web site: www.larrysdive.com

Mermaid's Dive Center (☎ 038-232219, fax 232221) Soi White House, Hat Jomtien

Millennium Divers (☎ 038-427185) Soi Pattay Land 1, South Pattaya

Paradise Scuba Divers (☎ 038-710567) Siam Bayview Resort

Scuba Professionals (☎ 038-221860, fax 221618) 3 Thanon Naklua
Scuba Tek Dive Center (☎ 038-361616, ⓔ rickr@loxinfo.co.th) Weekender Hotel, Thanon Pattaya 2
Seafari Sports Center (☎ 038-429253, fax 424708) Soi 5, North Pattaya

Other Sports
Other recreational activities available include bowling, snooker, archery, tennis, target-shooting, golf and horse riding. Among the several gyms and fitness centres around town is Gold's Gym in South Pattaya's Julie Complex. Gold's has a second branch in North Pattaya just past Soi 1 on Thanon Naklua-Pattaya.

Places to Stay – Budget
The number of places to stay in Naklua, Pattaya and Jomtien is mind-boggling – close to 200 hotels, guesthouses and bungalows. Because of low occupancy rates, some hotels offer special deals, especially mid-week; bargaining for a room may also net a lower rate. On weekends and holidays the cheaper rooms tend to book out.

In Pattaya, North Pattaya and Naklua are quieter and better places to stay if you want to avoid the full-on nightlife of South Pattaya. Overall Hat Jomtien is much better, with clean water and beach, and no obvious sex scene.

An average hotel room costs 350B to 2000B, and for guesthouses the prices range from around 300B to 450B.

Pattaya You'll find the cheapest places in town are the guesthouses in South Pattaya along Thanon Pattaya 2, the street parallel to Thanon Hat Pattaya. Most are clustered near Soi 6, 10, 11 and 12. Opposite Soi 11, the modern four-storey *Apex Hotel* (☎ 038-429233, fax 421184, 216/2 Thanon Pattaya 2) has rooms with air-con, hot water, TV and fridge for 400B in the new building and 350B in the older wing at the back – great value. There's also a pool on the premises. Almost next door, the *Diana Inn* (☎ 038-429675, fax 424566) has large rooms with air-con and hot-water bathroom for 650B, plus a restaurant and a pool with bar service.

The *Honey Lodge* (☎ 038-429133, fax 710185, 597/8 Mu 10, Thanon Pattaya Tai)

has air-con rooms with hot water, fridge and phone for 500B. It also has a restaurant and pool.

In a lane south of Soi 12, the family-run *BR Inn* (☎ 038-428229) offers single rooms for 250B, double rooms for 350B and an air-con room that sleeps three for 400B. All rooms have TV. Many Japanese budget travellers stay here. On Soi 13, the *Malibu Guest House* (☎ 038-428667) was undergoing renovation at last visit, but will reopen in the 350B to 500B range for air-con rooms. The rest of the many guesthouses on Soi 13 are in the 300B to 350B range, but rooms are usually cramped and without windows. An exception is *Ma Maison* (☎ 038-429318, fax 426060), which offers chalet-style air-con rooms around a swimming pool for 850B, including breakfast; as the name suggests, it's French managed and there's a French restaurant on the premises. Advance reservations are highly recommended, as it's often booked out.

Down in South Pattaya on Soi Viking, the *Viking* (☎ 038-423164, fax 425964) has been a long-time favourite for its quiet 350B (fan) and 450B (air-con) rooms and pool. *Pattaya Land Hotel* (☎ 038-429569, fax 421945, 325/42–45 Soi 1, Thanon Pattaya Land) sits right smack in the middle of 'Boys' Town' and has air-con rooms for 400B. Not surprisingly, the majority of the hotel's clientele didn't come for a night's sleep.

Wedged between North and Central Pattaya on Thanon Hat Pattaya, the three-storey *BJ Guest House* (☎ 038-421147) sits across from the beach and has air-con rooms with TV and fridge for 400B. BJ's restaurant serves Thai and German dishes.

Another German-oriented place is *Welkom Inn* (☎ 038-422589, fax 361193, Soi 3, Thanon Hat Pattaya), where air-con rooms cost 450B to 650B; a large pool, Thai garden restaurant and Franco-Belgian restaurant are pluses.

Hat Jomtien At Hat Jomtien, the budget category consists of several places around the mid-range Surf House International Hotel at the northern end of the beach. *Moonshine Place Guest House* (☎ 038-231956) has rooms for 500B; the popular old west–style bar/restaurant downstairs could make it noisy at night. Next to Surf

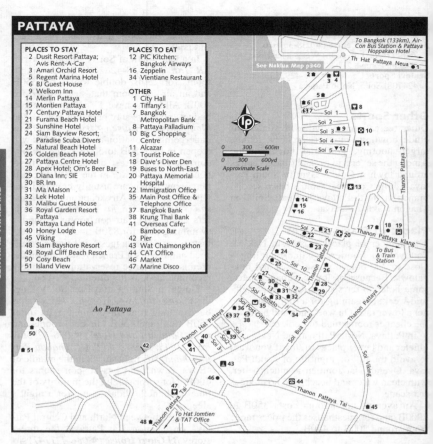

PATTAYA

PLACES TO STAY
2 Dusit Resort Pattaya;
   Avis Rent-A-Car
3 Amari Orchid Resort
5 Regent Marina Hotel
6 BJ Guest House
9 Welkom Inn
14 Merlin Pattaya
16 Montien Pattaya
17 Century Pattaya Hotel
21 Furama Beach Hotel
23 Sunshine Hotel
24 Siam Bayview Resort;
   Paradise Scuba Divers
25 Natural Beach Hotel
26 Golden Beach Hotel
27 Pattaya Centre Hotel
28 Apex Hotel; Orn's Beer Bar
30 Diana Inn; SIE
31 Ma Maison
32 Lek Hotel
33 Malibu Guest House
36 Royal Garden Resort
   Pattaya
39 Pattaya Land Hotel
40 Honey Lodge
45 Viking
48 Siam Bayshore Resort
49 Royal Cliff Beach Resort
50 Cosy Beach
51 Island View

PLACES TO EAT
12 PIC Kitchen;
   Bangkok Airways
16 Zeppelin
34 Vientiane Restaurant

OTHER
1 City Hall
4 Tiffany's
7 Bangkok
   Metropolitan Bank
8 Pattaya Palladium
10 Big C Shopping
   Centre
11 Alcazar
13 Tourist Police
18 Dave's Diver Den
19 Buses to North-East
20 Pattaya Memorial
   Hospital
22 Immigration Office
35 Main Post Office &
   Telephone Office
37 Bangkok Bank
38 Krung Thai Bank
41 Overseas Cafe;
   Bamboo Bar
42 Pier
43 Wat Chaimongkhon
44 CAT Office
46 Market
47 Marine Disco

House is **Sunlight Seafood & Hotel** (☎ 038-231835), with similar 500B air-con rooms and rooms with fan for 250B to 300B; most have private balconies.

The **DD Inn** (☎ 038-232995, 410/50 Thanon Hat Jomtien) is also at the northern end of the beach (sometimes referred to separately as Hat Dong Tan or 'Sugar Palm Beach'). Very clean air-con rooms with TV cost 350B, 400B for a room with a balcony. Almost next door, the **Sugar Palm Beach Hotel** (☎ 038-231386, fax 231713) offers rooms with air-con, TV and refrigerator for 650B (850B for a sea view) in a small but well-kept beachfront property.

Nearby **JB Guest House** (☎ 038-231581) takes the prize, with excellent singles/doubles with fan and cold-water bathroom for 250B;

air-con rooms with TV and hot water for 350B; rooms with a fridge and a sea view for 450B; and larger rooms for 600B. **Seaview Villa** (Chom Thaleh; ☎ 038-231070), farther south on Thanon Hat Jomtien, has nicely appointed bungalows starting at 1800B.

The friendly four-storey **Villa Navin** (☎ 038-231066, fax 231318, 350 Mu 12, Thanon Hat Jomtien) has doubles from 500B and three-bedroom air-con bungalows from 3200B. An outdoor restaurant specialises in seafood.

One of the cheapest places to stay is the tidy **RS Guest House** (☎ 038-231867), which sits at the southern end of the beach, near Thanon Chaiyapreuk. Reasonable, smallish rooms cost 250B with fan, 350B with air-con; all have cold-water showers.

You can also find unnamed *rooms for rent* in 'condotels' along Hat Jomtien for about 200B to 400B a night with fan and 400B to 600B with air-con. These are little more than concrete cubes filled with box-like rooms, often lacking in ventilation and plumbing efficiency.

Jomtien Hotel (☎ *038-251606, fax 251097, 403/74 Mu 12, Thanon Hat Jomtien*), at the northern end of Jomtien off the road leading to South Pattaya, stands well away from the beach. It's basically a low-end tourist hotel. The fan rooms look rather neglected but are cheap – only 200B. Air-con rooms go for up to 1200B, but discounts are sometimes given. There is a small rectangular pool on the roof. The fan rooms are OK value if you don't mind staying in a cement box.

The *Pattaya Noppakao Hotel* (☎/fax 038-370582, 10/17 Mu 6, Thanon Hat Pattaya Neua), next to the station for air-con buses to Bangkok, offers spacious, clean rooms with air-con, hot-water shower and satellite TV starting at 450B – good value for Pattaya.

Places to Stay – Mid-Range

Pattaya Good mid-range places can be found in Naklua, North Pattaya and Jomtien. In Pattaya the *Sunshine Hotel* (☎ *038-429247, fax 421302*) is tucked away at 217/1 Soi 8, where all rooms come with air-con, TV and mini-fridge for a well-priced 500B. The hotel also has two pools and a restaurant that stays open until midnight.

On Soi 11 the *Natural Beach Hotel* (☎ *038-710121, fax 429650*) overlooks the beach and has good air-con rooms for 750B. This modern, breezy, two-storey hotel also contains a small restaurant.

Farther south, on the corner of Thanon Pattaya 2 and Soi 13, is the high-rise *Lek Hotel* (☎ *038-425551/2, fax 426629*) with decent air-con rooms with TV for 560B.

In North Pattaya, *Regent Marina Hotel* (☎ *038-428015, fax 423296, 463/31 Thanon Pattaya Neua; in Bangkok* ☎ *02-390 2511*) bridges the mid-range to top-end gap with rooms from 800B to 1500B. Rooms come with air-con, TV, phone and fridge.

Furama Beach Hotel (☎ *038-428580, fax 428580, 164 Mu 9, Thanon Pattaya Klang*), a couple of blocks back from the beach, is a worn but clean hotel with all the

basic resort amenities. The rooms here cost 600B per night. On the premises are a coffee shop (open until midnight), seafood restaurant and swimming pool.

Naklua The two-storey *Garden Lodge* (☎ *038-429109, fax 421221*), built around a circular drive just off Thanon Naklua, features air-con rooms for 700B, plus a clean pool and good service

Seaview Resort Hotel (☎ *038-429317, fax 423668, Soi 18, Thanon Naklua*), on a quiet soi off Thanon Naklua, is an L-shaped four-storey hotel with decent air-con rooms for 750B per night, 850B with breakfast. Families and small groups may like the quieter *Pattaya Lodge* (☎ *038-225464; in Bangkok* ☎ *02-238 0230*), which is farther off Thanon Naklua, right on the beach and far from Pattaya's noise, pollution and bars. Two-storey, air-con bungalows cost 2700B (two bedrooms, sleeps six), 3300B (three bedrooms, sleeps nine) and 3800B (four bedrooms, sleeps 12). Discounts of 20% are given during the week.

The *Riviera Hotel Pattaya* (☎ *038-225230, fax 225764, 157/1 Soi Wat Pa Samphan, Thanon Naklua*) stands between the road and the beach and has cosy, quiet air-con rooms for 300B and from 400B with fridge and TV. The Riviera also boasts a large garden area and pool.

Hat Jomtien Peaceful Hat Jomtien has mostly mid-range condotel places with prices ranging from 500B to 800B. Set back from the main drag, the *Silver Sand Villa* (☎ *038-231288/9, fax 232491*) has spacious double air-con hotel rooms for 800B in the old wing and 1500B in the new wing. Prices include breakfast and there's a swimming pool on the premises. Farther north, the *Jomtien Bayview* (☎ *038-251889*) has air-con rooms with TV for 390B to 690B.

The friendly *Surf House International Hotel* (☎ *038-231025/6*), next to the Thai Farmer's Bank, has air-con rooms for 400B, 500B with a sea view and 600B with a bath tub as well. All rooms come with TV and fridge.

The *Marine Beach Hotel* (☎ *038-231129–31, 131/62 Thanon Hat Jomtien*) charges 500B to 1200B for air-con rooms. The well-run *Sea Breeze Hotel* (☎ *038-231056–8, fax 231059*) charges 800B to

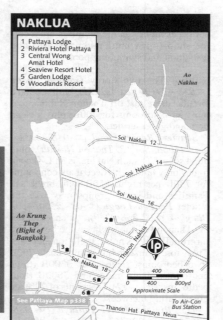

NAKLUA

1 Pattaya Lodge
2 Riviera Hotel Pattaya
3 Central Wong Amat Hotel
4 Seaview Resort Hotel
5 Garden Lodge
6 Woodlands Resort

Ao Naklua

Ao Krung Thep (Bight of Bangkok)

Soi Naklua 12
Soi Naklua 14
Soi Naklua 16
Soi Naklua 18

Thanon Naklua

0   400   800m
0   400   800yd
Approximate Scale

See Pattaya Map p338

To Air-Con Bus Station

Thanon Hat Pattaya Neua

1200B for air-con rooms. A good-value place is the friendly five-storey *Summer Beach Inn* (☎ 038-231777, fax 231778), near the Marine Beach Hotel, where fairly new air-con rooms cost 700B, including satellite TV and fridge in all rooms.

Another good deal is the pink-walled *Furama Jomtien Beach Inn* (☎ 038-231545), on Thanon Hat Jomtien south of Thanon Chaiyapreuk, where standard rooms with TV and air-con cost 500B to 600B and larger rooms cost 700B. The Furama caters particularly to Japanese, Chinese and Korean package tourists.

Jomtien Chalet (☎ 038-231205–8, 57/1 Mu 1, Thanon Hat Jomtien) offers simple, clean, air-con bungalows for 1800B. Two rooms in an old refurbished railway car go for 700B to 900B, depending on number of people and season; a restaurant serves Thai and Western food.

Places to Stay – Top End

Pattaya is really a resort for package tourists and convention goers, so the vast majority of its accommodation is in this price bracket. All of the following hotels have air-con rooms and swimming pools (unless otherwise noted). In most cases the upper end of the price range represents suites, while the lower end are standard doubles. Many of the top-end hotels have reduced rates on standard singles and doubles, so it's worth asking if anything cheaper is available when requesting a rate quote. Rooms are also often cheaper when booked through a Bangkok travel agency, or via the Internet.

Pattaya Among the reigning monarchs of Pattaya luxury hotels is the 500-room *Dusit Resort Pattaya* (☎ 038-425611, fax 428239, 240/2 Thanon Hat Pattaya Neua; in Bangkok ☎ 02-236 0450), in North Pattaya. It has two pools, tennis and squash courts, a health centre, a semiprivate beachfront and exceptional dim sum in the rooftop restaurant. It charges 4102B to 10,255B.

Nearby, another excellent choice in this category is the 234-room *Amari Orchid Resort* (☎ 038-428161, fax 428165, [e] amorchid@loxinfo.co.th; in Bangkok ☎ 02-267 9708), set on four lush hectares in North Pattaya, with an Olympic-size swimming pool, two tennis courts, children's playground, minigolf, garden chess and one of the best Italian restaurants in Pattaya. The Amari quotes only in US dollars: US$58 to US$190, plus 10% service charge and 7% value-added tax (VAT).

Royal Garden Resort Pattaya (☎ 038-412120, fax 429926, 218/2–4 Mu 10, Thanon Hat Pattaya; in Bangkok ☎ 02-476 0021), one of Pattaya's most well-established resorts, sits on three hectares of palms in Central Pattaya and has lotus ponds and Thai-style pavilions. It's attached to a relatively new four-storey shopping centre as well as a Ripley's Believe It or Not Museum. Also on the premises are a fitness centre, two tennis courts, two cinemas and a pool. The resort's rooms start at 4120B a night.

Another older luxury property is the *Royal Cliff Beach Resort* (☎ 038-250421–30 fax 250522; in Bangkok ☎ 02-282 0999), on Thanon Cliff at the southern end of Pattaya. It is really three hotels in one: a central section for package tours and conventions, a family wing and the very upmarket Royal Wing. The Royal Cliff's rooms start at 5297B.

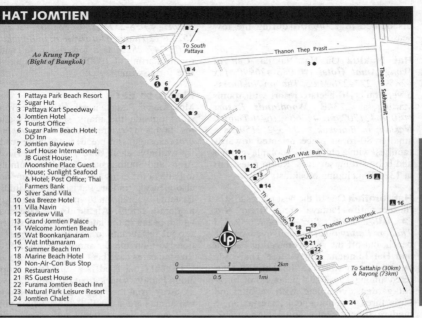

HAT JOMTIEN

Ao Krung Thep (Bight of Bangkok)

To South Pattaya

Thanon Thep Prasit

Thanon Sukhumvit

Thanon Wat Bun

Thanon Chaiyapreuk

Th. Hat Jomtien

To Sattahip (30km) & Rayong (73km)

1 Pattaya Park Beach Resort
2 Sugar Hut
3 Pattaya Kart Speedway
4 Jomtien Hotel
5 Tourist Office
6 Sugar Palm Beach Hotel; DD Inn
7 Jomtien Bayview
8 Surf House International; JB Guest House; Moonshine Place Guest House; Sunlight Seafood & Hotel; Post Office; Thai Farmers Bank
9 Silver Sand Villa
10 Sea Breeze Hotel
11 Villa Navin
12 Seaview Villa
13 Grand Jomtien Palace
14 Welcome Jomtien Beach
15 Wat Boonkanjanaram
16 Wat Inthamaram
17 Summer Beach Inn
18 Marine Beach Hotel
19 Non-Air-Con Bus Stop
20 Restaurants
21 RS Guest House
22 Furama Jomtien Beach Inn
23 Natural Park Leisure Resort
24 Jomtien Chalet

CENTRAL THAILAND

Once one of Pattaya's finest hotels, the *Merlin Pattaya* (☎ 038-428755–9, fax 421673; in Bangkok ☎ 02-253 2140), on Thanon Hat Pattaya, now seems rather plain beside more elegant properties, but caters to the growing wave of Russian tourists. Rooms cost 1580B. The *Montien Pattaya* (☎ 038-428155/6, fax 423155; in Bangkok ☎ 02-233 7060), on Thanon Hat Pattaya, is a bit better. Rooms cost 3531B to 10,711B.

Moving south, the top-enders drop in price a bit. Each of the following offers comfortable air-con rooms with phone, TV and fridge, plus other amenities on the premises such as a coffee shop or restaurant, travel agent and swimming pool.

Century Pattaya Hotel (☎ 038-427800, fax 428069, 129/16 Thanon Pattaya Klang) charges from 800B to 1413B. *Pattaya Centre Hotel* (☎ 038-425877, fax 420491, Soi 12, Thanon Hat Pattaya) charges 1400B for singles/doubles, including breakfast. *Golden Beach Hotel* (☎ 038-422331, 519/29 Thanon Pattaya 2; in Bangkok ☎ 02-254 5102) charges from 800B, including breakfast.

Right in the thick of Central Pattaya, *Siam Bayview Resort* (☎ 038-423871, fax 423879, e siamcity@siamhotels.com, 310/2 Thanon Hat Pattaya) features rooms from 2500B (1750B if you're Thai) plus a lovely pool, garden and terrace cafe.

The labyrinthine *Siam Bayshore Resort* (☎ 038-428678–81, fax 428730; in Bangkok ☎ 02-221 1004), on Thanon Pattaya Tai, is set at South Pattaya's quieter edge and charges 2943B for a cut above the standard.

Hat Cliff or Cliff Beach, named for the Royal Cliff Beach Resort, bears a few other places, including the *Asia Pattaya Beach Hotel* (☎ 038-250602, fax 259496; in Bangkok ☎ 02-215 0808), on Thanon Cliff, with 'golf view' rooms costing from 2438B and sea-view rooms for 3980B. Discounts of up to 50% are readily given. *Cosy Beach* (☎ 038-250801, fax 422818), on Thanon Cliff, has rooms from 850B in the old wing to 1500B in the new building. *Royal Cliff Hotel* (☎ 038-250421), on Thanon Cliff, has rooms from 5297B to 7651B. *Island View* (☎ 038-250813, fax 250818; in Bangkok ☎ 02-249 8941), on Thanon Cliff, offers rooms from 1200B to 1500B; they're discounted to 750/950B during the low season.

Hat Naklua On Hat Naklua, *Central Wong Amat Hotel* (☎ 038-426990, fax 428599, 277–278 Mu 5, Thanon Naklua) is a very quiet 10-hectare resort with rooms starting at 2234B. *Woodlands Resort* (☎ 038-421707, fax 425663, 164/1 Thanon Naklua; in Bangkok ☎ 02-392 2159) is a smaller 80-room place oriented towards families, with a children's pool, playground and baby-sitting services. Room rates start at 1320B, including breakfast.

Hat Jomtien One of the best places to stay in the entire Pattaya area, *Sugar Hut* (☎ 038-251686, fax 251689, 391/18 Thanon Pattaya Tai) is not even on the beach, but off the road connecting Pattaya and Hat Jomtien. Thirty-three Thai-style bungalows on stilts are thoughtfully scattered among 15 râi (2.4 hectares) of tropical gardens, complete with rabbits and birds, three swimming pools, a restaurant, a modern fitness centre and jogging track. The bungalows feature partially open bathrooms inspired perhaps by upmarket Balinese resorts. A standard bungalow costs 3280B plus tax and service, while a deluxe bungalow (with a separate living room) costs 4850B. Bungalows with two bedrooms and a living room go for 8120B.

Pattaya Park Beach Resort (☎ 038-251201, fax 251209, 345 Thanon Hat Jomtien; in Bangkok ☎ 02-511 0717) is a huge cement entertainment and hotel complex oriented towards package tourists or families, with such attractions as a tailor shop, huge 'fun complex', beer garden, diving shop and water park. The rooms start at 2825B. If you're in need of a thrill, you can slide down a cable that stretches from the top of the resort's 55-storey tower to the ground.

The 14-storey *Grand Jomtien Palace* (☎ 038-231405, fax 231404, 356 Thanon Hat Jomtien; in Bangkok ☎ 02-271 3613) has rooms from 1210B; it's popular with German and Russian package tourists. Nearby, *Welcome Jomtien Beach* (☎ 038-232701–15, fax 232716; in Bangkok ☎ 02-252 0594) also caters to package tourists (especially Russians), with rooms from

1600B. The nicer *Natural Park Leisure Resort* (☎ 038-231561, fax 231567, fax 247 1676, 412 Thanon Hat Jomtien; in Bangkok ☎ 02-247 2825) is a low-rise hotel with rooms starting at 1000B and an attractive free-form swimming pool.

Places to Eat

Most food in Pattaya is expensive. The front signs outside the many snack bars and restaurants in town reveal that *bratwurst mit brot* (sausage with bread) is far more readily available than *khâo phàt* (fried rice). Arabs and South Asians have been coming to Pattaya for many years now, so there are also plenty of Indian, Pakistani and Middle Eastern restaurants in town, some with fairly moderate prices. An influx of Russians, which began in the late 1990s, has inspired several restaurants to add Russian translations to their menus; more recently a few Russian cafes have been added to the scene.

Decent Thai food is available in shops along Pattaya's backstreet (Thanon Pattaya 2), away from the beach. The best seafood restaurants are in South Pattaya, where you pick out the sea creatures and are charged by their weight. Prices tend to be sky-high by Thai standards. *Savoey Seafood* (☎ 038-428580/1), part of the Furama Beach Hotel in Central Pattaya, is one of the better places for fresh seafood without breaking the bank.

One moderately priced yet well-appointed Pattaya restaurant is the *PIC Kitchen,* on Soi 5 (second entrance on Soi 4). The Thai-style sǎalaa have low wooden tables and cushions for dining and the emphasis is on Thai food with a limited selection of Western dishes; prices are 70B to 140B per dish. The upstairs bar area features live jazz nightly. It's open from 8 am to midnight. Another interesting place to eat is *Vientiane Restaurant* (☎ 038-411298, 485/18 Thanon Pattaya 2), opposite Soi Yamato. The 503-item menu includes mostly Thai and Lao dishes for 60B to 120B, plus lunch specials for 30B to 50B. It opens from 11 am to midnight.

For a splurge, *La Gritta* (☎ 038-428161) on Thanon Hat Pattaya near the Amari Orchid Resort, does Italian-style seafood with some flair. Prices are moderate to expensive but there's a pianist to keep you entertained. It's open 6 am to 11 pm.

Moonshine Place Guest House, on Thanon Hat Jomtien, specialises in Mexican and southern-Thai food; you can also buy a picnic lunch here.

Zeppelin (☎ 038-420016), in the Nova Hotel on Thanon Hat Pattaya, is one of many German restaurants in Pattaya. It's open at 9 am for breakfast and stays open till 2 am. The Royal Garden Plaza shopping centre, attached to Royal Garden Resort Pattaya, contains several *fast-food* franchise restaurants. as does the Big C shopping centre on Thanon Pattaya 2.

On Hat Jomtien, opposite the bus station on the corner of Thanon Hat Jomtien and Thanon Chaiyapreuk, there are a few basic and cheap *restaurants* serving the usual Thai and Chinese dishes.

Entertainment

Eating, drinking and merry-making are the big pastimes once the sun goes down. Merry-making in Pattaya, aside from the professional sex scene, means everything from hanging out in a video bar to dancing all night at one of the discos in South Pattaya. Two transvestite palaces, *Alcazar* (☎ 038-429694, *78/14 Thanon Pattaya 2*) and *Tiffany's* (☎ 038-421701), also on Thanon Pattaya 2, have drag-queen shows; the Alcazar is the best and puts on three shows nightly at 6.30, 8 and 9.30 pm. Tickets cost 400B to 600B.

Among the several discos in town, the very glitzy *Pattaya Palladium* (☎ 038-424922, *78/33–35 Thanon Pattaya 2)* is a large entertainment complex featuring 12 snooker tables, a 200-bed massage parlour, a Chinese restaurant, karaoke bar, cocktail lounge and a 360-degree Panorama cinema. The disco has a capacity of 6000 customers and is reportedly the largest in Thailand. It opens 9.30 pm to 2 am. The older *Marine Disco* on Thanon Pattaya Tai is still popular.

One of the best things to do in the evening is to stroll down Thanon Hat Pattaya and check out the amazing variety of bars – there's one for every proclivity, including a couple of outdoor *muay thai* (Thai boxing) bars featuring local talent. Truly the 'garden of earthly delights', in the most Boschean sense, 'Pattaya Land', encompassing Soi 1, 2 and 3 in South Pattaya, is one of the most concentrated bar areas. The many gay bars on Soi 3 are announced by a sign reading 'Boys Town'.

Pattaya's civic leaders are attempting to clean up the town's seamy nightlife image. Although the bars and discos are still tolerated, public soliciting is discouraged outside the part of South Pattaya known as 'the village'. This area attracts a large number of transvestite or transsexual prostitutes known as kàthoey – some from as far afield as Laos – who pose as female hookers and ply their trade among the droves of well-heeled European tourists. There is also a prominent gay scene. Incidentally, the easiest way to tell a kàthoey is by the Adam's apple – a scarf covering the neck is usually a dead giveaway. Nowadays, though, some kàthoey have their Adam's apples surgically removed.

After the collapse of the Soviet Union and its satellite states a decade ago, significant numbers of Russian and Eastern European women began coming to Pattaya on tourists visas in order to sell their services to moneyed tourists from Taiwan, Hong Kong and Singapore. Their numbers have since dwindled due to a swift crackdown by Thai police, who were horrified at the thought of having to compete for kickbacks with Russian pimps and mobsters.

With all the emphasis on girlie bars, there's precious little in the way of live music in Pattaya. One of the few places you can find it is at one of the town's original nightspots, the *Bamboo Bar*, on Thanon Pattaya Tai near the intersection with Thanon Hat Pattaya. There are two bands each night (the second act, starting around midnight, is usually better). There are of course plenty of hostesses happy to keep you company, but no one minds if you just want to knock back a few drinks and take in the music. A smaller place with live tunes is *Orn's Beer Bar*, next to the Apex Hotel. The quality of the music varies, but the place has a good feel to it, and if you feel you can do justice to a song, you might be able to take to the stage yourself.

Delaney's Pattaya (☎ 038-710641, *Thanon Pattaya 2)* brings Bangkok's popular Irish pub to Pattaya with all the usual trimmings, including Guinness on tap.

A *cinema* in the Big C shopping centre on Thanon Pattaya 2 shows first-run English-language movies.

Getting There & Away

Air Bangkok Airways (☎ 038-412382) has daily flights between Ko Samui and

U-Taphao airfield (about 30km south of Pattaya) four times weekly. The fare is 1920B one way to Ko Samui and 2250B in the reverse direction due to Ko Samui's higher departure tax. Children fly for half price. Bangkok Airways also operates flights between Pattaya and Phnom Penh, Cambodia, for 3970B. Its office is located at PIC Plaza, Soi 4, Thanon Pattaya 2.

Bus Air-con buses from Bangkok's Eastern bus station leave every 30 minutes from 4.30 am to 7.30 pm (79B, 2½ hours). Air-con buses to Pattaya are also available from Bangkok's Northern and North-Eastern bus station for the same fare. In Pattaya the air-con bus station is on Thanon Pattaya Neua, near the intersection with Thanon Sukhumvit. Several hotels and travel agencies in Bangkok also run thrice-daily air-con tour buses to Pattaya for around 100B to 150B. Cramped minivans from Thanon Khao San typically cost 170B per person. These buses take around two hours in either direction. Once you reach the main Pattaya bus station, waiting red săwngthăew will take you to the main beach road for 20B per person.

From Si Racha you can grab a public bus on Thanon Sukhumvit to Pattaya for 12B.

There are also buses between Pattaya and several North-Eastern towns, including Nakhon Ratchasima (178B air-con), Khon Kaen (125B ordinary, 225B air-con), Nong Khai (165B, 297B) and Ubon Ratchathani (150B, 275B).

Pattaya has a separate bus stop for buses to the North-East near the intersection of Thanon Pattaya Klang and Thanon Pattaya 3.

Train The No 283 train goes from Bangkok's Hualamphong station to Pattaya (31B) via Chachoengsao at 6.55 am, arriving at 10.37 am daily. In the opposite direction train No 240 departs Pattaya at 2.15 pm and arrives at Hualamphong at 6.35 pm. Although this is an hour longer than the typical bus ride from Bangkok, it beats biting your nails in traffic jams along the highway from Bang Na to Trat. The Pattaya train station is just north of the T-junction of Thanon Pattaya Klang and Thanon Sukhumvit.

Getting Around
To/From the Airport If you've just flown into Bangkok and need to get to Pattaya

right away, there are airport minibuses that go directly to Pattaya (200B) at 9 am, noon and 7 pm daily. In the reverse direction, the THAI minibus (also 200B) leaves from next to the Gulf Siam Hotel in Pattaya at 6.30 am and 2 and 6.30 pm. It takes around 2½ hours to reach the airport. Some hotels in Pattaya also run their own buses to Bangkok for 160B to 300B one way.

Car & Motorcycle Jeeps can be hired for around 2000B per day, and cars start at 1200B (as low as 800B for a 4WD Suzuki in the low season) depending on size and model; insurance and tax cost up to 160B more. All vehicle rentals in Pattaya are on a 24-hour basis.

Avis Rent-A-Car (☎ 038-361627/8, 425611) has an office at the Dusit Resort, and is by far the most expensive option. Of course, if something goes wrong you don't have to worry about any hassles (like a formerly unseen disclaimer popping up in your insurance policy). Avis also offers a pick-up and drop-off service at your hotel.

SIE (☎ 038-410629), located near the Diana Inn on Thanon Pattaya 2, is pretty good, and has competitive rates. Although SIE has signs claiming it's 'European managed' don't expect smooth sailing if anything goes wrong with the car, or you decide to return it early. There are no refunds, no matter what.

Motorcycles cost 150B to 200B per day for an 80cc or 100cc; a 125cc to 150cc will cost 300B, and you'll even see a few 750cc to 1000cc machines for hire for 500B to 1000B. There are motorcycle hire places along Thanon Hat Pattaya and Thanon Pattaya 2. Pattaya is a good place to purchase a used motorcycle – check the rental shops.

Săwngthăew Săwngthăew cruise up and down Hat Pattaya and Thanon Pattaya 2 frequently – just hop on and when you get out pay 10B anywhere between Naklua and South Pattaya, 20B as far as Jomtien. Don't ask the fare first as the driver may interpret this to mean you want to charter the vehicle. A chartered săwngthăew to Jomtien should be no more than 40B. It's usually easier to get a share săwngthăew from Jomtien to central Pattaya rather than vice versa.

Many readers have complained about having ridden the 10B săwngthăew with local passengers and then been charged a higher 'charter' price of 20B to 50B or more when they got off. In some instances drivers have threatened to beat fàràng passengers when they wouldn't pay the exorbitant fares. It's little use complaining to the tourist police unless you can give them the licence-plate number of the offending driver's vehicle. A refund is highly unlikely but perhaps if the tourist police receive enough complaints, they'll take some action to reduce or eliminate the rip-offs.

AROUND PATTAYA

Farther south and then east from Pattaya are more beaches and more resorts. The more upmarket places may, in the future, restructure themselves in favour of more middle-class tourists and convention goers.

In quiet Bang Sareh, *Khum Det* (☎ 038-437304, 472 Thanon Ban Na) offers 25 simple rooms with cold-water shower for 150B to 400B. *Bang Saray Villa* (☎ 038-436070) has air-con bungalows for 750B, plus air-con rooms in a hotel for a reasonable 300B to 500B, the latter with TV and fridge. The *Bang Saray Fishing Lodge* is a small hotel with air-con rooms for 550B to 850B. *Nong Nooch Village* (☎ 038-429342) has a choice of rooms from 300B and bungalows from 1600B. *Sea Sand Club* (☎ 038-435163, fax 435166) has 46 air-con bungalows that cost 880B, 1040B with TV.

There are still some good seafood restaurants for local Thais in Bang Sareh – something Pattaya hasn't seen for years.

Rayong Province

RAYONG & AROUND

อ.เมือง จ.ระยอง

postcode 21000 • pop 46,400

Rayong lies on the Gulf of Thailand coast 220km from Bangkok by the old highway (Hwy 3) or 185km on Hwy 36. The province produces fine fruit (especially durian and pineapple) and *náam plaa* (fish sauce). Rayong itself is not worth visiting, but nearby beaches are fair and Ko Samet is a favourite island getaway for Bangkok residents. Except for Ko Samet, this area has not received many foreign visitors, but it has been popular with Thai tourists for several years.

Estuarial beaches at **Laem Charoen**, about 2km south of the provincial capital of Rayong, aren't that great, but there are some reasonable seafood restaurants. Better are the beaches near **Ban Phe**, a seaside town around 25km south-east of Rayong (this is also the departure point for Ko Samet). If sun and sand are what you've come to Rayong for, head straight for Ban Phe. Then pick out a beach or board a boat bound for Ko Samet.

Another much smaller island near Rayong is **Ko Saket**, which is a 20-minute boat ride from the beach of Hat Sai Thong (turn south off Hwy 3 at the 208km marker).

Suan Son (Pine Park), 5km farther down the highway from Ban Phe, is a popular place for Thai picnickers and has white sand beaches as well.

Suan Wang Kaew is 11km east of Ban Phe and has more beaches and rather expensive bungalows. **Ko Thalu**, across from Suan Wang Kaew, is said to be a good diving area – the proprietors of Suan Wang Kaew, a private park, can arrange boats and gear. Other resort areas along the Rayong coast include **Laem Mae Phim** and **Hat Sai Thong**. **Hat Mae Rampeung**, a 10km strip of sand between Ban Taphong and Ban Kon Ao (11km east of Rayong), is part of Laem Ya–Ko Samet National Park. See the Ko Samet section later in this chapter for more information.

Khao Chamao–Khao Wong National Park is inland about 17km north of the 274km marker off Hwy 3. Although less than 85 sq km, the park is famous for limestone mountains, caves, high cliffs, dense forest, waterfalls, and freshwater swimming and fishing. The park service here rents bungalows, longhouses and tents. To get here from Ban Phe take a săwngthăew to the 274km marker for 24B, and another săwngthăew to the park.

Many more resort-type places are popping up along Rayong's coastline. Bangkok developers envisage a string of Thai resorts all the way to Trat along the eastern seaboard, banking on the increasing income and leisure time of Bangkok Thais.

One nonresort development is the deep-water port at Maptaphut, which, along with Chonburi's Laem Chabang port, catches the large shipping overflow from Bangkok's Khlong Toey port.

Information

Tourist Offices TAT (☎ 038-655420, 01-943 5214, e tatry@infonews.co.th) has an office at 153/4 Thanon Sukhumvit in Rayong. The staff can provide maps and fairly up-to-date lists of accommodation and sights in Rayong and Chanthaburi Provinces.

Money Several banks along Rayong's main drag, Thanon Sukhumvit, have exchange services, including Bangkok Bank, Thai Farmers Bank and Bank of Ayudhaya. Opening hours are 8.30 to 3.30 pm weekdays and 8.30 to noon Saturday. Besides Rayong, there are also banks with currency-exchange service in Ban Phe. Travellers heading for Ko Samet should know that there are no banks on the island.

Places to Stay & Eat

Rayong Should you somehow get caught overnight in Rayong, there are a few inexpensive hotels near the bus station off Thanon Sukhumvit. The *Rayong Otani* (☎ 038-611112, *69 Thanon Sukhumvit*) has rooms with fan for 230B and with air-con from 400B. Across the street and tucked down a small alley, the *Asia Hotel* looks a bit dubious, but has rooms with fan from 120B to 180B. To get to either place, walk south from the bus station out to Thanon Sukhumvit, turn left and proceed past Rayong hospital; soon after that you'll see signs for both places.

If you're looking for a more upmarket stay, try the *Rayong President Hotel* (☎ 038-611307), which has fairly new air-con rooms from 550B to 600B. The hotel is located down a small side street, so it's quiet at night. From the bus station, cross to the other side of Thanon Sukhumvit, turn

A Request

The Rayong tourist police request that visitors refrain from hiring jet skis on Ko Samet beaches because they are harmful to coral and dangerous to swimmers. They're hard on the ears, too. The local police don't seem to do much about them, even though they're illegal, so you'll be doing Ko Samet a favour by avoiding the use of these polluters.

right and after about three minutes' walk you'll see a sign pointing down a side street to the hotel. There are plenty of other places along Thanon Sukhumvit with simple rooms with fan for 150B to rooms with air-con and hot water for 700B.

For cheap food, check the *market* near the Thetsabanteung cinema, or the string of *restaurants* and *noodle shops* on Thanon Taksin Maharat just south of Wat Lum Mahachaichumphon. If you have plenty of time, take a sǎwngthǎew (3B) south from Thanon Sukhumvit to the mouth of Mae Nam Rayong at Laem Charoen, where the well-established **Laem Charoen** and **Ocharos** (Ocha Rot) serve moderately priced seafood. Sǎwngthǎew (7B) from the bus station take you to a small wooden bridge that crosses Mae Nam Rayong onto a long spit of land. After crossing the bridge you can catch a motorcycle taxi (10B) to the restaurants.

Ban Phe There are several hotels in Ban Phe near the central market and within walking distance of the pier. *TN Place* (☎ 038-825638), about 100m from the pier,

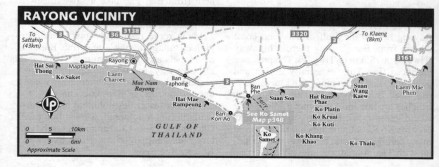

RAYONG VICINITY

has decent rooms with fan for 250B and with air-con for 300B to 500B. The owners are friendly and provide plenty of information, but the hotel can get a bit noisy.

The *Queen* (☎ 038-651018) is up the lane from the pier, near the central market, and has rooms for 150B (no bathroom), 200B (bathroom), and 400B (air-con); the painted ladies on hand testify to its mainly short-time clientele, although it's basically an OK place. Also close to the pier is the six-storey *Hotel Diamond Phe* (☎ 038-651826, fax 651757). It has fan rooms with private bathroom for 300B and good-value air-con rooms with TV, hot-water shower and fridge for only 500B.

The *Thale Thong* restaurant, where the tour bus from Bangkok stops, has good Thai seafood dishes – especially recommended is the *kŭaytĭaw thá-leh* (seafood noodle soup). The shop across the street is a good place to stock up on food, mosquito coils and the like to take to Ko Samet. You'll most likely spend some time in this spot waiting for the boat to leave the nearby pier for Ko Samet or for the bus to arrive from Bangkok.

Nearby Islands Two small islands off the coast of Rayong offer accommodation packages that include boat transport from the nearest pier along with four meals a day. These can be arranged only by phone in advance through Bangkok reservation numbers. *Mun Nork Resort (Bangkok ☎ 02-860 3025, fax 860 3028)* on Ko Man Nok, charges 2590B per person for a one-night, two-day package. The island is 15km off Pak Nam Prasae (53km east of Ban Phe).

Eight kilometres off Laem Mae Phim (27km east of Ban Phe) on Ko Man Klang, the *Raya Island Resort (Bangkok ☎ 02-316 6717)* offers 15 bungalows for 1200B each (one night and two days costs 1400B per person), boat transport and four meals included. Tiny Ko Saket, a 15-minute boat ride from Hat Sai Thong, used to have accommodation, but it has been razed as the island is now being adapted for industrial purposes.

Ko Man Klang and Ko Man Nok, along with Ko Man Nai to their immediate west, are part of Laem Ya–Ko Samet National Park. This official designation has not kept away all development, only moderated it.

The islands are in fair condition ecologically, the main threat to surrounding corals being the arrival of jet skis.

Getting There & Away
Public transport to the pier departure points for the two small islands off Rayong can be arranged in Ban Phe. On weekends and holidays there may be share taxis (or sǎwng-thǎew) out to the piers; otherwise you'll have to charter a vehicle from the market for 60B to 100B one way – be sure to make a pick-up appointment for your return.

See Getting There & Away under Ko Samet later in this chapter for details on transport to and from Rayong.

KO SAMET
เกาะเสม็ด

This T-shaped island earned a permanent place in Thai literature when classical Thai poet Sunthorn Phu set part of his epic *Phra Aphaimani* on its shores. The story follows the travails of a prince exiled to an undersea kingdom ruled by a lovesick female giant. A mermaid aids the prince in his escape to Ko Samet, where he defeats the giant by playing a magic flute. Formerly Ko Kaew Phitsadan or 'Vast Jewel Isle' – a reference to the abundant white sand – this island became known as Ko Samet or 'Cajeput Isle' after the cajeput tree that grows in abundance here and is very highly valued as firewood throughout South-East Asia. Locally, the *samet* tree has also been used in boat building.

In the early 1980s, the 13.1-sq-km Ko Samet began receiving its first visitors interested in more than cajeput trees and sand – young Thais in search of a retreat from city life. At that time there were only about 40 houses on the island, built by fisherfolk and Ban Phe locals. Rayong and Bangkok speculators saw the sudden interest in Ko Samet as a chance to cash in on an up-and-coming Phuket and began buying up land along the beaches. No-one bothered with the fact that Ko Samet, along with Laem Ya and other nearby islands, had been a national marine park since 1981.

When fàràng started coming to Ko Samet in greater and greater numbers, spurred on by rumours that Ko Samet was similar to Ko Samui '10 years ago' (one always seems

CENTRAL THAILAND

KO SAMET

To Ban Phe
Laem Noi Na
To Ban Phe
To Ban Phe
Laem Phra
Ao Wiang Wan
Ao Kham
Na Dan
Ao Phrao
Laem Ya/Ko Samet National Park
Hat Laem Yai
Laem Yai
Hat Sai Kaew
Ao Hin Khok
Ao Phai
Ao Phutsa
Laem Rua Taek
Ao Nuan
Ao Cho
Ao Wong Deuan
Hat Saeng Thian
Ao Thian
Ao Wai
GULF OF THAILAND
Ao Kiu Na Nai
Ao Kiu Na Nok
Laem Khut
Ao Karang

1	Samed Hut
2	Pu Dam Shrine
3	Tha Na Dan
4	Ao Prao Resort
5	Dome Bungalows
6	Hat Sawahn Paradise Beach
7	Ko Samet Health Centre; Police Substation
8	Buddhist Temple
9	Pineapple Bungalow
10	Laem Yai Hut Home
11	Ploy Resort
12	Diamond Beach; Samet Beach Restaurant
13	Coconut House
14	National Park Office
15	Saikaew Villa; Toy Restaurant
16	Ploy Talay
17	White Sand Bungalow; White Sand Restaurant
18	Naga Bungalows; Post Office
19	Tok's Little Hut
20	Jep's Inn
21	Ao Phai Hut
22	Sea Breeze
23	Silver Sand
24	Anchalee Hut
25	Samed Villa
26	Pudsa Bungalow
27	Tub Tim
28	Ao Nuan
29	Wonderland Resort
30	Tarn Tawan; Bamboo Restaurant
31	National Park Branch Office
32	Malibu Garden Resort
33	Seahorse Bungalow
34	Vongdeuan Resort
35	Vongdeurn Villa
36	Candlelight Beach
37	Lung Dam
38	Sametville Resort
39	Ao Kiu Coral Beach

to miss it by a decade, eh?), the National Parks Division stepped in and built a visitors office on the island, ordered that all bungalows be moved back behind the tree line and started charging a 5B admission into the park.

This entry fee has since risen to 200B for foreigners (100B for children 14 and under) and 20B for Thais. There are separate park units at each beach in charge of fees collection. There are now plenty of vehicles on the island, more frequent boat services from Ban Phe and a much improved water situation. Ko Samet is a very dry island (which makes it an excellent place to visit during the rainy season). Before they started trucking water to the bungalows you had to bathe at often-muddy wells. Now most of the bungalows have proper Thai-style bathrooms and Ko Samet is a much more comfortable place to visit, although it sometimes becomes overcrowded. Because of a ban on new accommodation (except where it replaces old sites), bungalows are spread thinly over most of the island, with the north-east coast being the most crowded. The beaches really are lovely, with the whitest, squeakiest sand in Thailand. There is even a little surf occasionally (best months are December to January). However, we still think the accommodation on Ko Samui and Ko Pha-Ngan is better value overall, although of course these islands are much more expensive and time-consuming to reach from Bangkok.

In spite of the fact that the island is supposedly under the protection of the National Parks Division, on recent trips to Ko Samet we have been appalled at the runaway growth in the Na Dan and Hat Sai Kaew areas. Piles of rubbish and construction materials spoil the island's charm at the northern end. Once you get away from this end of the island, however, things start looking a bit better.

Accommodation on Ko Samet can be very crowded during Thai public holidays: early November (Loi Krathong Festival); 5 December (King's Birthday); 31 December to 1 January (New Year); mid to late February (Chinese New Year); and mid-April (Songkran Festival). During these times people sleep on beach restaurant floors, on the beach, everywhere. September gets the lowest number of visitors (average 2500);

March the most (around 40,000, approximately 36,000 of them Thai). Thais in any month are more prevalent than foreigners, but many are day visitors; most stay at Hat Sai Kaew or Ao Wong Deuan in the more upmarket accommodation.

It should also be pointed out that Ko Samet has what is probably Thailand's largest and most loathsome collection of stray dogs, many of them with advanced cases of mange. The crusty curs can be especially disturbing during meal times when, hopeful for a handout, they park themselves nearby and stare longingly at your food. As if that wasn't enough, once night falls the dogs sometimes raise such an astounding din that some visitors find that only by drinking large quantities of alcohol are they able to fall asleep.

The Royal Forest Department has temporarily closed the park to all visitors a couple of times in an effort to halt encroachment on national park lands; so far it's always reopened the island within a month or less in response to protests by resort operators. Developers reasonably objected that if Ko Samet is to be closed then so must Ko Phi Phi. Court hearings continue; until a decision is reached, a permanent moratorium on new developments remains in place in order to preserve the island's forested interior.

Information

The park has a main office near Hat Sai Kaew, and a smaller one at Ao Wong Deuan. An excellent guide to the history, flora and fauna of Ko Samet is Alan A Alan's *Samet,* published by Asia Books. Instead of writing a straightforward guidebook, Alan has woven the information into an amusing fictional travelogue involving a pair of Swedish twins on their first trip to the island.

Post & Communications A small post office next to Naga Bungalows has poste restante. It's open 8.30 am to noon and 1 to 4.30 pm weekdays, and 8.30 am to noon Saturday. There is Internet access at a shop next to the post office.

Travel Agencies Near Na Dan and on Hat Sai Kaew and Ao Wong Deuan are several small travel agencies that can arrange long-distance phone calls as well as bus and train reservations – they even do air ticketing.

CENTRAL THAILAND

Medical Services The Ko Samet Health Centre, a small public clinic, is located midway between the village harbour in Na Dan and Hat Sai Kaew. English-speaking doctors are on hand to help with problems like heat rash or bites from poisonous sea creatures or snakes.

Malaria A few years ago, if you entered the park from the northern end near the village, you'd see a large English-language sign warning visitors that Ko Samet was highly malarial. The sign is gone now but the island still has a bit of malaria. If you're taking malarial prophylactics you have little to worry about. If not, take a little extra care to avoid being bitten by mosquitoes at night. Malaria is not that easy to contract, even in malarial areas, unless you allow the mosquitoes open season on your flesh. It's largely a numbers game – you're not likely to get malaria from just a couple of bites (that's what the experts say anyway), so make sure you use repellent and mosquito nets at night.

Activities

Several bungalows on the island can arrange boat trips to nearby reefs and uninhabited islands. Ao Phutsa, Ao Hin Khok, Hat Sai Kaew and Ao Wong Deuan have windsurfer-rental places that do boat trips as well. Typical day trips to Ko Thalu, Ko Kuti etc cost about 400B per person, including food and beverages (minimum of 10 people). Sailboards, boogie boards and inner tubes can be rented from a number of guesthouses.

Places to Stay

Every bungalow operation on the island has at least one restaurant and most have running water and electricity. Most places have electric power from 5 or 6 pm till 6 am; only the upmarket places have 24-hour power.

On less popular beaches you may come across abandoned bungalow sites and some of the most expensive places even during the high season offer discounts for accommodation to attract customers. Very basic small huts cost 100B to 120B; similar huts with fan and bathroom cost 150B to 200B; bungalows with furniture and air-con start at 600B. Most places offer discounts for

stays of four or more days, while on weekends and public holidays most will raise their rates to meet the demand – sometimes dramatically.

Some resorts, mostly around the Hat Sai Kaew area, have also been known to boot out foreigners without warning to make room for free-spending Thai tour groups. You won't need to worry about this at the more reputable spots, like Naga Bungalows and Samed Villa. Even so, if possible avoid Ko Samet during the high season, especially public holidays.

Since this is a national park, camping is allowed on any of the beaches. In fact, this is a great island to camp on because it hardly ever rains. There is plenty of room; most of the island is uninhabited and, so far, tourism is pretty much restricted to the north-eastern and north-western beaches.

East Coast The two most developed (overdeveloped) beaches are Hat Sai Kaew and Ao Wong Deuan. All of the other spots are still rather peaceful.

Hat Sai Kaew Ko Samet's prettiest beach, 'Diamond Sand', is a kilometre or so long and 25m to 30m wide. The bungalows here happen to be the most commercial on the island, with video in the restaurants at night and lots of electric lights. They're all very similar and offer accommodation, from 120B (in the low season) for simple huts without fan or bathroom, 200B to 600B for one with fan and private bathroom, and as high as 2500B with air-con.

Coconut House (☎ 038-651661) has 30 bungalows for 350B with fan to 800B with air-con, TV and fridge. *Diamond Beach* (☎ 038-652514) offers fan bungalows for 350B and air-con bungalows for 500B to 900B. Another option is *Ploy Talay* (☎ 01-218 7636), with rooms for 400B to 800B, all with private bathroom. There is also a disco but it doesn't seem to get much use. The *White Sand Bungalow* (☎ 038-653154) charges 300B for a fan room and 400B to 1500B for air-con. Also on this stretch, the *Ploy Resort* has concrete bungalows, with private bathroom, for 300B with fan and 600B to 800B with air-con and breakfast. A better choice is *Laem Yai Hut Home* (☎ 038-651956), which has spacious wooden bungalows with verandas. Rooms with fan and bathroom are 700B.

Saikaew Villa (*☎/fax 038-651852*) is a huge complex off the beach, with fan rooms for 700B to 1300B, and rooms with air-con and TV from 1650B. It's the top-end place near the prettiest part of the beach. Breakfast is included and the establishment boasts 24-hour power – try to get a room away from the noisy generators. Discounts for long-term stays are available.

Ao Hin Khok The beach here is about half the size of Sai Kaew but just as pretty – the rocks that give the beach its name add a certain character. Ao Hin Khok is separated from Hat Sai Kaew by a rocky point surmounted by a mermaid statue. Ao Hin Khok and Ao Phai, the next inlet south, offer the advantage of having among the least expensive huts on the island along with reasonably priced restaurants serving good food.

Two of Samet's original bungalow operations still reign here – *Naga Bungalows* (*☎ 01-218 5372*) and *Tok's Little Hut*. Naga offers simple bungalows set on a hill overlooking the sea for 100B and decent ones with a good mattress from 120B. The restaurant at Naga sells great bread (it is distributed to several other bungalows on the island), cookies, cakes, pizzas and other pastries. There is also Internet access, a bar and a tatty pool table. Bungalows at Tok's Little Hut are a little more solid, have fan and bathroom and go for 200B to 300B, depending on proximity to the generator.

Farther down the road is *Jep's Inn*, with nicely designed, clean bungalows with bathroom and fan for 350B and 500B. The restaurant (no videos) here is also quite good, and there's a nice shaded dining area right at the edge of the beach.

Ao Phai Around the next headland is another shallow bay with a nice wide beach, although it can get fairly crowded. At the northern end is the friendly *Ao Phai Hut* (*☎ 01-213 6392*), which has screened bungalows with bathroom and fan for 300B, 400B and 1000B, depending on size. Air-con bungalows cost 700B, 800B and 2000B; add 200B on weekends and holidays. Electricity is available from 5 pm to 6 am. The staff organise tours around the island and have an international telephone service, as well as basic postal services. The next place is *Sea Breeze* (*☎/fax 01-239 4780*), with rather closely spaced bungalows, all with bathroom, for 400B with fan and 650B with air-con. Adjacent is a small shop and a bookshop and library (no exchanges) that also has international phone and fax services. Next is *Silver Sand* (*☎ 01-218 5195*), which has fan bungalows for 250B to 300B and air-con bungalows for 400B to 800B; all have attached bathroom and 24-hour electricity.

Swiss-run *Samed Villa* (*☎ 01-494 8090*) has very clean, screened, well-maintained tree-shaded bungalows with large verandas from 600B for smaller units with private bathroom and up to 1000B for family accommodation. It has 24-hour electricity and quite good food, and some of the bungalows have great sea views. This is also one of the few places in the area that doesn't screen videos at night. About 30m behind Samed Villa in a small compound is *Anchalee Hut*, with clean wooden bungalows with fan and bathroom for 150B to 300B.

Ao Phutsa On Ao Phutsa, also known as Ao Thap Thim, you'll find *Pudsa Bungalow* (*☎ 01-663 1371*), where huts with fan and bathroom cost 350B and 400B. Some of the huts are close to the water, making them good value for money. At the southern end of the beach *Tub Tim* (*☎ 01-218 6425*) has fan bungalows on a hillside for 200B to 700B, while air-con bungalows cost 1200B. All bungalows have attached bathroom.

Ao Nuan If you blink, you'll miss this beach, which is one of the more secluded places to stay without having to go to the far south of the island. The bungalows at *Ao Nuan* have shared bathroom and intermittent electricity and vary in size. Some are little more than bamboo huts. Prices range from 150B to 400B. The food is quite good here and the eating area is set in an imaginatively arranged garden. It's a five-minute walk over the headland from Ao Phutsa.

Ao Cho A five-minute walk across the next headland from Ao Nuan, Ao Cho (Chaw) has its own pier and can be reached directly from Ban Phe on the boat *White Shark* or aboard the supply boat. Although just north of crowded Ao Wong Deuan, it's fairly quiet here, although the beach is not among Samet's best.

At the northern end of the beach **Wonderland Resort** (☎ 01-438 8409) has basic, rather scruffy bungalows with shower and toilet for 150B to 500B (more on weekends and holidays). Huts with fan and bathroom at **Tarn Tawan** are quite OK and cost 400B to 600B. The restaurant at Tarn Tawan specialises in Isan food.

Ao Wong Deuan This once-gorgeous bay is now filled with speedboats and jet skis, and there's a lot of accommodation packed into a small area, making things a bit cramped. The crescent-shaped beach is still nice, but it is noisy and often crowded. The best of the lot is **Vongdeuan Resort** (☎ 038-651777, fax 651819) with bungalows for 800B, complete with running water, flush toilet and fan. The air-con ones cost 1100B to 1200B.

Vongduern Villa (☎ 038-652300) is similar in amenities but all rooms have air-con and cost 650B to 2500B.

The **Malibu Garden Resort** (☎ 038-651057) has well-built brick or wooden bungalows for 800B to 1100B with fan and 1500B to 2200B with air-con; the more-expensive rooms have TV. Breakfast is included and if you tire of the scene at the beach this place even has a swimming pool.

Seahorse Bungalow (☎ 01-451 5184) has practically taken over the beachfront with two restaurants, a travel agency and 600B bungalows with fan and bathroom. Air-con bungalows go for 800B to 1000B.

Three boats go back and forth between Ao Wong Deuan and Ban Phe – the *Malibu*, *Seahorse* and *Vongduern*.

Ao Thian From this point south things start to get much quieter. Better known by its English name Candlelight Beach, Ao Thian is quite scenic, with stretches of sand and rocky outcrops.

On the bay's northern end is **Candlelight Beach** (☎ 01-218 6934) with fan and bathroom bungalows ranging from 400B to 700B, depending on proximity to the beach. Electricity is on from 6 pm to 6 am. At the southern end of the bay **Lung Dam** (☎ 01-458 8430) charges 200B for quite roughly built huts with shared bathroom and 400B for ones with attached bathroom. There is also an interesting treehouse you can rent for 150B per night. Keep in mind you'll have the choice of only two guesthouse kitchens here; you may want to bring some of your own food.

Other Bays You really have to be determined to get away from it all to go farther south on the east coast of Ko Samet, but it can be well worth the effort. Lovely Ao Wai is about 1km from Ao Thian, but can be reached by the boat *Phra Aphai* from Ban Phe, which sails once a day (50B).

There's only one bungalow operation here, the very private **Sametville Resort** (☎ 038-651681; in Bangkok ☎ 02-246 3196), which offers a fine combination of upmarket accommodation and isolation. Two-bed bungalows with bathroom cost 800B to 900B with fan and up to 1300B with air-con. Most bookings are done by phone, but you can try your luck by contacting someone on the *Phra Aphai* at the Ban Phe piers.

A 20-minute walk over the rocky shore from Ao Wai, Ao Kiu Na Nok also had only one place to stay at the time of writing – the friendly and clean **Ao Kiu Coral Beach** (☎ 01-218 6231). Bamboo huts cost 200B, while unattractive but better-equipped cement huts cost 300B to 600B. Tents may be rented for 100B a night. The beach here is gorgeous, one of the nicest on the island. Another plus is that it's a mere five-minute walk to the western side of the island and a view of the sunset.

West Coast Hat Ao Phrao is the only beach on the western side of the island, and it has nice sunset views. The name means Coconut Bay Beach, but for marketing reasons bungalow operators tend to use the clichéd Paradise Beach moniker. So far there are no jet skis on this side of the island, so it tends to be quieter than the island's east coast. Bungalow operators also do a good job of keeping the beach clean.

At the northern end of the beach is **Ao Prao Resort** (☎ 02-438 9771), where attractive air-con bungalows with large verandas are surrounded by lush landscaping. Amenities include cable TV and hot-water, attached bathroom and perhaps the best restaurant on the island. Rates range from 1878B to 3130B. Add 500B on weekends and holidays. Ao Prao Divers at the resort offers diving, windsurfing, kayaking and boat trips.

In the middle of the beach is ***Dome Bungalows*** (☎ *038-651377, fax 652600)*, which has nice fan and bathroom bungalows on the hillside for 800B to 900B, 1000B to 1100B with air-con. Breakfast is included. A pleasant restaurant on the premises features Thai and international dishes.

At the southern end near the cross-island trail is the friendly ***Hat Sawahn Paradise Beach*** (☎ *01-912 4587)*, where rustic wooden bungalows with fan and bathroom cost 400B. Electricity is on from 6 pm to 8 am. An attached restaurant serves Thai and international food.

There is a daily boat between Ban Phe and Ao Phrao for 80B per person.

Na Dan & Around To the north-west of Ko Samet's main pier (Tha Na Dan) is a long beach called Ao Wiang Wan, where several rather characterless bungalows are set up in straight lines facing the mainland. Here you get neither sunrise nor sunset. The best place is ***Samed Hut*** (☎ *01-818 3051; in Bangkok* ☎ *02-678 4645)*, which is shady and 'New Mexican' in style, with fan singles/doubles for 800B to 900B and air-con rooms for 1000B to 1100B. All rooms have attached bathroom.

Between Na Dan and Hat Sai Kaew, along the north-eastern corner of the island, are a couple of small beach bays with bungalow operations. Hardly anyone seems to stay here. ***Pineapple Bungalow*** at Hat Laem Yai (also known as Ao Yon) charges 300B per bungalow. On last pass this looked like it was soon to be abandoned.

Places to Eat
All bungalows except Anchalee Hut, Laem Yai Hut Home and Pineapple Bungalow have restaurants offering mixed menus of Thai and traveller food; prices are typically 30B to 50B per dish. Fresh seafood is almost always available and costs around 60B to 150B per dish. The pleasant ***Bamboo Restaurant*** at Ao Cho, behind Tarn Tawan, offers inexpensive but tasty food and good service. It's open for breakfast, lunch and dinner. ***Naga Bungalows*** on Ao Hin Khok has a very good bakery with all kinds of breads and cakes. Ao Wong Deuan has a cluster of restaurants serving Western and Thai food: ***Oasis***, ***Nice & Easy*** and ***Tom's Restaurant***. At the southern tip of the beach

the ***Vongduern Villa*** restaurant is a bit more expensive, but both the food and the location are quite nice.

On Hat Sai Kaew, the ***White Sand Restaurant*** has good seafood in the 100B range. For cheaper fare on this beach, try the popular ***Toy Restaurant***, next to Saikaew Villa. ***Samet Beach Restaurant*** next to Diamond Beach has also been recommended for good food with reasonable prices and friendly staff.

Probably the best eatery on the island is the fancy open-air terrace restaurant at ***Ao Prao Resort***.

Getting There & Away
Bus Many Thanon Khao San agencies in Bangkok provide transport to Ko Samet, including boat, for 170B (300B return). This is more expensive than doing it on your own, but for travellers who don't plan to go anywhere else on the east coast it's very convenient.

For those who want the flexibility and economy of arranging their own travel, the way to go is to take a bus to Ban Phe in Rayong Province, then catch a boat out to Ko Samet. There are buses to Rayong (87B, 4½ hours; 101B, 3½ hours air-con) throughout the day from the Eastern bus station, but if your destination is Ban Phe you'd do better to take one of the direct Ban Phe buses, which only cost 7B more (a săwngthăew to Ban Phe from Rayong costs 15B). Buses from Bangkok stop in Ban Phe in front of Saphan Nuan Tip. Air-con buses between Rayong and Bangkok's Eastern bus terminal take around 3½ hours, ordinary buses about an hour longer.

Ordinary buses go to Chanthaburi from Rayong (52B, 2½ hours). To get one of these, you need to catch a motorcycle taxi (10B) to the bus stop on Thanon Sukhumvit (Hwy 3).

Minibuses to Bangkok's Thanon Khao San and Pattaya can be arranged through several of the guesthouses on Ko Samet or through travel agencies in Ban Phe. Minibuses to Bangkok leave at 10 am and 2 pm (200B). Minibuses to Pattaya leave at 10 am and 1.30 and 5 pm (150B). All leave from the vicinity of Saphan Sri Ban Phe pier.

Boat There are various ways to get to and from the island by boat.

To Ko Samet There are three piers in Ban Phe: Saphan Nuan Tip for the regularly scheduled passenger boats; Saphan Mai for supply boats; and Saphan Sri Ban Phe for tour groups. Saphan Nuan Tip is usually the only one you'll need, but if you arrive between passenger-boat departure times you can try for a ride aboard one of the cargo boats from Saphan Mai (you must still pay the regular passenger fare).

Passenger boats to Ko Samet leave at regular intervals throughout the day starting around 8 am and ending around 5 pm. How frequently the boats depart depends on whether they have enough passengers or cargo to make the trip profitable. Obviously there will be more frequent trips in the high season (December to March). Still, there are always at least three or four boats a day going to Na Dan and Ao Wong Deuan.

It can be difficult to find the boat you need, as agents and boat owners want you to go with them rather than with their competitors. In most cases they'll be reluctant to tell you about another boat if they will not be making any money from you.

Some travellers have reported being hassled by 'agents' who show them photo albums of bungalows on Ko Samet, claiming that they must book a bungalow for several days in order to get onto the island. This is false; ignore these touts and head straight for the boats. Report any problems with the touts to the TAT office in Rayong.

Probably the best place to head is the Saphan Nuan Tip ticket office, behind all the food and souvenir stalls. The staff sell tickets for a number of different boat operators, and also are willing to tell you about private resort boats.

For Hat Sai Kaew, Ao Hin Khok, Ao Phai and Ao Phutsa, catch a boat to Na Dan; the return-trip fare is 80B. These generally leave as soon as there are at least 20 passengers. Ignore touts or ticket agents who claim the fare is 100B or more; simply buy a ticket from Saphan Nuan Tip ticket office. From Na Dan you can either walk to these beaches (10 to 15 minutes) or take one of the trucks that go round the island.

The Saphan Nuan Tip ticket office also has boats to Ao Wong Deuan (50B one way), Ao Phrao (80B) and Ao Wai (80B). All boats need at least seven people before they'll depart.

The Saphan Sri Ban Phe ticket office sells tickets for Na Dan (40B) as well as Ao Wong Deuan (50B), Ao Wai (80B), Ao Kiu Na Nok (100B), Ao Phrao (80B), Ao Nuan and Ao Thian (50B). Again, go directly to the ticket office and ignore what touts tell you.

If you arrive in Ban Phe at night and need a boat to Ko Samet, you can usually charter a one-way trip at the Ban Phe pier, but prices are steep: plan on about 1500B to Na Dan.

From Ko Samet Samet Tour seems to run a monopoly on return trips from Na Dan and the boats leave only when full. Some boats require a minimum of 18 people, while for others it's as high as 25 people. If the boat is underloaded anyone wanting to leave immediately may want to contribute more to the passage. The usual fare is 40B.

These days it is so easy to get boats back from the main beaches to Ban Phe that few tourists go to Na Dan to get a boat. There are four daily boats each from Ao Wong Deuan and Ao Cho, plus at least one daily boat from Ao Wai, Ao Kiu Na Nok and Ao Phrao.

While waiting for a boat back to the mainland from Na Dan, you may notice a shrine not far from the pier. This *săan jâo phâw* is a spirit shrine to Pu Dam (Grandfather Black), a sage who once lived on the island. Worshippers offer statues of *reusĭi* (hermit sages), flowers, incense and fruit.

Getting Around

If you take the boat from Ban Phe to Na Dan, you can easily walk the distance to Hat Sai Kaew, Ao Phai or Ao Phutsa. Don't believe the taxi operators who say that these beaches are a long distance away. If you're going farther down the island, or have a lot of luggage, you can take the taxi (which is either a truck or a three-wheeled affair with a trailer) as far as Ao Wong Deuan.

Set fares for transport around the island from Na Dan are posted on a tree in the middle of a square in front of the Na Dan harbour. Exactly how many people it takes to constitute 'public service' rather than a 'charter' is not a hard and fast number. Figure on 30B per person for six to eight people to anywhere between Na Dan and Ao Cho. If they don't have enough people to fill the vehicle, they either won't go, or passengers will have to pay up to 200B to charter the vehicle.

There are trails from Ao Wong Deuan all the way to the southern tip of the island, and a few cross-island trails as well. Near Sea Breeze bungalows in Ao Phai, the main road south to Ao Wong Deuan turns inland and heads down the middle of the island. A little farther along the road from here is where the cross-island road to Ao Phrao on the west coast starts.

After Ao Phutsa, the remaining beaches south are separated from one another by fairly steep headlands. To get from one to the next, you have a choice of negotiating rocky paths over the hilly points or walking west to the main road that goes along the centre of the island, then cutting back on side roads to each beach.

Taxis will make trips to Ao Phrao from Na Dan when the road isn't too muddy.

Motorbikes can be rented from a number of bungalow operations on Hat Sai Kaew, Ao Phai and Ao Phrao. Figure on about 500B per day or an hourly rate of 150B.

Chanthaburi Province

CHANTHABURI
อ.เมืองจันทบุรี

postcode 22000 • pop 40,900
Situated 330km from Bangkok, the 'City of the Moon' is a busy gem trading centre, particularly noted for sapphires and rubies from all over South-East Asia and farther afield. Chanthaburi (Chan'buri) is also renowned for tropical fruit (rambutan, durian, langsat and mangosteen) and rice noodles – Chanthaburi noodles are in fact exported all over the world.

A significant proportion of the local population comprises Vietnamese Christians who fled religious or political persecution in Vietnam years ago. The first wave arrived in the 19th century as refugees avoiding anti-Catholic persecution in Cochin China (southern Vietnam); the second came between the 1920s and 1940s, fleeing French rule; and the third wave arrived after the 1975 communist takeover of southern Vietnam.

From 1893 to 1905, while negotiating with the Siamese over the borders for Laos and Cambodia, the French occupied the town.

Chanthaburi's most recent claim to fame arose in 1993 when 1500 tonnes of war material were found cached in 12 warehouses throughout the province. The arms were thought to have been destined for the Khmer Rouge communist rebels, who held parts of western Cambodia at the time. The allegations were never proven, but it is almost certain the arms were in the control of certain factions in the Thai military.

Things to See & Do
Vietnamese-French influence has resulted in Chanthaburi having some interesting shophouse architecture – particularly along the river. The French-style **cathedral** here is the largest in Thailand. A small missionary chapel was built on this site in 1711, but after undergoing four reconstructions between 1712 and 1906 (the last carried out by the French) the structure has changed into its current form.

The **gem dealers** in town are found mostly along Thanon Si Chan and along Trok Kachang and Thanon Thetsaban 4, off Thanon Si Chan in the south-east quarter. All day long buyers and sellers haggle over little piles of blue and red stones. During the first week of June every year there is a gem festival and Chanthaburi can get very crowded. Most of the gems bought and sold here come from places other than Chanthaburi – chiefly Cambodia, Vietnam, Myanmar and Australia. The sapphires and rubies can be very good buys if (and only if) you know what you're buying.

King Taksin Park is a large public park with gazebos and an artificial lake near the centre of town – nice for an evening stroll. A few kilometres north of town off Rte 3249 is **Khao Phloi Waen** (Sapphire-Ring Mountain), which is only 150m high but features a Sri Lankan-style chedi on top, built during the reign of Rama IV. Tunnels dug into the side of the hill were once gem-mining shafts.

Wat Khao Sukim, a fairly well-known meditation centre, is 16km north of Chanthaburi off Rte 3322. A museum on the wát grounds contains all manner of valuables donated to the temple, such as jade carvings, ceramics and antique furniture, as well

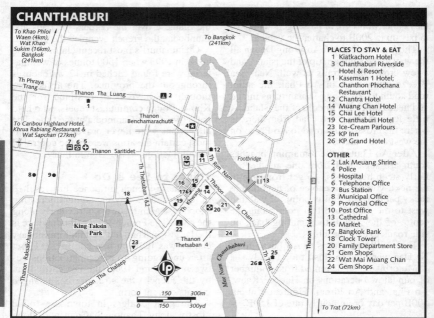

CHANTHABURI

PLACES TO STAY & EAT
1 Kiatkachorn Hotel
3 Chanthaburi Riverside Hotel & Resort
11 Kasemsan 1 Hotel; Chanthon Phochana Restaurant
12 Chantra Hotel
14 Muang Chan Hotel
15 Chai Lee Hotel
19 Chanthaburi Hotel
23 Ice-Cream Parlours
25 KP Inn
26 KP Grand Hotel

OTHER
2 Lak Meuang Shrine
4 Police
5 Hospital
6 Telephone Office
7 Bus Station
8 Municipal Office
9 Provincial Office
10 Post Office
13 Cathedral
16 Market
17 Bangkok Bank
18 Clock Tower
20 Family Department Store
21 Gem Shops
22 Wat Mai Muang Chan
24 Gem Shops

as resin figures of some of Thailand's most-revered monks. Another meditation centre is at **Wat Sapchan**, 27km west of Chanthaburi in Tha Mai district; Wat Sapchan is a branch of Sunyataram Forest Monastery in Kanchanaburi.

Places to Stay

The three-storey ***Kasemsan 1 Hotel*** (☎ 039-312340, 98/1 Thanon Benchamarachutit) has large, clean rooms for 200B with fan, private shower and toilet, and 300B with air-con. As usual, rooms off the street are quieter than those on it, but it's the best deal in town and very convenient to the city centre.

Down by the river at a nice spot on Thanon Rim Nam is the smaller ***Chantra Hotel*** (☎ 039-312310), with rooms for 80B, 120/150B singles/doubles with bathroom; some rooms have a river view. It's a bit run-down and has a slightly sleazy feel, but it's the cheapest place in town and rooms with windows on the river catch a breeze.

The ***Chai Lee Hotel*** (no Roman-script sign) on Thanon Khwang has large, clean singles/doubles for 170/210B with fan and

300B with air-con. In the same area, the ***Chanthaburi Hotel*** on Thanon Tha Chalaep has rooms for 170/250B with fan and bathroom, 290/330B with air-con.

On Thanon Si Chan is the friendly ***Muang Chan Hotel*** (sign on door reads 'hotel'), with adequate rooms with fan, bathroom and TV for 230/280B. Air-con rooms with TV go for 350/400B. Out on Thanon Tha Luang at the northern end of town, away from everything, the ***Kiatkachorn Hotel*** (☎ 039-311212) has rooms for 220B with fan, 300B with air-con, and 350B with VIP air-con. The latter includes TV, phone and fridge; all rooms have private baths.

Business travellers – at least those who are into buying gems – tend to stay at the 18-storey ***KP Grand Hotel*** (☎ 039-323201–13, fax 323214/5, 35/200–201 Thanon Trirat). Rooms with amenities start at 1250B. Across the street, ***KP Inn*** (☎ 039-301888) is condo-style and has rooms with air-con and hot-water showers for 480B to 700B.

The six-storey ***Caribou Highland Hotel*** (☎ 039-323431), west of the town centre on

Thanon Chawan Uthit, offers the best accommodation in town – large air-con rooms with TV, IDD phone and fridge – for 2000B, often discounted to 990B including breakfast. One- and two-bedroom suites are available from 4000B (discounted to 1980B).

A 30B taxi ride from town is the *Chanthaburi Riverside Hotel & Resort* (☎ 039-311726, 63 Mu 9, Thanon Chanthanimit 5), between Thanon Sukhumvit (Hwy 3) and the eastern bank of Mae Nam Chanthaburi. Originally planned to be super luxurious, the hotel must have run out of development money as it has turned out to be no more than a four-star establishment on 42 rather unkempt râi (6.7 hectares). On the premises are a swimming pool, coffee shop, nightclub and conference facilities. Rates are 700B in the hotel section and from 800B for lodgings in separate single, double and triple Thai-style cottages.

Places to Eat

For those famous Chanthaburi noodles, *kŭaytĭaw sên jan,* head for the Chinese/ Vietnamese part of town along Mae Nam Chanthaburi and you'll see variations on the basic rice noodle theme, including delicious crab with fried noodles. The popular *Chanthon Phochana* restaurant beneath the Kasemsan I Hotel has a good variety of Thai and Chinese dishes.

Khrua Rabiang, beside the Caribou Highland Hotel at Chawan Uthit 3, is a very nice, medium- to high-priced open-air restaurant serving mostly Thai food.

The *Family Dept Store* on Soi Sri Sakhon 1, off Thanon Si Chan, has a 2nd-floor food centre and ice-cream shop. There are also several good *rice and noodle shops* just west of the department store. On the south-eastern corner of King Taksin Park are a couple of outdoor *ice-cream parlours* that also serve a few standard Thai dishes.

Getting There & Away

From Bangkok, air-con buses cost 130B, regular buses 93B; from Rayong it's 52B. Direct buses between Nakhon Ratchasima and Chanthaburi on the south-east coast run hourly between 4.30 am and 4 pm (104B ordinary, 187B air-con, eight hours). Ordinary buses go to Trat (26B, 1½ hours), as do share taxis (60B).

If you have your own set of wheels, take Rte 317 north to Sa Kaew, then Hwy 33 west to Kabinburi and Rte 304 north to Khorat. From Sa Kaew you can also head east and reach Aranya Prathet on the Thailand-Cambodia border after just 46km. Now that this border crossing is open you can (if you have a Cambodian visa) take a share taxi from Poipet on the Cambodian side of the border to Siem Reap (near Angkor Wat). The trip takes approximately six hours.

AROUND CHANTHABURI

Two small national parks are within an hour's drive of Chanthaburi. Both are malarial, so take the usual precautions.

Khao Khitchakut National Park is about 28km north-east of town off Rte 3249 and is known for Nam Tok Krathing. There's a series of trails to the falls but no established trails or footpaths in the rest of the park.

Across the road from the park headquarters (☎ 039-431983) are *bungalows* costing 600B for six people to 1200B for 14 people. Camping costs 40B in a hired tent and 5B if you bring your own. A very basic *restaurant* sells various snacks and a few rice dishes.

To get to Khao Khitchakut by public transport, take a săwngthăew from the northern side of the market (20B, 50 minutes). The săwngthăew stops 1.5km from the park headquarters on Rte 3249, from which point you'll have to walk.

Khao Sabap National Park off Hwy 3 is only about 14km south-east of Chanthaburi and features the **Nam Tok Phliu**. There are three park *bungalows* near the park headquarters (Bangkok ☎ 02-579 4842) at Nam Tok Phliu that cost 600B to 800B and sleep eight to 10 people. A simple food service is available.

To get to the park, catch a săwngthăew from the northern side of the market in Chanthaburi to the park entrance (25B, 30 minutes), or get out 2.5km from the park entrance on Thanon Sukhumvit (8B), from where you will have to walk (this is how you will have to depart if there are no taxis). Entry fees are collected at both parks (see under National parks, Reserves & Wildlife Sanctuaries in the Facts about Thailand chapter).

Trat Province

About 400km from Bangkok, Trat Province borders Cambodia and, as in Chanthaburi, gem mining and gem trading are important occupations. *Tàlàat phloi* (gem markets) are open intermittently at the **Hua Thung** and **Khlong Yaw** markets in the Bo Rai district, about 40km north of Trat on Rte 3389. A smaller market is sometimes open all day in **Khao Saming** district only 20km north-west of Trat. There has been a drop in activity in the gem markets due to the dwindling supply of local gem stock. A sad by-product of gem mining has been the destruction of vast tracts of land – the topsoil is stripped away, leaving hectares of red-orange mud.

If the gem business doesn't interest you, another attraction Bo Rai district offers is **Nam Tok Salak Tai** (15km north-west of Bo Rai). The other big industry in Trat is the smuggling of consumer goods between Cambodia and Trat. For this reason, travelling alone along the border, or around the offshore islands that serve as conduits for sea smuggling, requires caution. More and more people have discovered the beaches and islands of Trat, however, and as the locals and the police have begun to see the benefits of hospitality to outsiders, security has apparently improved. One relatively safe spot for observing the border trade is at the Thai-Cambodian market in Khlong Yai, near the end of Rte 318/Hwy 3 south of Trat. As much as 10 million baht changes hands in these markets daily.

As Rte 318 goes east and then south from Trat on the way to Khlong Yai district, the province thins to a narrow sliver between the Gulf of Thailand and Cambodia. Along this sliver are a number of little-known beaches, including Hat Sai Si Ngoen, Hat Sai Kaew, Hat Thap Thim and Hat Ban Cheun. Hat Ban Cheun has a few bungalows, but there was no accommodation at the other beaches at the time of writing.

At the 70km marker, off Rte 318, is **Jut Chom Wiw** (Lookout Point), where you can get a panorama of the surrounding area, including Cambodia. Trat Province's southeasternmost point is at **Hat Lek**, which is also a jumping-off point for trips to the Cambodian coast. Although there are Thai military checkpoints between Trat and Hat Lek (two at last count), foreign tourists are no longer turned back. The border crossing is now open to all and, if you have a Cambodian visa, you will be allowed to visit Cambodia's Koh Kong and beyond.

TRAT & AROUND
อ.เมืองตราด

postcode 23000 • pop 14,400
The provincial capital of Trat has little to offer except as a jumping-off point for the Ko Chang island group or forays into outlying Cambodian markets. The locals are friendly, however, and there are certainly worse places to spend a few days. Market fans will note that Trat seems to have more markets for its size than almost any other town in Thailand, partly due to Cambodian coastal trade.

Information
There is no immigration office in Trat – you must go to the provincial offices in Khlong Yai or Laem Ngop for visa extensions or other immigration matters. Khlong Yai is where you have to go to have your passport stamped upon return from Cambodia.

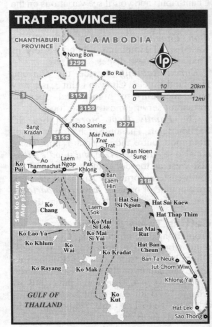

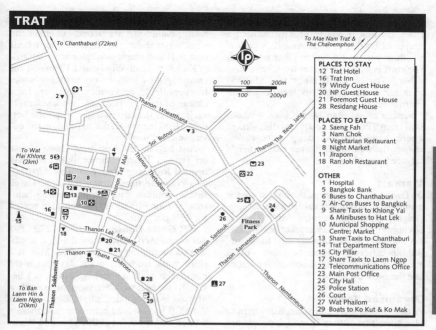

TRAT

To Chanthaburi (72km)

To Mae Nam Trat &
Tha Chaloemphon

Thanon Wiwatthana

Sot Buthoi

Thanon Tha Reua Jang

Thanon Tat Mai

Thanon Thetsaban 1

To Wat
Plai Khlong
(2km)

Thanon Lak Meuang

Thanon Santisuk

L Thanon Santisuk

Thanon Samammit

Thanon Thana Charoen

Thanon Nemtameuw

Thanon Sukhumvit

To Ban
Laem Hin &
Laem Ngop
(20km)

Fitness
Park

0   100   200m
0   100   200yd

PLACES TO STAY
12 Trat Hotel
16 Trat Inn
19 Windy Guest House
20 NP Guest House
21 Foremost Guest House
28 Residang House

PLACES TO EAT
2 Saeng Fah
3 Nam Chok
4 Vegetarian Restaurant
8 Night Market
11 Jiraporn
18 Ran Joh Restaurant

OTHER
1 Hospital
5 Bangkok Bank
6 Buses to Chanthaburi
7 Air-Con Buses to Bangkok
9 Share Taxis to Khlong Yai
   & Minibuses to Hat Lek
10 Municipal Shopping
   Centre; Market
13 Share Taxis to Chanthaburi
14 Trat Department Store
15 City Pillar
17 Share Taxis to Laem Ngop
22 Telecommunications Office
23 Main Post Office
24 City Hall
25 Police Station
26 Court
27 Wat Phailom
29 Boats to Ko Kut & Ko Mak

CENTRAL THAILAND

Bangkok Bank and Krung Thai Bank on Thanon Sukhumvit have foreign-exchange windows open 8.30 am to 3.30 pm daily.

The main post office is a long walk from the city centre on Thanon Tha Reua Jang. It's open 8.30 am to 4.30 pm weekdays and 9 am to noon weekends. The telecommunications office is on the corner a few doors down from the post office and offers international phone and fax services 7 am to 10 pm daily.

Medical Services Rates of infection for malaria are significantly higher for rural Trat (including Ko Chang) than for much of the rest of Thailand, so take the usual precautions. There is a malaria centre on the main road through Laem Ngop (20km south-west of Trat); here you can get the latest information on the disease. This office can also assist with testing and treatment of malaria.

Trat Canal & Estuary
คลองตราด

Trat town's older homes and shophouses lie along the canal. Windy Guest House offers

guests a free canoe to paddle around for a water-level look. During high tide it's possible to boat from the canal to the Trat estuary on the Gulf. This can also be done from Mae Nam Trat, north of the city; inquire at Tha Chaloemphon (also known simply as *thâa reua* or boat pier).

Wat Plai Khlong
วัดปลายคลอง(วัดบุปผาราม)

Wat Plai Khlong (Wat Bupharam), 2km west of the city centre, is over 200 years old and worth a visit if you're looking to kill an hour or so. Several of the wooden buildings date to the late Ayuthaya period, including the wíhǎan, bell tower and *kùtì* (monk's quarters). The wíhǎan contains a variety of sacred relics and Buddha images dating from the Ayuthaya period and earlier.

Trat is famous for *náam-man lěuang* (yellow oil), a herb-infused liquid touted as a remedy for everything from arthritis to stomach upsets. It's produced by a resident, Mae Ang-Ki (Somthawin Pasananon), using a secret pharmaceutical recipe that has been handed down through her

Chinese-Thai family for generations. The Thais say that if you leave Trat without a couple of bottles of Mae Ang-Ki's yellow oil, then you really haven't been to Trat. The stuff is available direct from her house at No 5 Thanon Rat Uthit (☎ 039-511935) or at NP Guest House, as well as all the pharmacies in town.

Farther afield, **Ban Nam Chiaw** – about 8km from Trat – is a mostly Muslim village where hemispherical straw hats called *ngâwp,* the traditional Khmer rice-farmer's hat, are hand woven.

Markets

Of Trat's several markets, the largest are the relatively new day market beneath the municipal shopping centre off Thanon Sukhumvit; the old day market off Thanon Tat Mai; and the day market next to the aircon bus office. The latter becomes a night market in the evening. Look for novelties like deep-fried lizards.

Organised Tours

Windy Guest House can arrange day trips to Mae Nam Trat estuary if enough people are interested. Boats leave from the canal in town for the Trat estuary to gather clams (in season) – the price depends on the number of people. It's not clear how long this will last, however, as locals claim that the number of clams has dropped sharply in the last few years.

Places to Stay

The city has a small but growing guesthouse scene. Any of the guesthouses can arrange boat trips along Mae Nam Trat if enough people are interested.

The friendly ***Windy Guest House*** (☎ *039-523644, 64 Thanon Thana Charoen)* consists of a traditional Thai wooden house with a porch built on stilts over the canal and a cosy outdoor lounge area with a small library, travel information and games. Singles/doubles cost 70/100B, or you can sleep under a mosquito net on the porch for 40B. Ask about borrowing canoes for exploring the canal (no charge to guests) – it depends on who's managing the guesthouse at the time and whether canoes are available.

Foremost Guest House (☎ *039-521270, 49 Thanon Thana Charoen),* also near the canal, offers rooms upstairs in an old shophouse; bathrooms are shared but clean and a hot-water shower is available. Dorm beds cost 50B and singles/doubles are 70/100B.

Kudos to both Windy and Foremost for encouraging guests to tap drinking water from refillable, recyclable containers for a charge of only 1B per litre – a considerable saving over the cost of a typical plastic bottle of drinking water, not to mention the environmental merit.

Just beyond the Foremost Guest House on Thanon Thana Charoen is the recently opened ***Residang House*** (☎ *039-530103),* in a concrete three-storey building. Large singles/doubles with fan and shared bathroom go for 120/180B. Bicycles are rented for 20B per hour.

NP Guest House (☎ *039-512270, 1–3 Soi Luang Aet),* down a soi that is a southwest continuation of Thanon Tat Mai, is a short walk from the main day and night markets as well as local bus stops. It's basically an old wooden shophouse with a glassed-in downstairs; singles/doubles cost 80/100B with shared bathroom, and there's a three-bed room for 200B. Thai and Western food is available.

Most of the hotels in Trat are along or just off Thanon Sukhumvit. The ***Trat Inn*** (☎ *039-511208, 1–5 Thanon Sukhumvit),* though housed in a run-down concrete shell, has a friendly Thai-speaking staff and rooms from 120B to 200B. Downstairs is Trat's only Internet access point.

More comfortable than the foregoing is the renovated ***Trat Hotel*** (*Meuang Trat;* ☎ *039-511091),* off Thanon Sukhumvit, which has standard rooms for 220B to 550B with fan and from 370B with air-con. This is the only hotel in town with a lift.

Eleven kilometres south-east of town at Ban Laem Hin, the ***Ban Pu Resort*** (☎*/fax 039-542355)* stands adjacent to Suan Pu, a famous seafood restaurant/crab farm. Large, well-appointed wooden bungalows connected by a boardwalk surrounding a large crab pond start at 1200B for a one-bedroom unit with two double beds or one king-size bed. A larger one-bedroom unit with six beds costs 2600B. All of these come with air-con, TV and a fridge. There are also deluxe VIP two-bedroom bungalows with TV, VCR and private karaoke room for 3400B, and there's a health club on the premises. It's a 20B, 15-minute săwngthăew ride from town. Ban Pu can arrange speedboat transport to Ko Chang and other Trat islands for 6000B to 8000B, including life jackets and snorkelling gear.

Places to Eat

With all the markets in Trat, you're hardly ever more than 50m away from something good to eat. The *indoor market* beneath the shopping centre has a food section with cheap, good noodle and rice dishes from early morning to early evening. Another good spot for a cheap breakfast is the ancient *coffee stand* in the old day market on Thanon Tat Mai.

In the evenings, there's a good *night market* next to the air-con bus station. On Mae Nam Trat in the northern part of town is another smaller but atmospheric *night market* – a good choice for long, leisurely meals. Trat is a good city for seafood, which is cheaper here than in Bangkok or in more well-touristed cities around the country (it's not the international tourists who drive up the seafood prices but the Thais, who spend huge sums of money eating out).

One of the longest-running Thai-Chinese restaurants in town is the *Jiraporn*, a small cafe-style place a few doors up from the Trat Hotel where older regulars hang out over tea and coffee every morning. As it's mostly a breakfast place, the main menu offerings are toast and eggs with ham, *jók* (rice gruel) and *khâo tôm* (rice soup), but it also serves fried rice or noodles.

The *Nam Chok*, a tin-roofed, Christmas-light–trimmed open-air restaurant on the corner of Soi Butnoi and Thanon Wiwatthana, is another local institution. Around lunchtime a good find is *Ran Joh* (no Roman-script sign) at 90 Thanon Lak Meuang. It's the place diagonally opposite the Trat Inn making *khànŏm bêuang* (a Khmer vegie crepe prepared in a wok). Ran Joh also serves other local specialities – it's very inexpensive, but open lunchtime only.

A good mid-range restaurant, the air-con *Saeng Fah* (☎ 039-511222, 157–159 Thanon Sukhumvit) has a menu with Thai specialities from 30B to 100B. The food is good, and there are plenty of seafood dishes. Try the 'jellyfish soup' or 'bloody clam salad'. The staff also serve breakfast, when you might (or might not) want to try the house speciality – 'rice with curdled pig's blood'.

A *Thai vegetarian restaurant,* down a lane behind the area where the night market is held, offers seven or eight pots of fresh vegie dishes daily from around 6 am to 2 pm, or until the food runs out. A plate of rice with your choice of toppings costs only 20B.

The best place in the whole province for seafood is *Suan Pu* (Crab Farm) in Ban Laem Hin, on the way to Laem Sok, 11km south-east of town (a 20B săwngthăew ride each way). Tables are atmospherically arranged on wooden piers over Ao Meuang Trat. All seafood is served fresh; crab, raised on the premises, is of course the house speciality and prices are moderate to high (still considerably cheaper than Bangkok). The menu is in Thai only, so bring along a Thai friend to translate.

Getting There & Away

Bangkok For Trat, air-con buses (169B 1st class, 132B 2nd class, five to six hours) or ordinary buses (113B, eight hours) leave from Bangkok's Eastern bus station.

Three bus companies operate a Trat to Bangkok service: Sahamit-Cherdchai, on Thanon Sukhumvit near the Trat Hotel and night market, has the best and most frequent (14 trips a day) air-con buses.

Chanthaburi Ordinary buses between Chanthaburi and Trat (26B, 1½ hours, 66km) leave every 30 minutes from 5.50 am to 2.30 pm and at 3.45, 4.20 and 5.30 pm.

You can also take the quicker share taxis between Trat and Chanthaburi (60B, 45 minutes). During the middle of the day, however, it may take up to an hour to gather the seven passengers necessary for a departure; try to schedule your departure from Trat to between 7 and 9 am or 4 and 6 pm for the shortest wait.

Khlong Yai, Hat Lek & Bo Rai Săwngthăew and share taxis go to Khlong Yai (35B, 400B chartered, 45 minutes) and leave from the back of the municipal shopping centre market. Săwngthăew go from Khlong Yai to Hat Lek (20B, 180B chartered, 16km); motorcycle taxis also make this journey (50B). Săwngthăew go to Bo Rai (50B).

Direct minibuses from Trat to Hat Lek (100B, one hour) leave every half-hour from Thanon Sukhumvit in front of the municipal shopping centre market.

Getting Around
Săamláw around town should cost 10B per person. Small săwngthăew cost 5B per person on a share basis or 20B to 40B for the whole vehicle.

BEACHES
The sliver of Trat Province that extends south-eastward along the Cambodian border is fringed by several Gulf of Thailand beaches. **Hat Sai Si Ngoen** (Silver Sand Beach) lies just north of the 41km marker off Hwy 3; a billboard says a resort will be constructed here but so far there's no sign of development. Nearby, at the 42km marker, is **Hat Sai Kaew** (Crystal Sand Beach) and at the 48km marker, **Hat Thap Thim** (Sapphire Beach); neither quite lives up to its name, but they're OK to walk along the water's edge or picnic in the shade of casuarina and eucalyptus trees.

The only beach with accommodation is **Hat Ban Cheun**, a very long stretch of clean sand near the 63km marker. The 6km road that leads to the beach passes a defunct Cambodian refugee camp. There are the usual casuarina and eucalyptus trees, a small restaurant and *basic bungalows* (200B) set on swampy land behind the beach. Travellers have reported that the friendly family that runs the operation is quite accommodating.

LAEM NGOP
แหลมงอบ

Laem Ngop is where you have to go for ferries to Ko Chang (see Getting There & Away under Ko Chang National Marine Park later) and for visa extensions. TAT (☎ 039-597259, 01-904 4623) has an office at 100 Mu 1, Thanon Trat-Laem Ngop.

A Thai Farmers Bank (between Chut Kaew Guest House and the pier) has an exchange counter open 8.30 am to 3.30 pm weekdays.

Places to Stay & Eat
There's usually no reason to stay here, since most boats to Ko Chang leave in the morning and early afternoon and it's only 20km from Trat. However, there are a couple of good accommodation choices. A five-minute walk from the harbour on the right is the **Chut Kaew Guest House** (☎ 039-597088), which is run by a nurse, teacher and university student – local, somewhat dated information (including hiking information for Ko Chang) is available in thick notebooks compiled by guests. Rooms with fan and bamboo-thatch walls cost 80B per person and are relatively clean; facilities are shared. Food and laundry services are also available.

The **Laem Ngop Inn** (☎ 039-597044, fax 597144) is farther up the road and down a side lane about 300m. The 31 clean, concrete bungalows (each with separate garage) come with fan, phone and TV for 300B and with air-con for 450B. For 600B add a refrigerator, bathtub and hot water. The **Paradise Inn** (☎ 039-597131), about 300m from the hospital, has concrete bungalows with air-con for 400B to 600B.

Near the pier in Laem Ngop are several rustic seafood places with views of the sea and islands. One of the more popular spots with local Thais and Thai tourists is the inexpensive **Ruan Talay**, a wooden place on stilts over the water.

Also good are **Kung Ruang Seafood**, **Tamnak Chang** and **Krua Rim Nam**, all moderately priced.

Getting There & Away
Share taxis to Laem Ngop (20B, 150B chartered) leave Trat from a stand on Thanon Sukhumvit next to the municipal shopping centre market. They depart regularly throughout the day, but after dark you will have to charter. Travel agents at Tha Laem Ngop arrange daily minibuses to Thanon Khao San in Bangkok (250B, five to six hours, 11 am departure); Pattaya (350B, three hours, 1 pm departure); and Ban Phe (120B, two hours, 11 am departure).

There are direct minivans from Thanon Khao San in Bangkok to Laem Ngop (250B).

KHLONG YAI
คลองใหญ่

Khlong Yai consists of a cluster of older wooden buildings west of the highway, surrounded by modern structures on both sides of the highway. There's a large market in the centre of town, as well as the moderately priced Suksamlan Hotel and two banks with foreign-exchange services. Just south of town is a large shrimp farm.

Places to Stay

The *Suksamlan Hotel* (☎ 039-581109), an old-fashioned Thai-Chinese–style place on a street between the market and the highway, offers rooms with fan from 120B, 250/300B with air-con. Out of town a bit off Hwy 3, *Bang In Villa* (☎ 039-581401) has nicer bungalows, but with less character, for 150B to 350B.

Getting There & Away

See Getting There & Away under Trat for information on public transport to Khlong Yai.

HAT LEK TO CAMBODIA

The small Thai border outpost of Hat Lek is the southernmost part on the Trat mainland. Untaxed goods travel back and forth between Cambodia and Thailand at this point; at the small market just before the border crossing itself, next to the pier for boats travelling to Cambodia, US Budweiser beer and other untaxed contraband is often available.

Opposite Hat Lek on Cambodian turf (Sao Thong) there's a cockfighting arena and casino popular with residents from both sides of the border.

There are two military checkpoints along Hwy 3 between Trat town and Hat Lek. These are serious checkpoints where searches by the military are common, especially since this area between Khlong Yai and Hat Lek was discovered to harbour a clandestine paramilitary force allegedly training to overthrow Vietnam's communist government.

Motorcycle and automobile taxis are available from Hat Lek across the border into Cambodia for 30B and 50B. There is very basic accommodation on the island of Koh Kong in Cambodia. If you plan to continue farther, you can embark on a 4½-hour boat ride (600B) to Sihanoukville. There is only one boat per day to Sihanoukville and it leaves at 8 am, so if you don't get across the border early, you'll have to spend a night on Koh Kong. Basically, if you want

to get from Trat to Sihanoukville in one day, you should be on the 6 am minibus to Hat Lek and at the border with passport in hand as soon as it opens at 7 am. This border crossing closes at 5 pm.

A Cambodian visa is necessary, and obtainable in Bangkok, not at the border. If you are going into Cambodia for a day trip, you might need to have a valid Thai visa on which you can return to Thailand. Nowadays Thailand grants most nationalities a one-month visa on arrival. If your nationality is not on the instant-visa list, you will find yourself stuck in Cambodia.

See Getting There & Away under Trat for transport information to Hat Lek.

Warning

Travel into Cambodia is potentially dangerous and many embassies advise against it. You may like to check with your embassy in Thailand first before making plans for Cambodian travel. Although the death of Pol Pot seems to have signalled the demise of the Khmer Rouge, banditry is still rife in many parts of rural Cambodia. It's best to contact the Foremost or Windy guesthouses in Trat for the latest information on travel in Cambodia.

KO CHANG NATIONAL MARINE PARK
อุทยานแห่งชาติเกาะช้าง

Forty-seven of the islands off Trat's coastline belong to a national park named after **Ko Chang** (Elephant Island), which at 492 sq km is the second-largest island in Thailand after Phuket. The entire park officially encompasses 192 sq km of land surface, and 458 sq km of sea. Ko Chang itself is about 70% undisturbed island rainforest – the best preserved in Thailand and perhaps in all South-East Asia – with steep hills and cliffs reaching as high as the 744m-high Khao Jom Prasat.

Beach forest and mangrove are also found in abundance. Notable wildlife includes the stump-tailed macaque, small Indian civet, Javan mongoose, monitor lizard, water monitor, Burmese and reticulated pythons, king cobra, barking deer and wild pig. Avian species (61 resident species, plus 12 migratory species) include Pacific reef egret, nightjar, green imperial pigeon,

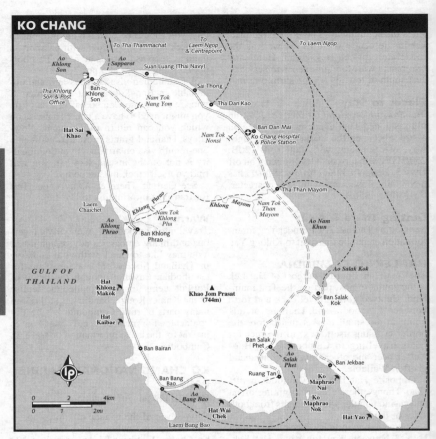

KO CHANG

CENTRAL THAILAND

white-winged tern, blue-winged pitta, hooded pitta and three hornbill species. An endemic amphibian, *Rana kohchang* (Ko Chang frog), is also found here.

Other major islands in the park include Ko Kut and Ko Mak. Ko Chang is ringed with small bays and beaches, among them Ao Khlong Son, Hat Sai Khao, Ao Khlong Phrao, Hat Kaibae, Ao Bang Bao and Ao Salak Phet. Near each of these beaches and bays are small villages.

Until rather recently there wasn't a single paved road on Ko Chang, only red dirt roads between Ban Khlong Son and Hat Kaibae on the western coast of the island, and between Ban Khlong Son and Ban Salak Phet on the eastern side, plus walking trails passable by motorcycle from

Hat Kaibae to Ban Bang Bao and Ban Salak Kok to Ban Salak Phet. A paved section now exists between Ban Dan Mai and Ban Bang Bao, and Trat authorities say the island will have a paved ring road within the next two or three years. Electricity now comes from the mainland to the northern part of the island via a cable beneath the sea, and power lines will probably continue to follow the sealing of the roads around the island.

Ko Chang receives around 75,000 visitors a year. Most of these are Thai. Thai visitors tend to come to the island on weekends and holidays only, stay for 24 hours or less, and stay in the more expensive kinds of accommodation. The average stay for non-Thai visitors is around five days; a small number of visitors take up residence for weeks on end.

A combination of steep terrain and year-round streams creates several scenic waterfalls. A series of three falls along the stream of Khlong Mayom in the interior of the island, **Nam Tok Than Mayom**, can be reached via Tha Than Mayom or Ban Dan Mai on the east coast. The waterfall closest to the shore can be climbed in about 45 minutes via a well-marked footpath. The view from the top is quite good and there are two inscribed stones bearing the initials of Rama VI and Rama VII nearby. The second waterfall is about 500m farther east along Khlong Mayom and the third is about 3km from the first. At the third waterfall is another inscribed stone, this one with the initials of Rama V. At the lower levels are public picnic areas.

A smaller waterfall on the west coast, **Nam Tok Khlong Phu**, can be visited from Ao Khlong Phrao (45 minutes on foot) or from Hat Kaibae (one hour) by following Khlong Phrao 2km inland. Or pedal a bicycle along the main road until you see the sign on the eastern side of the road. Ride up to the restaurant near the falls, from where it is only a 15-minute walk to the falls themselves. A pool beneath the falls is a good spot for a refreshing swim, and it is possible to stay in the bungalows or camp here.

On **Ko Kut** you'll find beaches mostly along the western side, at Hat Tapho, Hat Khlong Chao and Hat Khlong Yai Ki. A dirt road runs between Ban Khlong Hin Dam, the island's main village on the west coast, and Ao Salat along the north-east shore. Other villages on the island include Ban Ta Poi, Bang Ao Salat, Ban Laem Kluai, Bang Khlong Phrao and Ban Lak Uan. Nam Tok Tan Sanuk and Khlong Chao offer inland water diversions. The nearby small islands of Ko Rang and Ko Rayang have good coral in spots. Ko Kut can be reached from Khlong Yai on the mainland or from Ko Mak.

Ko Mak, the smallest of the three main islands, has a beach along the north-west bay and possibly others as yet undiscovered. Monsoon forest covers 30% of the island while coconut plantations take up another 60%. A few tractors or jeeps travel along the single paved road that leads from the pier to the main village. It is possible to rent motorbikes and organise diving trips from the resorts on the island.

Ko Wai has some of the best coral and is excellent for snorkelling and diving. The island has two bungalow operations. **Ko Kham** is also recommended for underwater explorations; accommodation is available. **Ko Lao Ya** has natural attributes similar to those at Ko Wai, with one rather expensive place to stay. The tiny **Ko Rang** archipelago, south-west of Ko Chang, is a primary nesting ground for the endangered hawksbill sea turtle.

As with other national marine parks in Thailand, park status versus resort development is a hot issue. On Ko Chang, so far, everyone seems to be in agreement about what is park land and what isn't. Any land that was planted before the conferral of park status in 1982 can be privately, bought, sold and developed – this includes many beach areas used for coconut plantations, or about 15% of the island. The Royal Forest Department makes regular flights over the island to check for encroachment on the 85% belonging to the national park – mostly in the interior – and the staff are said to be very strict with interlopers.

Information

The park headquarters are divided into four units, found at Tha Than Mayom, Ban Khlong Son, Tha Khlong Plu and Ban Salak Phet. All offer roughly the equivalent information, but the Tha Than Mayom visitors centre features informative displays on park flora and fauna.

Entry fees are collected at any one of the four park headquarters. Be sure to keep your receipt as rangers may demand payment from visitors who don't have one. Standard national park admission fees apply (see under Sai Yok National Park earlier in this chapter).

Money There is no bank on Ko Chang, but moneychangers will change US dollars and travellers cheques at very unfavourable rates. Ask around at places of accommodation. Those at Hat Sai Khao seem to have the best rates. The only post office is near the pier at Ban Khlong Son, where there is a telegram service but no international phone. On Hat Sai Khao and Hat Kaibae, a few places offer an international telephone service at very high rates.

Medical Services Ko Chang Hospital is located at Ban Dan Mai and can handle most minor emergencies. Another choice is the hospital at Laem Ngop on the mainland. There are health clinics at Ban Khlong Son, Hat Sai Khao and Hat Kaibae.

Dangers & Annoyances The local police headquarters is in Ban Dan Mai, where there is a jail that detains an average of three visitors each month caught smoking dope on the island.

Nudity and topless sunbathing are forbidden by law in Ko Chang National Marine Park; this includes all beaches on Ko Chang, Ko Kut, Ko Mak, Ko Kradat etc.

Diving & Snorkelling

Ko Chang and its vicinity is a new frontier compared with other marine locales in Thailand. With regard to climate and visibility, November to April is the best diving season. The better dive sites are at islets and seamounts off the southern tip of the island, stretching between Ko Chang and Ko Kut. In this area **Hin Luk Bat** and **Hin Lap** are both coral-encrusted seamounts with depths of around 18m to 20m. A few kilometres farther south, the northern end of **Ko Rang Yai** gets scenic at 10m to 25m, while **Hin Phrai Nam** (between Ko Wai and Ko Rang) has coral and white-tip reef sharks visible to around 20m. A small islet near Ko Rang Yai's northern tip, **Ko Kra**, has good snorkelling in depths of 4m to 5m near the islet's southern end. The islets around Ko Rang are favoured nesting grounds for sea turtles – this is one of the better opportunities to see them in Thailand.

South-west of Ao Salak Phet, reef-fringed **Ko Wai** features a good variety of colourful hard and soft corals at depths of 6m to 15m.

Near the mouth of Ao Salak Phet, at the south-eastern tip of the island, lies a **Thai warship** wreck at a depth of 15m. The ship was supposedly sunk by the French in 1941 during a dispute over whether these islands belonged to Thailand or to the French colony of Cambodia. Thai historians claim there should be a second wreck nearby but divers have yet to report on it. This site should not be dived without a guide.

Dive Services Ko Chang Divers has two branches, one next to Bamboo Bungalows and another near Aranee's Resort, both at Hat Sai Khao, and specialises in PADI certification for novice divers. Prices for instruction in beginning and advanced diving range from US$70 to US$250 per person. Instruction material is available in English, French, German, Italian and Japanese. Dive trips typically include two dives with all guiding, transport, equipment and food, and cost US$50. SeaHorse Dive Centre, located at the Kaibae Hut at Hat Kaibae, has similar instruction ranging from 6500B to 8000B. All-inclusive dive trips cost 1200B to 1500B per person. Eco-Divers, located in the Banpu Ko Chang Resort at Hat Sai Khao, offers diving instruction for US$70 to US$280 and dive trips for US$45 to US$60.

You can also hire boats from Ko Chang's western beaches for around 1500B a day, but there's no guarantee the boat pilots will be able to locate dive sites.

Walking on Ko Chang

The more interesting hikes are in the southern half of the island where there are fewer roads. At the northern end you can walk from Ban Khlong Son to Hat Sai Khao in about 1½ to two hours; from Hat Sai Khao to Ao Khlong Phrao in about two hours; and from Ao Khlong Phrao to Hat Kaibae in about two hours. All three are straightforward walks along the main road.

If you're looking for more of a grunt, just head for the interior – the steep, forested hills will have you sweating in no time. A footpath connects Ban Khlong Phrao on the west coast with Khlong Mayom on the east, but this all-day cross-island route shouldn't be undertaken without a local guide. Hedi at the White House Bakery at Hat Sai Khao has information on guides.

Don't try Ban Bang Bao to Ao Salak Phet unless you're an experienced tropical hiker with moderate orienteering skills – there are a lot of hills and many interconnecting trails. A Swede who hiked the perimeter of the island suggested that for this part of the island you carry a note in Thai reading 'I would like to go to Salak Phet. I like very much to walk in the jungle and have done it before. Please show me the start of this trail'.

If you don't get lost, this hike will take four to six hours; should you decide to attempt it, carry enough food and water for an overnight stay, just in case.

If you do get lost, climb the nearest hill and try to locate the sea or a stream to get a bearing on where you are. Following any stream will usually take you either to a village or to the sea. Then you can either follow the coast or ask directions. This advice is also good for hiking anywhere across the island, as it is very easy to get lost on the many intersecting, unmarked trails.

At the south-eastern end of Ao Bang Bao, around a headland that leads to Ao Salak Phet, is a beautiful and secluded beach, **Hat Wai Chek**.

On the eastern side of the island it's a one-hour walk between Ban Dan Mai and Tha Than Mayom; two hours between Ban Dan Mai and Sai Thong; and two hours between Sai Thong and Ao Khlong Son. Salak Kok to Salak Phet is straightforward and takes around three hours. The **estuary** at Ao Salak Kok's western end boasts one of the best mangrove systems in Thailand, although like other coastal wetlands it's threatened by increased shrimp farming.

A hike around the entire island can be done at a comfortable pace in a week to 10 days. Remember to carry plenty of water and watch out for snakes – a few poisonous varieties live on the island.

Other Activities

Some of the guesthouses at Hat Sai Khao and to a lesser extent Hat Kaibae rent out kayaks, sailboards, masks and snorkels, and boogie boards. Mountain bikes can be rented for 150B per day at several places on the island, including Muk Hut Restaurant and Ban Nuna Restaurant-Cafe at Hat Sai Khao and Coral Resort at Hat Kaibae.

Several bungalow operations along Ko Chang's west coast beaches (as well as Bang Bao Blue Wave on Ao Bang Bao) offer day trips to nearby islands for 150B to 1000B. Overnight trips can also be arranged and cost 1500B to 2000B per person.

Places to Stay

Ko Chang Many beach huts on the island have been open for years and others have just popped up, so standards vary quite a bit. Some of the older and simpler bungalow complexes are in the process of being upgraded. A few close down during the

rainy season (June to October), but as the island has become more popular, most places stay open and offer low season prices, sometimes as low as 60% off the normal rate. During the rainy season, boats will usually only go as far as Ao Sapparot, Ban Dan Mai and Tha Than Mayom. Note that the surf farther south along the east coast can be impassable during heavy rains.

Even during dry months, the trend is for boats to drop off at Ao Sapparot so that visitors can continue on to the beaches by săwngthăew.

West Coast As the island's better beaches are along the west coast, this is where most of the beach accommodation is. Most huts and bungalows have one double mattress on the floor or on a raised platform plus a mosquito net. If you are staying longer than a few days all places will discount their rates, even in high season. Most of the island now has electricity; if your bungalow isn't on the grid yet, kerosene or gas lanterns are usually provided. Only a few places have music and, blessedly, even fewer have TVs and videos.

At the northern tip of the island is the largest village, Ban Khlong Son, which has a network of piers at the mouth of the *khlawng* (canal; also written 'khlong'), a wát, a school, several noodle shops and a health clinic. A bit south of the northern cape of Ao Khlong Son, **Premvadee Resort** (☎ 01-933 5455) has simple bungalows with electricity and shared bathroom for 150B, larger bungalows with fan and bathroom from 400B, and large two-room houses with bathroom and fan for 1600B.

At Hat Sai Khao, 5km away, and separated from other Hat Sai Khao bungalow developments by a couple of small rocky points, is the nicely landscaped **White Sand Beach Resort** (☎ 01-218 7526). Simple thatched huts along the beach (no fan, shared bathroom) cost 200B. Behind these are wooden bungalows (shared bathroom) for 250B and more upmarket tiled-roof bungalows with bathroom and fan for 500B to 600B.

Next south is a more isolated spot, **Rock Sand Bungalow**, which has rustic wooden huts on a rocky outcrop surrounded by beach for 150B; nicer huts cost from 350B. There's a neat two-storey restaurant/bar with hammocks on the premises. *KC (☎ 01-833 1010)* has bamboo-thatch huts located behind a row of palms for 230B (no fan, shared bathroom). KC's herbal sauna is looking rather forlorn these days, but at night its beachside bar blasts techno music onto the beach until 2 am – avoid it if you've come for peace and quiet.

Yakah Bungalows is run by a friendly Thai/US couple. Clean bamboo huts with spacious verandas cost 200B to 500B. There are swings for children and a well-stocked library. Across the road from Yakah, *Aranee's Resort (01-827 1326)* offers rooms in a wooden hotel-style building for 250B with bathroom and fan. Arunee's offers international call and fax services and can arrange visas for Cambodia and Vietnam.

Farther south along Hat Sai Khao is a string of huts that have gradually gone up-market (and up in price) over the past few years. A host of newcomers have sprouted up, making this beach Ko Chang's most populated. *Tantawan* offers bamboo huts with shared facilities for 150B and brick bungalows with fan and bathroom for 400B. Nearby *Bamboo Bungalows* has simple bamboo-and-thatch huts with shared facilities for 250B. Both places – like several other bungalow operations along this coast – organise trips to other islands.

Cookie Bungalow (☎ 01-219 3859) is well run by a friendly staff and has concrete bungalows for 500B with fan and bathroom, 800B with air-con. Cookie also has a large and popular beachside restaurant. *Mac Bungalow (☎ 01-219 3056)* has similar bungalows with fan and bathroom for 500B.

South of Cookie on the beach, the *Sabay Beach Bungalow (☎ 01-949 3256)* features three rows of cottages that descend in price as you back away from the sand: 450B to 800B in the first row, 350B to 600B in the second and 250B to 450B in the third. The accompanying Sabay Bar is the local full-moon party headquarters.

The newer *Koh Chang Lagoon Resort (☎ 01-219 3830)* is more upmarket than the rest and offers fan and bathroom bungalows near the beach for 900B and air-con units for 1600B to 2000B. *Apple* offers huts for 300B with shared facilities and 350B with fan and bathroom.

In a quiet location, *Best Garden Beach Resort (☎ 039-529632)* has rooms for 300B with fan and shared bathroom and 700B with private bathroom. Larger air-con cabins cost 2000B to 2500B. The semi-outdoor restaurant does seafood barbecues in the evenings. *Banpu Ko Chang Resort (☎ 01-942 2964)* has both hotel accommodation and wooden bungalows set in a nicely landscaped garden that slopes down to the beach. The hotel rooms feature air-con, hot water and TV and go for 2000B. Bungalows have the same amenities and go for 2500B. This place is often packed out with Thai tourists on the weekends.

Sunsai Bungalow (☎ 01-219 1542), set above a rocky area with no beach, has friendly staff and well-kept, well-separated huts for 150B with fan and shared bathroom and 300B to 800B with private bathroom. Air-con huts go for 1600B. *Moonlight Resort (☎ 039-597198)* has huts from 100B (shared bathroom, no fan) to 500B and 600B (fan and private bathroom). Cost also depends on their proximity to the beach.

The German-owned *Plaloma Cliff Resort (☎ 01-863 1395)* is south of Sunsai on the other side of a rocky headland, spread over a rocky cliff. Quiet, spacious tile-and-cement bungalows cost 700B or 1000B with fan and private bathroom, 1500B with air-con. Up the cliff, Plaloma has some sturdy bamboo-and-thatch huts with private bathroom for 250B a night; the interspersed coconut palms and sea views are pluses.

Perched above Plaloma is *Dog Hut*, with just four wooden huts with fan and shared bathroom. Each hut has a small balcony and awesome view and costs 150B. There is no restaurant, so you'll have to hike when you get the munchies.

About 4km south of Hat Sai Khao is Ao Khlong Phrao (Coconut Bay). It stretches south of Laem Chaichet and encompasses Khlong Phrao and the village of Ban Khlong Phrao. On the northern side of the canal is *Chaichet Bungalows (☎ 01-940 5988)*, with A-frame wooden huts facing north-west from 150B and concrete bungalows with private bathroom for 400B to 500B. The bungalows are strung out along Laem Chaichet, a gently curving cape, although there's no beach to speak of.

Near Ban Chaichet south of Ao Khlong Phrao is *Coconut Beach Bungalows (☎ 01-*

CENTRAL THAILAND

949 3838), where wooden bungalows cost 200B and concrete bungalows with bathroom 500B. The bungalows are well kept, if somewhat close together.

About a 10-minute walk farther south along the beach is the pricey *Rooks Ko Chang Resort (☎ 039-529000).* Upmarket bungalows cost from 2300B to 2800B and include air-con, hot water and satellite TV. The majority of the guests are Thai businesspeople on vacation, many on incentive travel packages. Prices are 20% cheaper on weekdays. The resort owns the Centrepoint pier in Laem Ngop; private boats between that pier and the resort are available for 200B per person. Nearby *Klong Plow Resort (☎ 039-597216)* has wooden bungalows around a lagoon for 700B to 900B with fan, 1400B to 1600B with air-con. A two-storey house that can accommodate 15 people goes for 4000B.

It is possible to cross Khlong Phrao in a long-tail boat but you need to call for one on the southern bank. If you are staying at the PSS Bungalow the service costs 5B, but if you're staying anywhere else it's 10B. The *PSS Bungalow* has simple wooden huts for 150B to 250B. About a 10-minute walk farther south near Wat Ban Khlong Phrao is *KP Bungalows (☎ 01-863 7262),* where well-spaced basic thatched huts cost 150B to 200B and larger ones with bathroom cost 300B to 800B. Family bungalows cost 1000B to 3000B.

About 700m past the turn-off for Nam Tok Khlong Phu, off the main road in Ban Khlong Phrao, is the *Hobby Hut (☎ 01-213 7668).* It is secluded and a favourite with Thais associated with the music and art business. Hobby Hut has four simple huts and rates depend on length of stay and number of guests. It's 300m to the nearest beach; a small inland lagoon is good for canoeing. There's live music Wednesday to Friday evenings.

Around another headland to the south are two beach areas separated by a canal – Hat Khlong Makok and Hat Kaibae (15km south of Khlong Son). These beaches tend to disappear during high tide but they're OK – lots of coconut palms. *Magic (☎ 01-861 4829),* on Hat Khlong Makok, has A-frame bungalows with fan and shared bathroom for 200B and concrete bungalows with private bathroom for 400B and 500B.

Larger fan bungalows that sleep six go for 800B, 1200B with air-con. Magic has a pier, telephone service and scuba diving. The owner has a private boat service from Laem Ngop so is able to funnel many passengers directly to this beach. Magic's best feature is its restaurant built over the bay.

Next door is *Pikanade Resort (☎ 01-2910 9052),* with clean thatched huts with shared bathroom for 80B and concrete bungalows with fan and bathroom for 200B to 300B. It is set amid coconut palms but has no beach to speak of.

Hat Kaibae is an area that has become quite developed, with a new pier and bungalows with electricity. Heading south, the first place you come to is the German-run *Palm Beach-Comfortable Bar Resort.* Here, concrete bungalows with fan and bathroom cost 200B to 300B. The food here is reportedly good.

Coral Resort (☎ 01-219 3815) is set amid a bumper crop of coconut palms and costs 400B for bungalows with fan and private bathroom. It also has an international telephone service.

A khlawng separates Coral Resort from the *Nang Nual Resort,* where relatively new natural-looking bungalows start at 300B. The resort restaurant serves Thai and French dishes. Canoes are available for rent. This area is a bit trashed out in places and the adjacent shrimp farm is a definite detraction.

Kaibae Hut (☎ 01-862 8426), also on the southern side of the khlawng, has a nicely laid-out restaurant and fair bungalows, plus a bit of a beach even at high tide; rates are 300B to 500B for bungalows with bathroom. A large deluxe air-con bungalow (with TV, fridge and fan) that can fit up to eight people is available for 2500B. It's quiet and has a security gate that's locked at night. SeaHorse Dive Centre offers dive trips and instruction during the dry season. Next south is *KB Bungalows (☎ 01-862 8103),* on a grassy bank above the beach. Prices are 500B to 800B, with bathroom and fan.

On a better beach, *KaiBae Beach Bungalow (☎ 01-940 5102)* has clean, well-separated huts and bungalows for 150B to 500B. Walk another 100m to *Porn's (☎ 01-864 1608),* which offers basic huts with shared bathroom for 150B, fan and

CENTRAL THAILAND

bathroom huts for 300B and tents for 80B. The disco on the premises is the most popular night spot on Hat Kaibae. Beyond Porn's is the large **Siam View Resort** (☎ 039-529022), with bungalows costing 1250B with fan, 1700B with air-con. A 10-person bungalow costs 3500B. There are also hotel rooms for 900B to 1700B. The last place on the beach is the secluded and friendly **Siam Bay Resort** (☎ 01-829 5529), with huts for 250B and bungalows with private bathroom from 400B. Fancier concrete bungalows cost up to 600B. At low tide you can walk out to Ko Man Nai opposite. This is the last place on the west coast with electricity; accommodation farther south uses generators.

A 30-minute walk along the path to Ao Bang Bao will bring you to **Tree House Lodge** (☎ 01-847 8215), in a rocky area near a secluded white-sand beach. Simple thatched huts on stilts in a coconut grove start at 60B. There is a very good restaurant and a small library. During high season the lodge operates a taxi boat from Laem Ngop (50B).

South Coast The south coast places tend to close during the rainy season, from May to November, when regular transport is difficult. Nevertheless, this is the place to go if you want to get a feel for the life of Thai fisherfolk or to explore beautiful jungle paths and nearby islets.

On Ao Bang Bao you'll find the friendly **Bang Bao Blue Wave**, which has huts with private bathroom for 150B per person and 180B for two. The generator electricity is on from 6 to 10 pm. The owner also has a boat for hire. In the village of Ban Bang Bao is the optimistically named **Bang Bao Resort**, located on a pier over the water. Simple rooms with shared bathroom cost 100B and there are good seafood restaurants nearby.

At the head of the road near the pier at Ao Salak Phet, **Salakpet Seafood Restaurant & Resort** has clean rooms built over the water for 300B with fan and bathroom, plus some air-con rooms that house four people and cost 1200B.

Nearby **Sang Aroon Restaurant** (☎ 01-650 2658) has rooms for 100B. The same family owns **Sang Aroon Bungalows** at Ban Jaekbae, a 20-minute boat ride across

the bay (provided free by the restaurant). Rooms at the latter cost 200B to 500B.

Right at the tip of the cape, is the friendly **Tantawan Resort** on a rocky outcrop. Huts cost 100/200B single/double. The beach is only a two-minute swim away. To get here take a boat from Ao Salak Phet (30B).

East Coast There are a couple of mediocre places to stay near the nicely landscaped national park headquarters at Tha Than Mayom. Privately managed, **Koh Chang Cabana** (☎ 01-663 6352), near the Dan Kao pier, rents out rooms in a long rowhouse for 400B with fan. Separate air-con bungalows cost 1500B. Tour groups are the main clientele here. **Than Mayom Bungalows**, about 500m from the park offices, charges 500B for a large and comfortable two-room house and 2200B for a house that can accommodate 30 people.

If you have camping gear, it might be better to hike up and **camp** near Nam Tok Than Mayom.

Other Islands Ko Kut, Ko Mak, Ko Kradat, Ko Kham and Ko Wai are quieter and more secluded than Ko Chang, but transport can be a little tricky – although from December to April there are daily boats. Also, you can't just pick up and walk down the beach to another bungalow if you don't like the one you've landed at. Except at the package places, room rates overall are less expensive than on Ko Chang.

From May to November, it's a good idea to call in advance to make sure boat transportation is available. Most places of accommodation close down from June to September.

Ko Kut As on Ko Chang, the best beaches are found along the west coast, particularly at Hat Tapho. It is possible to visit the island on your own, but you will find it next to impossible to get accommodation without being on a package tour. The bungalow operations on this island include **Ko Kut Sai Khao Resort** (☎ 039-511824), 3200B; **Kut Island Resort** (in Bangkok ☎ 02-374 3004), 4150B; **Khlong Hin Hut** (☎ 039-530236), 3000B; **Ko Kut Cabana** (☎ 039-522955), 3800B to 4200B; and **Khlong Jaow Resort** (☎ 039-520337), 3600B. All of these places offer the usual amenities of a Thai-style 'resort'. All rooms have attached bathroom and air-con, and each resort has its own restaurant. The clientele is mostly Thai.

Ko Mak On the western bay, amid a coconut and rubber plantation, the friendly *Ko Mak Resort (☎ 01-219 1220; in Bangkok ☎ 02-319 6714/5)* has bungalows with fan and bathroom from 350B to 650B, or pay 1000B for large, two-room bungalows. A windsurfing school on the beach offers courses and rents out equipment. Also nearby is a post office and a minimart that rents out motorbikes and mountain bikes for 60B and 30B per hour. Not far away is *Fantasia (☎ 01-219 1220)*, which has colourful A-frame huts among the coconut palms for 100B; bamboo huts along the beach for 150B (shared facilities); and concrete bungalows with private bathroom for 250B. To the west, *TK Huts (☎ 039-521631)* has bungalows with fan and bathroom for 300B to 400B. Nearby is the *Holiday Beach Resort (☎ 01-255 7011)*, offering simple but clean bungalows with veranda (no fan, shared bathroom) for 150B to 200B. The location is very quiet and there is an unspoilt beach just 30m away. *Ao Kao Resort (☎ 01-647 5484)* offers comfortable bungalows with fan and private bathroom for 350B to 950B. Smaller basic huts go for 150B to 700B. Diving equipment and instruction are available from Lagona Divers located on the premises. Nearby is the aptly named *Lazy Days*, where tepees made from bamboo and palm fronds cost 80B, and larger huts are 100B to 150B. Facilities are shared and there is a small library.

As on Ko Kut, all of these tend to close during the rainy season.

Ko Kradat The *Ko Kradat Resort (☎ 01-432 8027)* is only open to people on a prearranged package tour. Air-con bungalows with attached bathroom are 1800B.

Ko Kham Run by a friendly ex-cop, *Ko Kham Resort* offers bamboo bungalows for 150B. More upmarket huts are available for up to 700B.

Ko Wai At *Ko Wai Paradise (☎ 039-597131)*, simple wooden bungalows go for 150B to 250B with shared facilities, 400B with private bathroom. Larger bungalows cost 600B.

Places to Eat
Menus at all the bungalows on Ko Chang are pretty similar. On Hat Sai Khao, highest marks go to the kitchens at *Sunsai Bungalow* and *Cookie Bungalow*. Several small *eateries* along the eastern side of the main road in Hat Sai Khao offer options, and *Ban Nuna Restaurant-Cafe*, an upstairs place where you sit on cushions, is good for Thai lunches and dinners, pizza and Western breakfasts.

Swedish-managed *White House Bakery*, across the road from Sabai Beach Bungalow, offers a variety of baked goods, fruit shakes and plenty of information on island activities.

The *Salakpet Seafood Restaurant*, at Ao Salak Phet, Ko Chang, serves the very best seafood on the island; prices are moderate. Also worth trying are the *seafood restaurants* on the pier at Ban Bang Bao.

At the end of a small pier at Tha Than Mayom is a very casual *restaurant* with rice and noodle dishes.

Getting There & Away
Ko Chang Take a sǎwngthǎew (20B, 25 minutes) from Trat to Laem Ngop on the coast, then a ferry to Ko Chang. There are now three piers serving Ko Chang – the main one at the end of the road from Trat, called Tha Laem Ngop; another 4km northwest of Laem Ngop called Tha Ko Chang Centrepoint (operated by Rooks Ko Chang Resort); and a newer one called Tha Thammachat at Ao Thammachat, farther west of Laem Ngop.

Tha Laem Ngop (look for the sign that reads 'Eastern Apex') is the best jumping-off point as there are boats to all the islands from here. Boats go to Tha Dan Kao on Ko Chang year-round; this is the boat most people take. During the high season – roughly December to April – boats depart hourly from 7 am to 5 pm (50B, one hour). The remainder of the year the schedule is reduced to about every two hours, although departures ultimately depend on weather, number of passengers and any number of other factors. You should check on fares in advance – sometimes the boat crews may overcharge fàràng. At Tha Dan Kao, săwng-thăew will be waiting to take you to any of the various beaches along the west coast or to Ao Salak Phet.

One boat leaves Tha Laem Ngop at 3 pm daily for Hat Sai Khao (80B, two hours) on Ko Chang's west coast. It returns at 9.30 am.

From the gleaming Tha Ko Chang Centrepoint, there are three or four boats to Ko Chang from 7 am to 4 pm daily (70B, 45 minutes). The fare includes the cost of a săwngthăew ride to one of the beaches. Round-trip tickets are also sold (120B), but be sure you board the right boat upon your return, otherwise you'll be charged again.

The newest way to get to Ko Chang is via a vehicle ferry from Ao Thammachat. The ferry leaves four times daily (400B for a vehicle and driver, plus 30B per passenger or pedestrian, 30 minutes). Custom is often restricted to people doing business on the island, but in the future this service could very well supplant the Laem Ngop tourist ferry as well.

Ko Mak From November to May, boats to Ko Mak (170B, three to 3½ hours) leave from Tha Laem Ngop at 3 pm daily, with additional departures at 10 am on Monday, Thursday and Saturday. In the reverse direction the boats depart at 8 am daily, with additional departures at 1 pm on Wednesday, Friday and Sunday. During the rainy season the departure schedule is cut back to every other day – except in high surf when boats may be cancelled altogether for several days.

Coconut boats also go to Ko Mak from the pier near the slaughterhouse in Trat once a week (170B, five hours) – if you can get on.

Ko Kut Most people get to Ko Kut from Ko Mak (150B). There are no direct boats from Laem Ngop to Ko Kut, but the 10 am boat to Ko Mak (leaves Monday, Thursday and Saturday) carries on to Ko Kut after making a stop at Ko Mak and departing at 1 pm. The cost is 170B and the trip takes three hours. Return boats from Ko Kut to Laem Ngop via Ko Mak leave on Friday and Saturday at noon.

Although it's a less dependable way to get there (but more adventurous for sure),

two or three fishing boats a week go to Ko Kut (100B to 150B, six hours) from Tha Chaloemphon on Mae Nam Trat towards the eastern side of Trat. Similar boats leave slightly less frequently (six to eight times a month) from Ban Nam Chiaw, a village about halfway between Trat and Laem Ngop. Departure frequency and times from either pier depend on the weather and the fishing season – it's best to inquire ahead of time.

Coconut boats go to Ko Kut once or twice a month from a pier next to the slaughterhouse in Trat (100B to 150B, six hours).

If you want to charter a boat to Ko Kut from the mainland, the best place to do so is from Ban Ta Neuk, near the 68km marker south-east of Trat, about 6km before Khlong Yai off Rte 318. A long-tail boat, capable of carrying up to 10 people, can be chartered here (1500B, one hour). During the rainy season these boats may suspend service.

Other Islands Daily boats to Ko Kham depart from Laem Ngop around 3 pm (170B, three hours). From Ko Mak to Ko Kham, it's a short hop from the pier at Ko Mak Resort; boats leave at 10 am and 1 and 2 pm daily (50B to 80B). A boat from Laem Ngop to Ko Wai leaves at 3 pm and arrives at 5.30 pm (120B). Both boats return the next day at around 8 am.

Getting Around

Motorcycle Bungalow operators along the west coast charge 60B per hour or 400B per day for motorbike hire; elsewhere on the island rental bikes are scarce. The owners claim they have to charge these rates because the island roads are so hard on the bikes.

Săwngthăew The săwngthăew meeting the boats at Tha Dan Kao charge 30B per person to Hat Sai Khao, Hat Kaibae and Ban Khlong Phrao on the west coast. Between Tha Dan Kao and Ban Salak Phet, the local price is only 30B per person, although tourists may be charged more.

Boat Charter trips to nearby islands average 500B to 800B for a half-day, or 1000B to 2000B all day, depending on the boat and distances covered. Make sure that the charter includes all 'user fees' for the islands – sometimes the boat operators demand 200B on top of the charter fee for 'using' the beach.

On the southern end of the island, you can charter a long-tail boat or fishing boat between Hat Kaibae and Ao Bang Bao for 1000B or around 150B per person shared by a boatful of passengers. Similar charters are available between Ao Bang Bao and Ao Salak Phet and Long Beach Bungalows on Hat Yao for around 150B.

Boat rides up Khlong Phrao to the falls cost 50B per person and can be arranged through most bungalows.

Prachinburi & Sa Kaew Provinces

Lying roughly halfway between Bangkok and the Cambodian border, the largely rural provinces of Prachinburi and Sa Kaew are peppered with many small Dvaravati and Khmer ruins. The latter province's name, in fact, means 'Jewel Pool', a reference to various Mon-Khmer reservoirs in the area. Little more than loose collections of laterite blocks, most will be of little interest to the casual visitor. The provincial capitals and larger towns lie next to the banks of Mae Nam Prachin – now paralleled by the eastern railway line and Hwy 33 – in the midst of a rice-growing region crossed by canals. The eastern districts of Prachinburi centred around *amphoe* Sa Kaew attained separate provincial status in January 1994.

NATIONAL PARKS

North of Prachinburi, Rte 3077 leads to Khao Yai National Park (see Nakhon Ratchasima Province in the North-Eastern Thailand chapter). North and north-east of Kabinburi, along the southern escarpment of the Khorat Plateau, are the contiguous Thap Lan National Park and Pang Sida National Park. Together these parks encompass 3084 sq km, one of the largest protected natural areas in Thailand.

Thap Lan National Park is well known as a habitat for the abundant *tôn laan* (talipot palm), the leaves of which were once used for Buddhist manuscripts. Wildlife seen in the park includes elephants, gaur, tigers,

sambar, barking deer, palm civets, hornbills and gibbons. Lowland bird varieties are particularly well represented here. This area was an important refuge for Thailand's communist guerrillas during the 1960s and 1970s, and remnants of their camps can be seen along the streams Khlong Nam Brang and Khlong Sam Son.

Facilities in the park are minimal; anyone who would like to explore the interior should contact the rangers at park headquarters in Thap Lan village, Amphoe Na Di. The rangers can arrange for a tour of the park and provide camping permits.

There is no public transport to the park entrance, which is around 32km north of Kabinburi via Rte 304 (the road to Nakhon Ratchasima).

Pang Sida National Park, around 30km south-east of Thap Lan near Sa Kaew, is smaller but hillier than Thap Lan. Streams that cut through the park form several scenic waterfalls, including **Nam Tok Pang Sida** and **Nam Tok Na Pha Yai** near the park headquarters, and the more difficult to reach **Suan Man Suan Thong** and **Nam Tok Daeng Makha**.

National park entry fees are collected at each of these parks (20B for Thais, 200B for foreigners, half price for children).

SA MORAKOT & SA KAEW
สระมรกต/สระแก้ว

South-east of Prachinburi provincial capital via Rtes 319 and 3070, in the village of Ban Sa Khoi (between Khok Pip and Sa Maha Pho on Rte 3070), is the Angkor-period Sa Morakot. Thai for 'Emerald Pool', this was an important Khmer reservoir during the reign of Angkor's Jayavarman VII. Original laterite-block sluices next to the dam, along with assorted *sĕmaa* (boundary stones), naga sculptures, pedestals and a sandstone lingam, can still be seen here.

Water from this reservoir is considered sacred and has been used in Thai coronation ceremonies.

Sa Kaew or 'Jewel Pool', another historic reservoir site, is just south of Khok Pip off Rte 3070. This one features a Dvaravati-period laterite quarry with some surviving bas-relief on the walls.

There are a number of other Dvaravati and Angkor laterite foundations in the area.

CENTRAL THAILAND

ARANYA PRATHET
อรัญประเทศ

postcode 27120 • pop 56,700

This district next to the Thailand-Cambodia border has long been an important trade and transport centre. After the Khmer Rouge took over Cambodia in 1975, and again when the Vietnamese invaded Cambodia in 1979, Aranya Prathet became a major recipient of Cambodian refugees. Until 1997, random skirmishes between Khmer Rouge guerrillas and the Phnom Penh government continued to send Cambodian citizens scurrying over the border from time to time. Now with the Khmer Rouge 'defeated' (it's too early to count them out altogether), the area is considered safe and the border between Aranya Prathet and the Cambodian town of Poipet is fully open to all visitors with the proper visas.

There isn't a lot to see around town; the refugee-camp business changed its relatively sleepy nature seemingly forever, and a slow increase in border trade has surrounded the older town centre with a smattering of modern auto dealers and office buildings. Convoys of shining Toyota Landcruisers flying UN flags ply the main streets on their way to and from Cambodia. A huge army base on the Thai side of Aranya Prathet houses a battalion of Thailand's 3rd Infantry.

Talat Rong Kleua, a large market consisting of rows of warehouse-like sheds at the northern edge of town, attracts a ragtag crowd of Cambodians who sell gems, textiles, basketry, brass and other handicrafts to the Thais. It's a fascinating spot to visit just to observe the steady stream of Cambodians crossing the border with huge hand-pulled carts piled high with market goods. Rickety rickshaws made of wood and bicycle tyres transport up to six passengers at a time between the market and the border crossing. There are several simple restaurants serving Thai food in the market.

Theft and banditry are common in the area, so take care with night travel. Although it's relatively safe to cross the border directly to Poipet, areas to the north and south of the district seat are heavily mined. You should also keep in mind that Poipet regularly experiences outbreaks of cholera and dengue fever, especially during the rainy season.

Places to Stay & Eat

The **Aran Garden 1** (*59/1–7 Thanon Rat Uthit*) is an older, somewhat seedy central hotel with acceptable rooms with fan and bathroom for 140B to 180B. The newer and larger **Aran Garden 2** (*110 Thanon Rat Uthit*) offers clean, quiet rooms for 200B with fan, 400B with air-con.

Catering to visiting, comparatively wealthy border traders and nongovernment-organisation (NGO) employees, **Aran Park** (☎ *037-232588, fax 232115*), on the main highway leading into Aranya Prathet from the west, offers clean modern rooms with air-con, phone, satellite TV and fridge for 700B to 1300B. The better-located (for anyone who wants to see the town on foot) **Inter Hotel** (☎ *037-231291, fax 231848*) is tucked away in a quiet residential area near the town centre on Soi Ban Aran. Nice rooms with satellite TV and private bathrooms with hot water cost 650B to 800B.

The air-con **Little Home Restaurant**, in the town centre, serves pizza, salads, sandwiches, ice cream and Thai and Chinese food from 7.30 am to 9.30 pm. A block south-east of Little Home is a small **night market** with a cluster of food vendors.

Getting There & Away

Ordinary buses from Bangkok's Northern and North-Eastern bus station to Aranya Prathet (81B, five hours) leave hourly from 5.30 am to 4.30 pm; air-con buses (150B) leave hourly from 5.30 to 10.30 am and from noon to 5 pm. Buses to/from Prachinburi cost 37B ordinary, 60B air-con.

Trains on the 3rd-class-only eastern railway line between Bangkok and Aranya Prathet leave Bangkok's Hualamphong station twice daily at 5.55 am and 1.05 pm (48B, 5½ hours).

If you have your own wheels you could also reach Aranya Prathet from Chanthaburi Province to the south via Rte 317, or from Buriram Province to the north via Rte 3068. Before taking the latter road in either direction, check the current security situation with a reliable local; renewed bandit activity in the area could precipitate the temporary closing of the road.

Border Crossing (Cambodia) The SRT train continues on for another half-hour east of Aran (as Aranya Prathet is commonly known) to the border for 5B. From Poipet on the Cambodian side you can take a pick-up truck to Siem Reap, for Angkor Wat, or to Sisophon. From Sisophon it is possible to catch a train all the way to Phnom Penh.

Phetchaburi Province

PHETCHABURI (PHETBURI)
อ.เมืองเพชรบุรี

postcode 76000 • pop 36,000

Situated 160km south of Bangkok, Phetchaburi (more commonly called by its short name Phetburi, and also Meuang Phet) is worth a stopover for its many old temples spanning several centuries. Six or seven temples can be seen via a circular walk of two or three hours through the city. These temples have made very few concessions to the 20th and 21st centuries and thus provide a glimpse of the traditional Siamese urban wát.

Also noteworthy is Khao Wang, just west of the city centre, which has the remains of a King Rama IV palace and several wát, plus a good aerial view of the city. Phra Ratchawang Ban Peun, a European-style palace built for King Rama V, and the underground Buddhist shrine at the Khao Luang Caves, north of the city, are also worth seeing.

Orientation & Information

If you arrive at the train station, follow the road south-east of the tracks until you come to Thanon Ratchadamnoen, then turn right. Follow Thanon Ratchadamnoen south to the second major intersection and turn left for central Phetchaburi, or take a sǎamláw from the train station to Saphan Chomrut for 20B.

Money The Siam Commercial Bank has an exchange office at 2 Thanon Damnoen Kasem, just south of the post office. Several other banks in the vicinity offer foreign exchange and have ATMs.

Post & Communications The post office, on the corner of Thanon Ratwithi and Thanon Damnoen Kasem, opens from 8.30 am to 4.30 pm. An international telephone office, upstairs in the same building, is open from 7 am to 10 pm daily.

Khao Wang & Phra Nakhon Khiri Historical Park
เขาวัง/อุทยานประวัติศาสตร์
พระนครคีรี

Just west of the city, a 20B sǎamláw ride from the bus station, is Khao Wang. Cobblestone paths lead up and around the hill, which is studded with wát and various components of King Rama IV's palace on Phra Nakhon Khiri. The views are great, especially at sunset. The walk up looks easy but is fairly strenuous. Fat monkeys loll about in the trees and on top of the walls along the main paths. In 1988 Phra Nakhon Khiri was declared a national historical park, so there is an entry fee of 40B. A tram has been installed to save you walking up to the peak (30/10B for adults/children one way). The park is open 8.15 am to 5 pm weekdays and to 5.30 pm weekends.

Phra Ratchawang Ban Peun
พระราชวังบ้านปืน

Located just over 1km south of the city centre is Phra Ratchawang Ban Peun (Ban Peun Palace). Construction began in 1910 at the behest of King Rama V, who passed away not long after the project was started. Completed in 1916, the German architects who were hired to do the job used it as an opportunity to showcase contemporary German innovations in construction and interior design. The structure is typical of the early 20th century, a period that saw a Thai craze for erecting European-style buildings – seemingly in an effort to keep up with the 'modern' architecture of its colonised neighbours. While the exterior of this two-storey palace promises little excitement, the exquisite glazed tile-work in the interior, particularly the columns in the domed foyer, is a must see. Ban Peun palace is situated on a Thai military base but is open to the general public from 8.30 am to 4.30 pm weekdays.

CENTRAL THAILAND

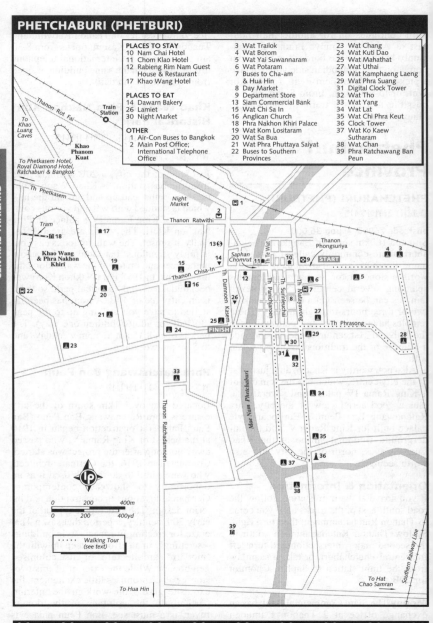

PHETCHABURI (PHETBURI)

PLACES TO STAY
10 Nam Chai Hotel
11 Chom Klao Hotel
12 Rabieng Rim Nam Guest
   House & Restaurant
17 Khao Wang Hotel

PLACES TO EAT
14 Dawarn Bakery
26 Lamiet
30 Night Market

OTHER
1 Air-Con Buses to Bangkok
2 Main Post Office;
  International Telephone
  Office

3 Wat Trailok
4 Wat Borom
5 Wat Yai Suwannaram
6 Wat Potaram
7 Buses to Cha-am
  & Hua Hin
8 Day Market
9 Department Store
13 Siam Commercial Bank
15 Wat Chi Sa In
16 Anglican Church
18 Phra Nakhon Khiri Palace
19 Wat Kom Lositaram
20 Wat Sa Bua
21 Wat Phra Phuttaya Saiyat
22 Buses to Southern
   Provinces

23 Wat Chang
24 Wat Kuti Dao
25 Wat Mahathat
27 Wat Uthai
28 Wat Kamphaeng Laeng
29 Wat Phra Suang
31 Digital Clock Tower
32 Wat Tho
33 Wat Yang
34 Wat Lat
35 Wat Chi Phra Keut
36 Clock Tower
37 Wat Ko Kaew
   Sutharam
38 Wat Chan
39 Phra Ratchawang Ban
   Peun

Walking Tour – Phetchaburi Temples

Wat Yai Suwannaram

After you've crossed Mae Nam Phetchaburi by Saphan Chomrut and passed the Nam Chai Hotel on the left, walk about 300m farther along Thanon Phongsuriya until you see a big temple on the right. This is Wat Yai Suwannaram, originally built in the 17th century and renovated during the reign of King Rama V (reigned 1868–1910). The main *bòt* (central sanctuary) is surrounded by a cloister filled with sombre Buddha images. The murals inside the *bòt* date to the 1730s and are in good condition. Next to the *bòt*, in the middle of a pond, is a beautifully designed old *hăw trai*, or Tripitaka library.

Wat Borom & Wat Trailok

These two *wát* are next to one another on the opposite side of Thanon Phongsuriya from Wat Yai Suwannaram, a little to the east. They are distinctive for their monastic halls and long, graceful, wooden 'dormitories' on stilts. Turn right onto the road heading south from Wat Trailok, passing a bamboo fence on the right to the entrance for Wat Kamphaeng Laeng.

Wat Kamphaeng Laeng

This is a 13th-century Khmer site with five *prang* (Khmer-style tower) and part of the original laterite wall *(kamphaeng laeng)* still standing. The front prang contains a Buddha footprint. Of the other four, two contain images dedicated to famous *lŭang phâw* (venerated monks), one was in ruins (but is being restored) and the last has recently been uncovered from a mound of dirt. The structures were built as Hindu monuments, so the Buddhist symbols are late additions.

Wat Phra Suang & Wat Lat

Follow Thanon Phrasong beside Wat Kamphaeng Laeng, heading west back towards the river until you pass Wat Phra Suang on the left, undistinguished except for one very nice Ayuthaya-style *prasat*. Turn left immediately after this *wát*, heading south again until you come to the clock tower at the southern edge of town. You'll have passed Wat Lat on the left-hand side of the street along the way, but it's not worth breaking your momentum for; this is a long walk.

Wat Ko Kaew Sutharam

Turn right at the clock tower and look for signs leading to the Ayuthaya-period Wat Ko Kaew Sutharam (Wat Ko). Two different soi on the left lead to the *wát*, which is behind the shops along the curving street. The *bòt* features early 18th-century murals that are among the best conceived in Thailand. One panel depicts what appears to be a Jesuit priest wearing the robes of a Buddhist monk, while another shows other foreigners undergoing Buddhist conversions. There is also a large wooden monastic hall on stilts similar to the ones at Wat Borom and Wat Trailok, but in much better condition.

Wat Mahathat

Follow the street in front of Wat Ko north (back towards central Phetchaburi) and walk over the first bridge you come to on the left, which leads to Wat Mahathat. Alternatively, you can cross the river at Wat Ko, near the clock tower, and take the street on the other side of the river around to Wat Mahathat. The large white prang of this *wát* can be seen from a distance – a typical late Ayuthaya/early Ratanakosin adaptation of the Khmer prang of Lopburi and Phimai. This is obviously an important temple in Phetchaburi, judging from all the activity here.

Khao Luang Caves
ถ้ำเขาหลวง

Five kilometres north of Phetchaburi is the cave sanctuary of Khao Luang. Concrete steps lead down into an anteroom then into the main cavern, which is filled with old Buddha images, many of them put in place by King Rama IV. Sunlight from two holes in the chamber ceiling spray light on the images, which are a favourite subject for photographers. To the rear of the main cavern is an entrance to a third, smaller chamber. On the right of the entrance is Wat Bunthawi, with a săalaa designed by the abbot of the wát himself and a bòt with impressively carved wooden door panels.

Admission to the caves is free (although donations are accepted). A săamláw trip from the centre of Phetchaburi to Khao Luang costs 50B, while a motorcycle taxi costs 30B.

Places to Stay
On the eastern side of Saphan Chomrut, on the right bank of Mae Nam Phetchaburi, is the 30-room *Chom Klao Hotel* (☎ 032-425398), an ordinary, fairly clean Chinese hotel with friendly staff. Rooms cost 120B with fan and shared bathroom and 160B with private bathroom.

The *Nam Chai Hotel (no Roman-script sign)* is a block east of the Chom Klao Hotel, and has rooms for 120B with shared bathroom and 150B with attached bathroom, but is not as good value as the Chom Klao.

Better than both of these is the *Rabieng Rim Nam Guest House* (☎/fax 032-425707, 1 Thanon Chisa-In), attached to the restaurant of the same name. Cosy singles/doubles with fan and clean shared bathroom cost 120/240B.

The 50-room *Khao Wang Hotel* (☎ 032-425167), opposite Khao Wang, is a favourite among travelling salesmen and not as sleazy as the town's other Chinese hotels. A fairly clean room with fan and bathroom costs 220B. Air-con rooms are 320B. Most rooms have TV.

The best-value hotel is the friendly and clean 50-room *Phetkasem Hotel* (☎ 032-425581, 86/1 Thanon Phetkasem), which is on the highway north to Bangkok on the western edge of town. Rooms cost from 150B for a single with fan and bathroom to 450B

Fair Enough

The Phra Nakhon Khiri Fair takes place in early February and lasts for about eight days. Centred on Khao Wang and Phetchaburi's historic temples, the festivities include a sound-and-light show at the Phra Nakhon Khiri Palace, temples festooned with lights and performances of Thai classical dance-drama, *lákhon chatrii*, *lí-keh* (see explanations in the Music, Theatre & Dance special section of the Facts about Thailand chapter) and modern-style historical dramas. A twist on the usual beauty contest provides a showcase for Phetchaburi widows.

for a double with air-con and TV. Nearby *Royal Diamond* (☎ 032-411062, 555 Mu 1, Thanon Phetkasem) is a more upmarket place, with air-con rooms for 800B to 1500B.

Places to Eat
Local dishes for which Phetchaburi is famous include *khànŏm jiin thâwt man* (thin noodles with fried spicy fish cake), *khâo châe phétbùrii* (moist chilled rice served with sweetmeats, a hot-season speciality) and *khànŏm mâw kaeng* (egg custard). You'll find these along with a range of standard Thai and Chinese dishes at several good restaurants in the Khao Wang area. A variety of cheap eats is available at the *night market* at the southern end of Thanon Surinleuchai, under the digital clock tower. Another very good *night market* sits along Thanon Rot Fai between the train station and the town centre. Near the Khao Wang Hotel, a small *restaurant* sets up in the evenings offering decent *khâo man kài* (Hainanese chicken and rice) and *khâo mŭu daeng* ('red' pork and rice).

Other good eating places can be found in the town centre along the main street to the clock tower. Across from Wat Mahathat, *Lamiet* sells really good khànŏm mâw kaeng and *făwy thawng* (sweet shredded egg yolk), which the Lamiet also ships to Bangkok. This shop also has a branch near Khao Wang, where a whole group of *egg custard places* serve tourists.

The *Rabieng Rim Nam*, on the southern side of Thanon Chisa-In near Saphan

Chomrut, features a Thai and English menu that boasts over 100 items, including seafood and 30 kinds of *yam* (spicy salads); most nonseafood dishes cost 25B to 50B, while seafood and some soups cost from 70B.

Dawarn Bakery, corner of Thanon Chisa-In and Thanon Damnoen Kasem, offers a decent assortment of baked goods.

Getting There & Away

Bus From Bangkok, buses leave regularly from the Southern bus station in Thonburi (2½ hours). Fares are 50B (ordinary) on the new road or 46B on the old road (via Ratchaburi and Nakhon Pathom); 60B for 2nd-class air-con; and 75B for 1st-class air-con.

Buses go to Phetchaburi from Cha-am (18B ordinary, 20B air-con, one hour) and Hua Hin (22B, 30B, 1½ hours). The distance is actually not that great but buses make an obligatory 20-minute stop just north of Cha-am so Thai tourists can load up on local sweets. Other ordinary bus fares are: Ratchaburi 18B (45 minutes); Nakhon Pathom 29B (two hours); Prachuap Khiri Khan 40B (three hours); and Phuket 210B ordinary, 304B air-con (12 hours). Buses to the southern provinces leave from the bus station just south-west of Khao Wang. Buses to Bangkok leave from the northern end of Thanon Damnoen Kasem. Buses to Hua Hin and Cha-am leave from Thanon Matayawong opposite the day market.

Train Trains leave Bangkok's Hualamphong station at 12.25 pm (rapid), 2.20 and 2.45 pm (special express), 3.50, 5.35 and 6.20 pm (rapid), 7.15 pm (express), and 10.30 and 10.50 pm (express diesel railcar). All of these trains offer 1st-, 2nd- and 3rd-class seating except for the 2.35 pm special express (1st and 2nd class only) and the 10.30 and 10.50 pm express diesel railcar (2nd class only). The trains take about three hours to reach Phetchaburi. Fares are 34/78/153B for 3rd/2nd/1st class, not including rapid or express surcharges. The bus is faster, unless you count getting out to Bangkok's Southern bus station.

There is no ordinary train between Hualamphong and Phetchaburi, but there is one ordinary 3rd-class train daily from Thonburi (Bangkok Noi) station at 1.05 pm (34B, no surcharges).

Getting Around

Săamláw and motorcycle taxis go anywhere in the town centre for 20B; you can charter one for the whole day for 150B. Share săwngthăew cost 6B around town, including to and from the train station.

KAENG KRACHAN NATIONAL PARK
อุทยานแห่งชาติแก่งกระจาน

This 3000-sq-km park is Thailand's largest, covering nearly half of Phetchaburi Province along the Myanmar border. In spite of its size and proximity to Bangkok, Kaeng Krachan doesn't seem to get many visitors (or perhaps its huge size just swallows them up). Because this part of Phetchaburi receives some of the heaviest rainfall in Thailand, the rainforest is particularly abundant in places. There are also areas of savanna-like grasslands, mountains, steep cliffs, caves, waterfalls, long-distance hiking trails and two rivers, the Phetchaburi and the Pranburi, which are suitable for rafting.

Above the **Kheuan Kaeng Krachan** is a large reservoir stocked with fish. Animals living in Kaeng Krachan include wild elephants, deer, tigers, bears, gibbons, boars, hornbills, bantengs, dusky leaf langurs, gaurs and wild cattle. Small Karen settlements here have taken their toll on the park via illegal farming and poaching. According to Piprell & Graham's *National Parks of Thailand*, 'Kaeng Krachan...could become one of the world's premier reserves if properly managed in the future'.

Hiking and camping are excellent as long as you have your own food, water and camping gear. Forestry officials at the park headquarters can sometimes be hired as guides for overnight trekking in the park. The standard guide fee is 200B per day. Very little English is spoken so this option is best for those who know some Thai or who don't need any commentary.

Eighteen-tiered **Nam Tok Tho Thip** is a three-hour hike from the 33km marker on the road into the park; longer hikes can reach the headwaters of Mae Nam Phetchaburi or the summit of **Phanoen Thung**, the park's highest point. Deeper into the park, near La-U Reservoir, are the twin waterfalls of **Pa La-U Yai** and **Pa La-U Noi**; reaching the heights of this cascade requires several days of trekking for which an experienced guide is necessary. There is a Karen village near the latter. The best hiking and camping months are November to April.

You can rent boats on Kaeng Krachan Reservoir for 350B per hour and 800B for three hours. Standard national park admission fees apply (see under Sai Yok National Park earlier in this chapter).

Places to Stay & Eat

It costs 100B to stay in the 11 bungalows near the park headquarters. You can also set up your own tent for 5B per person per night. Near the visitors centre is a modest restaurant.

Kaeng Krachan Riverside (☎ 032-461244) has fan bungalows with private bathroom for 800B. *Kaeng Krachan Country Club* (☎ 032-459260) offers high-end bungalows with all the amenities for 2500B.

As malaria is a definite risk in the park, be sure to take precautions against mosquito bites.

Getting There & Away

Kaeng Krachan is about 60km from Phetchaburi. The turn-off is at Tha Yang on Hwy 4, about 18km south of Phetchaburi. The park headquarters is 8km past Kheuan Kaeng Krachan where the road ends.

There is no regular transport all the way to the park, but you can get a săwngthăew from Phetchaburi as far as the village of Ban Kaeng Krachan (also known as Fa Prathan), 4km from the park. The săwngthăew leave from near the digital clock tower in Phetchaburi every half-hour between 7 am and 4 pm and cost 20B; there's a half-hour stopover in Tha Yang. From Ban Kaeng Krachan you should be able to hitch or charter a ride from the locals.

If you have your own vehicle, you can explore the dirt roads of Kaeng Krachan National Park.

CHA-AM

ชะอำ

postcode 76120 • pop 22,700

A growing town 178km from Bangkok, 38km from Phetchaburi and 25km from Hua Hin, Cha-am is known for its casuarina-lined beach, a favourite getaway for provincial Thai families. Every weekend and holiday they arrive by the score in multihued buses that are seemingly powered by groups of inebriated young men who dance in the aisles while pounding drums and clapping cymbals (Thais call these junkets 'ching chap tours', after the rhythmic noise the musicians produce: ching-chap-ching-chap).

Once on the beach, the families plant themselves comfortably in the shade and spend the day snacking while a few brave souls risk exposure to the sun's rays to ride jet skis and banana boats. It's really a Thai scene: While some westerners will find it diverting for an afternoon, eventually most will be driven off by the public-address system. Strung along the shore to blare announcements with a ding-dong prelude, it gives the beach all the ambience of an airport departure lounge. Of course it should also be said that if you come during a weekday, you're likely to have the beach to yourself.

Beach umbrellas and sling chairs are available for hire and there are public bathhouses where you can bathe in fresh water for 5B to 7B.

The old town centre is on the opposite side of Phetkasem Hwy, where you'll find the main post office, market, train station and government offices. The road that fronts the beach, Thanon Ruamjit, is a long line of hotels, restaurants and souvenir stalls catering mostly to Thai tourists.

Inland from the beach (follow the signs) at **Wat Neranchararama** is a fat, white, six-armed *phrá phákháwam* statue; the six hands cover the nine bodily orifices in a symbolic gesture denying the senses.

Information

Tourist Offices A TAT office (☎ 032-471005, 01-486 4936, ⓔ tatphet@tat.or.th) has been established on Phetkasem Hwy just 500m south of town. The staff are very helpful; they distribute information on Cha-am, Phetchaburi, Hua Hin, Prachuap Khiri Khan and Ratchaburi. This TAT office is open 8.30 am to 4.30 pm weekdays and 9 am to 4.30 pm weekends and holidays. A smaller tourist information office is located on the beach near the intersection of Thanon Ruamjit and Thanon Narathip.

Money Several banks maintain foreign-exchange booths along the beach and typically are open from 10 am to 8 pm. In the town centre, west of Hwy 4, are a number of banks with exchange services and ATMs.

Post & Communications There is a post office on the main beach strip between Khan Had Restaurant and Sam Resort. The post office is open 8.30 am to 4.30 pm weekdays and 9 am to noon on Saturday.

International telephone services are available at the post office.

Peggy's Pub (see Places to Eat later in this section) offers pay-as-you-go email and Internet services. Jolly & Jumper guesthouse and restaurant offers free email to its guests.

Places to Stay – Budget & Mid-Range

Hat Cha-am has two basic types of accommodation: Tacky apartment-style hotels built of cheap materials with faulty plumbing, right on the beach road (Thanon Ruamjit); and more expensive 'condotel' developments. New places are going up all the time at the northern and southern ends. Bungalow operations, once common, are now quite rare. Expect a 20% to 50% discount on posted rates for weekday stays.

Thanon Narathip leads to the beach from the highway; if you turn right at the beach you'll find the places listed under 'South'; turn left and you'll see those listed under 'North'.

South Near the air-con bus station, a couple of *guesthouses* that change name from time to time can be found in a row of modern shophouses similar to the scourge of Pattaya, Hua Hin and Phuket's Patong Beach – they all look the same. Rooms cost from 300B with fan and shared bathroom to 500B with air-con.

The following places are listed in progression heading south along the beach. South of the air-con bus station, the *Anantachai Guest House* (☎ 032-471980) has nice rooms with a beach view, air-con, TV, shower and toilet for 400B to 500B. It also provides information about the area and has a cheap Thai restaurant. *Savitree Resort* (☎ 032-434088), next door, offers rooms with air-con and TV in semidetached brick bungalows for 600B.

The slightly cheaper *Best House* (☎ 032-433401) has clean air-con rooms with TV for 500B.

Santisuk Bungalows & Beach Resort (☎ 032-471212) is a long-time favourite with tourists. It has early Cha-am–style wooden cottages and a newer, but equally tasteful, hotel section. An air-con room in the hotel-style section with bathroom costs 800B. Larger two-bedroom cottages cost 1500B with fan, bathroom and sitting area and 2000B with air-con. It costs 3000B for a three-bedroom, two-bathroom cottage. The *Niran Resort* (☎ 032-471038) has similar cottages for 300B with fan and 500B with air-con, TV and hot water.

The *Sea Pearl Hotel* (☎ 032-471118) is a well-maintained apartment-style place, with rates of 500B for a room with fan and private bathroom, 600B with air-con and 700B for larger rooms with carpet, bathtub and TV.

Nalumon Bungalows (☎ 032-471440) is an old-style place with large three-bedroom bungalows that can sleep 10 to 12 people. None have a sea view, but all have a big sink and shower outside as well as a toilet inside, TV and a large porch and carport. Bungalows with fan cost 1200B while ones with air-con and a fridge cost 1700B.

North Heading north along the beach from Thanon Narathip, *Thiptari Place* (☎ 032-471879) is a fairly reasonable place with air-con rooms from 800B to 1200B. Farther up, *Rua Makam Villa* (☎ 032-471073) has old-style wood-and-concrete cottages, which are spacious and off the road, for 400/1000B single/double with fan, 1700B with air-con.

The next cheapest places are the *Jitravee Resort* (☎ 032-471382) and *Cha-am Villa* (☎ 032-471241); both offer rooms for 300B to 600B. Better value again is the relatively new *Prathonchok House* (☎ 032-471215), which has clean rooms for 150B to 200B with fan and shared facilities, 250B with private bathroom and 300B with TV. Air-con rooms cost 300B with private bathroom, 400B with TV and fridge.

The clean and well-run *Jolly & Jumper* (☎ 032-433887, 274/3 Thanon Ruamjit), operated by a Dutch couple, has singles/doubles for 150/250B with fan and 400/500B with air-con. There is also free email and use of bicycles for guests.

Happy Home (☎ 032-471393), also known as Ban Sabai Dee, has older-style cement cottages for 300B with fan and from 400B with air-con and TV.

The *Inthira Plaza* complex, off Thanon Narathip, is striving to become a Pattaya-style 'entertainment centre'. A couple of the bars have apartment-style rooms upstairs for 250B to 300B with fan and bathroom and 350B to 400B with air-con. They could be noisy at night.

Places to Stay – Top End

Many places in Cha-am call themselves 'resorts', but only two places in the central area come close. First is the *Cha-am Methavalai Hotel* (☎ 032-471028, fax 471590). It has well-kept, modern rooms with flowers spilling from every balcony, plus a pool (available to nonguests for 50B from 7 am to 7 pm) and a small beach area of its own. Walk-in rates are 1850B to 4200B including tax, but discounts apply even on weekends unless it's a major holiday.

The second, next door to Happy Home on Thanon Ruamjit, is the towering 19-storey *Mark-Land Hotel* (☎ 032-433833, fax 433834), which offers large, luxurious rooms from 2400B. Facilities include pool, sauna, fitness room and various food outlets.

For roughly the same price, the seven-storey *Gems Cha-am* (☎ 032-434060, fax 434002) is a resort-style hotel in which all rooms have ocean views and amenities, from satellite TV to IDD phones; there's also a business centre. Rates start at 2500B per room plus tax and service, but even on weekends you can usually get a 25% discount.

Down a nearby soi, *Long Beach Cha-am Hotel* (☎ 032-472442, fax 472287; in Bangkok ☎ 02-243 8920, fax 241 3995) offers luxury rooms from 2389B, although the 'official' rate is 3000B. All rooms come with fridge, TV with in-house movies, hairdryer and private balcony.

On the beach north of town is the posh *Dusit Resort & Polo Club* (☎ 032-520009, fax 520296, ⓔ polo@dusit.com), where rates start at 3872B. The Dusit offers a fitness centre, minigolf, horse riding, pool, tennis and squash courts and, of course, polo.

Springfield Beach Resort (☎ 032-451181, fax 451194), south of town at the 210km marker off Phetkasem Hwy, is a newer, luxury hotel with rooms and suites all with sea views and balconies. Rates are 3000B to 6000B for a family room. All rooms have phone, air-con, refrigerator, electronic safe box, long bathtubs and hairdryers. On the premises are a terrace coffee shop overlooking the ocean, swimming pool and Jacuzzi, tennis court, putting green, 10-hole Jack Nicklaus–designed golf course, exercise room, sauna, steam room and karaoke.

Places to Eat

Opposite the beach are a few good *seafood restaurants*, which are reasonably priced – unlike the bungalow restaurants. The *food vendors* on the beach sell all manner of barbecued and fried seafood.

Near the entrance to Gems Cha-am hotel is *Poom Restaurant*, an outdoor place that is hugely popular among visiting Thais. Moderately priced *Khan Had Restaurant* has an extensive menu. *Anantachai Guest House* is a good place for inexpensive to moderately priced Thai and seafood dishes, while the *Jolly & Jumper* does reasonable Western food and has a special menu for kids. Several small restaurants catering to westerners are located on the soi leading down to the Long Beach Cha-am Hotel, including *Peggy's Pub*, which serves Thai and Scandinavian dishes.

The luxury hotels have generally fine Thai, seafood and Western cuisine at the standard high prices. Seafood and Thai cuisine are especially good at the Cha-am Methavalai Hotel's *Sorndaeng Restaurant*, a branch of the famous Bangkok restaurant of the same name.

Getting There & Away

Buses from Phetchaburi cost 18B, 20B aircon. From Hua Hin, take a Phetchaburi-bound bus and ask to be let off at Hat Cha-am (Cha-am Beach; 10B).

Buses from Bangkok's Southern bus station to Cha-am (55B ordinary, 101B aircon) stop on Phetkasem Hwy, from where you can take a motorcycle taxi (20B) or a share taxi (5B) out to the beach. A few hundred metres south of the corner of Thanon Narathip and Thanon Ruamjit, a private bus company operates six air-con buses to Bangkok daily (97B).

The train station is on Thanon Narathip, west of Phetkasem Hwy and a 20B motorcycle ride to/from the beach. There's only

one train from Hualamphong station, the
No 169 Rapid at 3.50 pm. There is also one
departure from the Sam Sen station in
Bangkok at 9.28 am, and one 1.05 pm departure from Thonburi's Bangkok Noi station. The train is slower than the bus by one
hour (taking about four hours) and costs
40B 3rd class. First- and 2nd-class seats are
also available on the No 169 (183B and 91B
respectively). Cha-am isn't even listed on
the English-language train schedule.

Getting Around
Standard prices for motorcycle taxi and
public săwngthǎew are 20B and 10B (40B
to charter) respectively. You can rent
motorcycles for 200B to 300B a day. Avis
Rent-A-Car (☎ 032-520009) has an office
at the Dusit Resort & Polo Club.

AROUND CHA-AM
A sandy beach between Cha-am and
Phetchaburi, **Hat Peuktian** has the usual casuarina trees and food vendors favoured by
Thai beach goers, and hardly a fàràng in
sight. Three rocky islets are within wading
distance of shore, one with a sǎalaa for
shade. Also standing knee-deep just offshore
is a 6m statue of Phi Seua Samut, the undersea female deity that terrorised the protagonist of *Phra Aphaimani* (see under Ko Samet
earlier in this chapter). A statue of the prince
sits on a nearby rock playing a flute.

A tasteless two-storey, townhouse-style
development has been built off the beach.
Designed in the pseudo-classical style
prevalent in modern city blocks all over
Thailand, it looks rather incongruous with
the natural beach surroundings.

Just before the border between Phetchaburi and Prachuap Khiri Khan Provinces is
reached – 9km south of Cha-am – stands
Phra Ratchaniwet Marukhathayawan, a
summer palace built during the reign of
King Rama VI. The collection of one- and
two-storey buildings are constructed of
prime golden teak and interlinked by covered boardwalks, all raised high above the
ground on stilts. Along with the high, tiled
roofs and tall, shuttered windows, this design allows for maximum air circulation – a
tropical building technique sorely missing
in most modern Thai architecture. Unlike
the current summer palace situated farther
south at Hua Hin, this one is open daily to
the public. It's surrounded by the grounds
of Camp Rama VI, a military post, but with
proper check-in at the gate you should have
no trouble receiving permission to tour the
palace from 8.30 am to 4.30 pm. Call
☎ 032-472482 for information.

Prachuap Khiri Khan Province

Pineapples and fishing are the main livelihoods of the Thais living in this narrow
province along the upper part of the Gulf of
Thailand peninsula. Along the Gulf coast
are a variety of small seaside resorts, most
of them very low-key.

CENTRAL THAILAND

HUA HIN
หัวหิน

postcode 77110 • pop 35,500

The beaches of Hua Hin first came to the country's attention in 1926, when King Rama VI's royal architect MJ Ithithepsan Kreudakon constructed Phra Ratchawang Klai Kangwon (Far-From-Worries Palace), a seafront summer palace of golden teak just north of what was then a small fishing village. Rama VII learned of Thailand's first coup d'etat in 1932 while playing golf at the Royal Hua Hin Golf Course. Once endorsed by the royal family, Hua Hin remained a traditional favourite among Thais long after the beaches of Pattaya and Phuket had been taken over by foreign tourists. The palace is still used by the royal family from time to time.

Hua Hin's 5km of beaches are studded with large, smooth boulders, enough to give the beach a scenic appeal but not enough to hinder **swimming**. The surf is safe for swimming year-round, although jellyfish are an occasional problem during the rainy season (May to October). **Water sports** are limited to sailing and jet-skiing. Overall Hua Hin is still a fairly quiet, economical place to get away from it all, and is less than four hours by train from Bangkok.

Hua Hin, like Cha-am, has traditionally been the domain of domestic beach tourism, but most visitors to Hua Hin are Bangkok Thais with some disposable income. The renovation of the 1923-vintage, colonial-style Hua Hin Railway Beach Hotel by a major French hotel group in the late 1980s attracted overseas attention. Now a number of cafes and bistros offer Spanish, French, Italian and German cuisine to an older polyglot bunch who are enjoying two-week Thai beach holidays at bargain rates.

Perhaps the major sign that Hua Hin has arrived on the international beach scene was the construction of a high-rise property belonging to Spain's Meliá hotel chain. Still, most visitors – Thai or foreign – stay at the numerous smaller hotels, inns and guesthouses located a couple of blocks west of the beach. There is accommodation for every budget, and the area now attracts a mix of Thais and older fàràng tourists who are seeking a comfortable beach holiday close to Bangkok but don't want the sleaziness that the sex industry creates in Pattaya.

Unfortunately, Hua Hin may already be moving in that direction. Already appearing are a lot of the same kind of cheap, unsightly shophouse apartment buildings with plumbing problems seen in Pattaya and Phuket's Hat Patong, as well as an invasion of girlie bars. Hua Hin has almost entirely lost its fishing-village atmosphere – the fishing fleet has been moved out and the town's infamous squid-drying piers have been replaced by hotels.

On the bright side, a relatively new sewage treatment plant and municipal sewer system have been constructed and the beach is cleaner than ever. The main swimming beach still has thatched umbrellas and long chairs; vendors from the nearby food stalls will bring loungers steamed crab, mussels, beer etc and there are pony rides for the kids. The Hotel Sofitel Central Hua Hin has successfully campaigned to have the vendors removed from the beach fronting the hotel – a minus for atmosphere but a plus for cleanliness. Vendors are now restricted to a small area near the public entrance to the beach, and to another short string south of the Sofitel.

Beer, soft drinks and seafood are reasonably cheap and umbrellas and sling chairs are free if you order food.

Information

Tourist Offices Tourist information on Hua Hin and the surrounding area is available at the municipal office (☎ 032-511047, 532433), on the corner of Thanon Phetkasem and Thanon Damnoen Kasem about 200m east of the train station. The *Welcome to Hua Hin* brochure contains a lot of useful information on hotels, restaurants and transport. The office is open 8.30 am to 4.30 pm daily.

The home-grown *Hua Hin Observer,* an expat-published newsletter with short features in English (and a few in German), contains snippets on eating out, culture and entertainment.

Money There are several banks around town. Most convenient to the beach is the Bank of Ayudhya's exchange booth on Thanon Naretdamri, near the corner of Thanon Damnoen Kasem.

Houses along Mae Nam Chanthaburi, Chanthaburi

A village clustered along the water's edge on Ko Chang

A boat heads upriver to the Ayuthaya Historical Park.

Bungalows at Ao Klong Phrao, Ko Chang, Trat Province

Elephant rides in Kanchanaburi Province

A floating restaurant in Kanchanaburi town

Post & Communications The post office is on Thanon Damnoen Kasem near the corner of Thanon Phetkasem. The attached CAT office offers Home Country Direct international phone service from 8 am to midnight daily.

Cyber Lounge, off Thanon Naretdamri in the Pavilion Village shopping centre opposite the Sofitel, offers Internet phone calls as well as access to email.

Beaches

Thanon Damnoen Kasem leads east directly from the train station to the main beach, which runs about 2km along the southern half of town. The nicest stretch of sand lies in front of the Sofitel. Smooth granite boulders pierce the surf and are the source of the town's name, which means 'Stone Head'.

Eight to 13km south of Hua Hin along Ao Takiap are the beaches of **Hat Khao Takiap, Suan Son** and **Khao Tao**, all of which are undergoing resort development. Two hilltop temples can be visited here. **Wat Khao Thairalat** is well off the beach on a rocky hill and is nothing special. At the end of the bay is the more well-endowed **Wat Khao Takiap**; climb the steps for a good bay view.

The southern end of Ao Takiap is now one big construction site as one high-rise after another goes up, blocking the sea view from all points inland. North along the bay, however, are several quiet, wooded spots with cabins and beach houses.

If you're driving, the turn-off for Ao Takiap is 4km south of Hua Hin. There are regular săwngthăew to and from town.

Places to Stay – Budget

Prices are moving up quickly for places near the beach. Hotels in town are still inexpensive and it's only a five-or 10-minute walk to the beach from most of them.

Guesthouses Near the beach, the cheapest places are along or just off Thanon Naretdamri. A room glut has kept rates low. Several small hotels and guesthouses in this area have rooms from 150B to 200B with fan and bathroom, 300B to 500B with air-con. On Thanon Damnoen Kasem, the *Thai Tae Guest House* offers rooms for 200B with fan and bathroom, 400B with air-con. Rooms at *Khun Daeng's House* on Thanon Naretdamri cost 150B with shared bathroom, 220B with private bathroom. The *Parichart Guest House* (☎ 032-513863), next to Khun Daeng's, is a slightly more up-market, modern, multistorey place with rooms for 150B with fan and private bathroom, 300B with air-con; rates increase in the high season.

The *Europa* (☎ 032-513235, 158 Thanon Naretdamri) has rooms over a shop for 150B with bathroom. *Sunee Guest House*, next door, is an old wooden building with rooms for 150B with shared bathroom.

Along Soi Kanjanomai, off Thanon Naretdamri just north of Thanon Damnoen Kasem, is the *Hare & Hound Guest House* (☎ 032-533757), which seems to change owners every year or two. Rooms cost 150B to 180B, some with bathroom.

On the same soi are the similar *Maple Leaf*, *Usaah* and *MP* Guest Houses, which all have small rooms in the 150B to 200B range. The Usaah has a bar downstairs open until 2 am, so is likely to be quite noisy during the night.

Som Waan Guest House, on the same soi, has basic but clean rooms for 150B to 250B with fan and toilet and 250B to 450B with air-con.

Along the next soi north off Thanon Naretdamri are a string of guesthouses in old wooden buildings. The soi has unfortunately become something of a bar scene, complete with freelance Thai hookers, so can no longer be recommended for anyone wanting a good night's sleep. *Phuen Guest House & Happy Bar* (☎ 032-512344) has rooms for 200B with fan, 450B with air-con; the downstairs bar can be a hindrance to an early night. *Relax Guest House* (☎ 032-513585), down an alley just before Phuen, charges 300B for four medium-size rooms with fan and bathroom in a private home. *Sukvilay Guest House* has quiet rooms for 150B to 200B with fan and 350B to 400B with air-con and hot-water showers; it's a bit more respectable than others on this soi. *Joy Guest House*, opposite, has rooms with fan for 150B and a 24-hour bar downstairs. Also on this soi is the modern, apartment-style *Ban Pak Hua Hin* (☎ 032-511653, fax 533649). It's quiet and exceptionally clean; rooms cost 200B with fan and bathroom and 300B with air-con.

Farther up Thanon Naretdamri is a string of wooden motel-like places built on piers

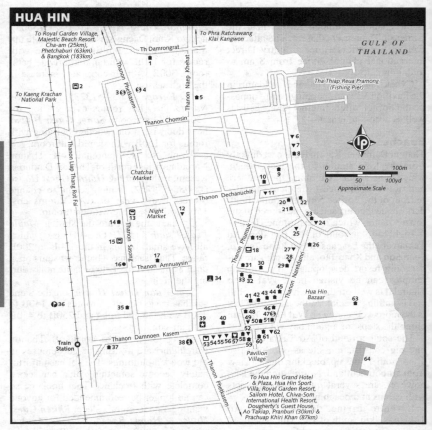

HUA HIN

over the edge of the sea. *Mod Guest House* has a variety of rooms, some of which have sea views, air-con and TV, for 200B to 1500B. Next-door, *Sirima* (☎ 032-511060) has rooms for 350B with fan and 500B to 600B with air-con. In the same area, *Rom Ruen Guest House* has small but clean rooms going for 200B with fan, 400B with air-con.

North of Rom Ruen Guest House on the beachfront is *Karoon Hut* (☎ 032-530242), with basic rooms for 400B with fan, 500B with air-con.

The *Pattana Guest House* (☎ 032-513393, fax 530081, 52 Thanon Naret-damri) has 13 comfortable fan rooms in two wooden houses costing from 200B. A bar and restaurant are on the premises.

Opposite Rom Ruen Guest House, in a two-storey building, is *Memory Guest House* (☎ 032-511816). It's super-clean and also has a locked entrance gate; rates are 550B to 850B. Nearby *Fulay Guest House* offers large, comfortable rooms with air-con, cable TV, fridge and balcony for 750B.

West off Thanon Naretdamri on Thanon Dechanuchit (east of Thanon Phunsuk) is the friendly and clean *All Nations* (☎ 032-512747), where rooms cost 150B to 250B depending on the size. Each room in the tall, narrow building comes with its own balcony and fan; each floor has a bathroom shared by two or three rooms.

Located off Thanon Phetkasem in a quiet neighbourhood south of the city centre is the newly opened *Dougherty's Guest*

HUA HIN

PLACES TO STAY
1 Thananchai Hotel
5 Phananchai Hotel
8 Karoon Hut
9 Pattana Guest House
10 All Nations
14 Siripetchkasem (Siri Phetkasem) Hotel
17 Subhamitra (Suphamit) Hotel
19 Sand Inn
20 Memory Guest House
21 Fulay Guest House
22 Rom Ruen Guest House; Piaf Restaurant
23 Sirima; Mod Guest House
26 Melia Hua Hin
29 Fresh Inn
30 Phuen Guest House & Happy Bar; Relax Guest House
31 Joy Guest House
32 Ban Pak Hua Hin
33 Sukvilay Guest House
35 Srichan Hua Hin (Top Boss)Hotel
37 Golf Inn
40 City Beach Resort

41 Hare & Hound Guest House
42 Maple Leaf Guest House
43 Usaah Guest House; MP Guest House
44 Som Waan Guest House
45 Europa; Sunee Guest House
46 Parichart Guest House; Khun Daeng's House
48 Ban Boosarin
50 Sirin Hotel
51 Thai Tae Guest House
58 Jed Pee Nong Hotel
59 Ban Somboon
60 Patchara House
61 Puangpen Villa Hotel; PP Villa Guest House
63 Mercure Resort Hua Hin
64 Hotel Sofitel Central Hua Hin

PLACES TO EAT
6 Seafood Restaurants
7 Le Chablis
11 Fa Mui
12 Chinese-Thai Restaurants
24 Taj Mahal
25 Luciano's Pizza House

27 Sunshine Restaurant & Bakery
28 Lo Stivale
49 La Villa
52 Tee Cuisine
54 Italian Ice Cream
55 Capo's; Al Fresco
56 Buffalo Bill's Steak & Grill
62 Lucky Restaurant

OTHER
2 Bus Station
3 Thai Farmers Bank
4 Bank of Ayudhya
13 Sawngthaew to Ao Takiap
15 Pran Tour; Air-Con Buses
16 Top Center Supermarket
18 Rockestra Cafe
34 Wat Hua Hin
36 Royal Hua Hin Golf Course
38 Tourist Information
39 Police
47 Bank of Ayudhya Exchange Booth
53 Main Post Office; CAT Office
57 Stone Town

CENTRAL THAILAND

House (☎ *032-532715, 236/72 Thanon Jamjuri*). It's good value for families, with clean double rooms for 600B to 800B, and a pool and restaurant on the premises.

Hotels Just off Thanon Phetkasem on Thanon Amnuaysin is *Subhamitra Hotel* (*Suphamit*; ☎ *032-511280, fax 511508*), where clean singles/doubles with fan and bathroom start at 250/300B; air-con triples cost 800B, a little more with TV and fridge. There's a pool on the premises. On Thanon Sasong, the *Siripetchkasem Hotel (Siri Phetkasem*; ☎ *032-511394, fax 511464*) is similar to the hotels along Thanon Phetkasem. Rooms cost 300B with fan and 400B with air-con and TV.

South of the Siripetchkasem, and on the same side of Thanon Sasong, is the *Srichan Hua Hin Hotel (Top Boss*; ☎ *032-513130*), which charges 500B to 600B for rooms with carpet and air-con – a bit overpriced.

Sand Inn (☎ *032-533667, fax 533669, 38–38/4 Thanon Phunsuk*) has spacious fan rooms with TV, phone and hot water for 400B, 500B with air-con. A restaurant and coffee shop are included in the complex.

In the northern part of town, *Thananchai* (☎ *032-511755, 11 Thanon Damrong-*

rat) has rooms for 350B with fan and bathroom and 600B with air-con. It's a bit far from the town centre if you're on foot.

Places to Stay – Mid-Range
Hua Hin's mid-range places are typically small, sedate, modern hotels with air-con rooms and such luxuries as telephones. The forerunner of this trend, *Ban Boosarin* (☎ *032-512076*), calls itself a 'minideluxe hotel' and although it costs 950B (discounted to 800B in the low season), all rooms come with air-con, hot water, telephone, TV, fridge and private terrace. It's super clean and rates don't rise on weekends. There's a 10% discount for stays of a week or more.

Along Soi Kasem Samphan are a couple of Ban Boosarin clones. *Patchara House* (☎ *032-511788*) has rooms with air-con, TV and video, telephone, hot water and fridge for 700B. *Ban Somboon* (☎ *032-511538*), has nicely decorated rooms for 450B with fan, TV and hot-water showers, and 700B with air-con, TV and fridge; all rates include breakfast and there is a pleasant garden on the premises. On the corner of Soi Kasem Samphan and Thanon Damnoen Kasem are the *Puangpen Villa Hotel* and the *PP Villa Guest House* (☎ *032-511216*), which share a garden, pool and reception area; clean, air-con rooms cost 780B with hot water, TV and fridge in the former, 600B with hot water in the latter. These hotels are about 200m from the beach. The PP Villa was undergoing renovation at last visit.

Nearby, the popular *Jed Pee Nong Hotel* (☎ 032-512381), on Thanon Damnoen Kasem, has modern and clean but otherwise unimpressive rooms for 600B with fan, TV and hot-water bathroom and 800B with air-con. The air-con rooms by the swimming pool behind the hotel cost 1000B to 1200B.

On Thanon Naretdamri, the modern *Fresh Inn* (☎ 032-511389) has all air-con rooms for 750B to 850B; downstairs is the restaurant Lo Stivale.

Running north from Thanon Chomsin (the road leading to the fishing pier) is Thanon Naep Khehat. The *Phananchai Hotel* (☎ 032-511707, fax 530157, 71 Thanon Naep Khehat) has rooms for 400B to 500B with fan, 600B with carpet and air-con. It's a bit of a walk from the swimming beaches, but all rooms come with hot water, TV and telephone. The hotel also has a restaurant.

Places to Stay – Top End

The air-con *Sirin Hotel* (☎ 032-511150, fax 513571), on Thanon Damnoen Kasem towards the beach, has well-kept rooms with hot water and fridge, and a pleasant semi-outdoor restaurant area. Doubles cost 890B to 1500B, including breakfast. The *City Beach Resort* (☎ 032-512870–75, 16 Thanon Damnoen Kasem) offers quiet, semiluxurious rooms with the usual service and extras from 1300B (discounted from the 2600B rack rate).

Near the train station and Royal Hua Hin Golf Course, off Thanon Damnoen Kasem, is the *Golf Inn* (☎ 032-512473), where air-con rooms cost 720B to 840B.

Hua Hin has several super-luxury hotels. *Hotel Sofitel Central Hua Hin* (☎ 032-512021, fax 511014; in Bangkok ☎ 02-233 0980) is a magnificent two-storey colonial-style place on the beach at the end of Thanon Damnoen Kasem. Rooms in the original L-shaped colonial wing cost 5440B; rooms in the new wing are more expensive. Discounts may be possible. Across the road is the *Mercure Resort Hua Hin* (☎ 032-512036, fax 511014), a collection of charming one- and two-bedroom wooden

beach bungalows, which cost 4200B to 6300B. From 20 December to 20 February there's a 1300B high-season supplement on all room charges at both the Mercure and the Sofitel hotels.

The plush *Meliá Hua Hin* (☎ 032-512879, fax 511135; in Bangkok ☎ 02-271 3435, fax 271 3689), off Thanon Naretdamri, is part of the Spanish-owned Meliá hotel chain and was the first high-rise to mar the Hua Hin skyline. Room prices are listed at 5179B, although it usually charges less, except during high season (20 December to 10 January) when there's a 900B supplement on all room rates. There's not much of a beach in front of the hotel at high tide, but the adjacent free-form swimming pool area is designed to encompass views of the ocean. Other facilities at the hotel include two tennis courts, two air-con squash courts, a fitness centre, sauna and massage facilities.

Along Hua Hin's southern beach, the *Royal Garden Resort* (☎ 032-511881, fax 512422, 107/1 Thanon Hat Phetkasem) offers rooms and suites, all with sea views, in a modern high-rise complex. Spacious rooms cost from 3800B (usually discounted to 2400B), including breakfast, rising to 13,000B for penthouse suites with Jacuzzis and private rooftop gardens.

On the northern side of town, the laid-back *Royal Garden Village* (☎ 032-520250, fax 520259, 43/1 Thanon Hat Phetkasem; in Bangkok ☎ 02-476 0021, fax 476 1120) features rooms and suites in Thai-style villas on six landscaped hectares; rooms cost from 2750B to 3250B. Both Royal Garden resorts offer tennis courts and swimming pools, nearby golf-course privileges, Thai massage services and water sports. The Royal Garden Resort also has a golf driving range.

The US$26 million *Chiva-Som International Health Resort* (☎ 032-536536, fax 511154, 74/4 Phetkasem Hwy) features 40 ocean-view rooms and 17 Thai-style pavilions on three beachside hectares south of town (before Nong Khae and Ao Takiap). The name means 'Haven of Life' in Thai-Sanskrit. The staff of 200 fuses Eastern and Western approaches to health with planned nutrition; you can get a 10-year membership, which entitles you to a 40% discount on use of the facilities, for US$8000, or pay US$420 single, US$630 double per day, a rate that includes three meals (with wine at dinner) along with health and fitness consultations, massage and all other activities. One-week, 10-day and two-week packages are also available.

There are a few more top-end places on beaches just north and south of town. Rooms at *Hua Hin Grand Hotel & Plaza* (☎ *032-512684, 511499, fax 511765, 222/2 Thanon Phetkasem; in Bangkok* ☎ *02-254 7675*) cost from 2000B to 3000B (discounted to 1000B low season). *Hua Hin Sport Villa* (☎ *032-512158, 10/95 Thanon Phetkasem*) charges 1800B. *Majestic Beach Resort* (☎ *032-520162, fax 520477*), on Hat Klai Kangwon, charges 3060B (1350B to 1750B discounted). Rooms at *Sailom Hotel* (☎ *032-511890/1, fax 512047, 29 Thanon Phetkasem; in Bangkok* ☎ *02-258 0652*) cost 1500B to 1999B. Some of these hotels add high-season supplements in December and January.

Places to Stay – Out of Town
South of Hua Hin around Hat Takiap and Nong Khae you'll find a mixture of high-rise condo-style hotels and low-rise cottages. In Hat Takiap, the *Fangkhlun Guest House* (☎ *032-512402*) has rooms for 600B with fan and 700B with air-con. The *Khao Ta-kiap Resort* (☎ *032-512405*) offers eight air-con cottages for 1500B a night, while *Ta-kiab Beach Resort* (☎ *032-512639, fax 515899*), south of Khao Takiap, has air-con rooms from 900B and a pool.

In a forested area called Nong Khae at the northern end of Ao Takiap is the quiet and comfortable low-rise *Nern Chalet* (☎ *032-511288*), with 14 air-con rooms with TV, hot water and phone for 1500B discounted to 1200B. Between Nong Khae and Hat Takiap, *Hua Hin Bluewave Beach Resort* (☎ *032-511036*) is a condotel-style place with rooms for 2354B discounted to 1926B including breakfast; on the grounds are a pool and fitness centre.

In Hat Suan Son, south of Hat Takiap, the modern *Suan Son Padiphat* (☎ *032-511239*) has rooms for 400B to 600B with fan and 500B to 800B with air-con.

In low-key Pranburi, the *Pransiri Hotel* (☎ *032-621061, 283 Thanon Phetkasem*) and *Pranburi Hotel* (☎ *032-622042, 30/9–10 Thanon Phetkasem*) have rooms from 150B.

At water-sports oriented *Club Aldiana* (☎ *032-631235*), resort-style accommodation in bungalows and hotel rooms goes for 2400/4800B. This includes three buffet meals, all sports activities and entertainment. Among the amenities on the grounds are eight quartz-sand tennis courts.

Places to Eat
One of Hua Hin's major attractions has always been the colourful and inexpensive Chatchai Market in the centre of town, where vendors gather nightly to cook fresh seafood for hordes of hungry Thais. During the day many of these same vendors prepare seafood snacks on the beach; cracked crab and cold Singha beer can be ordered without leaving one's sling chair.

The best seafood to eat in Hua Hin is *plaa sămlii* (cotton fish or kingfish), *plaa kràphong* (perch), *plaa mèuk* (squid), *hăwy málaeng phûu* (mussels) and *puu* (crab). The various forms of preparation include:

dìp	raw
nêung	steamed
phǎo	grilled
phàt	sliced, filleted and fried
râat phrík	smothered in garlic and chillies
thâwt	fried whole
tôm yam	in a hot and tangy broth
yâang	roast (squid only)

The best seafood in Hua Hin is found in three main areas. Firstly, there are some medium-priced restaurants along Thanon Damnoen Kasem near the Jed Pee Nong Hotel and City Beach Resort, and off Damnoen Kasem, on Thanon Phunsuk and Thanon Naretdamri. Secondly, there's excellent and inexpensive food in the *night market*, off Thanon Phetkasem on Thanon Dechanuchit, and in the nearby *Chinese-Thai restaurants*. The third area is next to *Tha Thiap Reua Pramong*, the big fishing pier at the end of Thanon Chomsin. The fish is, of course, fresh off the boats but not necessarily the cheapest in town. One of the places near the pier, *Saeng Thai*, is the oldest seafood restaurant in Hua Hin and quite reliable if you know how to order. The best value for money is in the smaller eating places on and off Thanon Chomsin and in the night market. There is also a *night market* on Thanon Chomsin.

CENTRAL THAILAND

Two Chinese/Thai seafood places along Thanon Phetkasem are **Khuang Seng** and **Thara Jan**, neither of which bear Roman-script signs; all are fairly good value.

Chatchai Market is excellent for Thai breakfasts – it sells very good jók and khâo tôm (rice soups). Fresh-fried *paa-thâwng-kŏh* (Chinese doughnuts) in the Hua-Hin-style – small and crispy, not oily – cost 2B for three. A few vendors also serve hot soy milk in bowls (5B) – break a few paa-thâwng-kŏh into the soy milk and drink free *náam chaa* (tea) – a very tasty and filling breakfast.

Tee Cuisine, on Thanon Damnoen Kasem next to the Jed Pee Nong Hotel, caters mostly to fàràng but the Thai food is generally good. **Lucky Restaurant**, nearby, is very similar.

Fa Mui, on Thanon Dechanuchit near All Nations, is a cosy, atmospheric place serving Thai cuisine and seafood to a hip crowd of local and visiting Thais; prices are inexpensive to moderate.

The **Taj Mahal**, on Thanon Naretdamri next to Bird guesthouse, serves decent Indian food. On a nearby pier is the **Thanachote**, which specialises in seafood and has a view of the ocean.

Thanon Phunsuk and Thanon Naretdamri are becoming centres for fàràng-oriented eateries; there must be more Italian restaurants per capita here than anywhere else in Thailand. The popular **Lo Stivale** (☎ 032-513800, 132 Thanon Naretdamri) serves the usual Italian dishes as well as pizza. The new **Luciano's Pizza House** (☎ 032-530709, 7A Soi Selakam), just off Thanon Naretdamri, also does Italian food.

Piaf (23 Thanon Naretdamri) is a German/Austrian restaurant that also offers Thai cuisine. **Le Chablis** (88 Thanon Naretdamri) serves French food and wine (accompanied by live piano in the evenings). The Italian **La Villa** (☎ 032-513435), on the corner of Thanon Damnoen Kasem and Thanon Phunsuk, has pizza, spaghetti, lasagne and so on. **Sunshine Restaurant & Bakery**, on Thanon Naretdamri, serves German food and fresh baked goods.

Al Fresco and **Italian Ice Cream**, both on Thanon Damnoen Kasem, offer home-made Italian-style ice cream. **Capo's**, in the same building as Al Fresco, specialises in steak and spare ribs. Meat lovers can also get their fill at **Buffalo Bill's Steak & Grill** (☎ 032-532727), nearby on Thanon Damnoen Kasem.

Hua Hin also has a number of British-style pubs that offer 'home cooking', including **Berny's Inn** (The Golfer's 19th Hole) at the Hua Hin Bazaar, which is off Thanon Naretdamri and Thanon Damnoen Kasem and is open from 2 pm to 2 am. **Baan Farang** is also at the Hua Hin Bazaar and offers breakfasts of generous proportions.

Entertainment

Several fàràng bars under European management can be found at the Hua Hin Bazaar. Many of these offer the familiar Thai hostess atmosphere but a few bill themselves as 'sports bars' and have a wide-screen TV tuned to sporting events.

The open-air **Rockestra Cafe**, off Thanon Phunsuk, has a house band on weekdays and guest bands on weekends.

Stone Town, an old-west–style pub next to Jed Pee Nong Hotel on Thanon Damnoen Kasem, features live folk and country music nightly. There's no cover charge and drinks are no more expensive than at any of the town's fàràng bars.

Getting There & Away

Bus Air-con buses go to Hua Hin station from Bangkok's Southern bus station (190B 1st class, 136B 2nd class, 3½ hours).

Buses for Hua Hin leave from Phetchaburi (22B ordinary, 30B air-con) or Cha-am (10B, 20B). Buses also depart/arrive at Hua Hin's main station at the northern end of Thanon Liap Rot Fai for/from Prachuap Khiri Khan (30B, 42B), Chumphon (77B, 108B), Surat Thani (136B, 190B), Phuket (198B, 277B), Krabi (177B, 248B) and Hat Yai (251B, 392B).

Pran Tour (☎ 032-511654), on Thanon Sasong near the Siripetchkasem Hotel, runs air-con buses to Bangkok about every two hours from 3 am to 9 pm (63B 2nd-class, 110B 1st-class).

Train The same trains described in the Phetchaburi Getting There & Away section also run to Hua Hin. Trains run to Hua Hin from Bangkok (202B 1st-class rapid and express, 102B 2nd-class rapid and express, 44B 3rd-class, 3¾ hours) and other stations on the southern railway line.

Getting Around

Local buses/sǎwngthǎew from Hua Hin to the beaches of Khao Takiap, Khao Tam and Suan Son cost 7B per person although for-eigners are sometimes charged 10B. These buses run from around 6 am until 5.50 pm; the ones to Hat Takiap leave from opposite the main bus station on Thanon Sasong, while the latter two leave from Thanon Chomsin opposite the wát.

Buses to Pranburi are 10B and leave from the same area on Thanon Chomsin.

Sǎamláw fares in Hua Hin have been set by the municipal authorities, although that doesn't keep sǎamláw drivers from attempt-ing to gouge. Fares include the train station to the beach for 20B; the bus station to Thanon Naretdamri for 30B to 40B (de-pending on size of your bags); Chatchai Mar-ket to the fishing pier for 20B; and the train station to the Royal Garden Resort for 40B.

Motorcycles and bicycles can be rented from a couple of places on Thanon Damnoen Kasem. Motorcycle rates are reasonable: 200B per day for 100cc, 250B to 300B for 125cc. Occasionally, larger bikes – 400cc to 750cc – are available for 500B to 600B a day. Bicycles cost 30B to 70B per day.

Avis Rent-A-Car (☎ 032-512021–38) has an office at Hotel Sofitel Central Hua Hin. There are also more inexpensive places in Hua Hin renting out sedans for 2300B to 2943B a day (depending on whether standard or automatic transmis-sion), or Suzuki Caribians for 1980B.

Mai Thai Cruise (☎ 032-515919, 47/2 Thanon Dechanuchit) operates a beautifully restored and modified Thai fishing boat for cruises into the gulf and to a nearby island. Cruises, which include shuttle to and from hotel and lunch cost 1950B per person.

At the fishing pier you can hire boats out to Ko Singtoh for 800B a day. On Hat Takiap you can get boats for 700B. To get these prices you will have to haggle.

KHAO SAM ROI YOT NATIONAL PARK
อุทยานแห่งชาติเขาสามร้อยยอด

Its name means 'Three Hundred Mountain Peaks', and this 98-sq-km park (established in 1966) has magnificent views of the coast-line if you can stand a little climbing. The hill known as Khao Daeng is only about a

half-hour walk from the park headquarters, and from here you can see the ocean as well as some brackish lagoons. If you have the time and energy, climb the 605m **Khao Kra-chom** for even better views. If you're lucky, you may come across a serow (Asian goat-antelope). The lagoons and coastal marshes are great places for bird-watching. Along the coast you may see the occasional pod of *plaa lohmaa hǔa bàat* (Irrawaddy dolphins).

Be sure to bring insect repellent along. King Rama IV and a large entourage of Thai and European guests convened here on 18 August 1868 to see a total solar eclipse – pre-dicted, so the story goes, by the monarch himself – and enjoy a feast prepared by a French chef. Two months later the king died from malaria, contracted from mosquito bites inflicted here (see the boxed text 'The Wrath of Rahu?'). The risk of malaria in the park is relatively low, but mosquitoes can be pesky.

Fauna

Notable wildlife around Khao Sam Roi Yot includes crab-eating macaque, dusky lan-gur (the park is considered one of the best spots in the world for viewing dusky lan-gurs), barking deer, slow loris, Malayan pangolin, fishing cat, palm civet, otter, serow, Javan mongoose and monitor lizard.

Because the park lies at the intersection of the East Asian and Australian fly ways, as many as 300 migratory and resident bird species have been recorded, including yel-low bittern, cinnamon bittern, purple swamp hen, water rail, ruddy-breasted crake, bronze-winged jacana, grey heron, painted stork, whistling duck, spotted eagle and black-headed ibis. The park protects Thailand's largest freshwater marsh (along with mangroves and mudflats), and is one of only three places in the country where the purple heron breeds.

Waterfowl are most commonly seen in the cool season. Encroachment by shrimp farmers in the vicinity has sadly destroyed substantial portions of mangroves and other wetlands, thus depriving the birds of an im-portant habitat.

Beaches, Canals & Marshes

A sandy beach flanked on three sides by dry limestone hills and casuarinas, **Hat Laem Sala** is the location for a small visitors centre, restaurant, bungalows and camping

The Wrath of Rahu?

King Mongkut (Rama IV) had a keen interest in science and despite, or perhaps with the support of, the many years His Majesty spent as a Buddhist monk (prior to ascending to the throne upon the death of his half-brother, Rama III), felt that one of his duties as Siam's monarch was to replace Thai superstition with logic and reason wherever possible.

One of the king's scientific passions was the study of astronomy, and in early 1868 His Majesty calculated the timing of the upcoming 18 August solar eclipse, as well as its exact path over Siam. The king decided to make the event a public lesson in astronomy by organising a large expedition to a spot on the Thai coast where the eclipse could be viewed in totality. According to *Katya and the Prince of Siam* by Eileen Hunter and Narisa Chakrabongse, Rama IV chose 'a wild and uninhabitable spot about 140 miles south of Bangkok'. That translates to 228.4km, almost exactly where Khao Sam Roi Yot shows up in today's atlases, although other chronicles claim the spot was 50km to 60km farther south near Wa Kaw, near the town of Prachuap Khiri Khan.

At the king's invitation, a French expedition travelled all the way overland (the Suez Canal hadn't yet been built) to Siam to join Rama IV in convincing his subjects that:

…contrary to their belief, the eclipse would not be caused by the dragon Rahu making a meal of the sun and disgorging it only when frightened by beating of gongs and letting off of fireworks, but could be predicted beforehand and explained by rather more rational methods.

According to the French expedition leader:

The King of Siam with all his court, part of his army and a crowd of Europeans, arrived by sea on 8th August in twelve steamboats of the Royal Navy, while by land came troops of oxen, horses and fifty elephants.

Also in attendance were Mongkut's sons Damrong and Chulalongkorn, along with the court astrologers, 'who could hardly be blamed if they concealed a certain lack of enthusiasm'.

Although a thick layer of clouds threatened to spoil the event – much to the chagrin of the French who had travelled 16,000kms and spent a fortune to support this royal endeavour – the sky cleared 20 minutes before totality and the event became a grand success.

Unaccounted for in the king's calculations was the fact that the chosen viewing spot was a low-lying swamp. Both Rama IV and 15-year-old Prince Chulalongkorn contracted malaria during their 10-day astronomical sojourn; the king died shortly after his return to Bangkok, on the day he turned 64.

---

area. Boats with a capacity of up to 10 people can be hired from Bang Pu to the beach for 150B return. You can also reach the beach from Bang Pu via a steep trail, about a 20-minute walk.

Hat Sam Phraya, 5km south of Hat Laem Sala, is a 1km-long beach with a restaurant and washrooms. The park headquarters is located just past Ban Khao Daeng, about 4km south-west of Hat Sam Phraya.

A larger visitors centre at the headquarters features well-curated exhibits, and binoculars or telescopes can be rented for bird-watching; there are several bird hides nearby on the nature trails. September to March are the best bird-watching months for waterfowl.

A 4km canal trip in a 10-person boat along **Khlong Khao Daeng** can be arranged in Ban Khao Daeng (200B, 1½ hours). The boat passes mangrove remnants and waterfowl habitats; the birds are most active in early morning or late afternoon. You might also spot monitor lizards and monkeys.

Caves

The other attractions at Sam Roi Yot are the Tham Kaew, Tham Sai and Tham Phraya Nakhon caves. **Tham Phraya Nakhon** is the

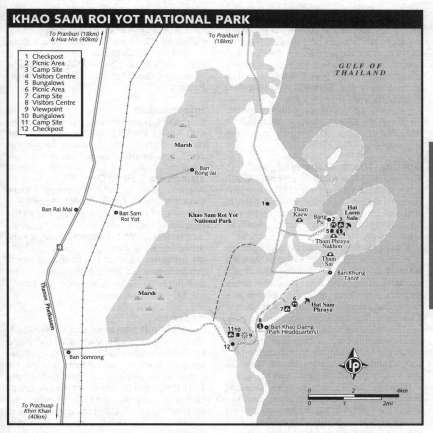

KHAO SAM ROI YOT NATIONAL PARK

1 Checkpost
2 Picnic Area
3 Camp Site
4 Visitors Centre
5 Bungalows
6 Picnic Area
7 Camp Site
8 Visitors Centre
9 Viewpoint
10 Bungalows
11 Camp Site
12 Checkpost

most visited and can be reached by boat or on foot. The boat trip only takes about half an hour return, while it's half an hour each way on foot along a steep, rocky trail. There are two large caverns, with sinkholes that allow light in. In one cave is a royal sǎalaa built for King Rama V, who would stop off when travelling between Bangkok and Nakhon Si Thammarat.

Tham Kaew, 2km from the Bang Pu turn-off, features a series of chambers connected by narrow passageways; you enter the first cavern by means of a permanent ladder. Stalactites and other limestone formations, some of which glitter with calcite crystals as if diamond encrusted (hence the cave's name, 'Jewel Cave'), are plentiful. Lamps can be rented for 100B, but Tham Kaew is

best visited in the company of a park guide because of the dangerous footing.

Tham Sai is ensconced in a hill near Ban Khung Tanot, about 2.5km from the main road between Laem Sala and Sam Phraya beaches. Villagers rent out lamps for around 30B at a shelter near the cave mouth. A 280m trail leads up the hillside to the cave, which features a large single cavern. Be careful of steep drop-offs in the cave.

Guides can be hired at the park office for 100B per hike; not much English is spoken but they're accustomed to leading non-Thai as well as Thai visitors.

Places to Stay

The Forestry Department hires out large **bungalows** near the larger visitors centre and at Hat Laem Sala. The bungalows sleep four to 20 people and cost 400B to 1000B per night or 100B per person. Three-person tents are available for 40B a night. You can also pitch your own tent for 10B per person at *camp sites* at the park headquarters, Hat Laem Sala or Hat Sam Phraya. There are restaurants at all three places.

For accommodation reservations, contact the Forestry Department in Bangkok on ☎ 02-561 4292 ext 747. National park entry fees apply.

Getting There & Away

The park is 37km south of Pranburi. Catch a bus or train to Pranburi (10B from Hua Hin) and then a săwngthăew to Bang Pu for 20B – these run between 6 am and 4 pm. From Bang Pu you must charter a vehicle, hitch or walk.

You can save the hassle of finding a ride in Bang Pu by chartering a săwngthăew for 300B or a motorcycle taxi for 150B from Pranburi all the way to the park. Be sure to mention you want to go to the national park (*ùtháyaan hàeng châat*) rather than Ban Khao Sam Roi Yot.

Most convenient of all would be to rent a car or motorbike in Hua Hin. If you're coming by car or motorcycle from Hua Hin, it's about 25km to the park turn-off, then another 38km to park headquarters.

If you're coming straight from Bangkok, another option is to catch an air-con bus bound for Prachuap Khiri Khan. Ask to get off at Ban Somrong (half a kilometre past the 286km marker) and then hitch a ride 13km to the park headquarters at Ban Khao Daeng.

PRACHUAP KHIRI KHAN
อ.เมืองประจวบคีรีขันธ์

postcode 77000 • pop 14,900
Roughly 80km south of Hua Hin, Prachuap Khiri Khan serves as the capital of the province of the same name, although it is somewhat smaller than Hua Hin. There are no real swimming beaches in town, but the 8km-long bay of Ao Prachuap is pretty enough. Better beaches can be found north and south of town. The seafood is fantastic and cheaper than in Hua Hin. Fishing is still the mainstay of the local economy.

Prachuap Khiri Khan (specifically Ao Manao) was one of seven points on the Gulf of Thailand coast where Japanese troops landed on 8 December 1941 during their invasion of Thailand. Several street names around town commemorate the ensuing skirmish: Phitak Chat – Defend Country; Salachip – Sacrifice Life; Suseuk – Fight Battle.

Information

Prachuap has its own city-run tourist office next to the Thaed Saban Bungalows. The staff are very friendly and they have maps and photos of all the attractions in the area.

Things to See & Do

At the northern end of Ao Prachuap is **Khao Chong Krajok** (Mirror Tunnel Mountain – named after the hole through the side of the mountain that appears to reflect the sky). At the top is **Wat Thammikaram**, established by King Rama VI. You can climb the hill for a view of the town and bay – and entertain the hordes of monkeys who live here. A ladder leads into the tunnel from the wát grounds.

Beaches

South of Ao Prachuap, around a small headland, is the scenic **Ao Manao**, a bay ringed by a clean white-sand beach with small islands offshore. A Thai air force base guards access to the bay (a possible legacy of the 1941 Japanese invasion), and the beach was closed to the public until 1990, when the local authorities decided to open the area to day visitors. The beach is 2km to 3km from the base entrance.

There are several săalaa along the beach, a hotel, one restaurant, toilets and a shower. Beach vendors offer chairs, umbrellas and inner tubes for rent (10B), plus seafood, north-eastern Thai dishes and beverages.

You must show your passport at the gate and sign in; the beach closes at 8 pm except for military and guests at the hotel.

Each year in September, on the air force base at Ao Manao, the Thai air force sponsors an impressive sound-and-light show commemorating Thai WWII heroes; it's open to the public and free.

Eight kilometres south of Ao Manao, **Hat Wa Kaw** is a pleasant, casuarina-lined beach that is even quieter and cleaner than Ao Manao. A small museum of astronomy (no English labels) and a Rama IV monument commemorate the 1868 solar eclipse that the king and his 15-year-old son Prince Chulalongkorn came south to witness. Both were stricken with malaria during their visit and Rama IV died soon after returning to Bangkok. (Whether the eclipse viewing event really happened here, or at Khao Sam Roi Yot as other chronicles say, is a matter of debate.) Also on display on the museum grounds is a US-built steam locomotive (Baldwin Locomotive Works, 1925).

Organised Tours
Local resident Pinit Ounope arranges popular day tours to Khao Sam Roi Yot National Park, Dan Singkhon (see Around Prachuap Khiri Khan later in this chapter) and to nearby beaches, other national parks and waterfalls. He lives at 144 Thanon Chai Thaleh near the beach in town and invites travellers to visit him. His house is rather difficult to find, so take a túk-túk or a motorcycle taxi. The typical day tour costs 500B (on the back of a motorcycle) or 1000B for two people (in a pick-up truck).

Places to Stay
Prachuap Khiri Khan The *Yuttichai Hotel* (☎ 032-611055, 35 Thanon Kong Kiat) has fair one/two-bed rooms with fan and shared bathroom for 120/180B, 180/240B with private bathroom; the latter are quieter since they're towards the back of the hotel. The proprietors lock the front door at 11 pm; after that you'll have to ring a doorbell to get in.

Around the corner, the eight-room *Inthira Hotel* (☎ 032-611418, 118–120 Thanon Phitak Chat) has similar singles/doubles with bathroom for 200B.

Prachuapsuk Hotel (☎ 032-601019, fax 601711, 63–65 Thanon Suseuk), in a two-storey shophouse near the municipal market, is a friendly, family run place with 11 rooms costing 150B with fan and bathroom and 250B with air-con. There is no English sign.

The three-storey *King Hotel* (☎ 032-611170, 203 Thanon Phitak Chat) has larger rooms with fan for 200B. There is no English sign. Facing Ao Prachuap is the *Suksan* (☎ 032-611145, 11 Thanon Suseuk), with rooms with fan for 270B to 320B and air-con bungalows from 370B to 450B.

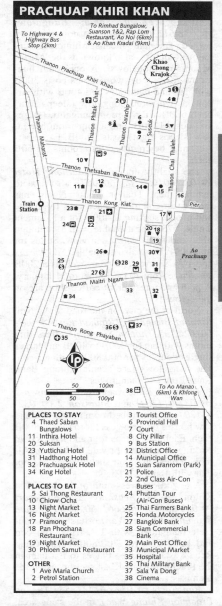

PRACHUAP KHIRI KHAN

PLACES TO STAY	3 Tourist Office
4 Thaed Saban Bungalows	6 Provincial Hall
11 Inthira Hotel	7 Court
20 Suksan	8 City Pillar
23 Yuttichai Hotel	9 Bus Station
31 Hadthong Hotel	12 District Office
32 Prachuapsuk Hotel	14 Municipal Office
34 King Hotel	15 Suan Saranrom (Park)
	21 Police
PLACES TO EAT	22 2nd Class Air-Con Buses
5 Sai Thong Restaurant	24 Phuttan Tour (Air-Con Buses)
10 Chiow Ocha	25 Thai Farmers Bank
13 Night Market	26 Honda Motorcycles
16 Night Market	27 Bangkok Bank
17 Pramong	28 Siam Commercial Bank
18 Pan Phochana Restaurant	29 Main Post Office
19 Night Market	33 Municipal Market
30 Phloen Samut Restaurant	35 Hospital
	36 Thai Military Bank
OTHER	37 Sala Ya Dong
1 Ave Maria Church	38 Cinema
2 Petrol Station	

CENTRAL THAILAND

Also facing the bay are the plain but well-kept ***Thaed Saban Bungalows*** (☎ *032-611204), which are now privately owned. The name means 'Municipal Bungalows', but it is also known as the 'Mirror Mountain Bungalows'. A one-room bungalow for one or two persons costs 300B with fan and bathroom and 400B with aircon; a two-room bungalow (sleeps four) costs 600B; a three-room bungalow (sleeps six) costs 1200B; and a four-room bungalow (sleeps eight) costs 1500B. Extra persons may be crammed into rooms for 50B each.

The slightly upmarket ***Hadthong Hotel*** (☎ *032-601050, fax 601057), also next to the bay near Thanon Maitri Ngam, has modern air-con rooms, each with TV, fridge and phone, starting at 400B for a basement single, 675B for a double with a mountain view and 819B with a sea view. Suites for up to 1349B are also available. Add 7% tax and 10% service charge as well as a 200B surcharge from 20 December to 31 January. A pool and a restaurant/coffee shop are on the premises.

North of the city, on the road to Ao Noi, ***Rimhad Bungalow*** (*Rimhad Rest;* ☎ *032-601626, 35 Thanon Suanson)* offers tiny rooms with fan for 300B to 400B and larger singles/doubles for 600/800B with air-con. The bungalows face scenic Khlong Bang Nang Lom and mangroves.

Along the same road are the ***Suanson 1*** (☎ *032-611204)* and ***Suanson 2*** (☎ *032-611204)*, with two-bedroom bungalows and row houses on a treeless lot for about 300B each. Each unit sleeps four and has its own parking space and private bathroom. Although these are a bit shabby, they're popular with Bangkok Thais.

A few kilometres south of Ao Manao at Khlong Wan, ***Seasand House Resort*** (☎ *032-661483, fax 661250, 409/1 Thanon Prachuap-Khlong Wan)* offers small, concrete bungalows with TV, fridge, air-con and hot water for 700/800B. The Chao Reua Restaurant (see Places to Eat later in the Prachuap Khiri Khan section) is on the premises.

Ban Forty (☎ *032-661437, 555 Thanon Prachuap-Khlong Wan)*, in the same area, offers four concrete bungalows located on 8 râi (1.2 hectares) of land with a private coconut-palm–lined beach. Owned by a

friendly retired Thai air force officer of Thai/English descent, the simple but clean units cost 700B to 800B. Meals can be arranged ahead of time and served in a săalaa near the beach.

Ao Noi In Ao Noi there are several rooms and small 'weekend inns', most catering to Thai visitors. ***Aow Noi Beach Resort*** (☎ *032-601350, 206 Tambon Ao Noi)* offers 12 rather run-down cottages with private bathroom for 400B to 600B with fan, 800B with air-con. The current owners of this place are claiming that the bungalows will soon be replaced by a hotel building, so things may change.

Places to Eat
Because of its well-deserved reputation for fine seafood, Prachuap Khiri Khan has many restaurants for its size. One of the seafood specialities that you shouldn't miss is *plaa sămlii dàet diaw* –whole cottonfish that's sliced lengthways and left to dry in the sun for half a day, then fried quickly in a wok. It's often served with mango salad on the side. It may sound awful, but the taste is sublime.

The best place for the money is the ***night market*** that convenes near the district office in the middle of town. On Thanon Chai Thaleh in front of the Suan Saranrom (public park) is a smaller ***night market*** that's also quite good; tables set up along the sea wall sometimes get a good breeze.

Of the many seafood restaurants, the best are the ***Pan Phochana Restaurant*** (☎ *032-611195, 11 Thanon Suseuk)*, behind Susskan Hotel, and the ***Sai Thong Restaurant*** (*Chiow Ocha 2;* ☎ *032-550868)*, on Thanon Chai Thaleh near the Thaed Saban Bungalows. Both serve great-tasting seafood at reasonable prices. Sai Thong serves Carlsberg draught beer and imported wine, and is a popular stop for tour buses. The Pan Phochana is famous for its *hàw mòk hăwy* (ground fish curry steamed in mussels on the half-shell). Just south of the Pan Phochana is a good ***night market*** with many seafood stalls.

Other good restaurants include the ***Chiow Ocha*** (☎ *032-611118, 100 Thanon Phitak Chat)*, the ***Pramong*** (☎ *032-611168, 36 Thanon Chai Thaleh)* and the ***Chao Reua*** (☎ *032-661482)*, located at the Seasand House Resort (see Places to Stay earlier).

There is no Roman-script sign to indicate either the Chiow Ocha or the Pramong. The **Phloen Samut Restaurant** (☎ *032-611115, 44 Thanon Chai Thaleh),* adjacent to Hadthong Hotel, is a good outdoor seafood place, although it doesn't have everything that's listed on the menu.

Several good seafood restaurants can also be found along the road north of Ao Prachuap on the way to Ao Noi. **Rap Lom** (☎ *032-601677)* is the most popular – look for the Carlsberg Beer sign.

Across from the Inthira Hotel is a small morning market with tea stalls that serve cheap curries and noodles.

Entertainment

Sala Ya Dong (no Roman-script sign) on Soi Phun Samakhi (opposite the Thai Military Bank) is a low-key, open-air, old west–style bar with *phleng phêua chii-wít* (live Thai folk music). Although the place touts its namesake *yaa dawng* (herbal liquor), which can be bought by the bottle or by the shot, beer is also available. A small khâo tôm stall next door supplies the bar with eats.

Getting There & Away

Bus From Bangkok, buses (93B ordinary, 122B 2nd-class air-con, four to five hours) leave the Southern bus station frequently between 3 am and 9.20 pm (ordinary), or 7 am and 1 am (air-con). Phuttan Tour operates 15 1st-class air-con buses a day in both directions between 6.15 am and 1 am (155B). In the opposite direction, Phuttan Tour air-con buses to Bangkok leave from 182 Thanon Phitak Chat at similar intervals.

From Hua Hin buses (30B ordinary, 42B air-con, 1½ to two hours) leave from the bus station on Thanon Sasong every 20 minutes from 7 am to 3 pm.

Ordinary/2nd-class air-con buses go from Prachuap Khiri Khan to Chumphon (55/77B), Surat Thani (110/240B), Nakhon Si Thammarat (150/210B), Krabi (170/240B), Phang-Nga (150/210B), Don Sak (for Ko Samui, 128/193B) and Phuket (173/242B).

The air-con bus from Bangkok to Ko Samui stops on the highway in Prachuap Khiri Khan between midnight and 1 am – if seats are available you can buy a through ticket to Ko Samui for 240B. It's a five-minute, 30B motorcycle taxi ride from the town centre to the highway bus stop.

Train For departure details from Bangkok, see the Phetchaburi Getting There & Away section earlier in this chapter: the same services apply. Fares from Bangkok are 272B for 1st class, 135B for 2nd class and 58B for 3rd class; to these add the appropriate rapid or express charges. The ordinary train between Hua Hin and Prachuap Khiri Khan costs 14B; from Hua Hin it leaves at 5.28 pm, arriving in Prachuap Khiri Khan at 6.55 pm. There are also several rapid and express trains between the two towns, but the time saved is negligible. A 3rd-class ticket to Chumphon costs 24B.

Getting Around

Prachuap is small enough to get around on foot, or you can hop on a túk-túk – actually more akin to the Isan-style *sàkailáep,* here called *sǎaleng* – for 10B anywhere on the main roads.

A sǎaleng to Ao Noi costs 30B to 40B. The Honda dealer on Thanon Salachip rents 100cc motorcycles for 200B a day plus 20B for a helmet.

A motorcycle taxi to Ao Manao costs 20B to 25B. They aren't permitted past the gate unless both driver and passenger are wearing helmets. Without a helmet you'll have to walk the 3km to the beach.

AROUND PRACHUAP KHIRI KHAN

If you continue north from Prachuap Khiri Khan around Ao Prachuap to the headland you'll come to a small boat-building village on **Ao Bang Nang Lom** where they still make wooden fishing vessels using traditional Thai methods. It takes about two months to finish a 12m boat, which will sell for around 400,000B without an engine. The industrious folks at Bang Nang Lom also catch a fish called *plaa ching chang,* which they dry beside the roads and then store for Sri Lankan traders who arrive by ship at certain times of the year specifically to buy up the catch.

West of the beach at Ao Bang Nang Lom is a canal, **Khlong Bang Nang Lom,** lined with picturesque mangroves. A few kilometres north of Ao Prachuap is another bay, **Ao Noi,** the site of a small fishing village with a few rooms to let.

Wat Khao Tham Khan Kradai
วัดเขาถ้ำคานกระได

About 8km north of town, following the road beyond Ao Noi, is this small cave wát at one end of **Ao Khan Kradai** (also known as Ao Khan Bandai – a long, beautiful bay).

A trail at the base of the limestone hill leads up and around the side to a small cavern and then to a larger one that contains a reclining Buddha. If you have a torch you can proceed to a larger second chamber also containing Buddha images.

From this trail you get a good view of Ao Khan Kradai. The beach here is suitable for swimming and is virtually deserted. It's not far from Ao Noi, so you could stay in Ao Noi and walk to the beach. Or you could stay in town, rent a motorcycle and make a day trip to Ao Khan Kradai.

Dan Singkhon
ด่านสิงขร

Just south of Prachuap Khiri Khan is a road leading west to Dan Singkhon, on the Myanmar border. This is the narrowest point in Thailand between the Gulf of Thailand and Myanmar – only 12km across. The Myanmar side changed from Karen to Yangon control following skirmishes in 1988–9. The border is open to Thai/Burmese citizens only. On the Thai side is a small frontier village and a Thai police camp with wooden semi-underground bunkers built in a circle.

Off the road on the way to Dan Singkhon are a couple of small cave hermitages. The more famous one at **Khao Hin Thoen**, surrounded by a park of the same name, has some interesting rock formations and sculptures – but watch out for the dogs.

The road to Khao Hin Thoen starts where the paved road to Dan Singkhon breaks left. **Khao Khan Hok** (also known as Phutthakan Bang Kao) is a less well-known cave nearby where an elderly monk, Luang Phaw Buaphan Chatimetho, lives.

THAP SAKAE & BANG SAPHAN
ทับสะแก/บางสะพาน

These two districts lie south of Prachuap Khiri Khan and together they offer a string of fairly good beaches that get few tourists.

The town of Thap Sakae is set back from the coast and isn't much, but along the seashore there are a few places to stay. The beach opposite Thap Sakae isn't anything special either, but north and south of town are the beaches of **Hat Wanakon** and **Hat Laem Kum**. There is no private accommodation at these beaches at the moment, but you could ask permission to camp at Wat Laem Kum, which is on a prime spot right in the middle of Hat Laem Kum. Hat Laem Kum is only 3.5km from Thap Sakae and at the northern end of the beach is the fishing village of Ban Don Sai, where you can buy food and supplies.

Hat Wanakon is part of Hat Wanakon National Marine Park, which covers 22.6 sq km of coastline and 15.4 sq km of marine resources.

Bang Saphan Yai (Bang Saphan) is no great shakes as a town either, but the long beaches here are beginning to attract some speculative development. In the vicinity of Bang Saphan Yai you'll find the beaches of **Hat Sai Kaew**, **Hat Ban Krut**, **Hat Khiriwong**, **Hat Ban Nong Mongkon**, **Hat Bo Thong Lang**, **Hat Pha Daeng** and **Hat Bang Boet**, all of which are worth looking up. Getting around can be a problem as there isn't much public transport between these beaches.

There are also islands off the coast, including **Ko Thalu** and **Ko Sing**, where there is good snorkelling and diving from the end of January to mid-May. Coral Resort and Suan Luang Resort in Bang Saphan can arrange half-day diving excursions to these islands for 500B to 700B.

Places to Stay & Eat
Thap Sakae The *Chaowarit* (*Chawalit*; ☎ 032-671010), right off the highway near the southern end of town, has simple but clean rooms for 170B with shared bathroom, 200B to 300B with fan and bathroom – good value. Around the corner less than 100m from Chaowarit, the *Sukkasem* (☎ 032-671598) has basic rooms for 100B to 120B.

A relatively new place at the northern end of town on the highway is *Thap Sakae Hotel* (☎ 032-546242), offering clean singles/doubles with fan for 400/500B and air-con bungalows for 1000B.

On the coast opposite Thap Sakae are a couple of accommodation options with concrete block–style bungalows for 200B to

450B, including the **Chan Reua Hotel** (☎ 032-671890, 671930, fax 671401).

Hat Ban Krut The **Reun Chun Seaview** (☎/fax 032-695061) has one-bedroom bungalows for 800B, and two-bedroom, two-bathroom ones for 1800B. All have air-con, TV and fridge – not bad for families. A seafood restaurant is on the premises. Nearby **Rim Haad Bungalow** (☎ 032-695205) offers bungalows in a nicely landscaped garden adjacent to a large coconut grove. Rooms have air-con, TV and fridge and the restaurant serves Isan cuisine and seafood. Rates are 800B for a double and 1500B for a larger bungalow (sleeps 10).

The **Ban Klang Aow Beach Resort** (☎ 032-695086; in Bangkok ☎ 02-463 7908) is an upmarket place on the beach with a nice pool. Standard bungalows cost 1000B; larger ones cost 2000B. All have air-con, TV and fridge. **Suan Ban Krut Resort** (☎ 032-695103, ☎/fax 695217) is a similar affair with 21 bungalows (a bit smaller than the ones at Ban Klang Aow Beach Resort) for 1500B to 3000B as well as a number of beach homes for sale or rent. Facilities include a pool, a fitness centre and a golf putting green.

Hat Khiriwong The **Tawee Beach Resort** (also Tawees, Tawee Sea) has simple thatched bungalows with private scoop showers (large basins from which you scoop water over yourself) for 100B single/double plus a few concrete bungalows with fans for 200/400B.

Sai-Eak Beach Resort (☎ 01-213 0317) opened in 1996 and is the nicest resort in the area. It's right on the beach and features a swimming pool and a variety of bungalows with satellite TV and fridge for 2000B to 4000B, depending on whether they face the pool or sea. Low-season discounts of up to 50% are available May to November.

Take a train or bus to the nearby town of Ban Krut, then a motorcycle taxi (30B daytime, 50B night) to Hat Khiriwong.

Bang Saphan Along the bay of Ao Bang Saphan are several beach hotels and bungalows. At Hat Sombun, the **Hat Somboon Sea View** (☎ 032-548344, fax 548345) has singles/doubles with private hot-water bathroom, TV, fridge and air-con for 400/500B; bungalows cost 400B. The cheaper **Boon-**

som Guest House (☎ 032-291273) has eight wooden bungalows with fan for 200B to 300B. The **Van Veena Hotel** (☎ 032-691251), also in this area, has rooms with TV and fridge for 250B with fan and 350B with air-con. The slightly run-down **Bangsaphan Resort** (☎ 032-691152/3) has rooms for 280B with fan and 550B with air-con, as well as 'VIP' rooms for 700B.

Karol L's (☎ 01-290 3067), 6km south of Bang Saphan Yai, has rustic, old Samui–style bungalows for 100B (shared bathroom) and 120B (private bathroom). If you call from the train or bus station, the staff will provide free transport. Meals here are very reasonably priced and free maps for exploring the area are provided.

The **Suan Luang Resort** (☎ 032-691663, fax 691664, 13 Mu 1) is 600m from the beach, just up from Karol L's. The staff will also pick up customers from the train station if you call. The resort is run by a friendly and helpful Thai-French couple, a combination reflected in the dining-room menu. Spacious bungalows with mosquito proofing cost 300B for wooden ones with fans and 500B for concrete ones with hot water, TV and air-con. There are discounts for longer stays. It rents out four motorbikes (250B for guests, 300B for nonguests) and windsurfing, diving and sailing equipment. The staff can organise boat trips to nearby islands or motorbike trips to surrounding areas, including Myanmar if the border is open.

The going rate for a half-day snorkel trip to Ko Sing is 500B to 700B per person, depending on the number in the group. Overnight camping trips to Ko Thalu can also be arranged.

The French-managed **Bang Saphan Coral Hotel** (☎ 032-691667, 171 Mu 9) offers beautiful bungalows with terracotta-tile roofs in a garden setting. All rooms have air-con, TV, fridge and hot water and cost 1860B to 2350B, plus tax and service. The hotel restaurant serves pricey US and continental breakfasts. It also has a pool and offers windsurfing, sailing, canoeing, diving and fishing equipment for rent, as well as day trips to Ko Thalu.

On the beach next to the Coral Hotel is a **cafe** selling inexpensive noodle and seafood dishes. A path leading inland from the beach leads to **Waree**, an open-air restaurant with good Thai Muslim fare.

CENTRAL THAILAND

Hat Bo Kaew Eight kilometres south of Hat Bang Saphan Yai (15km south of Bang Saphan town), this up-and-comer boasts the *Suan Annan Resort* (☎ 032-699118), with 10 bungalows around 300m from the beach costing 400B a night with air-con, TV and fridge.

Getting There & Away
Buses from Prachuap Khiri Khan to Thap Sakae are 12B and 8B from Thap Sakae to Bang Saphan Yai. If you're coming from farther south, buses from Chumphon to Bang Saphan Yai are 35B.

You can also get 3rd-class trains between Hua Hin, Prachuap Khiri Khan, Thap Sakae, Ban Koktahom, Ban Krut and Bang Saphan Yai for a few baht each leg, as all of these beach-side destinations have train stations (the rapid and express lines do not stop in Thap Sakae, Ban Krut or Bang Saphan). Each of these train stations is around 4km from the beach, with motor-cycle taxis the only form of public transport available.

It's possible to rent 100cc motorbikes in the small and nondescript town of Bang Saphan for 200B per day.

Northern Thailand

The first true Thai kingdoms (Lanna, Sukhothai, Nan, Chiang Mai and Chiang Saen) arose in what is now Northern Thailand, hence this region is endowed with a wide range of traditional culture and architecture, including the country's most beautiful Thai temple ruins. It is also the home of Thailand's hill tribes, whose cultures are dissolving rapidly in the face of the country's modernisation and foreign tourism. Despite this, the scenic beauty of the North has been fairly well preserved – the region boasts more natural forest cover than any other – and Chiang Mai is still arguably Thailand's most livable city.

Northern Thais *(khon meuang)* are known for their relaxed, easy-going manner, which shows up in their speech – the northern dialect *(kham meuang)* has a slower rhythm than Thailand's three other main dialects. Northern Thais are very proud of their local customs, considering northern ways to be part of Thailand's 'original' tradition and culture. Symbols frequently displayed by northern Thais to express cultural solidarity include clay water jars placed in front of homes, *kàlae* (carved wooden 'X' motifs) that decorate house gables, Shan or hill-tribe-style shoulder bags and the ubiquitous *sêua mâw hâwm* (indigo-dyed rice farmers' shirt) worn on Friday at many banks, universities and other institutions throughout the North.

Northern Thailand also has its own cuisine, featuring a wide variety of vegetables (the region's mountain slopes are well suited to vegetable cultivation). Sticky rice is preferred over the white rice favoured in Central and Southern Thailand and, as in North-Eastern Thailand and Laos, it is eaten with the hands. *Sôm-tam,* a tart, spicy salad usually made with green papaya (northern Thais also use a variety of other fruits and vegetables to make this dish) is very popular in the North but, unlike north-eastern Thais, northern Thais tend to eat it as a between-meals snack rather than as part of a main meal.

The mountainous North is part of the infamous 'Golden Triangle', a region where Myanmar, Laos and Thailand meet and where most of the world's illicit opium poppies are grown, although Thailand itself is today very much a minority producer.

Highlights

- Sukhothai & Si Satchanalai-Chaliang Historical Parks – World Heritage sites containing the finest collection of monuments to Thailand's 'golden age'

- Chiang Mai – vibrant northern capital with 300 temples and celebrated arts and crafts

- Doi Inthanon National Park – home to 400 bird species and featuring Thailand's tallest peak

- Mae Hong Son – crossroads province with dense forests, trekking and rafting

- Nan – rural province with fertile river valleys and Thai Lü communities

- Border crossing – trips to Myanmar's historic Kengtung with crumbling Buddhas and colonial architecture

- Tham Lot & Tham Nang Lang – limestone caves

The Northern Loop

While the normal way of travelling north is to head directly from Bangkok to Chiang Mai, there are many interesting alternatives.

Starting north from Bangkok, visit the ancient capitals of Ayuthaya, Lopburi and Sukhothai, or take a less-travelled and longer route by going west to Nakhon

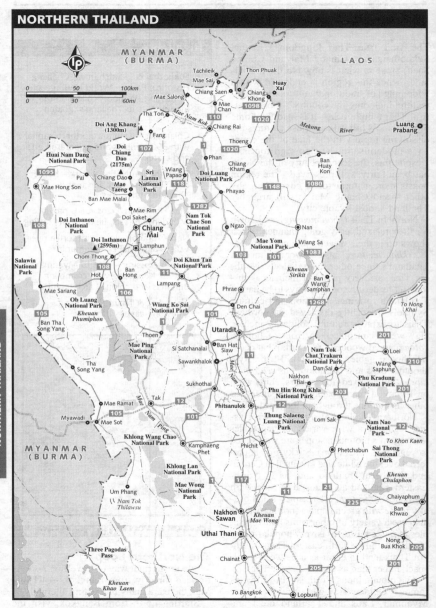

NORTHERN THAILAND

MYANMAR
(BURMA)

LAOS

Tachileik
Mae Sai
Thon Phuak
Mae Salong
Chiang Saen
Huay Xai
Chiang Khong
1098
Luang Prabang

Mae Chan
110
Chiang Rai
1020
Mekong River

Tha Ton
Doi Ang Khang (1300m)
Fang
107
Thoeng
1020

Huai Nam Dang National Park
Doi Chiang Dao (2175m)
Chiang Dao
Phan
Chiang Kham
Ban Huay Kon

1095
Pai
Mae Taeng
Sri Lanna National Park
Wiang Papao
Doi Luang National Park
1080

Mae Hong Son
Ban Mae Malai
118
Phayao
1148

Doi Inthanon National Park
Mae Rim
Mae Saket
1282
Nam Tok Chae Son National Park
Ngao
Nan
Wiang Sa

108
Chiang Mai
Lamphun
Mae Yom National Park
101
1083

Doi Inthanon (2595m)
Chom Thong
Ban Hong
Doi Khun Tan National Park
103
Kheuan Sirikit
Ban Wang Samphan

Salawin National Park
Mae Sariang
108
Hot
11
Lampang

106
Wiang Ko Sai National Park
Phrae
1268
To Nong Khai

Ob Luang National Park
Kheuan Phumiphon
101
Den Chai

105
Ban Tha Song Yang
Thoen
1
Utaradit
Ban Hat Siaw
11
Nam Tok Chat Trakarn National Park
201
Loei
Wang Saphung
210

Tha Song Yang
Mae Ping National Park
Si Satchanalai
Sawankhalok
Dan Sai
Phu Kradung National Park
201

Mae Ramat
Tak
Sukhothai
Nakhon Thai
203

Myawadi
Mae Sot
105
12
Phitsanulok
Phu Hin Rong Khla National Park
Nam Nao National Park
12
To Khon Kaen

MYANMAR
(BURMA)
101
Khlong Wang Chao National Park
Kamphaeng Phet
Phichit
Thung Salaeng Luang National Park
Lom Sak
Phetchabun
Sai Thong National Park

Khlong Lan National Park
117
21
Kheuan Chulaphon

Mae Wong National Park
11
225
Chaiyaphum

Um Phang
Nam Tok Thilawsu
1
Nakhon Sawan
Kheuan Mae Wong
Ban Khwao

Three Pagodas Pass
Uthai Thani
Nong Bua Khok
205

Chainat
205
201
2

Kheuan Khao Laem
To Bangkok
Lopburi

0   50   100km
0   30   60mi

Pathom and Kanchanaburi and then north-east by bus to Lopburi (backtracking to Ayuthaya if desired).

From Lopburi, either head north to Chiang Mai, or stop at Phitsanulok for side trips to Sukhothai, Tak and Mae Sot. It is possible to travel by road from Mae Sot to Mae Sariang, then on to Mae Hong Son or Chiang Mai.

Once you're in Chiang Mai, the usual route is to continue on to Fang for the Mae Nam Kok (Kok River) boat ride to Chiang Rai, then on into the Golden Triangle towns of Mae Sai and Chiang Saen. Travellers with more time might add to this the Chiang Mai to Mae Hong Son to Chiang Mai circle. A very rough but traversable road between Tha Ton and Doi Mae Salong (Mae Salong Mountain) is an alternative to the Mae Nam Kok trip once you get to the Fang area.

From Chiang Mai, proceed to North-Eastern Thailand via Phitsanulok and Lom Sak, entering the North-East proper at either Loei or Khon Kaen. From there, Nong Khai, Udon Thani and Khon Kaen are all on the railway back to Bangkok, but there are several other places in the area worth exploring before heading back to the capital.

A Northern Thailand–Laos loop, starting with the crossing of the Mekong River at Chiang Khong, Thailand, to Huay Xai, Laos, and then continuing by river to Luang Prabang and Vientiane, has become very popular over the last couple of years. From Vientiane you can loop back into North-Eastern Thailand or continue on to Vietnam or China by road or air. This loop can be done in reverse, of course, from Bangkok to Vientiane, Luang Prabang and Huay Xai, then back into Thailand via Chiang Khong to Chiang Rai and eventually Chiang Mai.

Chiang Mai Province

CHIANG MAI
อ.เมืองเชียงใหม่

postcode 50000 • pop 160,000

One of the many questions Thais may ask a foreigner visiting Thailand is 'Have you been to Chiang Mai yet?', underscoring the feeling that Chiang Mai is a keystone of any journey to Thailand. Along with

Sukhothai farther south, it was the first South-East Asian polity to make the historic transition from domination by Mon and Khmer cultures to a new era ruled by Thais. Although Thais idealise their beloved northern capital as a quaint, moated and walled city surrounded by mountains with legendary, mystical attributes, the truth is Chiang Mai has all but left that image behind to become a modern, cosmopolitan city exhibiting many of the hallmarks of contemporary world culture and technology.

More than 700km north-west of Bangkok, Chiang Mai has over 300 temples (121 within the *thêtsàbaan* or municipal limits) – almost as many as in Bangkok – a fact which makes it visually striking. Auspicious Doi Suthep rises 1676m above and behind the city, providing a picturesque backdrop for this fast-developing centre. Many visitors stay in Chiang Mai longer than planned because of the high quality and low price of accommodation, food and shopping, the cool nights (compared with Central Thailand), the international feel of the city and the friendliness of the people.

Another advantage is that the city is small enough to get around by bicycle. And with the increasing number of cultural and spiritual learning experiences available in Chiang Mai these days – Thai massage, Thai cooking, Thai language, yoga and *vipassana* (insight meditation) – Chiang Mai has become much more than just a quick stop on the Northern Thailand tourist circuit.

Not all the foreigners you see in Chiang Mai are tourists – many live in Chiang Mai part time or year-round. Chiang Mai residents often comment that living here has all the cultural advantages of being in Bangkok, but fewer of the disadvantages such as traffic jams and air pollution. In recent years, however, traffic has increased and the city's main avenues have become a bit noisy and polluted, particularly along major thoroughfares.

To preserve the city's character, it has been proposed that a 'twin city' be built nearby to channel development away from the old city – possibly at San Kamphaeng to the east. Conservation measures include a 1991 ban on the building of any high-rise

NORTHERN THAILAND

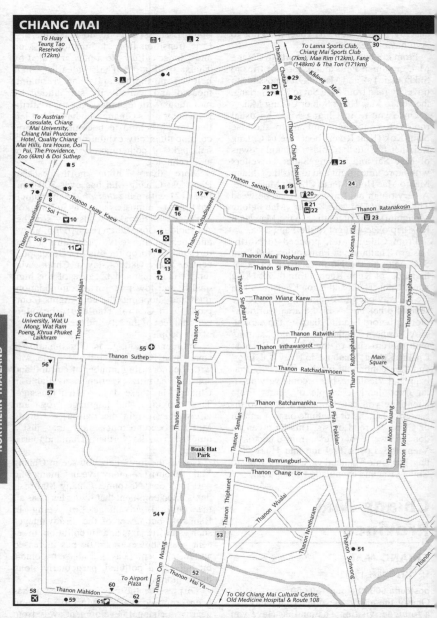

CHIANG MAI

To Huay Teung Tao Reservoir (12km)

To Lanna Sports Club, Chiang Mai Sports Club (7km), Mae Rim (12km), Fang (148km) & Tha Ton (171km)

Thanon Chotana

Khlong Mae Kha

To Austrian Consulate, Chiang Mai University, Chiang Mai Phucome Hotel, Quality Chiang Mai Hills, Isra House, Doi Pui, The Providence, Zoo (6km) & Doi Suthep

Thanon Chang Pheuak

Thanon Santitham

Thanon Ratanakosin

Thanon Huay Kaew

Thanon Nimanhaemin

Soi 1

Soi 9

Thanon Hutsadisawee

Th Soman Kla.

Thanon Mani Nopharat

Thanon Si Phum

Thanon Singharat

Thanon Wiang Kaew

Thanon Chaiyaphum

Thanon Sirimankhalajan

To Chiang Mai University, Wat U Mong, Wat Ram Poeng, Khrua Phuket Laikhram

Thanon Arak

Thanon Ratwithi

Thanon Inthawarorot

Thanon Ratchaphakhinai

Main Square

Thanon Suthep

Thanon Ratchadamnoen

Thanon Bunreuangrit

Thanon Samlan

Thanon Ratchamankha

Thanon Phra Pokklao

Thanon Moon Muang

Thanon Kotchasan

Buak Hat Park

Thanon Bamrungburi

Thanon Chang Lor

Thanon Thiphanet

Thanon Wualai

Thanon Nontharam

Thanon Sunwong

Thanon Om Muang

Thanon Hai Ya

To Airport Plaza

Thanon Mahidon

To Old Chiang Mai Cultural Centre, Old Medicine Hospital & Route 108

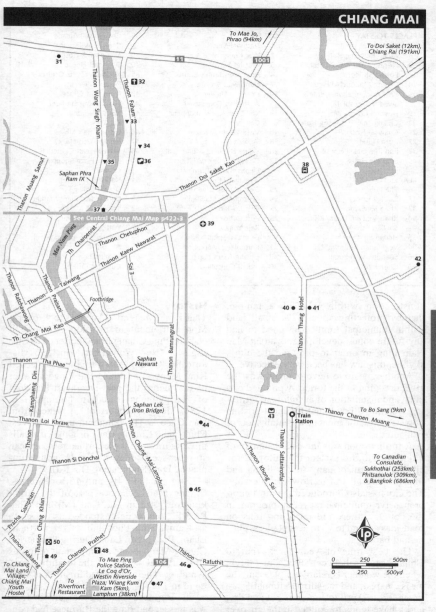

CHIANG MAI

To Mae Jo,
Phrao (94km)

To Doi Saket (12km),
Chiang Rai (191km)

11

1001

31

Thanon Wang Singh Kham

Thanon Faham

32

33

34

35

36

Thanon Muang Samut

Saphan Phra
Ram IX

Thanon Doi Saket Kao

38

37

39

Mae Nam Ping

Th Charoenrat

Thanon Chetuphon

Thanon Kaew Nawarat

Soi 3

42

Thanon Praisani

Taiwang

Thanon Ratchawong

Thanon

Footbridge

40 ● ● 41

Thanon Thung Hotel

Th Chang Moi Kao

Thanon Bamrungrat

Saphan
Nawarat

Thanon

Tha Phae

Saphan Lek
(Iron Bridge)

To Bo Sang (9km)

43

Train
Station

Thanon Charoen Muang

Thanon Kamphaeng Din

Thanon Loi Khraw

● 44

Thanon Chiang Mai Lamphun

Thanon Sattanirothai

Thanon Khong Sai

To Canadian
Consulate,
Sukhothai (253km),
Phitsanulok (309km),
& Bangkok (686km)

Thanon Si Donchai

● 45

Pracha Samphan

Thanon Chang Khlan

50

49

Thanon Chang Khian

48

Thanon Charoen Prathet

To Mae Ping
Police Station,
Le Coq d'Or,
Westin Riverside
Plaza; Wiang Kum
Kam (5km),
Lamphun (38km)

Thanon
Ratuthit

106

46 ●

To Chiang
Mai Land
Village;
Chiang Mai
Youth
Hostel

To
Riverfront
Restaurant

● 47

0   250   500m

0   250   500yd

NORTHERN THAILAND

See Central Chiang Mai Map p422-3

CHIANG MAI

PLACES TO STAY
5 Amity Green Hills
8 Amari Rincome Hotel
9 Hillside Plaza & Condotel
12 Lotus PSK Hotel
14 Chiang Mai Orchid Hotel
16 YMCA International Hotel;
   Swedish Consulate
19 Novotel Chiang Mai
21 Chiang Mai Phu Viang Hotel
26 Chawala Hotel
27 Iyara Hotel
37 Pun Pun Guest House
49 Empress Hotel

PLACES TO EAT
6 The Pub
17 Sa-Nga Choeng Doi
33 Khao Soi Samoe Jai
34 Khao Soi Lam Duan; Khao
   Soi Ban Faham
35 Heuan Sunthari
54 Vegetarian Restaurant
56 Suandok Vegetarian
60 Chez John

OTHER
1 National Museum
2 Wat Khuan Sing
3 Wat Jet Yot
4 Anantasiri Tennis Courts
7 Nantawan Arcade
10 Drunken Flower
11 Australian Consulate
13 Kad Suan Kaew Shopping
   Centre
15 Vista 12 Huay Kaew
18 Velocity
20 White Elephant Monument
22 Chang Pheuak (White
   Elephant) Bus Terminal
   (Provincial Buses)
23 Devi Mandir Chiang Mai
24 Chiang Mai Stadium
25 Wat Ku Tao
28 Post Office
29 Raja Yoga
30 Lanna Hospital
31 Kamthiang Market
32 Chiang Mai Church
36 Indian Consulate

38 Chiang Mai Arcade
   (New) Bus Terminal
39 McCormick Hospital
40 Duangjitt House
41 Northern Crafts Centre
42 Payap University
43 Main Post Office
44 Thai Boxing Stadium
45 Kawila Military
   Barracks
46 Gymkhana Club
47 Foreign Cemetery
48 Sacred Heart Cathedral
50 Season Plaza Shopping
   Centre
51 National Theatre;
   Drama College
52 Chiang Mai Plant Market
53 Thiphanet Market
55 Maharaj Hospital
57 Wat Suan Dok
58 Chiang Mai International
   Airport
59 Immigration
61 Customs Office

construction within 93m of a temple, thereby protecting about 87% of all land within municipal limits. Designed to halt any future condo developments along Mae Nam Ping in order to preserve the city's skyline, this law has been very effective.

Another positive development was the 1992 dredging of the formerly polluted city moat and installation of an automatic filtering system. Although not the most pristine of waterways, the moat now contains lots of fish and turtles.

A further boon was the establishment of a one-way traffic system that allowed the city to extinguish many traffic lights and improve overall traffic flow considerably. The city has also introduced the most comprehensive municipal recycling program in the country; there are recycling bins on roadsides around town to accept glass, plastic and paper.

The best time of year for a visit to Chiang Mai is between July and March, when the weather is relatively pleasant, the air is clearest, and the surrounding hills are green. From April to June it is hot and dry, and a haze tends to collect in the air over the surrounding valley. September is the rainiest month, although even then there are clear days.

History

Thai King Mengrai (Mangrai) took over a Mon settlement to develop Nopburi Si Nakhon Ping Chiang Mai (shortened to Chiang Mai, 'New Walled City') in 1296. Historically, Chiang Mai Province succeeded King Mengrai's Chiang Rai kingdom after he conquered the post-Dvaravati kingdom of Hariphunchai (modern Lamphun) in 1281. Mengrai, reportedly a prince from Nan Chao, a Thai kingdom in South-West China, built Chiang Mai's original city walls in 1296; traces of these earthen ramparts can still be seen today along Thanon Kamphaeng Din (Kamphaeng Din Rd).

Later, in the 14th and 15th centuries, Chiang Mai became a part of the larger kingdom of Lan Na Thai (Million Thai Rice Fields), which extended as far south as Kamphaeng Phet and as far north as Luang Prabang in Laos. During this period Chiang Mai became an important religious and cultural centre – the eighth world synod of Theravada Buddhism was held there in 1477.

The Burmese capture of the city in 1556 was the second time the Burmese had control of Chiang Mai Province: before King Mengrai's reign, King Anawrahta of Pagan (present-day Bagan) had ruled Chiang Mai

Province in the 11th century. The second time around, the Burmese ruled Chiang Mai for over 200 years.

In 1775 Chiang Mai was recaptured by the Thais under King Taksin, who appointed Chao Kavila, a *jâo meuang* (chieftain) from nearby Lampang principality, as viceroy of Northern Thailand. In 1800 Kavila built the monumental brick walls around the inner city, and expanded the city in southerly and easterly directions, establishing a river port at the end of what is today Thanon Tha Phae (*thâa phae* means 'raft pier').

Under Kavila, Chiang Mai became an important regional trade centre. Many of the later Shan and Burmese-style temples seen around the city were built by wealthy teak merchants who emigrated from Burma during the late 19th century.

The completion of the northern railway to Chiang Mai in 1921 finally linked the North with Central Thailand. Word soon spread among the Thais and foreign visitors that the quaint northern capital was a great place for shopping and recreation. Tourism has since replaced commercial trade as Chiang Mai's number one source of outside revenue. A close second is the manufacture and sale of local handicrafts.

Long before tourists began visiting the region, Chiang Mai was an important centre for handcrafted pottery, weaving, umbrellas, silverwork and woodcarving. In handicraft shops anywhere in Thailand, chances are at least someone working there will hail from the Chiang Mai area.

Orientation

The old city of Chiang Mai is a neat square bounded by moats and partial walls. Thanon Moon Muang (Mun Meuang), along the eastern moat, is the centre for inexpensive accommodation and places to eat. Thanon Tha Phae runs straight from the middle of this side and crosses Mae Nam Ping, where it changes into Thanon Charoen Muang.

The train station and the main post office are farther down Thanon Charoen Muang, a fair distance from the centre. There are several bus terminals around Chiang Mai, so make sure you go to the right one.

Several of Chiang Mai's important temples are within the moat area, but there are others to the north and west. Doi Suthep

rises up to the west of the city and its temples give you a fine view over the city.

Maps Finding your way around Chiang Mai is fairly simple, although a copy of Nancy Chandler's *Map of Chiang Mai*, sold in bookshops, is a very worthwhile investment for 140B. It shows all the main points of interest, shopping venues and oddities that you'd be most unlikely to stumble upon by yourself.

The Tourism Authority of Thailand (TAT) also puts out a sketchy city map that is free and available from the TAT office on Thanon Chiang Mai-Lamphun.

Information

Tourist Offices Chiang Mai has a friendly TAT office (☎ 053-248604) on Thanon Chiang Mai-Lamphun opposite the Saphan Lek (Lek Bridge) just south of Saphan Nawarat. It's open 8 am to 4.30 pm daily.

Chiang Mai's Tourist Police (☎ 053-248130, 248974, 1155), who have a reputation for honesty and efficiency, have an office about 100m north of the TAT office on Thanon Chiang Mai-Lamphun. It's open 6 am until midnight. Call ☎ 1155 in case of emergency (24 hours).

Foreign Consulates Chiang Mai has several foreign consular posts where you may be able to arrange visas. The Indian consulate here is a familiar stopping-off point for travellers on their way to India; it takes about four days to process a visa.

Australia (☎ 053-221083, fax 219726) 165 Thanon Sirimankhalajan
Austria (☎ 053-400231, fax 400232) 15 Mu 1, Thanon Huay Kaew
Canada (☎/fax 053-850147) 151 Thanon Chiang Mai-Lampang (Hwy 11)
China (☎ 053-276125, 200424, fax 274614) 111 Thanon Chang Lor
Finland (☎ 053-234777, fax 251512) 104–112 Thanon Tha Phae
France (☎ 053-281466, fax 821039) 138 Thanon Charoen Prathet
India (☎ 053-243066, 242491, fax 247879) 344 Thanon Faham (Charoen Rat)
Japan (☎ 053-203367, fax 203373) 104–107 Airport Business Park, 90 Thanon Mahidon
Sweden (☎ 053-220844, fax 210877) YMCA International Hotel, 11 Thanon Soemsuk
UK & Northern Ireland (☎ 053-263015, fax 263016) 198 Thanon Bamrungrat
USA (☎ 053-252629–31, fax 252633) 387 Thanon Wichayanon

Immigration The Thai immigration office (☎ 053-277510) is off Rte 1141 (Thanon Mahidon) near the airport.

Money All major Thai banks have several branches throughout Chiang Mai, many of them along Thanon Tha Phae; most are open 8.30 am to 3.30 pm.

In the well-touristed areas – for example, the Night Bazaar, Thanon Tha Phae and Thanon Moon Muang – there are automated teller machines (ATMs) and the banks also operate foreign-exchange booths that are open as late as 8 pm.

SK Moneychanger (☎ 053-271864) on the eastern side of Thanon Charoen Prathet, between Thanon Si Donchai and Soi Anusan (Anusan Lane) near the Diamond Riverside Hotel, specialises in cash exchanges in several currencies (although travellers cheques are also accepted) – sometimes at better rates than the banks. It's open 8 am to 6 pm Monday to Saturday.

Post & Communications The main post office is on Thanon Charoen Muang near the train station. It's open 8.30 am to 4.30 pm weekdays and 9 am to noon on weekends.

More convenient to visitors staying west of the river towards the old city, the Mae Ping post office, on Thanon Praisani near the flower market, is open 8.30 am to 4.30 pm weekdays, 9 am to noon Saturday. The old Mae Ping post office, which is across the street from the new post office, houses the Chiang Mai Philatelic Museum (open 9 am to 4 pm weekends and holidays only).

Other useful branch post offices can be found at Thanon Singarat/Samlan, Thanon Mahidon, Thanon Phra Pokklao, Thanon Chotana, Thanon Chang Khlan, and at Chiang Mai University and Chiang Mai International Airport.

Mail Boxes Etc (MBE) on Thanon Chang Khlan near the Night Bazaar and on Thanon Inthawarorot near Wat Phra Singh (Pra Singh Temple) offers the usual private mail services, including rental boxes, mailing supplies, packing services, stationery and a courier service. It also does passport photos and photocopies.

DHL International (☎ 053-418501) has an office on Thanon Mani Nopharat east of Pratu Chang Pheuak (Chang Pheuak Gate).

Overseas telephone calls and faxes can be arranged from 7 am to 10 pm in the telecommunications office around the side and upstairs from the main post office on Thanon Charoen Muang. International calls can also be made from larger hotels for a service charge (up to 30%), at many Internet cafes and at MBE on Thanon Chang Khlan. A few Internet cafes can arrange inexpensive Internet phone hook-ups.

Home Country Direct phones, with easy one-button connection with foreign operators in a number of countries around the world, are available at: Chiang Inn Plaza, 100/1 Thanon Chang Khlan, near the Night Bazaar; Chiang Mai International Airport; the main post office on Thanon Charoen Muang; the Thai Airways International (THAI) office on 240 Thanon Phra Pokklao; and the TAT office.

The list of places to log on in Chiang Mai is rapidly growing and you'll find plenty of Internet centres along the following streets: Tha Phae, Moon Muang, Ratchadamnoen, Ratchadamri, Huay Kaew, Suthep and Chang Khlan.

Chiang Mai Disabled Center (☎ 053-213941, ✉ assist@loxinfo.co.th), at 133/1 Thanon Ratchaphakhinai in the old city, offers several terminals with email and Internet access, along with fax and scanning services. Prices are the same as most other Internet centres in town, and all proceeds go to help local disabled people. The Foundation to Encourage the Potential of Disabled Persons, which runs the centre, has a Web site at www.infothai.com/disabled.

Internet Resources Chiang Mai Online (www.chiangmai-online.com) is a commercial site with an overall uneven information flow, although the accommodation listings are quite comprehensive and include room rates from guesthouses as well as hotels. Chiang Mai Newsletter (www.chiangmainews.com) shows great potential as well and posts articles on culture and art.

Books Lonely Planet will soon be coming out with a *Chiang Mai & Northern Thailand* guide. Local English expat Oliver Hargreave has written a colourful and authoritative guidebook to Chiang Mai entitled *Exploring Chiang Mai,* available around town for 350B.

Rip-Offs

Upon arrival in Chiang Mai – whether by bus, plane or train – you'll quite likely be crowded by touts trying to get you to a particular hotel or guesthouse. As elsewhere in Thailand, the touts get a commission for every prospective guest they bring to a guesthouse or hotel. Commissions run as high as 150B per head; the better guesthouses refuse to pay any commission to touts. At any rate, if you call a guesthouse from the bus or train station, staff will be delighted to arrange a ride to avoid paying such exorbitant commissions.

At the train station, ignore any official-looking, uniformed attendants who may try to funnel you into hotels and guesthouses paying commissions – they'll say that anything not on their list is either full, dirty or closed.

Another scam to be aware of is the bus or minivan services from Thanon Khao San in Bangkok, which often advertise a free night's accommodation in Chiang Mai if you buy a Bangkok–Chiang Mai ticket. What usually happens on arrival is that the 'free' guesthouse demands you sign up for one of the hill treks immediately; if you don't, the guesthouse is suddenly 'full'. Sometimes they levy a charge for electricity or hot water. The better guesthouses don't play this game.

The old gem scam has also reached Chiang Mai. The same modus operandi used in Bangkok is employed here: a well-dressed Thai man strikes up a seemingly harmless conversation that ends with you buying worthless sapphires at inflated prices in a local gem shop. Refuse all offers of 'free' sightseeing or shopping assistance.

Chiang Mai has several bookshops, the biggest being Suriwong Book Centre at its newly expanded location at 54 Thanon Si Donchai, and DK Book House on Thanon Kotchasan. A smaller place with a decent selection of books is The Book Zone (☎ 053-252418) on Thanon Tha Phae, directly opposite Wat Mahawan.

Bookazine (☎ 053-281370), in the basement of Chiang Inn Plaza, carries European and American newspapers and magazines, travel guides, maps and other English-language publications.

The American University Alumni (AUA) library on Thanon Ratchadamnoen has a large selection of English-language newspapers and magazines. The library is open 10 am to 6 pm weekdays, 9 am to 1 pm Saturday. Entry requires an annual 400B membership fee (100B for AUA students, 200B for other students) or a one-month temporary 150B membership fee for visitors. The British Council (☎ 053-242103, fax 244781) at 198 Thanon Bamrungrat also has a small English-language library. The Chiang Mai University library has a good collection of foreign-language titles.

Chiang Mai also has several shops specialising in used books. Lost Book Shop on the northern side of Thanon Ratchamankha (between Thanon Moon Muang and Thanon Ratchaphakhinai) and The Bookshop on Thanon Loi Kroh, in an alley next to L'Elephant Blanc, have especially good selections, going far beyond the usual airport pulp to include many books on arts and culture, including hardcovers. Most books for sale are in English, but books in French and German are also available. The Library Service, next to New Saitum Guest House at 21/1 Soi 2, Thanon Ratchamankha, not far from Pratu Tha Phae, also offers used paperbacks for sale or trade, as does Gecko Books on Thanon Chang Moi Kao.

Media Several free English-language publications are distributed at tourist spots throughout the city. The tourism-oriented *Guidelines Chiang Mai, Chiangmai Travel Holiday, Welcome to Chiangmai & Chiangrai* and *Good Morning Chiangmai* contain the usual assortment of brief cultural essays and maps embedded among stacks of advertisements for bars, pubs, restaurants and antique shops. All contain bus, train and airline timetables, which are updated perhaps once a year. *Guidelines* is arguably the best in terms of the writing content. A

NORTHERN THAILAND

portion of *Good Morning Chiangmai* is written in Japanese.

Chang Puak/L'Elephant Blanc appears occasionally and is printed almost entirely in French. *Trip Info* is a very useful booklet (published monthly), with extensive listings of government agencies, banks, churches, apartments, condos and current bus, train and plane schedules.

The monthly *Chiang Mai Newsletter* runs articles on local culture and politics as well as a listing of local events and regular columns such as 'The Pub Crawl'.

Cultural Centres Several foreign cultural centres in Chiang Mai host film, music, dance, theatre and other cultural events.

Alliance Française (☎ 053-275277) 138 Thanon Charoen Prathet. French films (subtitled in English) are screened at 4.30 pm every Tuesday and 8 pm Friday; admission is free to members, 10B students, 20B general public.

American University Alumni (AUA; ☎ 053-278407, 211377) 73 Thanon Ratchadamnoen. AUA offers English and Thai language courses (see Language & Culture under Courses later in this chapter).

British Council (☎ 053-242103) 198 Thanon Bamrungrat. The council features a small English-language library and the services of an honorary consul.

Medical Services McCormick Hospital (☎ 053-241311, 240832), an old missionary hospital on Thanon Kaew Nawarat, is good for minor treatment and is not expensive. As at most hospitals in Chiang Mai, many of the doctors speak English. Chiang Mai Ram Hospital (☎ 053-224861), on Thanon Bunreuangrit near the Sri Tokyo Hotel, is the most modern hospital in town. It's full of gleaming new equipment and costs a bit more than the other Chiang Mai hospitals.

Other recommended medical facilities include Chiang Mai University Hospital, in the university on Thanon Suan Dok, and Lanna Hospital (☎ 053-357234) on Thanon Chang Khlan. The Malaria Centre (☎ 053-221529) at 18 Thanon Bunreuangrit can do blood checks for malaria.

Chip Aun Tong Dispensary (☎ 053-234187), at 48–52 Thanon Chang Moi, offers traditional Chinese medicine and has a Chinese doctor on staff. Mungkala (☎ 053-278494, fax 208432), at 21–25 Thanon

Ratchamankha, is another good traditional Chinese clinic that offers acupuncture, massage and herbal therapy.

Alcoholics Anonymous (☎ 053-241311 ext 235) holds open meetings at 6.30 pm every evening at House No 11 behind McCormick Hospital. Closed meetings are held on Sunday at 9.30 am.

Film & Processing Outside of Bangkok, Chiang Mai has the best supply of quality photographic film in the country. Broadway Photo (☎ 053-251253), on Thanon Tha Phae about 100m east of Pratu Tha Phae, has a good selection of slide film, including hard-to-find (in Chiang Mai) Fujichrome slide films. Souvenir print processing is fine, but professional photographers will do better to wait till they're in Bangkok or back home for processing, as Chiang Mai's photo labs are notoriously unreliable.

Wat Chiang Man
วัดเชียงมั่น

The oldest *wát* (temple) in the city, Wat Chiang Man was founded by King Mengrai in 1296 and features typical northern-Thai temple architecture, with massive teak columns inside the *bòt* (central sanctuary), which in northern Thai is called a *sĭm*. Two important Buddha images are kept in a glass cabinet in the smaller *wíhǎan* (Buddhist image sanctuary) to the right of the sĭm.

The Phra Sila is a marble bas-relief Buddha standing 20cm to 30cm high. According to legend, it's supposed to have come from Sri Lanka or India 2500 years ago, but since no Buddha images were produced anywhere before around 2000 years ago it must have arrived later. The well-known Phra Satang Man, a crystal seated Buddha image, was shuttled back and forth between Thailand and Laos like the Emerald Buddha (see the boxed text 'Travels of the Emerald Buddha' in the Bangkok chapter). It's thought to have come from Lavo (Lopburi) 1800 years ago and stands just 10cm high. A very interesting silver Buddha sits in front of the cabinet among a collection of other images.

The sĭm containing the venerated images is open 9 am to 5 pm daily. Wat Chiang

Man is off Thanon Ratchaphakhinai in the north-eastern corner of the old city.

Wat Phra Singh
วัดพระสิงห์

Started by King Pa Yo in 1345, the wíhǎan that houses the Phra Singh image was completed between 1385 and 1400. It is a perfect example of the classic northern-Thai or Lanna style that was followed during this period from Chiang Mai to Luang Prabang. The Phra Singh Buddha supposedly comes from Sri Lanka, but it is not particularly Singhalese in style. As it is identical to two images in Nakhon Si Thammarat and Bangkok, and has quite a travel history (Sukhothai, Ayuthaya, Chiang Rai, Luang Prabang – the usual itinerary for a travelling Buddha image, involving much royal trickery), no-one really knows which image is the real one, nor can anyone document its place of origin. The sǐm was finished in about 1600.

Wat Phra Singh is at the end of Thanon Ratchadamnoen near Pratu Suan Dok.

Wat Chedi Luang
วัดเจดีย์หลวง

This temple complex, the name of which means 'Monastery of the Great Stupa', stands off Thanon Phra Pokklao. The centrepiece of the compound is a very large and venerable Lanna-style *chedi* (stupa) dating from 1441. It's now in partial ruins, damaged either by a 16th-century earthquake or by the cannon fire of King Taksin in 1775 during the recapture of Chiang Mai from the Burmese. The Phra Kaew ('Emerald' Buddha) – now in Bangkok's Wat Phra Kaew – sat in the eastern niche here in 1475. The làk meuang (guardian deity post) for the city is within the wát compound in the small building to the left of the main entrance. There are also some impressive dipterocarp trees (so named because of their 'twin winged' seed pods which come helicoptering down to the ground in the hot season) in the grounds.

A restoration of the great chedi, financed by Unesco and the Japanese government, has so far thankfully stopped short of creating a new spire, since no-one knows for sure how the original superstructure looked. New Buddha images have been placed in three of the four directional niches. In the eastern niche sits a jade replica of the original Phra Kaew; its official name is Phra Phut Chaloem Sirirat, but it's more commonly known locally as the Phra Kaew Yok Chiang Mai (Chiang Mai Holy Jade Image). The image was financed by the Thai king and carved in 1995; the placement of the image celebrated the 600th anniversary of the chedi (according to some reckonings), and the 700th anniversary of the city.

New porticoes and *naga* (serpent being) guardians for the chedi lack the finesse of the originals. On the southern side of the monument, six elephant sculptures in the pediment can be seen. Five are cement restorations; only the one on the far right – without ears and trunk – is original brick and stucco.

Wat Phan Tao
วัดพันเถา

Diagonally adjacent to Wat Chedi Luang, this wát contains a large, old teak wíhǎan that is one of the unsung treasures of Chiang Mai. Constructed of moulded wooden teak panels fitted together and supported by 28 gargantuan teak pillars, the wíhǎan features naga bargeboards inset with coloured mirror mosaic. On display inside are old temple bells, some ceramics, a few old northern-style gilded wooden Buddhas and antique cabinets stacked with old palm-leaf manuscripts. Also in the compound are some old monastic quarters.

There's a wall dividing Wat Phan Tao from Wat Chedi Luang, but you can walk through small gates from one to the other. Across Thanon Ratchadamnoen from here, at the Thanon Phra Pokklao intersection, is an uninteresting monument marking the spot where King Mengrai was struck by lightning!

Wat Jet Yot
วัดเจ็ดยอด

Out of town on the northern highway loop near the Chiang Mai National Museum, this wát was built in the mid-15th century to host the eighth World Buddhist Council in 1477. Based on the design of the Mahabodhi

Temple in Bodhgaya, India, the proportions for the Chiang Mai version are quite different from the Indian original, so it was probably modelled from a small votive tablet depicting the Mahabodhi in distorted perspective. The seven spires (*jèt yâwt*) represent the seven weeks Buddha was supposed to have spent in Bodhgaya after his enlightenment.

On the outer walls of the old wíhǎan is some of the original stucco relief. There's an adjacent stupa of undetermined age and a very glossy wíhǎan. The entire area is surrounded by well-kept lawns. It's a pleasant, relaxing temple to visit, although curiously it's not very active in terms of worship.

Wat Jet Yot is a bit too far from the city centre to reach on foot; by bicycle it's easy or you can take a red *sǎwngthǎew* (also written *songthaew*).

Wat Suan Dok
วัดสวนดอก

Built in 1383, the large , open wíhǎan was rebuilt in 1932. The bòt contains a 500-year-old bronze Buddha image and vivid *jataka* (Buddha's past-life stories) murals. Amulets and Buddhist literature printed in English and Thai can be purchased at quite low prices in the wíhǎan.

In the grounds is a group of whitewashed Lanna stupas, framed by Doi Suthep. The large central stupa contains a Buddha relic that supposedly self-multiplied. One relic was mounted on the back of a white elephant (commemorated by Chiang Mai's Pratu Chang Pheuak), which was allowed to wander until it 'chose' a site on which a wát could be built to enshrine it. The elephant stopped and died at a spot on Doi Suthep, where Chiang Mai residents built Wat Phra That Doi Suthep (see Doi Suthep under Around Chiang Mai later in this chapter).

Wat Ku Tao
วัดกู่เต้า

North of the moat, near Chiang Mai Stadium, Wat Ku Tao dates from 1613 and has a unique chedi that looks like a pile of diminishing spheres, said to be of possible Yunnanese design. Note the amusing sculptures on the outer wall of the wát.

Wat U Mong
วัดอุโมงค์

This forest wát was first used during King Mengrai's rule in the 14th century. Brick-lined tunnels in an unusual large, flat-topped hill were supposedly fashioned around 1380 for the clairvoyant monk Thera Jan. The monastery was abandoned at a later date and wasn't reinstated until a local Thai prince sponsored a restoration in the late 1940s. The late Ajahn Buddhadasa, a well-known monk and teacher at Southern Thailand's Wat Suanmok, sent several monks to re-establish a monastic community at U Mong in the 1960s. One building contains modern artwork by various monks who have resided at U Mong, including several foreigners. A marvellously grisly image of the fasting Buddha – ribs, veins and all – can be seen in the grounds on top of the tunnel hill, along with a very large chedi. Also in the grounds is a small lake.

A small library/museum with English-language books on Buddhism is also on the premises. Resident foreign monks give talks in English on Sunday afternoons at 3 pm by the lake.

To get to Wat U Mong, travel west on Thanon Suthep for about 2km and take the signed left turn past Phayom Market (Talat Phayom), then follow the signs for another 2km to Wat U Mong. Sǎwngthǎew to Doi Suthep also pass the turn-off.

Wiang Kum Kam
เวียงกุมกาม

These excavated ruins are near Mae Nam Ping, 5km south of the city via Hwy 106 (Thanon Chiang Mai-Lamphun). Apparently this was the earliest historical settlement in the Chiang Mai area, established by the Mon in the 11th or 12th century (before King Mengrai's reign, although the city's founding is often mistakenly attributed to Mengrai) as a satellite town for the Hariphunchai kingdom. The city was abandoned in the early 18th century due to massive flooding, and visible architectural remains are few – only the four-sided Mon-style chedi of Wat Chedi Si Liam and the layered brick pediments of Wat Kan Thom (the Mon name; in Thai the temple was known as Wat Chang Kham) are left. Chedi Si

Liam is said to have been inspired by the similar chedi at Wat Kukut in Lamphun.

Altogether, over 1300 inscribed stone slabs, bricks, bells and stupas have been excavated at the site – all are currently being translated at Chiang Mai University. So far, the most important archaeological discovery has been a four-piece inscribed stone slab now on display in the Chiang Mai National Museum. These early 11th century inscriptions indicate that the Thai script actually predates King Ramkhamhaeng's famous Sukhothai inscription (introduced in 1293) by 100 or more years.

The stones display writing in three scripts of varying ages; the earliest is Mon, the latest is classical Sukhothai script, while the middle-period inscription is proto-Thai. Historical linguists studying the slabs now say that the Thai script was developed from Mon models, later to be modified by adding Khmer characteristics. This means Ramkhamhaeng was not the 'inventor' of the script as previously thought, but more of a would-be reformer. His reformations appear on only one slab and weren't accepted by contemporaries – his script, in fact, died with him.

An ideal way of getting to Wiang Kum Kam is to hire a bicycle; follow Thanon Chiang Mai-Lamphun south-east about 3km and look for a sign to the ruins on the right. From this junction it's another 2km to the ruins. You could also hire a túk-túk (motorised săamláw, a three-wheeled vehicle) or red săwngthăew to take you there for 50B or 60B (one way). Once you're finished looking around you can walk back to Thanon Chiang Mai-Lamphun and catch a săwngthăew or a blue Chiang Mai-Lamphun bus back into the city.

Other Temples, Shrines & Mosques

Temple freaks looking for more wát energy can check out **Wat Pheuak Hong**, behind Buak Hat Park off Thanon Samlan. The locally revered **Chedi Si Pheuak** is over 100 years old and features the 'stacked spheres' style seen only here and at Wat Ku Tao. Another unique local temple is the Burmese-built **Wat Chiang Yeun** on the northern side of the moat (across Thanon Mani Nopharat), between Pratu Chang Pheuak and the north-eastern corner of the old city.

Besides the large northern-style chedi here, the main attraction is an old Burmese colonial gate and pavilion on the eastern side of the school grounds attached to the wát. It looks like it dropped out of the sky from Yangon or Mandalay.

Three wát along Thanon Tha Phae, **Chetawan**, **Mahawan** and **Bupparam**, feature highly ornate wíhăan and chedi designed by Shan or Burmese artisans; most likely they were originally financed by Burmese teak merchants who immigrated to Chiang Mai 100 years ago or more. Evidence of Burmese influence is easily seen in the abundant peacock symbol (a solar symbol common in Burmese and Shan temple architecture) and the Mandalay-style standing Buddhas found in wall niches. At Wat Mahawan no two guardian deity sculptures are alike; the whimsical forms include monkeys or dogs playing with lions and various mythical creatures. Wat Bupparam contains a precious little bòt constructed of teak and decorated in the Chiang Mai style. In one corner of the compound sit two spirit shrines, one for Jao Phaw Dam, another for Jao Phaw Daeng (Holy Father Black and Holy Father Red).

Wat Chai Phra Kiat, on Thanon Ratchadamnoen a block-and-a-half east of Wat Phra Singh, contains a huge bronze Buddha cast by order of a Burmese military commander in 1565. **Wat Sisuphan**, on Thanon Wualai south of the moat, was founded in 1502 but little remains of the original structures except for some teak pillars and roof beams in the wíhăan. The murals inside show an interesting mix of Taoist, Zen and Theravada Buddhist elements. Wat Sisuphan is one of the few wát in Chiang Mai where you can see the Poy Luang (Poy Sang Long) Festival, a Shan-style group ordination of young boys as Buddhist novices, in late March.

Muslim, Hindu & Sikh Of the 12 mosques in Chiang Mai, the oldest and most interesting is **Matsayit Chiang Mai** (Chiang Mai Mosque, sometimes called Ban Haw Mosque) on Soi 1, Charoen Prathet, between Thanon Chang Khlan and Thanon Charoen Prathet, not far from the Night Bazaar. Founded by jiin haw (Yunnanese Muslims) over a hundred years ago, it still primarily caters to this unique ethnic

NORTHERN THAILAND

group; you'll hear Yunnanese spoken as often as Thai within the compound. Along this *soi* (lane) are several Yunnanese Muslim restaurants that serve *khâo sàwy kài* (curried chicken and noodles) as a speciality.

The most colourful of Chiang Mai's two Hindu temples is the brightly painted, traditional mandir and sikhara **Devi Mandir Chiang Mai** on Thanon Ratanakosin, opposite Chiang Mai Stadium. At **Siri Guru Singh Sabha**, a Sikh temple off Thanon Charoenrat (behind Wat Ketkaram), free *prasada* (blessed vegetarian food) is distributed to temple-goers on Friday morning.

Namdhari Sikh Temple, on Thanon Ratchawong between Thanon Chang Moi and Thanon Tha Phae, is the place of worship for the Namdhari sect of Sikhism.

Chiang Mai National Museum
พิพิธภัณฑสถานแห่งชาติเชียงใหม่

The museum has a good selection of Buddha images in all styles, including a very large bronze Buddha downstairs. Pottery is also displayed downstairs (note the 'failed' jar on the stairs), while upstairs there are household and work items. Look for the amusing wooden 'dog' used for spinning thread.

The museum is open 9 am to 4 pm Wednesday to Sunday. Admission is 20B. The museum is close to Wat Jet Yot on Hwy 11 (also called Superhighway Rd), which curves around the city.

Tribal Museum
พิพิธภัณฑ์ชาวเขา

Originally established in 1965 on the ground floor of the Tribal Research Institute on Chiang Mai University campus, this teaching museum moved to its new location overlooking a lake in Ratchamangkhala Park on the northern outskirts of the city in 1997. The new, octagonal facility houses a large collection of handicrafts, costumes, jewellery, ornaments, household utensils, agricultural tools, musical instruments and ceremonial paraphernalia, along with various informative displays concerning the cultural features and backgrounds of each of the major hill

tribes in Thailand. There is also an exhibition on activities carried out by the Thai royal family on behalf of the hill tribes, as well as various bits of research and development sponsored by governmental and nongovernmental agencies.

Slide and video shows are presented daily from 10 am to 2 pm. General museum hours are 9 am to 4 pm weekdays except public holidays. Admission is free.

Night Bazaar
The Night Bazaar, arguably Chiang Mai's biggest tourist attraction, is in fact the legacy of the original Yunnanese trading caravans that stopped over here along the ancient trade route between Simao (in China) and Mawlamyaing (on Myanmar's Gulf of Martaban coast).

Today the market sprawls along Thanon Chang Khlan between Thanon Tha Phae and Thanon Si Donchai every night of the year, rain or dry, holiday or no. Made up of several different roofed areas, ordinary glass-fronted shops and dozens of street vendors, the market offers a huge variety of Thai and northern-Thai goods, as well as designer goods (both fake and licensed, so look carefully) at very low prices – if you bargain well. Many importers buy here because the prices are so good, especially when buying in large quantities. You'll also find a smaller selection of goods from India, Nepal and China.

Other Attractions
At the **Old Chiang Mai Cultural Centre** (OCMCC; ☎ 053-274093, 275097, fax 274094), at 185/3 Thanon Wualai, half a kilometre south of the town centre, northern-Thai and hill-tribe dances are performed nightly from 7 to 10 pm. Performances include a *khan tòk* dinner (northern-style food eaten from low round tables) and cost 270B per person. It's a touristy affair but done well. Several big hotels around town offer similar affairs, but the OCMCC was the first and is still the best.

Anusawari Sam Kasat (Three Kings Monument) on Thanon Phra Pokklao towards the THAI office, is a set of three bronze sculptures depicting Phaya Ngam Meuang, Phaya Mengrai and Phaya Khun Ramkhamhaeng, the three northern

Caravans of Northern Thailand

Dating from at least the 15th century, Chinese-Muslim caravans from Yunnan Province (China) used Chiang Mai as a 'back-door' entry and exit for commodities transported between China and the Indian Ocean port of Mawlamyaing (Moulmein) in Myanmar (Burma) for international seagoing trade.

British merchant Ralph Fitch, the first person to leave an English-language chronicle of South-East Asian travel, wrote of his 1583 to 1591 journey through Thailand: 'To the town of Jamahey (Chiang Mai) come many merchants out of China, and bring a great store of Muske, Gold, Silver, and many other things of China worke'.

The main means of transport for the Yunnanese caravaneers were mules and ponies, beasts of burden that contrasted with the South-East Asian preference for oxen, water buffalo and elephants. The Chinese Muslims who dominated the caravan traffic owed their preferred mode of conveyance, as well as their religious orientation, to mass conversions effected during the Mongol invasions of Yunnan in the 13th century. The equestrian nature of the caravans led the Thais to call the Yunnanese *jiin haw*, 'galloping Chinese'.

Three main routes emanated from the predominantly Thai Xishuangbanna (Sipsongpanna) region in southern Yunnan into Northern Thailand, and onward to the Gulf of Martaban via Mawlamyaing. The western route proceeded south-west from Simao to Chiang Rung (now known as Jinghong), then went on through Chiang Tung (Kengtung) to Fang or Chiang Rai.

The middle route went south to Mengla near the border of China and Laos, crossed Laos via Luang Nam Tha, and entered what is today Thailand at Chiang Khong (which was an independent principality at the time) on the Mekong River. At this point the middle route merged with the western route at Chiang Rai Province, and formed a single route through Chiang Mai to Mae Sariang, a line that continued along the Salawin River to Mawlamyaing in present-day Mayanmar.

The third route went from Simao to Phongsali in northern Laos then via Luang Prabang (Laos), crossing the Mekong River to Meuang Nan and Meuang Phrae (now Nan and Phrae Provinces) before curving north-westward via Lampang and Lamphun to Chiang Mai.

Principal southward exports along these routes included silk, opium, tea, dried fruit, lacquerware, musk, ponies and mules, while northward the caravans brought gold, copper, cotton, edible birds' nests, betel nut, tobacco and ivory. By the end of the 19th century many artisans from China, northern Burma and Laos had settled in the area to produce crafts for the steady flow of regional trade. The city's original transhipment point for such trade movements was a market district known as Ban Haw, a stozne's throw from today's Night Bazaar in Chiang Mai.

NORTHERN THAILAND

Thai–Lao kings most associated with early Chiang Mai history.

Buak Hat Park, in the south-western corner of the moat, is Chiang Mai's miniature counterpart to Bangkok's Lumphini Park, with very pleasant grass expanses, fountains and palms; many people jog here. The **Chiang Mai University** campus on Thanon Huay Kaew is another quiet place to wander around. It's also interesting in the evenings, with a busy night bazaar of its own.

Out towards Doi Suthep, 6km from the town centre, are the shady, nicely landscaped, hilly Chiang Mai Zoo (☎ 053-221179) and the nearby Chiang Mai Arboretum. Zoo admission costs 30B for adults, 5B for children; you can drive a vehicle through the zoo grounds for 30B per car or truck and 10B for a motorcycle or bicycle. Except for the name of each species, most signs are in Thai only. Apparently over 5000 birds (150 species) fly about the zoo's Nakhon Ping Birdwatching Park.

A few snack vendors scattered around the park offer simple rice and noodle dishes. The park is open daily from 8 am to 5 pm. The quiet, lush arboretum is a favourite local jogging spot.

Along the same road nearby are the **Huay Kaew Fitness Park** and **Nam Tok Huay Kaew** (Huay Kaew Falls).

The slightly spooky **Foreign Cemetery** off Thanon Chiang Mai-Lamphun near the Gymkhana Club, contains some 100-year-old headstones bearing American, English and European names marking the remains of traders, missionaries and various other expats who have died in Chiang Mai. A bronze statue of Queen Victoria, imported from Calcutta, India, during the Raj era, stands sentinel.

Aeronautics

The Chiang Mai Flying Club (☎/fax 053-200515, ✉ alpharom@samart.co.th), based at an airstrip in Lamphun but with a Chiang Mai office at 185/12 Thanon Wualai, offers pilot training as well as sightseeing flights. The latter run a half to 1½ hours, depending on the route (most are in the Lampang and Lamphun areas).

These flights cost from 1500B to 5500B per person, depending on the length of the flight and number of people. The cost includes transfers from Chiang Mai to Lam-

phun, the services of the pilot (also the guide) and membership in the club.

Overnight trips to Chiang Rai and Mae Hong Son are also offered for 8480B to 11,460B, depending on the number of people. The price includes transfers from Chiang Mai, a day tour of the region by road, and accommodation.

The planes appear to be in fine condition. A basic six-month flying course costs 12,000B; other programs are also available. Sightseeing flights can also be booked through Chiang Mai Newsletter (☎ 053-225201).

An ultralight-aircraft operation calling itself Microlite offers 15-minute flights over the Doi Saket area for 1200B per person. Contact Khun Prayot at ☎ 01-993 6861.

Bowling

Bully Bowl (☎ 053-224444 ext 19015) is a new bowling alley on the 4th floor of the Kad Suan Kaew shopping centre on Thanon Huay Kaew. Games cost 60B to 90B per person. UFO Bowling (☎ 053-801446), the first bowling alley in Chiang Mai, is behind the Mae Ping Police Station on Thanon Chiang Mai-Lamphun.

Cycling

The Chiang Mai Bicycle Club (☎ 053-943018) organises a trip almost every Sunday, starting between 7 and 7.30 am from the square in front of Pratu Tha Phae. These trips typically take routes outside of town.

Jogging

Top spots for joggers are Buak Hat Park, the Chiang Mai Arboretum and the fitness park at Maharaj Hospital on Thanon Suthep. There are also tracks at Chiang Mai Stadium and at Chiang Mai University.

Hash House Harriers The Chiang Mai Harriers (☎ 053-206822) meet each Saturday at the H3 Pub on the corner of Thanon Moon Muang and Soi 2, Thanon Moon Muang, and organise a 'hash' (foot race) at various locations in the area. Call for times.

Lanna Wedding Ceremonies

A traditional northern-Thai wedding ceremony (or renewal-of-vows ceremony) with full Lanna costuming, a temple blessing,

Túk-túk in front of the Y2K Pub in Phitsanulok

A night market in Chiang Mai

Talat Warorot (Warorot market), Chiang Mai

A great place to shop – the Night Bazaar, Chiang Mai

Elephants used to be the superweapons of the Thai army; now even log-pushing is a rare job.

A farmer tends his corn crops, Chiang Mai Province.

Memento of a tragic past – the Bridge on the River Kwai, Kanchanaburi Province

Muay thai (Thai boxing) – a great spectacle, but don't go to see it if you're squeamish.

elephant ride and khan tòk dinner in an old house by Mae Nam Ping, can be arranged through Chiang Mai Travel Centre (☎ 053-221692, 217450) at 5 Thanon Nimanhemin.

Muay Thai

Lanna Muay Thai (☎/fax 053-221621, 📧 andyboxing@hotmail.com), also known by its Thai name, Kiatbusaba, at 64/1 Soi Chiang Khian, off Thanon Huay Kaew, is a boxing camp that offers authentic *muay thai* (Thai boxing) instruction to foreigners as well as Thais. Several Lanna students have won stadium bouts, including the famous *kàthoey* (male transvestite) boxer Parinya Kiatbusaba (it's a tradition in Thailand for fighters to take the camp name as their ring surname), who wore lipstick and pink nail polish to his national weigh-in, then triumphed at Lumphini stadium in Bangkok. For nonresident boxers, training is held from 4 to 8 pm daily, while resident trainees also have morning sessions. Rates are 250B a day or 7000B a month; simple camp accommodation is available for 3000B a month. Thai food is available at low cost, Western food more expensively. According to the camp's management: 'Foreign boxers are much sought after and we offer match-ups with local boxers for all levels of competition'. Lanna Muay Thai maintains a Web site at www.asiaplus.com/lannamuaythai/.

Swimming

Landlocked Chiang Mai can get very hot, particularly from March to July. Fortunately, local opportunities for a refreshing swim – providing an alternative to the usual tourist solution (vegetating in refrigerated rooms most of the day) – are many.

City Pools Chiang Mai has several swimming pools for public use; you can pay on a per-day basis, or buy an annual membership. Typical per-use fees range from 20B to 50B (public pools are cheaper than hotel or private pools), while annual memberships start at around 200B and go up to 300B.

Amari Rincome Hotel (☎ 053-894884) Thanon Huay Kaew at Thanon Nimanhemin
Chiang Mai University (☎ 053-221699)
    Faculty of Education, Thanon Huay Kaew
Maharaj (Suandok) Hospital (☎ 053-221699)
    Faculty of Medicine, Thanon Suthep
Physical Education College (☎ 053-213629)
    Chiang Mai Stadium, Thanon Sanam Kila
Pongpat Swimming Pool (☎ 053-212812) 73/2 Thanon Chotana
Top North Guest House (☎ 053-278900) 15 Soi 2, Thanon Moon Muang

Huay Teung Tao Reservoir This sizable lake about 12km north-west of the city is a great place for an all-day swim and picnic, especially during the hotter months. Windsurfing equipment can be rented for around 150B an hour. By car or motorcycle you can get to Huay Teung Tao by driving 10km north on Rte 107 (follow signs towards Mae Rim), then west 2km past an army camp to the reservoir.

Cyclists would do best to pedal to the reservoir via Thanon Chonlaprathan. Head west on Thanon Huay Kaew, then turn right just before the canal. Follow Thanon Chonlaprathan north until it ends at a smaller road between the reservoir and the highway; turn left here and you'll reach the lake after another kilometre or so of pedalling. From the north-western corner of the moat, the 12km bike ride takes about an hour.

If you don't bring your own, food is available from vendors at the lake, who spread mats out for people to sit on. Fishing is permitted if you'd like to try your luck at hooking lunch.

Tennis

Anantasiri Tennis Courts (☎ 053-222210), off Hwy 11 and opposite the Chiang Mai National Museum, is the best public tennis facility in Chiang Mai. The eight courts are illuminated at night, and you can hire a 'knocker' (tennis opponent) for a reasonable hourly fee in addition to the regular court fee.

Other places with public tennis courts include:

Chiang Mai Land Village (☎ 053-272821)
Thanon Chiang Mai Land
Gymkhana Club (☎ 053-241035) Thanon Rat
Uthit
Lanna Sports Club (☎ 053-221911) Thanon
Chotana

There are also public tennis courts at the Amari Rincome Hotel on Thanon Huay Kaew.

Courses

Language & Culture The basic Thai course at American University Alumni (AUA; ☎ 053-278407, 211377, fax 211973), at 73 Thanon Ratchadamnoen, consists of three levels with 60 hours of instruction; there are also 30-hour courses in 'small talk', reading and writing and northern Thai. Costs range from 2700B for the reading and writing and northern-Thai courses to 3500B per level for the 60-hour courses. Private tutoring is also available at 220B per hour.

The Australia Centre (☎ 053-810552, fax 810554), at Soi 5, Thanon Suthep, at the back of Chiang Mai University in an old traditional Thai house, offers a 30-hour course in 'survival Thai' over a two-week period.

Payap University (☎ 053-304805 ext 250/251, fax 245353) offers intensive 30- and 60-hour Thai language courses at beginning, intermediate and advanced levels; these focus on conversational skills, as well as on elementary reading and writing, and Thai culture. Costs for each course are 3000B (30 hours) and 6000B (60 hours). Payap University also offers a Thai Studies Certificate Program, which involves two semesters of classroom lectures and field trips. These consist of 12 hours of Thai language study and an additional 18 hours of electives such as Foundations of Thai Music, Thai Drama and Dance, Survey of Thai History, Buddhist Traditions and Contemporary Thai Politics. Costs include a US$40 application fee, plus US$1500 for tuition. Single courses can be taken for 3500B each.

Cooking The central Chiang Mai Thai Cookery School (☎ 053-206388, fax 399036, ℮ nabnian@loxinfo.co.th), at 1–3 Thanon Moon Muang opposite Pratu Tha Phae, offers one-, two- and three-day courses in Thai cooking, starting at 800B.

The classes come highly recommended and include an introduction to Thai herbs and spices, a local market tour, cooking instructions and a recipe booklet. Of course, you get to eat the delicious Thai food as well – everything from Chiang Mai–style chicken curry to steamed banana cake.

The success of the Chiang Mai Thai Cookery School has inspired the establishment of several similarly named cooking classes in the city, and virtually every guesthouse in Chiang Mai offers to arrange cooking classes for rates of 700B to 800B a day.

We've also received good reports about the following:

Baan Thai (☎ 053-357339, ℮ baanthai@
yahoo.com) 11 Soi 5, Thanon Ratchadamnoen
Gap's Thai Culinary Art School (☎/fax 053-
278140, ℮ gap_house@hotmail.com) 3 Soi
4, Thanon Ratchadamnoen
Siam Thai Cookery School (☎ 053-271169,
fax 208950) 5/2 Soi 1, Thanon Loi Kroh
Sompet Thai Cookery School (☎/fax 053-
280901, ℮ sompet41@chmai.loxinfo.co.th)
Chiang Inn Plaza, 100/1 Thanon Chang
Khlan

Traditional Massage Over the years Chiang Mai has become a centre for Thai massage studies. Not all of the places purporting to teach massage are equally good. The oldest and most popular place to study is the Old Medicine Hospital (OMH; ☎ 053-275085) on Soi Siwaka Komarat off Thanon Wualai, opposite the Old Chiang Mai Cultural Centre. The 11-day course runs daily from 9 am to 4 pm and costs around 3180B, including all teaching materials. There are two courses a month year-round except for the first two weeks of April.

The OMH curriculum is very traditional, with a northern-Thai slant (the Thai name for the institute actually means Northern Traditional Healing Hospital). Classes tend to be large during the months of December to February.

Another highly recommended source of instruction is Lek Chaiya (☎ 053-278325, ✉ tanavid@loxinfo.co.th) at 25 Thanon Ratchadamnoen. Khun Lek is a Thai woman who has been massaging and teaching for 40 years, specialising in *jàp sên* (nerve-touch healing massage) and the use of medicinal herbs. Classic Touch vegetarian restaurant is on the premises.

A unique, one-on-one course is available at Ban Nit, Soi 2, Thanon Chaiyaphum. The teacher is Nit, an older woman who is a specialist in deep-tissue, nerve and herbal massages. Her methods were handed down from a long line of ancestral Chinese healers. Length of study and payment for Nit's tutelage is up to the individual – according to what you can afford – but all studies begin with an offering of nine flowers to nine Chinese deities. Nit doesn't speak English so you must know some Thai, although much of the teaching is unspoken. Most students live in and eat meals with Nit and her family while studying. If you want to try Nit's massage talents, you have to pay a minimum of 9B to the same deities; most people pay 100B an hour.

International Training Massage (☎ 053-218632, ✉ itm@infothai.com) at 171/7 Thanon Morakot in Santitham features another OMH-inspired curriculum with a five-day, 1800B course. Reports suggest that large class sizes can be a problem here.

Buddhist Meditation Not far from Wat U Mong, Wat Ram Poeng is a large monastery that supports the well-known Northern Insight Meditation Centre (☎ 053-278620), where many foreigners have studied vipassana. One-month individual courses are taught by a Thai monk, with Western students or bilingual Thais acting as interpreters. A reasonably large *Tripitaka* (Buddhist scriptures) library houses versions of the Theravada Buddhist canon in Pali, Thai, Chinese, English and other languages.

The formal name for this wát is Wat Tapotaram. To get there by public transport, take a sǎwngthǎew west on Thanon Suthep to Phayom Market. From Phayom Market, take a sǎwngthǎew south along Thanon Khlong Chonlaprathan about a kilometre and get off when you see the wát entrance on the right. Or charter a sǎwngthǎew or túk-túk all the way.

Meditation can also be learned from the monks at Wat U Mong. The best way to arrange something is to attend one of the Sunday talks (see the Wat U Mong entry earlier in this chapter).

Monk Chat Every Monday, Wednesday and Friday from 5 to 7 pm, a room at Wat Suan Dok is set aside for foreigners to meet and chat with novice monks studying at the monastic university on the monastery grounds. It's free, and provides an opportunity for the monastic students to practise their English and for foreigners to learn about Buddhism and Thai life. To reach the room, enter the wát from the main entrance on Thanon Suthep and walk straight past the large wíhǎan to a smaller building 100m or so into the temple grounds. Turn right at this smaller temple, and watch for the 'Monk Chat' signs pointing out the way. The monastery asks that visitors dress modestly – covered shoulders, no shorts or short skirts – and that women visitors take care not to make physical contact with the monks.

Yoga & Hindu Meditation Hatha yoga classes with Marcel Kraushaar (☎/fax 053-271555, ✉ marcelandyoga@hotmail.com), at 129/79 Chiang Mai Villa 1, Pa Daet intersection, meet from 5.30 to 7.30 am and 5 to 7 pm weekdays only.

Brahma Kumari's Raja Yoga (☎ 053-214904) has a centre at 218/6 Thanon Chotana in northern Chiang Mai. Raja Yoga (literally meaning 'kingly yoga', which is a Hindu version of meditation and self-inquiry) teaches a seven-step course involving the essential topics of self, god, karma, cycles, lifestyles and powers. Founded in northern India in the 20th century, this version of meditation study is basically an adaptation of Upanishad-inspired Hinduism. 'Creative meditation', held every Wednesday evening, mixes group therapy, visualisation, inquiry and other noncontemplative activities.

Informal Northern Thai Group

The 16-year-old Informal Northern Thai Group (INTG) meets every second Tuesday of the month at 7.30 pm at the Alliance Française, 138 Thanon Charoen Prathet. The usual evening format involves a lecture from a resident or visiting academic on some aspect of Thailand or South-East Asia, followed by questions and answers and an informal drink afterwards at a local bar or restaurant. Some of the more recent topics have included 'Community Forestry in Northern Thailand' and 'Is Thailand One of the Few Non-Homophobic Countries in the World?' A donation of 20B is requested for operational expenses.

River Cruises

From a small pier on Mae Nam Ping behind Wat Chaimongkhon on Thanon Charoen Prathet, you can take a two-hour tour of the river in a roofed boat for 300B per person. The boat stops at a small fruit farm about 40 minutes away where free samples and a beverage are provided. The tours run from 8.30 am to 5 pm daily. There is also a Thai dinner cruise from 7.15 to 9.30 pm, with a set menu for 400B per person. Alcoholic drinks cost extra. Call ☎ 053-274822 for more information.

Ferries also depart for river tours six times daily between 10 am and 3 pm from a landing north of Saphan Nawarat, just south of the Riverside Bar & Restaurant. The fare is 100B per person return. Call ☎ 01-885 0663 for more details.

Events

The week-long Winter Fair (thêtsàkaan ngaan reuduu nǎo) in late December and early January is a great occasion, as is the April Songkran Water Festival, which is celebrated here with an enthusiasm bordering on pure pandemonium. In late January the Bo Sang Umbrella Festival (thêtsàkaan rôm) features a colourful umbrella procession during the day and a night-time lantern procession. Although it sounds touristy, this festival is actually a very Thai affair; one of the highlights is the many northern-Thai music ensembles that give performances in shopfronts along Bo Sang's main street.

Perhaps Chiang Mai's most colourful festival is the Flower Festival (thêtsàkaan mái dàwk mái pràdàp), also called the Flower Carnival, which is held annually in February (actual dates vary from year to year). Events occur over a three-day period and include displays of flower arrangements, a long parade of floats decorated with hundreds of thousands of flowers, folk music, cultural performances and the Queen of the Flower Festival contest. Most activities are centred at Buak Hat Park near the south-western corner of the city moats. People from all over the province and the rest of the country turn out for this occasion, so book early if you want a room in town.

In May the Intakin Festival (ngaan tham bun sǎo inthákin), held at Wat Chedi Luang and centred around the city làk meuang, propitiates the city's guardian deity to ensure that the annual monsoon will arrive on time. Also in May – when the mango crop is ripe – a Mango Fair (thêtsàkaan mámûang) is celebrated in Buak Hat Park with lots of mango eating and the coronation of the Mango Queen.

During the festival of Loi Krathong, usually celebrated in late October or early November, Chiang Mai's river banks are crowded with people floating the small lotus-shaped boats that mark this occasion. In Chiang Mai this festival is also known as Yi Peng, and some khon meuang celebrate by launching cylindrical-shaped hot-air balloons, lighting up the night skies with hundreds of pinpoints of light.

Places to Stay – Budget

At any one time there are about 300 hotels and guesthouses operating in Chiang Mai. Room prices range from 50B for a single room at Isra House to US$320 for a garden-view room at the Regent Chiang Mai. As elsewhere in Thailand, at the cheaper hotels 'single' means a room with one large bed (big enough for two) while 'double' means a room with two beds; the number of people staying in the room is irrelevant.

Guesthouses These are clustered in several areas: along Thanon Moon Muang (the inside of the east moat) and on streets of Thanon Moon Muang; along several sois running south off Thanon Tha Phae; along Thanon Charoen Prathet, parallel to and west of Mae Nam Ping; and along Thanon

Charoenrat east of Mae Nam Ping. Several others are scattered elsewhere around the western side of Chiang Mai.

The best Chiang Mai guesthouses are those owned and managed by local families, rather than Bangkok Thais out for a quick buck. There are basically two kinds of budget guesthouse accommodation – old family homes converted into guest rooms (these usually have the best atmosphere although the least privacy) and hotel- or apartment-style places with rows of cell-like rooms. In both, the furnishings are basic – a bed and a few sticks of furniture. Usually you must supply your own towel and soap; the rooms are cleaned only after guests leave. You can assume that rooms under 100B will not have a private bathroom but will probably have a fan.

The cheaper guesthouses make most of their money from food service and hill-tribe trekking rather than from room charges, hence you may be pressured to eat and to sign up for a trek. Places that charge 250B or more don't usually hassle guests in this way.

Many of the guesthouses can arrange bicycle and motorcycle rental. If you phone a guesthouse, most will collect you from the train or bus terminal for free if they have a room (this saves them having to pay a commission to a driver).

The following list is not exhaustive but covers most of the more reliable, long-running places. Guesthouses that belong to the Chiangmai Northern Guest House Club (☎ 053-217513) are probably more secure in terms of theft than those that are not. As members pay government taxes, they are generally more interested in long-term operation. Members also meet regularly to discuss tourism issues, accommodation standards and room rates. The TAT office on Thanon Chiang Mai-Lamphun can provide an up-to-date list of members.

Inner Moat Area Banana Guest House (☎ 053-206285, fax 275077, 4/9 Thanon Ratchaphakhinai), near Pratu Chiang Mai, is a small but friendly place with dorm beds for just 70B, plus rooms with private hot-water shower for just 100/120B single/double. Banana Guest House is often full in high season. Call for free transport. ***Pha Thai*** (☎ 053-278013, fax 274075, 48/1

Thanon Ratchaphakhinai), in the same quiet south-eastern corner of the inner moat area, has clean rooms with fans in a modest three-storey building with private solar-heated showers for 200B to 250B a night.

Near the Library Service off Soi 2, Thanon Moon Muang, ***New Saitum Guest House*** (☎ 053-278575) offers basic, well-worn but relatively livable wooden bungalows with private bathroom and balconies in a quiet setting for a bargain 90B to 150B. Almost opposite on the same soi, ***Somwang Guest House*** (☎ 053-278505) used to have rooms in some older buildings for 80/150B, but they've recently been torn down, and will probably be replaced with something more expensive. They still have rooms in a newer, two-storey building for 150B with private hot-water shower.

Farther along this soi, almost at the corner with Thanon Ratchamankha, rooms at ***Smile House*** (☎ 053-208661, fax 208663), in an old Thai house surrounded by a row of newer rooms, cost 250B single/double with fan, 400B single/double air-con with TV. The charming outdoor eating area attached to the renovated house is a plus. Historical footnote: This house once served as the 'safe house' of infamous Shan-Chinese opium warlord Khun Sa whenever he came to Chiang Mai. The guesthouse rents motorcycles and bicycles and offers other travel services as well.

The friendly and centrally located ***Chiang Mai Garden Guest House*** (☎/fax 053-278881, 82–86 Thanon Ratchamankha) has clean rooms in an ageing two-storey building close to Heuan Phen, Mit Mai and several other restaurants. Wat Chedi Luang is in the next block. Singles/doubles cost 120B with fan and bathroom, 350B with air-con. There's also one large room with a fan that will sleep three/four for 150/200B. The Thai woman owner speaks French, German and English. Chiang Mai Garden will not pay commissions to túk-túk or săwngthăew drivers; call the guesthouse for free transport.

Eagle House 2 (☎ 053-210620, fax 216368, 26 Soi 2, Thanon Ratwithi), right around the corner from Irish Pub and convenient to several Thai bars along Thanon Ratwithi, is a newer, nicer branch of the original Eagle House (see under Pratu Tha Phae to the River later in this section). The three-storey, modern building has a pleasant garden

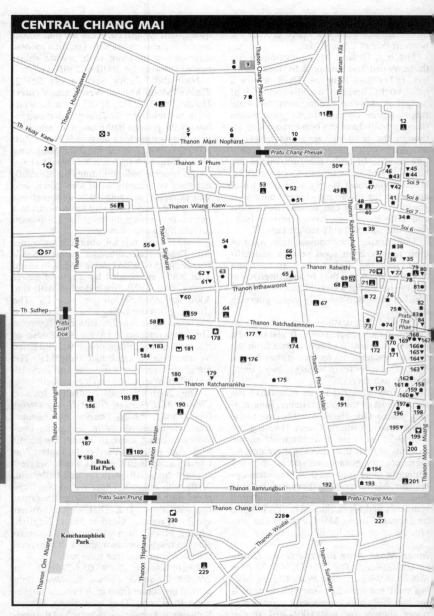

CENTRAL CHIANG MAI

Thanon Chang Pheuak

Thanon Sanam Kila

Thanon Hutbadsawee

Th Huay Kaew

Thanon Mani Nopharat

Thanon Si Phum

Thanon Wiang Kaew

Thanon Arak

Thanon Singharat

Thanon Ratchaphakhinai

Thanon Ratwithi

Thanon Inthawararot

Thanon Ratchadamnoen

Thanon Phra Pokklao

Thanon Moon Muang

Thanon Ratchamankha

Thanon Bunreuangrit

Thanon Samlan

Th Suthep

Pratu Suan Dok

Pratu Chang Pheuak

Pratu Tha Phae

Pratu Chiang Mai

Pratu Suan Prung

Buak Hat Park

Kanchanaphisek Park

Thanon Om Muang

Thanon Thiphanet

Thanon Chang Lor

Thanon Wualai

Thanon Sunwong

Soi 9
Soi 8
Soi 7
Soi 6

CENTRAL CHIANG MAI

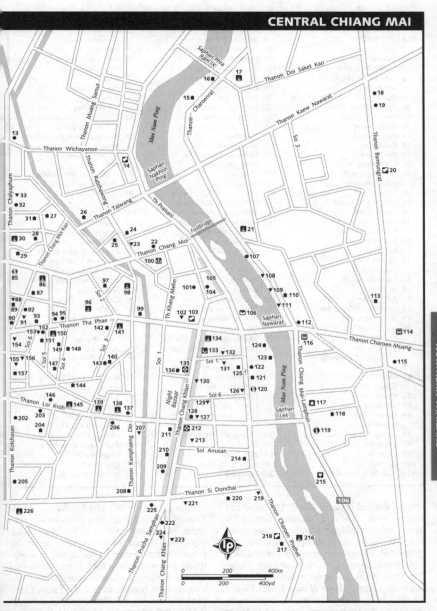

NORTHERN THAILAND

CENTRAL CHIANG MAI

PLACES TO STAY

2   Sri Tokyo Hotel
6   Northern Inn
7   Chang Peuk Hotel
9   Novotel Chiang Mai
15 Je t'Aime
16 Pun Pun Guest House
24 New Mitrapap Hotel
25 New Asia Hotel
26 Prince Hotel
27 Eagle House 1
28 Pao Come
29 Lek House
31 Orchid House
34 CM Apartments;
    Chiang Mai SP Hotel
36 Eagle House 2
38 Your House Guest House
39 Sumit Hotel
41 Northlands House;
    Lamchang House
43 Supreme House;
    SUP Court
44 SK and Libra
    Guesthouses
47 Paneeda House
48 RCN Court
72 Safe House Court
73 Rendezvous Guest House
75 Nice Apartment
76 Amphawan House, Kavil
    House; Chiang Mai
    White House;
    Chiangmai Kristi House
78 Rama House
82 Moon Meuang
    Golden Court
83 Montri Hotel
87 VK Guest House
89 Daret's House;
    Happy House
93 Roong Ruang Hotel
97 Veerachai Court
99 Tapae Inn
110 Le Pont
113 C&C Teak House

118 Ben Guest House
121 Diamond Riverside Hotel
123 River View Lodge
124 Galare Guest House
125 Porn Ping Tower Hotel
128 Royal Lanna
136 Chiang Inn
140 Fang Guest House
142 Tapae Place Hotel
143 Ratchada Guest House
144 Flamingo
147 Sarah Guest House
148 Midtown House; Thana;
    Baan Jongcome
149 Thapae
151 Living House
157 Little Home Guest House
158 Somwang Guest House
161 Smile Guest House
162 New Saitum Guest House;
    Library Service
171 Gap's House
175 Chiang Mai Garden
    Guest House
180 Felix City Inn
184 Wanasit Guest House
191 Anodard Hotel
193 Pha Thai Guest House
194 Banana Guest House
198 Muang Thong Hotel;
    Queen Bee
200 Top North Guest House
204 Center Place Guest House
205 Lai Thai Guest House
208 Imperial Mae Ping Hotel
210 Royal Princess
211 Suriwongse Hotel
214 Chiangmai Souvenir
    Guest House
    (Viking Guest House)
217 Baan Kaew Guest House
220 Chiang Mai Plaza Hotel

PLACES TO EAT

5   Asma Restaurant
23 Han Yang Hong Kong

33 Somphet Market
35 Irish Pub
42 Indian Restaurant
    Vegetarian Food
45 Biaporn
46 Kai Yang Isaan
    (SP Chicken)
50 Jok Somphet
52 The Amazing Sandwich
60 Si Phen Restaurant
61 Mangsawirat Kangreuanjan
62 Khao Soi Suthasinee
77 Kitchen Garden
80 Kafé
84 JJ Bakery & Restaurant
88 Thanam Restaurant
91 Da Stefano
102 Bacco
108 The Gallery
109 Good View
111 Riverside Bar & Restaurant
126 Rot Neung
127 Red Lion English Pub &
    Restaurant; German
    Hofbräuhaus; Café
    Benelux; Haus München
129 Shere Shiraz
130 Galare Food Centre
131 Sophia
132 Khao Soi Fuang Fah;
    Khao Soi Islam
153 Dara Steakhouse
154 Art Café
155 Aroon (Rai) Restaurant
156 El Toro
159 Kuaytiaw Reua Koliang
    Restaurant
163 Bierstube;
    Pinte Blues Pub;
    Sax Music Pub
164 Jerusalem Falafel;
    Libernard Café
165 AUM Vegetarian Food
167 Salom Joy
169 Easy Diner
173 Mitmai Restaurant

sitting area and is fairly quiet. Medium-sized rooms with fan and shower cost 170/200/270B single/double/triple, add hot water for 240/320B double/triple, air-con for 290/360B. Dorm beds are also available for 70B. Eagle House 2 offers a cooking course for 700B. A bit farther north along this same soi is the friendly *Your House Guest House* (☎ 053-217492, fax 419093, ⓔ yourhous@ cm.ksc.co.th), with rooms in a teak house for 140/160B single/double (shared hot-water bathroom), or in a cement building for 150/190B (private bathroom).

Along the little, red-bricked soi off Thanon Moon Muang is a plethora of other cheap places in several tacky, newer buildings. Soi 9, off Moon Muang near the north-eastern corner of the moat, is a particularly good area to look if you're having trouble finding a vacant room during festivals such as Songkran and the Flower Festival. On this soi, *SK House* (☎ 053-210690) is OK, with rooms for 150/250B, but if you don't sign up for a trek first, good luck getting a room. Next door, the clean and friendly *Libra Guest House* (☎/fax 053-

CENTRAL CHIANG MAI

177 La Villa Pizzeria
179 Heuan Phen
183 Ta-Krite
188 Rot Sawoei
192 Pratu Chiang Mai
     Night Market
195 Pum Pui Italian Restaurant
207 Kuaytiaw Kai Tun Coke
213 Anusan Market
219 Piccola Roma Palace
221 Whole Earth Restaurant
223 Vihara Liangsan
224 Khao Soi Suthasinee 2

WATS

4   Wat Lokmoli
11   Wat Chiang Yuen
12   Wat Pa Pao
17   Wat Chetuphon
21   Wat Ketkaram
30   Wat Chomphu
40   Wat Lam Chang
49   Wat Chiang Man
53   Wat Hua Khwang
56   Wat Pa Phrao Nai
58   Wat Phra Singh
59   Wat Thung Yu
64   Wat Chai Phra Kiat
67   Wat Duang Dii
68   Wat U Mong Klang
     Wiang
71   Wat Pan Ping
79   Wat Dawk Euang
86   Wat U Sai Kham
96   Wat Chetawan
98   Wat Saen Fang
134 Wat Upakhut
138 Wat Chang Khong
139 Wat Loi Khraw
141 Wat Bupparam
145 Wat Phan Tawng
150 Wat Mahawan
172 Wat Phan An
174 Wat Phan Tao
176 Wat Chedi Luang;
     Wat Phan Tao

182 Wat Si Koet
185 Wat Meun Ngoen Kong
186 Wat Meh Thang
189 Wat Pheuak Hong
190 Wat Phra Jao Mengrai
201 Wat Sai Mun Myanmar
216 Wat Chaimongkhon
226 Wat Pugchang
227 Wat Muang Mang
229 Wat Sisuphan

OTHER

1   Chiang Mai Ram
     Hospital
3   Computer Plaza
8   Velocity
10   DHL
13   Tui Big Bike
14   US Consulate
18   Thai Tribal Crafts
19   British Council
20   UK & Northern Ireland
     Consulate
22   Chip Aun Thong
     Dispensary
32   Ban Nit
37   Yoy Pocket
51   THAI Office
54   Chiang Mai Central
     Prison
55   School
57   Malaria Centre
63   District Offices
65   Anusawari Sam Kasat
66   Post Office
69   Chiang Mai Disabled
     Center (Internet)
70   Voodoo Lounge; X Chap
74   American University Alumni
     (AUA) Library
81   North Wheels
85   Money Exchange
90   Elephant Lightfoot
92   Gecko Books
94   Wild Planet
95   Book Zone

100 Namdhari Sikh Temple
101 Warorot Market
103 Finnish consulate
104 Lamyai Market
105 Flower Market
106 Mae Ping Post Office
107 Brasserie
112 Raintree Resource Centre
114 Buses to Baw Sang &
     San Kamphaeng
115 San Pa Khoi Market
116 Buses to Lamphun, Pasang,
     Chiang Rai & Lampang
117 Tourist Police
119 TAT
120 SK Moneychanger
122 Wild Planet
133 Matsayit Chiang Mai
135 Chiang Inn Plaza
137 Hangdong Rattan
146 The Bookshop
152 Broadway Photo
160 Lost Book Shop
166 Chiang Mai Cookery
     School
168 Lek Chaiya Massage
170 AUA
178 Police (Inside the quadrangle
     on Thanon Ratchadamnoen)
181 Post Office
187 Mengrai Kilns
196 The Loom
197 Mungkala
199 H3 Pub
202 DK Book House
203 Woven Dreams
206 Success Silk Shop
209 Mail Boxes etc
212 Chiangmai Pavilion
215 Gi Gi's
218 Alliance Française;
     French Consulate
222 DHL
225 Suriwong Book Centre
228 Chiang Mai Flying Club
230 Chinese Consulate

NORTHERN THAILAND

210687) has decent rooms with fan and cold-water shower for 100B single/double, 150B with hot water, although they're often full, even in the low season. ***Paneeda House*** (*☎ 053-213156),* a newer three-storey guesthouse on Soi 9 run by an elderly Thai couple, offers clean rooms for 150B per person with fan and shower; this may be a bit overpriced for the area, but the couple are very friendly and they don't push treks, food or anything else.

Others on or off Soi 9, Thanon Moon Muang include ***Supreme House*** (*☎ 053-*

222480, fax 218545), which has rooms in the 100B to 250B range, all with inside bathroom. Nearby, ***SUP Court*** (*☎ 053-210625, 224652)* offers rooms on a monthly basis only, starting at 2000B.

On parallel Soi 7, west of Chiang Mai SP Hotel and CM Apartments, the hotel-like ***Northlands House*** (*☎/fax 053-218860)* offers rooms in the 250B to 350B range. A little farther west on this soi, the more atmospheric ***Lamchang House*** (*☎ 053-210586, 211435)* is a wooden Thai-style house run by a Thai family. Simple rooms with shared toilet, fan and hot-water shower cost 80B to 150B. There is a small garden restaurant and information service.

On Soi 5 off Thanon Moon Muang, modern **Rama House** (☎ *053-216354, fax 225027)* has clean rooms with private facilities in a secure three-storey building for 120B single/double (cold water, fan) and 280B (hot water, air-con).

Wanasit Guest House (☎ *053-814042)* is down a quiet soi next to Ta-Krite restaurant, near Wat Phra Singh. Rooms in a two-storey, modern Thai house cost 150B single/double with bathroom, more with air-con.

Bridging the gap between budget and mid-range places are a couple of comfortable guesthouses in the 180B to 400B range. **Gap's House** (☎/fax *053-278140,* @ *gap_house@hotmail.com, 3 Soi 4, Thanon Ratchadamnoen)*, behind the AUA Thai Language Centre, has northern Thai–style houses built around a quiet garden filled with antiques. All rooms have carpet, air-con and private hot-water showers; rates are 250/390B single/double and include a filling breakfast. Gap's offers a Thai cooking course, as well as a tasty 80B vegetarian buffet from 7 to 9 pm nightly.

On the other side of Thanon Ratchadamnoen down Soi 5 a bit, **Rendezvous Guest House** (☎ *053-213763, fax 419009)* is a three-storey inn costing 180/250B for rooms with fan, 300B for air-con rooms; all with hot water, TV, phone and fridge. Farther north along the same soi is a short string of three- and four-storey apartment-style places: **Kavil Guest House & Restaurant** (☎/fax *053-224740,* @ *kavilgh@chmai .loxinfo.co.th)*, 180B to 360B a night; **Amphawan House** (☎ *053-210584)*, 200B to 250B, less for long-term stays; **Chiang Mai White House** (☎ *053-357130)*, fan rooms 250B, air-con with cable TV 350B, both with attached hot shower; and **Chiangmai Kristi House** (☎ *053-418165)*, 150B to 180B. We especially liked Chiang Mai White House, with its spotless rooms and public areas, nice garden and security; the checkout time is an early 10 am. An advantage of these last four is their quiet location.

Top North Guest House (☎ *053-278900, 278684, fax 278485, 15 Soi 2, Thanon Moon Muang)* is a popular, efficiently run place where rooms cost 300B with fan,

400B with air-con, 500B with TV and bathtub; all rooms come with private hot-water shower. Facilities include a pretty swimming pool and a travel agency.

Safe House Court (☎ *053-418955, 178 Thanon Ratchaphakhinai)*, opposite Wat U Mong Klang Wiang, features very clean air-con rooms with phone, fridge, toilet and hot-water shower, plus daily maid service, for 350B to 400B a night. Monthly rates are available. The semi-classical architecture at Safe House Court is of a more pleasing design than most apartment courts in Chiang Mai.

Head north along Thanon Ratchaphakhinai past Sumit Hotel, then right on Soi 7, to find friendly **RCN Court** (☎ *053-418280–2, 224619, fax 211969,* @ *rcncourt@chm .cscoms.com)*. Although the building exterior isn't as pleasing as that of Safe House Court, it's very clean and offers fax and laundering services, an attached minimart and a small restaurant. The security seems very good. Depending on the season, daily rates run from 300B to 350B (fan), 400B to 480B (air-con), although most residents are staying long term and it can be difficult to find a vacancy. Basic monthly rates of 4000B (fan) to 5500B (air-con), not including electricity and phone charges, are available. Rooms come with private toilet and hot-water shower and medium-sized fridge. A terrace with exercise equipment is available for guest use.

Pratu Tha Phae to the River Across the moat, quite close to Pratu Tha Phae, **Daret's House** (☎ *053-235440, 4/5 Thanon Chaiyaphum)* has stacks of basic, well-worn rooms costing 70/100B single/double for private bathroom with cold-water shower, 80/120B with hot-water shower. The large sidewalk cafe in front is popular. Around the corner on narrow Thanon Chang Moi Kao is the similar-looking but quieter **Happy House** (☎ *053-252619, fax 251871, 11/1 Thanon Chang Moi Kao)*. Large, well-tended rooms with hot-water bathrooms are 100/180B single/double with fan, 280B with air-con.

Down an alley off Thanon Chang Moi Kao is the fairly basic but adequate **VK Guest House** (☎ *053-252559)*, with singles/doubles costing 80B; a triple room with bathroom is available for 40B per person.

Another Chiang Mai original is *Lek House* (☎ 053-252686, e lekhouse@chmai.loxinfo .co.th, 22 Thanon Chaiyaphum), near the Thanon Chang Moi Kao intersection on the soi to Wat Chomphu. Reviews of this place seem to ride a roller coaster; recent renovations and new management should make a difference. Rooms with fan and bathroom are 80/100B downstairs, 100/120B in the larger rooms upstairs. Near Lek House is the OK standby *Pao Come* (☎ 053-252377, 9 Soi 3, Thanon Chang Moi Kao). Singles/ doubles cost 70/100B.

A bit farther north on Soi 3 Thanon Chang Moi Kao, *Eagle House 1* (☎ 053-235387, fax 216368) has simple rooms with private bathroom for 90B single, 120B to 150B double. The staff boast French, German, English and Spanish language skills. The rooms could use some additional maintenance, but at these prices it's hard to complain. Trekking is big here. Farther north at Soi 2, Thanon Chaiyaphum, friendly *Orchid House* (☎ 053-874127) has simple rooms with private shower and balcony in a modern four-storey building for 100B to 150B.

Soi 4, farther east (towards the river) along Thanon Tha Phae, has several newer, two-storey brick guesthouses with downstairs sitting areas: *Midtown House* (☎ 053-273191), *Thapae* (☎ 053-271591) and *Sarah Guest House* (☎ 053-208271), each with good rooms in the 100B to 200B range. All are fine – a step up from the Pratu Tha Phae places – but we'd choose Midtown House for its friendly service and sense of privacy. *Thana Guest House* (☎ 053-279794, fax 272285) caters to Israeli travellers (the management boasts 80% Israeli occupancy), with all signs in Thai and Hebrew. Good rooms with fan and hot water are 160/180B (250/300B with air-con) and there is a small restaurant on the premise serving kosher food. Three-storey *Baan Jongcome* (☎ 053-274823) is a little more upmarket, with comfortable rooms with fan for 350B, air-con 450B. A bit farther down the soi as it turns to the east is *Flamingo*, with four basic rooms in the 120B to 180B range; there's a bar and restaurant with a European menu.

Fang Guest House (☎ 053-282940, 46–48 Soi 1, Thanon Kamphaeng Din) is nearby in a newer, four-storey building well away from traffic. Clean rooms with fan and bathroom are 200/250B single/double and 300B with air-con and carpet. All rooms have solar-heated hot-water showers, but hot water is available in the afternoon only. The small restaurant serves fàràng (Western) food. Over on Soi 3 is *Ratchada Guest House* (☎ 053-275556, 55 Soi 3, Thanon Tha Phae), where quiet rooms with fan and hot-water shower cost 100/150B. On Soi 5, Thanon Tha Phae, about 70m in on the right is *Living House* (☎ 053-275370, e livinghouse@ hotmail.com), with fan rooms in a newer, three-storey building for 150B, air-con rooms for 250B, all with private hot-water facilities.

Towards the mid-range, the efficient *Little Home Guest House* (☎/fax 053-273662, e littleh@loxinfo.co.th, 1/1 Soi 3, Thanon Kotchasan), not far from the moat and DK Book House, offers large, clean, comfortable rooms in a modern Thai-style building for 200/280B single/double. All rooms have air-con and hot-water showers, and the upstairs rooms have private balconies.

Center Place Guest House (☎ 053-271169, fax 208950, e centerplace99@ hotmail.com, 17/2 Soi 1, Thanon Loi Kroh) can be found on a soi off Thanon Loi Kroh, a good street for textile shopping and within walking distance of both the inner moat area and the Night Bazaar. This well-run guesthouse features rooms for 150B single/double with fan and bathroom; the proprietors also offer instruction in Thai cooking.

Chiangmai Souvenir Guest House (☎ 053-818786, 116 Thanon Charoen Prathet), also known as Viking Guest House, is one block east of the Night Bazaar and right around the corner from the Anusan Night Market. It's a pleasant and inexpensive urban haven, complete with an attractive outdoor eating area. Room prices run from 130B to 180B with fan, 330B with air-con.

East of the River South of Saphan Nawarat and down a very narrow soi near the TAT office is the friendly *Ben Guest House* (☎ 053-244103, 4/11 Soi 2, Thanon Chiang Mai-Lamphun), which offers very clean rooms with fan and private hot-water shower in a quiet compound for 150B a

NORTHERN THAILAND

night. Food service is available in an adjacent garden, and the staff can arrange bicycle rentals. Although it's on the eastern side of the river, Ben Guest House is within walking distance of the Night Bazaar.

There is a string of guesthouses along Thanon Charoenrat, parallel to the river – a bit far from the centre of town but recommended for those who are seeking a quiet atmosphere or the scenic river setting. Opposite the Riverside Bar & Restaurant near Saphan Nawarat, *Le Pont* (*☎ 053-241712, fax 243673*) looks impressive, with its office, sitting area and restaurant housed in a 120-year-old teak residence. Air-con guest rooms in an adjacent modern wing cost 550B single/double, or 450B per day for stays of a week or more. The only drawback is that you can hear the live music from the Riverside until the bands shut down around 1 am.

The long-running *Je t'Aime* (*☎ 053-241912, 247–249 Thanon Charoenrat*) has a variety of rooms in separate several-storey buildings on secure, landscaped grounds for 80B to 120B single, 100B to 160B double. The owner, a Thai artist, has placed paintings or some kind of original artwork in every room.

The American-owned *Pun Pun Guest House* (*☎ 053-243362, fax 246140, ⓔ armms@iname.com, 321 Thanon Charoenrat*) has very tidy bungalows with shared hot-water shower for 150B to 200B. Rooms with private bathroom in a quaint two-storey wooden Thai-style house are 200B to 275B, depending on the number of people and the time of year. Assets include a fully stocked bar, snooker table and riverfront promenade.

C&C Teak House (*☎ 053-246966, 39 Thanon Bamrungrat*), closer to the train station than Mae Nam Ping (rather far from the old city), has quiet, comfortable rooms in a 100-year-old teak house in a secure, gated compound for a bargain 80/150B single/double. Bathroom facilities are shared; the upstairs shower has hot water.

Thanon Chang Khlan *Night Bazaar Guest House* (*☎ 053-272067, 89/2 Thanon Chang Khlan*), adjacent to the Galare Food Centre in the heart of the Night Bazaar neighbourhood, might be just the place to stay if you're buying wholesale in the area.

Fan or air-con rooms with private toilet and hot-water shower facilities range from 200B to 450B.

Chiang Mai Youth Hostel (*☎ 053-276737, fax 204025, ⓔ chiangmai@tyha.org, 21/8 Thanon Chang Khlan*) has rooms for 150B with fan and bathroom; 350B with air-con. A Hostelling International membership is required to stay here; a temporary membership valid for one night costs 50B. Call them for free pick-up.

Thanon Huay Kaew This area north-west of the old city generally contains Chiang Mai's more expensive hotels and restaurants, hence few guesthouses have so far opened up here. One that has been here several years is *Isra House* (*☎ 053-214924, 109/24 Thanon Huay Kaew*), which despite its street address is actually on a soi off Huay Kaew, north of The Pub. There are only nine rooms. The main virtue of Isra House is that it's the cheapest place to stay in the city – 50/70B single/double, with shared facilities. Because it's so cheap, some people stay long-term, and some elect to pay by the month. If you do much sightseeing or dining in the old city, however, any savings over a slightly more expensive but more centrally located place will quickly disappear in săwngthăew fares.

Hotels In Chiang Mai's small Chinatown, between the east moat and Mae Nam Ping, the *New Mitrapap Hotel* (*☎ 053-235436, fax 251260, 94–98 Thanon Ratchawong*) features adequate rooms for 320B single /double with fan, 400B with air-con; the latter are a better deal. It's close to several good, inexpensive Chinese restaurants, as well as the Warorot Market. A little farther north, the all air-con *Prince Hotel* (*☎ 053-252025, fax 251144, 3 Thanon Taiwang*) offers good, if time-worn, rooms starting at 440B. There's a restaurant, coffee shop and swimming pool.

Near the Chang Pheuak bus terminal, *Chiang Mai Phu Viang Hotel* (*☎ 053-221632, 5–9 Soi 4, Thanon Chotana*) has small but clean rooms with fan and bathroom starting at 200B, while more spacious rooms with TV and air-con go for 280B. A restaurant and coffee shop are on the premises.

The funky, old Thai-style **Muang Thong Hotel** (☎ 053-208135, fax 274349) at the corner of Thanon Ratchamankha and Thanon Moon Muang, a good location inside the city moat, has singles with fan and bathroom from just 120B, and doubles for 180B. Street noise from busy Thanon Moon Muang could be a problem.

Roong Ruang Hotel (Roong Raeng; ☎ 053-236746, fax 252409, 398 Thanon Tha Phae) is situated in a prime location, near Pratu Tha Phae, on the eastern side of the city moat. The service is good and the rooms, which face an inner courtyard and are therefore quiet, have been renovated with the addition of pleasant sitting areas. Rooms with fan and bathroom are 250/280B downstairs/upstairs; with air-con, cable TV and hot-water shower they are 350/400B. This is a good place to stay for the Flower Festival in February as the Saturday parade passes right by the entrance. There's another entrance on Thanon Chang Moi Kao. **Tapae Inn** (☎ 053-234640), just west of the canal on the northern side of Thanon Tha Phae, is a good budget choice, with fan rooms for 150B, 220B for air-con.

Sumit Hotel (☎ 053-211033, ☎/fax 214014), on a relatively quiet section of Thanon Ratchaphakhinai inside the old city, offers very clean, large rooms in the classic Thai/Chinese style. You can choose a room with one big bed or two twin beds for the same rate; with fan the rooms cost 200B single/double, with air-con 300B. All have private toilet and shower; air-con rooms have hot water. This is very good value for anyone avoiding the guesthouse scene – it's probably the best hotel deal in the old city.

YMCA International Hotel (☎ 053-221819, fax 215523, 11 Thanon Mengrairasmi) is above the north-western corner of the moat. Singles/doubles in the old wing are 130/190B with fan and shared bathroom, 220B with fan and private bathroom and 250/350B with air-con. Dorm beds in the old wing are 75B. In the fully air-con new wing, singles/doubles with private bathroom, telephone and TV are 500/600B. Facilities include a travel agency, handicraft centre and cafeteria.

The five-storey **Montri Hotel** (☎ 053-211069, fax 217416, ✉ am-intl@cm.ksc .co.th), on the corner of Thanon Moon Muang and Thanon Ratchadamnoen, has overpriced singles with air-con and bathroom for 595B. Small, recently remodelled rooms are 714B single/double with air-con and cable TV. Street-facing rooms are bombarded with noise from Thanon Moon Muang, which reflects off Tha Phae wall. One advantage is that JJ Bakery & Restaurant is downstairs.

The well-run **Nice Apartment** (☎ 053-210552, fax 419150, 15 Soi 1, Thanon Ratchadamnoen), on a soi behind the Montri Hotel, has clean, simple rooms with private hot-water bathroom, fan and cable TV for 200B to 250B (depending on season and length of stay); 300B to 350B with air-con. Discounted monthly rates, also depending on length of stay, are also available. **VIP** (☎ 053-418970, fax 419199), on the same soi almost directly behind JJ Bakery & Restaurant, is similar. On Soi 7 off Thanon Moon Muang are a couple of good apartment-style places: **CM Apartments** (☎ 053-222100) and **Chiang Mai SP Hotel** (☎ 053-214522, fax 223042), each with rooms in the 250B to 450B range, with monthly rates of 2500B to 3000B. **Veerachai Court** (☎ 053-251047, fax 252402, 19 Soi Tha Phae 2) features a nine-storey building on the eastern side of the soi, and a four-storey one on the western side. Clean, quiet, if smallish, rooms with air-con, TV and hot-water showers cost 400B a night here, with monthly rates of 3500B.

The apartment-style **Moon Meuang Golden Court** (☎ 053-212779), off Thanon Moon Muang north of Pratu Tha Phae, features clean doubles with fan and hot-water shower for 200B, air-con for 300B. A small coffee shop is attached.

Anodard Hotel (☎ 053-270755, fax 270759, 57–59 Thanon Ratchamankha) stands off by itself in the inner-city area. Well-kept rooms with air-con in a building that would have been called 'modern' 30 years ago start at 450B. There are a restaurant and swimming pool on the premises.

Pratu Chang Pheuak Area There are very few hotels north of the city walls. Far from the Tha Phae action, but near the Chang Pheuak bus terminal (for Chiang Dao, Fang and Tha Ton), one option is **Chawala Hotel**

(☎ 053-214939, 214453, 129 Thanon Chotana), where basic rooms cost 150B with fan and bathroom, 250B with air-con.

Chang Peuk Hotel (☎ 053-217513, fax 223668, 133 Thanon Chotana), near the Chang Pheuak bus terminal, has clean, air-con rooms for 250B, 350B with TV. There's a good coffee shop on the premises.

Places to Stay – Mid-Range

In this range you can expect daily room cleaning, the option of air-con (some places have rooms with fan also) and – in the hotels – TV and telephone. If anything marks a guesthouse, it's the absence of these latter appliances.

Some of the places in this price category (500B to 1500B for Chiang Mai) really blur the line between 'hotel' and 'guesthouse', the difference often being in name only. The well-managed *Galare Guest House* (☎ 053-821011, fax 279088, 7/1 Soi 2, Thanon Charoen Prathet), for example, is fully air-con and has spacious rooms with private hot-water shower, TV and refrigerator for 680B. It's popular with repeat visitors for its Mae Nam Ping location and proximity to both the Night Bazaar and post office.

Almost next door to the Galare Guest House, the *River View Lodge* (☎ 053-271110, fax 279019, 25 Soi 2, Thanon Charoen Prathet) offers 36 well-appointed rooms in a two-storey, L-shaped building on spacious, landscaped grounds with a swimming pool, for 1420B to 2200B (up to 40% discount from May to August). The friendly owner has a small collection of classic cars on display in the parking lot.

A little farther south along Thanon Charoen Prathet, the *Diamond Riverside Hotel* (Phet Ngam; ☎ 053-270080, fax 271482) has air-con rooms in the newer wing for 950B (800B low season) including breakfast, plus an older wing with rooms for 500B not including breakfast. On the premises are a pool (the pool is clean, but the pool toilet rooms are filthy) and coffee shop. Asian budget-package tourists are the main clientele here. The Thai name for this hotel is how most săwngthăew and túk-túk drivers know it.

Almost opposite the Diamond Riverside Hotel on Thanon Charoen Prathet, the much better *Porn Ping Tower Hotel* (☎ 053-

270099, fax 270119) has rooms that list for 1766B but at the time of research they were going for 790/890B single/double. From the ambience of the reception area, one might expect to pay much more. The Porn Ping is most famous for Bubble, still the most popular disco in town.

The relatively new *Royal Lanna* (☎ 053-818773, fax 818776, 119 Thanon Loi Kroh) towers over the Night Bazaar and rents clean rooms with air-con, hot-water shower and bathtub, TV, phone and medium-sized refrigerator for 900B a night including a breakfast buffet, with discounts for monthly rentals. There's a medium-sized swimming pool on the 4th floor.

Farther down Thanon Charoen Prathet, opposite Wat Chaimongkhon and two doors south of the Alliance Française, *Baan Kaew Guest House* (☎ 053-271606, fax 273436, 142 Thanon Charoen Prathet) is set far back off the road, so it's very quiet. Well-maintained rooms with cross-ventilation and outdoor sitting areas cost 350B with fan and hot-water shower, 450B with air-con. Meals are available in a small outdoor dining area. This place would be perfect if it wasn't for the inexplicably cold, suspicious owners, who demand room payment every morning or even days in advance if they can get it – unusual for a guesthouse in this price range.

Off Thanon Tha Phae in the centre of town, *Tapae Place Hotel* (☎ 053-270159, 281842, fax 271982, 2 Soi 3, Thanon Tha Phae) offers air-con rooms in a large, modern, L-shaped building for 700B to 1600B. Although it's a bit worn, the hotel's main drawcard is that it's only a few steps away from the banks, shops and restaurants of Thanon Tha Phae.

Inside the old city, the friendly and efficient *Felix City Inn* (☎ 053-270710, fax 270709, ✉ felix@cm.ksc.co.th, 154 Thanon Ratchamankha) offers 134 comfortable rooms for 1900B, including breakfast, during high season, or 800B from July to October.

The business-like *Lai Thai Guest House* (☎ 053-271725, 271534, fax 272724, 111/4 Thanon Kotchasan), facing the eastern side of the moat, has well-kept rooms for 290B to 390B (up to 590B during high season). There's also a swimming pool and garden on the grounds.

If you'd like to stay in Chiang Mai's bustling Chinatown, *New Asia Hotel* (☎ 053-252426, fax 252427, 55 Thanon Ratchawong) is a very Chinese place, with decent air-con rooms for 266B to 406B.

Close to the Japanese embassy, and next door to Chiang Mai Ram Hospital, is *Sri Tokyo Hotel* (☎ 053-213899, fax 211102, 6 Thanon Bunreuangrit), which has OK air-con rooms for 350B, plus suites for 590B to 690B. Street noise can be a problem in the front rooms.

Strung out along Thanon Huay Kaew to the immediate north-west of the old city are perhaps a dozen mid-range and top-end hotels. Once the best hotel in the city, the *Chiang Mai Phucome Hotel* (☎ 053-211026, fax 216412, 21 Thanon Huay Kaew) is now very middle-of-the-road but a fair deal at 680B for a room with all amenities. On the premises are a restaurant, coffee shop and traditional massage centre. This hotel remains a favourite with visiting Thais. Nearby, *Quality Chiang Mai Hills* (☎ 053-210030, fax 210035, 18 Thanon Huay Kaew) has 249 well-appointed air-con rooms for 1600B to 1900B, including breakfast. Farther out on Huay Kaew, *The Providence* (☎ 053-893123, fax 221750, 99/9 Thanon Huay Kaew) has air-con rooms for 380B single/double, plus a restaurant, coffee shop and lobby bar.

Close to Pratu Chang Pheuak and the Chang Pheuak bus terminal, the *Northern Inn* (☎ 053-210002, fax 215828, 234/18 Thanon Mani Nopharat) charges 450B for OK air-con rooms. Middle-budget package tourists use this hotel extensively. Several long blocks farther north of Pratu Chang Pheuak, opposite the teacher's college, the *Iyara Hotel* (☎ 053-222245, 214227, fax 214401, 126 Thanon Chotana) offers good air-con accommodation for 500B to 700B.

Places to Stay – Top End

The biggest single area in town for top-end hotels is Thanon Huay Kaew, a broad, straight avenue running north-westward from the north-western corner of the moat. In general, hotel rates for luxury hotels are lower in Chiang Mai than in Bangkok. You can expect to pay 1500B to 5000B for large, well-maintained rooms with air-con, TV, IDD telephone, restaurant (usually more than one), fitness centre and swimming pool.

Booking through a travel agency or via the Internet almost always means lower rates, or try asking for a hotel's 'corporate' discount.

Not far from the Night Bazaar, the friendly *Chiang Mai Plaza Hotel* (☎ 053-270036, fax 272230, 92 Thanon Si Donchai) has rack rates starting at 2500B single/double for a standard room, including breakfast, but a discounted rate of 1800B is easy to come by most of the time. The hotel has a spacious lobby with live northern-Thai music in the evenings, a lobby bar, restaurant, wood-panelled sauna, fitness centre and a well-kept pool area with shade pavilions. Nonsmoking rooms are available, which is unusual for a place charging less than 3000B.

Also near the Night Bazaar, the *Imperial Mae Ping Hotel* (☎ 053-270160, fax 270181, e maeping@loxinfo.co.th, 153 Thanon Si Donchai) charges 3000/3500B for well-outfitted standard rooms. Deluxe rooms run 3750/4250B. A coffee shop, three restaurants and pool are on the premises.

Behind the centre of the Night Bazaar, off Thanon Chang Khlan, the *Chiang Inn* (☎ 053-270070, fax 274299, e chianginn@ chiangmai.a-net.net.th) features comfortable rooms costing 1719B including breakfast. Amenities include a restaurant, popular disco and swimming pool. The Thanon Chang Khlan branch of JJ Bakery & Restaurant is just opposite the front of the hotel, in the Chiang Inn Plaza shopping centre.

On Thanon Chang Khlan itself, in the middle of where the Night Bazaar vendors set up nightly, stands *Royal Princess* (☎ 053-281033, fax 281044, e rpc@dusit.com), where rooms with all amenities start at 3000B. Facilities include three restaurants, a lobby bar and a swimming pool. This one is mainly used by package tourists.

Around the corner from the Royal Princess, on Thanon Loi Kroh, is *Suriwongse Hotel* (☎ 053-270051, fax 270063, e suriwongse_htl_cnx@hotmail.com; in Bangkok ☎ 02-541 5275, fax 541 5278). Rates are 1292/1420B for large singles/doubles (including tax, service and breakfast); on the premises are a coffee shop, restaurant, swimming pool and massage centre.

Farther south down Thanon Chang Khlan near Lanna Hospital, *Empress Hotel*

(☎ 053-270240, fax 272467, ℮ reservations @empresshotels.com, 199 Thanon Chang Khlan) offers plusher surroundings starting at 3146/3630B single/double including tax and service charges. The hotel facilities include a restaurant, coffee shop, swimming pool, fitness centre and disco.

Across Saphan Mengrai from this area, on the east bank of Mae Nam Ping, the **Westin Riverside Plaza** (☎ 053-275300, fax 275299, ℮ westincm@loxinfo.co.th, 318/1 Thanon Chiang Mai-Lamphun) is the city's top property at the moment. Rates start at 5200B for capacious rooms commensurate in quality with the international reputation enjoyed by this management group. Facilities include three restaurants, a coffee shop, fitness centre, swimming pool, sauna and beauty salon.

Along Thanon Huay Kaew, the most expensive option is the **Amari Rincome Hotel** (☎ 053-221130, fax 221915, ℮ rincome@ amari.com, 301 Thanon Huay Kaew), offers standard rooms starting at US$88/96 single/double. Amenities include a well-received Italian restaurant, coffee shop, lobby bar, conference facilities, tennis court and pool.

Next down the ladder, **Amity Green Hills** (☎ 053-220100, fax 221602, ℮ amity@ chmai.loxinfo.co.th, 24 Thanon Chiang Mai-Lampang) is actually a short distance north-east off Thanon Huay Kaew, on Hwy 11. The well-appointed rooms list for around 2589B to 3388B, but discounts to 2200B are available for the asking. Facilities include a restaurant, coffee shop, lobby bar, business centre, conference room, fitness room and swimming pool.

Two other top-drawer spots on Thanon Huay Kaew stand near Kad Suan Kaew shopping centre, not far from the corner of the moat: the **Chiang Mai Orchid Hotel** (☎ 053-222091, fax 221625, 100 Thanon Huay Kaew), charging from 2825B, and the **Lotus Pang Suan Kaew Hotel** (PSK; ☎ 053-224444, fax 224493, 99/4 Thanon Huay Kaew), behind Kad Suan Kaew shopping centre, which charges from 1000B to 2783B. PSK has the most extensive facilities, including a beer garden, restaurant, coffee shop, fitness centre, nightclub, tennis and squash courts, swimming pool and, of course, sheltered access to the shopping centre.

North of Pratu Chang Pheuak, the reliable **Novotel Chiang Mai** (☎ 053-225500, fax 225505, ℮ novotel-res@cmnet.co.th, 183 Thanon Chang Pheuak) offers spacious and well-decorated rooms for 2904/3146B. You may be able to negotiate these rates downward, as this isn't the most popular part of town to stay in.

Out of Town North of the city in the Mae Rim/Mae Sa area is a string of plush countryside resorts. Most offer free shuttle vans back and forth from the city. The creme de la creme of these, **The Regent Chiang Mai** (☎ 053-298181, fax 298190), features 64 vaulted pavilion suites (each around 75 sq metres), plus two- and three-bedroom residences spread amid eight hectares of landscaped gardens and rice terraces worked by water buffalo. On the premises are a health club, Thai herbal steam rooms, massage facilities, a pool, two illuminated tennis courts and a gym. Rates, quoted in dollars only, start at US$320 (plus tax and service) for a garden-view suite.

Chiang Mai Sports Club (☎ 053-298326, fax 297897, ℮ cshotel@loxinfo .co.th), 7km from town on Thanon Mae Rim, has 45 rooms and three two-storey luxury suites on 71 râi (one râi equals 1600 sq metres). Living up to its name, the resort boasts air-con squash courts, a badminton hall, grass- and hard-court tennis, fitness centre, sauna, gymnasium and swimming pool; you have to pay extra for the badminton, squash and tennis facilities, but everything else is free for guests. Official room rates are 2400B single/double or 6500B for a suite (plus a 400B high-season surcharge on holidays), although you may find that discounts of up to 50% are available.

Places to Eat

Chiang Mai has the best variety of restaurants of any city in Thailand outside of Bangkok. Most travellers seem to have better luck here than in Bangkok, though, simply because it's so much easier to get around and experiment.

Chiang Mai's guesthouses serve a typical menu of Western food along with a few pseudo-Thai dishes. If you're interested in authentic Thai cuisine, you'll have to leave the guesthouse womb behind.

Northern & North-Eastern Thai One of Chiang Mai's oldest and best known restaurants is the large, open-air *Aroon (Rai) Restaurant* (☎ 053-276947, 45 *Thanon Kotchasan), across the moat near Pratu Tha Phae. Aroon specialises in both northern- and central-Thai dishes and has a huge menu; prices are inexpensive to moderate. Look for Chiang Mai specialities like *kaeng hang-leh, kaeng awm* and *kaeng khae*. Despite the Thai word *kaeng* (curry) in these dish names, only the first is a curry by the usual definition – that is, made from a thick, spicy paste; the latter two dishes are more like stews and rely on local roots and herbs for their distinctive, bitter-hot flavours. Aroon's standard, Indian-inspired chicken curry – *kaeng kàrìi kài* – is the best in town. Downstairs you'll find more exotic dishes in trays near the cashier, including bamboo grubs and other forest goodies. The spacious open-air dining area upstairs is favoured by night-time clientele, and in hot weather it's cooler than downstairs. As it's open daily from 8 am to 10 pm, Aroon is a good choice for a Thai breakfast of curry and rice.

The smaller and super-clean *Thanam Restaurant* on Thanon Chaiyaphum, north from Pratu Tha Phae, leans more towards central-Thai cuisine, with a few northern-Thai dishes as well. Hallmark dishes include *phàk náam phrík* (fresh vegetables in chilli sauce), *plaa dùk phàt phèt* (spicy fried catfish), *kaeng sôm* (hot and sour vegetable ragout), as well as local dishes like *khâo sàwy* (Shan-Yunnanese curry soup with noodles) and *khànŏm jiin náam ngíaw* (Chinese noodles with spiced chicken curry). Thanam has a small, Roman-script sign inside. The restaurant closes at about 8 pm, doesn't serve alcohol and won't serve people wearing beach clothes (such as tank tops and singlets).

The inexpensive *Si Phen Restaurant* (no Roman-script sign), at 103 Thanon Inthawarorot near Wat Phra Singh, specialises in both northern and north-eastern style dishes. The kitchen prepares some of the best *sôm-tam* (spicy papaya salad) in the city, including a variation made with pomelo fruit. The *kài yâang khâo nĭaw* combo (grilled chicken and sticky rice) – another Isan favourite – is also very good, as is the *khâo sàwy* and *khànŏm jiin*

(Chinese noodles) with either *náam yaa* (fish sauce) or *náam ngíaw* (sweet, spicy sauce) – always incredible. Si Phen is open from 9 am to 5 pm only.

Another highly regarded place for northern-Thai food is the classier *Heuan Phen* (☎ 053-277103, 112 *Thanon Ratchamankha), east of the Felix City Inn. Among the house specialities here are Chiang Mai and jiin haw dishes such as khànŏm jiin náam ngíaw, khâo sàwy, lâap khûa (northern-style minced-meat salad), náam phrík nùm (chilli sauce made with roasted eggplant), kaeng hang-leh, kaeng awm, kaeng khae, and other *aahăan phéun meuang* (local food). There's no Roman-script sign, but it's almost opposite a kindergarten. Daytime meals (8.30 am to 3 pm) are served in a large dining room out front, while evening meals (5 to 10 pm) are served in an atmospheric antique-decorated house at the back. Prices are moderate.

In the north-eastern corner of the old city on Thanon Si Phum, inside the moat is *Kai Yang Isan* (the English sign reads 'SP Chicken'), which specialises in tasty Isan-style grilled chicken and is only open from 4 to 9 pm.

Heuan Sunthari is an atmospheric open-air restaurant built on several levels on the west bank of the river, a little north of Saphan Phra Ram IX. The owner – the famous northern-Thai singer Khun Sunthari – performs at the restaurant nightly. The menu is a pleasant blend of northern, north-eastern and central-Thai specialities.

Central & Southern Thai If you tire of northern- and north-eastern-Thai cuisines or if you just want a little coconut in your curry, check out *Khrua Phuket Laikhram* (Classical Phuket Kitchen), a small family-run restaurant at 1/10 Thanon Suthep, near Chiang Mai University. It's worth hunting down for the delicious, cheap, yet large portions of authentic home-style southern-Thai cooking. If there are no seats downstairs, try the upstairs dining room. Specialities include *yâwt máphráo phàt phèt kûng* (spicy stir-fried shrimp with coconut shoots), *hèt hŭu nŭu phàt khài* (eggs stir-fried with mouse-ear mushrooms) and *yam phuukèt laikhraam* (a delicious salad of cashew nuts and squid). The restaurant has daily specials, too.

Inside the moat, *Ta-Krite* (Ta-Khrai), on Soi 1 (the soi that runs along the southern side of Wat Phra Singh), Thanon Samlan, is a nice indoor-outdoor place with iron-work chairs in a garden setting. The kitchen focuses on central Thai food for the most part, and prices are very reasonable. *Nám phrík* (thick chilli sauce) is a house speciality, along with *khâo tang nâa tâng* (sticky rice with meat, shrimp and coconut). Ta-Krite is open 10 am to 11 pm daily; there are a few other Ta-Krite branches around town.

Noodles Noodles in Chiang Mai are wonderful and the variety is astounding. Khâo sàwy – a Shan–jiin haw concoction of chicken (or, less commonly, beef), spicy curried broth and flat, squiggly, wheat noodles – is one of the most characteristic northern-Thai noodle dishes. It's served with small saucers of shallot wedges, sweet-spicy pickled cabbage and a thick red chilli sauce.

The oldest area for khâo sàwy is Ban Haw, the jiin haw area around the Matsayit Chiang Mai on Soi 1, Thanon Charoen Prathet, around the corner from the Diamond Riverside Hotel and Galare Guest House and not far from the Night Bazaar (in fact this is where the jiin haw caravans of yore used to tie up). Yunnanese-run **Khao Soi Fuang Fah** and **Khao Soi Islam** (no Roman-script signs for either), both on Soi 1 near Matsayit Chiang Mai, serve khâo sàwy (25B) as well as Muslim curries, khànŏm jiin (choice of two sauces, náam yaa or náam ngíaw) and *khâo mòk kài* (the Thai-Muslim version of chicken biryani). Most khâo sàwy places are open from around 10 am till 3 or 4 pm, although Khao Soi Islam and Khao Soi Fuang Fah are open 5 am to 5 pm. Khao Soi Islam also serves *khâo mòk pháe* (goat biryani).

Inside the old city, the best choice is **Khao Soi Suthasinee**, on Soi 1, Thanon Inthawarorot opposite the district office; this restaurant serves exemplary khâo sàwy. There's another branch at 164/10 Thanon Chang Khlan, near Lanna Commercial College, and yet a third at 267–269 Thanon Chang Khlan. Other khâo sàwy places can be found around the city – just look for the distinctive noodle shape and orange-brown broth.

One of the more famous khâo sàwy places in Chiang Mai is **Khao Soi Lam Duan** on Thanon Faham (an extension of Thanon Charoenrat, and sometimes called by the latter name), just north of Saphan Phra Ram IX. Large bowls of beef, pork or chicken khâo sàwy cost 30B. Also on the menu are kao-lǎo (soup without noodles), mǔu sà-té (grilled spiced pork on bamboo skewers), khâo sàwy with beef or pork instead of chicken, *khànŏm rang phêung* (literally, beehive pastry, a coconut-flavoured waffle), Mekong rice whisky and beer. Two more very good khâo sàwy places along this same stretch of Thanon Faham are **Khao Soi Samoe Jai** and **Khao Soi Ban Faham**.

Unassuming **Rot Sawoei**, on Thanon Arak around the corner from Buak Hat Park, is famous for very delectable kǔaytǐaw kài tǔn yaa jiin, rice noodles with Chinese herb–steamed chicken that practically melts off the bone. A normal bowl costs 25B, while a *phísèht* (special) order with extra chicken costs 35B. *Khâo nâa kài* (sliced chicken over rice) is also good. In addition, Rot Sawoei serves juices made from fresh toddy palm, coconut, orange and guava. It's open 11 am to 2.30 am daily, and makes the perfect late-night spot for a snack.

A simpler take on the same idea substitutes Coca-Cola for the Chinese herbs at **Kuaytiaw Kai Tun Coke**, a small food stall directly opposite the main entrance to the Imperial Mae Ping Hotel on Thanon Kamphaeng Din. Here the chicken is marinated in cola and spices overnight before being steamed then served with rice noodles for 40B a bowl.

Kuaytiaw Reua Koliang Restaurant, on the corner of Ratchamankha and Thanon Moon Muang, has been serving authentic kǔaytǐaw reua ('boat noodles' – rice noodles served in a dark broth seasoned with ganja leaves) for many years now.

Rot Neung ('One Taste', but no English sign), opposite the Diamond Riverside Hotel on Thanon Charoen Prathet, serves some of the best kǔaytǐaw lûuk chín plaa (rice noodle soup with fish balls) in Chiang Mai. If you thought you didn't like fish balls – ground fish rolled into balls – give them a second try here, as this place makes them fresh and sells them to many other stands in town. A bowl filled with noodles, fish balls, plus strips of fishcake and even delicious fish wonton, costs 30B. Or you can buy a kilo of fish balls or fish strips to take away for 200B.

Chinese Chiang Mai has a small Chinatown in an area centred around Thanon Ratchawong north of Thanon Chang Moi. Here you'll find a whole string of Chinese rice and noodle shops, most of them offering variations on Tae Jiu (Chao Zhou) and Yunnanese cooking.

Han Yang Hong Kong (Hong Kong Roast Goose), next to the New Mitrapap Hotel on Thanon Ratchawong, does succulent roast duck, pork and goose, as well as dim sum. There are several other inexpensive Chinese restaurants along this street.

The clean, simple and spacious *Mitmai Restaurant* (☎ 053-275033, 42/2 Thanon Ratchamankha) is a Yunnanese place specialising in delicious vegetable soups made with pumpkin, taro, mushrooms, snowpeas or other Chinese vegetables. Especially tasty is the *tôm sôm plaa yâwt máphráo* (hot and sour fish soup with coconut shoots). The bilingual menu also includes *yam* (tangy, Thai-style salad) made with Chinese vegetables, as well as Yunnanese steamed ham, Chinese medicine chicken and many vegetarian dishes. Prices are moderate, no MSG is used in the cooking and it's open 9 am to 9 pm daily.

For a quick Chinese breakfast, try the food stall opposite JJ Bakery on Thanon Ratchadamnoen, *Salom Joy* (no Romanscript sign). It has held out against the development of Pratu Tha Phae for many years and still serves cheap *jók* (rice congee), *paa-thâwng-kŏh* (Chinese 'doughnuts') and *náam tâo hûu* (hot soy milk). This is one of the few places in the Pratu Tha Phae area that opens for breakfast – around 6 am. Later in the day noodle and rice plates are available. You can also get great congee, with a choice of chicken, fish, shrimp or pork, from the *jók vendor* next to the Bangkok Bank on Thanon Chang Moi.

Jok Somphet, on the corner of Thanon Ratchaphakhinai and Thanon Si Phum, facing the northern moat, is popular for its namesake *jók*. The friendly proprietors also make decent khâo sàwy kài and other noodles – *bà-mìi, kŭaytǐaw* – with chicken, beef or pork.

Probably the best place to totally splurge on Chinese food is the Westin Riverside Plaza's *China Palace* (☎ 053-275300), which specialises in excellent, if slightly pricey, Cantonese cuisine.

Indian, Muslim & Israeli Along Soi 1, Charoen Prathet, between Thanon Chang Khlan and Thanon Charoen Prathet and near the Chiang Mai (Ban Haw) Mosque, are a number of simple restaurants and alley vendors selling inexpensive but tasty Muslim curries and khâo sàwy. *Sophia*, on the opposite side of the soi from Khao Sawy Islam and Khao Soi Fuang Fah (see under Noodles earlier in this section), serves good curries and khâo mòk kài. *Néua òp hǎwm* ('fragrant' Yunnanese Muslim-style dried beef), a speciality of Chiang Mai, is also sold along the lane. A *rotii vendor stall* on this same soi does delicious *rotii* (Indian flat bread) and chicken martabak (*mátàbà kài; rotii* stuffed with chicken).

The friendly, family-owned *Indian Restaurant Vegetarian Food* (☎ 053-223396, 27/3 Soi 9, Thanon Moon Muang) serves cheap and adequate (but not brilliant) vegetarian thalis as well as individual Indian dishes. There's also a second branch (☎ 053-278324, 85/2 Thanon Ratchaphakhinai).

Shere Shiraz (☎ 053-276132, Soi 6, Thanon Charoen Prathet) serves mostly north-Indian food, with a few south-Indian dishes. The extensive menu includes many vegetarian dishes. It's open 9.30 am to 11 pm daily. *Asma Restaurant* (☎ 053-404506, 248/55–56 Thanon Mani Nopharat), in a row of relatively new shophouses off Thanon Mani Nopharat, west of Pratu Chang Pheuak, serves Indian and Thai food in a clean, air-con setting. It offers a daily buffet for 90B per person, and is open 11.30 am to 2 pm and 5 to 8 pm.

Arabia (☎ 053-818850), in the Anusan Night Market, does north-Indian/Pakistani/Arab-style cuisine very well, perhaps better than any of the foregoing in terms of the freshness of the flavours. Don't let the fact that it's often empty or nearly so throw you off the trail; Arabia has a steady and discerning, if small, clientele.

Jerusalem Falafel (☎ 053-270208, 35/3 *Thanon Moon Muang)* is a restaurant and bakery serving a selection of falafels, shaslik, hummus, and other Israeli specialities, as well as Thai and vegetarian food, baguette sandwiches, pizza, soups, salads, gelato and delicious home-made cakes and pies. It's closed Friday.

If you happen to be near the YMCA in the Santitham district, *Sa-Nga Choeng Doi* on Thanon Charoensuk, a five-minute walk from the Y, has probably the best khâo mòk kài and mátàbà in town. The home-made, unsweetened yogurt here is also highly recommended. The restaurant is only open from around 10 am to 2 pm, and it has no Roman-script sign – just look for the appropriate dishes on the tables.

Italian Several enterprising Italians own and operate restaurants around town, and all of them have their strong points. In a large, old Thai house on Thanon Ratchadamnoen, *La Villa Pizzeria* (☎ 053-277403) serves delicious pizzas baked in a wood-fired oven, and the rest of the Italian food on the menu is tops.

Da Stefano (☎ 053-874189, 2/1–2 *Thanon Chang Moi Kao)* is an intimate, well-decorated, air-con place that focuses on fresh Italian cuisine, with one of the better wine lists in town. Prices are moderate, and the food and service are very good. Da Stefano is closed Monday.

The more casual *Pum Pui Italian Restaurant* (☎ 053-278209, 24 Soi 2, *Thanon Moon Muang)*, near Top North Guest House, features a low-key garden setting and moderate prices; the menu includes olive pate and other antipasto, along with salads, Italian wines, several vegetarian selections, ice cream, breakfast and espressos. The complimentary Italian breads served at the beginning of all meals are excellent.

Bacco (☎ 053-251389), in a very old Thai building towards the eastern end of Thanon Tha Phae, is the least expensive Italian restaurant in town and has quite an enjoyable menu. Bacco is open noon to 10.30 pm Monday to Saturday.

The luxurious new *Piccola Roma Palace* (☎ 053-271256, 144 Thanon Charoen Prathet)* is more of a splurge setting, with subdued lighting, sharp service and great attention to culinary detail. It also

has very high prices (for Chiang Mai), the best salads in town and an excellent wine list – overall a good spot to celebrate an anniversary or the firing of your evil boss back home. Piccola Roma Palace offers free transportation to and from the restaurant – just call. It's open 11 am to 2 pm and 5 to 11 pm.

The Amari Rincome Hotel's *La Gritta* (☎ 053-221130) serves good, authentic Italian food at international prices. You can sample a wide variety of international and Thai dishes at La Gritta's daily buffet (11.30 am to 2 pm) for 240B, including tax and service.

Although it's hardly Italian, *OK Pizza* (☎ 053-818499) gets a thumbs up for its fresh, light pizzas, good mixed salad, extreme cleanliness and friendly service. It's at the intersection of Thanon Chang Khlan and Loi Kroh, in the Chiangmai Pavilion.

International Parallel to Thanon Loi Kroh is *El Toro* (☎ 01-882 0345, 6 Soi 1 Thanon Kotchasan)*. The menu boasts 19 Mexican dishes, six Thai, four Indian, five pastas, plus a list of sandwiches, salads, desserts, beers and cocktails including margaritas and piña coladas. If Elvis showed up here, he'd order the chimichanga and a chicken vindaloo. A pool table and a good collection of recorded Latin tunes make this a good spot to party with friends.

Art Cafe (☎/fax 053-206365), at the corner of Thanon Tha Phae and Thanon Kotchasan, facing Pratu Tha Phae, is an air-con place offering a combination of vegetarian and nonvegetarian Italian, as well as Thai, Mexican and American food, including pizza, sandwiches, pasta, enchiladas, tacos, salads, ice cream, tiramisu, pies, shakes, fruit juices and coffees. Art Cafe is the perfect place to go if you have a small group who can't decide what kind of food they want to eat. It occasionally hosts 190B Mexican buffets on Saturday. This restaurant is 100% smoke-free.

The amazing *JJ Bakery & Restaurant*, on the corner of Thanon Moon Muang and Thanon Ratchadamnoen, offers a very diverse menu of Western, Thai and Chinese dishes, all of them consistently good. JJ has very good coffee, inexpensive cocktails and a great selection of pies, cakes, croissants and cookies. Vegetarians may drool over the well-made brown-rice salad from the macrobiotic section of the menu. There's a second branch of JJ at the rear ground floor of Chiang Inn Plaza, off Thanon Chang Khlan near the Night Bazaar. Both branches are open 6.30 am to 11.30 pm daily.

Next door to the Chiang Inn Plaza branch of JJ, *Foccacia* is a smaller place that specialises in sandwiches made with freshly baked breads, including olive-studded foccacia (a foccacia sandwich costs 75B). Fillings include organically grown vegetables. Foccacia also has cappuccino, flat white and other coffees.

The friendly *Libernard Cafe* (☎ 053-234877), on Thanon Moon Muang just south of the Bar Beer Centre near Pratu Tha Phae, serves possibly the best fresh roasted coffee in town. The banana pancakes also deserve much acclaim. Libernard Cafe is open 7.30 am to 5 pm.

Irish Pub (☎ 053-214554), on Thanon Ratwithi, offers baked goods, good coffee, yogurt, muesli, sandwiches, pasta, pizza, vegetarian dishes, baked potatoes, ice cream, some Thai food, beer on tap, and fruit and vegetable juices. The homy indoor section is decorated with Irish kitsch and there's pleasant garden seating out the back. It's open 9 am to 1 am.

Across the street from Irish Pub, down a soi behind the Trekking Collective, is the outdoor *Kitchen Garden* (☎ 053-419080, 25/1 Thanon Ratwithi). Another entrance faces Soi 5, Thanon Moon Muang. The set breakfast plates include sausage, ham, eggs, toast, French toast and tea or filtered coffee. Kitchen Garden also offers fresh orange juice, home-made scones, continental breakfast, set vegetarian dishes, chicken liver pate, mixed fruit, sandwiches and Thai dishes. A full assortment of beverages, including beer, is available. It's open 8 am to 5 pm daily.

The new *Easy Diner* (☎ 053-208989, 27/29 Thanon Ratchadamnoen) is an air-con place west of Pratu Tha Phae that specialises in American diner fare such as burgers (vegetarian and chicken burgers included), hot dogs, ribs, chicken, salads, milk shakes and apple pie. Breakfast (including British style) is served all day, and there's a takeaway and delivery service. Easy Diner is closed Sunday.

The Pub (☎ 053-211550, 189 Thanon Huay Kaew), close to some of the large hotels on Thanon Huay Kaew, is one of the oldest fàràng-oriented pubs in Chiang Mai. Nowadays it serves both international and Thai cuisines and draws Thais as well as westerners. *Newsweek* magazine named it 'one of the world's best bars' in 1986 and although its glory days may have passed, it's still got a homy kind of class. European wines and draught beer are available, and there's also a dart board. One of the best things going at The Pub is the annual traditional Christmas dinner offered on the evenings of 24 and 25 December.

Dara Steakhouse, on Thanon Tha Phae across from Roong Ruang Hotel, is a very casual spot, with an extensive Thai and Western menu and low prices.

The Amazing Sandwich (☎ 053-218846, 252/3 Thanon Phra Pokklao), three doors north of the THAI office, is a small, very clean air-con place specialising in fresh baguette sandwiches with your choice of a dozen fillings, as well as lasagne, vegetable pie and quiche, plus juices, beers, wine, spirits and cocktails. It's open 9 am to 8.30 pm, closed Sunday.

Popular among German expats and visitors are the *Bierstube* at 33/6 Thanon Moon Muang (good French fries, but lots of fearless cockroaches) near Pratu Tha Phae, and *Haus München* (☎ 053-274027, 115/3 Thanon Loi Kroh), east of Chiangmai Pavilion. Next to Haus München are three more European eateries, all in a row along Thanon Loi Kroh: *Red Lion English Pub & Restaurant*, *German Hofbräuhaus* and *Cafe Benelux*, each serving the type of cuisine their names imply.

Chez John (☎ 053-201551, 18/1 Thanon Mahidon), near the airport and opposite the customs office, offers moderately priced French cuisine and a large selection of wines. More expensive and formal, the long-standing *Le Coq d'Or* (☎ 053-282024, 68/1 Thanon Ko Klang) serves French haute cuisine in a lavishly decorated mansion off Thanon Chiang Mai-Lamphun east of the river.

The main fast-food district in Chiang Mai runs along Thanon Chang Khlan, in the Night Bazaar area. This strip features the usual Western fast-food outlets, most of which are clustered within the Chiang Inn

Plaza shopping centre. Similar franchise-style places can be found in the Kad Suan Kaew shopping centre on Thanon Huay Kaew and at Airport Plaza near the airport.

Vegetarian Chiang Mai is blessed with over 25 vegetarian restaurants, most of them very inexpensive. Long popular with travellers because of its easy location is *AUM Vegetarian Food* (☎ 053-278315), on Thanon Moon Muang near Pratu Tha Phae. The all-vegie menu features a varied list of traditional Thai and Chinese dishes, including northern and north-eastern Thai dishes, prepared without meat or eggs. There is an upstairs eating area with cushions on the floor and low tables. It's open 8 am to 9 pm daily.

On Soi 1, Thanon Inthawarorot, a few doors down from Khao Soi Suthasinee towards Chiang Mai Central Prison, is *Mangsawirat Kangreuanjam* (the difficult-to-see English sign reads 'Vegetarian Food'; look for a cluster of stainless steel pots). The cooks put out 15 to 20 pots of fresh, 100%-Thai vegetarian dishes daily between 8 am and early afternoon (till everything's sold). The dishes feature lots of bean curd, squash, peas, pineapple, sprouts and potato, and the desserts are good. Very good and very cheap – three items over rice cost just 15B to 20B, or figure 40B to 50B for three large bowls of food, two plates of rice, and two bottles of water, more than enough to engorge two hungry stomachs.

Also within the old city quadrangle, just north of SK Guest House on Soi 1, Thanon Si Phum, is *Biaporn*, an OK, very inexpensive Thai vegetarian place with a more limited selection of dishes; it's open midday only.

The Asoke Foundation–sponsored Vegetarian Centre of Chiang Mai (☎ 053-271262) operates an extremely cheap Thai *vegetarian restaurant* on Thanon Om Muang south of the south-western corner of the city walls. The food is served cafeteria-style – you push a tray down a rack and point at what you want. Warning: brown rice only. A small health-food section to one side of the restaurant offers dried gluten, nuts, beans, herbs, vegetarian chilli sauces, natural beauty products, herbal medicines and Dharma books (mostly in

Thai). It's open 6 am to 2 pm Sunday to Thursday only. From Thursday afternoon to Saturday it's closed so that the staff can visit retreat centre belonging to the Santi Asoke Buddhist sect in the *amphoe* (district) of Mae Taeng.

On Thanon Suthep just west of the entrance to Wat Suan Dok, *Suandok Vegetarian* offers a similar array of inexpensive, wholesome Thai vegetarian dishes and brown rice.

Out along Thanon Si Donchai, past the Thanon Chang Khlan intersection, is the *Whole Earth Restaurant* (☎ 053-282463), associated with a Transcendental Meditation centre. The food is Thai and Indian (vegetarian and nonvegetarian) and the atmosphere is suitably mellow, although the food may be a bit overpriced and under-spiced.

Around the corner from Whole Earth and south down Thanon Chang Khlan, take a left into a small soi past the all-white Season (Sii Suan) Plaza shopping centre, and you'll come to the *Vihara Liangsan* (☎ 053-818094) on your right. At this one you serve yourself from a long buffet table (the food is a mix of Chinese and Thai vegetarian, with lots of tofu and gluten), then place your plate – including rice – on a scale, and pay by weight. A heaped plate ends up costing around 25B; it's best to get here between 11 am and 1 pm.

There's a small vegetarian restaurant on *Chiang Mai University* campus open limited daytime hours only.

All of the Indian restaurants mentioned earlier in this section feature short vegetarian sections on their menus; one, the Indian Restaurant Vegetarian Food, is all vegie.

The Vegetarian Chiang Mai Club collects and disperses information on the international vegetarian movement; call ☎ 053-222571 for further information. Also look for the brown 'Vegetarian Restaurant Map', drawn by an expat American and available at many vegie spots around town.

Food Centres A food centre on the 3rd floor of the Kad Suan Kaew shopping centre on Thanon Huay Kaew gathers together vendors selling all kinds of Thai and Chinese dishes at reasonable prices. *Galare Food Centre*, a large indoor/outdoor cluster of permanent food vendor booths opposite the main Night Bazaar building on Thanon Chang Khlan, is also good; free Thai classical dancing is featured every evening. Airport Plaza also has a good food centre.

Night Markets Chiang Mai is full of interesting day and night markets stocked with very inexpensive and very tasty foods. The *Somphet Market* on Thanon Moon Muang, north of the Thanon Ratwithi intersection, sells cheap takeaway curries, yam, *lâap* (spicy minced meat), *thâwt man* (fried fish cakes), sweets and seafood. On the opposite side of the moat, along Thanon Chaiyaphum north of Lek House, is a small *night market* (sometimes called 'Somphet night market') where you can get everything from noodles and seafood to the specialities of Yunnan. A lot of travellers eat here, so prices are just a bit higher than average, but the food is usually good.

Another good hunting ground is the very large and popular *Pratu Chiang Mai night market* near Pratu Chiang Mai along Thanon Bamrungburi. People tend to take their time here, making an evening of eating and drinking – there's no hustle to vacate tables for more customers. Over on the eastern side of the city, a large *fruit and vegetable market* assembles nightly along Thanon Chang Moi near the Charoen Prathet intersection; several rice and noodle vendors coexist alongside fruit stalls.

In the upstairs section of *Warorot Market* (on the corner of Thanon Chang Moi and Thanon Praisani) are a number of great stalls for *khâo tôm* (rice soup), *khâo man kài*, (chicken rice), *khâo mǔu daeng* ('red' pork with rice), *jók* and *khâo sàwy*, with tables overlooking the market floor. It's not the best cooking in Chiang Mai by a long shot, but it's cheap. A set of vendors on the ground floor specialise in inexpensive noodles – this area is particularly popular. The market is open 6 am to 5 pm daily.

Anusan Night Market, near the Night Bazaar, attracts both tourists and Thais. If you wander over here, look for the stalls that are crowded – they're usually the best. All of the places have English menus. The large khâo tôm place near the market entrance, *Uan Heh-Hah*, still packs in the customers; the most popular dish is the *khâo tôm plaa* (fish and rice soup), but other specialities worth trying include curried fish balls and curry-fried crab. *San Pa Khoi Market*, midway between the river and the train station on Charoen Muang, has a better selection and lower prices than Anusan. A curry stand in San Pa Khoi Market is probably the only place in Chiang Mai where you can find fresh Thai curries past 11 pm. It stays open till around 5 am and is very popular with late-night partiers.

On the River Over the years, the most consistent riverside place has been the *Riverside Bar & Restaurant* (☎ 053-243239), on Thanon Charoenrat, 200m north of Saphan Nawarat. The food is always good, and it's as popular with Thais as with fàràng. The atmosphere is convivial and there's live music nightly. Another plus is that you can choose from indoor and outdoor dining areas. There's also an 8 pm dinner cruise – you can board the boat any time after 7.30 pm. Nearby *Good View* (☎ 053-241866) is newer, with more open-air areas, and it is more popular with Thais than fàràng. The 122-item menu covers everything Thai. There's live music here, also. Good View is open 6 pm to 1 am daily.

Another elegant eatery a little farther north along the river on Thanon Charoenrat is *The Gallery* (☎ 053-248601), a converted Chinese temple that's half art gallery, half restaurant. The quality of the food goes up and down here, however; sometimes it's great, other times so-so. Ditto for service. The Gallery is open noon to 1 am.

The Riverfront Restaurant (Tha Nam; ☎ 053-275125), on Thanon Chang Khlan along the west bank of Mae Nam Ping, is housed in an old, northern Thai–style building and is also quite good; a northern-Thai folk ensemble performs in the evenings.

See Northern & North-eastern Thai earlier in this section for a description of Heuan Sunthari, on the west bank of the river.

Entertainment
Bars & Pubs A section of Thanon Ratwithi extending a couple of blocks west of Thanon Moon Muang has become a good area for pubs where Thais and foreigners, women as well as men, meet for drinks and conversation. Mixed in among

the pubs are a large art supplies store, a couple of homespun print shops, and other vaguely 'media-industrial' endeavours, some of them rather old. Walking from Thanon Moon Muang, first is the long-running *Irish Pub* on the right, which has nothing particularly Irish about it other than some kitsch on the walls. The beers are all Thai-brewed, but it's quiet and the comfortable upstairs is even suitable for solo reading or writing. Next, at the corner of Ratwithi and the soi that leads around the corner to Eagle House 2, sits the diminutive *Yoy Pocket*, a funky spot reminiscent of some of the homier cafes/pubs on Thanon Phra Athit in Bangkok. Directly opposite Yoy Pocket is the *Voodoo Lounge*, a bar with a pool table and a decent sound system, then next up on the same side of the street is *X Chap*, a small Thai bar. Look for other abandoned shopfronts along this street to give birth to more Thai pubs with creative decor – if the sagging economy permits.

The happy hour at *Kafé* on Thanon Moon Muang, between Soi 5 and Soi 6 near Somphet Market, is popular among expats and Thais. Farther south along Thanon Moon Muang, between Thanon Ratchadamnoen and Soi 3, is a string of small bars, some strongly male-oriented in their over-abundance of female staff, others good all-round places for a drink.

The long-running *Pinte Blues Pub*, at 33/6 Thanon Moon Muang, serves espresso and beer, and plays tapes from a huge blues collection *Bierstube* features German grub and beer, while *John's Place* and *Spotlight* (on the opposite side of the moat on Thanon Kotchasan) are go-go bars frequented almost exclusively by men, both Thai and foreign. *Sax Music Pub* in this same area plays a wide variety of pre-recorded tapes, DJ style. The Pinte Blues Pub is the only bar in the Pratu Tha Phae vicinity where you generally see couples or fàràng women, although during high season the crowd at the Sax Music Pub can be relatively mixed.

Farther south along Thanon Moon Muang is the *H3 Pub*, a rustic open-air bar that serves as the local Hash House Harriers headquarters.

Drunken Flower, at the end of Soi 1 off Thanon Nimanhemin, is a cosy indoor/outdoor bar and restaurant with a mixed Thai and expat crowd, especially local non-government organisation (NGO) staffers.

Discos All the flashy hotels have discos with hi-tech recorded music. The most active hotel discos in town are still *Fantasy Discotheque* (Chiang Inn), *Stardust* (Westin Riverside Plaza), *Crystal Cave* (Empress Hotel) and the ever popular *Bubble* (Porn Ping Tower Hotel). The cover charge at each is around 100B, which includes one drink, with the usual 'ladies free' nights sprinkled throughout the week. Bubble (actually the name has been 'updated' to Space Bubble, but everyone in town still calls it by the old name, which in Thai is pronounced 'Bubben') has the most regular local clientele.

One of the most popular non-hotel discos is *Gi Gi's* on Thanon Chiang Mai-Lamphun east of the river, along with *Discovery* on the ground floor of Kad Suan Kaew shopping centre. All Chiang Mai discos are legally required to close at 2 am, although Gi Gi's sometimes stays open later. In Thai parlance, these are 'kitchen discos' (*disco khrua*), which means customers stand next to small, round, waist-height tables on the dance floor so that they dance close to their drinks and pocketbooks. Another popular spot is the relatively newer *Nice Illusion* on Thanon Chaiyaphum near the moat, where it gets so crowded some nights there's barely room to move. At all three, the crowd tends to be very young.

Gay Venues Chiang Mai has several gay men's bars, including the relaxed *Coffee Boy Bar* (☎ 053-247021, 248 Thanon Thung Hotel) in a 70-year-old teak house not far from the Arcade bus terminal. On weekends there's a cabaret show.

Other popular gay meeting places include *Circle Pub* (☎ 053-214996, 161/7–8 Soi Erawan, Thanon Chotana) and *Doi Boy* (☎ 053-404361, 27/1–2 Soi 4, Thanon Chang Pheuak), both not far from the Novotel, and both featuring weekend cabarets. The three-storey *Adam's Apple* (☎ 053-220381, 132/46–47 Soi Wiang Bua, Thanon Chotana) has a massage centre, go-go bar, gay pub and karaoke lounge; it's open 7 pm to 2 am daily. *House of Male* (☎ 053-894133, 269/2 Soi 3, Thanon

Sirimangkhalajan) has a similar orientation but focuses on a pool, steam room and gym.

Live Music One of the longest-running live music venues in Chiang Mai is the *Riverside Bar & Restaurant* (☎ 053-243239), on Thanon Charoenrat, on Mae Nam Ping. It has good food, fruit shakes, cocktails and live music nightly – a variety of covers from The Beatles to reggae, as well as some Thai pop. It's usually packed with both foreigners and Thais on weekends, so arrive early to get a table on the veranda overlooking the river. There are two indoor bars, both full of regulars, with separate bands. It usually stays open till 2 or 3 am. Next door, *Good View Bar & Restaurant* features a good covers band and is also quite popular.

A block or so north of the Rim Ping at 37 Thanon Charoenrat, *Brasserie* (☎ 053-241665) has become a favourite late-night spot (11.15 pm to 2 am) to listen to a talented Thai guitarist named Took play energetic versions of Hendrix, Cream, Dylan, Marley, the Allmans and other 1960s and 1970s gems. A couple of other local bands warm up the house before Took comes on, often to a packed house. Food service is available inside the bar or out the back by the river.

Massage All of the places that teach massage (see under Courses earlier in this chapter) offer massage services as well, usually for around 200B per hour. There are also dozens of *nûat phǎen boraan* (traditional massage) centres all around the city, often doing massage for as little as 100B per hour, but most people find that the massage schools give the best service.

Massages given by *Let's Relax* (☎ 053-818498), on the second floor of the small Chiangmai Pavilion shopping centre on Thanon Chang Khlan in the Night Bazaar strip, are generally of superior quality, and are performed in a very clean and professional atmosphere. In addition to full-body massage, Let's Relax offers 30-minute back and shoulder massage, arm massage and foot massage.

Cinema Movies with English soundtracks are frequently shown at the *Vista* chain of cinemas at two shopping centres opposite one another on Thanon Huay Kaew: Kad Suan Kaew and Vista 12 Huay Kaew. Raintree Resource Center's 'movieline' (☎ 053-262661) carries a recorded message in English giving weekly program information for these two cinemas.

Shopping

Hundreds of shops all over Chiang Mai sell hill-tribe and northern-Thai craftwork, but a lot of it is commercial and touristy junk churned out for the undiscerning. So bargain hard and buy carefully! The nonprofit outlets often have the best quality, and although the prices are sometimes a bit higher than at the Night Bazaar, a higher percentage of your money goes directly to the hill-tribe artisans.

Thai Tribal Crafts (☎ 053-241043) at 208 Thanon Bamrungrat, near the McCormick Hospital, is run by two church groups on a nonprofit basis and has a good selection of quality handicrafts. Hill-Tribe Products Promotion Centre (☎ 053-277743) at 21/17 Thanon Suthep, near Wat Suan Dok, is a royally sponsored project; all profits go to hill-tribe welfare programs. The YMCA International Hotel also operates a nonprofit handicrafts centre.

The two commercial markets with the widest selections of northern-Thai folk crafts are Warorot Market at the eastern end of Thanon Chang Moi Kao and the Night Bazaar off Thanon Chang Khlan. Warorot (also locally called *kàat lǔang* or 'great market') is the oldest market in Chiang Mai. A former royal cremation ground, it has been a marketplace site since the reign of Chao Inthawararot (1870–97). Although the huge enclosure is quite dilapidated (the escalator and lifts don't work any more), it's an especially good market for fabrics. Across the street is the similar Lamyai Market.

Other markets on the outskirts of town include Kamthiang, San Pa Khoi and Thiphanet, all worth a visit if you like Thai markets. Just south of Thiphanet Market is the Chiang Mai Plant Market, the perfect place to pick up some greenery to feather your Chiang Mai nest if you're settling in long term.

As Chiang Mai is Thailand's main handicraft centre, it's ringed by small cottage factories and workshops where you can watch craftspeople at work. In general, though, merchandise you see at factories outside the city will cost more than it would in Chiang Mai unless you're buying in bulk.

Night Bazaars The Chiang Mai Night Bazaar, the mother of all tourist markets, stretches along Thanon Chang Khlan from Thanon Tha Phae to Thanon Si Donchai. Good buys include Phrae-style sêua mâw hâwm, northern- and north-eastern Thai hand-woven fabrics, *yâam* (shoulder bags), hill-tribe crafts (many tribespeople set up their own stalls here; the Akha wander around on foot), opium scales, hats, silver jewellery, lacquerware, woodcarvings, iron and bronze Buddhas and many other items.

In the main Night Bazaar building, which is called Chiangmai Night Bazaar shopping centre, are a couple of dozen permanent shops selling antiques, handicrafts, rattan and hardwood furniture, textiles, jewellery, pottery, basketry, silverwork, woodcarving and other items of local manufacture. Prices can be very good if you bargain hard.

If you're in need of new travelling clothes, this is a good place to look. A light cotton dress, trousers or yâam can be bought for less than 150B, and sêua mâw hâwm cost between 80B and 100B, depending on size. Spices – everything from a *tôm yam* (soup made with lemongrass, chilli, lime and usually seafood) herbal mix to pure saffron – are available from several vendors. Cashew nuts, roasted or raw, are often less expensive here than in Southern Thailand where they're grown.

One of our favourite shops along the entire strip is Chiang Mai (118 Thanon Chang Khlan), which carries a selection of well-made cotton T-shirts silk-screened with more than 30 different old Chiang Mai designs, along with equally well-designed silver-and-bead jewellery and a changing selection of interesting accessories.

Except in the few shops with fixed prices (like the aforementioned Chiang Mai), you must bargain patiently but mercilessly. The fact that there are so many different stalls selling the same items means that competition effectively keeps prices low, if you haggle. Look over the whole bazaar before you begin buying. If you're not in the mood or don't have the money to buy, it's still worth a stroll, unless you don't like crowds – most nights it's elbow to elbow.

Several restaurants and many food trolleys feed the hungry masses. Down Soi Anusan at the southern end of Thanon Chang Khlan, the Anusan Night Market has lots of good Thai and Chinese food at night, and in the early morning (from 5 to 9 am) you'll find fresh produce and noodle vendors.

Shopping Centres & Department Stores Chiang Mai had 17 shopping centres with department stores at last count. The Kad Suan Kaew shopping centre on Thanon Huay Kaew, centred around a branch of Bangkok's Central department store, is the best, with Airport Plaza a close second. There are several upmarket shops in both complexes. Computer Plaza on Thanon Mani Nopharat near the north-western corner of the moat is the place to go for computer supplies.

Antiques You'll see lots of antiques in the city. Check prices in Bangkok first, as Chiang Mai's shops are not always cheap. Also remember that worldwide there are a lot more instant antiques than authentic ones. The Night Bazaar area is probably the best place to look for fake antiques. Inside the Nakhon Ping Night Bazaar building, towards the back on the second floor, are a few small shops with real antiques. Among the best is The Lost Heavens (☎ 053-278185), which specialises in Mien tribal artefacts. It's located at Stall 2, on the 2nd floor of the main Night Bazaar building, in the 'antiques corner' towards the back left. The Lost Heavens also has a store at 234 Thanon Tha Phae (☎ 053-251555) opposite Wat Bupparam. There is also Under the Bo (☎ 053-818831) at Stall 22–23, which carries many unique pieces, in the form of furniture, antique bronze and wood figures, old doors, woodcarvings and weaving from Africa, South Asia and South-East Asia. Neither is cheap, but many items are one-of-a-kind. Under the Bo has another shop out on the road to Hang Dong, about 5km south-west of Thanon Mahidon.

Many more antique shops can be found along Thanon Tha Phae and especially along Thanon Loi Kroh. Burmese antiques are becoming more common than Thai, as most of the Thai stuff has been bought by collectors. You can get some great buys of antique Burmese furniture from the British colonial period.

Hang Dong, 25km south of Chiang Mai, is even better for antique furniture of all kinds, especially the string of shops just east of Hang Dong on Thanon Thakhilek (the road to Ban Thawai), an area usually called Ban Wan. A couple of shops in Ban Wan make reproductions of Thai and Burmese antique furniture using salvaged old teak – these can be very good buys. One of the better ones is a small shop, Srithong Thoprasert (☎ 053-433112), about 500m from the main Hang Dong intersection on Thanon Thakhilek.

A few hundred metres towards Ban Thawai from Srithong Thoprasert, Nakee's Asia Treasures (☎ 053-441357) has contemporary Thai furniture and design accessories based on older themes updated for form and function (including some fusion with Santa Fe styles). It also sells good antiques – all very tasteful and of high quality, if a bit pricey. Ban Thawai itself is a woodcarving village offering mostly new pieces, and very little of high quality.

Bamboo Saxophones Perhaps because Northern Thailand is one of Asia's major locales for both wild and cultivated bamboo, Chiang Mai has attracted interest in the crafting of 'saxophones' from bamboo (although the first such instruments seem to have taken shape some 40 years ago in Jamaica). Actually a sort of hybrid between the saxophone and the recorder (sax shape and sax reed, recorder fingering), the instruments come in two keys, G and F. For each saxophone the bamboo must be carefully selected, cut into short rings, which are roasted over a fire to temper them, and then fitted and glued into the familiar curved shape. The sonic characteristics of the bamboo perfectly compliment the traditional cane sax reed to produce a very mellow, slightly raspy sound.

Two Chiang Mai residents make these delightful little instruments, which produce amazing volume considering their relatively small size. Joy of Sax sells bamboo saxes through The Lost Heavens (see under Antiques for contact details). You can also contact the Joy of Sax workshop directly on

☎ 053-222505. A sax in the key of G costs 4500B, the slightly larger F sax 4800B; an instruction sheet and colourful hemp bag are included. Elephant Lightfoot (☎ 053-879191) has a shopfront at 4/1 Thanon Chaiyaphum (near Pratu Tha Phae) and makes F, G, Bflat and Eflat models, for about the same price as Joy of Sax.

Ceramics Thai Celadon, about 6km north of Chiang Mai, turns out ceramics modelled on the Sawankhalok pottery that used to be made hundreds of years ago at Sukhothai and exported all over the region. With their deep, crackle-glaze finish, some ceramic pieces are very beautiful and the prices are often lower than in Bangkok. The factory is closed on Sunday.

Mengrai Kilns (☎ 053-272063), 79/2 Thanon Arak in the south-western corner of the inner moat area near Buak Hat Park, is reliable. Other ceramic stores can be found close to the Old Chiang Mai Cultural Centre.

There are also several celadon operations in the nearby town of Hang Dong.

Clothes All sorts of shirts, blouses and dresses, plain and embroidered, are available at very low prices, but make sure that you check the quality carefully. The Night Bazaar and shops along Thanon Tha Phae and Thanon Loi Kroh have good selections. Also see under Tailors and Textiles later in this section for other clothing options.

Lacquerware Decorated plates, containers, utensils and other items are made by building up layers of lacquer over a wooden or woven bamboo base. Burmese lacquerware, smuggled into the North, can often be seen, especially at Mae Sai. There are several lacquerware factories in San Kamphaeng.

Rattan Two cheaper rattan shops can be found along the northern side of Thanon Chang Moi two blocks east of the moat. This is the place to buy chairs, small tables, chaise longues, planters, floor screens, settees, bookshelves and other everyday household items. Most of the cheaper pieces, eg, a bookshelf or low-quality chair, cost around 800B, while a rattan chair of better, longer-lasting workmanship will cost 2000B to 5000B.

For higher-quality furniture and accessories made from this jungle vine, check out Hangdong Rattan (☎ 053-208167) at 54–55 Thanon Loi Kroh. In addition to the many items on display, Hangdong takes custom orders.

Silverwork There are several silverwork shops on Thanon Wualai close to Pratu Chiang Mai. Sipsong Panna (☎ 053-216096), in the Nantawan Arcade opposite the Amari Rincome Hotel on Thanon Nimanhemin, is a more upmarket place for jewellery collected in Thailand, Laos, Myanmar and South-West China. Hill-tribe jewellery, which is heavy, chunky stuff, is very nice.

Tailors There are several tailor shops off Thanon Kotchasan near Aroon (Rai) Restaurant, including Florida, Chao Khun, Chaiyo and Progress. Another strip of tailors, catering mostly to tourists, can be found along Thanon Chang Khlan in the Night Bazaar area. Prices are reasonable, and often cheaper than in Bangkok. City Silk (☎ 053-234388) at 336 Thanon Tha Phae, more or less opposite Wat Mahawan, specialises in silk tailoring for women. English is spoken here, and service is friendly and professional. Ask to see some finished work before choosing a shop.

Textiles Very attractive lengths of material can be made into all sorts of things. Thai silk, with its lush colours and pleasantly rough texture, is a particularly good bargain and is usually cheaper here than in Bangkok. Warorot Market is one of the best and least expensive places to look for fabrics, but take care as many items said to be silk are actually polyester.

Several individual shops in town focus on high-quality traditional (sometimes antique) Thai and Lao fabrics, sold by the metre or made up into original-design clothes. A list of the best places in town would have to include Sbun-Nga and Nandakwang, both in a strip of shops opposite the Amari Rincome Hotel.

Studio Naenna (☎/fax 053-226042), at 138/8 Soi Chang Khian, Thanon Huay Kaew, is operated by Patricia Cheeseman, an expert on Thai-Lao textiles who has written extensively on the subject. It's open 8.30 am to 5 pm Monday to Saturday. The Loom, near Soi 3 at 27 Thanon Ratchamankha, carries very fine fabrics from Northern and North-Eastern Thailand, Laos and Cambodia.

Another good source of textiles is Duangjitt House, on a soi off Thanon Thung Hotel opposite the Northern Crafts Centre building – call ☎ 053-242291 or 243546 for an appointment.

You'll also find several shops selling antique Thai and Lao textiles along Thanon Loi Kroh, including Woven Dreams (☎ 053-272569) at No 30/1, and Success Silk Shop (☎ 053-208853) at No 56 (the sign out the front says 'Silk Patchwork – Textile – Mut-Mee Collection'), which features Thai silk ready-made and made-to-order clothes using fabrics from Thailand, Laos and Cambodia. Many are patched together from old hand-woven textiles and made into dresses, skirts, shirts and jackets. They also offer silk scarves, woven hats and yâam – all more or less sized for fàràng.

If you want to see where and how the cloth is made, go to the nearby town of San Kamphaeng for Thai silk, or to Pasang, south of Lamphun, for cotton.

Umbrellas At Bo Sang, the 'umbrella village', you'll find hand-painted paper umbrellas of all kinds, from simple traditional brown ones to giant rainbow-hued parasols.

Woodcarving Many types of carvings are available, including countless elephants. Teak salad bowls are good and very cheap. Many shops along Thanon Tha Phae and near the Night Bazaar stock wood crafts, or go to the source – Hang Dong and Ban Thawai.

Getting There & Away

Air Chiang Mai International Airport (☎ 053-270222) lands regularly scheduled international flights from the following countries as well as domestic flights from several other cities in Thailand:

Kuala Lumpur (Malaysia Airlines; ☎ 053-276523)
Kunming, Hong Kong (THAI; ☎ 053-211044–7)
Siem Reap (Bangkok Airways; 053-281519)
Taipei (Mandarin Airlines; ☎ 053-205187)
Vientiane, Luang Prabang (Lao Aviation; ☎ 053-418258)
Yangon, Mandalay (Air Mandalay; ☎ 053-818049)

The THAI office is within the city moat area at 240 Thanon Phra Pokklao, behind Wat Chiang Man. THAI operates 11 one-hour flights between Bangkok and Chiang Mai daily (plus additional flights on certain days of the week). The fare is 1900B one way in economy class.

Air fares between Chiang Mai and some other Thai cities are:

destination	fare
Chiang Rai	505B
Mae Hong Son	420B
Mae Sot	765B
Nan	605B
Phitsanulok	65B
Phrae	485B
Phuket	3950B

Bangkok Airways (☎ 053-281519, fax 281520) also operates daily flights to and from Bangkok via Sukhothai for 1530B. The 30-minute flight to/from Sukhothai costs only 680B. Fares for children are half the adult price.

Although rather small, Chiang Mai International Airport is well equipped with facilities for the traveller. Upstairs on the departure level is a branch of Suriwong Book Centre, with magazines and newspapers as well as books, and a large restaurant operated by THAI, with Thai, Chinese and international food. On the ground floor there's an espresso bar, Dairy Queen, Pizza Hut, post office, international (IDD and Home Country Direct) phone office (open from 8.30 am to 8 pm), a few speciality gift shops, a car-rental booth, money changers, ATMs, a tourist information booth and a taxi service.

Bus From Bangkok's newer Northern and North-Eastern bus terminal (also known as Moh Chit) there are five ordinary buses daily to Chiang Mai, departing from 5.25 am to 10 pm. The 12-hour trip costs 205B via Nakhon Sawan and 193B via Ayuthaya. First-class air-con buses leave every 30 minutes between 7 am and 8.45 pm. These air-con buses cost 369B one way and take from 10 to 11 hours to reach Chiang Mai, depending on the traffic.

There are 13 2nd-class air-con buses a day between 6.30 am and 10 pm for 290B.

The public buses from the Northern and North-Eastern bus terminal are generally more reliable and on schedule than the private ones booked in Banglamphu and other tourist-oriented places.

Ten or more private tour companies run air-con buses between Bangkok and Chiang Mai, departing from various points throughout both cities. Return tickets are always somewhat cheaper than one-way tickets. The fares range from 260B to 360B, depending on the bus. VIP buses are the most expensive as these have fewer seats per coach to allow for reclining positions. The government VIP bus fare is 570B. Similar buses can be booked in the Soi Ngam Duphli area of Bangkok and also near the Indra Hotel in Pratunam.

Several Thanon Khao San agencies offer bus tickets to Chiang Mai for as little as 200B, including a night's free stay at a guesthouse in Chiang Mai. Sometimes this works out well, but the buses can be substandard and the 'free' guesthouse may charge you 40B for electricity or hot water, or apply heavy pressure for you to sign up for one of its treks before you can get a room. Besides, riding in a bus or minivan stuffed full of foreigners and their bulky backpacks is not the most cultural experience.

A couple of years ago a bus driver on a Thanon Khao San bus bound for Chiang Mai attacked a passenger with a machete when he asked why the promised air-con wasn't working. Several readers have complained that they purchased tickets for large air-con or even VIP buses and at the last minute were shunted into cramped minivans. We recommend avoiding these buses altogether; use public buses from Bangkok's Moh Chit terminal instead.

Public buses between Chiang Mai and other northern towns have frequent departures throughout the day (at least hourly), except for the Mae Sai, Khon Kaen, Udon, Ubon and Khorat buses, which have morning and evening departures only. (See the table for public fares and destinations for public buses.)

For buses to destinations within Chiang Mai Province use the Chang Pheuak terminal (☎ 053-211586), while for buses outside the province use the Chiang Mai Arcade terminal (☎ 053-242664).

Northern Thailand to Yunnan, China

It's possible to travel from Thailand to China's Yunnan Province by road via Laos, a land route that ties together the Golden Triangle and Yunnan's Xishuangbanna district (called Sipsongpanna in Thailand) in South-West China. The Thais, Shan and Lao all consider Xishuangbanna to be a cultural homeland.

One can now cross into Laos from Thailand via at least six legal border crossings. Once in Laos, head to Luang Nam Tha or Udomxai, then proceed north to the Lao village of Boten on the Chinese border, close to the Xishuangbanna town of Mengla (Mong La). From Mengla, an existing road leads to Jinghong. To reach Luang Nam Tha from Northern Thailand you may cross by ferry from Chiang Khong on the Thai side to Huay Xai on the Lao side. This crossing is fully operational; foreigners may enter Laos here with the proper visa. The Boten crossing is legal for all nationalities.

Another way to reach Boten is via Pakbeng in Laos' Udomxai Province. Pakbeng is midway along the Mekong River route between Huay Xai and Luang Prabang; from Pakbeng a Chinese-built road system continues all the way to Boten. To facilitate trade and travel between China and Thailand, the Chinese have offered to build a new road directly south to the Thai border (Nan Province) from the river bank opposite Pakbeng. For now, Thai authorities are not too happy about this proposed road extension, which is seen as an 'invasion' of Thailand. During the years of Thai communist insurgency, Communist Party of Thailand cadres used the Pakbeng road to reach Kunming, China, for training in revolutionary tactics.

Another land route to China begins at the Burmese border town of Tachileik (opposite Mae Sai on the Thai side) and proceeds 164km northward to Myanmar's Kengtung (known as Chiang Tung to the Thais) Shan State. At present the road from Kengtung to Thakhilek is a rough track that takes all day to cover when road conditions are good; permission to cross here can be arranged in Mae Sai on the Thai side. From Kengtung the road continues another 100km north to Myanmar's Mengla (opposite Daluo on the Chinese border); this latter section is now approved for tourist travel upon registration in Kengtung. The Chinese have improved the Daluo to Kengtung section of the road in return for limited mineral and logging rights in Myanmar, so this section is much better than the longer stretch between Kengtung and Thakhilek. From Daluo it's 300km to Jinghong, capital of Xishuangbanna. If you have a valid Chinese visa, you can now cross the Chinese border by land from Myanmar at Mengla/Daluo.

In the long term, the river route is also promising. Chinese barges weighing up to 100 tonnes now ply the Mekong River eight months a year; from the Chinese border to Chiang Khong, Thailand, the trip takes about five days. During the drier months, however, river transport north of Luang Prabang is hampered by rocks and shallows. Blasting and dredging could make way for boats of up to 500 tonnes to travel year-round, but could have devastating effects on the watercourse and lands downstream.

From the town centre, a túk-túk or chartered sǎwngthǎew to the Chiang Mai Arcade terminal should cost 30B to 40B; to the Chang Pheuak terminal you should be able to get a sǎwngthǎew at the normal 10B per person rate.

Train Chiang Mai–bound rapid trains leave Bangkok's Hualamphong station daily at 7.45 am (non-air-con 2nd class and 3rd class) and 10 pm (non-air-con 2nd-class sleeper and 3rd class), arriving at 10.20 and 1.05 pm respectively. One rapid train offering 1st- and 2nd-class air-con sleeper and 3rd-class service departs daily at 3 pm, arriving in Chiang Mai at 5.35 am. Express diesel railcars depart at 8.25 am and 7.25 pm (2nd-class air-con only) and arrive at 7.35 pm and 7.20 am. Special express trains depart at 6 (1st- and 2nd-class air-con sleeper and 2nd-class non-air-con sleeper) and 7.40 pm (1st- and 2nd-class air-con only), reaching Chiang Mai at 7.10 and 9.05 am respectively.

The basic 2nd-class one-way fare is 321B, plus either the special express (80B),

Bus Destinations from Chiang Mai

destination	fare	duration (hrs)	destination	fare	duration (hrs)
Chiang Dao*	25B	1½	Mae Sariang	66B	4-5
Chiang Khong	108B	6½	(1st class air-con)	106B	4-5
(air-con)	151B	6	Mae Sot	115B	6½
(1st class air-con)	194B	6	(1st class air-con)	207B	6
Chiang Rai	66B	4	Nan	100B-114B	6
(air-con)	92B	3	(air-con)	140B-160B	6
(1st class)	119B	3	(1st class air-con)	180B	6
Chiang Saen	86B	4	Pai	51B	4
(1st class air-con)	155B	3½	(air-con	71B	4
Chom Thong*	19B	1	Phayao	59B	3
Fang*	48B	3½	(air-con)	83B	2½
Hang Dong*	6B	30 min	(1st class air-con)	106B	2½
Khon Kaen (via Tak)	230B	12	Phrae	65B	4
(air-con)	322B	12	(air-con)	91B	3½
(1st class air-con)	414B	12	(1st class air-con)	117B	3½
Khon Kaen			Phitsanulok	114B-126B	5-6
(via Uttaradit)	205B	11	(air-con)	160B-176B	5
(air-con)	287B	11	(1st class air-con)	205B-227B	5
(1st class air-con)	369B	11	Sukhothai	109B	6
Khorat	218B	12	(air-con)	153B	5
(1st class air-con)	392B	12	(1st class air-con)	196B	5
(VIP)	458B	12	Tak	60B	4
Lampang	23B	2	(air-con)	90B	4
(air-con)	48B	2	Tha Ton	55B	4
(1st class air-con)	61B	2	Ubon Ratchathani	300B	16
Lamphun	10B	1	(air-con)	540B	15
Mae Hong Son			(VIP)	630B	15
(via Mae Sariang)	133B	8	Udon Thani	205B	12
(air-con)	239B	8	(air-con)	287B	12
(via Pai)	93B	7	(1st class air-con)	480B	12
(air-con)	130B	7			
Mae Sai	83B	5	*Leaves from Chang Pheuak bus terminal. All
(air-con)	116B	5	other buses leave from the Chiang Mai Arcade
(1st class air-con)	149B	5	bus terminal (also called New Terminal) off Thanon Kaew Nawarat.

express (60B) or rapid (40B) surcharges. Add 100B for an upper berth and 150B for a lower berth in a non-air-con 2nd-class rapid train (130B and 200B respectively on the special express). For air-con 2nd-class rapid trains, add 220/270B for upper/lower sleepers (250/320B on special express trains). For example, if you take a non-air-con 2nd-class upper berth on a rapid train, your total fare will be 461B (321+ 100+40B). Tickets for the 'express diesel railcar' (Nos 9 and 11) cost the same as 2nd-class air-con seats on an express.

The basic 1st-class fare is 593B; berths are 520B per person and are available on the special express and rapid trains only.

Trains leave Lopburi for Chiang Mai at 10.52 am (rapid), 10.41 am (express diesel railcar), 5.56 pm (rapid) and 8.45 pm (special express), arriving at the times listed for the same trains from Bangkok. Fares are 257/277B for 2nd-class rapid/express seats and 133B for 3rd-class rapid, including express/rapid surcharges.

Berths on sleepers to Chiang Mai are increasingly hard to reserve without booking well in advance; tour groups sometimes book entire cars. The return trip from Chiang Mai to Bangkok doesn't seem to be as difficult, except during the Songkran (mid-April) and Chinese New Year (late February to early March) holiday periods.

Chiang Mai's neat and tidy train station (☎ 053-244795, 247462) has an ATM and two advance booking offices, one at the regular ticket windows outdoors (open 5 am to 9 pm daily), the other in a more comfortable air-con office (open 6 am to 8 pm daily). The booking office has a computerised reservation system through which you can book train seats for anywhere in Thailand up to 60 days in advance. There is also a left-luggage facility that is open 4.50 am to 8.45 pm daily. The cost is 10B per piece for the first five days and 15B per piece thereafter, with a 20-day maximum.

Getting Around
To/From Chiang Mai International Airport There are two legal airport taxi services, both of which charge 100B for sedan cars that can take up to four or five people and their luggage. Pick up a ticket at either of the taxi kiosks just outside the baggage claim area, then present your ticket to the taxi drivers outside by the main arrival area exit. The airport is only 2km to 3km from the city centre. You can charter a túk-túk or red săwngthăew from the centre of Chiang Mai to the airport for 50B or 60B.

Bus Chiang Mai cancelled all bus services in the city in 1997, a lamentable but understandable fact, given the general lack of passengers. Most Chiang Mai residents now take săwngthăew and many also have their own bicycles or motorcycles.

Car & Motorcycle Cars, 4WDs and minivans are readily available at several locations throughout the city. Be sure that the vehicle you rent has insurance (liability) coverage – ask to see the documents and carry a photocopy with you while driving.

Two of the best agencies in town for service and price are North Wheels (☎ 053-216189, fax 221709, e sales@northwheels.com), at 127/2 Thanon Moon Muang near Somphet Market, and Queen Bee (☎ 053-275525, fax 274349), next to Muang

Thong Hotel on Thanon Moon Muang. Both offer hotel pick-up and delivery as well as 24-hour emergency road service; North Wheel's rates include insurance, while Queen Bee charges extra for insurance. Sample rentals at North Wheels include Suzuki Caribians for 1000B per 24-hour day, and Toyota Mighty-X 4WDs for 1500B a day. Discounted weekly and monthly rates are available.

It's important to choose a car rental agency carefully, by reputation rather than what's on paper. Also realise that whatever happens you're still responsible for personal injury and medical payments of anyone injured in connection with a traffic accident.

Other prominent rental agencies include:

Avis (☎ 053-221316) 14/14 Thanon Huay Kaew; (☎ 053-201574, 201798/9) Chiang Mai International Airport
Budget (☎ 053-202871) Chiang Mai International Airport
Journey Car Rent (☎ 053-208787, fax 273428) 283 Thanon Tha Phae
National Car Rental (☎ 053-210118) Amari Rincome Hotel

If you're looking to hire a motorcycle, Honda Dream 100cc step-throughs can be rented for 100B to 200B a day, depending on the season, the condition of the motorcycle and length of rental. Prices are very competitive in Chiang Mai because there's a real glut of motorcycles. For two people, it's cheaper to rent a small motorcycle for the day to visit Doi Suthep than to go up and back in a săwngthăew. Occasionally you'll see slightly larger 125cc to 150cc Hondas or Yamahas for rent for 200B to 250B a day.

Availability of bikes bigger than 150cc varies from year to year but you can usually find Honda XL600s or Yamaha XT600s (800B to 900B a day), Honda AX-1 250s (500B, 350B low season), Honda Baja 250s (500B, 350B low season) and Honda XR 250s (400B) at a few of the agencies.

Motorcycle hire places come and go with the seasons. Many of them are lined up along the eastern side of the moat on Thanon Moon Muang, Thanon Chaiyaphum and Thanon Kotchasan. Among the more established and more reliable are:

C&P Service (☎ 053-271161) 51 Thanon Kothchasan. Honda Baja 250s and Honda Dreams.

CVA Suzuki Co Ltd (☎ 053-216666) 85/1–4 Thanon Kamphaeng Din.

Dang Bike Hire (☎ 053-271524) Thanon 23 Kotchasan. Big bikes.

Jaguar (☎ 053-214694) 131 Thanon Moon Muang. Honda MRX 125s and Honda Baja 250s.

Lek Big Bike (☎ 053-251830) 74/2 Thanon Chaiyaphum. Large fleet from 250cc to 750cc.

Mr Mechanic 4 Soi 5 Thanon Moon Muang. Small motorcycles, Suzuki 4WD vehicles (insurance included).

Pop Rent-A-Car (☎ 053-276014) Near Soi 2 Thanon Kotchasan. Motorcycles, cars (insurance included).

Tui Big Bike (☎ 053-876227) Corner of Thanon Wichayanon and Thanon Chaiyaphum. Big bikes.

These agencies offer motorcycle insurance for around 50B a day, not a bad investment considering you could face a 25,000B to 60,000B liability if your bike is stolen. Most policies have a high deductible (excess), so in cases of theft you're usually responsible for a third to half of the bike's value – even with insurance. More casual rental places that specialise in quick, easy and cheap rentals of 100cc bikes can be found along Thanon Moon Muang, including Mr Beer at 2 Thanon Moon Muang near Somphet Market.

Several car-rental places also rent motorcycles. See the Getting Around chapter for information on motorcycle touring.

Bicycle This is by far the best way to get around Chiang Mai. The city is small enough so that everywhere is accessible by bike, including Chiang Mai University, Wat U Mong, Wat Suan Dok and the Chiang Mai National Museum on the outskirts of town.

Basic Chinese- or Thai-manufactured bicycles can be rented for around 30B to 50B a day from several of the guesthouses or from various places along the east moat.

Bike and Bite (☎ 053-418534) Thanon Si Phum. This is a combination Thai restaurant and mountain bike rental/tour company.

SP Bike Rental (☎ 053-357559) 99/1 Thanon Moon Muang, near Pratu Tha Phae.

Velocity (☎ 053-410665) 177 Thanon Chang Pheuak. Velocity rents mountain and racing bikes, offers guided tours and carries all kinds of cycling accessories.

The Wild Planet-Contact Travel (☎ 053-277178, fax 279505, ✉ planet@thailine.com) 73/7 Thanon Charoen Prathet between Thanon Loi Kroh and Thanon Tha Phae. This outfit rents rugged 21-speed mountain bikes for 200B a day. The company also operates cycling tours around the province.

Săwngthăew, Túk-túk & Săamláw
Hordes of săwngthăew ply the streets of Chiang Mai looking for passengers. Flag one down, state your destination, and if it is going that way you can ride for 10B. Săwngthăew come in various sizes and conditions – all based on small pick-ups – and take anywhere from 12 to 20 passengers. It's best to board one that already has passengers if you're worried about getting overcharged. Some drivers try to charge lone passengers (both Thais and fàràng) 20B instead of the usual 10B. If you're the only passenger and you're going to an out-of-the-way place, that may be reasonable, but if you're going, say, from Pratu Tha Phae to Warorot Market – a relatively short and well-travelled distance – you shouldn't have to pay more than the normal 10B fare. You can charter (*măo*) a săwngthăew anywhere in the city for 60B or less.

Túk-túk work only on a charter or taxi basis, at 30B for short trips and 40B to 60B for longer ones. After midnight in entertainment areas such as along Thanon Charoenrat near the Riverside and the Brasserie, or down towards Gi Gi's, most túk-túk charge a flat 50B for any trip back across the river.

Chiang Mai still has loads of săamláw (also spelled samlor), especially in the old city around Warorot Market. Săamláw cost around 20B to 30B for most trips.

AROUND CHIANG MAI
Doi Suthep
ดอยสุเทพ

Sixteen kilometres north-west of Chiang Mai is Doi Suthep, a 1676m peak named after the hermit Sudeva, who lived on the mountain's slopes for many years. Near its summit is **Wat Phra That Doi Suthep**; first established in 1383 under King Keu Naone, it is one of the North's most sacred temples.

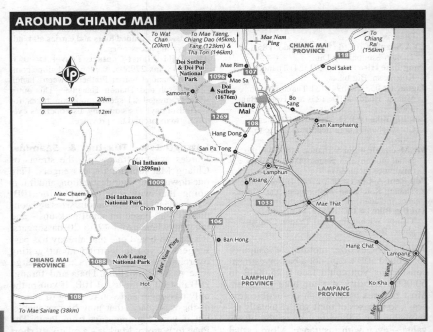

AROUND CHIANG MAI

A naga staircase of 300 steps leads to the wát at the end of the winding road up the mountain. Until a fatal 1997 accident forced its closure, you also had the option of riding a tram from the parking lot to the wát grounds for 5B; no word yet on whether the tram will be repaired and reopened.

At the top, weather permitting, there are some fine views of Chiang Mai. Inside the cloister is an exquisite, Lanna-style, copperplated chedi topped by a five-tiered gold umbrella – one of the holiest chedi in Thailand.

About 4km beyond Wat Phra That Doi Suthep is **Phra Tamnak Phu Phing**, a winter palace for the royal family; the palace gardens are open on weekends and holidays from 8.30 am to 12.30 pm and 1 to 4 pm. The road that passes the palace splits off to the left, stopping at the peak of Doi Pui. From there a dirt road proceeds for a couple of kilometres to a nearby Hmong hill-tribe village. If you won't have an opportunity to visit remote villages, it's worth visiting this one, even though it is well touristed. You can buy Hmong handicrafts here and see traditional homes and costumes, although these are mostly posed situations.

If you're cycling or driving to the summit, you can stop off along the way at **Nam Tok Monthathon**, 2.5km off the paved road to Doi Suthep. The trail is well marked; if you're interested in checking the falls out, have the săwngthăew driver drop you off on the way up the mountain. Pools beneath the falls hold water year-round, although swimming is best during or just after the annual monsoon. The falls can be a little crowded on weekends. In 2000 admission to the falls went from free to 200B for foreigners, raising quite a ruckus locally. The 200B fee allows you to visit other waterfalls on the road to Suthep; it appears that the fees will be used to build cement parking lots and other infrastructure for the park, which could be a negative or a positive, depending on your point of view.

Doi Suthep & Doi Pui National Park

Most visitors do a quick tour of the temple, the Hmong village and perhaps the winter palace grounds, altogether missing the surrounding park. This 261-sq-km reserve is home to more than 300 bird species and nearly 2000 species of ferns and flowering plants. Because of its proximity to urban Chiang Mai, development of the park has become a very sensitive issue. The western side of the park has been severely disturbed by poachers and land encroachers, including around 500 hill-tribe families. In 1986 a Bangkok company tried to establish a cable-car system through the park to the temple, but protests, petitions and marches by the Group for Chiang Mai (Chomrom Pheua Chiang Mai) stopped the plan.

There are extensive hiking trails in the park, including one that climbs 1685m Doi Pui; the summit is a favourite picnic spot. Other trails pass Hmong villages that rarely get fàràng visitors. Bungalow and dormitory accommodation is available near the park headquarters (past the temple car park on the right). Depending on who's on duty at the park headquarters, there are also maps available here. Mountain bikers will find lots of fat-tyre fun.

A 4km trail also leads to the scenic and more isolated **Nam Tok Sai Yai**, and connects with a trail to Nam Tok Monthathon.

Entry fee is 20B for Thais and 200B for foreigners, half that for children under 14.

Getting There & Away Săwngthăew to Doi Suthep leave Chiang Mai throughout the day from the western end of Thanon Huay Kaew in front of Chiang Mai University. Doi Suthep săwngthăew fares are 30B per person. Departures are from Pratu Chang Pheuak and the Chiang Mai Zoo. To Phra Tamnak Phu Phing and Doi Pui add 20B in each direction.

Bo Sang
บ่อสร้าง

Bo Sang (often spelt 'Baw Sang' or 'Bor Sang'), 9km east of Chiang Mai on Rte 1006, is usually called the Umbrella Village because of its many umbrella manufacturers. Almost the entire village consists of craft shops selling painted umbrellas, fans, silverware, straw handiwork, bamboo and teak, statuary, china, celadon and lacquerware, along with tacky Chiang Mai and northern-Thai souvenirs and some quality items.

The larger shops can arrange overseas shipping at reasonable rates. As at Chiang Mai's Night Bazaar, discounts are offered for bulk purchases here. Some of the places will also pack and post parasols, apparently quite reliably.

One of the best times to visit Bo Sang is during the annual Umbrella Festival, which is quite local in flavour and features lots of northern-Thai music, food and colourful processions. It's usually held in late January.

San Kamphaeng
สันกำแพง

Four or 5km farther down Rte 1006 is San Kamphaeng, which flourishes on cotton and silk weaving. Stores offering finished products line the main street, although the actual weaving is done in small factories down side streets. There are some good deals to be had here, especially in silk. For cotton, you'd probably do better in Pasang, a lesser-known village near Lamphun, although you may see shirt styles here not available in Pasang.

Getting There & Away Buses to Bo Sang and San Kamphaeng leave Chiang Mai frequently during the day from the northern side of Thanon Charoen Muang, east of Mae Nam Ping. The bus stop is towards the main post office and the train station and across from San Pa Khoi Market. The fare is 5B to Bo Sang and 6B to San Kamphaeng. White săwngthăew leave from Chang Pheuak bus terminal and make the trip to either destination for 4B.

Hang Dong, Ban Wan & Ban Thawai
หางดง

Fifteen kilometres south of Chiang Mai on Rte 108 is Hang Dong, which is well known for ceramics, woodcarving and antiques. Many of the shops here deal in wholesale as well as retail, so prices are low. Catch a bus from Pratu Chiang Mai to Hang Dong (6B fare). The shops are actually strung out along Rte 108, starting about 2km before Hang Dong.

Immediately east of Hang Dong there are more antique and furniture shops in Ban Wan, and beyond that, in Ban Thawai. Ban Wan generally has the best-quality furniture and antiques.

Trekking in Northern Thailand

Thousands of foreign travellers each year take part in treks into the hills of the North. Most come away with a sense of adventure, but there are a few who are disillusioned by the experience. The most important ingredient in a good trek is having a good leader/organiser, followed by a good group of trekkers. Some travellers finish a tour complaining more about the other trekkers than about the itinerary, food or trek leader.

Before Trekking

Hill-tribe trekking isn't for everyone. First, you must be physically fit to cope with the demands of sustained up and down walking, exposure to the elements and spotty food. Second, many people feel awkward walking through hill-tribe villages and playing the role of voyeur.

In cities and villages elsewhere in Thailand, Thais and other lowland groups are quite used to foreign faces and foreign ways (from TV if nothing else), but in the hills of Northern Thailand the tribes lead largely insular lives. Hence, hill-tribe tourism has pronounced effects, both positive and negative. On the positive side, travellers have a chance to see how traditional subsistence-oriented societies function. (See the special Hill Tribes section later in this chapter.) Also, since the Thai government is sensitive about the image of their minority groups, tourism may actually have forced it to review and sometimes improve its policies towards hill tribes. On the negative side, trekkers introduce many cultural items and ideas from the outside world that may erode tribal customs to varying degrees.

If you have any qualms about interrupting the traditional patterns of life in hill-tribe areas, you probably should not go trekking. It is undeniable that trekking in Northern Thailand is marketed like soap or any other commodity. Anyone who promises you an authentic experience is probably exaggerating at the very least, or at worst contributing to the decline of hill-tribe culture by leading travellers into untouristed areas.

Choosing a Company

Because of the inherent instability of the trekking business, it's difficult to make specific recommendations for particular trekking companies in Chiang Mai. Many of the trekking guides are freelance and go from one company to the next, so there's no way to predict which companies are going to give the best service at any time. Many guesthouses that advertise their own trekking companies actually act as brokers for off-site operations; they collect a commission for every guest they book into a trek.

The Tourism Authority of Thailand (TAT) office in Chiang Mai maintains and distributes a list of licensed agencies. It is also making efforts to regulate trekking companies operating out of Chiang Mai and recommends that you trek only with members of the Professional Guide Association of Chiang Mai or the Jungle Tour Club of Northern Thailand. Still, with more than 150 companies, it's very difficult to guarantee any kind of control. Ultimately the best way to shop for a trek is to talk to travellers who have just returned from one.

If you decide to do a trek keep these points in mind: choose your trek operator carefully, try to meet the others in the group (suggest a meeting) and find out exactly what the tour includes and does not include, as usually there are additional expenses beyond the basic rate. In the cool season, make sure sleeping bags are provided, as the thin wool blankets available in most villages are not sufficient for the average visitor. If everything works out, even an organised tour can be worthwhile. A useful check list of questions to ask are:

- How many people will there be in the group? (Six to 10 is a good maximum range.)
- Can the organiser guarantee that no other tourists will visit the same village on the same day, especially overnight?
- Can the guide speak the language of each village to be visited? (This is not always necessary, as many villagers can speak Thai nowadays.)

Trekking in Northern Thailand

- Exactly when does the tour begin and end? (Some three-day treks turn out to be less than 48 hours in length.)
- Do they provide transport before and after the trek or is it just by public bus (which may mean long waits)?

In general, the trekking business has become more conscious of the need to tread carefully in hill-tribe villages than in previous decades. Most companies now tend to limit the number of visits to a particular area and are careful not to overlap areas used by other companies. Everyone benefits from this consciousness: the hill tribes are less impacted by trekkers, the trekkers have a better experience and the trekking industry runs at a sustainable rate. Opium smoking among guides continues to be a problem with some companies: A few companies are now advertising drug-free treks to avoid the pitfalls of opium-addicted guides and also to avoid the adverse influences the sight of constant opium smoking has on young hill-tribe members.

These days there are plenty of places apart from Chiang Mai where you can arrange treks. You might find these organisations offer better and less expensive tours from more remote and less trekked areas. Also, they are generally smaller, friendlier operations and the trekkers are usually a more determined bunch since they're not looking for an easy and quick in-and-out trek. The treks are often informally arranged, usually involving discussions of duration, destination, cost etc.

You can easily arrange treks out of the following northern-Thai towns: Chiang Rai, Mae Hong Son, Pai, Mae Sai and Tha Ton. If you have a little time to seek out the right people, you can also go on organised treks from Mae Sariang, Khun Yuam, Soppong (near Pai), Mae Sot, Um Phang and various out-of-the-way guesthouses that are springing up all over the North.

The down side, of course, is that companies outside of Chiang Mai are generally subject to even less regulation than those in Chiang Mai, and there are fewer guarantees with regard to trekking terms and conditions.

Costs

Organised treks out of Chiang Mai average from 1800B for a three-day, two-night trek to 6000B for a deluxe seven-day, six-night trek, both of which include transport, guide, accommodation, meals and rafting and/or elephant riding. Rates vary, so it pays to shop around – although these days so many companies are competing for your business that rates have remained pretty stable for the last few years. Elephant rides actually become quite boring and even uncomfortable after an hour or two. Some companies now offer quickie day treks or one-night, two-day programs.

Don't choose a trek by price alone. It's better to talk to other travellers in town who have been on treks. Treks out of other towns in the north are usually less expensive.

The Professional Guide Association in Chiang Mai meets monthly to set trek prices and to discuss problems, and issues regular, required reports to the TAT about individual treks. All trekking guides and companies are supposed to be government-licensed and bonded. As a result, a standard for trekking operators has emerged whereby you can expect the price you pay to include: transport to and from the starting/ending points of a trek (if outside Chiang Mai); food (three meals a day) and accommodation in all villages visited; basic first aid; predeparture valuables storage; and sometimes the loan of specific equipment, such as sleeping bags in cool weather or water bottles.

Not included in the price are beverages other than drinking water or tea, lunch on the first and last days and personal porters.

Seasons

Probably the best time to trek is November to February, when the weather is refreshing with little or no rain and poppies are in bloom everywhere. Between March and May the hills are dry and the weather is quite hot. The second-best time is early in the rainy season, between June and July, before the dirt roads become too saturated.

Trekking in Northern Thailand

Safety

Every year or so there's a trekking robbery or two in Northern Thailand – the likelihood of this occurring to you is low. However, if it does happen often the bandits are armed with guns, which they will use if they meet resistance. Once they collect a load of watches, money and jewellery, many bandit gangs hightail it across the border into Myanmar. In spite of this, police have had a good arrest record so far and have created hill-country patrols. Still, gangs can form at any time and anywhere. The problem is that most people living in the rural North believe that all foreigners are very rich (a fair assumption in relation to hill-tribe living standards). Most of these people have never even been to Chiang Mai and, from what they have heard about the capital, consider Bangkok to be a virtual paradise of wealth. So don't take anything that you can't afford to lose, and don't resist robbery attempts.

If you leave your valuables with a guesthouse, make sure you obtain a fully itemised receipt before departing on a trek.

Conduct

There are several other guidelines to minimise the negative impact your trekking may have on the local people:

- Always ask for permission before taking photos of tribespeople and/or their dwellings. You can ask through your guide or by using sign language. Because of traditional belief systems, many individuals and even whole tribes may object strongly to being photographed.
- Show respect for religious symbols and rituals. Don't touch totems at village entrances or any other object of obvious symbolic value without asking permission. Keep your distance from ceremonies being performed unless you're asked to participate.
- Exercise restraint in giving things to tribespeople or bartering with them. If you want to give something to the people you encounter on a trek, the best thing is to make a donation to the village school or other community fund. Your guide can help arrange this. While it's an easy way to get a smile – giving sweets to children contributes to tooth decay – remember they probably don't have toothbrushes and toothpaste like you do.
- Set a good example to hill-tribe youngsters by not smoking opium or using other drugs.
- Don't litter while trekking or staying in villages.

You might also want to check the 'Guidelines for Visitors to Northern Thailand's Mountain Peoples' through the Internet home page at www.lanna.com.

Opium Smoking

Some guides are very strict now about forbidding the smoking of opium on treks. This seems to be a good idea, since one of the problems trekking companies have had in the past is dealing with opium-addicted guides! Volunteers who work in tribal areas also say opium smoking sets a bad example for young people in the villages.

Opium is traditionally a condoned vice of the elderly, yet an increasing number of young people in the villages are now taking opium, heroin and amphetamines. This is possibly due in part to the influence of young trekkers who may smoke once and a few weeks later be hundreds of kilometres away while the villagers continue to face the temptation every day. Addiction has negative effects for the village as well as the individual's health, including a reduced male labour force and corresponding increase in women's workloads (most addicts are men) and reduced overall agricultural production. Also, an increase in the number of villagers injecting heroin (needles are often shared) has led to sky-rocketing rates of HIV infection in hill-tribe villages. Given the already high incidence of HIV infection among northern-Thai prostitutes some welfare groups say that entire tribal communities will be wiped out unless the rate of infection can be stopped.

Trekking in Northern Thailand

Independent Trekking

You might consider striking out on your own in a small group of two to five people. Gather as much information as you can about the area you'd like to trek in from the Tribal Museum in Chiang Mai. Browsing the displays will help you identify different tribes, and the inscriptions offer cultural information. Don't bother staff with questions about trekking as this is not their area of expertise. Maps, distributed mostly by guesthouses outside of Chiang Mai, pinpoint various hill-tribe areas in the North.

Be prepared for language difficulties. Few people will know any English. Usually someone in a village will know some Thai, so a Thai phrasebook can be helpful. Lonely Planet publishes a *Hill Tribes phrasebook* with phrase sections for each of the six major hill-tribe languages.

As in Himalayan trekking in Nepal and India, many people now do short treks on their own, staying in villages along the way. It is not necessary to bring a lot of food or equipment, just money for food that can be bought en route at small Thai towns and occasionally in the hill-tribe settlements. (Obviously, be sure to take plenty of water and some high energy snacks.) However, the TAT strongly discourages trekking on your own because of the safety risk. Check with the police when you arrive in a new district so they can tell you if an area is considered safe or not. A lone trekker is an easy target for robbers.

San Pa Tong
สันป่าตอง

Farther south down Rte 108, this village is known for its large water buffalo and cattle market, held each Saturday morning from 5.30 am till around 10 am. In addition to livestock, the lively market purveys used motorcycles. If you want breakfast, there are also plenty of food vendors. You can catch a bus or săwngthăew to San Pa Tong from the bus queue near Pratu Chiang Mai.

Mae Sa & Samoeng
แม่สาและสะเมิง

This forested loop north-west of Chiang Mai via Mae Rim and/or Hang Dong makes a good day or overnight trip. Although dotted with tourist developments – resorts, orchid farms, butterfly parks, snake farms, elephant camps, botanic gardens, antique and handicraft shops – the Rte 1096/1269 loop through the Mae Sa Valley is very scenic in spots. **Nam Tok Mae Sa** is only 6km from the Mae Rim turn-off from Rte 107, which in turn is 12km north of Chiang Mai. Farther along the loop are several Hmong villages.

There are at least four places along the loop that call themselves elephant 'camp', 'farm', or 'village'. Best of the bunch is the **Maesa Elephant Camp** near Nam Tok Mae Sa, where it costs 80B per person for the one-hour elephant shows at 8 and 9.40 am daily (there's also a 1.30 pm show during high season). You can feed the elephants sugar cane and bananas, and visit the baby elephants in their nursery and training school. Call ☎ 053-297060 for more information.

Samoeng, at the westernmost extension of the loop (35km from Mae Rim), is the most peaceful area for an overnight stay, since it's 5km north of the main loop junction between the highways to/from Mae Rim and Hang Dong via Rte 1269. The *Samoeng Resort* (☎ 053-487072), about 1.5km outside Samoeng village itself, has 15 quiet, well-designed bungalows from 700B with fan, more for air-con.

Getting There & Away You can get a săwngthăew to Samoeng from the Chang Pheuak bus terminal in Chiang Mai for 20B.

Since it's paved all the way, the winding loop road makes a good ride by bicycle or motorcycle. From Samoeng you can take a north-west detour along Rte 1265 to Rte 1095 for Pai and Mae Hong Son; the 148km road (136km unpaved, 12.2km paved) breaks north at the Karen village of Wat Chan, where fuel is available. This is the longest stretch of unpaved road remaining

NORTHERN THAILAND

in Northern Thailand and is recommended for experienced off-highway bikers only (and only in the dry season). The road passes a few Hmong and Karen villages.

CHOM THONG & AROUND
จอมทอง

Chom Thong (pronounced 'jawm thawng') is a necessary stop between Chiang Mai and Doi Inthanon, Thailand's highest peak, if you're travelling by public transport. The main temple is worth an hour's stop for its ancient bòt, or longer if you're interested in meditation.

Wat Phra That Si Chom Thong
วัดพระธาตุศรีจอมทอง

If you have time, walk down Chom Thong's main street to Wat Phra That Si Chom Thong. The gilded Burmese chedi in the compound was built in 1451 and the Burmese-style bòt, built in 1516, is one of the most beautiful in Northern Thailand. Inside and out it is an integrated work of art, and the whole is well looked after by the local Thais. Fine woodcarving can be seen along the eaves of the roof and inside on the ceiling, which is supported by massive teak columns. The impressive altar is designed like a small *prasat* (enclosed shrine), in typical Lanna style, and is said to contain a relic from the right side of the Buddha's skull.

Nearby is a glass case containing ancient Thai weaponry. Behind the prasat altar is a room containing religious antiques.

A few doors up from the wát compound, the **Vegetarian Restaurant** *(Watjanee)* offers simple one-plate rice and noodle dishes that substitute tofu and gluten for meat. All dishes cost 25B. Look for the yellow pennants out front.

Meditation Retreats Under the direction of Ajahn Thong, formerly of Wat Ram Poeng in Chiang Mai, meditation retreats in the style of the late Mahasi Sayadaw are held regularly. Meditation students are asked to stay a minimum of two weeks; the optimum course lasts 26 days. Students dress in white, and stay in a group of *kùtì* (meditation huts) at the back of the wát. The schedule is very rigorous.

Some students continue individual practice at a forest monastery in the Chom Thong district known as **Wat Tham Thong**, 5km before the town of Hot (west of Chom Thong) off Rte 108. The abbot at the latter monastery, Ajahn Chuchin Vimaro, teaches the same style of vipassana.

Doi Inthanon National Park
อุทยานแห่งชาติดอยอินทนนท์

Doi Inthanon (often called Doi In; 2595m), Thailand's highest peak, has three impressive waterfalls cascading down its slopes. Starting from the bottom, these are **Nam Tok Mae Klang**, **Nam Tok Wachiratan** and **Nam Tok Siriphum**. The first two have picnic areas and food vendors. Nam Tok Mae Klang is the largest waterfall and the easiest to get to; you must stop here to get a bus to the top of Doi Inthanon. Nam Tok Mae Klang can be climbed nearly to the top, as there is a footbridge leading to rock formations over which the water cascades. Nam Tok Wachiratan is also very nice and less crowded.

The views from Inthanon are best in the cool dry season from November to February. You can expect the air to be quite chilly towards the top, so take a jacket or sweater. For most of the year a mist, formed by the condensation of warm humid air below, hangs around the highest peak. Along the 47km road to the top are many terraced rice fields, tremendous valleys and a few small hill-tribe villages. The mountain slopes are home to around 4000 Hmong and Karen tribespeople.

The entire mountain is a national park (482 sq km), despite agriculture and human habitation. One of the top destinations in South-East Asia for naturalists and bird-watchers, the mist-shrouded upper slopes produce a bumper crop of orchids, lichens, mosses and epiphytes, while supporting nearly 400 bird varieties, more than any other habitat in Thailand. The mountain is also one of the last habitats of the Asiatic black bear, along with the Assamese macaque, Phayre's leaf-monkey and a selection of other rare and not-so-rare monkeys and gibbons, plus the more common Indian civet, barking deer and giant flying squirrel – around 75 mammalian species in all.

Most of the park's bird species are found between 1500m and 2000m; the best bird-watching season is from February to April, and the best spots are the *beung* (bogs) near the top.

Phra Mahathat Naphamethanidon, a chedi built by the Royal Thai Air Force to commemorate the king's 60th birthday in 1989, is off the highway between the 41km and 42km markers, about 4km before reaching the summit of Doi Inthanon. In the base of the octagonal chedi is a hall containing a stone Buddha image.

The 200B entry fee for foreigners collected for Nam Tok Mae Klang near the foot of the mountain is good for all stops on the Doi Inthanon circuit; be sure to keep your receipt. At the park headquarters, 31km from Chom Thong, you can book park *bungalows* for 100B per person or tents for 40B. Blankets may be hired for 10B each.

Getting There & Away

Buses to Chom Thong leave regularly from just inside Pratu Chiang Mai at the south moat as well as from the Chang Pheuak bus terminal in Chiang Mai. Some buses go directly to Nam Tok Mae Klang and some go only as far as Hot, although the latter will let you off in Chom Thong. The fare to Chom Thong, 58km from Chiang Mai, is 19B.

From Chom Thong there are regular săwngthăew to Mae Klang, about 8km north, for 15B. Săwngthăew from Mae Klang to Doi Inthanon leave almost hourly until late afternoon and cost 30B per person. Most of the passengers are locals who get off at various points along the road, thus allowing a few stationary views of the valleys below.

For another 15B you can go from Chom Thong to Hot, where you can get buses on to Mae Sariang or Mae Hong Son. However, if you've gone to Doi Inthanon and the waterfalls, you probably won't have time to make it all the way to Mae Sariang or Mae Hong Son in one day, so you may want to stay overnight in the park or in Chom Thong. Forestry service bungalows near the park headquarters (past the Chom Thong park entrance) cost 800B (sleeps eight), 900B (sleeps 10) and 1000B (sleeps 10) a night. In Chom Thong, inquire at the wát for a place to sleep. Call ☎ 053-311608 for more information.

NORTH TO THA TON
Mae Taeng & Chiang Dao
แม่แตง/เชียงดาว

The mountainous area around Mae Taeng – especially south-west of the junction of Rtes 107 and 1095 – has become a major trekking area because of the variety of Lisu, Lahu, Karen and Hmong villages in the region. Rafting along Mae Taeng is so popular these days that there's a permanent rafting centre, Maetaman Rafting, west of Rte 107. For the most part, the centre handles rafting groups on trips out of Chiang Mai.

The **Elephant Training Centre Taeng-Dao**, off Rte 107 between Mae Taeng and Chiang Dao, is one of several training centres in the area that puts on elephant shows for tourists. If you haven't seen the one in Lampang Province (in Thung Kwian), this one's a reasonable alternative.

Fang Dao Forest Monastery, off the highway south of Chiang Dao near the 52km marker, is a meditation wát in the north-eastern forest tradition.

From the main four-way junction at Chiang Dao, those with their own wheels – preferably a mountain bike, motorcycle or truck – can head east to visit Lahu, Lisu and Akha villages within a 15km ride. Roughly 13.5km from Rte 107 is the Lisu village of **Lisu Huay Ko**, where rustic accommodation is available.

Tham Chiang Dao The main attraction along the way to Fang and Tha Ton is this cave complex 5km west of Rte 107 and 72km north of Chiang Mai.

The complex is said to extend some 10km to 14km into 2285m Doi Chiang Dao; the interconnected caverns that are open to the public include Tham Mah (7365m long), Tham Kaew (477m), Tham Phra Nawn (360m), Tham Seua Dao (540m) and Tham Nam (660m).

Tham Phra Nawn and Tham Seua Dao contain religious statuary and are electrically illuminated (and thus easily explored on one's own), while Tham Mah, Tham Kaew and Tham Nam have no light fixtures. A guide with a pressurised gas lantern can be hired for 60B for up to eight people. The interior cave formations are quite spectacular in places – over 100 of them are named.

Local legend says this cave complex was the home of a *reusii* (hermit) for a thousand years. As the legend goes, the sage was on such intimate terms with the deity world that he convinced some *thewádaa* (the Buddhist equivalent of angels) to create seven magic wonders inside the caverns: a stream flowing from the pedestal of a solid-gold Buddha; a storehouse of divine textiles; a mystical lake; a city of nagas; a sacred immortal elephant; and the hermit's tomb. No, you won't find any of the seven wonders; the locals say these are much deeper inside the mountain, beyond the last of the illuminated caverns.

The locals also say that anyone who attempts to remove a piece of rock from the cave will forever lose their way in the cave's eerie passages.

Admission to the overall complex is 5B. There is a wát complex outside the cavern and a collection of vendors selling roots, herbs and snacks (mostly noodles).

The surrounding area is quite scenic and largely unspoiled. From the summit of Doi Chiang Dao there are spectacular views. Beyond Tham Chiang Dao along the same rural road is a smaller sacred cave called **Tham Pha Plong**.

Places to Stay Under Thai and German management, *Malee's Nature Lovers Bungalows* (☎ 01-961 8387), about 1.5km past Tham Chiang Dao on the right, has dorm beds for 100B and thatch-and-brick bungalows with private bathroom for 300B a double. Malee's can arrange trekking, rafting and bird-watching trips in the area.

Traveller Inn Hotel, on the highway in Mae Taeng, is a well-run place with rooms in the 300B to 500B range. *Pieng Dao*, an old wooden hotel in Chiang Dao village, has rooms for 90B.

Chiang Dao Hill Resort (☎ 053-236995), off the highway between the 100km and 101km markers, offers good tourist bungalows for 700B to 1800B, and a restaurant open 7 am to 10 pm. The *Royal Ping Garden Resort*, off the highway south of Chiang Dao, has more expensive luxury rooms.

Getting There & Away Buses to Chiang Dao from Chiang Mai's Chang Pheuak terminal depart every 30 minutes between 5.30 am and 5.30 pm and cost 25B. The trip takes 1½ hours.

Doi Ang Khang
ดอยอ่างขาง

About 20km before Fang is the turn-off for Rte 1249 to Doi Ang Khang, Thailand's 'Little Switzerland'. Twenty-five kilometres from the highway, this 1300m peak has a cool climate year-round and supports the cultivation of flowers, as well as fruits and vegetables that are usually found only in more temperate climates.

A few hill-tribe villages (Lahu, Lisu and Hmong) can be visited on the slopes. You can pick up a free map of the area at the main military checkpoint on Rte 1249. Some interesting do-it-yourself treks can be made in the area.

The Yunnanese/KMT (Kuomintang; Chinese Nationalist Army) village of **Ban Khum** on Doi Ang Khang rents hillside bungalows for around 200B to 300B.

Nineteen kilometres before the turn-off to Doi Ang Khang you can make a 12km detour west on a dirt road to visit **Ban Mai Nong Bua**, another KMT village with an atmosphere like that of Doi Mae Salong.

FANG & THA TON
ฝาง/ท่าตอน

The present city of Fang was founded by King Mengrai in the 13th century, although as a human settlement and trading centre for jiin haw caravans the locale dates back at least 1000 years. North from Chiang Mai along Rte 107, Fang doesn't look particularly inviting, but the town's quiet backstreets are lined with interesting little shops in wooden buildings. The Shan/Burmese-style **Wat Jawng Paen** (near the Wiang Kaew Hotel) has a very impressive stacked-roof wíhǎan.

There are Mien and Karen villages nearby that you can visit on your own, but for most people Fang is just a road marker on the way to Tha Ton, the starting point for Mae Nam Kok trips to Chiang Rai, and for treks to the many hill-tribe settlements in the region. Most people prefer Tha Ton's more rural setting for spending the night. It's only half an hour or so by sǎwngthǎew to the river from Fang or vice versa.

Two banks along the main street in Fang offer currency exchange. Through the Wiang Kaew Hotel in Fang you can arrange tours to local villages inhabited by Palaung (a Karennic tribe that arrived from Myanmar around 14 years ago), Black Lahu, Akha and Yunnanese.

About 10km west of Fang at Ban Meuang Chom, near the agricultural station, is a system of **hot springs**, which are part of Doi Fang National Park. Just ask for the *bàw náam ráwn* (*baw nâam hâwn* in northern Thai). On weekends there are frequent săwngthăew carrying Thai picnickers from Fang to the hot springs.

Tha Ton has a săwngthăew stand and a collection of river boats, restaurants, souvenir shops and tourist accommodation along a pretty bend in Mae Nam Kok. For something to do, climb the hill to **Wat Tha Ton** and the Chinese shrine for good views of the surrounding area. A large temple bell, which sounds every morning at 4 am (wake-up call for monks) and again at 6 am (alms-round call) can be heard throughout the valley surrounding Tha Ton.

Tourist Police
Near the bridge is a Tourist Police office open 8.30 am to 4.30 pm daily.

Trekking & Rafting
There are some pleasant walks along Mae Nam Kok. Within 20km of Fang and Tha Thon you can visit Lahu and Palaung villages on foot, mountain bike or motorcycle.

Treks and raft trips can be arranged through Thip's Travellers House, Mae Kok River Lodge or the Thaton River View, all in Tha Ton. Thip's arranges economical bamboo house-rafts with pilot and cook for three days for 1500B per person (minimum four people), including all meals, lodging and rafting.

On the first day you'll visit several villages near the river and spend the night in a Lisu village; on the second day rafters visit hot springs and more villages, and spend the second night on the raft; and on the third day you dock in Chiang Rai.

You could get a small group of travellers together and arrange your own house-raft with a guide and cook for a two- or three-day journey down river, stopping off in villages of your choice along the way. A house-raft generally costs 400B to 500B per person per day including simple meals and takes up to six people – so figure on 1200B

to 1500B for a three-day trip. Police regulations require that an experienced boat navigator accompany each raft – the river has lots of tricky spots and there have been some mishaps.

Near the pier you can rent inflatable kayaks to do your own paddling in the area. Upstream a few kilometres the river crosses into Myanmar.

Places to Stay & Eat
Fang A good choice is the *Wiang Kaew Hotel*, behind the Fang Hotel off the main street. Basic but clean rooms with private bathroom are 100B, 140B with hot water.

Around the corner on Thanon Tha Phae, the *Ueng Khum Hotel (UK Hotel; ☎ 053-451268)* has large bungalow-style accommodation around a courtyard for 180/280B single/double with fan, 380B single/double with air-con; all rooms have hot-water showers. Slightly more upmarket digs near the market on the highway are available at the *Chok Thani* and *Roza*; both have rooms with fan from 200B, with air-con from 350B.

The *Fang Restaurant* (its Thai sign reads 'Khun Pa'), next to the defunct Fang Hotel entrance, has a bilingual menu and quite decent food, including the speciality of the house, *khâo mŭu daeng* (barbecued pork over rice). *Parichat Restaurant*, on the northern side of Thanon Rawp Wiang near the highway market, serves khâo sàwy with chicken or beef, plus *kŭaytĭaw* (rice noodles), *khâo phàt* (fried rice) and other standards. Farther down this same road is a row of cheap Isan restaurants and *lâo dawng* (herbal liquor) bars.

A few *food vendors* – not quite enough to make a true 'night market' – set up near the bus terminal at night.

Tha Ton If you want to spend the night near the pier in Tha Ton, there are several options. The old standby *Thip's Travellers House* is a short walk from the pier, quite near the bridge where the road from Fang meets the river. Rates are 80B for thin-walled rooms without bathroom, 100B with cold-water bathroom. There's a nice little cafe out front.

Chan Kasem (☎ 053-459313), down near the pier, has a restaurant on the river and a variety of none-too-clean rooms: 80B with shared bathroom in the older wooden section; 100B for singles/doubles with fan and bathroom; 120B to 200B with hot water and 300B for a brick bungalow. Nearby, the friendly **Naam Waan Guest House** offers 10 tidy rooms, all with fan and private cold-water shower for 150B.

Opposite the boat landing in a new, two-storey building is the **Apple Guest House**, with an upmarket restaurant on the ground floor and spacious light-filled rooms above. All have attached hot-water showers and go for 300B, or 400B with a small TV. Credit-card symbols on the front door seem to be merely decorative, as this place only accepts cash.

Farther along the river, the newish **Maekok River Village Resort** (☎ 053-459328, 459189, fax 459329, ✉ rooms@ track-of-the-tiger.com) offers four-bed rooms for 813B per person as well as two-bed poolside rooms for 1125B per person. On the grounds are a pool and restaurant. A variety of activities, including massage, cooking classes, trekking, rafting, mountain biking and caving can be arranged through the resort. The resort has several options for groups who want to use the facility; in fact the orientation is slanted towards school groups from around Thailand and abroad.

On the opposite side of the river there are three other places to choose from. Along the river about 150m from the bridge, the tranquil **Garden Home** (☎ 053-373015) offers very clean thatched-roof bungalows spaced well apart among lots of litchi trees and bougainvillea for 300B with private hot-water shower – most visitors will probably agree that this is the best deal in Tha Ton. Garden Home also offers a few stone bungalows for 400B, and three larger, more luxurious bungalows on the river with small verandas, TV and refrigerator for 1000B. From the bridge, turn left at the Thaton River View Hotel sign to find it.

Next is the new **Riverside House** (☎ 053-373214, fax 373215), featuring small cement air-con bungalows with terraces back from the river (500B), fan rooms in a cement building, also back off the river (300B) and a couple of large air-con wooden bungalows with terraces right on the river (1000B). All rates include breakfast. The grounds are beautifully landscaped, and an attached restaurant overlooks the river.

Farther along the river, the well-designed **Thaton River View Hotel** (☎ 053-373173, fax 459288) has 33 immaculate, spacious rooms facing the river and joined by wooden walkways for 1320B including breakfast, a better value at this price than Maekok River Lodge. The hotel's restaurant is the best in the area, with Shell Chuan Chim honours (see the 'Thai Cuisine' special section earlier in this book) for four different dishes on the menu. Facilities include a herbal sauna, massage, safe-deposit boxes, library, game room and jogging track.

The **Thaton Garden Riverside** (☎ 053-459286), also on the river, offers good bungalows with fans and hot-water showers for 300B to 400B a night. The attached **Rim Nam Restaurant** is good.

The four-storey stone-facade **Thaton Chalet** (☎ 053-373155, fax 373158) is right on the river next to the bridge. All rooms have carpet, air-con, TV and hot water. The hotel features a pleasant beer garden right on the river, as well as an indoor restaurant. Officially published room prices are 1000/1200B superior, 2000B deluxe, although when we asked, we were told that the starting rate was 950B.

Several little noodle stands can be found in the vicinity of the bus queue and there are several rustic food stalls near the pier and near the bridge. **Racha Roti** in front of Thip's Travellers House features 16 flavours of rotii. A local culinary speciality is *lûu*, a northern-Thai salad made with pig's blood.

About 15km north-east of Tha Ton, in Lou-Ta, the nearest Lisu village, **Asa's Guest Home** offers two basic bamboo-walled rooms for 150B per person per night including two meals. The friendly family who owns the house can arrange one- and two-day jungle trips in the area. To get to Asa'a Guest Home take a yellow săwng-thăew from Tha Ton for 15B (or motorcycle taxi for 30B) and ask to get off in Lou-Ta.

Getting There & Away

Bus & Săwngthăew Buses to Fang leave from the Chang Pheuak bus terminal in Chiang Mai every 30 minutes between 5.30 am and 5.30 pm. The trip takes 3½ hours and costs 48B. Air-con minivans make the trip to Fang every 30 minutes between 7.30 am and 4.30 pm, leaving from behind the

Chang Pheuak bus terminal on the corner of Soi Sanam Kila. The fare is 80B.

From Fang it's 23km to Tha Ton. A săwngthăew does the 40-minute trip for 12B; the larger orange buses from Fang leave less frequently and cost 10B. Buses leave from near the market, or you can wait in front of the Fang Hotel for a bus or săwngthăew. Both operate from 5.30 am to 5 pm only.

Buses to Mae Sai cost 33B from Tha Ton, 39B from Fang.

The river isn't the only way to get to points north from Tha Ton. Yellow săwngthăew leave from the northern side of the river in Tha Ton to Mae Salong in Chiang Rai Province every 30 minutes or so between 7 am and 3 pm. The trip takes about 2½ hours and costs 45B per person. You can charter an entire săwngthăew for 400B one way, 600B round trip. Hold tight – the road is steep and winding.

If you're heading to or coming from Mae Hong Son Province, it's not necessary to dip all the way south to Chiang Mai before continuing westward or eastward. At Ban Mae Malai, the junction of Rte 107 (the Chiang Mai-Fang highway), you can pick up a bus to Pai for 45B; if you're coming from Pai, be sure to get off here to catch a bus north to Fang.

Motorcycle Motorcycle trekkers can also travel between Tha Ton and Doi Mae Salong, 48km north-east along a fully paved but sometimes treacherous mountain road. There are a couple of Lisu and Akha villages along the way. The 27km or so between Doi Mae Salong and the village of Hua Muang Ngam are very steep and winding – take care, especially in the rainy season. When conditions are good, the trip can be accomplished in 1½ hours.

For an extra charge, you can take a motorcycle on most boats to Chiang Rai.

RIVER TRIP TO CHIANG RAI

From Tha Ton you can make a half-day longtail boat trip to Chiang Rai down Mae Nam Kok. The regular passenger boat takes up to 12 passengers, leaves at 12.30 pm and costs 200B per person. You can also charter a boat all the way for 1600B, which between eight people works out to the same per person but gives you more room to move. The trip is a bit of a tourist trap these days as the passengers are all tourists (what local will pay 200B to take the boat when they can catch a bus to Chiang Rai for less than 40B?), and the villages along the way sell cola and souvenirs – but it's still fun. The best time to go is at the end of the rainy season in November when the river level is high.

To catch one of these boats on the same day from Chiang Mai you'd have to leave by 7 or 7.30 am and make no stops on the way. The 6 am bus is the best bet. The travel time down river depends on river conditions and the skill of the pilot, taking anywhere from three to five hours. You could actually make the boat trip in a day from Chiang Mai, catching a bus back from Chiang Rai as soon as you arrive, but it's better to stay in Fang or Tha Ton, take the boat trip, then stay in Chiang Rai or Chiang Saen before travelling on. You may sometimes have to get off and walk or push the boat if it gets stuck on sand bars.

Some travellers take the boat to Chiang Rai in two or three stages, stopping first in **Mae Salak**, a large Lahu village that is about a third of the distance, or **Ban Ruammit**, a Karen village about two-thirds of the way down. Both villages are well touristed these days (charter boat tours stop for photos and elephant rides), but from here you can trek to other Shan, Thai and hill-tribe villages, or do longer treks south of Mae Salak to **Wawi**, a large multiethnic community of jiin haw, Lahu, Lisu, Akha, Shan, Karen, Mien and Thai peoples. The Wawi area has dozens of hill-tribe villages of various ethnicities, including the largest Akha community in Thailand (Saen Charoen) and the oldest Lisu settlement (Doi Chang).

Another alternative is to trek south from Mae Salak all the way to the town of **Mae Suai**, where you can catch a bus on to Chiang Rai or back to Chiang Mai. You might also try getting off the boat at one of the smaller villages (see the boat fares table later). Another alternative is to make the trip (much more slowly) upriver from Chiang Rai – this is possible despite the rapids.

Near Ban Ruammit on the opposite river bank (90 minutes by boat from Chiang Rai, 50B) are some very pretty **hot springs**. Don't even think about entering the water – it's scalding hot. From here you can hike about an hour to *Akha Hill House* (☎ 01-460 7450, *fax 053-715451,* ⓔ *apaehouse@hotmail .com),* wholly owned and managed by Akha tribespeople. This rustic guesthouse is in a beautiful setting overlooking a mountain valley; a waterfall and several other villages (Akha, Mien, Lisu, Karen and Lahu) are within walking distance. It can organise overnight trips into the forest with guides who build banana-palm huts and cook meals using sections of bamboo. Rates are 40B for a dorm bed, 50B to 60B for a single and 80B to 90B a double with shared facilities, and 70B single and 100B to 120B double for a hut with private bathroom. Akha Hill House can also be reached by road from Chiang Rai, 26km away. Call for free pick-up (once daily between 3.30 and 4 pm).

Several of the guesthouses in Tha Ton now organise raft trips down the river – see Fang & Tha Ton earlier in this chapter.

A boat leaves once daily from Tha Ton at 12.30 pm. The following table shows boat fares from Tha Ton:

destination	fare
Ban Mai	50B
Mae Salak	60B
Pha Tai	75B
Jakheu	90B
Kok Noi	110B
Pha Khwang	110B
Pha Khiaw	170B
Hat Wua Dam	160B
Ban Ruammit	185B
Chiang Rai	200B

Lamphun Province

This tiny province south-east of Chiang Mai is very much one small city, Lamphun, surrounded by farms and villages.

LAMPHUN
อ.เมืองลำพูน

postcode 51000 • pop 15,200
Most often visited as a day trip from Chiang Mai, Lamphun was, along with Pasang, the centre of the small Hariphunchai principality (AD 750–1281) originally ruled by the semi-legendary Mon princess Chama Thewi. Long after its progenitor, Dvaravati, was vanquished by the Khmer, Hariphun-

chai succeeded in remaining independent of both the Khmer and the Chiang Mai Thais.

This oval-shaped provincial capital on the western bank of the Nam Mae Kuang is fairly quiet but there are a few places to stay if you want to get away from the hustle and bustle of Chiang Mai or want to study the temples here in depth. The number of historic temples in the capital is many times greater than the two described below.

The village just north of Lamphun, **Nong Chang Kheun**, is known for producing the sweetest *lamyai* (longan) fruit in the country. During the second week of August, Lamphun hosts the annual Lam Yai Festival, which features floats made of the fruit and, of course, a Miss Lam Yai contest.

Wat Phra That Hariphunchai
วัดพระธาตุหริภุญชัย

This wát, which was built on the site of Queen Chama Thewi's palace in 1044 (1108 or 1157 according to some datings), is on the western side of the main road into Lamphun from Chiang Mai. The temple lay derelict for many years until Khruba Siwichai, one of Northern Thailand's most famous monks, made renovations in the 1930s. It has some interesting post-Dvaravati architecture, a couple of fine Buddha images and two old chedi of the original Hariphunchai style. The tallest stupa, Chedi Suwan, dates from 1418; although not built during the Hariphunchai period, it was styled after Hariphunchai models. The chedi's 46m height is surmounted by a nine-tiered umbrella made with 6.5kg of pure gold. Thais consider this to be one of the eight holiest stupas in Thailand.

The world's largest bronze gong hangs in a reddish pavilion on the grounds. Towards the back of the grounds is a very nice Lanna-style *hăw trai* (Tripitaka library) and a small stupa labelled 'Mount Meru'.

Wat Chama Thewi
วัดจามเทวี

A more unusual Hariphunchai chedi can be seen at Wat Chama Thewi (popularly called Wat Kukut), which is said to have been erected in the 8th or 9th century as a Dvaravati monument, then rebuilt by the Hariphunchai Mon in 1218. As it has been

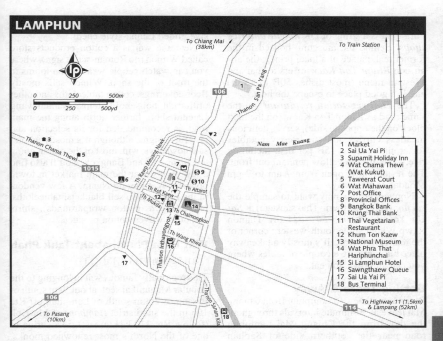

LAMPHUN

1	Market
2	Sai Ua Yai Pi
3	Supamit Holiday Inn
4	Wat Chama Thewi (Wat Kukut)
5	Taweerat Court
6	Wat Mahawan
7	Post Office
8	Provincial Offices
9	Bangkok Bank
10	Krung Thai Bank
11	Thai Vegetarian Restaurant
12	Khum Ton Kaew
13	National Museum
14	Wat Phra That Hariphunchai
15	Si Lamphun Hotel
16	Sawngthaew Queue
17	Sai Ua Yai Pi
18	Bus Terminal

restored many times since then it is now a mixture of several schools. The stepped profile bears a remarkable resemblance to the 12th-century Satmahal Prasada at Polonnaruwa in Sri Lanka.

Each side of the chedi – known as Chedi Suwan Chang Kot – has five rows of three Buddha figures, diminishing in size on each higher level. The standing Buddhas are in Dvaravati style, although made recently.

Wat Chama Thewi is on the opposite side of town from Wat Phra That Hariphunchai. To get there, walk west down Thanon Mukda, perpendicular to the Chiang Mai-Lamphun road (opposite Wat Hari), passing over the town moat, then past the district government offices until you come to the wát on the left.

Lamphun National Museum
พิพิธภัณฑสถานแห่งชาติลำพูน

Across the street from Wat Phra That Hariphunchai, Lamphun's National Museum has a small collection which includes artefacts from the Dvaravati, Hariphunchai and Lanna kingdoms. Opening hours are from 9 am to 4 pm Wednesday to Sunday; admission is 30B for foreigners.

Places to Stay & Eat

The easiest accommodation to find is the *Si Lamphun Hotel* (*no Roman-script sign;* ☎ 053-511176) at Soi 5 on the town's main street, Thanon Inthayongyot. It's a real dive – singles with grotty bathrooms cost 100B, doubles 200B. This place needs an overhaul, and traffic noise is a problem.

Across from Wat Chama Thewi is the relatively new 50-room *Supamit Holiday Inn* (☎ 053-534865, fax 534355) – no relation to the international hotel chain. Clean, simple rooms cost with fan and attached bathroom cost 250/300B single/double and 350/400B with air-con. All rooms come with hot water and balconies. An open-air restaurant on the 5th floor is quite good and offers a nice view of Lamphun. There's a karaoke lounge on the 5th floor.

Taweerat Court (☎ 053-534338), on Thanon Chama Thewi near Wat Mahawan, is a clean, apartment-style place with rooms for 150B with fan, 300B with air-con and TV.

Along Thanon Inthayongyot south of Wat Phra That is a string of OK *noodle and rice shops*. Behind the museum, housed in the former teak palace of a local prince, the all-air-con *Khum Ton Kaew* offers a Thai and Western menu (most dishes 50B to 150B) and is a good place to escape the heat.

The *Thai vegetarian restaurant*, on the same road as Khum Ton Kaew (on the next block on the opposite side), serves delicious meatless curries and stir-fried vegetables for around 10B to 15B per dish including rice. Look for the yellow pennant out front. The restaurant is open from 7 am to 7 pm Monday to Saturday.

Nonvegetarians may want to sample the *sâi ùa:* (spicy northern-Thai sausage) at *Sai Ua Yai Pi (☎ 053-561381)* off Thanon Rawp Wiang at the south-western corner of the main city 'oval'. It's mostly a takeaway place but there are a couple of tables where you can sit down and eat.

Getting There & Away

Blue săwngthăew to Lamphun from Chiang Mai leave at 30-minute intervals throughout the day from the Chiang Mai-Lamphun road near the southern side of Saphan Nawarat. In the reverse direction, săwngthăew leave Lamphun from the queue near the intersection of Thanon Inthayongyot and Thanon Wang Khwa. The 26km ride (10B) goes along a beautiful country road, parts of which are bordered by tall *yaang* (a kind of dipterocarp) trees.

Ordinary buses to Chiang Mai (10B) leave from the bus terminal on Thanon Sanam Kila, and in the reverse direction, from the Chang Pheuak bus terminal or along the Chiang Mai-Lamphun road in Chiang Mai. Green buses on the Chiang Mai-Chiang Rai route also stop in Lamphun, but only leave from the Arcade terminal in Chiang Mai. From Lamphun, green buses depart for Lampang about 13 times a day between 6 am and 5 pm for 29B.

PASANG
ป่าซาง

Don't confuse this village with Bo Sang, the umbrella village. In Pasang, cotton weaving is the cottage industry. **Wat Chang Khao Noi Neua**, off Rte 106 towards the southern end of town, features an impressive gilded Lanna-style chedi.

Near the *wát* is a cotton products store called Wimon (no Roman-script sign), where you can watch people weaving on looms in the front of the shop. Wimon sells mostly floor coverings, cotton tablecloths and other utilitarian household items. Nandakwang Laicum shop, farther north along the main road, is recommended for its selection and tasteful designs, although it's mostly whole-sale nowadays, with most of the output going to Chiang Mai and Bangkok. You'll also find a few shops near the main market in town, opposite Wat Pasang Ngam. A few vendors in the market also sell blankets, tablecloths, *phâakhamáa* (cotton wraparounds), shirts and other woven cotton products.

Wat Phra Phutthabaht Tahk Phah
วัดพระพุทธบาทตากผ้า

This regionally famous *wát* belonging to the popular Mahanikai sect, about 9km south of Pasang or 20km south of Lamphun off Rte 106 in the subdistrict *(tambon)* of Ma-Kok (follow Rte 1133 1km east), is a shrine to one of the North's most renowned monks, Luang Pu Phromma. It contains a lifelike resin figure of the deceased monk sitting in meditation.

One of his disciples, Ajahn Thirawattho, teaches meditation to a large contingent of monks who are housed in *kùti* of laterite brick. Behind the spacious grounds is a park and a steep hill mounted by a chedi. The *wát* is named after an unremarkable Buddha footprint *(phrá phútthábàat)* shrine in the middle of the lower temple grounds and an-other spot where Buddha supposedly dried his robes *(tàak phâa)*.

A săwngthăew from Lamphun to the *wát* costs 20B.

Getting There & Away

A săwngthăew will take you from Lamphun to Pasang for 8B.

If you're heading south to Tak Province under your own power, traffic is generally much lighter along Rte 106 to Thoen than on Hwy 11 to Lampang; a winding 10km section of the road north of Thoen is particularly scenic. Both highways intersect Hwy 1 south, which leads directly to Tak's capital.

DOI KHUN TAN NATIONAL PARK
อุทยานแห่งชาติดอยขุนตาล

This park receives only around 10,000 visitors a year, one of Northern Thailand's lowest park visitation rates. It's unique in that the main access is from the Khun Tan train station (four daily trains from Chiang Mai, 15B, 1½ hours). Once at the Khun Tan station, cross the tracks and follow a steep, marked path 1.5km to park headquarters. By car take the Chiang Mai-Lampang highway to the Mae Tha turn-off, then follow signs along a steep unpaved road for 18km.

The park covers 255 sq km and ranges in elevation from 350m at the bamboo forest lowlands to 1363m at the pine-studded summit of Doi Khun Tan. Wildflowers, including orchids, ginger and lilies, are abundant. In addition to a well-marked trail covering the mountain's four peaks, there's also a trail to **Nam Tok Tat Moei** (7km round trip). Thailand's longest train tunnel (1352m), which opened in 1921 after six years of manual labour by a thousand Lao workers (several of whom are said to have been killed by tigers), intersects the mountain slope.

Bungalows which can accommodate six to nine people are available for around 600B to 1200B near the park headquarters and at Camp 1 on the first peak. At Camp 2 on the second peak it's 250B per person, or you can pitch your own tent for 10B; food is available at a small shop near the park headquarters. There's the usual national park entry fee (see under Doi Suthep & Doi Pui National Park earlier in this chapter). The park is very popular on cool season weekends. Call ☎ 055-242492 for more information.

Lampang Province

LAMPANG
อ.เมืองลำปาง

postcode 52000 ● pop 44,700
One hundred kilometres from Chiang Mai, Lampang was inhabited as far back as the 7th century in the Dvaravati period and played an important part in the history of the Hariphunchai kingdom. Legend says the city was founded by the son of Hariphunchai's Queen Chama Thewi.

Like Chiang Mai, Phrae and other older northern cities, Lampang was built as a walled rectangle alongside a river (in this case Mae Wang). At the end of the 19th and beginning of the 20th centuries Lampang, along with nearby Phrae, became an important centre for the domestic and international teak trade. A large British-owned timber company brought in Burmese supervisors familiar with the teak industry in Burma to train Burmese and Thai loggers in the area. These well-paid supervisors, along with independent Burmese teak merchants who plied their trade in Lampang, sponsored the construction of more than a dozen impressive temples in the city. Burmese and Shan artisans designed and built the temples out of local materials, especially teak. Their legacy lives on in several of Lampang's best-maintained wát, now among the city's main visitor attractions.

Many Thais visit Lampang for a taste of urban Northern Thailand without the crass commercialism of Chiang Mai. Although the central area is quite busy, the shophouses provide a more traditional feel.

Information
At the north-western corner of the clock tower circle there's a tourist information office staffed by members of the private Lampang Tourist Association Office. The city also maintains a tourist office in the new provincial complex a good distance outside of town, not very convenient for most visitors, even those who arrive by car.

Wat Phra Kaew Don Tao
วัดพระแก้วดอนเต้า

This wát, on the northern side of the Mae Wang, was built during the reign of King Anantayot and housed the Emerald Buddha (now in Bangkok's Wat Phra Kaew) from 1436 to 1468. The main chedi shows Hariphunchai influence, while the adjacent mondòp (a square, spire-topped shrine room) was built in 1909. The mondòp, decorated with glass mosaic in typical Burmese style, contains a Mandalay-style Buddha image. A display of Lanna artefacts (mostly religious paraphernalia and woodwork) can be viewed in the wát's **Lanna Museum**. A small admission fee is charged.

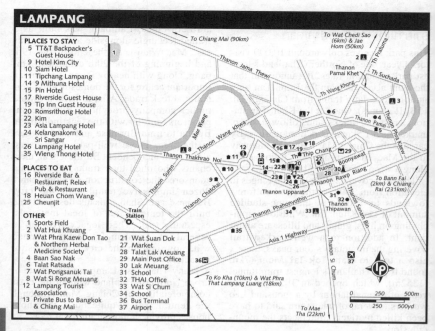

LAMPANG

PLACES TO STAY
5 TT&T Backpacker's Guest House
9 Hotel Kim City
10 Siam Hotel
11 Tipchang Lampang
14 9 Mithuna Hotel
15 Pin Hotel
17 Riverside Guest House
19 Tip Inn Guest House
20 Romsrithong Hotel
22 Kim
23 Asia Lampang Hotel
24 Kelangnakorn & Sri Sangar
26 Lampang Hotel
35 Wieng Thong Hotel

PLACES TO EAT
16 Riverside Bar & Restaurant; Relax Pub & Restaurant
18 Heuan Chom Wang
25 Cheunjit

OTHER
1 Sports Field
2 Wat Hua Khuang
3 Wat Phra Kaew Don Tao & Northern Herbal Medicine Society
4 Baan Sao Nak
6 Talat Ratsada
7 Wat Pongsanuk Tai
8 Wat Si Rong Meuang
12 Lampang Tourist Association
13 Private Bus to Bangkok & Chiang Mai
21 Wat Suan Dok
27 Market
28 Talat Lak Meuang
29 Main Post Office
30 Lak Meuang
31 School
32 THAI Office
33 Wat Si Chum
34 School
36 Bus Terminal
37 Airport

Other Temples

Two wát built in the late 19th century by Burmese artisans are **Wat Si Rong Meuang** and **Wat Si Chum**. Both have temple buildings constructed in the Burmese 'layered' style, with tin roofs gabled by intricate woodcarvings. The current abbots of these temples are Burmese.

Besides the wíhǎan at Wat Phra That Lampang Luang (see Around Lampang later), the mondòp at **Wat Pongsanuk Tai** is one of the few remaining local examples of original Lanna-style temple architecture, which emphasised open-sided wooden buildings.

Wat Chedi Sao, about 6km north of town towards Jae Hom, is named for the 20 whitewashed Lanna-style chedi on its grounds (*sao* is northern Thai for 20). It's a pretty, well-endowed wát, landscaped with bougainvillea and casuarina. At one edge of the wát stands a very colourful statue of Avalokiteshvara, while a pavilion in the centre features a gilded Buddha similar in style to the Phra Chinnarat in Phitsanulok. But the wát's real treasure is a solid-gold, 15th-century seated Buddha on display in a

glassed-in pavilion built over a square pond. The image weighs 1507g, stands 38cm tall and is said to contain a piece of the Buddha's skull in its head and an ancient Pali-inscribed golden palm leaf in its chest; precious stones decorate the image's hairline and robe. A farmer reportedly found the figure next to the ruins of nearby Wat Khu Kao in 1983. Monks stationed at Wat Chedi Sao make and sell herbal medicines; the popular *yaa màwng* is similar to tiger balm. The pavilion with the gold Buddha is open 8 am to 5 pm daily.

Baan Sao Nak
บ้านเสานัก

Baan Sao Nak (Many Pillars House), built in 1895 in the traditional Lanna style, is a huge teak house in the old Wiang Neua (north city) section of town, and is supported by 116 square teak pillars. The local *khun yǐng* (a title equivalent to 'Lady' in England) who owned the house died recently and left the house to the Thai government to be used as a museum. The entire house is furnished with Burmese and Thai antiques; three rooms display antique silverwork, lacquerware, bronzeware, ceramics and other northern-Thai crafts. The area beneath the house is sometimes used for khan tòk ceremonial dinners.

The house is supposed to be open 10 am to 5 pm daily, but hours can be erratic. The admission fee of 30B includes a soft drink. Call ☎ 054-227653 for more information.

Horse carts
Lampang is known throughout Thailand as Meuang Rot Mah (Horse Cart City) because it's the only town in Thailand where horse carts are still used as public transport. These days, Lampang's horse carts are mainly for tourists. Trying to get a good price is difficult. A 20-minute horse cart tour around town costs 150B; for 200B you can get a half-hour tour that goes along the Mae Wang, and for 300B a one-hour tour that stops at Wat Phra Kaew Don Tao and Wat Si Rong Meuang. If there's little business you may be able to negotiate to bring the price down to 120B per half-hour or 200B per hour. The main horse cart stands are in front of the provincial office and the Tipchang Lampang and Wieng Thong Hotels.

Traditional Massage
The **Samakhom Samunphrai Phak Neua** (Northern Herbal Medicine Society) at 149 Thanon Pratuma, next to Wat Hua Khuang in the Wiang Neua area, offers traditional northern-Thai massage and herbal saunas. The massage costs 100B for half an hour and 150B per hour; 1½ hours is a recommended minimum for best effect. The outdoor sauna room is pumped with herbal steam created by heating a mixture of several medicinal herbs; it costs 100B per use. Once you've paid, you can go in and out of the sauna as many times as you want during one visit. The massage service and sauna are open from 8 am to 8 pm daily.

Places to Stay – Budget & Mid-Range
There are several economical choices in Lampang along Thanon Boonyawat, which runs through the centre of town. The centrally located **Sri Sangar** *(Si Sa-Nga; ☎ 054-217070),* at No 213–215, has clean rooms with fan and bathroom for 100/180B single/double.

The recently repainted **9 Mithuna Hotel** *(☎ 054-217438),* off Thanon Boonyawat (with a second entrance off Thanon Rawp Riang), is a standard Thai-Chinese place with rooms for 143B with fan, 260B with air-con – not as good a deal as Sri Sangar. **Lampang Hotel** *(☎ 054-227311, 696 Thanon Suan Dok)* is similar at 180B with fan and bathroom, 280B with air-con and a bit more with TV.

Some more upmarket options are the three-storey **Kim** *(☎ 054-217721, fax 226929, 168 Thanon Boonyawat)* and the **Kelangnakorn** *(☎ 054-217137)* diagonally across the street. At Kim, clean, comfortable rooms with air-con, hot water and TV cost 320B. Popular with travelling salesmen, the Kelangnakorn is farther off the road and has been refurbished; rooms with fan are 280B, air-con rooms with TV and phone are 420B. The new **Romsrithong** *(☎ 054-217254, 142 Thanon Boonyawat)* is a three-storey place built on the site of the old Romsri Hotel at the corner of Thanon Boonyawat and Thanon Upparat. Rooms cost 200B with fan and cold-water shower, 300B with air-con.

Riverside Guest House *(☎ 054-227005, fax 322342),* tucked away on narrow Thanon Talat Kao near the river, provides comfortable rooms in old teak buildings surrounded by beautiful landscaping. Fan rooms with outside bathroom are 150B, rooms with private bathroom start at 250B, and rooms with balconies overlooking the river cost 350B. One air-con room with a large living area is also available for 600B. The guesthouse offers continental breakfast, fax service, international calls, motorcycle rental, laundering service and sightseeing tours.

Nearby **Tip Inn Guest House** *(☎ 054-221821, 143 Thanon Talat Kao)* features nine quiet rooms off the street. Adequate rooms are 100B for a single with shared bathroom, 160B for a double with private hot-water bathroom (270B if you run the air-con). A small restaurant is downstairs. The English-speaking Thai owners have a Thai silk shop nearby on Thanon Thip Chang. The hotel is down a small alley marked by a small green sign reading 'Hotel'.

The friendly **Siam Hotel** *(☎ 054-217472, fax 217277),* south-west of the clock circle on Thanon Chatchai, has clean, well-kept rooms

NORTHERN THAILAND

for 250B with fan and private bathroom or 380B with air-con, TV, phone and hot water.

TT&T Backpacker's Guest House (☎ 054-225361, 01-951 5154), on the northern side of the river off Thanon Pamai, has fairly clean, basic multibed rooms for 80B per person, singles for 120B or larger doubles for 200B, all with shared hot-water showers. A săwngthăew ride from the bus station to the guesthouse should cost about 20B per person.

About 2km outside of town on Hwy 1, ***Bann Fai*** (☎/fax 054-224602) offers large rooms in a charming teak house decorated with Thai antiques and cotton hand-woven on the premises. The landscaped grounds around the house encompass 300 plant species and river frontage, plus views of nearby rice fields and mountains. Rates are 220B a double – the four hot-water bathrooms are shared. Motorcycles are available for rent.

Places to Stay – Top End

The long-running ***Asia Lampang Hotel*** (☎ 054-227844, fax 224436, 229 Thanon Boonyawat) has good rooms facing the street for 350B and nicer rooms for 450B to 500B; the latter are large suite-style rooms on the 5th floor. All rooms have air-con, TV and fridge. The Asia's pleasant street-level cafe is its best feature.

The four-storey ***Pin Hotel*** (☎ 054-221509, fax 322286, 8 Thanon Suan Dok), right behind the Kim Hotel in the town centre, has spacious, well-maintained air-con rooms in an older section for 450B, or in a very new wing for 650B deluxe, 900B for a suite. All 59 rooms come with air-con, satellite TV, phone and hot water. The Evergreen Restaurant is attached.

The ***Tipchang Lampang Hotel*** (☎ 054-226501, fax 225362, 54/22 Thanon Thakhrao Noi) has rooms for 840B to 1500B, including American breakfast. The facilities include a coffee shop, cafe, supper club, cocktail lounge, tennis courts and pool. The ***Hotel Kim City*** (☎ 054-310238, fax 226635, 274/1 Thanon Chatchai) falls into this same category and costs 500B to 900B a room.

The modern ***Wieng Thong Hotel*** (☎ 054-225801, fax 225803, 138/109 Thanon Phahonyothin) is a multistorey hotel with air-con rooms costing from 883B.

Places to Eat

Near the Kim and Asia Lampang Hotels are several good ***rice and noodle shops***. Just east of the Kelangnakorn Hotel is a little row of ***jók and noodle shops*** open early morning. ***Cheunjit*** on Thanon Boonyawat, across from Wat Suan Dok, has good curries, especially *kaeng kàrìi* (mild, Indian-style curry) and khâo sàwy. It's open late morning to early afternoon.

The ***Riverside Bar & Restaurant*** (same owners as the Riverside Guest House) is in an old teak structure at 328 Thanon Thip Chang on the river. It's a good choice for a drink or meal, with live folk music nightly and reasonable prices considering the high quality of the food and service. A bit farther west, the more modern ***Relax Pub & Restaurant*** also has good food and live music.

The atmospheric ***Heuan Chom Wang*** can be found by walking east from the Riverside Guest House on Thanon Talat Kao about 100m, then north down an alley on the left. This open-air restaurant is set in a beautiful old teak building overlooking the river. Ceramic pots filled with fragrant flower blossoms line the stairway leading into the restaurant. The local menu features northern-Thai food as well as more typical central-Thai fare.

Getting There & Away

Air The THAI office (☎/fax 054-217078) is at 314 Thanon Sanam Bin. THAI has two daily flights to Lampang from Bangkok for 1680B one way.

Bus Air-con buses to Lampang from Phitsanulok's main bus terminal cost 135B via the new route and take four hours. The trip takes five hours via the old longer route and costs 136B. From Chiang Mai, buses for Lampang leave from the Chiang Mai Arcade terminal about every half-hour during the day and also from next to Saphan Nawarat in the direction of Lamphun. The fare is 23B and the trip takes two hours; there are also air-con buses available for 48B to 61B, depending on the company and service. Buses from Lamphun are 29B. Ordinary buses to/from Bangkok (four daily departures each way) cost 176B. There are also three 2nd-class air-con buses (246B), six 1st-class buses (317B) and one 24-seat VIP bus (490B) to/from Bangkok each day. The bus terminal in Lampang is some way out of town – 10B by shared săwngthăew.

To book an air-con bus from Lampang to Bangkok or Chiang Mai there is no need to go out to the bus terminal because the tour bus companies have offices in town along Thanon Boonyawat near the clock tower roundabout. Sombud, Thanjit Tour and Thaworn Farm each have 1st-class air-con buses to Bangkok for 330B that leave nightly around 8 pm. In the same vicinity, New Wiriya organises nine daily air-con departures to Bangkok between 9.30 am and 10 pm for 317B.

Train Third-class train tickets from Lampang to Chiang Mai cost 15B. The trip takes about two hours.

AROUND LAMPANG
Wat Phra That Lampang Luang
วัดพระธาตุลำปางหลวง

Probably the most magnificent temple in Northern Thailand, Wat Phra That Lampang Luang is also the best compendium of Lanna-style temple architecture.

The centrepiece of the complex is the open-sided **Wihan Luang**. Thought to have been built in 1476, the impressive wíhăan features a triple-tiered wooden roof supported by teak pillars. It's considered to be the oldest existing wooden building in Thailand. A huge gilded mondòp in the back of the wíhăan contains a Buddha image cast in 1563; the faithful leave small gold-coloured Buddha figures close to the mondòp and hang Thai Lü weavings behind it.

Early 19th-century **jataka murals** are painted on wooden panels around the inside upper perimeter of the wíhăan. The tall **Lanna-style chedi** behind the wíhăan, raised in 1449 and restored in 1496, measures 24m at its base and is 45m high. The small, simple **Wihan Ton Kaew** to the right of the main wíhăan was built in 1476 (standing with your back to the main gate). The oldest structure in the compound is the smaller 13th-century **Wihan Phra Phut** to the left of the main chedi; the wíhăan to the right of the chedi (Wihan Nam Taem) was built in the early 16th century and, amazingly, still contains traces of the original murals.

The **Haw Phra Phutthabaht**, a small white building behind the chedi, has a sign that reads 'Women don't step on this place', meaning women are forbidden to climb the steps. You're not missing much – it's just a bare room containing an undistinguished Buddha footprint sculpture. The bòt or sĭm to the left of the Haw Phra dates from 1476 but was reconstructed in 1924.

The lintel over the entrance to the compound features an impressive dragon relief – once common in northern temples but rarely seen these days. This gate supposedly dates back to the 15th century.

Wat Phra That Lampang Luang is located 18km south-west of Lampang in Ko Kha. To get there by public transport from Lampang, catch a blue săwngthăew south on Thanon Praisani to the market in Ko Kha (10B), then a Hang Chat–bound săwngthăew (5B) 3km north to the entrance of Wat Phra That Lampang Luang. A chartered motorcycle taxi from the Ko Kha săwngthăew station to the temple costs around 20B to 30B.

If you're driving or cycling from Lampang, head south on the Asia 1 highway and take the Ko Kha exit, then follow the road over a bridge and bear right. Note the police station on your left and continue for 2km over another bridge until you see the temple on the left. If you're coming from

WAT PHRA THAT LAMPANG LUANG

1 Wihan Nam Taem
2 Wihan Ton Kaew
3 Wihan Phra Jao Sila
4 Main Chedi
5 Wihan Luang
6 Naga Gate
7 Haw Phra Phutthabaht
8 Wihan Phra Phut
9 Bòt
10 Entrance Stairway

NORTHERN THAILAND

Elephants in Thailand

The elephant is one of the most powerful symbols in Thai culture, and until 1917 a white elephant appeared on the Thai national flag. Historically Thais have worked side-by-side with elephants on farms and in the jungle, and elephants were the superweapons of South-East Asian armies before the advent of tanks and big guns. Today elephants are still revered in Thai society and are a strong drawcard for Western tourists.

Current estimates put the number of wild elephants in Thailand at 1300 to 2000, more than India but less than Myanmar. The number of domesticated elephants hovers at around 3800. However, numbers of both wild and domestic animals is steadily dwindling. Around the year 1900 it was estimated that there were at least 100,000 elephants working in Thailand; by 1952 the number had dropped to 13,397. Today Tak Province has the highest number of elephants and is one of only three provinces (the other two are Mae Hong Son and Surin) where the elephant population has actually increased over the last 20 years.

Elephant mothers carry their calves for 22 months. Once they are born, working elephants enjoy a brief childhood before they begin training at around three to five years of age. The training, which is under the guidance of their *mahouts* (a Hindustani term for elephant caretakers) takes five years. Tasks they learn include pushing, carrying and piling logs, as well as bathing and walking in procession.

Working elephants have a career of about 50 years; hence when young they are trained by two mahouts, one older and one younger – sometimes a father-and-son team – who can see the animal through its lifetime. Thai law requires that elephants be retired and released into the wild at age 61. They often live for 80 years or more.

Today the elephant is still an important mode of jungle transport as it beats any other animal or machine for moving through a forest with minimum damage – its large, soft feet distribute the animal's weight without crushing the ground. Interestingly, an adult can run at speeds of up to 23km/h but put less weight on the ground per square centimetre than a deer!

Recently logging was banned in Thailand, resulting in much less demand for trained elephants. The plight of these unemployed creatures is becoming an issue of national concern. Many domesticated elephants are increasingly neglected, mistreated or abandoned by owners who often cannot

Chiang Mai via Hwy 11, turn south onto Rte 1034 18km north-west of Lampang at the 13km marker – this route is a 50km short cut to Ko Kha that avoids much of Lampang.

Thai Elephant Conservation Center
ศูนย์ฝึกลูกช้าง

In Hang Chat district north-west of Lampang, outside Thung Kwian at the 37km marker, is the Thai Elephant Conservation Center. Its main objectives are to conserve Thai elephants, to promote ecotourism, to provide medical treatment and care for sick elephants, and to train young elephants. This camp has moved from its previous location in Ngao, between Lampang and Chiang Rai; the Ngao centre remains in use as a care facility for old tuskers.

In addition to the standard tourist show, the centre offers exhibits on the history and culture of elephants as well as elephant rides (8 am to 3.30 pm) through the surrounding forest. At 9.45 am you can see the elephants bathing in the river. The animals appreciate pieces of fruit – 'feels like feeding a vacuum cleaner with a wet nozzle', said one visitor.

Training takes place daily between 7 and 11 am, with public shows daily at 10 and 11 am, as well as 1.30 pm on weekends and holidays (except during the elephants' summer vacation from March to May). Show times seem to change from year to year.

To reach the camp, you can take a bus or sǎwngthǎew from Lampang's main bus terminal bound for Chiang Mai and get off at the 37km marker. Be forewarned, the showgrounds are about 2km off the highway and no túk-túk or motorcycle taxis are available. Call ☎ 054-229042 for more information.

Elephants in Thailand

afford to care for them. Meanwhile, destruction of forests and ivory-trade poaching are placing the wild elephant population in increasing jeopardy.

Of course, some owners continue to work their elephants in the illegal logging industry along the Thai-Myanmar border. Sadly, some animals are pumped full of amphetamines so they can work day and night.

Motala, one of the elephants working here, become something of a celebrity when she trod on a landmine – common in that area – which shattered her left foot. Conservation group Friends of the Asian Elephant (FAE), with the assistance of Chiangmai University, devised a plan to amputate her foot with the aim of eventually fitting a prosthetic limb. Around US$100,000 was raised for the operation which took place with the help of a crane and enough anaesthetic to knock out 70 people. The procedure has been a long and painful one for Motala.

TOM COCKREM

Rising numbers of unemployed elephants also means unemployed mahouts; many elephant owners have begun migrating with their elephants to large Thai cities, even Bangkok, in search of money, which can be earned simply by walking the animal through the streets and selling bananas and vegetables to people to feed it. In these urban environments, the elephants often suffer; in 1998 an elephant died in Bangkok after getting one of its legs caught in a sewer culvert.

For more information about the state of elephants in Thailand check the FAE Web site (www .elephant.tnet.co.th).

Thung Kwian Market
ตลาดป่าทุ่งเกวียน

The famous **Thung Kwian Market** (*tàlàat pàa thûng kwian*) at Thung Kwian in Hang Chat district (off Hwy 11 between Lampang and Chiang Mai) sells all manner of wild flora and fauna from the jungle, including medicinal and culinary herbs, wild mushrooms, bamboo shoots, field rats, beetles, snakes, plus a few rare and endangered species like pangolin. Officials are said to be cracking down on the sale of endangered species. The market meets every Wednesday from around 5 am till noon. If you're coming from Lampang, the market is before the Thai Elephant Conservation Center.

The nearby **Thung Kwian Reforestation Centre** protects a 353-râi (56.5-hectare) forest under the Forest Industry Organisation.

Other Attractions

North and east of Lampang are the cotton-weaving villages of **Jae Hom** and **Mae Tha**. You can wander around and find looms in action; there are also plenty of shops along the main roads.

Tham Pha Thai is 66km north of Lampang, between Lampang and Chiang Rai about 500m off Hwy 1. Besides the usual formations (stalagmites and stalactites), the cave has a large Buddha image.

The province is well endowed with waterfalls. Three are found within Wang Neua district, roughly 120km north of the provincial capital via Rte 1053: **Wang Kaew**, **Wang Thong** and **Than Thong** (Jampa Thong). Wang Kaew is the largest, with 110 tiers. Near the summit is a Mien hill-tribe village. This area became part of the 1172-sq-km **Doi Luang National Park** in 1990; animals protected by the park include serow, barking deer, pangolin and the pig-tailed macaque.

In Meuang Pan district, about halfway to Wang Neua from Lampang, is another waterfall, **Jae Son**, part of the 593-sq-km **Jae Son National Park**. Elevations in the park reach above 2000m. Jae Son has six drops, each with its own pool; close to the falls are nine hot springs. Small huts house circular baths, recessed into the floor and lined with clay tiles, that are continuously filled with water direct from the spring. For 20B you can take a 20-minute soak, preceded and followed by an invigorating cold-water shower.

Camping is permitted in both Jae Son and Doi Luang National Parks.

Phitsanulok Province

PHITSANULOK
อ.เมืองพิษณุโลก

postcode 65000 • pop 82,400
Phitsanulok is often abbreviated as 'Phi-lok'. Under the reign of Ayuthaya King Borom Trailokanat (1448–88), Phitsanulok served as the capital of Thailand for 25 years. The town straddles Mae Nam Nan near a junction with Mae Nam Khwae Noi, hence it's sometimes referred to as Song Khwae (Two Tributaries), and it's the only city in Thailand where it's legal to reside on a houseboat within municipal boundaries. No new houseboats are permitted, however, so it's likely that they will gradually disappear.

This vibrant city makes an excellent base from which to explore the lower north. Besides the temples of Wat Phra Si Ratana Mahathat and Wat Chulamani, you can explore the attractions of historical Sukhothai, Kamphaeng Phet and Si Satchanalai, as well as the national parks and wildlife sanctuaries of Thung Salaeng Luang and Phu Hin Rong Kla, the former strategic headquarters of the Communist Party of Thailand (CPT). All of these places are within 150km of Phitsanulok.

Information
Tourist Offices The TAT office (☎/fax 055-252742/3, ✉ tatphs@loxinfo.co.th) at 209/7–8 Thanon Borom Trailokanat has knowledgeable and helpful staff (some of TAT's best) who give out free maps of the town and a sheet that describes a walking tour. The office also has information on Sukhothai and Phetchabun Provinces. It's open 8.30 am to 4.30 pm daily.

If you plan to do the trip from Phitsanulok to Lom Sak, ask for the sketch map of Hwy 12 that marks several waterfalls and resorts along the way.

Money Several banks in town offer foreign-exchange services and ATMs; only the Bangkok Bank, at 35 Thanon Naresuan, has an after-hours exchange window (usually open till 8 pm). There's also an ATM inside the Wat Yai compound.

Post & Communications The main post office on Thanon Phuttha Bucha is open 8.30 am to 4.30 pm weekdays, 9 am to noon weekends. The attached Communications Authority of Thailand (CAT) phone office offers Internet services and is open from 7 am to 11 pm daily.

Shops offering Internet access dot the central area of town near the railway station. The highest concentration of Internet cafes is on the western bank of the river near Saphan Ekathotsarot. Internet House, opposite Naresuan University, is the closest spot to the Phitsanulok Youth Hostel, although it probably won't be long before the hostel itself offers email services to guests.

Wat Phra Si Ratana Mahathat
วัดพระศรีรัตนมหาธาตุ

The full name of this temple is Wat Phra Si Ratana Mahathat, but the locals call it Wat Phra Si or Wat Yai. The wát is next to the bridge over Mae Nam Nan (on the right as you're heading out of Phitsanulok towards Sukhothai). The main wíhǎan contains the Chinnarat Buddha (Phra Phuttha Chinnarat), one of Thailand's most revered and copied images. This famous bronze image is probably second in importance only to the Emerald Buddha in Bangkok's Wat Phra Kaew. In terms of total annual donations collected (about 12 million baht a year), Wat Yai follows Wat Sothon in Chachoengsao.

The image was cast in the late Sukhothai style, but what makes it strikingly unique is the flame-like halo around the head and torso that turns up at the bottom to become dragon-serpent heads on either side of the image. The head of this Buddha is a little wider than standard Sukhothai, giving the statue a very solid feel.

The story goes that construction of this wát was commissioned under the reign of King Li Thai in 1357. When it was completed, King Li Thai wanted it to contain three high-quality bronze images, so he sent for well-known sculptors from Si Satchanalai, Chiang Saen and Hariphunchai (Lamphun), as well as five Brahman priests. The first two castings worked well, but the third required three attempts before it was decreed the best of all. Legend has it that a white-robed sage appeared from nowhere to assist in the final casting, then disappeared. This last image was named the Chinnarat (Victorious King) Buddha and it became the centrepiece in the wíhǎan. The other two images, Phra Chinnasi and Phra Si Satsada, were later moved to the royal temple of Wat Bowonniwet in Bangkok. Only the Chinnarat image has the flame-dragon halo.

The walls of the wíhǎan are low to accommodate the low-swept roof, typical of northern temple architecture, so the image takes on larger proportions than it might in a central or north-eastern wát. The brilliant interior architecture is such that when you sit on the Italian marble floor in front of the Buddha, the lacquered columns draw your vision towards the image and evoke a strong sense of serenity. The doors of the building are inlaid with mother-of-pearl in a design copied from Bangkok's Wat Phra Kaew.

Another sanctuary to one side has been converted into a museum displaying antique Buddha images, ceramics and other historic artefacts. It's open 9 am to 4 pm Wednesday to Sunday; admission is free. Dress appropriately when visiting this most sacred of temples – no shorts or sleeveless tops.

Near Wat Yai, on the same side of the river, are two other temples of the same period – **Wat Ratburan** and **Wat Nang Phaya**.

Wat Chulamani
วัดจุฬามณี

Five kilometres south of the city (a 4B trip on bus No 5 down Thanon Borom Trailokanat) is Wat Chulamani, the ruins of which date from the Sukhothai period. The original buildings must have been impressive, judging from what remains of the ornate Khmer-style *prang* (tower). King Borom Trailokanat was ordained as a monk here and there is an old Thai inscription to that effect on the ruined wíhǎan, dating from the reign of King Narai the Great.

The prang itself has little left of its original height, but Khmer-style door lintels remain, including one with a Sukhothai walking Buddha and a *dhammacakka* (Buddhist wheel of law) in the background.

Besides the prang and the wíhǎan, the only original structures left are the remains of the monastery walls. Still, there is a peaceful, neglected atmosphere about the place.

Buddha-Casting Foundry
โรงหล่อพระ

On Thanon Wisut Kasat, not far from the Phitsanulok Youth Hostel, is a small factory where bronze Buddha images of all sizes are cast. Most are copies of the famous Phra Chinnarat Buddha at Wat Yai. Visitors are welcome to watch and there are even detailed photo exhibits describing step by step the lost-wax method of metal casting. Some of the larger images take a year or more to complete. The foundry is owned by Dr Thawi, an artisan and nationally renowned expert on northern-Thai folklore.

There is a small gift shop at the foundry where you can purchase bronze images of various sizes. The foundry is open to the public 8.30 am to 4.30 pm Wednesday to Sunday; to get here take city bus No 8.

Folk Museum
พิพิธภัณฑ์พื้นบ้าน

Across the street and a short distance north of the foundry is a folk museum established by Dr Thawi. Exhibits include items from his personal collection of traditional farm implements, hunting equipment, musical instruments, cooking utensils and other folkloric artefacts from throughout the northern region. It's the best collection of its kind in the country and many of the objects on display are virtually nonexistent in modern Thai life. If you're lucky, Dr

Thawi may be around to offer you an impromptu demonstration of rustic devices used for calling birds and other animals, including elephants! The museum is open 8.30 am to 4.30 pm Tuesday to Sunday; entrance is by donation. City bus No 8 passes by the museum.

Places to Stay – Budget

Phitsanulok has good coverage in the budget accommodation category.

Guesthouses & Hostels The *Phitsanulok Youth Hostel* (☎ *055-242060,* e *phitsanulok @tyha.org, 38 Thanon Sanam Bin)* stands well above all other Thai hostels associated with Hostelling International. Set amid a lush garden with aromatic jasmine vines and a

spring, a 50-year-old house has been converted into a restaurant featuring Thai and European food. A lofty teak-wood *săalaa* (*sala;* open-sided pavilion) behind the house is built of salvaged timber from seven old Tak Province teak houses to create a pleasant, open-air sitting and dining area – a good place to sit back and relax over a glass of wine or freshly brewed locally grown coffee while listening to the cadence of frogs and crickets.

Row house rooms behind the săalaa, each furnished with northern-Thai antiques and featuring unique semi-outdoor bathrooms, cost 200/300/450/600B single/double/triple/quad. There are also a few rooms with shared bathroom for 120B. All rates include breakfast. From the train station you can

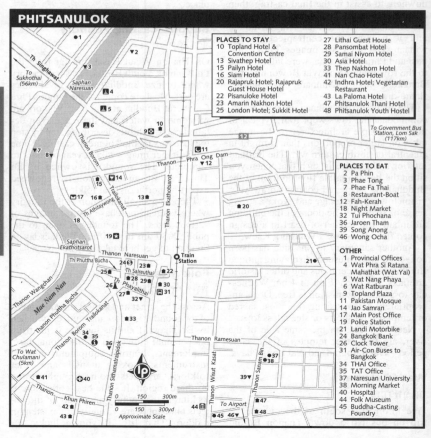

PHITSANULOK

PLACES TO STAY
10 Topland Hotel & Convention Centre
13 Sivathep Hotel
15 Pailyn Hotel
16 Siam Hotel
20 Rajapruk Hotel; Rajapruk Guest House Hotel
22 Pisanuloke Hotel
23 Amarin Nakhon Hotel
25 London Hotel; Sukkit Hotel
27 Lithai Guest House
28 Pansombat Hotel
29 Samai Niyom Hotel
30 Asia Hotel
33 Thep Nakhorn Hotel
41 Nan Chao Hotel
42 Indhra Hotel; Vegetarian Restaurant
43 La Paloma Hotel
47 Phitsanulok Thani Hotel
48 Phitsanulok Youth Hostel

PLACES TO EAT
2 Pa Phin
3 Phae Tong
7 Phae Fa Thai
8 Restaurant-Boat
12 Fah-Kerah
18 Night Market
32 Tui Phochana
36 Jaroen Tham
39 Song Anong
46 Wong Ocha

OTHER
1 Provincial Offices
4 Wat Phra Si Ratana Mahathat (Wat Yai)
5 Wat Nang Phaya
6 Wat Ratburan
10 Topland Plaza
11 Pakistan Mosque
14 Jao Samran
17 Main Post Office
19 Police Station
21 Landi Motorbike
24 Bangkok Bank
26 Clock Tower
31 Air-Con Buses to Bangkok
34 THAI Office
35 TAT Office
37 Naresuan University
38 Morning Market
40 Hospital
44 Folk Museum
45 Buddha-Casting Foundry

get to the hostel by săamláw (20B to 30B) or on a No 4 city bus. From the airport take a túk-túk (30B) or a No 4 bus that passes by the hostel (on the right). From the bus terminal, take a săamláw (30B) or a No 1 city bus (get off at Thanon Ramesuan and walk the last 300m or so).

Lithai Guest House (☎ *055-219626, fax 219627*) is in the Lithai Building, a large office building towards the middle of Thanon Phayalithai. Sixty clean, quiet rooms with plenty of light are strung out over three floors, giving more the feel of an apartment complex than a guesthouse. Fan rooms with shared bathroom cost 150/180B single/double, while the same with private bathroom and TV cost 180/200B. Standard air-con rooms with TV, hot shower and a la carte Thai or European breakfast go for 300/330B; add a fridge for 440B single/double. This might be a good choice for a long-term stay and, in fact, the Lithai offers one night free for every 15 you pay for. There's a low-key coffee shop downstairs, and parking at the back.

Hotels Near the train station are several inexpensive hotels and places to eat. The classic *Pisanuloke Hotel* (☎ *055-247555, 247999*) is in an old two-storey building, conveniently located right next to the train station. One-bed fan rooms run to 180B, two-bed rooms are 280B and air-con rooms are 380B. There's a *khâo kaeng* (rice-and-curry) vendor downstairs in the lobby, and plenty of places to eat nearby.

Not far from the train station on Thanon Ekathotsarot is the four-storey *Asia Hotel* (☎ *055-258378, fax 230419*), with quite decent single/double rooms for 200B, air-con for 300B. Street noise can be deafening, so ask for a room towards the back of the hotel. Across the street is the *Samai Niyom Hotel*, a three-storey place with OK air-con rooms for 280/380B single/double.

If you turn left out of the station and then take the first right turn on to Thanon Saireuthai, you'll come to *Pansombat Hotel* on the left side of the road. Rooms 100/200B with private shower and shared toilet, and 150/300B with toilet. It's noisy and has a bit of night traffic, however. The *Sukkit* (☎ *055-258876, 20/1–2 Thanon Saireuthai*) is a better deal at 150B for a

clean room with fan and private bathroom. Although it's strictly basic and a little dark, it's centrally located a block from the river and is less noisy than hotels towards the station.

If you keep walking towards the river, Thanon Saireuthai changes name to Soi 1, Thanon Phuttha Bucha, where you'll find the best cheapie in this area, the *London Hotel* (☎ *055-225145, 21–22 Soi 1, Thanon Phuttha Bucha*). It's an old wooden Thai-Chinese hotel that has been spruced up and painted in cheery colours; clean rooms with shared cold-water facilities are 120B.

The friendly *Siam Hotel* (☎ *055-258844, 4/8 Thanon Athitayawong*) is an old-fashioned four-storey place a half-block from the river and main post office. Large rooms, all with private bathroom and ceiling fan, cost 150B single, 200B double; those towards the back are considerably quieter. You might want to have a look at the rooms before taking one – some are cleaner than others; if you get a clean, quiet one, this is good value.

Places to Stay – Mid-Range
Behind the more upmarket Rajapruk Hotel on Thanon Phra Ong Dam is the *Rajapruk Guest House Hotel* (☎ *055-259203*), where rooms with fan and hot-water showers go for 280B (great value), air-con 360B. Guests may use the Rajapruk Hotel swimming pool. *Rajapruk Hotel* (☎ *055-258477, fax 251395, 99/9 Thanon Phra Ong Dam*) itself offers good upper mid-range value. All rooms come with air-con, hot-water showers, carpeting, TV and telephone for 500B single/double; there are also more-expensive suites.

Also good is the 45-room *Indhra Hotel* (☎ *055-217934, 103/8 Thanon Sithamataipidok*), next to La Paloma Hotel. Clean air-con singles/doubles are 300B, 350B with TV.

The *Sivathep Hotel* (☎ *055-244933, 110/21 Thanon Prasongprasat*) was once the top end in Phitsanulok. It offers clean rooms with fan or air-con and TV ranging from 230B to 400B.

Places to Stay – Top End
Prices at Phitsanulok's upper-end hotels all start at 1000B or less, making it one of Thailand's bargain provincial capitals. This

is also where the main hotel growth is, so a room glut will probably keep prices stable or even slightly depressed, especially at the older places.

The six-storey *Thep Nakhorn Hotel* (☎ 055-244070, fax 251897, 43/1 Thanon Sithamatraipidok) offers quiet air-con rooms for 500B and suites for 1500B, American breakfast included. The centrally located *Pailyn Hotel* (☎ 055-252411, fax 258185, 38 Thanon Borom Trailokanat) has rooms starting at 792/924B single/double, including breakfast. Others in this category – places that were once Phitsanulok's flashiest digs but are now a little worn at the edges yet still quite comfortable – include *Nan Chao Hotel* (☎ 055-244702/5, fax 244794), which has rooms from 900B, and *Amarin Nakhon Hotel* (☎ 055-219069–75, fax 219500, 3/1 Thanon Chao Phraya Phitsanulok), which has rooms from 550B. A 24-hour restaurant attached to the hotel serves Chinese and north-eastern Thai cuisine.

The *Topland Hotel & Convention Centre* (☎ 055-247800, fax 247815) is connected to Topland Plaza shopping centre at the intersection of Thanon Singhawat and Thanon Ekathotsarot. It's a luxurious place with a beauty salon, cafe, snooker club, fitness centre, several restaurants and other facilities. The room rates start at 1400/1600B single/double, which is a bargain compared with Bangkok or Chiang Mai prices for similar quality. Free airport transfer is available.

La Paloma Hotel (☎ 055-217930, fax 217937, 103/8 Thanon Sithamatraipidok), just a little way south of the Indhra Hotel, is a six-storey, 249-room luxury hotel with a bit of family orientation – it will arrange day care for children with advance notice. Rooms with all the amenities start at 800B single/double.

Right next door to the Phitsanulok Youth Hostel stands the relatively new *Phitsanulok Thani Hotel* (☎ 055-211065, fax 211071; in Bangkok ☎ 02-314 3168), part of the Dusit chain. It features 110 air-con rooms, 21 of which are luxury rooms designed for business travellers. The regular rate for a standard room is 1600B, although it offers an 'Amazing Thailand' discount rate of 800B. Suites run as high as 4000B, including breakfast for two.

Places to Eat

Phitsanulok is a great town for eating – there must be more restaurants per capita here than in just about any other town in Thailand.

Excellent, inexpensive Thai food can be had at *Tui Phochana*, on Thanon Phayalithai east of the Lithai Building. It makes fabulous *yam khànǔn* (curried jackfruit) at the beginning of the cool season, plus many other outstanding Thai curries year-round. There are plenty of other cheap Thai restaurants in this area too.

Close to the Phitsanulok Youth Hostel are several small noodle and rice shops. South around the corner from the hostel, a permanent vendor stand called *Wong Ocha* (no Roman-script sign) sells delicious kài yâang, khâo nǐaw and *yam phàk kràchèt* (water mimosa salad).

Across from the Naresuan University campus on Thanon Sanam Bin is the very popular and very inexpensive *Song Anong* outdoor restaurant, open 9 am to 3 pm daily. It has a great selection of curries, noodles and Thai desserts, all priced at less than 25B. Try the *sǎo náam*, a mixture of pineapple, coconut, dried shrimp, ginger and garlic served over khànǒm jiin (Chinese noodles) – it's delicious. Also good is the *kaeng yûak*, a curry made from the heart of a banana palm, and *kǔaytǐaw sùkhǒthai*, thin rice-noodles served dry in a bowl with peanuts, barbecued pork, spices, green beans and bean sprouts.

Early risers can try the small but lively *morning market* next to Naresuan University. Vendors serve inexpensive khâo nam kài, *saalaapao* (Chinese steamed buns), paathâwng-kǒh and jók from 6 to 10 am daily.

There's a cluster of inexpensive market-style *food stalls* just west of the London Hotel near the cinema.

Near the mosque on Thanon Phra Ong Dam are several Thai-Muslim cafes. One very famous one, *Fah-Kerah*, has thick rotii served with *kaeng mátsàmàn* (Muslim curry), which is unusual this far north. Ask for *rotii kaeng* to get the set plate. This small cafe also has fresh milk and yogurt.

A small *Thai vegetarian restaurant* next to the Indhra Hotel offers very inexpensive vegetable dishes. *Jaroen Tham*, around the corner from TAT, is similar. Both are open 8 am to noon only.

If you're out past midnight, your best bet is the very good, 24-hour *khâo tôm place* next to the train station. At Topland Plaza next to the Topland Hotel there's *KFC*, *Pizza Hut* and *Swensen's*.

On the River Floating restaurants light up Mae Nam Nan at night. Some good choices include the *Phae Fa Thai*, which has a talented chef, and *Phae Tong*. South of the main string of floating restaurants is a pier where you can board a *restaurant-boat*, owned by Phae Fa Thai, that cruises Mae Nam Nan every night. You pay a small fee – 20B to 40B – to board the boat and then order from a menu as you please – there is no minimum charge.

Also along the river is a popular *night market* area with dozens of food vendors, a couple of whom specialise in *phàk bûng lawy fáa* (literally, floating-in-the-sky morning glory vine), which usually translates as 'flying vegetable'. This food fad originated in Chonburi but has somehow taken root in Phitsanulok. There are several of these places in town as well as along the river. The dish is nothing glorious – basically morning glory vine stir-fried in soya bean sauce and garlic – but there is a performance thrown in: The cook fires up a batch of phàk bûng in the wok and then flings it through the air to a waiting server who catches it on a plate. The eating places on the river are now so performance-oriented that the server climbs to the top of a van to catch the flying vegetable! Tour companies bring tour groups here and invite tourists to try the catch – it's just as amusing watching the tourists drop phàk bûng all over the place as it is to watch the cook. During the day this area is a sundries market.

In the same riverside night market, *Midnight Kai Tawn* prepares excellent khâo man kài. Most vendors here close around midnight, although a couple of khâo tôm vendors stay open till 2 am.

The old and established *Pa Phin*, just back from the river and north of Wat Phra Si Ratana Mahathat, is famous for *kǔaytǐaw hâwy khǎa* (literally, legs-hanging rice noodles). The name comes from the way customers sit on a bench facing the river, with their legs dangling below. It's open from 10 am to 4 pm daily.

Entertainment

Along Thanon Borom Trailokanat near the Pailyn Hotel is a string of really popular Thai pubs. *Jao Samran*, on this street, features live Thai-folk and pop. The food service starts around 5 or 6 pm and the music comes on around 8 pm.

More or less across from the Siam Hotel, the *Kamikaze Pub* is a good spot for a quiet drink.

Getting There & Away

Air The THAI office (☎ 055-258020, fax 251671) is at 209/26–28 Thanon Borom Trailokanat, near the TAT office. THAI has four 55-minute flights to Phitsanulok from Bangkok daily for 1110B one way. There are also flights between Phitsanulok and Chiang Mai (765B, four weekly), Nan (680B, four weekly), Lampang (680B, two daily) and Phrae (495B, four weekly).

Phitsanulok's airport is just out of town. Sǎwngthǎew leave the airport for town every 20 minutes (10B); otherwise, you can catch the No 4 city bus (4B). The big hotels in town run free buses from the airport, and THAI has a door-to-door van service for 30B per person.

Bus Phitsanulok lies about 390km from Bangkok. Transport choices out of Phitsanulok are very good, as it's a junction for bus lines running both north and north-east. Bangkok is six hours away by bus and Chiang Mai 5½ hours. Buses leave Bangkok's Northern and North-Eastern bus station for Phitsanulok several times daily (108B ordinary, 160B 2nd class air-con, 194B 1st class air-con).

Be sure to get the new route *(sǎi mài)* bus via Nakhon Sawan (Rte 117), as the old route *(sǎi kào)* via Tak Fa (Hwy 11) takes six hours and costs more. Phitsanulok Yan Yon Tour and Win Tour both run VIP buses between Bangkok and Phitsanulok for 230B.

Buses between Phitsanulok and Loei via Dan Sai cost 75B (97B air-con) and take four hours.

Buses to destinations in other northern and north-eastern provinces leave several times a day from the Baw Khaw Saw (government bus station) just outside town, except for the air-con buses that may depart only once or twice a day.

NORTHERN THAILAND

destination	fare	duration (hrs)
Chiang Mai (via Den Chai)		
ordinary	114B	5½
air-con	176B, 227B (VIP)	5
Chiang Mai (via Tak)		
ordinary	126B	6
air-con	176B, 227B(1st)	6
Chiang Rai (via Utaradit)		
ordinary	139B	6½
air-con	195B, 250B (VIP)	6
Chiang Rai (via Sukhothai)		
ordinary	139B	7½
air-con	195B	7
Khon Kaen		
ordinary	110B	6
air-con	153B, 196B(1st)	6
Mae Sot		
air-con minivan	104B	5
Nakhon Ratchasima (Khorat)		
ordinary	133B	6
air-con	221B, 258B (VIP)	6
Nan		
ordinary	91B	9
air-con	127B	8
Udon Thani		
ordinary	110B	7
air-con	175B	7

Buses to the following points leave on the hour (*), every two hours (**) or every three hours (***) from early morning until 5 or 6 pm (except for Sukhothai buses, which leave every half-hour):

destination	fare	duration (hrs)
Dan Sai**		
ordinary	50B	3
Kamphaeng Phet*		
ordinary	37B	3
air-con	52B	2
Lom Sak*		
ordinary	40B	2
Phetchabun**		
ordinary	56B	3
Sukhothai		
ordinary	19B	1
air-con	27B, 40B (VIP)	1
Tak*		
ordinary	44B	3
air-con	62B	3
Utaradit*		
ordinary	40B	3
air-con	60B	2

Train Two ordinary trains (69B 3rd class only, eight to nine hours) leave Bangkok for Phitsanulok at 7.05 am (or Ayutthaya at 8.52 am) and 8.35 am (Ayuthaya 10.25 am). For most people this is a more economical and convenient way to reach Phitsanulok from Bangkok than with the bus, since you don't have to go out to Bangkok's Northern and North-Eastern bus station.

Rapid trains from Bangkok depart at 7.45 am and 3, 6.10, 8 and 10 pm (about seven hours). The basic fare is 159B for 2nd class or 69B for 3rd class, plus a 40B surcharge for the rapid service. There are also three all air-con, 2nd-class express diesel trains ('Sprinter' Nos 3, 5 and 7), at 10.55 am and 4.35 and 11.10 pm daily, that are about an hour quicker than the rapid service.

First class is available on the 3 pm rapid train (2nd and 3rd class also available) and 6 pm special express train (2nd class also available). The basic 1st-class and 2nd-class fares are 324B and 159B, not including the rapid and special express surcharges of 40B and 80B, plus any berth arrangements. Other basic 3rd-, 2nd- and 1st-class train fares to and from Phitsanulok include: Chiang Mai 52/122/269B; Lopburi 41/95/201B; and Ayuthaya 54/124/258B.

If you're going straight on to Sukhothai from Phitsanulok, a túk-túk ride from the train station to the bus station 4km away costs 30B to 40B. From there you can get a bus to Sukhothai, or you can catch a Sukhothai-bound bus in front of the Topland Hotel on Thanon Singhawat; a túk-túk to Thanon Singhawat costs 20B from the train station.

Getting Around

Săamláw rides within the town centre should cost 20B to 30B per person. Ordinary city buses cost 4B, and there are 13 lines making the rounds, so you should be able to get just about anywhere by bus. A couple of the lines also feature air-con coaches for 6B. The station for city buses is near the train station, off Thanon Ekathotsarot.

Motorcycles can be rented at Landi Motorbike (☎ 055-252765) at 57/21–22 Thanon Phra Ong Dam. Rates are 150B a day for a 100cc and 200B for a 125cc or 150cc.

PHU HIN RONG KLA NATIONAL PARK

อุทยานแห่งชาติภูหินร่องกล้า

From 1967 to 1982, the mountain known as Phu Hin Rong Kla served as the strategic headquarters for the CPT and its tactical arm, the People's Liberation Army of Thailand (PLAT). The remote, easily defended summit was perfect for an insurgent army. Another benefit was that the headquarters was only 50km from the Lao border, so lines of retreat were well guarded after 1975 when Laos fell to the Pathet Lao. China's Yunnan Province is only 300km away and it was here that CPT cadres received their training in revolutionary tactics (until the 1979 split between the Chinese and Vietnamese communists, when the CPT sided with Vietnam).

For nearly 20 years the area around Phu Hin Rong Kla served as a battlefield for Thai troops and the communists. In 1972 the Thai government launched a major offensive against the PLAT in an unsuccessful attempt to rout them from the mountain. The CPT camp at Phu Hin Rong Kla became especially active after the Thai military killed hundreds of students in Bangkok during the October 1976 student-worker uprising. Many students subsequently fled here to join the CPT, setting up a hospital and a school of political and military tactics. By 1978 the PLAT ranks here had swelled to 4000. In 1980 and 1981 the Thai armed forces tried again and were able to recapture some parts of CPT territory. But the decisive blow to the CPT came in 1982, when the government declared an amnesty for all the students who had joined the communists after 1976. The departure of most of the students broke the spine of the movement, which had by this time become dependent on their membership. A final military push in late 1982 effected the surrender of the PLAT, and Phu Hin Rong Kla was declared a national park in 1984.

Orientation & Information

The park covers about 307 sq km of rugged mountains and forest. The elevation at park headquarters is about 1000m, so the park is refreshingly cool even in the hot season. The main attractions on the main road through the park are the remains of the CPT stronghold, including a rustic meeting hall, the school of political and military tactics and

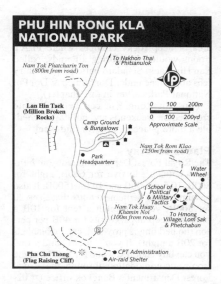

PHU HIN RONG KLA NATIONAL PARK

To Nakhon Thai & Phitsanulok

Nam Tok Phatcharin Ton (800m from road)

Lan Hin Taek (Million Broken Rocks)

Camp Ground & Bungalows

Park Headquarters

Nam Tok Rom Klao (250m from road)

Water Wheel

School of Political & Military Tactics

Nam Tok Huay Khamin Noi (100m from road)

To Hmong Village, Lom Sak & Phetchabun

Pha Chu Thong (Flag Raising Cliff)

CPT Administration
Air-raid Shelter

0   100   200m
0   100   200yd
Approximate Scale

the CPT administration building. Across the road from the school is a water wheel designed by exiled engineering students.

Things to See & Do

A trail leads to **Pha Chu Thong** (Flag Raising Cliff, sometimes called Red Flag Cliff), where the communists would raise the red flag to announce a military victory. Also in this area are an **air-raid shelter**, a **lookout** and the remains of the main **CPT headquarters** – the most inaccessible point in the territory before a road was constructed by the Thai government. The buildings in the park are made out of wood and bamboo and have no plumbing or electricity – a testament to how primitive the living conditions were.

At the park headquarters is a small **museum** that displays relics from CPT days, including medical instruments and weapons. At the end of the road into the park is a small White Hmong village. When the CPT was here, the Hmong were its ally. Now the Hmong are undergoing 'development' at the hands of the Thai government. One wonders what would have happened if the CPT had succeeded in its revolutionary goal. Maybe the Thai army's headquarters in Phitsanulok would now be a museum instead.

If you're not interested in the history of Phu Hin Rong Kla, there are **hiking trails**, **waterfalls** and **scenic views**, plus some interesting **rock formations** – an area of jutting boulders called Lan Hin Pum, and an area of deep rocky crevices where PLAT troops would hide during air raids, called Lan Hin Taek. Standard national park entry fees apply (see under Doi Suthep & Doi Pui National Park earlier in this chapter).

Phu Hin Rong Kla can become quite crowded on weekends and holidays; schedule a more peaceful visit for mid-week.

Places to Stay
The Royal Forest Department rents out *bungalows* that sleep five for 600B, eight for 800B, 10 for 1000B and 14 for 1500B. It also has three large permanent *tents* that sleep 20 for 800B; you can pitch a tent for 10B a night or sleep in park tents for 40B per person (no bedding is provided, except blankets for 20B a night). If you want to build a fire, you can buy chopped wood for 150B a night. Book accommodation through the Royal Forest Department's Bangkok office (☎ 02-561 4292), the provincial office (☎ 055-389002) or Golden House Tour Company (☎ 055-259973, 389002) in Phitsanulok.

Places to Eat
Near the camp ground and bungalows are some vendors. The best are *Duang Jai Cafeteria* – try its famous sôm-tam – and *Rang Thong*.

Getting There & Away
The park headquarters is about 125km from Phitsanulok. To get here, first take an early bus to Nakhon Thai (30B, two hours, hourly from 6 am to 6 pm). From there you can catch a săwngthăew to the park (25B, three times daily from 7.30 am to 4.30 pm).

A small group can charter a pick-up and driver in Nakhon Thai for about 600B to 800B for the day. This is a delightful trip if you're on a motorbike as there's not much traffic along the way. A strong engine is necessary to make it up the hills to Phu Hin Rong Kla.

PHITSANULOK TO LOM SAK
Along Hwy 12 between Phitsanulok and Lom Sak (the scenic 'gateway' to North-Eastern Thailand) there are several resorts and waterfalls. As in Phu Hin Rong Kla, the sites here tend to be more popular on weekends and holidays.

The Phitsanulok TAT office distributes a sketch map of attractions along this 130km stretch of road that marks the resorts and three waterfalls. You may want to bypass the first two waterfalls, **Nam Tok Sakhunothayan** (at the 33km marker) and **Kaeng Song** (at the 45km marker), which are on the way to Phu Hin Rong Kla and hence get overwhelmed with visitors. The third, **Kaeng Sopha** at the 72km marker, is a larger area of small falls and rapids where you can walk from rock formation to rock formation – there are more or fewer rocks depending on the rains. *Food vendors* provide inexpensive sôm-tam and kài yâang.

Farther east along the road is 1262-sq-km **Thung Salaeng Luang Wildlife Sanctuary** (entrance at the 80km marker), one of Thailand's largest and most important protected areas. Thung Salaeng Luang encompasses vast meadows and dipterocarp forests, and once was home to the PLAT. Among birdwatchers it's known as a habitat for the colourful Siamese fireback pheasant.

If you have your own wheels, you can turn right at the 100km marker onto Rte 2196 and head for **Khao Kho (Khao Khaw)**, another mountain lair used by the CPT during the 1970s. About 1.5km from the summit of Khao Kho, you must turn onto the very steep Rte 2323. At the summit, 30km from the highway, stands a tall obelisk erected in memory of the Thai soldiers killed during the suppression of the communist insurgency. The monument is surrounded by an attractive garden. Gun emplacements and sandbagged lookout posts perched on the summit have been left intact as historical reminders. On a clear day, the 360-degree view from the summit is wonderful.

If you've made the side trip to Khao Kho you can choose either to return to the Phitsanulok–Lom Sak highway, or take Rte 2258, off Rte 2196, until it terminates at Rte 203. On Rte 203 you can continue north to Lom Sak or south to Phetchabun. On Rte 2258, about 4km from Rte 2196, you'll pass **Khao Kho Palace**. One of the smaller royal palaces in Thailand, it's a fairly uninteresting, modern set of structures but has a quite nice rose garden. Still, if you've come all the way to Khao Kho you may as well take a look.

Continued on page 486

Sukhothai Period Ruins

Sukhothai Period Ruins

ANDERS BLOMQVIST

MARY LOU JANSON

MANFRED GOTTSCHALK

TOM COCKREM

Title Page: Ancient stupa looms majestically over a lotus pond at Sukhothai Historical Park. (Photograph by Glenn Beanland)

Top Left: The main chedi of Wat Mahathat with its lotus-bud finial

Middle Left: Buddha statue at Wat Mahathat

Bottom Left: This tall *prang* at Wat Phra Phai Luang shows Khmer influence.

Near Left: The huge Buddha at Wat Si Chum still evokes a feeling of awe.

SUKHOTHAI HISTORICAL PARK

GLENN BEANLAND

The original capital of the first Thai kingdom was surrounded by three concentric ramparts and two moats bridged by four gateways. Today the remains of 21 historical sites and four large ponds can be seen within the old walls, with an additional 70 sites within a 5km radius. The Sukhothai ruins are one of Thailand's World Heritage sites.

The ruins are divided into five zones – central, north, south, east and west – each of which has a 30B admission fee, except for the central section, which costs 40B. For 150B you can buy a single ticket that allows entry to all the Sukhothai sites, plus Sawanwaranayok National Museum, Ramkhamhaeng National Museum and the Si Satchanalai and Chaliang ruins in nearby Sawankhalok. The ticket is good for repeated visits over 30 days. There are additional charges for bicycles (10B), motorcycles (20B), *săamláw/túk-túk* (30B) and cars or vans (50B). The park's official hours are from 6 am to 6 pm.

Sukhothai temple architecture is most typified by the classic lotus-bud stupa, which features a conical spire topping a square-sided structure on a three-tiered base. Some sites also exhibit other rich architectural forms introduced and modified during the period – bell-shaped Singhalese and double-tiered Srivijaya stupas.

See under Getting Around in the Sukhothai section in this chapter for details on the best way to tour the park.

SUKHOTHAI HISTORICAL PARK

To Tak (65km)

To New Sukhothai (15km) & Phitsanulok (71km)

1 Wat Sang Khawat	16 Wat Mahathat
2 Thuriang Kiln	15 Ramkhamhaeng
3 Wat Phra Pai Luang	National Museum
4 Archaeology Centre	14 Wat Trapang Thong
5 Information Centre	18 Wat Si Sawai
6 Wat Si Chum	19 Tourist Police
7 Wat Saphan Hin	20 Main Gate
8 Wat Chang Rop	21 Vitoon Guest House
9 Wat Paa Mamuang	22 Wat Chang Lom
10 Wat Si Thon	23 Wat Trapang Thong
12 Ramkhamhaeng	Luang
Monument	24 Wat Mumlangka
13 Wat Mai	25 Wat Ton Jan
11 Wat Sa Si	26 Wat Wihan Thong
17 Wat Trapang Ngoen	27 Wat Chetuphon

Ramkhamhaeng National Museum

พิพิธภัณฑสถานแห่งชาติรามคำแหง

The museum provides a good starting point for an exploration of the ruins. A replica of the famous Ramkhamhaeng inscription (see Wiang Kum Kam under Chiang Mai earlier in this chapter) is kept here among a good collection of Sukhothai artefacts.

The museum is open daily except public holidays from 9 am to 4 pm and admission is 30B.

Wat Mahathat

วัดมหาธาตุ

The largest *wát* in the city, circa 13th-century Wat Mahathat is surrounded by brick walls (206m long and 200m wide) and a moat, said to represent the outer wall of the universe and the cosmic ocean. The stupa spires feature the famous lotus-bud motif, and some of the original stately Buddha figures still sit among the ruined columns of the old *wíhǎan* (main hall). There are 198 *chedi* (stupa) within the monastery walls – a lot to explore in what many consider was the spiritual and administrative centre of the old capital.

Wat Si Sawai

วัดศรีสวาย

Just south of Wat Mahathat, this shrine (dating from the 12th and 13th centuries) features three *prang* (Khmer-style towers) and a picturesque moat. It was originally built by the Khmers as a Hindu temple.

Wat Sa Si

วัดสระศรี

Wat Sa Si, or 'Sacred Pond Monastery', sits on an island west of the bronze monument of King Ramkhamhaeng (the third Sukhothai king). It's a simple, classic Sukhothai-style *wát* with one large Buddha, one chedi and the columns of the ruined *wíhǎan*.

Wat Trapang Thong

วัดตระพังทอง

Next to the museum, this small, still inhabited *wát* with its fine stucco reliefs is reached by a footbridge across the large lotus-filled pond that surrounds it. This reservoir, the original site of Thailand's Loi Krathong Festival, supplies the Sukhothai community with most of its water.

Wat Phra Phai Luang

วัดพระพายหลวง

Outside the city walls in the northern zone, this somewhat isolated *wát* features three 12-century Khmer-style prang, bigger than those at Wat Si Sawai. This may have been the centre of Sukhothai when it was ruled by the Khmers of Angkor prior to the 13th century.

Wat Si Chum
วัดศรีชุม

This wát is north-west of the old city and contains an impressive, much-photographed *mondòp* (a square, spired shrine hall) with a 15m, brick-and-stucco seated Buddha. Archaeologists theorise that this image is the 'Phra Atchana' mentioned in the famous Ramkhamhaeng inscription. A passage in the mondòp wall that leads to the top has been blocked so that it's no longer possible to view the *jataka* (stories of the Buddha's past lives) inscriptions that line the tunnel ceiling.

Wat Chang Lom
วัดช้างล้อม

Off Highway 12 in the east zone, Wat Chang Lom (Elephant Circled Monastery) is about a kilometre east of the main park entrance. A large bell-shaped chedi is supported by 36 elephants sculpted into its base.

Wat Saphan Hin
วัดสะพานหิน

Wat Saphan Hin is a couple of kilometres to the west of the old city walls in the west zone, on the crest of a hill that rises about 200m above the plain. The name of the wát, which means 'stone bridge', is a reference to the slate path and staircase leading to the temple, which are still in place. The site affords a good view of the Sukhothai ruins to the south-east and the mountains to the north and south.

All that remains of the original temple are a few chedi and the ruined wíhǎan, consisting of two rows of laterite columns flanking a 12.5m-high standing Buddha image on a brick terrace.

Wat Chang Rop
วัดช้างรอบ

On another hill west of the city, just south of Wat Saphan Hin, this wát features an elephant-base stupa, similar to that at Wat Chang Lom.

ight: Main Buddha and supporting columns of Wat Mahathat, ukhothai Historical Park

HERMANN MOLL

SI SATCHANALAI-CHALIANG HISTORICAL PARK

The 13th- to 15th-century ruins in the old cities of Si Satchanalai and Chaliang, about 50km north of Sukhothai, are in the same basic style as those in the Sukhothai Historical Park. The park covers roughly 720 hectares and is surrounded by a 12m-wide moat. Chaliang, a kilometre to the south-east, is an older city site (dating to the 11th century), though its two temples date to the 14th century. This historical park has also been classified as a World Heritage Site.

The ruins at Si Satchanalai are set among hills and are very attractive in the sense that they're not as heavily visited as the Sukhothai ruins. Some people actually prefer the more unrestored atmosphere at Si Satchanalai over Sukhothai. Those listed below represent only the more distinctive of the numerous Si Satchanalai ruins.

The park is open from 8 am to 6 pm. There are bicycles for rent near the entrance to the park for 20B. Admission to the historical park is 40B per person, plus 50B per car, 10B per bicycle, 30B per motorcycle and 40B per sǎamláw. For details on getting to the park, see under Getting There & Away in the Around Sukhothai section in this chapter.

Wat Chang Lom
วัดช้างล้อม

This fine temple, marking the centre of the old city of Si Satchanalai, has elephants surrounding a bell-shaped stupa but is somewhat better preserved than its counterpart in Sukhothai. An inscription says the temple was built by King Ramkhamhaeng between 1285 and 1291.

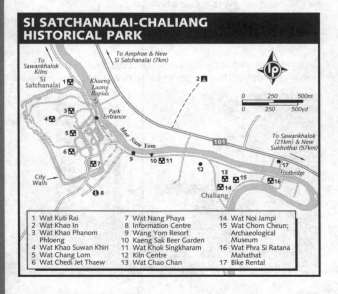

SI SATCHANALAI-CHALIANG HISTORICAL PARK

To Amphoe & New Si Satchanalai (7km)
To Sawankhalok Kilns
Si Satchanalai
Khaeng Luang Rapids
Park Entrance
Mae Nam Yom
City Walls
Chaliang
To Sawankhalok (21km) & New Sukhothai (57km)
Footbridge

1 Wat Kuti Rai	7 Wat Nang Phaya
2 Wat Khao In	8 Information Centre
3 Wat Khao Phanom Phloeng	9 Wang Yom Resort
4 Wat Khao Suwan Khiri	10 Kaeng Sak Beer Garden
5 Wat Chang Lom	11 Wat Khok Singkharam
6 Wat Chedi Jet Thaew	12 Kiln Centre
	13 Wat Chao Chan

14 Wat Noi Jampi	
15 Wat Chom Cheun; Archaeological Museum	
16 Wat Phra Si Ratana Mahathat	
17 Bike Rental	

Wat Khao Phanom Phloeng
วัดเขาพนมเพลิง

On the hill overlooking Wat Chang Lom to the right are the remains of Wat Khao Phanom Phloeng, including a large seated Buddha, a chedi and stone columns that once supported the roof of the *wíhǎan*. From this hill you can make out the general design of the once great city. The slightly higher hill west of Phanom Phloeng is capped by a large Sukhothai-style chedi – all that remains of Wat Khao Suwan Khiri.

Wat Chedi Jet Thaew
วัดเจดีย์เจ็ดแถว

Next to Wat Chang Lom, these ruins contain seven rows of chedi, the largest of which is a copy of one at Wat Mahathat in Sukhothai. An interesting brick-and-plaster wíhǎan features barred windows designed to look like lathed wood (an ancient Indian technique used all over South-East Asia). A prasat and chedi are stacked on the roof.

Wat Nang Phaya
วัดนางพญา

South of Wat Chang Lom and Wat Chedi Jet Thaew, this stupa is Singhalese in style and was built in the 15th or 16th century, a bit later than other monuments at Si Satchanalai. Stucco reliefs on the large laterite wíhǎan in front of the stupa – now sheltered by a tin roof – date to the Ayuthaya period when Si Satchanalai was known as Sawankhalok. Goldsmiths in the district still craft a design known as *nang phaya*, modelled after these reliefs.

Wat Phra Si Ratana Mahathat
วัดพระศรีรัตนมหาธาตุ

These ruins at Chaliang consist of a large laterite chedi (dating from 1448–88) between two wíhǎan. One wíhǎan contains a large seated Sukhothai Buddha image, a smaller standing image and a bas-relief of the famous walking Buddha, so exemplary of the flowing, boneless Sukhothai style. The other wihǎan contains some less distinguished images.

There's a separate 10B admission for this wát.

Wat Chao Chan
วัดเจ้าจันทร์

These wát ruins are about 500m west of Wat Phra Si Ratana Mahathat in Chaliang. The central attraction is a large Khmer-style prang similar to later prang in Lopburi and probably built during the reign of Khmer King Jayavarman VII (1181–1217). The prang has been restored and is in fairly good shape. The roofless wíhǎan on the right contains the laterite outlines of a large standing Buddha that has all but melted away from weathering.

Continued from page 480

Places to Stay & Eat

There are several resorts just off Hwy 12 west of the Rte 2013 junction for Nakhon Thai. Best of the lot is the ***Rainforest Resort*** (☎ 055-293085, fax 293086, 🖃 rnforest@ loxinfo.co.th), at the 44km marker. Spacious, tastefully designed cottages spread over a hillside facing Mae Nam Khek cost 1000B to 1800B for up to four people, and there is also one cottage for up to seven people for 2400B. All cottages come with air-con and hot water. An indoor-outdoor restaurant serves locally grown coffee and good Thai food. Other resorts in the area, ***Wang Nam Yen*** and ***Thanthong***, are similarly priced. ***SP Huts*** (☎ 055-293402, fax 293405) is a bit cheaper, with rooms starting at 500B.

Stop at ***Blue Mountain Coffee***, at the 42km marker, ***Rainforest Resort***, at the 44km marker, or ***Thawee Fresh Coffee***, at the 45km marker, all on Hwy 12 near Ban Kaeng Song (close to Nam Tok Kaeng Song). These restaurants serve some of the best fresh coffee outside of Bangkok; the beans are locally grown *kaafae jàak rái* (literally, coffee from the fields) but have names like Blue Mountain and Brazil. Freshly brewed coffee costs 15B to 25B, but it's worth it for 100% Arabica or Robusta beans.

Getting There & Away

Buses between Phitsanulok and Lom Sak cost 48B each way, so any stop along the way will cost less. During daylight hours it's easy to flag down another bus to continue your journey, but after 4 pm it gets a little chancy.

Sukhothai Province

SUKHOTHAI
อ.เมืองสุโขทัย

postcode 64000 • pop 25,800
As Thailand's first capital, Sukhothai (Rising of Happiness) flourished from the mid-13th century to the late 14th century. The Sukhothai kingdom is viewed as the 'golden age' of Thai civilisation – the religious art and architecture of the era are considered to be the most classic of Thai styles.

The new town of Sukhothai is almost 450km from Bangkok and is undistinguished except for its good municipal market in the town centre. The *meuang kào* (old city) of Sukhothai features around 45 sq km of ruins (which have been made into a historical park) making an overnight stay in New Sukhothai worthwhile, although you can make a day trip to the old city ruins from Phitsanulok.

See the 'Sukhothai Period Ruins' special section for more details about the ruins.

Information

The tourist police maintain an office in the Sukhothai Historical Park directly across from the Ramkhamhaeng National Museum.

Money Siam Commercial Bank, on the south-western corner of Thanon Singhawat and Thanon Tri Chat, has an ATM, as do several other banks in the vicinity.

Post & Communications The post office on Thanon Nikhom Kasem is open 8.30 am to noon weekdays, 1 to 4.30 pm on weekends and 9 am to noon on holidays. The attached CAT office offers international phone services 7 am to 10 pm daily.

There are several Internet centres in the vicinity of the Chinnawat Hotel.

Swimming

Suan Nam Premsuk, at the 4km marker on Route 101, is a modest sports complex with a clean swimming pool, tennis courts and ping pong table. It's open 7 am to 9 pm and costs 40B to use the facilities. Look for a couple of tall brick pillars supporting a blue-and-white sign.

Places to Stay

Guesthouses Most of the guesthouses in New Sukhothai offer reasonably priced accommodation in family homes (dorms and/or private rooms) and all rent out bicycles and motorcycles. Places continue to multiply, and competition keeps the prices low. The local taxi mafia has its hooks in the guesthouse proprietors, so expect lots of opinions about where you want to go from the săamláw drivers.

The ***Lotus Village*** (☎ 055-621484, fax 621463, 🖃 lotusvil@yahoo.com, 170 Thanon Ratchathani), on the east bank of Mae Nam Yom, is set in spacious grounds with a garden sitting area, and is quite suitable for long-term stays. Rooms with shared toilet in a teak house cost 120B per person (480B for the whole house). Teak bungalows with private hot-water shower cost 400B single/double, while deluxe rooms in another building cost 500B with fan and 800B with air-con; all have hot water. An attractive lobby/restaurant area with stacks of magazines and books is a pleasant place to hang out if you don't mind mosquitoes. The multilingual staff are friendly and knowledgeable.

Yupa House (☎ 055-612578, Soi Mekhapatthana, 44/10 Thanon Prawet Nakhon) is near the west bank of Mae Nam Yom. The family that runs it is friendly and helpful and often invites guests to share family meals. Dorm beds cost 40B;

rooms of various sizes cost 80B to 100B. There's a nice view of the city from the roof. *Somprasong Guest House (☎ 055-611709)* is on the way to Yupa House along the same road, at No 32. The rooms are arranged hotel-like on the 2nd floor of a large family house; singles/doubles cost 120B with fan and shared bathroom, and 300B with air-con and private facilities. It rents out bicycles and has ample off-road parking. Next door to the Somprasong is the newer *Ban Thai (☎ 055-610163)*. It's run by yet another friendly family, and has rooms for 120B with shared bathroom, and bungalows with private bathroom for 200B. Ban Thai is a good place for reliable information on things to see and do in the Sukhothai area.

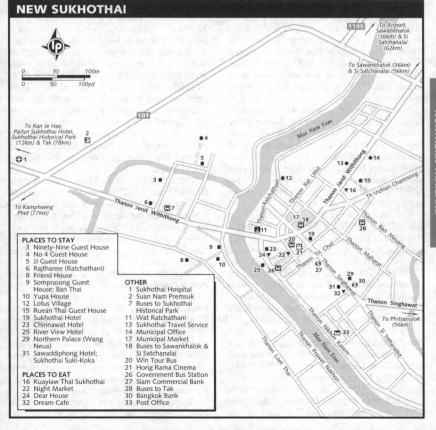

NEW SUKHOTHAI

NORTHERN THAILAND

0   50   100m
0   50   100yd

To Ran Je Hae,
Pailyn Sukhothai Hotel,
Sukhothai Historical Park
(12km) & Tak (78km)

To Kamphaeng
Phet (77km)

To Airport,
Sawankhalok
(36km) & Si
Satchanalai
(62km)

To Sawankhalok (36km)
& Si Satchanalai (56km)

Mae Nam Yom

Thanon Jarot Withithong
Thanon Ratchathani
Thanon Rat Uthit
Thanon Jarot Withithong
Th Vichian Chamnong
Thanon Ban Meuang
Thanon Maharat
Thanon Singhawat
Thanon Nikhon Kasem
Mae Nam Yom
Thanon Prawet Nakhon
Thanon Loet Thai
Thanon Si Intharathit

To Phitsanulok
(56km)

PLACES TO STAY
3 Ninety-Nine Guest House
4 No 4 Guest House
5 JJ Guest House
6 Rajthanee (Ratchathani)
8 Friend House
9 Somprasong Guest
   House; Ban Thai
10 Yupa House
12 Lotus Village
15 Ruean Thai Guest House
19 Sukhothai Hotel
23 Chinnawat Hotel
25 River View Hotel
29 Northern Palace (Wang
   Neua)
31 Sawaddiphong Hotel;
   Sukhothai Suki-Koka

PLACES TO EAT
16 Kuayiaw Thai Sukhothai
22 Night Market
26 Dear House
32 Dream Cafe

OTHER
1 Sukhothai Hospital
2 Suan Nam Premsuk
7 Buses to Sukhothai
   Historical Park
11 Wat Ratchathani
13 Sukhothai Travel Service
14 Municipal Office
17 Municipal Market
18 Buses to Sawankhalok &
   Si Satchanalai
20 Win Tour Bus
21 Hong Rama Cinema
26 Government Bus Station
27 Siam Commercial Bank
28 Buses to Tak
30 Bangkok Bank
33 Post Office

At *Friend House* (☎ *055-610172, 52/7 Soi Nissan)*, off Thanon Loet Thai (parallel to Thanon Prawet Nakhon), all rooms come with private bathroom and cost 100/120B for a single/double with fan, 250B with air-con. Discounts for stays of more than two nights are available. The guesthouse has a small garden dining area, free bikes, and motorcycles for rent. The proprietor teaches English to Thais so it's a good place to meet students.

No 4 Guest House (☎ *055-610165, 140/4 Soi Khlong Mae Ramphan, Thanon Jarot Withithong)*, the first guesthouse in Sukhothai, has moved a couple of times and is now in its third location. Rustic bamboo-thatch bungalows, with private, open-air, cold-water bathrooms, fan and nicely furnished outdoor lounging areas, go for 150B each; slightly larger ones cost 180B. There are several sitting areas on the property. The guesthouse offers information and a local area map as well as a two-day Thai cooking course and a five-day Thai massage course. Next door, to the south, is *JJ Guest House*, with basic rooms in a wood-and-cement house for 150B with shared cold-water bathroom.

About 150m south-west on the opposite side of the canal, the friendly *Ninety-Nine Guest House* (☎ *055-611315, 01-972 9308, 234/6 Soi Panitsan)* offers rooms in a clean two-storey teak house surrounded by gardens. Dorm beds cost 80B in a three-bed room, while singles/doubles go for 120/150B with shared cold-water facilities upstairs, hot water downstairs.

The *Dream Cafe* (☎ *055-612081, fax 622157, 86/1 Thanon Singhawat)* offers a few charming guest rooms in a wooden building behind the restaurant; all have fan and attached hot-water shower and cost 250/350B. The owner has used recycled architectural features from old Thai houses throughout, and the rooms are nicely decorated with local crafts and antiques. More rooms will be added in the near future.

On a soi between Thanon Jarot Withithong and Thanon Vichian Chamnong, in a nice residential neighbourhood, is the new *Ruean Thai Guest House* (☎ *055-612444, 181/20 Soi Pracha Ruammit, Thanon Jarot Withithong)*. Done in a traditional Thai style but with modern facilities, the house contains large and well-spaced guest rooms, with lots of inviting sitting areas in between. Prices range from 250B for a fan room up to 600B for a huge air-con room (less if you don't use the air-con). All have modern, private hot-water facilities. The guesthouse rents out bicycles for 15B.

In the old city close to the main entrance of the Sukhothai Historical Park, *Vitoon Guest House* offers fan rooms for 250B with attached cold-water bathroom, and large, comfortable air-con rooms with TV and hot water for 500B. Vitoon also rents out bicycles.

Hotels The friendly *Sawaddiphong Hotel* (☎ *055-611567, 56/2–5 Thanon Singhawat)* has good singles/doubles with fan and private bathroom for 150/180B, and doubles for 220B with TV or 260B to 400B with air-con – good value.

Sukhothai Hotel (☎ *055-611133, 15/5 Thanon Singhawat)*, once a travellers' favourite, is now very much an also-ran. Singles/doubles with fan cost 170/250B and air-con rooms cost 280B; all have cold-water bathroom. *Chinnawat Hotel* (☎ *055-611385, 1–3 Thanon Nikhon Kasem)* is in need of renovation. Rooms with fan and bathroom cost 150B to 180B, depending on whether they are in the old or new wing – the old wing is cheaper and a bit quieter. Air-con rooms cost from 350B. Be sure to check that the air-con works before booking in.

The all air-con *River View Hotel* (☎ *055-611656, fax 613373)*, on Thanon Nikhon Kasem near Mae Nam Yom, remains a favourite among small traders. Clean air-con rooms cost 350/450B with one/two beds, while slightly nicer rooms with TV cost 500B. There is a large sing-song coffee shop downstairs.

Once the top hotel in town, the *Rajthanee* (Ratchathani; ☎ *055-611031, fax 612583, 229 Thanon Jarot Withithong)* has seen better days. Standard air-con rooms cost 300B with hot water, while rooms with TV and refrigerator cost 600B. *Northern Palace* (Wang Neua; ☎ *055-613522, fax 612038, 43 Thanon Singhawat)* charges 450B for OK rooms with air-con, small TVs and refrigerators. The hotel has a coffee shop and swimming pool.

About 8km from the city centre on the road between the old and new cities of

Sukhothai, the huge **Pailyn Sukhothai Hotel** (☎ 055-613310, fax 613317; in Bangkok ☎ 02-215 7110, fax 215 5640) caters mostly to tour groups and has a disco, health centre and several restaurants. Rooms start at 800B.

Places to Eat

The **night market** across from Win Tour and the **municipal market** near the town centre are great places to eat; rice and noodle dishes are quite inexpensive and the night market has a vendor with good fruit shakes. **Sukhothai Hotel** and Chinnawat Hotel have restaurants that prepare Thai and Chinese food for Western tastes. Attached to the Chinnawat Hotel, **Rainbow** has a variety of noodle dishes, Thai curries, sandwiches, Western breakfasts and ice cream at very reasonable prices. Just south-east of the Chinnawat on Thanon Nikhon Kasem is **Dear House**, a place serving sandwiches, burgers, Western breakfasts and Thai and Chinese food in wagon-wheel decor. **Sukhothai Suki-Koka**, in front of the Sawaddiphong Hotel, specialises in Thai-style sukiyaki.

On Thanon Singhawat opposite Bangkok Bank, **Dream Cafe** is an air-con cafe decorated with 19th-century Thai antiques. Despite catering primarily to tourists, the cafe serves very good food and the staff is attentive. The extensive menu includes a long list of herbal liquors ('stamina drinks'), ice cream and very well-prepared Thai and Chinese food. Unlike many Thai restaurants, most of the Thai menu items are also on the bilingual menu. One dish that isn't listed in English is *thâwt man khâo phôht* (tasty corn fritters with a dipping sauce).

On the northern side of Thanon Jarot Withithong about 350m west of Rte 101 is **Ran Je Hae**, a place specialising in Sukhothai-style kǔaytǐaw – pork, coriander, green onions, pickled cabbage, pork skins, peanuts, chilli and green beans are added to the basic kǔaytǐaw recipe. Another good spot to try Sukhothai-style kǔaytǐaw is **Kuaytiaw Thai Sukhothai**, on Thanon Jarot Withithong about 20m south of the turn-off for Ruean Thai Guest House. The restaurant is in a nice wooden building with a fountain fashioned from ceramic pots out front.

Getting There & Away

Air The so-called 'Sukhothai' airport is 27km outside of town off Route 1195 about 11km from Sawankhalok. It's privately owned by Bangkok Airways, and, like its Ko Samui counterpart, is a beautifully designed small airport that uses tropical architecture to best advantage. Bangkok Airways (☎ 055-633266/7, fax 610908; at the airport ☎ 055-612448), with an office at 10 Mu 1, Thanon Jarot Withithong, operates a daily flight from Bangkok (1820B including 30B departure tax, one hour and 10 minutes). In the reverse direction, the flight costs 1890B (including the 100B domestic/international 'airport tax' charged at this airport). Bangkok Airways charges 80B to transport passengers between the airport and Sukhothai.

Bangkok Airways flies daily from Chiang Mai to Sukhothai (680B), or from Sukhothai to Chiang Mai (750B); prices include tax. Fares for children are half the adult price. Bangkok Airways also has a flight to Siem Reap (Cambodia; 8500B including airport tax). Tickets can be purchased from any travel agency in town.

Bus Sukhothai can be reached by road from Phitsanulok, Tak or Kamphaeng Phet. If you arrive in Phitsanulok by rail or air, take a city bus No 1 to the air-con bus station in the centre, or to the Baw Khaw Saw (government bus) station, for buses out of town. The bus to Sukhothai (19B ordinary, 27B air-con, one hour) leaves regularly throughout the day.

From Tak, get a Sukhothai bus at the Baw Khaw Saw station just outside town (40B, 1½ hours); at last count there were 10 departures daily. Buses from Kamphaeng Phet cost 38B (one to 1½ hours).

Baw Khaw Saw buses to/from Chiang Mai via Tak (the shortest, fastest route) cost 109B ordinary, 153B air-con (4½ to five hours). Buses between Bangkok and Sukhothai cost 128B or 179B air-con (seven hours). Buses to Chiang Rai cost 126B or 171B air-con (six hours); there are two departures a day of both air-con and ordinary buses.

Phitsanulok Yan Yon Tour has six daily VIP buses (with reclining seats) to Bangkok for 230B. Win Tour has nine departures for the same price. Ordinary buses to destinations outside Sukhothai Province leave from the government bus station; tour buses leave from Win Tour or Phitsanulok Yan Yon Tour near the night market area. Buses to Tak leave from Thanon Ban Meuang, two streets east of Thanon Singhawat.

Buses to Sawankhalok (18B, 45 minutes) and Si Satchanalai (20B, one hour) leave hourly between about 6 am and 6 pm from the intersection of Thanon Singhawat and Thanon Jarot Withithong.

Getting Around
Around New Sukhothai, a săamláw ride should not cost more than 20B to 30B. Săwngthăew run frequently from 6.30 am to 6 pm between New Sukhothai and Sukhothai Historical Park, leaving from Thanon Jarot Withithong near Mae Nam Yom; the fare is 10B (check with locals first to see if there's been a price increase) and it takes 20 to 30 minutes from the river to the park.

The best way to get around the historical park is by bicycle; these can be rented at shops outside the park entrance for 20B a day, or you can borrow or rent one at any guesthouse in New Sukhothai. Don't rent the first bikes you see at the bus stop at meuang kào (old city), as the better bikes tend to be found at shops around the corner, closer to the park entrance.

If you rent a bike in town, instead of taking Hwy 12 straight to the park consider a more scenic (if slower) way to reach the ruins: Turn right (north) off the highway about 2.5km west of the main junction of Hwy 12 and Rte 101. The best place to turn off is right into the compound of Wat Kamphaeng Ngam, in the village of Ban Kluay. Pedal through the wát compound and out the back entrance, where you'll see a canal. Follow the road along the canal – sometimes you must cross a canal bridge as the road changes sides from time to time. You shouldn't get lost as long as you can keep the canal in sight, and along the way you'll get a taste of village life. When you reach the ruins of Wat Chang Lom (the one with elephants along the base), continue another 200m or so and look for a bridge on the left that will take you back to Hwy 12 and the main entrance to the park.

The park operates a tram service through the old city for 20B per person.

AROUND SUKHOTHAI
Si Satchanalai-Chaliang Historical Park
อุทยานประวัติศาสตร์ศรีสัชชนาลัย/
ชะเลียง

See the special section 'Sukhothai Period Ruins' for information on the major ancient sites in this 7.2-sq-kilometre park. The nearby town of Sawankhalok is the main supply centre for the area.

Sawankhalok Kilns
เตาเผาสังคโลก

The Sukhothai–Si Satchanalai area has long been famous for its beautiful pottery, much of which was exported to countries throughout Asia. In China – the biggest importer of Thai pottery during the Sukhothai and Ayuthaya periods – the pieces came to be called 'Sangkalok', a mispronunciation of Sawankhalok. Particularly fine specimens of this pottery can be seen in the national museums of Jakarta and Pontianak in Indonesia.

At one time, more than 200 huge pottery kilns lined the banks of Mae Nam Yom in the area around Si Satchanalai. Several have been carefully excavated and can be viewed at the **Si Satchanalai Centre for Study & Preservation of Sangkalok Kilns**, which opened in 1987. So far the centre has opened two phases of its construction to the public: a small museum in Chaliang with excavated pottery samples and one kiln; and a larger outdoor kiln site 2km northwest of the Si Satchanalai ruins. The exhibits are very well presented, although there are no English labels. More phases are planned, including one featuring a working kiln.

Sawankhalok pottery rejects, buried in the fields, are still being found. Shops in Sukhothai and Sawankhalok sell misfired, broken, warped and fused pieces. The **Sawanwaranayok Museum** near Sawankhalok's **Wat Sawankhalam** on the western bank of the river, exhibits pottery and Buddha images unearthed by local villagers and donated to the wát. Thai Celadon near Chiang Mai is a ceramics centre producing a modern interpretation of the old craft.

Ban Hat Siaw
บ้านหาดเสี้ยว

Ban Hat Siaw is a colourful village south-east of Si Satchanalai. It is home to the Thai Phuan, a Thai tribal group that immigrated from Xieng Khuang Province in Laos about 100 years ago when the Annamese and Chinese were in North-Eastern Laos.

The local Thai Phuan are famous for **hand-woven textiles** (*phâa hàat sîaw*), which have patterns of horizontal stripes bordered by brocade.

Traditionally every Thai Phuan woman is taught weaving skills, which are passed on from generation to generation. Practically every stilt house in the village has a loom beneath it; cloth can be purchased at the source or from shops in Sawankhalok. Vintage Hat Siaw textiles 80 to 200 years old can be seen at the Village Old Clothes Museum in central Si Satchanalai.

Another Thai Phuan custom is the use of **elephant-back processions** in local monastic ordinations; these usually take place in early April.

If you can't make it to Ban Hat Siaw but are interested in buying Hat Siaw textiles, you'll find small shops and vendors selling them along the main road through the town of Si Satchanalai.

Places to Stay & Eat

Just outside the Si Satchanalai Historical Park, 400m before the south-eastern corner of the old city, *Wang Yom Resort (Sunanthana; ☎ 055-631380)* has bungalows and a 'handicraft village' set amid beautifully landscaped grounds along Mae Nam Yom. Spacious bungalows are overpriced with 1200B with fan, 1500B with air-con. Bargaining is in order. Wang Yom's large restaurant is reportedly very good. Food and drink are also available at a *coffee shop* in the historical park until 6 pm.

Kaeng Sak Beer Garden, by the river near the park entrance, shares a compound with several 'antique' shops. It's open only from 9 am to 3.30 pm and features a moderately priced Thai and Chinese menu. This is a popular tour bus stop.

Sawankhalok This charming town on Mae Nam Yom, about 11km south of the historical park, has a couple of more-economical possibilities for visitors wishing to explore the area. The *Saengsin Hotel (☎ 055-641259, fax 641828, 2 Thanon Thetsaban Damri 3)* is centrally located on the main street that runs through Sawankhalok. It has clean and comfortable singles/doubles costing 150/210B with fan, or 280/320B with air-con. It also has a coffee shop.

Muang Inn Hotel (☎ 055-641622, 21 Thanon Kasemrat) has rooms for 160B with fan and 350B with air-con. There is a dark coffee shop and sing-song cafe downstairs from the hotel.

This isn't a big town for eating; most food places sell noodles and khâo man kài and not much else. There is a *night market* in Sawankhalok, which is held along the main streets. This night market is bigger than the one in New Sukhothai.

Ko Heng is an old riverside Chinese restaurant that's well past its prime and is now primarily a place for old Chinese cronies to sit and drink tea.

Probably the best spot for eating is *Kung Nam*, a Thai and Chinese garden restaurant on the outskirts of Sawankhalok towards Sukhothai. Kung Nam is not far from the Muang Inn Hotel.

Getting There & Away

Bus Si Satchanalai-Chaliang Historical Park is off Rte 101 between Sawankhalok and New Si Satchanalai. From New Sukhothai, take a Si Satchanalai bus (22B ordinary, 28B air-con) and ask to get off at *meuang kào*.

There are two places along the left side of the highway where you can get off the bus and reach the ruins in the park; both involve crossing Mae Nam Yom. The first leads to a footbridge over Mae Nam Yom to Wat Phra Si Ratana Mahathat at Chaliang; the second crossing is about 2km farther northwest just past two hills and leads directly into the Si Satchanalai ruins.

Train King Rama VI had a 60km railway spur built from Ban Dara (a small town on the main northern trunk) to Sawankhalok just so that he could visit the ruins. The original train station in Sawankhalok is one of the main local sights. A vendor in the station sells real filtered coffee.

Amazingly, there is a daily special express from Bangkok to Sawankhalok, No 7, which leaves the capital at 11.10 pm (about eight hours) Don't look for this train on your English train schedule, as it's only listed on the Thai timetable. It's a 'Sprinter', which means 2nd class air-con, no sleepers, and the fare is 372B (this includes dinner and breakfast). You can also pick up this train in Phitsanulok at 5.32 am; expect to pay about 33B for this shorter distance. In the reverse direction, No 4 leaves Sawankhalok at 7.40 am.

There is also one local train a day, No 405, originating from Taphan Hin (73km north of Nakhon Sawan). It leaves Phitsanulok at 11.50 am and arrives in Sawankhalok at 1.45 pm (21B 3rd class). The No 406 leaves Sawankhalok at 2 pm and arrives at Sila-at at 3.15 pm.

Getting Around
Bicycle is the best way to see the ruins. You can rent bikes from outside a barber shop at the gateway to Wat Phra Si Ratana Mahathat; rates are 20B a day.

Kamphaeng Phet Province

KAMPHAENG PHET
อ.เมืองกำแพงเพชร

postcode 62000 • pop 24,500
Formerly known as Chakangrao or Nakhon Chum, Kamphaeng Phet (Diamond Wall) was once an important front line of defence for the Sukhothai kingdom but is now mostly known for producing the tastiest *klûay khài* ('egg banana', a delicious kind of small banana) in Thailand. It's a nice place to spend a day or two wandering around the ruins and experiencing a small northern provincial capital that receives few tourists.

Information
A privately sponsored tourist information centre (the sign reads 'Chamber of Commerce'), a block south of the Chakungrao hotel on Thanon Thesa, can answer general queries about accommodation and restaurants. It also has a good map of the town.

Money Thai Farmers Bank and Siam Commercial Bank have branches with ATMs on Thanon Charoensuk, the road coming into town from Phitsanulok. Most of

the major banks also have branches with ATMs along the main streets along the river.

Post The main post office is just south of the old city on Thanon Thesa.

Old City
เมืองเก่า

Only a couple of kilometres off the Bangkok-Chiang Mai road are some ruins within the old city area of Kamphaeng Phet, as well as some very fine remains of the long city wall.

The Kamphaeng Phet Historical Park has been established at the old city site and the area is now cared for by the Fine Arts Department. The park was declared a Unesco World Heritage site in 1991. The entry fees to the ruins within the city wall are 40B per person (plus 10B per bicycle, 20B per motorcycle, 30B per túk-túk, or 50B per car). The park's hours are 6 am to 6 pm daily. Here you'll find **Wat Phra Kaew**, which used to be adjacent to the royal palace (now in ruins). The weather-corroded Buddha statues have assumed slender, porous forms that remind many visitors of Giacometti sculptures. About 100m south-east of Wat Phra Kaew is **Wat Phra That**, distinguished by a large round-based chedi surrounded by columns. This park is a popular spot for joggers and walkers.

Kamphaeng Phet National Museum
พิพิธภัณฑสถานแห่งชาติกำแพงเพชร

Across the road and south 100m or so from these temples is a national museum. Downstairs has the usual survey of Thai art periods while upstairs has a collection of artefacts from the Kamphaeng Phet area, including terracotta ornamentation from ruined temples and Buddha images in the Sukhothai and Ayuthaya styles. The museum is open from 9 am to 4 pm Wednesday to Sunday; admission is 30B.

Kamphaeng Phet Museum
พิพิธภัณฑ์กำแพงเพชร

Just south of the Kamphaeng Phet National Museum is the similarly named Kamphaeng Phet Museum, which consists of a series of

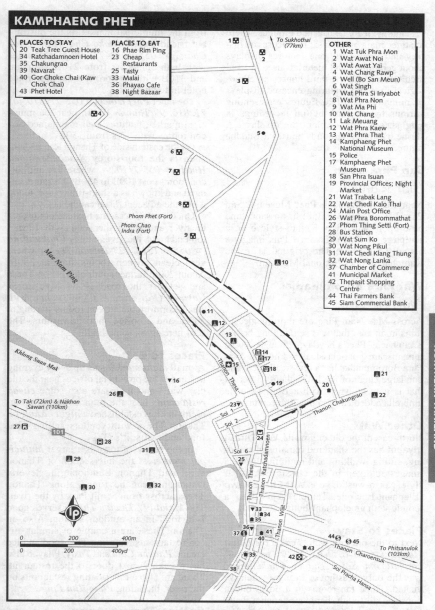

KAMPHAENG PHET

PLACES TO STAY
20 Teak Tree Guest House
34 Ratchadamnoen Hotel
35 Chakungrao
39 Navarat
40 Gor Choke Chai (Kaw Chok Chai)
43 Phet Hotel

PLACES TO EAT
16 Phae Rim Ping
23 Cheap Restaurants
25 Tasty
33 Malai
36 Phayao Cafe
38 Night Bazaar

OTHER
1 Wat Tuk Phra Mon
2 Wat Awat Noi
3 Wat Awat Yai
4 Wat Chang Rawp
5 Well (Bo San Meun)
6 Wat Singh
7 Wat Phra Si Iriyabot
8 Wat Phra Non
9 Wat Ma Phi
10 Wat Chang
11 Lak Meuang
12 Wat Phra Kaew
13 Wat Phra That
14 Kamphaeng Phet National Museum
15 Police
17 Kamphaeng Phet Museum
18 San Phra Isuan
19 Provincial Offices; Night Market
21 Wat Trabak Lang
22 Wat Chedi Kalo Thai
24 Main Post Office
26 Wat Phra Borommathat
27 Phom Thing Setti (Fort)
28 Bus Station
29 Wat Sum Ko
30 Wat Nong Pikul
31 Wat Chedi Klang Thung
32 Wat Nong Lanka
37 Chamber of Commerce
41 Municipal Market
42 Thepasit Shopping Centre
44 Thai Farmers Bank
45 Siam Commercial Bank

To Sukhothai (77km)

Mae Nam Ping

Phom Phet (Fort)
Phom Chao Indra (Fort)

Khlong Suan Mak

To Tak (72km) & Nakhon Sawan (110km)

Thanon Thesa

Thanon Chakungrao

Soi 1
Soi 2
Soi 6

Thanon Ratchadamnoen

Thanon Thesa

Thanon Wijit

To Phitsanulok (103km)

Thanon Charoensuk

Soi Pracha Hansa

0   200   400m
0   200   400yd

NORTHERN THAILAND

central Thai–style wooden structures on stilts set among nicely landscaped grounds. There are three main buildings: One focuses on history and prehistory, one features displays about geography and materials used in local architecture, and the third houses an ethnological museum featuring encased displays of miniature doll-like figures representing various tribes. Push-button recordings in English and Thai explain the displays. A shrine hall in the grounds houses a Buddha figure. Admission is free.

San Phra Isuan
ศาลพระอิศวร

Near the Kamphaeng Phet Museum, San Phra Isuan (Shiva Shrine) has a sandstone base upon which is a Khmer-style bronze sculpture of Shiva (Isvara). This image is actually a replica: The original is in the Kamphaeng Phet National Museum.

Wat Phra Borommathat
วัดพระบรมธาตุ

Across Mae Nam Ping are more neglected ruins in an area that was settled long before Kamphaeng Phet's heyday, although visible remains are post-classical Sukhothai. Wat Phra Borommathat has a few small chedi and one large chedi of the late Sukhothai period that is now crowned with a Burmese-style umbrella added early in the 20th century.

Other Wát
North-east of the old city walls, **Wat Phra Si Iriyabot** has the shattered remains of standing, sitting, walking and reclining Buddha images sculpted in the classic Sukhothai style. North-west of here, **Wat Chang Rawp** (Elephant-Encircled Temple) is just that – a temple with an elephant-buttressed wall.

Places to Stay
Next to the old city wall, ***Teak Tree Guest House*** (☎ 01-675 6471, @ teakkpp@ hotmail.com, Soi 1 Thanon Chakungrao) was the only guesthouse in town when we visited. Three fan rooms in a tidy wooden house on stilts with shared modern hot-water bathroom cost 130/200B single/double. The guesthouse is only 10 minutes' walk from the historical park. Bicycles are available for 30B per day.

In the centre of the new town, not far from the municipal market, is the bustling but friendly ***Gor Choke Chai*** (Kaw Chok Chai; ☎ 055-711247). Singles/doubles with bathroom cost from 210B with fan and 310B with air-con; it's the best-value hotel in town.

The nicer ***Phet Hotel*** (☎ 055-712810, fax 712816, 99 Thanon Wijit), near the municipal market, features well-maintained air-con rooms with TVs from 350B.

On the eastern side of Thanon Ratchadamnoen is the four-storey ***Ratchadamnoen Hotel*** (☎ 055-711029), where fan and air-con rooms cost 100B to 450B. It's rather tattered and known as a short-time place; to top it off, the adjacent disco can be noisy.

On Thanon Thesa, the next street towards the river, and a bit farther south, is the town's top-end hotel, the seven-storey ***Chakungrao*** (☎ 055-711315, 123 Thanon Thesa), where very clean air-con rooms start at 350B. About 200m farther south on Thanon Thesa and set off the road is the five-storey ***Navarat*** (Nawarat; ☎ 055-711211), with clean, comfortable air-con rooms starting at 500B, and a coffee shop downstairs. The staff here speak some English.

Places to Eat
A small **night market** sets up every evening in front of the provincial offices near the old city walls and there are also some **cheap restaurants** near the roundabout. The municipality has established a **night bazaar** on Thanon Thesa with vendors selling Thai food and crafts; it's OK.

In the centre of town is a larger **municipal market** at the intersection of Thanon Wijit and Thanon Banthoengjit. Several restaurants can be found along Thanon Thesa across from Sirijit Park by the river. The **Malai** (77 Thanon Thesa) serves good Isan food in an outdoor setting. Also on Thanon Thesa are a couple of similar air-con restaurants featuring Thai food and ice cream, **Phayao Cafe** and **Tasty**. Phayao also has a bakery next door to the restaurant. There are also a few floating restaurants on the river, including ***Phae Rim Ping***.

Getting There & Away
The bus fare from Bangkok is 105B ordinary and 147B air-con. Most visitors arrive from Sukhothai (38B), Phitsanulok (37B

ordinary, 52B air-con) or Tak (25B). The government bus station is located across the river from town.

Getting Around

The least-expensive way to get from the bus station into town is to take a shared săwngthăew (4B per person) to the roundabout across the river, and from there take a săamláw anywhere in town for 20B.

Tak Province

Tak, like Loei, Nan, Phetchabun, Krabi and certain other provinces, has traditionally been considered a 'remote' province, ie, one that the central Bangkok government has had little control over. In the 1970s the mountains of western Tak were a hotbed of communist guerrilla activity. Since the 1980s the former leader of the local CPT movement has been involved in resort-hotel development and Tak is very much open to outsiders, but the area still has an untamed feeling about it. The province has a population of only around 350,000. It also has Thailand's largest population of domesticated elephants, which are still commonly used by Karen villagers in western Tak for transport and agricultural tasks.

Western Tak has always presented a distinct contrast with other parts of Thailand because of strong Karen and Burmese cultural influences. The Thailand-Myanmar border districts of Mae Ramat, Tha Song Yang and Mae Sot are dotted with refugee camps, an outcome of the firefights between the Karen National Union (KNU) and the Myanmar government, which is driving Karen civilians across the border. As of mid-1998 there were an estimated 10,000 Burmese and Karen refugees along the border.

The main source of income for people living on both sides of the border is legal and illegal international trade. The main smuggling gateways on the Thailand side are Tha Song Yang, Mae Sarit, Mae Tan, Wangkha, Mae Sot and Waley. One important contraband product is teak, cut by the Karen or the Karenni (Kayah) and brought into Thailand from Myanmar on big tractor trailers at night. Up to 200,000B in bribes per truckload is distributed among local Thai authorities who conveniently look the other way. None of the trade is legal since the Thai government cut off all timber deals with the Burmese military in 1997.

Most of the province is forested and mountainous and is excellent for trekking. Organised trekking occurs, some farther north out of Chiang Mai, most of it locally organised. There are Hmong, Musoe (Lahu), Lisu and White and Red Karen settlements throughout the west and north.

In Ban Tak, 25km upstream along Mae Nam Tak from Tak, you can visit **Wat Phra Boromathat**, the original site of a Thai chedi that, according to legend, was constructed during the reign of King Ramkhamhaeng (1275–1317) to celebrate his elephant-back victory over King Sam Chon, ruler of an independent kingdom once based at or near Mae Sot. The wát's main feature is a large, slender, gilded chedi in the Shan style surrounded by numerous smaller but similar chedi. Many Thais flock to the temple each week in the belief that the chedi can somehow reveal to them the winning lottery numbers for the week.

Approximately 45km north of Meuang Tak via Rte 1 and then 17km west (between the 463km and 464km markers), via the road to Sam Ngao, is Kheuan Phumiphon (Bhumibol Dam), which impounds Mae Nam Ping at a height of 154m, making it the tallest dam in South-East Asia and the eighth-tallest in the world. The shores and islands of the reservoir are a favourite picnic spot for local Thais.

TAK

อ.เมืองตาก

postcode 63000 • pop 21,600
Lying along the eastern bank of Mae Nam Ping, Tak is not particularly interesting except as a point from which to visit the Lan Sang and Taksin Maharat National Parks to the west or Kheuan Phumiphon to the north. Travellers heading to the Thailand-Myanmar border town of Mae Sot occasionally find themselves here for a few hours or overnight.

Although most of Tak exhibits nondescript, cement-block architecture, the southern section of the city harbours a few old teak homes. Residents are proud of the suspension bridge (for motorcycles, pedicabs, bicycles and pedestrians only) over Mae Nam Ping, which flows quite broadly here even in the dry season. There's also a larger highway bridge (Saphan Kittikachon) over the river.

Information

TAT (☎ 055-514341) has an office in a beautiful new building, at 193 Thanon Taksin off Thanon Mahat Thai Bamrung, where you can ask questions or pick up tourist pamphlets and brochures. Its hours are 8.30 am to 4.30 pm daily.

Several banks have branches along Thanon Mahat Thai Bamrung and Thanon Taksin, all with ATMs.

Places to Stay & Eat

Most of Tak's hotels are lined up on Thanon Taksin or Thanon Mahat Thai Bamrung in the town centre. The slightly worn *Mae Ping* (*☎ 055-511807, 619 Thanon Taksin*) has large clean rooms with fan and bathroom in an old wooden building for 110B; air-con rooms cost 250B. It's surprisingly quiet considering its location opposite the market.

One street west of the Mae Ping Hotel is the old wooden two-storey *Sa-Nguan Thai* (*☎ 055-511155*). There is no sign, but this classic can be identified by the red Chinese lanterns on the 2nd-floor veranda. Singles/doubles cost 170/200B with fan and 300/350B with air-con. There's a decent Chinese-Thai restaurant downstairs.

The eight-storey *Viang Tak 2* (*☎ 055-511910*), on Thanon Chumphon by Mae Nam Tak, has comfortable standard rooms for a discounted 550B and deluxe rooms for 800B to 900B – although listed rates are higher. Amenities include a coffee shop, karaoke bar and swimming pool. The hotel's older, bigger sibling, *Viang Tak* (*☎ 055-511950, 25/3 Thanon Mahat Thai Bamrung*), features 100 recently renovated rooms at roughly the same rates. The less expensive *Racha Villa* (*☎ 055-512361*), at the intersection of Rte 105 and Hwy 1, is better value. Fairly well-appointed rooms with air-con, carpet, TV, video and hot water start at 230B.

Near the intersection of Hwys 1 and 12, *Panasan Hotel* (*☎ 055-511436*) has basic but clean bungalows for 110B to 160B with fan and bathroom and 250B with air-con. The Panasan is good value, if a little removed from town.

Cheap food can be bought in the *market* across the street from the Mae Ping Hotel. Nearby is *Pond*, a simple place specialising

TAK

1 TAT Office
2 King Maha Taksin Shrine
3 Wat Botmani Sibunruang
4 Vegetarian Restaurant
5 Provincial Hall
6 Bus Station
7 Police Station
8 Thanjit Tour
9 Siam Commercial Bank
10 Viang Tak Hotel
11 Thai Military Bank
12 Sa-Nguan Thai
13 Bangkok Bank
14 Pond
15 Market
16 Mae Ping
17 Wat Mani Banphot
18 Taksin Hospital
19 Viang Tak 2
20 Fire Station
21 Wat Sitalaram

in Thai curries. On the south-eastern corner of Thanon Taksin and Thanon Charot Withi Thong you'll find a *vegetarian restaurant* (no Roman-script sign).

Getting There & Away

Tak airport, 15km out of town towards Sukhothai on Hwy 12, isn't operating at the moment; the nearest functioning airports are in Phitsanulok and Mae Sot. THAI provides a free shuttle van a few times a day between Phitsanulok airport and Tak. In Tak the vans stop at the Viang Tak 2 Hotel.

There are frequent buses to Tak from Sukhothai (40B ordinary, one to 1½ hours). The Tak bus station is just outside town, but a túk-túk will take you to the town centre for around 20B.

Ordinary government buses depart for Bangkok three times daily (123B, 10 hours), while a 2nd-class air-con bus leaves once each day (172B, eight hours). There are four daily 1st-class air-con departures from Tak to Bangkok and one 10 pm departure in the reverse direction (221B, six hours). Thanjit Tour and Choet Chai Tour offer 1st-class air-con buses with similar departures and fares.

Air-con buses to Mae Sot (46B) leave at 2, 4 and 5 pm. Minivans to Mae Sot leave much more frequently from the main station in Tak (33B).

AROUND TAK
Taksin Maharat & Lan Sang National Parks
อุทยานแห่งชาติตากสินมหาราช

These small national parks receive a steady trickle of visitors on weekends and holidays, but are almost empty during the week. Taksin Maharat (established in 1981) covers 149 sq km; the entrance is 2km from the 26km marker on Rte 105/Asia Rte 1 (the so-called Pan-Asian Hwy, which would link Istanbul and Singapore if all the intervening countries allowed land crossings) to Mae Sot.

The park's most outstanding features are the 30m, nine-tiered **Nam Tok Mae Ya Pa** and a record-holding *tàbàak,* a dipterocarp that is 50m tall and 16m in circumference. Bird-watching is said to be particularly good here; known resident and migratory species include the tiger shrike, forest wagtail and Chinese pond heron.

Nineteen kilometres from Tak, Lan Sang National Park preserves 104 sq km surrounding an area of rugged, 1000m-high granite peaks, part of the Tenasserim Range. A network of trails leads to several **waterfalls**, including the park's 40m-high namesake. To reach the park entrance, take Rte 1103 3km south off Rte 105.

National park entry fees apply (200B for foreigners, 20B for Thais, half price for children).

Places to Stay Lan Sang National Park has *bungalows* for rent for 150B to 600B, and also *tents*. Taksin Maharat National Park offers rustic *rooms* for 250B each, and has a *camp ground*. Food service can be arranged in both parks.

Kheuan Phumiphon
เขื่อนภูมิพล

This huge reservoir is a favourite canoeing, swimming, fishing and picnicking destination for Tak residents. The Electrical Generating Authority of Thailand (EGAT) maintains several **bungalows** and **longhouses** for visitors, costing 400B to 1000B per multibed unit. For information or reservations, call Ban Phak Rap Rong Kheuan Phumiphon (☎ 055-549509), or EGAT in Bangkok (☎ 02-436 3179).

Between the provincial capital and the reservoir, in Ban Tak, *Ban Tak Youth Hostel (☎/fax 055-591286,* 🖂 *bantak@tyha.org, 9/1 Mu 10)* offers a few rooms in a house with a large garden and a view of the mountains. The hostel can accept only eight visitors at a time. Rates are 120B per person. Bikes are available for hire. The hostel is on the western side of the village adjacent to Mae Nam Yom.

MAE SOT
แม่สอด

Mae Sot is 80km from Tak on Rte 105. This Burmese-Chinese-Karen-Thai trading outpost has become a small but simmering tourist destination. A decade or so ago, several public billboards in town carried the warning (in Thai): 'Have fun, but if you carry a gun, you go to jail', underscoring Mae Sot's reputation as a free-swinging, profiteering wild-East town. The billboards are long gone but the outlaw image lingers. Black-market trade between Myanmar and Thailand is the primary source of local revenue, with most transactions taking place in the districts of Mae Ramat, Tha Song Yang, Phop Phra and Um Phang. Mae Sot has also become the most important jade and gem centre along the border, with most of the trade controlled by Chinese and Indian immigrants from Myanmar.

Border skirmishes between Myanmar's central government and the weakening Karen and Kayah ethnic insurgencies can break out at any time, sending thousands of refugees – and the occasional mortar rocket – across the Thai-Myanmar border, elements that add to the area's perceived instability.

Walking down the streets of Mae Sot, you'll see an interesting mixture of ethnicities

NORTHERN THAILAND

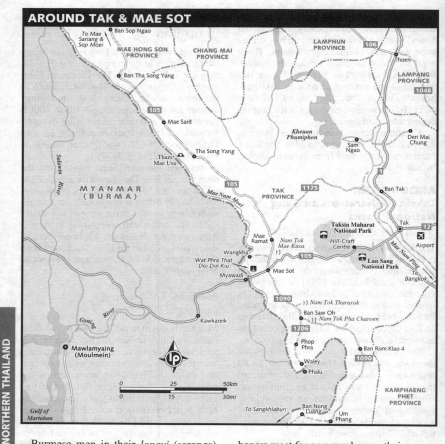

AROUND TAK & MAE SOT

To Mae Sariang & Sop Moei
Ban Sop Ngao
MAE HONG SON PROVINCE
CHIANG MAI PROVINCE
LAMPHUN PROVINCE
106
Thoen
LAMPANG PROVINCE
1048
Ban Tha Song Yang
105
Mae Sarit
Kheuan Phumiphon
Den Mai Chung
Sam Ngao
Tha Song Yang
Tham Mae Usu
M Y A N M A R (B U R M A)
Salawin River
105
Mae Nam Moei
TAK PROVINCE
1175
Ban Tak
1
Tak
12
Airport
Taksin Maharat National Park
Mae Ramat
Nam Tok Mae Kasa
Hill-Craft Centre
Wangkha
105
Wat Phra That Doi Din Kiu
Myawadi
Mae Sot
Lan Sang National Park
Mae Nam Ping
To Bangkok
Gyaing River
Kawkareik
1090
Nam Tok Thararak
Ban Saw Oh
Nam Tok Pha Charoen
1206
Phop Phra
Ban Rom Klao 4
1090
Waley
Phalu
Mawlamyaing (Moulmein)
KAMPHAENG PHET PROVINCE
Gulf of Martaban
0   25   50km
0   15   30mi
To Sangkhlaburi
Ban Nong Luang
Um Phang

NORTHERN THAILAND

– Burmese men in their *longyi* (sarongs), Hmong and Karen women in traditional hill-tribe dress, bearded Indo-Burmese men and Thai army rangers.

Shop signs along the streets are in Thai, Burmese and Chinese. Most of the temple architecture in Mae Sot is Burmese. The town's Burmese population is largely Muslim, while those living outside town are Buddhist and the Karen are mostly Christian.

The large municipal market in Mae Sot, behind the Siam Hotel, sells some interesting stuff, including Burmese clothing, cheap cigarettes, roses, Indian food, sturdy Burmese blankets and velvet thong slippers from Mandalay.

A big **Thai-Burmese gem fair** is held in April. Around this time Thai and Burmese

boxers meet for an annual muay thai competition held somewhere outside town in the traditional style. Matches are fought in a circular ring and go for five rounds; the first four rounds last three minutes, the fifth has no time limit. Hands bound in hemp, the boxers fight till first blood or knockout. You'll have to ask around to find the changing venue for the annual slugfest, as it's not exactly legal.

The Thai-Myanmar Friendship Bridge was completed in 1996, linking Mae Sot with Myawadi and the highway west to Mawlamyaing (Moulmein) and Yangon, an exciting prospect for overland travel. At the moment foreigners can go no farther than Myawadi however, although there are rumours that the route to Hpa-an and Mawlamyaing will soon be open.

Information

Tourist Police The tourist police (☎ 055-533523, 534341) have an office 100m south-west of No 4 Guest House.

Money Thai Military Bank, Siam Commercial Bank and Krung Thai Bank offer ATMs in the centre of town.

Email & Internet Access You can check your email at Cyber Space on the southern side of Thanon Prasat Withi, just a bit before the THAI office. It's open 10 am to 10 pm.

Books DK Book House, attached to the DK Hotel, has a branch in Mae Sot on Thanon Intharakhiri. The only English-language books it stocks so far are Penguin classics, but there are a few maps of the area for sale, including a detailed Thai military-surveyed topographic map (1:250,000) of the border area entitled *Moulmein*. This map covers as far north as Mae Ramat, to the south almost to Um Phang, west to Mawlamyaing and only about 50km east of Mae Sot.

Herbal Sauna

At Wat Mani men can take a herbal sauna between 3 and 7 pm for 20B. The sauna volunteers also sell herbal medicines made by the monks. The sauna is towards the back of the monastery grounds, past the monks' kùtì.

Ban Mae Tao
บ้านแม่เฒ่า

Wat Wattanaram (Phattanaram) is a Burmese temple at Ban Mae Tao, 3km west of Mae Sot on the road to the Thailand-Myanmar border. A fairly large alabaster sitting Buddha is in a shrine with glass-tile walls – it's very Burmese in style. In the main wíhǎan on the 2nd floor is a collection of Burmese musical instruments, including tuned drums and gongs.

Wat Phra That Doi Din Kiu (Ji)
วัดพระธาตุดอยดินกิว(จี)

Wat Phra That Doi Din Kiu (Ji) is a forest temple 11km north-west of Mae Sot on a 300m-high hill overlooking Mae Nam Moei and Myanmar. A small chedi mounted on what looks like a boulder that has been balanced on the edge of a cliff is one of the attractions, and is reminiscent of the Kyaik-tiyo Pagoda in Myanmar.

The trail that winds up the hill provides fairly good views of the thick teak forests across the river in Myanmar. On the Thai side, a scattering of smaller trees is visible. There are a couple of small limestone caves in the side of the hill on the way to the peak. The dirt road that leads to the wát from Ban Mae Tao passes through a couple of Karen villages.

During Myanmar's dry-season offensives against the KNU, this area is sometimes considered unsafe and the road to the temple is occasionally blocked by Thai rangers. Ask in town about the current situation before heading up the road.

Border Market & Myawadi

Sǎwngthǎew frequently go to the border, 6km west of Mae Sot: Ask for Rim Moei (Edge of the Moei). The trip costs 10B and the last sǎwngthǎew back to Mae Sot leaves Rim Moei at 5 pm.

A market about 100m from the river on the Thai side legally sells Burmese goods – dried fish and shrimp, dried bamboo shoots, mung beans, peanuts, woven-straw products, teak carvings, thick cotton blankets, lacquerware, tapestries, jade and gems. Dried and preserved foods are sold by the *pan* (the pound), the Burmese/Karen unit of weight measure, rather than by the kilogram, the usual measure in Thailand. You can also buy black-market kyat (Burmese currency) here at very favourable rates.

As of our last visit, the border was officially open to foreigners – it is now possible to cross the international bridge to Myawadi for day visits. Travel isn't yet permitted beyond Myawadi. The prospect that the road all the way from Myawadi to Mawlamyaing on the Gulf of Mottama (Martaban) will open is probably still a year or two away.

If your Thai visa is about to expire, you can cross the border here, turn around, and walk back into Thailand for an instant 30-day visa. Immigration procedures are taken care of at the Thai immigration booth at the bridge, although if you have any problems there's a larger immigration office in nearby Mae Moei Shopping Bazaar. It takes about 15 minutes to finish all the

MAE SOT

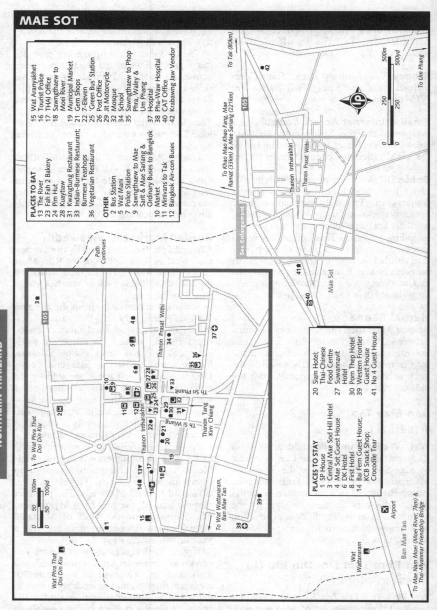

PLACES TO EAT
13 The River
23 Fah Fah 2 Bakery
24 Pim Hut
28 Kuaytiaw
31 Kwangtung Restaurant
33 Indian-Burmese Restaurant;
   Burmese Teashops
36 Vegetarian Restaurant

OTHER
2 Bus Station
5 Wat Mani
7 Police Station
9 Sawngthaew to Mae
   Sarit & Mae Sariang &
   Ordinary Buses to Bangkok
10 Market
11 Minivans to Tak
12 Bangkok Air-con Buses

15 Wat Aranyakhet
16 Tourist Police
17 THAI Office
18 Sawngthaew to
   Moei River
19 Municipal Market
21 Gem Shops
22 7-Eleven
25 'Green Bus' Station
26 Post Office
29 Jit Motorcycle
32 Mosque
34 School
35 Sawngthaew to Phop
   Phra, Waley &
   Um Phang
37 Hospital
38 Pha-Waw Hospital
40 CAT Office
42 Krabawng Jaw Vendor

PLACES TO STAY
1 SP House
3 Central Mae Sod Hill Hotel
4 Mae Sot Guest House
6 DK Hotel
8 First Hotel
14 Bai Fern Guest House;
   KCB Snack Shop;
   Crocodile Tear

20 Siam Hotel;
   Thai-Chinese
   Food Centre
27 Suwannavit
   Hotel
30 Pom Thep Hotel
39 Western Frontier
   Guest House
41 No 4 Guest House

NORTHERN THAILAND

paperwork to leave Thailand officially, and then you're free to walk across the arched bridge. The bridge is open 6 am to 6 pm daily.

At the other end of the bridge is a rustic Myanmar immigration booth where you'll fill out permits for a one-day stay, pay a US$10 fee and leave your passports as a deposit. Then you're free to wander around Myawadi as long as you're back at the bridge by 5 pm to pick up your passport and check out with immigration.

Myawadi Myawadi is a fairly typical Burmese town with a number of monasteries, schools, shops and so on. The most important temple is **Shwe Muay Wan**, a traditional bell-shaped stupa gilded with many kilos of gold and topped by over 1600 precious and semiprecious gems. Surrounding the main stupa are 28 smaller stupas, and these in turn are encircled by 12 larger ones. Colourful shrines to Mahamuni Buddha, Shin Upagot and other Buddhist deities follow the typical Mon and central Burman style, with lots of mirrored mosaics. Another noted Buddhist temple is **Myikyaungon**, called Wat Don Jarakhe in Thai and named for its crocodile-shaped sanctuary. A hollow stupa at Myikyaungon contains four marble Mandalay-style Buddhas around a central pillar, while niches in the surrounding wall are filled with Buddhas in other styles, including several bronze Sukhothai-style Buddhas.

Myawadi's 1000-year-old earthen city walls, probably erected by the area's original Mon inhabitants, can be seen along the southern side of town.

If you're looking for a good traditional Burmese meal, one of the best places is the inexpensive *Daw Y Bon* on the left-hand side of the main street leading away from the bridge. Look for a row of curry pots and an English sign reading 'Tea House'.

Because of long-time commercial, social and religious links between Mae Sot and Myawadi, many local residents speak some Thai. The Riverside Club, a casino on the river about 1km north of town, serves a mostly Thai clientele.

Organised Tours

SP House, Mae Sot Guest House and Western Frontier Guest House (see Places to

Stay later) can arrange trekking and rafting trips north and south of Mae Sot.

Places to Stay – Budget

Guesthouses At the time of writing Mae Sot had five guesthouses. The *Mae Sot Guest House* on Thanon Intharakhiri offers not-so-great singles/doubles with shared bathroom for 80/120B, and nicer air-con rooms with cold-water showers in a row house for 280B. The guesthouse's best feature is the pleasant open-air sitting area at the front. Local maps and information are available and the owner speaks English quite well.

The new *Bai Fern Guest House* (☎ 055-533343), on Thanon Intharakhiri near Crocodile Tear, offers basic rooms with shared hot-water showers for 100/150B in a rambling Thai house.

Farther west is the simple but well-run *No 4 Guest House* (☎/fax 055-544976, 736 Thanon Intharakhiri), a large teak house well off the road. Rates are 50B for a dorm bed and 80/100B for singles/doubles with shared hot-water bathroom.

In the southern part of town, the *Western Frontier Guest House* (☎ 055-532638, 18/2 Thanon Bua Khun), near Pha-Waw Hospital, has six rooms in a two-storey brick-and-wood house for 100B per room. The staff boasts language skills in English, Japanese, Thai, Karen and Burmese and can arrange local trekking and rafting trips. Rental bikes are also available.

On the north-western outskirts of town, *SP House* (☎ 055-531409, 14/21 Thanon Asia) offers adequate wooden rooms for 50B per person. Although it's a bit far from the centre of town, good travel information is available. The staff can arrange various treks around the province.

Hotels The cheapest hotel in town is the *Suwannavit Hotel* (☎ 055-531162) on Soi Wat Luang. Rooms with fan and bathroom cost 100B in the old wooden wing and 120B in the newer concrete one.

Siam Hotel (☎ 055-531376, fax 531974), on Thanon Prasat Withi, has adequate rooms for 200B with fan, 250B with fan and TV, 350B with air-con and 500B with carpet and TV. Although it's basically a truckers' and gem traders' hotel, local rumour has it that Myanmar intelligence agents hang out at the Siam.

NORTHERN THAILAND

Places to Stay – Mid-Range

The clean and efficiently run *Porn Thep Hotel* (☎ *055-532590, 25/4 Thanon Si Wiang)* is off Thanon Prasat Withi near the day market. In the rear wing of the hotel, air-con singles/doubles with hot water cost 400B, while rooms with fan and cold-water bathroom cost 250B. A few deluxe rooms with TV and hot water are available for 700B in the newer front wing. Porn Thep has security parking.

At the *First Hotel* (☎ *055-531233)*, off Thanon Intharakhiri near the police station, large comfortable rooms start at 270B with fan and bathroom; air-con rooms cost up to 450B. All rooms come with TV. Like the Siam, it's favoured by Thai truckers. The hotel is still undergoing renovations, so prices may change.

A three-storey hotel attached to DK Book House on Thanon Intharakhiri, the *DK Hotel* (☎ *055-531699)* has smallish apartment-style rooms with fan and private bathroom for 250B; you'll pay 450B to 800B for larger air-con rooms. The rooms tend to vary a lot in quality, so it might be best to look at a few before checking in.

Places to Stay – Top End

The *Central Mae Sod Hill Hotel* (☎ *055-532601–8, Bangkok 02-541 1234)* is on the highway to Tak, just outside the town centre. It has a swimming pool, tennis courts, a good restaurant, a disco and a cocktail lounge. All rooms come with air-con, hot water, fridge, TV, video and telephone. Standard rooms cost 900B, suites start at 1200B.

Places to Eat

Mae Sot has an unusually good selection of places to eat. Near the Siam Hotel on Thanon Prasat Withi are several choices, including an adjacent *Thai-Chinese food centre* with several different vendors serving noodles and curry. It's open morning to afternoon only. You can also try the rambling *market* behind the Siam Hotel for cheap Thai takeaway.

An *Indian-Burmese restaurant* opposite the mosque (the sign reads 'Tea Shop') has good rotii kaeng, fresh milk, curries and khâo sàwy. On the same side of the street about 50m south, a *Burmese Muslim teashop* does cheap and tasty samosas, curries and naan; a meal of curry, dhal,

vegetables, two naan, two plates of rice, two teas and two coffees costs only 70B.

A favourite local snack is *krabawng jaw* (Burmese for 'fried crispy'), a sort of vegetable tempura. The best place to eat it is at the small *vendor stand* 1km east of Mae Sot Guest House on the southern side of Thanon Intharakhiri, where the same family has been supplying Mae Sot residents with 'fried crispy' for many years. You can sit at a small table near the wok and order fresh chunks of squash, pumpkin or papaya fried in egg batter and dipped in a delicious sauce of peanuts, tamarind, molasses and dried chilli. If you don't want to eat it here they'll wrap for takeaway in two portion sizes, costing 5B or 10B. The family fires up the wok from 4.30 pm and keeps cooking until 8 pm or until they've run out of ingredients.

Another local specialty is *kŭaytĭaw meuang*, a rich bowl of rice noodles covered with sliced pork, greens, peanuts, chilli and green beans very similar to kŭaytĭaw sùkhŏthai. Look for rice-noodle vendors along Thanon Prasat Withi; the best place is the *vendor* on the western side of Soi Sapphakan, running north off Thanon Prasat Withi.

The best Chinese restaurant in town is the air-con *Kwangtung Restaurant* (no English sign), which specialises in Cantonese cooking. It's around the corner from the Porn Thep Hotel, south of Thanon Prasat Withi.

There are a few fàràng restaurants along Thanon Tang Kim Chiang and Thanon Intharakhiri. On the former you'll find *Pim Hut*, with decent pizza, steak, Thai and Chinese dishes, ice cream and international breakfasts at moderate prices, and brightly lit *Fah Fah 2 Bakery*, with a similar but slightly less expensive menu. Both cater to tourists, foreign volunteer workers (from nearby refugee camps) and upper-middle-class Thais.

On Thanon Intharakhiri, *The River* (☎ *055-534593)* is a cosy place in an old wooden building serving good fresh-ground coffee, excellent banana pancakes, Thai and vegetarian dishes, ice cream, fruit shakes and beer. It's also a good place to pick up a map and some information about the area. It's open 6 am to 9 pm daily.

Next west is *Crocodile Tear*, which serves Thai food but is really more of a bar scene, with live Thai and Western music. A bit farther west past Soi Ruam Jai is the friendly *KCB Snack Shop*, and finally, *Bai Fern*, next to the guesthouse of the same name, both with the usual mix of Thai and fàràng dishes.

A small, no-name *vegetarian restaurant* next to the Um Phang săwngthăew stop offers good, inexpensive Thai vegetarian food from around 7 am to 7 pm or until the food is sold out.

If you're looking for an atmospheric evening out, try *Khao Mao Khao Fang*, which is a little north of town between the 1km and 2km markers on the road to Mae Ramat. A Thai botanist designed this open-air restaurant to make it feel as if you're dining in the forest, with lots of common and not-so-common live plants from around Northern Thailand. The Thai cuisine is equally inventive, with such specialities as *yam hèt khon* (a spicy salad made with forest mushrooms available in September and October only) and *mŭu khâo mâo* (a salad of home-cured sausage, peanuts, rice shoots, lettuce, ginger, lime and chilli).

Getting There & Away

Air THAI flies to Mae Sot from Bangkok (1625B) four times a week, and four times from Chiang Mai (765B). The THAI office in Mae Sot (☎ 055-531730) is in the town centre at 76/1 Thanon Prasat Withi.

Bus & Săwngthăew The ordinary green bus *(rót meh khĭaw)* leaves at 6 am daily from a dirt lot on the southern side of Thanon Intharakhiri, one block west of the post office. The air-con bus departs at 8 am. Destinations include Tak (60B air-con), Lampang (86B ordinary, 155B air-con), Chiang Mai (115B, 207B), Chiang Rai (176B, 317B) and Mae Sai (193B, 348B). An orange bus to Mae Sot leaves every day at 2, 4 and 5 pm from the Tak bus station and costs 46B.

The more frequent orange-and-white minivans along the same route cost 33B per person and usually arrive a little quicker than the bus. The minivans depart from the roadside in front of the First Hotel in Mae Sot. The trip takes about 1½ hours on a beautiful winding road through mountains.

Ordinary buses between Bangkok and Mae Sot (151B) depart from Bangkok at 8.20 pm and from Mae Sot at 9.30, 10 and 10.30 pm. First-class air-con buses leave Mae Sot five times daily for 272B (the Bangkok departure is at 9 pm), while 2nd-class air-con buses with similar departures cost 211B. Similarly priced Choet Chai Tour has a 1st-class bus leaving Bangkok at 10.15 pm, and Mae Sot at 10 pm; its 2nd-class air-con bus departs at 8.40 pm in both directions.

VIP buses (24 seats) to/from Bangkok leave four times daily (420B, about eight hours). Thanjit Tour offers 32-seat VIP buses to Bangkok for only 317B, departing at 10 pm. In Mae Sot, Bangkok-bound air-con and VIP buses leave from the northern side of Thanon Inthakhiri just west of the police station; ordinary buses to Bangkok leave from the bus station near the market north of the police station.

Săwngthăew to destinations north of Mae Sot, such as Mae Sarit (60B, 2½ hours), Tha Song Yang (50B, 1½ hours) and Mae Sariang (150B, five to six hours) leave frequently between 6 am and noon from the rót meh khĭaw station west of the post office.

Săwngthăew heading to Um Phang (100B, five hours) leave hourly between 7 am and 3 pm.

Myawadi to Mawlamyaing (Myanmar)

Theoretically it's possible to cross the river to Myawadi and catch a bus to Mawlamyaing via Kawkareik. Each leg takes about two hours; the Myawadi-Kawkareik stretch can be dicey when fighting between Yangon and KNU troops is in progress, while the Kawkareik-Mawlamyaing stretch is generally safe although the road itself is quite rough. Another way to reach Mawlamyaing is to get off the road at Kyondo and continue by boat along the Gyaing River. At the moment it's not legal to travel beyond Myawadi, but it's very conceivable that this road will open to foreigners within the next couple of years.

Getting Around

Most of Mae Sot can be seen on foot. Jit Motorcycle, a motorcycle dealer on Thanon Prasat Withi, rents out motorcycles for 160B a day. Make sure you test-ride a bike before renting; some of its machines can be in rather poor condition. Cars and vans can be rented for around 1200B a day; ask at any hotel. Motorcycle taxis charge 10B for trips around town.

AROUND MAE SOT
Karen & Burmese Refugee Camps
ค่ายผู้อพยพชาวกะเหรี่ยงและพม่า

A couple of refugee camps have been set up along the eastern bank of Mae Nam Moei in either direction from Mae Sot. Most of the refugees in these camps are Karen fleeing battles between Burmese and KNU troops across the border. The camps have been around for over a decade but the Thai government has generally kept their existence quiet, fearing the build-up of a huge refugee 'industry' such as the one that developed around the Indo-Chinese camps in eastern Thailand in the 1970s.

Although many Thai and foreign volunteers have come to the refugees' aid, the camps are very much in need of outside assistance. Tourists are no longer permitted to visit the camps, although if you meet a camp volunteer in Mae Sot you might be able to visit by invitation. Donations of clothes and medicines (to be administered by qualified doctors and nurses) may be offered to the camps via No 4 Guest House in Mae Sot.

Waley
บ้านวะเลย์

Thirty-six kilometres from Mae Sot, Rte 1206 splits south-west off Rte 1090 at Ban Saw Oh and terminates 25km south at the border town of Waley, an important smuggling point.

The Burmese side was once one of the two main gateways to Kawthoolei, the Karen nation, but in 1989 the Yangon government ousted the KNU. Until the Thai government cut off all timber trade with Myanmar's military government, teak was the main border trade. Nowadays there's a brisk trade in teak furniture instead.

One can visit hill-tribe villages near **Ban Chedi Kok**, and, if invited, the large Mawker refugee camp, both off Rte 1206 on the way to Waley. Opium is cultivated extensively in this area, much to the chagrin of Thailand's authorities, who send rangers in every year to cut down the production. There is a small **hotel** in Phop Phra with rooms for 50B.

Getting There & Away Săwngthăew to Phop Phra (30B) and Waley (35B) depart frequently between 6 am and 6 pm from a stop south-east of the mosque in Mae Sot. If you go by motorcycle or car, follow Rte 1090 south-east towards Um Phang and after 36km take Rte 1206 south-west. From this junction it's 25km to Waley; the last 10km of the road are unpaved. Your passport may be checked at a police outpost before Waley.

UM PHANG & AROUND
อุ้มผาง

Rte 1090 goes south from Mae Sot to Um Phang, 150km away. This stretch of road used to be called the 'Death Highway' because of the guerrilla activity in the area that hindered highway development. Those days ended in the 1980s, but lives are still lost because of brake failure or treacherous turns on this steep, winding road through incredible mountain scenery.

Along the way – short hikes off the highway – are two waterfalls, **Nam Tok Thararak** (26km from Mae Sot) and **Nam Tok Pha Charoen** (41km). Nam Tok Thararak streams over limestone cliffs and calcified rocks with a rough texture that makes climbing the falls easy. It's been made into a park of sorts, with benches right in the stream at the base of the falls for cooling off and a couple of outhouse toilets nearby; on weekends food vendors set up here.

The eucalyptus-lined dirt road leaves the highway between the 24km and 25km markers. A side road at the 48km marker leads to a group of government-sponsored hill-tribe villages (Karen, Lisu, Hmong, Mien, Lahu). Just beyond Ban Rom Klao 4 (previously Um Piam) – roughly midway between Mae Sot and Um Phang – is a very large **Karen and Burmese refugee camp** and several Hmong villages.

Um Phang is an overgrown village populated mostly by Karen people at the junction of Mae Nam Mae Klong and Huay Um Phang. Many Karen villages in this area are very traditional – elephants are used as much as oxen for farm work. *Yaeng* (elephant saddles) and other tack used for elephant wrangling are a common sight on the verandas of Karen houses outside of town. You'll also see plenty of **elephants** in other Karen villages throughout the district. The name for the district comes from the Karen word *umpha*, a type of bamboo

UM PHANG

PLACES TO STAY
2 Gift House
4 Umphang Country Huts
11 Phudoi Camp Site
12 Thawatchai TJ Tour (Trekker Hill)
13 Suan Ruen Kaew Resort
14 Tu Ka Su Cottage
15 Umphang Hillside Pension
16 Umphang Hill Resort
18 Garden Huts
19 Veera Tourism
20 Um Phang House
21 Um Phang Guest House

PLACES TO EAT
1 Ban Kru Sun
23 Phu Doi Restaurant
24 Tom Restaurant

OTHER
3 Border Police
5 District Gate
6 Umphang Conservation & Tourism Society
7 Meteorology Station
8 Post Office
9 Umphang Hospital
10 Market
17 Checkpoint
22 Wat Nilaman
25 District Office
26 Public Health Office

0   100   200m
0   100   200yd
Approximate Scale

Mae Nam Klong

Huay Um Phang

Bridge

Airstrip

Bridge

To Palatha

container in which Karen who were travelling carried their documents to show to Thai border authorities.

An interesting **hike** can be done that follows the footpaths south-east of the village through rice fields and along a stream called Huay Um Phang to a few smaller Karen villages.

At the border where Um Phang district meets Myanmar, near the Thai-Karen villages of Ban Nong Luang and Ban Huay, is a Karen **refugee village**. It's inhabited by over 500 Karen who originally hailed from Htikabler village on the other side of border.

South of Um Phang, towards Sangkhlaburi in Kanchanaburi Province, Um Phang Wildlife Sanctuary links with the Thung Yai Naresuan and Huay Kha Kaeng Reserves as

well as Khlong Lan and Mae Wong National Parks to form Thailand's **largest wildlife corridor** and one of the largest intact natural forests in South-East Asia.

Nam Tok Thilawsu
น้ำตกทีลอซู

In Um Phang district you can arrange trips down Mae Nam Mae Klong to Nam Tok Thilawsu and Karen villages – inquire at any guesthouse. Typical three-day excursions include a raft journey along the river from Um Phang to the falls, then a two-day trek from the falls through the Karen villages of **Khotha** and **Palatha**, where a 4WD picks trekkers up and returns them to Um Phang (25km from Palatha by road). Some people prefer to spend two days on the river, the first night at a cave or hot springs along the river before Thilawsu and a second night at the falls. On the third day you can cross the river by elephant to one of the aforementioned villages to be met by a truck and returned to Um Phang. Or you can continue south along the road to Palatha 20km farther to the Hmong village of **Kangae Khi**. On the way back to Um Phang from Palatha you can stop off at **Nam Tok Thilawjaw**, which tumbles over a fern-covered cliff.

The scenery along the river is stunning, especially after the rainy season (November and December), when the 200m to 400m limestone cliffs are streaming with water and Nam Tok Thilawsu is at its best. This waterfall is Thailand's largest, measuring an estimated 400m high and up to 300m wide in the rainy season. There's a shallow cave behind the falls and several levels of pools suitable for swimming. The Thais consider Nam Tok Thilawsu to be the most beautiful waterfall in the country; it is now part of Um Phang Wildlife Sanctuary, declared a Unesco World Heritage site in 1999.

You can *camp* at the Um Phang Wildlife Sanctuary headquarters near the falls any time of year, and between December and May there are also rooms available for 100B per person. You must bring your own food. The 1.5km trail between the Um Phang Sanctuary headquarters and the falls has been transformed into a self-guided nature tour with the addition of well-conceived educational plaques. Surrounding the falls

NORTHERN THAILAND

on both sides of the river are Thailand's thickest stands of natural forest, and the hiking in the vicinity of Nam Tok Thilawsu can be superb. The forest here is said to contain over 1300 varieties of palm; giant bamboo and strangler figs are commonplace, and the orchid tree *(Bauhinia variegata)* can even be seen along the road to Palatha.

Between 1 December and 1 June you can also drive to the falls via a rough 47km road from Um Phang suitable for 4WD or a skilled dirt-bike rider only. Or follow the main paved road south of Um Phang to the 19km marker; the walk to the falls is a stiff four hours from here via **Mo Phado** village. A săwngthăew goes to the 19km marker from Um Phang once a day; ask for *kii-loh sìp kâo* and expect to pay 15B to 20B per person.

Letongkhu to Sangkhlaburi

From Ban Mae Khlong Mai, a few kilometres east of Um Phang via the highway to Mae Sot, a graded dirt road (Rte 1167) heads south-west along the border to **Beung Kleung** (sometimes spelt Peung Kleung), a Karen, Burmese, Indo-Burmese, Talaku and Thai trading village where buffalo carts are more common than motorbikes. The picturesque setting among spiky peaks and cliffs is worth the trip even if you go no farther. Impressive **Nam Tok Ekaratcha** is an hour's walk away. Săwngthăew from Um Phang usually make a trip to Beung Kleung once a day, and it's possible to put up at the village clinic or in a private home for a donation of 100B per person. On the way you can stop off at the small, traditional Karen village of **Ban Thiphochi**.

Four hours' walk from here along a rough track (passable by 4WD in the dry season), near the Myanmar border on the banks of Mae Nam Suriya next to Sam Rom mountain, is the culturally singular, 109-house village of **Letongkhu** (Leh Tawng Khu). The villagers are for the most part Karen in language and dress, but their spiritual beliefs are unique to this area. They will eat only the meat of wild animals and hence do not raise chickens, ducks, pigs or beef cattle. They do, however, keep buffalo, oxen and elephants as work animals.

According to what little anthropological information is available, the villagers belong to the Lagu or Talaku sect, said to represent a form of Buddhism mixed with shamanism and animism. Letongkhu is one of only six such villages in Thailand; there are reportedly around 30 more in Myanmar. Each village has a spiritual and temporal leader called a *pu chaik* (whom the Thais call *reusǐi* – 'rishi' or 'sage') who wears his hair long – usually tied in a topknot – and dresses in white, yellow or brown robes, depending on the subsect.

According to Christian Gooden, author of *Three Pagodas: A Journey Down the Thai Border,* the residents of Letongkhu were chased out of Myanmar in the mid-19th century. The current 48-year-old pu chaik at Letongkhu is the 10th in a line of 'white-thread' priests dating back to their residence in Myanmar. The reusǐi's many male disciples also wear their hair in top-knots (often tied in cloth) and may wear similar robes. All reusǐi abstain from alcohol and are celibate. The priests live apart from the village in a temple and practise traditional medicine based on herbal healing and ritual magic. Antique elephant tusks are kept as talismans.

An altercation between the Thai border police and another group of reusǐi (said to be a rival sect, known as the 'yellow-threads' for the colour of their robes) over hunting rights resulted in the knifing deaths of five policemen. Hence the Thai border police can be a little touchy about outsiders, and there are several checkpoints along the way (as frequently as every 3km in some areas); in fact you need permission from the Border Patrol Police before going to Letongkhu.

At the same time evangelistic Christian missionaries have infiltrated the area and have tried to convert followers of the Talaku sect; this has made the Talaku more sensitive to outside visitation. If you visit Letongkhu, take care not to enter any village structures without permission or invitation. Likewise, do not take photographs without permission. If you treat the villagers with respect, then you shouldn't have a problem.

Opposite Letongkhu on the Myanmar side of the border, the KNU has set up its latest tactical headquarters. Yangon government offensives against the KNU can break out in this area during the dry months of the year, but when this is happening or is likely to happen, Thai military checkpoints will turn all trekkers back. It wouldn't hurt to make a few inquiries in Um Phang first, just to make sure.

Sangkhlaburi (Kanchanaburi Province; see the Central Thailand chapter) is 90km or four to five days' walk from Beung Kleung. On the way (11km from Beung Kleung), about 250m off the road, is the extensive cave system of **Tham Takube**. From Ban Mae Chan, 35km on the same route, there's a dirt road branching across the border to a KNU-controlled village. The route to Sangkhlaburi has several branches; the main one crosses over the border into Myanmar for some distance before crossing back into Thailand. There has been discussion of cutting a newer, more direct road between Um Phang and Sangkhlaburi.

Because of the overall sensitive nature of this border area, and the very real potential for becoming lost, ill or injured, a guide is highly recommended for any sojourn south of Um Phang. You may be able to arrange a guide for this route in either Um Phang or Beung Kleung. Umphang Hill Resort in Um Phang can also arrange a trek but you need to give it a couple of weeks' notice. The best time of year to do the trek is October to January.

Organised Tours

Several of the guesthouses in Um Phang can arrange trekking and rafting trips in the area. The typical three-night, four-day trip costs from 2000B per person (seven or more people) to 3500B (two people). The price includes rafting, an elephant ride, food and guide service.

Longer treks of up to 12 days may also be available, and there are day trips to Nam Tok Thilawsu as well. It is worth checking to see what kind of rafts are used; most places have switched to rubber as bamboo rafts can break up in the rough rapids. Choose rubber, unless you are really looking for adventure – like walking to your camp site rather than rafting there.

In Um Phang, Umphang Hill Resort (see Places to Stay later) appears to have the best equipment and trip design. It offers basic three- to six-day rafting and hiking trips to Nam Tok Thilawsu and beyond, including one itinerary that takes rafters through 11 different sets of rapids on Mae Nam Mae Klong. Longer or shorter trips may also be

arranged, and elephant riding instead of walking is always an option. BL Tour, at Um Phang Guest House, Thawatchai TJ Tour and most other lodgings in Um Phang can arrange similar trips.

Companies based in Mae Sot, such as SP Tour (☎ 055-531409) at SP House, do Um Phang trips for about 1500B to 2000B more per person than local Um Phang agencies. This adds private transport between Mae Sot and Um Phang to the trip, but nothing more. The typical Nam Tok Thilawsu–Palatha trip, for example, costs 4000B to 5000B per person for a four-day trip in which two half-days are spent in transit from Mae Sot.

Places to Stay

Accommodation in Um Phang is plentiful, and the majority of visitors to the area are Thai.

Thawatchai TJ Tour (Trekker Hill; ☎ 055-561090), on a hillside near the village centre, charges 60B per person for beds in rustic thatched-roof shelters with shared facilities.

Phudoi Camp Site (☎ 055-561049, 01-886 8783, fax 561279), around the corner from Trekker Hill towards the market, is a well-landscaped place on another hillside. You can pitch your own tent at the camp ground for 50B, or you can rent one of four clean wooden bungalows for 100B per person. Additional bungalows were under construction when we visited.

Um Phang House (☎ 055-561073), owned by the local *kamnan* (precinct officer), offers a few motel-like rooms with private bathroom that sleep up to three for 150B, and nicer wood-and-brick cottages with hot water and ceiling fans that sleep up to four for 300B (a solo traveller might be able to negotiate the price down a bit). There's a large outdoor restaurant in an open area near the cottages.

Farther east away from Huay Um Phang, on the same side of the road, is *Um Phang Guest House* (☎ 055-561021, fax 561322). Owned by BL Tour, it has rooms sleeping five to six in Thai-style houses for 500B, rooms in a cottage that sleep up to six for 300B and thatched huts for up to six people for 100B – a real bargain, but of course they hope you'll take one of their trekking/rafting trips (no hard sell, though, as yet). Farther west toward Huay Um Phang, *Veera*

Tourism (☎ 055-561239) offers rooms in a wooden house for 100B per person.

Continuing west, next to Huay Um Phang, are a couple of other guesthouses (referred to as 'resorts' in typical Thai fashion). *Garden Huts* (also known as Boonyaporn Guest House or Thaphae Resort, no Roman-script sign) features five levels of accommodation ranging from 300B for bamboo huts with shared cold-water bathroom up to 700B for bungalows with attached hot-water bathroom; most of these rooms will sleep up to four people. The place is run by a nice Thai lady who brews good Thai-grown Arabica coffee.

Overlooking the stream on the opposite bank is friendly *Umphang Hill Resort* (☎ 055-561063, fax 561065, ⓔ *umphanghill @thaimail.com; in Mae Sot* ☎ 055-531409; *in Bangkok* ☎ 02-573 7942), where large wood-and-thatch bungalows with two or even three bathrooms cost around 2000B, depending on the season; these are usually rented by Thai groups, and can accommodate up to 20 people. When not full, the resort will rent out beds in these bungalows for 50B per person. There are also a few very solid wooden bungalows for 500B single/double with attached hot-water shower, small TV and refrigerator. This is one of the best places in Um Phang to book treks or raft trips.

Tu Ka Su Cottage (☎ 055-561295, 01-487 1643), south of the checkpoint and west of Huay Um Phang, is a set of Japanese-owned, tin-roofed wooden bungalows surrounded by flowers. Each bungalow sleeps up to 10 persons and costs 1500B.

Farther west of the checkpoint near the bridge, past Huay Um Phang on the road to Palatha, *Suan Ruen Kaew Resort* (☎ 055-561119), overlooking a stream, has nice cottages or rooms in a house with private bathroom for 100B per person.

In the same area, *Umphang Hillside Pension* (☎ 055-561315), owned by a local policeman, has rooms for 80B per person. The rooms are basic and worn, but the owners are civil and keep the place clean. Information about the area is posted around the place. Follow a road through Umphang Hill Resort to reach Umphang Hillside Pension.

About 3km before town coming from Mae Sot, *Gift House* (☎ 055-561181) features simple timber huts for 80B to 100B a night – it's very quiet. *Umphang Country Huts*, off the highway 1.5km before Um Phang, is in a nice hilly setting. Rooms in a wood and thatch, two-storey building facing Huay Mae Klong share a common veranda with benches. A downstairs room with bathroom costs 400B, while a larger upstairs room sleeping up to four costs 700B. Larger, more atmospheric rooms in another two-storey building come with private verandas and cost 500B and 700B. Every room has a private cold-water shower. Umphang Country Huts can arrange raft trips; it gets lots of Thai tour groups.

By the time you arrive in Um Phang other guesthouses will surely have opened as the area's popularity continues to grow.

Places to Eat

Um Phang has three or four simple noodle and rice shops plus a morning market and a small sundries shop. *Phu Doi Restaurant*, on the main street into town, has very good food, especially the *phánaeng* (mild curry) dishes, but there are also rice dishes, noodles, *tôm yam* and cold beer. Phu Doi has a bilingual menu and seems to be virtually the only place open past 8 pm.

There is a short string of noodle shops along the main road. *Tom Restaurant* also does rice dishes.

About 2.5km out of town near Gift House and off the main road, *Ban Kru Sun* is a small indoor-outdoor place owned and operated by local teacher Sompong Meunjit. Sompong is also a composer and performer of Thai folk music inspired by the beauty of the Um Phang area; he usually performs live on weekends. The pub serves typical Thai and northern-Thai dishes.

Getting There & Away

Săwngthăew to Um Phang cost 100B and leave several times a day from Mae Sot, starting around 7 am and finishing around 3 pm. It takes five to six hours to complete the 164km journey. Săwngthăew usually stop for lunch at windy **Ban Rom Klao 4** along the way. In the reverse direction, săwngthăew depart between 7 am and 2.30 pm.

If you decide to try to ride a motorcycle from Mae Sot, be sure it's one with a strong engine as the road has lots of fairly steep grades. Total drive time is around 3½ to four hours. The only petrol pump along the way is in Ban Rom Klao 4, 80km from Mae Sot, so you may want to carry 3L or 4L of extra fuel. The road is barely 1½ lanes wide and roughly sealed in some spots. The stretch between Ban Rom Klao 4 and Um Phang passes impressive stands of virgin monsoon forest.

MAE SOT TO MAE SARIANG

Route 105 runs north from Mae Sot all the way to Mae Sariang in Mae Hong Son Province. The section of the road north of Tha Song Yang has finally been sealed and public transport is now available all the way to Mae Sariang (226km), passing through **Mae Ramat**, **Mae Sarit**, **Ban Tha Song Yang** and **Ban Sop Ngao** (Mae Ngao). In Mae Ramat a temple called **Wat Don Kaew**, behind the district office, houses a large Mandalay-style marble Buddha. Other attractions on the way to Mae Sariang include **Nam Tok Mae Kasa**, between the 13km and 14km markers, and extensive limestone caverns at **Tham Mae Usu**, at the 94km marker near Ban Tha Song Yang. From the highway it's a 2km walk to Tham Mae Usu; note that in the rainy season, when the river running through the cave seals off the mouth, it's closed.

Instead of doing the Myanmar border run in one go, some people elect to spend the night in **Mae Sarit** (118km from Mae Sot), then start fresh in the morning to get to Ban Tha Song Yang in time for a morning săwngthăew from Ban Tha Song Yang to Mae Sariang.

Săwngthăew to Mae Sarit cost 60B and leave hourly between 6 am and noon from the market north of the police station in Mae Sot (four hours). Mae Sarit to Ban Tha Song Yang costs 20B; from there to Mae Sariang costs 50B (three hours). If you miss the morning săwngthăew from Mae Sarit to Mae Sariang, you can usually arrange to charter a truck for 150B to 200B.

If you decide not to stay overnight in Mae Sarit you can take a direct Mae Sariang săwngthăew from Mae Sot for 150B. These large orange săwngthăew have the same departure times as the Mae Sot–Mae Sarit săwngthăew (about six hours).

Along the way you'll pass through thick forest, including a few stands of teak, and see Karen villages, the occasional work elephant and a large Thai ranger post.

Places to Stay

The **Mae Salid Guest House**, in Mae Sarit, offers very basic rooms with private toilet and shared shower for 70B/100B single/double.

There are no guesthouses yet in Ban Tha Song Yang but it would probably be easy to arrange a place to stay by inquiring at the main market (where the săwngthăew stop) in this prosperous black-market town.

Mae Hong Son Province

Mae Hong Son Province is 368km from Chiang Mai by the southern route through Mae Sariang (on Rte 108), or 270km by the northern road through Pai (on Rte 1095). Thailand's most north-western province is a crossroads for ethnic minorities (mostly Karen, with some Hmong, Lisu and Lahu), Shan (known locally as Thai Yai) and Burmese immigrants, and opium traders living in and around the Mae Pai valley. Reportedly 75% of the province consists of mountains and forest.

As the province is so far from the influence of sea winds and is thickly forested and mountainous, the temperature seldom rises above 40°C, while in January the temperature can drop to 2°C. The air is often misty with ground fog in the winter and smoke from slash-and-burn agriculture in the hot season.

The province has undergone a tourist mini-boom over the last decade, with many resorts opening in the area around the capital. So far few visitors seem to leave the beaten Mae Hong Son-Soppong-Pai track.

MAE SARIANG & KHUN YUAM
แม่สะเรียง/ขุนยวม

postcode 58110 • pop 7800
Many of the hill-tribe settlements in Mae Hong Son Province are concentrated in the districts and towns of Khun Yuam, Mae La Noi and Mae Sariang, which are good departure points for treks to Hmong, Karen and Shan villages. Of these three small towns, Mae Sariang is the largest and offers the most facilities for use as a base. Khun Yuam is also a good place to start from.

Mae Sam Laep, south-west of Mae Sariang on the Myanmar border, can be reached by săwngthăew or motorcycle, and from there you may be able to hire boats for journeys along the quite scenic **Mae Nam Salawin**.

Although there is little to see in Mae Sariang, it's a pleasant riverside town with a small travel scene. Two Burmese/Shan temples, **Wat Jong Sung** (Uthayarom) and **Wat Si Bunruang**, just off Mae Sariang's main street (not far from the Mae Sariang bus station), are worth a visit if you have time. Built in 1896, Wat Jong Sung is the more interesting of the two temples and has slender, Shanstyle chedi and wooden monastic buildings.

The Riverside Guest House (see Places to Stay, later) can arrange day and overnight **boat trips** on Mae Nam Salawin that include stops in Karen villages and Mae Sam Laep. During the dry season, a truck from the Riverside leaves every morning at around 6.30 am for Mae Sam Laep, where a boat takes visitors two hours down Mae Nam Salawin (locally called Mae Nam Khong) to a sand beach at Sop Moei. The total cost is 100B per person.

You can take a boat upriver from Mae Sam Laep to **Salawin National Park**, a 722-sq-km protected area established in 1994. The boat trip takes about half an hour to reach the park headquarters. There are no lodgings, but in the dry season you can pitch a tent for free on a white-sand beach, called Hat Thaen Kaew, along the river in front of the park offices. There are good views of the river and Myanmar from the

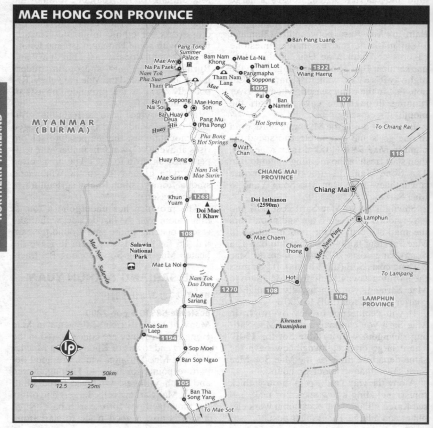

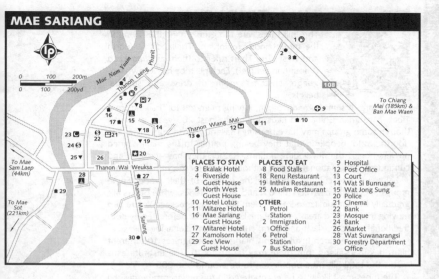

MAE SARIANG

PLACES TO STAY	PLACES TO EAT	9 Hospital
3 Ekalak Hotel	8 Food Stalls	12 Post Office
4 Riverside	18 Renu Restaurant	13 Court
Guest House	19 Inthira Restaurant	14 Wat Si Bunruang
5 North West	25 Muslim Restaurant	15 Wat Jong Sung
Guest House		20 Police
10 Hotel Lotus	OTHER	21 Cinema
11 Mitaree Hotel	1 Petrol	22 Bank
16 Mae Sariang	Station	23 Mosque
Guest House	2 Immigration	24 Bank
17 Mitaree Hotel	Office	26 Market
27 Kamolsorn Hotel	6 Petrol	28 Wat Suwanarangsi
29 See View	Station	30 Forestry Department
Guest House	7 Bus Station	Office

park headquarters. The park is heavily forested in teak, Asian redwood and cherry-wood. In the last couple of years Karen refugees have logged the park illegally but in 1998 the Thai government ordered all non-Thai residents to leave the park.

About 36km south-east of Mae Sariang at **Ban Mae Waen** is Pan House, where a guide named T Weerapan (Mr Pan) leads local treks. To get to Ban Mae Waen, take a Chiang Mai–bound bus east on Rte 108 and get out at the 68km marker. Ban Mae Waen is a 5km walk south along a mountain ridge and (during the rainy season) across a couple of streams. If you're driving, 4WD will be necessary if the road is wet. Pan House charges 50B per person to spend the night in a big wooden house. Ban Mae Waen is a mixed Thai/Karen village in the middle of a heavily Karen district.

On the slopes of **Doi Mae U Khaw**, 25km from Khun Yuam via upgraded Rte 1263, is a Hmong village (Ban Mae U Khaw) and the 250m **Nam Tok Mae Surin** (50km north-east of Khun Yuam), reportedly Thailand's highest cataract. The area blooms with scenic *bua thawng* ('golden lotus', more like a sunflower than a lotus) in November; this is also the best time to view the waterfall.

The North West and Riverside Guest Houses in Mae Sariang lead rafting and elephant-riding tours to local Karen villages and waterfalls for 1000B per day per person – less if you do it all on foot and by truck.

Places to Stay
Mae Sariang Out on Rte 108, *Ekalak Hotel* (☎ 053-681052) charges 150B for a fairly clean room with ceiling fan, air-con and private bathroom with hot water. It has an attached restaurant as well.

Mae Sariang's oldest hotel, *Mitaree Hotel* (☎ 053-681022), near the bus station on Thanon Mae Sariang, has singles/doubles for 120/200B in the old wooden wing (called the Mitaree Guest House) or for 250B with hot-water shower in the new wing; air-con rooms in the new wing cost 400B. The old wing is popular with Thai truckers.

On Thanon Wiang Mai near the post office you'll find another *Mitaree Hotel* (☎ 053-681109), run by the same family and sometimes referred to as 'New Mita-ree'. Rooms cost 120/150B with fan and cold-water shower, 190/200B to 250B with hot water and fan and 300/400B with hot-water shower and air-con. There is also a set of newer wooden 'resort' cottages at the back with sitting areas in front, air-con and TV for 600B to 1200B.

Continued on page 513

NORTHERN THAILAND

HILL TRIBES

The 'hill tribes' are the ethnic minorities living in the mountainous regions of Thailand's far north and west. The Thais refer to them as *chao khǎo* ('mountain people'). Each hill tribe has its own language, customs, mode of dress and spiritual beliefs.

Most are of semi-nomadic origin, having migrated to Thailand from Tibet, Myanmar, China and Laos during the past 200 years or so, although some groups may have been in Thailand much longer. They are 'fourth world' people in that they belong neither to the main aligned powers nor to the developing nations. Rather, they have crossed and continue to cross national borders without regard for recent nationhood.

Language and culture constitute the borders of their world. Some groups are caught between the 6th and 21st centuries, while others are gradually being assimilated into modern life. Many tribespeople are also moving into lowland areas as montane lands become deforested by both traditional swidden (slash-and-burn) cultivation and illegal logging.

The Tribal Research Institute in Chiang Mai recognises 10 different hill tribes in Thailand, but there may be up to 20. The institute estimates the total hill-tribe population to be around 550,000.

The tribes most likely to be encountered in the region can be divided into three main linguistic groups: the Tibeto-Burman (Lisu, Lahu, Akha), the Karenic (Karen, Kayah) and the Austro-Thai (Hmong, Mien). Within each group there may also be several subgroups, eg, Blue Hmong, White Hmong; these names usually refer to predominant elements of clothing.

The Shan (Thai Yai, meaning large Thai) are not included in the descriptions below as they are not a hill-tribe group per se – they have permanent habitations and speak a language similar to Thai. Thai scholars consider them to have been the original inhabitants of the area. Nevertheless, Shan villages are often common stops on hill-tribe treks.

The following comments on dress refer mostly to the female members of each group, as hill-tribe men tend to dress like rural Thais. Population figures are taken from 1995 estimates. For more detailed descriptions on Thailand's hill tribes, see some of the recommendations in the Books section of the Facts for the Visitor chapter. The Tribal Research Institute in Chiang Mai maintains an informative Web site at www.tribal.or.th.

PATRICK HORTON

Left: The world comes a hill-tribe village satellite di⟨

Akha tribeswoman

Akha *(I-kaw)*
Pop 48,500
Origin: Tibet
Present locations: Thailand, Laos, Myanmar, Yunnan
Economy: rice, corn, opium
Belief system: animism, with an emphasis on ancestor worship
Distinctive characteristics: headdress of beads, feathers and dangling silver ornaments. Villages are along mountain ridges or on steep slopes from 1000m to 1400m in altitude. The well-known Akha Swing Ceremony takes place from mid-August to mid-September, between planting and harvest. The Akha are among the poorest of Thailand's ethnic minorities and tend to resist assimilation into the Thai mainstream. Like the Lahu, they often cultivate opium for their own use.

Red Lahu village

Lahu *(Musoe)*
Pop 73,200
Origin: Tibet
Present locations: south China, Thailand, Myanmar
Economy: rice, corn, opium
Belief system: theistic animism (supreme deity is Geusha); some groups are Christian
Distinctive characteristics: black-and-red jackets with narrow skirts for women, bright green or blue-green baggy trousers for men. The Lahu tend to live at about 1000m altitude. Their intricately woven shoulder bags *(yâam)* are prized by collectors. There are five main groups – Red Lahu, Black Lahu, White Lahu, Yellow Lahu and Lahu Sheleh.

A Lisu girl near Chiang Mai

Lisu *(Lisaw)*
Pop 28,000
Origin: Tibet
Present locations: Thailand, Yunnan
Economy: rice, opium, corn, livestock
Belief system: animism with ancestor worship and spirit possession
Distinctive characteristics: the women wear long multicoloured tunics over trousers and sometimes black turbans with tassels. Men wear baggy green or blue pants pegged in at the ankles. Premarital sex is said to be common, along with freedom in choosing marital partners. Patrilineal clans have pan-tribal jurisdiction, which makes the Lisu unique among hill-tribe groups (most of which have power centred with either a shaman or a village headman). Lisu villages are usually in the mountains at about 1000m.

Mien *(Yao)*

Pop 40,300

Origin: central China

Present locations: Thailand, south China, Laos, Myanmar, Vietnam

Economy: rice, corn, opium

Belief system: animism with ancestor worship and Taoism

Distinctive characteristics: women wear trousers and black jackets with intricately embroidered patches and red fur-like collars, along with large dark blue or black turbans. The Mien have been heavily influenced by Chinese traditions and use Chinese characters to write their language. They tend to settle near mountain springs at between 1000m and 1200m. Kinship is patrilineal and marriage is polygamous. The Mien are highly skilled at embroidery and silversmithing.

Mien woman at a traditional wedding

Hmong *(Meo or Maew)*

Pop 124,000

Origin: south China

Present locations: south China, Thailand, Laos, Vietnam

Economy: rice, corn, opium

Belief system: animism

Distinctive characteristics: tribespeople wear simple black jackets and indigo or black baggy trousers with striped borders or indigo skirts and silver jewellery. Most women wear their hair in a large bun. They usually live on mountain peaks or plateaus above 1000m. Kinship is patrilineal and polygamy is permitted. The Hmong are Thailand's second-largest hill-tribe group and are especially numerous in Chiang Mai Province.

Hmong women sewing

Karen *(Yang or Kariang)*

Pop 322,000

Origin: Myanmar

Present locations: Thailand, Myanmar

Economy: rice, vegetables, livestock

Belief system: animism, Buddhism, Christianity, depending on the group

Distinctive characteristics: thickly woven V-neck tunics of various colours (unmarried women wear white). Kinship is matrilineal and marriage is monogamous. They tend to live in lowland valleys and practise crop rotation rather than swidden agriculture. There are four distinct Karen groups – the Skaw (or White) Karen, Pwo Karen, Pa-O (or Black) Karen and Kayah (or Red) Karen. These groups combined form the largest hill tribe in Thailand, numbering about half of all hill-tribe people.

Karen girl, Thai/Myanmar border

Continued from page 511

If you turn left out of the bus station and then take the first right you'll come to the small *Mae Sariang Guest House* on Thanon Mongkhonchai, opposite the entrance to Wat Jong Sung. Rooms cost 80/150B with/ without bathroom but it's nothing special.

Around the corner from the Mae Sariang Guest House, on Thanon Laeng Phanit (incorrectly spelt on local street signs as 'Rang Phanich') by Mae Nam Yuam, is the efficiently run *Riverside Guest House* (☎ 053-681188), where basic singles/doubles cost 80/160B. There's a pleasant sitting and dining area overlooking the river. Nearby on the opposite side of the street, and under the same ownership, *North West Guest House* (☎ 053-681956, fax 681353) offers rooms in a large wooden house for 90B/160B. North West also has a separate leaf-thatched cottage across the road facing the river, usually reserved for groups.

The *See View Guest House* (☎ 053-681556), on the western side of Mae Nam Yuam, offers rooms with private hot-water shower in a row house far back from the river for 150B with fan, 300B with air-con. Less attractive overpriced bungalows closer to the river are available for 250B. The management says these rates are negotiable in the low season and offers free transport to and from the bus station. The open-air Old House restaurant on the premises sometimes features live Thai country music during high season – a plus or minus depending on your sleeping schedule.

The *Kamolsorn Hotel* (☎ 053-681204), on Thanon Mae Sariang just south of Thanon Wai Weuksa, is a newer multi-storey place with rooms for 350B with private bathroom, fan and TV, for 450B with air-con, and for 600B with air-con and TV.

Hotel Lotus (Lotus Guest House; ☎ 053-681048, 73/5 Thanon Wiang Mai) is an odd little complex in a cul-de-sac with a restaurant, karaoke, massage and barber shop. Clean rooms cost 120/250B with fan and private hot-water bathroom and 350B with air-con.

Khun Yuam The *Mit Khun Yuam Hotel* (☎ 053-691057) is an old wooden hotel on the main road through the town centre with upstairs singles for 100B with shared facilities. A three-bed room in a new building towards the back of the property costs 200B with fan and cold-water shower; rooms with air-con and hot-water showers cost 400B. Watch out for the owner's dog, which has been known to nip a guest or two.

Off the main road towards the northern end of town (look for the signs) is the clean and friendly *Ban Farang* (☎ 053-622086, 691023). Dorm beds cost 50B, rooms in a row house with private facilities 200B and new bungalows 250B to 350B.

Rustic accommodation is available at the Hmong village of Mae U Khaw, between Khun Yuam and Nam Tok Mae Surin.

Places to Eat

The *Riverside Guest House* on Thanon Laeng Phanit in Mae Sariang has a pleasant restaurant area upstairs overlooking the river, serving inexpensive Thai and fàràng dishes.

The *Inthira Restaurant*, on Thanon Wiang Mai near Thanon Mae Sariang, is well known for its batter-fried frogs, although you won't see them on the English menu. It has added an indoor air-con section. Across the street is the *Renu Restaurant*, decorated with 10 photos of King Bhumibol playing saxophone, and offering such menu delights as nut-hatch curry. Both restaurants have English menus, and both are very good.

The *food stall* next to the bus station on Thanon Mae Sariang serves excellent khâo sàwy and khànŏm jiin for less than 10B – it's only open from morning till early afternoon. A *Muslim restaurant* on Thanon Laeng Phanit near the main market in the town centre serves good curries and khâo mòk kài.

In Khun Yuam, your best bets are the open-air dining area at the *Mit Khun Yuam Hotel* or the cosy restaurant at *Ban Farang*. Just west of Wat Photaram at the southern end of Khun Yuam are several *food stalls* with khâo man kài.

Getting There & Around

Ordinary buses to Mae Sariang leave Chiang Mai's Arcade terminal at 8 am and 1.30, 3 and 8 pm (66B, four hours). First-class air-con buses depart at 6.30 and 11 am and 9 pm (106B). From Mae Sariang to Khun Yuam it's another 42B, or to Mae Hong Son 70B (four to five hours). An air-con bus to Mae Hong Son costs 120B but there's no way to reserve a seat – you must wait for the bus from Chiang Mai and hope there's a vacant seat. There's one bus daily between Mae Sot and Mae Sariang (150B, six hours).

Destinations anywhere in town are 10B by motorcycle taxi.

One săwngthăew goes to Mae Sam Laep on Mae Nam Salawin every morning (60B) or you can charter a truck (400B).

See the Mae Sot to Mae Sariang section earlier in this chapter for details on săwngthăew between Mae Sot and Mae Sariang.

Motorcycle Next to the petrol station across from the bus station is a small motorcycle rental place.

MAE HONG SON
อ.เมืองแม่ฮ่องสอน

postcode 58000 ● pop 6800

Surrounded by mountains and punctuated by small but picturesque Nong Jong Kham (Jong Kham Lake), this provincial capital is still relatively peaceful despite the intrusion of daily flights from Chiang Mai. Much of the capital's prosperity is due to its supply of rice and consumer goods to the drug lords across the border. It has also become part of Northern Thailand's standard tourist scene, with plenty of guesthouses, hotels and resorts in the area, most of them catering to Thais. The town's population is predominantly Shan. Several Karen and Shan villages in the vicinity can be visited as day trips, and farther afield are Lisu, Lahu and Musoe villages.

Two Hollywood films were shot in the immediate area: *Volunteers,* a comedy-adventure starring Tom Hanks and John Candy about the Peace Corps, and *Air America,* a Mel Gibson vehicle loosely based on events that occurred during the secret US war in Laos during the 1960s.

Mae Hong Son is best visited between November and March when the town is at its most beautiful. During the rainy season (June to October) travel in the province can be difficult because there are few paved roads. During the hot season, the Mae Pai valley fills with smoke from slash-and-burn agriculture. The only problem with going in the cool season is that the nights are downright cold – you'll need at least one thick sweater and a good pair of socks for mornings and evenings and a sleeping bag or several blankets. If you're caught short, you might consider buying a blanket at the market (the Chinese acrylic blankets are cheap) and cutting a hole in the middle for use as a poncho.

The **Sun Silapachip** (Vocational Arts Centre), a kilometre south of Rooks Resort on Rte 108, has a small collection of local handicrafts on display.

Information

Tourist Police Tourist brochures and maps can be picked up at the fledgling tourist police office (☎ 053-611812, 1155) on Thanon Singhanat Bamrung. Office hours are 8.30 am to 9.30 pm, but you can call 24 hours a day to report mishaps such as theft or to lodge complaints against guesthouses and trek operators.

Money Foreign-exchange services are available at Bangkok Bank, Thai Farmers Bank and Bank of Ayudhya, all located along Thanon Khunlum Praphat in the centre of town. Bangkok Bank and Thai Farmers Bank have ATMs.

Post & Communications The Mae Hong Son main post office, towards the southern end of Thanon Khunlum Praphat, is open 8.30 am to 4.30 pm weekdays except holidays. International telephone service is available at the attached CAT office – hours are the same as the post office. All other times you can use public phones –there's a Lenso phone (see International Phonecards in the Facts for the Visitor chapter) as well as a Home Country Direct phone outside the entrance to the CAT office. A separate CAT office on Thanon Udom Chow, west of Pa Dim restaurant, also offers international phone service, along with Internet access.

Several places around town, including Sunflower Cafe, provide Internet access by the minute.

Wat Phra That Doi Kong Mu
วัดพระธาตุดอยกองมู

Climb the hill west of town, Doi Kong Mu (1500m), to visit this Shan-built wát, also known as Wat Phai Doi. The view of the sea of fog that collects in the valley each morning is impressive; at other times of the day you get a view of the town. Two Shan stupas, erected in 1860 and 1874, enshrine the ashes of monks from Myanmar's Shan State. Around the back of the wát you can see a tall, slender standing Buddha and catch views west of the ridge. No shorts or miniskirts are permitted in the wát grounds, but you can rent cover-ups.

Wat Jong Kham & Wat Jong Klang
วัดจองคำ/วัดจองกลาง

Next to Nong Jong Kham in the southern part of town are a couple of mildly interesting Burmese-style wát – Wat Jong Kham and Wat Jong Klang.

Wat Jong Kham was built nearly 200 years ago by Thai Yai (Shan) people, who make up about 50% of the population of Mae Hong Son Province. Wat Jong Klang houses 100-year-old glass jataka paintings and has small rooms full of wooden reliefs and figures depicting the Vessantara Jataka (the popular jataka in which the Bodhisattva develops the Perfection of Giving) – all very Burmese in style. The wíhǎan containing these is open 8 am to 6 pm daily. Wat Jong Klang has several areas that women are forbidden to enter – not unusual for Burmese/Shan Buddhist temples.

Wat Hua Wiang
วัดหัวเวียง

Although its wooden bòt is in an advanced state of decay, a famous bronze Buddha in the Mandalay style, called **Chao Phlalakhaeng**, can be seen in this wát, on Thanon Phanit Wattana east of Thanon Khunlum Praphat.

Trekking

Trekking out of Mae Hong Son can be arranged at several guesthouses and travel agencies; Mae Hong Son Guest House has some of the most dependable and experienced guides. Guides at Don Enterprise (in the back of the night market building) and Sunflower Cafe have also received good reviews. Typical rates for most treks are 500B to 600B per day per person (if there are four or more people), with three to five days the normal duration. Popular routes

include the Mae Pai valley, Khun Yuam district and north of Soppong. A six-day trek from east of Mae Hong Son to near Soppong costs 400B per day per person. As with trekking elsewhere in the North, be sure to clarify when a trek starts and stops or you may not get your money's worth. Nearby Karen villages can be visited without a guide by walking two hours outside of town – several guesthouses in town can provide a map.

Rafting

Raft trips on the nearby Mae Pai are gaining in popularity, and the same guesthouses and trekking agencies that organise treks from Mae Hong Son can arrange the river trips. The most common type of trip sets off from Tha Mae Pai (Pai river pier) in **Ban Huay Deua**, 8km south-west of Mae Hong Son, for a day-long upriver journey of 5km. From the same pier, down-river trips to the 'long-neck' village of **Kariang Padawng Kekongdu** (Hawy Sen Thao) on the Thailand-Myanmar border are also possible. Another popular raft route runs between **Sop Soi** (10km north-west of town) and the village of **Soppong** to the west (not to be confused with the larger Shan trading village of the same name to the east). These day trips typically cost 500B per person if arranged in Ban Huay Deua, or 800B to 1200B if done through a Mae Hong Son agency.

The Mae Pai raft trips can be good fun if the raft holds up – it's not uncommon for rafts to fall apart or sink. The Myanmar trip, which attracts travellers who want to see the Padaung or 'long-necked' people, is a bit of a rip-off and, to some, exploitative – a four-hour trip through unspectacular scenery to see a few Padaung people who have fled to Mae Hong Son to escape an ethnic war in Myanmar. When there is fighting between Shan armies and Yangon troops in the area this trip may not be possible.

Special Events

Wat Jong Klang and Wat Jong Kham are the focal point of the Poi Sang Long Festival in March, when young Shan boys are ordained as novice monks during the school holidays in the ceremony known as *bùat lûuk kâew*. Like elsewhere in Thailand, the ordinands are carried on the shoulders of friends or relatives and paraded around the wát under festive parasols, but in the Shan custom the boys are dressed in ornate costumes (rather than simple white robes) and wear flower headdresses and facial make-up. Sometimes they ride on ponies.

Another important local event is the Jong Para Festival, held towards the end of the Buddhist Rains Retreat in October (three days before the full moon of the 11th lunar month – so it varies from year to year). The festival begins with local Shan bringing offerings to monks in the temples in a procession marked by the carrying of models of castles (prasat) on poles. An important part of the festival is the folk theatre and dance which is performed on the wát grounds, some of it unique to northwest Thailand.

During Loi Krathong – a national holiday usually celebrated by floating kràthong (small lotus floats) on the nearest pond, lake or river – Mae Hong Son residents launch balloons called kràthong sàwăn (heaven kràthong) from Doi Kong Mu.

Places to Stay – Budget
Guesthouses With more than 20 guesthouses in town, the accommodation scene in Mae Hong Son is very competitive – most rooms cost 50B to 80B with shared bathroom and 80B to 100B with private bathroom.

The original **Mae Hong Son Guest House** (☎ 053-612510, 295 Thanon Makasanti) has a secluded location on the north-western outskirts of town (about 700m west of Thanon Khunlum Praphat). Rooms in a wooden longhouse cost 100B to 150B without bathroom; bungalows with private bathroom cost 250B to 500B. The guesthouse is a good source of information and inexpensive meals.

'Longnecked' Padaung Villages

Near Mae Hong Son are several Padaung refugee villages where 'longneck' women are a local tourist attraction. The brass ornaments the Padaung women wear around their necks and limbs, which look like separate rings but are actually continuous coils, may weigh up to 22kg (though 5kg is a more common maximum) and stand 30cm in height. The neck coils depress the collarbone and rib cage, making it look as if their necks have been unnaturally stretched. A common myth says that if the coils are removed, the women's necks will fall over from atrophy and they'll die, but the women attach and remove the coils at will with no such problems.

No-one knows for sure how the coil custom got started. One theory says it was conceived to make the women's appearance strange enough that men from other tribes wouldn't pursue them. Another story says it was so tigers wouldn't carry them off by their throats. The Padaung themselves tell an apocryphal story claiming their ancestors were the offspring of a liaison between the wind and a beautiful female dragon, and that the coil-wearing custom pays tribute to their dragon progenitor. The women also wear thin hoops made of cane or lacquered cord in bunches around their knees and calves. As fewer and fewer Padaung women adopt the custom, the coil-wearing tradition is gradually dying out.

As a tourist attraction, the longneck village business is for the most part controlled by the Karenni National Progressive Party (KNPP), a Kayah (Karenni) insurgent group whose reported objective is to establish an independent Kayah state in eastern Myanmar. The Padaung are, in fact, an ethnolinguistic subgroup of the Kayah. Of the 7000 Padaung thought to be residents of Myanmar, around 300 have fled to Thailand as refugees.

The biggest of the Padaung villages is Nai Soi (also known as Nupa Ah), 35km north-west of the capital. Independent interviews with the 'longneck' women have ascertained that they earn around 3000B a month from selling handicrafts and from a small portion of the 250B entrance fee collected from foreigners. On average 1200 tourists a year visit this village (as many as 50 per day in the high season), and the bulk of the entry fees is thought to go to the KNPP. The typical tourist visit consists of extended photography sessions during which the coil-adorned Padaung women pose while weaving, or standing next to visitors. The women tell reporters they aren't bothered by the

In the hills nearby are the equally se-cluded **Sang Tong Huts** (☎ 053-620680, 🄴 *sangtonghuts@hotmail.com*), which have panoramic views. The setting is pretty and the huts have been recently renovated. Rates are 200B for smaller huts with shared facilities to 1000B for nicely furnished huts with balcony, hot-water shower and fridge. Set dinners are available in the dining area, with menus in English and German. Hill-tribe coffee and wine are also available.

Head north from the airport on Thanon Khunlum Praphat; just over a little bridge turn left onto Thanon Sirimongkhon and you'll come to **Chan Guest House** (☎ 053-620432). It's a large house with a few small but clean rooms for 150B with fan and pri-vate cold-water shower, plus four common hot-water showers. The high ratio of bath-rooms to guest rooms and fairly quiet loca-tion are pluses. If you continue north-west along this same road another 300m, past a

wát, you'll come to **Yok Guest House** (☎ 053-611532, 14 Thanon Sirimongkhon) on the right. It's a small, very quiet, family-run place with nine super-clean rooms around a courtyard parking area for 250B with fan, 400B with air-con. The rooms have private hot-water shower and fans.

In the area of Nong Jong Kham are sev-eral very pleasant guesthouses. **Jong Kam Guest House** (☎ 053-611150) overlooks the lake from the north and has slightly worn but clean rooms in a row house plus some newer thatched huts, all with shared facili-ties, for 100/200B single/double. One hut with fan and attached hot-water shower is available for 250B. The nearby **Friend House** (☎ 053-620119, fax 620060) has large clean rooms in a teak house for 100B single/double with fan and shared hot-water shower, 250B double with fan and attached bathroom, and 300B for up to four. Upstairs rooms have a view of the lake. Friend

'Longnecked' Padaung Villages

photography, which they consider to be part of their livelihood. As Nai Soi's Ma Nang was quoted in one of several stories the Bangkok Post has run on the Padaung, 'We had nothing in Myanmar. I had to work relentlessly in the rice fields. We miss our homes, but we don't want to go back.'

Other Padaung women have not been as fortunate. In 1991 a Shan man brought seven longneck women into Thailand and tried to 'sell' them to a resort in Soppong. Thai police arrested the man and freed the women, who immediately went to Nai Soi. One occasionally hears of other such tales; the same thing goes on in Myanmar as well, particularly in the Shan State around Inle Lake.

Opinions are sharply divided as to the ethics of 'consuming' the Padaung as a tourist attraction. Obviously there's the claim that the viewing of the longnecked Padaung in Thailand amounts to crass exploitation, but those who have taken the time to interview these people and learn about their lives have pointed out that this is the best opportunity they have available for making a liv-ing under current social conditions in Myanmar and Thailand. One thing seems certain: They are usually in Thailand by choice, having fled a potentially worse fate in Myanmar amid ethnic war. Thai authorities view Nai Soi as a self-sustaining refugee camp.

We see the longneck phenomenon as sitting squarely on the same cline of ethno-tourism as tribal trekking, one of the crasser forms to be sure, but only differing in degree from paying an Akha or a Guatemalan Indian to pose for a photo. Ethically it surely beats paying a trek operator for the privi-lege of photographing tribals on a trek when the latter receive nothing.

If you want to see any of the Padaung settlements, you can choose among Hawy Sen Thao (11km west of Mae Hong Son, 20 minutes by boat from the nearby Huay Deua landing), Nai Soi (35km north-west) and Huay Ma Khen Som (about 7km before Mae Aw). Travel agencies in Mae Hong Son arrange tours to these villages for 700B to 800B per person, which means they take in 450B to 550B over the village entry fees to pay for transport and expenses.

If you go to Nai Soi on your own, it's possible to arrange overnight accommodation in the village for 50B per person a night. At the entrance to the village your name, passport number and country of residence will be noted on a payment receipt issued by the 'Karenni Culture Department'. A couple of hundred metres beyond Nai Soi is a large Kayah refugee settlement, also controlled by the KNPP.

House also rents out motorcycles. Northeast of Nong Jong Kam is **Johnnie House**, a wooden row house with clean rooms for 80/100B with shared facilities, or 120B with private hot-water shower.

On the south-western side of the lake, **Piya Guest House** (☎ 053-611260) features rooms built around a garden, with a bar/restaurant in front; room rates are 150B with fan and 250B with air-con. All rooms have private hot-water showers; cleanliness, service and food continue to get mixed reports, however. Farther north on Thanon Udom Chaonithet is the basic **Sabanga House** (☎ 053-612280), a bamboo row house with eight rooms with a mattress on the floor, fan and shared hot-water shower, for 100B.

On the southern side of the lake is **Rim Nong Guest House** (☎ 053-611052), a friendly place with a little restaurant on the water's edge. Dorm beds cost 60B; private rooms with shared hot-water bathroom cost 100B to 150B. Across the street, away from the lake, is the very basic **Joe Guest House** (☎ 053-612417), which charges 100B for rooms with shared hot-water shower in an old teak house and up to 250B for newer rooms with private hot-water shower.

Pen Porn House (☎/fax 053-611577), on the road to Wat Phra That Doi Kong Mu, sits in a residential neighbourhood on a slope on the western side of town. Clean spacious rooms in a row house cost 250B a double, 400B for a four-bed room; all have fan and private hot-water shower.

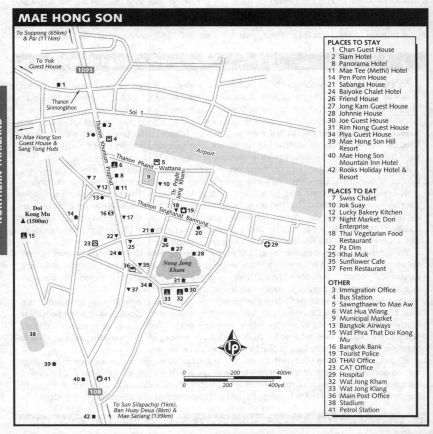

MAE HONG SON

To Soppong (65km) & Pai (111km)

To Yok Guest House

1095

Thanon Sirimongkhon

To Mae Hong Son Guest House & Sang Tong Huts

Thanon Khunlum Praphat

Soi 1

Thanon Phanit Wattana

Th Pradit Jong Kham

Airport

Thanon Singhanat Bamrung

Doi Kong Mu ▲ (1500m)

Nong Jong Kham

38

39

40   41

108

To Sun Silapachip (1km), Ban Huay Deua (8km) & Mae Sariang (139km)

0   200   400m
0   200   400yd

PLACES TO STAY
1 Chan Guest House
2 Siam Hotel
8 Panorama Hotel
11 Mae Tee (Methi) Hotel
14 Pen Porn House
21 Sabanga House
24 Baiyoke Chalet Hotel
26 Friend House
27 Jong Kam Guest House
28 Johnnie House
30 Joe Guest House
31 Rim Nong Guest House
32 Piya Guest House
39 Mae Hong Son Hill Resort
40 Mae Hong Son Mountain Inn Hotel
42 Rooks Holiday Hotel & Resort

PLACES TO EAT
7 Swiss Chalet
10 Jok Suay
12 Lucky Bakery Kitchen
17 Night Market; Don Enterprise
18 Thai Vegetarian Food Restaurant
22 Pa Dim
25 Khai Muk
35 Sunflower Cafe
37 Fern Restaurant

OTHER
3 Immigration Office
4 Bus Station
5 Sawngthaew to Mae Aw
6 Wat Hua Wiang
9 Municipal Market
13 Bangkok Airways
15 Wat Phra That Doi Kong Mu
16 Bangkok Bank
19 Tourist Police
20 THAI Office
23 CAT Office
29 Hospital
32 Wat Jong Kham
33 Wat Jong Klang
36 Main Post Office
38 Stadium
41 Petrol Station

NORTHERN THAILAND

Other less-convenient places can be found around Mae Hong Son – the touts will find you at the bus station.

Hotels Most of the hotels in Mae Hong Son are along the main north-south road, Thanon Khunlum Praphat. *Siam Hotel* (☎ *053-612148*), next to the bus station, is overpriced at 170/250B for ordinary rooms with fan, 350B with air-con. Farther south at No 55, *Mae Tee Hotel (Methi;* ☎ *053-612141, 611141)* is slightly cheaper but better; one/two-bed rooms with fan cost 150/160B; one/three-bed rooms with air-con cost 300/400B.

Places to Stay – Mid-Range & Top End

The *Panorama Hotel* (☎ *053-611757, fax 611790, 51 Thanon Khunlum Praphat)* charges 400/500B single/double with fan and hot-water shower, or 800B for a simple clean room with fridge, TV, air-con and hot-water shower.

Towards the southern end of town near the post office, *Baiyoke Chalet Hotel* (☎ *053-611486, fax 611533, 90 Thanon Khunlum Praphat)* offers all the typical amenities for 1330B. Low-season rates are 40% less, and breakfast is included. Farther south, the larger *Mae Hong Son Mountain Inn Hotel* (☎ *053-612284, fax 611309, 112 Thanon Khunlum Praphat)* charges 800B (500B to 600B in low season) for clean, medium-sized air-con singles/doubles, with hot water, around a courtyard. The price also includes breakfast. The Mountain Inn has well-kept, nicely landscaped public areas.

Mae Hong Son Hill Resort (☎/fax 053-612475, 106/2 Thanon Khunlum Praphat), near the stadium, is a quiet spot with 22 well-kept bungalows in a semigarden area for 400B, 500B with air-con.

A bit farther south, the *Rooks Holiday Hotel & Resort* (☎ *053-612324, fax 611524,* e *rooksgroup@hotmail.com, 114/5–7 Thanon Khunlum Praphat)* definitely represents the top end in town. Rooms and bungalows cost 1800B to 2200B. Facilities include a swimming pool, tennis courts, disco, snooker club, bakery, coffee shop and restaurant.

Out of Town South-west of town a few kilometres towards Ban Huay Deua and Ban

Tha Pong Daeng on the river are several 'resorts', which in the Thai sense of the term means any hotel near a rural or semirural area. Here you'll find the upmarket *Imperial Tara Mae Hong Son Hotel* (☎ *053-611021, fax 611252,* e *pomanote@loxinfo.co.th),* with doubles from 3500B (less if you request a discounted rate) along with a pool, sauna and fitness centre.

About 5km south-west of town via Rte 108 and a turn-off for Ban Hua Nam Mae Sakut, the ecofriendly *Fern Resort* (☎ *053-611374, fax 612363,* e *ferngroup@ softhome.net)* features Shan-style wooden bungalows adjacent to rice paddies for 950B to 1500B; low-season discounts are readily available, and there are good walks in the vicinity.

Farther off the highway, a couple more mid-range places worth considering are *Mae Hong Son Riverside Hotel* (☎ *053-611504, 611406),* with doubles from 1150B (discounted to 750B), and *Sam Mork Villa* (☎ *053-611478),* with doubles from 500B with fan, 800B with air-con.

Places to Eat

Mae Hong Son isn't known for its food, but there are a few decent places to eat besides the guesthouses. *Khai Muk*, an outdoor restaurant just off Thanon Khunlum Praphat, is one of the better Thai-Chinese restaurants in town. Another excellent, long-running spot is *Fern Restaurant*, south of the post office on Thanon Khunlum Praphat. Specialities at Fern include *chùu-chìi kûng* (shrimp in a succulent curry sauce) and *hèt hǎwm òp sii-íu* (mushrooms baked in soy sauce and served with a roasted garlic sauce).

Pa Dim, diagonally opposite Khai Muk, is a restaurant with dishes from every region in Thailand; it's popular because of its reasonable prices and good-size portions. The *morning market* behind the Mae Tee Hotel is a good place to buy food for trekking. Get there before 8 am.

The best place in town for jók is *Jok Suay*, opposite the municipal market on Soi Niwet Phisatn and open 5 to 9.30 am daily.

The *Thai Vegetarian Food Restaurant*, next to the tourist police office, serves inexpensive vegetarian Thai (as well as some nonvegetarian dishes) from around 9 am till 3 or 4 pm.

Lucky Bakery Kitchen, west of Thanon Khunlum Praphat on Thanon Singhanat Bamrung, does 'cowboy steak' and baked goods. Next door, *Swiss Chalet* (☎ 053-612050) serves cheese fondue, roesti and pasta, and is open from 7 to 1 am daily. *Sunflower Cafe*, near the post office, offers fresh-baked whole wheat breads and cakes, pizzas and coffee, plus information on local trekking.

Getting There & Away
Air THAI flies to Mae Hong Son from Chiang Mai three times daily (420B, 35 minutes). For many people, the time saved flying to Mae Hong Son versus bus travel is worth the extra money. Mae Hong Son's THAI office (☎ 053-611297, 611194) is at 71 Thanon Singhanat Bamrung.

Bus From Chiang Mai there are two bus routes to Mae Hong Son: the northern route through Pai (93B ordinary, 130B air-con, seven to eight hours) and the southern route through Mae Sariang (133B, 239B, eight to nine hours). The fare is 70B as far as Mae Sariang.

Although it may be longer, the southern route through Mae Sariang is a much more comfortable ride because the bus stops every two hours for a 10- to 15-minute break and larger buses – with large seats – are used. Buses to Mae Hong Son via Mae Sariang leave Chiang Mai's Arcade bus station five times daily between 6.30 am and 9 pm.

The northern route through Pai, originally built by the Japanese in WWII, is very winding and offers spectacular views from time to time. Because the buses used on this road are smaller, they're usually more crowded and the younger passengers tend to get motion sickness. The Pai bus leaves the Chiang Mai Arcade station four times a day at 7, 9 and 10.30 am and 12.30 pm. The 4 pm bus only goes as far as Pai.

Buses to Soppong cost 35B, to Pai 48B.

Getting Around
It is pretty easy to walk around most of Mae Hong Son. Motorcycle taxis within town cost from 10B to 20B; to Doi Kong Mu it's 30B one way or 50B return. Motorcycle drivers will also take passengers farther afield but fares out of town are expensive. There are now a few túk-túk in town, charging 20B to 30B per trip.

Several guesthouses rent out bicycles (20B to 30B) and motorcycles (150B for 24 hours). Avis Rent-a-Car (☎ 053-620457/8) has an office at the Mae Hong Son airport.

AROUND MAE HONG SON
Pha Bong Hot Springs
บ่อน้ำร้อนผาบ่อง
Eleven kilometres south of the capital at the 256km marker on Rte 108, this public park with hot springs covers 8 rai (1.2 hectares). Facilities include bathing rooms and a couple of simple restaurants.

Mae Aw
แม่ออ
Another day trip you can do from the provincial capital is to Mae Aw, 22km north of Mae Hong Son on a mountain peak at the Myanmar border. Mae Aw is a Chinese KMT settlement, one of the last true KMT outposts in Thailand, although it's not as interesting as Doi Mae Salong or Ban Mai Nong Bua near Doi Ang Khang. There's no feeling of 'wow an exciting place filled with old renegade fighters', just a quiet place with people who basically ignore you, but it's an interesting trip.

The town lies along the edge of a large reservoir and the faces and signs are very Chinese. Occasionally there is fighting along the border between the KMT and the Mong Tai Army, formerly led by the infamous opium warlord Khun Sa but now operating as four splinter units under separate leaderships. When this happens, public transport to these areas is usually suspended and you are advised against going without a guide. The modern Thai name for Mae Aw is Ban Rak Thai (Thai-Loving Village).

Accommodation in thatched huts is available at *Roun Thai Guest House* in the Chinese/Hmong village of Na Pa Paek, 7.3km south-west of Mae Aw, for 40B per person or 150B including two meals. Two small tea shops set up for tourists serve tea, cola and snacks of dubious sterility. You can also purchase a cool souvenir here – a section of bamboo filled with tea labelled 'special blend tea, made by KMT' in English, Thai and Chinese. The better of the two is *Mr Huang Yuan Tea & Restaurant*.

From Na Pa Paek a rough dirt road leads south-west to the Hmong village of Ma Khua Som (3.5km) and the KMT village of Pang Ung La (6km) on the Myanmar border. Pang Ung La also has a guesthouse.

Since the sealing of the 22km road to Na Pa Paek, trips to Mae Aw are easier, although it's still a steep, winding route. The final unsealed 7km to Mae Aw can be very troublesome in the wet season.

There are rather irregular săwngthăew going back and forth from Mae Hong Son for 50B per person, but it's so unpredictable these days that you're better off getting a group of people together and chartering a săwngthăew. It will cost you 500B to 1300B (depending on whether the drivers have any paid cargo). This option lets you stop and see the sights along the way. Check Thanon Singhanat Bamrung near the telephone office at around 9 am to see if there are any săwngthăew going.

The trip takes two hours and passes Shan, Karen and Hmong villages, the **Pang Tong Summer Palace** and waterfalls. Mae Aw is also included on some day tours operated out of Mae Hong Son.

If you have your own transport, you can stop off at **Nam Tok Pha Sua** on the way to Mae Aw. About 17km north of Rte 1095, turn onto a marked dirt road. The multi-levelled cataract has water year-round; during the rainy season swimming can be dangerous due to thundering water flow. Facilities include picnic tables and toilets.

Tham Pla National Park A trip to Mae Aw could be combined with a visit to this recently established national park centred on the animistic Tham Pla or Fish Cave, a water-filled cavern where hundreds of *tor soro* (soro brook carp) thrive. These fish grow up to 1m in length and are found only in the provinces of Mae Hong Son, Ranong, Chiang Mai, Rayong, Chanthaburi and Kanchanaburi. The fish eat vegetables and insects, although the locals believe them to be vegetarian and feed them only fruit and vegetables (which can be purchased at the park entrance).

You can see the fish through a 2-sq-metre rock hole at the base of an outer wall of the cave. A statue of a Hindu rishi called Nara,

said to protect the holy fish from danger, stands nearby.

A path leads from the park entrance to a suspension bridge that crosses a stream and continues to the cave. The park is a shady, cool place to hang out; picnic tables are available. You can pitch a tent for free on the grounds. Last we checked admission to the park was still free, although the recent general increase in national park entry fees may mean the rangers will begin charging. The park is 17km north-east of Mae Hong Son on the northern side of Hwy 1095.

Mae La-Na
แม่ละนา

Between Mae Hong Son and Pai, Rte 1095 winds through an area of forests, mountains, streams, Shan and hill-tribe villages and limestone caves. Some of Mae Hong Son's most beautiful scenery is within a day's walk of the Shan village of Mae La-Na (6km north of Rte 1095 via a half-sealed road), where overnight accommodation is available. From here you can **trek** to several nearby Red and Black Lahu villages and to a few caves within a 4km to 8km radius.

It's possible to walk a 20km half loop all the way from Mae La-Na to Tham Lot and Soppong, staying overnight in Red Lahu villages along the way. Ask for a sketch map at the Mae Lana Guest House (see Places to Stay under Around Mae Hong Son). Experienced riders can accomplish this route on a sturdy dirt bike – but not alone or during the rainy season.

Local guides will lead visitors to nearby **caves** for set prices per cave. **Tham Mae La-Na**, 4km from the village, is largest and most famous – it's threaded by a 12km length of river – and a journey to the cave and through it costs 600B. Tham Pakarang (Coral Cave), Tham Phet (Diamond Cave), Tham Khao Taek (Broken Rice Cave) and Tham Khai Muk (Pearl Cave) all feature good wall formations and cost 200B each for guides. Rates are posted at a small săalaa near a noodle stand and petrol barrel pumps in the centre of the village; this is also where you may contact the guides during the day. If no-one's at the săalaa when you go there, just mention *thâm* (cave) to someone at the petrol pumps.

Even if you don't go trekking or caving, Mae La-Na can be a peaceful and mildly interesting cul-de-sac to stay for a short while. Beyond a Shan-style temple, a school, some houses and the aforementioned 'downtown' area around the noodle shops and petrol pumps, there's little to see, but the surrounding montane scenery is quite pleasing.

Twenty-seven kilometres west of Pangmapha is a short turn-off for **Wat Tham Wua Sunyata**, a peaceful forest monastery.

The Mae La-Na junction is 55km from Mae Hong Son, 10km from Soppong and 56km from Pai. The village is 6km north of the junction. Infrequent săwngthăew from the highway to the village cost 20B per person – mornings are your best bet.

Tham Lot
ถ้ำลอด

About 8km north of Soppong is Tham Lot (pronounced *thâm lâwt* and also known as *thâm náam lâwt*), a large limestone cave with a wide stream running through it. Along with Tham Nam Lang farther west, it's one of the longest known caves in mainland South-East Asia (although some as yet unexplored caves in Southern Thailand may be even longer). It is possible to hike all the way through the cave (approximately 200m) by following the stream, although it requires some wading back and forth. Apart from the main chamber, there are three side chambers that can be reached by ladders – it takes two to three hours to see the whole thing. Where the stream exits the cave, thousands of bats and swifts leave the cave at dusk.

At the park entrance you must hire a gas lantern and guide for 100B (one guide can lead up to four people) to take you through the caverns; they no longer permit visitors to tour the caves alone. The guide fee includes visits to the first and third caverns; to visit the second cavern you must cross the stream. Raft men waiting inside the cave charge 10B per person per crossing; in the dry season you may be able to wade across. For 100B you can stay on the raft through the third cavern. If you decide to book a Tham Lot day tour from Mae Hong Son, ask if the tour cost includes guide, lamp and raft fees.

The park is open from 8 am to 5.30 pm every day. A row of outdoor restaurants outside the park entrance offers basic Thai fare.

Soppong
สบปอง

Soppong is a small but relatively prosperous market village a couple of hours northwest of Pai and about 70km from Mae Hong Son. Since the paving of Rte 1095, Soppong and Tham Lot have become popular destinations for minivan tours from Mae Hong Son and Chiang Mai.

Close to Soppong are several Shan, Lisu, Karen and Lahu villages that can easily be visited on foot. Inquire at the Jungle Guest House or Cave Lodge in Soppong for reliable information. It's important to ask about the current situation as the Myanmar border area is somewhat sensitive due to the opium trade and smuggling.

Soppong has a post office opposite the main market area on the highway.

The rough back road between Soppong and Mae La-Na is popular with mountain bikers and off-highway motorcyclists.

Coffin Caves
ถ้ำผี

A 900-sq-km area of Pangmapha and adjacent districts may contain more caves than any other region in the world. Over 30 of these limestone caverns are known to contain very old wooden coffins carved from solid tree logs. Up to 6m long, the coffins are typically suspended on wooden scaffolds inside the caves and bound with ceremonial tassels (very few of which have been found intact). The coffins – which number in the dozens – are of unknown age and origin, but Thai anthropologists have classified them into at least 14 different design schemes. Pottery remains associated with the sites have also been found.

The local Thais know these burial caves as *thâm phĭi* (spirit caves), or *thâm phĭi maen* (coffin caves). The eight coffin caves that scientists are investigating at the moment are off limits to the public, but you may be able to find guides in the Pangmapha district willing to tour others. **Tham Nam Lang**, 30km north-west of Soppong near Ban Nam Khong, is 9km long and said to be one of the largest caves in the world in terms of volume.

Places to Stay

Mae La-Na & Vicinity Run by Mae La-Na's village headman, *Top Hill* sits on a hill overlooking the village and offers OK bungalow accommodation with shared facilities for 40B per person. A little farther below towards the valley bottom is *Mae Lana Guest House*, which rents out four large doubles with mosquito nets for 80B and a four-bed dorm for 40B per person. Mae Lana Guest House closes during the rainy season.

At Ban Nam Khong, the *Wilderness Lodge* is run by the same family that owns the Cave Lodge in Tham Lot. Huts are 50B per person. The Rte 108 turn-off for Wilderness Lodge is located 25km west of Pangmapha village.

About 12km north of Mae La-Na in the Black Lahu village of Ban Huay Hea (close to the Myanmar border) is the *Lahu Guest House*, run by a village teacher who speaks English. Simple lodging costs 50B and the money goes to a community fund.

Soppong Most accommodation in the area is concentrated around Soppong, which has developed into an important stop for both day and overnight package tours. Just off the highway near the bus stop, *Lemon Hill Guest House* features nice huts facing the Nam Lan stream and with bougainvillea tumbling over the roofs. Rooms cost 200B with private hot-water shower or 100B with shared hot-water shower.

On the opposite side of the road, a narrow lane leads to *Kemarin Garden Lodge*, which was closed when we visited. The owners say they plan to renovate and reopen – but they didn't say when. If you continue along this track another kilometre (the last half kilometre is accessible by foot or bicycle only) and cross a footbridge over a stream you'll come to *Charming Home*. Two well-designed, well-spaced huts with private bathroom sit on a breezy hillside backed by primary forest; rates are 120/150B singles/doubles per hut. There are many birds in this area and you can easily hike to Lisu and Lahu villages nearby.

The friendly *Jungle Guest House* (☎ 053-617099), 1km west on the road to Mae Hong Son, offers well-designed huts for 80/100B with shared hot-water shower and 200/250B with private facilities. The new restaurant overlooking the river serves better fare than most of the other guesthouses in the area. The nearby *Pangmapa Guest House,* north-west of the Jungle Guest House on the same road, is similar.

Well off the road in a nice river setting, *T Rex House* (☎ 053-617054, fax 617053) is run by a German/Thai couple and features solar water heating and a swimming pool. Nine A-frame bungalows are available, all with private toilet and hot-water shower, for 350B. Two VIP rooms in the main house cost 450B. Discounts may be available during the rainy season.

Tham Lot Near Tham Lot, several guesthouses have come and gone. Royal Forest Department officials have on occasion cracked down on illegal accommodation encroaching on the forest area, although we haven't heard of that happening lately. At the moment there are only two, both within a few hundred metres of the cave.

The long-running *Cave Lodge* offers dorm beds for 60B, bungalows with shared bathroom for 120B to 250B, a few newer and more spacious two-person bungalows with attached bathroom for 350B, and four-person bungalows with attached bathroom for 280B.

Guided day hikes are available for a very reasonable 350B, inflatable kayak trips for 500B.

On the banks of the stream that runs through the cave, west of the park entrance, the relaxed and friendly *Lang River Guest House* has a large shed-like dormitory back from the river with raised, partitioned sleeping platforms, each fairly wide with a mattress, mosquito net and built-in shelves. It costs 70B per person. Bungalows by the river cost 120/150B single/double, while two nicer bungalows are now reserved for tour groups. Trekking guides can also be arranged here.

You may also be able to rent a room from villagers at Ban Tham, the village closest to Tham Lot.

On foot it takes about 1½ hours along a well-marked, half-sealed road to reach Ban Tham, Cave Lodge and Lang River Guest House from Soppong. Nowadays there's plenty of vehicular traffic so you should also be able to hitch a ride fairly easily.

Ban Nam Rin At this Lisu village 10km south of Soppong towards Pai, between the 132km and 133km markers, you can stay at *Lisu Village Guest House* for 70/100B.

Getting There & Around

Pai to Mae Hong Son buses stop in Soppong and there are two or three each day in either direction. From Mae Hong Son to Soppong, buses take about 2½ hours and cost 35B. The trip between Pai and Soppong costs 25B (28B air-con) and takes from 1½ to two hours.

Motorcycle taxis stationed at the bus stop in Soppong will carry passengers to Tham Lot or the Cave Lodge for 50B per person; private pick-up trucks will take you and up to five other people for 200B. If you have your own wheels, the road from Soppong to Ban Tham is graded until the 7km marker, after which it's rough dirt all the way to the cave.

PAI
ปาย

postcode 58130 • pop 3000

It first appears that there's not a lot to see in Pai (pronounced like the English word 'bye', *not* 'pie'), a peaceful crossroads town about halfway between Chiang Mai and Mae Hong Son on Rte 1095. But if you stick around a few days and talk to some of the locals, you may discover some beautiful spots in the surrounding hills.

Most of the town's population are Shan and Thai, but there's also a small but visible Muslim population – mostly jiin haw. North-west of town, a Shan, a Lahu and a Lisu village, a KMT village called **Ban Santichon** (San Ti Chuen in Yunnanese) and **Nam Tok Maw Paeng** can all be visited on foot. The Shan, Lisu and KMT villages lie within 4km of Pai, while the Lahu village is near Nam Tok Maw Paeng, another 4km farther from town (8km total).

You can cut the hike in half by taking a Mae Hong Son–bound bus north about 5km and getting off at a signpost for the falls; from the highway it's only 4km (about 2km beyond the Pai Mountain Lodge). A couple of pools at the base of the falls are suitable for swimming – best just after the rainy season, October to early December.

Across the Mae Pai and 8km south-east of town via a paved road is **Tha Pai Hot Springs**, a well-kept local park 1km from the road. A scenic stream runs through the park; it mixes with the hot springs in places to make pleasant bathing areas. There are also small public bathing houses to which hot spring water is piped. Entry to the park is free.

Information

The Krung Thai Bank located on the eastern side of Thanon Rangthiyanon (the main road through town) has an ATM.

Several places around town offer Internet services, all for about 1B per minute.

Wat Phra That Mae Yen
วัดพระธาตุแม่เย็น

This temple sits atop a hill with a good view overlooking the valley. Walk 1km east from the main intersection in town, across a stream and through a village, to get to the stairs (a decent climb – 353 steps) that lead to the top. Or take the 400m sealed road that follows a different route to the top.

Trekking, Rafting & Elephant Riding

Any of the guesthouses in town can provide information on local trekking and a few do guided treks for as little as 500B per day if there are no rafts or elephants involved. Among the more established local agencies are Duang Trekking and Northern Green, both near Duang Guest House and the bus station.

Raft trips on the nearby Mae Pai operate from July to December, sometimes longer in rainy years; September is usually the best month. Most outfits use flimsy bamboo rafts but it's fun anyway if you don't mind getting wet.

Thai Adventure Rafting (☎/fax 053-699111, ℮ rafting@activethailand.com) leads excellent two-day white-water rafting trips in sturdy rubber rafts from Pai to Mae Hong Son for 1800B per person including food, rafting equipment, camping gear, dry bags and insurance. Along the way rafters visit a waterfall, a fossil reef and hot springs; one night is spent at the company's permanent riverside camp. The main rafting season is July to December; after that the trips aren't normally run. It has offices in

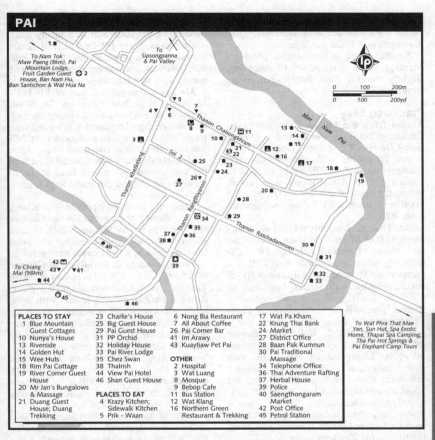

PAI

To Nam Tok
Maw Paeng (8km), Pai
Mountain Lodge,
Fruit Garden Guest
House, Ban Nam Hu,
Ban Santichon & Wat Hua Na

To
Sipsongpanna
& Pai Valley

Mae Nam Pai

Thanon Chaisongkhram

Thanon Khetkelang

Soi 2

Thanon Rangthiyanon

Thanon Ratchadamnoen

To Chiang
Mai (98km)

To Wat Phra That Mae
Yen, Sun Hut, Spa Exotic
Home, Thapai Spa Camping,
Tha Pai Hot Springs &
Pai Elephant Camp Tours

PLACES TO STAY		
1 Blue Mountain Guest Cottages	23 Charlie's House	6 Nong Bia Restaurant
13 Riverside	25 Big Guest House	7 All About Coffee
14 Golden Hut	29 Pai Guest House	26 Pai Corner Bar
15 Wee Huts	31 PP Orchid	41 Im Arawy
18 Rim Pai Cottage	32 Holiday House	43 Kuaytiaw Pet Pai
19 River Corner Guest House	33 Pai River Lodge	
20 Mr Jan's Bungalows & Massage	35 Chez Swan	**OTHER**
	38 Thalrish	2 Hospital
21 Duang Guest House; Duang Trekking	44 View Pai Hotel	3 Wat Luang
	46 Shan Guest House	8 Mosque
		9 Bebop Cafe
10 Nunya's House	**PLACES TO EAT**	11 Bus Station
	4 Krazy Kitchen; Sidewalk Kitchen	12 Wat Klang
	5 Prik - Waan	16 Northern Green Restaurant & Trekking

17 Wat Pa Kham	34 Telephone Office
22 Krung Thai Bank	36 Thai Adventure Rafting
24 Market	37 Herbal House
27 District Office	39 Police
28 Baan Pak Kumnun	40 Saengthongaram Market
30 Pai Traditional Massage	42 Post Office
	45 Petrol Station

Pai (Thanon Rangthiyanon) and in Chiang Mai (Thanon Charoen Prathet).

Pai Elephant Camp Tours (aka Thom's Elephant Camp Tours) offers jungle rides year-round at its camp south-east of Pai near the hot springs. The cost is 300B to 550B per person (minimum of two persons) for a one- to three-hour ride that includes a visit to the hot springs. It can also arrange bamboo or rubber rafting trips down the Mae Pai. Combination elephant-trekking and river-rafting tours cost 1000B per person, and include lunch and transport. Other combination tours and treks are available, including overnight stays in hill-tribe villages. Contact the office (☎/fax 053-699286) on Thanon Ratdamrong, about 20m south of Thanon Rangthiyanon.

Traditional Massage

Pai Traditional Massage (☎ 053-699121), in a house near the river on Thanon Sukhapiban 1, has very good northern-Thai massage for 150B an hour, or 230B for 1½ hours, as well as a sauna where you can steam yourself in *sàmŭn phrai* (medicinal herbs) for 50B per visit. The couple that do the massages are graduates of Chiang Mai's Old Medicine Hospital. A three-day massage course is available for around 1800B. Massage and sauna services are available from 4.30 to 8.30 pm weekdays and 8.30 am to 8.30 pm weekends.

Herbal House, next to ThaIrish Guesthouse on Thanon Rangthiyanon, offers foot massage, oil massage and Thai traditional massage in a spacious massage hall.

Three-day courses and/or traditional Thai herbal medicine are also available. Most massage costs 150B per hour.

Another place in town called Mr Jan's Massage. at Soi Wanchalerm 18, employs a slightly rougher Shan/Burmese massage technique.

Places to Stay

Across from the bus station on Thanon Chaisongkhram is the friendly *Duang Guest House* (☎ 053-699101, fax 699581), where 26 rooms with shared hot-water showers cost 60B to 70B a single, 120B to 130B a double. A few rooms with private hot-water shower are also available for 200B; one room with TV and refrigerator costs 400B.

On Thanon Rangthiyanon, two doors south-west of Krung Thai Bank, is the clean and secure *Charlie's House* (☎ 053-699039), where dorm beds cost 60B and rooms around a large courtyard cost 60/100B a single/double with shared bathroom or 200B to 250B with attached hot-water shower (plus 40B for a third person). Charlie's is often full during the high season.

Nearby on Soi 2, *Big Guest House* (☎ 053-699080) has small A-frame huts for 60/100B, larger rooms for 120B with shared toilet and hot-water shower, plus a few nicer rooms with private shower for 150B single/double. *Chez Swan* (☎ 053-699111), on Thanon Rangthiyanon, has a row of large rooms behind the restaurant with private hot-water showers and thick mattresses for 200B per night.

Farther south along the street, the *ThaIrish* (☎ 053-699149) is housed in the former Wiang Pai Hotel, once Pai's only commercial accommodation. Spacious rooms in a wooden building cost 100/150B with shared bathroom. There's a bar downstairs.

Along the Mae Pai in the eastern part of town is a string of quiet bungalow operations. *Pai River Lodge,* south of Thanon Ratchadamnoen, has simple huts arranged in a large circle with a dining and lounge area on stilts in the middle. The older A-frames cost 80B single/double; pay 100B for a couple of slightly larger nicer ones. Because of its quiet, scenic location it's often full. Rates may be higher in peak season. *Holiday Guest House*, to the immediate north, is similar.

PP Orchid, close to the river, offers basic bungalows for 100/150B in a nicely land-scaped area. Near PP Orchid, *Pai Guest House* has singles/doubles for 70/90B, 80/100B with bathroom; all are very basic rooms with thin mattresses on the floor.

Mr Jan's Bungalows, part of Mr Jan's Massage, is tucked away on Soi Wan-chaloem 18 and features 10 simple bamboo huts set among a large herb garden and fruit trees. Huts with shared bathroom cost 70B single/double, while two units with private cold-water shower go for 150/200B (less in the low season). All guests have access to facilities where you can bathe with heated, herb-infused water.

Down the soi that's opposite Wat Klang, the new *Baan Pak Kunmun* has bungalow or row-house rooms for 80B and 120B; all have shared bathroom. The rooms are separated from the road by a large expanse of grass.

The upmarket (for Pai) *Rim Pai Cottage* (☎ 053-699133, 235931) is farther north on Thanon Chaisongkhram along the river. Rim Pai's clean, quiet A-frames with bathroom, electricity and mosquito nets go for 400B, while rooms in a nice row house are 300B. One large bungalow is available by the river for 600B; rates include breakfast. Nearby *River Corner Guest House* has simpler bamboo-and-thatch cottages with private bathroom from 120B in the low season to 250B in the high season. A larger cottage costs 500B to 750B.

North of Rim Pai Cottage around a bend in the river is the well-landscaped *Golden Hut*, which offers simple thatched huts on stilts lined up along the river. Dorm beds cost 50B, double rooms with shared bathroom 100B, separate bungalows with shared hot-water bathroom 120B, and singles/doubles/triples with private bathroom 200/250/300B. A path continues along the river to *Riverside*, with simple thatched bungalows scattered around a large area on the river for 80/120B single/double with shared bathroom. On the road that leads to Golden Hut, you'll pass the very basic *Wee Huts* on the left. The huts here are a little close together and cost the same as at Riverside.

On the southern edge of town, off Thanon Rangthiyanon, is the quiet, well-run *Shan Guest House* (☎ 053-699162). Solid bungalows with private hot-water showers and comfortable beds cost 200B. A separate dining and lounging building sits on stilts in the middle of a large pond. Long-term discounts are available.

Farther south towards Chiang Mai, past the petrol stations, the three-storey *View Pai Hotel* (☎ 053-699174) is a rather plain place with overpriced rooms for 300B with fan, or 500B with air-con.

Towards the western end of Thanon Chaisongkhram near the hospital, *Blue Mountain Guest Cottages* offers several simple, small wooden bungalows for 50B. Three larger cottages cost 80/100B to 100/150B. Farther out on this road, about 50m past Wat Hua Na, is a turn-off onto a narrow 200m dirt road that leads to *Fruit Garden Guest House*. Six bamboo bungalows are thinly scattered over hillsides around a stream and cost 100B.

Across the Mae Pai south-east of town are a number of places to stay along the road that leads to the hot springs. Most offer simple thatched-roof huts for about 50B to 100B. Best of the bunch is *Sun Hut* (☎ 053-699730), a new place with nicely spaced bamboo huts, plus one tree house, for 100/120B with shared bathroom. Nicer units with private shower go for 120B to 200B. The turn-off for *Sun Hut* comes right before a bridge over a stream, about 200m before the entrance to Wat Phra That Mae Yen.

Farther down this road are a couple of small resorts that take advantage of the local hot springs by piping the mineral-rich water into the facilities. *Spa Exotic Home* (☎ 053-699035, 699145, fax 699462) features comfortable wooden bungalows with private hot-water shower for 500B with one large bed or 700B with two large beds. You can get a 40% discount from May to August. You can also pitch a tent on the property for 100B a night. On the well-landscaped premises are a nicely designed set of outdoor hot tubs for the use of guests and a restaurant serving good Thai and Western food.

Nearby *Thapai Spa Camping* (*in Chiang Mai* ☎ 053-218583, fax 219610) offers 15 wood-and-stone cottages with natural hot mineral-water showers for 600B to 800B. There's also an outdoor hot-water pool. Visitors may use the mineral baths here for 50B without staying overnight.

Out of Town A couple of kilometres north of town in the village of Ban Wiang Neua, *Sipsongpanna* (also known as Artist Homestay) is a small but charming collection of wood-and-bamboo bungalows alongside the river. The Thai artist-owner has designed the units with lots of deft little touches, such as private but separate toilet/shower facilities for each. Rates are a reasonable 150B a night. There are sitting areas sprinkled throughout the compound, along with a vegetarian cafe and art studio. Thai vegetarian cooking lessons are available.

Pai Mountain Lodge (☎ 053-699068) is 7km north-west of Pai near Nam Tok Maw Paeng and several hill-tribe villages. Well maintained spacious A-frames with hot-water showers and stone fireplaces sleep four and cost from 500B to 600B – good value. A few VIP bungalows are under construction, which will probably cost 1000B per night. In town you can book a room or arrange transport at 89 Thanon Chaisongkhram, near Northern Green Restaurant & Trekking.

Pai Valley, 2km out of town on the road to Mae Hong Son, offers six rooms in one long building. Each room has private facilities and its own sitting area out front, and costs 300B. The building is surrounded by 20 rái (3.2 hectares) of mango, lychee and papaya orchards. The proprietors claim that they use no pesticides in guest rooms but rather plant and herb extracts.

Places to Eat

The *Nong Bia Restaurant* (☎ 053-699103) on Thanon Chaisongkhram serves a good variety of inexpensive Thai and Chinese standards, as well as khâo sàwy. Across from Nong Bia, the more up-scale *Prik-Waan* (☎ 053-699519) offers Bangkok-style specialities such as spicy poached river fish salad and quail stir-fried with curry paste, all in the 50B to 70B range.

Every evening a row of local *food vendors* sets up in front of the day market. During the day, takeaway food can also be purchased at the larger *Saengthongaram Market* on Thanon Khetkelang. Also on this street you'll find a row of *noodle shops* near the post and telegraph office including *Kuaythiaw Pet Pai* (Pai Duck Noodles), just south of the post office, and *Im Arawy*, opposite, which specialises in *khâo râat kaeng* (curry over rice).

Krazy Kitchen and *Sidewalk Kitchen*, on Thanon Khetkelang, and *Pai Corner Bar*, on Thanon Rangthiyanon, serve OK Thai and Western food. *All About Coffee* on Thanon Chaisongkhram does the best fàràng breakfast and lunch menu in town. It serves very nice but pricey pastries, coffees, teas, fruit drinks and egg breakfasts. It opens 8.30 am to 6 pm Monday to Saturday.

Good French food – including several cheeses – is available at the nicely decorated *Chez Swan* (☎ 053-699111) on Thanon Rangthiyanon.

Entertainment
Bebop Cafe and *Blue Mountain Guest Cottages* have live blues, rock and jazz some nights – mainly Thai musicians transplanted from Bangkok or Chiang Mai.

Getting There & Away
Buses (51B ordinary, 71B air-con) depart Chiang Mai's Arcade bus station at 8.30 and 11 am and noon, 2 and 4 pm daily. The distance is only 134km but the trip takes about three hours due to the steep and winding road. From Mae Hong Son there are also five buses a day with the same departure times as the buses from Chiang Mai. This winding, 111km stretch takes three to four hours (48B, 67B). In the other direction, buses depart Pai for Chiang Mai and Mae Hong Son at 8.30 and 10.30 am and noon, 2 and 4 pm. Buses from Pai to Soppong cost 25B ordinary, 28B air-con.

Getting Around
All of Pai is accessible on foot. For local excursions you can rent bicycles or motorcycles at several locations around town. A place next door to Duang Guest House rents out bicycles for 50B per day (80B for newer bikes). Motorcycles can be rented at MS Motorcycle Rent just south of Pai Elephant Camp Tours office – 100cc bikes for 150B per 24 hours, larger bikes for 200B. All motorcycle rental places keep your passport as collateral.

Motorcycle taxis can be hired from the taxi stand at the bus stop. Typical fares are 20B to Ban Nam Hu and Ban Wiang Neua, 30B to Nam Hu Lisaw and Nam Hu Jin, and 40B to Tha Pai.

AROUND PAI
Pai can be used as a base for excursions to hill-tribe villages, as described earlier in the Pai section. Farther afield, the area northeast of Pai has so far been little explored. A network of unpaved roads – some little more than footpaths – skirts a mountain ridge and the Mae Taeng valley all the way to the Myanmar border near **Wiang Haeng** and **Ban Piang Haeng**, passing several villages along the way. Near Ban Piang Luang is a Shan temple built by Khun Sa, the opium warlord.

This area can also be visited by road from Chiang Dao in Chiang Mai Province.

Chiang Rai Province

Chiang Rai, the northernmost province in Thailand, is one of the country's most rural areas. Half of its northern border, separating province and nation from Laos, is formed by the Mekong River. Mountains form the other half, cleaving Myanmar from Thailand, with the junction of the Nam Ruak and Mekong River at Thailand's peak. The fertile Mekong flood plains to the east support most of the agriculture in the province; to the west the land is too mountainous for most crops. One crop that thrives on steep mountain slopes is opium, and until recently Chiang Rai was the centre for most of the opium in Thailand.

Crop substitution and other development projects sponsored by the late Princess Mother (the king's mother), along with accelerated law enforcement, have pushed much of the opium trade over the border into Myanmar and Laos. While there are undoubtedly still pockets of the trade here and there, even a few poppy patches, Chiang Rai's Golden Triangle fame is now mostly relegated to history books and museums.

CHIANG RAI
อ.เมืองเชียงราย

postcode 57000 • pop 37,600
About 180km from Chiang Mai, Chiang Rai (called 'Siang Hai' in northern-Thai dialect) is known in tourist literature as 'the

gateway to the Golden Triangle'. Most visitors to the town are interested in trekking or have just arrived after having taken the boat trip down Mae Nam Kok from Tha Ton. Few people stay more than a night or two.

King Mengrai founded Chiang Rai in 1262 as part of the Lao–Thai Lanna kingdom. It became a Siamese territory in 1786 and a province in 1910. The city's most historic monument, Wat Phra Kaew, once hosted the Emerald Buddha during its travels (the image eventually ended up at the wát of the same name in Bangkok). It now houses a replica of Chiang Mai's Wat Phra Singh Buddha image and a new 'Emerald Buddha' of its own.

Lots of wealthy Thais began moving to Chiang Rai in the 1980s and in the early 1990s the area saw a development boom as local entrepreneurs speculated on the city's future. Things have calmed down a bit and a few guesthouses have closed down, although having an airport has increased its potential as a major tourist destination. From a tourism marketing point of view, Chiang Rai is becoming a touted alternative to Chiang Mai, although it's not nearly as colourful and there's less to do in town. On the other hand it's a little more laid-back, and anyone interested in trekking will find they can reach village areas quicker than from Chiang Mai.

Information
Tourist Offices The TAT office (☎ 053-744674, 711433) on Thanon Singkhlai, north of Wat Phra Singh, distributes maps of Chiang Rai as well as useful brochures on accommodation and transport. It's open daily from 8.30 am to 4.30 pm.

Money Chiang Rai is well supplied with banks, especially along Thanon Thanalai and along Thanon Utarakit. Bangkok Bank on Thanon Thanalai has an ATM, as do several other banks in town.

Post & Communications The main post office, on Thanon Utarakit south of Wat Phra Singh, is open from 8.30 am to 4.30 pm weekdays, and 9 am to noon on Saturday, Sunday and public holidays.

A CAT office at Thanon Ratchadat Damrong and Thanon Ngam Meuang offers international telephone, telegram, telex and fax services from 7 am to 11 pm weekdays.

There are several Internet cafes in the city centre, particularly in the vicinity of the Wang Come Hotel. The CAT and main post offices also offer Internet service.

Wat Phra Kaew
วัดพระแก้ว

Originally called Wat Pa Yia (Bamboo Forest Monastery) in local dialect, this is the city's most revered Buddhist temple. Legend says that in 1434 lightning struck the temple's octagonal chedi, which fell apart to reveal the Phra Kaew Morakot or Emerald Buddha (actually made of jade).

Around 1990 Chiang Rai commissioned a Chinese artist to sculpt a new image from Canadian jade. Named the Phra Yok Chiang Rai (Chiang Rai Jade Buddha), it was intentionally a very close but not exact replica of the Phra Kaew Morakot in Bangkok, with dimensions of 48.3cm across the base and 65.9cm in height, just 0.1cm shorter than the original. The image is housed in the impressive Haw Phra Kaew, which sits towards the back of the wát compound.

The main wíhăan is a medium-sized, nicely preserved wooden structure with unique carved doors. The chedi behind it dates to the late 14th century and is typical Lanna style.

Wat Jet Yot
วัดเจ็ดยอด

The namesake for this wát is a seven-spired chedi similar to the chedi in Chiang Mai's Wat Jet Yot but without stucco ornamentation. Of more aesthetic interest is the wooden ceiling of the front veranda of the main wíhăan. This wooden ceiling features a unique Thai astrological fresco.

Wat Phra Singh
วัดพระสิงห์

Housing yet another copy of a famous Buddha image, this temple was built in the late 14th century during the reign of Chiang Rai's King Mahaphrom. A sister temple to Chiang Mai's Wat Phra Singh, its original buildings are typical northern-style

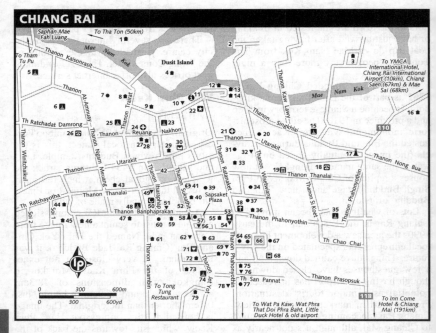

CHIANG RAI

wooden structures with low, sweeping roofs. The impressive dragon-carved gate looks to be of Thai Lü design. The main wíhǎan houses a copy of Chiang Mai's Phra Singh Buddha.

Other Temples

Wat Phra That Doi Chom Thong is a hilltop wát north-west of Wat Phra Kaew with views of the river and an occasional river breeze. The Lanna-style stupa here was supposedly built in 940. **Wat Pa Kaw**, near the entrance to the old Chiang Rai airport south of town, is a Shan-built temple with distinctive Burmese designs. Also near the old airport is **Wat Phra That Doi Phra Baht**, a northern-style temple perched on a hillside.

Hilltribe Museum & Education Center

ศูนย์การศึกษาชาวเขา

The nonprofit Population & Community Development Association (PDA) operates this combination museum/handicrafts centre at 620/1 Thanon Thanalai (☎ 053-

719167, 711475, fax 718869). Crafts for sale are displayed on the ground floor. The 3rd floor of the facility serves as a museum with typical clothing for six major tribes, folk implements and other anthropological exhibits. The museum hours are 9 am to 8 pm daily. The centre also offers a 25-minute slide show on Thailand's hill tribes with narration in English, French, German, Japanese and Thai. Admission to the slide show is 20B per person.

If you've already been to the Tribal Research Institute at Chiang Mai University, you'll have seen it all before; otherwise, it's a good place to visit before undertaking any hill-tribe treks. A branch of Bangkok's Cabbages & Condoms restaurant is on the premises (see Places to Eat). See Trekking for information on the PDA's trekking agency.

Tham Tu Pu If you follow the road across Saphan Mae Fah Luang to the northern side of Mae Nam Kok, you'll come to a turn-off for Tham Tu Pu 800m from the bridge. Follow this dirt road 1.2km to arrive at this network of caves in the side of a limestone

CHIANG RAI

PLACES TO STAY		
1	Rimkok Resort	
3	Chian House	
4	Dusit Island Resort	
8	Chat House	
9	Mae Kok Villa	
12	Bowling Guest House	
13	Lotus Guest House	
14	Mae Hong Son Guest House of Chiang Rai	
16	Wang Din Place	
27	Ruang Nakhon	
28	Kijnakorn Guest House	
29	Siriwattana (Closed for Renovations)	
33	Pintamorn Guest House	
36	Golden Triangle Inn	
40	Chiengrai (Chiang Rai) Hotel	
43	Paowattana Hotel	
44	Lek House	
45	Ben Guest House	
46	Ya Guest House	
47	Saenphu Hotel	
55	Siam Hotel	
59	Suknirand Hotel	
61	Krung Thong Hotel	
63	Wang Come Hotel	
70	Baan Bua	
72	Boonbundan Guest House	
73	Boonbundan Inn	

75	Wiang Inn	
79	Tourist Inn	
PLACES TO EAT		
10	Cham Cha	
32	Vegetarian Restaurant	
49	Thai-Muslim Restaurant	
51	Phetburi Restaurant; Ratburi Restaurant	
52	Rice and noodle restaurants	
54	Nakhon Pathom	
56	La Cantina; Cladia	
62	Khao Sawy Po Sai	
66	Night Market	
69	Ga-re Ga-ron	
76	Muang Thong Restaurant	
78	Bierstube	
OTHER		
2	Tha Mae Nam Kok	
5	Wat Phrat That Doi Chom Thong	
6	Wat Ngam Meuang	
7	Government Office; Town Hall	
11	TAT Office	
15	Wat Bunreuang	
17	King Mengrai Monument	
18	TOT Office	
19	Hilltribe Museum & Education Center	

20	Chiang Rai Business School	
21	Provincial Health Centre	
22	Police Station	
23	Wat Phra Singh	
24	Hospital	
25	Wat Phra Kaew	
26	CAT Office	
30	Main Post Office	
31	School	
34	Old Jail	
35	Wat Si Koet	
37	AUA	
38	Chiang Rai First Church	
39	District Office	
41	Bangkok Bank	
42	Market	
48	Wat Ming Meuang	
50	Daru Aman Mosque	
53	Teepee Bar	
57	ST Motorcycle	
58	Clock Tower	
60	DK Books	
64	THAI Office	
65	Night Bazaar	
67	Rama II Theatre	
68	Bus Terminal	
71	Tossers Bar	
74	Wat Jet Yot	
77	KM Car Rent	

NORTHERN THAILAND

cliff. At the base of the cliff is Tham Tu Pu Meditation Centre (Samnak Vipassana Tham Tu Pu), where you'll find a steep set of stairs leading up to one of the main chambers.

Trekking

More than 20 travel agencies, guesthouses and hotels offer trekking, typically in the Doi Tung, Doi Mae Salong and Chiang Khong areas. Chiang Rai's guesthouses were the first places to offer treks in the area and generally have the most experienced guides. Many of the local travel agencies merely act as brokers for guides associated with one of the local guesthouses; hence it may be cheaper to book directly through a guesthouse. As elsewhere in Northern Thailand, you're more assured of a quality experience if you use a TAT-licensed guide.

Trek pricing depends on the number of days and the number of participants, but averages 3000B per person for a four-day trek in a group of five to seven people (and

as high as 3500B to 4500B per person in a smaller group of two to four people). PDA Tours & Travel (☎ 053-740088), at the Hilltribe Education Center, claims to be the only company in Chiang Rai where profits from the treks go directly to community development projects. You'll find it open daily from 9 am to 8 pm on the centre's 2nd floor.

From Tha Mae Nam Kok (Kok River pier), boats can take you upriver as far as Tha Ton. (See Fang & Tha Ton earlier in this chapter.) An hour's boat ride from Chiang Rai is **Ban Ruammit**, which is a fair-sized Karen village. From here you can trek on your own to Lahu, Mien, Akha and Lisu villages – all of them within a day's walk. Inexpensive room and board (40B per person, meals 25B to 40B) are available in many villages in the river area. Another popular area for do-it-yourself trekkers is **Wawi**, south of the river town of Mae Salak near the end of the river route. (See the River Trip to Chiang Rai section earlier in this chapter.)

Places to Stay – Budget & Mid-Range

Guesthouses Near Mae Nam Kok (for boats from Tha Ton) is *Mae Kok Villa* (☎ 053-711786, 445 Thanon Singkhlai), which has dorm beds for 80B, bungalows with fan and cold-water bathroom for 120/150B and large singles/doubles with fan and hot-water shower for 140/190B. The owner, who speaks good English, keeps over 10 dachshunds on the property. Another nice place near Mae Nam Kok is *Chat House* (☎ 053-711481, 1 Thanon Trairat). It's an old Thai house with singles/doubles at 80B with shared bathroom, 100B to 150B with private hot-water shower, and 60B for a dorm. There are bicycles and motorcycles for rent, and 4WD and car rentals as well as guided treks can be arranged.

A bit east of here in a network of soi off Thanon Singkhlai are a couple of small family-run guesthouses. First is the clean and friendly *Bowling Guest House* (☎ 053-712704), which has five rooms with attached cold-water shower for 80/100B. A hot-water shower is available. Next is the very pleasant *Mae Hong Son Guest House of Chiang Rai* (☎ 053-715367), so named because it was once run by the same family as the original guesthouse in Mae Hong Son. Now under Dutch-Thai management, rooms start at 100/120B with shared hot-water showers, 150/180B with private ones. This guesthouse has a very nice garden cafe; the owners also rent motorcycles, teach cooking courses and organise treks.

Nearby, the new *Lotus Guest House* has 16 well-kept rooms in row houses surrounding a grassy courtyard. Simple rooms cost 80/100B without bathroom, 120/150B with attached cold shower. One room with attached hot shower is available for 150B single, and there are hot showers outside that anyone can use.

North of here on a large island separated from the city by a Mae Nam Kok tributary, *Chian House* (☎ 053-713388, 172 Thanon Si Bunruang) has simple but nicely done rooms and bungalows with private hot-water showers for 100B to 200B. There's a pool on the premises, unusual for a place this inexpensive.

Lek House (☎ 053-713337, 95 Thanon Ratchayotha) near the city centre has rooms in an old house for 70B a single/double with shared bathroom, or small bungalows with private bathroom for 120B. A row house has rooms with private bathroom for 130B. Lek rents motorcycles and a 4WD.

If you follow Soi 1 Ratchayotha south till it ends, then turn left, you'll come to the ambitious *Ben Guest House* (☎ 053-716775, 351/10 Soi 4 Thanon Sankhong Noi). Clean rooms with fan and hot-water shower in a northern-style building made of salvaged teak cost 120B downstairs and 160B upstairs, while fan rooms with private bathroom in a newer brick building go for 200B. A few rooms without facilities are available above the reception area for 80B single, 100B double. The owners speak English very well and can arrange treks with licensed guides. They also offer motorcycle and 4WD rentals.

Pintamorn Guest House (☎ 053-714161, 715427, fax 713317, 509/1 Thanon Ratanaket) has moved to a new location in the city centre. Fan rooms with shared facilities are 100B, while those with private bathroom cost 200/250/300B single/double/triple. Air-con rooms go for 350B double, and there are also two adjoining air-con rooms that sleep six for 600B.

In the southern part of town is the *Boonbundan Guest House* (☎ 053-717040, fax 712914) in a walled compound at 1005/13 Thanon Jet Yot. The choice of accommodation here includes small rooms off the garden, in huts or in the air-con building overlooking the garden – something to suit all budgets. Small dingy rooms with hot-water shower and fan are 140B but not such good value compared with other budget places in town. Better value are the large singles/doubles with a fan in the new building for 200/250B, 300/350B with air-con. If you take a left at the end of the soi and go down about 50m, you'll find the related *Boonbundan Inn* (☎ 053-752413). Rooms in the two-storey L-shaped building cost 250B with fan and 350B with air-con and TV.

Also in this vicinity is the very friendly and efficient *Tourist Inn* (☎ 053-714682, 1004/5–6 Thanon Jet Yot). Clean, large rooms are 150B with fan and private bathroom in the old house, 200/400B fan/air-con in a new building; the proprietors speak

English, Thai and Japanese, and there is a good bakery on the premises. Car and motorcycle rentals can be arranged.

In the town centre, a few steps away from Ruang Nakhon Hotel but set back from the road in a modern four-storey building, *Kijnakorn Guest House* (☎ 053-744150/1, 24 *Thanon Reuang Nakhon*) has rooms with fan for 300B and with air-con for 400B to 500B. All rooms come with TV, fridge and phone as well as hot-water showers. It's clean and new, although not very atmospheric. Friendly *Baan Bua* (☎ 053-718880), in a quiet spot off Thanon Jet Yot, offers 10 large, very clean rooms with fan for 180/200B, air-con for 300B, all in a cement row house. The well-designed rooms feature screen doors on either side to allow for insect-free cross-ventilation.

Ya Guest House (☎ 053-717090), nestled about 50m down a soi at the end of Thanon Banphaprakan, has basic rooms in a wooden building with shared facilities for 80B single/double, or 120B with private shower. A quiet garden and a lending library with hundreds of used paperbacks are Ya's main advantage.

Hotels On Thanon Suksathit near the clock tower and district government building is the well-run *Chiengrai Hotel* (Chiang Rai; ☎ 053-711266), a favourite with Thai truck drivers and travelling salespeople. Clean rooms with fan and bathroom cost 165/220/350B single/double/triple. Also centrally located is the recently renovated *Suknirand* (☎ 053-711055, fax 713701, 424/1 *Thanon Banphaprakan*), between the clock tower and Wat Ming Meuang, and near the Chiengrai Hotel. Prices start at 300B for rooms with fan, 500B for air-con. The *Siam Hotel* (☎ 053-711077, 531/6–8 Thanon Banphaprakan) is funkier and cheaper, with rates of 250/300B with fan and bathroom. *Ruang Nakhon* (☎ 053-745000, fax 745003, 25 *Thanon Reuang Nakhon*), near the hospital, allows four people to share a room with fan and bathroom for 200B, air-con doubles 300B to 400B.

If you favour the old Thai-Chinese type of hotel, check out the classic *Paowattana* (☎ 053-711722, 150 Thanon Thanalai), which has spacious, worn but clean rooms for 150B to 200B – a real find. The similarly old-fashioned *Siriwattana* (☎ 053-

711466, 485 Thanon Utarakit) next to the main post office, was closed for renovations when we visited. The clean and efficient *Krung Thong Hotel* (☎ 053-711033, fax 717848, 412 Thanon Sanambin) has large singles/doubles with fan and bathroom for 250/290B; air-con rooms cost 340B. Out of town, at 70 Thanon Phahonyothin (the highway to Mae Sai), is the *YMCA International Hotel Chiangrai* (☎ 053-713785, fax 714336). This is a very modern establishment with dorm beds for 90B and singles/doubles with fan and private bathroom for 300/400B, 400/500B with air-con. All rooms come with hot water and a telephone. Facilities include a restaurant, convention room, daycare centre and a small swimming pool. Thai massage and herbal sauna are recent additions.

Places to Stay – Top End

The *Golden Triangle Inn* (☎ 053-711339, 716996, fax 713963, 590/2 Thanon Phahonyothin) has 39 tasteful rooms with tile floors, air-con and hot water (even bathtubs) for 650/900B, including American breakfast. During the low season, April to October, the Golden Triangle knocks 100B off these rates. Also on the landscaped grounds are a cafe, a Japanese-Thai garden, a branch of AUA, a Budget car rental office and an efficient travel agency. It's a popular place, so book in advance to ensure you get in.

Of similar value in this range is the centrally located *Saenphu Hotel* (☎ 053-717300, fax 717309, 389 Thanon Banphaprakan). Rooms with all the amenities – air-con, TV, phone, fridge – start at a bargain 500B for a single or double. The hotel's basement nightclub has live music and is a very popular local rendezvous spot. *Inn Come Hotel* (☎ 053-717850, fax 717855, 176/2 Thanon Ratbamrung), south of the city centre, offers similar rooms for 650B and has a restaurant, coffee shop, karaoke and a popular disco.

The *Wiang Inn* (☎ 053-711533 e wianginn@samart.co.th, 893 Thanon Phahonyothin; in Bangkok ☎ 02-513 9804/5, fax 513 2926,) has modestly luxurious standard rooms priced at 1400/1600B (deluxe rooms are 1800/2000B), but they are readily discounted by 200B to 500B. Facilities include a swimming pool, massage parlour, bar, restaurant, coffee shop and karaoke.

Nearing the top of the Chiang Rai room-rate scale is *Wang Come Hotel* (☎ 053-711800, fax 712973, 869/90 Thanon Premawiphat; in Bangkok ☎ 02-252 7750) in the Chiang Rai Trade Centre. Comfortable rooms range from 1060B to 1600B and come with air-con, carpet, TV, fridge and phone. Suites are available for 2000B to 5500B. The hotel has a pool, banquet room, disco, coffee shop, two restaurants and a nightclub. It also rents golf clubs and provides transport to a golf course for 100B.

Perched on its own island in Mae Nam Kok (you can't miss seeing its stacked white facade if you arrive in Chiang Rai by boat), the *Dusit Island Resort* (☎ 053-715777–9, fax 715801, ⓔ chiangrai@dusit.com; in Bangkok ☎ 02-636 3333) is an island unto itself, insulating its guests from the rigours of laid-back Chiang Rai. Rooms start at 2800B, but since occupancy rates often run below 60%, the Dusit offers discounts to attract prospective guests. Facilities include Chinese and European restaurants, a coffee shop, pub, swimming pool and fitness centre.

Opposite the Dusit Island Resort on the other side of the river, the Thai-style *Rimkok Resort* (☎ 053-716445, fax 715859; in Bangkok ☎ 02-279 0102) is probably Chiang Rai's most beautiful hotel. Set in lush grounds, 256 spacious rooms with all the amenities start at 1700B. One drawback is the lack of a nearby bridge, so it's a 15-minute trip back and forth from Chiang Rai via the highway bridge at the eastern end of town. Another good choice in this range is *Wang Din Place* (☎ 053-713363, fax 716790, 341 Thanon Khae Wai), in the north-eastern corner of town near the river. Sturdy, Thai-style bungalows with fridge, TV, air-con and private hot-water shower are 800B.

The *Little Duck Hotel* (☎ 053-715620, fax 715639, ⓔ chitpong@loxinfo.co.th, 199 Thanon Phahonyothin; in Bangkok ☎ 02-691 5941/6), south of the city past the old airport, has picked up a regular clientele of Thai politicos and entrepreneurs in spite of its distance from the new airport and town. Rooms start at 1200B. Amenities include a pool and a restaurant.

Places to Eat

Thai The food scene in Chiang Rai continues to improve, and you'll find plenty of restaurants, especially along Thanon Banphaprakan

and Thanon Thanalai. *Phetburi* and *Ratburi* on Thanon Banphaprakan are cheap and good. The Phetburi has a particularly good selection of curries and other Thai dishes.

Nakhon Pathom (no English sign), yet another local restaurant named after a Central Thailand city, is very popular for inexpensive khâo man kài (Hainanese chicken rice) and kǔaytǐaw pèt yâang (roast duck with rice noodles). The restaurant is on Thanon Phahonyothin near the Banphaprakan intersection; it closes around three in the afternoon.

Muang Thong Restaurant (☎ 053-711162), just south of the Wiang Inn, has an extensive Thai and Chinese menu that includes a frog section. The house speciality is kaeng pàa pèt, a delicious duck curry made without coconut milk.

Next to the mosque on Thanon Itsaraphap is a *Thai-Muslim restaurant* with delicious khâo mòk kài, a Thai version of chicken biryani. Near the bus terminal are the usual *food stalls*; the *night market* next to the station and Rama I cinema is also good. There's a string of inexpensive *rice and noodle restaurants* along Thanon Jet Yot between Thanon Thanalai and Wat Jet Yot, near the Chiengrai Hotel. A khâo sàwy vendor called *Khao Soi Po Sai*, not far from the Wang Come Hotel in this stretch, is particularly recommended. *Mayura Bakery & Cafe*, attached to the Wang Come, sells baked goods and a selection of Thai and Western dishes.

Cham Cha, beside the TAT office, is a very good place for breakfast or lunch if you arrive at TAT tired and hungry. It has all the usual Thai and Chinese standards, along with a few Isan dishes such as lâap and sômtam not on the English menu – ice cream, too. It's open daily 7 am to 4 pm only.

For northern Thai, try the semi-outdoor *Tong Tung Restaurant* (☎ 053-756403, 1/1 Thanon Sanambin), on the western side of the road about 1km south of Thanon Banphaprakan. Most evenings the restaurant presents a program of northern-Thai dancing. So far the clientele is mostly Thai, and there's no English sign; look for a small fountain in front of the bar pavilion.

Ga-re Ga-ron (☎ 053-714165, 869/18 Thanon Phahonyothin) serves good, moderately priced international food. Well-made Thai rice and noodle dishes cost 35B; the menu also offers a good selection of Thai yam, including yam made of guava, coconut shoots and apple. Western breakfasts are available, as well as lassis and vegetarian dishes. The restaurant also has books, tapes and videos for sale.

Cabbages & Condoms (☎ 053-740784), on the grounds of the Hilltribe Museum & Education Center, serves northern-Thai food in a casual indoor/outdoor eating area. Profits from the restaurant are used by the PDA for HIV/AIDS education with the intention to make condoms as easy to find as cabbages (we'd say that objective has been achieved, as any corner store in Thailand now has condoms and you have to visit a vegetable market to find cabbage!).

There's a small, pleasant family-run Thai *vegetarian restaurant* on Thanon Wisetwiang between Utarakit and Thanalai; it's open 7 am to 3 pm only.

There are several restaurants and food vendors adjacent to the night market near the bus station.

International *Bierstube* (☎ 053-714195) on Thanon Phahonyothin south of the Wiang Inn has been recommended for German food, and there are several other Western-style pubs along here and on Thanon Suksathit/Jet Yot near the Wang Come Hotel.

Two Italian restaurants, *La Cantina* and *Cladia*, can be found side-by-side on Thanon Wat Jet Yot. Both have long menus featuring a variety of Italian dishes. Cladia offers genuine Italian espresso and cappuccino. La Cantina is open for breakfast.

Entertainment

Chiang Rai is pretty quiet at night. *Teepee Bar*, next to the Nakhon Pathom restaurant on Thanon Phahonyothin, is a hang-out for backpackers and Thai hippies, a good place to exchange information. *Sapkaset Plaza*, an L-shaped soi between Thanon Banphaprakan and Thanon Suksathit, has become a go-go bar centre.

Free northern-Thai music and dance performances are given nightly on a stage set in the *night market* area.

Shopping

Prices for antiques and silverwork are sometimes lower in Chiang Rai than in Chiang Mai. Several shops worth checking for handicrafts, silver and antiques can be found along Thanon Phahonyothin, including Gong Ngoen at No 873/5, Silver Birch at No 891 and Chiangrai Handicrafts Center at No 237. Ego, at 869/81 Thanon Premawiphak, carries upmarket items like antique textiles.

It's cheaper to buy direct from the craft vendors who set up on the sidewalk in front of the northern entrance to the bus station nightly. Adjacent to the bus station is a tourist-oriented night market that resembles Chiang Mai's but on a much smaller scale.

Getting There & Away

Air Chiang Rai International Airport is 10km north of the city. The terminal has several snack vendors, souvenir shops, a Chinese tea shop, a money exchange, a post office (open 7 am to 7 pm daily) and rental car booths. THAI has a restaurant on the upper floor. THAI flies twice daily between Chiang Rai and Chiang Mai; the flight takes 35 minutes and costs 505B. Daily flights are also available to/from Bangkok (1¼ hours, 2230B). There is talk of flights from Hong Kong, Kunming, Vientiane and Mandalay, but as long as Chiang Mai's airport fields flights from these cities it's not likely.

Chiang Rai's THAI office (☎ 053-711179, 222279) is at 870 Thanon Phahonyothin, not far from the Wang Come Hotel.

Taxis into town from the airport cost 150B. Out to the airport you can get a túk-túk for 80B to 100B.

Bus There are two routes to Chiang Rai from Chiang Mai: an old and a new. The old route (*săi kào*) heads south from Chiang Mai to Lampang before heading north through Ngao, Phayao and Mae Chai to Chiang Rai. If you want to stop at these cities, this is the bus to catch, but the trip will take up to seven hours. In Chiang Mai the bus leaves from Thanon Chiang Mai-Lamphun, near Saphan Nawarat; the fare is 83B (ordinary only).

The new route (*săi mài*) heads north-east along Rte 118, stopping in Doi Saket and Wiang Papao, and takes about four hours. The fare is 66B ordinary, 92B 2nd-class aircon or 119B for 1st-class air-con. New-route 'green buses' (*rót meh khĭaw*) leave from Chiang Mai's Arcade bus terminal. Chiang Mai to Chiang Rai buses are sometimes stopped for drug searches by police.

The bus terminal is on Thanon Prasopsuk, several blocks south of Thanon Phahonyothin.

NORTHERN THAILAND

Other bus services from Chiang Rai include:

destination	fare	duration (hrs)
Bangkok		
ordinary	241B	11
air-con	337B	10
1st class	439B	10
VIP	640B	10
Ban Huay Khrai (for Doi Tung)		
ordinary	14B	1
Ban Pasang		
ordinary	10B	¾
Chiang Saen		
ordinary	20B	1½
Chiang Khong		
ordinary	37B	2½
Khon Kaen		
ordinary	226B	13
air-con	264B	13
1st class	339B	13
Lampang		
ordinary	30B	2½
air-con	47B	2
1st class	71B	2
Mae Chan		
ordinary	10B	¾
Mae Sai		
ordinary	20B	1½
air-con	37B	1½
Mae Sot		
ordinary	176B	7½
air-con	317B	7½
Mae Suai		
ordinary	16B	1¼
air-con	30B	1
1st class	35B	1
Nan		
ordinary	90B	6
Phayao		
ordinary	15B	1¾
air-con	25B	1¾
1st class	30B	1¾
Phitsanulok		
ordinary	139B	6
air-con	195B	5
Phrae		
ordinary	74B	4
air-con	104B	4
1st class	134B	4
Tak		
ordinary	148B	6½
air-con	176B	6½

Boat One of the most popular ways of getting to Chiang Rai is the river trip from Tha Ton (see the River Trip to Chiang Rai section earlier in this chapter).

For boats heading upriver on Mae Nam Kok, go to the pier in the north-western corner of town. The boats leave daily at 10.30 am. Regular long boats from Chiang Rai stop at the following villages along the Kok (times are approximate for ideal river conditions):

destination	fare	duration (hrs)
Ban Ruammit	50B	1
Hat Yao	80B	2¼
Kok Noi	100B	3
Mae Salak	150B	4
Phah Khwang	90B	2½
Pong Nam Rawn	60B	1½
Tha Ton	200B	5

You can charter a boat to Ban Ruammit for 650B or all the way to Tha Ton for 1600B. Call Chiang Rai Boat Tour (☎ 053-750009) for further information.

Getting Around

A săamláw ride anywhere in central Chiang Rai should cost 20B to 30B. Túk-túk cost twice as much. A city săwngthăew system (10B fare) circulates along the main city streets; there are also route túk-túk that charge 15B to 20B.

Several small agencies near the Wang Come Hotel rent cars (around 1200B a day), vans (1300B to 1500B) and Suzuki Caribian 4WDs (800B). The following charge a little more than the local offices:

Avis Rent-A-Car (☎ 053-793827) Chiang Rai
  International Airport
Budget Rent-A-Car (☎ 053-740442/3) 590
  Thanon Phahonyothin, Golden Triangle Inn
  complex
National Car Rental (☎ 053-793683) Chiang
  Rai International Airport; Dusit Island Resort

Bicycles and motorcycles can be hired at ST Motorcycle (☎ 053-713652), who appear to take good care of their motorcycles. They are near the clock tower on Thanon Banphaprakan, but get there early as they often run out in the morning. Daily bike rental costs 60B to 100B a day. Motorcycle rentals start at 150B per day for older

Honda Dreams (200B for newer ones) up to 660B per day for a 250cc Yamaha TTR. ST has a second location (☎ 053-752526) on Thanon Wat Jet Yot. Motorcycles can also be rented at many of the guesthouses.

MAE SALONG
แม่สลอง(สันติคีรี)

postcode 57240

The village of Mae Salong (Santikhiri) was originally settled by the 93rd Regiment of the KMT, which fled to Myanmar from China after the 1949 Chinese revolution. After futile intermittent rear guard action against the Chinese communists, the renegades were forced to flee Myanmar in 1961 when the Yangon government decided they wouldn't allow the KMT to remain legally in northern Myanmar. Crossing into Northern Thailand with their pony caravans, the ex-soldiers and their families settled into mountain villages and re-created a society much like the one they left behind in Yunnan.

After the Thai government granted the KMT refugee status in the 1960s, efforts were made to incorporate the Yunnanese

KMT and their families into the Thai nation. Until the late 1980s they didn't have much success, as many ex-KMT persisted in involving themselves in the Golden Triangle opium trade in a three-way partnership with opium warlord Khun Sa and the Shan United Army (SUA). Because of the rough, mountainous terrain and lack of sealed roads, the outside world was rather cut off from the goings-on in Mae Salong. Hence the Yunnanese were able to ignore attempts by Thai authorities to suppress opium activity and tame the region.

Infamous Khun Sa made his home in nearby Ban Hin Taek (now Ban Theuat Thai) until the early 1980s when he was finally routed by the Thai military. Khun Sa's retreat to Myanmar seemed to signal a change in local attitudes and the Thai government finally began making progress in its pacification of Mae Salong and the surrounding area.

In a further effort to separate the area from its old image as an opium fiefdom, the Thai government officially changed the name of the village from Mae Salong to Santikhiri (Hill of Peace). Until the 1980s

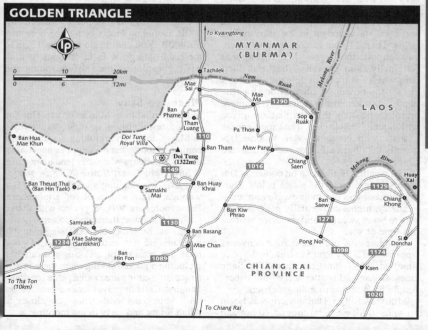

GOLDEN TRIANGLE

pack horses were used to move goods up the mountain to Mae Salong, but today the 36km road from Basang (near Mae Chan) to Santikhiri is paved and well travelled. The Yunnanese immigrants' equestrian history, alien to the Thais, has led the latter to refer to them as *jiin haw* ('galloping Chinese').

Despite the ongoing 'Thai-isation' of Mae Salong, the town is unlike any other in Thailand. The combination of pack horses (still used locally), hill tribes (Akha, Lisu, Mien, Hmong) and southern Chinese–style houses conjures up images of a small town or village in Yunnan Province in China. It's not unusual for hotels and restaurants in Mae Salong to boast satellite reception of three TV channels from China and three from Hong Kong. Although the Yunnanese dialect of Chinese remains the lingua franca, the new generation of young people look more to Bangkok than Taipei for their social and cultural inspirations. Many have left for greater educational and career opportunities.

One of the most important government programs is the crop-substitution plan to encourage hill tribes to cultivate tea, coffee, corn and fruit trees. This seems to be quite successful, as there are plenty of these products for sale in the town markets, and tea and corn are abundant in the surrounding fields. There is a **tea factory** in town where you can taste the fragrant Mae Salong teas (originally from Taiwan). The local illicit corn whisky is much in demand – perhaps an all-too-obvious substitution for the poppy. Another local speciality is Chinese herbs, particularly the kind that are mixed with liquor (*yaa dawng*). Thai and Chinese tourists who come to Mae Salong frequently take back a bag or two of assorted Chinese herbs.

The weather is always a bit cooler on **Doi Mae Salong** than on the plains below. During the cool and dry months, November to February, nights can actually get cold – be sure to bring sweaters and socks for visits at this time of year.

An interesting morning market convenes from around 5 to 7 am (5 to 6 am is the peak time) at the T-junction near Shin Sane Guest House and is attended by hill tribespeople from the surrounding districts.

Minivans full of Thai day-trippers begin arriving in Mae Salong around 10 am and leave by 4 pm. If you can stay overnight you'll pretty much have the place to yourself in the mornings and evenings.

Trekking

Shin Sane Guest House has a wall map showing approximate routes to Akha, Mien, Hmong, Lisu, Lahu and Shan villages in the area. Nearby Mien, Akha and Lisu villages are less than half a day's walk away.

The best hikes are north of Mae Salong between Ban Theuat Thai and the Myanmar border. Ask about political conditions before heading off in this direction (towards Myanmar), however. Shan and Wa armies competing for control over this section of the Thailand-Myanmar border occasionally clash in the area. A steady trade in amphetamines and, to a lesser extent, heroin, flows across the border via several conduit villages.

It's possible to walk south from Mae Salong to Chiang Rai in three or four days, following trails that pass through fairly remote hill-tribe villages. There are also several easily reached hill-tribe villages along the highway between Ban Basang and Mae Salong, but these days they're full of day tourists from Chiang Rai.

Shin Sane Guest House arranges six-hour horseback treks to four nearby villages for 600B, including lunch, or a three-hour trek for 400B. You could also trek the 12km to the Lahu village of Ja-Ju on your own. A basic guesthouse there offers rooms and two meals a day for 50B per person.

Places to Stay

Since the road from Mae Salong to Tha Ton opened, fewer visitors are opting to overnight in Mae Salong. The resulting surplus of accommodations often make prices negotiable, except at holidays when they tend to increase.

Shin Sane Guest House (Sin Sae; ☎ 053-765026), Mae Salong's original hotel, is a wooden affair with a bit of atmosphere. Basic rooms are 50B per person with shared hot-water shower; there are also some newer cabins at the back for 200B single/double with private hot-water showers and good beds. Information on trekking is available, including a good trekking map; there is also a nice little eating area and a place for doing laundry. Calls to prayer from a mosque behind Shin Sane will bring you closer to Allah bright and early in the morning.

The **Golden Dragon Inn** (☎ 053-765009), directly opposite the mosque, offers clean bungalows with balconies and private hot-water showers for 200B. Recently added hotel-type rooms cost 300B; each with two double beds and private hot shower.

Mae Salong Villa (☎ 053-765114–9, fax 765039), just below the town centre, has clean rooms and bungalow-style accommodation in a garden setting from 600B to 1200B – this is better value than the Mae Salong Resort. The restaurant offers a nice view of the mountains, and the food is quite good. High-quality tea, grown on the proprietor's tea estate, can be purchased here.

At the top of the price range is the 59-room **Mae Salong Resort** (☎ 053-765014, fax 765135), where a variety of so-so rooms and bungalows (they look good from a distance but are none too clean) cost 500B to 2000B. An exhibit hall on the grounds displays interesting old photographs, captioned in English, from the KMT era. The Yunnanese restaurant here is very good – especially tasty are the fresh mushroom dishes.

On the opposite side of town near the afternoon market, on the road to Tha Ton, the once-upmarket **Khum Nai Phol Resort** (☎ 053-765001–3, fax 765004) is under new management and not as well kept as it once was. Modern hotel-style rooms are available for 500B single/double.

Places to Eat

Paa-thâwng-kŏh and hot soybean milk at the morning market are a good way to start the day. Don't miss the many street noodle vendors who sell khànŏm jiin náam ngíaw, a delicious Yunnanese rice-noodle concoction topped with a spicy pork sauce – Mae Salong's most famous local dish and a gourmet bargain at 15B per bowl.

Around town you'll find a variety of places serving simple Chinese snacks like fluffy mantou (plain steamed Chinese buns) and saalaapao (pork-stuffed Chinese buns) with delicious pickled vegetables. Many of the Chinese in Mae Salong are Muslims, so you'll find several **Muslim Chinese restaurants** serving khâo sàwy.

Salema Restaurant, located halfway between the Shin Sane Guest House and the day market, serves tasty Yunnanese dishes using locally grown shitake mushrooms at moderate prices.

Of the hotel restaurants, the Mae Salong Villa's is best. Try the local speciality of black chicken steamed in Chinese medicinal herbs

Several **tea houses** in town selling locally grown teas offer complimentary tastings in very traditional, elaborate procedures involving the pouring of tea from a tall, narrow cup into a round cup to enhance the experience of the tea's fragrance.

Getting There & Away

Mae Salong is accessible via two routes. The original road, Rte 1130, winds west from Ban Basang, about 2km north of Mae Chan. Newer Rte 1234 approaches from the south, allowing easier access from Chiang Mai. The older route is definitely more spectacular.

To get to Mae Salong by public transport, take a bus from Mae Sai or Chiang Rai to Ban Basang, just north of Mae Chan. From Ban Basang, there are săwngthăew up the mountain to Mae Salong for 50B per person (down again costs 40B); the trip takes about an hour. This service stops at around 5 pm; you can charter a săwngthăew in either direction for 300B.

The bus fare from Chiang Rai to Ban Basang is 16B. You can also reach Mae Salong by road from Tha Ton. See the earlier Fang & Tha Ton section for details.

MAE SAI

แม่สาย

postcode 57130 • pop 60,000

The northernmost point in Thailand, Mae Sai is a good place from which to explore the Golden Triangle, Doi Tung and Mae Salong. It's also a good spot to observe border life, as Mae Sai is one of the few official land crossings open between Myanmar and Thailand. Don't come expecting bags of atmosphere; the town is little more than a modern trading post.

Foreigners are permitted to cross the border to Tachileik (the town opposite Mae Sai, spelt Thakhilek by the Thais) and continue as far as Kengtung, 163km from Thailand and 100km short of China. Within a few years, the road should be open all the way to the Chinese border – already the town seems to be gearing up for Thailand-China traffic.

NORTHERN THAILAND

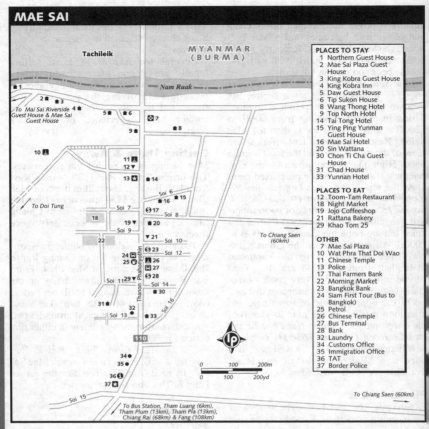

MAE SAI

PLACES TO STAY
1 Northern Guest House
2 Mae Sai Plaza Guest House
3 King Kobra Guest House
4 King Kobra Inn
5 Daw Guest House
6 Tip Sukon House
8 Wang Thong Hotel
9 Top North Hotel
14 Tai Tong Hotel
15 Ying Ping Yunman Guest House
16 Mae Sai Hotel
20 Sin Wattana
30 Chon Ti Cha Guest House
31 Chad House
33 Yunnan Hotel

PLACES TO EAT
12 Toom-Tam Restaurant
18 Night Market
19 Jojo Coffeeshop
21 Rattana Bakery
29 Khao Tom 25

OTHER
7 Mae Sai Plaza
10 Wat Phra That Doi Wao
11 Chinese Temple
13 Police
17 Thai Farmers Bank
22 Morning Market
23 Bangkok Bank
24 Siam First Tour (Bus to Bangkok)
25 Petrol
26 Chinese Temple
27 Bus Terminal
28 Bank
32 Laundry
34 Customs Office
35 Immigration Office
36 TAT
37 Border Police

(See the Around Mae Sai section for current details on this trip.) In spite of the opening, Thai tourists are much more commonly seen in Mae Sai than fàràng.

Burmese lacquerware, gems, jade and other goods from Laos and Myanmar are sold in shops along the main street. Many Burmese come over during the day from Tachileik to work or do business, hurrying back by sunset. Gem dealers from as far away as Chanthaburi frequent the **gem market** opposite the police station.

Take the steps up the hill near the border to **Wat Phra That Doi Wao**, west of the main street, for superb views over Myanmar and Mae Sai. This wát was reportedly constructed in memory of a couple of thousand Burmese soldiers who died fighting

KMT here in 1965 (you'll hear differing stories around town, including a version wherein the KMT are the heroes). There are also some interesting trails in the cliffs and hills overlooking the Mae Sai Guest House and the river. A persistent rumour says there's a gated cave tunnel that crosses to Myanmar beneath the Nam Ruak; the entrance is supposedly within the grounds of Wat Tham Phah Jom.

Mae Sai is a base for exploring the nearby caves of **Tham Luang**, **Tham Pum** and **Tham Pla**, as well as the trip to Doi Tung (see Around Mae Sai).

In February 2001, as this book was going to press, Burmese forces, apparently in pursuit of Shan State Army rebels, shelled and fired on parts of Mae Sai, invoking retaliatory shelling from the Thai army. During the fighting the whole of Mae Sai was evacuated and the border area was subsequently closed for a time. Check the current situation before travelling to Mae Sai.

Places to Stay

Guesthouses Near the town entrance and the bus terminal is *Chad House* (☎ 053-732054, fax 642496), off the main street a bit in a residential neighbourhood. The English-speaking Thai-Shan family that runs it is friendly and helpful, and the food is good. Simple rooms are 100/150B with shared hot-water shower. There are a couple of 200B bungalows with private bathroom, and space on a bamboo floor is 50B per person.

On Soi 14 off Thanon Phahonyothin is *Chon Ti Cha Guest House* (☎ 053-732068) with 12 clean, well-worn motel-style rooms – all with Thai-style toilet and cold-water shower. Fan rooms are 180B; rooms with air-con and TV are 300B. A Thai restaurant is attached, but very little English is spoken.

Farther down the same soi as Mae Sai Hotel, the *Ying Ping Yunnan Guest House* (☎ 053-640507) offers 12 very clean rooms with fan, TV, phone and hot-water shower for 200B to 250B – good value. There's a Chinese restaurant on the premises. Not much English is spoken.

Right on the Nam Ruak (Ruak River) west of the international bridge is the friendly *Northern Guest House* (☎ 053-731537), where a variety of rooms and huts are available from 60/80B for basic singles/ doubles with shared bathroom, or up to 300B (350B air-con) for a double with hot-water shower and river view. A new air-con building has fancier rooms for 350B. Add 50B to 100B to these rates in the high season. The guesthouse maintains a nicely landscaped sitting area along the river; a restaurant on the premises offers room service, and is open from 7 am to midnight.

East of the Northern Guest House on the southern side of the road (no river frontage), *King Kobra Guest House* (☎ 053-733055, e kkmaesai@chmai.loxinfo.co.th) features apartment-style rooms with private hot-water shower and fans costing 150/250B, plus more inexpensive rooms with shared facilities costing 100/120B. King Kobra Guest House offers trekking and motor-cycle tours in the Mae Sai area and into

Myanmar as far as Kengtung and Mengla (Mong La), as well as 4WD tours. A minimum of four people is necessary for the Myanmar journeys. Next door to King Kobra Guest House, the affiliated *King Kobra Inn* has air-con rooms for 350B, or nicer VIP rooms for 450B, including breakfast. Email service is available.

In the same vicinity, the Yunnanese-owned *Daw Guest House* (☎ 053-640476) has five very large rooms for 160/200B with fan and hot-water shower. The proprietor speaks excellent English. A bit east of Daw Guest House is the new three-storey *Tip Sukon House* (☎ 053-642816, 01-883 7318). All rooms are spotless and have private hot-water showers. One-bed rooms on the first floor are 200B, while air-con VIP rooms on the second floor are 400B, each with TV and a balcony overlooking the street. The third floor houses 300B doubles with fan and TV.

Farther west, and just back from the river, is the rambling, 71-room *Mae Sai Plaza Guest House* (☎ 053-732230). This huge hillside bamboo and wood complex has a laid-back atmosphere and a cafe overlooking the road but we've received complaints about the general lack of cleaning and maintenance here. There are three levels with room rates ranging from 80B to 120B. Add 50B to these rates during high season. Between Mae Sai Plaza and Mae Sai Guest House, next to the river landing for local Thai-Burmese trade, the *Mae Sai Riverside Guest House* (☎ 053-732554) offers clean, secure rooms for 150B with fan and private bathroom, 200B with hot water.

Another 150m west, *Mae Sai Guest House* (☎ 053-732021) has a nicely landscaped and scenic location on the river across from Myanmar. It's a walk of about a kilometre from the end of Mae Sai's main road and thus very quiet. Nicely designed bungalows with shared hot-water shower cost 100/200B, while bungalows with private bathroom cost 200B to 500B. There's a restaurant and treks can be arranged.

Hotels *Mae Sai Hotel* (☎ 053-731462), off Thanon Phahonyothin on Soi 6 in the centre of town, isn't a bad budget choice. Rooms with fan and private bathroom are 200B single/double, while air-con rooms with hot-water shower are 350B. *Sin Wattana*

(☎ 053-731002) is on the same side of Thanon Phahonyothin across from the market; fairly well-kept rooms cost from 200B with private cold-water shower and fan, 300B with air-con.

About 100m before the turn-off for Chad Guest House is the friendly but somewhat gaudy-looking *Yunnan Hotel* (☎ 053-642169), with a beer garden in front. Nice rooms sleeping up to three people cost 350B and come with fan, hot water and TV; air-con VIP rooms with the same plus sofa and fridge cost 500B.

Top North Hotel (☎ 053-731955, fax 732331), on the western side of Thanon Phahonyothin towards the bridge, has comfortable singles/doubles with private bathroom for 300/400B; add hot water for 500B, air-con for 550B or air-con, fridge and TV for 600B.

Tai Tong Hotel (Thai Thong; ☎ 053-731975, fax 640988, 6 Thanon Phahonyothin) has smaller standard rooms for 300B, somewhat larger rooms for 500B and suites for 900B. The rates for the larger rooms and suites include breakfast for two. All come with air-con and hot water.

The nine-storey *Wang Thong Hotel* (☎ 053-733389, fax 733399), off Thanon Phahonyothin in the northern part of town, entertains brisk traffic among business travellers. Spacious, international-class rooms with all the amenities are 900B single/double, while suites are available for up to 1500B, not including tax and service. Facilities include a swimming pool, pub, disco and restaurant. Off-street parking is available in a guarded lot behind the hotel.

Places to Eat

Many *food stalls* offering everything from khâo sàwy to custard set up at night on the sidewalks along Thanon Phahonyothin. The *night market* is rather small but the Chinese vendors do excellent *kǔaytǐaw phàt sii-íu* (rice noodles stir-fried in soy sauce) and other noodle dishes. You can also get fresh paa-thâwng-kǒh and hot soy milk.

Jojo Coffeeshop on Thanon Phahonyothin serves very good Thai curries and Thai vegetarian dishes, plus ice cream and Western snacks. You'll eat well while contemplating the collection of Lanna-style wooden Buddhas along the walls; note that it's only open from 6.30 am to 4.30 pm.

For late eats your best bet is *Khao Tom 25* near Chad House, open from about noon to 4 am nightly. South of the Chinese temple and north of the police station is *Toom-Tam Restaurant*, a Muslim place with good curries and *khâo mòk*.

Rattana Bakery, north of Soi 10 on the main drag, offers Thai-style pastries and cakes. It's open 8 am to 5 pm.

Getting There & Away

Buses to Mae Sai leave frequently from Chiang Rai and cost 20B (37B air-con) for the 1½-hour trip. To/from Chiang Saen by bus costs 20B via Mae Chan. See Getting Around in the Chiang Saen section for details on different routes between Mae Sai and Chiang Saen.

To/from Chiang Mai it's 83B by ordinary bus (three departures a day) or 116/149B 2nd/1st-class air-con (seven a day); this trip takes about four to five hours. VIP buses to Bangkok leave Mae Sai at 6.30, 7 and 7.10 pm.

There are also direct buses to Mae Sai from Fang (39B) and Tha Ton (33B) via the paved Tha Ton-Mae Chan road. Other destinations include Doi Tung (35B), Mae Chan (12B), Mae Salong (55B) and Sop Ruak (30B). Mae Sai's main bus terminal (☎ 053-646403) is 2km south of the immigration office, a 5B shared sǎwngthǎew ride.

Bangkok Siam First Tour operates VIP 'sleeper' buses from Mae Sai to Bangkok that leave at about 5.30 or 6 pm daily for 450B to 640B depending on the number of seats; the journey takes around 13 hours.

Ordinary government buses to Bangkok cost around 245B and depart from the main street at 5.30 am and 4, 5 and 5.30 pm. Second-class air-con (343B), 1st-class air-con (441B) and VIP (685B) buses are also available.

Getting Around

Sǎwngthǎew around town are 5B shared. Túk-túk cost 20B to 30B and motorcycle taxis 10B to 20B. Guesthouses in Mae Sai have stopped renting motorcycles, but Honda Dreams can be rented at Pornchai on Thanon Phahonyothin between Siam First Tour and the petrol station for 150B per day. Thong Motorbike, across from Tip Sukon House, also rents motorcycles for 150B.

AROUND MAE SAI

Tham Luang
ถ้ำหลวง

About 6km south of Mae Sai off Rte 110 is Tham Luang, which is a large cave that extends into the hills for at least a couple of kilometres, possibly more. The first cavern is huge, and a narrow passage at the back leads to a series of other chambers and side tunnels of varying sizes. The first kilometre is fairly easy going but after that you have to do some climbing over piles of rocks to get farther in. At this point the roof formations become more fantastic and tiny crystals make them change colour according to the angle of the light. For 30B you can borrow a gas lantern from the caretakers in front of the cave or you can take someone along as a guide (for which there's no fixed fee; just give them whatever you want). Guides aren't always available during the week.

Tham Pum & Tham Pla
ถ้ำปุ่ม/ถ้ำปลา

Only 13km south of Mae Sai, just off Rte 110 at Ban Tham, are a couple of caves with freshwater lakes inside. Bring a torch to explore the caves as there are no lights. Another attraction here is the unique cake-like chedi in front of the cave entrance. It's a very large, multi-tiered structure stylistically different from any other in Thailand.

Doi Tung
ดอยตุง

About halfway between Mae Chan and Mae Sai on Rte 110 is the turn-off west for Doi Tung. The name means 'Flag Peak', from the northern-Thai word for flag (tung). King Achutarat of Chiang Saen ordered a giant flag to be flown from the peak to mark the spot where two chedi were constructed in AD 911; the chedi are still there, a pilgrimage site for Thai, Shan and Chinese Buddhists.

But the main attraction at Doi Tung is getting there. The 'easy' way is via Rte 149, which is mostly paved to the peak of Doi Tung. But it's winding, steep and narrow, so if you're driving or riding a motorcycle, take it slowly.

Along the way are Shan, Akha and Musoe (Lahu) villages. Opium is cultivated near Doi Tung and this can be a dangerous area to explore alone if you go far off the main roads. Travelling after 4 pm – when traffic thins out – is not advised except along the main routes. It is not safe to trek in this area without a Thai or hill-tribe guide simply because you could be mistaken for a USDEA agent (by the drug traders) or drug dealer (by the Thai army rangers who patrol the area). You may hear gunfire from time to time, which might indicate that the rangers are in pursuit of MTA or Karen rebels or others who have been caught between two hostile governments.

On the theory that local hill tribes will be so honoured by a royal presence that they will stop cultivating opium, the late Princess Mother (the king's mother), who passed away in 1995, built the **Doi Tung Royal Villa**, a summer palace, on the slopes of Doi Tung near Pa Kluay Reservoir. The beautifully landscaped **Mae Fah Luang Garden** is open to the public, and the royal villa itself has been converted into a museum that preserves everything in the house almost exactly as it was before the Princess Mother's death.

Another royal project nearby, **Doi Tung Zoo**, covers an open space of over 32 hectares. The zoo was first established as a wildlife breeding and animal conservation station, to help reintroduce many species to a reforested Doi Tung. These include Siamese fireback pheasants, peacocks, bears, sambar deer, barking deer and hog deer.

At the peak, 1800m above sea level, **Wat Phra That Doi Tung** is built around the twin Lanna-style chedi. The chedi were renovated by famous Chiang Mai monk Khruba Siwichai early in the 20th century.

Pilgrims bang on the usual row of temple bells to gain merit. Although the wát isn't that impressive, the high forested setting will make the trip worthwhile. From the walled edge of the temple you can get an aerial view of the snaky road you've just climbed.

A walking path next to the wát leads to a spring, and there are other short walking trails in the vicinity. A bit below the peak is the smaller **Wat Noi Doi Tung**, where food and beverages are available from vendors.

Places to Stay Part of the Doi Tung Development Project, **Baan Ton Nam** (☎ 053-767003, fax 767077) opened in 2000 and offers 45 deluxe twin rooms with attached hot-water shower, air-con, refrigerators and satellite TV for 1500B. A semi-outdoor restaurant offers excellent meals made with local produce, including lots of fresh mushrooms.

Getting There & Away Buses to the turn-off for Doi Tung are 12B from either Mae Chan or Mae Sai. From Ban Huay Khrai, at the Doi Tung turn-off, a săwngthăew to Ban Pakha is 25B, or 60B all the way to Doi Tung, 18km away.

Road conditions to Doi Tung vary from year to year depending on the state of repair; during bad spells, the section above Pakha can be quite a challenge to climb, whether you're in a truck, 4WD or motorcycle.

You can also travel by motorcycle between Doi Tung and Mae Sai along an even more challenging 16km unevenly sealed road that starts in the Akha village of Ban Phame, 8km south of Mae Sai (4km south along Rte 110, then 4km west), and joins the main road about two-thirds of the way up Doi Tung – about 11km from the latter. You can also pick up this road by following the dirt road that starts in front of Mae Sai's Wat Doi Wao. West of Ban Phame the road has lots of tight curves, mud, rocks, precipitous drops, passing lorries and occasional road repair equipment – figure on at least an hour by motorcycle or 4WD from Mae Sai. Although now paved this is a route for experienced bikers only. The road also runs high in the mountains along the Myanmar border and should not be travelled alone or after 4 pm. Ask first in Mae Sai about border conditions. If you want to do a full loop from Mae Sai, ride/drive to Doi Tung via Rte 110 south of Mae Sai, then Rte 1149 up to Doi Tung. Once you've had a look around the summit, return to Mae Sai via the Bang Phame aforementioned roads; this means you'll be running downhill much of the way.

Cross-Border Trips to Tachileik & Beyond

Foreigners are ordinarily permitted to cross the bridge over the Nam Ruak into Tachileik. On occasion – such as in May 1994 when the MTA bombed the Tachileik dyke (draining the reservoir that supplied the town with water) – the border closes for a while for security reasons, so be prepared for possible disappointment if the situation deteriorates again.

For now you can enter Myanmar at Tachileik and travel to Kengtung or Mengla for two weeks upon payment of a US$10 fee and the exchange of US$100 for 100 FEC (foreign exchange certificates), the phoney money Myanmar's government uses to dampen black-market currency exchange. You can use the FEC to pay for hotel rooms and plane tickets, but that's about all. Or change them for Myanmar kyat at the going black-market rate. Your two-week tourist visa can be extended for another two weeks at the immigration office in Kengtung.

If you only want to cross the border into Tachileik for the day, the cost is US$5 or 250B. There is no FEC exchange requirement for day trips. Besides shopping for Shan handicrafts (about the same price as on the Thai side, and everyone accepts baht) and eating Shan/Burmese food, there's little to do in Tachileik. About 4000 people cross the bridge to Tachileik daily, most of them Thais shopping for dried mushrooms, herbal medicines, cigarettes and other cheap imports from China. Be wary of cheap cartons of Marlboros and other Western-brand cigarettes, as many are filled with Burmese cigarettes instead of the real thing.

Three-night, four-day excursions to the town of Kengtung (called Chiang Tung by the Thais and usually spelt Kyaingtong by the Burmese), 163km north, may be arranged through King Kobra Guest House in Mae Sai or you can do it on your own as described earlier.

Kengtung is a sleepy but historic capital for the Shan State's Khün culture – the Khün speak a northern-Thai language related to Shan and Thai Lü and use a writing script similar to the ancient Lanna script. It's a bit more than halfway between the Thai and Chinese borders – eventually the road will be open all the way to China but for now Kengtung is the limit. Built around a small lake, and dotted with ageing Buddhist temples and crumbling British colonial architecture, it's a much more scenic town than Tachileik, and one of the most interesting towns in Myanmar's entire Shan

State. About 70% of all foreign visitors to Kengtung are Thais seeking a glimpse of ancient Lanna. Few westerners are seen around town save for contract employees working for the UNDCP (United Nations Drug Control Project).

The road trip allows glimpses of Shan, Akha, Wa and Lahu villages along the way. *Harry's Guest House & Trekking* (☎ 101-21418), at 132 Mai Yang Rd in Kengtung, rents basic rooms in a large house for US$5 per person. Harry is an English-speaking Kengtung native who spent many years as a trekking guide in Chiang Mai. The *Noi Yee Hotel* near the centre of town costs US$8 to US$15 per person per night in large multibed rooms.

For a complete description of Kengtung and the surrounding area, see Lonely Planet's *Myanmar* guidebook.

Beyond Kengtung Eighty-five kilometres north of Kengtung lies the Sino-Burmese border district of Mengla (or Mong La as it's sometimes spelt). Although Mengla is mainly a Thai Lü district, in a deal worked out with the Myanmar military it's currently controlled by ethnic Wa, who once fought against Yangon troops but who now enjoy peaceful relations with Yangon (in return for a sizable share in the Wa's thriving amphetamine and opium trade, it is suspected). A Drug Free Museum contains an exhibit on how to refine heroin from opium. The district receives lots of Chinese tourists, who come to peruse Mengla's well-known wildlife market and to gamble in the district's several casinos. The largest and plushest, the Myanmar Royal Casino, is an Australian-Chinese joint venture. There are also plenty of karaokes, discos and other staples of modern Chinese entertainment life. The main currency used in town is the Chinese yuan.

In order to proceed to Mengla from Kengtung, you must first register at the Kengtung immigration office. The staff at Harry's Guest House can help you accomplish this, or if you take a tour via King Kobra Guest House, these details will be taken care of for you.

The obvious question is, can you cross the border from Mengla into Daluo, China? The simple answer is we haven't tried, and we don't know anyone who has.

Getting There & Away The cheapest form of transport to Kengtung is the săwngthăew that leave each morning from Tachileik, but reports say Myanmar authorities aren't allowing foreigners to board these. Give it a try anyway, as this sort of situation tends to change. You can rent 4WDs on either side of the border, but Thai vehicles with a capacity of five or fewer passengers are charged a flat US$50 entry fee, US$100 for vehicles with a capacity of over five. Burmese vehicle hire is more expensive and requires the use of a driver. Whatever the form of transport, count on at least six to 10 gruelling hours (depending on road conditions) to cover the 163km stretch between the border and Kengtung.

The road is slowly being improved and will eventually be paved all the way to the Chinese border.

CHIANG SAEN
เชียงแสน

postcode 57150 • pop 54,698
A little more than 60km from Chiang Rai, Chiang Saen is a small crossroads town on the banks of the Mekong River. Scattered throughout the town are the ruins of the Chiang Saen kingdom, a Lanna principality founded in 1328 by King Mengrai's nephew Saenphu. Surviving architecture includes chedi, Buddha images, wíhǎan pillars and earthen city ramparts. A few of the old monuments still standing predate Chiang Saen by a couple of hundred years; legend says this pre-Chiang Saen kingdom was called Yonok. Formerly loosely affiliated with various northern-Thai kingdoms, as well as 18th-century Myanmar, Chiang Saen didn't really become a Siamese possession until the 1880s. A 19th-century American missionary wrote that the city was:

... admirably situated for purposes of trade, at the intersection of routes leading from China, Burmah, Karenni, the Shan States, Siam, Tonquin and Annam. It forms, in fact, a centre of intercourse between all the Indo-Chinese races and the point of dispersion for caravans along the diverging trade routes.

Yunnanese trade routes extended from Simao, Yunnan, through Laos to Chiang Saen and then on to Mawlamyaing in Burma, via Chiang Rai, Chiang Mai and

Mae Sariang. A lesser-used route proceeded through Utaradit, Phayao and Phrae.

The sleepy town hasn't changed too much in spite of Golden Triangle commercialisation, which is concentrated in nearby Sop Ruak. Practically everything in Chiang Saen closes down by 9 pm. Chiang Saen is an official border crossing for Thai and Lao citizens travelling by ferry to and from the Lao PDR town on the opposite side of the river, Thon Phuak.

Information

Tourist Offices The visitors centre on the left-hand side as you come into town from the west has a good relief display showing the major ruin sites as well as photos of various stupas before, during and after restoration. The centre is open 8.30 am to 4.30 pm Monday to Sunday.

Immigration Chiang Saen's immigration office is on the south-western corner of the main intersection in town.

Money Siam Commercial Bank has an ATM and currency exchange.

Chiang Saen National Museum
พิพิธภัณฑสถานแห่งชาติเชียงแสน

Near the town entrance, a small museum displays artefacts from the Lanna period and prehistoric stone tools from the area, as well as hill-tribe crafts, dress and musical instruments. It's open 9 am to 4 pm Wednesday to Sunday and the admission fee is 30B.

Wat Chedi Luang
วัดเจดีย์หลวง

Behind the museum to the east are the ruins of Wat Chedi Luang, which features an 18m octagonal chedi in the classic Chiang Saen or Lanna style. Archaeologists argue about its exact construction date but agree it dates to some time between the 12th and 14th centuries.

Wat Pa Sak
วัดป่าสัก

About 200m from the Pratu Chiang Saen are the remains of Wat Pa Sak, where the ruins of seven monuments are visible. The

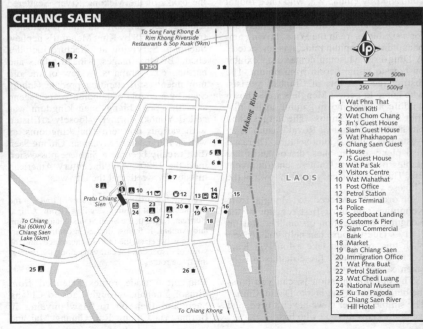

CHIANG SAEN

To Song Fang Khong & Rim Khong Riverside Restaurants & Sop Ruak (9km)

1290

Mekong River

LAOS

To Chiang Rai (60km) & Chiang Saen Lake (6km)

Pratu Chiang Sien

To Chiang Khong

1 Wat Phra That Chom Kitti
2 Wat Chom Chang
3 Jin's Guest House
4 Siam Guest House
5 Wat Phakhaopan
6 Chiang Saen Guest House
7 JS Guest House
8 Wat Pa Sak
9 Visitors Centre
10 Wat Mahathat
11 Post Office
12 Petrol Station
13 Bus Terminal
14 Police
15 Speedboat Landing
16 Customs & Pier
17 Siam Commercial Bank
18 Market
19 Ban Chiang Saen
20 Immigration Office
21 Wat Phra Buat
22 Petrol Station
23 Wat Chedi Luang
24 National Museum
25 Ku Tao Pagoda
26 Chiang Saen River Hill Hotel

NORTHERN THAILAND

main mid-14th century stupa combines elements of the Hariphunchai and Sukhothai styles with a possible Burmese Bagan influence. Since these ruins form part of a historical park, there is a 20B admission fee.

Wat Phra That Chom Kitti
วัดพระธาตุจอมกิตติ

About 2.5km north of Wat Pa Sak on a hill top are the remains of Wat Phra That Chom Kitti and Wat Chom Chang. The round chedi of Wat Phra That is thought to have been constructed before the founding of the kingdom. The smaller chedi below it belonged to Wat Chom Chang. There's nothing much to see at these chedi, but there's a good view of Chiang Saen and the river from the top of the hill.

Wat Phakhaopan
วัดผ้าขาวป้าน

Inside the grounds of this living wát near the river stands a magnificent Lanna-period chedi. The large square base contains walking Lanna-style Buddhas in niches on all four sides. The Buddha facing east is sculpted in the so-called 'calling for rain' mudra, with both hands held straight at the image's sides – a pose common in Laos and not so common in Thailand.

Mekong River Trips

A relatively new boat landing and customs station stand alongside the Chiang Saen waterfront. Boats from China, Laos and Myanmar can be seen unloading their cargoes in the mornings.

Six-passenger speedboats (reua rehw) will go to Sop Ruak (half an hour) for 400B per boat one way or 700B return, or all the way to Chiang Khong (1½ to two hours) for 1300B one way or 1700B return, depending on your bargaining skills.

See Mekong River Cruises in the Sop Ruak section later in this chapter for information on services from that town.

Places to Stay

Chiang Saen does not have any accommodation standouts. With a few exceptions, guesthouse rooms are in need of repair and bathrooms need better maintenance. An exception is the *JS Guest House* (☎ 053-777060), about 100m off the main road near the post office. Tidy, simple rooms in a long concrete building cost 100B single/double with clean shared bathroom; beds in a dorm are 60B. A solar hot-water shower is available in the proprietor's house, and vegetarian Thai meals can be arranged. The guesthouse also rents bicycles for 40B per day.

Faded *Chiang Saen Guest House* offers singles/doubles with shared bathroom in a house for 70/90B. A-frame bungalows in need of repair with private bathroom cost 200B – not a good value. It's on the road to Sop Ruak, opposite the river.

A bit farther along this road on the same side, *Siam Guest House* offers singles/doubles in huts with mosquito nets for 70/120B with shared bathroom, 130/160B with private bathroom. Oddly enough, none of the rooms have fans. This guesthouse also has a pleasant-looking cafe.

Farther north on the edge of town (about 1.5km from the bus terminal) is the secluded *Jin's Guest House* (☎ 053-650847) with a variety of accommodation possibilities (all with attached bathroom) and a variety of prices ranging from 200B to 300B. An upstairs veranda is a good place to watch the Mekong flow by. Mountain bike and motorcycle rentals are available. Visas for Laos can be arranged; Jin also puts together custom tours with car, driver and guide according to the interests of guests.

The clean, four-storey *Chiang Saen River Hill Hotel* (☎ 053-650826, fax 650830, 714 Mu 3 Tambon Wiang; in Bangkok ☎ 02-748 9046–8, fax 748 9048) features good service and some nice northern-Thai touches to the furnishings. All the rooms cost 1000B single/double (down to 850B in low season) and contain a fridge, TV and phone, along with a floor sitting area furnished with Thai axe pillows, a Thai umbrella and a small rattan table.

Places to Eat

Cheap noodle and rice dishes are available at *food stalls* in and near the market on the river road and along the main road through town from the highway, near the bus stop. A small *night market* sets up each evening at the latter location and stays open till around midnight.

During the dry months, *riverside vendors* sell sticky rice, green papaya salad, grilled chicken, dried squid and other fun foods for people to eat while sitting on grass mats along the river bank in front of Chiang Saen Guest House – a very pleasant way to spend an evening. Local specialities include fish or chicken barbecued inside thick joints of bamboo, eaten with sticky rice and sôm-tam.

Ban Chiang Saen is a friendly little wooden pub in the centre of town with cold beer and Thai *kàp klâem* (drinking snacks).

Two *sŭan aahǎan* (food garden)–style riverside restaurants off the river road out of Chiang Saen towards Sop Ruak, ***Song Fang Khong*** and ***Rim Khong***, offer extensive menus of Thai, Chinese and Isan food. Bring your Thai-language skills.

Getting There & Away

There are frequent buses from Chiang Rai to Chiang Saen for 20B. The trip takes between 40 minutes and 1½ hours, depending on traffic, number of passengers getting on and off etc.

From Chiang Mai, ordinary/air-con buses cost 73B/130B and take up to five hours. In either direction, be sure to ask for the new route (sǎi mài) via Chiang Rai. The old route (sǎi kào) passes through Lamphun, Lampang, Ngao, Phayao and Phan, a trip that takes from seven to nine hours. You can also take a bus first to Chiang Rai then change to a Chiang Saen bus, a trip of about 4½ hours.

Buses to Bangkok depart Chiang Saen at 3 pm (261B ordinary) and 5 pm (470B 1st class air-con). A VIP bus (730B) also leaves Chiang Saen at 5 pm.

Laos A 30B ferry service between Thon Phuak, Laos, and Chiang Saen is open only to Thai and Lao citizens. The crossing is open 8 am to 6 pm.

Getting Around

A good way to see the Chiang Saen–Mae Sai area is on two wheels. Mountain bikes (50B a day) and motorcycles (15B to 200B) can be rented at Jin's Guest House, while JS rents regular bicycles for 40B.

From Mae Sai to Chiang Saen there's a choice of two scenic paved roads (one from the centre of Mae Sai and one near the town entrance), or a wider, busier paved road via Rte 110 to Mae Chan and then Rte 1016 to Chiang Saen.

The roads out of Mae Sai are considerably more direct but there are several forks where you have to make educated guesses on which way to go (there are occasional signs). The two roads join near the village of Mae Ma, where you have a choice of going east through Sop Ruak or south through Pa Thon. The eastern route is more scenic.

AROUND CHIANG SAEN
Sop Ruak
สบรวก

Nine kilometres north of Chiang Saen is Sop Ruak, the official 'centre' of the Golden Triangle where the borders of Myanmar, Thailand and Laos meet, at the confluence of Nam Ruak and the Mekong River. In historical terms, 'Golden Triangle' actually refers to a much larger geographic area, stretching thousands of square kilometres into Myanmar, Laos and Thailand, within which the opium trade is prevalent. Nevertheless hoteliers and tour operators have been quick to cash in on the name by referring to the tiny village of Sop Ruak as 'the Golden Triangle', conjuring up images of illicit adventure even though the adventure quotient here is close to zero. In northern Thai this village is pronounced 'Sop Huak'; many out-of-town Thais don't know either Thai name and simply call it 'Sam Liam Thong Kham' (sǎam lìam thawng kham; Thai for 'Golden Triangle').

Tourists have replaced opium as the local source of gold. Sop Ruak has in fact become something of a tourist trap, with souvenir stalls, restaurants, a massage place and bus loads of package-tour visitors during the day. In the evenings things are quieter.

One place worth a visit is the **House of Opium**, a small museum with historical displays pertaining to opium culture. Exhibits include all the various implements used in the planting, harvest, use and trade of *Papaver somniferum* resin, including pipes, weights, scales and so on, plus photos and maps. Most labels are in Thai only. The museum is at the 30km marker, at the southeastern end of Sop Ruak. A little shop at the front of the museum sells souvenir opium pipes for 80B, more authentic ones from China for 1500B to 1800B, and antique ones for 10,000B or more. The museum is open 7 am to 6 pm daily; admission is 20B.

On the southern edge of town a huge pier and attached Thai-Lao-Chinese-Myanma Department Store shopping centre complex is under construction. The pier is meant to serve passenger-boat traffic between Sop Ruak and China – once the red tape has cleared and such a service becomes established.

On the Burmese side of the river junction stands the Golden Triangle Paradise Resort, a huge hotel and casino financed by Thai and Japanese business partners who have leased nearly 3000 rài (480 hectares) from the Myanmar government. Only two currencies – baht and dollars – are accepted at the hotel.

Ten kilometres north of Chiang Saen on a plot of about 40 hectares opposite Le Meridien Baan Boran, the Mah Fah Luang Foundation is building a 5600-sq-metre **Opium Exhibition Hall**. This educational centre intends to become the world's leading exhibit and research facility for the study of the history of opiate use around the world; the expected completion date is 2002.

Mekong River Cruises Local long-tail boat or speedboat trips can be arranged through several local agents. The typical trip involves a 40-minute circuit around a large island and upriver for a view of the Burmese casino hotel for 400B per person. Longer trips head down river as far as Chiang Khong for 1800B per person return.

On longer trips you can stop off at a Lao village on the large river island of Don Sao, roughly halfway between Sop Ruak and Chiang Saen. The Lao immigration booth here is happy to allow day visitors onto the island without a Lao visa. A 20B arrival tax is collected from each visitor. There's not a lot to see, but there's an official post office where you can mail letters or postcards with a Lao PDR postmark, a few shops selling T-shirts and Lao handicrafts, and the *Sala Beer Lao*, where you can drink Lao beer and munch on Lao snacks.

Places to Stay & Eat Most budget travellers stay in Chiang Saen these days. Virtually all the former budget places in Sop Ruak have given way to souvenir stalls and larger tourist hotels. *Akha Guest House*, a kilometre south of Sop Ruak on the road to Chiang Saen, has simple huts for 200B per night. Just south of Akha Guest House is *Bamboo Hut* (☎ 053-650077, 769084), a cluster of bamboo huts near the Mekong with a central bar area and shared bathroom for 190B single/double.

Jumping right into the top-end hotel category, *Imperial Golden Triangle Resort* (☎ 053-784001–5, fax 784006; in Bangkok ☎ 02-653 2201) is on a hillside overlooking the river and offers 1st-class accommodation costing from 2500B including buffet breakfast.

Also at the top end, the 110-room *Le Meridien Baan Boran Hotel* (☎ 053-784084, fax 784096; in Bangkok ☎ 02-653 2201) is on a secluded hillside spot off the road between Sop Ruak and Mae Sai. Designed by Thai architect ML Tridhosyuth Devakul, the Baan Boran melds classic northern-Thai design motifs with modern resort hotel tricks like cathedral ceilings and skylights. To fit the naughty Golden Triangle image, one of the restaurants is called *Suan Fin* (Opium Field) and is decorated with poppy motifs; windows off the dining area serve up a view of Myanmar and Laos in the distance. The hotel bar is called Trafficker Rendezvous. A swimming pool, jacuzzi, tennis and squash courts, gym, sauna, medical clinic, karaoke and two restaurants round out the amenities. What does it cost to stay amid this glorification of the regional narcotics trade? Rates range from 4180B to 10,260B, plus tax and service.

Of the several tourist-oriented restaurants overlooking the Mekong in Sop Ruak, the best is *Sriwan*, opposite the Imperial Golden Triangle Resort.

Getting There & Away From Chiang Saen to Sop Ruak, a săwngthăew/share taxi costs 10B; these leave every 20 minutes or so throughout the day. It's an easy bike ride from Chiang Saen to Sop Ruak.

Chiang Khong
เชียงของ

postcode 57140 • pop 9000
At one time Chiang Khong was part of a small river-bank meuang (city-state) called Juon, founded in AD 701 by King Mahathai. Over the centuries Juon paid tribute to Chiang Rai, then Chiang Saen and finally Nan before being occupied by the Siamese in the 1880s. The territory of Chiang Khong

CHIANG KHONG

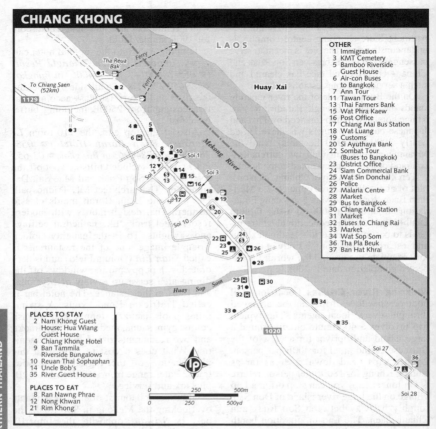

OTHER
1 Immigration
3 KMT Cemetery
5 Bamboo Riverside
  Guest House
6 Air-con Buses
  to Bangkok
7 Ann Tour
11 Tawan Tour
13 Thai Farmers Bank
15 Wat Phra Kaew
16 Post Office
17 Chiang Mai Bus Station
18 Wat Luang
19 Customs
20 Si Ayutthaya Bank
22 Sombat Tour
  (Buses to Bangkok)
23 District Office
24 Siam Commercial Bank
25 Wat Sin Donchai
26 Police
27 Malaria Centre
28 Market
29 Bus to Bangkok
30 Chiang Mai Station
31 Market
32 Buses to Chiang Rai
33 Market
34 Wat Sop Som
35 Tha Pla Beuk
36 Ban Hat Khrai

PLACES TO STAY
2 Nam Khong Guest
  House; Hua Wiang
  Guest House
4 Chiang Khong Hotel
9 Ban Tammila
  Riverside Bungalows
10 Reuan Thai Sophaphan
14 Uncle Bob's
35 River Guest House

PLACES TO EAT
8 Ran Nawng Phrae
12 Nong Khwan
21 Rim Khong

extended all the way to Yunnan Province in China until the French turned much of the Mekong River's northern bank into French Indochina in 1893.

More remote yet more lively than Chiang Saen, Chiang Khong is an important market town for local hill tribes and for trade with northern Laos. Nearby are several villages inhabited by Mien and White Hmong. Among the latter are contingents who fled Laos during the 1975 communist takeover and who are rumoured to be involved in an organised resistance movement against the current Lao government.

The current town of Chiang Khong has several northern Thai–style wát of minor interest. **Wat Luang**, on the main road, was once one of the most important temples in Chiang Rai Province and features a chedi dating to the 13th century (restored in 1881).

On a hill overlooking the town of Chiang Khong and the river is a **Nationalist Chinese Soldiers Cemetery** where over 200 KMT soldiers have been buried. The grave mounds are angled on the hill so that they face China. A shrine containing old photos of KMT soldiers-in-arms stands at the top of the hill.

The village of **Ban Hat Khrai**, about 1km south of Chiang Khong, is famous as being one of the few places where *plaa bèuk* (giant Mekong catfish) are still caught (see the 'Plaa Bèuk' boxed text). During the plaa bèuk season, April and May, you can watch the small fishing boats coming and going

Plaa Bèuk

The Mekong River stretch that passes Chiang Khong is an important fishing ground for the *plaa bèuk* (giant Mekong catfish, *pangasianodon gigas* to ichthyologists) probably the largest freshwater fish in the world. A plaa bèuk takes at least six and possibly 12 years (no-one's really sure) to reach full size, when it will measure 2m to 3m in length and weigh up to 300kg. Locals say these fish swim all the way from Qinghai Province (where the Mekong originates) in northern China. In Thailand and Laos its flesh is revered as a delicacy; the texture is very meaty but has a delicate flavour, similar to tuna or swordfish, only whiter in colour.

These fish are only taken between mid-April and May when the river depth is just 3m to 4m and the fish are swimming upriver to spawn in Erhai Lake, Yunnan Province, China. Before netting them, Thai and Lao fishermen hold a special annual ceremony to propitiate Chao Mae Pla Beuk, a female deity thought to preside over the giant catfish. Among the rituals comprising the ceremony are chicken sacrifices performed aboard the fishing boats. After the ceremony is completed, fishing teams draw lots to see who casts the first net, and then take turns casting.

Anywhere from 15 to 60 catfish are captured in a typical season, and the catfish hunters guild is limited to 40 men, all natives of Ban Hat Khrai. Fishermen sell the meat on the spot for up to 500B per kilo (a single fish can bring up to 100,000B in Bangkok); most of it ends up in Bangkok or Chiang Mai restaurants, since local restaurants in Huay Xai and Chiang Khong can't afford such prices. Sometimes you can sample the catfish during harvest season in a makeshift restaurant near the fishermen's landing in Ban Hat Khrai.

Although the plaa bèuk is on the CITES list of endangered species, there is some debate as to just how endangered it is. Because of the danger of extinction, Thailand's Inland Fisheries Department has been taking protective measures since 1983, including a breed-and-release program. Every time a female is caught, it's kept alive until a male is netted, then the eggs are removed (by massaging the female's ovaries) and put into a pan; the male is then milked for sperm and the eggs are fertilised in the pan. As a result, well over a million plaa bèuk have been released into the Mekong since 1983. Of course, not all of the released fish survive to adulthood.

from **Tha Pla Beuk**, about 2km south of Chiang Khong on the Mekong; the turn-off is near the 137km marker.

Huay Xai, opposite Chiang Khong on the Lao side of the river, is a legal point of entry for Laos. Anyone with a valid Laos visa may cross by ferry. From Huay Xai it's 250km to Luang Nam Tha, a short distance from Boten, a legal border crossing to and from China – see Border Crossing (Laos) later in this section for more information.

Trade between Thailand and China via Chiang Khong is steady. Thai goods going north include dried and processed food and beverages, cosmetics, machinery, spare parts and agro-industrial supplies.

The Si Ayuthaya, Thai Farmers and Siam Commercial Banks have branches in town with ATMs and foreign exchange services.

Places to Stay There are several guesthouses at the northern end of town in a neighbourhood called Ban Wiang Kaew. Near the old ferry pier, *Nam Khong Guest House (053-655102, fax 655277, [e] phayao98@hotmail.com)* and *Hua Wiang Country Guest House* have a variety of simple hut accommodations overlooking the Mekong for 40B to 150B, with separate hot showers.

A little farther south-east, *Bamboo Riverside Guest House (☎ 053-791621, 791629)* offers thatched huts with dorm beds for 70B, or private units for 150B to 250B, all with fan and attached hot shower. A restaurant perched on a deck overlooks the river.

Old standby *Ban Tammila Riverside Bungalows (☎ 053-791234)* offers simpler huts overlooking the river for 100B with shared bathroom, 200B with private bathroom; there's also a very pleasant sitting/ dining area by the river. Ban Tammila receives a lot of repeat business.

Next door to Ban Tammila Riverside Bungalows is the more upmarket **Reuan Thai Sophaphan** (☎ 053-791023), which has rooms in a wooden hotel-like building for 100B with shared bathroom, 150B to 200B with hot-water shower. A new wing by the river has rooms for 350B to 500B, while fancier rooms in the main building with TV cost up to 600B.

Farther north and towards the river road from Chiang Saen is the **Chiang Khong Hotel** (☎ 053-791182). Plain but nicely kept singles/doubles with hot-water shower and fan are 150/200B.

A little north-west of Wat Phra Kaew, **Uncle Bob's** has six rooms in an old wooden building for 80/120B with shared facilities (including a hot-water shower).

South of town in an area known as Ban Sop Som, on the way to Tha Pla Beuk, is **River Guest House** with nicely designed multilevel wooden structures with rooms for 150B with fan, mosquito net and shared bathroom, 250B with attached bathroom.

Places to Eat There are a number of rice and noodle shops along the main street, none of them particularly good. Just north-west of the entrance to Ban Tammila Riverside Bungalows **Ran Nawng Phrae** serves good khâo sàwy, Western breakfasts, kǔaytǐaw and *aahǎan taam sàng* (food made to order). Just opposite the entrance to Ban Tammila, **Nong Khwan** does vegetarian food.

The **Rim Khong**, on a narrow road down by the river, is a simple indoor/outdoor restaurant overlooking the river. The bilingual menu is much shorter than the Thai menu; yam are the house speciality, but the kitchen can make just about anything.

Getting There & Away From Chiang Saen, graded and paved 52km-long Rte 1129 is the quickest way to come from the west. A second 65km road curving along the river has also been paved and provides a slower but less trafficked alternative. With mountains in the distance and the Mekong to one side, this road passes through picturesque villages and tobacco and rice fields before joining Rte 1129 just outside Chiang Khong.

Buses leave hourly between Chiang Rai and Chiang Khong from around 4 am to 5 pm; ditto to/from Chiang Saen. Buses from Chiang Rai and beyond use roads from the south (primarily Rte 1020) to reach Chiang Khong. The Chiang Rai bus costs 37B and takes about 2½ hours; there are hourly departures approximately from 6 am to 5 pm daily. These stop more or less opposite the Bamboo Riverside Guest House.

First-class government air-con buses to/from Bangkok cost 470B, depart at 7 am and 3.30 pm and take around 13 hours. Second-class air-con buses depart six times between 7 am and 7 pm and cost 370B. Ordinary buses leave Chiang Khong at 5.30 pm and cost 250B. There's also a private company with a 4 pm 1st-class bus for 450B.

Boats taking up to 10 passengers can be chartered up the Mekong River from Chiang Khong to Chiang Saen for 1800B. Boat crews can be contacted near the customs pier behind Wat Luang, or farther north at the pier for ferries to Laos.

Border Crossing (Laos) Ferries to Huay Xai, Laos, leave frequently between 8 am and 5.30 pm from Tha Reua Bak, a pier at the northern end of Chiang Khong, for 20B each way. A new pier was recently built about 100m south-east of the Tha Reua Bak, but when we visited it wasn't yet in use.

As long as you hold a visa valid for Laos, there should be no problem crossing. If you don't already have a visa, Ann Tour (☎ 053-655198, fax 791218), on the main road in town near Ban Tammila Guest House, can arrange a 15-day visa in one day (except on weekends and holidays) for US$50 or the baht equivalent; if you submit your passport to the office at 8 am, they'll have it back to you, complete with visa, by 3 pm – in time to get across the river and start your Laos journey. If you can wait three working days, your visa will only cost 1300B. A 30-day visa takes three to five days to process; the fee ranges from 1450B to 2050B depending on your nationality. Ann Tour can also arrange vehicle permits to take cars (7000B) or motorcycles (4000B to 5000B) into Laos.

Plans to build a bridge across the Mekong here were aborted in 1997 following the baht crash. If the bridge ever gets built, it will, of course, replace the ferry service. Completion of a bridge might also affect the visa situation. Either way there is talk of allowing visas on arrival in Huay Xai. Ask at the local guesthouses for the latest information.

Once on the Lao side you can continue on by road to Luang Nam Tha and Udomxai or by boat down the Mekong to Luang Prabang and Vientiane. Lao Aviation flies from Huay Xai to Vientiane a couple of times a week.

Phrae Province

Phrae Province is probably most famous for the distinctive sêua mâw hâwm, the indigo-dyed cotton farmer's shirt seen all over Thailand. 'Made in Phrae' has always been a sign of distinction for these staples of rural Thai life, and since the student-worker-farmer political solidarity of the 1970s, even Thai university professors like to wear them. The cloth is made in Ban Thung Hong outside the town of Phrae. A good place to buy mâw hâwm clothes in Phrae is **Maw Hawm Anian**, a shop about 60m from the south-eastern gate (Pratu Chai) into the old city.

The annual Rocket Festival kicks off the rice-growing season in May. In Phrae the biggest celebrations take place in **Long** and **Sung Men** districts. Look for launching towers in the middle of rice fields for the exact location.

Sung Men district is also known for **Talat Hua Dong**, a market specialising in carved teak wood. Phrae has long been an important teak centre. Along Rte 101 between Phrae and Nan you'll see a steady blur of teak forests (they are the thickest around the 25km marker). Since the 1989 national ban on logging, these forests are all protected by law. Most of the provincial teak business now involves recycled timber from old houses. Specially licensed cuts taken from fallen teak wood may also be used for decorative carvings or furniture (but not in house construction).

The province of Phrae and its neighbouring province of Nan have been neglected by

tourists and travellers alike because of their remoteness from Chiang Mai, but from Den Chai – on the northern train route – they're easily reached by bus along Rte 101.

PHRAE
อ.เมืองแพร่

postcode 54000 • pop 21,600
Like Chiang Mai and Lampang, Phrae has an old city partially surrounded by a moat alongside a river (here, Mae Nam Yom). Unlike Chiang Mai, Phrae's old city still has lots of quiet lanes and old teak houses – if you're a fan of traditional Thai teak architecture, you'll find more of it here than in any other city of similar size anywhere in Thailand. The local temple architecture has successfully resisted Central Thai influence over the centuries as well. It's a bit unusual since you'll find a mix of Burmese, northern-Thai (Nan and Lanna) and Lao styles.

South-east of the old city, the newer, more modern Phrae looks like any other medium-sized town in Thailand.

If you're in the market for baskets or woven mats, a shop called Kamrai Thong (no Roman-script sign) near Pratu Chai carries a fine selection of hand-woven basketry.

Information
Phrae's main post office stands near the centre of the old city near the traffic circle; hours are 8.30 am to 4.30 pm weekdays and 9 am to noon on Saturday. Long-distance calls can be made at the CAT office (attached to the main post office) daily from 8 am to 8 pm.

Bangkok Bank and Krung Thai Bank, both on Thanon Charoen Meuang, offer foreign exchange services during normal banking hours (8.30 am to 3.30 pm weekdays); both also have ATMs.

Wat Luang
วัดหลวง

This is the oldest wát in the city, probably dating to the founding of the city in the 12th or 13th century. **Phra That Luang Chang Kham**, the large octagonal Lanna-style chedi, sits on a square base with elephants supporting it (cháang khám) on all

NORTHERN THAILAND

four sides, surrounded by kùtì and coconut palms. As is sometimes seen in Phrae and Nan, the chedi is usually swathed in Thai Lü fabric.

The veranda of the main wíhǎan is in the classic Luang Prabang–Lan Xang style but has unfortunately been bricked in with laterite. Opposite the front of the wíhǎan is **Pratu Khong**, part of the city's original entrance gate. No longer used as a gate, it now contains a statue of Chao Pu, an early Lanna ruler. The image is sacred to local residents, who leave offerings of fruit, flowers, candles and incense.

Also on the temple grounds is a **museum** displaying temple antiques, ceramics and religious art dating from the Lanna, Nan, Bago and Mon periods. A 16th-century, Phrae-made sitting Buddha on the 2nd floor is particularly exquisite. There are also some 19th-century photos with English labels on display, including some gruesome shots of a beheading. The museum is usually open weekends only, but the monks will sometimes open it on weekdays upon request.

Wat Phra Non
วัดพระนอน

South-west a few hundred metres from Wat Luang is a 300-year-old wát named after its highly revered reclining Buddha image (phrá nawn). The bòt was built around 200 years ago and has an impressive roof with a separate two-tiered portico and gilded carved wooden facade with Ramayana scenes. The wíhǎan behind the bòt contains the Buddha image, swathed in Thai Lü cloth with bead and foil decoration.

Wat Jom Sawan
วัดจอมสวรรค์

Outside the old city on Thanon Ban Mai, this temple was built by local Shan in the late 19th and early 20th centuries, and shows Shan and Burmese influence throughout. The well-preserved wooden wíhǎan and bòt have high, tiered, tower-like roofs like those found in Mandalay. A large copper-crowned chedi has lost most of its stucco to reveal the artful brickwork beneath. A prized temple possession in the main wíhǎan is a Tripitaka section consisting of 16 ivory 'pages' engraved in Burmese.

Other Temples
Across from the post office in the old city, **Wat Phra Baht Ming Meuang** houses a Buddhist school, an old chedi, an unusual octagonal drum tower made entirely of teak and the highly revered Phra Kosai, which closely resembles the Phra Chinnarat in Phitsanulok. Just outside the north-eastern corner of the moat, **Wat Sa Baw Kaew** is a Shan-Burmese–style temple similar to Wat Jom Sawan. **Wat Phra Ruang**, inside the old city, is typical of Phrae's many old city wát, with a Nan-style, cruciform-plan bòt, a Lao-style wíhǎan and a Lanna chedi. Or is this unique mix a coherent design of local (Nan-Phrae) provenance that has yet to be identified?

Vongburi House
บ้านวงศ์บุรี

Opened as a private museum in 1997, this two-storey teak house was constructed between 1897 and 1907 for Luang Phongphibun (the last prince of Phrae) and his wife Chao Sunantha, who once held a profitable teak concession in the city. Elaborate carvings on gables, eaves, balconies and above doors and windows are in very good condition. Inside, many of the house's 20 rooms display late 19th-century teak antiques, documents (including early 20th-century slave concessions), photos and other artefacts from the bygone teak dynasty era. Most are labelled in English as well as Thai.

The house is open 8 am to 5 pm daily. Call ☎ 054-620153 for further information,

Ban Prathup Jai
บ้านประทับใจ

On the outskirts of town is Ban Prathup Jai (bâan pràtháp jai; Impressive House), also called Ban Sao Roi Ton (Hundred Pillar-Filled House), a large northern-style teak house that was built using more than 130 teak logs, each over 300 years old. Opened in 1985, the house took four years to build, using timber taken from nine old rural houses. The interior pillars are ornately carved. It's also filled with souvenir

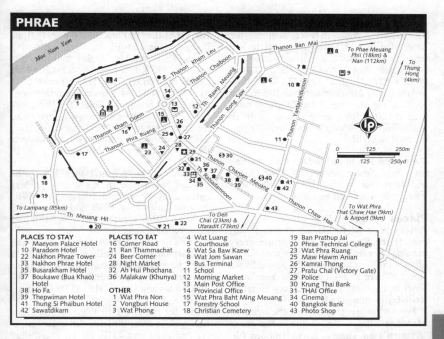

PHRAE

Mae Nam Yom

Thanon Ban Mai

To Phae Meuang
Phii (18km) &
Nan (112km)

To
Thung
Hong
(4km)

Thanon Kham Leu

Thanon Chaiboon

Thanon Kham Doem

Th Rawp Meuang

Thanon Rong Saw

Thanon Yantarakitkoson

Thanon Phra Ruang

Thanon Charoen Meuang

Thanon Ratsadamnoen

Th Meuang Hit

Thanon Chaw Hae

To Lampang (85km)

To Den
Chai (23km) &
Utaradit (73km)

To Wat Phra
That Chaw Hae (9km)
& Airport (9km)

0   125   250m
0   125   250yd

PLACES TO STAY	PLACES TO EAT		4 Wat Luang	19 Ban Prathup Jai
7 Maeyom Palace Hotel	16 Corner Road		5 Courthouse	20 Phrae Technical College
10 Paradorn Hotel	21 Ran Thammachat		6 Wat Sa Baw Kaew	23 Wat Phra Ruang
22 Nakhon Phrae Tower	24 Beer Corner		8 Wat Jom Sawan	25 Maw Hawm Anian
33 Nakhon Phrae Hotel	28 Night Market		9 Bus Terminal	26 Kamrai Thong
35 Busarakham Hotel	32 Ah Hui Phochana		11 School	27 Pratu Chai (Victory Gate)
37 Boukawe (Bua Khao)	36 Malakaw (Khunya)		12 Morning Market	29 Police
Hotel			13 Main Post Office	30 Krung Thai Bank
38 Ho Fa	**OTHER**		14 Provincial Office	31 THAI Office
39 Thepwiman	1 Wat Phra Non		15 Wat Phra Baht Ming Meuang	34 Cinema
41 Thung Si Phaibun Hotel	2 Vongburi House		17 Forestry School	40 Bangkok Bank
42 Sawatdikarn	3 Wat Phong		18 Christian Cemetery	43 Photo Shop

NORTHERN THAILAND

vendors and is rather tackily decorated, re-inforcing the fact that 'impressive' is a relative term. It's open 8 am to 5 pm daily; admission is 20B. Call ☎ 054-511008 for information.

Places to Stay – Budget

Several inexpensive hotels can be found along Thanon Charoen Meuang, including *Ho Fa* (no Roman-script sign; ☎ 054-511140) and *Thepwiman* (☎ 054-511103), both of which have rooms starting in the 100B to 160B range; Thepwiman is still the better of the two.

The friendly *Thung Si Phaibun* (Toongsri Phaibool; ☎ 054-511011, 84 Thanon Yantarakitkoson) has clean rooms with fan and bathroom for 130B to 180B, air-con for 300B. *Sawatdikarn* at No 76–78 is similar to the Thung Si Phaibun but not as well kept; rooms start at 100B.

South-east of the Nakhon Phrae Hotel on the same side of Thanon Ratsadamnoen is the *Busarakham Hotel* (☎ 054-511437), a low- to medium-priced place with decent rooms with fan for 180B per person, 300B per person for air-con.

Places to Stay – Mid-Range & Top End

Nakhon Phrae Hotel (☎ 054-511122, fax 521937, 29 Thanon Ratsadamnoen) is a mere two-minute walk from the old city. Large singles/doubles with fan and hot water cost 200B in the old wing (250B with TV); across the street in the new wing, standard rooms with fan and TV are 350B, air-con rooms with TV are 500B, and rooms with TV and fridge are 560B. Local tourist information is available in the lobbies of both wings.

Paradorn Hotel (Pharadon; ☎ 054-511177, 177 Thanon Yantarakitkoson) has OK-priced singles/doubles with fan and bathroom for 200/250B and air-con rooms for 350B. Information on local attractions is available in the lobby, but the hotel is looking a bit run-down these days.

Towards the top of the scale in Phrae is the *Maeyom Palace Hotel* (☎ 054-521028–38, fax 522904), on Thanon Yantarakitkoson 100m north-east of the Paradorn. Rooms with air-con, carpet, TV, phone and fridge cost from 1000B to 2000B, although low occupancy rates mean you can easily get a room for 600/800B. Hotel facilities include a pool and two restaurants; the hotel also provides free transport to and from the Phrae bus terminal and airport.

A luxury hotel, *Nakhon Phrae Tower* (☎ *054-521321, fax 521937, 3 Thanon Meuang Hit*) offers quality similar to that found at the Maeyom Palace. Official rates start at 1200B for a standard room with all the amenities, although this is readily discounted to 660B.

Den Chai If you are in Den Chai waiting for a train, *Saeng Sawang* (☎ *054-613367*) and *Yaowarat* (☎ *054-613293*) offer adequate rooms for 80B to 120B.

Places to Eat
A very good *night market* convenes just outside the Pratu Chai intersection every evening. Several *food vendors* also set up nightly in the soi opposite the Sawatdikarn Hotel. There's another *night market* a block or two behind the Paradorn Hotel on weekday evenings only.

For a slow evening repast, the open-air *Malakaw* (the name on the menu reads 'Khunya') on Thanon Ratsadamnoen (diagonally opposite the Busarakham Hotel) offers good-quality Thai food and drink in a rustic ambience of rough-cut wooden tables and chairs beneath lots of hanging plants. It's open daily from 3.30 pm to midnight.

Also on Thanon Ratsadamnoen, near the Nakhon Phrae Hotel and Busarakham Hotel, are several other eating spots. A Chinese coffee shop next to the Nakhon Phrae Hotel, *Ah Hui Phochana*, offers strong coffee and various noodle and rice dishes in the evening.

Corner Road, an indoor/outdoor place two blocks south-west of the traffic circle in the old city on Thanon Kham Doem, is decorated with lots of wood and old movie photos and serves good rice and noodle dishes for 40B to 50B and Thai dishes for 60B to 90B. The indoor section is air-con. An English menu is available, and there's live music in the evenings. *Beer Corner* near the night market is similar but more rustic.

On Thanon Saisibut is *Ran Thamachat* (no Roman-script sign), a Thai vegetarian place open from 7 am to 7 pm.

Getting There & Away
Air THAI flies to Phrae thrice weekly from Bangkok for 1530B; the flight takes 1½ hours. There are also flights to/from Phitsanulok (495B, four times weekly) and Nan (370B, once daily). The THAI office (☎ 054-511123) is at 42–44 Thanon Ratsadamnoen, near the Nakhon Phrae Hotel. The Phrae airport is 9km south-east of town via the same road that goes to Wat Phra That Chaw Hae; THAI operates a free shuttle service between the airport and the THAI office.

Bus Ordinary buses from Bangkok's Northern and North-Eastern bus terminal depart twice daily (9 am and 10 pm) for 160B. Air-con buses cost 288B and leave twice nightly; VIP (sleeper) buses cost 445B and leave twice nightly.

From Chiang Mai's Arcade bus terminal, ordinary buses leave daily at 6.30 and 9 am (65B, four hours). Air-con buses leave from the same terminal several times daily between 8 am and 10 pm (91B, 117B 1st class).

Train By train to Den Chai station from Bangkok it costs 90B for 3rd class, 207B for 2nd class and 431B for 1st class, plus supplementary charges. Trains that arrive at a decent hour are the No 101 rapid (2nd and 3rd class only, departs Bangkok at 7.45 am and arrives in Den Chai at 5.44 pm), the No 205 ordinary (3rd class only, leaves at 7.05 am and arrives at 6.10 pm), the No 9 express diesel (2nd class only, leaves at 8.25 am and arrives at 3.48 pm) and the No 109 rapid (2nd and 3rd class, departs at 10 pm and arrives at 8.25 am). On the latter you can get a 2nd-class sleeper.

Blue săwngthăew and red buses leave the Den Chai station frequently for the 23km jaunt to Phrae and cost 20B. You can catch them anywhere along the southern end of Thanon Yantarakitkoson.

Getting Around
A săamláw anywhere in the old town costs 20B to 30B; farther afield to somewhere like Ban Prathup Jai it can cost up to 40B. Motorcycle taxis are available at the bus terminal; a trip from here to, say, Pratu Chai should cost around 20B.

Shared săwngthăew ply a few of the roads – mainly Thanon Yantarakitkoson – and cost 5B to 10B depending on the distance.

AROUND PHRAE
Wat Phra That Chaw Hae
วัดพระธาตุช่อแฮ

On a hill about 9km south-east of town off Rte 1022, this wát is famous for its 33m-high gilded chedi. Chaw Hae is the name of the cloth that worshippers wrap around the chedi – it's a type of satin thought to have originated in Xishuangbanna (Sipsongpanna, literally 12,000 Rice Fields, in northern Thai). Like Chiang Mai's Wat Doi Suthep, this is an important pilgrimage site for Thais living in the North. The **Phra Jao Than Jai** Buddha image here – similar in appearance to Phra Chinnarat in Phitsanulok – is reputed to impart fertility to women who make offerings to it.

The bòt has a gilded wooden ceiling, rococo pillars and walls with lotus-bud mosaics. Tiered naga stairs lead to the temple compound; the hill top is surrounded by a protected forest of mature teak trees.

Săwngthăew between the city and Phra That Chaw Hae are frequent and cost 12B.

Phae Meuang Phii
แพะเมืองผี

The name means 'Ghost-Land', a reference to this strange geological phenomenon about 18km north-east of Phrae off Rte 101. Erosion has created bizarre pillars of soil and rock that look like giant fungi. The area has recently been made a provincial park. There are shaded tables and food vendors near the entrance – you may need a drink after wandering around the baked surfaces between the eroded pillars.

Getting there by public transport entails a bus ride 9km towards Nan, getting off at the signposted turn-off for Phae Meuang Phii, and then catching a săwngthăew another 6km to a second right-hand turn-off to the park. From this point you must walk or hitch about 2.5km to reach the entrance.

Mabri Hill Tribe
ชนเผ่ามาบรี

Along the border of Phrae and Nan Provinces live the remaining members of the Mabri (sometimes spelt Mrabri or Mlabri) hill tribe, whom the Thais call *phĭi tawng lěuang* ('spirits of the yellow leaves'). The most nomadic of all the tribes in Thailand, the Mabri customarily move on when the leaves of their temporary huts turn yellow, hence their Thai name. Now, however, their numbers have been greatly reduced (possibly to as few as 150) and experts suspect that few of the Mabri still migrate in the traditional way.

Traditionally, the Mabri are strict hunter-gatherers but many now work as field labourers for Thais, or other hill-tribe groups such as the Hmong, in exchange for pigs and cloth. Little is known about the tribe's belief system, but it is said that the Mabri believe they are not entitled to cultivate the land for themselves. A Mabri woman typically changes partners every five or six years, taking any children from the previous union with her. The Mabris' knowledge of medicinal plants is said to be enormous, encompassing the effective use of herbs for fertility and contraception, and for the treatment of snake or centipede poisoning. When a member of the tribe dies, the body is put in a tree top to be eaten by birds.

In Phrae Province there is a small settlement of around 40 Mabri living in Rong Khwang district (north-east of the provincial capital, near Phae Meuang Phii) under the protection (control) of American missionary Eugene Long. Long calls himself 'Boonyuen Suksaneh' and the Mabris' village 'Ban Boonyuen' – a classic scenario right out of Peter Mathiessen's *At Play in the Fields of the Lord*. Ban Boonyuen can only be reached on foot or by elephant; the nearest village, which is linked by road, is about 12km away.

Several Mabri families abandoned Ban Boonyuen in early 1992 and are now living in Hmong villages in Phrae and Nan. The remaining 100 or so Mabri live across the provincial border in Nan.

The Thai government operates a 'Pre-Agricultural Development of Mabri Society Project' in both provinces to ease the Mabri into modern rural society without an accompanying loss of culture.

According to project leaders, the effort is necessary to protect the Mabri from becoming a slave society within Northern Thailand's increasingly capitalist rural economy. Because of their anti-materialist beliefs, the Mabri perform menial labour for the Hmong and other hill tribes for little or no compensation.

Nan Province

One of Thailand's formerly government-designated 'remote provinces', Nan before the early 1980s was so choked with bandits and PLAT insurgents that travellers were discouraged from visiting.

With the successes of the Thai army and a more stable political machine in Bangkok during the last two decades, Nan has opened up considerably. The roads that link the provincial capital with the nearby provinces of Chiang Rai, Phrae and Utaradit pass through exquisite scenery of rich river valleys and rice fields. Like Loei in the North-East, this is a province to be explored for its natural beauty and its likeable people.

Nan remains a largely rural province with not a factory or condo in sight. Most of the inhabitants are agriculturally employed, growing sticky rice, beans, corn, tobacco and vegetables in the fertile river plains. Nan is also famous for two fruits: *fai jiin* (a Chinese version of Thailand's indigenous *máfai*) and *sôm sǐi thawng,* golden-skinned oranges. The latter are Nan's most famous export, commanding high prices in Bangkok and Malaysia. Apparently the cooler winter weather in Nan turns the skin orange (lowland Thai oranges are mostly green) and imparts a unique sweet-tart flavour. Thung Chang district supposedly grows the best sôm sǐi thawng in the province. Nan is also famous for its *phrík yài hâeng,* long hot chillies similar to those grown in China's Sichuan Province. During the hot season, you'll see lots of these chillies drying by the roadside.

Geography

Nan shares a 227km border with Laos. Only 25% of the land is arable (and only half of that actively cultivated), as most of the province is covered by heavily forested mountains; **Doi Phu Kha**, at 2000m, is the highest peak. Half the forests in the province are virgin upland monsoon forest. Most of the province's population of 364,000 live in the Mae Nam Nan valley, a bowl-shaped depression ringed by mountains on all sides.

The major river systems in the province include the Nan, Wa, Samun, Haeng, Lae and Pua. At 627km, Mae Nam Nan is Thailand's third-longest river after the Mekong and the Mun.

People

Nan is a sparsely populated province, and the ethnic groups found here differ significantly from those in other northern provinces. Outside the Mae Nam Nan valley, the predominant hill tribes are Mien (around 8000), with smaller numbers of Hmong. During the Vietnam War, many Hmong and Mien from Nan (as well as Chiang Rai and Phetchabun) were recruited to fight with the Communist Pathet Lao, who promised to create a Hmong-Mien king following a Pathet Lao victory in Laos. Some of these so-called 'Red Meos' even trained in North Vietnam.

Along the south-western provincial border with Phrae are a few small Mabri settlements. What makes Nan unique, however, is the presence of three lesser-known groups seldom seen outside this province: the Thai Lü, Htin and Khamu.

Thai Lü Originally from Xishuangbanna (Sipsongpanna) in China's Yunnan Province, the Thai Lü migrated to Nan in 1836 in the wake of a conflict with a local jâo meuang (lord). Phra Jao Atityawong, ruler of the Nan kingdom at the time, allowed the Thai Lü to stay and grow vegetables in what is now Tha Wang Pha district. Their influence on Nan (and to a lesser extent, Phrae) culture has been very important. Like most Siamese Thai, the Thai Lü are Theravada Buddhists, and the temple architecture at Wat Phra That Chae Haeng, Wat Phumin and Wat Nong Bua – typified by thick walls with small windows, two- or three-tiered roofs, curved pediments and naga lintels – is a Thai Lü inheritance. Thai Lü fabrics are among the most prized in Northern Thailand and the weaving motifs show up in many Nan handicrafts.

The Thai Lü build traditional wooden or bamboo-thatched houses on thick wooden stilts, beneath which they place their kitchens and weaving looms. Many still make all their own clothes, typically sewn from indigo-dyed cotton fabrics. Many Thai Lü villages support themselves by growing rice and vegetables. In Nan

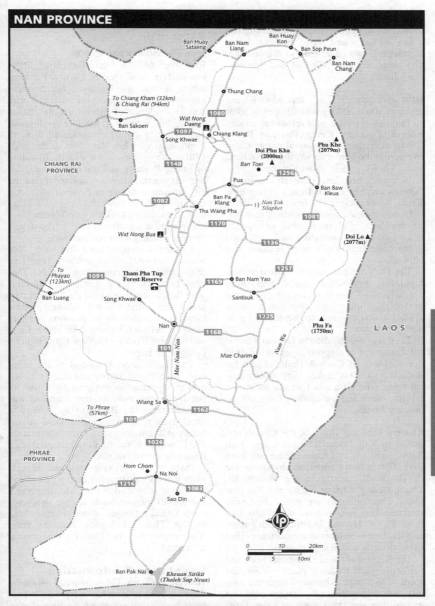

NAN PROVINCE

Ban Huay Sataeng
Ban Nam Liang
Ban Huay Kon
Ban Sop Peun
Ban Nam Chang

Thung Chang

To Chiang Kham (32km) & Chiang Rai (94km)

1080

Wat Nong Daeng

1097 Chiang Klang

Ban Sakoen

Song Khwae

Doi Phu Kha (2000m)

Phu Khe (2079m)

CHIANG RAI PROVINCE

1148

Ban Toei

Pua

1256

Ban Baw Kleua

1082

Ban Pa Klang

Tha Wang Pha

Nan Tok Silaphet

1081

Wat Nong Bua

1170

1136

Doi Lo (2077m)

To Phayao (123km)

1091

Tham Pha Tup Forest Reserve

1257

Ban Luang

Song Khwae

1169 Ban Nam Yao

Santisuk

LAOS

Nan

Mae Nam Nam

101

1168

1225

Phu Fa (1750m)

Mae Charim

Nam Wa

NORTHERN THAILAND

To Phrae (57km)

Wiang Sa

101

1162

1026

PHRAE PROVINCE

Hom Chom

Na Noi

1216

1083

Sao Din

0   10   20km
0   5   10mi

Ban Pak Nai

Kheuan Sirikit (Thaleh Sap Neua)

they maintain a strong sense of tradition; most Thai Lü communities still recognise a jâo meuang and *mǎw meuang* (state astrologer), two older men in the community who serve as political and spiritual consultants.

Htin Pronounced 'Tin', this Mon-Khmer group of about 3000 live in villages of 50 or so families spread across remote mountain valleys of Chiang Klang, Pua and Thung Chang districts. A substantial number also live across the border in Sayaburi Province, Laos. They typically subsist by hunting for wild game, breeding domestic animals, farming small plots of land and, in Ban Baw Kleua, by extracting salt from salt wells.

Htin houses are usually made of thatched bamboo and raised on bamboo or wooden stilts. No metal – including nails – is used in the construction of houses because of a Htin taboo.

The Htin are particularly skilled at manipulating bamboo to make everything needed around the house; for floor mats and baskets they interweave pared bamboo with a black-coloured grass to create bold geometric patterns.

They also use bamboo to fashion a musical instrument of stepped pipes – similar to the *angklung* of Central Thailand and Indonesia – which is shaken to produce musical tones. The Htin don't weave their own fabrics, often buying clothes from neighbouring Miens.

Khamu Like the Thai Lü, the Khamu migrated to Nan around 150 years ago from Xishuangbanna and Laos. There are now over 5000 in Nan (more than anywhere else in Thailand), mostly in the Wiang Sa, Thung Chang, Chiang Klang and Pua districts. Their villages are established near streams; their houses have dirt floors like those of the Hmong but their roofs sport crossed beams similar to the northern-Thai kàlae (locally called *kapkri-aak*).

The Khamu are skilled at metalwork and perform regular rituals to placate Salok, the spirit of the forge. Khamu villages are usually very self-sufficient; villagers hold fast to tradition and are known to value thrift and hard work. Ban Huay Sataeng in Thung Chang district is one of the largest and easiest Khamu villages to visit.

NAN

อ.เมืองน่าน

postcode 55000 • pop 25,800

Just over 668km from Bangkok, little-known Nan is steeped in history. For centuries it was an isolated, independent kingdom with few ties to the outside world. Ample evidence of prehistoric habitation exists, but it wasn't until several small meuang (city-states) consolidated to form Nanthaburi on Mae Nam Nan in the mid-14th century – concurrent with the founding of Luang Prabang and the Lan Xang (Million Elephants) kingdom in Laos – that the city became a power to contend with. Associated with the powerful Sukhothai kingdom, the meuang took the title Waranakhon and played a significant role in the development of early Thai nationalism.

Towards the end of the 14th century Nan became one of the nine northern Thai–Lao principalities that comprised Lan Na Thai (now known simply as Lanna) and the city-state flourished throughout the 15th century under the name Chiang Klang (Middle City), a reference to its position roughly midway between Chiang Mai (New City) and Chiang Thong (Golden City, today's Luang Prabang).

The Burmese took control of the kingdom in 1558 and transferred many inhabitants to Myanmar as slaves; the city was all but abandoned until western Thailand was wrested from the Burmese in 1786. The local dynasty then regained local sovereignty and remained semi-autonomous until 1931 when Nan finally accepted full Bangkok sponsorship.

Parts of the old city wall and several early wát dating from the Lanna period can be seen in present-day Nan. Meuang Nan's wát are distinctive: Some temple structures show Lanna influence, while others belong to the Thai Lü legacy brought from Xishuangbanna, the Thai Lü's historical homeland.

Orientation & Information

Tourist Offices The provincial office on Thanon Suriyaphong has a friendly tourist centre, although not much English is spoken. Maps are sometimes available. It's open weekdays from 9 am to 4.30 pm and Saturday from 9 am to noon.

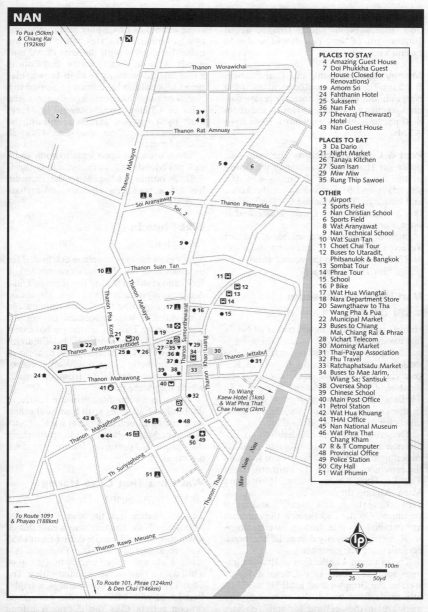

NAN

To Pua (50km) & Chiang Rai (192km)

Thanon Worawichai

Thanon Rat Amnuay

Thanon Mahayot

Soi Aranyawat

Thanon Premprida

Sol. 2

Thanon Suan Tan

Thanon Pha Kong

Thanon Mahayot

Thanon Sumonthewarat

Thanon Anantaworarittidet

Thanon Khao Luang

Thanon Jettabut

Thanon Mahawong

To Wiang Kaew Hotel (1km) & Wat Phra That Chae Haeng (2km)

Thanon Mahaphrom

Th Suriyaphong

Thanon Thai

Mae Nam Nan

Thanon Rawp Meuang

To Route 1091 & Phayao (188km)

To Route 101, Phrae (124km) & Den Chai (146km)

NORTHERN THAILAND

PLACES TO STAY
4 Amazing Guest House
7 Doi Phukkha Guest House (Closed for Renovations)
19 Amorn Sri
24 Fahthanin Hotel
25 Sukasem
36 Nan Fah
37 Dhevaraj (Thewarat) Hotel
43 Nan Guest House

PLACES TO EAT
3 Da Dario
21 Night Market
26 Tanaya Kitchen
27 Suan Isan
29 Miw Miw
35 Rung Thip Sawoei

OTHER
1 Airport
2 Sports Field
5 Nan Christian School
6 Sports Field
8 Wat Aranyawat
9 Nan Technical School
10 Wat Suan Tan
11 Choet Chai Tour
12 Buses to Utaradit, Phitsanulok & Bangkok
13 Sombat Tour
14 Phrae Tour
15 School
16 P Bike
17 Wat Hua Wiangtai
18 Nara Department Store
20 Sawngthaew to Tha Wang Pha & Pua
22 Municipal Market
23 Buses to Chiang Mai, Chiang Rai & Phrae
28 Vichart Telecom
30 Morning Market
31 Thai-Payap Association
32 Fhu Travel
33 Ratchaphatsadu Market
34 Buses to Mae Jarim, Wiang Sa; Santisuk
38 Oversea Shop
39 Chinese School
40 Main Post Office
41 Petrol Station
42 Wat Hua Khuang
44 THAI Office
45 Nan National Museum
46 Wat Phra That Chang Kham
47 R & T Computer
48 Provincial Office
49 Police Station
50 City Hall
51 Wat Phumin

0   50   100m
0   25   50yd

Immigration One of the closest immigration offices is in Thung Chang, about 100km north of Nan. You should be able to extend visas here.

Money Bangkok Bank and Thai Farmers Bank on Thanon Sumonthewarat, near the Nan Fah and Dhevaraj hotels, operate foreign exchange services. Hours are from 8.30 am to 3.30 pm weekdays. Both have ATMs.

Post & Communications The main post office on Thanon Mahawong in the centre of the city is open 8.30 am to 4.30 pm weekdays and 9 am to noon on weekends and holidays. The attached CAT office offers a Home Country Direct Phone and is open 7 am to 10 pm daily.

Internet services are available at Vichart Telecom on Thanon Anantaworarittidet and at R&T Computer on the corner almost opposite Fhu Travel Service.

Nan National Museum
พิพิธภัณฑสถานแห่งชาตินาน

Housed in the 1903-vintage palace of Nan's last two feudal lords (Phra Jao Suriyapongpalidet and Jao Mahaphrom Surathada), this museum first opened its doors in 1973. Recent renovations have made it one of the most up-to-date provincial museums in Thailand. Unlike most provincial museums in the country, this one also has English labels for many items on display.

The ground floor is divided into six exhibition rooms with ethnological exhibits covering the various ethnic groups found in the province, including the northern Thais, Thai Lü, Htin, Khamu, Mabri, Hmong and Mien. Among the items on display are silverwork, textiles, folk utensils and tribal costumes. On the 2nd floor of the museum are exhibits on Nan history, archaeology, local architecture, royal regalia, weapons, ceramics and religious art.

The museum's collection of Buddha images includes some rare Lanna styles as well as the floppy-eared local styles. Usually made from wood, these standing images are in the 'calling for rain' posture (with hands at the sides, pointing down) and they show a marked Luang Prabang influence. The astute museum curators posit a Nan style of art in Buddhist sculpture; some examples on display seem very imitative of other Thai styles, while others are quite distinctive, with the ears curve outwards. Also on display on the 2nd floor is a rare 'black' (actually reddish-brown) elephant tusk said to have been presented to a Nan lord over 300 years ago by the Khün ruler of Chiang Tung (Kengtung). Held aloft by a wooden garuda sculpture, the tusk measures 97cm long and 47cm in circumference.

The museum is open 9 am to noon and 1 to 4 pm Monday to Saturday; admission is 30B. A building adjacent to the museum has a few books on Thai art and archaeology for sale.

Wat Phumin
วัดภูมินทร์

Nan's most famous temple is celebrated for its cruciform bòt that was constructed in 1596 and restored during the reign of Chao Anantavorapitthidet (1867–74). Murals on the walls depicting the Khatta Kumara and Nimi jatakas were executed during the restoration by Thai Lü artists; the bòt exterior exemplifies the work of Thai Lü architects as well. The murals have historic as well as aesthetic value since they incorporate scenes of local life from the era in which they were painted.

The ornate altar sitting in the centre of the bòt has four sides with four Sukhothai-style sitting Buddhas in *maan wíchai* ('victory over Mara' – with one hand touching the ground) posture, facing in each direction.

Wat Phra That Chae Haeng
วัดพระธาตุแช่แห้ง

Two kilometres past the bridge that spans Mae Nam Nan, heading south-east out of town, this very old temple dating from 1355 is the most sacred wát in Nan Province. It is set in a square, walled enclosure on top of a hill with a view of Nan and the valley. The Thai Lü–influenced bòt features a triple-tiered roof with carved wooden eaves, and dragon reliefs over the doors. A gilded Lanna-style chedi sits on a large square base next to the bòt with sides 22.5m long; the entire chedi is 55.5m high.

Wat Phra That Chang Kham
วัดพระธาตุช้างค้ำ

This is the second-most important temple in the city after Wat Phra That Chae Haeng; the founding date is unknown. The main wíhǎan, reconstructed in 1458, has a huge seated Buddha image and faint murals in the process of being painstakingly uncovered. (Sometime in the mid-20th century an abbot reportedly ordered the murals to be whitewashed because he thought they were distracting worshippers from concentrating on his sermons!)

Also in the wíhǎan is a collection of Lanna-period scrolls inscribed (in Lanna script) not only with the usual Buddhist scriptures but with the history, law and astrology of the time. A *thammâat* (a 'dharma seat' used by monks when teaching) sits to one side.

The magnificent chedi behind the wíhǎan dates to the 14th century, probably around the same time the temple was founded. It features elephant supports similar to those seen in Sukhothai and Si Satchanalai.

Next to the chedi is a small, undistinguished bòt from the same era. Wat Chang Kham's current abbot tells an interesting story involving the bòt and a Buddha image that was once kept inside. According to the venerable abbot, in 1955 art historian AB Griswold offered to purchase the 145cm-tall Buddha inside the small bòt. The image appeared to be a crude Sukhothai-style walking Buddha moulded of plaster. After agreeing to pay the abbot 25,000B for the image, Griswold began removing the image from the bòt – but as he did it fell and the plaster around the statue broke away to reveal an original Sukhothai Buddha of pure gold underneath. Needless to say, the abbot made Griswold give it back, much to the latter's chagrin. The image is now kept behind a glass partition, along with other valuable Buddhist images from the area, in the abbot's kùtì. Did Griswold suspect what lay beneath the plaster? The abbot refuses to say.

Wat Chang Kham is also distinguished by having the largest hǎw trai (Tripitaka library) in Thailand. It's as big as or bigger than the average wíhǎan, but now lies empty.

The wát is opposite the Nan National Museum on Thanon Phá Kong.

Wat Hua Khuang
วัดหัวข่วง

Largely ignored by art historians, this small wát diagonally opposite Wat Chang Kham features a distinctive Lanna/Lan Xang–style chedi with four Buddha niches, a wooden Tripitaka library (now used as a kùtì) and a noteworthy bòt with a Luang Prabang–style carved wooden veranda.

Inside are a carved wooden ceiling and a huge naga altar. The temple's founding date is unknown, but stylistic cues suggest this may be one of the city's oldest wát.

Wat Suan Tan
วัดสวนตาล

Reportedly established in 1456, Wat Suan Tan (Palm Grove Monastery) features an interesting 15th-century chedi (40m high) that combines prang and lotus-bud motifs of obvious Sukhothai influence. The heavily restored wíhǎan contains an early Sukhothai-style bronze sitting Buddha.

Wat Suan Tan is on Thanon Suan Tan, near the north-eastern end of Thanon Pha Kong.

Trekking

Nan has nothing like the organised trekking industry found in Chiang Rai and Chiang Mai, but there is one company that leads two- or three-day excursions into the mountains. Fhu Travel Service (☎ 054-710636, 710940, 01-472 8951, fax 775345) at 453/4 Thanon Sumonthewarat offers treks to Mabri, Hmong, Mien, Thai Lü and Htin villages.

A one-day 'soft' trek costs 700B to 1200B per person depending on the number of participants (two-person minimum); a two-day, one-night journey costs 1200B to 2000B per person; and three days and two nights costs 1500B to 2700B per person. The trekking fees include transport, meals, accommodation, sleeping bag and guide services.

Fhu also runs boat trips on Mae Nam Nan in December and January when the water level is high enough. White-water rubber rafting trips on the Nam Wa in Mae Charim are offered all year. The prices run from 1300B per person (for trips of seven to eight people) to 2500B per person (for trips of two people). This price includes transport, guide, lunch and safety equipment. Three-day rubber-rafting trips are 3000B to 6000B per person, depending on the number of people. Elephant tours are also available.

Tours of the city and surrounding area cost 500B for up to five people.

Places to Stay

Guesthouses An old favourite, *Doi Phukha Guest House* (☎ 054-751517, 94/5 Soi 1 Thanon Sumonthewarat), was closed for renovation when we stopped by. The *Nan Guest House* (☎ 054-771849, 57/16 Thanon Mahaphrom) is in a large house at the end of a soi off Thanon Mahaphrom, closer to town and near the THAI office. Clean singles/doubles/triples with shared bathroom cost 70/100/130B; for rooms with private bathroom add 20B per person. Nan Guest House also does tours and rents mountain bikes for 30B.

In a tidy two-storey house on a quiet soi off Thanon Rat Amnuay, the friendly *Amazing Guest House* (☎ 054-710893, 23/7 Thanon Rat Amnuay) offers five fan rooms upstairs, all with wooden floors, clean beds and hot shared showers. Rates run 100/160/210/260B single/double/triple/ quadruple. Discounts are available for long-term stays.

Hotels *Amorn Sri* (no Roman-script sign; ☎ 054-710510, 62/1 Thanon Anantaworarittidet) has very basic single/double rooms with fan for 170/250B, which is a bit overpriced. The hotel is at a very busy intersection so it may not be the quietest choice. *Sukasem* (☎ 054-710141, fax 771581, 29/31 Thanon Anantaworarittidet) has much better rooms costing 200B to 300B with fan and bathroom, 350B with air-con.

The *Dhevaraj Hotel* (Thewarat; ☎ 054-710094, fax 771365, 466 Thanon Sumonthewarat) is a four-storey place built around a tiled courtyard with a fountain. It's not really fancy but it's a pleasant place and is one of the best hotels Nan has to offer. Parts of the hotel were undergoing renovation when we visited. Large, clean rooms on the 2nd floor, with fan and private bathroom, are 300/400B – a bit steep due to the lack of competition, but the

rooms are a cut above the usual room with fan. Rooms towards the back of the hotel are quieter than those towards the front. Rooms on the 3rd floor are all air-con and cost 500/600B. On the top floor are newly renovated 'VIP' rooms with double-glazed windows, carpet, cable TV and minifridge; these cost 700B single/double. The attached Dhevee coffee shop is open 6 am to 2 am.

The all-wood *Nan Fah* (☎ 054-710284, 438–440 Thanon Sumonthewarat), next to the Dhevaraj Hotel, is well known for a supporting teak pillar that extends for three storeys. All rooms come with air-con and hot-water showers and cost 440B single, 540B double. Breakfast is included.

The friendly *Wiang Kaew Hotel* (☎ 054-750573, fax 774573) is at the 1km marker on Rte 1168, 1km from the bridge on the road that leads to Wat Phra That Chae Haeng. Although the rooms are in row houses, they have the appearance of separate bungalows. There's no lounge or karaoke, so it's quiet at night. Fan rooms cost 240B, air-con 380B. Both types of rooms come with hot water, TV, refrigerator and phone.

The new seven-storey *Fahthanin Hotel* (☎ 054-757321, fax 757324, 303 Thanon Anantaworarittidet), offers rooms with TV, air-con, hot shower and minifridge for 700B or slightly larger versions with bathtubs for 800B. Rates include breakfast. The restaurant/coffee shop has very good Thai food.

Places to Eat

A *night market* assembles on the corner of Thanon Pha Kong and Thanon Anantaworarittidet every night; it's not that spectacular, but the vendors along the sidewalks nearby have fairly good food. Another group of food vendors sets up along the soi opposite the Dhevaraj Hotel.

The most dependable Thai-Chinese restaurant in the vicinity of the Nan Fah and Dhevaraj hotels is the old brick and wood *Rung Thip Sawoei*, open 7 am to 9 pm daily. *Miw Miw* (no Roman-script sign), opposite the Thai Farmers Bank, is a bit cleaner than Rung Thip Sawoei and has good jók, noodles and real coffee.

If you turn left at the soi next to Rung Thip Sawoei and follow it about 200m, you'll come to the semi-outdoor *Suan Isan*, the best choice in town for Isan food.

At 75/23–24 Thanon Anantaworarittidet, the clean *Tanaya Kitchen* serves a range of reasonably priced vegetarian dishes (plus non-veg).

Da Dario (☎ 054-750258, 37/4 Thanon Rat Amnuay), next to Amazing Guest House, is a Swiss-run Italian/Thai restaurant; prices are reasonable and the food and service are very good. It's open 10 am to 2 pm and 5 to 10 pm Monday to Saturday and 5 to 10 pm Sunday.

Shopping

Good buys include local textiles, especially the Thai Lü weaving styles from Xishuangbanna. Typical Thai Lü fabrics feature red and black designs on white cotton in floral, geometric and animal designs; indigo and red on white is also common. A favourite is the 'flowing-water design' *(lai náam lǎi)* showing stepped patterns representing streams, rivers and waterfalls.

Local Mien embroidery and Hmong applique are of excellent quality. Htin grass-and-bamboo baskets and mats are worth a look, too.

The nonprofit Thai-Payap Association (☎ 054-710230), one of Thailand's most successful village self-help projects, has a shop at 24 Thanon Jettabut near the morning market and Nan bus terminal. Supported by Britain's Ockenden Venture from 1979 to 1990, the association now involves over 20 villages and has become totally self-sufficient. The handiwork offered through Thai-Payap is among the highest quality available, often including intricate, time-consuming designs. All proceeds go directly to the participating villages – even the administrative staff are trained village representatives.

There are several small artisan-operated shops along Thanon Sumonthewarat and along Thanon Mahawong and Thanon Anantaworarittidet.

Getting There & Away

Air You can fly to Nan on THAI from Chiang Mai (605B, four departures weekly), Phitsanulok (680B, four departures weekly), Phrae (370B, daily) or Bangkok (1765B, thrice weekly). The THAI office (☎ 054-710377) is at 34 Thanon Mahaphrom. THAI offers free transport from its office to the airport.

Bus Baw Khaw Saw (government) buses run from Chiang Mai, Chiang Rai and Phrae to Nan. The fare from Chiang Mai's Arcade bus terminal is 114B (140B to 160B air-con, 180B 1st class air-con) and the trip takes from six to seven hours. From Chiang Rai there's one daily bus at 9.30 am (No 611, 90B) that takes six to seven gruelling hours via treacherous mountain roads – get a window seat as there's usually lots of motion sickness. Buses from Phrae to Nan leave frequently, cost 39B (55B air-con) and take from two to 2½ hours.

From Nan, buses to Chiang Mai, Chiang Rai and Phrae leave from a terminal west of the large market along Thanon Anantaworarittidet.

Ordinary buses to Bangkok leave from the Baw Khaw Saw terminal off Thanon Khao Luang every other day at 5.30, 6.30 and 7.30 pm and cost 214B.

Regular government-run air-con buses to Bangkok cost 273B (daily at 8 and 8.30 am and 7 pm), 1st-class air-con is 351B (daily 8 am and 7 pm) and 24-seat VIP buses are 545B (daily 7 pm). The journey takes 10 to 13 hours.

Private 1st-class and VIP Bangkok buses leave from offices located along the eastern end of Thanon Anantaworarittidet, not far from the Baw Khaw Saw terminal. Sombat Tour and Phrae Tour both run VIP buses to Bangkok for as low as 350B – check the number of seats before booking, although. Choet Chai Tour offers 1st-class air-con buses to Bangkok. Most of these private buses depart between 6.15 and 6.45 pm

Train The northern railway makes a stop in Den Chai, which is a 46B, three-hour bus ride from Nan.

A Bangkok-bound rapid train leaves Den Chai at 7 and 7.38 pm (arriving at Bangkok's Hualamphong station at 5.40 and 5.55 am respectively); to be sure of meeting either of these trains, take an early afternoon (1 or 2 pm) Den Chai–bound bus from Nan's Baw Khaw Saw bus terminal. To Chiang Mai there's a train that departs Den Chai at 3.48 pm, arriving at Chiang Mai at 7.35 pm. The 3rd-class fare to/from Chiang Mai is 31B, plus the rapid surcharge.

See Getting There & Away in the Phrae section for more Den Chai train information.

Săwngthăew Pick-ups to districts in the northern part of the province (Tha Wang Pha, Pua, Phah Tup) leave from the petrol station opposite Sukasem hotel on Thanon Anantaworarittidet. Southbound săwng-thăew (for Mae Charim, Wiang Sa, Na Noi) depart from the car park opposite the new Ratchaphatsadu Market on Thanon Jettabut.

Getting Around
P Bike (no Roman-script sign; ☎ 054-772680), opposite Wat Hua Wiangtai at 331–333 Thanon Sumonthewarat, rents Honda Dreams for 150B a day including helmet and third-party insurance. Bicycles are also available, and P Bike does repair work.

Oversea Shop (☎ 054-710258) at 488 Thanon Sumonthewarat (a few doors down from the Dhevaraj Hotel) rents bicycles and motorbikes and can also handle repairs.

Săamlâw around town cost 20B to 30B. Green săwngthăew circulating around the city centre charge 5B to 10B per person depending on distance.

AROUND NAN
Doi Phu Kha National Park
อุทยานแห่งชาติดอยภูคา

This national park is centred around 2000m-high Doi Phu Kha in the Pua and Baw Kleua districts of north-eastern Nan (about 75km from Nan). There are several Htin, Mien, Hmong and Thai Lü villages in the park and vicinity, as well as a couple of caves and waterfalls and endless opportunities for forest walks.

The *park* offers 14 bungalows that rent for 250B per double room. You must bring food and drinking water in from town, as the park office no longer offers food service.

A much better choice is *Bamboo Hut* (*103 Mu 10, Tambon Phu Kha, Amphoe Pua, Nan 55120*) in Ban Toei, a Lawa-Thai village near the summit at the edge of the park. Opened in 2000 by an English- and Dutch-speaking Lawa and his Thai wife, Bamboo Hut offers five clean, well-spaced bamboo-thatch huts with shared bathroom and stupendous mountain and valley views for 100B single/double. The owner is happy

to lead guests on one- to three-day treks for 500B per day, including all meals. Treks visit local waterfalls, limestone caves (Tham Lawng is the biggest cave – about a one-day walk from the guesthouse) and hill-tribe villages. This area gets quite cool in the winter months – evening temperatures of 5°C to 10°C are not uncommon – so dress accordingly.

The standard national park entry fees apply (see under Doi Suthep & Doi Pui National Park earlier in this chapter).

To reach the park by public transport you must first take a bus or săwngthăew north of Nan to Pua (20B), and then pick up one of the infrequent săwngthăew to the park headquarters or Bamboo Hut (25B). The one from Nan to Pua leaves about 6 am, the one from Pua to Ban Toei at about 7 am.

Ban Baw Kleua is a Htin village south-east of the park where the main occupation is the extraction of salt from local salt wells (*bàw kleua*). Rte 1256 meets Rte 1081 near Ban Baw Kleua; Rte 1081 can be followed south back to Nan (107km) via a network of unpaved roads.

Nong Bua
หนองบัว

This neat and tidy Thai Lü village near the town of Tha Wang Pha, approximately 30km north of Nan, is famous for Lü-style **Wat Nong Bua**. Featuring a typical two-tiered roof and carved wooden portico, the bòt design is simple yet striking – note the carved naga heads at the roof corners. Inside the bòt are some noteworthy but faded jataka murals; the building is often locked when religious services aren't in progress, but there's usually someone around to unlock the door. Be sure to leave a donation for temple upkeep and restoration at the altar.

You can also see Thai Lü weaving in action in the village. The home of Khun Janthasom Phrompanya, near the wát, serves as a local weaving centre – check there for the locations of looms, or to look at fabrics for purchase. Large yâam are available for just 45B, while nicely woven neck scarves cost more. There are also several weaving houses just behind the wát.

Getting There & Away Săwngthăew to Tha Wang Pha (15B) leave from opposite

Nan's Sukasem hotel. Get off at Samyaek Longbom, a three-way intersection before Tha Wang Pha, and walk west to a bridge over Mae Nam Nan, then left at the dead end on the other side of the bridge to Wat Nong Bua. It's 3.1km from the highway to the wát.

If you're coming from Nan via your own transport on Rte 1080, you'll cross a stream called Lam Nam Yang just past the village of Ban Fai Mun but before Tha Wang Pha. Take the first left off Rte 1080 and follow it to a dead end; turn right and then left over a bridge across Mae Nam Nan and walk until you reach another dead end, then left 2km until you can see Wat Nong Bua on the right.

Tham Phah Tup Forest Reserve
ถ้ำผาตูบ

This limestone cave complex is about 10km north of Nan and is part of a relatively new wildlife reserve. Some 17 caves have been counted, of which nine are easily located by means of established (but unmarked) trails.

From Nan, you can catch a săwngthăew bound for Pua or Thung Chang; it will stop at the turn-off to the caves for 10B. The vehicles leave from the petrol station opposite the Sukasem hotel.

Sao Din
เสาดิน

Literally 'Earth Pillars', Sao Din is an erosional phenomenon similar to that found at Phae Meuang Phii in Phrae Province – tall columns of earth protruding from a barren depression. The area covers nearly 20 râi (3.2 hectares) off Rte 1026 in Na Noi district about 60km south of Nan.

Sao Din is best visited by bicycle or motorcycle since it's time consuming to reach by public transport. If you don't have your own wheels, take a săwngthăew to Na Noi from the southbound săwngthăew station opposite the Ratchaphatsadu Market in Nan. From Na Noi you must get yet another săwngthăew bound for Fak Tha or Ban Khok, getting off at the entrance to Sao Din after 5km or so. From here you'll have to walk or hitch 4km to Sao Din itself. There are also occasional direct săwngthăew from Na Noi.

North-west of Sao Din, off Rte 1216, is a set of earth pillars called **Hom Chom**.

Other Attractions

There are a couple of interesting destinations in and around the Thai Lü village of **Pua**, roughly 50km north of Nan. In Pua itself you can check out another famous Thai Lü temple, **Wat Ton Laeng**, which is admired for its classic three-tiered roof. **Nam Tok Silaphet** is south-east of Pua just off the road between Pua and Ban Nam Yao. The water falls in a wide swath over a cliff and is best seen at the end of the monsoon season in November. On the way to the falls and west of the road is the Mien village of **Ban Pa Klang**, worth a visit to see silversmiths at work. This village supplies many silver shops in Chiang Mai and Bangkok. Other silverwork Mien villages can be found on Rte 101 between Nan and Phrae.

Off Rte 1148, north of the village of Ban Sakoen, is a huge, 200m-wide cave called **Tham Luang**. The path to the cave is not signposted, but if you ask at the police checkpoint in Ban Sakoen you should be able to get directions or you might even find a guide.

Thaleh Sap Neua (Northern Lake) formed by Kheuan Sirikit is an important freshwater fishery for Nan, as well as a recreational attraction for Nan residents. **Ban Pak Nai** on its north-western shore is the main fishing village. Just before Mae Nam Nan feeds into the lake at its extreme northern end, there is a set of river rapids called **Kaeng Luang**.

Border Crossing (Laos)

Ban Huay Kon (140km north of Nan) in Thung Chang District is now a legal border crossing for Lao and Thais, and it may be promoted to an international crossing in the foreseeable future. From this crossing it's just 152km to Luang Prabang or about 300km to the Chinese border at Boten, Laos. From the Lao side of the border crossing, a dirt road leads north–north-east about 45km to the banks of the Mekong River in Laos' Udomxai Province. From here you can either take a boat down river to Luang Prabang or cross the river and pick up Rte 2 to Muang Xai, the provincial capital. From Muang Xai it's only a couple of hours to the international border with China's Yunnan Province.

Nan residents with an interest in history are excited by the prospect of linking again the five *chiang* (cities) of the Lanna-Lan Xang-Xishuangbanna diaspora: Chiang Mai, Chiang Rai, Chiang Thong (the original name for Luang Prabang), Chiang Rung (Yunnan's Jinghong) and Chiang Klang (Nan).

There is an immigration office in the district capital of Thung Chang, 100km north of Nan; if you find out that the border crossing is open to foreigners, you should stop in to get a Thai exit stamp in your passport.

Every Saturday morning from around 5 to 11 am there's a lively Lao-Thai market in Thung Chang.

North-Eastern Thailand

In many ways, the north-eastern region of Thailand is the kingdom's heartland. Partly due to the area's general nondevelopment, the older Thai customs remain more intact here than elsewhere in the country.

The region also hosts fewer tourists – in a typical year only 2% of the country's annual international arrivals venture into North-Eastern Thailand.

Compared to the rest of Thailand the pace is slower, the people friendlier and inflation is less effective in the Isan provinces; and although fewer people speak or understand English, travel in the North-East is relatively easy.

Sites of historical and archaeological significance abound in the North-East and many of them have been restored or excavated. Scattered around the region are 202 known *prasat, prang* and *ku,* 182 of which are of Khmer origin. Most of these sites are found in four provinces: Buriram (61 sites), Nakhon Ratchasima (26), Surin (33) and Si Saket (12).

Generally speaking, prasat (from the Sanskrit architectural term *prasada*) refers to large temple sanctuaries with a cruciform floor plan, while prang refers to a Khmer-style tower that may constitute an entire *chedi* (or stupa) or part of a chedi and ku is a smaller chedi that is partially hollow and open. However, many Thais use these terms interchangeably. Prasat is sometimes translated in Thai tourist literature as 'castle' or 'palace', but these Khmer monuments were never used as royal residences.

The Khorat Plateau extends across most of North-Eastern Thailand and is divided by the Phu Phan mountain range into two wide drainage basins, the Sakon Nakhon Basin in the upper North-East (fed by the Mekong River and its tributaries) and the Khorat Basin in the lower North-East (fed by the Chi and Mun Rivers).

Isan (or *isăan,* the collective term for the north-eastern region) officially consists of an amalgamation of 19 provinces: Amnat Charoen, Buriram, Chaiyaphum, Kalasin, Khon Kaen, Loei, Mahasarakham, Mukdahan, Nakhon Phanom, Nakhon Ratchasima, Nong Bualamphu, Nong Khai, Roi Et, Sakon Nakhon, Si Saket, Surin, Ubon Ratchathani, Udon Thani and Yasothon.

History

The region has a long history, beginning with the 4000-year-old bronze culture of Ban Chiang, which predates both Mesopotamia and China as a metallurgical and agricultural site.

Thais use the term *isăan* to classify the region *(phâak isăan),* the people *(khon isăan)* and the food *(aahăan isăan)* of North-Eastern Thailand. The name comes from Isana, the Sanskrit name for the Mon-Khmer kingdom that flourished in what is now North-Eastern Thailand and pre-Angkor Cambodia; Isana was a precursor to the Funan empire (1st to 6th centuries AD). Funan was in turn absorbed by the Chenla

NORTH-EASTERN THAILAND

569

NORTH-EASTERN THAILAND

empire during the late 6th to 8th centuries and divided into Upper (Water) and Lower (Land) Chenla, which corresponded with parts of modern-day Isan, southern Laos and north-western Cambodia. After the 9th century, Chenla was superseded by the Angkor empire, which extended into Isan and beyond.

Isan remained more-or-less autonomous from early Thai kingdoms until the coming of the French in the 18th century created the Indochinese state of Laos, thus forcing Thailand to define its north-eastern boundaries. Rama V divided the region into four *monthon* (Thai pronunciation of the Pali-Sanskrit *mandala*), or semi-autonomous satellite states, including Lao Phuan (north-eastern Isan), Roi Et (central Isan), Lao

Klang (south-western Isan) and Ubo (south-eastern Isan). The monthon syster was changed to the *jangwàt* (province system in 1933.

Traditionally Thailand's poorest regior due to the infertility of the soil and lack o rain in comparison with the rest of the coun try, the North-East was fertile ground fo the communist movement. Ho Chi Min spent 1928–29 proselytising in Udon Than Sakon Nakhon and Khorat (Nakho Ratchasima's more common name); in th 1940s a number of Indochinese Communi Party leaders fled to Isan from Laos an helped strengthen the Communist Party o Thailand. From the 1960s until 1982 or sc Isan was a hotbed of guerrilla activity, e pecially in the provinces of Buriram, Loe

Ubon Ratchathani, Nakhon Phanom and Sakon Nakhon. Almost immediately following the amnesty of 1982, the north-eastern strongholds of the Communist Party dissolved rapidly. The process was hastened by a decade of economic growth that drew large numbers of Isan peasants from the forests and rice fields to various provincial capitals and to Bangkok.

During the boom years only the larger cities of the North-East were able to ride the coat-tails of Thailand's rising income. The rural areas have the lowest per-capita income of the country's four major regions.

Culture

Isan culture and language are marked by a mixture of Lao and Khmer influence. The Khmers left behind Angkor Wat–like monuments near Surin, Khorat, Buriram and other north-eastern towns. Along the Mekong River/Lao border are several Lao-style temples, including Wat Phra That Phanom. Many of the people living in this area speak Lao – or Thai dialects which are very close to Lao dialects spoken in Laos – and in fact there are more people of Lao heritage in North-Eastern Thailand than in all of Laos. In certain areas of the lower North-East, Khmer is the most common language.

Isan food is famous for its pungency and choice of ingredients. Well-known dishes include *kài yâang* (grilled spiced chicken) and *sôm-tam* (spicy salad made with grated papaya, lime juice, garlic, fish sauce and fresh chillies). North-easterners eat glutinous rice with their meals, rolling the almost translucent grains into balls with their hands.

The music of North-Eastern Thailand is highly distinctive in its folk tradition, using instruments such as the *khaen,* a reed instrument with two long rows of bamboo pipes strung together; the *ponglaang,* which is like a xylophone and made of short wooden logs; and the *phin,* a type of small three-stringed lute played with a large plectrum. The most popular song forms are *lûuk thûng* (literally, children of the fields) types – a very rhythmic style in comparison to the classical music of Central Thailand.

The best silk in Thailand is said to come from the North-East, particularly Khorat, Khon Kaen and Roi Et. A visit to north-eastern silk-weaving towns can uncover bargains, as well as provide an education in Thai weaving techniques. Cotton fabrics from Loei, Nong Khai and Nakhon Phanom are highly regarded, especially those woven using *mát-mìi* methods (in which cotton threads are tie-dyed before weaving, similar to Indonesian *ikat*).

For real antiquity, Udon Thani Province offers prehistoric cave drawings at Ban Pheu, north of Udon Thani, and a look at the ancient ceramic and bronze culture at Ban Chiang to the east. The latter harbours remains of what appears to be the world's oldest agricultural society and first bronze metallurgy.

Travellers who want to know more about North-Eastern Thailand should read the works of Pira Sudham, a Thai author born in Buriram. His autobiographical *People of Esarn* is especially recommended.

The humble buffalo – friend, worker, transport and dinner to many Thai farmers.

Getting There & Away

The main train and bus lines in the North-East are between Bangkok and Nong Khai, and between Bangkok and Ubon Ratchathani. The North-East can also be reached from Northern Thailand by bus or from Phitsanulok, with Khon Kaen as the gateway.

Nakhon Ratchasima Province

Thailand's largest province (20,500 sq km) is most well known for silk weaving. Some of the country's best silk is made in the village of Pak Thong Chai, 30km south-west of Khorat on Rte 304. Many of the Bangkok silk houses have their cloth made there, so don't expect to get any special bargains just because you went all that way. There are also a couple of silk shops in Khorat that are just as good – sometimes better – for their selection and price. Still, Pak Thong Chai is worth a trip if you're interested in observing Thailand's silk-weaving methods.

Nakhon Ratchasima's other big attraction is the Angkor-period Khmer ruins scattered about the province. Most are little more than a jumble of stones or a single prang, but the completed restoration at Prasat Hin Phimai and ongoing work at Prasat Phanomwan are very impressive. In addition to Khmer religious shrines, there are some 192 ancient city sites – Mon, Lao and Khmer – scattered around the province. Most are visible only to archaeologists trained to look for the odd earthen rampart, boundary stone or laterite (red clay) foundation.

Not much is known about the early history of the province except that, as indicated by an AD-937 inscription, it was part of a kingdom known as Sri Janas (Si Janat), which apparently extended over the entire Khorat Plateau. The inhabitants of Sri Janas – or at least its elite royal inhabitants – practised a mixture of Mahayana Buddhism and Brahmanist Shiva worship, hence it was quite possibly an Angkor satellite.

NAKHON RATCHASIMA (KHORAT)
อ.เมืองนครราชสีมา(โคราช)

postcode 30000 • pop 208,500

Exactly 250km from Bangkok, *amphoe meuang* (provincial capital) Nakhon Ratchasima was once the capital of Lao Klang, a Thai monthon that covered present-day Khorat, Chaiyaphum and Buriram Provinces. Up until the mid-Ayuthaya era it was actually two towns, Sema and Khorakpura, which merged under the reign of King Narai. To this day, Khorat has a split personality of sorts, with the older, less commercial half to the west, and the newer central half inside the city moats to the east. Sema and Khorakpura were originally built in present-day Sung Noen (35km to the south-east).

No longer the quaint Isan town it once was, busy Khorat has become an important transportation hub and burgeoning industrial centre, and is Thailand's second largest city. Between 1988 and 1997 new factory registrations averaged 1300 per year. Yet only in 1992 did the city get its first international-class hotel. Often cited only as a train or bus stop from which one reaches the nearby Phimai ruins, Khorat is a fairly interesting place if you don't mind putting up with the grubby air, which can be almost as bad as Bangkok's. Those who prefer a quieter setting might want to spend the night in Phimai instead, making day trips to Khorat; those who like city life might consider the opposite tactic.

One of seven air bases in Thailand used by the US armed forces to launch air strikes on Laos and Vietnam in the 1960s and 1970s was just outside Khorat. A few retired GIs still live in the area with their Thai families, and the Veterans of Foreign Wars Cafeteria is still open on Thanon Phoklang (Phoklang Rd). But the heavy US influence that was obvious in the late 1970s after the base was closed has all but faded away. Yes, the big massage parlours are still there, but the clientele is almost exclusively Thai.

Khorat's most popular annual event is the Thao Suranari Festival, a celebration of Thao Suranari's victory over the Lao (see Thao Suranari Memorial later). It's held from late March to early April and features parades, *lí-keh* (Thai folk dance-drama), *phleng khorâat* (Khorat folk song) and a beauty contest. (See the 'Music, Theatre & Dance' special section.) Thousands of participants from around Nakhon Ratchasima Province and beyond attend the festivities.

Orientation

Central Khorat is contained within a road loop formed on the west and north by the Friendship Hwy (Hwy 2), also known as Thanon Mittaphap; and connecting routes to the east and south. A historic moat further subdivides the city in two, with the more densely developed half to the east of the Khun Ying Mo Memorial and a slightly more low-key section to the west, around the train station and bus terminal. Khorat has expanded in all directions well beyond these main areas, but the parts of the city most visitors deal with are found in these central sections.

Information

Tourist Offices The Tourism Authority of Thailand office (TAT; ☎ 044-213666, fax 213667) at 2102–2104 Thanon Mittaphap (western edge of town) is worth a visit. The friendly staff have plenty of information about Khorat as well as Buriram, Surin and Chaiyaphum, so if you're headed to one of those provinces you can stop here and get maps and advice. To get to the TAT office, walk straight across from the entrance of the Khorat train station to Thanon Mukkhamontri, turn left and walk west until you reach the highway to Bangkok – this is Thanon Mittaphap. The TAT is just across the road, on the south-western corner. The office is open from 8.30 am to 4.30 pm daily.

A tourist police office (☎ 044-341777–9, 1155) is located opposite bus terminal 2, off the highway to Nong Khai north of the city centre.

Money The best area for banks is Thanon Chumphon, where you'll find Bangkok Bank, Thai Farmers Bank and Siam Commercial Bank, all of which offer foreign exchange services from 8.30 am to 3.30 pm on weekdays. Bangkok Bank of Commerce, opposite the Fah Thai Hotel on Thanon Phoklang, has an exchange window open from 8.30 am to 8 pm daily.

Post & Communications A conveniently located main post office on Thanon Mittaphap is open from 8.30 am to 4.30 pm weekdays and 9 am to 1 pm Saturday. There is a branch on Thanon Jomsurangyat between Klang Plaza 2 shopping centre and the Chao Phraya Inn, and another on Thanon Atsadang. International telephone calls are best made from the Communications Authority of Thailand (CAT) office attached to the Atsadang post office; it's open from 7 am and 11 pm daily.

TP Internet 2000 (☎ 044-261533) is located next to the train station.

Mahawirawong National Museum
พิพิธภัณฑสถานแห่งชาติมหาวีรวงศ์

In the grounds of Wat Sutchinda, directly across from the government buildings off Thanon Ratchadamnoen and just outside the city moat, this museum has a good collection of Khmer art objects, especially door lintels, as well as objects from other periods. It's open from 9 am to 4 pm daily. Admission is 10B.

Thao Suranari Memorial
อนุสาวรีย์ท้าวสุรนารี

At the Chumphon Gate to central Khorat, on the western side, is this much-worshipped memorial shrine to Thao Suranari (also known as Khun Ying Mo), a courageous Thai woman who led the local citizens in a battle against Lao invaders from Vientiane during the rule of Rama III (1824–51).

Hundreds of unique offerings, such as a miniature model of a bus donated by local bus drivers, find their way to the shrine in the hope that Khun Ying Mo's spirit will protect the supplicants from danger or any ill will.

Khorat Song In the evenings you can see performances of phleng khorâat, the traditional Khorat folk song, in an area opposite the shrine near some shops selling *năem* (preserved pork). It's usually performed by groups of four singers hired by people whose supplications to Thao Suranari have been honoured. To show gratitude to the spirit, they pay for the performance. Over 100 groups are for hire, usually for 300B to 600B per performance.

NAKHON RATCHASIMA (KHORAT)

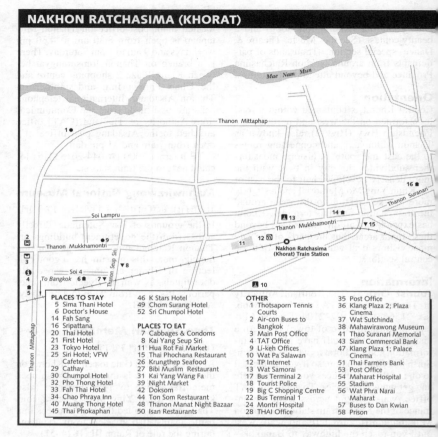

PLACES TO STAY
5 Sima Thani Hotel
6 Doctor's House
14 Fah Sang
16 Sripattana
20 Thai Hotel
21 First Hotel
23 Tokyo Hotel
25 Siri Hotel; VFW Cafeteria
29 Cathay
30 Chumpol Hotel
32 Pho Thong Hotel
33 Fah Thai Hotel
34 Chao Phraya Inn
40 Muang Thong Hotel
45 Thai Phokaphan

46 K Stars Hotel
49 Chom Surang Hotel
52 Sri Chumpol Hotel

PLACES TO EAT
7 Cabbages & Condoms
8 Kai Yang Seup Siri
11 Hua Rot Fai Market
15 Thai Phochana Restaurant
26 Krungthep Seafood
27 Bibi Muslim Restaurant
31 Kai Yang Wang Fa
39 Night Market
42 Doksom
44 Ton Som Restaurant
48 Thanon Manat Night Bazaar
50 Isan Restaurants

OTHER
1 Thotsaporn Tennis Courts
2 Air-con Buses to Bangkok
3 Main Post Office
4 TAT Office
9 Li-keh Offices
10 Wat Pa Salawan
12 TP Internet
13 Wat Samorai
17 Bus Terminal 2
18 Tourist Police
19 Big C Shopping Centre
22 Bus Terminal 1
24 Montri Hospital
28 THAI Office

35 Post Office
36 Klang Plaza 2; Plaza Cinema
37 Wat Sutchinda
38 Mahawirawong Museum
41 Thao Suranari Memorial
43 Siam Commercial Bank
47 Klang Plaza 1; Palace Cinema
51 Thai Farmers Bank
53 Post Office
54 Maharat Hospital
55 Stadium
56 Wat Phra Narai Maharat
57 Buses to Dan Kwian
58 Prison

Wat Phra Narai Maharat

วัดพระนารายณ์มหาราช

This monastery is of interest for two main reasons: It has a Khmer sandstone sculpture of Phra Narai (Narayana or Vishnu), and it also houses Khorat's *làk meuang,* or city pillar. The wát is on Thanon Prajak between Thanon Atsadang and Thanon Chumphon.

Wat Sala Loi

วัดศาลาลอย

This modern 'Temple of the Floating Pavilion' is 400m east of the north-eastern corner of the moat and has a *bòt* (central chapel) shaped like a Chinese junk.

Wat Pa Salawan

วัดป่าสาละวัน

A Thammayut 'forest monastery' once surrounded by jungle, Wat Pa Salawan has been engulfed by the city, but it's still a fairly quiet escape. The late abbot, Luang Phaw Phut, was quite well known as a meditation teacher and has developed a strong lay following in the area. A few relics belonging to the legendary Ajahn Man are on display in the main *wíhǎan* (hall), a large but simple wooden affair. A cemetery on the grounds has a couple of markers with photos of US veterans who lived their later years in Khorat. Wat Pa Salawan is in the south-western sector of the city behind Khorat's train station.

Places to Stay – Budget

Guesthouses Nakhon Ratchasima's longest-running guesthouse, *Doctor's House* (☎ 044-255846, 78 Soi 4, Thanon Seup Siri) is in the western area of the city. The house is quiet and comfortable, and has five large singles/doubles for 180B. The proprietors are friendly and speak English. A No 1 yellow *săwngthăew* (pick-up truck) will take you past here. On the down side, it is far from the city centre and the gate is locked at 10 pm.

Hotels Visit the TAT office for a map and complete list of Khorat's hotels.

Fah Sang (☎ 044-242143, 112–114 Thanon Mukkhamontri), not far from Khorat train station, has OK rooms and friendly staff, although the location is noisy. Rooms

with fan and bathroom are 150B in the old wooden section, and 240B single/double in the newer section. Air-con rooms with hot water cost 350/380B.

Pho Thong (☎ 044-242084, 658 Thanon Phoklang) has rooms with fan and bathroom from 170B to 220B, 300B with air-con and TV. It's on the corner of Thanon Ratchadamnoen at the west city gate, right in the centre of things, and is overall better value than the Fah Sang.

In the same vicinity is the quiet and friendly – and even better value – *Siri Hotel* (☎ 044-242831, 241556, 167–168 Thanon Phoklang), well located a couple of blocks west of the city moats. Rooms cost 130B to 200B with a fan and 300B to 400B with air-con. The VFW Cafeteria is next door.

Chumpol Hotel (☎ 044-242453, 701–702 Thanon Phoklang) charges 220B for a basic but clean single/double, 300B for an air-con double, and 350B for an air-con room with TV that sleeps three.

Muang Thong Hotel (☎ 044-242090, 46 Thanon Chumphon) is a classic old wooden hotel that's seen better days – look for the green-painted building inside the moat near the Thao Suranari Memorial. Rooms are a cheap 120B a night without bathroom, 220B with cold-water shower – be sure to get a room off the street; and stay away if you're bothered by its reputation as the town brothel.

The *Thai Phokaphan* (☎ 044-242454, 104–106 Thanon Atsadang) is inside the city moats, across the street from the more expensive K Stars Hotel and the KR massage parlour. Good one- and two-bed rooms cost 180B with fan and cold-water shower, 360B with air-con and hot water. Thai Phokaphan is near the night market but well off the street and not too noisy.

The *Cathay* (☎ 044-252067, 3692/5–6 Thanon Ratchadamnoen) has basic rooms with cold-water baths for 140/180B and is not far from the bus terminal for Buriram, Surin, Ubon Ratchathani and Chiang Mai. Closer still is the five-storey *First Hotel* (☎ 044-255117, 132–136 Thanon Burin) with cheap, clean rooms with fan starting at 250B; add 110B more for air-con, refrigerator and attached bathroom. A small attached restaurant serves basic Thai food at reasonable prices.

The *Sri Chumpol Hotel* (☎ 044-242460, 133 Thanon Chumphon) is a bit quieter than the other Thai-Chinese places on Thanon Phoklang and Thanon Ratchadamnoen, and it's cleaner than most. Rooms with fan and cold-water bathroom and one bed cost 160B; two beds cost 220B. Rooms with air-con and hot water are 240B.

The *Tokyo Hotel* (☎ 044-242873, 257179, fax 242788, 329–333 Thanon Suranari) has OK rooms – quieter than most of those on Thanon Phoklang – for 120B with fan and cold-water bathroom, 400B with air-con and hot water. Opposite the Tokyo Hotel on Thanon Suranari is the *Tokyo 2 Hotel* (☎ 044-242788), which is actually an extension of the Tokyo Hotel. Large rooms cost 120B to 200B with a bathroom, and 300B to 400B with air-con.

Places to Stay – Mid-Range

The *Fah Thai Hotel* (☎ 044-267390, fax 252797, 3535 Thanon Phoklang) charges 250/350B for a single/double room with fan and private bathroom, 350B for air-con. It's good for a Thanon Phoklang Thai-Chinese place. A small attached restaurant is open from from 7 am to 8 pm.

The well-located *Chao Phraya Inn* (☎ 044-243825, 62/1 Thanon Jomsurangyat), near the Klang Plaza 2 shopping centre, charges 350B for simple but comfortable air-con rooms with cold-water bathroom. There's a 24-hour coffee shop on the premises.

Thai Hotel (☎ 044-270727, fax 241613, 644–650 Thanon Mittaphap), not far from the main city centre bus terminal, has similar digs for 320B to 380B, plus less-expensive rooms with fans for 250B to 300B.

Places to Stay – Top End

At the bottom of the top end, *Sripattana* (☎ 044-251652, fax 251655, 346 Thanon Suranari) has air-con rooms with hot-water bathroom and TV for 510B. Suites are available for 1200B but are often discounted to around 900B. This circa-1965 hotel has a pub, 24-hour coffee shop and a swimming pool.

Chom Surang (☎ 044-257088, fax 252897, 2701/2 Thanon Mahat Thai) has all air-con rooms from 850B, and also has a pool.

The multistorey *K Stars Hotel* (☎/fax 044-257057, 191 Thanon Atsadang) has clean, comfortable air-con rooms ranging from 500B (or 650B including buffet breakfast) to 1500B for a deluxe suite. The hotel offers a 24-hour coffee shop, minimart, massage, snooker and nightclub.

The *Sima Thani Hotel* (☎ 044-213100, fax 213121) originally opened in 1992 as a Sheraton but is now owned by a Thai hotel group. Superior rooms start at 900B, while deluxe rooms cost 1300B to 1800B. All rooms have air-con, IDD phone, satellite TV, fridge and safe. The hotel has a lobby bar, restaurant, pub and pool.

Not to be outdone, Thailand's Dusit Group has opened its own *Royal Princess Khorat* (☎ 044-256629, fax 256601, 1137 Thanon Suranari) on the north-eastern outskirts of the city. Rates begin at 1200B for a standard room, including an excellent breakfast buffet featuring Chinese, Thai and Western food. All rooms have a fridge, bathroom, satellite TV and air-con. The list of amenities includes a lobby bar, restaurant, large pool and a business centre.

Places to Eat

Khorat has many excellent Thai and Chinese restaurants, especially along Thanon Ratchadamnoen near the Thao Suranari Memorial and western gate to central Khorat. The *Hua Rot Fai Market* on Thanon Mukkhamontri near the Khorat train station is a great place to eat in the evening, as is the *Thanon Manat night bazaar*; both are at their best from 6 to 10 pm.

The air-con, well-known *Thai Phochana* (142 Thanon Jomsurangyat) has a mix of standard Thai and local specialities, including *mìi khorâat* (Khorat-style noodles) and *yam kòp yâang* (roast frog salad). Also good here is *kaeng phèt pèt* (duck curry).

Just around the corner from Doctor's House is a branch of Bangkok's *Cabbages & Condoms* (C & C). Like the original it's a nonprofit operation sponsored by the Population & Community Development Association; the food is good but a bit pricey for Khorat. It's open from 10.30 am to 10 pm.

For good, fresh seafood visit *Krungthep Seafood* (☎ 044-256183) on Thanon Phoklang, not far from the Siri Hotel; it's open from 6 pm to midnight. On the same side of Thanon Phoklang, a little farther east, *Bibi Muslim* does tasty halal curries and *khâo mòk kài* (chicken biryani).

On Thanon Chumphon near the Thanon Suranari Memorial, the air-con *Doksom* (☎ 044-252020) is a good place to cool off with some delicious ice cream or cold drinks.

Backing up to Doksom on Thanon Wacharasarit is the upmarket Thai restaurant *Ton Som Restaurant* (☎ 044-252275), which is open until midnight.

Isan Two very unassuming Isan places along the eastern side of Thanon Wacharasarit between Thanon Saphasit and Thanon Kamhaeng Songkhram, *Suan Sin* and *Sam-ran Lap*, serve locally popular Isan fare such as *plaa chonnábòt* (freshwater fish steamed with vegetables and served with a tart, spicy sauce), *súp hǎang wua* (oxtail

soup) and *lín yâang* (barbecued tongue). It also serves *lâap* (spicy minced-meat salad) and other Isan standards.

For the best *kài yâang* (grilled spiced chicken) and sôm-tam (grated papaya salad) in town, check out *Kai Yang Seup Siri*, near Doctor's House on Thanon Seup Siri. There are two Isan places next door to each other here – look for the one with chickens on the grill out the front. It starts serving around 10.30 am and is usually sold out by 3 or 4 pm.

Also good, and open longer hours, is *Kai Yang Wang Fa*, on Thanon Ratchadamnoen opposite the shrine.

International *VFW Cafeteria* next to the Siri Hotel on Thanon Phoklang has cheap American-style breakfasts, as well as steaks, ice cream, pizzas and salads. It gets mixed reviews, however, so let's just say it's a good imitation of a US 'greasy spoon', for all that term implies. The central tables are often taken by a tight-knit group of US Vietnam War veterans chatting about the good old days.

Cleaner and more reliable – if more expensive – are the American-style restaurants in Klang Plaza 2 shopping centre, including *KFC, Dunkin' Donuts, Black Canyon Coffeeshop* and *Royal Home Bakery*. Klang Plaza also has a large supermarket, should you want to shop for groceries.

Entertainment

Khorat is a regional headquarters for lí-keh troupes, who maintain several offices along Thanon Mukkhamontri near the Thanon Seup Siri intersection. Hired performances start at 1000B for a small ensemble – you provide the venue and the troupe will bring its costumes, stage sets and so on – much like a travelling carnival.

The *Phlap-Phla Dawan Restaurant* in the Sima Thani Hotel hosts a well-executed cultural performance of Thai, Lao and Khmer dancing every night – check with the hotel for the times.

Several *cinemas* in town show motion pictures daily. The better movies, including occasional foreign flicks, seem to turn up at the *Plaza*, which is behind the Klang Plaza 2 shopping centre off Thanon Ratchadamnoen and Thanon Jomsurangyat.

The city boasts seven *massage parlours*, three Thai-style *nightclubs* and a couple of hotel *discos*. You can get a complete list of nightlife venues from the TAT office.

Shopping

A night bazaar along Thanon Manat features cheap clothes, fruit, flowers, sunglasses, watches and food vendors – nothing spectacular, but it's a fine place to spend time.

Klang Plaza 2 shopping centre on Thanon Jomsurangyat offers five floors of shops purveying everything from videos to housewares. There's another Klang Plaza on Thanon Atsadang near the Thai Phokaphan Hotel.

Big C shopping centre, near the Thai Hotel, has two floors of small stores, a good pharmacy and restaurants, including a KFC.

Khorat has many shops that specialise in silk. Several can be found along Thanon Ratchadamnoen near the Thao Suranari Memorial.

Getting There & Away

Air Thai Airways International (THAI) flies to Khorat from Bangkok twice daily; the fare is 660B one way. There is also a flight to/from Buriram for 450B. The THAI office (☎ 044-252114) is at 40–44 Thanon Suranari.

Bus Ordinary buses leave the Northern bus terminal in Bangkok every hour from 5 am to 8 pm. The fare is 77B and the trip takes four hours. Air-con buses cost 139B. In Khorat, air-con buses from/to Bangkok arrive at and depart from the air-con bus terminal on Thanon Mittaphap.

For buses to other places in Thailand, there are two main bus terminals. Bus terminal 1, off Thanon Burin in the city centre near the intersection of the Thanon Mittaphap loop and the highway north to Nong Khai, has buses to Khon Kaen, Phitsanulok, Chiang Mai and Chiang Rai, plus a few buses to Bangkok. This terminal can be extremely congested. Buses between Khorat and Khon Kaen cost 58B and leave throughout the day.

Buses to other points in the North-East or in eastern Central Thailand leave from bus terminal 2, off the highway to Nong Khai north of the city centre. Direct buses between Khorat and Chanthaburi on the southeast coast run hourly between 4.30 am and 4 pm. The fare is 104B (187B air-con) and the trip takes about eight hours. The following table lists buses to and from Khorat.

destination/class	fare	duration (hrs)
Chiang Mai*		
ordinary	218B	12
air-con	392B	12
VIP	458B	10
Chiang Rai*		
ordinary	258B	10
air-con	464B	9
Loei		
air-con	209B	3
Nakhon Phanom		
air-con	250B	4½
Nong Khai		
ordinary	105B	4
air-con	189B	3½
Pattaya		
air-con	178B	5½
Phitsanulok*		
ordinary	133B	5
air-con	221B	4
VIP	258B	4
Rayong		
air-con	201B	4
Roi Et		
air-con	140B	2½
Sakon Nakhon		
ordinary	111B	4½
air-con	200B	4
Ubon		
ordinary	105B–121B	6
air-con	175B–220B	5
Udon		
ordinary	90B	4
air-con	126B	3
Yasothon		
ordinary	79B	5
air-con	145B	3

* Leaves from bus terminal 1; all others in list leave from bus terminal 2.

Train An express train bound for Ubon Ratchathani departs Bangkok's Hualamphong station at 9 pm, arriving in Khorat at 2.19 am.

Rapid trains on the Ubon line depart from Bangkok at 6.50 am and 6.45 and 10.45 pm, arriving in Khorat at 12.12 pm and 12.20 and 4.51 am respectively.

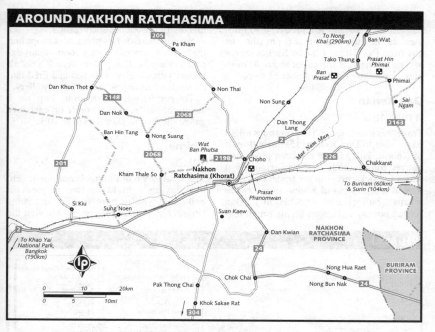

AROUND NAKHON RATCHASIMA

There are also four ordinary trains (3rd class only) that depart from Bangkok at 9.10 and 11.45 am and 3.25 and 11.25 pm, arriving in Khorat about 5½ to six hours after departure. Express diesel railcars (aka 'Sprinters'; 2nd-class air-con only) depart from Hualamphong at 11.05 am and 9.50 pm and arrive in Khorat at 4.06 pm and 2.55 am respectively.

A special express train (1st and 2nd class) leaves at 5.45 am and arrives in Khorat at 10.18 am.

The 1st-class fare (express train only) is 230B, 2nd class is 115B and 3rd class 50B. Add 40B for the rapid trains, 60B for the express and 80B for the special express. The train passes through some great scenery on the Khorat Plateau, including a view of the enormous white Buddha figure at Wat Theppitak on a thickly forested hillside.

Getting Around
Săamláw (three-wheeled pedicabs) around the city cost 20B; túk-túk (motorised săamláw) cost 40B to most places around town (30B for a short hop), 50B to 60B for longer trips.

The city also has a fairly extensive bus system. From the Khorat train station, bus No 1 heads east along Thanon Phoklang; No 2 heads east along Thanon Mukkhamontri and No 3 goes east along Thanon Jomsurangyat. In the opposite direction, bus Nos 1, 2 and 3 all end up heading west on Thanon Mukkhamontri towards the TAT office. The fare on each line is 3B. Comfortable air-con versions of bus No 2 are also available for 5B.

AROUND NAKHON RATCHASIMA
Pak Thong Chai
ปักธงชัย

Thirty-two kilometres south of Khorat on Rte 304 is Pak Thong Chai, one of Thailand's most famous **silk-weaving** villages. Several varieties and prices of silk are available, and most weavers sell directly to the public. However, prices are not necessarily lower than in Khorat or Bangkok. There are around 70 silk factories in the district.

Achan Pan and *Pak Thong Chai* hotels are both on the main road through town and have rooms from 70B.

Bus No 1303 to Pak Thong Chai leaves bus terminal No 1 in Khorat every 30 minutes, the last trip leaving at 6 pm (the last bus from Pak Thong Chai to Khorat leaves at 5 pm). The 12B trip takes about 40 minutes, depending on the number of stops.

Dan Kwian
ด่านเกวียน

Travellers interested in Thai **ceramics** might pay a visit to Dan Kwian, 15km south-east of Khorat. This village has been producing pottery for hundreds of years; originally it was a bullock-cart stop for traders on their way to markets in old Khorat (*dàan kwian* means 'bullock-cart checkpoint'). Dan Kwian pottery is famous for its rough tex-

ture and rust-like hue – only kaolin from this district produces such results.

Several more-or-less permanent shops line the highway. Prices are very good – many exporters shop for Thai pottery here. It's not all pottery either – clay is shaped and fired into all kinds of art objects, including jewellery.

To get here from Khorat, hop on a sǎwngthǎew from the south or east city gates; the fare to Dan Kwian is 10B.

Phimai
พิมาย

The small town of Phimai is nothing much, but staying a night or two is pleasant enough if you're here to visit the ruins (Prasat Hin Phimai). If you want to visit the

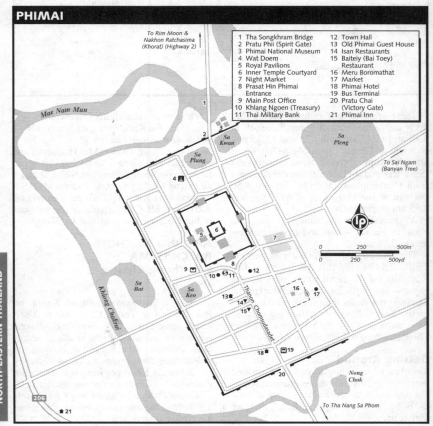

PHIMAI

To Rim Moon & Nakhon Ratchasima (Khorat) (Highway 2)

1 Tha Songkhram Bridge
2 Pratu Phii (Spirit Gate)
3 Phimai National Museum
4 Wat Doem
5 Royal Pavilions
6 Inner Temple Courtyard
7 Night Market
8 Prasat Hin Phimai Entrance
9 Main Post Office
10 Khlang Ngoen (Treasury)
11 Thai Military Bank
12 Town Hall
13 Old Phimai Guest House
14 Isan Restaurants
15 Baiteiy (Bai Toey) Restaurant
16 Meru Boromathat
17 Market
18 Phimai Hotel
19 Bus Terminal
20 Pratu Chai (Victory Gate)
21 Phimai Inn

Mae Nam Mun

Sa Kwan
Sa Plung
Sa Pleng

To Sai Ngam (Banyan Tree)

Khlong Chakrai

Sa Bot
Sa Keo

Thanon Chomsudasadet

Nong Chok

To Tha Nang Sa Phom

206

ruins as a day trip from Khorat, the 8 am bus will give you plenty of wandering time at the ruins with time to spare for the return bus trip in the late afternoon. If Khorat's not your cup of tea, do it the other way around; stay in Phimai and take a day trip to Khorat.

Outside the town entrance, a couple of kilometres down Rte 206, is Thailand's largest and oldest banyan tree, a megaflorum spread over an island in a large pond (actually a state irrigation reservoir). The locals call it **Sai Ngam** (Beautiful Banyan); you can walk through the banyan branches via walkways built over the pond. Food vendors and astrologers offer their services to picnickers in the vicinity.

Around town you'll see one of North-Eastern Thailand's trademarks, the *rót kàsèt,* or farm truck. These low-tech vehicles – painted with technicolour sunsets, swaying palms and bright geometric patterns – feature cheap Kubota engines in an open engine housing. The engines are easily detached to run ploughs, water pumps or long-tail boats. U Prasan, around the corner from the Phimai Hotel, specialises in the painting and repair of these oddities.

Since 1991 the town has hosted a festival during November to celebrate Prasat Hin Phimai history. The events vary, but typically include a sound-and-light show at the ruins, historical and cultural exhibits, classical dance-drama performances and a lamp-lit procession between temples.

Information The Baiteiy (Bai Toey) restaurant distributes a town map; the owner speaks English. There's a Thai Farmers Bank next door to the restaurant, and a branch of the Thai Military Bank near the Prasat Hin Phimai Historical Park entrance. Banking hours are 8.30 am to 3.30 pm weekdays. The post office is open from 8.30 am to 4.30 pm weekdays and 9 am to noon Saturday.

Prasat Hin Phimai National Historical Park The Angkor-period Khmer shrine monument in this park, 60km north-east of Khorat, makes Phimai worth a visit. Originally started by Khmer King Jayavarman V in the late 10th century and finished by King Suriyavarman I (reigned AD 1002–49) in the early 11th century, this Hindu–Mahayana Buddhist temple projects a majesty that transcends its size.

The 28m-tall main shrine, of cruciform design, is made of white sandstone, while the adjunct shrines are of pink sandstone and laterite. The sculptures over the doorways to the main shrine are particularly impressive.

The Phimai temple, like many other Khmer monuments in this part of Thailand, predates the famous Angkor Wat complex in Cambodia. When the Angkor empire was at its peak, and encompassed parts of Thailand, Phimai was directly connected to the Angkor capital by road.

Reconstruction work by the Fine Arts Department has been completed, and although the pieces do not quite fit together as they must have originally, this only seems to add to the monument's somewhat eerie quality. Between the main entrance and the main street of the small town is a ruined palace and, farther on, an open-air museum features Khmer sculpture.

The complex is open from 6 am to 6 pm daily; admission is 40B.

Phimai National Museum The exhibits at this nicely designed new museum are mostly dedicated to Isan sculpture, with many of the best lintels and statues from Phimai, Phanom Rung, Phanomwan and other Khmer sites in Thailand as well as ceramics from nearby Ban Prasat.

The museum's most prized possession, a stone sculpture of Angkor King Jayavarman VII, comes from Prasat Hin Phimai National Historical Park – it looks very much like a sitting Buddha.

An open-air sculpture garden, next to the main hall, displays ornate boundary stones and other Khmer figures from Phimai. A small bookshop is attached to the museum.

The museum is open from 9 am to 4 pm daily and admission is 30B. There's a small souvenir shop and a restaurant that serves simple Thai dishes and ice cream.

Places to Stay *Old Phimai Guest House* (☎ 044-471918), a spartan but comfortable guesthouse on an alley off the main street leading to the ruins, has dorm beds for 90B. Singles/doubles/triples/quads cost 150/200/250/350B. All rooms have a fan and shared bathroom in a large house. One air-con room is available for 350B. The staff provide a basic self-serve breakfast and old bicycles are available to rent for 10B per hour.

The *Phimai Hotel* (☎ 044-471940), around the corner from the bus terminal, is a bit dingy. Clean, adequate rooms, but not as good value as the guesthouses, cost 220/250B single/double with fan and cold water and 350/380B for air-con, satellite TV and hot water.

The newer and better *Phimai Inn* (☎/fax 044-471175) is about 2km south-west of the old town (20B by sǎamláw) on Rte 206. Clean and comfortable rooms cost 250B with fan, TV and private cold-water bathroom, 350B with air-con and hot water. Deluxe 600B rooms have carpet and a minibar. The hotel rents bicycles, and has a refreshing pool with a snack bar.

Places to Eat Good Thai and Chinese food is available at the *Baiteiy Restaurant* (*Bai Toey;* ☎ 044-471725) near the hotel and guesthouse. Daily lunch specials are just 30B; there are also more-expensive a la carte items, several vegetarian dishes, Western breakfasts and ice cream.

Around the corner from the Baiteiy, on a smaller east-west street, are two modest *restaurants* specialising in lâap and kâwy (spicy Isan-style salads made with meat, poultry or fish) and sticky rice. There is also a decent collection of food vendors at a *night market* just north of the regular day market; it operates from around 6 pm to midnight.

On a tributary of the Mae Nam Mun (Mun River) about 2km north-west of town, the *Rim Moon* is a typical upcountry garden restaurant. Open daily, in the evenings it features a live band.

Getting There & Away Bus No 1305 leaves for Phimai every half-hour during the day from Khorat's bus terminal 2. The trip to Phimai (34B) takes from one to 1½ hours, depending on the number of passengers that are picked up along the way. The bus terminal in Phimai is around the corner from the Phimai Hotel and down the street from Prasat Hin Phimai. The last Phimai bus leaves Khorat bus terminal at about 10 pm; from Phimai the last bus is at 6 pm.

Getting Around Phimai is small enough to walk easily between the bus terminal, Phimai Hotel, guesthouses and the ruins. Sǎamláw

trips in town cost 10B to 20B one way. If you would like to see more of the town and environs (eg, Sai Ngam), you can rent bicycles from Old Phimai Guest House for 10B per hour. Baiteiy Restaurant also rents bikes.

The guesthouse can also arrange day trips to the ruins of Phanom Rung, Meuang Tam (see the Phanom Rung Historical Park special section in this chapter) or Khao Phra Wihan for 400B to 800B per person (minimum of four people). The trip to the latter ruin is a good four hours each way, so it might be better explored from Surin or Si Saket.

Prasat Phanomwan
ปราสาทพนมวัน

Although not as large as Prasat Hin Phimai, the 11th-century ruins at Prasat Phanomwan are nonetheless impressive. The sanctuary is on the grounds of a temple (Wat Phanomwan) that seems to have been temporarily abandoned while restoration work on the sanctuary takes place. Once adorned with Shivalingam (phallus images) and a Nandi (Shiva's bull mount), which indicated that the Khmers originally built Phanomwan as a Hindu temple, the sanctuary now looks more like a construction site, with large cranes being used to put massive sandstone blocks back into place. Fine Arts Department staff estimate that the restoration work will take around four years to complete. In the meantime, a visit to Prasat Phanomwan is a lesson in the extensive modern efforts needed to rebuild an ancient Khmer monument.

Getting There & Away There are direct buses from Khorat's bus terminal 2 every hour from 7 am to 5.30 pm. The fare is 7B.

Ban Prasat
บ้านปราสาท

Forty-five kilometres north-east of the city of Nakhon Ratchasima near the banks of Lam Than Prasat (Than Prasat River; off Hwy 2 between Non Sung and Phimai), Ban Prasat is the oldest archaeological site in the Khorat Basin. Excavations completed in 1991 show that the site, which is also known as the Ku Tan Prasat Mound, was inhabited by an agricultural-ceramic culture at least 3000 years ago. This culture lasted around 500 years and may even have pre-dated Udon Thani Province's Ban Chiang by 1000 years.

Archaeological evidence suggests the Ban Prasat culture spun thread for weaving cloth, made sophisticated coloured pottery, planted rice, raised domestic animals and – towards the end of the culture's 500 years of prosperity – developed bronze metallurgy. Other layers uncovered indicate the site was later taken over by a pre–Dvaravati Mon city, followed by a 10th-century settlement whose main legacy is a small brick sanctuary known locally as **Ku Than Prasat**. This structure shows both Dvaravati and Khmer characteristics, and may have been a cultural transition point between Mon kingdoms to the west and the Khmer principalities to the east.

Several excavation pits are on display; the visitors centre houses pottery and skeletons found in the pits and is open from 8.30 am to 4 pm Wednesday to Sunday.

Ordinary buses between Phimai and Khorat will stop in Ban Prasat for 9B. In Ban Prasat a motorcycle taxi can take you 1.5km to all three excavation sites for 50B.

KHAO YAI NATIONAL PARK
อุทยานแห่งชาติเขาใหญ่

Established in 1961, this is Thailand's oldest national park; it covers 2172 sq km and includes one of the largest intact monsoon forests in mainland Asia. Considered by many experts to be among the world's best national parks, Khao Yai was designated an Association for South East Asian Nations (Asean) National Heritage Site and has been nominated for international status by the UN. More recently, millions of movie-goers unknowingly gazed upon one of Khao Yai's landmarks while watching the 2000 film *The Beach*: the waterfall that appears repeatedly in the film is Nam Tok Hew Suwat (Hew Suwat Falls). The park's terrain covers five vegetation zones: evergreen rainforest (100m to 400m); semi-evergreen rainforest (400m to 900m); mixed deciduous forest (northern slopes at 400m to 600m); hill evergreen forest (over 1000m); and savannah and secondary-growth forest in areas where agriculture and logging occurred before it was protected.

Some 200 to 300 wild elephants reside within the park boundaries; other mammals

recorded include sambar deer, barking deer, gaur, wild pig, Malayan sun bear, Asiatic black bear, tiger, leopard, serow and various gibbons and macaques. In general these animals are most easily spotted during the rainy season from June to October. Khao Yai also has Thailand's largest population of hornbills, including the great hornbill (*nók kòk* or *nók kaahang* in Thai), king of the bird kingdom; as well as the wreathed hornbill (*nók ngaa cháang;* literally, elephant-tusk bird), Indian pied hornbill (*nók khàek*) and rhinoceros hornbill (*nók râet*). Hornbills breed from January to May, the best time to see them. They also feed on figs, so ficus trees are good places to find them. Caves in the park are home to rare wrinkle-lipped bats and Himalayan ribbed bats.

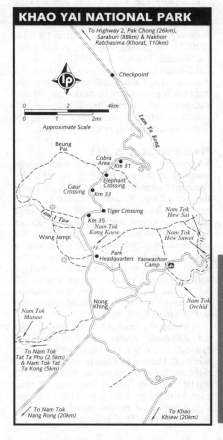

KHAO YAI NATIONAL PARK

To Highway 2, Pak Chong (26km), Saraburi (88km) & Nakhon Ratchasima (Khorat, 110km)

Checkpoint

0   2   4km
0   1   2mi
Approximate Scale

Lam Ta Kong

Beung Pai

Cobra Area   Km 31

Elephant Crossing

Gaur Crossing   Km 33

Lam Ta Tiw   Tiger Crossing   Nam Tok Hew Sai

Km 35
Nam Tok Kong Kaew

Wang Jampi   Nam Tok Hew Suwat

Park Headquarters   Yaowachon Camp

Nong Khing   Nam Tok Orchid

Nam Tok Manao

To Nam Tok Tat Ta Phu (2.5km) & Nam Tok Tat Ta Kong (5km)

To Nam Tok Nang Rong (20km)   To Khao Khiew (20km)

NORTH-EASTERN THAILAND

The park has over 50km of hiking trails, many of them formed by the movement of wildlife. Elevations range from 100m to 1400m where the western edge of Cambodia's Dangrek mountain range meets the southern edge of the Khorat Plateau. You can get a rather inaccurate trail map from the park headquarters. It's easy to get lost on the longer trails so it's advisable to hire a guide. Rangers may be able to act as guides for 100B per day. If you do plan to go walking, it is a good idea to take boots as leeches can be a problem – although mosquito repellent does help to keep them away. There are also three wildlife-watching towers in the park.

You can buy a colour topographical map of the park at the visitors centre for just 10B.

In nearby Pak Chong, you can arrange tours from two or three different agencies. Currently the most reputable seem to be those organised by Wildlife Safari (☎ 044-312922), 39 Thanon Pak Chong; and Khao Yai Wildlife Tours (☎ 044-365167), at Khao Yai Garden Lodge (see Places to Stay & Eat later). Package tours lasting 1½ days cost from 850B per person, including guides and transport; meals and lodging are extra. Standard national park entry fees apply (200B for adults, half price for children).

Places to Stay & Eat

All commercial visitor accommodation was removed at the end of 1992. Forestry department *bungalows* that sleep 12 are available for 1500B. Reservations can be made by calling Bangkok ☎ 02-561 4292. There is also a very basic *dorm* shelter for 30B per person at Yaowachon (Youth) Camp but you need to supply your own bedding; a sleeping bag is a must during the cooler months. Two-person *tents* can be rented for 80B, or you can pitch your own tent for 5B per person per night. A small *restaurant* here serves reasonably priced Thai food from 6 am to 6 pm daily.

In the nearby market town of Pak Chong, the *Phubade Hotel* (*Phubet; ☎ 044-314964, 781/1 Soi 15, Thanon Thetsaban*) is just off Thanon Mittaphap – walk past the night market towards the road to Khao Yai and take a left at Thanon Thetsaban 15, then a left at the sign that reads 'Hotel'. Clean, well-maintained rooms catering to businesspeople and Thai government officials cost 180B to 240B with fan and private bathroom, 300B to 330B with air-con.

Khao Yai Garden Lodge (☎ 044-365167) is 7km out of town (just past the International School) on the way to Khao Yai. Take a blue săwngthăew from the market for 6B or a regular Khao Yai bus for 8B. You can also call the lodge and someone will pick you up in town for free. The Thai-German couple who run the lodge claim there are over 200 species of botanical and hybrid orchids in their garden. Rooms with fan and shared bathroom are 350B. There are also more-expensive rooms with garden views and tasteful decor for 500B with fan, 900B to 1200B with air-con. The affiliated Khao Yai Wildlife Tours offers well-run, full-day Khao Yai trips for 950B.

Also along this road, from 17km to 25km out of Pak Chong, there are at least a dozen 'resorts', including the *Wan-Ree Resort*, *Golden Valley Resort* and *Juldis Khao Yai Resort*, which offer upmarket bungalows in the 1000B to 5000B range on weekends. During the week you should be able to haggle the rates down by half.

Near the main highway intersection in Pak Chong is an excellent **night market** purveying a wide range of Thai and Chinese food from around 5 to 11 pm. There are also a few decent *Thai restaurants* on the highway through town. *Krua Sonont*, on the *soi* (lane) leading to the train station off the main highway through town, is a clean, air-con place with a good Thai/Chinese menu. The owner speaks excellent English and is helpful with local information.

Getting There & Away

From Bangkok take a bus (38B ordinary, 70Bair-con, every 15 minutes from 5 am to 10 pm) from the Northern bus terminal to Pak Chong. From Pak Chong you can catch a săwngthăew to the park gates for 10B from in front of the 7-Eleven store. You may also be able to take a direct bus from Bangkok at certain times of year – inquire at the Northern bus terminal. Minivans to the terminal are available from next to Pak Chong's air-con bus terminal for 100B.

From Khorat take a Bangkok-bound bus and get off in Pak Chong (28B ordinary).

You can also easily get to Pak Chong from Ayuthaya by ordinary train (25B 3rd class, 56B 2nd class; around three hours).

From Bangkok the train costs 36B in 3rd class and 82B in 2nd class, not including the surcharge (40B) for rapid trains. The ordinary train takes around four hours from Bangkok; the rapid is half an hour shorter.

Hitchhiking in the park is usually easy.

Buriram Province

Buriram is a large province (the 18th-largest of 76) with a small capital and a long history. During the Angkor period this area was an important part of the Khmer empire. The restored ruins at Phanom Rung (formally known as Prasat Hin Khao Phanom Rung) are the most impressive of all Angkor monuments in Thailand; other lesser-known ruins in the province include Prasat Meuang Tam, Ku Rasi, Prasat Ban Khok Ngiu, Prasat Nong Hong, Prasat Ban Thai Charoen, Prasat Nong Kong, Prang Ku Samathom, Prang Ku Khao Plaibat, Prang Ku Suwan Taeng, Prang Ku Khao Kadong and many others. If one includes all ancient city sites (including Dvaravati and pre-Dvaravati), the province contains 143, second in number only to Nakhon Ratchasima Province.

Most of the ruins in Buriram are little more than piles of bricks by the side of a road or out in a field. As the Fine Arts Department and/or the local communities continue restoration in the province, more of the Khmer monuments mentioned here may become worth seeing.

Contemporary Buriram Province is famous among Thais for the 320-hectare **Dong Yai Forest**, once protected by monk Prajak Kuttajitto, who 'ordained' trees with monastic robes and sacred thread so people wouldn't cut them down. In 1991 he and his followers were finally run out of the forest by the Thai military, but not without the sustained protests of thousands of sympathetic Thai citizens.

BURIRAM
อ.เมืองบุรีรัมย์

postcode 31000 • pop 30,400
Buriram is a small provincial capital where there is not a great deal to do. Nevertheless, the town is a good base for visiting Khmer temple ruins around the province, such as Phanom Rung. See the Phanom Rung Historical Park special section for details about these fine Khmer ruins.

Information
The post office is open from 8.30 am to 4.30 pm weekdays; the overseas phone inside is accessible from 7 am to 10 pm daily. There is an international phone-card telephone in front of the post office.

Buriram Comnet, on Thanon Nivas west of the clock tower, is Buriram's sole Internet access centre.

Places to Stay
Buriram's choice of accommodation is a bit on the sleazy side. Nearly all of the establishments in the provincial capital double as brothels. If you are put off by this, consider staying in nearby Nang Rong (see later).

Several cheap hotels are within walking distance of the Buriram train station. *Chai Jaroen Hotel* (☎ 044-601559, 114–116 Thanon Nivas), in front of the station, has dreary rooms from 120B single/double with fan and bathroom.

Cheaper but definitely a step or three down in quality is the *Nivas Hotel (Niwat; ☎ 044-611640)*, on a desolate soi just off Thanon Nivas. Its barely adequate singles/doubles are 60/80B. The *Grand Hotel* (☎ 044-611179), along Thanon Nivas in the other direction, has fair rooms with fan and cold-water bathroom for 160B a single, 200B a double, and doubles with air-con for 300B. A small restaurant is attached.

Farther south of the train station is the friendly *Prachasamakhi Hotel* (☎ 044-611198), a four-storey Chinese hotel with a restaurant downstairs on Thanon Sunthonthep. Simple but adequate rooms cost 120/100B with/without bathroom.

The fairly nice *Thai Hotel* (☎ 044-611112, fax 612461, 38/1 Thanon Romburi) has clean single/double rooms with fan and bathroom for 180/220B, and rooms with air-con and TV for 350/390B. There is also a larger 450B 'deluxe' room.

The *Buriram Hotel* (☎ 044-611740), near the town entrance from Rte 218, seems to always be in a state of semi-renovation. It charges 300B for fan rooms and 450B for air-con, but it is known for its bad plumbing and was completely deserted on last visit.

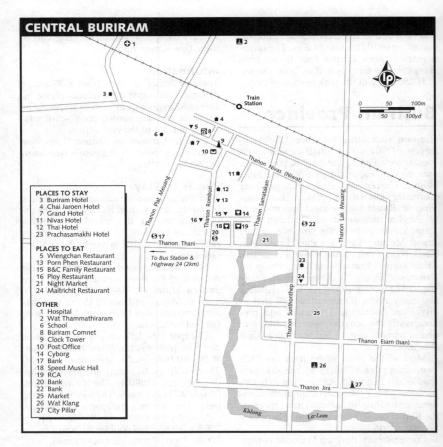

CENTRAL BURIRAM

Train Station

Thanon Nivas (Niwat)

Thanon Plat Meuang

Thanon Romburi

Thanon Samatakan

Thanon Lak Meuang

Thanon Thani

To Bus Station &
Highway 24 (2km)

Thanon Sunthonthep

Thanon Esarn (Isan)

Thanon Jira

Khlong La-Lom

PLACES TO STAY
3 Buriram Hotel
4 Chai Jaroen Hotel
7 Grand Hotel
11 Nivas Hotel
12 Thai Hotel
23 Prachasamakhi Hotel

PLACES TO EAT
5 Wiengchan Restaurant
13 Porn Phen Restaurant
15 B&C Family Restaurant
16 Ploy Restaurant
21 Night Market
24 Maitrichit Restaurant

OTHER
1 Hospital
2 Wat Thammathiraram
6 School
8 Buriram Comnet
9 Clock Tower
10 Post Office
14 Cyborg
17 Bank
18 Speed Music Hall
19 RCA
20 Bank
22 Bank
25 Market
26 Wat Klang
27 City Pillar

Nang Rong You can also stay closer to Phanom Rung by spending the night at this tiny town off the highway. *Honey Inn* (☎ 044-622825, 8/1 Soi Si Kun) is a world away from the provincial capital's unwholesome hotels. Run by a local schoolteacher who speaks English, it contains large, clean rooms which go for 150/200B. To find it, walk 100m from the bus stop to the main road, turn east and go 100m past a petrol station on the left, then turn left just before the hospital, and it's about 150m farther on the right (past a reservoir). Or take a săamláw for 30B. Good food is available here also. A couple of motorbikes can be rented for 200B per day – very handy for visiting the Phanom Rung and Meuang Tam ruins.

The run-down and peephole-ridden *Nang Rong Hotel* (☎ 044-631014) has rooms costing 140B single/double with fan and 300B with air-con, plus an attached restaurant.

Places to Eat

In front of the train station there are a few restaurants that are open during the day for breakfast and lunch. The *restaurant* on the corner of the clock tower opens early in the morning and sells coffee, tea and *paa-thâwng-kŏh* (Chinese doughnuts).

At the Thanon Samatakan and Thanon Thani intersection there is a large *night market* that has mostly Chinese as well as a few Isan vendors. More Isan food can be found at the *Wiengchan Restaurant* on Thanon Nivas near the Grand Hotel.

The *Maitrichit Restaurant* on Thanon Sunthonthep near the Prachasamakhi Hotel has a large selection of Thai and Chinese standards that are served from morning until night. It offers bakery items as well.

Ploy Restaurant on Thanon Romburi, opposite and about 100m south of the Thai Hotel, serves very good Thai food and Western breakfasts with real coffee, and even has a selection of wines.

Also good for basic Thai food is the *Porn Phen* (Phawn Phen) near the Thai Hotel on Thanon Romburi.

Nearby, on a road off Thanon Romburi, is the *B&C Family Restaurant Buriram Chicken Pizza* (☎ 044-613069). As the name suggests, it offers a variety of pizza and chicken dishes, as well as spaghetti and Thai food.

Just after you turn left (east) from Ban Don Nong Nae on the way to Phanom Rung via Rte 2221 there is a nice little family-owned place called *Ban Nit* (Nit's House) where you can get good home-cooked local food. Nit only has a few tables, but out in this area there's not a lot of choice.

Entertainment

For a small town, Buriram actually has a good selection of nightlife options. On a road off Thanon Thani just opposite Ploy restaurant, you'll find *RCA*, where you can enjoy a beer or some Thai food while listening to a live band play decent covers of *fàràng* (Western) favourites.

Across the street from the RCA is the *Speed Music Hall*, a modern dance club with state-of-the-art sound equipment and an impressive light show. .

Nearby, *Cyborg* has an excellent sound system and funky decor, featuring a live DJ from Khorat every night from 9 pm to 6 am.

Getting There & Away

Air THAI flies Bangkok-Buriram five times a week (1060B, one hour and 10 minutes). There's also a flight to/from Nakhon Ratchasima (450B). The THAI office is at Phusiam Tours, 24/23 Thanon Romburi.

Bus Ordinary buses from Khorat to Buriram leave every 20 minutes between 4.30 am and 8 pm (48B, about 2½ hours). From Surin ordinary buses head for Buriram at a similar frequency (32B, about an hour).

From Bangkok's Northern bus terminal there are five 1st-class air-con departures (205B), nine 2nd-class air-con buses for 168B, and ordinary buses for 120B.

Train Buriram is on the Bangkok–Ubon Ratchathani line. Fares are 67B in 3rd class, 155B in 2nd class and 316B in 1st class, not including supplementary charges for rapid (40B) or express (60B) service. Express diesel railcars or 'Sprinters' (2nd class air-con only) to Buriram from Bangkok depart at 11.05 am and 9.50 pm. Ordinary 3rd-class trains depart at 11.45 am and 3.25 and 11.25 pm. All of these take around seven hours to reach Buriram. Rapid and express trains are only about 50 minutes faster than these – see the Nakhon Ratchasima (Khorat) Getting There & Away section later for information on the departure times from Bangkok.

From Khorat there are 13 trains to Buriram (17B 3rd class, 40B 2nd class, 1¾ hours, departures at 12.30, 2.26, 3.05, 5.01, 5.34, 7.50, 10.28 and 10.55 am, and 12.22, 2.25, 4.21, 6.19 and 9.52 pm). Trains from Surin take only 50 minutes and cost just 6B in 3rd class.

Getting Around

Săamláw and túk-túk going from the Buriram train station to the town centre charge 20B.

Chaiyaphum Province

Bounded by Phetchabun, Lopburi, Nakhon Ratchasima and Khon Kaen Provinces, right in the centre of Thailand, Chaiyaphum might as well be in the middle of nowhere considering its low tourist profile. The least visited of any province in the country, it's so remote from national attention that even many Thai citizens can't tell you exactly where it is – or even whether it's in the northern or the north-eastern region.

The several Khmer shrine ruins in the province – none of which are major sites – indicate that the territory was an Angkor, and later Lopburi, satellite during the 10th and 11th centuries.

CHAIYAPHUM

อ.เมืองชัยภูมิ

postcode 36000 • pop 26,400

During the late 18th century a Lao court official brought 200 Lao from Vientiane to settle this area, which had been abandoned by the Khmers 500 years earlier. The community paid tribute to Vientiane but also cultivated relations with Bangkok and Champasak. When Prince Anou (from Vientiane) declared war on Siam in the early 19th century, the Lao ruler of Chaiyaphum, Jao Phraya Lae, wisely switched allegiance to Bangkok, knowing that Anou's armies didn't stand a chance against the more powerful Siamese. Although Jao Phraya Lae lost his life in battle in 1806, the Siamese sacked Vientiane in 1828 and ruled most of western Laos until the coming of the French near the end of the 19th century. Today a statue of Jao Phraya Lae (renamed Phraya Phakdi Chumphon by the Thais) stands in a prominent spot in central Chaiyaphum.

Chaiyaphum residents celebrate a week-long festival in Jao Phraya Lae's honour each year in mid-January. Activities focus on his statue and on a **shrine** erected on the spot where he was killed by Vientiane troops in 1806 – at the base of a tamarind tree about 3km west of town off the road to Ban Khwao (Rte 225).

The town itself is a typical, medium-grade Thai trade centre with little to hold most visitors for more than a day or so. The districts around Chaiyaphum (especially Kut Lalom to the south) are known for trained **elephants** and elephant trainers, and it's not uncommon to see an elephant or two walking down the capital streets. Since work demand for elephants in Thailand is steadily declining due to the timber ban, many Chaiyaphum elephants are being sold to 'elephant camps' for tourists in the North, or to circuses in Europe. The city started an annual elephant round up a few years ago that gained in popularity until the provincial governor had a nightmare in which elephants were injuring people. The round up has since been cancelled.

The main reason people visit Chaiyaphum nowadays is to tour **Ban Khwao** (15km west) and other nearby silk villages. Silk can also be purchased at Chaiyaphum shops or in the

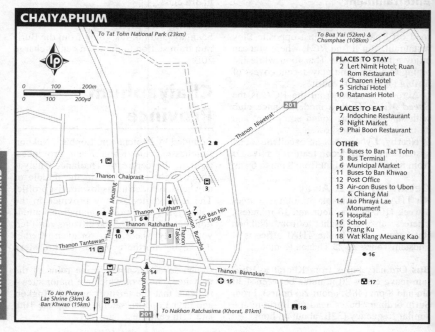

CHAIYAPHUM

To Tat Tohn National Park (23km)

To Bua Yai (52km) &
Chumphae (108km)

Thanon Niwetrat

Thanon Chaiprasit

Thanon Non Meuang

Thanon Yutitham

Soi Ban Hin Tang

Thanon Ratchathan

Thanon Burapha

Thanon Taksin

Thanon Tantawan

Th. Haruthai

Thanon Bannakan

To Jao Phraya
Lae Shrine (3km) &
Ban Khwao (15km)

To Nakhon Ratchasima (Khorat, 81km)

PLACES TO STAY
2 Lert Nimit Hotel; Ruan Rom Restaurant
4 Charoen Hotel
5 Sirichai Hotel
10 Ratanasiri Hotel

PLACES TO EAT
7 Indochine Restaurant
8 Night Market
9 Phai Boon Restaurant

OTHER
1 Buses to Ban Tat Tohn
3 Bus Terminal
6 Municipal Market
11 Buses to Ban Khwao
12 Post Office
13 Air-con Buses to Ubon & Chiang Mai
14 Jao Phraya Lae Monument
15 Hospital
16 School
17 Prang Ku
18 Wat Klang Meuang Kao

NORTH-EASTERN THAILAND

municipal market in the centre of town. Buses to Ban Khwao leave from the bus terminal every 20 minutes between 6 am and 6 pm and the fare is 6B. If you've never observed the silk process – from the cultivation of mulberry trees and propagation of silkworms to the dyeing and weaving of silk thread – you're in for an interesting day.

Information

The post office is located on Thanon Bannakan, near the corner of Thanon Non Meuang, and is open from 8.30 am to 4.30 pm.

Prang Ku
ปรางค์กู่

This hollow Khmer *prang* (tower) was constructed during the reign of the final Angkor king, Jayavarman VII (AD 1181–1219) as a 'healing station' on the Angkor temple route between the Angkor capital in Cambodia and Prasat Singh in Kanchanaburi Province. Chaiyaphum residents consider this a very holy spot; many make daily offerings of flowers, candles and incense. The Buddha figure inside the *ku* (hollow, cave-like stupa) purportedly hails from the Dvaravati period (6th to 10th centuries). Also on the small grounds are a Shivalingam pedestal and a venerable tamarind tree.

Prang Ku is about 1km east of the Jao Phraya Lae monument.

Tat Tohn National Park
อุทยานแห่งชาติตาดโตน

Eighteen kilometres north-west of Chaiyaphum via Rte 2051, this seldom-visited, 218-sq-km park at the edge of the Laen Da mountain range is centred on the scenic waterfalls of **Tat Tohn**, **Tat Klang** and **Pha Phiang**. Tat Tohn Falls are the largest, reaching a width of 50m during the May-to-October monsoon. Most of the vegetation in the park is dry dipterocarp forest. Little wildlife research has been carried out in the park, but since it lies halfway between Nam Nao National Park on the Chaiyaphum-Phetchabun border and Khao Yai National Park on the Nakhon Nayok–Nakhon Ratchasima–Prachinburi border, it's bound to harbour an interesting variety of resident and migratory species.

Park bungalows are available for 250B (sleeps up to six), 500B (sleeps up to 15) and 800B (sleeps up to 20). If you have your own equipment, you can camp for 5B per night. Tents can also be rented for 30B per night.

It's best to have your own vehicle to find the park since there's no regular public transport from Chaiyaphum. Alternatively, you can get a sǎwngthǎew from Chaiyaphum as far as Ban Tat Tohn (around 6B), then hire a pick-up truck on to the park for about 100B one way.

Places to Stay

The ***Ratanasiri Hotel*** (☎ *044-821258*), on the corner of Thanon Non Meuang and Thanon Ratchathan, is an efficiently run place with one floor of rooms with fan for 200B to 280B and two floors with air-con and hot water for 350B to 400B. All rooms come with TV.

The friendly ***Sirichai Hotel*** (☎ *044-811461, fax 812299*), on the opposite side of Thanon Non Meuang farther north, has slightly more upmarket rooms, all with TV. Fan single/double rooms go for 220/320B, double rooms with air-con for 400B. The restaurant serves American breakfasts and good Thai food. Farther east off Thanon Yutitham at 196/7 Soi 1, the run-down ***Charoen Hotel*** (☎ *044-811194*) has rooms with fan and cold water for 160B, air-con for 250B.

Top end for Chaiyaphum is the popular five-storey ***Lert Nimit Hotel*** (☎ *044-811522, fax 822335*) on Thanon Niwetrat east of the bus terminal on the road to Chumphae (Rte 201). Well-kept rooms with fan and attached bathroom are available for 200B to 250B, and there are nicer carpeted air-con bungalows for 550B to 600B, including breakfast.

Places to Eat

Phai Boon, next to the Ratanasiri Hotel on Thanon Ratchathan, serves the usual Thai and Chinese standards.

If you're into kài yâang, look no further than the cluster of ***vendors*** in front of the hospital on Thanon Bannakan (food is only served during the day). Chaiyaphum has a splendid ***night market*** off Thanon Taksin.

Indochine on Thanon Burapha, near the corner of Soi Ban Hin Tang, serves an interesting blend of Isan and Vietnamese food. It's open from 10 am to 10 pm. The **Ruan Rom** at the back of the Lert Nimit Hotel serves good Thai and Western food.

Getting There & Away
Chaiyaphum can be reached by bus from Khon Kaen and Khorat, both of which are about two hours away, for about 36B.

Buses from Bangkok's Northern bus terminal cost 176B for lst class air-con (five hours; 14 buses daily); 137B for 2nd class air-con (five hours; six times daily); and 93B ordinary (six hours; every half-hour from 6.15 am to 11 pm).

Getting Around
A túk-túk should cost no more than 20B for any destination in town.

Khon Kaen & Roi Et Provinces

Khon Kaen and Roi Et are mostly rural provinces where farming and textiles are the main occupations. At the heart of the Isan region, these provinces are good places to explore Isan culture – its language, food and music.

KHON KAEN
อ.เมือง ขอนแก่น

postcode 40000 • pop 134,200
Khon Kaen is about a 2½-hour bus trip from either Khorat or Udon Thani, and 450km from Bangkok. It is also the gateway to the North-East if you are coming from Phitsanulok in Northern Thailand.

The fourth-largest city in Thailand, Khon Kaen is an important commercial, financial, educational and communications centre for Isan. **Khon Kaen University**, the largest university in the North-East, covers 5000 *rai* (8.1 sq km) in the north-western part of Khon Kaen.

The city has grown fantastically over the last decade, with lots of added neon and the heaviest automotive traffic in the North-East after Khorat. Unlike in Khorat, the air is fairly clean.

With its international cuisine restaurants, air-con hotels and modern banking facilities, Khon Kaen makes a good spot to take a rest from small-town and village travel in the North-East. It can also be used as a base for day trips to Chonabot (57km south-west), which is a centre for good quality mát-mìi silk, and the Khmer ruins of Prasat Peuay Noi (66km south-east). See those sections later for information.

History
The city is named after Phra That Kham Kaen, a revered chedi at Wat Chetiyaphum in the village of Ban Kham in Nam Phong district, 32km to the north-east. Legend says that early in the last millennium a *thâat* (reliquary stupa) was built over a tamarind tree stump that miraculously came to life after a contingent of monks carrying Buddha relics to Phra That Phanom (in today's Nakhon Phanom Province) camped here overnight. There was no room at That Phanom for more relics, so the monks returned to this spot and enshrined the relics in the new That Kham Kaen (Tamarind Heartwood Reliquary). A town developed nearby but was abandoned several times until 1789, when a Suwanna-phum ruler founded a city at the current site, which he named Kham Kaen after the chedi. Over the years the name changed to Khon Kaen (Heartwood Log).

Information
Tourist Offices The TAT (☎ 043-244498, fax 244497) has a branch office in Khon Kaen at 15/5 Thanon Prachasamoson. It is open from 8.30 am to 4.30 pm daily.

The English-speaking staff distribute good maps of the city and can answer general queries on Khon Kaen and the surrounding provinces.

Khon Kaen's tourist police (☎ 043-236937, 1155) have an office next door to TAT.

Consulates in Khon Kaen The Lao People's Democratic Republic operates a consulate (☎ 043-223689, 221961) at 123 Thanon Photisan. This consulate issues 30-day visas for Laos in one to three days.

The Vietnamese consulate (☎ 043-242190, fax 241154) at 65/6 Thanon Chatapadung issues visas for Vietnam in seven days.

Money Every major Thai bank has a branch in Khon Kaen, most of which are clustered along the southern side of Thanon Si Chan west of Thanon Na Meuang, and along Thanon Na Meuang between Thanon Si Chan and Thanon Reun Rom. Bangkok Bank on Thanon Si Chan has an ATM (automated teller machine) and foreign exchange.

Post & Communications The main post office, on the corner of Thanon Si Chan and Thanon Klang Meuang, is open from 8.30 am to 4.30 pm on weekdays and 9 am to noon on Saturday. There is a CAT international phone office attached; you can also make international phone calls at the CAT office on Thanon Lang Sunratchakan in the northern part of town.

Hyperlink, on the eastern side of Thanon Klang Meuang, one block north of Saen Samran hotel, has 15 terminals. Other Internet centres can be found opposite the Villa Hotel on Thanon Klang Meuang and near the corner of Thanon Na Meuang and Thanon Prachasamoson.

Things to See

About the only tourist attraction is the very well-curated **Khon Kaen National Museum**, which features Dvaravati objects, *sĕmaa* (ordination-precinct marker stones) from Kalasin and Meuang Fa Daet, and bronze and ceramic artefacts from Ban Chiang. It's open from 9 am to noon and 1 to 5 pm, Wednesday to Sunday. Admission is 30B.

On the banks of Khon Kaen's 603-rai (100-hectare) **Beung Kaen Nakhon** (Kaen Nakhon Pond) is **Wat That**, with the

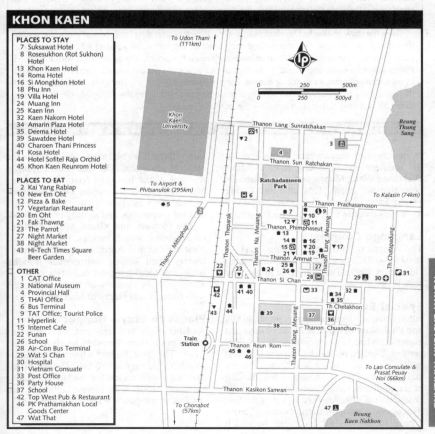

KHON KAEN

PLACES TO STAY
7 Suksawat Hotel
8 Rosesukhon (Rot Sukhon) Hotel
13 Khon Kaen Hotel
14 Roma Hotel
16 Si Mongkhon Hotel
18 Phu Inn
19 Villa Hotel
24 Muang Inn
25 Kaen Inn
32 Kaen Nakorn Hotel
34 Amarin Plaza Hotel
35 Deema Hotel
39 Sawatdee Hotel
40 Charoen Thani Princess
41 Kosa Hotel
44 Hotel Sofitel Raja Orchid
45 Khon Kaen Reunrom Hotel

PLACES TO EAT
2 Kai Yang Rabiap
10 New Em Oht
12 Pizza & Bake
17 Vegetarian Restaurant
20 Em Oht
21 Fak Thawng
23 The Parrot
37 Night Market
38 Night Market
43 Hi-Tech Times Square Beer Garden

OTHER
1 CAT Office
3 National Museum
4 Provincial Hall
5 THAI Office
6 Bus Terminal
9 TAT Office; Tourist Police
11 Hyperlink
15 Internet Cafe
22 Funan
26 School
28 Air-Con Bus Terminal
29 Wat Si Chan
30 Hospital
31 Vietnam Consuate
33 Post Office
36 Party House
37 School
42 Top West Pub & Restaurant
46 PK Prathamakhan Local Goods Center
47 Wat That

To Udon Thani (111km)
Khon Kaen University
To Airport & Phitsanulok (295km)
Thanon Mittaphap
Train Station
To Chonabot (57km)
Thanon Lang Sunratchakan
Thanon Sun Ratchakan
Ratchadanuson Park
Thanon Theparak
Thanon Na Meuang
Thanon Prachasamoson
Thanon Phimphaseut
Thanon Ammat
Thanon Si Chan
Thanon Klang Meuang
Th Chatapadung
Thanon Chuanchun
Th Chetakhon
Thanon Reun Rom
Thanon Kasikon Samran
Beung Thung Sang
To Kalasin (74km)
Beung Kaen Nakhon
To Lao Consulate & Prasat Peuay Noi (66km)

NORTH-EASTERN THAILAND

Bai Sĭi Ceremony

North-eastern Thais commonly participate in *bai sĭi* (sacred thread) ceremonies on auspicious occasions such as birthdays, farewells and times of serious illness, and during certain festivals such as Khon Kaen's annual *phùuk sìaw,* or 'tying friends' festival. In the bai sĭi ceremony, the 32 guardian spirits known as *khwăn* are bound to the guest of honour by white strings tied around the wrists. Each of the 32 khwăn are thought to be guardians over different organs or functions in a person's body.

Khwăn occasionally wander away from their owner, which isn't considered much of a problem except when that person is about to embark on a new project or on a journey away from home, or when they're very ill. At these times it's best to perform the bai sĭi to ensure that all the khwăn are present and attached to the person's body. A *măw phawn,* or 'wish doctor' – usually an elder who has spent some time as a monk – presides over the ritual. Those participating sit on mats around a tiered vase-like centrepiece, or *phakhuan,* which is decorated with flowers, folded banana leaves and branches with white cotton strings hanging down; pastries, eggs, bananas, liquor and money are placed around the base as offerings to the spirits in attendance.

After a few words of greeting, the măw phawn chants in a mixture of Isan and Pali to convey blessings on the honoured guest, while all in attendance place their hands in a prayer-like, palms-together pose. For part of the chanting segment, everyone leans forward to touch the base of the phakhuan; if there are too many participants for everyone to reach the base, it's permissible to touch the elbow of someone who can reach it, thus forming a human chain.

Once the măw phawn has finished chanting, each person attending takes two of the white strings from the phakhuan and ties one around each wrist of the honoured guest(s) while whispering a short, well-wishing recitation. When all have performed this action, the guest is left with a stack of strings looped around each wrist. Small cups of rice liquor are passed around, sometimes followed by an impromptu *ram wong* (circle dance). For the intended effect, the strings must be kept around the wrists for a minimum of three full days. Some Isan people believe the strings should be allowed to fall off naturally rather than cut off – this can take weeks.

extra-elongated spires typical of this area. At the southern end of Beung Kaen Nakhon, **Wat Nong Wang Muang** features a relatively new nine-tier chedi. This lake and **Beung Thung Sang** in the north-eastern section of town are favourite venues for evening strolls.

Language Courses
The American University Alumni (AUA; ☎ 043-241072) has a branch at Khon Kaen University where Thai-language instruction may be available.

Special Events
Khon Kaen's biggest annual event is the **Silk and Phuk Siaw Festival**, held for 10 days and nights from late November through early December. Centred on Ratchadanuson Park and in the field in front of the Sala Klang (Provincial Hall), the festival celebrates the planting of the mulberry tree, a necessary step in the production of silk. Another aspect of the festival is *phùuk sìaw,* or 'friend-bonding', a reference to the *bai sĭi* ceremony in which

sacred threads are tied around one's wrists for spiritual protection. The ritual also implies a renewal of the bonds of friendship and re-affirmation of local tradition. Other activities include parades, Isan music, folk dancing, and the preparation and sharing of Isan food.

The **Flowers and Khaen Music Festival** takes place during Songkran, the Thai lunar New Year in mid-April. Along with the customary ritual bathing of important Buddha images at local temples, activities in Khon Kaen include parades of floats bedecked with flowers and plenty of Isan music.

Places to Stay – Budget
As Khon Kaen is a large city and important transit point, there are many hotels to choose from. The best budget choice is the all-wooden *Si Mongkhon (61–67 Thanon Klang Meuang),* with rooms for 100B with shared bathroom, 150B with private bathroom and 300B with air-con, TV and hot water.

Continued on page 597

Phanom Rung Historical Park

Phanom Rung Historical Park

JOE CUMMINGS

JOE CUMMINGS

Title Page: The 12th-century Khmer temple, Prasat Hin Khao Phanom Rung (Photograph by John Elk III)

Top: The much-travelled Phra Narai Lintel has finally returned to Thailand.

Bottom: Khao Phanom Rung during the annual Phanom Rung Festival

JOHN ELK III

PHANOM RUNG HISTORICAL PARK
อุทยานประวัติศาสตร์เขาพนมรุ้ง

Phanom Rung is on an extinct volcanic cone (383m above sea level) that dominates the flat countryside for some distance in all directions. To the south-east you can clearly see Cambodia's Dongrek mountains and it's in this direction that the capital of the Angkor empire once lay. The temple complex is the largest and best restored of all the Khmer monuments in Thailand (it took 17 years to complete the restoration) and, although it's not the easiest place to reach, it's well worth the effort.

During the week of the nationwide Songkran Festival in April, the local people have their own special celebration, Phanom Rung Festival, which commemorates the restoration of Phanom Rung. During the day there is a procession up Phanom Rung Hill and at night sound-and-light shows and dance-dramas are performed in the temple complex.

Phanom Rung is Khmer for 'Big Hill', but the Thais have added their own word for hill (khǎo) to the name as well as the word for stone (hǐn) to describe the prasat (a large temple sanctuary with a cruciform floor plan). Its full name is Prasat Hin Khao Phanom Rung.

Phanom Rung

The temple was built between the 10th and 13th centuries, the bulk of it during the reign of King Suriyavarman II (reigned AD 1113–50), which by all accounts was the apex of Angkor architecture. The complex faces east, towards the original Angkor capital. Of the three other great Khmer monuments of South-East Asia, Cambodia's Angkor Wat faces west, its Prasat Khao Wihan faces north and Thailand's Prasat Hin Phimai faces south-east. Nobody knows for sure whether these orientations have any special significance, especially as most smaller Khmer monuments in Thailand face east (towards the dawn – typical of Hindu temple orientation).

A small museum on the grounds contains some sculpture from the complex and photographs of the 17-year restoration process.

There is a 40B admission fee (between 8 am and 5.30 pm) to the Phanom Rung Historical Park. *The Sanctuary Phanomrung*, by Dr Sorajet Woragamvijya, is an informative booklet put out by the Lower North-East

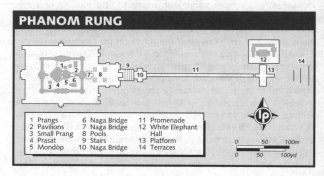

PHANOM RUNG

1 Prangs
2 Pavilions
3 Small Prang
4 Prasat
5 Mondòp
6 Naga Bridge
7 Naga Bridge
8 Pools
9 Stairs
10 Naga Bridge
11 Promenade
12 White Elephant Hall
13 Platform
14 Terraces

0   50   100m
0   50   100yd

Study Association (LNESA). Sometimes it is available for sale near the entrance to the complex for 20B (vendors may ask 50B, but the LNESA says visitors shouldn't pay more than 20B). Several English-speaking guides also offer their services at the complex – fees are negotiable.

Downhill a bit from the main sanctuary, a number of new structures have been built to house collections of art and artefacts found on the site. When finished, the buildings will become part of a museum complex that may have a separate admission fee – for now they're free.

The best time to visit Phanom Rung is before 10 am – this beats most bus tours, and it's cooler and the light is better for photography.

Design One of the most remarkable design aspects of Phanom Rung is the promenade leading to the main gate. This is the best surviving example in Thailand. It begins on a slope 400m east of the main tower, with three earthen terraces. Next comes a cruciform base for what may have been a wooden pavilion. To the right of this is a stone hall known locally as the White Elephant Hall (Rohng Cháng Phèuak). On the northern side of this hall are two pools that were probably once used for ritual ablutions before entering the temple complex. Flower garlands to be used as offerings in the temple may also have been handed out here. After you step down from the pavilion area, you'll come to a 160m avenue paved with laterite and sandstone blocks, and flanked by sandstone pillars with lotus-bud tops, said to be early Angkor style (AD 1100–80). The avenue ends at the first and largest of three *naga* (serpent) bridges.

These naga bridges are the only three that have survived in Thailand. The first is flanked by 16 five-headed naga in the classic Angkor style – in fact these figures are identical to those found at Angkor Wat. After passing this bridge and climbing the stairway you come to the magnificent east gallery leading into the main sanctuary. The central prasat has a gallery on each of its four sides and the entrance to each gallery is itself a smaller version of the main tower. The galleries have curvilinear roofs and false balustraded windows. Once inside the temple walls, have a look at each of the galleries and the *gopura* (entrance pavilion), paying particular attention to the lintels over the porticoes. The craftsmanship at Phanom Rung represents the pinnacle of Khmer artistic achievement, on a par with the reliefs at Angkor Wat in Cambodia.

Sculpture The Phanom Rung complex was originally built as a Hindu monument and exhibits iconography related to the worship of Vishnu and Shiva. Excellent sculptures of both Vaishnava and Shaiva deities can be seen in the lintels or pediments over the doorways to the central monuments and in various other key points on the sanctuary exterior.

On the east portico of the *mondòp* is a Nataraja (Dancing Shiva), in the late Baphuan or early Angkor style, while on the south entrance are the remains of Shiva and Uma riding their bull mount, Nandi. The central cell of the prasat contains a Shivalingam (phallus images).

Several sculpted images of Vishnu and his incarnations, Rama and Krishna, decorate various other lintels and cornices. Probably the most beautiful is the **Phra Narai lintel** (see the boxed text 'Phra Narai Lintel' in this section), a relief depicting a reclining Vishnu (Narayana) in the Hindu creation myth. Growing from his navel is a lotus that branches into several blossoms, on one of which sits the creator god Brahma. On either side of

Phra Narai Lintel

A tale of intrigue goes with the Phra Narai (Lord Narayana/Vishnu) lintel. In the 1960s local residents noticed the lintel was missing from the sanctuary and an investigation determined that it must have disappeared between 1961 and 1965. A mysterious helicopter was reportedly seen in the vicinity during this period. The lintel was later discovered on display at the Art Institute of Chicago, a donation by one James Alsdorf.

The Thai government, as well as several private foundations, tried unsuccessfully for many years to get the artwork returned to its rightful place. As the Phanom Rung complex was reaching the final stages of restoration in preparation for the official opening in May 1988, a public outcry in Thailand demanded the return of the missing lintel. In the USA, Thai residents and US sympathisers demonstrated in front of the Chicago museum. The socially conscious Thai pop group Carabao recorded an album entitled Thap Lang (Lintel), with a cover that featured a picture of the Statue of Liberty cradling the Phra Narai lintel in her left arm! The chorus of the title song went: 'Take back Michael Jackson – Give us back Phra Narai'.

In December 1988 the Alsdorf Foundation returned the Phra Narai lintel to Thailand in exchange for US$250,000 (paid by private sources in the USA) and an arrangement whereby Thailand's Fine Arts Department would make temporary loans of various Thai art objects to the Art Institute of Chicago on a continual basis. Rumour in Thailand has it that of the seven Thai people involved in the original theft and sale of the lintel, only one is still alive. The other six are supposed to have met unnatural deaths.

Vishnu are heads of Kala, the god of time and death. He is asleep on the milky sea of eternity, here represented by a naga. This lintel sits above the eastern gate (the main entrance) beneath the Shiva Nataraja relief.

Prasat Meuang Tam & Other Ruins

About 5km south of Phanom Rung, and outside the historical park complex, this Khmer site dates to the late 10th century and was sponsored by King Jayavarman V. The laterite wall is still in fair condition, and the tumbled-down prasat has been well restored. Admission is 30B.

North of Meuang Tam and east of Phanom Rung are the harder-to-find Khmer ruins of **Kuti Reusi Nong Bua Lai** and **Prasat Khao Praibat**. East of these are **Prasat Lalomthom**, **Prasat Thong** and **Prasat Baibaek**. South of Prasat Meuang Tam is **Kuti Reusi Khok Meuang**. We haven't explored any of these but they're spotted on the Vicinity of Phanom Rung map in case anyone is interested in taking a look. To find these it would be best to hire a local guide from the Phanom Rung complex or in the village of Prasat Meuang Tam.

From Prasat Meuang Tam you can continue south-east via Ban Kruat and Ban Ta Miang (along Rtes 2075 and 2121) to **Prasat Ta Meuan**, a secluded Khmer ruins complex on the Thai-Cambodian border (see the Surin section later in this chapter for details). From Ta Miang you can then proceed north to Surin town or continue east along the border to Si Saket and Ubon provinces.

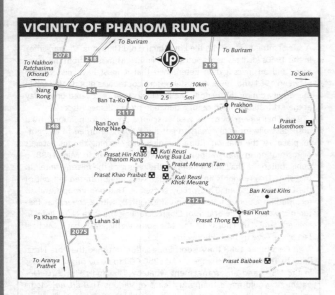

VICINITY OF PHANOM RUNG

Getting to the Ruins

Phanom Rung can be approached from Nakhon Ratchasima (Khorat), Buriram or Surin. From Khorat, take a Surin-bound bus and get out at Ban Ta-Ko, which is a few kilometres past Nang Rong (the turn-off north to Buriram). The fare should be about 35B; Ban Ta-Ko is well marked as the turn-off for Phanom Rung. Once in Ta-Ko you have several options. At the Ta-Ko intersection you can wait for a săwng-thǎew that's going as far as the foot of Phanom Rung (12km, 18B) or one that's on the way south to Lahan Sai. If you take a Lahan Sai truck, get off at the Ban Don Nong Nae intersection (you'll see signs point-ing the way to Phanom Rung to the east). From Ta-Ko to Don Nong Nae will cost 6B. From Don Nong Nae, get another săwngthǎew to the foot of the hill for 10B or charter a pick-up for 50B one way.

If you don't have the patience to wait for a săwngthǎew, take a motorcycle taxi from Ta-Ko to Don Nong Nae (40B) or all the way to Phanom Rung for 100B each way. A return trip will cost 150B; for an extra 50B the drivers will add Meuang Tam. These rates include waiting for you while you tour the ruins.

It's easier from Buriram. You can take a bus direct from Buriram to Nang Rong for 18B, then continue as above. You can also work the whole thing out from Nang Rong, even though it's farther away. Săwngthǎew going to Phanom Rung from Buriram, although they're rather infrequent, will pick up passengers in Nang Rong for 8B. Or you can rent a motorcycle from the Honey Inn for 200B all day. This beats chartering a motorcycle taxi or săwngthǎew, either of which will cost 300B to 500B.

From Surin, take a Khorat-bound bus and get off at Ban Ta-Ko on Hwy 24, then follow the directions as from Khorat.

Continued from page 592

Suksawat (☎ 043-236472), off Thanon Klang Meuang, is quieter as it's a bit off the main streets. It has clean rooms for 80B with shared facilities and 100B to 160B with fan and bathroom.

The friendly, long-running **Roma Hotel** (☎ 043-237177, fax 242450, 50/2 Thanon Klang Meuang) has large rooms with fan for 230B, plus refurbished air-con rooms for 330B. The coffee shop serves basic Thai dishes at reasonable prices.

Prices at the clean and modern **Sawatdee** (☎ 043-221600, fax 320345, 177–179 Thanon Na Meuang) range from 200/250B for single/double rooms with fan to 520/600B for air-con rooms. All rooms have hot water; air-con rooms have bathroom, minibar, large TV, private balcony and carpet.

The **Villa Hotel** (☎ 043-241545, fax 237720), on the corner of Thanon Klang Meuang and Thanon Ammat, is mostly a short-time place attached to a massage parlour/'entertainment complex', but it has rooms with air-con and hot water for 300B to 350B.

Places to Stay – Mid-Range

Khon Kaen excels in this category, with a fine selection of accommodation in the 400B to 600B range.

Deema Hotel (☎ 043-321562, fax 321561, 133 Thanon Chetakhon), near the Khon Kaen bus terminal and market, is a good deal. It has clean rooms with private hot-water bathroom and fan for 250B. Air-con rooms with satellite TV cost 450B.

The **Muang Inn** (☎ 043-245870, fax 334411), at a convenient location on Thanon Na Meuang, offers tidy air-con single/double rooms with telephone and TV for 490B, and VIP rooms with refrigerator for 550B; there's an excellent bakery and restaurant on the ground floor.

The modern, six-storey **Amarin Plaza Hotel** (☎ 043-321660) off Thanon Lang Meuang has nice air-con rooms with hot water for 450B to 600B.

Phu Inn (☎ 043-243174, fax 243176), a similar mid-range spot near the market, has 98 air-con rooms for 400B to 500B. The slightly more expensive rooms on the upper floors are in better condition than those on the ground floor.

The **Khon Kaen Reunrom Hotel** (☎ 043-223522, fax 220567, 335 Thanon Reun Rom), near the train station, has 72 well-kept air-con rooms for 500B; all rooms come with TV, minibar, carpet and hot water – good value in this range.

Towards the eastern end of Thanon Si Chan, the **Kaen Nakorn Hotel** (☎ 043-224268, fax 224272) has clean and comfortable air-con rooms for 200B to 600B.

Places to Stay – Top End

More-expensive places include the seven-storey **Khon Kaen Hotel** (☎ 043-244881, fax 242458) on Thanon Phimphaseut, which has 130 clean, comfortable air-con singles/doubles with private balcony and refrigerator for 690/700B.

The similar **Rosesukhon Hotel** (Rot Sukhon; ☎ 043-238576, fax 238579), near the Khon Kaen Hotel on Thanon Klang Meuang, has air-con rooms for 700/800B, less in the low season. Both hotels also have more-expensive suites in the 2000B-to-2500B range.

The popular **Kosa Hotel** (☎ 043-225014, 320320, fax 225013) on Thanon Si Chan has rooms with all the amenities for 900B to 2300B; suites range from 3000B to 15,000B. The attached karaoke club attracts a steady flow of Thai businessmen.

Nearby, the **Hotel Sofitel Raja Orchid** (☎ 043-322155, fax 322150, [e] sofitel@ kkaen.loxinfo.co.th) has well-decorated rooms for 3000B and suites starting at 3300B. There are nonsmoking floors and facilities for the disabled and the hotel has several restaurants. The Underground entertainment complex beneath the hotel even has a German brauhaus where it brews its own 'Kronen beer'.

Until recently the top hotel in the city was the friendly **Kaen Inn** (☎ 043-245420, fax 239457, 56 Thanon Klang Meuang). Singles/doubles cost 800B with air-con, TV, telephone and fridge. On the premises are Chinese and Japanese restaurants, a karaoke lounge, coffee shop, barber room and snooker club. This hotel is often full.

The **Charoen Thani Princess** (☎ 043-220400, fax 220438, [e] princess@icon.co.th; in Bangkok ☎ 02-281 3088) towers over the city at 260 Thanon Si Chan. Well-appointed rooms with all the mod-cons start at 2160B plus tax and service charge.

Places to Eat

Thai & Isan Khon Kaen has a lively night market with plenty of good food stalls next to the air-con bus terminal; look for the busy *Khun Aem* *jók* stall, which serves exemplary broken-rice congee.

A good spot for local Isan food is *Kai Yang Rabiap*, on Thanon Theparak near the corner of Thanon Lang Sunratchakan.

The upmarket *Hi-Tech Times Square Beer Garden* (☎ 043-321310), on Thanon Theparak near the Hotel Sofitel Raja Orchid, contains numerous outdoor restaurants and beer gardens among nicely landscaped gardens and waterfalls, mostly catering to an upper-class Thai clientele. Dishes range from 50B to 80B each, more for seafood.

Opposite Kaen Inn on Thanon Lang Meuang, the inexpensive *Fak Thawng* (no Roman-script sign) is a popular spot for breakfast. It's a clean, simple Thai place. Another good place for breakfast is *Em Oht* across from the Roma Hotel. It serves real coffee and specialises in *kài kàthá* (eggs served in a cooking pan with local sausages). The smaller *New Em Oht*, just north of Hyperlink, is similar.

A good *night market* convenes along Thanon Reun Rom between Thanon Klang Meuang and Thanon Na Meuang each evening from around sunset to 11 pm.

International *The Parrot* (☎ 043-244692), on Thanon Si Chan near Kosa Hotel, offers good Western breakfasts (with wholemeal toast and Dutch coffee) for 40B to 55B. The lengthy menu includes grilled salmon, submarine sandwiches, hamburgers, pizza and good Thai food. Open from 7.30 am to 10 pm daily, this restaurant is popular with the local expat crowd as well as with well-to-do Thais.

The family-oriented *Pizza & Bake* has two locations, one near the THAI office on Thanon Maliwan west of the railway and another on the corner of Thanon Phimphaseut and Thanon Klang Meuang. Pizza is the main focus, but the restaurant also prepares a variety of other European and Thai dishes, as well as a full line of espresso drinks. It's open from 6.30 am to 11.30 pm.

Vegetarian The *Vegetarian Restaurant* on Thanon Lang Muang serves Thai vegetarian dishes for 15B to 25B and is open from 8 am to 9 pm daily.

Entertainment

The lively *Party House* is an outdoor beer garden next to the Amarin Plaza Hotel. It serves beer and snacks in surroundings decorated in a safari-style decor.

Funan (☎ 043-239628), on Thanon Si Chan near the railway line, is a wooden shophouse where local college and university students hang out and listen to live *phleng phêua chii-wít* (modern Thai folk songs) and occasional jazz; it opens at 6 pm. *Top West Pub & Restaurant*, down a soi on the opposite side of the street, has duplicated the 'old-west' theme found all over the country.

Heaven Dance Club, on the premises of the Hi-Tech Times Square Beer Garden (and owned by the Hotel Sofitel Raja Orchid), charges an 80B admission.

Shopping

Khon Kaen is a good place to buy hand-crafted Isan goods such as silk and cotton fabrics (you can get mát-mìi cotton as well as silk), silver and basketry. A speciality of the North-East is the *măwn khwăan* ('axe pillow'), a stiff triangle-shaped pillow used as an elbow support while sitting on the floor. These come in many sizes, from small enough to carry in a handbag to large enough to fill your entire backpack. Perhaps the most practical way to acquire axe pillows while on the road is to buy them unstuffed (*mâi sài nûn*, 'no kapok inserted') – the covers are easily carried and you can stuff them when you get home.

If textiles are your main interest, try PK Prathamakhan Local Goods Center (☎ 043-224080) at 79/2–3 Thanon Reun Rom just west of Thanon Na Meuang – a local handicraft centre with a small museum.

Also good are Rin Mai Thai (☎ 043-221042) at 412 Thanon Na Meuang, and Prae Pan (☎ 043-337216) at 131/193 Thanon Chatapadung. Prae Pan is run by the Handicraft Centre for Northeastern Women's Development.

Several shops selling local preserved foods and other Isan products can be found along Thanon Klang Meuang between Thanon Prachasamoson and Thanon Si Chan, including Jerat, Naem Laplae and

Heng Nguan Hiang. The emphasis in these shops is *năem* (a kind of sausage made of raw pickled pork) and other types of sausage or processed meats such as *sâi krâwk, mǔu yaw, kun siang mǔu* and *kun siang kài*. Still, behind the stacks of sausage you can often ferret out some good handicraft purchases.

Getting There & Away

Air THAI flies five times daily between Bangkok and Khon Kaen (1230B one way, 55 minutes).

The Khon Kaen THAI office (☎ 043-227701) is at 9/9 Thanon Prachasamoson. The airport (☎ 043-236523, 238835) is a few kilometres west of the city centre off Hwy 12; minivan shuttles between the airport and the city are available through THAI.

Bus Ordinary buses arrive at and depart from a terminal on Thanon Prachasamoson (☎ 043-237300), while air-con buses use a depot near the market off Thanon Klang Meuang (☎ 043-239910).

A 1st-class air-con bus from Bangkok's Northern bus terminal costs 232B. Departures are approximately every half-hour between 7.30 am and 11.30 pm. Ordinary buses (129B) leave several times between 8.40 am and 10.45 pm. There are also a couple of VIP bus departures daily that cost 295B. This is a seven- to eight-hour bus trip.

The Phitsanulok-to-Khon Kaen road runs through spectacular scenery, including two national parks. Ordinary buses to Khon Kaen from Phitsanulok leave several times throughout the day, take about six hours and cost 110B. Air-con buses leave Phitsanulok less frequently (153B to 196B, depending on the company).

Air-con night buses from Khon Kaen to Chiang Mai depart from the terminal on Thanon Prachasamoson at 8 pm for the old route via Tak (414B), and 9 pm for the new route via Utaradit (369B). A 2nd-class air-con bus (322B) departs from Khon Kaen at 8 am. An ordinary bus (eight departures daily, 5 am and 5.45 pm) takes 11 to 13 hours and costs 205B to 230B, depending on the route.

Other air-con bus destinations that you can reach from Khon Kaen include: Chiang Rai (339B, 13 hours), Nakhon Phanom (129B, five to six hours), Ubon (125B, five hours), Nong Khai (79B, three hours), Loei (95B, four hours), Udon Thani (53B to 68B, two hours), Roi Et (55B, two hours) and Sakon Nakhon (90B, three to four hours).

Ordinary buses leave Khon Kaen for Khorat at 5.30, 6.15 and 6.50 am (58B, 2½ to three hours). Other destinations include Udon Thani (38B, two hours), Chaiyaphum (34B, two hours) and Surin (69B, 5½ hours).

Train Rapid train Nos 137 and 133 (2nd and 3rd class) depart from Bangkok's Hualamphong station at 6.15 am and 7 pm, arriving in Khon Kaen at 3.10 pm and 4.02 am respectively. The only overnight sleeper train that arrives at a semi-decent hour is express No 69 (77B 3rd class, 179B 2nd class, 368B 3rd class, express and rapid surcharges not included), which leaves Bangkok at 8.30 pm and arrives in Khon Kaen at 5.37 am.

Getting Around

A regular săwngthăew system plies the central city for 4B per person, and colour-coded city bus routes cost 5B. If you want to charter a vehicle you usually have to pay a săwngthăew or túk-túk driver 30B to 60B.

AROUND KHON KAEN
Chonabot

ชนบท

This small town located south-east of the provincial capital of Khon Kaen is famous for mát-mìi cotton and silk. Mát-mìi is a method of tie-dyeing the fabric threads before weaving and is similar to Indonesian ikat. The easiest place to see the fabrics is at **Sala Mai Thai** (Thai Silk Exhibition Hall), on the campus of Khon Kaen Industrial & Community Education College (Withayalai Kan Achip Khon Kaen). This resource centre for the local silk industry contains a well-organised exhibit of silk products. There are a couple of traditional north-eastern wooden houses next to the exhibition hall. The campus is 1km west of Chonabot on Rte 229, near the 12km marker.

AROUND KHON KAEN

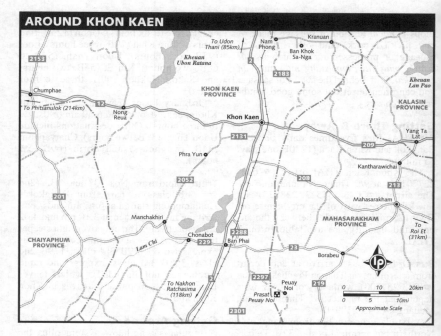

Textiles can be purchased directly from silk-weaving houses along Chonabot's off-highway streets – look for the tell-tale looms beneath the wooden homes. Even if you're not interested in buying, it's worth wandering around to take a look at the amazing variety of simple wooden contraptions devised to spin, tie, weave and dry silk.

Some of the more reputable weaving households include those belonging to Khun Songkhram, Khun Suwan, Khun Thongsuk and Khun Chin. Very little English is spoken in Chonabot so it helps considerably if you bring someone who can speak Thai along.

Getting There & Away Săwngthăew to Chonabot leave the ordinary bus terminal in Khon Kaen hourly between 5.30 am and 5.30 pm (15B, 45 minutes to an hour); the last one back from Chonabot leaves the market around 3.30 or 4 pm.

Chonabot can also be reached from the south (eg, Khorat) by taking either a bus or train to Ban Phai. Ban Phai is 167km northeast of Khorat.

Prasat Peuay Noi
ปราสาทเปื่อยน้อย

Also known as Ku Peuay Noi, and locally known as That Ku Thong, this 12th-century Khmer temple ruin is undergoing restoration at Khon Kaen–government expense. About the size of Buriram's Prasat Meuang Tam, the monument consists of a large central sandstone sanctuary surmounted by a Lopburi-style prang and surrounded by stone-slab walls with two major gates. The site is rich in sculpted lintels; during restoration many of them have been gathered together to one side of the monument in a sort of impromptu sculpture garden.

Getting There & Away Although Prasat Peuay Noi can be time-consuming to approach if you don't have your own transport, it's a rewarding visit because of the quiet scenery along the way, even if you're not a Khmer temple buff. On your own from Khon Kaen, proceed 44km south on Hwy 2 to Ban Phai, then east on Hwy 23 (signposted to Borabeu), 11km to Rte 2297. Follow Rte 2297 for 24km south-east through a scenic tableau of rice fields and grazing cattle to the town of Peuay Noi. The ruins are at the western end of town on the southern side of the road; you can't miss their grey eminence on your right as you enter the town.

By public transport from Khon Kaen, take a bus or train to Ban Phai, then a săwngthăew to Peuay Noi. Start early in the morning if you plan to do this in one day; the last săwngthăew back to Ban Phai from Peuay Noi leaves around 3 pm. Hitching may be possible. See the Chonabot Getting There & Away entry earlier for details on transport to Ban Phai.

King Cobra Conservation Project
โครงการอนุรักษ์งูจงอาง

North-east of Khon Kaen via Hwy 2 and Rte 2039, this labour of love in the village of Ban Khok Sa-Nga seeks to protect and breed Thailand's endangered king cobra (*nguu jong aang* in Thai). Dozens of king cobras, including one over 4.5m in length, can be seen in their cages here. Other snakes, including the python *(nguu lǎam)* are also on display. For a donation, the staff will put on a show that includes 'snake parades', snake 'bai sǐi' (where snakes are wrapped around your body!) and so on. If you arrive at the right time of day you may be able to watch the snakes being fed small rodents.

If you're driving from Khon Kaen, just after passing through Nam Phong take the turnoff marked 'Kranuan', near the 33km marker. Along the way to Kranuan you should begin seeing English signs for the 'King Cobra Club'.

ROI ET
อ.เมืองร้อยเอ็ด

postcode 45000 • pop 35,000

Roi Et is the fairly small but growing capital of a province which, three centuries ago, probably served as a buffer between Thai and Lao political conflict. Old Roi Et had 11 city gates and was surrounded by its 11 vassal colonies. The name Roi Et means 'one hundred and one'; this could be an exaggeration of the number 11.

The capital is now on an entirely new site, with the large **Beung Phlan Chai** artificial lake in the centre. Paddleboats are

The king cobra's venom is less deadly than the cobra's – but because of the snake's size, it injects enough in one bite to kill 20 people.

available for hire on the lake. An island in the middle, reached by north, west and south causeways, features a fitness park surrounding a tall walking Buddha – demonstrating perhaps that even the Buddha walked for health?

Roi Et Province is known for the crafting of the quintessential Isan musical instrument, the **khaen**, a kind of panpipe made of the *mái kuu* reed and wood. The best khaen are reputedly made in the village of Si Kaew, 15km north-west of Roi Et. It generally takes about three days to make one khaen, depending on its size. The straight, sturdy reeds, which resemble bamboo, are cut and bound together in pairs of six, eight or nine. The sound box that fits in the middle is made of *tôn pràduu*, a hardwood that's resistant to moisture.

Silk and cotton fabrics from Roi Et are high in quality and generally cheaper than in Khorat and Khon Kaen.

A Bangkok Bank branch, near the Ban Chong Hotel, has foreign-exchange services.

Wat Neua
วัดเหนือ

This *wát* (temple), in the northern quarter of town, is worth seeing for its 1200-year-old chedi from the Dvaravati period, Phra Satup Jedi. This chedi exhibits an unusual four-cornered bell-shaped form that is rare in Thailand. Around the bòt are a few old Dvaravati *sěmaa* (ordination-precinct

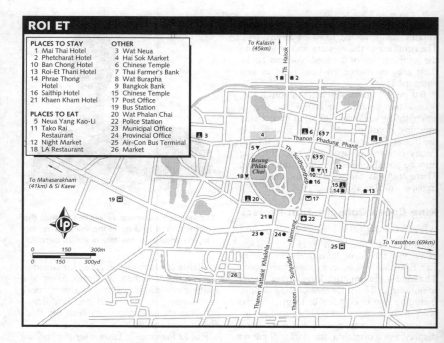

ROI ET

PLACES TO STAY
1 Mai Thai Hotel
2 Phetcharat Hotel
10 Ban Chong Hotel
13 Roi-Et Thani Hotel
14 Phrae Thong Hotel
16 Saithip Hotel
21 Khaen Kham Hotel

PLACES TO EAT
5 Neua Yang Kao-Li
11 Tako Rai Restaurant
12 Night Market
18 LA Restaurant

OTHER
3 Wat Neua
4 Hai Sok Market
6 Chinese Temple
7 Thai Farmer's Bank
8 Wat Burapha
9 Bangkok Bank
15 Chinese Temple
17 Post Office
19 Bus Station
20 Wat Phalan Chai
22 Police Station
23 Municipal Office
24 Provincial Office
25 Air-Con Bus Terminal
26 Market

To Kalasin (45km)

Th Haisok

Thanon Phadung Phanit

Th Sunthonthep

Beung Phlan Chai

Thanon Rattakit Khlaikhla

Bamrung

Thanon

Suriyadet

To Mahasarakham (41km) & Si Kaew

To Yasothon (69km)

0   150   300m
0   150   300yd

marker stones) and to one side of the wát is an inscribed pillar, erected by the Khmers when they controlled this area during the 11th and 12th centuries.

Wat Burapha
วัดบูรพา

The tall, standing Buddha that towers above Roi Et's minimal skyline is the Phra Phuttha-ratana-mongkon-mahamuni (Phra Sung Yai for short) at Wat Burapha. Despite being of little artistic significance, it's hard to ignore. From the ground to the tip of the *ùtsànít* (flame-shaped head ornament) it's 67.8m high, including the base. You can climb a staircase through a building that supports the figure to about as high as the Buddha's knees and get a view of the town.

Places to Stay

Accommodation in Roi Et costs less than in many other provincial capitals. The friendly *Ban Chong Hotel* (Banjong; ☎ 043-511235, 99–101 Thanon Suriyadet Bamrung) has clean rooms with fan and

cold-water bathroom from 150B to 200B. On the same street at No 133 is the *Saithip Hotel* (☎ 043-511985), where semi-clean rooms with fan cost 260B to 280B, air-con and hot water 340B to 360B; this one's often full.

The *Khaen Kham Hotel* (☎ 043-511508, 52–62 Thanon Rattakit Khlaikhla) has clean but very worn rooms with fan and bathroom for 180B to 220B, air-con 300B to 340B. A coffee shop is attached.

The noisy *Phrae Thong Hotel* (☎ 043-511127, 45–47 Thanon Ploenchit), next to a Chinese temple, has comfortable rooms for 130B to 220B with fan.

Mai Thai Hotel (☎ 043-511038, fax 512277, 99 Thanon Haisok) has well-worn air-con rooms with TV and hot-water bathroom for 442B a double. 'VIP' rooms with a bath tub go for 750B. The *Phetcharat Hotel* (☎ 043-511741, 514058, fax 511837) opposite the Mai Thai has clean mid-range rooms with air-con and hot water for 350B to 450B. Ask for a room off the road – they're quieter.

The *Roi-Et Thani Hotel* (☎ 043-520387, fax 520401), near the Phrae Thong Hotel,

Măw Lam and the Khaen

Among villages in Isan *(isăan)*, the up-tempo Lao-Thai musical tradition of *măw lam* – roughly 'master of verse' – rules. Performances always feature a witty, topical combination of singing and improvised or recited speech that ranges across themes as diverse as politics and sex. Very colloquial, even bawdy language is employed; this is one art form that has always bypassed government censors and provides an important outlet for grass-roots expression. Măw lam is most commonly performed at temple fairs and local festivals native to Isan, such as Dan Sai's Phi Ta Khon.

There are four basic types of măw lam. The first, *măw lam lŭang* (great măw lam), involves an ensemble of performers in costume, on stage. *Măw lam khûu* (couple măw lam) features a man and woman who engage in flirtation and verbal repartee. *Măw lam jòt* (duelling măw lam) has two performers of the same gender who 'duel' by answering questions or finishing an incomplete story issued as a challenge. Finally, *măw lam dìaw* (solo măw lam) involves only one performer.

The backbone of măw lam is the *khaen*, a wind instrument consisting of a double row of bamboo-like reeds fitted into a hardwood soundbox with beeswax. The rows can be as few as four or as many as eight courses (for a total of 16 pipes), and the instrument can vary in length from around 80cm to 2m in length. Around the turn of the 20th century there were also nine-course khaen but these have all but disappeared. Melodies are almost always pentatonic; ie, they feature five-note scales. The khaen player blows (as with a harmonica, sound is produced whether the breath is moving in or out of the instrument) into the soundbox while covering or uncovering small holes in the reeds that determine the pitch for each. An adept player can produce a churning, calliope-like music that inspires dancing. The most popular folk dance is the *ram wong* (*lam wong* in Isan), the 'circle dance', in which couples dance circles around one another until there are three circles in all: a circle danced by the individual, the circle danced by the couple, and one danced by the whole crowd.

Traditionally the khaen was accompanied by the *saw*, a bowed string instrument, although the plucked *phin* is nowadays much more common. In modern măw lam, the khaen and phin are electrically amplified and electric bass and drums are added to the ensemble to produce a sound enjoyed by Isan people young and old.

has 167 single/double rooms for 900B, all with air-con, bathroom, IDD phone (with dataports), TV, fridge and carpet; plus nicer VIP rooms for 1700B. Breakfast is included and there are two restaurants on the premises.

Places to Eat

Around the edge of Beung Phlan Chai are several medium-priced garden restaurants. The *Neua Yang Kao-Li* is on the north-western side and has a pleasant atmosphere, a menu in English and good food; the namesake house speciality is cook-it-yourself Korean beef. Another good lake-side place is the *LA Restaurant*, offering an English menu including soups, sandwiches and English breakfast, as well as Thai dishes.

You'll find a string of cheaper *restaurants* along Thanon Ratsadon Uthit, which runs east off the lake from the north-eastern corner.

Tako Rai, on Thanon Sukkasem around the corner from the Ban Chong Hotel, serves some of the best Isan food in town. The *night market* area is a couple of streets east of the Ban Chong and Saithip Hotels. A decent *night market* also assembles each evening along a street a block south of the post office.

Shopping

If you want to buy local handicrafts, the best place to go is the shopping area along Thanon Phadung Phanit, where you'll find shops selling măwn khwăan, *phâa mát-mìi* (thick cotton or silk fabric woven from tie-dyed threads), sticky-rice baskets, traditional musical instruments and Buddhist paraphernalia. Phaw Kan Kha, at 377–379 Thanon Phadung Phanit, has a particularly good selection of fabrics but, as always, you must bargain skillfully to get good prices. Charin (Jarin), at 383–385 Thanon Phadung Phanit, is also good; the owner speaks some English and he also sells gourmet Thai groceries.

Roi Et's street fabric vendors have better prices but less of a selection (and lower quality) than the shops. On the street, 4m of yeoman-quality cotton mát-mìi costs as little as 150B.

Weavers themselves buy from a weaving supply shop at 371 Thanon Phadung Phanit; here you may see local betel-munchers squatting on the floor checking out dyes, pattern books and pre-knotted skeins.

Getting There & Away

Buses to Roi Et cost 36B from Udon Thani to Roi Et (air-con 81B), 32B from Khon Kaen (air-con 55B) and 57B from Ubon Ratchathani (74B to 95B air-con). If you're coming straight from Bangkok's Northern bus terminal, you can catch an air-con bus for 266B (7 hours, three times in the morning and eight times in the evening between 7.45 and 10.45pm). VIP buses cost 410B and leave at 9 and 9.30 pm nightly.

Ordinary-bus destinations include Surin (41B) and Yasothon (22B).

Getting Around

It costs from 10B to 15B to take a sǎamláw around Roi Et. To take a túk-túk, you'll be paying from 20B to 30B.

AROUND ROI ET
Ku Phra Khuna
กู่พระกู่นา

Around 60km south-east of Roi Et town, in Suwannaphum district, are the ruins of an 11th-century Khmer shrine. The monument comprises three brick prang facing east from a sandstone pediment, surrounded by a sandstone-slab wall with four gates. The middle prang was replastered in 1928 and Buddha niches were added. A Buddha footprint shrine, added to the front of this prang, is adorned with the Khmer monument's original Bayon-style *naga* (serpent) sculptures.

The two other prang have been restored but retain their original forms. The northern prang has a Narai (Vishnu) lintel over one door and a *Ramayana* relief on the inside gable. Watch out for monkeys looking for something to eat – it's best not to carry any food.

Getting There & Away Suwannaphum can be reached by frequent buses (20B) and sǎwngthǎew (12B) from the provincial capital via Rte 215. From Suwannaphum it's another 6km south via Rte 214 to Ku Phra Khuna; any Surin-bound bus can stop at Ban Ku, which is at the T-intersection with Rte 2086 east to Phon Sai. The ruins are in a wát compound known locally as Wat Ku.

The ruins can also be approached from Surin, 78km south. From Surin to Ban Ku costs 25B on an ordinary bus and takes about two hours. These buses run more-or-less hourly from about 8 am to 5.30 pm, and there is plenty of time to go out and back in one day.

Udon Thani Province

UDON THANI
อ.เมืองอุดรธานี

postcode 41000 ● pop 104,500
Just over 560km from Bangkok, Udon (often spelt Udorn) is one of several north-eastern cities that boomed virtually overnight when US air bases were established nearby during the Vietnam War.

Udon is an important transport hub and an agricultural market centre for surrounding provinces. Except as a base for touring nearby Ban Chiang, Ban Pheu or *khít*-weaving villages, the city has little to offer, unless you've spent a long time already in the North-East and are seeking Western amenities like air-con coffee houses, flashy ice-cream parlours or fàràng food.

Information
Tourist Offices The TAT (☎ 042-325406, fax 325408) has an office at 16/5 Thanon Mukkhamontri near Nong Prajak (there's another entrance off Thanon Thesa). This office has printed material on Udon, Loei and Nong Khai Provinces, and is open from 8.30 am to 4.30 pm daily.

Money Several banks along the main avenues provide foreign-exchange services and ATMs. Only the Bangkok Bank branch on Thanon Prajak Silpakorn has an after-hours exchange window, usually open until 8 pm.

CENTRAL UDON THANI

PLACES TO STAY
13 Ton Koon Hotel
14 Udon Hotel
22 Ban Chiang Hotel
27 King's Hotel
28 Charoensri Palace Hotel
29 Tang Porn Dhiraksa Hotel
30 Krung Thong Hotel
32 Chai Porn
35 Maphakdi Hotel
41 Srisawat Hotel
44 Prachapakdee Hotel
47 Queen Hotel
51 Siri Udon
65 Charoensri Grand Royal Hotel
70 Malasri Sangden Hotel
73 Charoen Hotel; Yellow Strike

PLACES TO EAT
2 Rim Nam
4 Rabiang Phatchani
26 Night Market
31 Mandarin Bakery
36 Chai Seng; Miss Cake
38 Em Oht
46 Rung Thong
53 Khao Tom Prasopchok
54 Mae Ya
64 Ban Issan
67 Kai Yang Mittaphap

OTHER
1 American University Alumni
3 Wattana Hospital
5 School
6 Main Post Office
7 Technical College
8 Wat
9 Rangsina Market
10 Buses to Nong Khai, Tha Bo & Ban Pheu
11 Telephone Office
12 Provincial Office
15 THAI Office
16 Lak Meuang (City Pillar Shrine)
17 TAT Office
18 Thung Si Meuang (City Field)
19 Central Hospital
20 Wat Pho
21 Regional Education Office
23 School
24 Jail
25 Market
33 Bank
34 Mae Lamun
37 Udon Ekaphanit (Skylabs)
39 Chinese Temple
40 Kannika Tour
42 407 Bus Co
43 Bangkok Bank
45 Clock Tower
48 Market
49 Fountain
50 Nevada Cinema
52 Post Office
55 Immigration Office
56 Traffic Police
57 Police
58 Mosque
59 Udon Thani Teachers College
60 Statue
61 Hospital
62 Thai-Isan Market
63 Petrol Station
66 Charoensri Complex
68 I-Kool Internet
69 Sheriff Pub; Nam Phu
71 407 Bus Co; Choet Chai Tour
72 No 1 Bus Station (Buses to Nakhon Ratchasima, Nakhon Phanom & Ubon)
74 Aek Udon International Hospital

To Nong Khai (55km)

Huay Mak Khaeng

Nong Prajak

To Ban Chiang & Sakon Nakhon (171km)

To Train Station

To Sleep Inn; Airport & Khon Kaen (111km)

To TJ's Family Restaurant (600m); Udon Sunshine (600m); No 2 Bus Station (1km), Loei (139m) & Phitsanulok (365km)

To Loei (139km) & Ban Pheu (42km)

NORTH-EASTERN THAILAND

Post & Communications The main post office on Thanon Wattananuwong (Wattana) is open from 8.30 am to 4.30 pm on weekdays and 9 am to noon on weekends and holidays. The upstairs telephone office is open from 7 am to 10 pm daily. There is a Lenso international card-phone right outside the TAT office. Phone calls can also be made at the telephone office on Thanon Wattanuwong.

I-Kool Internet (☎ 042-344229) provides Internet access at 277/68 Thanon Prajak, opposite Pizza Hut.

Medical Services The new Aek Udon International Hospital (☎ 042-342555) at 555/5 Thanon Pho Si is the best medical facility in the upper north-eastern region. Most employees are fluent in English, and there are translation services for all major languages. Wattana Hospital, on Thanon Suphakit Janya near Nong Prajak, is also a good choice.

Things to See & Do
In the north-eastern corner of the Thung Si Meuang (City Field) is the **Lak Meuang**, or city phallus-pillar, where the city's guardian deity is thought to reside. Encrusted with gold leaf and surrounded by offerings of flowers, candles and incense, the pillar shrine sits next to a smaller shrine containing Phra Phuttha Pho Thong, a Buddha stele of undetermined age. Next to this is a sacred banyan tree used as a repository for broken or abandoned spirit houses and Chinese house shrines.

To get away from the busy central area, walk around **Nong Prajak**, a reservoir and park in the north-western part of town. This is a favourite area for locals to go jogging, to picnic, and to meet and socialise.

Udon Sunshine This nursery just northwest of the city in Ban Nong Samrong is famous for producing 100% natural orchid perfumes. Recently it has become even more famous for cultivating a 'dancing plant' bred from several generations of Thai gyrants selected for their inexplicable propensity to sway and jitter when exposed to certain sounds. The mature gyrant (despite the way it has been described in the Thai press, it is not an orchid) has long oval leaves, plus smaller ones of similar shape. If you sing or talk to the plant in a high, gentle voice (saxophone or violin works even better), the smaller leaves will begin making subtle back-and-forth motions, sometimes quick, sometimes slow. This is no hype; we've seen it for ourselves. The experience of talking or singing to the plants is said to produce a calming influence on troubled spirits, and several local psychotherapists bring patients here for sessions.

The nursery is open to the public daily year-round. The plants are most active from November to February, the cool season. If you come in the hot or rainy seasons it's best to try to arrive between 6 and 9 am or 4.30 and 7 pm; midday is OK if it's cloudy. The owner speaks very good English and is happy to show people around the nursery for a donation of 30B. All proceeds earned from viewing the plant go to an HIV/AIDS project at Udon Hospital. The plants are not for sale, and the owner is careful to remove all flowers from plants on public display so that no-one can pilfer them and grow their own. You can, however, buy 'Miss Udon Sunshine', a rare orchid bred for fragrance (and the first ever to be made into a perfume). Call ☎ 042-242475 for further information.

To get here, follow signs to Ban Nong Samrong off Hwy 2024, then after 200m, follow the sign reading 'Udon Sunshine'. A túk-túk from Udon's city centre would cost about 50B each way.

Places to Stay – Budget
Udon has a plethora of hotels in all price ranges. The central **Krung Thong Hotel** (☎ 042-295299, 195–199 Thanon Pho Si) offers fair singles/doubles for 100B with shared bathroom, 150/200B with fan and bathroom, and 240/300B with air-con. Located in a busy market area, **Queen Hotel** (☎ 042-221451, 6–8 Thanon Udondutsadi) has 22 simple rooms from 120B to 160B with fan and bathroom, and 240B with air-con.

Srisawast Hotel (123 Thanon Prajak Silpakorn) charges 80B for a room with fan and shared bathroom in the old wooden building, and 180B for rooms with fan and private bathroom in the new building. It's a bit noisy, according to one report, charming according to others. It definitely has more character than most hotels in this range.

On Thanon Prajak Silpakorn, conveniently located near several cafes and bakeries, is the ancient-looking *Maphakdi Hotel*, a Thai-Chinese place built partially of wood, with a restaurant downstairs. Rooms with shared facilities cost 100/120B.

Nicer than any of these, yet not much more expensive, the *Tang Porn Dhiraksa Hotel* (☎ 042-221032) on Thanon Mak Khaeng has large, fairly quiet fan rooms for 140B with shared bathroom, 200B with attached bathroom.

Another decent place in this range is *Prachapakdee Hotel* (Prachaphakdi; ☎ 042-221804, 156/7–9 Thanon Prajak Silpakorn). Rooms cost 190B with fan and bathroom, 300B to 350B with air-con; it's very clean, friendly and relatively quiet for a central hotel – a great budget choice. Equally good is the friendly *Chai Porn* (☎ 042-221913, 222144, 209–211 Thanon Mak Khaeng), which charges 150B to 200B for rooms with fan and private bathroom, and 200B to 250B with air-con.

The *Siri Udon* (☎ 042-221658), on a soi between Thanon Pho Si and Thanon Sri Suk, has 98 clean rooms for 180B with fan, 280B with air-con.

There are several other small, inexpensive hotels along the eastern end of Thanon Prajak Silpakorn near Charoensri Complex shopping centre. A typical example is the *Malasri Sangden*, with nothing-special rooms for 120B to 150B.

Next to the Charoensri Palace Hotel on Thanon Pho Si, the nondescript *King's Hotel* (☎ 042-222919, 221634) offers average rooms off the street for 180B with fan and only 200B to 280B with air-con, all with hot-water shower.

Travellers preferring something quieter and calmer might consider staying in nearby Ban Chiang (see the Around Udon Thani Province section later).

Places to Stay – Mid-Range

Moving up a bit in quality and price, the enlarged and upgraded *Udon Hotel* (☎ 042-248160, fax 242782, 81–89 Thanon Mak Khaeng) has comfortable air-con rooms from 460B to 540B, including breakfast. A favourite with travelling businesspeople because it has a parking lot, this hotel is often full.

Next door, the newer six-storey *Ton Koon Hotel* (☎ 042-326336, fax 326349, 50/1 Thanon Mak Khaeng) offers air-con rooms with satellite TV, fridge and phone for 490B a single and 600B a double.

Charoensri Palace Hotel (☎ 042-242611–3, fax 222601, 60 Thanon Pho Si) has decent air-con rooms with hot water for 300B, and rooms with carpet and a minifridge for 360B.

The *Charoen Hotel* (☎ 042-248155, fax 241093, 549 Thanon Pho Si) has air-con rooms for 500B in its old wing, up to 800B in the new wing. Facilities include a pool, cocktail lounge, restaurant and disco.

Three kilometres outside of town, near the airport on Rte 210, the relatively new *Sleep Inn* (☎/fax 042-346223, 14 Mu 1, Thanon Udon-Nongbualamphu) is a modern, three-storey hotel with 121 rooms and suites. All feature air-con, minibar, cable TV and IDD phone and cost a reasonable 500/800B. Other amenities include a restaurant, beer garden, 16 hi-tech karaoke rooms, parking and free transportation to/from the Udon airport.

Places to Stay – Top End

At the Charoensri Complex, off the south-eastern end of Thanon Prajak Silpakorn, the 14-floor *Charoensri Grand Royal Hotel* (☎ 042-343555, fax 343550) offers luxury singles/doubles for 1100/1200B and suites for up to 2000B. Secure covered parking is available. The 10-storey *Ban Chiang Hotel* (☎ 042-327911, fax 223200, ℮ bchiang@ udon.ksc.co.th) on Thanon Mukkhamontri has deluxe rooms for 1000B single/ double, including breakfast. There's a convention centre attached to the hotel.

Places to Eat

Thai, Chinese & Isan There is plenty of good food in Udon, especially Isan fare. *Ban Issan* (☎ 042-248128, 177–179 Thanon Adunyadet) serves tasty kài yâang and sôm-tam, along with other north-eastern specialities. Across from the Charoensri Complex, the outdoor *Kai Yang Mittaphap*, is another good choice for grilled chicken.

Rung Thong, on the western side of the clock tower roundabout, sells excellent Thai curries and is also cheap; this is one of the longest-running curry shops in North-Eastern Thailand but it closes around 5 pm.

NORTH-EASTERN THAILAND

In addition to takeaway pastries, the roomy air-con *Mandarin Bakery*, adjacent to the Chai Porn Hotel on Thanon Mak Khaeng, serves Thai, Chinese and fàràng food at reasonable prices, and it's open until 11 pm. Several other small restaurants are scattered along nearly the entire length of Thanon Mak Khaeng.

On Thanon Prajak Silpakorn between Thanon Mak Khaeng and Thanon Si Sattha, *Chai Seng* is a popular breakfast place serving khài kàthá (eggs served in a pan) and real coffee. *Em Oht*, near the Chai Seng, is similar. In this same strip, *Miss Cake* is a small shop with cakes and pastries.

Near the post office on Thanon Ratchaphatsadu, *Khao Tom Prasopchok* is an open-air place specialising in khâo tôm (boiled rice soup) and Thai curries; it's open till late. The nearby *Mae Ya* (☎ 042-223889) is a clean two-storey air-con place serving a variety of Thai dishes.

On the banks of the Nong Prajak reservoir off Thanon Suphakit Janya are two decent open-air Thai restaurants, *Rim Nam* and *Rabiang Phatchani*.

There's a good *night market* on Thanon Mukkhamontri.

International The best place in town for fàràng food is *TJ's Family Restaurant*, almost opposite the turnoff for Udon Sunshine. Reminiscent of Khorat's VFW Cafeteria (but a lot cleaner), the small eatery offers hamburgers, sandwiches, American-style chili, steaks (175B to 235B), Southern fried chicken and huge breakfasts with grits and homefries. It's open from 9 am to 10 pm daily.

The Charoensri Complex at the southeastern end of Thanon Prajak Silpakorn contains *KFC, Mister Donut, Sunmerry Bakery, Pizza Hut, Swensen's* and a huge *supermarket*.

Entertainment

The *Nevada Cinema* has a sound room that plays original soundtracks of English-language films – probably the only such theatre in North-Eastern Thailand. For nightlife, the *Charoen Hotel* has a comfortable bar and also a disco. *La Reine* at the Udon Hotel is a popular cabaret-style club.

Behind the Charoen Hotel is a 'kitchen disco'-style dance club called *Yellow Strike*, featuring decent live bands. *Nam Phu* (no Roman-script sign) and nearby *Sheriff Pub* are small but popular Thai folk-music pubs, opposite the Charoensri Complex.

Thanon Mak Khaeng, near the Udon Hotel, has a few modern *massage parlours* (ahem) left over from the US GI era; nowadays the clientele is mostly Thai.

Shopping

Udon's main shopping district is centred on Thanon Pho Si, between the fountain circle and Thanon Mak Khaeng.

Mae Lamun is a good local craft shop on Thanon Prajak Silpakorn just east of Thanon Mak Khaeng; it's on the 2nd floor of a shop selling Buddhist paraphernalia. Mae Lamun has a selection of quality silks and cottons, silver, jewellery, Buddha images and ready-made clothes tailored from local fabrics. Prices start high but are negotiable. Another good craft shop – especially for pillows – is Thi Non Michai at 208 Thanon Pho Si.

The relatively new Charoensri Complex, off Thanon Prajak Silpakorn, is the largest shopping centre in Isan, with 22,000 sq m of retail space filled with standard Thai department stores, a huge supermarket, a flock of designer clothing boutiques, several restaurants and coffee shops (see Places to Eat earlier), and the attached Charoensri Grand Royal Hotel (see Places to Stay).

If you're in the market for a large túk-túk – a motorised three-wheel taxi known across the river in Vientiane as a 'jumbo', and called rót sàkailáep ('Skylab', named for the space capsule of many years ago) throughout Isan – Udon Thani is Thailand's manufacturing capital for the same. You can buy a new Skylab at Udon Ekaphanit, 117/2–4 Thanon Prajak, next door to Em Oht coffee shop. They come in several models depending on the engine, from one powered by a Honda 90cc to a 125cc job. Ekaphanit's motto: 'In Lampang, ride a horse cart – in Udon, ride a Skylab'.

Getting There & Away

Air THAI flies to Udon from Bangkok three times daily. The flight takes about an hour and costs 1515B. The Udon THAI office (☎ 042-246697, 243222) is at 60 Thanon Mak Khaeng.

Bus Buses for Udon leave Bangkok's Northern bus terminal throughout the day (227B 2nd-class air-con, 450B 24-seat VIP, 10 to 11 hours, 5 am to 11 pm).

Buses leave the main bus terminal in Khorat every half-hour during the day and arrive in Udon five hours later. The cost is 90B (126B air-con).

To get out of Udon by bus, you must first sort out the tangle of departure points scattered around the city. Ordinary buses to Nong Khai (17B, 15 buses a day, 5 am to 5 pm) leave from Rangsina Market on the northern outskirts of town; take city bus No 6 or a săwngthăew north along Thanon Udon-dutsadi to get to Talat Rangsina (Rangsina Market). You can also get buses to Tha Bo, Si Chiangmai and Ban Pheu from here.

The No 2 bus terminal is on the north-western outskirts of the city next to the highway, and has buses to Loei (45B ordinary, 81B air-con), Nakhon Phanom (73B, 107B), Chiang Rai (227B, 409B), Si Chiangmai (28B ordinary), Nong Khai (17B, 25B) and Bangkok (227B air-con).

The No 1 bus terminal is off Thanon Sai Uthit near the Charoen Hotel in the south-eastern end of town. Buses from here go mostly to points south and east of Udon, including Khorat, Sakon Nakhon, Nakhon Phanom, Ubon Ratchathani, Khon Kaen, Roi Et and Bangkok, and also to Beung Kan.

There are also private air-con buses to Bangkok. The company with the best local reputation is 407 Co (☎ 042-221121) at 125/3 Thanon Prajak Silpakorn. It has many daily departures to Bangkok (292B, 32-seat VIP) and Khon Kaen (58B, air-con). Nearby Choet Chai Tours (no Roman-script sign; ☎ 042-243243) has VIP buses to Bangkok departing at 8, 8.30 and 9 pm.

Train The 8.30 pm *Nong Khai Express* (No 69) from Bangkok arrives in Udon at 7.49 am the next day. Rapid trains leave Bangkok on the Nong Khai line at 6.15 am and 7 pm, arriving in Udon at 5.07 pm and 6.16 am. Two special diesel railcars (Nos 75 and 77) depart from Bangkok at 8.20 am and 8.40 pm, reaching Udon at 6 pm and 6.25 am. The 1st-class fare is 457B, 2nd class is 219B and 3rd class is 95B, plus applicable charges for sleeper and express service.

In the reverse direction, the No 70 express leaves Udon at 7.37 pm, while rapid trains (Nos 134 and 138) depart at 8.34 pm and 9.22 am, and special diesel railcars (Nos 76 and 78) leave at 7 am and 7.25 pm. To reach Nakhon Ratchasima from Udon, the only available train is the No 78 special diesel railcar which arrives in Khorat at 12.22 am.

Getting Around

Bus A hassle-free way to get around is by city bus. The most useful city bus for visitors is the yellow bus No 2, which plies a route from the No 2 bus terminal, south along Thanon Suphakit Janya, and then east along Thanon Pho Si past the Charoen Hotel. The No 6 bus runs between the No 2 bus terminal and Rangsina Market, while bus No 23 runs between bus terminal Nos 1 and 2. The fare for all city buses is 5B.

Car Three car-rental places opposite the Udon Hotel offer sedans, jeeps and vans for hire starting at around 1200B. Should you want to hire a car with driver, a cheaper alternative is to negotiate for one of the old four-door Nissan and Toyota taxis waiting along Thanon Phanphrao at the southern end of Thung Si Meuang. Figure on no more than 800B per day for one of these, including the services of a driver. These drivers are happy to go anywhere in the province, and as far out of the province as Nong Khai.

Túk-Túk & Săamláw Official túk-túk and săamláw rates are posted at the bus terminal. Basically, it's 20B to 40B anywhere in town via túk-túk and 10B to 30B by săamláw.

AROUND UDON THANI PROVINCE
Ban Chiang
บ้านเชียง

Ban Chiang, 50km east of Udon Thani, now plays host to a steady trickle of tourists. As well as the original excavation pit of an ancient Ban Chiang burial ground at **Wat Pho Si Nai** at the village edge (open to the public, 30B admission), there is a relatively new **national museum** with extensive Ban Chiang exhibits. The excavation pit displays 52 human skeletons, in whole or in

NORTH-EASTERN THAILAND

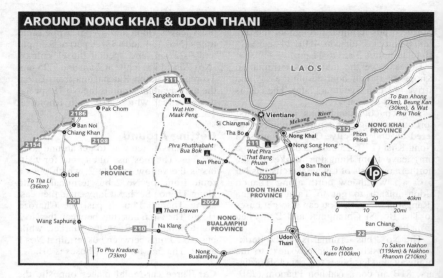

AROUND NONG KHAI & UDON THANI

part, along with lots of pottery. This is worth a trip if you're at all interested in the historic Ban Chiang culture, which goes back at least 4000 years. The well-conceived museum, open from 9 am to 4.30 pm daily, exhibits plenty of pottery from all Ban Chiang periods, plus myriad bronze objects recovered from the Pho Sin Nai excavation, including spearheads, sickles, axeheads, fish hooks, chisels, arrowheads, bells, rings and bangles. Entry is 30B.

The Ban Chiang culture, an agricultural society that once thrived in North-Eastern Thailand, is known for its early bronze metallurgy and clay pottery, especially pots and vases with distinctive burnt-ochre swirl designs, most of which were associated with burial sites. Seven layers of civilisation have been excavated; the famous swirl-design pottery comes from the third and fourth layers. The area was declared a Unesco World Heritage site in 1992.

The locals attempt to sell Ban Chiang artefacts, real and fake, but neither type will be allowed out of the country, so don't buy them. Some of the local handicrafts, such as thick hand-woven cotton fabric, are good buys; over 50 local families are involved in the spinning and weaving of such textiles, along with ceramics and basket-weaving. The other main local livelihoods are rice cultivation, fishing and hunting.

Places to Stay & Eat A five-minute walk from the museum is the nicely landscaped *Lakeside Sunrise Guest House* (☎ 042-208167), with upstairs rooms for 100B a single, 140B a double. One larger room is also available for 200B. Clean, shared facilities are downstairs, while the upper floor boasts a spacious wooden veranda overlooking the lake.

Across from the national museum entrance are a couple of restaurants. One is called *Nakhon Sawan*. It specialises in rice noodles that have been made with Thai pumpkin to produce bright-yellow noodles (*mìi lĕuang*); they're delicious when prepared *râat-nâa* style (with sauce poured over the top).

Getting There & Away Săwngthăew run regularly from Udon Thani to Ban Chiang from late morning until around 3.45 pm (22B). In the reverse direction they're frequent from around 6.30 am until 10.30 am. You can catch them from in front of the museum.

Alternatively, take a bus bound for Sakon Nakhon or Nakhon Pathom and get off at the Ban Pulu turn-off, a 10-minute săamláw ride from Ban Chiang. Buses leave in either direction several times a day, but the last leaves Ban Chiang in the late afternoon.

Ban Pheu
บ้านผือ

Ban Pheu district, 42km north-west of Udon Thani, has a peculiar mix of prehistoric cave paintings, bizarre geological formations and Buddhist shrines, the bulk of which are at **Phra Phutthabaht Bua Bok Park**, 12km outside Ban Pheu on Khao Phra Baht hill.

The formations are an interesting mix of balanced rocks, spires and whale-sized boulders, with several shrines and three wát built in and around them. A trail meandering through the park takes around two hours to negotiate at a normal walking pace.

At the entrance to the area is the largest temple in the historical park, **Wat Phra That Phra Phutthabaht Bua Bok**, with its namesake Lao-style chedi. Prehistoric paintings in several caves feature wild animals, humans and cryptic symbols. To the southeast of the main wát are the caves of **Tham Lai Meu** and **Tham Non Sao Eh**, and to the west are **Tham Khon** and **Tham Wua Daeng**. For Isan residents, this is an important place of pilgrimage. For visitors, the side-by-side progression from rock art to Buddhist temples represents a localised evolution of thought and aesthetics.

Entry to the park costs 30B. A crude trail map is available at the park entrance, although it doesn't include all the caves (nor all the trail branches).

Also in the Ban Pheu district – but outside the park – is **Wat Pa Ban Kaw**, a respected meditation temple under the tutelage of Ajahn Thun (Bhikkhu Khippapanyo).

Getting There & Away Ban Pheu has one hotel (100B with shared bathroom) if you want to spend some time here. Otherwise, Phra Phutthabaht can be visited as a long day-trip from either Udon or Nong Khai. From Udon it's an 18B săwngthăew ride to Ban Pheu; it's 26B from Nong Khai. From Ban Pheu, take a săwngthăew for 10B to the village nearest the site, Ban Tiu, then walk or hitch the 2km to Phra Phutthabaht. You could also charter a motorcycle in the Ban Pheu market to take you all the way to Phra Phutthabaht.

Easiest of all is to visit the park by bicycle or motorbike from Nong Khai.

Weaving Villages

Two villages renowned for khít-pattern fabrics are **Ban Na Kha** and **Ban Thon**, around 16km north of Udon via Hwy 2 on the way to Nong Khai. Khít is a geometric, diamond-grid minimal weft brocade commonly used for the centre square of măwn khwăan fabrics or other decorative items. Ban Na Kha is just east of Hwy 2, while Ban Thon is 2km farther east along a laterite road. Shops in Ban Na Kha that are used to dealing with foreigners include Songsi Isan Handicraft at 184/1 Mu 1; and Chanruan Nakha at 92 Mu 1.

Ban Nong Aw Tai, in the district of Nong Wua Saw, about 40km south-west of Udon via Rte 210, produces high-quality silk. In this same district is **Wat Tham Kok Du**, a famous meditation wát presided over by abbot Phra Ajahn Kham Fong, whose simple, direct style of teaching has attracted a large number of lay students. Nong Wua Saw is actually part of Nong Bualamphu Province.

Tham Erawan
ถ้ำเอราวัณ

If you happen to be travelling along Rte 210 between Loei Province and Udon, you can stop off and visit Tham Erawan, a large cave shrine high up on the side of a limestone mountain. A huge seated Buddha in the cave can be seen gazing out over the plains from several kilometres away.

The cave is at the back of **Wat Tham Erawan**, which is 2km north of a turn-off between the 31km and 32km markers on Rte 210. It's near the village of Ban Hong Phu Thawng, west of the town of Na Klang. There is a smaller cave wát near this turn-off – keep going north until you can see the larger, higher cave in the distance.

Nong Khai Province

Nong Khai Province is a narrow 300km strip along the Mekong River. At its widest point the province measures only 50km across. Even if you don't cross into Laos, Nong Khai is a fascinating province to explore, with long, open views of the Mekong River and Laos on the other side. The capital exhibits

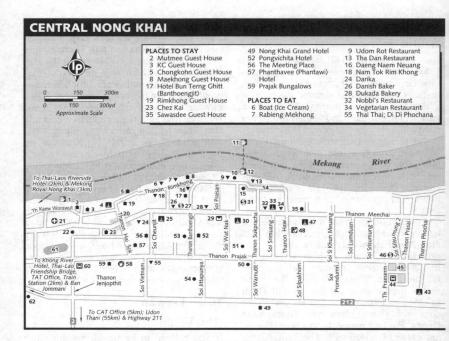

CENTRAL NONG KHAI

PLACES TO STAY
2 Mutmee Guest House
3 KC Guest House
5 Chongkohn Guest House
8 Maekhong Guest House
17 Hotel Bun Terng Ghitt (Banthoengjit)
19 Rimkhong Guest House
23 Chez Kai
35 Sawasdee Guest House

49 Nong Khai Grand Hotel
52 Pongvichita Hotel
56 The Meeting Place
57 Phanthavee (Phantawi) Hotel
59 Prajak Bungalows

PLACES TO EAT
6 Boat (Ice Cream)
7 Rabieng Mekhong

9 Udom Rot Restaurant
13 Tha Dan Restaurant
16 Daeng Naem Neuang
18 Nam Tok Rim Khong
24 Darika
26 Danish Baker
28 Dukada Bakery
32 Nobbi's Restaurant
34 Vegetarian Restaurant
55 Thai Thai; Di Di Phochana

vague touches of Lao influence, and one of Asia's most intriguing sculpture gardens is on the outskirts of the city.

NONG KHAI

อ.เมืองหนองคาย

postcode 43000 • pop 27,500
More than 620km from Bangkok and 55km from Udon Thani, Nong Khai is where Hwy 2 (also known as Mittaphap Hwy, Friendship Hwy and Asia 12) ends, at the Thai-Lao Friendship Bridge over the Mekong River. Across the river is the Lao People's Democratic Republic.

Nong Khai was once part of the Vientiane (Wiang Chan) kingdom, which for much of its history vacillated between independence and tribute to either Lan Xang (AD 1353–1694) or Siam (late 18th century–1893). In 1827 Rama III gave a Thai lord, Thao Suwothamma, the rights to establish Meuang Nong Khai at the present city site. In 1891, under Rama V, Nong Khai became the capital of monthon Lao Phuan, an early Isan satellite state that included what are now Udon, Loei, Khon

Kaen, Sakon Nakhon, Nakhon Phanom and Nong Khai Provinces, as well as Vientiane.

The area came under several attacks by Jiin Haw (Yunnanese) marauders in the late 19th century. The 1886-vintage **Prap Haw Monument** (*pràap haw* means 'defeat of the Haw') in front of the former Provincial Office (now used as a community college) commemorates Thai-Lao victories over Haw invasions in 1874, 1885 and 1886.

When western Laos was partitioned off from Thailand by the French in 1893, the monthon capital was moved to Udon, leaving Nong Khai to fade into a provincial backwater.

Today's Nong Khai has a row of old buildings of French-Chinese architecture along Thanon Meechai, east of Soi Si Khun Meuang and parallel to the river. Unfortunately, local developers have razed some of the most historic buildings in Nong Khai and have replaced them with the ugly eggcarton architecture common all over urban Asia. The construction of the Thai-Lao Friendship Bridge largely shifts the focus of international trade from Nong Khai's historic central area to the bridge area west of

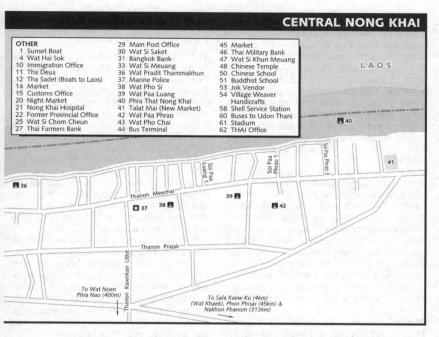

CENTRAL NONG KHAI

OTHER		
1 Sunset Boat	29 Main Post Office	45 Market
4 Wat Hai Sok	30 Wat Si Saket	46 Thai Military Bank
10 Immigration Office	31 Bangkok Bank	47 Wat Si Khun Meuang
11 Tha Deua	33 Wat Si Meuang	48 Chinese Temple
12 Tha Sadet (Boats to Laos)	36 Wat Pradit Thammakhun	50 Chinese School
14 Market	37 Marine Police	51 Buddhist School
15 Customs Office	38 Wat Pho Si	53 Jok Vendor
20 Night Market	39 Wat Paa Luang	54 Village Weaver
21 Nong Khai Hospital	40 Phra That Nong Khai	Handicrafts
22 Former Provincial Office	41 Talat Mai (New Market)	58 Shell Service Station
25 Wat Si Chom Cheun	42 Wat Paa Phrao	60 Buses to Udon Thani
27 Thai Farmers Bank	43 Wat Pho Chai	61 Stadium
	44 Bus Terminal	62 THAI Office

the city, so perhaps this will alleviate the pressure to replace older architecture.

The opening of the bridge on 8 April 1994 marked the beginning of a new era of development for Nong Khai as a regional trade and transport centre. New multistorey hotels and office buildings were built along the outskirts of town near the relatively new Hwy 2 (Mittaphap Hwy) bypass that leads to the Thai-Lao Friendship Bridge. The slowing down of the Thai and Lao economies, however, has brought development to a virtual halt.

The restaurant next to the immigration office and pier is a good place to sit and watch the ferry boats cross back and forth between Thailand and Laos. Since pedestrians aren't permitted on the bridge, this ferry will probably continue to operate until a regular bus service is established between Nong Khai and Vientiane.

The city is constructing a new riverside promenade for strolling along the Mekong. At present the promenade begins at the far eastern end of town and ends near Thanon Phochai. Shops along Thanon Meechai near the pier are jammed with Lao, Vietnamese and Chinese goods.

Like many other cities in the North-East, Nong Khai has a large Rocket Festival (ngaan bun bâng fai) during the full moon of May, and a Candle Festival (ngaan hàe thian) at the beginning of phansăa, or the Buddhist Rains Retreat, in late July. The city also holds a Nong Khai Festival in March.

Information

Tourist Offices A small TAT office (☎ 042-467844) is tucked away in a shopping centre next to the Thai-Lao Friendship Bridge checkpoint. The staff distribute information on Nong Khai and surrounding provinces, as well as some information on Vientiane.

Visas for Laos Nong Khai is one of five crossings open to non-Thai foreigners along the Thai-Lao border (the other five are Chiang Khong, Nakhon Phanom, Mukdahan and Chong Mek) and citizens of the two countries are allowed to cross at will for day trips.

The Lao government issues 15-day Tourist Visas on arrival on the Friendship Bridge, which spans the Mekong River near Nong

Khai. To receive this visa on arrival you must present the following: US$30 cash or the baht equivalent (travellers cheques and kip are not accepted); a passport photo; the name of a hotel you will be staying at in Vientiane; the name of a contact in Vientiane. Most people leave the latter unfilled with no problem but if you do know someone in Vientiane by all means write the name in.

It's important to note that you must have US$30 cash or the baht equivalent in hand when you arrive at the bridge. Change is not available.

If you want to save money or you'd like to stay in Laos longer than 15 days, you can obtain your visa ahead of time at the Lao embassy in Bangkok, which can usually issue a 30-day visa in 24 hours if you leave your passport overnight. Some travellers have reported being able to get the shorter visa on the same day of application. See the Khon Kaen section earlier for information on obtaining visas at the Lao consulate there.

Lonely Planet's *Laos* guidebook contains extensive visa and travel information.

Money Several banks along Thanon Meechai offer ATMs and foreign-exchange services.

Post & Communications The main post office on Thanon Meechai is open from 8.30 am to 4.30 pm weekdays, and 9 am to noon on weekends and holidays. Long-distance phone calls can no longer be placed here, but a new CAT office has opened 5km from the intersection of Rte 212 and Hwy 2, on the eastern side of the road to Udon Thani (Hwy 2); signs at the post office give directions.

Immigration Offices Should you need to extend your visa, the Nong Khai immigration office is on the highway bypass that leads to the Friendship Bridge, south of the bridge shuttle bus stop.

Bookshops Wasambe Bookshop (fax 042-460717, [e] wasambe@loxinfo.co.th) is located on the soi leading to Mutmee Guest House. It sells new and used English-language novels, books on spirituality, guidebooks (especially for Thailand and Laos), maps and a small but growing collection of German, French and Dutch titles. Fax and email services are also available here.

Thai-Lao Friendship Bridge
สะพานมิตรภาพไทยลาว

The US$30 million, Australian-financed Saphan Mittaphap Thai-Lao (Thai-Lao Friendship Bridge) spans the Mekong River from Ban Jommani (3km west of Nong Khai) to Tha Na Laeng (19km south-east of Vientiane) on the Lao side. An 8.2km highway bypass was added to link the bridge with Hwy 2/Asia 12 just south of Nong Khai.

The 1174m-long bridge opened in April 1994 amid much hoopla about how it would improve transport and communications between Thailand and Laos. It is only the second bridge to have been erected anywhere along the Mekong's entire length (the first is in the People's Republic of China).

In spite of its two 3.5m-wide traffic lanes, two 1.5m-wide footpaths and space for a railway down the centre, the bridge has done little to fulfil its design potential. City planners say that eventually a train link will extend from the Nong Khai railhead across the 12.7m-wide bridge. On the Lao side a new railway will skirt Vientiane to the south-east and terminate near That Luang.

For bridge transport information, see Laos under Getting There & Away later in this section.

Wat Pho Chai
วัดโพธิ์ชัย

Wat Pho Chai (Phra Sai), off Thanon Prajak in the south-eastern part of town, is renowned for its large Lan Xang–era sitting Buddha. The head of the image is pure gold, the body is bronze and the ùtsànìt (flame-shaped head ornament) is set with rubies. The altar on which the image sits features elaborately executed gilded wooden carvings and mosaics, while the ceiling bears wooden rosettes in the late Ayuthaya style.

Murals in the bòt depict the image's travels from the interior of Laos to the banks of the Mekong, where it was put on a raft. A storm capsized the raft and the image sat at the bottom of the river from 1550 to 1575, when it was salvaged and placed in a temple now called Wat Pradit Thammakhun on the Thai side of the river. The highly revered image was moved to Wat Pho Chai during the reign of King Mongkut (1852–68).

Mekong

The Thai name for the river is Mae Nam Khong. Mae Nam means river (literally, Water Mother) and Khong is its name (from the Sanskrit *ganga*). The Thais themselves sometimes shorten the name to 'Maekhong' (on the Laos side they prefer 'Nam Khong'), hence the Western term 'Mekong River' is, in some ways, redundant. By agreement between the Thai and Lao governments, all islands in the Mekong – including sandbars that appear only in the dry season – belong to Laos.

During the annual Songkran Festival (April), the Phra Sai image is taken out in procession around town.

The main wíhǎan (hall) is open from 7 am to 5 pm daily.

Phra That Nong Khai
พระธาตุหนองคาย

Also known as **Phra That Klang Nam** (Holy Reliquary in the Middle of the River), this Lao chedi is submerged in the Mekong River and can only be seen in the dry season when the Mekong lowers about 30m. The chedi slipped into the river in 1847 and continues to slide – it's near the middle now. For the best view of the chedi, walk east along Thanon Meechai past the marine police post, then past three wát on the right, then turn left on Soi Paphraw (Paa Phrao) 3. Follow this soi until it ends at the new riverside promenade and look for the chedi in the river off to your right. Once the top of the chedi has cleared the water during the dry season, coloured flags are fastened to the top to make it easier to spot.

You can get a closer look at the chedi by taking the nightly floating restaurant cruise from Tha Wat Hai Sok – see Places to Eat later for details.

Wat Noen Phra Nao
วัดเนินพระเนาว์

This forest wát at the south-eastern edge of town boasts a *vipassana* (insight meditation) centre on nice, tree-shaded grounds. Many westerners meditated here in the 1960s and 1970s. Some extremely ornate temple architecture, including perhaps the most rococo bell tower we've ever seen, stand in contrast with the usual ascetic tone of such forest monasteries. There's a Chinese cemetery on the grounds.

Sala Kaew Ku
ศาลาแก้วกู่

Also called Wat Khaek (Indian Temple) by locals, this strange Hindu-Buddhist shrine, established in 1978, is a tribute to the wild imagination of Luang Pu Bunleua Surirat. Luang Pu (Venerable Grandfather) was a Brahmanic yogi-priest-shaman who made a concoction of Hindu and Buddhist philosophy, mythology and iconography into a cryptic whole. He developed a large following in North-Eastern Thailand and Laos, where he lived for many years before moving to Nong Khai. He is supposed to have studied under a Hindu *rishi* in Vietnam; according to legend, Luang Pu was walking in the mountains when he fell through a sinkhole and landed in the rishi's lap! Luang Pu lived in this cave, called Kaew Ku, for years.

The temple has many bizarre cement statues of Shiva, Vishnu, Buddha and every other Hindu and Buddhist deity imaginable, as well as numerous secular figures, all supposedly cast by unskilled artists under Luang Pu's direction. The style of the figures is remarkably uniform, with faces that look like benign Polynesian masks. The tallest, a Buddha seated on a coiled naga with a spectacular multiheaded hood, is 25m high. Luang Pu died in 1996.

The main shrine building was recently demolished and replaced by a new structure with an onion-dome roof mounted with a cobra sculpture. As in the old building, there are two large rooms, upstairs and down, full of framed pictures of Hindu and Buddhist deities, temple donors, and Luang Pu at various ages, plus smaller bronze and wooden figures of every description and provenance, guaranteed to throw an art historian into a state of disorientation. Luang Pu's corpse is displayed under a glass dome in the upper room. The caretakers say this room will eventually be open to the public, but for now only the downstairs room is open.

NORTH-EASTERN THAILAND

The grounds are open from 7.30 am to 5.30 pm daily; entry is 10B for pedestrians and motorcycles, 20B per car or truck.

Getting There & Away To get to Sala Kaew Ku, board a sǎwngthǎew heading south-east towards Beung Kan and ask to get off at Wat Khaek, which is 4km to 5km outside of town, near St Paul Nong Khai School. The fare should be about 12B. A chartered túk-túk costs 50B.

Sala Kaew Ku is an easy 3km bike ride from town.

Hat Jommani
หาดจอมมณี

This sand 'beach' along the Mekong River only appears during the dry season. Next to the Thai-Lao Friendship Bridge in Ban Jommani, 3km west of Nong Khai, Hat Jommani is a favourite picnic destination for local Thais.

During the season a rustic thatched shelter with straw mats becomes a restaurant serving delicious kài yâang, *plaa pîng* (grilled fish), sôm-tam and cold beer.

Sunset Cruise

Sunset boat rides are available daily at around 5 pm aboard a floating restaurant behind Wat Hai Sok. There's no charge for the ride, as long as you order food and drink, and it's a wonderful way to soak up Mekong ambience.

Places to Stay – Budget

Guesthouses Just west of Wat Hai Sok, *Mutmee Guest House* (fax 042-460717, e mutmee@nk.ksc.co.th, 111/4 Thanon Kaew Worawut) has 25 rooms in a couple of old houses and in rustic bungalows. Rates start at 100B to 110B (single) for simple, unscreened rooms and go up to 130B to 280B (double) for a hut with one large bed, screened windows and shared bathroom. There's also one three-bed room with shared bathroom for 80B per bed, and a couple of larger, more private rooms with attached bathroom and private veranda for 360B. The guesthouse has a pleasant garden restaurant next to the river.

KC Guest House near the mouth of the soi takes the overflow from Mutmee Guest House for 140B per room, shared facilities.

It also rents motorcycles for 200B per day and bicycles for 50B. The soi leading to Mutmee Guest House has become a miniature travellers centre, with a well-stocked bookshop, art gallery and simple studios offering *taijiquan* (t'ai chi) and yoga instruction.

Chongkonh Guest House on Thanon Rimkhong is housed in an older two-storey wooden building on the river. Rooms with fan and shared bathroom cost 100B, and air-con rooms cost 300B.

Farther east along Thanon Rimkhong, the *Maekhong Guest House* (☎ 042-460689) has 16 basic but clean rooms overlooking the river for 100B per person, plus a couple of larger rooms for 150/250B single/double. Hot showers are available. In a new Thai-style wooden bungalow on an upstairs deck overlooking the river are two large air-con rooms with private hot-water shower for 500B. Between the Mekong and Mutmee guesthouses, on a quiet spot near the river, the *Rimkhong Guest House* (☎ 042-460625, fax 420967) has 12 decent rooms in three wooden houses with shared bathroom for 80/150B.

Sawasdee Guest House (☎ 042-412502, fax 420259, 402 Thanon Meechai) is in one of Nong Khai's old shophouses, restored and refurbished to provide small but very clean rooms for 80/120B with fan and shared bathroom, 280B with air-con and hot-water shower; VIP rooms are 380B. A small inner courtyard is pleasant for sitting. The house is opposite Wat Si Khun Meuang. It would be great if more historic Nong Khai shophouses could be preserved like this one.

Australian-managed *The Meeting Place* (☎ 042-421223, 1117 Soi Chuenjit) has a few rooms with shared facilities for 200B, plus an expat-oriented bar. Fifteen-day tourist visas for Laos are available here for 1500B, including transport to the Friendship bridge, plus maps and information. *Chez Kai* (☎/fax 042-460968, 1160 Soi Samoson), formerly Chez Pierrot, runs a similar guesthouse-bar-visa service; rooms cost 100/150B.

Hotels A cheapie on Thanon Banthoengjit is the *Hotel Bun Terng Ghitt* (Banthoengjit), with very simple two-bed rooms for 100B with shared bathroom, and 200B with private cold-water bathroom.

Pongvichita Hotel (Phong Vichitr; ☎ 042-411583, 1244/1–2 Thanon Banthoengjit), across the street from the Sukhaphan, is clean and businesslike, with one-/two-bed rooms for 200/250B with fan and bathroom, 450/500B with air-con.

Prajak Bungalows (☎ 042-412644, 1178 Thanon Prajak) has quiet off-street singles/doubles for 250B with fan and 300/350B with air-con and hot water.

Places to Stay – Mid-Range & Top End

The *Phanthavee Hotel (Phantawi; ☎ 042-411568, 1241 Thanon Hai Sok)* has tidy air-con rooms with hot water for 300B to 400B, plus a few rooms with fan for 250B. There's a decent coffee shop downstairs. Across the street is *Pantawee Bungalows*, under the same management and at the same rates.

The nine-storey *Nong Khai Grand Hotel (☎ 042-420033, fax 412026, e info@nongkhaigrand.com)* is on Rte 212 a bit south of the town centre. Modern rooms with all the amenities cost 2119B to 2354B, although discounts to around 800/900B single/double are readily available. On the premises are a restaurant, coffee shop, swimming pool, conference room and disco.

The modest *Khong River Hotel (☎ 042-465557)*, almost directly opposite the train station, has decent rooms with private facilities for 250B to 400B.

Built in hopes of reaping a profit from the bridge opening, the 208-room, nine-storey *Mekong Royal Nong Khai (☎ 042-420024, fax 421280)* sits on the highway bypass near Ban Jommani, east of the town centre. Plush rooms start at 1000B, including breakfast. Hotel facilities include a restaurant, coffee shop, cocktail lounge, pool, miniature golf, a jogging track and conference rooms. This hotel provides access (and one room) for the mobility impaired.

In the same general vicinity, the new seven-storey *Thai-Laos Riverside Hotel (☎ 042-460263, fax 460317, 051 Thanon Kaew Worawut)* has 72 rooms featuring air-con, IDD phone, satellite TV and minibar. Some upper-floor rooms have a river view. Rates range from 600B to 800B, including breakfast. Facilities include a restaurant, karaoke, Thai massage and parking.

Places to Eat

Out of all the guesthouses in town, the *Mutmee* has the best food, including many vegetarian dishes, home-baked bread and wine.

The *Dukada Bakery* on Thanon Meechai has Western breakfasts and Thai food, although the once-plentiful pastry selection has become a bit thin lately. In addition to an extensive selection of Thai and Chinese meals, the menu offers fried chicken, beef steak or pork chops with vegetables and potatoes for just 35B. Also on Thanon Meechai, next to the Thai Farmers Bank, is *Danish Baker*. They serve good coffee here, but there's not much on the menu that would appeal to vegetarians. It's open for breakfast, lunch and dinner.

Darika, on the same street, serves cheap egg-and-toast breakfasts, real Thai coffee, banana pancakes and Lao-style baguette sandwiches, plus *khànǒm jìip* (Chinese dumplings), *jók* (rice congee) and *kǔaytǐaw* (rice soup).

Very good Vietnamese food is available from *Daeng Naem Neuang* at the corner of Thanon Rimkhong and Thanon Banthoengjit; the house speciality is the namesake *nǎem neuang* – spicy pork sausage served with lettuce leaves, sliced starfruit and various condiments.

Udom Rot, which overlooks the Mekong and Tha Sadet (the ferry pier for boats to/from Laos), has good food and atmosphere, and Isan-Lao crafts for sale at the front. On the other side of the pier is the more expensive *Tha Dan* (Customs Pier) restaurant, which also has a souvenir shop at the front. If you wander east along Thanon Rimkhong into the covered part of Talat Tha Sadet, look for a Lao-style restaurant called *Nong Naen Pla Phao* on your left. This rustic but clean spot offers delicious salt-baked *plaa châwn* stuffed with herbs, plus *kài yâang*, *kaeng lao* (Lao-style bamboo-shoot soup), grilled sausage and grilled prawns (shrimp). The eating area overlooks the river.

Another riverside choice is the *Rabieng Mekhong*, next to the Maekhong Guest House. On the opposite side of the street is *Nam Tok Rim Khong*, a restaurant specialising in Isan dishes, including *néua náam tòk* (literally, waterfall beef) – a spicy, tart salad of barbecued beef served with sticky rice.

NORTH-EASTERN THAILAND

Boat, farther west on Thanon Rimkhong, serves ice cream, sundaes, milk shakes and good Thai food; you can choose to sit in the indoor air-con section or in the outdoor riverside section.

The popular *Thai Thai* (☎ 042-4203730, *1155/8 Thanon Prajak),* near Soi Cheunjit, has all the usual Thai and Chinese dishes. It's open all night. *Di Di Phochana,* just west of Thai Thai, is similar. Diagonally opposite the Pongvichita Hotel is a major *jók shop*, with a choice of chicken or pork jók.

At a pier behind Wat Hai Sok, a *floating restaurant* leaves around 5 pm nightly to view the sunset and Phra That Nong Khai (the latter visible in the dry season only) a little way down the Mekong River. The menu includes a few regional dishes as well as Thai standards; prices are reasonable and cold beer is available.

Night vendors set up each evening in front of the Buddhist school on Thanon Prajak, and in front of Wat Si Saket on Thanon Meechai.

Nobbi's Restaurant (☎ 042-460583), at the north-eastern corner of the intersection of Thanon Meechai and Thanon Sukpracha, caters to the older expat crowd in the city with European favourites such as home-made German sausage, goulash, bratwurst, steaks, sandwiches, salads, pizza and spaghetti.

Farther east, there's a *vegetarian restaurant* (an English sign reads 'Vegetarian Food') right next to Wat Si Meuang on Thanon Meechai.

Shopping

A shop called Village Weaver Handicrafts (☎ 042-411236, e village@udon.ksc.co.th) at 1151 Soi Jittapanya, off Thanon Prajak, sells high-quality, moderately priced woven fabrics and ready-made clothes. The staff can also tailor clothing in a day or two from pre-purchased fabric. The shop was established by the Good Shepherd Sisters as part of a project to encourage local girls to stay in the villages and earn money by weaving, rather than leaving home to seek work in urban centres. The hand-dyed mát-mìi cotton is particularly good here, and visitors are welcome to observe the methods in the weaving workshop behind the shop. The Thai name for the project is Hatthakam Sing Thaw.

The Good Shepherd Sisters have also recently established the Isan Weaving and Isan Pottery training centres to further provide alternative vocational skills and employment to local people. A new shop called Isan, located 6km outside Nong Khai on the road to Udon Thani, carries the items produced at these centres.

Art Studio Lisa Lippuner (☎ 042-461110, fax 460717, e mira@nk.ksc.co.th), on the same soi as Mutmee Guest House, houses a one-room gallery exhibiting the naturalistic paintings of a long-time Swiss resident.

Getting There & Away

Air The nearest airport is approximately 55km south at Udon Thani. THAI flies to Udon; see the Udon Thani Getting There & Away section earlier for flight details. THAI operates an express van direct from Udon airport to the THAI office (on the southern side of Rte 212, about 300m west of Hwy 2) in Nong Khai for 100B per person; the trip takes around 35 minutes. You can get a túk-túk to the office for about 20B.

Bus Nong Khai's main bus terminal, off Thanon Prajak, has buses to Si Chiangmai, Beung Kan, Loei, Udon Thani, Ubon Ratchathani, Tha Bo, Bangkok and Rayong.

Buses (No 221) to Nong Khai leave Udon Thani approximately every half-hour throughout the day from Udon's Rangsina Market bus terminal. The trip takes about 1¼ hours and costs 17B.

Buses to Loei (No 507) leave Nong Khai throughout the day between 6 am and 4 pm and cost 75B; Nakhon Phanom buses (No 224) depart 16 times each day between 6.30 am and 4.30 pm and cost 54B (95B air-con).

If you're coming from Loei Province, you can get buses from Chiang Khan or Pak Chom without having to double back to Udon Thani. From Nakhon Phanom you can travel via Beung Kan along the Mekong River or you can cut through Sakon Nakhon and Udon Thani.

Bangkok Ordinary buses to Nong Khai from Bangkok's Northern bus terminal leave seven times daily between 4.10 am and 10 am (177B, 11 to 12 hours). Second-class air-con buses cost 248B, and leave three times a day at 8.40 am and 9.15 am and 9 pm. First-class air-con and VIP buses leave nightly between 8 and 9.15 pm (there's one

1st-class departure at 8.30 am); 1st class costs 319B, while 24-seat VIP is 495B. Most people prefer to take the Bangkok–Nong Khai train – you can wander around a bit rather than sit on a narrow bus seat for 10 or more hours.

Laos Shuttle buses ferry passengers back and forth across the bridge from a designated terminal near the Thai-Lao Friendship Bridge for 10B per person; there are departures every 20 minutes from 6 am to 7.30 pm. You must arrange your own transport to the bridge bus terminal from Nong Khai; figure on around 30B by túk-túk. The bus stops at Thai immigration control on the bridge, where you pay 10B to have your passport stamped with an exit visa. You then reboard the bus and pay a fee of 20B to have your passport stamped (40B between noon and 2 pm and on weekends); after crossing the bridge, stop at Lao immigration and customs.

The bridge is open from 6 am to 8 pm. If you're driving, a toll of 20B is collected for cars; 30B for trucks under one tonne; 50B for mini or medium buses; 100B for bus coaches; and 100B to 300B for larger trucks, depending on the number of wheels.

Train From Bangkok, the Nong Khai express (No 69) leaves Hualamphong station daily at 8.30 pm, arriving in Nong Khai at 8.40 am – it's about the same speed as the bus but considerably more comfortable. Two rapid trains leave daily at 6.15 am and 7 pm, arriving at 6 pm and 7.10 am. One-way fares are 497B in 1st class, 238B in 2nd class and 103B in 3rd class, not including surcharges for express or rapid service (60B and 40B) or sleeping berths.

A more inexpensive way to go by train most of the way is to take a 3rd-class diesel railcar as far as Udon Thani (95B) and hop on a bus from there for another 17B – see the Udon Thani Getting There & Away section earlier for schedule information.

In the reverse direction, the Nong Khai express (No 70) departs Nong Khai at 6.35 pm and arrives in Bangkok at 6.10 am. There are also two Bangkok-bound rapid trains leaving Nong Khai at 7.25 pm and 8.10 am – both offer 2nd- and 3rd-class services only, but make only one more stop than the express.

Getting Around

Săamláw around the town centre cost 10B to 20B; túk-túk are 20B, or 30B to the Friendship Bridge shuttle-bus terminal and the train station.

AROUND NONG KHAI PROVINCE
Wat Phra That Bang Phuan
วัดพระธาตุบังเผือน

Twelve kilometres south of Nong Khai on Hwy 2 and then 11km west on Rte 211, Wat Phra That Bang Phuan is one of the most sacred sites in the North-East because of the old Indian-style stupa here. It's similar to the original chedi beneath the Phra Pathom Chedi in Nakhon Pathom, but no-one knows when either chedi was built. It's speculated that it must have been in the early centuries AD – the chedi supposedly enshrines some chest bones of the Buddha himself.

In 1559 King Jayachettha of Chanthaburi (not the present Chanthaburi in Thailand, but Wiang Chan – known as Vientiane – in Laos) extended his capital across the Mekong and built a newer, taller, Lao-style chedi over the original as a demonstration of faith (just as King Mongkut did in Nakhon Pathom). Rain caused the chedi to lean precariously and in 1970 it fell over. The Fine Arts Department restored it in 1976 and 1977. The current chedi stands 34.25m high on a 17.2-sq-m base.

But it is the remaining 16th-century Lao chedi in the compound (two contain semi-intact Buddha images in their niches) that give the wát its charm. There is also a roofless wíhăn with a large Buddha image, and a massive round brick base that must have supported another large chedi. A small museum displays site relics and a collection of old wooden spirit houses. Admission is free, although donations are appreciated.

Getting There & Away To get to Wat Phra That Bang Phuan, get a săwngthăew or bus in Nong Khai bound for Si Chiangmai or Sangkhom and ask for Ban Bang Phuan (15B). Most Sangkhom-bound buses automatically stop at Phra That Bang Phuan. Otherwise, get any bus south on Hwy 2 and get off in Ban Nong Song Hong, the junction for Rte 211. From there take the next bus (from either Udon or Nong Khai) that's going to Si Chiangmai and get off near the wát. The fare should be about 15B to the road leading off Rte 211; it's an easy walk to the wát from that point.

Tha Bo
ท่าบ่อ

postcode 43110 • pop 16,000

Along the Mekong River and Rte 211, between the town of Nong Khai and the Loei Province border, are several smaller towns and villages where life revolves around farming and (minimal) trade between Laos and Thailand.

Surrounded by banana plantations and vegetable fields flourishing in the fertile Mekong floodplains, Tha Bo is the most important market centre between Nong Khai and Loei. An open-air market along the main street probably offers more wild plants and herbs than any market along the Mekong, along with Tha Bo's most famous local product – tomatoes. Annual tomato exports from Tha Bo often exceed 80,000 tonnes. Tobacco is also grown in fairly impressive quantities.

The **Kheuan Huay Mong** (Huay Mong Dam), which crosses the Mekong at the western edge of town, irrigates 108 sq km of land around Tha Bo. This relatively small-scale pumping project is one of the most successful hydrology efforts in Thailand, running at higher efficiency than any of the country's larger dam facilities and with less-extreme environmental impact. There is a pleasant public park next to the dam.

Aside from the market and dam, the town's only other claim to fame is **Wat Ong Teu** (also known as Wat Nam Mong), an old Lao-style temple sheltering a 'crying Buddha'. According to local legend, the left hand of the 300-year-old bronze image was once cut off by art thieves; tears streamed from the Buddha's eyes until the hand was returned. The wát is 3km west of town off Rte 211.

Places to Stay & Eat *Suksan Hotel*, on the main street through town, has basic rooms for 60B to 100B. *Tha Bo Bungalow* (☎ 042-431196), on a back street not far from the town centre, has passable rooms with fan and bathroom for 140B to 200B.

Quieter accommodation is available at *Isan Orchid Guest Lodge* (☎ 042-431665,

87/9 Thanon Kaew Worawut), a large modern house in the middle of village-like surroundings near the river. Owned by a retired American and managed by Thais, the house has large, comfortable air-con rooms from 500B to 750B, including a European breakfast. A smaller bungalow next to the main house is available for 700B to 850B. The manager can arrange pick-ups from Udon airport as well as trips to Phra Phutthabaht Bua Bok; bicycles can be borrowed at no charge.

Getting There & Away All săwngthăew and buses from Nong Khai (25km to the east) bound for Si Chiangmai will drop passengers in Tha Bo for 10B to 12B. If you're cycling from Nong Khai, you have a choice of the scenic river road or the less scenic Rte 211.

Si Chiangmai
ศรีเชียงใหม่

Just across the river from Vientiane, Si Chiangmai has a large number of Lao and Vietnamese who make their living from the manufacture of rice-paper spring-roll wrappers. You can see the translucent disks drying in the sun on bamboo racks all over town. Si Chiangmai is one of the world's leading exporters of spring-roll wrappers! Many of the Vietnamese and Lao residents are Roman Catholic and there is a small cathedral in town. A local bakery prepares fresh French rolls every morning in an outdoor brick oven.

Wat Hin Mak Peng, Ban Pheu and various local villages can be visited from Si Chiangmai – inquire at Tim Guest House for the latest information.

Ferries now cross regularly to Vientiane – there are immigration and customs offices in town – but foreigners are usually referred to Nong Khai (see that section earlier) for river crossings.

Places to Stay & Eat *Tim Guest House* (☎/fax 042-451072), the only guesthouse in town, is run by a friendly Swiss-French man who speaks English, French, German and Thai. Rooms start at 60B a small single to 130B a large double with a river view. Simple Thai and fàràng food is served in a dining area downstairs. Maps of the vicinity, massage and herbal sauna, laundry service, and bicycle and motorcycle rental are available.

Boat trips along the Mekong to Nong Khai, Wat Hin Mak Peng and Sangkhom can also be arranged. The guesthouse is on Thanon Rim Khong, near the river in the centre of town – walk west from the bus terminal and turn right at Soi 17, then turn left at the end of the road and you'll find it on the left.

A bit south-east of Tim is the basic *Hotel Suthisuwan* (*☎/fax 042-451127*), with rooms for 150B to 200B. This hotel is in a historic building; check out the impressive upper floor.

About 700m south-east you'll find the new three-storey *Maneerat Resort* (*☎ 042-451311*), with air-con rooms for 350B, and a few special larger VIP rooms for 650B. The hotel has a restaurant with a few tables across the road on the river, as well as a karaoke lounge.

Getting There & Away Probably because of its importance as a spring-roll wrapper capital, Si Chiangmai has an abundance of public transport. Bus fares to/from Si Chiangmai are:

destination	fare	duration (hrs)
Bangkok		
air-con	335B	12
Khon Kaen		
ordinary	62B	4
air-con	117B	3½
Khorat		
ordinary	114B	6
air-con	210B	5½
Loei		
ordinary	60B	3
Nong Khai		
ordinary	16B–18B	¾
Pak Chom		
ordinary	40B	¾
Sangkhom		
ordinary	13B	½
Udon Thani		
ordinary	28B	1½

Wat Hin Mak Peng
วัดหินหมากเป้ง

Sixty-four kilometres north-west of Nong Khai between Si Chiangmai and Sangkhom, Wat Hin Mak Peng is worth a trip just for the scenery along Rte 211 from Nong Khai. This monastery is locally known for its *thúdong* (Pali: *dhutanga*) monks – monks who have taken ascetic vows in addition to the standard 227 precepts. These vows include, for example, eating only once a day and wearing only forest robes made from discarded cloth, plus a strong emphasis on meditation. There are also several *mâe chii* (Thai Buddhist nuns) living here. The place is very quiet and peaceful, set in a cool forest with lots of bamboo groves overlooking the Mekong. The *kùtì* (monastic huts) are built among giant boulders that form a cliff high above the river; casual visitors aren't allowed into this area, though. Below the cliff is a sandy beach and more rock formations. A Lao forest temple can be seen directly across the river. Fisherfolk occasionally drift by on house rafts.

The abbot at Wat Hin Mak Peng requests that visitors to the wát dress politely – no shorts or sleeveless tops. Those who don't observe the code will be denied entrance.

Getting There & Away To get here, take a săwngthăew from Nong Khai to Si Chiangmai (16B) and ask for a săwngthăew directly to Wat Hin (there are a few) or to Sangkhom, which is just past the entrance to the wát – the other passengers will let you know when the truck passes it (the săwngthăew usually makes a stop here anyway). The second săwngthăew is 18B. On the way to Wat Hin Mak Peng you might notice a large topiary garden at Ban Phran Phrao on the right-hand side of the highway.

Sangkhom
สังคม

The tiny town of Sangkhom could be used as a rest stop on a slow journey along the Mekong River from Loei to Nong Khai. Wat Hin Mak Peng is nearby and there are some good hikes to caves and waterfalls in the area. The guesthouses hand out maps.

Opposite the River Huts guesthouse, in the middle of the Mekong River, the Lao island of **Don Klang Khong** appears during the dry season. From around the beginning of December a couple of rustic outdoor eating areas with thatched-roof shelters and tables and chairs are set up in the river shallows. On the Thai side you can get local boys to paddle you across to the island in canoes – no visa necessary.

One of the largest local waterfalls is **Nam Tok Than Thip**, 3km from Rte 211 between the 97km and 98km markers, and a few kilometres west of Sangkhom. The waterfall has two major levels; the upper level is cleaner and has a deep pool (during or just after the rainy season) that is good for a dip. The falls are a long walk from the road – this is a trip best accomplished by motorcycle.

Nam Tok Than Thong, 11.5km east of Sangkhom at the 73km marker off the northern (river) side of Rte 211, is more accessible but can be rather crowded on weekends and holidays.

Wat Aranyabanphot is a forest wát on a nearby hilltop with a very good sunset-over-the-Mekong view. A recent addition to the wát is a Lanna-style gilded chedi.

Places to Stay & Eat The town's guesthouses are off the main road through town and near the river.

The friendly and efficient *River Huts* has a secluded location well off the main road, and thatched huts overlooking the river are 100B single/double. The food is good and there are bicycles for rent.

Out on the main road is the original *Bouy's Guest House* (☎/fax 042-441065), a very pleasant place with huts on the river for 100B single/double. Its better-than-average restaurant is worth a stop for lunch even if you're not staying overnight. Sandwiches, as well as Thai food, are available.

Two or three other guesthouses seem to come and go with the seasons, including *Mama's River View Lodge* and *Garden Home*. Outside of town a little bit, on the way to Si Chiangmai, are the similar *Dee Daeng Guest House* (just west of the 83km marker, opposite a PTT petrol station) and *Pak Som Guest House* (a bit farther east), neither of which is anything special.

There are a couple of riverside *restaurants*. Ask around and you may be able to find a taste of *náam yân,* the sweetest moonshine from Laos.

Getting There & Away Buses from Nong Khai are 35B, and the trip takes about two hours. From Loei it costs 59B (three or four hours) and from Pak Chom 24B (1½ hours). From nearby Si Chiangmai the fare is 13B.

West of Pak Chom, săwngthăew are less frequent because the road worsens; the fare to Chiang Khan is 17B.

BEUNG KAN
บึงกาฬ

This is a small dusty town on the Mekong River, 185km east of Nong Khai by Rte 212. You may want to break your journey here if you are working your way around the north-eastern border from Nong Khai to Nakhon Phanom (as opposed to the easier but less interesting Udon Thani–Sakon Nakhon–Nakhon Phanom route).

Between Nong Khai and Nakhon Phanom you'll pass many towns with 'Beung' or 'Nong' in their names; both terms refer to shallow bodies of fresh water fed by seasonal streams (a *beung* is usually larger than a *năwng*).

The closer you get to Nakhon Phanom Province, the more Vietnamese you will see working in the rice fields or herding cows along the road. Nearly all the farmers in this area, whether ethnic Vietnamese or Thai, wear a simple conical Vietnamese-style straw hat to fend off the sun and rain.

The district of Beung Kan itself isn't much but there are some mildly interesting spots, including a nicely landscaped promenade along the waterfront. During the dry season the Mekong River recedes from Beung Kan and reaches its narrowest point along the Thai-Lao border.

East of town is **Nam Song Si** (Two Colour River), where the broad, muddy Huay Songkhram replenishes the Mekong.

Information
Near the clock tower is a Thai Farmers Bank with an ATM.

Wat Phu Thok
วัดภูทอก(วัดเจดีย์คีรีวิหาร)

Travellers interested in north-eastern forest wát can visit Wat Phu Thok (Wat Chedi Khiri Wihan), a massive sandstone outcropping in the middle of a rather arid plain and a real hermit's delight. The entire outcropping, with its amazing network of caves and breathtaking views, belongs to the wát. The wát mountain is climbed by a seven-level series of stairs representing the seven factors of enlightenment in Buddhist psychology. Monastic *kùtì* (monks' dwellings) are scattered around the mountain, in caves and on cliffs. As you make the strenuous climb, each level is cooler than the one before. It is the cool and quiet isolation of this wát that entices monks and mâe chii from all over the North-East to come and meditate here.

This wát used to be the domain of the famous meditation master Ajahn Juan, a disciple of the fierce Ajahn Man who passed away in 1949. Ajahn Juan died in a plane crash about 20 years ago, along with several other highly revered forest monks who were flying to Bangkok for Queen Sirikit's birthday celebration.

To get to Wat Phu Thok you'll have to take an early morning săwngthăew south on Rte 222 to Ban Siwilai (10B, 25km), then another săwngthăew east (left) on a dirt road, 20km to the wát (15B). This săwngthăew carries merit-makers. Hitching might be possible if you miss the truck. Occasionally you can find a local túk-túk going to the wát in the afternoon from Siwilai for 15B. If solitude is your main objective, it's best to tour Phu Thok early in the morning before the crowds of Thai pilgrims arrive.

If you're driving or pedalling yourself, a more direct route to the monastery is to continue south-east along Rte 212 from Beung Kan (in the direction of Nakhon Phanom) until you reach the 61km marker, then turn right (south-east) at a road signed for Jet Si, Tham Phra and Chut Na waterfalls. After 17km make a right on another road heading south-west, signed (in Thai only) for Phu Thok. You'll come to a monastery gate on the right after another 3.5km.

Ban Ahong

บ้านอาฮง

This village at the 115km marker on Rte 212 between Beung Kan and Nong Khai (23km west of Beung Kan) makes an interesting alternative to staying overnight in Beung Kan. The friendly Hideaway Guest House (see Places to Stay & Eat later) next to the Mekong River is just a 200m walk from one of Isan's smallest and most intriguing wát. Set among giant boulders along the river, **Wat Pa Ahong Silawat** is a pretty riverside wát.

The narrow stretch of Mekong River opposite the wát has some refreshing pools for swimming during the dry season when the river is fairly clear. This area is also considered a highly auspicious spot to spend the evening of *wan àwk phansăa*, the end of the Buddhist Rains Retreat. According to the local legend, supernatural lights, *bâng fai pháyaa nâak* (dragon rockets), emerge from beneath the Mekong River on this evening each year and arc across the sky three times. Several hundred Thai and Lao residents gather along the river for the yearly event. At other times of year there's frequent talk of UFO appearances. Similar stories circulate at Phon Phisai farther south-west towards Nong Khai.

Hideaway Guest House can arrange boat trips to nearby river islands.

Places to Stay & Eat

Beung Kan The modest *Samanmit* (60B to 80B) and *Santisuk* (120B to 350B) are both on Thanon Prasatchai not far from the town clock tower; the Samanmit has the best overall appearance, while the Santisuk has a nice eating area downstairs.

The new two-storey *Mekong Guest House* (☎/fax 042-491341) sits across from the riverbank and offers clean rooms with private hot shower for 250B with fan, 350B air-con. The attached *Joy's Restaurant* downstairs serves reasonably priced tasty Thai dishes.

In addition to a few nondescript *food stalls* in town, the *Phloen Da* and *Mae Nam Restaurant*, both overlooking the river, offer decent Thai and Isan meals.

Ban Ahong The *Hideaway Guest House*, behind the village school next to the river (turn off at the 115km marker), has a circle of simple, quiet huts on stilts for 100/120B single/double with shared bathroom, 150B with private bathroom. Meals are available, there is a pleasant riverside sitting area nearby, and you can go for walks in the village.

Getting There & Away

The No 4193 bus from Nong Khai to Beung Kan (37B) departs every half-hour from 6 am to 6.30 pm. Buses from Nakhon Phanom to Beung Kan cost 45B, and buses between Beung Kan and Ban Ahong cost 10B.

NORTH-EASTERN THAILAND

Loei Province

Loei is one of Thailand's most beautiful and unspoiled provinces. The terrain is mountainous and the temperature goes from one extreme to the other – hotter than elsewhere in Thailand during the hot season and colder than anywhere else during the cold season. This is the only province in Thailand where temperatures can drop to as low as 0°C.

The culture is an unusual mixture of northern and north-eastern influences – a mixture that has produced more than one local dialect. Rural life outside the provincial capital has retained more of a traditional village flavour than many other places in Thailand, with the possible exceptions of Nan and Phetchabun, which were also once classified as remote or closed provinces.

Within the province, Phu Kradung and Phu Reua National Parks, in addition to the district of Chiang Khan, are worth a look and are good places to explore natural attractions.

LOEI

อ.เมืองเลย

postcode 42000 • pop 22,700

Nearly 520km from Bangkok, 140km from Udon Thani, 269km from Phitsanulok via Lom Sak and 200km via Nakhon Thai, the remote provincial capital of Loei has little to hold the interest of the ordinary traveller. Cotton is one of the province's major crops, so the town is a good place to buy cotton goods, especially the heavy cotton quilts (quite necessary during the chilly nights of Loei's cool months) made in Chiang Khan district – they're priced by the kilogram.

During the first week of February, Loei holds a **Cotton Blossom Festival** that culminates in a parade of cotton-decorated floats and, naturally, a Cotton Blossom Queen beauty contest. Loei also celebrates with fervour its own annual Rocket Festival, held in May. The city has even imported the colourful Phi Ta Khon procession from nearby Dan Sai district (see 'The Arrival of the Spirits' boxed text later in this chapter).

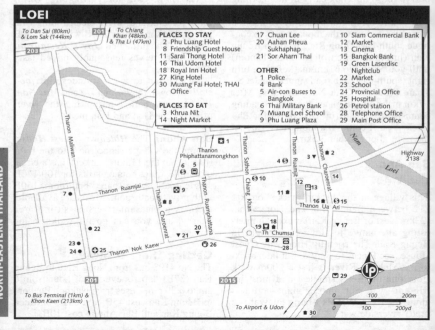

LOEI

To Dan Sai (80km) & Lom Sak (144km)

To Chiang Khan (48km) & Tha Li (47km)

PLACES TO STAY
2 Phu Luang Hotel
8 Friendship Guest House
11 Sarai Thong Hotel
16 Thai Udom Hotel
18 Royal Inn Hotel
27 King Hotel
30 Muang Fai Hotel; THAI Office

PLACES TO EAT
3 Khrua Nit
14 Night Market
17 Chuan Lee
20 Aahan Pheua Sukhaphap
21 Sor Aharn Thai

OTHER
1 Police
4 Bank
5 Air-con Buses to Bangkok
6 Thai Military Bank
7 Muang Loei School
9 Phu Luang Plaza
10 Siam Commercial Bank
12 Market
13 Cinema
15 Bangkok Bank
19 Green Laserdisc Nightclub
22 Market
23 School
24 Provincial Office
25 Hospital
26 Petrol station
28 Telephone Office
29 Main Post Office

Thanon Maliwan
Thanon Phiphattanamongkhon
Thanon Ruamjai
Thanon Charoenrat
Thanon Ruamphattana
Thanon Sathon
Thanon Chiang Khan
Thanon Ruamjit
Thanon Charoenrat
Thanon Ua Ari
Th Chumsai
Thanon Nok Kaew

Nam Loei

Highway 2138

To Bus Terminal (1km) & Khon Kaen (213km)

To Airport & Udon

0 100 200m
0 100 200yd

Very un-Isan, the Pu Ya Shrine in Udon Thani

Sounding the gong at Ban Chiang, Udon Thani

Hall at Wat Thung Si Muang, Ubon Rachathani

View from Wat Phu Thawk, Nong Khai Province

The main sanctuary at the Khmer-period Prasat Hin Phimai, Nakhon Ratchasima Province

Abandoned Khmer Rouge gun, Khao Phra Wihan, on the border of Sisaket Province and Cambodia

Ancient stone steps rising to the remote ruins of Khao Phra Wihan

Information
Money Directly opposite the Thai Udom Hotel on Thanon Charoenrat is a branch of Bangkok Bank with an ATM.

Post & Communications Loei's main post office is on Thanon Charoenrat, not far from the Muang Fai Hotel. The telephone office is located on the southern side of Thanon Chumsai, just east of Thanon Ruamjit.

Places to Stay – Budget
Friendship Guest House (☎ 042-832408), at a new location on Thanon Charoenrat, offers spacious rooms which can sleep up to five people for 200B. Toilet and shower facilities are shared. The owner, Khun Dum, speaks good English.

Sarai Thong Hotel, off Thanon Ruamjit, has 56 none-too-clean rooms in three buildings, costing 140B, all with fan and bathroom. The service isn't great, but it's off the street so it's usually quiet.

Places to Stay – Mid-Range & Top End
Phu Luang Hotel (☎ 042-811532/570, 55 Thanon Charoenrat), near the night market, charges 400B to 600B for air-con singles/doubles. On the premises are a so-so restaurant and nightclub.

Across from Bangkok Bank is the friendly *Thai Udom Hotel* (☎ 042-811763, fax 830187, 122/1 Thanon Charoenrat), where rooms with fan cost 240/320B for one/two beds and air-con rooms cost 350/500B; larger VIP air-con rooms are 600B to 800B. Overall it's a better choice than the Phu Luang, especially if you get a room away from the street.

Over on Thanon Chumsai near the Green Laserdisc nightclub is the well-run three-storey *King Hotel* (☎ 042-811701, fax 811235), where rooms cost 240/310B single/double with fan and bathroom, and 380/399B with air-con and hot water. An attached restaurant serves Thai, Vietnamese, Chinese and European dishes. Also in this vicinity, just off Thanon Chumsai, is the *Royal Inn Hotel* (☎ 042-812563, fax 830873), with nice modest apartments for rent with TV and air-con for 380/420B.

The four-storey *Muang Fai Hotel* (☎ 042-811302, fax 812353) is near the THAI office and main post office on Thanon Charoenrat. Although the official rack rates are much higher, it offers very pleasant fan rooms for 150B, standard air-con rooms for 300B and deluxe air-con rooms for 350B. It's a well-run place with a decent coffee shop.

Places to Eat
The *night market* near the intersection of Thanon Ruamjai and Thanon Charoenrat has cheap eats and other items of local provenance. Look for the local speciality, *khài pîng* (eggs-in-the-shell toasted on skewers).

Khrua Nit, opposite Phu Luang Hotel on Thanon Charoenrat, serves *hàw mòk* (food steamed in banana leaves) and other central-Thai dishes; it's inexpensive and open from 6 am to 8.30 pm daily. *Chuan Lee* is a traditional Chinese pastry and coffee shop on Thanon Charoenrat, not far from the Thai Udom Hotel and Bangkok Bank. It's very good and also serves a few curries at lunch and dinner.

Along Thanon Nok Kaew near the roundabout is a moderately priced Thai restaurant, *Sor Aharn Thai* (☎ 042-813436), serving all kinds of Thai dishes in an indoor-outdoor setting.

If you're looking for vegetarian fare, there is a Chinese vegetarian place called *Ahan Pheua Sukhaphap* (the English sign reads 'Vegetarian Food') at No 17 Thanon Nok Kaew, about 50m east of Sor Aharn Thai. It's open only during the day.

Entertainment
The town seems to be asleep by 10 pm. Opposite the King Hotel on Thanon Chumsai, the *Green Laserdisc* features live music and karaoke.

Getting There & Away
Air The Loei airport, 6km south of town on the road to Udon Thani, has closed for repairs. In the past THAI has operated flights between Loei and Phitsanulok. If or when the airport reopens there may be flights from Bangkok as well.

Bus Buses to Loei leave Udon regularly until late afternoon for 45B (81B air-con, 150km, four hours). From Nong Khai the fare is 75B (five or six hours).

A direct bus between Phitsanulok and Loei costs 75B (97B air-con) and takes four to five hours. Buses between Loei and Dan Sai cost 38B, and depart from Loei nine times between 5 am and 5 pm.

Air-con buses to Loei from Bangkok's Northern bus terminal leave several times daily (227B 2nd class, 292B 1st class, 10 hours, 5 am and 10.30 pm). A VIP bus leaves nightly at 8.40 pm and costs 450B. Ordinary buses cost 162B and leave several times daily. In Loei you can get air-con buses to Bangkok from the bus terminal at the south-western edge of town or from an agency in the lobby of the King Hotel.

Getting Around

You'll find plenty of túk-túk waiting at the bus station to take you into town. The fare is 5B per passenger, or about 30B for a chartered ride.

AROUND LOEI PROVINCE
Phu Kradung National Park
อุทยานแห่งชาติภูกระดึง

At 1360m, Phu Kradung is the highest point in Loei. On top of this bell-shaped mountain is a large plateau with 50km of marked trails to cliffs, meadows, waterfalls and montane forests of pine, beech and oak. The weather is always cool on top (average year-round temperature 20°C), hence the flora is more like that in a temperate zone. Lower down are mixed deciduous and evergreen monsoon forests as well as sections of cloud forest. The 359-sq-km park is a habitat for various forest animals, including elephants, Asian jackals, Asiatic black bears, barking deer, sambars, serows, white-handed gibbons and the occasional tiger. A Buddhist **shrine** near the park headquarters is a favourite local pilgrimage site.

The **main trail** scaling Phu Kradung is 6km long and takes about three hours to climb (or rather walk – it's not that challenging since the most difficult parts have bamboo ladders and stairs for support). The hike is quite scenic and there are rest stops with food vendors along the way. It's another 3km to the park headquarters. You can hire porters to carry your gear balanced on bamboo poles for 15B per kilogram.

During the hottest months, from March to June, it's best to start the climb about

dawn. Temperatures in December and January can drop as low as 3° to 4°C; blankets can be hired. Bring sweaters and thick socks.

Phu Kradung is closed to visitors during the rainy season from mid-July to early October because it is considered too hazardous, being slippery and subject to mud slides. The park can get crowded during school holidays (especially March to May, when Thai schools are closed).

A visitors centre at the base of the mountain distributes detailed maps and collects an admission fee of 200B for foreigners (100B for children under 14). This entrance is open only from 7 am to 3 pm.

Places to Stay & Eat Lots of young Thai people, mainly friendly college students, *camp* in the park. The park offers two-person tents for 100B a night, and boards for the bottom of the tents are available. Check the tents before paying – some are in quite ragged condition. Other *park accommodation* includes 10 different units that sleep eight each for 800B, a longhouse with four rooms (600B per room, sleeping 10 people each) and another longhouse with five rooms (300B per room, sleeping 30 each). A reader wrote in to say he also found A-frame cabins sleeping three for 300B.

Getting There & Away Buses on the Khon Kaen line go to the town (actually an amphoe) of Phu Kradung. Direct buses from Khon Kaen to the park are sometimes available for 42B – ask at the Khon Kaen government bus station. Departures from the Loei bus terminal are scheduled every half-hour from 6 am until 5.30 pm (but don't forget the park entrance closes at 3 pm) for the 28B, 77km trip. From amphoe Phu Kradung, hop on a săwngthăew (10B) to the park visitors centre at the base of the mountain, 7km away.

The last bus back to Loei from amphoe Phu Kradung leaves around 6 pm.

Phu Reua National Park
อุทยานแห่งชาติภูเรือ

This relatively small park of 121 sq km surrounds Phu Reua (Boat Mountain), so-named because a cliff jutting from the peak

AROUND LOEI

is shaped like a Chinese junk. The easy 2½-hour hike to the summit (1375m) passes from tropical forest to broad-leaf evergreen forest to pine forest. In December, temperatures near the summit approach freezing at night.

The park entrance is about 50km west of the provincial capital on Rte 203. The usual admission fees apply. Although there is public transport from Loei to the town of Phu Reua, it is difficult to find săwngthăew all the way to the park except on weekends and holidays. A well-marked 16km trail from the park visitors centre (3km off the highway) covers a good sample of what the park has to offer, including fine views of a mountain range in Sainyabuli Province, Laos.

Places to Stay & Eat The forestry department *bungalows* cost from 250B a night for up to five people.

On weekends and holidays, food is sometimes available from vendors in the park; at other times you may be able to arrange food through the park rangers.

In the nearby town of Phu Reua, you can stay at the *Phu Reua Chalet* for 250B to 500B; or *Rai Waranya* (☎ 042-899020), which offers large bungalows on the road to the park entrance for 400B to 2000B.

Getting There & Away Nine buses a day run between Loei and Dan Sai between 5 am and 5 pm, passing through Phu Reua town on the way. The fare should be around 25B.

The Arrival of the Spirits

Without a doubt, Dan Sai's three-day Bun Phra Wet Festival – also known as the Phi Ta Khon (phĭi taa khŏn) Festival – is one of the most colourful and unique annual events in Thailand. On the first day of the festival, the current village shaman – Jao Phaw Kuan – dons white clothing and a white headband, and, along with his shaman wife, Jao Mae Nang Tiam (also dressed in white with a white cloth wrapped around her hair), leads the propitiation of the all-important tiam. Tiam are a class of spirits similar to the Lao-Thai khwǎn but perceived to be at a higher level.

Assisting in the rites are a group of male and female lesser mediums. Ceremonies begin around 3.30 am in a procession from Dan Sai's Wat Phon Chai to the Man River. Rites are performed at the riverside to coax Phra Upakhut – a water spirit supposedly embodied in an invisible piece of white marble – to join the proceedings. Phra Upakhut is believed to have once been a monk with super-natural powers, who transformed himself into white marble 'to live a solitary and peaceful existence below the water', according to local descriptions. It's possible he is somehow related to the bodhi-sattva (Buddhist saint) Upagupta, who in Mahayana Buddhist mythology is thought to reside in the ocean. The procession – accompanied by the invisible spirit – then returns to the wát, where resident monks receive ceremonial food at around 7 am.

Shortly thereafter the summoning of additional spirits takes place at Jao Phaw Kuan's home, which doubles as the most important spirit shrine in Dan Sai. Villagers are invited to attend the cere-mony, and all present participate in a bai sĭi (sacred thread tying) ceremony. After some incanta-tions and lighting of candles, villagers crawl up to the Jao Phaw and Jao Mae, seated cross-legged on the floor in a semi-trance, and tie lots of sacred thread on their arms, which are propped up by pillows. The attendants also tie single loops of sacred thread around one wrist of everyone present. While all this is taking place, free food is served on round trays and everyone downs shots of lâo khǎo ('white spirit') to get in the mood for what comes next.

As the tying of threads finishes up, the shaman's attendants take down bundles of special cos-tuming kept on a high altar near the ceiling of the house, put the clothing on and gather in front of the house. Most of the costumes look like something from Shakespearian theatre meant for beg-gar or jester roles – ragged and tattered but very colourful. To complete the transformation into phĭi taa khŏn (an untranslatable term basically meaning 'Phra Wet spirits'), each attendant dons a huge mask made from a hûat (crescent-shaped basket used for steaming sticky rice), cut and re-shaped to fit atop the head, and a thick sheath from the base of a coconut palm frond. On the typical mask, small eye-openings have been cut into the palm sheath and a large, curving wooden nose added, and the whole affair is custom-painted to suit the wearer with all manner of designs. Brightly coloured cloth hangs from the basket top to cover the back of the head.

Two of the attendants, however, wear tall bamboo frames assembled in vaguely human shapes, covered with white cloth, and topped with giant heads standing perhaps 2m above their own heads.

Dan Sai
ด่านซ้าย

About 80km west of Loei is the small town of Dan Sai, which is famous for its unique form of the **Bun Phra Wet Festival**. The three-day festival occurs during the fourth lunar month (usually in June) and actually combines the Phra Wet Festival – during which recitations of the Mahavessantara Jataka are supposed to enhance the lis-tener's chance of being reborn in the life-time of the next Buddha – with the Bun Bang Fai or Rocket Festival. The latter usu-ally takes place a month or so earlier throughout the North-East in May.

Nobody seems to know how or when Dan Sai's distinctive festival first began, but an-other aspect to the festival has to do with tribal Thai – possibly Thai Dam – spirit cults. In fact the dates for the festival are divined by Jao Phaw Kuan, a local spirit medium who channels the information from Jao Saen Meuang, the town's guardian deity.

The festival has grown in popularity among outsiders and now has a steady fol-lowing among Thais from nearby provinces and as far away as Bangkok. A few

The Arrival of the Spirits

One figure is male, the other female, as is obvious from the huge, exaggerated sexual organs attached to the front of the figures – a giant penis (controlled from inside by a string that makes it flop up and down) for one, a large hairy vaginal triangle and conical breasts for the other. These are the *phǐi taa khǒhn yài* (big Phra Wet spirits), and exactly what they represent is anyone's guess nowadays. These figures, surrounded by regular phǐi taa khǒhn as well as 'civilians', then lead a boisterous procession from the Jao Phaw's house back to the monastery, with musical accompaniment supplied by khaen, pin and other Isan instruments.

More lâo khǎo is passed around and soon the knees and elbows get moving and everyone starts dancing down the road. Once the procession reaches the wát grounds, the participants begin circumambulating the main *wíhǎan* (hall) and continue for a couple hours, becoming increasingly rowdy with each turn. There's lots of sexual innuendo and older village women take turns grabbing the lengthy penis of the male phǐi taa khǒhn yài and giving it a few good shakes, laughing all the while. The whole thing ends around noon and people stagger back home to sleep it off.

On the second day all the locals get into costume and accompany Jao Phaw Kuan, Jao Mae Nang Tiam and the four female assistant mediums in a procession from Chum Chon Dan Sai School to the temple. In earlier years the Jao Phaw/Jao Mae and their shaman court rode on wood or bamboo palanquins, but nowadays they sit on colourful dais in the back of pick-up trucks. Bamboo rockets ride along with them. As on the first day, there's plenty of music and dancing but this time there are hundreds more participants, and spectators marvel at the many different costume designs cooked up for this year's event. Some show real creative genius. Many of the costumed phǐi taa khǒhn, both men and women, carry carved wooden phalli (or a knife or sword with a phallic handle) in one or both hands, waving them about as talismans or using them to tease the crowd while they dance and strut down the street. Tin cans and wooden cowbells may be hung from the costumes to create more of a racket.

Once again, when they reach the wát, the participants circumambulate the wíhǎan many times, dancing along the way. Fuelled by the consumption of much lâo khǎo, the rounds continue for hours and become more raucous and spontaneous as the day wears on. At the same time in the main courtyard in front of the wát there's live *mǎw lam* music, and lots more dancing and wooden penis antics. If it has rained recently, participants will revel in the mud. As one Western observer remarked, 'It's like Woodstock and Halloween rolled into one'.

In the late afternoon of the second day the bamboo rockets are fired. Be prepared to run for cover if one of the rockets loses its course and comes spiralling back into the crowd.

The third day is much more solemn as the villagers assemble at the temple to listen to Mahavessantara Jataka recitations and Dhamma sermons by local and visiting monks. By custom 13 sermons are delivered in a row.

westerners are beginning to find their way here as well. See the boxed text 'The Arrival of the Spirits' in this chapter.

About 1km outside town off Rte 2113 stands **Phra That Si Songrak**, a large Lao-style chedi with a very wide base, giving a much stronger-looking profile than the average Lao chedi. The most highly revered stupa in Loei Province, the whitewashed chedi stands 30m high and was built in AD 1560 as a gesture of national friendship between the Lao kingdom of Wiang Chan (Vientiane) and the Thai kingdom of Ayuthaya. A smaller stupa in front is semi-hollow and attached to a pavilion. The open repository contains a very old chest that supposedly contains an even older carved stone Buddha about 76cm long. Shoes can't be worn anywhere in the compound. The chedi's caretaker is none other than Jao Phaw Kuan, Dan Sai's main spirit medium.

Wat Neramit Wiphatsana, on a wooded hill just south-west of town, is a meditation wát where most of the buildings are made of unplastered laterite blocks. Famous Thai temple muralist Pramote Sriphrom has been painting images of *jataka* (past-life stories of the Buddha) tales on the interior walls of the bòt for the last seven years and estimates it will take him another five to finish the job. The wát is dedicated to the memory of the late Ajahn Mahaphan (also known as Khruba Phawana), a much-revered local monk.

Farther outside of town on Rte 203 near the 61km marker is the entrance for **Chateau de Loei Vineyards**, Thailand's most serious and respected vineyard. Visitors are welcome to tour the vineyards, after obtaining a pass at the Chateau de Loei store/restaurant about 30m from the vineyard entrance.

Na Haew district, about 30km north-west of Dan Sai, is separated from Laos by the Nam Heuang (also known locally as the Nam Man, although cartographers say the Man is a tributary of the Heuang and starts farther south). There is an official border crossing at the village of Meuang Phrae in Na Haew. A toll of 17B is collected from Lao and Thais who cross here. They cross either by wading across the river when the water level is low, or by raft when the water is high. For the moment foreigners cannot cross here legally.

Places to Stay & Eat *Yensuk Guest House,* very close to Wat Phon Chai, offers six featureless rooms in a row house, each with private bathroom but no ventilation. The rate is 200B except during the festival, when the owners ask as much as 400B. Farther away but still in town, *Wiang Kaew Guest House* has three larger rooms with ceiling fans and attached bathroom. It's off the road, so it's fairly quiet. Rates are the same – 200B normally, 300B during the festival. You may want to ask the staff to clean your room before checking in.

Nicer than either of these is *Phak Thanapho (T Guest House;* ☎ 042-891702), in a wooden house at the edge of town on Soi Thetsaban 4. Simple but clean and quiet rooms with shared bathroom cost 100B, possibly more during the mask festival.

Out on Rte 203 towards Loei, near the 61km marker, there's a good choice if you can spend a little more, and have your own transport. *Rangyen Resort (Rungyen Resort;* ☎ 042-891089, fax 891423) is spread out over several hectares of land that also hold a large pond, a swimming pool, bad-minton court and tennis courts. Large rooms with two beds, minibar and satellite TV cost 700B with fan, 925B with air-con, although even during the festival discounts to 475B and 825B are readily available. The resort also has two-, four- and five-bedroom bungalows. There's a large restaurant and a karaoke bar on the premises – the place seems to be geared toward Thai business or civil service conventions. Rangyen Resort is at least a 20-minute drive off the highway, so you can forget about using public transport to get here or to get from here to Dan Sai.

There are a few *noodle and rice stands* near Wat Phon Chai. One of the best places to eat is a small open-air roadside place called *Restaurant Je-Boy* on Rte 2114 just north of Dan Sai.

Getting There & Away A Phitsanulok–Udon Thani express bus stops in Dan Sai at 1.10 and 4 pm, and at noon and 2.20 in the opposite direction. The fare in either direction from Dan Sai is 50B. There are also several departures to Loei (38B).

Pak Chom
ปากชม

Pak Chom is the first town of any size you come to in Loei Province if travelling west along the Mekong River from Nong Khai. It owes much of its erstwhile development to nearby **Ban Winai Refugee Camp**. The camp consisted mostly of Hmong soldiers and families from the secret CIA/USAF base at Long Tieng (Long Chen), Laos, who were evacuated just before the 1975 Pathet Lao takeover. Ban Winai is officially closed and many of the 30,000 Hmong tribespeople at the camp have been voluntarily repatriated to Laos.

There is nothing much to do in Pak Chom except take walks along the river or to nearby villages. The town name means 'mouth of the Chom', a reference to the confluence of the Nam Chom and Mekong River here. During the dry season, locals pan for gold on Don Chom, a large island at the river junction.

Money There's a Thai Farmers Bank (with foreign-exchange) on Thanon Chiang Khan and a Bank of Ayudhya near the junction of Rtes 211 and 2108.

Places to Stay & Eat The very basic *Pak Chom Guest House* (☎ 042-881021), on the western edge of town next to the river, has a commanding view of the river and of limestone formations on the opposite banks. The couple who own it have added a few more huts and it's a suitable spot for long-term stays if you're seeking peace and quiet – no dogs or roosters in sight! Five simple bamboo huts on stilts and three rooms in a wooden building all cost 100B single/double, with shared cold-water bathroom; food and boat rentals are available.

To find the guesthouse coming from Chiang Khan on Rte 211, get off the bus at the 147km marker and walk along a dirt road to the left. Coming from Loei along Rte 2108, get off at the T-intersection in town, turn left and look for the 147km marker or follow the guesthouse signs. Coming from Nong Khai, walk straight across the intersection where the road makes a 90-degree turn left towards Chiang Khan, and walk about 500m until you see the sign pointing right to the Pak Chom Guest House. The huts are another 300m towards the river. If no-one is there, go by and check at the Boeng Khong Restaurant.

Nearby on the river, *Boeng Khong Restaurant* is a ramshackle wooden place with inexpensive noodle and rice dishes.

Getting There & Away From Chiang Khan, buses to Pak Chom cost 22B. Buses from Sangkhom or Loei cost 24B.

CHIANG KHAN
เชียงคาน

Chiang Khan is about 50km north of Loei, on the Mekong River in a large valley surrounded by mountains. The shophouses along the backstreets are wooden and give the place a bit of a frontier atmosphere and there are some nice views of the river.

Boat trips upriver as far as the Nam Heuang river junction or downriver to Kaeng Khut Khu can be arranged at Friendship Hotel (see Places to Stay later) for 150B to 200B per person, depending on the size of the group and length of the trip.

Chiang Khan comes alive during *wan àwk phansăa*, the end of the **Buddhist Rains Retreat** in late October and early November. There's a week-long festival that features displays of large carved wax prasat (shrines)

at each of the temples in town, as well as boat races on the river. At night there are performances of *măw lam* (Isan-style folk music) in the field facing the main post office.

Temples
The town's wát feature a style of architecture rarely seen in Thailand – wíhăan with colonnaded fronts and painted shutters that seem to indicate a French (via Laos) influence. A good example in the centre of town is **Wat Pa Klang**, which is about 100 years old and features a new glittery superstructure; in the grounds of this wát is a small Chinese garden with pond, waterfall and Chinese-style sculptures of Buddha and Kuan Yin.

Wat Mahathat in the centre of town is Chiang Khan's oldest temple; the bòt, constructed in 1654, has a new roof over old walls, with faded murals on the front. **Wat Si Khun Meuang**, between Soi 6 and Soi 7 on Thanon Chiang Khan, contains a Lao-style chedi and bòt (*sĭm* in Lao) plus a topiary garden.

Temple structures at **Wat Santi** and **Wat Thakhok** are similar to those at Wat Pa Klang (minus the Chinese garden). The walls of the temple buildings are stained red from all the dust and mud that builds up in the dry and rainy seasons.

Wat Tha Khaek is a 600- to 700-year-old temple, 2km outside town, on the way to Ban Noi. The seated Buddha image in the bòt is sacred and it is said that holy water prepared in front of the image has the power to cure any ailing person who drinks it or bathes in it.

Other well-known monastic centres in the area include **Samnak Song Phu Pha Baen**, 10km east of Chiang Khan, where monks meditate in caves and on tree platforms; and **Wat Si Song Nong**, west of Kaeng Khut Khu (within easy walking distance) on the river. The latter is a small forest wát where the highly respected Ajahn Maha Bun Nak resides.

Kaeng Khut Khu
แก่งคุดคู้

About 4km downstream from Chiang Khan is Kaeng Khut Khu, a stretch of rapids (best in the dry, hot season) with a park on the Thai side and a village on the Lao side. You can hire a boat to reach the rapids. The park

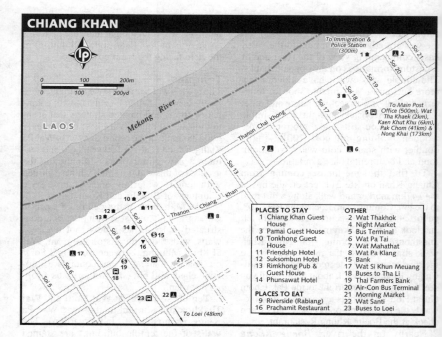

CHIANG KHAN

To Immigration & Police Station (300m)

To Main Post Office (500m), Wat Tha Khaek (2km), Kaen Khut Khu (6km), Pak Chom (41km) & Nong Khai (173km)

Mekong River

LAOS

Thanon Chai Khong

Thanon Chiang Khan

To Loei (48km)

PLACES TO STAY	OTHER
1 Chiang Khan Guest House	2 Wat Thakhok
3 Pamai Guest House	4 Night Market
10 Tonkhong Guest House	5 Bus Terminal
11 Friendship Hotel	6 Wat Pa Tai
12 Suksombun Hotel	7 Wat Mahathat
13 Rimkhong Pub & Guest House	8 Wat Pa Klang
14 Phunsawat Hotel	15 Bank
	17 Wat Si Khun Meuang
PLACES TO EAT	18 Buses to Tha Li
9 Riverside (Rabiang)	19 Thai Farmers Bank
16 Prachamit Restaurant	20 Air-Con Bus Terminal
	21 Morning Market
	22 Wat Santi
	23 Buses to Loei

has thatched-roof picnic areas with reed mats on raised wooden platforms. Vendors sell delicious Isan food – kài yâang, sôm-tam and khâo nǐaw (sticky rice) – as well as kûng tên (literally, dancing shrimp; fresh river prawns served live in a light sauce of lime juice and chillies), kûng thâwt (the same fried whole in batter) and drinks. One large restaurant called Khrua Nucha serves sit-down meals. This is a nice place to spend a few hours.

Nearby **Wat Noi** houses three very old stone Buddha images; they're placed on a ledge high above a larger, modern Buddha in the wát's new bòt.

Places to Stay

Chiang Khan The *Chiang Khan Guest House* (☎ 042-821691) has fair rooms for 100B, and rooms with two beds and shared bathroom for 120B. The dining area overlooks the river and inexpensive food is served. At night it's a bit of a Thai hang-out. It's between Soi 19 and Soi 20 on Thanon Chai Khong, which runs along the Mekong.

On Soi 18, *Pamai Guest House* offers two rooms in a private home for 50B per person.

On Thanon Chai Khong, in an older building between Soi 9 and Soi 10, is the *Tonkhong Guest House* (☎ 042-821187), an OK riverside place with rooms for 80/200B single/double with shared facilities. There's a nice view from the 2nd-storey vegetarian restaurant. Between Soi 8 and Soi 9, just south of the Suksombun Hotel in a two-storey wood, brick and stucco house on the river is the *Rimkhong Pub & Guest House* (☎ 042-821125), with clean rooms for 100/200B, all with shared hot-water bathroom.

The atmospheric *Suksombun Hotel* (☎ 042-821064), on Thanon Chai Khong just past Soi 9, has one-bed rooms for 150B to 200B and two-bed rooms for 250B to 300B. This hotel seems to be popular with Dutch and German budget bus-tours. Around the corner on Soi 9 is the *Phunsawat* (Poon-sawat), the cheapest place in town, which charges just 80B to 100B for rooms with shared bathroom; add 10B for hot water. Motorcycles are available for hire.

Opposite Tonkhong Guest House is the new *Friendship Hotel* (☎/fax 042-822052, e janchiangk@hotmail.com), with rooms

NORTH-EASTERN THAILAND

in a well-kept old wooden two-storey house for 150/200B. Hot-water showers are available. The hotel also offers bicycle and motorcycle rental and boat tours. One-hour trips on the Mekhong cost 400B for two people, or 150B per person for three to 10 people. A sunset trip is 150B per person. (See Getting There & Away later for other options.)

Kaeng Khut Khu For most people, visiting Kaeng Khut Khu as a day trip from Chiang Khan is sufficient, but accommodation is available near the rapids for those inclined to spend the night. *Chiang Khan Hill Resort* (☎ 042-821285) offers solid brick bungalows near the rapids starting at 420B for a fan room and going up to 2750B for an air-con suite.

Places to Eat
Riverside (Rabiang) and *Rimkhong Pub & Guest House* are modest Thai restaurants in old shophouses on the river.

A few more eating places are clustered on Soi 9 and around the intersection of Soi 9 and Thanon Chiang Khan. *Prachamit Restaurant,* on the south-western corner of the intersection, serves inexpensive Thai and Chinese dishes. For cheap breakfasts, head for the morning market off Soi 9 near Wat Santi. Between 5 and 7.30 am there are two *stalls* selling *kaafae thǔng* (Thai coffee), curries and paa-thâwng-kǒh (Chinese doughnuts). The *riverside restaurant* at the Suksombun Hotel serves good Thai and Chinese standards.

Getting There & Away
Sǎwngthǎew to Chiang Khan leave almost every hour from the Loei bus terminal for 18B (a one-hour trip). From Chiang Khan the bus to Loei departs from near the Shell petrol station.

For land transport between Chiang Khan and Nong Khai, see the Pak Chom, Sangkhom and Si Chiangmai sections in this chapter.

As an alternative to road travel, Friendship Hotel (☎/fax 042-822052, ✉ janchiangk@ hotmail.com – see Places to Stay earlier) offers boat trips to Nong Khai (eight hours) for 8500B for up to eight people, and to Pak Chom (two hours) for 1200B for three people and 2000B for three to 10 people.

NAM NAO NATIONAL PARK
อุทยานแห่งชาติน้ำหนาว

One of Thailand's most beautiful and valuable parks, Nam Nao (Cold Water) covers nearly 1000 sq km, at an average elevation of 800m, at the intersection of Chaiyaphum, Phetchabun and Loei Provinces. Although the park was first opened in 1972 it remained a People's Liberation Army of Thailand (PLAT) stronghold until the early 1980s. Marked by the sandstone hills of the Phetchabun mountains, the park features dense, mixed evergreen/deciduous forest on mountains and hills, open dipterocarp pine-oak forest on plateaus and hills, dense bamboo mountain forest with wild banana stands in river valleys, and savannah on the plains. A fair system of trails branches out from the park headquarters; the scenic and fairly level **Phu Khu Khao trail** cuts through pine forest and grass meadow for 24km. The park also features several waterfalls and caves. The park's highest peak, **Phu Pha Jit**, reaches 1271m.

Although it's adjacent to 1560-sq-km **Phu Khiaw Wildlife Sanctuary**, a highway bisecting the park has unfortunately made wildlife somewhat more accessible to poachers, so many native species are in decline. There are no villages within the park boundaries, however, so incidences of poaching and illegal logging remain fairly minor. Elephants and banteng (wild cattle) are occasionally spotted, as well as Malayan sun bears, tigers, leopards, Asian jackals, barking deer, gibbons, langurs and flying squirrels. Rumours of rhinoceros (last seen in 1971, but tracks were observed in 1979) persist, and the bizarre fur-coated Sumatran rhino may survive here. Phu Khiaw itself is a sandstone mountain in Khon San district covered with thick forest that harbours crocodiles, banteng, gaurs, tigers, elephants, serows, leopards and barking deer. Three rivers are sourced at Nam Nao: the Chi, Saphung and Phrom.

A small **museum** in the visitors centre contains a collection of confiscated guns and traps used by poachers, an ecological map and a bird list. Temperatures are fairly cool year-round, especially nights and mornings; the best time to go is from November to February, when morning frost occasionally occurs.

NORTH-EASTERN THAILAND

The Royal Forest Department operates *accommodation* including 500B units which sleep up to eight people, as well as 1000B units sleeping up to 24. Two-person tents are available for rent for 40B. *Vendors* next to the visitors centre offer noodles, Thai and Isan food.

Daily buses run through Nam Nao National Park from Chumphae or Khon Kaen (103km). Look for the park office sign on Hwy 12 at the 50km marker; the office is 2km from here. Standard national park entry fees apply (200B for adults, half price for children).

Nakhon Phanom Province

Nakhon Phanom Province has a strong Lao and Vietnamese presence, although its capital is largely ethnic Chinese. If you're visiting That Phanom, you'll probably have to stop here first to change buses, unless you go directly to That Phanom from Sakon Nakhon via Rte 223. The province is dotted with temples with Lao-style *thâat* (four-sided, curvilinear chedis).

NAKHON PHANOM
อ.เมืองนครพนม

postcode 48000 • pop 34,400
Nakhon Phanom is 242km from Udon Thani and 296km from Nong Khai. It's a rather ordinary town that just happens to have a panoramic view of the Mekong River and the craggy mountains of Laos beyond – in fact, the Sanskrit-Khmer name Nakhon Phanom means 'city of hills'.

A landscaped promenade was added along the river at either end of town to take advantage of the views. If you were choosing a north eastern–Thai capital to live in, Nakhon Phanom might make a good candidate since the streets are well laid-out, there are many green areas, the riverside is scenic and there's not much traffic – the only drawback is, there's almost nothing to do!

Just south of the Mae Nam Khong Grand View Hotel is a river 'beach', where locals and visitors gather to watch the sun set and buy snacks from the vendors. On hot, still days an upside-down mirror image of the

---

Nakhon Phanom Festival

On the full moon of the 11th lunar month (usually late October) at the end of the Buddhist Rains Retreat, Nakhon Phanom residents celebrate Wan Phra Jao Prot Lok – a holiday in honour of Buddha's descent from the Devaloka (Deity World), where legend says he had spent a Rains Retreat offering teachings. Besides the usual wát offerings, festival activities include the launching of *reua fai*, or fire boats, on the Mekong. Originally these 8m to 10m boats were made of banana logs or bamboo, but modern versions can be fashioned of wood or synthetic materials. The boats carry offerings of cakes, rice and flowers; at night the boats are launched on the river and illuminated in a spectacular display.

During this same festival in the daytime, the city hosts longboat races similar to those seen in many towns along the Mekong River.

---

river island **Don Don** appears to hang in the air above the real thing.

The interior murals of the bòt at **Wat Si Thep**, in town on the street of the same name, show jataka (past-life stories of the Buddha) along the upper part, and kings of the Chakri dynasty along the lower part. On the back of the bòt is a colourful triptych done in modern style.

The Lao town on the other side of the river is **Tha Khaek**. Foreigners with Lao visas are now permitted to cross by ferry. Thai and Lao government officials are currently mulling over the possibility of adding a bridge over the Mekong here. This would link Nakhon Phanom with the Vietnamese seaport of Vinh on the Gulf of Tonkin via the 240km Rte 12 across Laos and Vietnam.

Information
Tourist Offices The TAT (☎ 042-513490, fax 513492, ✉ tat.ne@npu.msu.ac.th) has an office in a beautiful colonial-style building on the corner of Thanon Sala Klang and Thanon Sunthon Wijit. The staff distribute information on Nakhon Phanom, Mukdahan and Sakon Nakhon Provinces. It's open from 8.30 am to 4.30 pm daily.

Post & Communications The main post office, on the corner of Thanon Ratchathan

NAKHON PHANOM

To Airport,
Beung Kan
& Nong Khai
(313km)

Thanon Sala Klang

To Somtam
Khun Taew
(300m)

Thanon Ratchathan

Thanon Sunthon Wijit

Th Luk Seua

Thanon Fuang Nakhon

Mekong River

Thanon Thamnong Prasit

Passenger
Ferry

Thanon Aphibun Bancha

Thanon Bamrung Meuang

Thanon Si Thep

Thanon Ruamjit

To Renu Nakhon (52km),
That Phanom (56km) &
Sakon Nakhon (94km)

Thanon Ruamjit Thawai

LAOS

To Mae Nam Khong
Grand View Hotel (300m)
& Nakhon Phanom River
View

Vehicle
Ferry

0   50   100m
0   50   100yd

PLACES TO STAY
16 Windsor Hotel
17 Charoensuk Hotel
19 First Hotel
24 Grand Hotel
28 Nakhon Phanom Hotel
33 Si Thep Hotel

PLACES TO EAT
8 Riverside Restaurants;
  Plag Beuk Thong; New
  Rapmit; Rim Nam; New
  Suan Mai
10 Rot Mai & Rot Isan
   Restaurants
11 Pho Thong Restaurant
26 Vietnam Restaurant

OTHER
1 Telephone Office
2 TAT Office
3 Provincial Office
4 Lak Meuang
5 Prison
6 Main Post Office
7 Police
9 Internet
12 Bus Terminal
13 Market
14 Local Buses
15 Market
18 Bangkok Bank
20 Clock Tower
21 Wat Okaat (Si Bua Ban)
22 Market
23 Bangkok Bank
25 Chinese School
27 Thepnakhon Cinema
29 Thai Farmers Bank
30 Siam Commercial Bank
31 THAI Office
32 Immigration & Customs
34 Wat Si Thep

and Thanon Sunthon Wijit, is open from 8.30 am to 4.30 pm weekdays, and 9 am to noon on weekends and holidays. The separate CAT telephone office on Thanon Sala Klang is open from 8.30 am to 4.30 pm weekdays.

Places to Stay – Budget

The cheapest place in town is the *Charoensuk Hotel* (no Roman-script sign) on Thanon Bamrung Meuang, directly opposite Bangkok Bank; simple but clean and surprisingly large rooms cost 160/200B with fan and bathroom. The hotel is set back from the street with off-street parking in front. Similar is the *Grand Hotel* (☎ 042-511526, fax 511283), on the corner of Thanon Si Thep and Thanon Ruamjit, which has simple but well-kept rooms for 170B, and from

370B with air-con. *First Hotel* (☎ 042-511253, 370 Thanon Si Thep) has well-worn rooms with fan and bathroom for 160B and with air-con for 280B.

Places to Stay – Mid-Range & Top End

The *Windsor Hotel* (☎ 042-511946, 692/19 Thanon Bamrung Meuang) is a former budget place that was recently upgraded a bit and now has fan rooms with attached shower for 250B, and air-con rooms for 350B.

The rambling *Si Thep Hotel* (☎ 042-511036, 708/11 Thanon Si Thep) charges 268B for rooms with fan and bathroom in the old wing and 330B for air-con rooms with hot water in the new wing. VIP rooms with fridge and TV are 550B.

The ***Nakhon Phanom Hotel*** (☎ 042-511455, 403 Thanon Aphiban Bancha) has ageing air-con rooms with carpet, TV and hot water for 400B and VIP rooms with fridge and nicer furnishings from 600B.

The all air-con ***Mae Nam Khong Grand View Hotel*** (☎ 042-513564, fax 511037), overlooking the river at the southern end of town, offers spacious rooms with all the amenities for 450B a night (550B for rooms with a river view and balcony). About 350m farther south along the same road, the even newer ***Nakhon Phanom River View*** (☎ 042-522333, fax 522777) is now the town's most luxurious hotel, with well appointed standard/superior rooms for 800/900B.

Places to Eat

Most of the better restaurants are along the river on Thanon Sunthon Wijit; they include ***Plaa Beuk Thong*** (Golden Giant Catfish), ***New Rapmit***, ***Rim Nam*** and ***New Suan Mai***. New Suan Mai, Plaa Beuk Thong (also open for breakfast) and Rim Nam are the best of the bunch; Rim Nam has an open-air, floating platform at the back that gets a breeze. At these restaurants, giant Mekong catfish is occasionally available and served *phàt phèt* (stir-fried with basil and curry paste), *tôm yam* (in a spicy lemon-grass broth), *phàt kràthiam* (garlic-fried) or *òp mǎw din* (baked in a clay pot). A sunset dining boat leaves from the back of Rim Nam at 5 pm for 40B per person plus the cost of whatever you order. Diners may hire a mǎw lam ensemble to entertain on special occasions.

There are several good, inexpensive restaurants serving dishes like noodles and curry-and-rice along Thanon Bamrung Meuang north of the Windsor and Charoensuk Hotels. Two small rice shops between the Charoensuk Hotel and Honey Massage, ***Rot Mai*** and ***Rot Isan***, serve local specialities, including *jàew hâwn*, a sukiyaki-style soup with noodles, beef and vegetables. Other popular dishes at these restaurants are *lâap pèt* (spicy duck salad) and *yâang sěua ráwng hâi* ('grill that would make a tiger cry' – beef grilled with chillies). ***Pho Thong*** on Thanon Fuang Nakhon is a larger place serving Isan food. ***Somtam Khun Taew*** on Thanon Suthon Wijit, two blocks north of the TAT office, is one of the most famous sôm-tam shops in Isan. Here Khun Taew will pound an order of the spicy green papaya salad made to your specifications. She also makes good *súp nàw mái* (spicy bamboo-shoot salad), *plaa châwn phǎo* (grilled serpentfish) and *hǎwy khǒm* (freshwater snails).

Vietnam Restaurant on Thanon Thamrong Prasit serves Vietnamese specialities, including *nǎem neuang* (barbecued pork meatballs) and *yáw* (spring rolls), usually sold in 'sets' *(sùt)*, with cold rice noodles, fresh lettuce leaves, mint, basil, various dipping sauces, sliced starfruit and sliced green plantain.

Opposite and south of the Si Thep Hotel are ***restaurants*** selling jók and khài kàthá.

Getting There & Away

Air THAI (☎ 042-512940) fields daily flights to/from Bangkok (1850B 1¼ hours). There are also flights from Sakon Nakhon to Nakhon Phanom (370B, 25 minutes), but not in the reverse direction. THAI runs a shuttle van between the airport, 16km away, and the city centre. The THAI office is at Bovon Travel, 13 Thanon Ruamjit Thawai.

Bus Regular buses run from Nong Khai to Nakhon Phanom via Sakon Nakhon for 54B. There are air-con buses hourly from 6 to 11 am for 95B. If you want to go through Beung Kan, you can get a bus to Beung Kan (37B) first, then change to a Nakhon Phanom bus. The journey all the way from Udon Thani costs 73/107B by ordinary/air-con bus.

Between Nakhon Phanom and Mukdahan there are hourly departures between 6 am and 5 pm for 34B (55B air-con); ordinary buses between Nakhon Phanom and Sakon Nakhon run on a similar schedule for 30B (33B air-con).

Air-con buses run between Khorat and Nakhon Phanom thrice daily for 250B.

From Bangkok's Northern and North-Eastern bus terminal there are several air-con buses to Nakhon Phanom each day between 6 am and 8.30 pm (2nd class 293B to 328B, 1st class 376B to 421B). There are also 6, 7, 7.40 and 8.15 pm VIP departures for 585B.

Boat A ferry boat across the Mekong River to Tha Khaek, in Laos, costs 40B per person; the fare is the same in the reverse direction. Anyone with a valid visa for Laos is permitted to cross here.

AROUND NAKHON PHANOM
Renu Nakhon
เรณูนคร

The village of Renu Nakhon is known for cotton- and silk-weaving, especially mát-mìi designs. The local Phu Thai, a Thai tribe separate from mainstream Siamese and Lao, also market their designs here. Each Saturday there's a big **handicraft market** near Wat Phra That Renu Nakhon. On other days you can buy from a string of shops and vendors near the temple or directly from weavers in the village. Prices for rough grades of mát-mìi are as low as 50B for a 170cm length.

The thâat at **Wat Phra That Renu Nakhon** exhibits the same basic characteristics as That Phanom but in less elongated proportions. Renu Nakhon is worth a visit if you're in the vicinity, even during the week.

During local festivals the Phu Thai sometimes hold folk-dance performances called *fáwn lákhon thai,* which celebrate their unique heritage. They also practise the *bai sïi* custom common in other parts of the North-East as well as in Laos, in which a shaman ties loops of sacred string around a person's wrists (see the 'Bai Sïi Ceremony' boxed text in this chapter). On Saturday at the handicraft market, the Phu Thai put on a music and dance performance for tourists, as well as an abbreviated version of the bai sïi ceremony, from 1 to 3 pm.

Getting There & Away The turn-off to Renu Nakhon is south of Nakhon Phanom at the 44km marker on Rte 212. Since it's only 10km farther to That Phanom, you could visit Renu on the way, or if you are staying in That Phanom, visit Renu as a day trip. From Rte 212, it's 7km west on Rte 2031 (7B by sǎwngthǎew from the junction).

Tha Khaek
ท่าแขก

This Lao town across the river from Nakhon Phanom traces its roots to French colonial construction in 1911–12. Before the war (and during the war until the North Vietnamese Army and Pathet Lao cut the road north to Vientiane), Tha Khaek was a thriving provincial capital and a gambling centre for day-tripping Thais. Today it's a quiet transport and trade outpost with French colonial architecture similar to that in Vientiane and Savannakhet.

If you hold a valid Lao visa, you can catch a 40B ferry ride across the river; the border is open from 8.30 am to 5 pm weekdays and until 12.20 pm Saturday. Buses from Tha Khaek to Vientiane cost 5000 kip and take 10 hours. The *Khammouane Hotel,* a large four-storey, white, curved-front building facing the Mekong, has clean rooms with TV, fridge, air-con, hot water and good mattresses for the Lao kip equivalent of US$8 to US$12. The *Thakhek May Hotel,* a few blocks away from the river on Thanon Vientiane, offers simple rooms in a two-storey square building for around US$6 to US$10. For more information see Lonely Planet's *Laos* guidebook.

THAT PHANOM
ธาตุพนม

That Phanom is 53km south of Nakhon Phanom and 70km south-east of Sakon Nakhon. The centre of activity in this small town is Wat Phra That Phanom.

The short road between Wat Phra That Phanom and the old town on the Mekong River passes under a large Lao arch of victory, which is a miniature version of the arch on Thanon Lan Xang in Vientiane (which leads to Vientiane's Wat That Luang). This section of That Phanom is interesting, with a smattering of French-Chinese architecture reminiscent of old Vientiane or Saigon.

Hundreds of Lao merchants cross the river for the **market** from around 8.30 am to noon on Monday and Thursday. There are two market locations in town, one on the highway near the wát and one on the river north of the pier. The latter is where the Lao congregate on their twice-weekly visits. Exotic offerings include Lao herbal medicines, forest roots, Vietnamese pigs and animal skins; the maddest haggling occurs just before the market closes, when Thai buyers try to take advantage of the Lao's reluctance to carry unsold merchandise back to Laos.

About 20km south of town (turn-off for Wan Yai, between the 187km and 188km markers) is a wooded park next to **Kaeng Kabao,** a set of rapids in the Mekong River. Nearby hills afford views over the river and to Laos on the other side. The usual food vendors make this a good spot for an

NORTH-EASTERN THAILAND

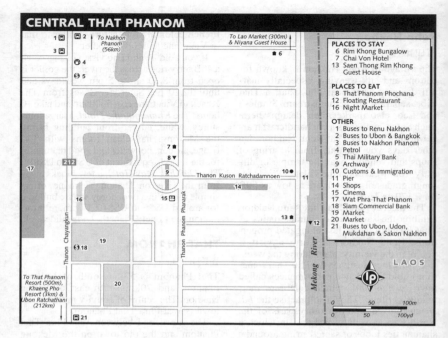

CENTRAL THAT PHANOM

To Nakhon Phanom (56km)

To Lao Market (300m) & Niyana Guest House

Thanon Kuson Ratchadamnoen

Thanon Chayangkun

Thanon Phanom Phanarak

Mekong River

LAOS

To That Phanom Resort (500m), Khaeng Pho Resort (3km) & Ubon Ratchathani (212km)

0   50   100m
0   50   100yd

PLACES TO STAY
6 Rim Khong Bungalow
7 Chai Von Hotel
13 Saen Thong Rim Khong Guest House

PLACES TO EAT
8 That Phanom Phochana
12 Floating Restaurant
16 Night Market

OTHER
1 Buses to Renu Nakhon
2 Buses to Ubon & Bangkok
3 Buses to Nakhon Phanom
4 Petrol
5 Thai Military Bank
9 Archway
10 Customs & Immigration
11 Pier
14 Shops
15 Cinema
17 Wat Phra That Phanom
18 Siam Commercial Bank
19 Market
20 Market
21 Buses to Ubon, Udon, Mukdahan & Sakon Nakhon

impromptu picnic – it's an easy and interesting bicycle ride from That Phanom.

During the **That Phanom Festival** in mid-February, hordes of visitors descend from all over Isan. Lao cross over to visit the wát, Thais cross over to Laos, and the town hardly sleeps for seven days.

Information

The Thai Military and Siam Commercial Banks, both on Thanon Chayangkun, offer foreign-exchange services and ATMs.

Wat Phra That Phanom
วัดพระธาตุพนม

The centrepiece of this wát is a huge thâat, or Lao-style chedi, more impressive than any chedi in present-day Laos. The monument, which caved in during heavy rains in 1975 and was restored in 1978, is a talismanic symbol of Isan and is highly revered by Buddhists all over Thailand. The age of the wát is disputed, but some archaeologists set it at about 1500 years. The chedi is 57m (or 52m, depending on whom you believe) high and the spire is decorated with 110kg

of gold. Surrounding the famous chedi is a cloister filled with Buddha images and behind the wát is a shady park.

Places to Stay & Eat

Niyana Guest House (☎ 042-540088, e niyanaguesthouse@hotmail.com), opposite Wat Hua Wiang at the northern end of town, offers rooms with shared bathroom in an old house for 120B single/double and a few dorm beds for 50B. There's a good information board and a nice upstairs sitting area. In addition to the usual Thai and traveller fare, English-speaking owner Niyana offers Lao coffee and *khâo jìi*, Lao-style French bread. She can also arrange bicycle rentals, short boat trips on the river and excursions to Phu Mu and Mukdahan's Indochina Market.

One block south is *Rim Khong Bungalow* (☎ 042-541634), with six OK rooms for 200B to 400B.

Near the boat landing, *Saeng Thong Rim Khong Guest House* (☎ 042-525614), with no Roman-script sign, features nine clean rooms in a modern L-shaped building with hard mattresses, ceiling fan and cold-water shower for 200/400B.

NORTH-EASTERN THAILAND

The friendly *Chai Von Hotel*, on Thanon Phanom Phanarak to the north of the arch (turn left as you pass under the arch), is an historic little Franco-Chinese-style place with lots of character, but pretty basic. Rooms cost 100B with shared bathroom, 120B with private Thai-style bathroom. One air-con room is available for 300B to 350B, depending on length of stay.

On the southern edge of town off Rte 212 on the river is the *That Phanom Resort* (☎ 042-541047), with uninspiring rooms in row buildings for 250/500B with fan/air-con. A better choice is the well-maintained *Khaeng Pho Resort* (☎ 042-541412), 3km south of That Phanom on Rte 212. Individual bungalows in a nicely land-scaped setting are 200B with fan and 500B with air-con.

During the February That Phanom Festival, hotel rooms soar in price and both hotel and guesthouse rooms are booked out well in advance.

A small *night market* convenes every evening on Thanon Chayangkun. *That Phanom Phochana* serves Thai and Chinese standards. A *floating restaurant* just south of the pier has a decent menu.

Getting There & Away

Bus From different points on Thanon Chayangkun, there are regular buses to Mukdahan (17B ordinary, 28B air-con), Ubon Ratchathani (65B, 119B), Sakon Nakhon (24B, 41B), Nakhon Phanom (17B, 30B) and Udon Thani (71B, 119B).

The air-con Khorat–Nakhon Phanom bus makes a stop at That Phanom. The fare (250B) is the same as all the way to Nakhon Phanom.

Săwngthăew Săwngthăew to That Phanom leave regularly from the intersection near the Nakhon Phanom Hotel in Nakhon Phanom and cost 17B. Stay on the bus until you see the chedi on the right. The trip takes about 1½ hours. The last săwngthăew to That Phanom leaves around 6 pm; the last vehicle leaves That Phanom for Nakhon Phanom at 8 pm.

Boat A ferry ride across to Laos costs 20B per person. At the moment only Thai and Lao citizens are permitted to cross the border here.

Sakon Nakhon Province

Sakon Nakhon Province is known among Thais as the one-time home of two of the most famous Buddhist monks in Thai history, Ajahn Man Bhuridatto and Ajahn Fan Ajaro. Both were ascetic thúdong monks who were thought to have attained high levels of proficiency in *vipassana* meditation. Ajahn Man is widely recognised among Thais as having been an *arahant,* or fully enlightened being. Although born in Ubon Ratchathani, Ajahn Man spent most of his later years at Wat Pa Sutthawat in Sakon Nakhon. He died in 1949, and his relics and possessions are now contained in a museum at the latter monastery.

The end of the Buddhist Rains Retreat in late October/November is fervently celebrated in Sakon with the carving and display of wax shrines (prasat), as well as parades.

One of Sakon's claims to fame is the relative popularity of dog-meat dishes. Contrary to a common Thai stereotype, not all natives of Sakon are fond of eating dog – in fact, it's a custom mostly restricted to the Soh ethnic minority of Tha Lae, around 42km northwest of Sakon Nakhon town. A dog market in Tha Lae slaughters up to 100 animals a day and purveys the meat for a price well below that of beef. The market also sells cooked dog in curries, satay, meatball soups and so on for on-site dining and takeaway. By national law, however, it's illegal to buy and sell live dogs for dining purposes.

SAKON NAKHON
อ.เมืองสกลนคร

postcode 47000 • pop 25,500
As the secondary agricultural market centre (after Udon Thani) for upper Isan, the provincial capital is mostly a collection of shops selling farm equipment. For most visitors, the only reason to stay in the city is to visit Wat Phra That Choeng Chum and Wat Phra That Narai Jaeng Waeng.

A **city monument** in a field in the north-western corner of the city centre was obviously inspired by Vientiane's Patuxai or That Phanom's gate. In this case the arch-like structure consists of four big, ornate, cement pillars standing over a bowl filled with naga (serpent) beings.

Along the eastern edge of town is **Nong Han**, Thailand's largest natural lake. *Don't swim in the lake* – it's infested with liver flukes, which can cause a nasty liver infection known as opisthorchiasis. The villagers around the lake have among the highest incidences of opisthorchiasis in the world, since many of them eat snails gathered from the lake. These snails play host to the flukes, which bore through human or animal skin and breed in the internal organs. (See Health in the Facts for the Visitor chapter.)

Ajahn Man Museum
พิพิธภัณฑ์พระอาจารย์มั่น

In the grounds of Wat Pa Sutthawat, on the south-western outskirts of town (off the road to Kalasin), this museum contains an exhibition of the personal effects of Thailand's most famous forest monk. The very modern building looks a bit like a modern Christian church, with arches and stained glass windows. A bronze image of Ajahn Man surrounded by flowers sits on a pedestal at one end. Articles and photos associated with the monk's history are on display behind glass. The museum building is usually open from 8 am to 6 pm daily.

Wat Phra That Choeng Chum
วัดพระธาตุเชิงชุม

Next to the Nong Han Lake in town, this wát features a 25m-high Lao-style chedi, which was erected during the Ayuthaya period over a smaller 11th-century Khmer prang. To view the prang you must enter through the adjacent wíhǎan. If the door to the chedi is locked, ask one of the monks to open it – they're used to having visitors. Around the base of the prang is a collection of Lao and Khmer Buddha images.

Also on the grounds is a small Lan Xang–era bòt and a wíhǎan built in the cruciform shape reminiscent of Lanna styles found in Northern Thailand. Lûuk nímít, spherical ordination-precinct markers that look like cannonballs, are arranged on the grass near the wíhǎan; next to the monastery's east gate is the base for an original Khmer Shivalingam (phallic object).

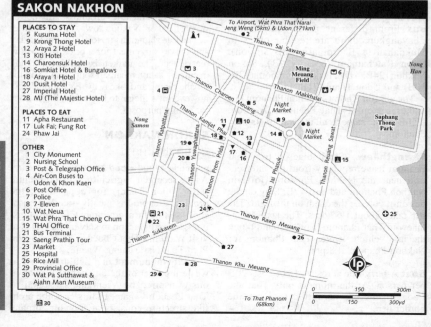

SAKON NAKHON

PLACES TO STAY
5 Kusuma Hotel
9 Krong Thong Hotel
12 Araya 2 Hotel
13 Kiti Hotel
14 Charoensuk Hotel
16 Somkiat Hotel & Bungalows
18 Araya 1 Hotel
20 Dusit Hotel
27 Imperial Hotel
28 MJ (The Majestic Hotel)

PLACES TO EAT
11 Apha Restaurant
17 Luk Fai; Fung Rot
24 Phaw Jai

OTHER
1 City Monument
2 Nursing School
3 Post & Telegraph Office
4 Air-Con Buses to Udon & Khon Kaen
6 Post Office
7 Police
8 7-Eleven
10 Wat Neua
15 Wat Phra That Choeng Chum
19 THAI Office
21 Bus Terminal
22 Saeng Prathip Tour
23 Market
25 Hospital
26 Rice Mill
29 Provincial Office
30 Wat Pa Sutthawat & Ajahn Man Museum

To Airport, Wat Phra That Narai Jeng Weng (5km) & Udon (171km)

Thanon Sai Sawang
Ming Meuang Field
Thanon Makkhalai
Nong Han
Thanon Charoen Meuang
Night Market
Nong Samon
Thanon Rapattana
Thanon Kamjat Phai
Thanon Prem Prida
Thanon Yuwaphattana
Night Market
Thanon Reuang Sawat
Saphang Thong Park
Thanon Jai Phasuk
Thanon Rawp Meuang
Thanon Sukkasem
Thanon Khu Meuang

To That Phanom (68km)

0   150   300m
0   150   300yd

A drum tower donated by the local Vietnamese population bears the inscription 'Viêt Kieu Luu Liem' – so this wát features Thai, Lao, Vietnamese and Khmer elements.

Wat Phra That Narai Jaeng Waeng

วัดพระธาตุนารายณ์แจงแวง

About 5km west of town at Ban That (3km past the airport), this wát has a 10th- to 11th-century Khmer prang in the early Bapuan style. Originally part of a Khmer Hindu complex, the five-level sandstone prang features a reclining Vishnu lintel over its eastern portico and a dancing Shiva over its northern one.

To get to the temple by public transport, catch a săwngthăew west towards the airport on Thanon Sai Sawang and get off at Talat Ban That Nawaeng (5B). From here it's a pleasant 1km walk to the wát through a village.

The wát is called Phra That Nawaeng (contraction of Narai Jaeng Waeng) for short.

Places to Stay

The *Araya 1*, at the corner of Thanon Prem Prida and Thanon Kamjat Phai, has one- and two-bed rooms with fan for 150/250B and air-con rooms for 300/350B; diagonally opposite is the wooden *Araya 2*, with rooms for only 150B with fan and 220B with attached bathroom. There is a Thai-Chinese restaurant below. Araya 1 can be difficult to find, as a large modern shophouse stands in front of it – look around the back.

On the same block as the Araya 2 are *Somkiat Hotel & Bungalows*, with rooms for 150/200B (a truck-driver favourite because of its inside parking lot); and *Kiti Hotel*, with basic but OK rooms for 200B. Somkiat's bungalow section is looking very run-down nowadays; the hotel rooms are better.

The *Krong Thong Hotel* (☎ 042-711097, 645/2 Thanon Charoen Meuang) has very decent rooms for 120B to 200B with fan, and 330B with air-con. Also along Thanon Charoen Meuang are several similar hotels in the 150B to 250B price range, including the *Kusuma* and *Charoensuk* (no Roman-script sign), both fair choices.

Moving upmarket a bit, the *Imperial* (☎ 042-711119, fax 713889, 1892 Thanon Sukkasem) has rooms in its old wing for 200B with fan and bathroom, 300B with air-con (add 50B to these rates for rooms with TV); in the new wing, carpeted VIP rooms with TV, refrigerator and breakfast are 590B.

The *Dusit Hotel* (☎ 042-711198, 1784 Thanon Yuwaphattana) is not associated with any of the Dusit Group hotels around the country. This one has rooms starting at 306B economy and up to 612B deluxe. The public areas have recently been totally redone and now look rather chic.

The new all air-con *MJ (The Majestic Hotel; ☎ 042-733771, fax 733616)* is a modern hotel offering 600B standard rooms and 700B superior rooms. The more expensive rooms have a small sitting area. Additional facilities include a restaurant, cocktail lounge, pub, cafe, massage, snooker club and karaoke.

Places to Eat

Night markets are open each evening near the roundabout at Thanon Charoen Meuang and Thanon Jai Phasuk, and also at the intersection of Thanon Charoen Meuang and Thanon Sukkasem. Both markets are very popular nightspots, and are open until late.

Along Thanon Prem Prida are several inexpensive Thai-Chinese restaurants with passable food at cheap prices. *Phaw Jai*, at the three-way intersection of Thanon Sukkasem, Thanon Prem Prida and Thanon Rawp Meuang, serves a good variety of Thai and Chinese dishes; as do *Luk Fai* (no Roman-script sign) and *Fung Rot*, both near Somkiat Hotel & Bungalows on Thanon Kamjat Phai.

About a block west on the opposite side of the street, *Apha Restaurant* is a clean place specialising in curries and other Thai dishes.

Getting There & Away

Air Should you wish to fly in or out of Sakon Nakhon, THAI operates one flight daily from Bangkok (1765B one way). There are also daily flights to Nakhon Pathom (370B, 25 minutes), though none in the reverse direction. The THAI office in Sakon (☎ 042-712259/60) is at 1446/73 Thanon Yuwaphattana.

Bus Direct buses to Sakon are available from Ubon Ratchathani (83B ordinary, 150B air-con, six hours), Nakhon Phanom (30B, 33B, 1½ hours), That Phanom (24B, 1½ hours),

Khon Kaen (60B, 90B 2nd-class air-con, 108B 1st-class air-con, four hours) and Udon Thani (50B, 70B air-con, 3½ hours). Buses from Sakon to Bangkok cost 182B ordinary, 255B air-con and 505B for 24-seat VIP.

A little bit south-west of the bus station is a company called Saeng Prathip Tour (☎ 042-711731), which offers private 1st-class buses to Bangkok for 328B, and 32-seat VIP buses for 382B.

Private air-con buses to Udon and Khon Kaen leave four times daily from the Udon Thani–Sakon Doen Rot bus terminal, next to the Esso petrol station on Thanon Ratpattana.

AROUND SAKON NAKHON
Tham Kham & Wat Pa Udom Somphon
ถ้ำขามและวัดป่าอุดมสมพร

Ajahn Fan Ajaro, a famous student of Ajahn Man, established a cave hermitage for the practise of meditation at Tham Kham on the mountain of Khao Phu Phan, 17km off Hwy 22 (the turnoff comes between the 125km and 126km markers on Hwy 22 on the way from Udon). He was also affiliated with Wat Pa Udom Somphon in his home district of Phanna Nikhom, 37km from Sakon Nakhon towards Udon Thani off Hwy 22. A **museum** well outside the wát compound at Ban Phanna commemorates the life of Ajahn Fan, who died in 1963. Unlike Wat Pa Sutthawat, which has become a *wát thîaw* (tourist wát), Wat Pa Udom Somphon is still a strict forest meditation monastery. Visitors are welcome to tour the museum, but only those with a serious interest in Buddhism or meditation should enter the compound of the adjacent monastery.

Phu Phan National Park
อุทยานแห่งชาติภูพาน

This 645-sq-km nature reserve is in the Phu Phan mountains near the Sakon Nakhon–Kalasin border. Deer, monkeys and other, smaller, forest animals are common to the park, and wild elephants and tigers are occasionally seen as well.

The mountain forests are thick and the area is fairly undeveloped. It has been used as a hiding spot by two guerrilla forces – the Thai resistance against the Japanese in WWII and the PLAT guerrillas in the 1970s.

The park has only a few hiking trails but there are good views along Rte 213 between Sakon Nakhon and Kalasin. Three waterfalls – **Tat Ton**, **Hew Sin Chai** and **Kham Hom** – can be visited fairly easily. Admission is 200B per person.

The **Tham Seri Thai** cave was used by the Thai Seri (see WWII & Postwar Periods in the Facts about Thailand chapter) during WWII as an arsenal and mess hall.

Yasothon & Mukdahan Provinces

YASOTHON
อ.เมืองยโสธร

postcode 35000 • pop 30,700

Yasothon is a bit out of the way, but if you happen to be in the area (say, in Ubon Ratchathani, which is about 100km away) during May, it might be worth the two-hour bus trip (from Ubon) to catch the annual **Rocket Festival** that takes place from 8 to 10 May. The festival (Bun Bang Fai in Thai) is prevalent throughout the North-East as a rain and fertility rite, and is celebrated most fervently in Yasothon, where it involves parades and fantastic fireworks. The name of the town, which has the largest Muslim population in the North-East, comes from the Sanskrit 'Yasodhara' (meaning 'preserver or maintainer of glory') and is also the name of one of Krishna's sons by Rukmini in the *Mahabharata*.

In town, **Phra That Phra Anon** (also known as Phra That Yasothon) at Wat Mahathat is a highly venerated Lao-style chedi. It's said to be over 1200 years old and to enshrine holy relics of Phra Anon (Ananda), the Buddha's personal attendant monk and one of his chief disciples.

The village of **Ban Si Than** in Pha Tiu district, about 20km east of Yasothon off Rte 202, is renowned for the crafting of firm, triangle-shaped măwn khwăn, which are said to rival those of Roi Et.

Phra That Kong Khao Noi, in Ban Tat Thong off Hwy 23 (between the 194km and 195km markers) heading towards Ubon Ratchathani, is a brick-and-stucco chedi dating from the late Ayuthaya period. It's name, *kawng khâo náwy* actually means 'small

Yasothon Rocket Festival

As a countdown is intoned over crackling loudspeakers, crowds of onlookers flee in all directions. A wooden launch platform, looking like some precarious stairway to the heavens, is the object of their terror. And soon it becomes apparent why. With a roar reminiscent of an F-16 fighter jet being catapulted from an aircraft carrier, a flag-pole-sized bamboo rocket is launched skyward on a huge plume of grey smoke. Seconds later it explodes with a loud boom and pieces of flaming bamboo tumble from the sky.

'That wasn't supposed to happen', says Wachara Bunsungnern as thousands of eyes scan the heavens, trying to gauge whether the falling debris is a personal threat.

'The whole idea is to keep your rocket airborne for as long as possible,' Wachara explains while leaning on another enormous bamboo rocket painted a sinister day-glow orange.

Welcome to Yasothon. For 363 days of the year the populace of this provincial backwater in North-Eastern Thailand leads a quiet existence. Then, at the height of the torrid hot season the town becomes temporarily gripped by a strange passion for pyrotechnics.

Originally an animist ritual thought to predate the arrival of Buddhism to this region, the festival, known locally as *bun bâng fai*, was a common annual event held all over North-Eastern Thailand and neighbouring Laos. Thick bamboo poles were packed with black powder and then launched skyward. The resulting clouds of white smoke and thundering reports seemed to herald the approach of a rain-heavy storm and, it was hoped, the appropriate spirits would be tricked into initiating the rainy season.

'In the old days this was a ceremony to call for rain', explains Wachara, who, dressed in a Hawaiian-print shirt and swigging a beer, seems to represent the ancient ritual's modern face.

'Nowadays we're not so much into the old spirit beliefs. I don't mean to say that we no longer believe', he says, pointing to a spirit offering of joss sticks and jasmine tied to the nose of the rocket with

JOE CUMMINGS

a length of silk, 'It's just that bun bâng fai has become more of a sporting event.'

While Wachara chats, his team, wearing identical T-shirts bearing the team logo, busily work to ready their rocket for a 3 pm launch. Measuring nearly 15m, the section of the rocket containing the fuel is actually a 5m piece of plastic pipe lashed to a bamboo pole.

'We compete to see whose rocket stays airborne longest and this takes a powerful booster to get the rocket up high and a brake to give it a slow descent. We've spent nearly 20,000B on this one and if it fails to clear the launch platform we'll be very disappointed', he laughs.

As the designated launch time approaches Wachara and his team pass around a bottle of rice liquor for a final toast before parading their rocket to the platform and inserting an electric fuse into its tail end. On signal the crude missile spirals into the cloudless sky with a deafening roar. For anxious seconds the team squints into the afternoon glare and comments cautiously as the rocket peaks and then plummets into a far-off paddy field.

Even before the official timekeepers make their announcement it is clear that this year's entry is not a winner. 'It doesn't matter', says Wachara with a good-natured shrug. 'Maybe we'll get some rain instead.'

sticky-rice basket', a reference to the chedi's unusual shape and a local legend. According to an old story, a young farmer who had toiled all morning in the hot sun murdered his mother in a fit of rage when she brought his lunch to the fields late – and in the smallest of sticky-rice baskets. The farmer, eating his lunch over his mother's body, realised that the small basket actually contained much more sticky rice than he could eat. To atone for his deed he then built the chedi.

Places to Stay

Udomphon (☎ *045-711564, 80/1–2 Thanon Uthairamrit)* and *Surawet Wattana (128/1 Thanon Changsanit)* each charge 150B to 250B for rooms with fan and bathroom. If you can't get into either of these, try the *Yot Nakhon* (☎ *045-711122, 141–143/1–3 Thanon Uthairamrit)*, where rooms cost from 220/300B with/without air-con.

JP Emerald Hotel (☎ *045-724851, fax 724855)*, on Thanon Jaeng Sanit, is Yasothon's newest and most expensive accommodation, offering air-con rooms with all the amenities for 880B to 1600B. There is a coffee shop and restaurant on the premises.

Getting There & Away

An ordinary bus to Yasothon from Ubon costs 33B (46B air-con); from Khorat it costs 79B (145B air-con).

MUKDAHAN

อ.เมืองมุกดาหาร

postcode 49000 • pop 25,800

Fifty-five kilometres south of That Phanom, 170km north of Ubon Ratchathani and directly opposite the city of Savannakhet in Laos, Mukdahan is known for its beautiful Mekong scenery and as a Thai-Lao trade centre. Among Thais it's most known for the **Talat Indojin**, or Indochina Market, a Thai-Lao-Vietnamese affair that gathers around Wat Si Mongkhon Tai near Tha Mukdahan. On weekends the market spills over onto nearby streets; you'll see khaen (Isan panpipes) and bolts of cloth from around Isan in addition to the usual Lao, Vietnamese and Chinese imports. The more formal **Danang Market**, in the town centre, contains shopfronts selling many of the same goods.

According to agreements between the Thai and Lao governments, a bridge between Mukdahan and Savannakhet on the opposite bank of the Mekong is planned to be built in the near future, although the economic situation in the region has delayed these plans for the time being. Vietnam, Laos and Thailand had likewise agreed to accelerate development of Laos' Rte 9 to link Mukdahan, Savannakhet and Danang along an east-west trade corridor. Such discussions had prompted lots of construction around town as speculators positioned themselves for an anticipated economic boom. South of Hotel Muk, the ambitious **Haw Kaew Mukdahan** (Mukdahan Jewel Hall) is a tall needle-shaped shopping and business centre.

For a view of the town, climb the 500m **Phu Narom** hill, 3km south of town. **Phu Mu**, a favourite local picnic spot with scenic views, is 34km south of the town of Mukdahan off Rte 212 – just south of Ban Taw Khet and the Mukdahan Province line between the 29km and 30km markers.

Information

The Bangkok Bank of Commerce on Thanon Samut Sakdarak in town has a currency exchange service.

Phu Pha Thoep National Park

อุทยานแห่งชาติภูผาเทิบ

Sixteen kilometres south of Mukdahan, off Rte 2034, begins a hilly area of caves and unusual mushroom-shaped rock formations protected by national park status. Besides the rock formations, the park is a habitat for barking deer, wild boar, monkeys and civets. The main entrance to the park can be found 25km south of town, just south of the Ubon Ratchathani provincial line. About 2km south-west into the park, next to a waterfall, is a collection of dozens of small **Buddha images**.

Places to Stay

None of the hotels in Mukdahan are great deals, but they're adequate. The *Hua Nam Hotel* (☎ *042-611197, 20 Thanon Samut Sakdarak)* charges 120B for rooms with fan and shared bathroom and 220B for rooms with fan and bathroom. Air-con singles/doubles with bathroom go for 280/350B. On the same road is *Banthom Kasem Hotel* (☎ *042-611235)*, which has fan singles with shared bathroom for 140B, but it's a real dive.

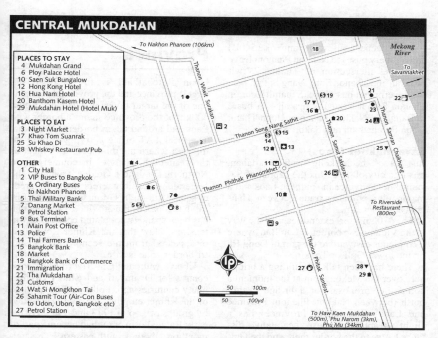

CENTRAL MUKDAHAN

PLACES TO STAY
4 Mukdahan Grand
6 Ploy Palace Hotel
10 Saen Suk Bungalow
12 Hong Kong Hotel
16 Hua Nam Hotel
20 Banthom Kasem Hotel
29 Mukdahan Hotel (Hotel Muk)

PLACES TO EAT
3 Night Market
17 Khao Tom Suanrak
25 Su Khao Di
28 Whiskey Restaurant/Pub

OTHER
1 City Hall
2 VIP Buses to Bangkok
 & Ordinary Buses
 to Nakhon Phanom
3 Thai Military Bank
7 Danang Market
8 Petrol Station
9 Bus Terminal
11 Main Post Office
13 Police
14 Thai Farmers Bank
15 Bangkok Bank
18 Market
19 Bangkok Bank of Commerce
21 Immigration
22 Tha Mukdahan
23 Customs
24 Wat Si Mongkhon Tai
26 Sahamit Tour (Air-Con Buses
 to Udon, Ubon, Bangkok etc)
27 Petrol Station

To Nakhon Phanom (106km)

Mekong River

To Savannakhet

Thanon Wiwit Surakan

Thanon Song Nang Sathit

Thanon Samut Sakdarak

Thanon Samran Chaikhong

Thanon Phithak Phanomkhet

Thanon Phitak Santirat

To Riverside Restaurant (800m)

To Haw Kaen Mukdahan (500m), Phu Narom (3km), Phu Mu (34km)

Hong Kong Hotel (☎ 042-611143, 161/1–2 Phitak Santirat) is similar in design to the Hua Nam but a bit nicer; its rates are 160B to 300B. Better still is *Saensuk Bungalow* (☎ 042-611124, 2 Thanon Phitak Santirat), which offers clean, quiet aircon rooms for 350B to 500B.

Mukdahan Hotel (Hotel Muk; ☎ 042-611619) is probably the best deal in town – it's a little away from the centre of town on Thanon Samut Sakdarak, and rooms cost 150B with fan and shared bathroom, and 350B to 600B with air-con.

A couple of posher places were built before the recent economic crisis to house the bigger players in Muk's anticipated Laos-Vietnam trade boom. The *Ploy Palace Hotel* (☎ 042-611329, fax 611883) on Thanon Phithak Phanomkhet features impressive marble-and-wood public areas and 150 rooms outfitted with stereo TV, fridge, air-con and hot water from 1500B, discounted to 900B when business is slow. The nearby *Mukdahan Grand* (☎ 042-612020, fax 616021) on Thanon Song Nang Sathit has similar but larger rooms starting at 1800B.

Places to Eat

The *night market* along Thanon Song Nang Sathit has kài yâang, sôm-tam, khâo jìi (Lao baguette sandwiches) and pàw-pía (Vietnamese spring rolls), either fresh (sòt) or fried (thâwt). *Khao Tom Suanrak*, next to Hua Nam Hotel, is a Chinese rice-soup place that's open all night. Another place that's open in the wee hours is the *Whiskey Restaurant/Pub* next to the Hotel Muk. House specialities are American-style breakfasts and khâo tôm.

South of the pier along the river is a string of moderately priced indoor-outdoor restaurants, including the well-patronised *Su Khao Di*. Also on the river, about 1km south of the pier, the *Riverside* has a shady outdoor area with a view of Savannakhet. The menu covers mostly Thai and Chinese dishes, but lâap (spicy minced meat salad) is also served. Prices are moderate and the beer is cold.

Getting There & Away

There are frequent buses from either direction – 34B ordinary (55B air-con) from Nakhon Phanom, half that price from That

NORTH-EASTERN THAILAND

Phanom and 49B (92B air-con) from Ubon Ratchathani.

VIP (sleeper) buses to Bangkok (540B) and ordinary buses to Nakhon Phanom leave from the intersection of Thanon Wiwit Surakan and Thanon Song Nang Sathit, near the government bus office. Sahamit Tour on Thanon Samut Sakdarak has air-con buses to Bangkok, Nakhon Phanom, Udon Thani, Ubon Ratchathani and Sakon Nakhon.

Savannakhet (Laos)

Just across the Mekong from Mukdahan, this Lao city of 45,000 is the capital of Savannakhet Province in southern Laos and a major relay point for trade between Thailand and Vietnam.

The 570km Rte 9 extends east all the way to the Vietnamese border at Lao Bao, where it continues eastward to the port of Dong Ha on the lower Gulf of Tonkin.

There has been talk of building a bridge here over the Mekong, but at the moment a competing proposal for a bridge farther north (between Nakhon Phanom Province and Laos' Khammuan Province) has a slight advantage because the relative distance between the border there and the Gulf of Tonkin is shorter.

Like Vientiane and Luang Prabang, Savannakhet has a number of French colonial and Franco-Chinese buildings, but with less of a Western presence and fewer tourists.

It's legal for foreigners to enter and exit the country via Savannakhet; other than a visa, no special permission is needed.

Places to Stay Near the centre of town on Thanon Latsawongseuk is the good-value *Sayamungkhun Guest House* (the sign out front reads simply 'Guest House'). All rooms in this well-kept villa come with bathroom and air-con and cost the Lao kip equivalent of US$5 to US$6.

Getting There & Away Ferries cross the Mekong between Savannakhet and Mukdahan frequently between 9 am and 3.30 pm Monday to Saturday, and 10.30 am to 3 pm on Sunday (50B). From Savannakhet it is possible to catch a bus north to Vientiane, south to Pakse or east to Vietnam. For more information on Savannakhet, see Lonely Planet's *Laos* guidebook.

Ubon Ratchathani Province

Ubon Ratchathani is the North-East's largest province and the provincial capital is one of the larger towns in Thailand. About 300km of the province shares a border with Laos and around 60km borders Cambodia. The local TAT office is trying to promote the area where the three countries meet as the 'Emerald Triangle' in counterpart to Northern Thailand's Golden Triangle. The 'emerald' ostensibly refers to the hundreds of square kilometres of intact monsoon forest in this part of the province – an area that has been sparsely populated because of war tensions. Now that the Khmer Rouge has disappeared from the scene, travel in the tri-border zone is safe.

Ubon's Mun and Chi River basins were centres for Dvaravati and Khmer cultures many centuries ago. Following the decline of the Khmer empires, the area was settled by groups of Lao in 1773 and 1792. By the early Ratanakosin era it had become part of monthon Ubon, a south-eastern Isan satellite state extending across what are now Surin, Si Saket and Ubon Provinces – as well as parts of southern Laos – with Champasak, Laos, as monthon capital. Today the Lao influence in the province predominates over the Khmer.

UBON RATCHATHANI

อ.เมืองอุบลราชธานี

postcode 34000 • pop 92,700

Ubon (sometimes spelt Ubol – the 'l' is pronounced like an 'n') is 557km from Bangkok, 271km from Nakhon Phanom and 311km from Khorat. Situated on the banks of the Mae Nam Mun – Thailand's second-longest waterway after the Mekong – Ubon is a financial, educational, communications and agricultural market centre for eastern Isan. Like Udon Thani and Khorat, it served as a US air base in the Vietnam War days. The main attractions are a few wát and a national museum. Now that the Thai/Lao border crossing at nearby Chong Mek is open to foreigners, Ubon is receiving more and more travellers who are finding it a good place to decompress after the comparatively rustic food and accommodation of southern Laos. Ubon's Candle Festival is actually a parade of gigantic, elaborately carved wax sculptures that is held during Khao Phansa, a Buddhist holiday marking the commencement of phansǎa, the Rains Retreat or Buddhist Lent, in July. The festival is very popular with Thai tourists and often all the city's hotel rooms are booked for the event.

Information

Tourist Offices The TAT (☎ 045-243770) has a very helpful branch office at 264/1 Thanon Kheuan Thani, opposite the Sri Kamol Hotel. The office distributes free maps of Ubon and information handouts about Si Saket and Yasothon Provinces as well. It's open from 8.30 am to 4.30 pm daily. The local tourist police office (☎ 045-245505, 1155) is located on Thanon Suriyat directly behind the police station.

Post & Communications Ubon's main post office is near the intersection of Thanon Luang and Thanon Si Narong. It's open from 8.30 am to 4.30 pm weekdays, and 9 am to noon on weekends. The telephone office is next door and is open from 7 am to 11 pm daily.

A handful of Internet access centres, including PC Net (☎ 045-254922), are located on Thanon Saphasit.

Medical Services The Rom Kao Hospital on Thanon Uparat near the bridge is the best medical facility in the lower North-East.

Ubon National Museum

พิพิธภัณฑสถานแห่งชาติอุบลราชธานี

Housed in a former palace of the Rama VI era, west of the TAT office on Thanon Kheuan Thani, Ubon National Museum is a good place to learn about Ubon's history and culture before exploring the city or province. Most of the exhibits have bilingual labels. Flanking the main entrance are a large Buddhist ordination-precinct stone from the Dvaravati period and some Pallava-inscribed pillars from the Khmer era. A prehistory room displays stone and bronze implements, burial urns, and 1500- to 3000-year-old pottery from the North-East. Another gallery contains many real treasures of mainland South-East Asian art, including Hindu-Khmer sculpture from the Chenla and Angkor eras, Lao Buddhas, Ubon textiles, local musical instruments and folk utensils (eg, rice containers, fish traps, and betel nut holders).

Among the museum's most prized possessions are a rare standing Dvaravati Buddha image and a Dong Son bronze drum. The museum is open from 9 am to 4 pm Wednesday to Sunday. Admission is 30B.

Just north of the museum is Thung Si Meuang Park, the centrepiece of which is a huge concrete replica of an elaborate votive candle. The park is the venue of Ubon's annual candle festival held in October.

Wat Thung Si Meuang

วัดทุ่งศรีเมือง

Off Thanon Luang, near the centre of town, this wát was originally built during the reign of Rama III (1824–51) and has a *hǎw trai* (tripitaka library) in good shape. Like many hǎw trai, it rests on tall, angled stilts in the middle of a small pond, surrounded by water to protect the precious scriptures from termites. Nearby is an old *mondòp* (square, spired building) with a Buddha footprint symbol. The bòt's interior is painted with 150-year-old jataka murals.

Wat Phra That Nong Bua

วัดพระธาตุหนองบัว

This wát on the road to Nakhon Phanom on the outskirts of town (catch a white city bus for 4B) is based almost exactly on the Mahabodhi stupa in Bodhgaya, India. It's a much better replica than Wat Jet Yot in Chiang Mai, which is also purported to be a Mahabodhi reproduction, but was designed by people who never saw the real thing. The jataka reliefs on the outside of the chedi are very good. Two groups of four niches on each side of the four-sided chedi contain Buddhas standing in stylised Gupta or Dvaravati closed-robe poses.

Wat Supatanaram

วัดสุปัฏนาราม

Called Wat Supat for short, the unique bòt at this temple features a mix of Khmer, European and Thai styles. In contrast to the

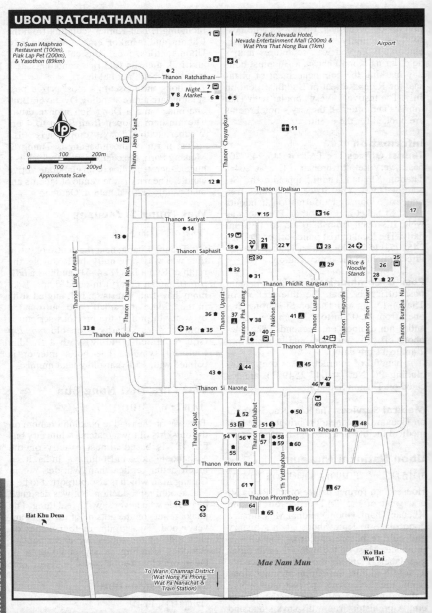

UBON RATCHATHANI

To Suan Maphrao
Restaurant (100m),
Piak Lap Pet (200m),
& Yasothon (89km)

To Felix Nevada Hotel,
Nevada Entertainment Mall (200m) &
Wat Phra That Nong Bua (1km)

Airport

Thanon Ratchathani

Night
Market

Thanon Jaeng Sanit

Thanon Chayangkun

Thanon Upalisan

Thanon Suriyat

Thanon Liang Meuang

Thanon Chawala Nok

Thanon Saphasit

Thanon Phichit Rangsan

Thanon Uparat

Thanon Pha Daeng

Th Nakhon Baan

Thanon Luang

Thanon Thepyothi

Thanon Phon Phaen

Thanon Burapha Nai

Rice &
Noodle
Stands

Thanon Phalo Chai

Thanon Phalorangrit

Thanon Si Narong

Thanon Ratchabut

Thanon Supat

Thanon Kheuan Thani

Th Yutthaphan

Thanon Phrom Rat

Thanon Phromthep

Hat Khu Deua

Mae Nam Mun

Ko Hat
Wat Tai

To Warin Chamrap District
(Wat Nong Pa Phong,
Wat Pa Nanachat &
Train Station)

Approximate Scale

0   100   200m
0   100   200yd

UBON RATCHATHANI

PLACES TO STAY		61	Aroi	26	Market No 5
6	Pathumrat Hotel; Cave	64	Night Market	29	Wat Pa Yai
9	Ruanrangsi Mansion Park			30	PC Net
12	Racha Hotel	**OTHER**		31	Khampun
27	Lai Thong Hotel; Night Fever	1	Buses for Mukdahan, Udon	34	Central Memorial
32	Tokyo Hotel		& Sakon Nakhon		Hospital
33	Tohsang Hotel	2	Ubon Teachers College	37	Wat Suthatsanaram
35	Bodin Hotel	3	Border Police	39	Mit Ying Mai Thai
36	Montana Hotel	4	Highway Police	40	Air-con buses to
47	Krung Thong Hotel; Choeng	5	THAI Office		Chiang Mai &
	Ubon Restaurant	7	Ordinary Bus Terminal		Phitsanulok
55	Ubon Hotel	10	Buses to Roi Et, Khon Kaen,	41	Wat Pa Noi
57	Ratchathani Hotel; Rim Mun		Udon & Yasothon	42	Cinema
	2 Restaurant	11	Airfield (Wing 21)	43	Province & District
59	Sri Kamol Hotel	13	Highway Department		Offices
60	New Nakornluang Hotel		Office	44	Giant Votive Candle
65	Sri Isan 1 & 2	14	Chaw Wattana	45	Wat Thung Si Meuang
			Motorcycles	48	Wat Liap
PLACES TO EAT		16	Tourist Police	49	Main Post Office
8	Fern Hut	17	Market	50	Fire Station
15	Kai Yang Wat Jaeng	18	Thai Massage Clinic	51	TAT Office
20	Indochine	19	Post Office	52	City Pillar
22	Sincere Restaurant	21	Wat Jaeng	53	Ubon National Museum
28	Log Home Restaurant	23	Police	58	Saiyan Tour
38	Sakhon	24	Saphasit Prasong	62	Wat Supatanaram
46	Yim Yim Restaurant		Hospital	63	Rom Kao Hospital
54	Khow Klong Restaurant	25	Buses to Phibun Mangsahan	66	Wat Luang
56	Chiokee (Jiaw Ki)		& Khong Jiam	67	Wat Klang

usual Thai- or Lao-style temple structures of the region, the bòt is made entirely of stone, like the early Khmer stone prasat, and the roof corners display dragons.

In front of the bòt is the largest wooden bell in Thailand.

Wat Jaeng
วัดแจ้ง

This wát on Thanon Saphasit has a typical Lao-style bòt (known locally by the Lao term *sĭm*). The carved wooden veranda depicts a *kotchasi,* a mythical cross between an elephant and a horse; above that is Airavata, Indra's three-headed elephant mount.

Warin Chamrap District Temples

Ubon city district is separated from Warin Chamrap to the south by the Mae Nam Mun. Two well-known wát in this district are forest monasteries *(wát pàa)* founded by the famous monk and meditation master Ajahn Cha. The venerable ajahn died in January 1992, aged 75, after a productive and inspirational life, but his teachings live on at these two hermitages.

Wat Nong Pa Phong About 10km past the train station, in Warin Chamrap district, is Wat Nong Pa Phong. This very famous forest wát was founded by Ajahn Cha, who also founded many other branch temples in Ubon Ratchathani Province and one in Sussex, England; monks in his lineage have founded monasteries in other parts of the world. All of these temples are known for their quiet discipline and daily routine of work and meditation.

Dozens of westerners have studied here during the past 20 years or so, and many live here or at branch temples as ordained monks.

Ajahn Cha, a former disciple of the most famous north-eastern teacher of them all, Ajahn Man, was known for his simple and direct teaching method that seemed to cross all international barriers. His funeral, which was held here in 1993, drew thousands of followers from around the world.

The wát features a small museum and a chedi where Ajahn Cha's ashes are interred. To get to the wát from Ubon, take a pink city bus No 3 to the Baw Khaw Saw terminal, then catch a săwngthăew going to the wát.

NORTH-EASTERN THAILAND

Wat Pa Nanachat Bung Wai The abbot here is English and most of the monks are European, American or Japanese. As English is the main language spoken here, Wat Pa Nanachat is a better place to visit than Wat Nong Pa Phong if you don't speak Thai and are interested in more than sightseeing. The wát is very clean, cool and quiet.

Generally only those with a serious interest in Buddhism – preferably with previous practical experience – are permitted to stay overnight. Both men and women are welcome, but men are required to shave their heads if they want to stay beyond three days. Write in advance to avoid disappointment (Wat Pa Nanachat, Ban Bung Wai, Amphoe Warin, Ubon Ratchathani 34310); during the March-to-May hot season monks go into retreat and overnight guests aren't usually accepted.

From Ubon, take a white city bus No 1 south down Thanon Uparat, cross the bridge over the Mae Nam Mun and get off as the bus turns right in Warin Chamrap for the train station. From there, catch any sǎwngthǎew heading south (though heading west eventually, on Rte 2193 towards Si Saket) and ask to be let off at Wat Pa Nanachat – everybody knows it. You can also get there by catching a Si Saket bus from Ubon for 6B to Bung Wai, the village across the road from Wat Pa Nanachat.

There is a sign in English at the edge of the road – the wát is in the forest behind the rice fields. You can also hire a túk-túk direct to the wát from town for about 100B.

Ko Hat Wat Tai
เกาะหาดวัดใต้

This is a small island in the Mae Nam Mun on the southern edge of town. During the hot and dry months, from March to May, it is a favourite picnic spot and there are 'beaches' where you can swim. You can get here by boat from the northern shore of the river.

Hat Khu Deua
หาดคูเดื่อ

Hat Khu Deua is a 'beach' area on the northern bank of the river west of town, off Thanon Lang Meuang. Several thatched

sǎalaa (pavilions) offer shade for picnicking or napping by the river; you can even stay overnight in simple raft houses at no charge.

Places to Stay – Budget
A good budget choice is the **Sri Isan 1 & 2** (☎ 045-254204, 242444, 60–66 Thanon Ratchabut), where singles/doubles are 100/150B with fan and private bathroom; in a separate building there are air-con rooms for 260B. The mosaic railing on the staircase in the old wing is worth a look.

The **New Nakornluang Hotel** (☎ 045-254768, 84–88 Thanon Yutthaphan) has decent rooms for 190B with fan and private bathroom, and 270B with air-con.

The well-kept **Tokyo Hotel** (☎ 045-241739, fax 263140, 178 Thanon Uparat), near the town centre, is preferable to all of the foregoing hotels if you can afford another 50B or so. Comfortable rooms in the old building cost 170/270B with fan and bathroom and 300/350B with air-con and TV. Fan rooms in the new building go for 350/500B, 800B for air-con, TV and fridge.

Places to Stay – Mid-Range
The friendly **Racha Hotel** (☎ 045-254155, 149/21 Thanon Chayangkun), north of the town centre, charges 280/350B for clean rooms with fan and bathroom, and 400/500B with air-con.

On Thanon Si Narong, near Wat Thung Si Meuang, is the clean and comfortable **Krung Thong** (☎ 045-254200), offering fan rooms with TV for 280B, and air-con doubles with TV for 450B.

The **Bodin** (Badin; ☎ 045-243000, 14 Thanon Phalo Chai) has singles/doubles with fan for 250B to 380B and air-con rooms for 450B. It's a bit overpriced for the hotel's shabby condition, although it's a favourite with the 'salespeople' crowd.

Ubon Hotel (Kao Chan; ☎ 045-241045, 333 Thanon Kheuan Thani) used to be the city's number-one lodgings but has gone steadily downhill over the years. Singles – some quite OK, others rather dank – cost 280B to 400B with fan and bathroom, and 350B to 450B with air-con. Similar in price but in better condition is the **Ratchathani Hotel** (☎ 045-244388, 297 Thanon Kheuan Thani), where decent rooms are 220/400B with fan and 450/600B with air-con. Another good one in this category is the **Montana**

Hotel (☎ 045-261752), where all rooms have air-con and cost 480B, 600B with breakfast included.

Ruanrangsi Mansion Park (☎ 045-244744), in the Ruanrangsi Complex off Thanon Ratchathani, offers air-con apartments for rent by the day (400B to 450B) or by the month (3800B to 4300B). The landscaped grounds are conveniently adjacent to the Fern Hut restaurant, various shops and a branch post office.

The *Sri Kamol Hotel* (Si Kamon; ☎ 045-241136, fax 243792, 22/2 Thanon Ubonsak), near the Ratchathani Hotel, has large rooms with all the amenities from 630B to 690B; discounts are available and all rates include a Thai or international breakfast.

The *Pathumrat Hotel* (☎ 045-241501, fax 242313, 337 Thanon Chayangkun), once the top-end hotel in Ubon, has slid into the midrange. Standard air-con rooms are 400B, 'deluxe' rooms are 700B and rooms with video are 2500B. Although the staff are friendly, the rooms are not good value.

Places to Stay – Top End

The *Tohsang Hotel* (☎ 045-241925, fax 244814, 251 Thanon Phalo Chai) offers large, pleasant rooms with air-con, TV and fridge for 880B to 990B, breakfast included. Facilities include a coffee shop and Chinese restaurant.

The *Lai Thong Hotel* (☎ 045-264271, fax 264270, 50 Thanon Phichit Rangsan) has comfortable rooms with all the amenities for 963B to 1650B, including breakfast. There's a swimming pool on the premises.

The *Felix Nevada Hotel* (☎ 045-280999, fax 283424, Thanon 434 Chayangkun) is a relatively new luxury hotel attached to the Nevada Entertainment Mall. Decked-out rooms cost from 990B to 1100B, including breakfast.

Places to Eat

Regional Ubon is famous for its Isan food – many Thai gourmets claim it has the best in all of Isan. Lâap pèt (spicy duck salad) is the local speciality, often eaten with *tôm fák* (squash soup) and Chinese mushrooms. Good places for lâap pèt include *Jak Kan Lap Pet* on Thanon Suriyat, *Piak Lap Pet* on Thanon Jaeng Sanit (next to a radio relay station) and *Suan Maphrao*, near the 288km marker on the road to Yasothon.

Ubon is also big on kài yâang (grilled Lao-style chicken) and everyone in town agrees that the best is at *Kai Yang Wat Jaeng*, a block north of Wat Jaeng on Thanon Suriyat. The chicken is sold from 9 am to 2 pm only, after which the vendor switches to curries. Other specialities include *hàw mòk* (soufflé-like curry steamed in banana leaves) – choice of fish (plaa), or chicken (kài).

A favourite with local Thai families, the simple *Sakhon*, on Thanon Pha Daeng near the provincial courthouse, is a long-running Ubon institution with a full array of Isan dishes available. There's also an English menu.

Indochine (Indojin) on Thanon Saphasit near Wat Jaeng specialises in tasty Vietnamese food, including good-value set meals. It's only open from 10 am to 6 pm. A little farther east along the same side of the road, the air-con *Sincere Restaurant* serves an interesting Thai-French cuisine. It's open from 9 am to 11 pm, and closed on Sunday.

Noodles & Rice On Thanon Si Narong, the *Choeng Ubon* (next to the Krung Thong hotel) and *Yim Yim* (oppesite the main post office) make good kǔaytǐaw.

Rim Mun 2 on Thanon Kheuan Thani (next to the Ratchathani Hotel) is a late-night khâo tôm place that can prepare just about any Thai or Chinese dish that you can name.

The *Aroi* (no Roman-script sign), towards the southern end of Thanon Ratchabut, has a good Thai-Chinese buffet.

The cheapest string of *rice and noodle places* in town runs along Thanon Saphasit just opposite Saphasit Prasong Hospital.

International Good pizza is available at the Italian-managed *Log Home*, near the Lai Thong Hotel on Thanon Phichit Rangsan.

Vegetarian Ubon has two vegetarian restaurants. One is in Warin, near the train station, and is called *Rom Pho*. The other is the newly opened *Khow Klong*, in front of the Ubon Hotel.

Breakfasts & Bakeries The French-Lao influence in Ubon means people are somewhat more accustomed to pastries and

Western breakfasts than in many parts of Thailand. *Chiokee* (Jiaw Ki) on Thanon Kheuan Thani is very popular among local office workers for both Chinese and Western breakfasts. Prices are good and it serves everything from khâo tôm to ham and eggs. Jók is a speciality.

Fern Hut, down a soi opposite the teachers' college *(wítháyaalai khruu)*, sells good cakes and other baked items.

In Warin, on Thanon Pathumthepphakdi near a Bangkok Bank branch, *Warin Bakery* offers decent baked goods, coffee and breakfasts.

Night Markets Ubon has two night markets that are open from dusk to dawn, one by the river near the bridge *(tàlàat yài* or big market), and the other near the bus terminal on Thanon Chayangkun – convenient to hotels on Thanon Chayangkun and Thanon Suriyat.

Entertainment
Nightclubs *Night Fever*, at the Lai Thong Hotel, and *Cave* at the Pathumrat Hotel were the favoured night spots at last visit.

The *Nevada Entertainment Mall*, at 434 Thanon Chayangkun, contains eight cinema screens in addition to the usual snooker, karaoke, massage and other favourite night-time activities of the mon-eyed and mindless.

Massage The *Thai Massage Clinic* (☎ 045-254746, *369–371 Thanon Saphasit)* offers traditional-style massage from 9 am to 9 pm daily. Rates are 100B per hour.

Ubon also has several *àap òp nûat* (bathe-steam-massage) places that probably got their start when a US air base was located outside town. The most notorious is the Pathumrat Hotel's *Long Beach*, which Ta Mok and other Khmer Rouge commanders visited regularly until rather recently.

Shopping
One of the major local specialities is silver betel-nut containers moulded using the lost-wax process. The Ubon National Museum on Thanon Kheuan Thani has a good exhibit of locally produced betel boxes; to see them being made visit Ban Pa-Ao, a silver-smithing village between Yasothon and Ubon off Hwy 23.

Phanchat (☎ 045-243433), at 158 Thanon Ratchabut, carries a range of Ubon handicrafts, including fabrics and silverware, as does Mit Ying Mai Thai on the corner of Thanon Phalorangrit and Thanon Pha Daeng. For locally woven fabrics that can be tailor-made into clothes, check out Khampun on Thanon Pha Daeng, near the corner of Thanon Phichit Rangsan.

Getting There & Away
Air THAI has two daily flights from Bangkok to Ubon. The fare is 1625B and the flight takes an hour and five minutes. The THAI office (☎ 045-313340–4) is at 364 Thanon Chayangkun. THAI operates a shuttle van between its city office and the airport.

Bus Two air-con buses go daily to Ubon Ratchathani from Nakhon Phanom, at 7 am and 2 pm, leaving from the intersection of Thanon Bamrung Meuang and Thanon Ratsadon Uthit near the Windsor Hotel in Nakhon Phanom. The fare is 144B. Ordinary buses from the Baw Khaw Saw terminal in Nakhon Phanom leave regularly from morning until late afternoon (81B). The trip takes 5½ hours on the tour bus and six to seven hours on the *rót thammádaa* (ordinary bus).

If you're coming from Northern Thailand, you'll find air-con buses to Ubon from both Phitsanulok (370B) and Chiang Mai (540B).

Ordinary buses to Ubon from Bangkok cost 180B to 193B (depending on the route) and leave the Northern bus terminal in Bangkok hourly from around 4.30 am to nearly midnight. First-class air-con buses cost 351B, and leave twice in the morning (8.30 and 9.30) and eight times in the evening between 7.45 and 11 pm. There is one 520B VIP departure nightly at 8 pm. From Ubon's main bus terminal on Thanon Chayangkun, three first-class air-con buses depart for Bangkok in the morning and four in the evening between 6 and 9 pm. Second-class air-con buses leave at 7 am and 7.30 pm and cost 248B.

Other fares to/from Ubon are in the following list. Some fares differ according to alternative routes taken between the same terminals – longer routes are usually cheaper – or class of air-con service.

destination	fare
Buriram	
ordinary	66B
air-con	148B
Kantharalak (for Khao Phra Wihan)	
ordinary	20B
Khong Jiam	
ordinary	35B
Khon Kaen	
ordinary	83B
air-con	116B–149B
Khorat	
ordinary	105B–121B
air-con	175B–220B
Mahasarakham	
ordinary	64B
air-con	90B–115B
Mukdahan	
ordinary	49B
air-con	92B
Phibun Mangsahan	
ordinary	20B
Prakhon Chai (for Phanom Rung)	
ordinary	84B
Roi Et	
ordinary	57B
air-con	74B–95B
Sakon Nakhon	
ordinary	83B
air-con	150B
Si Saket	
ordinary	22B
air-con	38B–50B
Surin	
ordinary	52B
air-con	96B
That Phanom	
ordinary	65B
air-con	119B
Udon Thani	
ordinary	116B
air-con	162B–210B
Yasothon	
ordinary	33B
air-con	46B

Train The Ubon Ratchathani express leaves Bangkok nightly at 9 pm, arriving in Ubon at 7.20 am the next morning.

The basic 1st-class fare is 460B and 2nd class is 221B, not including surcharges for express service or a sleeping berth.

Rapid trains leave at 6.50 am and 6.45 and 10.45 pm, arriving in Ubon about 11 hours later. There is no 1st class on the rapid trains. Ordinary trains take only about an hour longer to reach Ubon. There are two departures daily in either direction; the fare is 95B.

Rapid trains from Khorat leave at 12.30 and 5.01 am and at 12.22 pm, arriving in Ubon Ratchathani at 5.35 and 10.45 am and 6.10 pm respectively. The basic fares for rapid trains are 106B in 2nd class and 45B in 3rd class.

Ordinary trains to Bangkok leave Ubon at 6.50 am and 11.25 pm, arriving in Bangkok about twelve hours later. Rapid trains leave at 6.45 and 10.45 pm. One express train departs Ubon for Bangkok nightly at 9 pm. The basic fare is 95/221B for 3rd/2nd class.

Ubon's train station is in Warin Chamrap; take a white No 2 city bus (4B) to reach Thanon Chayangkun in the city centre.

Getting Around

A city bus system runs large buses along the main avenues (4B) – very convenient for getting from one end of town to the other cheaply. Săamláw around town cost around 30B per kilometre.

Motorcycles, vans and cars can be rented at Chaw Wattana (☎ 045-241906), 39/8 Thanon Suriyat.

AROUND UBON PROVINCE
Phibun Mangsahan to Khong Jiam

The small riverside district of Khong Jiam is 75km east of Ubon via Rte 217 – to Phibun Mangsahan and then over the Mae Nam Mun by bridge at the western end of Rte 2222. Visitors often stop in Phibun to see a set of rapids called **Kaeng Sapheu** next to the river crossing. Phibun Mangsahan is also the location of the Ubon immigration office; visa extensions as well as exit visas (for crossings into Laos) are available here. The office is about 1km from town on the way south to Chong Mek – look for a large communications antenna nearby.

Ban Khawn Sai, half a kilometre west of Phibun on Rte 217 between the 23km and 24km markers, is a small village whose main livelihood is the forging of bronze gongs for temples and classical Thai music ensembles. You can watch the gong-makers

NORTH-EASTERN THAILAND

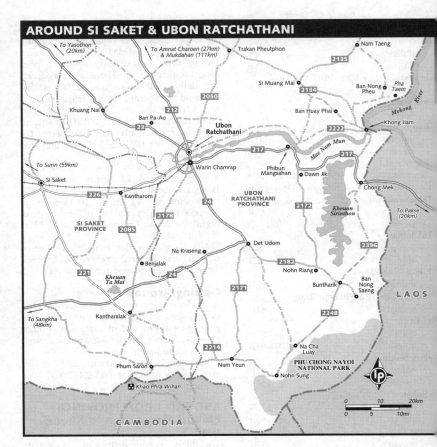

AROUND SI SAKET & UBON RATCHATHANI

hammering the flat metal discs into beautiful instruments and tempering them in rustic fires – often in temporary shelters just off the road. Should you care to make a purchase or two, small gongs cost 400B to 500B each, larger ones 4000B to 5000B; the huge 2m gongs run as high as 50,000B.

Ban Pa-Ao, north-west of Ubon on Hwy 23, is another village that produces household utensils of brass using the lost-wax casting method. The turn-off for the village is near the 19km marker on Hwy 23 – from there it is another 3km to the village. Nearly all buses to Yasothon pass this way.

Farther east along Rte 2222 you can stop at **Nam Tok Sae Hua Maew** and **Wat Tham Hew Sin Chai.** The latter is a cave temple with a waterfall cascading over the front of

the cave; it's just a 2km walk south-west of Khong Jiam. Other waterfalls in Ubon Province are **Nam Tok Pak Taew** in Nam Yeun district – a tall vertical drop – and the low but wide **Nam Tok Tat Ton.**

Khong Jiam itself sits on a picturesque peninsula formed by the confluence of the Mae Nam Mun and the Mekong. Huge conical fish traps are made here for local use; they look very much like the fish traps that appear in the 3000-year-old murals at Pha Taem (see later in this section). Thais visit Khong Jiam to see the so-called **Mae Nam Song Si** (Two Colour River), the contrasting coloured currents formed at the junction of the Mae Nam Mun and the Mekong. Along the Mekong side is a simple but pleasant park with benches and food vendors.

NORTH-EASTERN THAILAND

For 200B to 300B per hour you can charter 15-person capacity long-tail boats from a landing next to the Pak Mun Restaurant to see Two Colour River and various small river islands; Thais can cross the Mekong to Laos. While this is not an official crossing for foreigners, it is sometimes possible to persuade boatmen to take you to the Lao village across the river for an hour or two, especially during Buddhist festival days, when regulations get lax. (Foreigners are, however, officially permitted to cross into Laos 42km farther south at Chong Mek.)

Places to Stay & Eat In Phibun Mangsahan the *Phiboonkit Hotel* (☎ 045-441201), near the bus stop in the centre of town, has rooms with fan for 120B with shared bathroom, 150B with attached bathroom, and air-con rooms for 300B.

Three kilometres north of Phibun, *Sanamhai Guest House* (☎ 045-441289) has modern bungalows for 250B to 300B with fan, 300B with air-con. There's a pub and a garden restaurant opposite the guesthouse.

Near the bridge to Rte 2222 is a simple *restaurant* famous for *saalaapao* (Chinese buns) and *năng kòp* (frog skin, usually fried). Thais visiting Pha Taem like to stop here on the way to stock up on these items.

In Khong Jiam, the *Apple Guest House* (☎ 045-351160) on Thanon Kaewpradit has rooms in a couple of buildings off the main road. There are two large, clean rooms upstairs and six smaller rooms downstairs, all with shared bathroom. Rates are a reasonable 150B per room with fan, and 300B with air-con; windows are screened and soap and towels provided. Bicycles and motorcycles are available for rent and there is a restaurant nearby.

Near the river, the friendly, motel-like *Khong Jiam Guest House* (☎ 045-351074) has rooms with 150/200B with fan and bathroom, 350B with air-con and TV. Also on the river, *Ban Rim Khong* (☎ 045-351101) offers six timber bungalows overlooking the river for 1000B (or 800B with some bargaining), each with TV, fridge, bathroom and carpet. *Araya Resort* (☎ 045-351191), set back from the river on a back road, with its own waterfall and gardens, has bungalows with air-con, TV and fridge for 500B to 1000B. Two kilometres outside of town towards Phibun, *Khong Chiam*

Marina Resort (☎ 045-351145) features bungalows with air-con for 450B to 1000B, depending on size and amenities.

On the Mae Nam Mun side of Khong Jiam are two restaurants, the floating *Phae Rak Mae Mun*, with a good selection of freshwater fish dishes; and the *Hat Mae Mun* on a hillside overlooking the river. The latter has the better food – try the delicious *yam mét má-mûang săam sŭan*, a warm cashew-nut salad made with tomatoes, chillies and fresh green peppercorns.

Along the Mekong side, *Araya* is very popular on weekends and serves a variety of freshwater fish, Thai-Lao standards, river turtle *(tà-phâap náam)* and wild pig – depending on how you feel about eating wildlife versus penned protein, you may want to avoid this one.

Two other restaurants in this vicinity are *Pak Mun* and *Mae Nam Song Si*.

Getting There & Away From Ubon, direct buses to Khong Jiam (74km) cost 35B and leave from the Warin Market or the bus queue behind the Lai Thong Hotel.

When direct buses aren't running to Khong Jiam, catch a Phibun bus (20B) from Warin train station between 5 am and 3.30 pm, and change to a Khong Jiam bus (20B) in Phibun. Air-con buses from Khong Jiam to Bangkok depart at 4 pm/4.30 pm and cost 290/333B.

If you're driving or cycling to Khong Jiam from the Sirinthon Reservoir area via Rtes 217 and 2396, you'll have to cross the Mae Nam Mun by vehicle ferry (look for the sign that says 'ferpy boat'). The ferry is 30B per vehicle.

Pha Taem
ผาแต้ม

In Khong Jiam district, 94km north-east of Ubon, near the confluence of the Mae Nam Mun and the Mekong, is a tall stone cliff called Pha Taem. The cliff is about 200m long and features **prehistoric colour paintings** that are at least 3000 years old. Mural subjects include fish traps, *plaa bèuk* (giant Mekong catfish), turtles, elephants, human hands and a few geometric designs – all very reminiscent of prehistoric rock art found at widely separated sites around the world. The latest anthropological theory speculates that rock-art sites like this one

NORTH-EASTERN THAILAND

were created by shamans while they were in trance states, or immediately after leaving trance states.

A 500m trail descends from the cliff edge to the base, past two platforms where visitors can view the rock paintings; from the top of the cliff you get a bird's eye view of Laos. Vendors sell snacks and beverages near the top of the cliff. A cliff-top visitors centre contains exhibits pertaining to the paintings and local geology.

On the road to Pha Taem is **Sao Chaliang**, an area of unusual stone formations similar to Phu Pha Thoep in Mukdahan.

Places to Stay Both Pha Taem and Sao Chaliang are a part of the Pa Taem National Park. If you have your own equipment, *camping* is permitted in a designated area near the park headquarters between the turn-off from Rte 2112 and the visitors centre.

Getting There & Away Pha Taem is 20km beyond Khong Jiam via Rte 2112, but there's no direct public transport there. The bus from Ubon to Khong Jiam will pass the final turn-off to Pha Taem on request; then you can walk or hitch 5km to the cliff.

By car, bike or motorcycle from Ubon, go east on Rte 217 to Phibun Mangsahan, then turn left and head north across the Mae Nam Mun on Rte 2222 and follow this road to Khong Jiam.

From Khong Jiam, take Rte 2134 northwest to Ban Huay Phai and then go northeast at the first turn-off to Pha Taem.

Chong Mek & the Emerald Triangle
ช่องเม็กและสามเหลี่ยมมรกต

South of Khong Jiam via Rte 217 is the small trading town of Chong Mek on the Thai-Lao border. If you possess a valid Lao visa, Chong Mek has the distinction of being the only town in Thailand where you can cross into Laos by land (that is, you don't have to cross the Mekong). Some people report that you have to obtain a Thai exit stamp at the Thai immigration office in Phibun Mangsahan before you'll be allowed to leave Thailand at Chong Mek. We've never had a problem crossing here in either direction, but to be safe you might consider stopping in Phibun first. The southern Lao

capital of Pakse is about an hour by road and ferry from Ban Mai Sing Amphon, the village on the Lao side of the border.

Thai visitors come to Chong Mek to drink *oh-líang* (Chinese-style iced coffee) and to shop for Lao and Vietnamese souvenirs.

In July of 2000 an armed band of Lao nationals and ethnic Lao from Ubon staged an attack on the Lao border outpost here in which at least five were killed. The attackers, who had been using Ubon province as a base, were in possession of a flag of the defunct Kingdom of Laos when routed by the Lao army and forced to flee back into Thailand. At the time of writing it was still unclear who had sponsored the attack and what it was meant to achieve.

About 5km west of Chong Mek is the north-eastern shore of the huge **Sirinthon Reservoir**, an impoundment of a Mae Nam Mun tributary. On forested hills near the dam at the northern end of the reservoir is a recreation area frequented by local picnickers.

Farther south, near the intersection of the Lao, Thai and Cambodian borders (an area sometimes called the 'Emerald Triangle' for its relatively healthy forest cover) is the little-known **Phu Chong Nayoi National Park**. Established in 1987, the 687-sq-km park's predominant attractions include the **Bak Taew Yai Waterfall** (3.5km from the park headquarters), which plunges 40m over a cliff in two separate but parallel streams; a number of interesting rock formations; and a couple of fresh springs and some nice views of the surrounding countryside from a cliff called **Pha Pheung**. The park's highest point reaches 555m. Fauna includes the endangered white-winged wood duck. There is no accommodation at the park but camping is permitted in a designated area if you bring your own equipment. To get there from Ubon, take a bus from the Warin market to the town of Najaluay. Buses leave hourly between 10 am and 1 pm, cost 40B and the trip takes about an hour. From Najaluay, săwngthăew can be hired for 400B to 500B for the round-trip journey. If you have your own wheels, take Hwy 24 south, and turn onto Rte 2182 at the town of Det Udom. From there it's 45km to the town of Buntharik, where you turn south onto Rte 2248. The turn-off to Phu Chong Nayoi National Park is a few kilometres beyond Najaluay. The park headquarters is 7 km from the turn-off.

Getting There & Away Săwngthăew run between Phibun and Chong Mek for 20B. There are two daily air-con buses that run directly from Chong Mek to Bangkok and vice versa. They leave Chong Mek at 4 pm (280B) and at 5 pm (360B) and arrive at the Northern and North-Eastern bus terminal in Bangkok at about 6 am the next day.

Surin & Si Saket Provinces

These adjacent provinces between Buriram and Ubon border Cambodia and are dotted with the ruins of ancient Khmer structures built during the Angkor empire. The only other major attraction in the area is the Surin Annual Elephant Roundup. Few elephants are still used as work animals in Surin; they are brought out for ceremonial occasions such as parades and monastic ordinations.

SURIN
อ.เมืองสุรินทร์

postcode 32000 • pop 41,200
Surin, 452km from Bangkok, is a quiet provincial capital except during the **Elephant Roundup** in late November. At that time a carnival atmosphere reigns, with elephants providing the entertainment. If you have ever wanted to see a lot of elephants in one place (there are more elephants now in Thailand than in India), this is your opportunity.

Culturally, Surin represents an intersection of Lao, central Thai, Khmer and Suay peoples, resulting in an interesting mix of dialects and customs.

A fifth group contributing to the blend was the many volunteers and UN employees working with local refugee camps here during the 1970s and 1980s; with the huge refugee industry winding down, their influence has waned considerably.

To see Surin's elephants during the low season, visit **Ban Tha Klang** in Tha Tum district, or about 60km north of Surin. Many of the performers at the annual festival are trained here, but their presence is seasonable – inquire in Surin before making a trip.

Silk weaving can be observed at several local villages, including **Khwaosinarin** and **Ban Janrom**.

Prasat Ta Meuan
ปราสาทตาเหมือน

The most atmospheric – and most difficult to reach – of Surin's temple ruins is a series of three sites known collectively as Prasat Ta Meuan in Ban Ta Miang district on the Cambodian border. Ban Ta Miang is 25km east of Ban Kruat and 49km west of Kap Choeng via Rte 2121. The sites are 10.5km from Ban Ta Miang via a mediocre dirt road. This trip is best done by hired bicycle, motorcycle or car – Pirom's House (see the Places to Stay entry later) can also arrange day trips by Land Rover if you can get a small group together.

The first site, **Prasat Ta Meuan** proper, was built in the Jayavarman VII period (AD 1121–1220) as a rest stop for pilgrims. It's a fairly small monument with a two-door, eight-window sanctuary constructed of laterite blocks; only one sculpted sandstone lintel over the rear door remains.

To the south, about 500m along a winding road, is the more impressive **Prasat Ta Meuan Tot**, which is said to have been the chapel for a 'healing station' or 'hospital' like Prang Ku outside Chaiyaphum. The ruins consist of a *gopura* (entrance pavilion), mondòp and main sanctuary, which is surrounded by a laterite wall. This site has fairly recently been restored and the strangler figs cut away.

Farther south, right next to the Cambodian border, is the largest site, **Prasat Ta Meuan Thom**. Built mostly of sandstone blocks on a laterite base, on a slope that drops off at the southern end to face the Cambodian border, the walled complex has been rather badly reassembled into a jumble of sculpted blocks. Unfortunately, some of the sculpted blocks from the highly ornate southern gate have ended up haphazardly inserted into other structures in the compound. This temple was occupied by the Khmer Rouge in the 1980s and many of the best carvings were pried or blasted from the temple and sold to unscrupulous Thai dealers. Just beyond the southern gate the forest is cordoned off by barbed wire and red skull-and-crossbone signs (Khmer and English) warning of undetonated mines.

Mines and undetonated hand grenades around the Prasat Ta Meuan sites are a real danger; *don't* veer from the cleared paths around and between the monuments. In the not-so-distant past, firefights between the Khmer Rouge and Phnom Penh government troops could be heard almost daily during the dry season. The demise of the Khmer Rouge has brought peace to the border but banditry is still a possibility. A Thai military checkpoint along Rte 2121 screens all visitors and they may turn back nonresidents if the situation at the border is volatile.

Other Khmer Temple Ruins

The southern reach of Surin Province along the Cambodian border harbours several minor Angkor-period ruins, including **Prasat Hin Ban Phluang** (30km south of Surin). The solitary sandstone sanctuary, mounted on a laterite platform, exhibits well-sculpted stone lintels. A 30B admission fee is collected here.

A larger Khmer site can be seen 30km north-east of town at **Prasat Sikhoraphum**, 500m north of Rte 226 at the 34km marker. Sikhoraphum (or Si Khonphum) features five Khmer prang, the tallest of which reaches 32m. The doorways to the central prang are decorated with stone carvings of Hindu deities in the Angkor Wat style. Admission is 30B. Sikhoraphum can be reached by bus or train from Surin town.

The ruined **Prasat Phumpon** in Sangkha district (59km south-east of Surin via Rte 2077) is the oldest Khmer prasat in Thailand, dating from the 7th or 8th century AD. Unless you're adamant about ticking off every Khmer site in Thailand, you'll most likely be disappointed by this jumble of bricks.

Surin can also be used as a base for visiting the Khmer ruins at Phanom Rung and Prasat Meuang Tam, about 75km south-west of Surin in Buriram Province (see Buriram Province and the 'Phanom Rung Historical Park' special section in this chapter).

Places to Stay

Pirom's House (☎ 044-515140, 242 Thanon Krung Si Nai) has singles/doubles for 100/150B in a traditional wooden house. Pirom knows the area well and can suggest ideas for day trips around Surin, including excursions to lesser-known Khmer temple sites. He also owns a Land Rover

and can lead reasonably priced all-day tours of several Khmer temple sites along the Cambodian border (about 600B per person if you go in a group of four, including a Thai lunch prepared by his wife). Besides trips to Khmer temples, Pirom can also do tours of little-known weaving villages populated by ethnic Lao, Khmer and Suay people. If you're at all interested in getting an in-depth look at Isan culture, take advantage of Pirom's informative and flexible tours. At the time of our last visit, Pirom was building a new guesthouse in a quiet area about 1km west of the train station. A săwngthăew to the new guesthouse from the train station should cost about 30B. Pirom's wife (who speaks some French) will do the cooking at the new place.

Hotel rates may increase during the Elephant Roundup and hotels may fill up, but otherwise *Krung Si Nai* (☎ 044-511037, 185 Thanon Krung Si Nai) charges from 200B to 300B. *New Hotel* (☎ 044-511341), next to the train station at 22 Thanon Thanasan, starts at 160B for rooms with fan and has some air-con rooms from 380B. *Thanachai Hotel*, just off the roundabout on Thanon Thetsaban 1 near the post office, has somewhat dark and dingy rooms for 100B.

Moving upmarket just a bit, the very clean and well-run *Nid Diew Hotel* (☎ 044-512099, 279–283 Thanon Thanasan) offers rooms with fan for 150B and single/double rooms with air-con, TV and hot water for 320/390B. *Memorial Hotel* (☎ 044-511637), on Thanon Lak Meuang, just west of Thanon Thanasan, has good rooms for 300B with fan (add 50B with TV), and 500/600B with air-con, TV and fridge.

The business-like *Phetkasem Hotel* (☎ 044-511274/576, 104 Thanon Jit Bamrung) has all air-con rooms and rates are from 450B to 750B. Surin's top-end place to stay, the *Thong Tarin Hotel* (☎ 044-514281, 60 Thanon Sirirat), has 205 air-con rooms and rates starting at 780B with all the amenities, including breakfast.

Places to Eat

Along the northern end of Thanon Thanasan between the Saeng Thong Hotel and the train station are a number of good, inexpensive Thai and Chinese restaurants.

Along this stretch the long-running **Surin Phochana** serves dependable curries and noodles.

A small **night market** assembles in front of the Surin train station each evening. There is also a larger **night market** next to the main municipal market along Thanon Krung Si Nai, close to Pirom's House and the Krung Si Hotel.

Pai Ngun, located about 100m down the first soi on the right as you walk towards the centre of town from Pirom's House, does decent Thai-Chinese dishes and has cold beer.

Next to the Thong Tarin Hotel is the **Big Bite**, an air-con restaurant with a huge menu featuring Thai, European and Japanese dishes at reasonable prices; the sushi is surprisingly good.

Nearby, the **Old West Country Pub** has a good selection of Thai food and draught beer, plus live music in the evenings.

Getting There & Away

Bus Ordinary buses to Surin leave from Bangkok's Northern bus terminal (127B to 131B, 7.30, 9.15 and 9.45 pm). Second-class air-con buses cost 183B and leave 15 times a day between 7 am and 11 pm, while 1st-class air-con buses depart at 11 am and 9.40, 10 and 10.45 pm (229B).

During the Elephant Roundup there are many special air-con buses to Surin organised by major hotels and tour companies.

Surin lies about halfway between Ubon Ratchathani and Khorat; buses from either direction take around four hours and cost 52B ordinary, 96B air-con.

Train Most people travel to Surin by rapid train No 135, which leaves Bangkok at 6.50 am, arriving in Surin at 3.07 pm. The 2nd-class fare is 209B, including the rapid surcharge. Book your seats at least two weeks in advance for travel during November. If you prefer night train travel, the rapid No 141 leaves Bangkok at 10.45 pm and arrives in Surin at 7.48 am.

Ordinary 3rd-class trains take around nine hours from Bangkok, cost 73B and leave daily at 11.45 am and 3.25 and 11.25 pm. Surin can also be reached by train from any other station along the Ubon line, including Buriram, Si Saket and Ubon Ratchathani.

Getting Around

Săamláw around central Surin cost about 20B per kilometre.

SI SAKET
อ.เมืองศรีสะเกษ

postcode 33000 • pop 35,700

Si Saket's provincial capital has gained in size and wealth on Surin's; however, with nothing like Surin's Elephant Roundup, the town has less of a tourist infrastructure – a boon for visitors in search of laid-back, authentic Isan ways. Also, Si Saket Province has more Khmer ruins of significance within its borders than Surin Province.

When Khao Phra Wihan (a major Angkor site just over the provincial border in Cambodia) first opened the town's fortunes began to change as it became the gateway for visitors to the ruins.

Khao Phra Wihan
เขาพระวิหาร

For many years both Thailand and Cambodia claimed the territory on which this great temple complex is found. In 1963 the World Court finally awarded it to Cambodia. Privately many Thais still seethe at the concession, pointing out that Khao Phra Wihan sits in an upland valley attached to Thailand's Khorat Plateau and has little geographic connection with the Cambodian interior. Apparently the World Court was influenced by the argument that the Angkor-period complex represented Cambodian patrimony, in spite of the fact that there are over 2000 Khmer archaeological sites within Thailand's borders. Perhaps the court thought Thailand had enough Khmer ruins.

Lying just across the Cambodian border opposite Si Saket Province's Kantharalak district, the impressive Khao Phra Wihan (other common spellings include Kao Prea Vihar and Khao Phra Viharn) are virtually inaccessible from the Cambodian side and until a Khmer Rouge cease-fire was reached in Cambodia they were also off-limits from the Thai side. After a year of negotiations between the Cambodian and Thai governments, the ruins finally opened to the public in 1991, then closed down again during the 1993–97 Phnom Penh offensive against the Khmer Rouge. In August 1998, following the death of Pol Pot and the banishment of the Khmer Rouge from its nearby Anglong Veng base, the ruins once again opened to the public.

Khao Phra Wihan was built over two centuries under a succession of Khmer kings, beginning with Rajendravarman II in the mid-10th century and ending with Suryavarman II in the early 12th century – it was the latter who also commanded the construction of Angkor Wat. The hill itself was sacred to Khmer Hindus for at least 500 years before the completion of the temple complex, however, and there were smaller brick monuments on the site prior to the reign of Rajendravarman II.

One of the most impressive of all Angkor-period archaeological sites, Phra Wihan sits atop a 600m cliff at the edge of the Dangrek (Dong Rek) escarpment, commanding a dramatic view of the Cambodian plains to the east. Built originally as a Hindu temple in the classic Baphuon and early Angkor Wat styles, the complex extends a linear 850m, encompassing four gopura, and a large prasat or sanctuary surrounded by a courtyard and galleries. A stepped naga approach ascends approximately 120m from the foot of the hill to the sanctuary.

The temple complex is semi-restored – the general condition is somewhere between that of Prasat Phanomwan in Khorat and Phanom Rung in Buriram. During Khmer Rouge occupation it suffered a heavy loss of artefacts – lintels and other carvings in particular – although some of this smuggled art has been intercepted and will eventually be returned to the site. One naga balustrade of around 30m is still intact; the first two gopura have all but fallen down and many of the buildings are roofless, but abundant examples of stone carving are intact and visible. The doorways to the third gopura have been nicely preserved and one (the inner door facing south) is surmounted by a well-executed carved stone lintel depicting Shiva and his consort Uma sitting on Nandi (Shiva's bull), under the shade of a symmetrised tree. A Vishnu creation lintel is also visible on the second gopura; in contrast to the famous Phanom Rung lintel depicting the same subject, this one shows Vishnu climbing the churning stick rather than reclining on the ocean below.

The main prasat tower in the final court at the summit is in need of major restoration before the viewer can get a true idea of its former magnificence. Many of the stone carvings from the prasat are either missing or lie buried in nearby rubble. The galleries leading to the prasat have fared better and have even kept their arched roofs. Eventually the complex may undergo a total

KHAO PHRA WIHAN

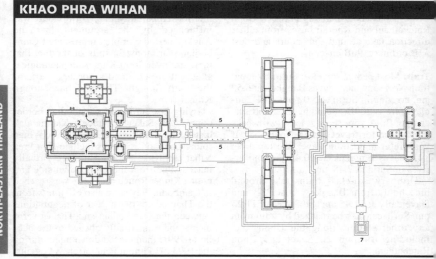

restoration but at the moment the money from entrance fees is supposedly going towards the improvement of the road to Phra Wihan from the Cambodian side (currently Cambodian officials must walk six to eight hours to reach the Thai border).

To enter the site you must first complete an entry form at the Thai army checkpoint and leave your passport or other picture ID as security. Admission fees for Thais are 5B for students, 50B for adults; for foreign visitors it's 200B.

From the Thai border, visitors must walk down and then up a rocky and sometimes steep slope. Visitors may tour only the immediate surroundings of the complex. There are still plenty of land mines and live ordnance in the fields and forests nearby; stick to the designated safety lanes leading to the ruins. The site closes at 4 pm. Avoid visiting on weekends, when the site is packed with hundreds of local Thai visitors.

Getting There & Away Rte 221 leads 95km south from Si Saket to Phum Saron – 11km short of the temple – via Kantharalak. Catch a săwngthăew from near the bus terminal adjacent to the main day market in Si Saket for 25B. If you miss the infrequent direct săwngthăew service, you may have to take a bus first to Kantharalak (24B) and pick up another săwngthăew to Phum Saron

(8B). Buses to Kantharalak leave every half-hour from around 6 am to 5 pm. From either Kantharalak or Phum Saron, you'll have to hire a motorcycle taxi to the border entrance to Khao Phra Wihan – figure on 200B return from Kantharalak or Phum Saron, with a couple of hours waiting time (100B one way). Motorcycle taxi drivers in Kantharalak seem to be much more reasonable than their grasping counterparts in Phum Saron, who are aware that visitors will be unwilling to backtrack to Kantharalak in search of a better deal. On weekends, when the temple complex is open, there are sometimes direct săwngthăew from Si Saket all the way to the border entrance for 25B.

Pha Maw I Daeng
ผามออีแดง

If border entry to Khao Phra Wihan is closed, you can still walk to the edge of this cliff, around 400m from the temple site on the Thai side. In addition to good views of the plains below and the Dangrek mountain range in the distance, you can also make out the Khao Phra Wihan ruins over a chasm on a hill opposite the cliff – binoculars will certainly enhance the view. In early 1994, we watched from the relative safety of this cliff as Phnom Penh troops bombarded a Khmer Rouge position on the plains below.

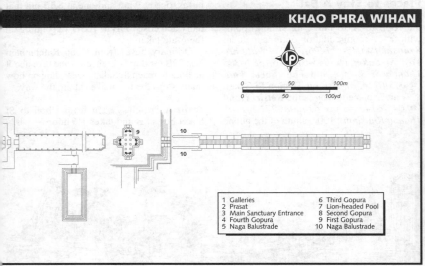

KHAO PHRA WIHAN

0   50   100m
0   50   100yd

1 Galleries	6	Third Gopura
2 Prasat	7	Lion-headed Pool
3 Main Sanctuary Entrance	8	Second Gopura
4 Fourth Gopura	9	First Gopura
5 Naga Balustrade	10	Naga Balustrade

NORTH-EASTERN THAILAND

A railed stairway cut into the edge of the cliff leads down to a well-sculpted relief executed directly onto the upper cliff face. The relief depicts three figures whose identities are an enigma to archaeologists and art historians. Although they give the general impression of representing deities, angels or kings, the iconography corresponds to no known figures in Thai, Mon or Khmer mythology. Stylistically the relief appears to date back to the Koh Ker (AD 921–45) period of Khmer art, when King Jayavarman IV ruled from his capital at Koh Ker.

For information on how to get here see the Khao Phra Wihan Getting There & Away section earlier.

Other Khmer Ruins

Forty kilometres west of Si Saket in Uthumphon Phisai district, **Prasat Hin Wat Sa Kamphaeng Yai** features a striking 10th-century sandstone prang with carved doorways. The ruined sanctuary can be found on the grounds of Wat Sa Kamphaeng Yai's modern successor.

About 8km west of town via Rte 226 is **Prasat Hin Wat Sa Kamphaeng Noi**, a hospital chapel.

Other minor Khmer sites in the province include **Prasat Prang Ku**, **Prasat Ban Prasat** and **Prasat Phu Fai**.

Places to Stay & Eat

Si Saket Most everything in Si Saket is in the 100B-to-220B range for simple rooms with fan. Accommodation options include: *Santisuk* (☎ 045-611496, 573 Soi Wat Phra To); *Si Saket* (☎ 045-611846, 384–385 Thanon Si Saket); and *Thai Soem Thai* (☎ 045-611458), also on Thanon Si Saket.

A nicer place to stay is the *Ketsiri Hotel* (☎ 045-614006, fax 614008, 1102–1105 Thanon Khukhan), 100m south of the phone office. It has stylish rooms that cost from 550B to 1600B, although discounts of up to 40% are readily available.

Phrom Phiman (☎ 045-612677, 849/1 Thanon Lak Meuang) has rooms with fan for 280B to 350B, and with air-con from 400B to 1300B. Security is lax here though – keep an eye on your belongings.

There are many *small restaurants* on the street in front of the train station. A *night market* convenes 200m east of the station, with good Isan and Thai food. The friendly *Chu Sin Than* is a vegetarian restaurant around the corner from the Thai Soem Thai Hotel, with good Thai vegie dishes for 15B to 20B.

Kantharalak This is the place to stay if you want to see Khao Phra Wihan early in the morning. The comfortable *Kantharalak Palace Hotel* (☎ 045-635157, 661084, 131 Thanon Sinpadit) is on the main street, with rates ranging from 200B to 550B for air-con rooms. The only eating options this town has are the usual *rice and noodle shops*.

Getting There & Away

Bus From Bangkok's Northern bus terminal there are two 1st-class air-con buses daily to Si Saket, one at 9.30 am and the other at 9 pm. The fare is 284B and the trip takes 8½ hours. There are also two 2nd-class air-con buses, one at 9 am and one at 8.15 pm that costs 217B. Ordinary buses leave five times daily and cost 159B to 165B, depending on the route taken.

Ordinary buses from Ubon Ratchathani cost 22B (38B to 50B air-con) and take about an hour to reach Si Saket, depending on how many stops the bus makes along the way.

Train A 3rd-class train from Ubon to Si Saket costs 8B and takes 1½ hours.

Andaman Coast

A heady mix of sandy beaches framed by soaring mountains of jagged limestone, Thailand's Andaman Coast offers some of South-East Asia's most striking scenery. Comprised of the provinces of Ranong, Phang-Nga, Phuket, Krabi, Trang and Satun, the Andaman Coast is bordered to the north by Myanmar and to the south by Malaysia. Culturally, it shares virtually all of the same characteristics as the neighbouring provinces of the Southern Gulf: an ethnic Chinese merchant class dominates the cities while Muslim Thais (many of whom are ethnic Malay) inhabit the rural areas.

For the visitor to Thailand's southern provinces and its famed beaches, the main concern is weather. The Andaman Coast gets more rain than the Southern Gulf provinces – with May through October being the months of heaviest rainfall. During this time passenger boats to some islands, such as the Surin and Similan groups, are suspended. On the other hand, the Southern Gulf provinces are comparatively dry until October, with rainfall heaviest in November. Of course the abundance of microclimates makes it difficult to generalise but, fortunately, the peninsula on which Southern Thailand sits is somewhat narrow. If you find the weather on the Andaman Coast not to your liking, you can always hop to provinces of the Southern Gulf without much effort.

Ranong Province

Thailand's least populous province is 80% forest and 67% mountains. Like much of Southern Thailand it undergoes two monsoons, but the mountains here tend to hold the rains over the area longer, so it gets the highest average annual rainfall in the country. Hence, it's incredibly green overall, with lots of waterfalls, although it's swampy near the coastline so there isn't much in the way of beaches. A reader who stopped over during the height of the rainy season decided that Ranong must be a corruption of the English 'Rained On'! Actually, it's pronounced 'ra-nawng'.

Highlights

- Ko Surin & Ko Similan – national marine parks with great coral colonies
- Phuket – Thailand's largest island with forested hills, great seafood and world class diving
- Krabi Province – some of Asia's hottest rock-climbing spots
- Than Bokkharani National Park – beautiful emerald-green waters flowing into waterfalls
- Hat Jao Mai National Park – opportunities to spot the endangered sea cow (dugong)
- Ko Phi-Phi – spectacularly scenic backdrop for the film *The Beach*
- Ao Phang-Nga – sea gypsy villages amidst impossibly vertical islands
- Ko Tarutao – prison ruins, wildlife and sea turtles
- Trang – ancient trading port and one of the cleanest cities in Thailand

The provincial economy is supported mainly by mineral extraction and fishing, along with rubber, coconut and cashew nut production. In Ranong they call cashews *ka-yuu* (in other Southern provinces the word is *ka-yii* and in the rest of Thailand it's *mét má-mûang*).

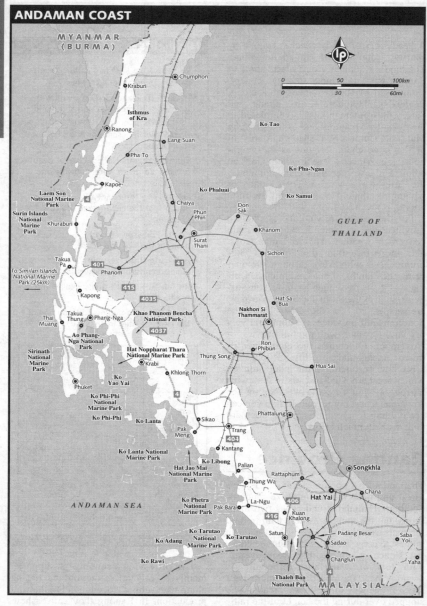

ANDAMAN COAST

MYANMAR
(BURMA)

Kraburi
Chumphon

Isthmus
of Kra

Ranong
Lang Suan

Ko Tao

Pha To

Kapoe

Ko Pha-Ngan

Laem Son
National Marine
Park
Chaiya
Ko Phaluai
Ko Samui

Surin Islands
National
Marine
Park
Khuraburi
Phun
Phin
Don
Sak

GULF OF
THAILAND

Khanom

Surat
Thani

Takua
Pa
401
Phanom
41
Sichon

To Similan Islands
National Marine
Park (25km)
Kapong
415

Hat Sa
Bua

4035

Takua
Thung
Phang-Nga
Khao Phanom Bencha
National Park
Nakhon Si
Thammarat

Thai
Muang
Ao Phang-
Nga National
Park
4037

Hat Nopparat Thara
National Marine Park
Ron
Phibun

Sirinath
National
Marine
Park
Krabi
Thung Song

Ko
Yao Yai
Khlong Thorn
Hua Sai

Phuket
4

Ko Phi-Phi
National
Marine Park

Ko Phi-Phi
Ko Lanta
Sikao
Phattalung

Pak
Meng
Trang
404

Ko Lanta National
Marine Park
Kantang

Hat Jao Mai
National Marine
Park
Ko Libong
Palian

Songkhla

ANDAMAN SEA
Rattaphum
Chana

Ko Phetra
National
Marine Park
Thung Wa

Pak Bara
La-Ngu
406
Hat Yai

416
Kuan
Khalong

Ko Tarutao
National
Marine Park
Ko Tarutao
Satun
Padang Besar
Saba
Yoi

Ko Adang
Sadao

Ko Rawi
Changlun
Yaha

Thaleh Ban
National Park
MALAYSIA

0   50   100km
0   30   60mi

RANONG

อ.เมืองระนอง

postcode 85000 • pop 18,500

The small capital and port of Ranong is only separated from Myanmar by Pak Chan, the estuary of Mae Nam Chan (Chan River). Burmese residents from nearby Kawthoung (Ko Song) hop across to trade in Thailand or to work on fishing boats. Although there is nothing of great cultural interest in the town, the buildings are architecturally interesting, since this area was originally settled by Hokkien Chinese. Tourists, mostly of Asian origin, are beginning to use Ranong as a gateway to Kawthoung and Thahtay Island, and there are rumours that an international dive tour operator will soon open shop in Ranong, in anticipation of leading dive trips to various islands and reefs off the southern tip of Myanmar.

Information

Ranong is about 600km south of Bangkok and 300km north of Phuket. Most of Ranong's banks are on Thanon Tha Meuang (Tha Meuang Rd, the road to the fishing pier), near the intersection with Thanon Ruangrat.

The main post office is on Thanon Dap Khadi, while the Communications Authority of Thailand (CAT) telephone office is off Thanon Phoem Phon in the south of town.

Chaon Thong Food & Drinks, at 8–10 Thanon Ruangrat, dispenses good travel information. The proprietor, Khun Thongsook, is quite knowledgeable and speaks English.

The proprietors of JT Food & Ice, also on Thanon Ruangrat, opposite the old post office, are also flush with information about accommodation possibilities on Ko Chang and Ko Phayam.

Email & Internet Access Kay-Kai (☎ 077-812967), a restaurant near the cinema on Thanon Ruangrat, has Ranong's fastest computers.

Nai Khai Ranong

ในค่ายระนอง

During the reign of King Rama V, a Hokkien named Koh Su Chiang became governor of Ranong (thus gaining the new name Phraya Damrong Na Ranong) and his former residence, Nai Khai Ranong, has become a combination clan house and shrine. It's on the northern edge of town and is worth a visit while you're in Ranong.

Of the three original buildings, one still stands and is filled with mementoes of the Koh family glory days. The main gate and part of the original wall also remain.

Koh Su Chiang's great-grandson Koh Sim Kong is the caretaker and he speaks some English. Several shophouses on Thanon Ruangrat preserve the old Hokkien style too. Koh Su Chiang's mausoleum is set into the side of a hill a few hundred metres farther north on the road to Hat Chandamri.

Places to Stay

As elsewhere in Thailand, at the cheaper hotels 'single' means a room with one large bed (big enough for two) while 'double' means a room with two beds.

Asia Hotel (☎ 077-811113, 39/9 Thanon Ruangrat), near the market, has spacious, clean rooms with fan and bathroom for 240B to 300B and air-con rooms for 620B. Information on local islands is posted in the lobby.

Across from the market is the not-very-friendly *Sin Ranong Hotel* (☎ 077-811454, 24/24 Thanon Ruangrat) with adequate rooms with fan for 180/200B single/double and air-con for 330/400B. North a bit, the *Sin Tavee Hotel* (Thawi; ☎ 077-811213, 81/1 Thanon Ruangrat) offers somewhat inferior fan rooms for 160/240B, plus air-con rooms for 280B.

Farther up Thanon Ruangrat is the multi-storey *Rattanasin Hotel* (no sign, look for a green building) on the right. It's a typical Thai-Chinese place that looks a bit worse for wear. Rooms with fan and bathroom cost 100/170B.

A few kilometres south of the town centre on the highway to Kapoe is the *Eiffel Inn* (☎ 077-823271) – you can't miss it, there's a 15m Eiffel Tower model in the parking lot – offers fancy bungalows with TV, fridge, phone and hot-water shower for 660B, and 880B with breakfast included.

Back towards town, just south of the river and on the road to the hot springs, is *Jansom Thara Ranong Hotel* (☎ 077-822516, fax 823250, 2/10 Thanon

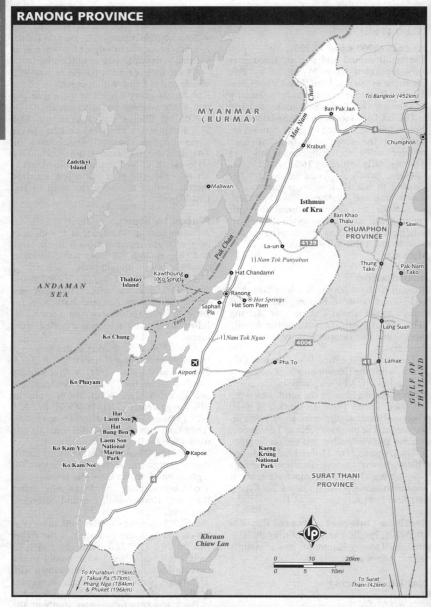

RANONG PROVINCE

MYANMAR (BURMA)

To Bangkok (452km)

Ban Pak Jan

Mae Nam Chan

Kraburi

4

Chumphon

Zadetkyi Island

Maliwan

Isthmus of Kra

Ban Khao Thalu

CHUMPHON PROVINCE

Sawi

Pak Chan

La-un

4139

)) Nam Tok Punyaban

Thung Tako

Pak Nam Tako

ANDAMAN SEA

Kawthoung (Ko Song)

Hat Chandamri

Thahtay Island

Ranong

Hot Springs

Hat Som Paen

Saphan Pla

Ferry

Lang Suan

Ko Chang

)) Nam Tok Ngao

4006

Pha To

41

Lamae

Airport

GULF OF THAILAND

Ko Phayam

Hat Laem Son

Hat Bang Ben

Laem Son National Marine Park

Ko Kam Yai

Kapoe

Kaeng Krung National Park

Ko Kam Noi

4

SURAT THANI PROVINCE

Kheuan Chiaw Lan

0   10   20km
0   5   10mi

To Khuraburi (15km), Takua Pa (57km), Phang Nga (184km) & Phuket (196km)

To Surat Thani (42km)

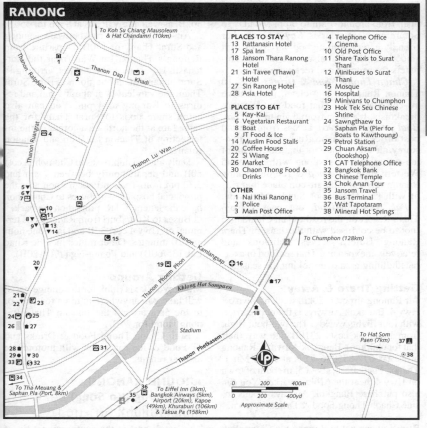

RANONG

To Koh Su Chiang Mausoleum & Hat Chandamri (10km)

PLACES TO STAY
13 Rattanasin Hotel
17 Spa Inn
18 Jansom Thara Ranong Hotel
21 Sin Tavee (Thawi) Hotel
27 Sin Ranong Hotel
28 Asia Hotel

PLACES TO EAT
5 Kay-Kai
6 Vegetarian Restaurant
8 Boat
9 JT Food & Ice
14 Muslim Food Stalls
20 Coffee House
22 Si Wiang
26 Market
30 Chaon Thong Food & Drinks

OTHER
1 Nai Khai Ranong
2 Police
3 Main Post Office
4 Telephone Office
7 Cinema
10 Old Post Office
11 Share Taxis to Surat Thani
12 Minibuses to Surat Thani
15 Mosque
16 Hospital
19 Minivans to Chumphon
23 Hok Tek Seu Chinese Shrine
24 Sawngthaew to Saphan Pla (Pier for Boats to Kawthoung)
25 Petrol Station
29 Chuan Aksam (bookshop)
31 CAT Telephone Office
32 Bangkok Bank
33 Chinese Temple
34 Chok Anan Tour
35 Jansom Travel
36 Bus Terminal
37 Wat Tapotaram
38 Mineral Hot Springs

Thanon Ratphant
Thanon Dap
Khadi
Thanon Ruangrat
Thanon Lu Wan
Thanon Kamlangsap
Thanon Phoem Phon
Khlong Hat Sompaen
Thanon Phoem Phon
Stadium
Thanon Phetkasem

To Chumphon (128km)

To Hat Som Paen (7km)

To Tha Meuang & Saphan Pla (Port, 8km)

To Eiffel Inn (3km), Bangkok Airways (5km), Airport (20km), Kapoe (49km), Khuraburi (106km) & Takua Pa (158km)

0   200   400m
0   200   400yd
Approximate Scale

Phetkasem), which has just about everything you could possibly want in a hotel. Standard rooms come with air-con and TV and there's in-house video, hot-water bathroom with spa (piped in from the hot springs), and a refrigerator stocked with booze. There are also two restaurants (one of which specialises in Chinese dim sum and noodles), two large mineral spas, fitness centre, disco, coffee shop/cocktail lounge, swimming pool and travel agency. Rates range from 600B for a standard room to 2313B for a suite, breakfast included. Near the Jansom Thara Ranong Hotel on Hwy 4 (Thanon Phetkasem), the *Spa Inn* (☎ 077-811715) charges 220B for rooms with fan, 430B to 550B for air-con rooms.

Places to Eat

For inexpensive Thai and Burmese breakfasts, try the *market* on Thanon Ruangrat. Also along Thanon Ruangrat are several traditional *Hokkien coffee shops* with marble-topped tables and enamelled metal teapots. A typical example of the genre is the *Si Wiang* next to the Sin Tavee Hotel. Between the Rattanasin and Sin Tavee Hotels (same side of Thanon Ruangrat as the Rattanasin) are three modest *Muslim food stalls* where you can get Malaysian-style curry, rice, roti, pickled cucumbers and tea for 30B. Around here also is the friendly *Coffee House*, a tiny place that serves Western-style breakfasts and light meals.

Just north of the cinema on Thanon Ruangrat is a *vegetarian restaurant* serving very inexpensive Thai vegie dishes; it's open from around 7 am to 6 pm Monday to Saturday. Next door is *Kay-Kai*, another friendly eatery with a good variety of fruit smoothies. Kay-Kai also has a row of computers for sending and receiving email.

Chaon Thong Food & Drinks, at 8–10 Thanon Ruangrat, is a clean, inexpensive air-con place with Thai food and Western breakfasts. It's open from 6 am to 9.30 pm. *Boat* (☎ 077-823996), across from the old post office on Thanon Ruangrat, is a two-storey air-con restaurant that does a lot of ice-cream business, along with Thai and Western food. *JT Food & Ice* on Thanon Ruangrat is a similar air-con place that fills up with Thai families on Sunday afternoon.

Pak Nam Seafood, out past Jansom Thara Resort on the road to Hat Chandamri (not to be confused with the Jansom Thara Ranong Hotel), serves delicious and relatively inexpensive Thai seafood in a terraced dining area overlooking the seaside.

Getting There & Away
Air Ranong airport is 20km south of town off Hwy 4. Bangkok Airways is the only carrier, with four flights weekly. The two-hour flight from Bangkok costs 2310B one way (half that for children). Bangkok Airways' Ranong office (☎ 077-835096–7) is at 50/18 Mu 1, Thanon Phetkasem, about 5km south of town on Hwy 4, near the 616km marker. You can also purchase Bangkok Airways tickets inside Chaon Thong Food & Drinks in town.

Bus You can get to Ranong via Chumphon (40/60B ordinary/air-con), Surat Thani (80/120B), Takua Pa (54/80B) and Phuket (91/170B). The bus terminal is on Hwy 4 about 800m south of the Jansom Thara Hotel, but buses stop in town on Thanon Ruangrat (passengers flag them anywhere on Thanon Ruangrat) before proceeding on to the terminal. *Săwngthăew* No 2 (small passenger trucks, also written songthaew) passes the terminal.

To/from Bangkok, ordinary buses cost 160B, 2nd class air-con 230B, 1st class air-con 302B and VIP 470B. Air-con buses don't depart that frequently, usually once in the morning and three or four times in the afternoon/evening. From Ranong, Chok Anan Tour (☎ 077-811337) on Thanon Phoem Phon, operates 1st-class air-con

buses to Bangkok at 8 am and 8 pm daily for 302B, as well as a VIP bus at 8 pm for 350B.

Air-con minivans run between Ranong and Surat Thani for 130B. Departure from Ranong's Thanon Lu Wan (near the Rattanasin Hotel) is at about 8 am, arriving in Surat Thani at about noon. From Surat Thani the van leaves at about 1 pm and returns to Ranong at 4 pm. You can also catch share taxis to Surat Thani for the same fare at the north-east corner of the intersection of Thanon Lu Wan and Thanon Ruangrat.

Daily air-con minibuses to Chumphon cost 80B and depart hourly between 7 am and 5.30 pm from Thanon Phoem Phon near the provincial hospital. Minibuses to Chumphon have the letters 'CTR' printed on the back.

Buses to Khuraburi from Ranong bus terminal on Hwy 4 cost 37B and take one hour and 20 minutes. Other routes include Khao Lak (35/60B) and Phang-Nga (70/120B).

Getting Around
Motorcycle taxis (look for the orange vests) will take you anywhere in town for 15B, or to the area around the Jansom Thara Ranong Hotel for 20B.

Both Chaon Thong Food & Drinks and JT Food & Ice can assist with motorcycle and car rentals.

AROUND RANONG
Kawthoung (Ko Song)
วิคตอเรียพอยท์ (เกาะสอง)

This small port at the southernmost tip of mainland Myanmar is separated from Thailand by Pak San, the broad estuary of Mae Nam Chan. To the British it was Victoria Point and to the Thais it's Ko Song, which means Second Island. Kawthoung, the Burmese name, is probably a corruption of the latter.

The main business here is trade with Thailand, followed by fishing. Among the Burmese, Kawthoung is perhaps best known for producing some of the country's best kickboxers. Most residents are bilingual, speaking Thai and Burmese. Many people born and raised around Kawthoung, especially Muslims, also speak Pashu, a dialect that mixes Thai, Malay and Burmese. Nearby islands are inhabited by bands of nomadic Moken, or sea gypsies.

At the moment Kawthoung is only accessible to foreigners by boat from Ranong, Thailand. It's probably not worth making a special trip to Ranong just to visit Kawthoung, but if you're in the area and decide to cross over, you'll find it's similar to Southern Thailand except that many more men wear the *longyi* (the Burmese sarong). It is now legal to travel from Kawthoung into the interior of Myanmar – eg, Dawei (Tavoy) or Yangon – by plane or by ship. Road travel north of Kawthoung, however, is forbidden by the Myanmar government due to security concerns – this is an area plagued by Mon insurgency.

Boats to Kawthoung leave Saphan Pla (Pla Bridge) in Ranong regularly from around 7 am until 6 pm for 50B per person. Take sǎwngthǎew No 2 from Ranong and when the vehicle stops to pay a toll at the entrance to the pier area, get off and walk down a *soi* (lane) to the right (you'll see a petrol station on your left). At the end of the soi are boats to Kawthoung. If you wish, you can charter a boat holding six to seven people for 500B round trip.

Once the boat is under way, there's an initial stop at Thai immigration, where your passport is stamped. Then upon arrival at the Kawthoung jetty, before leaving the boat, there's a stop at Myanmar immigration. At this point you must inform immigration authorities whether you're a day visitor – in which case you must pay a fee of US$5 or 300B for a day permit. If you have a valid Myanmar visa in your passport, you'll be permitted to stay up to 28 days, but are required to buy US$200 worth of foreign exchange certificates (FECs).

Yangon Airways sometimes flies an ATR-72 to Yangon for US$145. Its Kawthoung office is located at 1/1 Bogyoke Lan. By ship it's two nights (one night each is spent in Dawei and Myeik) – 36 hours total.

Organised Tours Jansom Travel (☎ 077-821576) on Thanon Phetkasem in Ranong offers Kawthoung and island tours aboard four boats, with capacities ranging from 15 to 200 people. A half-day tour costing 750B per person (minimum of 10) sails from Ranong, visits a couple of pagodas in Kawthoung and returns to Ranong around 11 am.

Places to Stay So far there are only two places in Kawthoung approved to accept foreigners. Closest to the pier is the modern and friendly *Honey Bear Hotel*, which offers 24-hour power and 39 clean air-con rooms with satellite TV and cold-water shower for 700B; not a great deal by Thai standards but it's a comfortable hotel. The other option is the mouldy *Kawthoung Motel* (Victoria Point Motel), about 300m beyond the main immigration office and about 500m from the pier. For simple double rooms with private cold-water shower, foreigners pay US$25 or 1000B, breakfast included.

On nearby Thahtay Island (Thahtay Kyun in Burmese, literally 'Rich Man's Island', also spelt Thahte or Thade), well-heeled Thai and Singaporean gamblers shack up at the *Andaman Club* (in Ranong ☎ 077-830463; in Bangkok ☎ 02-679 8389), a huge five-star hotel complex sporting a casino and a Jack Nicklaus-designed 18-hole golf course. All rooms come with sea views and start at 2880B, but promotional rates as low as 1700B are sometimes available. Guests with reservations are able to take a 250B boat direct from Jansom Thara Resort on Hat Chandamri, about 10km north-west of Ranong. If you're already in Kawthoung, you can catch a five-minute boat ride out to the island from the Kawthoung jetty for 100B.

Ko Chang
เกาะช้าง

Don't confuse this island with the larger Ko Chang in Trat Province. As with many of the islands in this area, estuarial effluent from Mae Nam Chan inhibits clarity in the Andaman waters surrounding Ko Chang, but natural mangroves on the east coast and a hilly, forested interior are attractions enough for some. Bird life includes hornbills, sea eagles and Andaman kites.

Two trails meander around the island and so far there is no electricity – the resorts on the island either do without or generate their own. Beaches are found along the western shore, but are not white-sand strands; however, regular visitors enjoy the laid-back atmosphere.

Bungalow operations on the island can arrange boat trips to Ko Phayam and other nearby islands for around 150B per person (including lunch) in a group of six or more.

Places to Stay & Eat Several beach places have opened up over the last few years, although for the most part they're only open from November to April. *Ko Chang Contex (Ranong ☎ 077-833137)* is run by a Thai family with huts for 100B to 200B a night, along with an a la carte restaurant menu.

South and west, the *Eden Bistro Cafe* offers a few small bungalows with shared bathroom for 100B each, and one large bungalow with attached shower for 150B. Just down the beach from Eden, *Sunset Bungalow* offers nicely built bungalows in a shady, breezy spot for 100B to 250B each.

Cashew Resort (☎ 077-824741), the oldest and largest place on the island, charges 200B for wooden A-frame bungalows and 600B for larger bungalows. Cashew, Eden and Sunset will pick prospective guests up at JT Food & Ice in Ranong.

A few hundred metres past the pier for boats from the mainland are the friendly *Chang Thong Bungalows (☎ 077-833820)* and *Pheung Thong*, side-by-side operations run by a brother and sister. Wooden or plasterboard huts here cost 100B, and 150B with attached bathroom; Chang Thong's *restaurant* serves decent Thai food. Chang Thong often picks visitors up at Chaon Thong Food & Drinks in Ranong. The nearby *Suphan Nee Paradise* is much the same.

Ko Chang Resort sits on a section of rocky headland and offers huts with shared bathroom for 100B, with attached bathroom for 150B. Sharing a small bay just beyond are newcomers *Lae Tawan* with wood-and-concrete bungalows, and *Ta Daeng Bay* with thatched huts, both for 100B to 200B.

At the southern end of the island at Ao Lek (Small Bay), *N & X Bungalows* offers thatched huts for 100B each.

Getting There & Away From Ranong take a săwngthăew (6B) to Saphan Pla, getting off by the petrol station towards the main pier. Look for signs advertising Ko Chang bungalows and follow them down a zigzag soi about 200m, where you'll find *reua hăang yao* (long-tail boats) that run to Ko Chang. If you have a heavy bag, a motorcycle taxi can bring you to this landing for 20B. Depending on the tides, two or three boats leave every morning from November to April; turn up around 9 am to see

when they're going, as they don't usually leave before this hour. During the high season – December to March – there's a consistent noon departure daily. Boats return to Ranong at 8 am the next day.

The cost is negotiable depending on how many passengers board; if you book a bungalow through Ranong Travel in town, you may get a free boat ride, along with a ride down to Saphan Pla. Otherwise count on paying up to 100B per person.

Phang-Nga Province

KHURABURI, TAKUA PA & THAI MUANG
คุระบุรี,ตะกั่วป่าและท้ายเหมือง

These districts of Phang-Nga Province are of minor interest in themselves but are departure points for other destinations. From Khuraburi you can reach the remote Surin and Similan Islands, or from Takua Pa you can head east to Khao Sok National Park and Surat Thani.

Takua Pa is also about halfway between Ranong and Phuket so buses often make rest stops here. Just off the highway is the *Extra Hotel (☎ 076-421412)* with fan rooms from 255B if you want to stop for the night.

In the district of Thai Muang is **Hat Thai Muang National Park**, where sea turtles come to lay eggs between November and February. **Thap Lamu**, about 23km north of Thai Muang, has a pier with boats to the Similan Islands.

The Tourism Authority of Thailand (TAT) has put out a revised, fairly accurate map of Phang-Nga Province and also has glossy pamphlets listing sights, accommodation and restaurants. However, you'll probably need to go to the office in Phuket to get this information, although the head office in Bangkok may have some.

HAT BANG SAK & HAT KHAO LAK
หาดบางสัก/หาดเขาหลัก

About 14km south of Takua Pa lies little-known Hat Bang Sak, a long sandy beach backed by casuarina trees. It's mainly a destination for locals out for a picnic or drinks and seafood at one of the little open-air places that line the shore. The gently curving beach offers good views of the coast to the south. The areas inland are cluttered with shrimp farms and are none too inviting. Still, if you have time on your hands, it might be fun to do like the locals and come for a meal or a drink at sunset.

About 154km south, the more touristy beach at Khao Lak is a pretty stretch of sand studded with granite boulders. An offshore coral reef suitable for snorkelling is 45 minutes away by boat, and some bungalow resorts offer dive excursions to this reef or to the Similan and Surin Islands.

The area to the immediate south of Hat Khao Lak is encompassed by the 125-sq-km **Khao Lak/Lam Ru National Park**, a beautiful collection of sea cliffs, 1000m-high hills, beaches, estuaries and mangroves. Wildlife seen in the area includes hornbills, drongos, tapirs, gibbons, monkeys and Asiatic black bears. The visitors centre, just off Hwy 4 between the 56km and 57km markers, has little in the way of maps or printed information, but there's a very nice open-air restaurant perched on a shady slope overlooking the sea. Entrance to the park for foreigners is 200B per adult, 100B for children aged 14 and under, or 20B for Thais.

Activities
Park ranger-guided treks along the coast or inland can be arranged, as well as long-tail boat trips up the scenic Khlong Thap Liang estuary. The latter affords an opportunity to view mangrove communities of crab-eating macaques.

Live coral formations can be found just off Hat Khao Lak and along the western tip of the bay. Sea Dragon Dive Service (☎/fax 01-229 2418), on Hwy 4 opposite Nang Thong Bay Resort, is the main diving operation in the area. In addition to selling and renting diving/snorkelling equipment, it offers PADI-certified scuba instruction and dive trips to the Similan Islands. Sea Dragon's four-day, four-night Similan and Surin excursion costs 15,000B for divers, including 11 dives, food, transport, accommodation and all equipment, or 7000B for nondivers. These are among the lowest rates available for dive excursions to the

Similans since most companies work out of Phuket. Local dive trips to nearby coral reefs cost 1200B per day including equipment and two tanks.

Between Khao Lak and Bang Sak is a network of sandy beach trails – some of which lead to deserted beaches – that are fun to explore on foot or by rented motorcycle.

Places to Stay & Eat
Hat Khao Lak Although Hat Khao Lak has moved steadily upmarket, there are still a couple of economical options to choose from. These cheaper places tend to shut down during the rainy season.

At the north end of Hat Khao Lak, the *Garden Beach Resort (☎ 076-420121)* has clean, small huts with bathroom and fan for 300B to 400B depending on proximity to the beach, or air-con for 1000B to 1200B. It has a relaxed atmosphere and the restaurant is good. This place also rents motorcycles (200B per day) and Suzuki jeeps (900B).

Towards the centre of Hat Khao is the well landscaped *Nang Thong Bay Resort (☎ 076-420084)*. This place is similar in style to the Garden Beach resort, with smaller bungalows (bathroom attached) away from the beach for 300B, and 600B for those closest to the beach. Motorcycles and jeeps are also available for rent here. Towards the southern end of the beach, *Nang Thong Bay II Bungalows (☎ 076-420078)* has larger and more attractive cottages with bathroom and fan for 500B.

Towards the southern end of the beach, the *Khao Lak Laguna Resort (☎ 076-420200)* features Thai-style cottages with all the amenities from 3200B. It's very popular, and commands a nice section of beach. During the low season prices drop by about half.

About 1km farther south along Hwy 4, *Khao Lak Sunset Resort (☎ 076-420075)* has upmarket air-con hotel rooms stacked against a cliff with balcony and sea views for 1800B to 2000B.

Nearby is the *Khao Lak Palm Beach Resort (☎ 076-420095)*, an upmarket place with multiroom bungalows boasting all the amenities. Prices start at 4500B. Similar but a bit cheaper is *Bay Front Resort (☎ 076-420111)* which has duplex-style bungalows for 2500B to 3000B, depending on proximity to the beach. Both places cut their rates by about half during the low season.

A cluster of simple thatched-roof *beach restaurants* towards the centre of the beach (just north of Nang Thong Bay Resort) offer reasonably priced Thai dishes and tasty seafood, as well as a fine view of the sea and sunset.

National Park Environs Khao Lak/Lam Ru National Park has four simple *bungalows* for 200B per night at its headquarters, 2km south of Hat Khao Lak. The restaurant nearby, in addition to its wonderful setting, has good food for pretty reasonable prices.

Getting There & Away

Any bus coming down Hwy 4 between Thai Muang and Takua Pa will stop at Hat Bang Sak or Hat Khao Lak if asked (for the latter, look for the Sea Dragon Dive Service on the eastern side of the highway). If you miss Khao Lak heading south, get off at the Thap Lamu highway junction and catch a motorcycle taxi for 40B.

SURIN ISLANDS NATIONAL MARINE PARK
อุทยานแห่งชาติหมู่เกาะสุรินทร์

A national park since 1981, the Surin Islands (Mu Ko Surin) are famous for excellent diving and snorkelling. The two main islands (there are five in all), Ko Surin Neua and Ko Surin Tai (North Surin Island and South Surin Island), lie about 70km north-west of Khuraburi and less than 5km from Thailand's marine border with Myanmar. The park office and visitors centre are on the south-western side of the north island at Ao Mae Yai, where boats anchor. Standard admission fees apply (20B for Thais, 200B for foreigners, half that for children 14 and under). Some of the best diving can be found in the channel between the two islands.

On the southern island is a village of *chao náam* (sea gypsies, also called *chao leh*). In April the chao náam hold a major ancestral worship ceremony, called Loi Reua, on Ko Surin Tai. The island may be off-limits during that time, so be sure to check first at the park office. Long-tail boats can be hired at Ao Mae Yai to ferry you to the south island for around 200B per person for the day.

Compared with the Similan Islands to the south, the Surin Islands is more suited to visitors who are interested in hiking and exploring rather than diving. There are several hiking trails, especially on the northern island. Also, getting to some of the best reefs doesn't require scuba gear, another plus for nondivers. Snorkelling gear can be rented at the park office for 150B per day.

Most visitors to the islands are Thai tourists, who tend to arrive in large numbers on national holidays. There also seems to be a fairly steady flow of tour groups, again mostly Thai, visiting from December to March, although most only stay a night or two. The main advantage of going at this time, especially if you're not a diver, is that you can probably catch a ride on one of the tour boats for 1000B return: at other times the only way out to the islands is by chartering your own boat (which is costly) or joining a diving trip. The disadvantage of course is that accommodation can easily get booked up.

Surrounding the Surin Islands are the most well developed coral colonies in Thai seas, according to Piprell & Boyd's *Diving in Thailand,* although the Similan Islands boast a richer variety of fish species. There are seven major dive sites in the immediate vicinity of the Surin Islands, of which the best are found at the south-eastern point of Surin Neua at **HQ Bay**; at **Ko Chi**, a small island off the north-eastern shore of Surin Neua; and at **Richelieu Rock**, a seamount about 14km south-east of Surin Tai. Whale sharks – the largest fish in the world – are reportedly spotted near Richelieu on 50% of dive trips, most commonly during the months of March and April. Snorkelling is excellent in many areas due to relatively shallow reef depths of 5m to 6m.

The little-explored **Burma Banks**, a system of submerged seamounts about 60km north-west of the Surin Islands, are so prized by Thai dive operations that they keep the GPS coordinates virtually secret. Actually the only way to visit the Burma Banks – unless you have your own boat – is by way of seven- to 10-day live-aboard dive trips out of Phuket. The three major banks, Silvertip, Roe and Rainbow, provide four- to five-star diving experiences, with fields of psychedelic coral laid over flat, underwater plateaus and loads of large oceanic as well as smaller reef marine species. Sharks – reef, silvertip, nurse, leopard and at least a half dozen other species – abound.

Many of the dive operators in Phuket have live-aboard diving excursions to the Surin Islands. Because of the distances involved, Surin is the most expensive dive destination in Thailand; rates start at around 9000B to 10,000B for a minimum two-night, three-day trip.

Ko Surin National Marine Park closes in early to mid-May every year and doesn't re-open until mid-November. The exact dates appear to vary from year to year, perhaps influenced by perceived weather patterns.

Places to Stay & Eat

Accommodation at the *park longhouses* is 100B per person or you can rent six- and eight-person bungalows for 1200B. At the camp site, two-person tents cost 300B a night or you can use your own (or camp without a tent) for 20B per night per person. The park also offers a daily package of three good meals (mostly seafood) for 350B, or you can order meals separately. Electric power is generated from 6 to 11 pm. It's strongly recommended that you make bookings in advance by calling the park's mainland office (☎ 076-491378).

Should you get stuck in Khuraburi, the *Nangnuan*, opposite the provincial offices, has adequate rooms for 250B. A couple of kilometres south of town is *Tararain River Hut Resort* with three-person bungalows for 300B to 500B.

At the park office in Ngan Yong is a good *outdoor restaurant* serving Thai seafood from 7 am to 8 pm daily.

Getting There & Away

The mainland office of Ko Surin National Park is in the messy fishing village of Ngan Yong, from where boats to the islands depart. The road to Ngan Yong turns off Hwy 4 at the 720km marker, 6km north of Khuraburi and 109km south of Ranong. The park office, which is also where the pier is located, is about 2km down the road on the right-hand side: from Hwy 4 a motorcycle taxi will take you there for 10B.

Buses between Khuraburi and Ranong cost 37B and take about an hour and 20 minutes; ask to be let off at Ngan Yong (saying 'Ko Surin' should also work). To/from Phuket, buses cost 55B and take about three hours. From Khuraburi to Ngan Yong costs 50B by motorcycle taxi.

The cheapest way to the island is to latch on to one of the tour-group boats heading there. To do this you'll need to call the Surin mainland office (☎ 076-491378) to find out when boats are making the trip. If so, park staff will try to book you seats: the price is usually 1000B per person return. Tour boats run from December to April, and the busiest time is between February and April.

You can charter a boat out to the Surin Islands from Ngan Yong through the park officers, who will serve as brokers/interpreters. A boat for up to 30 people can be chartered for 6000B return – it takes four to five hours each way. Ordinarily, boat travel is only considered safe between December and early May, between the two monsoons. The park is closed from mid-May to mid-November.

SIMILAN ISLANDS NATIONAL MARINE PARK
อุทยานแห่งชาติหมู่เกาะสิมิลัน

The Similan Islands (Mu Ko Similan) are world-renowned among diving enthusiasts for incredible underwater sightseeing at depths ranging from 2m to 30m. Beside attractive sand beaches, huge, smooth granite rock formations plunge into the sea and form seamounts, rock reefs and dive-throughs. As elsewhere in the Andaman Sea, the best diving months are December to May when the weather is good and the sea is at its clearest (and boat trips are much safer).

The Thais sometimes refer to the Similan Islands as Ko Kao, or Nine Islands, because there are nine of them – each has a number as well as a name. In fact, the word 'Similan' comes from the Malay word *'sembilan'* for nine. Counting in order from the north, they are Ko Bon, Ko Ba-Ngu, Ko Similan, Ko Payu, Ko Miang (which is actually two islands close together), Ko Payan, Ko Payang and Ko Hu Yong. They're relatively small islands and uninhabited except for park officials and occasional tourist groups.

Princess Chulabhorn, the present Thai monarch's youngest daughter, has a cottage on Ko Miang, a royal association that adds an extra layer of protection to the islands' national park status. The Thai navy operates a sea turtle preserve on Ko Ba-Ngu, another bonus for enforcement of park preservation.

Also on Ko Miang, which is second in size to Ko Similan, you'll find a visitors centre, the park headquarters and accommodation. Venturing inland from the beach, you should catch glimpses of the Nicobar pigeon or the hairy-legged mountain land crab. If you're not into aqualungs, the beaches on this island are good for snorkelling (as opposed to scuba diving), as is the channel between Ko Miang and Ko Payu. Ko Similan is also good for hiking and snorkelling. In a small bay on the Similan's western side you may be able to see spiny lobsters resting in rock crevices, along with sea fans and plume worms. The largest granite outcrop in the Similan Islands is also found on Ko Similan; scramble to the top to enjoy a sweeping view of the sea.

On the nine islands, there are 32 species of birds that can be seen including residents such as the Brahminy kite and the white-breasted waterhen. Migratory species of note include the pintail snipe, grey wagtail, cattle egret, watercock and the roseate tern. Fairly common mammal residents include the bush-tailed porcupine, common palm civet, flying lemur and bottlenose dolphin. Species of reptiles and amphibians found on the islands include the banded krait, reticulated python, white-lipped pit viper, common pit viper, hawksbill turtle, leather turtle, Bengal monitor lizard, common water monitor lizard and ornate froglet.

Admission to the Similan Islands National Marine Park is collected on Ko Miang (see the Facts about Thailand chapter for information on fees).

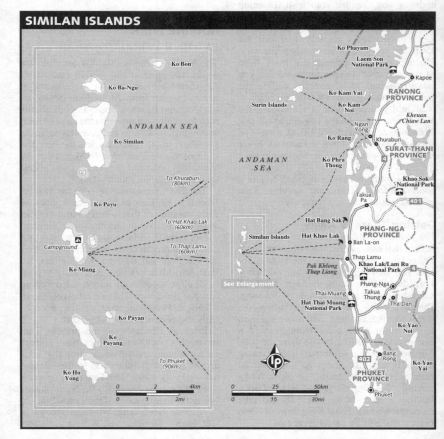

SIMILAN ISLANDS

Organised Tours

Hat Khao Lak Sea Dragon at Hat Khao Lak does four-day/four-night Similan and Surin Islands trips for 15,800B (7000B for nondivers). See the Activities entry in the Hat Khao Lak & Hat Bang Sak section earlier in this chapter for more details.

Phuket Overnight diving excursions leaving from Phuket are fairly reasonable in cost – about 5000B per day. These costs usually include food, accommodation, diving equipment and underwater guides. It may also be possible for nondivers to join these diving excursions for around half the cost – snorkellers are also welcome.

Package deals out of Phuket typically start at US$340 for a three-day/three-night dive trip, and go up to US$1225 for a seven-day/seven-night Similan and Burma Banks trip on Siam Diving Center's (☎ 076-330608) live-aboard MV *Sai Mai*. The latter sometimes offers longer, more exotic dive excursions such as a 10-day/10-night whale shark expedition.

Places to Stay & Eat

Accommodation, including camping, is only allowed on Ko Miang. The park has *bungalows* for 600B and four-bed rooms in a *longhouse* for 400B. If there are only one or two in your party, you may be able to get a per-person rate of 100B for the longhouse, but don't count on it. Tent rental costs 150B, and there's a 20B tent site fee if you bring your own. Bookings must be made in advance at the park's mainland office in Thap Lamu (☎ 076-411913–4).

The only source of food on Ko Miang is a privately run *restaurant*. Prices are ridiculously high (eg, 40B for a fried egg), and even then you need to let park staff know you're coming in advance if you want food to be there for you. Bringing your own food is strongly recommended, although occasional restrictions on open fires may force you to eat at the restaurant at least a few times.

Getting There & Away

The Similan Islands can be reached from the port at Thap Lamu (39km south of Takua Pa off Hwy 4, or 20km north of Thai Muang) and from Phuket.

From Thap Lamu the islands are 60km away, about three hours by boat. Met Sine Tours (☎ 076-443276) near the pier, is the place to go for boat bookings. At the time of research, boats ran daily, departing Thap Lamu at 11 am and heading back from Ko Miang at 3 pm the same day. The return (round trip) fare is 2000B. It would be best to call ahead just to check what's going on, as the situation seems rather fluid (there is at least one English speaker at Met Sine).

Boats run to the Similan Islands from November to May only; during the remainder of the year the seas are too rough. If the weather looks rough when you arrive give some thought to how badly you want to go: in recent years several boats operating out of Thap Lamu have foundered or become stranded, although no casualties have resulted.

AO PHANG-NGA & PHANG-NGA
อ่าวพังงา/อ.เมืองพังงา

postcode 82000 • pop 9300

Over 95km from Phuket, the area around Ao Phang-Nga is quite scenic – lots of limestone cliffs, odd rock formations, islands that rise out of the sea like inverted mountains, not to mention caves and quaint fishing villages. Phang-Nga would make a good motorcycle trip from Phuket, or, if you have time, you could spend a few days there.

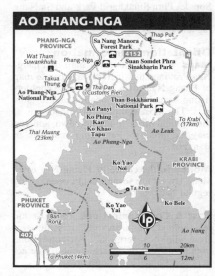

On the way north-east to Phang-Nga turn left off Hwy 4 at the 31km marker, just 5km past the small town of Takua Thung, to get to **Wat Tham Suwankhuha** (Heaven Grotto Temple), a cave shrine full of Buddha images. The shrine consists of two main caverns, a larger one containing a 15m reclining Buddha and tiled with *laikhraam* and *benjarong,* two coloured patterns more common in pottery, and a smaller cavern displaying spirit flags and a rishi *(reusǐi)* statue. Royal seals of several kings, including Rama V, Rama VII and Rama IX – as well as those of lesser royalty – have been inscribed on one wall of the latter cave.

Other caves in the province include **Tham Reusi Sawan** (Hermit Heaven; 3km south of Phang-Nga) and **Tham Phung Chang** (Elephant Belly Cave).

Phang-Nga Province's best beach areas are on the west coast facing the Andaman Sea. Between Thai Muang in the south and Takua Pa in the north are the beaches of Hat Thai Muang and Hat Bang Sak.

Phang-Nga is a small town wedged between verdant limestone cliffs, but there's little to see or do unless you happen to be there during the annual Vegetarian Festival in October (see the boxed text 'Vegetarian Festival' later in this chapter for information on this unusual festival). Nearby Suan Somdet Phra Sinakharin Park and Sa Nang Manora Forest Park are good places for hiking and picnicking.

Orientation & Information

Maps TAT distributes a map of Phang-Nga Province that includes a separate map of Phang-Nga town, as well as pamphlets listing sights, accommodation and restaurants. The most complete information is at the regional office in Phuket town, and you may be able to get some material in Bangkok.

Money In the centre of Phang-Nga town along Hwy 4 are several banks open during regular banking hours.

Post & Communications The post and telephone offices are about 2km south-west from the bus terminal. Air-con phone booths in front of the telephone office accept coins and Thai phonecards.

Bookshops The Books, at 265/1 Thanon Phetkasem, carries a small selection of English-language books and magazines.

Organised Tours

Boat Trips Between Takua Thung and Phang-Nga is the road to **Tha Dan** (Customs Pier), where you can find the Phang-Nga customs pier.

At an adjacent pier, boats can be hired (with driver) to tour Ao Phang-Nga National Park and visit a Muslim fishing village on stilts, half-submerged caves, strangely shaped islands (yes, including those filmed in *The Man with the Golden Gun*) and other local oddities.

While it's possible to charter a boat at the pier for a tour of the islands, unless you enjoy haggling with greedy boatmen, it's much easier to go with a local tour arranged through one of the two small agencies next to the bus terminal in Phang-Nga town. Sayan Tours (☎ 076-430348) has been doing overnight tours of Ao Phang-Nga for many years now, and these continue to receive good reviews from some travellers.

The overnight tour costs 450B per person and includes a boat tour of **Tham Lawt** (Tunnel Cave, a large water cave), **Ko Phing Kan** (Leaning Island, aka 'James Bond Island'), **Ko Khao Tapu** (Nail Mountain Island), **Khao Maju** (Poodle Mountain), **Tham Nak** (Dragon Cave), **Khao Khian** (Inscription Mountain; rock wall murals), a former mangrove charcoal factory and **Ko Panyi**, plus dinner, breakfast and very rustic accommodation in a Muslim fishing village on Ko Panyi.

Sayan also leads morning (rainy season) and afternoon (dry season) trips for 200B, as well as a full-day tour for 500B. Both include a seafood lunch and return in the afternoon. The overnight trip is recommended over either day trip; the latter tends to be a bit rushed. Sayan Tours can also arrange trips to nearby sites on land, including Sa Nang Manora Forest Park and the various caves near town.

The other tour agency at the bus terminal, Kean Tours, charges slightly cheaper rates for similar half-day, full-day and overnight tours. Kean Tours also operates a small office in the Ratanapong Hotel (☎ 076-411247).

These same tours are available out of Phuket, but cost at least 200B to 400B per person more. Whatever you do, try to avoid touring the bay in the middle of the day (from 10 am to 4 pm) when hundreds of package tourists crowd the islands.

Alternatively, you could do a canoe tour from Phuket. See under Paddling in the Phuket section.

See the Around Phang-Nga section for more extensive descriptions and information about Ao Phang-Nga National Park.

Places to Stay – Budget
Phang-Nga Phang-Nga has several small hotels. The *Thawisuk* (☎ *076-412100, 77–79 Thanon Phetkasem)* is right in the middle of town. It is a bright blue building with the English-language sign 'Hotel'. Simple but usually clean rooms upstairs go for 150/200B single/double with fan and bathroom, plus towel and soap on request. You can sit and have a beer on the roof of Thawisuk while watching the sun set over Phang-Nga's rooftops and the limestone cliffs surrounding the town.

The *Lak Meuang I* (☎ *076-412486, fax 411512)*, on Thanon Phetkasem just outside town towards Krabi, has rooms for 220B with fan and bathroom and 450B with air-con, plus an OK restaurant downstairs. On the same side of the street farther south-west is the *Ratanapong Hotel* (☎ *076-411247)*, which offers average single/twin/triple/quad rooms for 150/230/280/350B; air-con rooms are also available for 430B.

Farther down the road towards Phuket is the *Muang Thong* (☎ *076-412132, 128 Thanon Phetkasem)*, with grubby singles/doubles for 120/180B with fan, 250/320B with air-con.

Places to Stay – Mid-Range
On the outskirts of town in the direction of Phuket, is *Lak Meuang II* (☎ *076-411500, fax 411501, 540 Thanon Phetkasem)*, with all air-con single/double rooms from 450B to 672B. It's a convenient location for exploring the central area.

Sunimit Mansion (☎ *076-440400, ☎/fax 411130, 21/1 Thanon Sirirat)* is a 20-room four-storey hotel off the main drag in the centre of town with rates of 250B (fan), 350B (air-con), 400B (air-con, mid-sized refrigerator and TV) and 600B (same in a larger suite). Bread and coffee or Ovaltine are complimentary from 7 to 10 am.

Phang-Nga Bay Resort (☎ *076-412201, fax 411393, 5/5 Thanon Phetkasem)* is on the southern outskirts of town before you reach the highway to Krabi. Thirty-one rooms in large tile-roofed bungalows range from 450B to 560B.

Tha Dan On Rte 4144 towards Tha Dan, the faded *Phang-Nga Bay Resort Hotel* (☎ *076-412067–70)* costs 1300B in the low season and up to 3500B during holidays. Its facilities include a swimming pool and a decent restaurant. All 88 rooms come with TV, telephone and fridge. Hardly anyone ever seems to stay here except for the occasional surprised tour group.

Places to Eat
Duang Restaurant, next to Bangkok Bank on Thanon Phetkasem, has a bilingual menu and a good selection of Thai and Chinese dishes, including southern-Thai specialities. Prices have crept up a little higher than the standard of the food would indicate. *Suan Ahan Islam* (no Roman-script sign) on the left just north-east of Soi Langkai, serves simple Thai Muslim food, including *rotii kaeng* (flat bread and curry) in the morning. On the other side of Soi Langkai is a cafe called *Chai Thai* (no Roman-script sign) that's open early and specialises in *paa-thâwng-kŏh* (Chinese doughnuts).

South-west of the market, a little way past the bus terminal, the tidy *Bismilla* also does Thai Muslim food.

As the name suggests, *Phang-Nga Satay*, at 189 Thanon Phetkasem, specialises in Malay-style satay. The shrimp satay is highly recommended. It's open from early evening until late at night.

Several *food stalls* on the main street of Phang-Nga sell delicious *khànŏm jiin* (thin wheat noodles) with chicken curry, *náam yaa* (spicy ground-fish curry) or *náam phrík* (sweet and spicy peanut sauce). One vendor in front of the market (opposite Bangkok Bank) serves khànŏm jiin with an amazing 12 varieties of free vegetable accompaniments – but only from 1 to 8 pm Tuesday to Sunday; an adjacent *vendor* does *khâo mòk kài* (chicken biryani) from 6 am to noon.

Rotii kaeng is available in the *morning market* from around 5 to 10 am. There are also the usual Chinese *khâo man kài* (chicken and rice) places around town.

The *Lak Muang Hotel* has a decent and moderately priced open-air restaurant downstairs.

Getting There & Away
Buses for Phang-Nga leave from the Phuket bus terminal on Thanon Phang-Nga, near the Thanon Thepkasatri intersection, at 10.10 am, noon and 1.40, 3.30 and 4.30 pm. The trip to Phang-Nga takes 2½ hours and the one-way fare is 31B ordinary. Alternatively you can rent a motorcycle in Phuket. The Phang-Nga bus terminal is located just south of the market on Soi Bamrung Rat.

Buses to/from Krabi leave every half-hour, cost 36B and take 1½ hours; air-con buses leave hourly and cost 52B. To/from Surat Thani, ordinary buses cost 55B and take 3½ hours. Other air-con departures to/from destinations around Southern Thailand include Ranong (120B, two or three times per day), Hat Yai (196B, one per day), Trang (121B, 11 times) and Satun (198B, two per day).

There are 2nd-class air-con buses to/from Bangkok costing 326B which take a long 14 hours, while 1st-class air-con is 403B and VIP is 625B, taking 13 and 12 hours respectively.

Getting Around
Most of the town is easily accessible on foot. Sayan Tours at the bus terminal can assist with motorcycle rental. Săwngthăew between Phang-Nga and Tha Dan cost 15B.

AROUND PHANG-NGA
Suan Somdet Phra Sinakharin Park
สวนสมเด็จพระศรีนครินทร์

This public park has two entrances. The most dramatic entry is through a huge hole in a limestone cliff near Phang-Nga Bay Resort. A road goes through the cliff, so if you have a vehicle you can drive through it and into the park. The main entrance is towards the southern end of town, opposite the provincial transport department. Nearly the entire park is surrounded by limestone cliffs and bluffs, into which nature has carved a scenic network of caves and tunnels, some containing ponds. Wooden walkways link the water-filled caverns so that visitors can admire the ponds and

amazing limestone formations. One of the larger caves, **Tham Reusi Sawan**, is marked by a gilded statue of a *reusĭi* (Hindu sage) – complete with tiger skins and staff – outside the entrance. The other rather large cavern is known locally as **Tham Luk Seua** (Tiger Cub Cave). Entry is free.

Sa Nang Manora Forest Park
วนอุทยานสระนางมโนราห์

This recently established park (28.8 hectares) features lots of dense rainforest and a set of cool green cascades. The setting is truly impressive, with plenty of rattan vines, moss-encrusted roots and rocks and a many-levelled cascade with several pools suitable for swimming. The overall impression is similar to that of Krabi's Than Bokkharani National Park but it receives far fewer visitors, either Thai or foreign. As a result it's much cleaner, at least so far. Primitive trails follow the falls level after level and beyond – you could easily get a full day's hiking in without walking along the same path twice. Bring plenty of drinking water – although the shade and the falls moderate the temperature, the humidity in the park is quite high.

The park's name comes from a local folk belief that the mythical Princess Manora bathes in the pools of the park when no-one else is around. Facilities include some tables and chairs here and there, plus a small restaurant next to the car park. The park is north of town via Hwy 4 (turn-off 3.4km from the Shell station and the Lak Muang II Hotel, then 4.5km down a winding road through rubber plantations). Entry is free.

Ao Phang-Nga National Park
อุทยานแห่งชาติอ่าวพังงา

Established in 1981 and covering an area of 400 sq km, Ao Phang-Nga National Park is noted for its classic karst scenery, created by fault movement on the mainland that pushed massive limestone blocks into geometric patterns. As these blocks extend southward into Ao Phang-Nga, they form over 40 islands with huge vertical cliffs. The bay itself is composed of large and small tidal channels that originally connected with the mainland fluvial system. The main tidal channels – Khlong Ko

Phanyi, Khlong Phang-Nga, Khlong Bang Toi and Khlong Bo Saen – run through vast mangroves in a north-south direction and today are used by fisherfolk and island inhabitants as aquatic highways. These mangroves are the largest remaining primary mangrove forest in Thailand. Over 80% of the area within the park boundaries is covered by the Andaman Sea.

The biggest tourist spot in the park is so-called 'James Bond Island', known to the Thais as **Ko Phing Kan** (Leaning on Itself Island). Once used as a location setting for *The Man with the Golden Gun,* the island is now full of vendors hawking coral and shells that should have stayed in the sea, along with butterflies, scorpions and spiders encased in plastic – not exactly the stuff to inspire confidence in Thailand's national park system.

The Thai name for the island refers to a flat limestone cliff that appears to have tumbled sideways to lean on a similar rock face, which is in the centre of the island. Off one side of the island in a shallow bay stands a tall slender limestone formation that looks like a big rock spike that has fallen from the sky.

There are a couple of caves you can walk through on the island, and a couple of small sand beaches, often littered with rubbish from tourist boats. About the only positive development has been the addition of a concrete pier so that tourist boats don't have to moor directly on the island's beaches. Of course that hasn't stopped the boat operators from doing so when the water level is high and the pier is crowded with other boats.

Flora & Fauna Two types of forest predominate in the park; limestone scrub forest and true evergreen forest. The marine limestone environment favours a long list of reptiles, including the Bengal monitor, flying lizard, banded sea snake, dogface water snake, shore pit viper and Malayan pit viper. Keep an eye out for the two-banded (or water) monitor *(Varanus salvator),* which looks like a crocodile when seen swimming in the mangrove swamp and can measure up to 2.2m in length (only slightly smaller than the Komodo dragon, the largest lizard in the Varanidae family). Like its Komodo cousin, the water monitor (called *hîa* by the Thais, who generally fear or hate the lizard) is a carnivore that prefers to feed on carrion but occasionally preys on live animals.

Amphibians in the Ao Phang-Nga area include the marsh frog, common bush frog and crab-eating frog. Avian residents of note are the helmeted hornbill (the largest of Thailand's 12 hornbill species, with a body length of up to 127cm), the edible-nest swiftlet *(Aerodramus fuciphagus),* white-bellied sea eagle, osprey and Pacific reef egret.

In the mangrove forests and on some of the larger islands reside over 200 species of mammals, including the white-handed gibbon, serow, dusky langur and crab-eating macaque.

Rock Art Many of the limestone islands in Ao Phang-Nga feature prehistoric rock art painted or carved onto the walls and ceilings of caves, rock shelters, cliffs and rock massifs. In particular you can see rock art on Khao Khian, Ko Panyi, Ko Raya, Tham Nak, and Ko Phra At Thao. Khao Khian (Inscription Mountain) is probably the most visited of the sites. The images contain scenes of human figures, fish, crabs, shrimp, bats, birds and elephants, as well as boats and fishing equipment – it's obvious this was some sort of communal effort tied to the all-important harvesting of sustenance from the sea. Some drawings also contain rows of lines thought to be some sort of cabbalistic writing. The rock paintings don't fall on any one plane of reference, they may be placed right-side up, upside-down or sideways. Most of the paintings are monocoloured, while some have been repeatedly traced several times over in orange-yellow, blue, grey and black.

Places to Stay & Eat *National park bungalows* (☎ 076-412188) are available for rent next to the visitors centre parking lot. Small bungalows that sleep four persons go for 500B, while larger ones that sleep up to ten go for 900B. Camping is permitted in certain areas within park boundaries but you should ask permission at the visitors centre first. For foreigners, there's a 200B entry fee to the park (100B for children aged 14 and under). Thais pay 20B.

There's a small, clean restaurant in front of the visitors centre.

Getting There & Around To reach the park HQ and pier for Ao Phang-Nga trips, take a săwngthăew going from Phang-Nga to Tha Dan. Under your own steam, proceed 8km south-east of town on Hwy 4, then turn left onto Rte 4144; you'll reach park HQ after an additional 2km.

Boats can be hired to explore the bay from the *thâa reua nam thîaw* (tourist pier) opposite the visitors centre.

Ko Panyi & Muslim Stilt Villages
เกาะปันหยี

This small island towards the centre of Ao Phang-Nga is well known for its Muslim fishing village built almost entirely on stilts and nestled against a towering limestone cliff. The village appears very commercialised during the day when hordes of tourist boats invade to eat lunch at the village's many overpriced seafood restaurants and buy tacky souvenirs at the many stalls. Yet once the tourist boats depart, the village returns to its normal self.

The 200 households here – home to perhaps a total of 2000 people – are said to descend from two seafaring Muslim families that arrived here from Java around 200 years ago. Ko Panyi's primary livelihood remains fishing, since only during the dry season do a significant number of tourists visit the island. In addition to a big green mosque, a health clinic and a school, you'll find a market filled with small shops selling clothes, toiletries, medicines and all the other usual staples seen in markets all over Thailand – except for any type of alcoholic beverage. Besides alcohol, two other things forbidden on the island are dogs and pigs. Houses mixed in with the shops vary from grubby little shacks to homes with fancy tile fronts and curtained windows. The people are generally quite friendly, especially if you can speak a little Thai. Village men often gather to gossip and watch the sunset over the western side of the village near the mosque.

There's a pay phone at the island's northern pier.

If you fancy a look at similar but less well known Muslim stilt villages in Ao Phang-Nga, take a boat to one of these villages in the huge mangrove forests at the north end of the bay: **Ban Ling** (Monkey Village), **Ban Mai Phai** (Bamboo Village) or **Ban Sam Chong** (Three Channels Village).

Places to Stay & Eat Very basic accommodation with shared toilet and scoop shower is available at a tattered set of thin-walled rooms near the village's northern pier. Figure on 100B per night. Although the rooms aren't much, they do have windows that catch sea breezes. Some of the overnight tours from Phang-Nga use these rooms; if they're full you should be able to find a room in a village home for about the same or less. Ask at one of the restaurants.

Along with the more expensive seafood restaurants built out over the sea in front of the village (which are generally open for lunch only), there are some smaller cafes and restaurants along the interior alleys where locals eat. *Khâo yam* (southern-Thai rice salad) and roti are available in the morning. The villagers raise grouper in floating cages next to the island, selling them to the island and mainland restaurants. A local culinary speciality is *khànŏm bâo lâng,* a savoury dish made with black sticky rice, shrimp, coconut, black pepper and chilli steamed in a banana leaf – a breakfast favourite.

Getting There & Away Most visitors to the island arrive on tour boats, whether for brief day visits or overnight stays. You can also take a regular ferry from Tha Dan for 50B per person. These leave frequently from dawn to dusk, arriving and departing from the village's northern pier (the southern pier is mostly reserved for tourist boats). Or you can charter a long-tail boat from the pier opposite Ao Phang-Nga National Park HQ in Tha Dan direct to the island for 400B to 500B. During heavy monsoon weather boat services may be cancelled.

Ko Yao
เกาะยาว

Ko Yao Yai and Ko Yao Noi (Big Long Island and Little Long Island) are in the middle of the bay, directly south of the provincial capital, almost equidistant between the provinces of Phuket and Krabi. Together they encompass 137 sq km of forest, beaches and rocky headlands with views of the surrounding karst formations characteristic of Ao Phang-Nga. Contrary to first assumptions, Ko Yao Noi is the main population centre of the two, although even here fishing, coconuts and a little tourism sustains a relatively small group of year-rounders. **Hat Pa Sai** and **Hat Tha Khao**, both on Yao Noi, are the best beaches. Bring along a mountain bike if you want to explore the island's numerous dirt trails.

Ta Khai, the largest settlement on the island, is a subdistrict seat and a source of minimal supplies. Boat trips to neighbouring islands, birds'-nest caves and sea gypsy funeral caves are possible. **Ko Bele**, a small island east of the twin Ko Yai, features a large tidal lagoon, three white-sand beaches, and easily accessible caves and coral reefs around the entire island. Long-tail boats from Ko Yao Noi or from Ao Nang in Krabi can be chartered for around 600B to 1000B per day, depending on the size of the boat.

Places to Stay & Eat On Ko Yao Noi, the only island with regular visitor lodgings, *Sabai Corner Bungalow* (☎ 01-892 1827) has thatch-and-wood bungalows with bathroom for 350B to 700B a night, depending on size. The electricity is switched on in the evening and all day on weekends. Nearby *Long Beach Bungalow* (☎ 076-381623) is a bit more rustic; bungalows are 500B and some are in better shape than others.

Alone on the beach at Hat Tha Kao is the newly opened *Tha Khao Bungalow* (☎ 01-676 7726) which offers bamboo bungalows with bathroom and fan for 450B, and 900B for larger bungalows that sleep six. Electricity is on in the evening and weekends.

Another fairly new operation that is getting good reviews is *Nui's Place*, run by a Thai and his Canadian wife. Rustic but well-built bungalows with mosquito net are 300B or a room in the family's house is 200B. Toilet and bathing facilities are shared. For 200B per day three *meals* are provided and Nui is said to be quite a cook. There is no electricity and Nui's Place shuts down during the rainy season from June to October.

Getting There & Away Although both islands fall within the Phang-Nga Province boundaries, the easiest places to find boat transport to Ko Yao Noi are Phuket (Phuket Province), Ao Leuk and Ao Nang (both in Krabi Province).

In Phuket town, catch a sǎwngthǎew from in front of the Thanon Ranong market to Bang Rong on Ao Po for 25B. From the public pier at Ao Po there are usually two mail boats a day to Ko Yao Noi, one between 8 and 9 am and another around noon. The fare

is 50B per passenger and the trip takes about one hour. Between departures or after hours you can charter a long-tail boat out to the island for 600B to 1000B one way. Coming back to Phuket from Yao Noi, there's one boat back that leaves between 6 and 7 am.

You can also get boats from Ko Yao Noi north-east across Ao Phang-Nga to Tha Laem Sak at Ao Leuk, Krabi. These cost around 40B on regular ferries, or 600B to charter. From Krabi's Ao Nang you can charter a boat for about 600B to 1000B each way. Shared with five or six friends, this doesn't have to dent your budget much.

If you want to take a look around Ko Yao Yai, directly south of Ko Yao Noi, catch a shuttle boat from Ko Yao Noi's Tha Manaw for 20B each way.

Phuket Province

Dubbed 'Pearl of the South' by the tourist industry, Phuket (pronounced 'Poo-GET') is Thailand's largest island (810 sq km) and a province in itself. It is also Thailand's wealthiest province, and although tourism is its biggest source of income (along with tin, rubber and cashews), the island is still large enough to accommodate escapists of nearly all budget levels.

Formerly called Ko Thalang and before that Junk Ceylon (an English corruption of the Malay 'Tanjung Salang' or Cape Salang), Phuket has a culture all of its own, combining Chinese and Portuguese influences (like neighbouring western Malaysia) with that of the chao náam or the sea gypsies, an indigenous ocean-going people, and the southern Thais. About 35% of the island's population are Thai Muslims and mosques outnumber Buddhist *wát* (temples) 38 to 37.

Lying in the Andaman Sea off Southern Thailand's west coast, the island's terrain is incredibly varied, with rocky beaches, long, broad, sandy beaches, limestone cliffs, forested hills and tropical vegetation of all kinds. Great seafood is available all over the island and several offshore islands are known for good snorkelling and scuba diving.

Comparisons with Ko Samui, off the east coast, as well as with other Thai islands, are inevitable, of course. All in all, there is more to do in Phuket, but that means more to spend

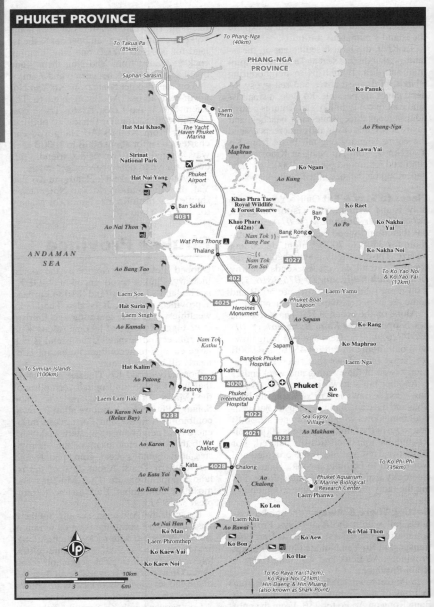

PHUKET PROVINCE

To Takua Pa (85km)

To Phang-Nga (40km)

PHANG-NGA PROVINCE

Ko Panuk

Saphan Sarasin

Laem Phrao

Hat Mai Khao

The Yacht Haven Phuket Marina

Ao Phang-Nga

Ao Tha Maphrao

Sirinat National Park

Ko Lawa Yai

Phuket Airport

Ko Ngam

Hat Nai Yang

Ao Kung

Khao Phra Taew Royal Wildlife & Forest Reserve

Ban Po

Ko Raet

Ban Sakhu

Khao Phara (442m)

Ao Po

Ko Nakha Yai

4031

Nam Tok Bang Pae

Bang Rong

Ao Nai Thon

Wat Phra Thong

Ko Nakha Noi

ANDAMAN SEA

Thalang

Nam Tok Ton Sai

4027

To Ko Yao Noi & Ko Yao Yai (12km)

402

Ao Bang Tao

Laem Son

4025

Laem Yamu

Hat Surin

Heroines Monument

Phuket Boat Lagoon

Laem Singh

Ao Sapam

Ao Kamala

Ao Sapam

Ko Rang

To Similan Islands (100km)

Nam Tok Kathu

Ko Maphrao

Hat Kalim

Bangkok Phuket Hospital

Laem Nga

Ao Patong

4029

Kathu

Sapam

4020

Patong

Phuket

Laem Lam Jiak

Phuket International Hospital

Ko Sire

Ao Karon Noi (Relax Bay)

4233

4022

Sea Gypsy Village

Karon

Ao Makham

Ao Karon

4021

4023

To Ko Phi Phi (35km)

Wat Chalong

Kata

4028

Chalong

Ao Kata Yai

Ao Chalong

Phuket Aquarium & Marine Biological Research Center

Ao Kata Noi

Ko Lon

Laem Phanwa

Ao Nai Han

Laem Kha

Ko Man

Ao Rawai

Ko Aew

Ko Mai Thon

Laem Phromthep

Ko Bon

Ko Kaew Yai

Ko Hae

Ko Kaew Noi

0   5   10km

0   3   6mi

To Ko Raya Yai (12km), Ko Raya Noi (21km), Hin Daeng & Hin Muang (also known as Shark Point)

your money on, too. There are more tourists in Phuket than on any other island, but they are concentrated at certain beaches – Patong, Karon and Kata. Beaches like Nai Han and Kamala are relatively quiet, in spite of major tourist developments at both, while Nai Yang, Nai Thon and Mai Khao to the north are still relatively pristine. The beaches of Ko Samui, by contrast, are highly developed around the entire perimeter of the island.

Development on Phuket has been influenced by the fact that it is connected to the mainland by a bridge, and hence it receives much more vehicular traffic than any other island in the country. And Phuket's high per-capita wealth means there's plenty of money available for investment. A turning point was reached when a Club Méditerranée (Club Med) was established at Hat Kata, followed by the construction of the more lavish Phuket Yacht Club on Hat Nai Han and Le Meridien on Karon Noi (Relax Bay). This marked an end to the decade-long cheap bungalow era, which started in the early 1970s when a 10B guesthouse was attached to a laundry on Hat Patong. The cheapies have long since been bought out and replaced by all manner of hotel and bungalow developments, some ill-conceived, others quite appealing.

The era of chasing quick money regardless of the cost to the environment has passed. Most beachside resorts are nowadays looking towards long-term, sustainable practices – not all of them, but a far greater percentage than on Ko Samui, Ko Pha-Ngan, Ko Tao, and even Ko Chang (although the total number of beach places on the latter is still small enough that the total impact of negative environmental practices is so far minimal). For this long-term outlook, the Phuket visitor pays a premium in terms of somewhat higher prices overall.

On the other hand, the general growth of commercialism along the island's main roads detracts from the island's appeal – there seems to be a snake farm, gaudy billboard, bungee-jumping operation, half-built condo project, travel agency or tacky craft shop every 500m in the southern half of the island. The island's beaches and relatively unspoiled northern interior remain its main attractions, and the provincial authorities as well as the business sector should do more to recognise and support these attractions.

The geography of Phuket is more varied than any other island in Thailand, and its large size has allowed microclimates to develop in different areas of the island. Check out the whole island if you have time. Don't ignore the interior of the island, which offers rice paddies, plantations of rubber, cashew nut, cacao, pineapple and coconut, as well as Phuket's last bit of island rainforest.

Dangers & Annoyances

Every year about twenty people lose their lives in drowning accidents off Phuket's beaches. Red flags are posted on beaches to warn bathers of riptides and other dangerous conditions. If a red flag is flying at a beach, don't go into the water.

Diving & Snorkelling

Although there are many, many places to dive around Thailand, Phuket is indisputably the primary centre for the Thai scuba-diving industry and one of the world's top 10 dive destinations. The island is ringed by good to excellent dive sites, including several small islands to the south– Ko Hae, Ko Raya (Noi & Yai), Hin Daeng and Hin Muang (known as Shark Point as it is a habitat for harmless leopard sharks, however Hin Muang literally means Purple Rock) – and to the east – Ko Yao (Noi & Yai). Excursions farther afield, to Ao Phang-Nga islands to the east and to the world-famous Surin and Similan Islands to the north-west, are also for the most part operated from Phuket. At least four outfits are now also providing live-aboard trips to islands in the Mergui archipelago off the southern coast of Myanmar.

Most Phuket diving operations are centred at Hat Patong, with a sprinkling of branch offices in town or on other beaches. Many companies stagger regularly scheduled dives throughout the week so that different dive groups don't bump into one another; eg, Santana might go to Ko Raya Yai on Monday and Shark Point on Tuesday, while Calypso might do Shark Point on Monday and Raya Yai on Tuesday, and so on. Typical one-day dive trips to nearby sites such as these cost around 1900B to 2600B, including two dives, tanks and weights, transport, dive master service, breakfast and lunch. Nondivers – including snorkellers – are often permitted to join such dive trips for a 30% to 50% discount. PADI open-water certification courses cost around 8000B to 11,000B for four days of instruction and all equipment.

A few companies – generally the larger, more well-established ones – offer extended three- to seven-day trips on live-aboard dive boats, ranging from 3000B to 5000B per day per person, to Ko Phi-Phi, Ko Similan and Ko Surin. Trips to the increasingly popular Burma Banks are also possible but are a bit more expensive, due to the extra paperwork involved.

Most dive shops also rent the following equipment: regulator (250B a day), buoyancy control device (BCD; 300B), mask, fins and snorkel (250B) and wetsuit (200B). Ask about equipment rental 'packages' that go for around 500B to 700B per day, with further discounts given to long-term renters.

Phuket boasts a large number of dive companies – at last count there were over 50. A list of the more reputable dive companies on the island follows (and, of these, Aqua Divers, Marina Divers and Paradise Diving have French-speaking staff):

Andaman Divers (☎/fax 076-341126) Hat Patong
Aqua Divers (☎ 076-327006, fax 327338) Pearl Village Resort
Web site: www.aquadivers.com
Calypso Divers (☎/fax 076-330869) Hat Kata-Karon
Fantasea Divers (☎ 076-340088, fax 340309) Hat Patong
Web site: www.fantasea.net
Marina Divers (☎ 076-330272/516) Hat Karon
Neptune Diving (☎/fax 076-340585) Hat Patong
PIDC Divers (☎ 076-280644, fax 381219) Ao Chalong
Web site: www.pidcdivers.com
Pioneer Diving Asia (☎/fax 076-342508) Hat Patong
Santana (☎ 076-294220, fax 340360, e diving@santanaphuket.com) Hat Patong
Scuba Cat Diving (☎ 076-293121, fax 293122) Hat Patong
Web site: www.scubacat.com
Sea Bees Diving (☎/fax 076-381765) Ao Chalong
Web site: www.sea-bees.com
Sea Hawk Divers (☎ 076-341179, fax 344151) Hat Patong
South East Asia Divers (☎ 076-344022, fax 342530) Hat Patong
Web site: www.phuketdive.net
South East Asia Live Aboard (☎ 076-340406, fax 340586) Hat Patong
Web site: www.sealiveaboards.com

It's a good idea to make sure that the dive shop you pick is affiliated with Sub-aquatic Safety Service (SSS; ☎ 076-342518, 01-606 1869, fax 076-342519), which operates a hyperbaric (recompression) chamber in Patong. This means the dive shop is insured should one of their customers need to use the chamber in an emergency. If a shop is not a member, and should you need Dive Safe Asia's services, you may ending up footing the bill (around US$3000).

Snorkelling is best along Phuket's west coast, particularly at rock headlands between beaches. Mask, snorkel and fins can be rented for around 250B a day. As with scuba diving, you'll find better snorkelling, with greater visibility and variety of marine life, along the shores of small outlying islands like Ko Hae, Ko Yao and Ko Raya.

As elsewhere in the Andaman Sea, the best diving months are December to May, when the weather is good and the sea is at its clearest (and boat trips are much safer).

The following shops have dive supplies:

Dive Supply (☎ 076-342511, e dsupply@loxinfo.co.th) 189 Thanon Rat Uthit, Hat Patong. Stocks a large variety of dive supplies and equipment.
Phuket Wetsuits (☎ 076-381818) Offers both custom and ready-made wet suits.
Sea Sports (☎ 076-381065) 1/11–12 Thanon Chao Fa, Phuket. Carries all manner of water sports equipment and supplies, along with canoes and kayaks.

Yachting

Phuket is one of South-East Asia's main yacht destinations and you'll find all manner of craft anchored along its shores, from 80-year-old wooden sloops that look like they can barely stay afloat, to the latest in hi-tech motor cruisers. Marina-style facilities with year-round anchorage are available at two locations on the protected east side of the island: Phuket Boat Lagoon (☎ 076-239055, fax 239056) at Ao Sapam, about 20km north of Phuket town on the east shore, and The Yacht Haven Phuket Marina (☎ 076-206705, fax 206706) at Laem Phrao at the north-east tip.

Phuket Boat Lagoon offers an enclosed marina with tidal channel access, serviced pontoon berths, 60- and 120-tonne travel lifts, hard-stand area, plus a resort hotel, laundry, coffee shop, fuel, water, repairs and maintenance services. The Yacht Haven boasts 130 berths, immigration facilities, restaurants and a health spa.

Port clearance is rather complicated; both Phuket Boat Lagoon and The Yacht Haven will take care of the paperwork (for a fee of course) if notified of your arrival in advance.

At the time of research, major disagreements between local yachting interests and the Phuket customs department were driving much of Phuket's yachting business down to Langkawi in Malaysia. Much, but not all, of the dissatisfaction was stemming from high customs taxes being collected by Phuket officials. Only time will tell if this is just a temporary wrinkle or whether corruption in the local customs department will cause the demise of yachting on Phuket.

Parts & Service The Yacht Haven and Phuket Boat Lagoon offer routine repair and maintenance services, along with limited parts and supplies. In Ao Chalong there are several smaller marine repair/supply shops. If you need sails, Rolly Tasker Sailmakers (☎ 076-280347, fax 280348) claims to have the lowest sail prices in Asia; riggings, spars and hardware are also available.

Charters For information on yacht charters – both bareboat and crewed – yacht sales and yacht deliveries, contact the following:

Asia Yachting (☎ 076-381615, 01-941 5660) Ao Chalong
Big A Yachting Swann 55 (☎ 076-381914, fax 381934) Ao Chalong
South East Asia Liveaboards (☎ 076-340406, fax 340586) Hat Patong
Sunsail Yacht Charters (☎ 076-239057, fax 238940, e sunthai@phuket.loxinfo.co.th) Phuket Boat Lagoon
Thai Marine Leisure (☎ 076-239111, e tml@thaimarine.com) Hat Patong
Yachtpro International (☎ 076-348117–8, fax 348119, e info@sailing-thailand.com) Yacht Haven Marina, Phuket
Web site: www.sailing-thailand.com

Charters aboard 32- to 44-foot yachts start at 900B a day, while larger ones (to 85-foot) start at 18,000B. Discounts of around 33% are available June to October. Day trips usually include boat, crew, lunch and soft drinks, plus snorkelling and fishing gear.

Paddling
Several companies based in Phuket offer inflatable canoe tours of scenic Ao Phang-Nga. Sea Canoe Thailand (☎ 076-212252, fax 212172, e info@seacanoe.com), a company based in Phuket at 367/4 Thanon Yaowarat, was the first and is still the most famous. The kayaks are able to enter semisubmerged caves (which Thai fishermen have called *hâwng* or 'room' for centuries) inaccessible by the long-tail boats. A day paddle costs 2970B per person and includes meals, beverages, equipment and transfer, while all-inclusive, three- or six-day camping trips are 20,900B and 37,600B per person, respectively. The three-day trips leave Wednesday and Sunday; six-day trips leave on Sunday. The day trips can also be booked from Ao Nang in Krabi for 1700B, but a different area without semisubmerged caves is explored.

Several other companies in the area offer similar inflatable canoe trips for less than half these prices, but Sea Canoe Thailand claims it is still the most ecologically conscious in terms of the way in which it organises and operates tours. Another company with experience navigating the hâwng and for which we've received good feedback from readers is Andaman Sea Kayak (☎ 076-235353, 235098). Almost any travel agency on the island can book trips with this outfit.

Soft Adventure Treks
Siam Safari (☎ 076-280116) and Adventure Safaris (☎ 076-341988) combine 4WD tours of the island's interior with short elephant rides and short hikes for around 1950B a day. Half-day trips are also available, although the difference in price is not that great.

Cooking
Pat Thienthong, who worked as a chef at a Thai restaurant in California for six years, is offering Thai cooking courses at her home, located just outside Phuket town. Pat lets her students choose their own course, either central Thai or traditional Phuket cuisine. Half-day courses cost 900B, and 1200B including transfer from anywhere on the island. She can be contacted by calling ☎ 01-397 5537 during the day, or by stopping in at Phuket Reminder (☎ 076-213765) at 85 Thanon Rasada, a souvenir shop in Phuket town.

ANDAMAN COAST

PHUKET

อ.เมืองภูเก็ต

postcode 83000 • pop 61,800

Centuries before Phuket began attracting sand-and-sea hedonists it was an important trade centre for Arab, Indian, Malay, Chinese and Portuguese traders who exchanged goods from the rest of the world for tin and rubber. Francis Light, the British colonialist who made Penang the first of the British Straits Settlements, married a native of Phuket and tried unsuccessfully to pull this island into the colonial fold as well. Although this polyglot, multicultural heritage has all but disappeared from most of the island, a few vestiges can be seen and experienced in the province's *amphoe meuang* (provincial capital), Phuket.

In the older town centre you'll see some Sino-Portuguese architecture, characterised by ornate two-storey Chinese *hâang thǎew* or 'row companies', fronted by Romanesque arched porticoes with 'five-foot ways' that were a 19th-century tradition in Malaysia, Singapore, Macau and Hainan Island. For a time it seemed this wonderful old architecture was all being torn down and replaced with modern structures but, in recent years, a preservation ethic has taken hold.

Information

Tourist Office TAT's office (☎ 076-212213, 211036, ⒺＥ tathkt@phuket.ksc.co.th), at 73–75 Thanon Phuket, has maps, brochures, a list of the standard sǎwngthǎew fares to the various beaches and also the recommended charter costs for a vehicle. It's open from 8.30 am to 4.30 pm daily. The tourist police can be reached at ☎ 076-355015, 254693 or 1155.

Maps Although it doesn't look like it, the advertisement-plastered *A-O-A Phuket Map* is probably the best one if you're planning to drive around. It's more accurate than the other freebies, and it has all the route numbers marked. The free Thaiways map isn't very good for island navigation, although the inset maps for Patong and Karon-Kata are better than the A-O-A's. You can pick up both maps at the TAT office and other places around the island.

Groovy Map's informative new *Phuket Day & Night Map 'n' Guide* (100B) fea-

tures five maps (Phuket Town, Phuket Island, Patong, Kata and Karon, and a boat route map) as well as a selection of short reviews of restaurants, pubs, nightclubs and beaches in Phuket and Krabi. Bus routes and fares are also included.

Money Several banks along Thanon Takua Pa, Thanon Phang-Nga and Thanon Phuket offer exchange services and ATMs (automated teller machines). Bank of Asia, opposite the TAT office on Thanon Phuket, has an exchange window open from 8.30 am to 8 pm daily.

Post The main post office, which is housed in a new building next to the smaller, older architectural gem on Thanon Montri, is open from 8.30 am to 4.30 pm weekdays and from 9 am to noon weekends and holidays.

Mail Boxes Etc (MBE; ☎ 076-256409, fax 256411) has a branch at 168/2 Thanon Phuket, almost opposite The Books. MBE rents private mail boxes, sells packaging and mailing materials and offers photocopying, laminating, binding, passport photo and business card services.

Two courier services in town are DHL World Wide Express (☎ 076-258500) at 61/4 Thanon Thepkasatri and UPS (☎ 076-263989) at 64/53 Thanon Chao Fa.

Telephone The Phuket Telecommunications Centre, on Thanon Phang-Nga, offers Home Country Direct service and is open from 8 am to midnight daily.

Email & Internet Access eBuzz Internet Cafe on Thanon Takua Pa, opposite Kra Jok See restaurant, is conveniently located near the On On Hotel. A quiet corner of The Books, at 53–55 Thanon Phuket, near the TAT office, also functions as an Internet access point.

Internet Resources Phuket Island Access (www.phuket.com) offers a sophisticated compendium of many kinds of information, including accommodation on the island. Phuket Net is an Internet service (ⒺＥ info@phuket.net) that provides forums for tourism and business-oriented exchange, and has limited listings. Check out their Web site at www.phuket.net.

ANDAMAN COAST

PHUKET

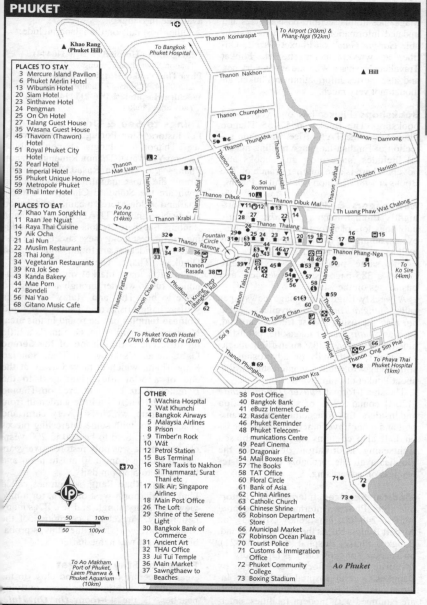

▲ Khao Rang
(Phuket Hill)

Thanon Komarapat

To Airport (30km) &
Phang-Nga (92km)

To Bangkok
Phuket Hospital

▲ Hill

Thanon Nakhon

PLACES TO STAY
3 Mercure Island Pavilion
6 Phuket Merlin Hotel
13 Wibunsin Hotel
20 Siam Hotel
23 Sinthavee Hotel
24 Pengman
25 On On Hotel
27 Talang Guest House
35 Wasana Guest House
45 Thavorn (Thawon)
   Hotel
51 Royal Phuket City
   Hotel
52 Pearl Hotel
53 Imperial Hotel
55 Phuket Unique Home
59 Metropole Phuket
69 Thai Inter Hotel

PLACES TO EAT
7 Khao Yam Songkhla
11 Raan Jee Nguat
19 Raya Thai Cuisine
21 Lai Nun
22 Muslim Restaurant
28 Thai Jong
34 Vegetarian Restaurants
39 Kra Jok See
43 Kanda Bakery
44 Mae Porn
47 Bondeli
56 Nai Yao
68 Gitano Music Cafe

Thanon Chumphon

Thanon Damrong

Thanon Narison

Thanon Mae Luan

Thanon Thungkha

Thanon Yaowarat

Thanon Theplastri

Thanon Suthat

Thanon Satun

Thanon Paiphat

To Ao
Patong
(14km)

Soi
Rommani

Thanon Dibuk

Thanon Dibuk Mai

Th Luang Phaw Wat Chalong

Thanon Krabi

Thanon Thalang

Thanon Montri

Thanon Phang-Nga

Fountain
Circle

Thanon
Ranong

To
Ko Sire
(4km)

Thanon Chao Fa

Thanon Pattana

Soi Phuthon

Th Krung Thep (Bangkok Rd)

Thanon
Rasada

Thanon Takua Pa

Thanon Tilok

Th Phuket

Uthit

To Phuket Youth Hostel
(7km) & Roti Chao Fa (2km)

Soi 9

Thanon Phunphon

Thanon Taling Chan

Thanon Kra

Thanon Ong Sim Phai

To Phaya Thai
Phuket Hospital
(1km)

To Ao Makham,
Port of Phuket,
Laem Phanwa &
Phuket Aquarium
(10km)

0   50   100m
0   50   100yd

Ao Phuket

OTHER
1 Wachira Hospital
2 Wat Khunchi
4 Bangkok Airways
5 Malaysia Airlines
8 Prison
9 Timber'n Rock
10 Wát
12 Petrol Station
15 Bus Terminal
16 Share Taxis to Nakhon
   Si Thammarat, Surat
   Thani etc
17 Silk Air; Singapore
   Airlines
18 Main Post Office
26 The Loft
29 Shrine of the Serene
   Light
30 Bangkok Bank of
   Commerce
31 Ancient Art
32 THAI Office
33 Jui Tui Temple
36 Main Market
37 Sawngthaew to
   Beaches

38 Post Office
40 Bangkok Bank
41 eBuzz Internet Cafe
42 Rasda Center
46 Phuket Reminder
48 Phuket Telecom-
   munications Centre
49 Pearl Cinema
50 Dragonair
54 Mail Boxes Etc
57 The Books
58 TAT Office
60 Floral Circle
61 Bank of Asia
62 China Airlines
63 Catholic Church
64 Chinese Shrine
65 Robinson Department
   Store
66 Municipal Market
67 Robinson Ocean Plaza
70 Tourist Police
71 Customs & Immigration
   Office
72 Phuket Community
   College
73 Boxing Stadium

The *Phuket Gazette* (see Newspapers & Magazines in this section) posts articles and updated information along with its searchable *Gazette Guide* on Phuket Gazette Online, at www.phuketgazette.net. Phuket Travellers Net has a Web site at www.trv.net, and also carries information on Phuket, although not very much.

Bookshops Phuket has one very good bookshop, The Books, at 53–55 Thanon Phuket near the TAT office. The wide selection of English-language reading material includes magazines, guidebooks and novels. There is also another branch of The Books at 198/2 Thanon Rat Uthit in Patong.

Newspapers & Magazines The fortnightly English-language *Phuket Gazette* publishes lots of information on activities, events, dining and entertainment in town, as well as around the island.

The same publisher issues *Gazette Guide,* a 385-page listing of services and businesses on the island.

A weekly English language newspaper called *Siangtai Times* is also available. There are also the usual tourist freebies around, such as *South. Phuket* magazine, published nine times yearly, is like an in-flight magazine that relies heavily on advertising but still manages to publish an interesting article about Phuket once in awhile.

The small-format *Phuket Holiday Guide* (120B) contains lots of solid information and insiders' tips on accommodation, transport and other travel practicalities on the island. It also contains the most unbiased sightseeing information of any of the glossies available, probably because it relies less on advertising.

Medical Services International doctors rate the Phuket International Hospital (☎ 076-249400, emergency 210935), on Airport Bypass Rd, as the best on the island. Bangkok Phuket Hospital (☎ 076-254421), on Thanon Yongyok Uthit, is reportedly the favourite with the locals, and is run by Bangkok General Hospital. Both Phuket International and Bangkok Phuket Hospitals are equipped with modern facilities, emergency rooms and outpatient-care clinics.

Feedback we've received about these hospitals indicates that, although they're well equipped, better treatment is readily available in Bangkok.

Other hospitals on the island include:

Patong/Kathu Hospital (☎ 076-340444)
  Thanon Sawatdirak, Patong
Phya Thai Phuket Hospital (☎ 076-252603–42) 28/36–37 Thanon Si Sena, Phuket
Wachira Hospital (☎ 076-211114) Thanon Yaowarat, Phuket

Things to See & Do

For historic **Sino-Portuguese architecture** see Thanon Thalang, Thanon Dibuk, Thanon Yaowarat, Thanon Ranong, Thanon Phang-Nga, Thanon Rasada and Thanon Krabi; the most magnificent examples in town are the Standard Chartered Bank – Thailand's oldest foreign bank – on Thanon Phang-Nga and the THAI office on Thanon Ranong, but there are lots of modest buildings of interest along these streets. The best restored residences are found along Thanon Dibuk and Thanon Thalang.

Phuket's main **market** on Thanon Ranong is fun to wander through and is a good place to buy Thai and Malay sarongs as well as baggy fisherman pants. A few old **Chinese temples** can be found in this area. Most are standard issue. One that's a little bit different is the **Shrine of the Serene Light**, or as it's known in Thai, San Jao Sang Tham, which is tucked away at the end of a 50m alley right next to the Bangkok Bank of Commerce on Thanon Phang-Nga. There's a little garden in front of the shrine, which is a very calm and peaceful spot with some interesting pieces of temple art. Said to be 100 to 200 years old, the shrine was only restored five years ago. It's open from 8.30 am to noon and from 1.30 to 5.30 pm daily.

Walk up **Khao Rang**, sometimes called Phuket Hill, north-west of town, for a nice view of the city, jungle and sea. If, as many people say, Phuket is a corruption of the Malay word *bukit* (hill), then this is probably the hill it was named after.

Places to Stay – Budget

Near the centre of town, and close to the săwngthăew terminal for most outlying beaches, is the 49-room *On On Hotel* (☎ 076-211154, 19 Thanon Phang-Nga). This hotel's old Sino-Portuguese architecture (established 1929) gives it real

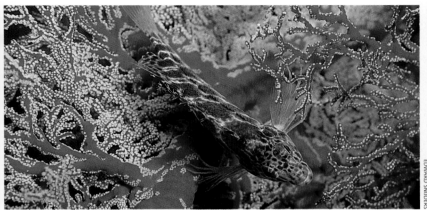

In a burst of brilliance, a Similan hawk fish swims over red coral.

Fishing on Patong beach, Phuket Province

Muay thai, Patong beach, Phuket Province

Patong town and beach, Phuket Province

Donald Duck Bay, Similan Islands, Phang-Nga

Repairing fishing nets, Phuket Province

Downtown Phuket

Canoeing at Phang-Nga National Park

character. Room rates are 120B for a single with fan and shared facilities, 180/250B single/double with fan and attached bathroom and 360B with air-con.

Nearby, the simple *Pengman* (☎ 076-211486 ext 169, 69 Thanon Phang-Nga) above a Chinese restaurant, costs 120B for basic but quite clean rooms with ceiling fan and shared bathroom.

The three-storey *Talang Guest House* (☎ 076-214225, 37 Thanon Thalang) is in a classic and tidy shophouse in the old city centre, rents large rooms with one bed and fan for 250B per day in the low season, 300B in the high season. Air-con rooms with three or four beds cost 400B. If you want a good street view, ask for No 31, a fan room on the third floor with a wide veranda.

Wasana Guest House (☎ 076-211754, 213385, 159 Thanon Ranong), next to Thanon Ranong Market, has clean rooms for 200B with fan and bathroom and 300B with air-con.

Thai Inter Hotel (☎ 076-220275, 22 Thanon Phunphon) is convenient to the airport shuttle drop-off in town if you've just flown into Phuket or are catching an early-morning flight. Rooms with fan cost 280B and air-con are 390B. Both have attached bathroom.

Phuket Youth Hostel (☎ 076-280806, 73/11 Thanon Chao Fa, Chalong) is located some 7km south of the city centre. The cost is 195B per person per night for fan rooms with attached bathrooms. Those without Hostelling International membership must pay 50B extra per night. The Phuket Youth Hostel is located on the left between Wat Chalong and the five-road intersection.

Places to Stay – Mid-Range

The *Thavorn Hotel* (Thawon; ☎ 076-211333, 74 Thanon Rasada) is a huge place consisting of an original, less expensive wing out the back and a flashier place up front. In the back wing, large rooms with ceiling fan and private bathroom cost 280B single/double, while in the front building, larger rooms come with TV, air-con, hot water and carpet and cost 550B. The best thing about the Thavorn is the lobby, which is filled with antiques and historic photos of Phuket.

The friendly and well-located *Imperial Hotel* (☎ 076-212311, fax 213155, 51 Thanon Phuket) has clean, comfortable rooms for 650B with air-con, TV, hair dryer and other amenities.

The *Sinthavee Hotel* (☎ 076-211186, fax 211400, 85–91 Thanon Phang-Nga) offers OK air-con rooms for 707B during the high season and 518B during the low season. Deluxe rooms go for 1272B in the high season and 809B in the low season. All rooms come with carpet, hot-water bathroom and refrigerator (add TV and video for deluxe); other facilities include a 24-hour coffee shop and business centre.

Places to Stay – Top End

The *Pearl Hotel* (☎ 076-211044, 212911, 42 Thanon Montri) has rooms from 1883B, but gives a 50% discount during the low season. The hotel boasts a rooftop restaurant, fitness centre, pool and so on. The *Phuket Merlin Hotel* (☎ 076-212866, fax 216429, 158/1 Thanon Yaowarat) has 180 rooms for 1531B and up again there's a 50% discount given in the low season. The hotel has a swimming pool and fitness centre.

One of the best-located top-enders is the plush 248-room *Metropole Phuket* (☎ 076-215050, fax 215990), right in the centre of things on Thanon Montri. 'Superior' rooms start at 1600B, deluxe from 2000B, American breakfast included. Facilities include two Chinese restaurants, a coffee shop, three bars, swimming pool, fitness centre, business centre and airport shuttle service. Another well-located spot is the *Mercure Island Pavilion* (☎ 076-210444, fax 210458, 133 Thanon Satul), where spacious, well-appointed rooms go for 1600B to 2100B.

A short walk east of the Phuket Telecommunications Centre at is the towering 251-room *Royal Phuket City Hotel* (☎ 076-233333, fax 233335, 154 Thanon Phang-Nga), where state-of-the-art rooms start at 4120B, although discounts down to 2884B are easily available.

Places to Eat

Town Centre If there's one thing the town of Phuket is known for, it's good food – even if you're staying at the beach it's worth a trip to the city to sample authentic, Phuket-style cooking (a blend of Thai, Malay and Straits Chinese influences). Meals in the city tend to cost at least 50% less (often many times less) than meals at the beach.

One long-running local institution is *Ran Jee Nguat*, a Phuket-style restaurant run by Hokkien Chinese, across the street from the now-defunct Siam Cinema on the corner of historic Thanon Yaowarat and Thanon Dibuk. Jee Nguat serves Phuket's most famous dish – delicious *khànǒm jiin náam yaa phuukèt* – Chinese noodles in a pureed fish and curry sauce, Phuket style, with fresh cucumbers, long green beans and other fresh vegetables on the side – for under 20B. Don't leave it too late, though; they open from early in the morning but close around 2 pm. A few doors south of Jee Nguat on Thanon Yaowarat, *Thai Jong* (no Roman-script sign) is a small Hokkien coffee shop serving southern-Thai food.

The inexpensive *coffee shop* below the Pengman Hotel specialises in seafood noodles and is very popular at lunchtime. *On On Cafe*, beside the On On Hotel, serves rice dishes and curries at reasonable prices; it's open from 7 am to 8 pm. In part of the same building is *On On Ice Cream*, an air-con ice-cream parlour that also serves cold beer.

Very popular with Thais and *fàràng* alike, and deservedly so, is the friendly *Mae Porn*, a restaurant on the corner of Thanon Phang-Nga and Soi Pradit, close to the On On and Sinthavee Hotels. There's an air-con room as well as outdoor tables. It sells curries, seafood, fruit shakes – you name it and Mae Porn has it – all at very reasonable prices. Another popular spot in town is *Kanda Bakery* on Thanon Rasada, just south of the Bangkok Bank of Commerce. It's open early in the morning with freshly baked whole-wheat bread, baguettes, croissants, cakes and real brewed coffee; they also serve a variety of *khâo tôm* (boiled rice) specialities any time of day.

Another good local discovery is the simple *Muslim restaurant* on the corner of Thanon Thepkasatri and Thanon Thalang – look for the star and crescent. This family-run place serves delicious and inexpensive *mátsàmàn kài* (chicken and potato curry), rotii kaeng (in the morning only) and khâo mòk kài (usually gone by 1 pm).

Lai Nun (no Roman-script sign, look for a sign with a red star) is a similar Muslim restaurant on the opposite side of Thanon Thalang, west of the intersection. Light breakfasts of real coffee and shredded roti topped with sweetened condensed milk are served in the morning.

A bit out of the city centre but well worth the effort to find is *Roti Chao Fa* (the sign simply says 'Muslim') on Thanon Chao Fa, a clean and spacious place run by Thai-Malays, open from 6 am to noon only. Besides superb rotii kaeng (curries served with flat bread instead of rice), this restaurant has a wide variety of teas, including what is known in Malaysia as *teh tarik* or 'pull tea' (*chaa ráwn máleh* in Thai). This frothy tea gets its Malay name from the process of aerating it, which involves an engaging show of pouring the tea from cup to cup at arm's length.

In the vicinity of Thanon Phang-Nga near the post office are two or three inexpensive Phuket-style *ráan khâo kaeng* (rice-and-curry shops), including the *Aik Ocha*; try the tasty cashew-nut curry.

Venerable *Nai Yao* is still hanging on in an old wooden building with a tin roof near the Honda dealer on Thanon Phuket. It features an excellent, inexpensive seafood menu (bilingual), cold beer and, at night, tables on the sidewalk. The house speciality is the unique and highly recommended *tôm yam hâeng* (dry tôm yam), which can be ordered with chicken, shrimp or squid. It's open evenings only.

A good place for an intimate night out, is *Kra Jok See* (☎ 076-217903), in an old shophouse on Thanon Takua Pa just south of Thanon Rasada on the west side of street. It's hard to spot as the front of the restaurant is screened by plants; look for Ban Boran Antiques next door. The restaurant specialises in a fàràng-friendly Phuket cuisine, including delicious *hàw mòk tháleh* (steamed seafood curry). Kra Jok See is open from 6 pm to midnight Tuesday to Sunday, but on slow nights the kitchen (but not the bar) may close as early as 10 pm.

Yet another place that takes advantage of old Phuket architecture is the tourist-oriented *Raya Thai Cuisine* (☎ 076-218155, 48/1 Thanon Dibuk Mai), on the corner of Thanon Thepkasatri. Housed in a Sino-Portuguese mansion, the high ceilings and tall windows provide lots of air flow and offer glimpses of the surrounding garden. The food is good, if a bit expensive by local standards.

A couple of *vegetarian restaurants* on Thanon Ranong east of the garish Jui Tui Chinese temple serve good Chinese vegetarian food during daylight hours.

Khao Yam Songkhla, on Thanon Thungkha, is very popular with the locals and specialises in khâo yam, the southern-Thai rice salad.

For a change from Phuket fare, try *Gitano Music Cafe*, located on Thanon Ong Sim Phai, near Robinson Ocean Plaza. Great Latin decor compliments a menu of Mexican and Thai dishes, as well as fruit shakes. The air-con *Bondeli* on the corner of Thanon Rasada and Thanon Thepkasatri, does sandwiches and pizza.

There's also a *KFC* in the Robinson Ocean Plaza, and a *McDonald's* in the same vicinity. Next door to the shopping complex is Phuket's municipal market where you can buy everything from fresh produce to inexpensive clothing. Around three sides of this market you'll find a *night market* that sells Thai and Chinese food.

Khao Rang At the top of Khao Rang (Phuket Hill) is the outdoor *Thungkha Kafae* (☎ 076-211500), which has a very pleasant atmosphere and good food. Try the *tôm khàa kài* (chicken coconut soup) or *khài jiaw hǎwy naang rom* (oyster omelette).

Ao Chalong Just past Wat Chalong (on the left past the five-road intersection) is *Kan Eang 1* (☎ 076-381212), a good fresh seafood place that used to sit on a pier over the bay. Now housed in an enclosed air-con restaurant (open-air dining is still available as well), it continues to set a standard for Phuket seafood, although prices have risen considerably. You order by weight, choosing from squid, oysters, cockles, crab, mussels and several kinds of fish, and then specify the method of cooking, whether grilled *(phǎo)*, steamed *(nêung)*, fried *(thâwt)*, parboiled *(lûak* – for squid), or in soup *(tôm yam)*. It also offers a decent wine list. At the other end of Ao Chalong is a second location, *Kan Eang 2* (☎ 076-381323).

Entertainment
The *Pearl Cinema*, on the corner of Thanon Phang-Nga and Thanon Montri near the Pearl Hotel, occasionally shows English-language films. *Alliance Française* (☎ 076-

222988, 3 Soi 1, Thanon Phattana) has weekly showings of French films (subtitled in English). It also has a library and a TV with up-to-date news broadcasts.

The bar/restaurant *Gitano Music Cafe*, run by a Colombian-born German, features an excellent collection of Latin CDs as well as tequila and Colombian coffee. It's located on Thanon Kra, near Robinson Ocean Plaza. The *Timber 'n Rock*, on the eastern side of Thanon Yaowarat just south of Thanon Thungkha, is a pub with an attractive rustic decor, lots of Phuket and Thai food and live music after 10 pm. The major hotels have discos and/or karaoke clubs.

Eight real bouts of **Thai boxing** can be viewed every Friday night at 8 pm at the boxing stadium near the pier on the southern edge of town. All seats are 500B and tickets can be purchased at the gate or, more conveniently, through a desk in the lobby of the On On Hotel (which includes transfer to/from the stadium).

Shopping
Although there are loads of souvenir shops and clothing boutiques surrounding the beach resorts of Patong, Kata and Karon, the best shopping bargains on the island are found in the provincial capital. There are two main markets, one off the south side of Thanon Ranong near the centre of town, and a second off the north side of Thanon Ong Sim Phai, a bit south-east of town centre. The Thanon Ranong (day) market traces its history back to the days when pirates, Indians, Chinese, Malays and Europeans traded in Phuket and offers a wide variety of sarongs and fabrics from Thailand, Malaysia, Indonesia and India. You'll also find inexpensive clothing and crafts here.

At the newer Thanon Ong Sim Phai market the focus is more on fresh produce.

Adjacent to the market is the large Robinson Ocean Plaza, which contains a branch of Robinson department store, as well as smaller shops with moderately priced clothing and housewares. Along Thanon Yaowarat, between Thanon Phang-Nga and Thanon Thalang, are a number of Indian-run tailor and fabric shops, while Chinese gold shops are lined up along Thanon Ranong opposite the Thanon Ranong market. Other shopping venues include the small Rasda Center/Phuket shopping centre on Thanon Rasada.

The Loft (☎ 076-258160), in a well-restored shophouse at 36 Thanon Thalang, sells Asian antiques and objets d'art downstairs, contemporary art upstairs. Other antique shops include Ancient Art (☎ 076-258043) on Thanon Yaowarat, and Ban Boran Antiques (☎ 076-212473) on Thanon Takua Pa, next to Kra Jok See restaurant.

Phuket Unique Home (☎ 076-212093), at 186 Thanon Phuket, opposite The Books and the Imperial Hotel, carries lots of original designs in silverware, dishware, home decor accessories and furniture, much of it a blend of old and new influences. Out of town on the way to Ao Chalong, Island Furniture (☎ 076-253707) on Thanon Chao Fa sells lounge and patio furniture made from farmed Indonesian teak, along with deluxe bamboo furniture and imported wood block flooring.

Getting There & Away

Air Phuket International Airport (☎ 076-327230–5) has a post office and bookshop in the domestic departure area, plenty of foreign exchange in both sections and, in the arrivals area, two ATMs and a TAT office.

THAI operates over a dozen daily flights from Bangkok for 2300B one way. The flight takes an hour and 25 minutes, except for departures that have a half-hour stopover in Hat Yai. There are also regular flights to/from Hat Yai (910B, 45 minutes). THAI also flies between Phuket and several international destinations, including Penang, Langkawi, Kuala Lumpur, Singapore, Hong Kong, Taipei and Tokyo.

Bangkok Airways flies between Ko Samui and Phuket twice daily (once a week in June and September) for 1560B each way. Bangkok Airways has recently started a new twice-weekly route between Phuket and Siem Reap, Cambodia (for excursions to Angkor Wat). The one-way fare is US$288.

International airlines with offices in Phuket are:

Bangkok Airways (☎ 076-225033–5) 58/2–3 Thanon Yaowarat
China Airlines (☎ 076-327099) Phuket International Airport
Dragonair (☎ 076-217300) 37/52 Thanon Montri

Malaysia Airlines (☎ 076-216675) 1/8–9 Thanon Thungkha
Silk Air (☎ 076-213891) 183/103 Thanon Phang-Nga
Singapore Airlines (☎ 076-213891) 183/103 Thanon Phang-Nga
THAI (☎ 076-258236) 78/1 Thanon Ranong

Bus From Bangkok, one government 1st-class air-con bus leaves the Southern bus terminal at 7 pm for 446B. Buses leave Phuket for the return journey at 5.30 pm. Two VIP buses (690B) run daily from Bangkok (Southern bus terminal) at 5.30 pm and 6 pm. Departure times from Phuket are 4 and 5 pm. The trip takes 14 hours. The ride along winding Hwy 4 between Ranong and Phuket can be hair-raising if you are awake. Ordinary buses leave three times a day at 3, 6 and 10.30 pm, for 248B to 356B (depending on the route), and take a gruelling 15 or 16 hours.

Two private tour buses run from Bangkok's Southern terminal to Phuket in the evening, with fares of 457/800B one way/return. From Phuket, buses to Bangkok leave between 3 and 6 pm. Several agencies have offices on Thanon Rasada and Thanon Phang-Nga.

The main bus terminal for government buses is off the northern side of Thanon Phang-Nga opposite the Royal Phuket City Hotel. Fares and trip durations for bus trips to/from Phuket's government terminal include:

destination	fare	duration (hrs)
Hat Yai		
ordinary	135B	8
air-con	233B to 243B	7
Krabi		
ordinary	56B	4½
air-con	101B	4
Nakhon Si Thammarat		
ordinary	115B	8
air-con	155B	7
Phang-Nga		
ordinary	31B	2½
Surat Thani		
ordinary	90B	6
air-con	140B to 165B	5
Takua Pa		
ordinary	45B	3
Trang		
ordinary	95B	6
air-con	132B to 169B	5

Taxi & Minivan There are share taxis between Phuket and other provincial capitals in the south; taxi fares are generally around double the fare of an ordinary bus. The taxi stand for Nakhon Si Thammarat, Surat Thani, Krabi, Trang and Hat Yai is on Thanon Phang-Nga, near the Pearl Cinema.

Some Bangkok travel agencies sell tickets for air-con minivans (rót túu) down to Ko Samui; the fare includes ferry transport. Air-con minivan services to Surat, Krabi and Ranong are also available. As in share taxis, fares are about double the public bus fares.

Getting Around
To/From the Airport There is a minibus service at the airport that will theoretically take you into town for 80B per person. However, if there aren't enough of you to fill the van, you'll most likely be directed towards a taxi. The same minibus also continues to Patong, Kata or Karon beaches for 120B, but again, unless there are enough of you, you're probably out of luck.

Taxis ask 360B for the trip from the airport to the city, 480B to 540B to the beaches; in the reverse direction you should be able to negotiate a fare of 300B from either place.

Car & Motorcycle Several agencies in town rent Suzuki jeeps for 900B per day, including insurance. If you rent for a week or more you can get the price down to 800B per day.

Avis Rent-A-Car (☎ 076-351243) Phuket International Airport. Charges a bit more (around 1500B a day) but has outlets around the island at Le Meridien, Dusit Laguna, Novotel Patong, Sheraton Grande Laguna Beach.
Pure Car Rent (☎ 076-211002) 75 Thanon Rasada. Your best choice in the centre of town.
Via Rent-A-Car (☎ 076-341660) 189/6 Thanon Rat Uthit, Patong. Offers similar rates to Pure, and can deliver to anywhere on the island.

Motorcycle taxis around town are 10B. You can hire motorcycles (usually 100cc Japanese bikes) in Phuket along Thanon Rasada between Thanon Phuket and Thanon Yaowarat or from various places at the beaches. Costs are in the 200B to 300B per day range. Bigger bikes (over 125cc) can be rented at a couple of shops at Patong and Karon.

You should think seriously about whether or not it's worth the convenience to rent a motorcycle on Phuket. Even Thais admit that driving on the island is dangerous. In 1999, 170 people were killed and 10,553 were injured in motorcycle accidents on Phuket. A significant number of these were foreign visitors. If you have an accident you're unlikely to find that medical attention is up to international standards. People who ride around in shorts, T-shirt and a pair of thongs are asking for trouble. A minor spill while wearing reasonable clothes would leave you bruised and shaken, but for somebody clad in shorts it could result in enough skin loss to end your travels right there.

Săwngthăew & Túk-Túk Large bus-size săwngthăew run regularly from Thanon Ranong near the market to the various Phuket beaches for 10B to 30B per person – see the Getting There & Away sections for the respective Beaches for details. Beware of tales about the tourist office being 5km away, or that the only way to reach the beaches is by taxi, or even that you'll need a taxi to get from the bus terminal to the town centre (the bus terminal is more or less *in* the town centre). Officially, beach săwngthăew run from 7 am to 5 pm; after that time you must charter a túk-túk to the beaches. The latter cost from 150B for Karon, Kata, Patong and Nai Han to 250B for Hat Kamala.

For a ride around town, smaller săwngthăew cost a standard 10B, túk-túk cost 20B.

AROUND PHUKET PROVINCE
Khao Phra Thaew Royal Wildlife & Forest Reserve
อุทยานสัตว์ป่าเขาพระแทว

This mountain range in the northern interior of the island protects 23 sq km of virgin island rainforest (evergreen monsoon forest). There are some nice jungle hikes in this reserve, along with a couple of **náam tòk** (waterfalls), **Ton Sai** and **Bang Pae**. The falls are best seen in the rainy season between June and November; in the dry months they slow to a trickle. Because of its royal status, the reserve is better protected than the average Thai national park.

A German botanist, Dr Darr, discovered a rare and unique species of palm in Khao Phra Thaew about 50 years ago. Called the white-backed palm or langkow palm, the fan-shaped plant stands 3m to 5m tall and is found only here and in Khao Sok National Park. The highest point in Khao Phra Thaew Royal Wildlife & Forest Reserve is 442m **Khao Phara**.

Tigers, Malayan sun bears, rhinos and elephants once roamed the forest here, but nowadays resident mammals are limited to humans, gibbons, monkeys, slow loris, langur, civets, flying foxes, squirrels, mousedeer and other smaller animals. Watch out for cobras and wild pigs.

Near Nam Tok Bang Pae (Bang Pae Falls), the **Phuket Gibbon Rehabilitation Centre** (☎ 076-381065, 260492) is open to the public from 10 am to 4 pm daily. Financed by donations, the centre cares for gibbons that have been kept in captivity and reintroduces them to the wild. Visitors who wish to help may 'adopt' a gibbon for 1500B, which will pay for one animal's care for a year. The program includes keeping you updated on your adopted gibbon's progress throughout the year of adoption. Park rangers may act as guides for hikes in the park on request; call ☎ 01-676 7864 and ask for Mr Phongchat. Payment for services is by donation.

To get to Khao Phra Thaew from the provincial capital, take Thanon Thepkasatri north about 20km to the district of Thalang, and turn right at the intersection for Nam Tok Ton Sai Waterfall 3km down the road.

Patong
ป่าตอง

Directly west of Phuket, Patong is a large curved beach around Ao Patong. During the 1990s, Hat Patong rapidly turned into another Pattaya in all respects. It is now a strip of hotels, upmarket bungalows, German and Italian restaurants, expensive seafood places, beer bars, nightclubs and coffee shops. It's also a major party scene; anyone looking for peace and quiet will be disappointed, while those looking for maximum nightlife need look no further. Ironically, although this began as Phuket's most expensive beach, the prices are stabilising, as the local accommodation market has become saturated with over 80 places to stay. As it becomes funkier, Patong is rapidly becoming the cheapest beach on the island for accommodation.

Information Patong has many foreign-exchange booths, plus its own post and telephone office off Soi Phoemphong Phattana and Thanon Thawiwong.

Email & Internet Access Several places in Patong offer terminals, including Pizzedelic on Thanon Thawiwong, next to the Banana Disco.

Dive Shops Patong is the diving centre of the island. See Diving & Snorkelling at the start of the Phuket Province section for a list of established dive shops.

Massage & Herbal Sauna The Hideaway (☎ 076-340591), on Thanon Na Nai in the foothills of east Patong, is an excellent sauna and massage centre. A two-hour Thai herbal massage/sauna package costs 950B. Massage or sauna alone is 500B per hour. Other treatments are available, including facials and aromatherapy. It's open from noon to 9 pm daily.

Places to Stay – Budget Rates on Patong vary according to season. In the high season (December to March, and August) you'll be doing very well to find something under 400B a night. On the beach there is nothing under 600B, but on and off Thanon Rat Uthit, especially in the Paradise Complex shopping arcade and along Soi Saen Sabai, there are several nondescript guesthouses with rooms for 300B to 500B. The best of the lot is the central but quiet *999 Peters Guest House* (☎/fax 076-340555), which has clean fan rooms with shared bathroom for 200B to 250B and rooms with private bathroom for 350B. The prices increase by 100B during the high season.

During the low season some of the 600B places will drop to as low as 400B, but that's about it. Budget places usually come with fan and shared bathroom; more expensive rooms in this category will have a private bathroom and perhaps air-con. During the rainy season, from May to November, you may be able to knock about 100B off rates.

Chanathip Guest House (☎ 076-294087, fax 294088), off Thanon Rat Uthit south of Thanon Sawatdirak (opposite the Pow Wow Pub) has rooms with fan, refrigerator, satellite TV, phone and hot-water shower for 450B, 700B with air-con. Private lockers are available. The **PS Bungalow** (PS II; ☎ 076-342207–8, 78/54 Thanon Rat Uthit) and **Shamrock Park Inn** (☎ 076-340991, 17/2 Thanon Rat Uthit) aren't bad backstreet places for 400B to 650B (add 100B in December). **Capricorn Village** (☎ 076-340390, 82/29 Thanon Rat Uthit) has good bungalows for 500B to 1000B and is often fully booked from mid-November through January, when the rates jump to 800B to 1500B.

Places to Stay – Mid-Range A large number of places in Patong fall into the 800B to 2000B range, which always includes air-con and private bathroom; the more expensive ones will have hot-water showers, lower priced ones cold water only. Room rates vary widely depending on the time of year. Besides high and low season, some establishments find it necessary to jack up their prices even higher during the 'peak' season, roughly December and January. On the bright side, prices in this category can usually be negotiated downwards substantially during the rainy season.

At the friendly, quiet and efficient **Sansabai Bungalows** (☎ 076-342948–9, fax 344888), at the end of Soi Saen Sabai off Thanon Rat Uthit, all rooms have hot water, fridge and TV. High-season prices are 1100B for rooms with fan, 1595B for deluxe rooms with air-con, 1430B to 1540B for superior rooms and 1980B for bungalows with air-con and kitchen. During the low season these drop to 550B fan, 750B deluxe, 850B to 980B superior and 1400B bungalow. These rates include breakfast but not tax (10%). The restaurant serves a range of Italian and Thai dishes.

Considering its central location facing the beach on Thanon Thawiwong, rooms at the friendly **Safari Beach Hotel** (☎ 076-341170, fax 340231) aren't too pricey at 900B in the low season and 2000B in the high season. There's also a small but pleasant pool and a good seafood restaurant.

Just a little farther south on the same stretch of Thanon Thawiwong, **Tropica Bungalow** (☎ 076-340204, fax 340206) offers similar rooms for 1300B in the low season and 2000B in the high season. The Banana Disco is next door.

The **Sky Inn** (☎ 076-342486, fax 340576) on the 9th floor of the Patong Grand Condotel, caters to a primarily gay

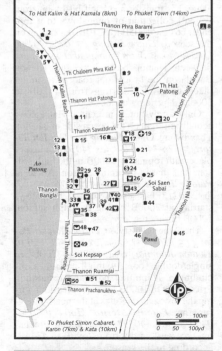

PATONG

PLACES TO STAY
1 Patong Lodge Hotel
2 Diamond Cliff Resort
6 PS Bungalow (PS II)
9 Shamrock Park Inn
10 Patong Grand Condotel; Sky Inn
11 Casuarina Patong Garden Resort
12 Phuket Cabana Resort
13 Patong Beach Bungalow
14 Patong Bay Garden Resort
15 Thara Patong
16 Chanathip Guest House
22 999 Peters Guest House
23 Capricorn Village
31 Safari Beach Hotel
33 Tropica Bungalow
38 Patong Beach Hotel
41 Baan Sukhothai Hotel
44 Sansabai Bungalows
51 Comfort Resort Patong
52 Patong Merlin Hotel

PLACES TO EAT
3 Da Maurizio Bar Ristorante
4 Otowa
5 Baan Rim Pa
18 Ngoen Lan
28 Restaurant 4
32 Sovoey

34 Pizzedelic
37 Seafood Stalls
39 Navrang Mahal
40 Le Croissant
47 Viva Mexico

OTHER
7 Mosque
8 Wat Suwan Khiri Wong
17 Pow Wow Pub
19 Hospital
20 Police Station
21 Paradise Complex
24 Bank
25 Valhalla
26 Soi Sunset Bars
27 Rock Hard a Go Go
29 Andaman Queen
30 Gonzo Bar
35 Banana Disco
36 Shipwreck
42 Shark Club
43 Tai Pan
45 The Hideaway
46 Market
48 Post & Telephone Office
49 Patong Shopping Centre
50 Buses to Phuket

clientele. Rooms cost 700B with fan to 1200B with air-con in high season and as low as 500B for fan and 700B for air-con during the rainy season.

Patong Lodge Hotel (☎ 076-341020–4, fax 340287), just north of Hat Patong in a more secluded and rocky area known as Hat Kalim, has well-kept rooms with all amenities starting from 900B to 2300B, depending on the season.

Places to Stay – Top End At the lower end of the top-end price range (roughly around 2000B to 3000B) you'll find a number of air-con places with swimming pools, modest room service, phones and most of the other amenities desired by the average mainstream visitor and package tourist.

Towards the north end of Thanon Thawiwong facing the beach, long-established *Casuarina Patong Garden Resort (☎ 076-341197, fax 340123, 77/1 Thanon Thawiwong)* has transformed itself bit-by-bit from a small collection of bungalows to a top-ender costing 1605B to 3210B, depending on the season. *Thara Patong (☎ 076-340135, fax 340446, ⓔ thara@sun.phuket.ksc.co.th)*, between Thanon Sawatdirak and Thanon Bangla on the beachfront road, is a similar place with rates starting from 1320B to 3000B, depending on the season.

Only a few hotels in central Hat Patong actually sit right on the beach side of Thanon Thawiwong. One is *Patong Bay Garden Resort (☎ 076-340297–8, fax 340560)*, a luxury place with rooms for 3000B in the high season, half that in the rainy season. Adjacent *Patong Beach Bungalow (☎ 076-340117, fax 340213)* has separate deluxe bungalows starting at 2000B during the high season, 1200B during the low season.

The American-style *Comfort Resort Patong (☎ 076-294130–4, fax 294143, 18/110 Thanon Ruamjai)* charges 2800/3200B for single/double rooms with all amenities, including a swimming pool and restaurant. Prices drop to 1600B for a double room during the low season. Rates at the nearby long-running *Patong Merlin Hotel (☎ 076-340037, fax 340394)*, on Thanon Prachanukhro, vary wildly from 2696B to 4244B, according to the season.

Moving up a couple of notches to places with true world-class standards, rates start at 3000B and reach epic proportions for large suites with the best bay views. Many top-end places add a 500B to 1000B peak-season surcharge between late December and mid-January.

Another place right on the beach, *Phuket Cabana Resort (☎ 076-340138, fax 340178, 41 Thanon Thawiwong)* has luxuriously appointed bungalows for 5800B (subtract 2000B in the low season), including breakfast. The independently owned and managed *Patong Beach Hotel (☎ 076-340301, fax 340541)*, which actually isn't on the beach but back off Thanon Thawiwong south of Thanon Bangla, starts at 4943B for large, luxurious rooms on landscaped grounds.

If you're looking for Thai ambience, the *Baan Sukhothai Hotel (☎ 076-314394, fax 340197)*, off Thanon Bangla, may be your best choice. Set on spacious grounds, the hotel uses lots of teak assembled in semi-open, central Thai architectural motifs – a bit out of place in Phuket perhaps, but a favourite with tour groups. Rack rates are 3884B but discounts down to 2119B are available in the low season.

Up on Hat Kalim, the *Diamond Cliff Resort (☎ 076-340501, fax 340507)* has units in spacious grounds with good sea views from 4235B to 7651B, depending on the season.

Places to Eat Patong has stacks of restaurants, some of them quite good. The seafood restaurants are concentrated along Thanon Bangla. Most are expensive; lobster in Patong is going for about 1000B per kilogram these days.

Restaurant 4, in a no-nonsense, fluorescent-lit shed off Thanon Bangla, is the best priced of the seafood places; add your name to the graffiti on the walls when you've finished dining. A couple more bargain *seafood stalls* can be found on the tiny soi opposite Soi Eric on Thanon Bangla. Walk a few metres down the soi and look for the push carts on the right.

Savoey is a big open-air seafood restaurant in front of the Safari Beach Hotel on Thanon Thawiwong with atmosphere and a good slay 'em and weigh 'em-style setup.

Around the intersection of Thanon Rat Uthit and Thanon Bangla are a few inexpensive Thai and fàràng cafes worth trying. *Le Croissant (☎ 076-342743)*, on Thanon Bangla, carries French pastries, French wines, sandwiches, salads, baguettes and imported cheeses. A couple of soi south, Soi Phoemphong Phattana offers a string of international eateries, including **Viva Mexico**, **Saloniki Greek** and a couple of German restaurants.

Pizzedelic on Thanon Thawiwong, next to the Banana Disco, does creative pizza toppings and killer Caesar salads.

Navrang Mahal, on Soi Patong Resort, has probably Patong's best Indian food.

Cheap and delicious lamb and beef gyros can be found at a little **stand** on the corner of Thanon Bangla and Thanon Rat Uthit.

For inexpensive noodle and rice vendors, check Thanon Sawatdirak. **Ngoen Lan** (no Roman-script sign), on the south-eastern corner of Thanon Sawatdirak and Thanon Rat Uthit, is an all night khâo tôm place that's good and inexpensive.

For a splurge you might try one of three classy restaurants on the northern edge of Patong at Ban Kalim. The location of **Baan Rim Pa** (☎ 076-340789), set above a thicket of mangrove trees on the beach, affords a stunning view of the ocean beyond. The restaurant serves Thai food, just slightly toned down for visitors' tastes. There is also a bar and cigar lounge. Next door is **Otowa** (☎ 076-344254), a Japanese restaurant situated just above the crashing waves, which specialises in Japanese barbecue and also has a sushi bar. Next door to Otowa is **Da Maurizio Bar Ristorante** (☎ 076-344079), an Italian restaurant with an equally spectacular setting.

Entertainment Dancing has become the main night-time activity in Patong as a new generation of tourists interested in more than just sitting on their bums in a bar has taken over the scene. **Banana Disco** (☎ 076-340301, 96 Thanon Thawiwong) is still one of the more popular dance clubs. The attached **Banana Pub** is very in at the moment, and offers a nonthreatening coffeehouse atmosphere where most Western women and couples should feel comfortable. Another such place is **Shipwreck** on Thanon Bangla. More of a bar but without the ubiquitous hostesses, its location opposite Soi Kathoey makes it a great place to peoplewatch. Two other popular dance clubs are the hi-tech **Shark Club** on Thanon Bangla and the nearby **Tai Pan**, on Thanon Rat Uthit where it intersects with Thanon Bangla. The Tai Pan is more of an after-hours place and doesn't get kicking until about 3 am. Some of these big clubs collect cover charges of 100B to 200B, which includes a drink coupon or two.

The **Pow Wow Pub** on Thanon Rat Uthit near the Paradise Complex is a typical old-west Thai bar with live country & western mixed with Thai folk rock.

There are dozens of simple bars around town, many of them little more than a collection of stools around a rectangular bar and a handful of female touts whose objective is to hook passersby and keep them drinking long enough to pay the rent. Thanon Bangla is the main 'zone' but they're also found all along Thanon Thawiwong and Thanon Rat Uthit – anywhere there isn't a hotel, restaurant or souvenir shop. **Rock Hard a Go Go** (☎ 076-340409) on the corner of Thanon Bangla and Thanon Rat Uthit is one of the larger and more popular go-go bars. Managed by an American woman, the Rock Hard welcomes couples and solo women. It also has a terrace bar that affords a fine view of the surrounding nightlife venues. On the same street, **Kangaroo Bar**, **Gonzo Bar** and **U2 Bar** get started late and go into the morning hours.

A string of bars on Soi Sunset (near the intersection of Thanon Rat Uthit and Thanon Bangla) doesn't get started until around midnight, and rocks until about 6 am. The crowd consists mainly of Western men and Thai women (many of whom will have just got off work), but it's still enough of a social scene that couples and female travellers can join in the partying with no real problem.

Valhalla, with something of a Nordic theme park for beer drinkers, is located at the end of Soi Sunset. The imaginatively decorated complex includes a stone watchtower and a miniature poolside bar within a Viking ship.

There's a strip of gay go-go bars on the various soi leading into the Paradise Complex. If you like transvestite shows, check out the well-done **Phuket Simon Cabaret** (☎ 076-342011), south of town on the way to Karon and Kata. Performances occur at 7.30 pm and 9.30 pm nightly. Sleazier but more of a hoot is the kàthoey go-go and cabaret show at **Andaman Queen** at the end of Soi Kathoey on Thanon Bangla.

Shopping A string of shops and stalls along the central part of Thanon Thawiwong sell clothing, silk, jewellery and souvenirs from all over Thailand. The prices here are higher than average.

Getting There & Away Săwngthăew from Phuket to Patong leave from Thanon Ranong, near the day market and fountain circle; the fare is 30B. The after-hours charter fare is 150B. Săwngthăew and buses from Patong to Phuket leave from the corner of Thanon Thawiwong and Thanon Prachanukhro until 7 pm.

Getting Around Túk-túk circulate Patong for 10B per ride. There are numerous places to rent 125cc motorcycles and jeeps. Patong Big Bike (☎ 076-340380) on Thanon Rat Uthit rents 250cc to 750cc bikes. Keep in mind that the law requiring all motorcycle riders to wear helmets is strictly enforced in Patong.

Motor yachts, sailboats and catamarans can sometimes be chartered with or without crew. Check with dive shops around Patong to find out who has what.

Several travel agencies on Patong do day cruises to nearby islands. For excursions to the Similan and Surin Islands off the Andaman Coast, see the Phang-Nga Province section earlier in this chapter.

Karon

กะรน

Karon is a long, gently curving beach with small sand dunes and a few palms and casuarina trees. Some insist on calling it two beaches: Karon Yai and Karon Noi. Karon Noi, also known as Relax Bay, can only be reached from Hat Patong and is almost entirely monopolised by Le Meridien Hotel. The main section of Karon now features a paved promenade with streetlights, and the entire area has blended with Hat Kata to the south to produce a self-contained village inhabited by a mixture of tourists, seasonal residents and year-rounders. It is still a fairly peaceful beach, where a few fisherfolk cast nets, and where you can occasionally buy fresh seafood from their boats. However, the rice fields between the beach and the surrounding hills have been abandoned or filled with high-rise hotels.

Karon's worst feature are the canals that feed into the sea; they badly need cleaning, not so much from the effluent they contain as the rubbish, which is allowed to collect in them year-round. Developers in Karon like to boast that this is one of Phuket's 'high end' beaches with an 'ecological' consciousness; the canal situation proves them dead wrong.

Dino Park (☎ 076-330625), next to Marina Cottage, features an 18-hole minigolf course with a Fred Flintstone-looking environment, along with a fake waterfall. There is also food (eg, Bronto Burgers), music in the Rock Garden and drinks at the Dino Bar. It's open all day and late into the night.

Places to Stay Karon is lined with inns and deluxe bungalows, along with a number of places with rooms or huts for under 400B. During the low season – May to November – you can often get a 400B room for as low as 200B to 250B, a 1000B room for 600B, and a 2000B room for 1000B.

Most of the places under 700B are well off the beach, often on small hillocks to the east of the main road. At the northern end of the beach, *Ann House* (no phone) has a row of 14 very basic fan rooms with private bathroom for 150B to 300B. Next door *Lume & Yai Bungalow* (☎/fax 076-396096) has the advantage of a hillside location; its 19 huts cost 300B to 500B. One advantage to both of these places is that beach săwngthăew usually pass right in front.

In the commercial centre of Karon, near the roundabout, the quiet *Karon Seaview Bungalow* (☎ 076-396798–9) offers OK concrete duplexes and row houses for 300B in the low season and 450B in the high season. On the main road near the beach is the popular and friendly *My Friend Bungalow* (☎ 076-396344), with 45 rooms for 200B to 350B during the low season, 600B to 900B during the high; the cafe out the front is a plus. *Fantasy Hill Bungalow* (☎ 076-330106), farther south on a small hill off the main road, has decent bungalows, some with air-con, for 350B to 600B, or as low as 200B to 400B in the rainy season. All rooms have small refrigerators.

In the mid-range (averaging 500B and up) is the *Crystal Beach Hotel* (☎ 076-396580–5, fax 336584), on the main road away from the beach. The air-con rooms are 1000B in the high season, but only half that during the low season.

The **Karon Village Bungalow** (☎ 076-396431), inland a bit on Thanon Patak, has all air-con rooms with fridge and hot-water shower for 1100B, discounted to 450B in the low season. **Karon Guest House** (☎ 076-396860), just east of the roundabout, has fan rooms for 800B in the high season and 500B in the low season, or air-con rooms for 1000B in the high season and 600B in the low season. You can knock 100B off all room rates if you stay more than one night.

Many of the remaining places on Karon are newer resort-type hotels with rooms starting at 1500B or above, with air-con, swimming pools, multiple restaurants etc. Prices at most places have come down a bit over the last two years due to competition, although a few places have raised their rates. Bargaining at the larger ones is worthwhile; as a rule of thumb the more rooms they have, the more they'll drop the price, especially during the south-west monsoon season, from May to October. Among the more reliable is the **Felix Karon Phuket** (☎ 076-396666, fax 396853), which has 81 rooms and is vaguely American south-western in style. Rates start at 4000B in the high season but plummet to 1800B for a double room, with breakfast included, in the low season.

Occupying a scenic spot on the southern end of Hat Karon, the **Karon Beach Resort** (☎ 076-330006, fax 330529) has 81 rooms with all the mod-cons, from 4400B in the high season, 2000B in the low.

On the beach road, the **Karon Villa & Karon Royal Wing** (☎ 076-396139, fax 396122, ✉ karon@phuket.ksc.co.th) has 'standard' two-bed bungalows for 4120B (2472B in the low season) and larger 'superior' two-bed bungalows for 4473B (2684B in the low season).

Up at Karon Noi (Relax Bay), the small bay around the northern headland of Karon, the top-end **Le Meridien Phuket** (☎ 076-340480, fax 340479, ✉ meridien@phuket.ksc.co.th) has 470 well-appointed rooms from US$210. Above Le Meridien on a hillside, a bit of a hike from the beach, the **Karon Hill** (☎/fax 076-341343) has simple but adequate rooms with private bathroom for 600B to 900B, depending on the season or your bargaining skills.

KARON & KATA

PLACES TO STAY
1 Felix Karon Phuket
2 Ann House
3 Lume & Yai Bungalow
6 Karon Guest House
7 Crystal Beach Hotel
9 My Friend Bungalow
10 Karon Villa & Karon Royal Wing
12 Karon Seaview Bungalow
13 Karon Village Bungalow
17 Karon Beach Resort
18 Marina Cottage
19 Kata Garden Resort
22 Lucky Guest House
25 Kata On Sea
26 Fantasy Hill Bungalow
29 Smile Inn
30 Peach Hill Hotel
31 Dome Bungalow; Sumitra Thai House
33 Club Méditerranée (Club Med)
36 Kata Beach Resort
37 The Boathouse
38 Friendship Bungalow
39 Cool Breeze
41 Pop Cottage
42 Kata Thani Resort
43 Katanoi Riviera
44 Kata Thani Resort (Kata Buri Wing)

PLACES TO EAT
4 Seafood Restaurants
5 Red Onion
8 The Little Mermaid
11 Seafood Restaurants
14 Old Siam
20 Raan Khao Kaeng
21 Bluefin Tavern
24 Bondeli Kata
27 Kampong-Kata Hill
28 Pizzedelic
32 Seafood Restaurants
40 Gung Café

OTHER
15 Maxim Supermarket
16 Dino Park
23 Post Office
34 Sawngthaew to Phuket
35 Bank

Places to Eat As usual, almost every place to stay provides some food. The cheapest Thai and seafood places are off the roundabout near the commercial centre, although overall you'll find more selection farther south at Hat Kata Yai and Hat Kata Noi.

The Little Mermaid, 100m east of the traffic circle, has a long, inexpensive, mostly Scandinavian menu written in 12 languages; it's open 24 hours.

Crossing the road and going another 100m in the same direction will bring you to *Red Onion* (Hawm Daeng), a simple, open-air Thai restaurant with good and cheap eats.

Old Siam, part of the Thavorn Palm Beach, is a large open-air place designed in central Thai style and producing Thai dishes for the tourist palate for 100B to 300B.

Getting There & Away See the Kata Getting There & Away section for details on transport to Karon.

Kata

กะตะ

Just around a headland south from Karon, Kata is a more interesting beach and is divided into two – Ao Kata Yai (Big Kata Bay) and Ao Kata Noi (Little Kata Bay). The small island of Ko Pu is within swimming distance of the shore and on the way are some OK coral reefs. Snorkelling gear can be rented from several of the bungalow groups. Although it has around 30 hotels and bungalow resorts, it is much less crowded than Patong, yet has a slightly urban feel. Concrete walls, protecting upmarket resorts from the riffraff, are a detraction. Contrary to rumour, the beach in front of Club Med is open to the public.

The Boathouse offers a two-day **Thai cooking class** each weekend from 10 am to 1.30 pm for 2200B per person including lunch, Boathouse recipes and a certificate.

Places to Stay – Budget The crowd of places to stay ranges from 150B at Kata On Sea, inland and between Kata Yai and Kata Noi, to 8710B for a suite at the classy Boathouse, a step above the Club Med on Kata Yai. In general the less expensive places tend to be off the beach between Kata Yai (to the north) and Kata Noi (to the south) or well off the beach on the road to the island interior.

Friendship Bungalow (☎ 076-330499), a popular place off the beach at the headland between Kata Yai and Kata Noi, is 350B for fan bungalow with attached bathroom, 750B for air-con.

Kata On Sea (☎ 076-330594), on a ridge off Thanon Thai Na east of Kata Yai, offers simple huts with ceiling fans, mosquito nets and attached bathroom for 150B to 300B, depending on the season.

One place worth checking out – basic but clean and friendly – is *Lucky Guest House* (☎ 076-330572, 110/44-45 Thanon Thai Na) with fan rooms for 250B, fan bungalows for 300B, and air-con bungalows for 600B. It's found towards the back road that runs parallel to the beach, north-east of Bondeli Kata restaurant.

Rooms at *Cool Breeze* (☎ 076-330484) in Kata Noi start at 350B for sturdy fan bungalows with fridge and hot water, to 700B for an air-con bungalow.

A couple of places conveniently near the beach and beachside seafood restaurants include *Dome Bungalow* (☎ 076-330270), which has fan bungalows with hot-water showers for 800B during the high season and 450B during the low season. Air-con bungalows are also available and prices vary according to size and condition, from 750B to 800B in the low season. During the high season the prices double. The nearby *Sumitra Thai House* (☎ 076-330515) has only eight rooms but is also located near the beach. Fan rooms with fridge and hot water go for 1000B in the high season and 400B in the low season. Air-con rooms are 1500B during the high season and 700B in the low season.

Places to Stay – Mid-Range As with many other mid-range places on the island, many of Kata's have almost doubled in price since the last edition. Recommended mid-range places (all air-con) in Kata are *Peach Hill Hotel* (☎ 076-330603, fax 330895). In a nice setting with a pool, it has rooms with TV, fridge and hot water starting at 1531B, breakfast included. *Smile Inn* (☎ 076-330926, fax 330925) is a clean, friendly place with a pleasant open-air cafe and rooms with hot-water showers, TV and fridge for 1100B (1200B including breakfast).

Other mid-range lodgings are available at *Pop Cottage* (☎ 076-330181, fax 330794, e popcott@loxinfo.co.th), which has units on a hill opposite the south end of Kata Yai costing from 963B to 1491B during the low season. Prices increase by 800B during the high season. *Kata Garden Resort* (☎ *076-330627, fax 330446*), opposite the Marina Cottage, has 50 stilted bungalows and lots of trees. Rates are 824/912B single/double with fan. 'Superior' bungalows with fridge and hot water are 1059/1177B. Larger 'deluxe' bungalows go for 1359/1471B. Prices increase by about 500B during the high season.

Across the road from the beach at Kata Noi, *Katanoi Riviera* (☎ *076-330726, fax 330294*) is a cluster of row houses and bungalows, with a bit of landscaping, costing 300B for a fan bungalow to 1000B for an aircon bungalow with hot water. During the high season the prices are 800B and 2000B. Much of its beach view is blocked by the Kata Thani, but the setting is still relaxing.

Places to Stay – Top End Moving up in price, one of the more exemplary places at the top end is the long-running *Marina Cottage* (☎ *076-330625, fax 330516*, e *info@ marina-cottage.com*), a medium-scale, low-rise, low-density place on shady, palm-studded grounds near the beach. During the high season, room rates range from US$100 to US$160, dropping to US$80 to US$112 during the low season. Some rooms have an ocean view while others are set back in a wooded area.

The Boathouse (☎ *076-330015, fax 330561*, e *the.boathouse@phuket.com; in Bangkok* ☎ *02-438 1123*), the brainchild of architect and Phuket resident ML Tri Devakul, is a 36-room boutique resort that manages to stay full year-round without resorting to low-season rates. In spite of rather ordinary-looking if spacious rooms, the hotel hosts a steady influx of Thai politicos, pop stars, artists, celebrity authors (the hotel hosts periodic poetry/fiction readings) and the ordinary rich on the strength of its stellar service, acclaimed restaurant and its scenic spot at the south end of Kata Yai. Rooms start at 8710B, plus tax and service.

The palatial 202-room *Kata Thani Resort* (☎ *076-330124–6, fax 330426*, e *katathani@phuket.com*) commands most of the beach at Kata Noi and is one of the choicest spots anywhere along Karon or Kata. Upmarket, well-appointed rooms on nicely landscaped grounds cost from 5082B

to 6292B, with a 30% drop in rates during the low season. There are two swimming pools at the main Kata Thani resort, and another across the road and south a bit at the Kata Buri Wing (which was formerly under separate management).

Close to Kata Yai and near Club Med, the *Kata Beach Resort* (☎ *076-330530, fax 330128*, e *katagrp@loxinfo.co.th*) is a three-storey concrete hotel on the access road to the beach. Its 262 rooms (not all have beach views) range from 5179B to 5650B, with a 50% discount in the low season. The *Club Med* (☎ *076-330455–9, fax 330461; in Bangkok* ☎ *02-253 9758*) occupies a large chunk of land near Kata Yai, as well as a fair swathe of beachfront. Per-person rates range from around 3800B to 6000B.

Places to Eat Most of the restaurants in Kata offer standard tourist food and service. The best restaurant in the entire area, including Karon and Patong to the north, is *The Boathouse Wine & Grill*, which is owned by ML Tri Devakul, the architect who is attempting to bring high culture, art and cuisine to Phuket.

The Boathouse Wine & Grill started out as an indoor/outdoor restaurant and now has 36 rooms attached to its original location at the south end of Kata Yai. It boasts a wine collection that so far is the only one in Thailand to have been cited for excellence by *Wine Spectator* magazine. The nightly seafood buffet is excellent. It's a pricey place but the atmosphere is casual and service is tops.

Next to The Boathouse, and under the same ownership, *Gung Cafe* (*Kang*; ☎ *076-330015*) features seafood by The Boathouse chefs, served in a more casual atmosphere.

Another standout, although considerably less expensive, is the *Kampong-Kata Hill* (☎ *076-330103*), a Thai-style place decorated with antiques and situated on a hill a bit inland from the beach. It's open only for dinner, from 4 to 11 pm. *Bondeli Kata* (☎ *076-396482*), on the same road, serves fresh pastries, four kinds of coffee and nine teas, while *Bluefin Tavern* (☎ *076-330856*) features Tex-Mex, pizza, burgers and Thai food.

Opposite and down the road towards the beach is *Pizzedelic*, with an eclectic selection of pizza and salad.

Towards the east end of Thanon Thai Na, well past the Kampong-Kata Hill, **Ran Khao Kaeng** (no Roman-script sign) is one of the few restaurants in Kata that an ordinary Thai person can afford to eat at. As the name suggests, it specialises in Thai curries over rice.

Getting There & Away Săwngthăew and buses to both Kata and Karon leave frequently from the Thanon Ranong market in Phuket from 7 am to 5 pm for 30B per person. After-hours charters cost 150B to 200B. The main săwngthăew stop is in front of Kata Beach Resort.

Nai Han
ในหาน

A few kilometres south of Kata, this beach around a picturesque bay is similar to Kata and Karon but, in spite of the 1986 construction of Le Royal Meridien Phuket Yacht Club, it's not as developed. This is mainly thanks to the presence of Samnak Song Nai Han, a monastic centre in the middle of the beach that claims most of the beachfront land. To make up for the loss of saleable beachfront, developers started cutting away the forests on the hillsides overlooking the beach. Recently, however, the development seems to have reached a halt.

This means that Nai Han is usually one of the least crowded beaches on the southern part of the island.

The TAT says Hat Nai Han is a dangerous place to swim during the monsoon season (May to October), but it really varies according to daily or weekly weather changes – look for the red flag, which means dangerous swimming conditions. Beach chairs and umbrellas can be rented for 60B.

Places to Stay & Eat Except for the Yacht Club, there's really not much accommodation available on or even near the beach.

Well back from the beach, near the road into Nai Han and behind a small lagoon, is the motel-like **Nai Han Beach Resort** (☎ 076-381810), with tidy rooms for 600B with fan, 800B with air-con; add 200B in high season from December to February. On the other side of the reservoir **Romzai Bungalows** (☎ 076-381338) has simple huts for 400B in the December to April high season and 300B the remainder of the year. Farther along the same road towards the interior of the island, **Orchid Bungalows** (☎ 076-381396) offers more motel-like rooms next to an orchid nursery for around 800B.

Le Royal Meridien Phuket Yacht Club (☎ 076-381156, fax 381164, ⓔ info@ phuket-yachtclub.com) sits on the western end of Hat Nai Han. Originally built at the

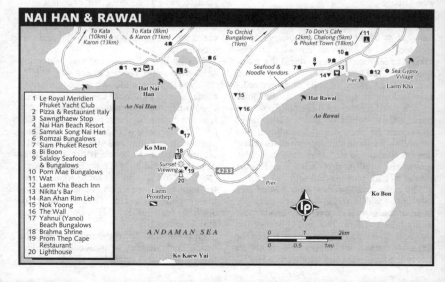

NAI HAN & RAWAI

1 Le Royal Meridien Phuket Yacht Club
2 Pizza & Restaurant Italy
3 Sawngthaew Stop
4 Nai Han Beach Resort
5 Samnak Song Nai Han
6 Romzai Bungalows
7 Siam Phuket Resort
8 Bi Boon
9 Salaloy Seafood & Bungalows
10 Porn Mae Bungalows
11 Wat
12 Laem Kha Beach Inn
13 Nikita's Bar
14 Ran Ahan Rim Leh
15 Nok Yoong
16 The Wall
17 Yahnui (Yanoi) Beach Bungalows
18 Brahma Shrine
19 Prom Thep Cape Restaurant
20 Lighthouse

astronomical cost of 145 million baht, the hotel has given up on the idea of becoming a true yacht club (apparently the bay currents aren't right for such an endeavour) and has removed the mobile pier. Luxurious rooms are still available for US$225 to US$928 a night. A line of bamboo-and-thatch huts housing cheap eateries and bars sits outside the gated entrance to Le Royal Meridien, tempting its guests to stray from their posh digs. Of these, *Pizza & Restaurant Italy* is Italian owned and has a wood-burning pizza oven. Nearby *Strand Charley's* and *Matahari Cafe* are clean and look promising as well.

On the other end of the bay from the Yacht Club, off the road to Rawai, *Yanui Beach Bungalows* (Yanoi; ☎/fax 076-238180) features a set of plain cottages, with ceiling fans and attached shower, on the opposite side of the road from the beach. Smaller bungalows cost 650B a night and somewhat nicer ones cost 850B. During the low season all bungalows cost 500B. A rustic restaurant enjoys a beautiful location on its own small sandy cove opposite the bungalows. It's a very quiet and peaceful spot among coconut palms, mangroves and casuarina trees; the cape and grassy hills nearby have lots of hiking potential. You'll need your own transport to get here.

Getting There & Away Nai Han is 18km from Phuket and a sǎwngthǎew (leaving from the intersection of Thanon Ranong and the fountain circle) costs 25B per person. Túk-túk charters are 150B to 200B one way.

Rawai & Laem Kha
ราไวย์

Rawai was one of the first coastal areas on Phuket to be developed, simply because it was near Phuket and there was already a rather large fishing community here. Once nicer beach areas like Patong and Karon were 'discovered', Rawai gradually began to lose popularity and today it is a spiritless place – but it's not crowded.

The beach is not so great, but there is a lot happening in or near Rawai: there is a local **sea-gypsy village**; Hat Laem Kha (better than Rawai) is to the north-east;

boats leave from the No 16 jetty and go to the nearby islands of Ko Lon, Ko Hae, Ko Aew, Ko Phi and others; and there's good snorkelling off **Laem Phromthep** at the southern tip of Phuket island, easy to approach from Rawai. In fact, most of the visitors who stay at Rawai these days are divers who want to be near Phromthep or boat facilities for offshore diving trips.

Laem Phromthep is also a popular viewing point at sunset, when busloads of Thai tourists come to pose for photos and enjoy the view. On a hill next to the viewpoint is a shrine to Phra Phrom (Brahma) as well as a lighthouse built to commemorate King Rama IX's 50th anniversary on the throne. On a clear day you can see Ko Phi-Phi from the back of the lighthouse.

The diving around the offshore islands is not bad, especially at Kaew Yai and Kaew Noi, off Phromthep and at Ko Hae. It's a good idea to shop around for boat trips to these islands to find the least expensive passage – the larger the group, the cheaper the cost per person.

If you're looking for a physical challenge, The Wall restaurant, on the road from Rawai north-west to Nai Han, has a **rockclimbing** wall as well as massage, herbal saunas and a jacuzzi.

Places to Stay The long-running *Salaloy Seafood & Bungalows* (☎ 076-381370, 52/2 Thanon Wiset) has bungalows for 350B with fan and up to 800B with air-con. Their seafood restaurant is one of the better – and more moderately priced – ones in the area. The whole operation closes down for the low season. Adjacent is the similar *Porn Mae Bungalows* (☎/fax 076-381300) with fan bungalows going for 350B, 500B in the high season. *Siam Phuket Resort* (☎ 076-381346, fax 381347) offers sturdy bungalows with air-con, hot water and fridge in the 650B to 900B range. These prices double during the high season.

Laem Ka Beach Inn (☎ 076-381305) has 20 thatched bungalows spread out among coconut groves starting at 500B for fan, and up to 900B for larger ones. During the high season the prices increase to 650B with fan and 1200B with air-con. The shoreline along this rounded cape is an interesting mix of clean sand and large boulders, and is a favourite local picnic spot. The swimming is good.

Places to Eat Besides the restaurants attached to the resorts in Rawai (Salaloy is the best), there are seafood and noodle vendors set up along the roadside near the beach, including *Ran Ahan Rim Leh* (no Roman-script sign), on the beach almost opposite Salaloy. Nearby is *Nikita's Bar*, which is interestingly decorated and very popular in the evenings. *Bi Boon*, between Salaloy and Siam Phuket Resort, offers an extensive breakfast menu including American, continental and German breakfasts. On the road from Rawai north-west to Nai Han is *The Wall*, with grilled seafood and salads as well as a rockclimbing wall and herbal sauna. *Nok Yoong*, just beyond The Wall, is an outdoor restaurant with reasonably priced Thai food. Just below the viewpoint for Laem Phromthep, *Prom Thep Cape Restaurant* offers simple Thai meals. *Don's Cafe* (☎ 076-288229), off Thanon Wiset between Rawai and Chalong, offers hearty meals of steak and ribs barbecued over a mesquite-wood fire. To get there from Phuket town, turn right at the Phuket Yacht Club sign just south of the Chalong roundabout. Don's Cafe is located 2km from the turn-off, just past the mosque.

Getting There & Away Rawai is about 16km from Phuket and costs 15B by săwngthăew from the circle at Thanon Ranong. Túk-túk charters cost at least 150B.

Laem Singh & Hat Kamala
แหลมสิงห์/หาดกมลา

Laem Singh (Cape Singh) is a beautiful rock-dominated beach north of Ao Patong and 24km from Phuket. You can camp here and eat at the rustic roadside seafood places at the northern end of Singh or in Ban Kamala, a village farther south.

More civilised is Hat Kamala, a lovely stretch of sand and sea south of Surin and Laem Singh. The northern end (the nicest area) is shaded by casuarina trees and features a small thatched-roof snack bar where free sling-chairs and beach umbrellas are available. The middle of the beach is now dominated by resorts and seafood restaurants. Most of the villagers here are Muslim, and there are a couple of rustic mosques towards the southern end of the main village, also known as Bang Wan. Visitors should

dress modestly when walking around the village in deference to local mores. Topless or nude beach bathing would be extremely offensive to the locals.

Phuket Fantasea (☎ 076-271222, fax 271333), a US$60 million 'cultural theme park' is located just north of Hat Kamala. Despite the billing, there aren't any rides but there is a truly magical show that manages to capture the colour and pageantry of traditional Thai dance and costumes and combine them with state-of-the-art light and sound techniques that rival anything found in Las Vegas. All of this takes place on a stage dominated by a full-scale replica of a Khmer temple reminiscent of Angkor Wat. Kids especially would be captivated by the spectacle. There is also quite a good and varied collection of souvenir shops in the park offering Thai-made handicrafts. Phuket Fantasea is open from 5.30 to 11.30 pm daily except Tuesday and admission is 1000B for the show and 1500B including a surprisingly good Thai buffet dinner. Tickets can be booked through most hotels and tour agencies. The park has a Web site at www.phuket-fantasea.com.

HAT KAMALA, SURIN & AO BANG THAO

1 Banyan Tree Phuket
2 Lotus Restaurant
3 The Allamanda Phuket
4 Sheraton Grande Phuket Laguna
5 Dusit Laguna Resort
6 Tatonka
7 Hideaway Day Spa
8 Laguna Beach Club
9 Royal Park Beach Resort
10 Bangtao Lagoon Bungalow
11 Amanpuri Resort

Ao Bang Thao

Choeng Thaleh

To Matsayit Mukaram & Heroines Monument (6km)

Laem Son

Hat Surin

Laem Singh

ANDAMAN SEA

Hat Kamala

To Patong

Ban Kamala

Approximate Scale

12 The Chedi
13 Surin Sweet Apartment
14 Taengthai Guesthouse & Restaurant
15 Phuket Fantasea
16 Nanork Seafood & Buffalo Bar
17 Malinee House
18 Bird Beach Bungalows
19 Kamala Seafood
20 Pa Pa Crab
21 Phuket Kamala Resort
22 Mosque
23 Kamala Beach Estate
24 Kamala Bay Terrace

Places to Stay The upmarket *Phuket Kamala Resort* (☎ *076-324396, fax 324399*) dominates the centre of the beach and prices start at 800B a night. High-season prices start at 1950B. The 40 bungalows have private balconies, air-con and TV; the coffee shop serves Thai and Western food.

Also on the other side of the road from the beach are several less-expensive options. Many eschew air-con, which is eminently sensible as Kamala hasn't become 'concrete-ised' enough yet to demand it. The quiet *Bird Beach Bungalows* (☎/fax 076-270669) has small, clean cottages with fan and shower for 650B, larger bungalows for 1200B. In this same area are several laundry services and minimarts, evidence that Kamala is attracting long-termers.

Other modest places to stay include the nearby *Malinee House* (☎ *076-271355*), which offers fan rooms for 350B and air-con rooms for 500B (high-season prices are 500B with fan and 700B with air-con), *Kamala Seafood* (☎ *076-324426*), with four rooms for 400B, and *Pa Pa Crab* (☎ *076-324315*), where a single/double room in a house costs 300B and a bungalow on the beach costs 500B. Towards the northern end of the beach near the police station, *Nanork Seafood & Buffalo Bar* (☎ *076-270668*) has clean rooms with fan for 500B. These last three places don't take guests from May to October.

At the southern end of the bay, overlooking but not on the beach, is *Kamala Beach Estate* (☎ *076-270756, fax 324115,* e *kamala .beach@phuket.com*), where fully-equipped, high-security, modern time-share apartments go for US$149 to US$425 in the high season and US$79 to US$215 in the low season. Around the headland farther south, the similar *Kamala Bay Terrace* (☎ *076-270801, fax 270818,* e *kamala@samart .co.th*) has more luxurious apartments and time-shares for 1999B to 3500B, depending on the season and size of the room.

Places to Eat The best value for eating is the friendly *thatched-roof restaurant* at the northern end of the beach. Near Bird Beach Bungalows are the decent *Kamala Seafood* and *Jaroen Seafood*, both family-run Thai seafood places that cater to fàràng. *Paul's Place* (☎ *076-270756*), next to Kamala Beach Estate at the southern end of the bay,

> ### Warning
>
> All of the western Phuket beaches, including Surin, Laem Singh and Kamala, have strong riptides during the monsoons. Take care when swimming, or don't go in the water at all if you're not a strong swimmer.
>
> Keep an eye out for jet skis when you're in the water. The Phuket governor declared jet skis illegal in 1997 and it looks like the ban has finally taken hold. Still, the situation may change at any time, so swimmers should always be aware of the potential danger.

is the most upmarket place to eat; it offers good views of the bay and reliable Thai and Western food.

For something more local, try one of the several *kopíi shops* (with strong coffee or *kopíi*) in the village.

Getting There & Away A regular săwngthăew between Kamala and Patong (from 7 am to 5 pm) costs 25B per person, while a charter can cost 250B.

Hat Surin

หาดสุรินทร์

A little north of Laem Singh, Surin has a long beach and sometimes fairly heavy surf. When the water is calm, there's fair snorkelling here. It's long been a popular place for local Thais to come to nibble at seafood snacks sold by vendors along the beach. Just before Surin, in Bang Thao Village No 2, is one of Southern Thailand's most beautiful mosques, **Matsayit Mukaram**, a large, whitewashed, immaculate structure with lacquered wooden doors.

Places to Stay Surin's northern end has been dubbed 'Pansea Beach' by developers and is claimed by the exclusive Amanpuri and Chedi resorts. *Amanpuri Resort* (☎ *076-324333, fax 324100,* e *amanpuri@ phuket.com*) plays host to Thailand's celebrity traffic, with each guest getting a 133-sq-metre pavilion or private two- to six-bedroom villa home and a personal attendant; the staff to guest ratio is 3½ to one. It's owned by Indonesian Adrian Zecha and designed by the architect who designed the former Shah of Iran's Winter Palace. Depending on the season, you can expect to pay US$400 to US$5040 for a night's accommodation. The resort offers about 20 cruisers for sailing, diving and overnight charters, six tennis courts, a gym, and Thai and Italian restaurants. The Amanpuri was once censured by the local community for the improper display of Buddha images.

The Chedi (☎ 076-324017, fax 324252, 🖃 info@chedi-phuket.com) offers 89 rooms and 21 two-bedroom cottages with teak floors and private verandas for US$160 to US$590, depending on the season and type of accommodation. The Chedi has its own golf course.

Towards the southern end of Surin, *Surin Sweet Apartment* (☎ 076-270863, fax 270865), *Sabai Guest House* (☎ 076-271146) and *Taengthai Guesthouse & Restaurant* (☎ 076-270259) offer simple but modern rooms in the 400B to 800B price range.

Getting There & Away A regular săwngthăew between Phuket's Thanon Ranong and Hat Surin costs 20B per person and túk-túk charter is 250B to 300B.

Ao Bang Thao
อ่าวบางเทา

North of Surin around the cape is Ao Bang Thao, an 8km sandy beach with an 18-hole golf course that has attracted much upmarket development. A steady breeze makes it a haven for sailboarders: since 1992 the annual Siam World Cup windsurfing championships have been held here (formerly at Pattaya's Hat Jomtien). A system of lagoons inland from the beach has been incorporated into the resorts and golf course, hence this is sometimes referred to as 'Laguna Beach'.

Massage & Herbal Sauna Hideaway Day Spa (☎ 076-271549), about 200m west of Tatonka restaurant, offers half-day programs of traditional Thai massage, herbal sauna and aromatherapy for 2500B to 3000B. The spa is located in a soothingly wooded setting next to one of Bang Thao's lagoons and is open from 11 am to 9 pm daily. Reservations are recommended.

Places to Stay With one exception, Bang Thao is strictly for the well-to-do nowadays. All the hotels in Bang Thao (except for Royal Park Beach Resort) are part of an integrated resort system, so if you stay at one of the hotels you can use any of the facilities at the other hotels. There is a shuttle that operates between all of the properties.

Least expensive is the quiet and secluded *Bangtao Lagoon Bungalow* (☎ 076-324483, fax 324168), at the southern end of the bay. It offers 50 private bungalows, with prices ranging from 600B to 1000B. Rates are 10% less in the low season. The restaurant on the premises serves Thai and European dishes.

The plush *Dusit Laguna Resort* (☎ 076-324320, fax 324174, 🖃 dusit@lagunaphuket .com; in Bangkok ☎ 02-238 4790) has 226 guest rooms and suites starting at US$85, with suites costing up to US$170, not including tax. From the November to April high-season, rates range from US$270 to US$430. Another top-end place towards the centre of the beach is the *Royal Park Beach Resort* (☎ 076-324021, fax 324243), where rooms start at 4740B in the low season. Add 600B in the high season.

Bringing yet more beachside luxury to the bay are the *Sheraton Grande Phuket Laguna* (☎ 076-324101, fax 324108, 🖃 sheraton@ phuket.com) and the *Banyan Tree Phuket* (☎ 076-324374, fax 324375, 🖃 banyanrs@ samart.co.th). The Sheraton features a sprawling 240 rooms (US$430 to US$460) and 84 'grande villas' (US$850 to US$1800). Low-season rates are US$350 to US$380 for rooms and US$700 to US$1200 for villas. The Sheraton is the only place on this beach with a fitness centre. The more exclusive Banyan Tree has 98 villas (all with open-air sunken bathtubs, 34 with private pool and spa bath) from US$480 to US$950 (US$260 to US$510 in the low season). The hotel boasts a golf course, full-service spa, three tennis courts, a lap pool and free-form swimming pool. The Banyan Tree specialises in spiritual and physical spa treatments, including massage, seaweed packs and meditation; in 1998 it was voted the world's best spa by readers of *Condé Nast Traveler*.

The Allamanda (☎ 076-324359, fax 324360, 🖃 allamanda@lagunaphuket.com) offers 94 units starting at US$95 for a junior suite in the low season to US$240 for a duplex villa in the high season; all suites come with kitchenette and satellite TV. The *Laguna Beach Club* (☎ *076-324352, fax 324353, reservation fax 270993,* e *beachclub@lagunaphuket.com)* rivals the Sheraton and Dusit in providing 252 rooms for US$159 to US$250 plus tax and service. Rooms are sometimes discounted to as low as US$99 in the low season. Set on eight hectares, the resort features a 1.6 hectare water park that incorporates waterfalls, water slides, whirlpools and a scuba pool.

Places to Eat Despite what local hoteliers would have you believe, there is some good food to be had outside the confines of Bang Thao's luxury hotels.

Tatonka (☎ *076-324349),* near the entrance to the Dusit Laguna Resort, features 'globetrotter' cuisine, which owner-chef Harold Schwarz developed by taking fresh local products and combining them with cooking and presentation techniques learned from his kitchen training in Europe and his experiences with the foods of Hawaii and the American South-West ('tatonka' is the Sioux word for American buffalo). Besides the eclectic regular menu, there are some creative vegetarian dishes to be sampled here and prices are quite reasonable. Tatonka is open from 5 pm daily except Wednesday; reservations are suggested in the high season.

Just beyond the entrance to Banyan Tree Phuket as you're coming from the direction of Patong, is a turn off for the beach. Follow this road into what looks like a shanty town but is actually a group of beachside Thai and seafood restaurants. Of these, the clean and breezy *Lotus Restaurant* stands out.

Getting There & Away A săwngthăew between Phuket's Thanon Ranong and Bang Thao costs 20B per person. In Ao Bang Thao săwngthăew can be caught along Rtes 4030 and 4025. Túk-túk charters are 200B.

Nearby Islands
At **Ko Hae**, a few kilometres south-east of Ao Chalong, the *Coral Island Resort* (☎ *076-281060, fax 381957,* e *coral_island@ phuket.com)* has upmarket bungalows with air-con for 2000B to 2400B, depending on proximity to the beach. During the high season prices are 3800B to 4000B. Sometimes the island itself is called Coral Island. It's a

good spot for diving and snorkelling if you don't plan on going farther out to sea, although jet skis and other pleasure craft can be an annoyance. The island gets lots of day-trippers from Phuket, but at night it's pretty quiet.

Ko Mai Thon, south-east of Laem Phanwa, is similar but slightly smaller. On this island *Maiton Resort* (☎ *076-214954, fax 214959)* rents luxurious hillside bungalows for 8000B and beachside bungalows for 11,200B, with breakfast included (in the high season add 20%).

Two islands about 1½ hours by boat south of Phuket, **Ko Raya Yai** and **Ko Raya Noi** (also known as Ko Racha Yai/Noi), are highly favoured by divers and snorkellers for their hard coral reefs. Because the coral is found in both shallow and deep waters, it's a good area for novice scuba divers and snorkellers, as well as accomplished divers. Visibility can reach 15m to 30m. The islands are inhabited by Muslim families who mainly fish and farm coconuts for a living. On Ko Raya Yai, accommodation is available at *Ban Raya* (☎ *076-354682, 01-828 6956,* e *banraya@phuket.com)* with sturdy, comfortable fan bungalows for 1000B or 1400B for air-con (1300B and 1900B in the high season). Diving instruction is also available. *Jungle Bungalow* (☎ *076-288550)* offers more rustic bungalows for 400B to 600B. *Raya Resort* (☎ *076-327084)* features simple palm-thatch bungalows for 350B to 500B; and *Raya Andaman Resort* (☎ *076-381710)* has air-con digs from 700B.

For information on attractions and accommodation on the island of Ko Yao Noi, off Phuket's north-western shore, see the Phang-Nga Province section earlier in this chapter.

Getting There & Away Boats leave Ao Chalong for Ko Hae once daily at 9.30 am, they take 30 minutes and cost 60B. Songserm Travel (☎ *076-222570)* runs passenger boats to Ko Raya Yai from Phuket town port at 9 am daily. The trip takes one half hour and costs 350/750B one way/ return. Pal Travel Service (☎ *076-344920)* runs a similar service. Both companies suspend service from May to October. You can also charter a long-tail boat or speed boat from Rawai or from Ao Chalong for 1500B.

Krabi Province

Krabi Province has scenic karst formations (similar to those in Phang-Nga Province) near the coast and even in the middle of Mae Nam Krabi (Krabi River). Over 150 islands offer excellent recreational opportunities; many of the islands belong to the Hat Noppharat Thara/Ko Phi-Phi National Marine Park. Hundreds of years ago, Krabi's waters were a favourite hideout for Asian pirates because of all the islands and water caves. Latter-day pirates now steal islands or parts of islands for development – land encroachment is reportedly taking place on Phi-Phi Don, Poda, Bubu, Jam (Pu), Po, Bilek (Hong), Kamyai and Kluang. About 40% of the provincial population is Muslim.

The interior of the province, noted for its tropical forests and the Phanom Bencha mountain range, has barely been explored. Bird-watchers come from far and wide to view Gurney's pitta (formerly thought to be extinct) and Nordmann's greenshank.

Krabi has a seldom-used deep-sea port financed by local speculators in tin, rubber and palm oil, which are Krabi's most important sources of income. The port's full potential has never been realised and there's now talk of developing a new, substitute deep-sea port farther south in Satun to spare Krabi's natural tourist attractions from shipping pollution.

Beach accommodation is inexpensive (although not as cheap as Ko Pha-Ngan) and there are regular boats to Ko Phi-Phi, 42km south-west. From December to March, the hotels and bungalows along Krabi's beaches can fill up. The beaches of Krabi are nearly deserted in the rainy season, so this is a good time to go.

KRABI
อ.เมืองกระบี่
postcode 81000 • pop 18,500
Nearly 1000km from Bangkok and 180km from Phuket, the fast-developing provincial capital, Krabi (pronounced 'gra-BEE', *not* 'crabby'), has friendly people, delicious food and some good nearby beaches. The capital sits on the banks of Mae Nam Krabi right before it empties into the Andaman Sea. Across from town you can see Bird, Cat and Mouse Islands, named for their shapes.

Most travellers breeze through town on their way to Ko Lanta to the south, Ko Phi-Phi to the south-west, or the beaches near Ao Nang to the west. Some elect to stay in town and make day trips to the latter.

Although Krabi is essentially more Taoist-Confucianist and Muslim than Theravada Buddhist, **Wat Kaew** contains some older buildings from the early 20th century and lots of large old trees.

Orientation
Maps Bangkok Guide publishes the handy *Guide Map of Krabi* (50B), which contains several minimaps of areas of interest throughout the province. Visid Hongsombud's *Guide Map of Krabi* (look for the picture of the bespectacled Mr Visid on the cover) is detailed and up to date, as well as being printed on waterproof paper. Frank Tour's *Krabi* (70B) is also quite good and is also printed on waterproof stock.

Information
Tourist Offices TAT (☎ 075-612740) maintains a small office on Thanon Utarakit near the waterfront. It has lots of useful printed information, including a few maps that depict the province, the capital and the islands of Ko Phi-Phi and Ko Lanta, along with accommodation lists.

Another 'tourist information booth' can be found near the night market on the waterfront; it's actually a ticket agency for buses and boats run by PP Family Co.

Immigration Visas can easily be extended at the immigration office, south of the main post office on Thanon Chamai Anuson.

Post & Communications The post and telephone office is on Thanon Utarakit past the turn-off for Saphan Jao Fah (Saphan Jao Fah pier); a separate poste restante entrance is at the side. The CAT office is located about 1km north of Krabi Hospital on Thanon Utarakit. Home Country Direct international phone service is available here from 7 am to midnight daily.

Vieng Thong Hotel, on Thanon Utarakit, offers email and Internet services.

Travel Agencies Krabi has dozens of fly-by-night travel agencies that will book accommodation at beaches and islands, as

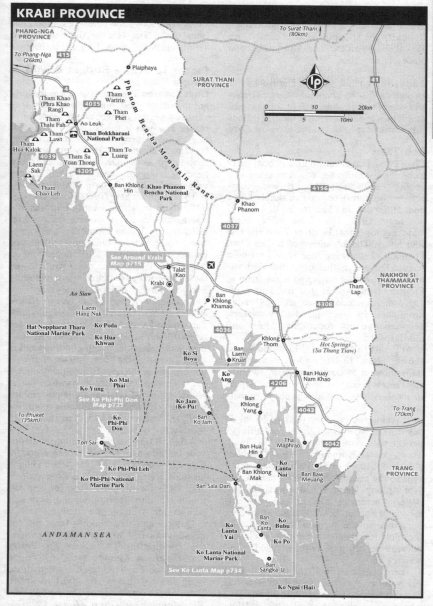

KRABI PROVINCE

PHANG-NGA
PROVINCE

To Phang-Nga
(26km)

415

Plaiphaya

To Surat Thani
(80km)

SURAT THANI
PROVINCE

41

4

Tham Khao
(Phra Khao
Rang)

4035

Tham
Waririn

Tham
Phet

Tham
Thalu Fah

Ao Leuk

Tham
Lawt

Than Bokkharani
National Park

Tham
Hua Kalok

4039

Tham Sa
Yuan Thong

Tham To
Luang

Laem
Sak

4205

Tham
Chao Leh

Ban Khlong
Hin

Khao Phanom
Bencha National
Park

Khao
Phanom

4156

4037

0   10   20km
0   5   10mi

NAKHON SI
THAMMARAT
PROVINCE

See Around Krabi
Map p715

Talat
Kao

Krabi

Tham
Lap

Ao Siaw

Ban
Khlong
Khamao

4

4308

Laem
Hang Nak

4036

Hot Springs
(Sa Thung Tiaw)

Hat Noppharat Thara
National Marine Park

Ko Poda

Ko Hua
Khwan

Ko Si
Boya

Ban
Laem
Kruat

Khlong
Thom

Ko
Ang

Ban Huay
Nam Khao

Ko Mai
Phai

4206

Ko Yung

See Ko Phi-Phi Don
Map p725

Ko Jam
(Ko Pu)

Ban
Khlong
Yang

4043

To Phuket
(35km)

Ko
Phi-Phi
Don

Ban
Ko Jam

To Trang
(70km)

Ton Sai

Ban Hua
Hin

Tha
Maphrao

4042

Ko Phi-Phi Leh

Ban Khlong
Mak

Ko
Lanta
Noi

Ban Baw
Meuang

TRANG
PROVINCE

Ko Phi-Phi National
Marine Park

Ban Sala Dan

ANDAMAN SEA

Ko
Lanta
Yai

Ban
Ko Lanta

Ko
Bubu

Ko Po

Ko Lanta National
Marine Park

See Ko Lanta Map p734

Ban
Sangka-U

Ko Ngai (Hai)

well as tour bus and boat tickets. Chan Phen Travel and Jungle Book, both on Thanon Utarakit, are still the most reliable. Jam Travel, between the two aforementioned places, is also good.

Bookshops Phuket-based The Books has an outlet at 78–80 Thanon Maharat. The selection of English-language books and magazines is rather slim, although it does carry same-day issues of the *Bangkok Post*.

Eco-Trips

Chan Phen Travel runs half-day boat tours to nearby estuaries for a look at mangrove ecology (300B to 350B per person – four-person minimum), or you can simply hire a boat at Saphan Jao Fah for 200B to 250B per hour. Chan Phen also offers bird-watching tours that begin at 7 am and last four hours. The advantage of taking Chan Phen's bird-watching tour versus hiring a boat at the pier is that Chan Phen's boat-man can point out birds and name them in English. Bird species that frequent mangrove areas include the sea eagle and ruddy kingfisher. In mud and shallow waters, keep an eye out for fiddler crabs and mudskippers.

At the Khao Nor Chuchi Lowland Forest Project (Naw Ju-Ji), visitors can follow trails through lowland rainforest, swim in clear forest pools and observe or participate in local village activities such as rubber-tapping.

Travel agencies in the town of Krabi do day trips to Khao Nor Chuchi for 650B per person, with visits to hot springs (Sa Thung Tiaw) near Khlong Thom, a rubber plantation, lunch at Sa Thung Tiaw and a visit to the recently renovated museum at Wat Khlong Thom. Besides weapons and pottery, the museum has an extensive collection of ancient beads that are still being unearthed in the surrounding fields. The fee includes air-con transport, lunch and beverages; bring a swimsuit and good walking shoes.

Travel agencies in Krabi (as well as at Ao Nang or Ao Phra Nang farther north) can also arrange trips to idyllic uninhabited isles nearby, all with coral reefs and luscious beaches set in tranquil sandy coves. Rates for such trips are 1300B to 1500B for up to eight people.

Sea Canoe Thailand operates sea canoe/kayak trips along the coast; it can be contacted on Ao Nang (see the Ao Nang & Laem Tham Phra Nang section later in this chapter).

Places to Stay – Budget & Mid-Range

Guesthouses The cheapest places in Krabi are the many guesthouses. Some only stay around a season or two, others seem fairly stable. The ones in the business district feature closet-like rooms above modern shop buildings, often with faulty plumbing or lacking windows – OK for one night before heading to a nearby beach or island but not very suitable for long-term stays.

The charming *Star Guest House* (☎ 075-630234) is in a rare example of Krabi's traditional wooden shophouse architecture. Located on Thanon Khongkha, just opposite the pier, Star has fan rooms with shared bathroom for 100B to 250B, depending on the season. Every room has a window and there are spacious common areas, including a wide veranda overlooking the river.

The small *River View Guest House* (☎ 075-612536), on Thanon Khongkha near Saphan Jao Fah and Customs House, has decent 80B and 120B rooms with shared facilities and a restaurant with good vegetarian food. There's also a terrace on the roof with good views of the river (hence the name).

On Thanon Prachacheun, *Swallow Guest House* (☎ 075-611645) is a popular place with fairly clean and comfortable rooms for 120B (no window) and 150B to 180B (with window).

You will find fairly clean rooms with private bathroom at *Grand Tower Hotel & Guest House* (☎ 075-612456–7) on Thanon Utarakit. Rates here are 300B for fan rooms and 450B for air-con. However, the fan rooms are on the fourth floor and, as there's no elevator, it's a bit of a climb.

Quieter and more comfortable are the guesthouses just south-west of town near the courthouse. The *Chao Fa Valley Guesthouse & Resort* (☎ 075-61249, 50 Thanon Jao Fah) has good-sized bamboo bungalows with fan for 200B to 400B. Next, on the same side of Thanon Jao Fah, *KR Mansion & Guest House* (☎ 075-612761) offers 40 hotel-style rooms for 150B with fan and shared bathroom, 250B with private bathroom. The KR will also

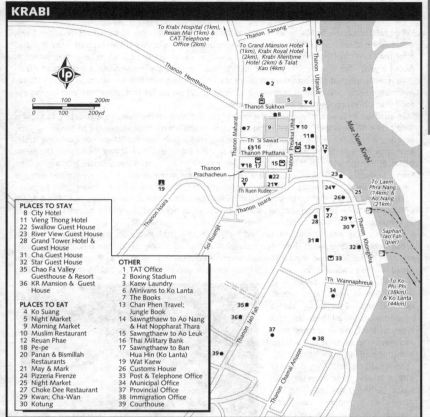

KRABI

PLACES TO STAY
8 City Hotel
11 Vieng Thong Hotel
22 Swallow Guest House
23 River View Guest House
28 Grand Tower Hotel &
   Guest House
31 Cha Guest House
32 Star Guest House
35 Chao Fa Valley
   Guesthouse & Resort
36 KR Mansion & Guest
   House

PLACES TO EAT
4 Ko Suang
5 Night Market
9 Morning Market
10 Muslim Restaurant
12 Reuan Phae
18 Pe-pe
20 Panan & Bismillah
   Restaurants
21 May & Mark
25 Night Market
27 Choke Dee Restaurant
29 Kwan; Cha-Wan
30 Kotung

OTHER
1 TAT Office
2 Boxing Stadium
3 Kaew Laundry
6 Minivans to Ko Lanta
7 The Books
13 Chan Phen Travel;
   Jungle Book
14 Sawngthaew to Ao Nang
   & Hat Nopparat Thara
15 Sawngthaew to Ao Leuk
16 Thai Military Bank
17 Sawngthaew to Ban
   Hua Hin (Ko Lanta)
19 Wat Kaew
26 Customs House
33 Post & Telephone Office
34 Municipal Office
37 Provincial Office
38 Immigration Office
39 Courthouse

rent rooms by the month. The rooftop beer garden provides a 360° view of Krabi – great for watching sunsets. The staff can arrange motorcycle rentals, local tours and boat tickets as well.

Along Thanon Utarakit, near the post office, *Cha Guest House* is a group of concrete bungalows (some windowless) with shared facilities for 80/120B single/double. For 200B you get a private bathroom. Even cheaper are the rooms at the back of *Jungle Book Tour & Guest House* (☎ 075-611148, 141 Thanon Utarakit), where tiny, older cubicles cost 50B while slightly bigger cubicles cost 80B. All come with fans, and the mattresses in both kinds of room are surprisingly good; bathroom/toilet facilities are shared.

Hotels In the centre of town, the *City Hotel* (☎ 075-621280, fax 621301, 15/2–3 Thanon Sukhon) also has pretty clean rooms at 300B with fan and 480B with air-con. Larger rooms with better TVs and air-conditioners are 500B to 750B; parking is available in a small car park next to the hotel.

The friendly and efficient *Vieng Thong Hotel* (☎ 075-620020, fax 612525, 155 Thanon Utarakit) has decent rooms for 350B with fan, 550B to 700B with air-con; all rooms have TV and phone; there's a car park attached.

The *Grand Mansion Hotel* (☎ 075-620833, 289/1 Thanon Utarakit) offers 58 plain but comfortable rooms with fan and hot-water shower for 300B or with air-con for 500B to 900B.

May & Mark

When husband and wife Matee and Kittiya Kulpanpinunt of Krabi opened a small restaurant in 1990, they had no idea to what culinary heights the endeavour would take them. Named 'May & Mark' after their two children, the eatery offered a selection of pre-cooked curries to be served over rice. About a year after opening, the couple first noticed foreign travellers strolling the streets of Krabi. 'The travellers would stop and stare at the pots of curries, but very few would come in and eat', remembered Kittiya. 'We didn't know why. Only later did we realise that many foreigners won't eat food that's been cooked and then left to cool'.

In an effort to cater to the visitors, the couple put pancakes on the menu. It was a start, but things didn't take off until they began renting out spare rooms above their restaurant to travellers. One boarder, a New Zealander named John Kean, stayed for two months. When not exploring Krabi, John took the time to teach Matee and Kittiya to bake bread and cook *fàràng* food. Soon the menu began to expand and reflect the tastes of other travellers who passed through and left behind their favourite recipes. 'A Californian taught us how to do some Mexican dishes, and we learned to make food from Sweden, Denmark, Germany and Italy from visitors from those countries', said Kittiya.

Yet it was John's bread-making skills and his willingness to share them that has put May & Mark on the map. 'John has been coming to Thailand for years now and every time he visits, he teaches us something new', said Matee.

Besides whole-wheat bread, Matee and Kittiya are now baking sourdough, French and Bavarian bread, which they serve at their own restaurant as well as supplying to over ten other establishments in Krabi. 'We have regular fàràng customers who come from as far as Phuket to stock up on bread. We're now using flour imported from Australia and we're the only bakery in southern Thailand making sourdough bread', said Matee. 'We've never been outside of Thailand. Everything we've learned to make, all these different types of food, we've learned from travellers who came in and wanted to eat something from home'.

So what's next for May & Mark? Kittiya is now experimenting with fusion cuisine. 'I've been using Thai curries as a topping for pizza. Fàràng love it – one taste and they're hooked!'

The **Krabi Royal Hotel** (☎ 075-611582, fax 611581, 403 Thanon Utarakit), near the more expensive Krabi Meritime at the northern edge of town, charges 960B for a comfortable air-con room with TV, fridge, phone and hot-water shower with tub, including breakfast for two. Discounts are available for stays of more than one night.

Places to Stay – Top End

The swanky **Krabi Meritime Hotel** (☎ 075-620028, 620046, fax 612992; in Bangkok ☎ 02-719 0034, fax 318 7687) is near the river on the way to Talat Kao, about 2km from central Krabi.

Rates for nicely decorated rooms with balconies and impressive views of the river and mountains start at 2200B.

Facilities include a swimming pool, artificial lake with swan-shaped paddleboats, nightclub, fitness centre and convention facilities. The pool is open to the public for a daily fee of 60/40B for adults/children.

Places to Eat

What Krabi lacks in good guesthouses it more than makes up for in good eating places. Along Thanon Khongkha is a **night market** near Saphan Jao Fah, with great seafood at low prices and a host of Thai dessert vendors. There's also another bigger *night market* near Ko Saung restaurant on Thanon Sukhon.

Quite a few of Krabi's travel agencies double as traveller-oriented restaurants, and the food will lead you to believe that the latter came about as an afterthought. *May & Mark* on Thanon Ruen Rudee is a welcome exception, offering excellent Thai and Western food as well as freshly baked bread. They're open from 6.30 am to 9 pm.

One of the better and most reasonably priced restaurants in town for standard Thai dishes and local cuisine is the *Kotung*, near Tha Saphan Jao Fah. The *tôm yam kûng* is especially good, as is anything else made with fresh seafood.

Pe-pe, on the corner of Thanon Maharat and Thanon Prachacheun, is a clean place that serves good, inexpensive noodles and *khâo man kài*; it's very popular at lunch time. Another good area for lunch-time eating is the three-way intersection at Thanon Preuksa Uthit and Thanon Sukhon (aka Soi 10, Thanon Maharat). You'll find several inexpensive *noodle and rice shops*, as well as the *Muslim Restaurant* which serves rotii kaeng (known as *roti chanai* in Malay), the Malaysian-style breakfast of flat bread and curry – but it's twice as expensive as Panan and Bismillah at the end of this section. *Ko Suang* (no Roman-script sign), also in this area, serves good, inexpensive khâo man kài, *khâo mǔu daeng, kǔaytǐaw* and *bà-mìi*. At the south-western corner of this intersection is a good *khànǒm jiin vendor*.

Pizzeria Firenze, at 10 Thanon Khongkha, does good pizza, pasta, wine, gelato and Italian bread. Around the bend on Thanon Khongkha, near Saphan Jao Fah, are a couple of other fàràng-oriented eateries, including *Kwan* and *Cha-Wan*, both of which specialise in Thai food for timid Western palates. Nicely decorated with modern art, both restaurants also serve pasta, salads, burgers, sandwiches and breakfasts; there are a few tables out the front.

Reuan Mai is a very good Thai-style *sǔan aahǎan* (garden restaurant) on Thanon Maharat near Krabi Hospital, about 1.6km north-north-east of the intersection of Thanon Maharat and Thanon Sukhon, 400m past the big Chinese temple on the left. It's mostly a locals' place but well worth seeking out for the high-quality Thai food.

Reuan Phae is an old floating restaurant on the river in front of town. Although the food at Reuan Phae is not that great overall, it's fine for a beer or rice whisky while watching the river rise and fall with the tide.

Opposite the Grand Tower Hotel is the *Choke Dee Restaurant* which offers wine and videos along with its travellers fare.

Places for spicy Thai-Malay Muslim cuisine continue to multiply as the earnings of the local population rise with tourism development. *Panan*, on the corner of Thanon Ruen Rudee and Thanon Maharat, has khâo mòk kài in the morning, inexpensive curries and kǔaytǐaw the rest of day. The Roman-script sign reads 'Makanan Islam' (Malay for 'Muslim food'). Next door is another decent Muslim place, *Bismillah*, with a sign in Thai only.

Getting There & Away

Air THAI and PB Air have daily flights to Krabi from Bangkok and vice versa for 2150B and 2250B respectively. Bangkok Airways has flights from Ko Samui to Krabi on Tuesday, Thursday and Saturday (2170B, 1870B in the reverse direction). Besides flying from Bangkok, PB Air also has flights to Krabi from Singapore and Medan (Indonesia) on Tuesday, Wednesday and Thursday. Bangkok Airways maintains an office at Krabi Airport (☎ 075-636543). Tickets for any of these airlines can be booked through Vieng Thong Travel, in the lobby of the Vieng Thong Hotel (☎ 075-620020).

Bus & Minivan Agents at Songserm Travel and PP Family Co (both on Thanon Khongkha opposite the pier) scoop up much of the naive tourist business in the city centre. It's easy buying tickets here but departure times and bus conditions are unreliable and at times unpredictable. If you use the Baw Khaw Saw terminal in nearby Talat Kao you'll save yourself the trouble of worrying about whether private buses booked in town really turn out to be what was advertised or whether they will leave at the scheduled time. Krabi's well-organised government bus terminal features separate ticket booths for each line (printed in English), a clean little restaurant, snacks and drinks for sale and clean toilets. The Talat Kao terminal is about 4km north of Krabi on the highway between Phang-Nga and Trang.

Government buses to/from Bangkok cost 248B ordinary, 328B to 347B 2nd-class air-con (no toilet), 446B 1st-class air-con and 550B VIP (655B for super 24-seat VIP). Air-con buses leave Bangkok's Southern bus terminal between 6 and 8 pm; they leave Krabi between 4 and 5 pm. Songserm and PP Family Co arrange air-con buses (or vans) to Thanon Khao San in Bangkok for 350B.

Buses to/from Phuket leave hourly during daylight hours, cost 56/101B ordinary/air-con and take three to four hours. Air-con minivans from PP Family Co cost 200B to Phuket airport or Phuket town, 250B to Patong, Karon or Kata beaches.

Buses for Krabi leave Phang-Nga hourly throughout the day for 36/52B. Most of these buses originate in Phuket and have Trang as their final destination. Government buses to/from Hat Yai cost 153B air-con and take five hours; from Trang it's 43/77B and 2½ hours. There are also share taxis to/from Trang, Hat Yai and Satun; fares are roughly twice the ordinary bus fare.

Ordinary buses between Surat Thani and Krabi make the four-hour trip 13 times daily between 5 am and 2.30 pm for 70B. Air-con buses depart three times a day between 7 am and 3.30 pm for 110B and take around three hours (it's the same price if you get out at Khao Sok National Park). Through various agencies in town you can pay 150B for a private air-con bus or minivan to Surat. These agencies also arrange minivans to Hat Yai, Trang or Phattalung, each for the same fare of 180B. There are no minivans from the Baw Khaw Saw terminal, so if you want to go by this method, you'll have to book through one of the many private agencies in town.

Săwngthăew to Ban Hua Hin (for Ko Lanta) leave from Thanon Phattana in town, with a second stop in Talat Kao, for 30B. They leave about every half-hour from 10 am to 2 pm and take 40 minutes to reach Ban Hua Hin. There are also air-con minivans available from Krabi travel agencies straight through to Ko Lanta for 150B.

Boat Krabi can be reached by sea from Ko Phi-Phi and Ko Lanta. See the respective Ko Phi-Phi and Ko Lanta sections for details.

Getting Around

Any place in town can easily be reached on foot, but if you plan to do a lot of exploring out of town, renting a motorcycle might be a good idea. Several travel agencies and guesthouses can arrange motorcycle rentals for 150B to 250B a day, with discounts for multiday rentals. Jeep rentals range from 800B (open-top) to 1200B (air-con) per day.

Most buses into Krabi terminate at Talat Kao, about 4km north of Krabi on the highway between Phang-Nga and Trang. You can catch a săwngthăew between Talat Kao and the centre of Krabi for 10B, or a motorcycle taxi for 30B.

From the airport, 17km from the city centre, you can catch a minivan for 60B, or hire a car for 300B. A car all the way to Ao Nang costs 500B. From town to the airport a taxi is 200B or, if you're travelling light, a motorcycle taxi will take you for 100B.

Săwngthăew to Ao Leuk (for Than Bokkharani National Park) leave from the intersection of Thanon Phattana and Thanon Preuksa Uthit for 30B. To Ao Nang (30B) they leave from Thanon Phattana opposite the New Hotel – departures are about every 15 minutes from 7 am to 6 pm during the high season (December to March), until 4 or 4.30 pm for the remainder of the year.

Boats to the islands and beaches mostly leave from Saphan Jao Fah. See the Ao Nang & Laem Tham Phra Nang Getting There & Away section for boat details.

AROUND KRABI
Su-San Hoi
สุสานหอย

Nineteen kilometres west of Krabi, on Laem Pho, is the so-called Su-San Hoi (Shell Fossil Cemetery; pronounced sù-săan hăwy), a shell 'graveyard' where 75-million-year-old shell fossils have formed giant slabs jutting into the sea.

To get there, take a săwngthăew from the Krabi waterfront for 20B – ask for the 'Su-San Hoi'.

Wat Tham Seua
วัดถ้ำเสือ

About 5km north and then 2km east of town, Wat Tham Seua (Tiger Cave Temple), is one of Southern Thailand's most famous forest

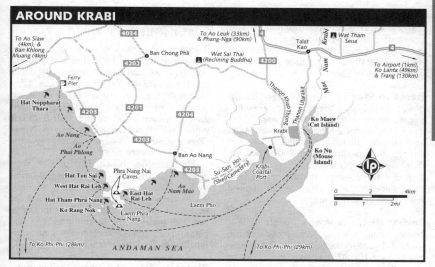

AROUND KRABI

To Ao Siaw
(4km), &
Ban Khlong
Muang (4km)

4034

To Ao Leuk (33km)
& Phang-Nga (90km)

Talat
Kao

Wat Tham
Seua

Ban Chong Phli

4202

Wat Sai Thai
(Reclining Buddha)

4200

To Airport (1km),
Ko Lanta (49km)
& Trang (130km)

Ferry
Pier

Hat Nopparat
Thara

4203

4201

4204

Ao Nang

Ao
Phai Phlong

4203

Ban Ao Nang

Ko Maew
(Cat Island)

Krabi

Thanon Khao Thong

Thanon Utarakit

Mae   Nam   Krabi

Ko Nu
(Mouse
Island)

Su-San Hoi
(Shell Cemetery)

Krabi
Coastal
Port

Hat Ton Sai

Phra Nang Nai
Caves

4203

West Hat Rai Leh

East Hat
Rai Leh

Ao
Nam Mao

Hat Tham Phra Nang

Ko Rang Nok

Laem Phra
Nang

Laem Pho

0   2   4km
0   1   2mi

To Ko Phi-Phi (28km)

ANDAMAN SEA

To Ko Phi-Phi (29km)

wát. The main *wíhǎan* (hall) is built into a
long, shallow limestone cave, on either side
of which dozens of *kùtì* (monastic cells) are
built into various cliffs and caves.

First, if you decide to head out for the
temple, please remember the dress protocol
for Thai monasteries.

Wat Tham Seua's abbot is Ajahn Jamnien Silasettho, a Thai monk aged in his
fifties who has allowed a rather obvious
personality cult to develop around him. In
the large, main cave the usual pictures of
split cadavers and decaying corpses on the
walls (useful meditation objects for coun-
tering lust) are interspersed with large portraits of Ajahn Jamnien, who is well known
as a teacher of *vipassana* (insight meditation) and *metta* (loving-kindness). It is
said that he was apprenticed at an early age
to a blind lay priest and astrologer who
practised folk medicine and that he has been
celibate his entire life. On the inside of his
outer robe, and on an inner vest, hang
scores of talismans presented to him by his
followers – altogether they must weigh several kilograms, a weight Ajahn Jamnien
bears to take on his followers' karma. Many
young women come to Wat Tham Seua to
practise as eight-precept nuns.

In the back of the main cave a set of marble stairs behind the altar leads up to a smaller
cavern (watch your head when you go up the

steps) known as the Tiger Cave. At the back
a Buddha footprint symbol sits on a gilded
platform, locked behind a gate. Near one of
the main cave entrances a life-size wax figure
of Ajahn Jamnien sits in a glass case. A sign
on the case in English and Thai says 'Not real
man', although the more you look at the figure, the more real it appears.

The best part of the temple grounds can be
found in a little valley behind the ridge where
the *bòt* is located. Follow the path past the
main wát buildings, through a little village
with nuns' quarters, until you come to a pair
of steep stairways on the left. The first leads
to an arduous climb of 1272 steps to the top
of a karst hill with another Buddha footprint
shrine and a good view of the area.

The second stairway, next to a large statue
of Kuan Yin (the Mahayana Buddhist Goddess of Mercy), leads over a gap in the ridge
and into a valley of tall trees and limestone
caves, 10 of which are named. Enter the
caves on your left and look for light switches
on the walls – the network of caves is wired
so that you can light your way chamber by
chamber through the labyrinth until you re-
join the path on the other side.

There are several *kùtì* in and around the
caves, and it's interesting to see the differences in interior decorating – some are very
spartan and others are outfitted like oriental
bachelor pads.

A path winds through a grove of 1000-year-old dipterocarps surrounded by tall limestone cliffs covered with a patchwork of foliage. If you continue to follow the path you'll eventually end up where you started, at the bottom of the stairway.

Places to Stay The friendly *Tiger House* (☎ 075-631625), on the access road just before the entrance to the temple grounds, offers 13 rooms for 200B with fan and 300B with air-con; all have attached cold-water shower. Rooms surround a shaded parking area. Spotlessly clean and nicely landscaped with potted plants, this might be a good place to stay if you want to explore Wat Tham Seua thoroughly.

Getting There & Away To get to Wat Tham Seua, take a săwngthăew from Krabi's Thanon Utarakit to the Talat Kao junction for 10B, then change to any bus or săwngthăew east on Hwy 4 towards Trang and Hat Yai and get off at the road on the left just after the 108km marker – if you tell the bus operators 'Wat Tham Seua' they'll let you off in the right place. It's a 2km walk straight up this road to the wát. In the morning a few săwngthăew from Thanon Phattana in town pass the turn-off for Wat Tham Seua (12B) on their way to Ban Hua Hin. Also in the morning there is usually a săwngthăew or two going direct to Wat Tham Seua from Talat Kao for around 20B. If you're in a group it might be easier to hail one of the blue or yellow mini-săwngthăew from anywhere around town and hire it (100B to 150B one way) for the trip all the way to Wat Tham Seua.

Wat Sai Thai
วัดไสไทย

A 15m reclining Buddha can be seen in a long rock shelter under a tall limestone cliff on the way to Ao Nang, about 7km from Krabi alongside Rte 4034 near the 7km marker. Though a wát in name only (there aren't enough monks in residence for official wát status, although a few monks look after the place), you can see an old bell-less bell tower, some *thâat kràdùuk* (reliquary stupas) and the foundation for a former cremation hall remaining from the time when it was an active monastery.

Hat Noppharat Thara
หาดนพรัตน์ธารา

Eighteen kilometres north-west of Krabi, this beach used to be called Hat Khlong Haeng (Dry Canal Beach) because the canal that flows into the Andaman Sea here is dry except during, and just after, the monsoon season. Former dictator Field Marshal Sarit gave the beach its current Pali-Sanskrit name, which means Beach of the Nine-Gemmed Stream. A royal residence was recently constructed here.

The 2km-long beach, part of Hat Noppharat Thara/Ko Phi-Phi National Marine Park, is a favourite spot for Thai picnickers. There are some government bungalows for rent and a recently upgraded visitors centre has wall maps of the marine park and displays on coral reefs and ecotourism; most are labelled in Thai, but a few have English.

Places to Stay At the park headquarters, *government bungalows* (☎ 075-637200) are available for 400B (three-person bungalow), and 1200B (nine people). They're quite OK, although on weekends the beach and visitors centre is thronged with local visitors. You can also rent tents for 200B (two people) to 300B (three people). A row of open-air restaurants and vendors strung out along the parking lot sell snacks and simple meals.

Boats at the park pier at the eastern end of Hat Noppharat Thara cross the canal to Hat Ton Soi, where the *Andaman Inn* (☎ 01-956 1173) has small huts with attached bathroom for 150B and larger huts with attached bathroom and double bed for 350B. Huts are well spaced and the grounds are well maintained. Long-tail boats ferry passengers across Khlong Haeng from Hat Noppharat Thara to the Andaman Inn for free.

Down the beach are the similar but even more secluded *Emerald Bungalows* (300B to 500B with attached bathroom), *Bamboo Bungalows* (150B with attached bathroom) and *Sara Cove*, which has rooms for 100B with shared bathroom, 250B with attached bathroom. Sara Cove can arrange inexpensive boating trips.

Farther west, around Laem Hang Nak (Dragon Tail Cape), *Pine Bungalow* (☎ 075-644332) on Ao Siaw is even more secluded and has simple but clean bungalows for 100B with shared facilities and 150B with attached bathroom. It's best approached by road via Rte 4034.

Getting There & Away Hat Noppharat Thara can be reached by săwngthăew that leave about every 15 minutes from 7 am to 6 pm (high season) or until 4 pm (low season) from Thanon Phattana (opposite the New Hotel) in Krabi town.

Boats from Saphan Jao Fah in Krabi also run to Hat Noppharat Thara frequently between 7 am and 4 pm. These cost 70B per person and take over an hour. There are also boats between Hat Noppharat Thara and Ao Nang, mainly in the high season, during the same hours (10B, 10 minutes).

Ao Nang & Laem Tham Phra Nang
อ่าวนาง/แหลมถ้ำพระนาง

South of Hat Noppharat Thara is a series of bays where limestone cliffs and caves drop right into the sea. The water is quite clear and there are some coral reefs in the shallows. The longest beach runs along Ao Nang, a lovely but fast-developing strand easily reached by road from Krabi. Judging from the signs in Ao Nang's ubiquitous Indian-owned tailor shops, this beach has become quite popular with Swedish package tourists.

Over the headlands to the south are the beaches of **Phai Phlong**, **Hat Ton Sai**, **West Hat Rai Leh**, and then the cape of Laem Phra Nang, which encompasses **Hat Tham Phra Nang** (Princess Cave Beach) on the western side, a mangrove-rimmed beach facing east usually called **East Hat Rai Leh** but also known as Hat Nam Mao, and finally **Hat Nam Mao** proper.

All these beaches are accessible either by hiking over the headland cliffs or by taking a boat from Ao Nang or Krabi – although for several years rumours of a tunnel road to be built to Hat Phai Phlong to provide access for a new resort hotel being constructed there have abounded. So far nothing has happened, and with local conservation groups growing stronger every day it's unlikely any such tunnel will be built in the near future.

Highway signs are beginning to refer to Ao Nang as 'Ao Phra Nang', which was its original full name (in typical southern-Thai fashion, the locals shortened it to Ao Nang), but it leads some people to confuse Ao Nang/Ao Phra Nang with Laem Phra Nang, the cape with the famous cave for which the bay was named, or Hat Tham Phra Nang, the beach near the cave.

Hat Tham Phra Nang This is perhaps the most beautiful beach in the area. At one end

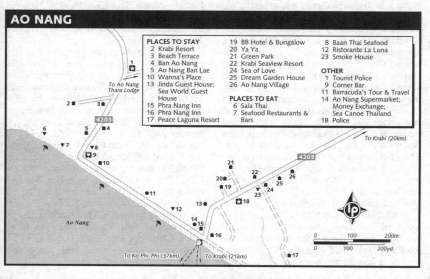

AO NANG

PLACES TO STAY
2 Krabi Resort
3 Beach Terrace
4 Ban Ao Nang
5 Ao Nang Ban Lae
10 Wanna's Place
13 Jinda Guest House;
   Sea World Guest
   House
15 Phra Nang Inn
16 Phra Nang Inn
17 Peace Laguna Resort

19 BB Hotel & Bungalow
20 Ya Ya
21 Green Park
22 Krabi Seaview Resort
24 Sea of Love
25 Dream Garden House
26 Ao Nang Village

PLACES TO EAT
6 Sala Thai
7 Seafood Restaurants &
   Bars

8 Baan Thai Seafood
12 Ristorante La Luna
23 Smoke House

OTHER
1 Tourist Police
9 Corner Bar
11 Barracuda's Tour & Travel
14 Ao Nang Supermarket;
   Money Exchange;
   Sea Canoe Thailand
18 Police

To Ao Nang Thara Lodge

4203

To Krabi (20km)

4203

Ao Nang

To Ko Phi-Phi (37km)   To Krabi (21km)

0   100   200m
0   100   200yd

is a tall limestone cliff that contains **Tham Phra Nang Nok** (Outer Princess Cave), a cave that is said to be the home of a mythical sea princess. Local legend says that during the 3rd century BC a passing royal barque carrying a charismatic Indian princess named Sri Guladevi (Si Kunlathewi in Thai) foundered in a storm. The princess' spirit came to inhabit a large cave near the wreck, using power gained through many past lives to grant favours to all who came to pay respect. Local fisherfolk place carved wooden phalli in the cave as offerings to the Phra Nang (Holy Princess) so that she will provide plenty of fish for them.

Inside the cliff is a hidden 'lagoon' called **Sa Phra Nang** (Holy Princess Pool) that can be reached by following a sometimes slippery cave trail into the side of the mountain. A rope guides hikers along the way and it takes about 45 minutes to reach the pool – guides are available from local guesthouses. If you turn left off the trail after 50m from the start, you can reach a 'window' in the cliff that affords a view of West Hat Rai Leh and East beaches. It's also possible to climb to the top of the mountain from here (some rock-climbing is involved) to get an aerial view of the entire cape and the islands of **Ko Poda** and **Ko Hua Khwan** (also known as Chicken Island) in the distance.

A second, larger cave on Laem Phra Nang was discovered only a few years ago. The entrance is in the middle of the peninsula near a batch of beach huts on East Hat Rai Leh. This one is called **Tham Phra Nang Nai** (Inner Princess Cave, called 'Diamond Cave' by the tourist industry) and consists of three caverns. All three contain some of the most beautiful limestone formations in the country, including a golden 'stone waterfall' of sparkling quartz. Local mythology says that this cave is the grand palace of the sea princess, while Tham Phra Nang on the beach is her summer palace. The cliffs around Ao Phra Nang have become a worldwide mecca for rock-climbers and it's easy to arrange equipment, maps and instruction from beach bungalows on (both east and west) Hat Rai Leh.

The islands off Laem Phra Nang are good areas for snorkelling. Besides Ko Poda and Ko Hua Khwan there is the nearer island of **Ko Rang Nok** (Bird Nest Island) and, next to that, a larger, unnamed island (possibly part of the same island at low tide) with an undersea cave. Some of the bungalows do reasonably priced day trips to these as well as other islands in the area.

Ao Phai Phlong This peaceful, palm-studded cove is worth boating to for the day. At the moment there is no accommodation here. Years ago a hotel conglomerate was rumoured to have purchased the land, but so far there are no signs of construction.

Rock-Climbing Limestone cliffs on the huge headland between Hat Tham Phra Nang and East Hat Rai Leh, and on nearby islands, offer practically endless rock-climbing. Most surfaces provide high-quality limestone with steep, pocketed walls, overhangs, and the occasional hanging stalactite. Over 460 routes have been identified and bolted by zealous climbers, most in the mid- to high-difficulty level (grades 16 to 25). They bear names like Lord of the Thais, The King and I, Andaman Wall, One-Two-Three, Sleeping Indian Cliffs and Thaiwan Wall. Novices often begin with Muay Thai, a 5m wall with around 20 climbs in the 17- to 21-grade range at the southern end of East Hat Rai Leh. According to King Climbers, during the high season as many as 300 visitors a day will climb this rock face. Certain areas are off-limits because they're part of Hat Noppharat Thara/Ko Phi-Phi National Marine Park, including the cliff next to the Rayavadee Premier resort and cliffs outside Tham Phra Nang Nai.

Most lodgings can arrange guided climbs or rock-climbing instruction. A half-day climb with instruction and guidance costs about 500B, while an all-day climb costs 1000B and three days costs 3000B; all equipment and insurance is included. Equipment rental rates for a two-person lead set are around 500B for a half-day, 800B for a full day. Along with King Climbers Rock Climbing School (e kingclimbers@iname.com), which has one branch in Ao Nang (☎ 075-639125) and another at East Hat Rai Leh (☎ 01-476 4035), the main local outfits are Tex Rock Climbing and Krabi Climbers (with the only female Thai teacher, Pung), both located near Ya-Ya, and Phra Nang Rock Climbers near East Hat Rai Leh's Viewpoint Resort. Most of these places shut down during the rainy season.

Diving & Snorkelling Phra Nang Divers at Railay Village, Coral Diving at Krabi Resort and Aqua Vision Dive Center on Ao Nang arrange day dives to local islands and live-aboard trips as far afield as Ko Bida Nok/Ko Bida Nai, the Maya Wall, Hin Daeng, Hin Muang, and the Surin and Similan Islands. Going rates are 1000B to 1800B for a day trip to nearby islands, while three- to four-day certification courses cost 8000B to 9000B. The most convenient local dive spots are Ko Poda Nai and Ko Poda Nok. At nearby Ko Mae Urai, a kilometre west of Poda Nok, two submarine tunnels lined with soft and hard corals offer lots of tropical fish and are suitable for all levels of divers.

Barracuda's Tour & Travel (☎ 075-637092) on Ao Nang operates four island trips daily for 280B, including snorkelling gear and a basic lunch.

You can also negotiate directly with the boat pilots along Ao Nang. To hire a boat that carries up to six people costs 800B for half a day, 1500B for the full day.

Paddling Tours of the coast, islands and semisubmerged caves by inflatable canoe or kayak can be arranged through Sea Canoe Thailand (☎ 075-637170), near Ao Nang Supermarket, and Sea, Land & Trek (☎ 075-637364), near Ao Nang Ban Lae on the Ao Nang beach road.

One of the best local paddles is the Tha Lin canyon river cruise, an estuary trip that cuts through 200m-high foliaged limestone cliffs, mangrove channels and tidal lagoon tunnels (euphemistically called 'hâwng', from the Thai word for 'room'). Birds frequently sighted in the mangroves include brown-winged kingfishers, Pacific reef egrets, Asian dowitchers and white-bellied sea eagles, while the most commonly seen mammals and reptiles are otters, macaques, gibbons and two-banded monitor lizards. Mudskippers and fiddler crabs abound.

Sea Canoe Thailand charges 1700B for a full-day excursion, 200B less in the low season. They also do an overnight to Ko Yao Noi for 7400B including accommodation. Sea, Land & Trek does cavern explorations for 1500B.

Places to Stay & Eat A large and growing number of **bungalows** and **inns** can be found along Ao Nang and nearby beaches.

Most of the cheap places are being edged out, but there are still a few to be found in the 200B to 300B range – mostly in the upper floors of shophouses. When choosing accommodation, scan around for open-air bars: these are often open until late and sound carries.

Ao Nang Because it's easily accessible by road, this beach has become fairly developed recently. The more expensive places usually have booking offices in amphoe meuang (provincial capital) Krabi. The oldest resort in the area, **Krabi Resort** (☎ 075-637051; in Bangkok ☎ 02-208 9165), at the northern end of Ao Nang, has luxury bungalows that cost 1792B to 4650B, depending on proximity to the beach and whether you stay in a bungalow or in the hotel wing. Most of the guests are with package tours or conferences. There are the usual resort amenities, including a swimming pool, bar and restaurant. Bookings can be made at the Krabi Resort office on Thanon Phattana in Krabi and guests receive free transport to the resort. We've received complaints that Krabi Resort bookings are not always honoured, however.

Off Rte 4203, the road leading to the beach's northern end, the **Beach Terrace** (☎ 075-637180, fax 637184) is a modern apartment-style hotel where rooms cost 2200B with air-con, hot water, TV and fridge; it's only 600B in the rainy season. The friendly **Ao Nang Ban Lae** (☎ 075-637189), about 150m south-west on the same side of Rte 4203, has a cluster of simple but well-maintained bungalows for 150B to 300B. On the opposite side of the road, **Ban Ao Nang** (☎ 075-637071) is a modern hotel with rooms for 1200B to 1600B; less in the rainy season.

Down on the beach heading south you'll come to **Wanna's Place** (☎ 01-476 7507), where simple huts with fan cost 700B (200B in the low season) or 900B with air-con in fairly simple bungalows. There's a **restaurant** in the front.

The beach road intersects Rte 4203 to Krabi just before you arrive at **Phra Nang Inn** (☎ 075-637130, fax 637134), a tastefully designed 'tropical hotel' with partial views of the bay and a small pool; streetside rooms can be noisy. Large air-con rooms start at 2900B a night in the high season (usually December to February) and 1500B the rest of the year. It has a good *restaurant*. A second, similarly designed branch is just across the road from the original.

Just around the corner from the beach on the left side of Rte 4203, *Jinda Guest House* and *Sea World Guest House* offer apartment-like rooms upstairs in two modern shophouses for 450B to 500B for fan rooms, 800B to 1200B for air-con. During the low season the prices drop by about half. Sea World has a good little restaurant as well as a few computers for sending email.

There are several other similar places in the immediate area that have smaller (sometimes windowless) rooms but are cheap for being this close to the beach (150B to 250B). These include *Angie's*, *Bernie's* and *Sea Beer*. About 100m or so from the beach, is *BB Hotel & Bungalow* (☎ 075-637147) with comfortable bungalows for 600B to 900B or hotel rooms for 1200B to 1500B. All rooms have air-con and TV. Prices drop by about half in the low season.

The *Ya Ya* (☎ 075-637176), next door (not to be confused with Ya-Ya on East Hat Rai Leh), has nicer bungalows with terraces for around 500B. Farther up the road about 200m from the beach, the *Green Park* (☎ 075-637300) is one of the better cheapies with well-maintained bamboo huts for 250B with shared bathroom and 700B for a cement bungalow with attached bathroom. This drops to as low as 100/200B single/double in the low season.

Moving farther away from the beach along Rte 4203 you'll find *Krabi Seaview Resort* (☎ 075-637242), with modern A-frames for 700B with fan and up to 2900B for a double with air-con.

On the opposite side of Rte 4203, set well back from the road next to a pond, the *Peace Laguna Resort* (☎ 075-637345) was in the middle of constructing a new hotel and facilities to go with its upmarket bungalows. Prices were 450B for rooms with fan and private bathroom, 600B to 1200B with air-con, but these are expected to increase. A trail leads directly to the beach from Peace Laguna so it's not necessary to walk out to the main road.

Farther east along Rte 4203 is *Ao Nang Village* (☎ 075-637109), with decent bungalows for 600B with fan and 1000B with air-con. Prices drop by 50% in the low season. The adjacent *Dream Garden House* (☎ 075-637338) offers more-upmarket rooms for 1000B with TV, fridge and hot water. Next door, the *Sea of Love* (☎ 075-637204) has just four rooms, but they're creatively done. The fan rooms are set atop spiral staircases and afford a terrific view of the mountains. Fan rooms cost 700B in the high season and 250B in the low season. Air-con rooms cost 1200B in the high season and 400B in the low season.

At the northern end of the beach, past where Rte 4203 turns inland, is a short string of thatched-roof bars and restaurants. *Sala Thai*, the last in the series, has the best Thai-style seafood, while most of the other restaurants serve pale cuisine. A short distance north along Rte 4203, around the corner from Wanna's, *Baan Thai Seafood* features a nice outdoor bar and decent barbecued seafood. *Smoke House*, opposite the Krabi Seaview Resort, is said to do delicious burgers and steaks. Out on the Ao Nang 'strip', *Ristorante La Luna* does pizza and pasta. The outdoor *Corner Bar*, near Wanna's, is a good place to have a beer and watch the action.

Hat Ton Sai Not to be confused with the Hat Ton Sai on Ko Phi-Phi, this 'Banyan Tree Beach' can only be reached by boat from Ao Nang, Ao Nam Mao or Krabi. Its beauty and relative isolation has made it the venue for small but increasingly popular alternative full-moon parties. There are three bungalow operations here so far. *Ton Sai Hut* has basic wooden bungalows, some with attached bathroom, for 200B to 350B. *Andaman Nature Resort* has newer bungalows with verandas and attached bathroom for 300B to 500B. Between them is *Dream Valley*, another newish place with similar rates.

West Hat Rai Leh At the centre of this pretty beach, *Railay Bay Bungalows* (☎ 01-228 4112) has a good selection of well-built concrete bungalows right across the peninsula to East Hat Rai Leh. Rates range from 500B to 1500B, depending on the size of the hut, number of beds and whether it has air-conditioning; rates can be negotiated down to 250B in the low season. The *Sand*

Peace Laguna Resort, Ao Nang, Krabi Province

Limestone pinnacles, Ao Nang, Krabi Province

Rock climbing, Hat Ton Sai, Krabi Province

Huts on Ko Phi-Phi, Krabi Province

Sea gypsy boy on Ko Lipe, Satun Province

Ao Jack Beach, Ko Tarutao, Satun Province

Bringing in the catch at Trang

Sea next door features two rows of cottages facing each other, some thatched and some with hard walls. It costs 600B to 900B for standard and deluxe bungalows with fan and cold water. Air-con will cost you up to 1500B, although all these rates should be less in the low season.

The similar *Railay Village* (☎/fax 01-228 4366, ☎ 464 6484) has small cottages with glass fronts in two facing rows for about 800B with fan and 2500B with air-con. In the low season it's 500B and 1500B. All three of these places have pleasant dining areas, but as Railay Village and Sand Sea are owned and operated by Muslim families, only Railay Bay serves alcohol – although the others don't mind if you buy alcohol outside for consumption on the premises. Railay Village cooks the best food and has the best atmosphere (all bamboo, no plastic).

At the northern end of the beach is *Railei Beach Club* (☎/fax 01-464 4338, fax 075-612914, e rbclub@phuket.ksc.co.th), also known as Langkha Daeng (Red Roof), a private home development where it's possible to rent one- to three-bedroom beach homes from the caretakers for 2400B to 7000B a night; a daily light housekeeping service is included. It's necessary to book several months in advance (several years in advance if you want to book in December).

West Hat Rai Leh can be reached by long-tail boat from Ao Nang, Ao Nam Mao or Krabi, or on foot from Hat Tham Phra Nang and East Hat Rai Leh, but these must be approached by boat as well.

The only place to eat not associated with overnight accommodation is *BoBo Bar & Restaurant*, next to Railay Village going north. Here you'll find a stand selling real coffee and a good assortment of herbal teas, plus a little bar. The restaurant, alas, is not very good and the service – provided by dope-smoking young Thais – is excruciatingly slow. During the high season the restaurant allows people to camp in the back for a modest fee. The *Sunset Bar* at Railay Bay Bungalows is still the most popular night-time scene.

Hat Tham Phra Nang The only place to stay at this beautiful beach is the *Rayavadee Premier* (☎ 075-620740), a tastefully designed and fairly unobtrusive resort with 179 luxurious rooms in domed cement-and-stucco or wooden 'pavilions' starting at 23,000B. The low-season price is 16,500B.

The beach is not the hotel's exclusive domain – a wooden walkway has been left around the perimeter of the limestone bluff so that you can walk to Hat Tham Phra Nang from East Hat Rai Leh. From West Hat Rai Leh a footpath leads through the forest around to the beach.

Hat Tham Phra Nang is accessible by boat or foot only.

East Hat Rai Leh Often referred to as Hat Nam Mao, even though another beach substantially farther east had the name first, the beach along here tends towards mud flats during low tide. The north-eastern end of the bay is vegetated with mangrove, so between the mangrove and the mudflats there's not much traditional beach scenery. Most people who stay here walk over to Hat Tham Phra Nang for beach activities.

Railay Bay Bungalows has another entrance on this side (see the West Hat Rai Leh entry, earlier). Right next door, the relatively small *Sunrise Bay Bungalows* (☎ 01-228 4236) has 15 fairly solid-looking cottages for 250B to 450B, 50B less in the low season. Videos are played nightly in Sunrise Bay's large restaurant.

Ya-Ya has some interesting bungalow designs, mostly two- and three-storey structures with brick downstairs, wood up top and integrated with coconut palms and such. A very few five-storey 'tree house' units remain; these are usually reserved for staff but you may be able to get in during the low season. Rates range from 300B to 600B, all rooms have attached bathroom. *Coco Bungalows*, farther north-east towards the mangrove area, is set back from the shoreline and offers thatched or concrete bungalows for 250B and one of the better restaurants in the area.

Farther along near the Phra Nang Nai caves, *Diamond Cave Bungalows* (☎ 01-477 0933) enjoys a beautiful setting and has nicely built concrete fan bungalows for 200B to 500B. There is also a large air-con cottage that sleeps four for 2800B.

On a hill overlooking East Hat Rai Leh and the mangrove, *Viewpoint Resort* (☎ 01-228 4115) offers fan rooms in clean, well-maintained two-storey cottages for 500B (down to 200B in the low season).

ANDAMAN COAST

Ao Nam Mao This large bay, around a headland to the north-east of East Hat Rai Leh, about 1.5km from Su-San Hoi (Shell Fossil Cemetery), has a coastal environment similar to that of East Hat Rai Leh – mangroves and shallow, muddy beaches.

The beach is sandier towards the bay's eastern end, where you'll find the environmentally friendly ***Dawn of Happiness Beach Resort*** *(01-464 4362, fax 075-612914)*. Natural, renewable, locally available building materials are used wherever possible and no sewage or rubbish ends up in the bay. Thatched bungalows with private bathrooms and mosquito nets cost 750B with a garden view, 950B with a sea view and 'family rooms' that can accommodate three to four people are 850B; low-season rates are 500B for all rooms. The staff can arrange trips to nearby natural attractions. Among many local excursions offered is an overnight camping safari to Khao Phanom Bencha National Park – a rare opportunity to see primary rainforest up close.

Ao Nam Mao is accessible by road via Rte 4204. The turn-off for the Dawn of Happiness Resort is exactly 4.2km south-east of the 0km marker on Rte 4203, the road to Su-San Hoi (the Shell Fossil Cemetery), where it splits from Rte 4204 on its way to Ao Nang. It's about 6km from Ao Nang. If you phone from Krabi, the Dawn of Happiness will arrange free transport.

Getting There & Away Hat Noppharat Thara and Ao Nang can be reached by săwngthăew that leave about every 15 minutes from 7 am to 6 pm (high season) or until 4 pm (low season) from Thanon Phattana in Krabi, opposite the New Hotel. The fare is 30B and the trip takes 30 to 40 minutes.

You can get boats to Ton Sai, West Hat Rai Leh and Laem Phra Nang at several places. For Ton Sai, the best thing to do is get a săwngthăew to Ao Nang, then a boat from Ao Nang to Ton Sai. It's 40B per person for two people or more, 100B if you don't want to wait for a second passenger to show up. Boats also go between Ao Nang and Ko Phi-Phi for 150B.

For West Hat Rai Leh or anywhere on Laem Phra Nang, you can get a boat direct from Krabi's Saphan Jao Fah for 50B. It takes about 45 minutes to reach Phra Nang.

However, boats will only go all the way round the cape to West Hat Rai Leh and Hat Tham Phra Nang from October to April when the sea is tame enough. During the other half of the year they only go as far as East Hat Rai Leh, but you can easily walk from there to West Hat Rai Leh or Hat Tham Phra Nang. You can also get boats from Ao Nang all year-round, but they only go as far as West Hat Rai Leh and Hat Tham Phra Nang (again, you can walk to East Hat Rai Leh from there). From Ao Nang you'll have to pay 40B per person for two or more passengers, 100B for just one.

Another alternative is to take a săwngthăew from Krabi as far as Ao Nam Mao, to the small fishing bay near the Su-San Hoi (Shell Fossil Cemetery), for 15B and then a boat to Laem Phra Nang for 50B (three or more people required).

Some of the beach bungalows have agents in Krabi who can help arrange boats – but there's still a charge.

THAN BOKKHARANI NATIONAL PARK
อุทยานแห่งชาติธารโบกขรณี

Than Bokkharani National Park was established in 1991 and encompasses nine caves throughout the Ao Leuk area in northern Krabi Province as well as the former botanical gardens for which the park was named.

The park is best visited just after the monsoons – when it has been dry a long time the water levels go down and in the middle of the rains it can be a bit murky. In December Than Bokkharani looks like something cooked up by Disney, but it's real and entirely natural. Emerald-green waters flow out of a narrow cave in a tall cliff and into a large lotus pool, which overflows steadily into a wide stream, itself dividing into many smaller streams in several stages. At each stage there's a pool and a little waterfall. Tall trees spread over 4000 *râi* (6.4 sq km) provide plenty of cool shade. Thais from Ao Leuk come to bathe here on weekends and then it's full of laughing people playing in the streams and pools – and shampooing their hair, which seems to be a favourite pastime here. During the week there are only a few people about, mostly kids fishing. Vendors sell noodles, excellent roast chicken, delicious batter-fried squid and *sôm-tam* (green papaya salad) under a roofed area to one side.

Watch out for aggressive monkeys in the park. Entry is 200B for foreigners.

Caves

Among the protected caves scattered around the Ao Leuk district, one of the most interesting is **Tham Hua Kalok**, set in a limestone hill in a seldom-visited bend of mangrove-lined Khlong Baw Thaw. Besides impressive stalactite formations, the high-ceilinged cave features 2000- to 3000-year-old cave paintings of human and animal figures and geometric designs.

Nearby **Tham Lawt** (Tube Cave) is distinguished by a navigable stream flowing through it – it's longer than Phang-Nga's Tham Lawt.

There are seven other similar limestone caves in Ao Leuk district – Tham Waririn, Tham Khao Phra, Tham Khao Rang, Tham Phet, Tham Thalu Fah, Tham Sa Yuan Thong, Tham To Luang and Tham Chao Leh – most of which require the services of a guide to find. Inquire at Than Bokkharani visitors centre for further information.

Places to Stay

There are a handful of places of accommodation around the entrance to the park. *Ao Leuk Bungalow* (☎ 075-681369), on the highway about 300m before Than Bokkharani, offers wood-and-concrete cottages for 250B with private bathroom.

Getting There & Away

Than Bok, as the locals call it, is near Ao Leuk. The entrance to the park is on Rte 4039, 1.3km south-west of Hwy 4 on the way to Laem Sak. To get there, take a săwngthăew from the intersection of Thanon Phattana and Thanon Preuksa Uthit in Krabi to Ao Leuk for 30B; get off just before town and it's an easy walk to the park entrance on the left.

To visit Tham Lawt and Tham Hua Kalok you must charter a boat from Tha Baw Thaw, around 6.5km west of Than Bokkharani. The tours are run exclusively by Ao Leuk native Uma Kumat and his son Bunma. They'll take one or two people for 100B; up to 10 can charter a boat for 300B. The boats run along secluded Khlong Baw Thaw and through Tham Lawt before stopping at Tham Hua Kalok. The pier at Tha Baw Thaw is 4.3km from Than Bok via Rte 4039, then 2km by dirt road through an oil palm plantation. You must provide your own transport to Tha Baw Thaw.

KHAO PHANOM BENCHA NATIONAL PARK
อุทยานแห่งชาติเขาพนมเบ็ญจา

This 50-sq-km park is in the middle of virgin rainforest along the Phanom Bencha mountain range. The main scenic attractions are the three-level **Nam Tok Huay To**, **Tham Khao Pheung** and **Nam Tok Huay Sadeh**, all within 3km of the park office. Other less well known streams and waterfalls can be discovered as well. Clouded leopard, black panther, tiger, Asiatic black bear, barking deer, serow, Malayan tapir, leaf monkey, gibbons and various tropical birds – including the helmeted hornbill, argus pheasant and extremely rare Gurney's pitta make their home here. Khao Phanom Bencha reaches 1350m in elevation, the highest point in Krabi Province. The name means Five-Point Prostration Mountain, a reference to the mountain's resemblance, in profile, to a man prostrating so that his knees, hands and head all touch the ground.

The park has a camping ground where you are welcome to pitch your own tent for 5B per person per night. Standard park admission fees apply (200B for foreigners, half price for children).

Getting There & Away

Public transport direct to Khao Phanom Bencha National Park from Krabi or Talat Kao is rare. Two roads run to the park off Hwy 4. One is only about 500m from Talat Kao – you could walk to this junction and hitch, or hire a truck in Talat Kao all the way for 100B or so. The other road is about 10km north of Krabi off Hwy 4. You could get to this junction via a săwngthăew or a bus heading north to Ao Leuk.

It would be cheaper to rent a motorcycle in Krabi for a day trip to Phanom Bencha than to charter a pick-up. Try to have someone at the park watch your bike while hiking to the falls – motorcycle theft at Phanom Bencha has been a bit of a problem in the past.

KO PHI-PHI

เกาะพีพี

Ko Phi-Phi actually consists of two islands about 40km from Krabi: Phi-Phi Leh and Phi-Phi Don. Both are part of Hat Nop-pharat Thara/Ko Phi-Phi National Marine Park, although this means little in the face of the blatant land encroachment now taking place on Phi-Phi Don.

Only parts of Phi-Phi Don are actually under the administration of the Park Division of the Royal Forest Department. Phi-Phi Leh and the western cliffs of Phi-Phi Don are left to the nest collectors, and the part of Phi-Phi Don where the chao náam live is also not included in the park.

After Phuket this is the most popular tourist destination along the Andaman Coast, especially during the peak months from December to March, when hordes descend on the island and snatch up every room and bungalow on Phi-Phi Don. Even so, the island still retains some of its original beauty, although to truly appreciate it usually means a fair hike to escape the crowds.

Ko Phi-Phi Don

เกาะพีพีดอน

Phi-Phi Don is the larger of the two islands, a sort of dumbbell-shaped island with scenic hills, awesome cliffs, long beaches, emerald waters and remarkable bird and sea life. The 'handle' in the middle has long, white-sand beaches on either side, only a few hundred metres apart.

The beach on the southern side curves around **Ao Ton Sai**, where the boats from Phuket and Krabi dock. There is also a very messy Thai Muslim village here. On the northern side of the 'handle' in the middle is **Ao Lo Dalam**.

The uninhabited (except for beach huts) western section of the island is called Ko Nok (Outer Island), and the eastern section, which is much larger, is Ko Nai (Inner Island). At the north of the eastern end is Laem Tong, where the island's chao náam population lives. The number of chao náam here varies from time to time, but there are generally about 100.

Hat Yao (Long Beach) faces south and has some of Phi-Phi Don's best coral reefs.

Ton Sai, Ao Dalam and Hat Yao all have beach bungalows.

Over a ridge north-east from Hat Yao is another very beautiful beach, **Hat Ranti**, with good surf. For several years the locals wouldn't allow any bungalows here out of respect for the large village mosque, situated in a coconut grove above the beach – but money talked, and the chao náam walked.

Farther north of Hat Ranti is the sizable bay of **Ao Bakao**, where there is a small resort, and near the tip of Laem Tong are three luxury resorts.

Park administrators have allowed development on Phi-Phi Don to continue fairly unchecked, although it's doubtful that they ever had the power or influence to stop the construction. Rumour has it that park officials won't dare to even set foot on Ko Phi-Phi for fear of being attacked by village chiefs and bungalow developers profiting from tourism.

Beautiful Ao Ton Sai has become more of a boat basin than a beach, and more and more bungalows have been crowded onto this section of the island. For solitude and scenery, this place falls short. On the other hand, those travellers in search of a more lively social scene will be rewarded by a wide choice of restaurants, beachfront bars and upmarket accommodation.

Other parts of Phi-Phi Don aren't this bad, although the once-brilliant coral reefs around the island are suffering from anchor drag and run-off from large beach developments. The least disturbed parts of the island so far are those still belonging to those chao náam who haven't cashed in.

Development on Ko Phi-Phi Don has stabilised to a significant degree over the last several years and it seems a near-truce between park authorities and greedy developers has come about. Still, there's much room for improvement in terms of rubbish collection and waste disposal.

A small power plant has been built in the centre of the island, but it doesn't have sufficient capacity to supply all of the resorts – even in Ao Dalam and Ao Ton Sai. Many resorts on this part of the island are forced to use generators on certain calendar days (odd or even depending on their location). Likewise, the single brackish reservoir on this island usually can't supply enough

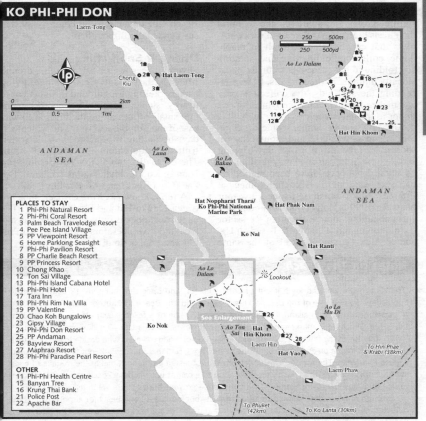

KO PHI-PHI DON

ANDAMAN
SEA

ANDAMAN
SEA

Laem Tong

Chong
Kiu

Hat Laem Tong

Ao Lo
Lana

Ao Lo
Bakao

Hat Noppharat Thara/
Ko Phi-Phi National
Marine Park

Hat Phak Nam

Ko Nai

Hat Ranti

Ao Lo
Dalam

Lookout

Ao Lo
Mu Di

Ko Nok

See Enlargement

Ao Ton
Sai

Hat
Hin Khom

Maphrao Resort

Laem Hin

Hat Yao

To Hin Phae
& Krabi (38km)

Laem Phaw

To Phuket
(42km)

To Ko Lanta (30km)

Ao Lo Dalam

Hat Hin Khom

PLACES TO STAY
1 Phi-Phi Natural Resort
2 Phi-Phi Coral Resort
3 Palm Beach Travelodge Resort
4 Pee Pee Island Village
5 PP Viewpoint Resort
6 Home Parklong Seasight
7 Phi-Phi Pavilion Resort
8 PP Charlie Beach Resort
9 PP Princess Resort
10 Chong Khao
12 Ton Sai Village
13 Phi-Phi Island Cabana Hotel
14 Phi-Phi Hotel
17 Tara Inn
18 Phi-Phi Rim Na Villa
19 PP Valentine
20 Chao Koh Bungalows
23 Gipsy Village
24 Phi-Phi Don Resort
25 PP Andaman
26 Bayview Resort
27 Maphrao Resort
28 Phi-Phi Paradise Pearl Resort

OTHER
11 Phi-Phi Health Centre
15 Banyan Tree
16 Krung Thai Bank
21 Police Post
22 Apache Bar

water, so some resorts have to turn their water supply off completely for certain hours of the day.

In 1997 and 1998 there was an extreme water shortage on the island due to a general lack of rain in Southern Thailand, and all the available tap water was quite brackish.

If you go to the island and want to air your opinion on what's going on there with regard to the environment, please contact one of the many organisations listed under the Ecology & Environment section in the Facts about Thailand chapter with your assessments, whether good or bad.

Money Krung Thai Bank has an exchange booth open from 8.30 am to 3.30 pm daily in the village next to Reggae Bar. Many of

the travel agents will also change money, although at predictably poor rates.

Medical Services Phi-Phi Health Centre, near Ton Sai Village, can handle minor emergencies and is open 24 hours.

Ko Phi-Phi Leh
เกาะพีพีเล

Phi-Phi Leh is almost all sheer cliffs, with a few caves and a sea lake formed by a cleft between two cliffs that allows water to enter into a bowl-shaped canyon. The so-called **Viking Cave** contains prehistoric paintings of stylised human and animal figures alongside later paintings of ships (Asian junks) no more than 100 years old.

The cave is also a collection point for swiftlet nests. The swiftlets like to build their nests high up in the caves in rocky hollows that can be very difficult to reach. Agile collectors build vine-and-bamboo scaffolding to get at the nests but are occasionally injured or killed in falls. Before ascending the scaffolds, the collectors pray and make offerings of tobacco, incense and liquor to the cavern spirits.

Ao Maya and Lo Sama, scenic coves on the island's western and south-eastern shores, are favourite stops for day-tripping snorkellers. Although once very pristine, the corals at these coves have been marred by bad anchoring and the beaches somewhat littered with rubbish jettisoned by tour boats. In 1999 a Hollywood film company spent about two months shooting scenes for the motion picture The Beach, based on UK author Alex Garland's novel of the same name. See the boxed text 'Notes on The Beach' for details on the controversy that surrounded the filming here.

Diving & Snorkelling

Several places in Ton Sai village – around fifteen at last count – can arrange diving and snorkelling trips around the island or to nearby islands. Several dive centres maintain small offices along the brick walkway east of the Ton Sai harbour. The typical all day snorkelling trip includes lunch, water, fruit and equipment for 360B to 400B. These usually stop at Ko Yung (Mosquito Island), Ko Mai Phai (Bamboo Island), Hin Pae (Goat Rock) and Ko Phi-Phi Leh.

A ferry, known as King Cruiser, sank between Ko Phi-Phi and Phuket in 1997. The uppermost deck is only 12m below the surface and dive operators from both Ko Phi-Phi and Phuket do dives on the wreck.

Notes on The Beach

'There's no way you can keep it out of Lonely Planet, and once that happens it's countdown to doomsday.' So says one of the backpacking characters in The Beach, UK author Alex Garland's controversial novel set in Thailand. Published in 1997, the tale of a failed beach utopia slowly caught fire in the Gen X book market and in 1999 was transformed into a US$40 million motion picture.

The story traces the fate of a small, loosely knit group of world travellers who decide to establish their own beach paradise on an island in Thailand's Ang Thong National Marine Park, not far from Ko Samui and Ko Pha-Ngan. The novel's selfish, Vietnam War-obsessed protagonist makes the mistake of passing on a map showing the beach's secret location to a pair of uninvited backpackers, whose island intrusion and subsequent confrontation with Thai dope growers brings the novel to its violent climax.

Although most readers seemed to agree that the book made a good beach or airport read, some quibbled about Garland's depiction of Thailand and the roving backpacker scene. Old Thai hands decried the attempts at Thai accents, which continually dropped the wrong consonants (resulting in an almost Cockney Thai, eg, 'le'er' for 'letter' and 'Mis'er' for 'Mister', when something more like 'let-tah' and 'Misatah' would have been more realistic). Furthermore, all the Thai characters seem rather dark and sinister. In interviews Garland has defended this criticism by pointing out that such portrayals were not intended to be realistic but were merely the perceptions of his characters. As Garland told Asiaweek magazine: 'I think it's fairly obvious this novel isn't about Thailand. It's about backpackers.'

More picky stuff: given his supposed long history of South-East Asian travel, the protagonist, Richard, seems to be incredibly naive about the use of Asian squat toilets. The beachclubbers gladly eat plain rice for breakfast, but with the abundant fishing described in the novel there was no motivation for them to do so. Finally, why does Richard never wonder (as every reader must) where the money comes from to pay for The Beach's periodic supply runs to Ko Pha-Ngan?

The novel's strengths include good fàràng dialogue and well-narrated settings. Noting the resemblance between a dipterocarp's buttressed root system and a rocket's stabilising fins, Garland coins the delightful 'rocketship trees'. Intriguing video-game references and a realistic travellers' conversation on Hat Rin also stood out. Although the novel's dip into backpacker culture and the Khao San Road scene hold up well enough (quote: 'You know, Richard, one of these days I'm going to find one of

Prices are more or less uniform at Phi-Phi's dive shops. Guided dive trips start at 900B for one dive and 1800B for two. An open-water certification course costs 9900B. Snorkelling trips can be arranged for 400B to 600B. You can rent masks, fins and snorkels for 100B a day. The best months are December to April. Phi Phi Scuba (☎ 01-228 4500) on Hat Ton Sai near the banyan tree is a reliable and long-running outfit. Check out its Web site at www.phiphi-scuba.com.

Paddling
You can rent kayaks on the beach along Ao Lo Dalam for 300B per hour, 600B per half day (700B for a double seater) or all day for 800B (1000B double).

Fishing
All day (from 8 am to 5 pm) fishing trips for marlin, sailfish, barracuda and other game-fish in nearby waters are available aboard long-tail boats for 1800B per boat, including soft drinks, lunch and fishing tackle. A half-day trip (from 9 am to 1 pm or from 1 to 5 pm) costs only 400B less. Look for signboards along the brick walkway in Ton Sai. Imperial Travel & Sport Fishing (☎ 01-894 1422) is a good bet.

Organised Tours & Boat Charters
From Ko Phi-Phi Don, boats can be chartered for a half-day trip to Ko Phi-Phi Leh or Bamboo Island for 600B. A full day costs 800B. Fishing trips average 1800B a day.

Places to Stay
During the high tourist months of December to February, July and August, nearly all the accommodation on Phi-Phi Don is booked out. As elsewhere during these months, it's best to arrive early in the morning to stake

---

Notes on *The Beach*

those Lonely Planet writers and I'm going to ask him, what's so fucking lonely about the Khao San Road?'), the novel really hits its stride once the story confines itself to the secret beach and lagoon.

Hollywood Invasion
Director Danny Boyle (of *Trainspotting* fame), teen idol Leonardo DiCaprio and a healthy Twenti-eth Century Fox crew turned up in Thailand in January 1999 to begin filming *The Beach* on the is-land of Ko Phi-Phi Leh. Almost immediately the film became embroiled in controversy when Bangkok protestors charged that the production's use of national park lands – with the express permission of the Royal Forest Department – was going to turn pristine Ao Maya into a wasteland.

The reality is that Ao Maya – like much of the rest of the Phi-Phi archipelago – has been under intense environmental pressure for many years now. First there were the dynamite and cyanide fish-ers, then came greedy resort developers and tour operators who over-ran Phi-Phi years ago and turned much of neighbouring Ko Phi-Phi Don into a trash heap. Ao Maya itself has received thou-sands of group snorkelling tours over the last 10 years. Although some concession to the bay's park status had been observed – there are no bungalows or other permanent developments at Ao Maya (most likely because the licensed bird's-nest collectors on the island won't allow it) – improper an-choring and the dumping of trash had toppled this beach from any 'pristine' status it may once have enjoyed years before 20th Century Fox arrived on the scene.

Many local and international observers who visit Ao Maya on a regular basis and who were able to visit the production set argue that Fox left the bay in better condition than it found it. For example, during the crew's first week on Phi-Phi Leh, they removed an estimated three to four tonnes of rubbish.

A strong monsoon season in 2000 seriously eroded the dunes at Ao Maya, leading many to sus-pect that Fox's beach 'renovation' may have weakened dune structure along the beach. However, we have seen other south-west-facing beaches suffer much worse monsoon damage (Ko Lanta's west coast is one good example), and have seen natural currents repair the damage within a year or two. In our opinion, the jury's still out. However, compared to the ongoing destruction one sees on adjacent Ko Phi Phi Don, whatever may have occurred on Ko Phi Phi Leh seems insignificant.

out a room or bungalow. During the low season, rates are negotiable.

During the last couple of years there has been a rash of break-ins at bungalows along Ao Lo Dalam and Ao Ton Sai. These typically occur during the early morning hours when occupants are asleep. The best way to foil thieves is to make sure your doors are locked at night.

Some bungalow operations provide lockers for guests to keep their valuables (although you must supply your own lock).

Ao Ton Sai Thirty comfortable bungalows are offered by *Ton Sai Village* (☎ *075-612434, fax 612196)* with air-con (but no fans), hot water, TV and minibar for 2100B including breakfast; it's also a little removed from others on this beach so is a bit quieter. Many Korean and Taiwanese tour groups make a stop at the beach chairs in front of this hotel.

Phi-Phi Island Cabana Hotel (☎ *075-620634, fax 612132)*, the oldest resort on the island, stretches across from Ton Sai to the beach at Ao Lo Dalam. Bungalows with fan start at 1600B while a standard room in the three-storey hotel building starts at 3400B. Amenities include a restaurant, coffee shop, snooker club, nightclub, tennis court, basketball court and a swimming pool overlooking the beach surrounded by pseudo-Greek statues and a large fountain that looks like it's been brought in from Las Vegas. Non-hotel guests may use the pool for a steep 300B.

In the back of the main restaurant-bar-diveshop strip, *Phi-Phi Hotel* (☎ *01-230 3138, 985 2667*, ✉ *phiphi@samart.co.th; in Bangkok fax 02-579 5764)* features 64 well-appointed rooms in a four-storey building. These rooms – probably the best on the island in terms of amenities as they include air-con, hot-water showers, satellite TV, minibars – cost 1800B (1500B in low season) including breakfast. *Chao Koh Bungalow* (☎ *075-611313)* consists of fairly basic but clean concrete bungalows with bathroom and fan for 500B (300B in the low season); air-con singles go for 700B, doubles for 900B. They're a bit off the beach on the way to Hat Hin Khom.

Ao Lo Dalam Set inland along a path connecting Ao Lo Dalam and Ao Ton Sai beaches is *Chong Khao*. Fairly quiet rooms

in a row house or bungalow among coconut palms range from 150B to 300B with fan and attached bathroom. This is still one of the best deals on the island as long as you don't need to be on the beach.

PP Princess Resort (☎/fax 075-622079) has large, well-spaced upmarket wooden bungalows with glass doors and windows for 1690B to 2990B. The bungalows feature deck areas and are connected by wooden walkways. Discounts down to 1290B are available from May to October.

The popular *PP Charlie Beach Resort* (☎ *075-620615)* features simple, clean thatched-roof bungalows, a pleasant restaurant and a beach bar in an atmospheric setting. Rooms with bathroom and fan cost 300B to 650B, depending on size and position on the beach. The 300B rooms are quite far back and near a generator. When the island gets crowded these prices jump to 500B and 1000B. *Phi-Phi Pavilion Resort* (☎ *075-620633)* is another thatched-roof place nicely situated in a coconut grove with bungalows with large windows, high ceilings and fan for 900B and air-con for 1400B in the high season. It costs 650B and 1000B in the low season. Security isn't the best, though, as it's impossible to lock the door-sized windows.

Home Parklong Seasight (☎ *01-671 7502)* consists of five rooms in the home of a local entrepreneur on the beach, just before you get to the end of Ao Lo Dalam and PP Viewpoint Resort. Small but clean rooms with fan and cold-water attached bathroom are 800B in the high season, while a much larger room with two double beds, two fans and a large bathroom is 1200B; prices drop to 550B and 800B in the low season. All rooms share a spacious covered wooden sitting area in front.

PP Viewpoint Resort (☎ *01-228 4111)* is set on a hillside approached by a small bridge over a canal. Units in front overlook Ao Lo Dalam while those at the back have no view. Rates range from 850B for a good wooden bungalow with fan to 1200B for a well-built concrete bungalow with air-con. In the low season the prices drop to 300B and 700B. The fan bungalows sit higher on the hill and their verandas make a great spot for a sunset cocktail. During the hot dry season from March to June, this hillside is hotter than most other locations.

Hat Hin Khom This beach a little east of Ton Sai has gone way downhill of late, with lots of rubbish floating on the water and collecting on land. Although many bungalows have been rebuilt and improved, bungalow owners here still don't seem to give a toss about keeping the area clean. *Phi-Phi Don Resort* (☎ 01-228 4083) has new cement-and-stucco bungalows and charges 300B to 500B with fan and bathroom and 800B to 900B with air-con. The service from staff is indifferent.

PP Andaman has newish but overpriced cement bungalows with bathroom and fan for 500B to 1800B. During the low season the prices drop to a much more reasonable 150B to 400B.

Behind the Andaman, well away from the beach, the well-kept *Gipsy Village* (☎ 01-229 0674) is a collection of cement bungalows arranged in a large 'U' shape amid coconut palms. They come with attached toilet and shower for 400B (150B low season). A second grouping of huts under the same name, farther back towards the interior of the island, costs about the same but is far inferior. Both of these places get very dark and lonely at night, so take care.

Bayview Resort (☎ 075-621223) is an upmarket place with modern-looking cottages geared to Thais, although plenty of faràng stay here as well. Clean, spacious, wood-floored cottages sit on a hillside and feature large decks overlooking the sea. With fan, fridge and hot-water shower, a cottage costs 1100B to 1400B, depending on the view. When the manager is present, the Thai cuisine at the restaurant can be quite good.

Interior A tourist village of sorts has developed in the interior of the island near Ao Ton Sai and Hat Hin Khom. Amid the gift shops, scuba shops and cafes, there are several budget-oriented places to stay (although none of these can be recommended as a first choice) as well as an upmarket place or two. *Tara Inn* (☎ 075-612402) has new rooms on a ridge overlooking the village. Fan rooms are 500B to 800B and air-con are 1500B to 2100B. Prices drop by almost half in the low season.

Out of the centre of the village towards the hills in the middle of the island, *PP Valentine* is a collection of thatched-roof huts with flowers growing around them for 250B to 350B. Friendly *Phi-Phi Rim Na Villa* costs 350B to 700B for rooms with fan and attached bathroom; the view of the reservoir isn't particularly inspiring. On the trail nearby are a bunch of cheapies that are really only a last resort, including *Banana House*, *Orchid House*, and *Lek's House*.

Hat Hin Khao Off by itself on a little cove that must be reached via a path over a headland to the south of Hin Khom, *Maphrao Resort* offers thatched huts in a natural setting for 250B to 350B.

Hat Yao Bungalows on this beach are practically piled onto one another, with very little space in between. A shortage of fresh water means most showers use salt water. The beach, however, is long and pretty. You can follow a trail over to a secluded beach at Lo Mu Di.

Phi-Phi Paradise Pearl Resort (☎ 075-622100) is the most substantial place on the beach, and consists of nearly 80 solid, well-kept bungalows in all shapes and sizes, ranging from 450B to 1050B in the high season; prices drop by half in the low season. All come with toilet, shower and fan. This one's a little tidier and more well spaced than others on Hat Yao.

Hat Ranti A Muslim family living on this beach offers a dozen thatched *huts* on stilts on a hillside overlooking the beach. All beds have mosquito nets. These cost 150B year-round – no dickering between high and low seasons. The huts are in varying condition so have a look around before choosing one, but basically it's a clean place. Toilets and showers are in separate huts.

It can be hard to get boat pilots from Ao Ton Sai to bring you to Hat Ranti, since the family here refuses to pay commissions. You can walk there via the lookout trail, however, once you get past the lookout the trail becomes overgrown and would be difficult to do with a large pack. Once you're on Hat Ranti the family can arrange boat trips anywhere around the island more cheaply than in Ton Sai. Note that the management at Phi-Phi Paradise Resort and other places on Hat Yao may tell you there are no bungalows on Hat Ranti, or that they've been torn down. Come see for yourself.

The family patriarch does a little farming and a little fishing, and one almost gets the impression he builds and lets these bungalows as much for company as for extra income. A nice little rustic restaurant overlooks the bay. The family cooks Thai Muslim food only and not much English is spoken; if you speak a little Thai you could very well learn a lot more here. There's decent snorkelling right off the beach.

Lo Bakao *Pee Pee Island Village (☎ 075-215014, fax 277 3990; in Bangkok ☎ 02-276 6056)* is the only resort on this beautiful, secluded stretch of sand. Limestone outcrops add a dramatic background, along with rock-climbing and hiking potential. During the high season standard rooms are 2500B and 'deluxe sea view' rooms go for 5000B. The rest of the year they cost 1800B to 2500B; air-con is available at the upper end of the price bracket.

Laem Tong This is another nice beach, with pricey resorts and its own pier. At the southernmost point, the European-managed *Palm Beach Travelodge Resort (☎ 075-214654, fax 215090)* consists of large Thai/Malay-style cottages on 2m stilts spread over spacious, landscaped grounds with lots of coconut palms. Oceanfront units have air-con, hot water and small refrigerators along with big two-level decks, while the mere deluxe ones have smaller decks, fans and cold water. High-season rates are 7415B for bungalows and 14,548B for a family cottage of two connecting rooms and two bathrooms accommodating up to six people maximum. Low-season rates start at 3900B and high-season surcharges of 17% of the room rate apply from 20 December to 31 January. On the grounds are a medium-size swimming pool and a well-equipped water sports centre.

Phi-Phi Coral Resort (☎/fax 075-214056; in Bangkok ☎ 02-270 1520) offers octagonal wood-and-bamboo cottages on the beach for 2200B to 2400B. During the low season, rates are 1800B to 2200B. One major drawback is that the resort caters to huge tour groups that visit the beach daily, and the beach is not very well maintained.

At the north end of the beach, with views over the rocky cape, *Phi-Phi Natural Resort (☎ 075-223636, fax 214301; in*

Bangkok ☎ 02-984 5600) offers very spacious grounds, a restaurant area overlooking the sea, and large split-level rooms with air-con and hot water. Although the rooms are very well maintained, maintenance in the public areas could be better. Standard rooms cost 1100B single/double, deluxe rooms cost 1500B and superior rooms cost 2500B. A surcharge of 1000B is added from 20 December to 10 January.

Between Phi-Phi Coral Resort and the Palm Beach Travelodge Resort is an area with beach chairs, a restaurant and a small dive centre with inexpensive snorkelling equipment for hire. A sea gypsy settlement at the end of that beach (signed 'Yipsae Village' in English), Mu Ban Thai Mai Pattana (New Thai Development Village) consists of shacks made of corrugated metal.

Places to Eat

Most of the resorts, hotels and bungalows around the island have their own restaurants. Cheaper and often better food is available at the restaurants and cafes in Ton Sai village, although virtually all of it is prepared for fàràng palates, so the Thai dishes aren't usually very authentic.

In the middle of the tourist village at Ao Ton Sai, the popular *Oasis* isn't bad for Thai food and offers a few European and American specialities besides. *Thai Cuisine* (Khrua Thai), on the brick walkway east of the pier, is also a good place to eat Thai.

Amico Resto, opposite the entrance to Phi-Phi Hotel, is possibly the best Italian food on the island, the seafood calzone being one of many excellent choices to be made. *Andaman Seafood*, across from the Reggae Bar, is one of several places offering good seafood.

Two branches of the friendly *Pee Pee Bakery*, one on the brick walkway east of the pier; the other at the back entrance to Phi-Phi Pavilion, offer a wide range of baked goods. The former branch stays open quite late and screens videos nightly.

A row of noodle shops and barbecued chicken stands, beyond Tin Tin's (down the soi and make a left), awaits those who tire of pasta, schnitzel and banana pancakes. A no name *khâo kaeng shop* set up in front of a wooden house just beyond Twin Palm Resort pulls no punches when it comes to mouth searing curries. However, while many local

Vegetarian Festival

Phuket's most important festival is the Vegetarian Festival, which takes place during the first nine days of the ninth lunar month of the Chinese calendar. This is usually in late September or October.

Basically, the festival celebrates the beginning of the month of 'Taoist Lent', when devout Chinese abstain from eating all meat and meat products. In Phuket, the festival activities are centred around five Chinese temples, with the Jui Tui temple on Th Ranong the most important, followed by Bang Niaw and Sui Boon Tong temples. Events are also celebrated at temples in the nearby towns of Kathu (where the festival originated) and Ban Tha Reua.

The Tourism Authority of Thailand (TAT) office in Phuket prints a helpful schedule of events for the Vegetarian Festival each year. If you plan to attend the street processions, consider bringing earplugs to make the noise of the firecrackers more tolerable. The festival also takes place in Trang, Krabi and other southern towns.

Besides abstention from meat, the Vegetarian Festival involves various processions, temple offerings and cultural performances and culminates with incredible acts of self-mortification – walking on hot coals, climbing knife-blade ladders, piercing the skin with sharp objects and so on. Shopkeepers along Phuket's central streets set up altars in front of their shopfronts offering nine tiny cups of tea, incense, fruit, candles and flowers to the nine emperor gods invoked by the festival.

Those participating as mediums bring the nine deities to earth for the festival by entering into a trance state and piercing their cheeks with all manner of objects – sharpened tree branches (with leaves still attached!), spears, slide trombones, daggers; some even hack their tongues continuously with saw or axe blades. During the street processions these mediums stop at the shopfront altars, where they pick up the offered fruit and either add it to the objects piercing their cheeks or pass it on to bystanders as a blessing. They also drink one of the nine cups of tea and grab some flowers to stick in their waistbands. The shopkeepers and their families stand by with their hands together in a *wâi* gesture, out of respect for the mediums and the deities by whom they are temporarily possessed.

The entire atmosphere is one of religious frenzy, with deafening firecrackers, ritual dancing, bloody shirt fronts and so on. Oddly enough, there is no record of this kind of activity associated with Taoist Lent in China. Some historians assume that the Chinese here were somehow influenced by the Hindu festival of Thaipusam in nearby Malaysia, which features similar acts of self-mortification. The local Chinese claim, however, that the festival was started by a theatre troupe from China that stopped off in nearby Kathu around 150 years ago. The story goes that the troupe was struck seriously ill because the members had failed to propitiate the nine emperor gods of Taoism. The nine-day penance they performed included self-piercing, meditation and a strict vegetarian diet.

---

at here, don't expect to get local prices – reckon on paying about 50B for a plate of curry over rice and a warm soft drink.

Entertainment

The most popular late night spots are *Tin-tin's Bar & Club* and the large *Reggae Bar*, both in the tourist village in the island centre. *Rolling Stoned Bar* is a laid-back place that has live music.

Apache Bar, an open-air place built up the side of a hill just beyond the police post, commands an impressive view of Ao Ton Sai and the mountains – of course you'll have to get there before dusk to enjoy it. Nearby *Blue Moon* has a similar view but cosier ambience.

Dive Cafe, above Phi Phi Scuba near the banyan tree, has beer and cocktails and features classic rock from the 1960s and 1970s.

Getting There & Away

Ko Phi-Phi is equidistant from Phuket and Krabi, but Krabi is the most economical point of departure. Until recently, boats travelled only during the dry season, from late October to May, as the seas are often too rough during the monsoons for safe navigation. Nowadays the boat operators risk sending boats year-round – we've received several reports of boats losing power and drifting in heavy swells during the monsoons. It all depends on the weather – some rainy season departures are quite safe, others are risky. If the weather looks chancy, keep in mind that there sometimes aren't enough life jackets to go around on these boats.

Most boats from Phuket and all boats from Krabi moor at the original pier at Ao Ton Sai. A few boats from Phuket, notably the *Jet Cruise*, use the new pier at Laem Tong.

Krabi From Krabi's Saphan Jao Fah, there are four departures daily at 10.30 and 11.30 am and 2.30 and 4 pm (in the reverse direction the times are 9 am and 1.30, 2.15 and 3.30 pm). The one-way fare is 160B and the trip takes 1½ hours. These fares are sometimes discounted by agents in town to as low as 120B. Departures are sometimes delayed because boats often wait for buses from Bangkok to arrive at the Krabi pier.

Ao Nang You can also get boats from Ao Nang on the Krabi Province coast for 250B from October to April; there's usually only one departure a day at around 9 am. The trip lasts 80 minutes. In the reverse direction, boats leave from Ko Phi-Phi to Ao Nang at 3.30 pm.

Phuket A dozen different companies operate boats from various piers on Phuket. These range in price from 250B or more for the boats that take an hour and 40 minutes to two hours. Any guesthouse or hotel on Phuket can arrange tickets; the more expensive fares include bus or van pick-up from your hotel. Boats leave frequently between 8.30 am and 1.30 pm. Boats from Phi-Phi to Phuket leave at 9 am and 2.30 pm and cost 250B.

Andaman Wave (☎ 075-222570) runs the 40-minute *Jet Cruise*, which leaves Phuket at 8.30 pm (Laem Tong at 3 pm) and costs 400B one way.

Various tour companies in Phuket offer day trips to Ko Phi-Phi for 500B to 950B per person, including return transport, lunch and a tour. If you want to stay overnight and catch another tour boat back, you have to pay another 100B. Of course, it's cheaper to book a one-way passage on the regular ferry service.

Other Islands As Ko Lanta is becoming more touristed, there are now fairly regular boats between that island and Ko Phi-Phi from October to April. Boats generally leave from the pier on Lanta Yai at around

8 am, arriving at Ko Phi-Phi Don around 9.30 am (sometimes there is a second boat departing at 1 pm). In the reverse direction the departure is usually at 2 pm (sometimes there is also a departure at 11 am). Passage costs 170B per person. It's also possible to get boats to/from Ko Jam; the same approximate departure time, fare and trip duration applies.

Getting Around

Transport on the island is mostly on foot, although fishing boats can be chartered at Ao Ton Sai for short hops around Ko Phi-Phi Don and Ko Phi-Phi Leh. Touts meet boats from the mainland to load people onto longtail boats going to Hat Yao (Long Beach) for 30B per person. Other boat charters around the island from the pier at Ton Sai include Laem Tong (400B), Lo Bakao (300B) and Viking Cave (200B).

KO JAM (KO PU) & KO SI BOYA
เกาะจำ(ปู)/เกาะศรีบอยา

These large islands are inhabited by a small number of fishing families and are perfect for those seeking complete removal from the videos, fàràng restaurants, beach bars and so on. About the only entertainment is watching the local villagers load and unload their fishing boats or collect cashews and coconuts, or to swim and take long walks on the beach.

Joy Bungalow (☎ 01-229 1502), on the south-western coast of Ko Jam, offers 37 spacious bungalows from 150B (bamboo) to 450B (wood).

New Bungalows (☎ 01-464 4230), also on Ko Jam, features more basic huts for 150B and nicer ones (including a couple of tree houses) cost up to 400B. During the rainy season this place sometimes shuts down, so it's a good idea to call in advance.

On nearby Ko Si Boya, the atmospheric *Siboya Bungalow* (☎ 01-229 1415) offers several sizes of bungalow in the 250B to 500B range. A generator provides electricity from 6 pm until midnight.

Getting There & Away

Boats to both islands leave once or twice a day from Ban Laem Kruat, a village about 30km from Krabi, at the end of Rte 4036 off Hwy 4. Passage costs 25B to Si Boya, 30B to Ban Ko Jam.

You can also take boats bound for Ko Lanta from Krabi's Saphan Jao Fah and ask to be let off at Ko Jam. There are generally two boats that leave at 10.30 am and 1.30 pm daily; the fare is supposed to be 150B as far as Ko Jam, although some boat operators will charge the full Ko Lanta fare of 170B. These latter boats only run November through May.

KO LANTA
เกาะลันตา

postcode 81150 • pop 18,000
Ko Lanta is a district of Krabi Province that consists of 52 islands. The geography here is typified by stretches of mangrove interrupted by coral-rimmed beaches, rugged hills and huge umbrella trees.

Twelve of the islands are inhabited and, of these, four are easily accessible: **Ko Klang**, **Ko Bubu**, **Ko Lanta Noi** and **Ko Lanta Yai**. You can reach the latter by ferry from Ban Hua Hin on the mainland across from Ko Lanta Noi, and from Ko Phi-Phi, Ko Jam and Krabi.

Modest beach accommodation is available on the group's largest island, Ko Lanta Yai, a long, slender portion of sand and coral with low, forested hills down the middle; accommodation and transport reservations are available through travel agencies in Krabi or Phuket. You can camp on any of the other islands – all have sources of fresh water.

Ban Sala Dan, at the northern tip of the island, is the largest settlement on the island and has a couple of ferry piers, tour outfits, dive shops and a Siam City Bank with exchange services. It's connected to the mainland by power lines.

The district capital **Ban Ko Lanta**, on the lower eastern coast, boasts a post office and long pier; there's not much to the town but the buildings are more solid-looking than those in Sala Dan.

The village of **Ban Sangka-U** on Lanta Yai's southern tip is a traditional Muslim fishing village and the people are friendly.

The people in this district are a mixture of Muslim Thais and chao náam who settled here long ago. Their main livelihood is the cultivation of rubber, cashew and bananas, along with a little fishing on the side.

A road nearly encircles the island – but only about half of its length is paved. Only the south-eastern tip around Ban Sangka-U is totally devoid of vehicles. In the centre of the island is **Tham Khao Mai Kaew**, a five- or six-cavern limestone cave complex.

Ko Lanta National Marine Park
อุทยานแห่งชาติเกาะลันตา

In 1990, 15 islands in the Lanta group (covering an area of 134 sq km) were declared part of Ko Lanta National Marine Park in an effort to protect the fragile coastal environment. **Ko Rok Nok** is especially beautiful, with a crescent-shaped bay featuring cliffs and a white-sand beach and a stand of banyan trees in the interior. The intact coral at **Ko Rok Nai** and limestone caves of **Ko Talang** are also worth seeing. Dive shops in Ban Sala Dan can arrange dives to these islands as well as coral-encrusted **Ko Ha**, **Ko Bida**, **Hin Bida** and **Hin Muang**. Camping is permitted on Ko Rok Nok.

Ko Lanta Yai itself is only partially protected since most of the island belongs to chao náam. As on Ko Phi-Phi, many bungalows have been built on shorelands under the nominal protection of the Royal Forest Department.

The interior of the island consists of rubber, cashew and fruit plantations, with a few stands of original forest here and there, mostly in the hilly southern section of the island. The park headquarters is at the southern tip of Ko Lanta Yai. Standard national park admission fees apply (200B for foreigners, half price for children).

Tham Khao Mai Kaew
ถ้ำเขาไม้แก้ว

A great break from the beach is a trip to this complex of caves in the centre of Ko Lanta Yai. Even the hike in, through original forest, is quite pleasant. But the real fun begins when you descend through a small, indistinct hole in the rocks and enter the series of diverse caverns.

Some sections are as large as church halls, others require you to squeeze through on hands and knees. Sights en route include impressive stalactites and stalagmites, bats and even a cavern pool that you can swim in. The latter is not recommended for the fainthearted, as access is via a long, slippery slope and a knotted rope that's almost as slimy – a bit of a challenge on the way back up.

ANDAMAN COAST

KO LANTA

PLACES TO STAY
1 Siboya Bungalow
2 Joy Bungalow
3 New Bungalows
5 Deer Neck Cabana
7 Kaw Kwang Beach Bungalows
9 Golden Bay Cottages
10 Diamond Sand Inn
11 Southern Lanta Resort
12 Lanta Villa; Chaba Lanta
13 Lanta Island Resort
14 Lanta Sea House; Lom Thalay
15 The Other Place
16 Lanta Garden Home
18 Otto's Bar & Bungalows
19 Lanta Palm Beach; Sandy Beach
20 Lanta Long Beach Bungalows
22 Lunta Marina Resort; Reggae House; Blue Marlin
23 The Sanctuary
24 Relax Bay Tropicana
25 Lanta New Beach Bungalow
26 Lanta Riviera
27 Lanta Emerald Bungalow
28 Lantas' Lodge
29 Where Else?
30 Lanta Coconut Green Field
31 Lanta Merry Hut
32 Klong Nin Resort
33 Nice Beach Bungalows
37 Lanta Nature Beach
38 Lanta Paradise
39 Lanta Miami
40 Dream Team; Lanta Coral Beach Resort
41 Sea Sun; Lanta Marine Park View Resort; Kantiang Seaview; Same Same
42 Waterfall Bay Resort

OTHER
4 Pier
6 Island View Restaurant
8 Hans
17 Triple Coconut Tree
21 Ko Lanta Hat Phra Ae Beach Park
34 Ko Lanta Meteorological Station
35 Tham Khao Mai Kaew
36 Police Station
43 Ko Lanta National Marine Park Headquaters

Ko Si Boya
1
Ko Jam
To Krabi
Ko Jam
2
3
Ban Ko Jam
0   2   4km
0   1   2mi
4206
Ban Hua Hin
ANDAMAN SEA
Ban Khlong Mak
To Ko Phi-Phi
Ban Lang Sot
Ko Lanta Noi
Ban Sala Dan
Hat Khlong Dao
Ban Lu Yong
Ko Klang
Ko Talabeng
Ban Phra Ae
Hat Phra Ae
Ban Thung Yi Pheng
Hat Thung Thaleh
Ban Phu Klom
Ko Kam
Ban Je Lii
Ko Bubu
See Enlargement
Ban Khlong Khong
Ban Khlong Tohp
32
33 34
35
36
Ko Paw
Hat Khlong Nin
37
38
39
Ban Khlong Nin
Ban Ko Lanta
Ban Hua Laem Klang
Ko Lanta National Marine Park
40
Ko Lanta Yai
Ban Hua Laem
Hat Khlong Hin
Ban Khlong Hin
Ao Kantiang
41
Ao Nui
42
Ban Sangkha-U
Ko Kluang
Ao Khlong Jak
43
Ko Lek
To Ko Rok Nai, Ko Rok Yai & Ko Ha
Laem Tanot

Laem Khaw Kwang
6 5
7
4
Ban Sala Dan
8
9
Hat Khlong Dao
10
11
12
Ban Lu Yong
13
14
15
16
17 18
19
20
21
Ban Phra Ae
Hat Phra Ae
22
23
24
Ban Phu Klom
25
26
27
28
Ban Khlong Khong
29
30
31
0   1   2km
0   0.5   1mi

A Muslim family living near the trail-head to the caves offers guide service, giving two-hour tours for 100B per person. You really need a guide to find your way around, particularly inside the caves, and the service is definitely worth it. The family also runs a very basic restaurant where you can buy a variety of snacks and drinks.

The caves are located off the lower of the two cross-island roads, down a narrow, 1.5km dirt track through a rubber plantation that ends up at the Muslim family's home. The best way to get there is by renting a motorcycle, although your bungalow may be willing to arrange transport.

Beaches

The western sides of all the islands have beaches, although in overall quality Lanta's beaches don't quite measure up to those found in Phuket or along Hat Tham Phra Nang. The best are along the north and south of Lanta Yai's west coast, with middle sections given over to rocky shores and reefs. There are coral reefs along parts of the western side of Lanta Yai and along Laem Khaw Kwang (Deer Neck Cape). A hill atop the cape gives a good aerial view of the island. During the rainy season high wind and waves sometimes leave the beach covered with trash and many of the bungalow operations shut down for the duration.

The little island between Ko Lanta Noi and Ko Klang has a nice beach called **Hat Thung Thaleh** – hire a boat from Ko Klang. Also worth exploring is Ko Ngai (Hai) – see the Trang Province section farther on for more details, as Ko Ngai is more accessible from that province.

Diving & Snorkelling

The uninhabited islands of Ko Rok Nai, Ko Rok Yai and Ko Ha, south of Ko Lanta Yai, offer plenty of coral along their western and south-western shores. According to Ko Lanta Dive Centre in Ban Sala Dan, the undersea pinnacles of Hin Muang and Hin Daeng farther south-west are even better, with visibility of up to 30m in good weather, hard and soft corals, and plenty of large schooling fish such as sharks, tuna and manta ray. Whale sharks have also been spotted in the area.

In any given season there may be as many as four dive operations on Ko Lanta,

all working out of Ban Sala Dan but often bookable at beach bungalows. Atlantis Dive Centre (☎ 075-612914) charges 2400B for a one-day dive trip, including equipment hire. Two-day trips with five dives start at 5000B.

Aquarius Diving (☎ 075-234201) has received some good reviews from travellers, as has Dive Zone, which also appears to be fairly well equipped. November to April is the best season for diving in these areas.

Massage

As on most other Thai beaches with a tourist presence, Ko Lanta has its share of wandering *măw nûat* (massage therapists). Typically the massage costs 100B to 200B per hour, but the quality of the massage varies, as many of the 'therapists' have received little or no formal training. An exception is Mr Boonsanong Banthisa (nicknamed Tou), who has been administering massage to beach-ridden *fàràng* for 12 years. If you are staying at one of the bungalows on Hat Khlong Dao, you can set up an appointment with Tou for an excellent massage by contacting the reception of the place you're staying.

Places to Stay

Ko Lanta Yai is now completely wired for electricity and air-con bungalows have become quite common. Surely videos and discos are on their way if we can judge by the lines of development followed in Phuket, Ko Samui and Ko Phi-Phi.

Ko Lanta has the opportunity of becoming a model for environmentally conscious island tourism if the beach developers here will cooperate to keep the island clean and noise-free. Deforestation has become a problem as unscrupulous developers cut down trees to build upmarket bungalows with hectares of wooden decks. The simple places catering to backpackers still use renewable bamboo. Typically, Ko Lanta's bungalow operations have a selection of two styles of accommodation: concrete bungalows with air-con, and more rustic fan accommodation built of wood or bamboo. Ironically, the air-con accommodation is always closest to the beach – blocking beach breezes – while the fan bungalows are farther inland. This practice is pushing everything more quickly in the direction of air-conditioning, an absolute non-necessity on any island beach in Thailand.

As seems obvious elsewhere in Thailand, the national park system cannot be relied upon to protect the lands, so it's really up to the local private sector to determine how it wants to handle tourism.

The prettiest beach areas are found along the north-western side of the island just south of Ban Sala Dan, and this is where all the development is concentrated. Because it's long, wide and flat, this is a perfect beach for walking and jogging. The majority of places on this end costs at least 500B a night during the high season (November to May). During low season, prices plummet to 200B a night. A handful of places are still in the 100B to 250B per night bracket even during the high season, but these tend to close during the low season. At this time proprietors make little effort to clean the beach of accumulating refuse and hence it's rather unappealing during that half of the year.

At the northernmost section of the beach near Ban Sala Dan is the long-running *Deer Neck Cabana*, a semicircle of solid-looking bungalows with roofs of corrugated fibre or tin, facing the western side of the small Laem Khaw Kwang peninsula that juts west from the island, on its own shallow beach – a particularly safe one for children. When the tide is in you can see trees seemingly growing out of the sea (rooted in submerged sand banks). Rates are low (around 150B to 250B), but on our last visit the land was up for sale, so it's unclear whether or not the situation will change.

The locally owned *Kaw Kwang Beach Bungalows* (☎ 01-228 4106) is the oldest of the beach places and still commands one of the best stretches of beach – and it's close to snorkelling areas, as well. It's actually on the south-eastern side of this tiny cape. Nicely separated thatched huts with private bathroom, fan and good cross-ventilation cost 100B to 800B, depending on size, time of year and proximity to the beach. Hammocks are strung from casuarina trees along the beach and snorkelling gear is available for rent. The proprietors offer fishing and snorkelling trips to nearby islands.

Starting about 2.5km south of Ban Sala Dan along the western side of the island are a cluster of places in higher price ranges along a wide stretch of sand known as Hat Khlong Dao. *Hans* comes up first with a collection of bungalows in different sizes and of different materials. These start at 300B for fan bungalows with attached bathroom. There's also a good restaurant here. *Golden Bay Cottages* (☎ 01-229 0879), next door, has clean, concrete bungalows with attached bathroom for 300B to 450B. *Diamond Sand Inn* (☎ 01-228 4473) is a very pleasant spot, with 20 new, large cottages with air-con for 1500B. The restaurant has very good Thai food, but it's not overpriced like the bungalows.

Next comes *Southern Lanta Resort* (☎ 075-218947, fax 218242), which has a pool and 65 air-con rooms costing 1600B to 2000B. *Lanta Villa* (☎ 075-620629) offers bungalows with distinctive high-pitched roofs for 400B to 600B with fan and 800B with air-con. It's open year-round and there's an Internet access place on the main road at its entrance. Just down the beach is *Chaba Lanta*, which has bamboo huts with shared facilities for just 120B. A cluster of open-air bars, known as the Lanta Night Plaza, is on the next lot. Next is the *Lanta Island Resort* (☎ 01-212 4183), where bungalows are 350B with fan and up to 1500B with air-con. It's popular with tour groups. This is followed by the slightly more upmarket *Lanta Sea House* (☎ 01-228 4160), with vaguely Malay-style bungalows for 600B to 800B with fan and 1500B with air-con and fridge; it's open year-round. Next is *Lom Thalay*, which charges 300B to 500B for its fan bungalows. An advantage to staying here is that there's a small supermarket nearby – no need to walk all the way to Ban Sala Dan if you run out of sunblock.

From here farther south accommodation becomes simpler and less expensive. *The Other Place* consists of just a few thatched and natural units with fan for 200B or a bit more in the December to February peak season. *Lanta Garden Home* next door has similarly basic huts with shared bathroom for 150B and up to 600B with private bathroom.

Just around a headland famous for a triple-trunked coconut palm Hat Phra Ae begins, where *Otto's Bar & Bungalows* offers five old-style thatched bungalows and four outside bathrooms for 80B in the low season and 120B in the high season. Around the headland are a couple of cheapies, *Sandy Beach* and *Lanta Palm Beach* has both wood and concrete huts with fan of widely varying quality for 80B to 150B.

Just before Ko Lanta Hat Phra Ae Beach Park, an access road leads 400m to *Lanta Long Beach Bungalows*, a group of rustic thatched bungalows on cement stilts with attached bathroom and nice decks. The huts are rather close together, but the open-air restaurant offers good beach views. Rates vary widely between low, high and 'peak' seasons.

Just beyond the small village of Ban Phra Ae is the *Lunta Marina Resort*, where for a rather steep 450B to 600B you'll get a wood-and-bamboo bungalow with an interesting elevated A-frame design. Nearby are the laid-back *Reggae House* and *Blue Marlin*, both of which are basic but cheap – 80B to 100B. In this same area, *The Sanctuary* offers rustic huts and good vegetarian food; it's a nice place but is almost always full (closed during the rainy season).

The nearby *Relax Bay Tropicana* (☎ 01-477 0077) features spacious bungalows with large decks for 800B; huts are perched around a rocky hillside overlooking the sea. The management can arrange day trips around the island and there's a dive shop on the premises. The beach along this stretch and for the next 2km is nothing special. It's followed a little farther south, near Ban Phu Klom, by *Lanta New Beach Bungalow*, where two rows of cement bungalows cost 250B to 400B a night. At the *Lanta Riviera*, very small but well-kept concrete cottages with attached bathroom cost 300B to 500B. They're in a nice coconut grove. There's a basic open-air restaurant here. This theme continues at the similarly priced *Lanta Emerald Bungalow*, which has bungalows for 250B to 300B.

The next place south towards Ban Khlong Khong (the beach here is also sometimes referred to as Hat Khlong Khong), *Lantas' Lodge* has thatched huts in a coconut grove for 500B to 700B in the high season and 200B to 300B in the low season. It's a little overpriced, but it's quiet and has a pleasant outdoor restaurant. Next comes *Where Else?*, with basic thatched huts on stilts for 300B to 450B, followed by *Lanta Coconut Green Field*, down a sandy

road that winds through coconut trees. The tidy thatched huts have cement foundations and small verandas. All have attached bathrooms and go for 350B to 500B. There's a restaurant on the beach in front. It's closed during the rainy season.

To reach the next one down, *Lanta Merry Hut*, take a dirt road to the right through a village and past a mosque, then through a wooden gateway past some private homes. The traditional thatch huts here number nine in all and come with attached bathroom for 300B to 400B in the high season. A simple open-air restaurant offers food. This is a good place to stay if you want to get involved in village life at Ban Khlong Khong.

Farther south (another kilometre or so) the beach changes name again to Hat Khlong Nin and the accommodation becomes even cheaper. *Khlong Nin Resort* has concrete bungalows with attached bathroom for 250B to 500B. It's got a good stretch of beach all to itself. About a kilometre down the beach is *Nice Beach Bungalows* (☎ 01-228 3162) which has concrete bungalows for 250B to 350B.

The next three are owned by the same local family. *Lanta Nature Beach* (☎ 01-397 0785) has both bamboo huts and concrete bungalows for 200B to 400B; *Lanta Paradise* offers OK wood and concrete bungalows with good beach frontage for 150B to 400B; *Lanta Miami* (☎ 01-228 4506) immediately south costs 150B to 650B. The management is quite friendly and flexible with their rates.

Sitting on a little headland with a rocky stretch of beach called Hat Khlong Hin is the friendly and well-landscaped *Dream Team* (☎ 01-228 4184), with well-kept, large, screened bungalows of bamboo as well as newer concrete air-con affairs. These cost 200B to 500B for fan (depending on proximity to the shoreline) and 1500B for large air-con rooms with bathroom tub and hot water. The newly established *Lanta Coral Beach Resort* is next door and has fan bungalows of both wood and concrete for 200B to 400B.

A better sand beach at Ao Kantiang is only about 10 minutes away on foot. Occupying a prime spot at the northern end of Ao Kantiang is *Lanta Marine Park View Resort*, which has both bamboo and concrete bungalows for 250B to 400B. *Sea Sun*, down the beach, has 80B to 120B concrete bungalows – but they're showing their age. Next is a newer cheapie, *Kantiang Seaview*, which has bamboo huts for 100B to 150B. The aptly named *Same Same*, has yet more bungalows of wood and concrete for 250B to 300B.

The next cove down, Ao Nui, is one of the most beautiful on the island and as yet has no bungalows – probably because it's a steep walk down to the beach.

At this point the road begins climbing and winding steeply as it approaches the southern tip of the island. Near the end of the road, on Ao Khlong Jak, *Waterfall Bay Resort* (☎ 01 836 4877) offers 18 well-spaced wooden bungalows with thatched roofs overlooking a secluded bay. Fan bungalows begin at 700B, and air-con bungalows cost up to 2500B – depending on their position relative to the beach and amenities provided. All have two rooms, one below and one above as a loft, making it very suitable for family stays. The namesake waterfall is a 30- to 40-minute walk. Call ahead and they will pick you up at Ban Sala Dan. The Waterfall Bay Resort recently underwent a change in ownership, so it remains to be seen if standards will be kept up.

Places to Eat

If you get tired of bungalow food there are a couple of basic places to eat in Ban Sala Dan at the northern end of Lanta Yai. *Seaview* and *Seaside* are two small, moderately priced restaurants over the water with Thai food and seafood. *Restaurants* on the beach near Lanta Garden Home come and go with the seasons but usually offer Swiss, French or Italian food.

Island View Restaurant sits on the crest of the hill between the two bungalow operations on either side of Laem Khaw Kwang and is only open in the high season. The food is standard but the view and surrounding cashew trees add novelty to the dining experience.

At the *Diamond Sand Inn*, try the excellent *kûng phàt náam mákhǎam* (shrimp stir-fried in tamarind sauce).

Otto's Bar & Bungalows serves good, inexpensive to moderately priced Thai and Western dishes. Occasionally during the high season the restaurant hosts a small full moon party with *muay thai* (Thai boxing) music, dancing and a seafood barbecue. *Hans* does delicious German-style steaks, as well as Thai specialities. *The Sanctuary* makes good vegetarian food, including a few Indian dishes.

Getting There & Away

Krabi Minibuses to Ko Lanta leave from Krabi's Thanon Sukhon at 11 am and 1 and 3.30 pm. The ride costs 150B and takes about 1½ hours. There is a vehicle ferry across the narrow channel between Ban Hua Hin on the mainland and Ban Khlong Mak on Ko Lanta Noi and another across the even narrower channel to Ban Sala Dan on Ko Lanta Yai. Both ferries cost 3B per pedestrian, 5B for a bicycle and one rider, 10B per motorcycle and 50B for a car or truck. If you take the minibus this is included in the fare. Going from Ko Lanta to Krabi, the minibus leaves from Anut Tour in Ban Sala Dan at 7.30 and 8 am and 12.30 pm. You can usually arrange for the minibus to pick you up at the bungalows where you're staying by informing the management of the bungalows about your intended departure a day ahead of time.

There are now two ferries sailing between Bang Lang Sot and Ban Sala Dan: a larger new one that lands a little south of Ban Sala Dan and the older, smaller one (two cars at a time only) that goes directly to Ban Sala Dan. Both ferries run frequently from 7 am to 8 pm. There is talk of building a bridge between Bang Lang Sot and Ban Sala Dan to supplant the ferry services.

Ban Hua Hin is 26km down Rte 4206 from Ban Huay Nam Khao, which is about 44km from Krabi along Hwy 4. If you're travelling by private car or motorcycle, the turn-off for Rte 4206 is near the village of Ban Huay Nam Khao, at the 64km marker on Hwy 4.

If you're coming from Trang, there's no direct public transport to Ban Hua Hin, but you can take a bus from Trang to Ban Huay Nam Khao (25B), then a sǎwngthǎew going south-west to the Tha Ban Hua Hin.

The quickest way to reach Ko Lanta from Krabi is to take a boat from Krabi's Saphan Jao Fah, only available from October to April. Boats usually depart at 10.30 am and 1.30 pm and take 1 to 1½ hours to reach Ban Sala Dan; the fare is 170B. In the reverse direction, boats leave at 10 am and 1 pm.

Ko Phi-Phi During the dry season from October to April, there are boats from Ko Phi-Phi at 2 pm daily (and sometimes 11 am) for 170B per person. They take about 80 minutes to reach Ban Sala Dan; in the opposite direction, boats leave Ko Lanta around 8 am (and sometimes 1 pm). There are also occasional boats to Lanta from Ko Jam.

Getting Around
Most of the bungalows on Ko Lanta will provide free transport to/from Ban Sala Dan. Motorcycle taxis are available from Ban Sala Dan to almost anywhere along the beaches for 15B to 50B depending on the distance. From Ban Ko Lanta, motorcycle taxi fares fall in the same range.

Motorcycles can be rented in Ban Sala Dan for a steep 250B a day.

Trang Province

The province of Trang has a geography similar to that of Krabi and Phang-Nga, with islands and beaches along the coast and limestone-buttressed mountains inland, but is much less frequented by tourists. Caves and waterfalls are the major attractions in the interior of the province – Trang seems to have more than its share.

To the north-west of the provincial capital is Thaleh Song Hong (Sea of Two Rooms), a large lake surrounded by limestone hills. Hills in the middle of the lake nearly divide it in half, hence the name.

TRANG
อ.เมืองตรัง

postcode 92000 • pop 50,900
Historically, Trang has played an important role as a centre of trade since at least the 1st century AD. It was especially important between the 7th and 12th centuries, when it was a sea port for ocean-going sampans sailing between Trang and the Straits of Malacca. Nakhon Si Thammarat and Surat Thani were major commercial and cultural centres for the Srivijaya empire at this time, and Trang served as a relay point for communications and shipping between the east coast of the Thai peninsula and Palembang, Sumatra. Trang was then known as Krung Thani and later as Trangkhapura (City of Waves), until the name was shortened during the early years of the Ratanakosin period.

During the Ayuthaya period, Trang was a common port of entry for seafaring Western visitors, who continued by land to Nakhon Si Thammarat or Ayuthaya. The town was then located at the mouth of Mae Nam Trang (Trang River), but King Mongkut later gave orders to move the city to its present location inland due to frequent flooding. Today Trang is still an important point of exit for rubber from the province's many plantations.

Information
Tourist Offices Trang has no TAT office but if you plan on spending a lot of time exploring Trang, it's worth dropping by the TAT office in Nakhon Si Thammarat, which is responsible for dispensing information about Trang.

Money Bangkok Bank, Thai Farmers Bank and Siam Commercial Bank have branches on Thanon Phra Ram VI. Bangkok Bank and Thai Farmers Bank have ATMs, as does the Thai Military Bank on Thanon Visetkul (Wisetkun).

Post & Communications The main post office and the telephone office are on the corner of Thanon Phra Ram VI and Thanon Kantang.

Things to See
Trang's main attractions are the nearby beaches and islands, plus the fact that it can be reached by train. Among Thais, one of Trang's claims to fame is that it often wins awards for 'Cleanest City in Thailand' – its main rival is Yala. One odd aspect of the city is the seeming lack of Thai Buddhist temples. Most of those living in the central business district are Chinese, so you do see a few joss houses but that's about it. Meun Ram, a **Chinese temple** between Soi 1 and Soi 2, Thanon Visetkul, sometimes sponsors performances of southern-Thai shadow theatre.

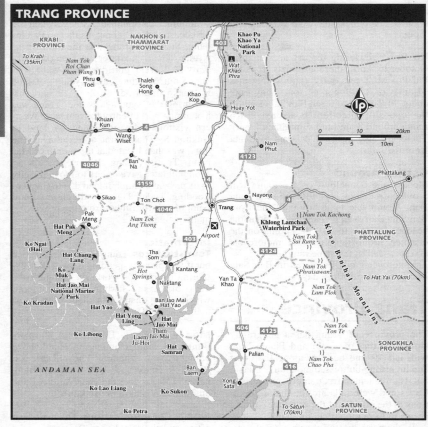

TRANG PROVINCE

Places to Stay

A number of hotels are found along the city's two main thoroughfares, Thanon Phra Ram VI and Thanon Visetkul, which run west and south from the clock tower. The long-running **Ko Teng Hotel** (☎ 075-218622), on Thanon Phra Ram VI, has large singles/doubles for a reasonable 180/300B, and a good restaurant downstairs. The front doors of the hotel are closed at 7 pm every day; there's another entrance around the back. **Wattana Hotel** (☎ 075-218184), on the same street, offers rooms for 170B with fan and bathroom, 300B with TV and phone and 330B with air-con. This is one of those hotels with lots of smoking men and painted ladies in the lobby.

On Thanon Visetkul, the **Queen Hotel** (☎ 075-218522) has large clean rooms with fan for 260B and 400B with air-con. The business-like **Trang Hotel** (☎ 075-218944), near the clock tower, has expansive air-con rooms (some with balcony) with TV, hot water, fan and phone for 470B, or with a bathtub for 520B. The downstairs coffee shop at the latter is a popular local spot.

Uppermost on the local scale is the **Thumrin Thana Hotel** (☎ 075-211211, fax 223288, 69/8 Thanon Trang Thana), a big fancy place not far from the bus terminal with a gleaming marbled lobby and spacious rooms, each with two beds, IDD phones with voice mail, fridge, TV and smoke detector, all for 1200B to 1500B (breakfast included). Other facilities include a small bakery, a

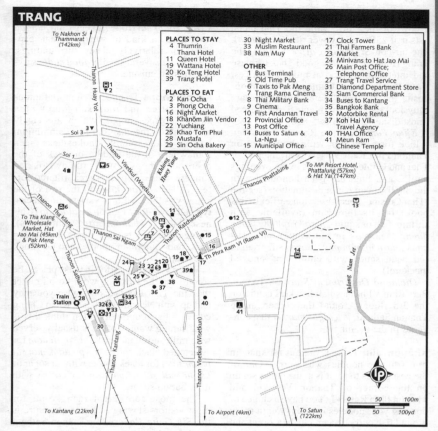

TRANG

PLACES TO STAY
4 Thumrin
 Thana Hotel
11 Queen Hotel
19 Wattana Hotel
20 Ko Teng Hotel
39 Trang Hotel

PLACES TO EAT
2 Kan Ocha
3 Phong Ocha
16 Night Market
18 Khanŏm Jiin Vendor
22 Yuchiang
25 Khao Tom Phui
28 Mustafa
29 Sin Ocha Bakery

30 Night Market
33 Muslim Restaurant
38 Nam Muy

OTHER
1 Bus Terminal
5 Old Time Pub
6 Taxis to Pak Meng
7 Trang Rama Cinema
8 Thai Military Bank
9 Cinema
10 First Andaman Travel
12 Provincial Office
13 Post Office
14 Buses to Satun &
 La-Ngu
15 Municipal Office

17 Clock Tower
21 Thai Farmers Bank
23 Market
24 Minivans to Hat Jao Mai
26 Main Post Office;
 Telephone Office
27 Trang Travel Service
31 Diamond Department Store
32 Siam Commercial Bank
34 Buses to Kantang
35 Bangkok Bank
36 Motorbike Rental
37 Koh Hai Villa
 Travel Agency
40 THAI Office
41 Meun Ram
 Chinese Temple

coffee shop, three restaurants, shopping centre, business centre, safety deposit boxes, pool, fitness centre, sauna room and spa bath.

Looking like a beached Titanic on the north-eastern outskirts of town, the **MP Resort Hotel** (☎ 075-214230, fax 211177, 184 Thanon Phattalung) is a huge sky-blue building designed to resemble a cruise ship from a distance. Despite the strange, kitschy exterior, the hotel has a classy lobby and the rates of 1200B to 1400B (prices start at 2500B for suites) are pretty good considering the luxuries: pool, poolside bar, sauna, spa bath, snooker, tennis court, golf driving range, games room, fitness centre, karaoke, restaurants and business centre. However, it's a bit far from town compared with the Thumrin Thara and lacks the polish of the latter.

Kantang If you happen to become stranded in nearby Kantang waiting for a boat to Hat Jao Mai or the islands, there are two inexpensive places to stay. **Siri Chai Hotel** (☎ 075-251172), on the main road leading to the port from the train station, has small but fairly clean singles/doubles for 180/280B – or you can have a room for two hours for 100B!

Near the main market near the waterfront, **JT Hotel** (☎ 075-251755) has rooms with fan for 250B or air-con for 350/450B.

Places to Eat
Plenty of good restaurants can be found near the hotels. The **Ko Teng Hotel** still serves some of the best kaeng kàrìi kài (chicken curry) in the city. The English

tourist menu prices it at 60B, which means a bowl of the stuff, while the Thai menu lists it at 25B, served over rice *(râat khâo).* The air-con *Si Trang Coffee Shop* in the Trang Hotel serves very good Thai, Chinese and international food at moderate prices. *Nam Muy* is a large Chinese restaurant opposite the Ko Teng Hotel; although Nam Muy looks fancy, the menu is mid-priced (most dishes are 30B to 50B).

Khao Tom Phui (no Roman-script sign – look for a red sign with chopsticks) on Thanon Phra Ram VI serves all manner of Thai and Chinese standards in the evenings until 2 am. Phui has been honoured with the Shell Chuan Chim designation (see the 'Thai Cuisine' special section earlier in this book) for its tôm yam (available with shrimp, fish or squid), *plaa kràphong náam daeng* (sea bass in red sauce) and *yâwt phàk khá-náa pûm pûy* (greens stir-fried in red bean sauce with chunks of smoked mackerel).

Diamond Department Store on Thanon Phra Ram VI has a small hawkers centre on the 3rd floor. Around the corner, along Thanon Sathani, is a *night market* that convenes in the evening.

Khànǒm Jiin Trang is famous for khànǒm jiin (Chinese noodles with curry). One of the best places to try it is at the tables set up on the corner of Thanon Visetkul and Thanon Phra Ram VI. You have a choice of dousing your noodles in *náam yaa* (a spicy ground fish curry), náam phrík (a sweet and slightly spicy peanut sauce), or *kaeng tai plaa* (a very spicy mixture of green beans, fish, bamboo shoots and potato). To this you can add your choice of fresh grated papaya, pickled vegies, cucumber and bean sprouts – all for just 10B per bowl.

Across the street from this vendor, in front of the municipal office, is a small night market that usually includes a couple of *khànǒm jiin vendors.*

Muslim The Malay culinary influence is strong in Trang. The *Muslim restaurant* opposite the Thamrin Hotel on Thanon Phra Ram VI serves inexpensive rotii kaeng, curries and rice. *Mustafa* (no Roman-script sign – look for the brightly lit place with curries in a glass cabinet at the front and a tiled interior), near the train station, serves

inexpensive Malay-style curries, rotii kaeng, *rotii khài* (roti with egg) and *mátàbà* (murtabak, a kind of stuffed Indian pancake) in relatively clean surroundings. Nearby are several smaller *food stalls* serving Muslim cuisine.

Ko-píi Shops Trang is even more famous for its coffee and *ráan kaa-fae* or *ráan ko-píi* (coffee shops), which are easily identified by the charcoal-fired aluminium boilers with stubby smokestacks seen somewhere in the middle or back of the open-sided shops. Usually run by Hokkien Chinese, these shops serve real filtered coffee (called *kaafae thǔng* in the rest of the country) along with a variety of snacks, typically paa-thâwng-kǒh, *saalaapao* (Chinese buns), *khànǒm jìip* (dumplings), Trang-style sweets, *mǔu yâang* (barbecued pork) and sometimes noodles and *jók* (thick rice soup).

When you order coffee in these places, be sure to use the Hokkien word ko-píi rather than the Thai kaa-fae, otherwise you may end up with Nescafé or instant Khao Chong coffee – the proprietors often think this is what fàràng want. Coffee is usually served with milk and sugar – ask for *ko-píi dam* for sweetened black coffee, *ko-píi dam, mâi sài náam-taan* for black coffee without sugar or *ko-píi mâi sài náam-taan* for coffee with milk but no sugar.

The most convenient ráan ko-píi for most visitors staying in the town centre is the *Sin Ocha Bakery*, on Thanon Sathani near the train station. Once the queen of Trang coffee shops (under its old name, Sin Jiaw), it was completely renovated a few years ago and made into a modern cafe. Ko-píi is still available here, along with international pastries and egg-and-toast breakfasts.

If you're more hard core, try *Yuchiang* (sign in Thai and Chinese only) at the corner of Thanon Phra Ram VI and Soi 6 (on the opposite corner from Khao Tom Phui). This is a real classic Hokkien coffee shop with marble-topped round tables in an old wooden building. It's open from early morning to mid-afternoon only.

On Thanon Huay Yot between the Thumrin Thana Hotel and the turn-off for the bus terminal, *Phong Ocha* (☎ 075-219918) does traditional ko-píi along with jók and *mìi sǔa kài tǔun* (super thin rice noodles with herb-steamed chicken). Phong Ocha is open from 7 am to 10 pm but is most active during the morning hours.

Farther north, along Thanon Huay Yot on the right, closer to the bus terminal, *Kan Ocha* catches the evening ko-pḯi shift.

Entertainment
Old Time Pub, off Thanon Huay Yot, is a cosy, air-con place with good service and no annoying *jík-kǒh* (Thailand's 'hoodlums').

Shopping
Trang is known for its wickerwork and, especially, mats woven of *bai toey* (pandanus leaves), which are called *sèua paa-nan,* or Panan mats. Panan mats are important bridal gifts in rural Trang, and are a common feature of rural households. The process of softening and drying the pandanus leaves before weaving takes many days. They can be purchased in Trang for about 100B to 200B.

The province also has its own distinctive cotton-weaving styles. The villages of Na Paw and Na Meun Si are the most highly regarded sources for these fabrics, especially the intricate diamond-shaped *lai lûuk kâew* pattern, once reserved for nobility.

The best place in town for good buys is the Tha Klang wholesale market, which is along Thanon Tha Klang.

Getting There & Away
Air THAI operates one flight daily from Bangkok (costing 2305B). The Trang THAI office (☎ 075-218066) is at 199/2 Thanon Visetkul. The airport is 4km south of Trang; THAI runs shuttle vans back and forth for 50B per person.

Bus & Share Taxi Ordinary buses from Satun or Krabi to Trang cost 43B. Share taxis from the same cities cost around 80B. Air-con buses from Satun cost 86B and take three hours. From Phattalung it's 20B by bus, 40B by share taxi.

You can get an air-con minivan to Hat Yai from the Trang bus terminal for 65B; they leave frequently between 5.30 am and 5.30 pm. Otherwise an ordinary bus to/from Hat Yai is 50B.

Air-con 1st-class buses to/from Bangkok are 443B (344B for air-con 2nd-class) and

685B for a VIP bus. The air-con buses take about 12 hours.

Trang's open-air bus terminal is on a back street off Thanon Huay Yot.

If you're coming from Ko Lanta, you can catch any north-bound vehicle and get off at Ban Huay Nam Khao, the junction for Hwy 4 and the road to Ko Lanta, then catch a bus south to Trang for 30B.

Minivans to Kantang leave from behind the train station in Trang several times a day for 35B.

Train Only two trains go all the way from Bangkok to Trang, the express No 83, which leaves Bangkok's Hualamphong station at 5.05 pm and arrives in Trang at 8.35 am the next day, and the rapid No 167, which leaves Hualamphong station at 6.20 pm, arriving in Trang at 10.45 am. Both trains offer all three classes of travel. The fare is 660B 1st class, 311B 2nd class and 135B 3rd class, not including rapid or express surcharges. From Thung Song in Nakhon Si Thammarat Province there are two trains daily to Trang, leaving at 7.03 and 9.05 am, arriving an hour and 45 minutes later.

Getting Around
Sǎamláw (also written samlor) and túk-túk around town cost between 10B to 20B per trip.

Big orange buses to the harbour at Kantang leave frequently from Thanon Kantang near the bus terminal for 10B. There are also air-con minivans that do the same trip every hour or so for 20B each; a motorcycle taxi will cost about 80B, but this is really too long a jaunt for a comfortable pillion ride.

TRANG BEACHES
Trang Province has several sandy beaches and coves along the coast, especially in the Sikao and Kantang districts. On Rte 403 between Trang and Kantang is a turn-off west onto a paved road that leads down to the coast through some interesting Thai Muslim villages.

At the end, the road splits north and south. The road south leads to Hat Yao, Hat Yong Ling and Hat Jao Mai. The road north leads to Hat Chang Lang and Hat Pak Meng. A more direct way to Hat Pak Meng from Trang is to take Rte 4046 via Sikao.

Hat Jao Mai & Ko Libong
หาดเจ้าไหมและเกาะลิบง

Hat Jao Mai and Ko Libong are in Kantang district, about 35km from Trang. The wide white-sand beach of Hat Jao Mai is 5km long and gets some of Thailand's biggest surf (probably the source of Trang's original unshortened name, City of Waves). Hat Jao Mai is backed by casuarina trees and limestone hills with caves, some of which contain prehistoric human skeletal remains.

Two large caves nearby can be reached by boat. You can charter a fisherman's long-tail for 100B an hour from Ban Jao Mai Hat Yao. Two hours is enough. Trangwaree Tours in Trang (☎ 075-219448) has kayak trips to the caves, including lunch, for 750B per person.

Tham Jao Mai is big enough to enter by boat, and contains at least three levels and many side caverns with extensive stalactites, stalagmites, crystal curtains and fossils. In a small chamber at the top level is a beautiful small spring.

This beach is part of the 231,000-sq-km **Hat Jao Mai National Park**, which includes Hat Chang Lang farther north and the islands of Ko Muk, Ko Kradan, Ko Jao Mai, Ko Waen, Ko Cheuak, Ko Pling and Ko Meng. In this area the endangered dugong (also called manatee or sea cow) can sometimes be spotted. In their only known appearance on the Thai-Malay peninsula, rare black-necked storks frequent Jao Mai to feed on molluscs and crustaceans.

More common wildlife that visitors may actually spot include sea otters, macaques, langurs, wild pigs, pangolins, little herons, Pacific reef-egrets, white-bellied sea eagles, monitor lizards and water monitors.

The park is also rich in evergreen forest, mangrove forest, beach forest and limestone crag forest.

National Park admission fees apply to all areas of Hat Jao Mai National Park (200B for foreigners, half price for children).

Ko Libong, Trang's largest island, lies opposite Hat Jao Mai. There are three fishing villages on the island, so it's easy to get a boat from Kantang port for the one-hour trip, or from Ban Jao Mai Hat Yao near Hat Jao Mai for the 15-minute ride.

Places to Stay & Eat A number of bungalows are available for rent at Hat Jao Mai National Park. Some are newly built and quite comfortable. The nicest goes for 2000B per night and sleeps eight people. There are also bungalows for 600B to 800B that sleep six. For reservations, call (☎ 075-210099) or contact the National Park Division, Royal Forest Department (☎ 02-561 4292). Camping is also permitted on the Jao Mai.

Sinchai's Chaomai Resort (☎ 01 396 4838) offers a couple of two-room wooden cottages with shared facilities for 200B and two more substantial bungalows with attached bathroom for 300B. Tents are available for rent during the dry season for 50B. Sinchai's wife is a good Thai cook and

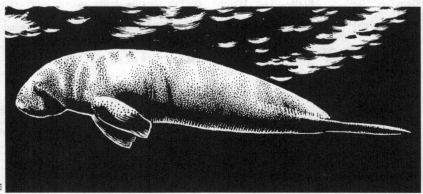

The dugong, or manatee, can sometimes be seen around the islands of Hat Jao Mai National Park.

meals are inexpensive. The family can also arrange boat trips to nearby caves and islands. It's a short walk from here to the village of Ban Jao Mai Hat Yao, where there's a local *coffee shop* and a *seafood restaurant* built on one of the village piers. There are also a few wooden *bungalows* on the pier for rent for an overpriced 200B.

On Ko Libong, the Botanical Department maintains free *shelters* on Laem Ju-Hoi, a cape on the eastern tip of the island. On the south-western side of the island is a beach where camping is permitted. The *Libong Beach Resort* (☎ *01 894 6936*) has A-frame thatched bungalows for 500B to 700B.

Getting There & Away The quickest way to reach Hat Jao Mai by public transport is via minivans from the Trang market, which leave every hour in the high season and less frequently in the low season. The journey costs 50B per person. If you are going to Sinchai's tell the driver and he'll drop you off near the resort.

You can also catch a bus, train or taxi from Trang to Kantang harbour, then hop onto one of the ferries across to Tha Som on the opposite shore of Mae Nam Trang estuary. The tickets cost 2B for pedestrians, 5B for motorcycles, 15B per car and 20B per pick-up truck. The ferry to Hat Jao Mai from Kantang harbour operates from 6 am to 8 pm daily.

From Tha Som there are frequent săwngthăew to Hat Jao Mai. Boats leave Ban Jao Mai Hat Yao for Ko Libong every half hour during daylight hours for 20B per person, or you can charter one to Ko Libong Resort for 200B.

Hat Yong Ling & Hat Yao
หาดหยงหลิง/หาดยาว

A few kilometres north-west of Hat Jao Mai are these two very long white-sand beaches separated by limestone cliffs. Hat Yong Ling is a short walk from the Hat Yong Ling park headquarters parking lot. It's a pretty bay and there are snack stands on weekends. There are some tidal pools off the beach at the base of the limestone cliffs, and you can camp nearby if you check in with the park officers first. Another curving beach nearby, **Hat San** can only be approached via a large cave that connects the two beaches. The access road into Hat Yong Ling park is 2km long.

Hat Chang Lang
หาดฉางหลาง

Hat Chang Lang is part of the Hat Jao Mai National Park, and this is where the main park office is located. The beach is about 2km long and very flat and shallow. At the northern end is Khlong Chang Lang, a stream that empties into the sea. On a cliff near the office is a series of ancient rock art sketched in ochre. There's also a freshwater spring and a grassy camp site beneath casuarina trees.

Ko Muk & Ko Kradan
เกาะมุก/เกาะกระดาน

Ko Muk is nearly opposite Hat Chang Lang and can be reached by boat from Kantang or Pak Meng. The coral around Ko Muk is lively, and there are several small beaches suitable for camping and swimming. The best beach, Hat Sai Yao, is on the opposite side of the island from the mainland and is nicknamed Hat Farang because it's 'owned' by a fàràng from Phuket.

Near the northern end is **Tham Morakot** (Emerald Cave), a beautiful limestone tunnel that can be entered by boat during low tide. The tunnel stretches for 80m to emerge in an open pool of emerald hue, hence the cave's name. At the southern end of the island is pretty Ao Phangkha and the fishing village of Hua Laem.

Ko Kradan is the most beautiful of the islands that belong to Hat Jao Mai National Park. Actually, only five of six precincts on the island belong to the park: one is devoted to coconut and rubber plantations. At both islands the water is so clear in places that the bottom is clearly visible from the surface. This clear water permits the growth of corals and good healthy reefs along the northern side of the islands, and the water is often shallow enough for snorkelling. There are fewer white-sand beaches on Ko Kradan than on Ko Muk, but the coral reef on the side facing Ko Muk is quite good for diving.

Ko Cheuak and **Ko Waen** are small islands between Ko Muk, Ko Kradan and the Trang coast. Both feature sand beaches and coral reefs. Ko Cheuak has a small cave that can be entered by boats at low tide.

Places to Stay & Eat *Ko Muk Resort (Trang office ☎ 075-214441, 25/36 Thanon Sathani)*, on Ko Muk facing the mainland next to the Muslim fishing village of Hua Laem, has simple but nicely designed bungalows for 300B with attached bathroom. The beach in front tends towards mud flats during low tide; the beach in front of the nearby village is slightly better but modest dress is called for. The resort organises boats to nearby islands including Ngai, Waen, Kradan and Lanta.

Ko Kradan Resort (☎ 075-211391; in Bangkok ☎ 02-392 0635) has OK bungalows and ugly cement shophouse-style rooms with fans and private bathroom for 700B to 900B a night and up. The beach isn't bad, but this resort still gets low marks for serving lousy, expensive food and for littering the area – a perfect example of the worst kind of beach resort development.

Getting There & Away The easiest place to get a boat to either Ko Muk or Ko Kradan is Kantang. Săwngthăew (20B), orange buses (10B) or air-con minivans (35B) from Trang to Kantang leave regularly. Once in Kantang you must charter another săwngthăew to the ferry pier for 20B, where you can get a regular long-tail boat to Ko Muk for 50B (or charter for 300B), to Ko Kradan for 100B or to Ko Libong for 25B. All boats leave around noon and return before sunset.

You can also get to the islands from Hat Pak Meng. There are two piers, one at the northern end of the beach and one at the southern end. Boats are more frequent from the southern pier, especially during the rainy season. Boats cost 30B to 60B per person to Ko Muk (depending on the number of passengers) and 120B to Ko Kradan.

Hat Pak Meng
หาดปากเมง

Thirty-nine kilometres from Trang in Sikao district, north of the beaches of Jao Mai, Yao and Chang Lang, is another long, broad, sandy beach near the village of Pak Meng. The waters are usually shallow and calm, even in the rainy season. A couple of hundred metres offshore are several limestone rock formations, including a very large one with caves. Several vendors and a couple of restaurants offer fresh seafood. You can use the sling-chairs and umbrellas on the beach, as long as you order something. A long promenade and sea wall runs along the middle and southern sections of the beach.

Around the beginning of November, locals flock to Hat Pak Meng to collect *hăwy tàphao*, a delicious type of sea mussel. The tide reaches its lowest ebb at this time of year, so it's fairly easy to pick up the shells.

About halfway between Pak Meng and Trang, off Rte 4046, is the 20m-high **Nam Tok Ang Thong**.

The *Pakmeng Resort (☎ 075-210321)* has sturdy bungalows with fan and bathroom for 300B to 700B. The more expensive rooms have sea views.

Pakmeng Resort operates one-day boat tours of Ko Cheuak, Ko Muk and Ko Kradan for 450B, including lunch and beverages.

Getting There & Away Take a van (20B) or săwngthăew (15B) to Sikao from the market at Trang, and then a săwngthăew (10B) to Hat Pak Meng. There are also one or two direct minivans daily to Pak Meng from Trang for 30B. These leave from the market.

If you're coming by your own transport from Trang, make a left before you get to the clock circle in Sikao, following a blue sign for Rte 2021. You'll come to a forked junction after 3.5km, where you should continue straight to get to Pak Meng, 6km farther.

A paved road now connects Pak Meng with the other beaches south, so if you have your own wheels there's no need to backtrack through Sikao.

Satun Province

Bordering Malaysia, Satun (or Satul) is the west coast's southernmost province. Besides crossing the Malaysian border by land or sea, the principal visitor attractions are Ko Tarutao National Marine Park and Thaleh Ban National Park.

Before 1813 Satun was a district of the Malay state of Kedah: the name 'Satun' comes from the Malay *setul*, a type of tree common in this area. At the time Kedah, along with Kelantan, Terengganu and Perlis, paid tribute to Siam. The Anglo-Siamese Treaty of 1909 released parts of these states to Britain and they later became part of independent Malaysia.

Satun didn't become a province of Siam until 1925. Today an estimated 66% of the population is Muslim, most of who speak Yawi (the language of the Malay Peninsula) or Malay as a first language, and there are 14 mosques for every wát in the province.

SATUN

อ.เมืองสตูล

postcode 91000 • pop 22,700

Satun itself is fairly interesting, and you may enter or leave Thailand here by boat via Kuala Perlis in Malaysia. Sixty kilometres north-west of Satun is the small port of Pak Bara, the departure point for boats to Ko Tarutao.

SATUN PROVINCE

As in the nearby provinces of Pattani and Narathiwat, one hears a lot of Yawi spoken in the streets of Satun. In the not-too-distant past, the Thai government maintained a loudspeaker system that would broadcast government programs at 6 am and 6 pm (beginning with a wake-up call to work and ending with the Thai national anthem, for which everyone had to stop and stand in the streets). Whether this was to instil a sense of nationalism in the typically rebellious southern Thais, or to try to drown out the prayer calls from local mosques, it was never quite certain. Now a government museum showcasing Thai Muslim culture has opened in Satun – evidence that Bangkok now views the deep south with much less suspicion.

A very few old Sino-Portuguese shop-houses, some said to date back as far as 1839, can be seen along Thanon Buriwanit. The modern, parachute-domed Bambang Mosque nearby was constructed in 1979.

Information

Immigration The Wang Prachan Customs complex at Tha Tammalang (the pier) south of town contains an immigration office where anyone arriving or departing Satun to/from Malaysia by boat will have their papers processed.

You can also use this office for extensions of your visa.

There is an immigration office in town but, compared to the Wang Prachan Customs complex, it's understaffed and if you

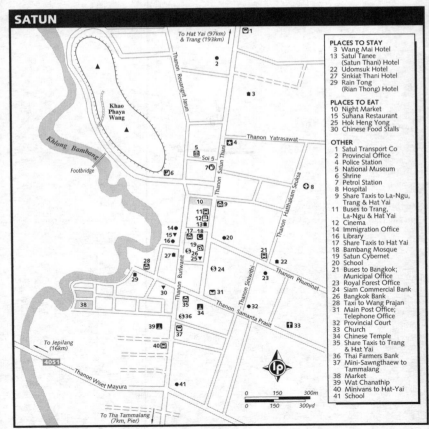

SATUN

PLACES TO STAY
3 Wang Mai Hotel
13 Satul Tanee (Satun Thani) Hotel
22 Udomsuk Hotel
27 Sinkiat Thani Hotel
29 Rain Tong (Rian Thong) Hotel

PLACES TO EAT
10 Night Market
15 Suhana Restaurant
25 Hok Heng Yong
30 Chinese Food Stalls

OTHER
1 Satul Transport Co
2 Provincial Office
4 Police Station
5 National Museum
6 Shrine
7 Petrol Station
8 Hospital
9 Share Taxis to La-Ngu, Trang & Hat Yai
11 Buses to Trang, La-Ngu & Hat Yai
12 Cinema
14 Immigration Office
16 Library
17 Share Taxis to Hat Yai
18 Bambang Mosque
19 Satun Cybernet
20 School
21 Buses to Bangkok; Municipal Office
23 Royal Forest Office
24 Siam Commercial Bank
26 Bangkok Bank
28 Taxi to Wang Prajan
31 Main Post Office; Telephone Office
32 Provincial Court
33 Church
34 Chinese Temple
35 Share Taxis to Trang & Hat Yai
36 Thai Farmers Bank
37 Mini-Sawngthaew to Tammalang
38 Market
39 Wat Chanathip
40 Minivans to Hat-Yai
41 School

To Hat Yai (97km) & Trang (193km)

Thanon Reuangrit Jarun

Khao Phaya Wang

Khlong Bambang

Footbridge

Thanon Satun Thani

Soi 5

Thanon Yatrasawat

Thanon Hatthakam Seuksa

Thanon Buriwanit

Thanon Siriwith

Thanon Phuminat

Thanon Samanta Prasit

To Jepilang (16km)

4051

Thanon Wiset Mayura

To Tha Tammalang (7km, Pier)

0   150   300m
0   150   300yd

try to extend your visa there you will probably be sent to Tammalang.

Money You can change money at Thai Farmers Bank, Bangkok Bank or Siam Commercial Bank, all of which have branches in the town centre either on Thanon Buriwanit or Thanon Satun Thani. The latter two banks have ATMs.

Post & Communications The main post and telephone office is on the corner of Thanon Samanta Prasit and Thanon Satun Thani.

Satun Cybernet, near the Bambang Mosque, is currently the only place in Satun where you can send email.

National Museum

The newly opened Satun National Museum is actually an early 20th-century 'palace' that was built by a local prince to accommodate King Rama V during a royal visit. Unfortunately, the king never stayed here, but the handsome two-storey structure served as the provincial office of Satun and later, during WWII, was sequestered by the Japanese and used as a military headquarters.

Built in a pseudo-European style common in nearby Malaysia, the building has been restored and its rooms arranged to give a surprisingly thorough introduction to the traditions and folkways of the Thai Muslim south. Most of the displays are miniature dioramas (with recorded narration in both Thai and English) that cover everything from southern mat weaving techniques to the traditional martial art called *sìlá*. Exhibits labelled in English also explain local marriage rites as well as male and female ritual circumcision. There are also narrated exhibits describing the Sakai, the tribal people who are believed to have inhabited the region long before the arrival of the Thai or Malay.

The museum is located on Soi 5, Thanon Satun Thani, just north of the Shell petrol station. It's open from 9 am to 4 pm Wednesday to Sunday and admission costs 30B.

Khao Phaya Wang

ขาพญาวัง

If, after the museum, you find yourself with more time to kill in Satun, you might con-

sider a visit to the park along the western side of Khao Phaya Wang, a limestone outcrop next to Khlong Bambang (sometimes referred to as Khlong Mambang). Steps lead up the vine-choked cliff on the *khlawng* (canal) side of the Phaya Wang and at the top there are views of the winding green khlawng, rice fields and coconut plantations. Pandan mats are available at the cool, bamboo-shaded picnic area next to the canal below. Vendors sell *sôm-tam, khâo nǐaw, kài thâwt, kûng thâwt* and *mîang kham* (pieces of ginger, onion, dried shrimp, toasted coconut, chilli, peanuts and lime placed into a wild tea leaf with a thick, sweet and salty tamarind sauce).

Places to Stay

The **Rain Tong Hotel** (Rian Thong) is a three-storey cube at the end of Thanon Samanta Prasit, next to the Tha Rian Thong, where small cargo boats go to/from Malaysia. Large, clean rooms with fan and attached shower and toilet cost 140B.

Near the municipal offices on Thanon Hatthakam Seuksa is the two-storey **Udomsuk Hotel** (☎ 074-711006), with reasonably clean rooms with fan and attached bathroom for 120/130B single/double.

The four-storey **Satul Tanee Hotel** (Satun Thani) near the centre of town is OK but noisy, with rooms with fan for 200/250B and air-con rooms for 350/400B.

At the upmarket **Wang Mai Hotel** (☎ 074-711607–8), near the northern end of town off Thanon Satun Thani, all rooms come with air-con, carpet, hot water and TV for 550/650B. It's 700B for deluxe and 1200B for VIP.

The **Sinkiat Thani Hotel** (☎ 074-721055, fax 721059) in the centre of town on Thanon Buriwanit has comfortable rooms similar to those at the Wang Mai but in better condition for 600/700B.

Places to Eat

Near the gold-domed Bambang Mosque in the centre of town are several cheap Muslim food shops, including the reliable **Suhana Restaurant**, almost opposite the mosque on Thanon Buriwanit. Two doors south of Suhana, a **roti food stall** with bright green walls serves light and fluffy roti with curry. A group of cheap **Chinese food stalls** are on Thanon Samanta Prasit near the intersection with Thanon Buriwanit. Lots of places serve khâo man kài and *kǔaytǐaw* around town, although none of them stand out.

Hok Heng Yong, across from the Siam Commercial Bank on Thanon Satun Thani, is a traditional Hokkien coffee shop with round marble-topped tables and a few snacks where older Chinese men sit around and chat. *Raya*, the coffee shop at the back of the Sinkiat Thani Hotel, has more Thai dishes than anywhere else in town.

A no-name *coffee shop* next to the Udomsuk Hotel is a good spot for Thai and Western breakfasts. For Chinese food, wander about the little Chinese district near the Rain Tong Hotel. There's nothing fancy, just a few *noodle shops* and small *seafood places*.

North of the Satul Tanee Hotel, along a short street running west off Thanon Satun Thani, a very good *night market* convenes every evening at around 5 pm. Many of the vendors sell Thai Muslim food and the prices are quite low. Considering the overall low quality of food in Satun, this is one of the best places to eat in town.

Getting There & Away

Bus & Share Taxi A share taxi or air-con van to Hat Yai costs 50B per person, while a bus costs 32/45B ordinary/air-con. Buses to Trang are 43/86B and share taxis to Trang are 80B. Share taxis to Hat Yai park in at least three places in Satun, near the Satul Tanee Hotel, near the mosque and on the corner of Thanon Samanta Prasit and Thanon Buriwanit. Air-con vans to Hat Yai park on Thanon Buriwanit, just south of Wat Chanathip.

The stand near the Satul Tanee Hotel also has taxis to La-Ngu for 30B and taxis to Trang leave from this spot as well. You can hire a whole taxi straight to Pak Bara for about 300B. Buses to Hat Yai also stop in front of the no-name, green-walled rotii kaeng place on Thanon Buriwanit.

An air-con bus from Bangkok's Southern bus terminal leaves once a day for Satun around 7 pm (2.30 pm in the reverse direction) and costs 511B for the 15-hour trip. A nightly VIP bus leaves at 6 pm, costs 795B and covers the distance an hour faster. A 2nd-class air-con bus (no toilet) leaves Bangkok at 6.30 pm for 398B, but this is really too long a bus trip for comfort – if you want to get to Satun from Bangkok, it would be better to take a train to Padang Besar on the Malaysian border and then a bus or taxi for the 60km trip to Satun. See the following Train entry for more details on this option.

Train The only train that goes all the way to Padang Besar is the special express No 35, which leaves Bankok's Hualamphong station at 2.20 pm and arrives in Padang Besar around 8 am the next day. The basic fare is 767B for 1st class, 360B for 2nd class and 156B for 3rd class, not including sleeper and special express surcharges.

Boat From Kuala Perlis in Malaysia, the boat ride costs RM5. All boats dock at the Wang Prachan Customs complex in Tammalang, the estuary 7.5km south of Satun. In the reverse direction the fare is 50B. Boats leave frequently in either direction between 9 am and 1 pm, then less frequently to around 4 pm, depending on marine conditions. You can charter a boat to Perlis for up to 20 people for 1000B.

From Pulau Langkawi (Langkawi Island) in Malaysia boats for Tammalang leave daily at 9.30 am, noon and 4 pm. The crossing takes 1½ to two hours and costs RM18 one way. Bring Thai money from Langkawi, as there are no moneychanging facilities at Tha Tammalang. Boats leave Tammalang for Langkawi at 9.30 am and 1.30 and 4 pm and cost 180B. Tickets for the Satun-Langkawi boat are sold at booths outside the immigration building at Wang Prachan.

Getting Around

Orange mini-sǎwngthǎew to Tha Tammalang (for boats to Malaysia) cost 10B per person from Satun. They run every 20 minutes between 8 am and 5 pm; catch one from opposite Wat Chanathip on Thanon Buriwanit. A motorcycle taxi from the same area costs 30B.

KO TARUTAO NATIONAL MARINE PARK

อุทยานแห่งชาติหมู่เกาะตะรุเตา

This park is a large archipelago of 51 islands, approximately 30km from Pak Bara in La-Ngu district, 60km north-west of Satun. Ko Tarutao, the biggest of the group, is only 5km from Pulau Langkawi in Malaysia. Only five of the islands (Tarutao, Adang, Lipe, Rawi and Klang) have any kind of regular boat service to them, and of these, only the first three are generally visited by tourists.

The Royal Forest Department has been considering requests from private firms to build hotels and bungalows in the marine park. This would be very unfortunate if it were to mean Ko Tarutao becoming like Ko Phi-Phi or Ko Samet, both of which are national parks that have permitted private development with disastrous results. At the time of writing, nothing had transpired.

Ko Tarutao
เกาะตะรุเตา

The park's namesake is about 151 sq km in area and features waterfalls, inland streams, beaches, caves and protected wildlife that includes dolphins, dugongs, sea turtles and lobster. Nobody lives on this island except for employees of the Royal Forest Department.

The island was a place of exile for political prisoners between 1939 and 1947, and remains of the prisons can be seen near Ao Talo Udang on the southern tip of the island, and at Ao Talo Wao on the middle of the east coast. There is also a graveyard, charcoal furnaces and fermentation tanks for making fish sauce.

Wildlife on the island includes dusky langur, mousedeer, wild pig, fishing cat and crab-eating macaque; dolphins and whales may be sighted offshore.

Four types of sea turtle swim the surrounding waters – Pacific ridley, hawksbill, leatherback and green. All four species lay eggs on the beaches here between September and April.

Tarutao's largest stream, Khlong Phante Malaka, enters the sea at the north-western tip of the island at Ao Phante Malaka; the brackish waters flow out of **Tham Jara-Khe** (Crocodile Cave – the stream was once inhabited by ferocious crocodiles, which seem to have disappeared). The cave extends for at least a kilometre under a limestone mountain – no-one has yet followed the stream to the cave's end. The mangrove-lined water-

Swiftlets' nests are considered throughout Asia to have medicinal value and are readily available in Thai supermarkets.

course should not be navigated at high tide, when the mouth of the cave fills.

The park pier, headquarters and **bungalows** are also here at **Ao Phante Malaka**. There is also a basic **restaurant** and a small general store. The standard national park admission fee is payable on arrival (200B for foreigners, half price for children). The best camping is at the beaches of **Ao Jak** and **Ao San**, two bays south of park HQ. For a view of the bays, climb Topu Hill, 500m north of the park office.

There is also camping at **Ao Makham** (Tamarind Bay), at the south-western end of the island, about 2.5km from another ranger station at Ao Talo Udang.

There is a road between Ao Phante Malaka in the north, and Ao Talo Udang in the south, of which 11km was constructed by political prisoners in the 1940s, and 12km was more recently constructed by the park division. The road is mostly overgrown, but park personnel have kept a path open to make it easier to get from north to south without having to climb over rocky headlands along the shore.

Ko Rang Nok (Bird Nest Island), in Ao Talo Udang, is another trove of the expensive swiftlet nests craved by Chinese diners around the world.

Good coral reefs are at the north-western part of Ko Tarutao at **Pha Papinyong** (Papillon Cliffs), at Ao San and in the channel between Ko Tarutao and Ko Takiang (Ko Lela) off the north-eastern shore.

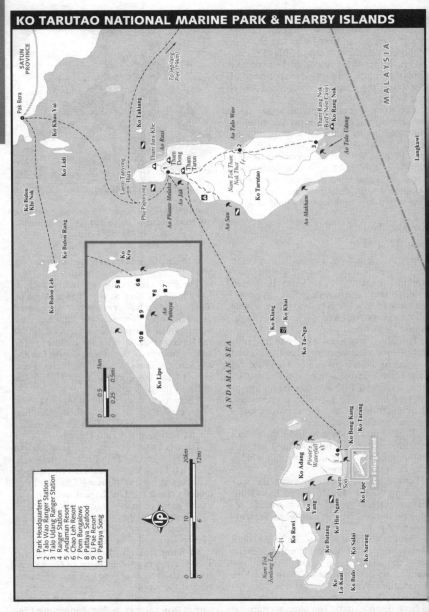

KO TARUTAO NATIONAL MARINE PARK & NEARBY ISLANDS

1 Park Headquarters
2 Talo Wao Ranger Station
3 Talo Udang Ranger Station
4 Ranger Station
5 Andaman Resort
6 Chao Leh Resort
7 Porn Bungalows
8 Pattaya Seafood
9 Li Pae Resort
10 Pattaya Song

Ko Adang
เกาะอาดัง

Ko Adang is 43km west of Tarutao, and about 80km from Pak Bara. Ko Adang's 30 sq km are covered with forests and freshwater streams, which supply water year-round. Green sea turtles lay their eggs here between September and December. At **Laem Son** (Pine Cape), on the southern tip of the island where the pier and park office are located, visitors can stay in a thatched longhouse. Camping is also allowed. The restaurant is a little expensive, considering the low quality of the food served – but then considering the transport problems, perhaps not. As on Tarutao, it's a good idea to bring some food of your own from the mainland.

An interesting hike can be undertaken along the island's east coast to a pretty beach 2km from the park ranger station. Inland a little way from the beach is a waterfall once used by passing pirate ships as a freshwater source. Around on the west coast, 3km from Laem Son, is another waterfall and the chao náam village of **Talo Puya**.

Ko Rawi & Ko Lipe
เกาะราวี/เกาะลิเป๊ะ

Ko Rawi is just west of Ko Adang, and a bit smaller. Off the west coast of Ko Adang, and the south-east coast of Ko Rawi, are coral reefs with many live species of coral and tropical fish.

Ko Lipe is immediately south of Ko Adang and is inhabited by about 500 chao náam (*orang rawot* or *orang laut* in Malay) who are said to have originated on Ko Lanta in Krabi Province. They subsist on fishing and some cultivation of vegetables and rice on the flatter parts of the island. You can camp here, or rent a hut from the chao náam for 150B to 300B a night at any of several bungalow operations in or near the main village along the east coast. There is a coral reef along the southern side of the small island and several small beachy coves. The chao náam can provide boat hire to nearby islets ringed by coral reefs. For some reason the chao náam on this island prefer to be called 'chao leh' – a term despised by other Moken on islands to the north, who prefer the term chao náam.

They also go by the term Thai Mai (New Thai), a nomenclature favoured by the Thai government.

Between Ko Tarutao and Ko Adang-Rawi is a small cluster of three islands called **Mu Ko Klang** (Middle Island Group), where there is good snorkelling. One of the islands, Ko Khai, also has a good white-sand beach. Boats from Ko Tarutao take about 40 minutes to reach Ko Khai.

Ko Phetra National Marine Park
อุทยานแห่งชาติหมู่เกาะเภตรา

Twenty-two islands stretching between Pak Bara and the boundaries of Ko Tarutao belong to the little-visited, 495-sq-km Ko Phetra National Marine Park. Uninhabited **Ko Khao Yai**, the largest in the group, boasts several pristine beaches suitable for camping, swimming and snorkelling. Crab-eating macaques are plentiful here, as local Muslims don't hunt them. There's a castle-shaped rock formation on one shore; during low tide boats can pass beneath a natural arch in the formation.

A park unit is on nearby **Ko Lidi** (sometimes spelt Lide), which features a number of picturesque and unspoiled caves, coves, cliffs and beaches. Camping facilities are available here.

Between Ko Lidi and Ko Khao Yai is a channel bay known as **Ao Kam Pu**, a tranquil passage with cascading waters during certain tidal changes and some coral at shallow depths.

A new park HQ, visitors centre and pier for Ko Phetra National Marine Park recently opened on the mainland at **Ban Talo Sai**, about 4km south-east of Pak Bara off Rte 4052. You can arrange boat transport to Ko Lidi here.

Standard national park entry fees apply. See the Facts about Thailand chapter for details.

Trees and plants on the park grounds are labelled in English, and there are nature trails through intact lowland evergreen forest just behind the park bungalows.

Other Islands
Ko Kabeng and **Ko Baw Jet Luk**, accessible by boat and bridge from Pak Bara, are of mild interest. The beaches here are often littered and murky, so it's basically just a

convenient place to stay in Pak Bara, but if you have time to kill, visit the charcoal factory at Khlong La-Ngu or check out the cashew orchards.

Paknam Resort on Ko Baw Jet Luk can also arrange boat trips to other, more pristine islands in the area, or if you speak enough Thai you could hire a fishing boat directly from Ko Kabeng's little harbour at the fishing village of Ban Jet Luk.

Places to Stay & Eat

Officially the Ko Tarutao park is only open from November to May. Visitors who show up on the islands during the monsoon season can stay in park accommodation, but they must transport their own food from the mainland unless staying with the chao náam on Ko Lipe.

Bungalows may be booked in advance at the park office in Pak Bara (☎ 074-711383, no English spoken) or through the Royal Forest Department (☎ 02-561 4292) in Bangkok. For Ko Tarutao and/or Ko Adang, bring as much of your own food as you can from Satun or Pak Bara – the park *restaurants* are expensive and not very good.

Ko Tarutao Park accommodation on Ko Tarutao costs 1000B for a large 'deluxe' two-room *bungalow* sleeping four. A four-bed room in a *longhouse* goes for 320B. Full rates for all rooms and bungalows must be paid, even if only one person takes a bed. Tents can be rented for 100B. If you have your own, the fee is 10B.

Ko Adang Laem Son has *longhouse accommodation* similar to that on Ko Tarutao for the same rates. A small *restaurant* provides basic meals and sundries; it's closed in the rainy season. You can pitch your own tent for 10B.

Ko Lipe There are basically five places to stay on the island. Two are in the chao leh village, on the north-eastern side of the island. At the northern side of the village the *Andaman Resort (in Satun ☎ 074-711313)* has good bungalows with attached bathroom for 250B to 350B and tents for 100B. You can also pitch your own tent here for 20B. At the other end of the village *Chao Leh Resort (☎ 074-729201)* has some pretty shaky

thatch huts for 150B, more solid ones for 250B with attached bathroom, and wood-and-thatch versions with glass windows overlooking the village backstreets for 300B. The beach is nicer in front of Andaman Resort than near Chao Leh Resort.

On Hat Pattaya, the biggest operation is the *Li Pae Resort (☎ 01 896 5491)*, which has spacious thatch bungalows for 300B with attached bathroom and shower. Although it has more amenities than its competitors, this place also wins the prize for the least personality. Down at the western end of the beach, *Pattaya Song* has small, simple huts on the beach with shared bathroom for 100B to 150B. On the adjacent hillside overlooking the bay are *Porn Bungalows*, which go for 150B to 200B depending on size.

Also on the beach, *Pattaya Seafood* is mainly a restaurant, but the owner also has three decent bungalows with attached bathroom for 100B. This seems to be the only operation on the island that's actually run by an islander. Even if you don't stay, stop by for dinner – the food is excellent.

See the following section for places to stay and eat in Pak Bara if you miss the boat.

Pak Bara & La-Ngu There is some accommodation in these jumping-off points for the park. In Pak Bara, *Bara Guest House* (no phone) has a travel agency and cafe downstairs, rooms upstairs and a couple of bungalows at the back. Rates are 80/150B single/double for a room and 200B to 250B for the bungalows. You can walk to the Tha Ko Tarutao from the guesthouse.

Just over 1km before the pier in Pak Bara, along the shore among the casuarina trees, are the *Diamond Beach Bungalows*, *Krachomsai Bungalows*, *Marina Bungalows*, *Sai Kaew Resort* and *Koh Klang Bungalows*, all with huts for about 200B to 350B a night. None are special; Diamond Beach is the top pick – only because it's newer and nearest to town.

On rocky, palm-fringed Ko Baw Jet Luk (often referred to as Ko Kabeng, though that's an adjacent island), a 10-minute drive north of Pak Bara over a relatively new bridge, the quiet *Paknam Resort (☎ 074-781129)* offers A-frame bungalows for 250/350B, or larger 'VIP' bungalows for 450B.

You can also stay in nicely designed *park bungalows* at the mainland headquarters for Ko Phetra National Marine Park, which are located near Ban Talo Sai, about 4km before you reach Pak Bara off Rte 4052. The turn-off is between the 5km and 6km markers on this highway; from here it's about 1.5km to the park headquarters. When asked the bungalow rates, park officials said it was up to the individual how much they wanted to pay, ie, by donation. This may change as park staff tires of visitors taking advantage of such policies.

There are several *food stalls* near the Tha Pak Bara that do fruit shakes and seafood.

La-Ngu has a couple of cheap hotels on its main street, but Pak Bara has a much better atmosphere.

Getting There & Away

Ko Tarutao Boats to Tarutao leave regularly between November and April from the pier in Pak Bara, 60km north-west of Satun and 22km from Ko Tarutao. During the rest of the year boat service is irregular, since the park is supposedly closed. Satun Province officials have discussed constructing a new pier in Tan Yong Po district, closer to Satun, that will serve tourist boats to Tarutao and other islands, possibly on a year-round basis.

For now, boats leave Pak Bara for Tarutao in season at 10.30 am and 3 pm daily. The return fare is 240B, and the one-way fare is 120B, and it takes 1½ to two hours, depending on the boat. Food and beverages are available on the boat. Departures back to Pak Bara are at 9 am and 1 pm.

If convenient, it would be best to buy one-way tickets for each leg of your journey, as this would allow a choice of routes back (say direct from Ko Lipe to Satun). Also if the boat you have a ticket for doesn't make it to the islands due to bad weather or an engine mishap, you won't have to worry about getting a refund for both tickets. Some companies will refuse to refund an unused return ticket.

There are also occasional tour boats out to Tarutao, but these usually cost several hundred baht per person, as they include a guided tour, meals etc. Your final alternative is to charter a boat with a group of people. The cheapest are the long-tail boats, which can take eight to 10 people from Pak Bara's commercial pier for 1000B. On holidays, boats may travel back and forth to Tarutao every hour or so to accommodate the increased traffic.

Other Piers It is also possible to hire boats to Ko Tarutao from three different piers on the coast near Satun. The nearest is the Tha Ko Nok, 4km south of Satun (40km from Tarutao). Then there is the Tha Tammalang, 9km from Satun, on the opposite side of the estuary from Tha Ko Nok. Tammalang is 35km from Tarutao. Finally there's the Tha Jepilang, 13km west of Satun (30km from Tarutao); this one seems most geared to boat charters.

Ko Adang & Ko Lipe There is no regularly scheduled boat between Pak Bara and Ko Adang or Ko Lipe. Between November and May a daily boat leaves Tarutao at 1 pm for Ko Adang and continues on to Ko Lipe. The cost is 230/440B one way/return. From Ko Lipe to Tarutao via Ko Adang, the boat leaves at 9 am daily.

Pak Bara From Hat Yai, there are three daily buses to La-Ngu and Pak Bara which cost 43B and take 2½ hours. If you miss one of the direct La-Ngu buses, you can also hop on any Satun-bound bus to the junction town of Chalung (28B, 1½ hours), which is about 15km short of Satun, then get a săwngthăew north on Rte 4078 for the trip to La-Ngu (12B, 45 minutes).

You could also take a share taxi from Hat Yai to La-Ngu for 50B.

There's also a minivan service from Hat Yai for 50B – a better deal since it goes all the way to Pak Bara.

To get to Pak Bara from Satun, you must take a share taxi or bus to La-Ngu, then a săwngthăew on to Pak Bara. Taxis to La-Ngu leave from a stand diagonally opposite a petrol station on Thanon Satun Thani, about 100m north of the Satul Tanee Hotel on the opposite side of the road, when there are enough people to fill them. It costs 30B per person. Buses leave frequently from a spot on the opposite side of the road, a little south towards the hotel, and cost 18B.

From La-Ngu, săwngthăew rides to Pak Bara are 10B and terminate right at the harbour; you can take a motorcycle taxi this same distance for 40B. You can also charter a taxi to Pak Bara from Satun for 300B.

You can also travel to La-Ngu from Trang by săwngthăew for 30B, or by share taxi for 50B.

THALEH BAN NATIONAL PARK
อุทยานแห่งชาติทะเลบัน

This 196-sq-km park on the Thailand-Malaysia border encompasses the best-preserved section of white meranti rainforest (named for the dominant species of dipterocarp trees) on either side of the border. Although the forest straddles the border, the Malaysian side has been deforested by agricultural development, so this park is crucial to the forest's continued survival. The terrain is hilly, with a maximum elevation of 740m at Khao Chin. The area east of Rte 4184 is primary forest on granitic rock reaching up to 700m high; there are many small streams in this section.

The park headquarters, situated on a lake in a valley formed by limestone outcrops, is only 2km from the border. Five kilometres north of the office and only 500m off Rte 4184 is **Nam Tok Yaroi**, a 700m, nine-tiered waterfall with pools suitable for swimming. Climb the limestone cliffs next to the park buildings for a view of the lake and surrounding area.

A network of trails leads to a number of other waterfalls and caves in the park, including **Nam Tok Rani**, **Nam Tok Chingrit**, **Tham Ton Din** and **Tham Lawt Pu Yu** (Pu Yu Tunnel Cave). Rangers will guide you along the trails for a small fee but little English is spoken. A new access road in the park also leads to **Nam Tok Ton Pliw**, cutting through secondary forest in the process of rehabilitation. There are vendor stands near the falls, which features several different levels with pools at the bottom of each. The turn-off for the falls comes 10km before the park entrance off Rte 4184 (10.5km from Rte 406).

Wildlife found within park boundaries tends to be of the Sundaic variety, which includes species generally found in Peninsular Malaysia, Sumatra, Borneo and Java. Common mammals include mouse deer, serow, tapir, chevrotain, chamois, various gibbons and macaques. Some of the rare bird species found here are the great argus hornbill, rhinoceros hornbill, helmeted hornbill, banded and bluewing pitta, masked finfoot, dusky crag martin and black Baza hawk. Honey bears and wild pigs are commonly seen near the park headquarters and up in the limestone are 150cm monitor lizards and 40cm tree geckos. More elusive residents include the clouded leopard and dusky leaf langur.

On Sunday morning a border market where produce, clothing and housewares are sold, convenes along both sides of the border; you're permitted to cross free of visa formalities for this occasion.

The park entrance is about 37km northeast of Satun's provincial capital or 90km south of Hat Yai via Rte 406 and 4184; coming from Malaysia it's about 75km from Alor Setar. Standard admission fees apply (200B for foreigners, half price for children). The road to Thaleh Ban is rather pretty and winds through several villages, rubber plantations and banana plantations.

To the south the park extends all the way to the Andaman Sea to a beach and mangrove area just 2km south of the Wang Prachan Customs complex at Tammalang.

The best time to visit is from December to March, between seasonal monsoons. It can rain any time of year here but the heaviest and longest rains generally fall in July, August, October and November. In January and February nights can be quite cool.

Places to Stay & Eat
Near the park office (☎ 074-797073) beside the lake are *longhouses* sleeping six to 20 people for 500B to 1000B per night. If you're in a group of less than six people and accommodation isn't already booked you can stay in more attractive *bungalows* for 100B per person. These can be booked in advance by calling the Royal Forest Department (☎ 02-561 4292) in Bangkok.

The park *restaurant* provides a nice view of the lake and simple Thai food from 30B per meal. It's open from 8 am to 8 pm daily. Next to the restaurant is a small shop selling a few toiletries and snacks.

Getting There & Away
The park is about 40km from Satun in *tambon* (precinct) Khuan Sataw. Take a săwngthăew or share taxi from near the Rain Tong Hotel in Satun to Wang Prajan on Rte 4184 for 24B. Wang Prajan is just

a few kilometres from the park entrance. Sometimes these vehicles take you to the park gate, otherwise you can hitch or hop on one of the infrequent sǎwngthǎew from Wang Prajan into the park. If you're coming from Hat Yai you can also pick these sǎwngthǎew up in Chalung; some are marked 'Thale Ban-Wangprachan' in English.

Sǎwngthǎew to Chalung and Hat Yai leave from the entrance nearly every hour from 8 am until 1 pm.

Southern Gulf

While the scenery of the Southern Gulf may not be as dramatic as that of the Andaman Coast, its vistas of coconut groves alongside azure seas evoke images of a tropical paradise in the classic sense. Composed of the provinces of Chumphon, Surat Thani, Nakhon Si Thammarat, Songkhla, Pattani, Yala and Narathiwat, it forms the eastern coast of Thailand's portion of the Malay Peninsula. As with the provinces of the Andaman Coast, there are large populations of Thai Muslims in the countryside, while ethnic Chinese dominate the cities. The former are, for the most part, fisherfolk and tillers of the soil, the latter merchants and professionals.

Except for landlocked Yala, the provinces of the Southern Gulf have an abundance of inviting beaches. Of course, the Southern Gulf isn't just about beaches. Inland you'll find protected areas that are home to endangered species inhabiting pockets of the primeval jungle that once covered much of South-East Asia. But if you're coming for the beach or for water sports such as diving, it's important to get your timing right.

Mid-September through to the end of November is the rainiest time along the Southern Gulf. The seas are choppy and hence visibility is poorest at this time of year. If somehow you find yourself on a rain-soaked beach, don't despair: The weather on the Andaman Coast might be bright and sunny – and it's a relatively short trip across the peninsula to find out.

Highlights

- Ko Samui – Thailand's legendary traveller beach destination, with a great laid-back feel
- Ko Pha-Ngan – Samui's famous neighbour, renowned for its full moon raves
- Khao Sok National Park – primeval rainforest, craggy limestone cliffs and rafflesia, the world's largest flower
- Nakhon Si Thammarat – manufacturing centre for life-sized shadow puppets
- Ang Thong National Marine Park – an archipelago dotted with small islands and sandy beaches, a perfect kayaking tour
- Southern-tip provinces – the Muslim cultures of Yala, Pattani and Narathiwat

Chumphon Province

CHUMPHON
อ.เมืองชุมพร

postcode 86000 • pop 15,500

About 500km south of Bangkok and 184km from Prachuap Khiri Khan, Chumphon is the junction town where you turn west to Ranong and Phuket or continue south on the newer road to Surat Thani, Nakhon Si Thammarat and Songkhla. In reference to its function as a crossroads, the name derives from the Thai *chumnumphon,* which means 'meeting place'. The provincial capital is a busy place, but of no particular interest except that this is where Southern Thailand really begins in terms of ethnic markers like dialect and religion.

Pak Nam, Chumphon's port, is 10km from Chumphon, and in this area there are a few beaches and a handful of islands with good reefs for diving. The best local beach is 4km-long Hat Thung Wua Laen (12km north of town), also known locally as 'Hat

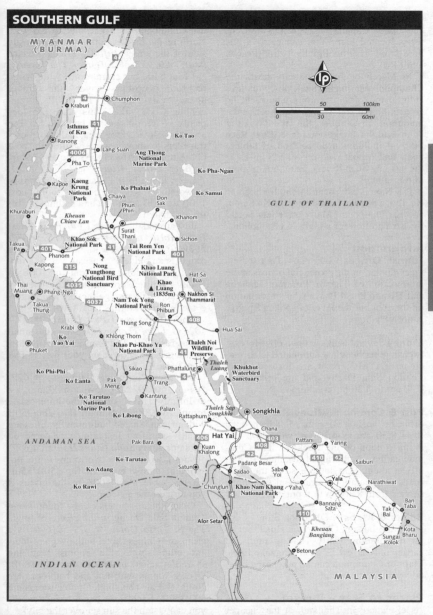

SOUTHERN GULF

MYANMAR
(BURMA)

Kraburi

Chumphon

Isthmus
of Kra

Ranong

Ko Tao

Lang Suan

Pha To

Ang Thong
National
Marine Park

Kapoe

Kaeng
Krung
National
Park

Ko Phaluai

Ko Pha-Ngan

Chaiya

Khuraburi

Kheuan
Chiaw Lan

Phun
Phin

Don
Sak

Ko Samui

GULF OF THAILAND

Khanom

Takua
Pa

Khao Sok
National Park

Surat
Thani

Sichon

Phanom

Tai Rom Yen
National Park

Kapong

Nong
Tungthong
National Bird
Sanctuary

Khao Luang
National Park

Hat Sa
Bua

Thai
Muang

Phang-Nga

Khao
Luang
(1835m)

Nakhon Si
Thammarat

Takua
Thung

Nam Tok Yong
National Park

Ron
Phibun

Krabi

Ko
Yao Yai

Khlong Thorn

Thung Song

Phuket

Khao Pu-Khao Ya
National Park

Thaleh Noi
Wildlife
Preserve

Hua Sai

Ko Phi-Phi

Ko Lanta

Sikao

Pak
Meng

Trang

Phatthalung

Thaleh
Luang

Khukhut
Waterbird
Sanctuary

Ko Tarutao
National
Marine Park

Kantang

Palian

Thaleh Sap
Songkhla

Songkhla

Ko Libong

Rattaphum

ANDAMAN SEA

Pak Bara

Chana

HAT YAI

Pattani

Yaring

Ko Tarutao

Kuan
Khalong

Satun

Padang Besar

Saba
Yoi

Saiburi

Ko Adang

Ko Rawi

Sadao

Yala

Narathiwat

Changlun

Khao Nam Khang
National Park

Yaha

Ruso

Bannang
Sata

Tak
Bai

Ban
Taba

Alor Setar

Kheuan
Banglang

Sungai
Kolok

Kota
Bharu

INDIAN OCEAN

Betong

MALAYSIA

SOUTHERN GULF

Cabana' because the long-running Chumphon Cabana Resort & Diving Center is located here. You can catch a bus here from Thanon Pracha Uthit (Pracha Uthit Rd).

In March or April the city hosts the **Chumphon Marine Festival**, which features cultural and folk-art exhibits, a windsurfing competition at Hat Thung Wua Laen and a marathon. In October, the five-day **Lang Suan Buddha Image Parade & Boat Race Festival** includes a procession of temple boats and a boat race on Mae Nam Lang Suan (Lang Suan River), about 60km south of the capital.

Pak Nam is a departure point for boats to Ko Tao, a popular island north of Ko Samui and Ko Pha-Ngan. Many travellers bound for Ko Tao stop for a night in Chumphon.

Information
Tourist Offices Chumphon Tourist Services Center, in the provincial offices at the intersection of Thanon Poramin Mankha and Thanon Phisit Phayap, has information on the area but the level of spoken English is not very high.

Money Several banks in town offer foreign exchange services and automated teller machines (ATMs); most are located along Thanon Sala Daeng and are open from 8.30 am to 3.30 pm weekdays.

Post & Communications The main post office on Thanon Poramin Mankha is open from 8.30 am to 4.30 pm weekdays and 9 am to noon on the weekend. The Communications Authority of Thailand (CAT) office, about 1km south-east on the same road, is open for international telephone service from 8.30 am to 9 pm daily.

Books & Maps A DK Book Store is opposite the Jansom Chumphon Hotel, but so far it's predominantly Thai-oriented and carries only a few English-language titles. Maps of Chumphon can be purchased here, however.

Places to Stay – Budget
As elsewhere in Thailand, at the cheaper hotels 'single' means a room with one large bed (big enough for two) while 'double' means a room with two beds.

Places continue to spring up as people use Chumphon as a gateway to Ko Tao. North of the bus terminal, on the opposite side of the street, *Infinity Travel Service* (☎ 077-501937, 68/2 Thanon Tha Taphao) has four basic but clean rooms with shared bathroom upstairs over the travel agency/restaurant for 100/150B single/double. Good value. This place provides plenty of information on boats to Ko Tao and things to do in the area, and also allows travellers to shower while waiting for boat or bus transfers. Under the same ownership, *Infinity Guest House* (224/37 Soi 1, Thanon Krom Luang) has six fan rooms in a two-storey wooden house. Rooms cost 100B to 150B and toilet and bathing facilities are shared.

Just around the corner, *Chumphon Guest House (also known as Miow House;* ☎ 077-502900) features clean, well-ventilated rooms in an old teak house as well as a row of simple cubicles out front for 100B to 150B. Facilities are shared. The friendly proprietors can arrange bicycle and motorcycle rental as well as local tours.

The *Sooksamer Guest House* (☎ 077-502430, 118/4 Thanon Suksamoe) has small rooms for 120B. The proprietors will allow you to use the shower on your way to Pak Nam for a Ko Tao boat.

Mayazes Resthouse (Mayaset; ☎ 077-504452, fax 502217), down a *soi* (lane) east of Infinity Travel, offers nine immaculate rooms for 200/250B with fan, 280/350B with air-con. Shared bathroom facilities are equally sparkling. Just around the corner on the same soi is *Suda Guest House* (☎ 077-504366), which rents two rooms in the upstairs of a row building for 250B/350B single/double. Add 100B to the prices if you turn on the air-con.

Other cheaper hotels can be found along Thanon Sala Daeng in the centre of town. The *Si Taifa Hotel* (☎ 077-501690) is a clean, old Chinese hotel built over a restaurant with single fan rooms featuring shared/attached bathroom for 140/180B. Double rooms with fan and bathroom are 260B, and air-con single/double rooms are 300/350B. Each floor has a terrace where you can watch the sun set over the city.

On Thanon Sala Daeng, the *Sri Chumphon Hotel* (☎ 077-511280, fax 504616, 127/22–24 Thanon Sala Daeng) is a clean and efficient Chinese hotel with rooms for 250B to 350B with fan and bathroom, 500B to 600B with air-con. The nearly identical *Suriwong Chumphon Hotel* (☎ 077-511203, fax 502699, 125/27–29 Thanon Sala Daeng) is better value at 210/280B for single/double rooms with fan and bathroom, and just 290/380B for air-con.

Tha Yang & Pak Nam Near the piers for boats to/from Ko Tao, the *Tha Yang Hotel* (☎ 077-553052) has decent air-con rooms for 250B to 350B. The adjacent *Tha Yang Guest House* offers fan rooms starting at 150B.

At Pak Nam the *Siriphet Hotel* (☎ 077-521304) has basic rooms with fan and shared toilet for 150B. *Mix Hotel* (☎/fax 077-502931–3, 108/8 Mu 1, Thanon Chumphon-Pak Nam) has rooms ranging from 400B to 900B.

Places to Stay – Mid-Range & Top End

The *Morakot Hotel* (☎ 077-503628, fax 570196), on Thanon Tawee Sinka, has very clean spacious rooms for 300B with fan, shower, cable TV and phone. Air-con rooms with hot-water showers start at 450B. Parking is available.

Although a bit newer, the *Jansom Chumphon Hotel* (☎ 077-502502, fax 502503, 118/138 Thanon Sala Daeng) is already looking a bit run down. Standard air-con rooms start at 495B; deluxe rooms cost 638B. The disco here is locally known as the

SOUTHERN GULF

CHUMPHON

To Prachuap Khiri Khan (184km) & Bangkok (500km)

Train Station

To Surat Thani

Thanon Tawee Sinka

Th Paradorn

Thanon Krom Luang Chumphon

Thanon Pracha Uthit

Thanon Sala Daeng

Thanon Tha Taphao

Thanon Phisit Phayaban

Thanon Suksamoe

Thanon Poramin Mankha

Thanon Phinit Khadi

Thanon Phisit Phayap

Thanon Tha Chang

Khlong Tha Taphao

To Highway 4

To CAT Office (1km), Pak Nam (10km), Tha Yang, Hat Thung Wua Laen (12km), Hat Sairi (21km) & Airport (35km)

0   100   200m
0   100   200yd

PLACES TO STAY
4 Infinity Guest House
5 Chumphon Guest House
6 Sooksamer Guest House
8 TC Super Mansion
9 Jansom Chumphon Hotel
14 Sri Chumphon Hotel
15 Suriwong Chumphong Hotel
16 Morakot Hotel
23 Mayazes Resthouse
24 Suda Guest House
25 Infinity Travel Service
33 Si Taifa Hotel

PLACES TO EAT
2 Night Market
12 Thai & Northeast Food Center
13 Curry Shops
28 Day & Night Market
30 Night Market
32 Tang Soon Kee

OTHER
1 Police
3 Minivans to Surat Thani
7 Provincial Hospital
10 Shopping Centre
11 DK Book Store
17 Cinema
18 Siam Commercial Bank
19 Sawngthaew to Ko Tao Boat Pier
20 Chok Anan Tour
21 Buses to Ao Thung Wua Laen
22 Bangkok Bank
26 Songserm Travel
27 Minivans to Ranong
29 Bus Terminal
31 Ban's Diving Center
34 Market
35 Municipal Office
36 District Office
37 Main Post Office
38 School
39 Chumphon Tourist Services Center
40 Provincial Hall
41 Hospital
42 Wat Suphannimit

'Khao Tom-theque' because of the *khâo tôm* (rice soup) meals served after midnight.

Places to Eat

Food vendors line the southern side of Thanon Krom Luang Chumphon between Thanon Sala Daeng and Thanon Suksamoe nightly from around 6 to 10 or 11 pm.

The *curry shops* along Thanon Sala Daeng are proof that you are now in Southern Thailand. Around the corner the *Thai & Northeast Food Center* serves inexpensive Isan food. Over on Thanon Tha Taphao is a small *night market* and a very popular Chinese place called *Tang Soon Kee*. Several *Isan-style places* can be found along Thanon Krom Luang Chumphon. The simple restaurant next to the Morakot Hotel has both *khâo man kài* (chicken rice) and *khâo mǔu daeng* (red pork and rice) in the evenings.

Chumphon Province is famous for *klûay lép meu naang,* or 'princess fingernail bananas'. They're very tasty and cheap – 25B will buy around a hundred.

Getting There & Away

Bus Ordinary buses depart from the Southern bus terminal in Bangkok once daily, at 6.30 am (136B).

First-class air-con buses are 245B and leave three times in the afternoon and evening; 2nd-class buses cost 190B and leave at 9 pm.

There are no government VIP departures from Bangkok to Chumphon, but Songserm Travel (☎ 077-506205, next to the Tha Taphao Hotel) has one at 10.30 pm and another at 11.30 pm each evening for 350B. At the time of writing there was a Songserm VIP bus departing for Bangkok at 2 pm daily for just 250B, although it was unclear how long the promotion would last.

Three different companies run air-con buses from Chumphon to Bangkok, the most reliable being Chok Anan Tour.

Minivans run regularly between Surat Thani and Chumphon (120B, 3½ hours) from Thanon Krom Luang Chumphon. From the Baw Khaw Saw (the Thai initials of Borisat Khon Song, the government bus company) terminal you can get buses to Bang Saphan Yai for 35B (or an air-con minivan for 80B), Prachuap Khiri Khan for 55B (77B air-con), Ranong for 40B (60B air-con) and Hat Yai for 230B. In Chumphon

the main terminal for these buses is found on the western side of Thanon Tha Taphao.

Air-con minivans run to/from Ranong daily every hour between 8 am and 5.30 pm for 80B from opposite Infinity Travel Service. There is also a minivan to Bangkok that meets the Ko Tao boat at the Tha Pak Nam (Pak Nam Pier), and leaves from Infinity Travel Service at noon and 5 pm (350B).

Train The rapid and express trains from Bangkok take about 7½ hours to reach Chumphon and cost 82B in 3rd class, 190B in 2nd class and 394B in 1st class; this does not include rapid or express surcharges.

There are four local 3rd-class trains daily to Prachuap Khiri Khan (24B), and one to Surat Thani (25B) that also continues on to Hat Yai (67B). Southbound rapid and express trains – the only trains with 1st and 2nd class – are much less frequent and can be difficult to book out of Chumphon.

Boat Ko Tao, a small island north of Ko Samui and Ko Pha-Ngan, can be reached by boat from Tha Reua Ko Tao (Ko Tao Boat Landing), 10km south-east of town in Pak Nam. The regular daily boat leaves at midnight (200B, about six hours). From Ko Tao the boat usually leaves at 10 am and arrives at Tha Reua Ko Tao around 3.30 pm. The ride can be very rough if seas are high – November is the worst month for stormy weather.

More expensive but faster is the Songserm express boat from Tha Yang (400B, 2½ hours). Depending on the weather, it usually departs at 7.30 am eastbound (to Ko Tao), 3 pm westbound (from Ko Tao). Faster still are speedboats that take about two hours to make the trip. These depart from Tha Yang at 7.30 am, and in the opposite direction at 10.30 am. The fare is 300B to 400B and transfer to/from the pier is usually included in the fare.

Sǎwngthǎew (also written *songthaew;* pick-up trucks) run to both piers frequently between 6 am and 6 pm for 10B. After 6 pm, Infinity and most other travel services and guesthouses can send a van to the pier around 10 pm for 50B per person. Going by van means you won't have to wait at the pier for six hours before the midnight boat departs. The only other alternative is an 80B motorcycle taxi ride to the pier.

Regular air-con minibuses (350B) to/from Bangkok's Thanon Khao San guesthouses and travel agencies also connect with the slow boat. Be extremely cautious about these, though, especially if they are offering the ride for only 50B to 100B. Basically there is no way a transport company can make any kind of profit on such low fares – unless they plan to steal from their passengers.

You can also charter a speedboat to Ko Tao from Pak Nam for 4000B to 5000B.

Getting Around

Motorcycle taxis around town cost a flat 10B per trip. Săwngthăew to Pak Nam Chumphon cost 13B per person, motorcycle taxis 80B to 100B. To Hat Sairi and Hat Thung Wua Laen they cost 20B (motorcycle 150B). Buses to Tako Estuary (for Hat Arunothai) are 40B. Infinity Travel Service can arrange rentals of motorcycles (200B per day) and cars (1000B per day).

Surat Thani Province

CHAIYA
ไชยา

About 640km from Bangkok, Chaiya is just north of Surat Thani and is best visited as a day trip from there. Chaiya is one of the oldest cities in Thailand, dating back to the Srivijaya empire. The name may in fact be a contraction of Siwichaiya, the Thai pronunciation of the city that was a regional capital between the 8th and 10th centuries. Previous to this time the area was a stop on the Indian trade route in South-East Asia. Many Srivijaya artefacts in the National Museum in Bangkok were found in Chaiya, including a famous Avalokiteshvara Bodhisattva bronze that's considered to be a masterpiece of Buddhist art.

Wat Suan Mokkhaphalaram
วัดสวนโมกข์พลาราม

Wat Suanmok (short for Wat Suan Mokkhaphalaram – literally, Garden of Liberation), west of Wat Kaew, is a modern forest *wát* (temple) founded by Ajahn

Buddhadasa Bhikkhu, arguably Thailand's most famous monk. Born in Chaiya in 1906, Buddhadasa was ordained as a monk when he was 21 years old, spent many years studying the Pali scriptures and then retired to the forest for six years of solitary meditation. Returning to ecclesiastical society, he was made abbot of Wat Phra Boromathat, a high distinction, but conceived of Suanmok as an alternative to orthodox Thai temples. During Thailand's turbulent 1970s he was branded a communist because of his critiques of capitalism, which he saw as a catalyst for greed. Buddhadasa died in July 1993 after a long illness.

Buddhadasa's philosophy was ecumenical in nature, comprising Zen, Taoist and Christian elements as well as the traditional Theravada schemata. Today the hermitage is spread over 120 hectares of wooded hillside and features huts for up to 70 monks, a museum/library, and a 'spiritual theatre'. This latter building has bas-reliefs on the outer walls that are facsimiles of sculptures at Sanchi, Bharhut and Amaravati in India. The interior walls feature modern Buddhist painting – eclectic to say the least – executed by the resident monks.

At the affiliated International Dhamma Hermitage (IDH), across the highway 1.5km from Wat Suanmok, resident monks hold meditation retreats during the first 10 days of every month. Anyone is welcome to participate; the cost is 1200B (120B per day for 10 days) and there is no advance registration or reservation required. Simply arrive in time to register on the final day of the month preceding the retreat. Registration takes place at the main monastery.

Other Attractions

The restored **Borom That Chaiya** at Wat Phra Boromathat, just outside town, is a *chedi* (stupa) that is a fine example of Srivijaya architecture and strongly resembles the *candi* (stupas) of central Java – a stack of ornate boxes bearing images of Kala, a peacock (a symbol for the sun), Airavata, Indra and the Buddha (facing east as usual). In the courtyard surrounding the chedi are several pieces of sculpture from the region, including an unusual two-sided *yoni* (the uterus-shaped pedestal that holds the Shivalingam, or phallic shrine), *reusii* (masters) performing yoga and several Buddha images.

A ruined stupa at **Wat Kaew** (also known as Wat Long), also from the Srivijaya period, shows central Javanese influence (or perhaps vice versa) as well as Cham (9th-century southern Vietnam) characteristics.

The **National Museum** near the entrance to Wat Phra Boromathat displays historic and prehistoric artefacts of local provenance, as well as local handicrafts and a shadow puppet exhibit. Admission to the museum is 30B; it's open from 9 am to 4 pm Wednesday to Sunday.

You can catch any sǎwngthǎew heading west from the main intersection south of the train station to Wat Boromathat for 5B. This same sǎwngthǎew route passes the turn-off for Wat Kaew, which is about 500m before the turn-off for Wat Boromathat. Wat Kaew is less than 500m from this intersection on the left, almost directly opposite Chaiya Witthaya School.

Places to Stay

Travellers can stay in Surat Thani for visits to Chaiya or request permission from the monks to stay in the guest quarters at Wat Suanmok. *Udomlap Hotel* (☎ 077-431123),

a Chinese-Thai hotel in Chaiya, has clean rooms in an old wooden building for 150B, while rooms in a modern multistorey air-con wing go for 250B to 450B.

Getting There & Away

If you're going to Surat Thani by train from Bangkok, you can get off at the small Chaiya train station, then later catch another train to Phun Phin, Surat's train station.

From Surat you can either take a sǎwngthǎew from Talat Kaset 2 in Ban Don (18B to Wat Suanmok, 25B to Chaiya) or get a train going north from Phun Phin. The trains between Phun Phin and Chaiya may be full but you can always stand or squat in a 3rd-class car for the short trip. The ordinary train costs 10B in 3rd class to Chaiya and takes about an hour. The sǎwngthǎew takes around 45 minutes. Or you can take a share taxi to Chaiya from Surat for 30B per person; in Chaiya, Surat-bound taxis leave from opposite the Chaiya train station.

Suanmok is about 7km outside Chaiya on the highway that runs to Surat and Chumphon. Until late afternoon there are sǎwngthǎew from the Chaiya train station to

Culture of the South

Although under Thai political domination for several centuries, the South has always remained culturally apart from the other regions of Thailand. Historically, the peninsula has been linked to cultures in ancient Indonesia, particularly the Srivijaya empire, which ruled a string of principalities in what is today southern Thailand, Malaysia and Indonesia. The influence of Malay-Indonesian culture is still apparent in the ethnicity, religion, art and language of the *Thai pàk tâi* (the southern Thais).

The Thai pàk tâi dress differently, build their houses differently and eat differently from Thais in the north. Many are followers of Islam, so there are quite a few mosques in southern cities; men often cover their heads and the long sarong is favoured over the shorter *phâa khǎo mǎa* worn in the northern, central and north-eastern regions. There are also a good many Chinese living in the south – their influence can be seen in the old architecture and in the baggy Chinese pants worn by rural non-Muslims.

Southern Thais speak a dialect that confounds even visitors from other Thai regions. Diction is short and fast and the clipped tones fly into the outer regions of intelligibility. In the provinces nearest Malaysia, many Thai Muslims speak Yawi, an old Malay dialect.

Southern architecture follows three basic threads. In rural areas, simple bungalows constructed from thatched palm leaves and bamboo strips affixed to wood or bamboo frames are common. A Malay style of construction emphasises sturdy houses of wood with square tile roofs. In the older cities you'll come across splendid examples of Sino-Portuguese architecture, featuring arched windows and porticoes and curved tiled roofs.

Southern Thai cuisine combines Chinese, Malay and Thai elements to create brightly coloured, heavily spiced dishes. Look for khànǒm jiin náam yaa, thin noodles doused in a fish curry sauce, and rotii kaeng, Malay-style flat bread served with a curry dip. Seafood is an everyday staple.

Wat Suanmok for 10B per passenger. From Chaiya you can also catch a Surat-bound bus from the front of the movie theatre on Chaiya's main street and ask to be let off at Wat Suanmok. (Turn right on the road in front of the train station.) The fare to Wat Suanmok is 5B. If buses aren't running you can hire a motorcycle taxi (20B) anywhere along Chaiya's main street.

SURAT THANI
อ.เมืองสุราษฎร์ธานี

postcode 84000 • pop 43,100
There is little of historical interest in Surat Thani, a busy commercial centre and port dealing in rubber and coconut, but the town's waterfront lends character nonetheless. It's 651km from Bangkok and the first point in a southbound journey towards Malaysia that really feels and looks like Southern Thailand. For most people Surat Thani (often known simply as 'Surat') is only a stop on the way to Ko Samui or Ko Pha-Ngan, luscious islands 32km off the coast – so the Talat Kaset bus terminal in the Ban Don area of Surat and the ferry piers to the east become the centres of attention.

If you find yourself with some time to kill in Surat, you can do a one- or two-hour tour of **Bang Ban Mai**, across Mae Nam Tapi from town. This easygoing village has changed remarkably little over the years, affording glimpses of the coconut plantation lifestyle as it once was on Ko Samui. Long-tail boats can be hired at the Tha Reua Klang (middle pier), near the night ferry pier, for 250B per hour.

In mid-October Chak Phra and Thawt Pha Pa celebrations occur on the same day (first day of the waning moon in the 11th lunar month) at the end of the Buddhist Rains Retreat and are major events for Surat Thani Province.

Thawt Pha Pa (Laying-Out of Forest Robes) begins at dawn with the offering of new monastic robes to the monks, while Chak Phra (Pulling of the Buddha Image) takes place during the day and evening. During Chak Phra, local lay devotees place sacred Buddha images on boats for a colourful procession along Mae Nam Tapi. A similar landborne procession uses trucks and hand-pulled carts. Lots of food stalls

and musical performances, including *lí-keh* (folk plays featuring dancing, comedy, melodrama and music) are set up for the occasion.

Information
Tourist Offices The friendly Tourism Authority of Thailand (TAT) office (☎ 077-288818/9, ℮ tatsurat@samart.co.th) at 5 Thanon Talat Mai near the south-western end of town, distributes plenty of useful brochures and maps. It's open from 8.30 am to 4.30 pm daily.

Money There's a string of banks – one on every block for five blocks – along Thanon Na Meuang south-west of Thanon Chonkasem; all have ATMs and most offer foreign exchange. Bangkok Bank at 193 Thanon Na Meuang has an exchange booth open from 8.30 am to 5 pm daily.

Post & Communications The main post office is on Thanon Talat Mai; Ban Don has its own post office on Thanon Na Meuang. The telecommunications centre on Thanon Don Nok, open from 7 am to 11 pm daily, is the place to make international calls.

Travel Agencies Several travel agents in town handle travel to the islands and elsewhere in Southern Thailand. These include Phantip Travel (☎ 077-272230) at 442/24–25 Thanon Talat Mai; and Songserm Travel (☎ 077-285124, fax 285127) at 30/2 Mu 3, Thanon Bangkoong. Songserm has another office opposite the pier. For the average transport transaction Phantip is the most reliable travel agent in town overall.

Due to the lucrative transport business here, shuttling travellers between Bangkok and nearby islands, Surat has attracted its share of shady travel agencies. One agency that should be avoided at all costs is Chaw Wang Tours. We've received several complaints from readers about rip-offs involving this company. According to TAT in Surat, travellers should also avoid Tam Thong Tour, Roi Koh Tour and CTV Travel.

Medical Services Surat has three hospitals but Taksin Hospital (☎ 077-273239) on Thanon Talat Mai is considered the most professional.

SOUTHERN GULF

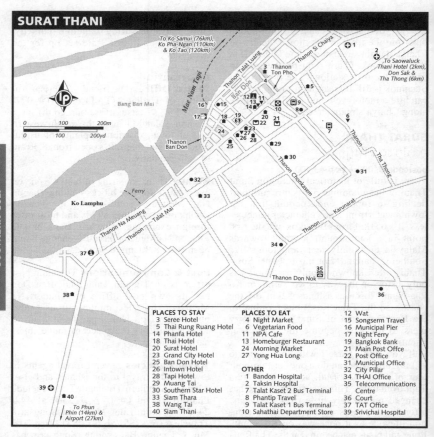

SURAT THANI

PLACES TO STAY
3 Seree Hotel
5 Thai Rung Ruang Hotel
14 Phanfa Hotel
18 Thai Hotel
20 Surat Hotel
23 Grand City Hotel
25 Ban Don Hotel
26 Intown Hotel
28 Tapi Hotel
29 Muang Tai
30 Southern Star Hotel
33 Siam Thara
38 Wang Tai
40 Siam Thani

PLACES TO EAT
4 Night Market
6 Vegetarian Food
11 NPA Cafe
13 Homeburger Restaurant
24 Morning Market
27 Yong Hua Long

OTHER
1 Bandon Hospital
2 Taksin Hospital
7 Talat Kaset 2 Bus Terminal
8 Phantip Travel
9 Talat Kaset 1 Bus Terminal
10 Sahathai Department Store

12 Wat
15 Songserm Travel
16 Municipal Pier
17 Night Ferry
19 Bangkok Bank
21 Main Post Offce
22 Post Office
31 Municipal Office
32 City Pillar
34 THAI Office
35 Telecommunications Centre
36 Court
37 TAT Office
39 Srivichai Hospital

Places to Stay – Budget

For many of Surat Thani's cheaper hotels, business is largely 'short-time' trade. This doesn't make them any less suitable as regular hotels – it's just that there's likely to be more noise, as guests arrive and depart with some frequency. In fact, in many ways it's better to zip straight through Surat Thani since there's nothing of interest to hold you. You're quite likely to sleep better on the night boat than in a noisy hotel. Another alternative is to stay near the train station in Phun Phin (see under Phun Phin later).

All of the following are within walking or *săamláw* (also written *samlor*; three-wheeled pedicab) distance of the Ban Don boat piers.

The *Surat Hotel* (☎ 077-272243, 496 Thanon Na Meuang), between the Grand City Hotel and bus terminal, charges 180B to 350B for spacious rooms with fan and bathroom, 380B to 480B with air-con. At the rear are some quiet, renovated rooms. Opposite the Surat, the *Phanfa Hotel* (☎ 077-272287, 247/2–5 Thanon Na Meuang) has similar rooms with fan and private bathroom for 180B to 280B.

The *Grand City Hotel* (☎ 077-272960, 428 Thanon Na Meuang) has plain but clean rooms with fan and bathroom costing 230/280B single/double, and air-con rooms costing 380/500B.

On Thanon Ton Pho, near the municipal pier, is the *Seree Hotel* (Seri; ☎ 077-272279). Adequate but somewhat airless rooms with fan and bathroom are 250/300B and air-con rooms cost 320/400B. There's a coffee shop on the premises.

One block from the night ferry pier on Thanon Si Chaiya is the **Thai Hotel** (☎ 077-272932), which charges 150B to 200B for dingy but fairly quiet singles/doubles with fan and bathroom.

The **Ban Don Hotel** (☎ 077-272167) on Thanon Na Meuang towards the morning market has clean singles/doubles with fan and bathroom for 200B, plus a few rooms with smaller bathrooms and squat toilets for 180B. Enter the hotel through a Chinese restaurant – quite a good one for inexpensive rice and noodle dishes.

The **Intown Hotel** (☎ 077-210145–9, fax 210422, 276/1 Thanon Na Meuang), close to the Ban Don Hotel, is a two-storey modern building with 48 rooms costing 220B to 260B with fan, 340B to 370B with air-con. All air-con rooms have TV, hot water and phone.

Phun Phin You may find yourself needing accommodation in Phun Phin, either because you've become stranded there due to booked-out trains or because you've come in from Ko Samui in the evening and plan to get an early-morning train out of Surat before the Surat–Phun Phin bus service starts. If so, there are a couple of cheap, dilapidated hotels just across from the train station. The **Tai Fah** has rooms for 120/150B with shared/attached bathroom. The **Si Meuang Thani** on the corner has a similar setup and similar rates.

If you can afford a few baht more, around the corner on the road to Surat, but still quite close to the train station, is the better **Queen** (☎ 077-311003), where rooms cost 180B to 250B with fan and 400B with air-con.

Places to Stay – Mid-Range

Although these don't cost much more than the budget places, the facilities and services (parking, bus- and boat-ticket booking, taxi service to the airport) are considerably better. Popular with travelling businesspeople, the **Tapi Hotel** (☎ 077-272575, 100 Thanon Chonkasem) has fan rooms for 280B to 300B and air-con for 320B to 400B. The recently renovated **Muang Tai** (☎ 077-272367, 390–392 Thanon Talat Mai) has fan rooms from 200B and air-con rooms from 320B.

The **Thai Rung Ruang Hotel** (☎ 077-273249, fax 286353, 191/199 Thanon Mitkasem), off Thanon Na Meuang near the bus terminal, is also good, with single/twin rooms from 280/300B (fan) and 320/400B (air-con, TV, phone).

Places to Stay – Top End

Surat Thani has a number of more expensive hotels, including the **Wang Tai** (☎ 077-283020/39, fax 281007, 1 Thanon Talat Mai). It's a big hotel with nearly 300 rooms, a swimming pool and prices from 850B. Rooms at the **Siam Thani** (☎ 077-273081–5, 180 Thanon Surat Thani-Phun Phin) start at 750B and climb up to 1700B for a double suite. It has a swimming pool, coffee shop and a good restaurant. The **Siam Thara** (☎ 077-273740), on Thanon Don Nok near the Thanon Talat Mai intersection, has air-con rooms ranging from 595B to 625B.

Southern Star Hotel (☎ 077-216414, fax 216427, 253 Thanon Chonkasem), south of the Muang Tai, is home to the biggest discotheque in Southern Thailand, the Star Theque. All 150 of the hotel's rooms feature sitting areas that have inspired it to call them 'suites'. A standard single/double room costs 1110B, and it's 2690B for a superior room. Other facilities include a coffee shop, restaurant, sky lounge and karaoke pub.

The newest top-end place in town, the 11-storey, 276-room **Saowaluk Thani Hotel** (☎ 077-213700, fax 213735, 99/99 Thanon Kanjanawithi) is on the northeastern city limits on the road to Don Sak. Rooms are listed as 1900/2100B single/ double but are readily available for 850/950B with breakfast. The hotel has a coffee shop, a lobby bar, a Chinese restaurant and several function rooms.

Places to Eat

The **Talat Kaset market** area, next to the bus terminal, and the **morning market**, between Thanon Na Meuang and Thanon Si Chaiya, are good food-hunting places. Many **stalls** near the bus terminal specialise in khâo kài òp (marinated baked chicken on rice), which is very tasty. During mango season, a lot of street vendors in Surat sell incredible khâo nĭaw mámûang (coconut-sweetened sticky rice with sliced ripe mango).

SOUTHERN GULF

The best of Surat's several *night markets* is one that runs along both sides of Thanon Ton Pho, near the Seree Hotel.

Just around the corner from the Bangkok Bank, off Thanon Na Meuang in an old wooden building, is an exemplary southern-style *khànŏm jiin place* (khànŏm jiin is curry noodles served with a huge tray of vegies).

NPA Cafe, an air-con place on Thanon Na Meuang between the Thai Military Bank and the Phanfa Hotel, has Western breakfasts, burgers, salads, macaroni, spaghetti, sandwiches, salads, Thai and Chinese food – plus Corona beer, Bud's Ice Cream, Geno's Pizza and an extensive list of appetisers. *Homeburger Restaurant,* next to the Phanfa Hotel, does hamburgers, pizza, steak and some Thai dishes.

Around the corner from the Grand City Hotel is the inexpensive and popular *Yong Hua Long* (no Roman-script sign), a decent Chinese restaurant with roast duck and a large buffet table.

Vegetarian Food, on the eastern side of Thanon Tha Thong, serves good vegetarian *kŭaytĭaw* (rice noodles) and some hot Thai curries. It's a bit pricier than the average for Thai vegetarian.

Phun Phin In Phun Phin, across from Queen is a good *night market* with cheap eats. The *Tai Fah* does Thai, Chinese and fàràng food at reasonable prices.

Opposite the northern end of the train station, *Oum's Restaurant* has an English menu and serves good Thai coffee, Western breakfasts and simple Thai dishes. Nearby is the similar *Wut,* which offers email and Internet services.

Getting There & Away
Air Thai Airways International (THAI) flies to Surat Thani from Bangkok twice daily (2055B, one hour and 10 minutes). The THAI office (☎ 077-272610, 273710) in Surat is at 3/27–28 Thanon Karunarat.

Bus, Share Taxi & Minivan First-class air-con buses leave Bangkok's Southern bus terminal in Thonburi three times in the morning, arriving in Surat 10 hours later; the fare is 346B. There is also one VIP departure at 7 pm for 535B.

Ordinary buses leave the Southern bus terminal once in the morning and once in the evening for 180B.

Take care when booking private air-con and VIP buses out of Surat. Some companies have been known to sell tickets for VIP buses to Bangkok, then pile hapless travellers onto an ordinary air-con bus and refuse to refund the fare difference. If possible get a recommendation from another traveller or inquire at the TAT office. See the Information section earlier in the chapter for a list of travel agencies we suggest you avoid.

Public buses and share taxis run from the Talat Kaset bus terminals 1 and 2. Phantip Travel handles minivan and bus bookings (as well as air, train and boat bookings).

Other fares to/from Surat are:

destination	fare	duration (hrs)
Hat Yai		
ordinary	103B	5
air-con	180B	4
share taxi or van	150B	3½
Krabi		
ordinary	70B	4
air-con	110B	3
share taxi or van	150B	2
Nakhon Si Thammarat		
ordinary	45B	2½
air-con	70B	2
share taxi	80B	2
Narathiwat		
air-con	160B	6
Phang-Nga		
ordinary	55B	4
air-con	110B	3
share taxi	90B	2½
Phuket		
ordinary	90B	6
air-con	140B–165B	5
share taxi or van	160B	4
Ranong		
ordinary	80B	5
air-con	120B	4
share taxi or van	130B	3½
Satun		
ordinary	85B	4
Trang		
ordinary	60B	3
van	120B	3
Yala		
ordinary	120B	6
van	160B	6

Train Trains for Surat (which don't really stop in Surat but in Phun Phin, 14km west of town) leave Bangkok's Hualamphong terminal at 12.25 pm (rapid), 2.20 and 2.45 pm (special express), 3.50 pm (rapid), 5.05 pm (express), 5.35 and 6.20 pm (rapid), 7.15 pm (express), and 10.30 and 10.50 pm (express diesel railcar), arriving 10½ to 11 hours later. The 6.20 pm train (rapid No 167) is the most convenient, arriving at 6.25 am and giving you plenty of time to catch a boat to Ko Samui, if that's your planned destination. Fares are 519B in 1st class, 248B in 2nd class and 107B 3rd class, not including the rapid/express/special express surcharges or berths.

The all-2nd-class express diesel railcars Nos 39 and 41 leave Bangkok daily at 10.30 and 10.50 pm and arrive in Phun Phin at 7.35 and 8.01 am. Tickets cost 368B. No sleeping berths are available on these trains.

The Phun Phin train station has a 24-hour left-luggage room that charges 10B a day for the first five days, 20B a day thereafter. The advance ticket office is open from 6 am to 6 pm daily.

It can be difficult to book long-distance trains out of Phun Phin; it may be easier to take a bus, especially if heading south. The trains are very often full and it's a drag to take the bus 14km from town to the Phun Phin train station and be turned away. You could buy a 'standing room only' 3rd-class ticket and stand for an hour or two until someone vacates a seat down the line. Advance train reservations can be made at Phantip Travel on Thanon Talat Mai in Ban Don, near the market/bus terminal. You might try making an onward reservation *before* boarding a boat for Ko Samui. On Samui, both Travel Solutions in Chaweng and Songserm Travel Service in Na Thon can assist with reservations.

Train/Bus/Boat Combinations It's possible to buy tickets from the State Railway of Thailand (SRT) that allow you to go straight through to Ko Samui or Ko Pha-Ngan from Bangkok on a train, bus and boat combination. The savings are typically little more than 50B.

Getting Around
Air-con vans from Surat Thani airport to town cost 80B per person. THAI runs a more-expensive 'limo' service for 150B.

Buses to Ban Don from Phun Phin train station leave every 10 minutes or so from 6 am to 8 pm (10B). Some of the buses drive straight to the pier (if they have enough tourists), while others terminate at the Talat Kaset 1 bus terminal, from where you must get another bus to Tha Thong (or to Ban Don if you're taking the night ferry).

If you arrive in Phun Phin on one of the night trains, you can get a free bus from the train station to the pier, courtesy of Songserm, Phantip or Samui Tour before the morning boat departures. If your train arrives in Phun Phin and the buses aren't running, then you'll have to hire a taxi to Ban Don for 80B to 100B, or hang out in one of the Phun Phin street cafes until buses start running around 5 am.

Orange buses run from Talat Kaset 1 bus terminal to Phun Phin train station every 10 minutes from 5 am to 7.30 pm (8B). Empty buses also wait at the Tha Thong pier for passengers arriving from Ko Samui on the express boat, ready to drive them directly to the train station or destinations farther afield. There are also share taxis to the Phun Phin station from Surat for 15B, but these leave only when full; otherwise, you'll have to hire the vehicle for 80B to 100B.

Around town, share săwngthăew cost 6B to 10B depending on the distance travelled. Săamláw rides cost 10B to 20B.

KHAO SOK NATIONAL PARK
อุทยานแห่งชาติเขาสก

Established in 1980, this 646-sq-km park lies in the western part of Surat Thani Province, off Rte 401 about a third of the way from Takua Pa to Surat Thani. The park has thick native rainforest with waterfalls *(náam tòk),* limestone cliffs, numerous streams, an island-studded lake, and many trails, mostly along rivers. According to Krabi resident Thom Henley, author of the highly informative *Waterfalls and Gibbon Calls,* the Khao Sok rainforest is a remnant of a 160-million-year-old forest ecosystem that is much older and richer than the forests of the Amazon and central Africa.

Connected to two other national parks, Kaeng Krung and Phang-Nga, along with the Khlong Saen and Khlong Nakha wildlife sanctuaries these form the largest contiguous nature preserve – around 4000 sq km – on the Thai peninsula. Khao Sok shelters a plethora of wildlife, including wild elephants, leopards, serow, banteng, gaur, dusky langurs, tigers and Malayan sun bears, as well as over 180 bird species.

A major watershed for the south, the park is filled with lianas, bamboo, ferns and rattan, including the giant rattan (*wǎi tào phráw*), with a stem over 10cm in diameter. One floral rarity found in the park is *Rafflesia kerri meyer*, known to the Thais as *bua phút* (wild lotus), the largest flower in the world. Found only in Khao Sok and an adjacent wildlife sanctuary (different varieties of the same species are found in Malaysia and Indonesia), mature specimens reach 80cm in diameter. The flower has no roots or leaves of its own; instead it lives parasitically inside the roots of the liana, a jungle vine. From October to December, buds burst forth from the liana root and swell to football size. When the bud blooms in January and February it emits a potent stench (said to resemble that of a rotting corpse), which attracts insects that are responsible for pollination.

Orientation & Information

The best time of year to visit Khao Sok is December to May, when trails are less slippery, river crossings are easier and riverbank camping is safer due to the lower risk of flash flooding. During the June to November wet season, on the other hand, you're more likely to see Malayan and Asiatic black bears, civets, slow loris, wild boar, gaur, deer and wild elephants – and tigers if you're very, very lucky – along the trail system. During dry months the larger mammals tend to stay near the reservoir in areas without trails.

The park headquarters is 1.5km off Rte 401 between Takua Pa and Surat Thani at the 109km marker. Besides the camping area and bungalows at the park headquarters, there are several private bungalow operations that feature 'tree house'–style accommodation outside the park.

As with all national parks in the kingdom, entry for foreigners costs 200/100B for adults/kids under 14. Thais pay 20B. At the visitors centre, as well as at various bookshops in Southern Thailand, you can purchase a copy of Henley's inspirational wildlife guide, *Waterfalls and Gibbon Calls*. The author pulls no punches when it comes to his critiques of park management and national policy.

A map of hiking trails within the park is available for 5B from the park headquarters near the park entrance.

Things to See & Do

Various trails lead to the waterfalls of **Mae Yai** (5.5km from park headquarters), **Than Sawan** (9km), **Sip-Et Chan** (4km) and **Than Kloy** (9km). Guesthouses near the park entrance can arrange guided hikes that include waterfalls, caves and river-running. Park rangers lead jungle tours and/or rafting trips, and can arrange elephant trekking. Prices depend on the distance travelled. Leeches are quite common in certain areas of the park, so take the usual precautions – wear closed shoes when hiking and apply plenty of repellent.

The 95m-high, 700m-long, shaled-clay Kheuan Ratchaprapha (Ratchaprapha Dam, also known as Kheuan Chiaw Lan), erected across Mae Nam Pasaeng in 1982, creates the vast **Chiaw Lan Lake**, which is 165km at its longest point. Limestone outcrops protruding from the lake reach a height of 960m, over three times the height of formations in Ao Phang-Nga (Phang-Nga Bay).

A limestone cave known as **Tham Nam Thalu** contains striking cavern formations and subterranean streams, while **Tham Si Ru** features four converging passageways used as a hideout by communist insurgents between 1975 and 1982. **Tham Khang Dao**, high on a limestone cliff face, is home to many bat species. All three caves can be reached on foot from the south-western shore of the lake. The dam is 65km from the visitors centre via a well-marked side road off Rte 401 (back towards Surat Thani). You can rent boats from local fishermen to explore the coves, canals, caves and cul-de-sacs along the lakeshore. On Chiaw Lan Lake, three floating raft houses belonging to the national park provide overnight accommodation.

Places to Stay & Eat

In the National Park Khao Sok has a camping area and several places to stay. The park no longer offers tents for rent; pitching your own tent costs 30B. Two *bungalows* near the visitors centre are available for 350B, and there's a *longhouse* that sleeps up to 12 people (on rice mats only), available for just 300B. Reservations can be made by calling ☎ 077-299150/1. A small cooperative *restaurant* near the entrance serves inexpensive meals but it's necessary to tell them a day in advance that you will be eating there.

Around the National Park Accommodation and food are also available at several places outside the park. All places offer guides for jungle trips. Next to the park entrance and 1.9km from the highway, the *Treetop River Huts* (☎ 077-421155, 421613 ext 107) has thatched-roof rooms with bathroom for 250/350B single/double, and a tree house with bathroom for 500B, plus meals for 40B to 70B. Khun Arun, the English-speaking owner, has lots of information about the surrounding area.

Bamboo House, off the main road to the park, has rustic but clean rooms for 200B with shared bathroom, 250B with private bathroom. Others in the 200B to 300B category include *Jampha House*, *Freedom Resort*, *Mountain Jungle View* and *Lotus Bungalows*, all near the park entrance or on the road leading past Bamboo House.

Art's Riverview Jungle Lodge (☎ 01-421 2394), beyond Bamboo House about 1km from the park, has rooms for 200B to 300B, tree houses for 400B, and two large houses with rooms with private bathroom and deck for 600B. Some of the newer tree houses are right on Mae Nam Sok and boast good views of nearby mountains. Art's seems to be well run, but success may be tempting the owner to overbuild, especially along the river. Despite the operation's obvious success, however, the owner still prefers a lamp-lit night-time ambience and has no plans to install electricity.

Past Art's and the Bamboo House *Our Jungle House* (☎ 01-893 9583, e our_jungle _house@hotmail.com) is run by a friendly Irishman and has nicely designed tree houses with private bathroom, set along the river facing a huge limestone cliff (good for gibbon-viewing). These cost from 400B to 600B, and there are less-expensive rooms set back away from the river for 250B. Overnight lake trips are available with lots of animal-viewing on the jungle's edge for 3150B per person (minimum two people), and full-day rainforest hikes with a guide are also offered. As at Art's, there are no noisy electricity generators here to drown out the sounds of the jungle.

Under the same management as the Dawn of Happiness in Krabi (see the Andaman Coast chapter), *Khao Sok Rainforest Resort* (☎ 01-676 2697) offers sturdy cottages on stilts, attached showers and toilets, and large verandas overlooking the forest. All the cottages have electricity, and thus fans, and cost 400B for a single, 600B for a double.

There are a couple of simple private *restaurants* along the park access road between the park entrance and the highway.

Chiaw Lan Lake At Substation 3 near the dam, two large *floating raft houses* contain screened rooms with two to three beds each and good toilet/shower facilities. Another *raft house* at Substation 4 offers seven small bamboo huts with mattresses on the floor and communal facilities outside. The price at both places is 500B per person per night, including meals.

Getting There & Away

From Phun Phin or Surat Thani catch a bus bound for Takua Pa and get off at the 109km marker (the park's entrance) on Rte 401. If you're having trouble seeing the kilometre markers, just tell the bus driver or ticket attendants 'Khao Sok' and they'll let you off at the right place. The bus will cost you 82B air-con, 33B ordinary. You can also come from the Phuket side of the peninsula by bus, but you'll have to go to Takua Pa first; Surat-bound buses from Phuket don't use Rte 401 any more.

To reach Chiaw Lan Lake and the park's floating raft houses, park rangers can arrange transportation from the park headquarters for 1200B to 1700B return (depending on which substation you go to). If you have your own vehicle, take the turn-off between the 52km and 53km markers on Rte 401, at Ban Takum. From here it's 14km north-west to Substation 2.

KO SAMUI
เกาะสมุย

postcode 84140 • pop 36,100
Ko Samui is part of an island group that was called Mu Ko Samui (Samui Archipelago), although you rarely hear that term now. Thailand's third-largest island at 247 sq km,

SOUTHERN GULF

it's surrounded by 80 smaller islands. Six of these, Pha-Ngan, Ta Loy, Tao, Taen, Ma Ko and Ta Pao, are also inhabited.

Samui's first settlers were islanders from Hainan Island (now part of the People's Republic of China) who took up coconut farming here around 150 years ago. You can still see a map of Hainan on the *săan jâo* (Chinese spirit shrine) near Siam City Bank in Na Thon, the oldest town on the island.

The island has had a somewhat legendary status among travellers to Asia for the past 20 years or so, but it wasn't until the late 1980s that it escalated to the touristic proportions of other similar getaways such as Goa and Bali. Since the advent of the Don Sak ferry and the opening of the airport in 1989, things have been changing fast. During the high seasons (late December to February, and July to August) it can be hard to find a place to stay, even though most beaches are crowded with bungalows and resorts. The port town of Na Thon teems with foreign travellers getting on and off the ferry boats, booking tickets onward, and collecting mail at the post office. There are nearly a dozen daily flights to Samui from Bangkok, and the island is rushing into top-end development.

Nevertheless, Samui is still an enjoyable place to spend some time, and more than a few people have been making regular visits for nearly 20 years. It still has some of the best-value accommodation in Thailand and a casual, do-as-you-please atmosphere that makes it quite attractive. Even with an airport, it has the advantage of being off the mainland and far away from Bangkok. Coconuts are still an important part of the local economy – up to two million are shipped to Bangkok each month.

But there's no going back to 1971, when the first two tourists arrived on a coconut boat from Bangkok, much to the surprise of a friend who had been living on the island for four years as a Peace Corps volunteer. The main difference is that there are now many more places to stay, most of them in the mid- to high range by Thai standards. And of course, with this 'something for everyone' climate have come more people, more traffic, more noise and more rubbish, but so far not in intolerable proportions. Samui residents are beginning to formulate policies to deal with these social and environmental challenges and the prognosis is, tentatively, optimistic – only time will tell.

Perhaps due to the Hainanese influence, Samui culture differs from that of other islands in Southern Thailand and its inhabitants refer to themselves as *chao samŭi* (Samui folk) rather than Thais. They can be even friendlier than the average upcountry Thai, in our opinion, and have a great sense of humour, although those who are in constant contact with tourists can be a bit jaded. Nowadays many of the resorts, restaurants, bars and other tourist enterprises are owned or operated by Bangkok Thais or Europeans, so you have to get into the villages to meet true chao samŭi.

The island has a distinctive cuisine, influenced by the omnipresent coconut, which is still the main source of income for chao samŭi, who have disproportionately less ownership in beach property than outsiders. Coconut palms blanket the island, from the hillocks right up to the beaches. The durian, rambutan and *langsat* (a small round fruit similar to rambutans) are also cultivated.

Ecology & Environment

Samui's visitors and inhabitants produce over 50 tonnes of garbage a day, much of it plastic. Not all of it is properly disposed of, and quite a few plastic bottles end up in the sea, where they wreak havoc on marine life. Remember to request glass water bottles instead of plastic, or to try to fill your own water bottle from the guesthouse or hotel restaurant's large, reusable canisters. On Ko Tao the TAT arranges monthly volunteer rubbish collections with half a dozen dive agencies that offer discounts to participating customers; ask your Samui dive shop if a beach cleanup is planned.

Orientation

The population of Ko Samui is mostly concentrated in the port town of Na Thon, on the western side of the island facing the mainland, and in 10 or 11 small villages around the island. One paved road forms a circuit around the island and several side roads extend into the interior, along with a couple of unpaved roads that lead right across the island. One road cuts diagonally across the middle from Bang Po in the

KO SAMUI

To Ko Pha-Ngan (34km)
To Ko Pha-Ngan (15km)
Ko Som
Chong Pha-Ngan
Ao Thong Son
Ao Bang Po
Wat Na Phalan
Laem Na Phra Lan
Ao Thong Sai
Hat Choeng Mon
Ban Tai
Hat Mae Nam
Laem Sai
Wat Phra Yai
Ko Fan Yai
Ko Fan
Causeway
Laem Yai
Ban Bang Po
Mae Nam
Hat Bo Phut
Hat Bang Rak
Ban Bo Phut
Hat Ang Thong
Viewpoint
Buffalo Fighting Stadium
Buffalo Fighting Stadium
Samui Monkey Centre
Airport
To Surat Thani (76km)
Viewpoint
▲ (467m)
Ko Mat Lang
Passenger Ferry
Na Thon
Viewpoint
Wat Pang Bua
Samui International Hospital
Ban Chaweng
North Chaweng
4169
▲ (465m)
Buffalo Fighting Stadium
To Ang Thong National Marine Park
Nam Tok Hin Lat
Viewpoint
Samui Highlands
Hat Chaweng
Hat Chaweng Noi
Ao Chon Khram
Khao Pom (630m)
4169
Laem Chon Khram
Ban Lipa Noi
Buffalo Fighting Stadium
Coral Cove
4174
Ao Thong Yang
Ban Saket
Nam Tok Na Muang
Ao Thong Ta Khian
Vehicle & Passenger Ferry
Thong Yang
4169
Khao Phlu (565m)
Ban Lamai
Ao Taling Ngam
Buffalo Fighting Stadium
Ban Hua Thanon
Hat Lamai
To Don Sak (30km), Khanom (35km) & Surat Thani (76km)
Ban Taling Ngam
Buffalo Fighting Stadium
Ban Thurian
Wat Khunaram
GULF OF THAILAND
Ao Phangkha
4170
Khao Khwang (410m)
Ban Bang Kao
Wat Samret
Ao Bang Nam Cheut
Ban Thong Krut
Ao Na Khai
Laem Hin Khom
Khao Thaleh
Ao Thong Krut
Wat Laem So
Ao Bang Kao
Laem Set

To Ko Taen (3km), Ko Mat Sum (6km), Ko Mot Daeng (7km) & Ko Rap (13km)

0   2.5   5km
0   1.5   3mi

SOUTHERN GULF

island's north-western corner all the way to Ban Lamai. Along the way are several hilltop vantage points that provide views of the surrounding hills and even the sea in the distance. At intervals along this road you'll find small restaurants that provide refreshment coupled with a view.

Maps In Surat Thani or on Ko Samui, you can pick up the TAT's helpful *Surat Thani* map, which has maps of Surat Thani, the province, Ang Thong National Marine Park and Ko Samui, along with travel information. A couple of private companies now do maps of Ko Samui, Ko Pha-Ngan and Ko Tao, which are available for 50B in the tourist areas of Surat and on the islands. Visid Hongsombud's *Guide Map of Koh*

Samui, Koh Pha-Ngan & Koh Tao is also good. If you fly into Samui airport, you may be handed the free Bangkok Airways island map, which isn't bad for a freebie.

Information
When to Go The best time to visit the Samui group of islands is during the hot and dry season, from February to late June. From July to October it can be raining on and off, and from October to January there are sometimes heavy winds. On the other hand, many travellers have reported fine weather (and fewer crowds) in September and October. November tends to get some of the rain that also affects the east coast of Malaysia at this time. Prices tend to soar from December to July, whatever the weather.

Tourist Offices The new and helpful TAT office (☎ 077-420504), at the northern end of Na Thon just off Thanon Thawi Ratchaphakdi, dispenses handy brochures and maps. The office is open from 8.30 am to 4.30 pm daily. The local tourist police can be reached by calling ☎ 077-421281 or ☎ 1155.

Immigration Offices Travellers can extend tourist visas by 30 days (or visa on arrival by 10 days) for a fee of 500B at the Ko Samui immigration office (☎ 077-421069). It's about 3km south of Na Thon at the intersection of the round-island road (Rte 4169) and the road that leads to the Samui Hospital (Rte 4172). Hours are 8.30 am to noon and 1 to 4.30 pm weekdays (closed public holidays).

Money Changing money isn't a problem in Na Thon, Chaweng or Lamai, where several banks or exchange booths offer daily exchange services. ATMs can be found in Na Thon and Chaweng.

Post The island's main post office is in Na Thon, but in other parts of the island there are privately run branches. The main office is open from 8.30 am to 4.30 pm weekdays and 9 am to noon on Saturday. Many bungalow operations also sell stamps and mail letters, but most charge a commission.

Telephone International telephone service is available on the 2nd floor of the CAT office, attached to Na Thon's main post office, from 7 am to 10 pm daily. Many private phone offices around the island will make a connection for a surcharge above the usual Telephone Organization of Thailand (TOT) or CAT rates.

Email & Internet Access There are several places in Na Thon, Chaweng and Lamai that allow you to send and receive email and surf the Web. In Chaweng, Travel Solutions, on the beach, and La Dolce Vita, next to Swensen's, are helpful and have some atmosphere.

Internet Resources The Web site Koh Samui Thailand at www.sawadee.com contains lists of information on dive centres, tours and accommodation, plus timetables for Bangkok Airways, ferries, trains and VIP buses.

Travel Agencies Efficient and reliable Travel Solutions (☎/fax 077-230706, ☎ 230202/3, e ttsolutions@hotmail.com), on Chaweng beach directly in front of Coconut Grove, can help with the usual international travel, accommodation and visa arrangements as well as helping with all national and local travel decisions, such as choosing between the many diving operations on Samui. Surat Thani travel agents Phantip (☎ 077-421221/2) and Songserm (☎ 077-421316) have offices in Na Thon.

Newspapers & Magazines A free home-grown, tourist-oriented newspaper with articles in German, English and Thai, *Samui Welcome* comes out monthly. *What's on Samui*, *Samui Guide* and the pocket-sized *Accommodation Samui* are free and contain listings of hotels, restaurants and suggestions of things to do, buried beneath scads of ads.

Medical Services
The following places are about the best places on Samui for medical treatment:

Muang Thai Clinic (☎ 077-424219) Hat Lamai; open from 9 to 11 am and 5 to 7 pm daily. House calls can be arranged if necessary.
Samui International Clinic (☎ 01-606 5833, 077-230186) Main Ring Road, Chaweng; open from 11 am to 7 pm daily. House calls are available from 9 am to 9 pm, and English and German are spoken.
Samui International Hospital (Chaweng Hospital; ☎ 077-422272, 230781) This is your best bet for just about any medical or dental problem. Emergency ambulance service is available 24 hours and credit cards are accepted for treatment fees. It's located opposite the Muang Kulaypan Hotel.

Dangers & Annoyances Several travellers have written to warn others to take care when making train and bus bookings. Bookings sometimes aren't made at all, the bus turns out to be far inferior to the one expected or other hassles develop. In another scam involving air tickets, agents say economy class is fully booked and that only business class is available; the agent then sells the customer an air ticket – at business-class prices – that turns out to be economy class.

As on Phuket, the rate of fatalities on Samui due to road accidents is quite high. This is due mainly to the large number of tourists who rent motorcycles only to find out that Samui's winding roads, stray dogs and coconut trucks can be lethal to those who have never dealt with them. If you feel you must rent a motorcycle, protect yourself by wearing a helmet, shoes and appropriate clothing when driving.

Waterfalls

Besides the beaches and rustic, thatched-roof bungalows, Samui has a couple of waterfalls. **Nam Tok Hin Lat** (Hin Lat Falls) is worth a visit if you're waiting in Na Thon for a boat back to the mainland. You can get here on foot – walk 3km or so south of town on the main road, turning left (east) at the road that leads to Samui Hospital in the opposite direction. Go straight along this road about 2km to arrive at the entrance to the waterfall. From here, it's about a half-hour walk along a trail to the top of the falls.

Nam Tok Na Muang, in the centre of the island (the turn-off is 10km south of Na Thon), is more scenic and less frequented. There are several levels. The lower falls is smaller but has a large pool suitable for swimming and is directly accessible from the road. To reach the upper falls requires a 1.5km hike – from the uppermost level the view extends to the sea. Săwngthăew from Na Thon cost about 20B – they can also be hired at Chaweng and Lamai beaches.

Temples

For temple enthusiasts **Wat Laem Saw**, at the southern end of the island near the village of Bang Kao, features an interesting and highly venerated old Srivijaya-style chedi. This chedi is very similar to the one in Chaiya (see that section earlier in this chapter).

At the northern end, on a small rocky island joined to Samui by a causeway, is the so-called **Temple of the Big Buddha**, or Wat Phra Yai. Erected in 1972, the modern image is about 12m high, and makes a pretty silhouette against the tropical sky and sea behind it. The image is surrounded by *kùtì* (meditation huts), mostly unoccupied. The monks prefer to receive visitors there. A sign in English requests that proper attire (no shorts or sleeveless shirts) be worn on the premises.

There is also an old semi-abandoned temple, **Wat Pang Bua**, near the northern end of Hat Chaweng, where 10-day *vipassana* (insight meditation) courses are occasionally held for fàràng; the courses are led by monks from Wat Suanmok in Chaiya.

Near the car park at the entrance to Nam Tok Hin Lat is another trail left to **Suan Dharmapala**, a meditation temple. Another attraction is the ghostly **mummified monk** at Wat Khunaram, south of Rte 4169 between Ban Thurian and Ban Hua Thanon. The monk, Luang Phaw Daeng, has been dead over two decades but his corpse is preserved sitting in a meditative pose and sporting a pair of sun glasses.

At **Wat Samret** near Ban Hua Thanon you can see a typical Mandalay sitting Buddha carved from solid marble – common in Northern Thailand but rarer in the south. A collection of antique Buddha images is housed in a hall on the monastery grounds. A number of the images were stolen recently, so if you want to view the Buddhas, ask one of the monks to unlock the hall and be prepared to leave a small donation.

Ang Thong National Marine Park
อุทยานแห่งชาติหมู่เกาะอ่างทอง

This archipelago of around 40 small islands combines sheer limestone cliffs, hidden lagoons, white-sand beaches and dense vegetation to provide a nearly postcard-perfect opportunity to enjoy gulf islands. The park encompasses 18 sq km of islands, plus 84 sq km of marine environments.

From Ko Samui, a couple of tour operators run day trips to the Ang Thong archipelago, 31km north-west of the island. A typical tour leaves Na Thon at 8.30 am and returns at 5.30 pm. Lunch is included, along with a climb to the top of a 240m hill to view the whole island group, and snorkelling in a sort of lagoon formed by the island from which Ang Thong (Golden Jar) gets its name. Some tours also visit **Tham Bua Bok**, a cavern containing lotus-shaped cave formations. Tours depart daily in the high season, less frequently in the rainy season. At least once a month there's an overnight tour. The tours are getting mostly good reviews, although one reader complained that the tour was 'not informative'. Bring hiking shoes (the 400m climb on Ko Wua demands some kind of reasonable footwear), snorkelling gear, a hat and plenty of sunscreen and drinking water. You may be able to book a passage alone to the Ang Thong islands; inquire at Travel Solutions in Chaweng (☎ 077-230706).

At the park headquarters (☎ 077-286025) on Ko Wat Ta Lap you can rent eight- to 10-person *bungalows* for 800B a night and large *tents* for 200B. Reservations can be made by calling the park headquarters. The usual national park entry fees apply (see the Facts about Thailand chapter for details).

You can also arrange to join a more active but more expensive Ang Thong kayak trip through Blue Stars at Gallery La Fayette (☎ 077-230497) in Hat Chaweng. The cost of 1990B per person includes several hours of paddling on stable open-top kayaks, light breakfast, lunch, nonalcoholic beverages, pick-up anywhere on Samui, as well as insurance.

Yet another alternative is to get a group together, charter your own boat and design your own Ang Thong itinerary. This is what Richard, Francoise, Etienne and the rest of the fictional crew in the novel/movie *The Beach* did.

Buffalo Fighting
Local villagers love to bet on duelling water buffaloes and events are arranged on a rotating basis at seven rustic fighting rings around the island in Na Thon, Saket, Na Muang, Hua Thanon, Chaweng, Mae Nam and Bo Phut. In these events two buffaloes face off and, at their owners' urging, lock horns and/or butt one another until one of the animals backs down. The typical encounter lasts only a few seconds, and rarely are the animals injured. As such events go, it's fairly tame – certainly far more humane than dogfighting, cockfighting or Spanish bullfighting. Tourists are charged 150B to 200B entry.

Samui Monkey Centre
Coconut plantation owners have been using trained macaques to climb coconut trees and harvest coconuts for decades. Despite the sign out front that reads 'Monkey Theatre', the Samui Monkey Centre (☎ 077-245140) is not a venue for *lákhon ling* (Thai drama that utilises monkeys as actors). Instead it's more like the 'working elephant' shows in Chiang Mai, with monkeys (and elephants) going through their work routines for the tourists.

Not a bad diversion if you're travelling with kids. Show times are at 10.30 am and 2 and 4 pm daily. The entrance fee is 150B per adult, 50B for kids under eight years old. The Samui Monkey Centre is located about half a kilometre south of Ban Bo Phut.

Diving
Those in the know say that the waters around Ko Tao are much more scenic than Samui's, but if you're only interested in getting certified, doing it on Samui is cheaper. Many dive operations have opened around the island. The franchised operations such as Easy Divers and SIDS get a large share of the business, but the smaller dive companies are often more flexible than their larger competitors.

Beach dives cost around 900B per day. Dives from boats start from 2000B, and a four-day certification course starts at 6500B and rises to 14,000B for the beach and boat option. An overnight dive trip to Ko Tao, including food and accommodation, can be done for as little as 4500B, plus 900B for each additional day.

The highest concentration of dive shops is at Hat Chaweng. Among the more established are:

Calypso Diving (☎ 077-422437) Hat Chaweng
Dive Indeep (☎ 077-230155, Ⓔindeep@ samart.co.th) Hat Chaweng
Easy Divers (☎ 077-413371, fax 413374) Hat Chaweng & Hat Lamai
Samui International Diving School (SIDS; ☎/fax 077-231242, 422386 Ⓔ cesareb@ samart.co.th) Na Thon, Hat Lamai, Bo Phut & Hat Chaweng
The Dive Shop (☎/fax 077-230232, Ⓔ diveshop@samart.co.th) Hat Chaweng

Muay Thai
In Na Thon and Chaweng there are *muay thai* (Thai boxing) rings with regularly scheduled matches. Admission to most fights is around 100B. The quality of the mostly local contestants isn't exactly top-notch.

Paddling
Blue Stars (☎/fax 077-230497), in Gallery La Fayette in Hat Chaweng, offers guided kayak trips in Ang Thong National Marine Park, along with cave exploring, snorkelling and speedboat transfer. These trips can also be booked through travel agencies.

Cooking Courses

Samui Institute of Thai Culinary Arts (SITCA; ☎/fax 077-413172) offers daily Thai cooking classes (including vegetarian dishes) as well as courses in the aristocratic Thai art of carving fruits and vegetables into intricate floral designs. One-day cooking classes cost 1650B and include a five-course group dinner for students and a companion of their choice. SITCA is located down the soi opposite the Central Samui Beach Resort.

Na Thon

หน้าทอน

Na Thon (pronounced *nâa thawn*), on the north-western side of the island, is where express and night passenger ferries from the piers in Surat Thani arrive. Car ferries from Don Sak and Khanom land at Ao Thong Yang, about 10km south of Na Thon. If you're not travelling on a combination ticket you'll probably end up spending some time in Na Thon on your way in or out, waiting for the next ferry. Or if you're a long-term beachcomber, it makes a nice change to come into Na Thon once in a while for a little town life.

Although it's basically a tourist town now, Na Thon still sports a few old teak Chinese shophouses and cafes along Thanon Ang Thong.

Places to Stay If you want or need to stay in Ko Samui's largest settlement (population 4000), there are several places to choose from.

The *Palace Hotel (Chai Thaleh; ☎ 077-421079)*, near the waterfront, has spacious rooms starting at 400B with fan and 550B with air-con. The friendly *Win Hotel (☎ 077-421500)* farther down the road has all air-con rooms with TV and hot water for 550B, plus a nice coffee shop downstairs. Around the corner from the Win Hotel is the similar four-storey *Seaview Hotel (☎ 077-421481)*, with good fan rooms for 300B, and rooms with air-con, TV, phone and fridge for 500B.

On the main road north out of town is the *Dum Rong Town Hotel (☎ 077-420359)*, which charges from 550B for double rooms with air-con and bathroom. *Chao Koh Bungalow (☎ 077-421157)*, just north of town nearer to the sea, has rooms for 350B with fan and attached bathroom, 700B with air-con.

SOUTHERN GULF

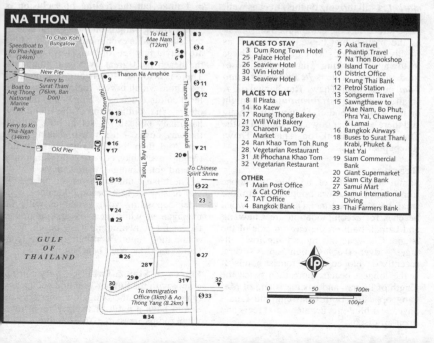

NA THON

PLACES TO STAY
3 Dum Rong Town Hotel
25 Palace Hotel
26 Seaview Hotel
30 Win Hotel
34 Seaview Hotel

PLACES TO EAT
8 Il Pirata
14 Ko Kaew
17 Roung Thong Bakery
21 Will Wait Bakery
23 Charoen Lap Day Market
24 Ran Khao Tom Toh Rung
28 Vegetarian Restaurant
31 Jit Phochana Khao Tom
32 Vegetarian Restaurant

OTHER
1 Main Post Office & Cat Office
2 TAT Office
4 Bangkok Bank

5 Asia Travel
6 Phantip Travel
7 Na Thon Bookshop
9 Island Tour
10 District Office
11 Krung Thai Bank
12 Petrol Station
13 Songserm Travel
15 Sawngthaew to Mae Nam, Bo Phut, Phra Yai, Chaweng & Lamai
16 Bangkok Airways
18 Buses to Surat Thani, Krabi, Phuket & Hat Yai
19 Siam Commercial Bank
20 Giant Supermarket
22 Siam City Bank
27 Samui Mart
29 Samui International Diving
33 Thai Farmers Bank

SOUTHERN GULF

Places to Eat There are several good restaurants and watering holes in Na Thon. On the road facing the harbour, the ***Roung Thong Bakery***, with home-made pastries and coffee as well as Thai standards, is a popular place to hang around while waiting for a boat. Nearby ***Ko Kaew*** also serves good Thai dishes and seafood.

Towards the Palace Hotel is a Thai rice and noodle place that's open all night, ***Ran Khao Tom Toh Rung*** (no Roman-script sign) – the cheapest place to eat on this strip. During the high season, many restaurants fill up at night with travellers waiting for the night ferry. After midnight the only place open is the Ran Khao Tom Toh Rung.

On the next street back from the harbour are a few old Chinese coffee shops. On Thanon Na Amphoe look for ***Il Pirata***, a tastefully decorated open-air restaurant/cafe serving pizza, pasta, Thai dishes, sandwiches, juices, coffee, wine and beer.

The third street back from the harbour mostly has travel agencies, photo shops and other small businesses. Two small supermarkets, ***Giant Supermarket*** and ***Samui Mart***, are also here. The ***Charoen Lap day market*** is still thriving on this street as well. The ***Will Wait Bakery***, to the north on the same street, has the same appetising menu as the branch in Chaweng – as well as freshly baked goods. One of the few places in town still serving Thai (and Chinese) food on a large scale is ***Jit Phochana Khao Tom*** on Thanon Thawi Ratchaphakdi. A small ***vegetarian restaurant*** opens at night on the southern end of Thanon Ang Thong and there's another down the soi next to the Thai Farmers Bank on Thanon Thawi Ratchaphakdi.

Beaches

Samui has plenty of beaches to choose from, with bungalows popping up at more small bays all the time. The most crowded beaches for accommodation are **Chaweng** and **Lamai**, both on the eastern side of the island. Chaweng has more bungalow 'villages' – over 80 at last count – plus several recently developed flashy tourist hotels. It is the longest beach, more than twice the length of Lamai, and has the island of **Mat Lang** opposite. Both Chaweng and Lamai have clear blue-green water, coral reefs and open-air discos.

Perhaps there's a bit more to do in Hat Lamai because of its proximity to two villages – Ban Lamai and Ban Hua Thanon. At the wát in Ban Lamai is the **Ban Lamai Cultural Hall**, a sort of folk museum displaying local ceramics, household utensils, hunting weapons and musical instruments. The drawback to Lamai is the rather sleazy atmosphere of the strip of beer bars behind the beach; Chaweng's bar-and-disco strip is decidedly more sophisticated and more congenial for couples or single women.

Chaweng is the target of current upmarket development because of its long beach. Another factor is that only Chaweng (and the northern part of Lamai) has water deep enough for swimming from October to April; at most other beaches on the island the water becomes very shallow during these months.

For more peace and quiet, try the beaches along the north, south and west coasts. **Mae Nam**, **Bo Phut** and **Bang Rak** (also known as Big Buddha or Phra Yai) are along the northern end; Bo Phut and Bang Rak are part of a bay that holds **Ko Fan** (the island with the Big Buddha), separated by a small headland. The water here is not quite as clear as at Chaweng or Lamai, but the feeling of seclusion is greater, and accommodation is cheaper.

Hat Thong Yang is on the western side of the island and is even more secluded. There are only a few sets of bungalows here, but the beach isn't great by Samui standards. There is also **Hat Ang Thong**, just north of Na Thon, which is very rocky but has more local colour (such as fishing boats) than the others. The southern end of the island now has many bungalows, set in little out-of-the-way coves – it's worth seeking them out. And then there's everywhere in between – every bay, cove or cape with a strip of sand gets a bungalow nowadays.

Theft isn't unknown on the island. If you're staying in a beach bungalow, consider depositing your valuables with the management while off on excursions around the island or swimming at the beach. Most of the theft reports continue to come from Lamai and Mae Nam beaches.

Places to Stay & Eat Prices vary considerably with the time of year and occupancy rates. Some of the bungalow operators on Samui have a habit of tripling room rates when rooms are scarce, so a hut that's 200B in June could be 600B in August. Rates given in this section can only serve as a guide – they could go lower if you bargain, or higher if space is tight.

Everyone has his or her own idea of the perfect beach bungalow. At Ko Samui, the search could take a month or two, with more than 250 licensed places to choose from. Most offer roughly the same services and accommodation for 300B to 500B, although some cost quite a bit more. The best thing to do is to go to the beach you think you want to stay at and pick one you like – look inside the huts, check out the restaurant, the menu, the guests. You can always move if you're not satisfied.

Beach accommodation around Samui now falls into four basic categories, chronicling the evolution of places to stay on the island. The first phase included simple bungalows with thatched roofs and walls of local, easily replaceable materials; the next phase introduced concrete bathrooms attached to the old-style huts; a transition to the third phase brought concrete walls and tile roofs – the predominant style now, with more-advanced facilities like fans and sometimes air-con. The latest wave is luxury rooms and bungalows that are indistinguishable from mainland inns and hotels.

For a pretty basic bungalow with private bathroom, 150B is the minimum you'll pay on Ko Samui. Generally anything that costs less than 150B a night will mean a shared bathroom.

Food is touch and go at all the beaches – one meal can be great, the next at the very same place not so great. Fresh seafood is usually best and the cheapest way to eat it is to buy it in one of the many fishing villages around the island, direct from the fisherfolk themselves, or in the village markets and have the bungalow cooks prepare it for you. Good places to buy are in the relatively large Muslim fishing villages of Mae Nam, Bo Phut and Hua Thanon.

The island has changed so much in the years between editions of this book that we hesitate to name favourites. Cooks come and go, bungalows flourish and go bankrupt, owners are assassinated by competitors – you never can tell from season to season. Prices have remained fairly stable here in recent years, but they are creeping up. With the establishment of several places

charging well over 3000B per night, the jet-set has discovered Samui. Finally, if Samui isn't to your liking, move islands! Think about Ko Pha-Ngan or Ko Tao.

What follows are some general comments on staying at Samui's various beaches, moving clockwise around the island from Na Thon.

Ban Tai
บ้านใต้(อ่าวบางปอ)

Ban Tai (Ao Bang Po) is the first beach area north of Na Thon with accommodation; so far there are just a handful of places to stay here. The beach has fair snorkelling and swimming. The *Axolotl Village* (☎/fax 077-420017, e info@axolotlvillage.com), run by an Italian-German partnership, caters to Europeans (the staff speak English, Italian and German) with tastefully designed, mid-range rooms for 350B to 450B, and 35 bungalows for 550B to 1500B. Meditation and massage rooms are available. A very pleasant restaurant area overlooking the beach has an inventive menu featuring vegetarian, Italian and Thai dishes.

Also at Ban Tai is *Sunbeam* (☎ 077-420600), a group of 500B bungalows in a nice setting, all with private bathroom.

At the extreme new-age end of the spectrum lies the *Healing Child Resort* (☎ 077-420124, fax 420145, e contactus@healingchild.com), a set of brick buildings with rooms costing from 150B to 250B in the low season and up to 400B to 600B in the high. You may order health food from a menu or join the communal meals for 75B. Among the many services offered are 'brain hemisphere tuning and balancing', 'small intestine cleaning' and 'vortex destiny astrology', along with pyramid-scheming invitations to become 'overseas reps, agents, distributors or business partners'.

Hat Mae Nam
หาดแม่น้ำ

Hat Mae Nam, 14km from Na Thon, is expanding rapidly in terms of bungalow development – there are still a few cheapies left but prices are going steadily up.

At the headland (Laem Na Phra Lan) where Ao Bang Po meets Hat Mae Nam is the *Home Bay Bungalows* (☎ 077-247214), with fan bungalows for 300B and air-con bungalows for 800B. Next is *Phalarn Inn* (☎ 077-247111), which has bungalows of wood and concrete for 200B, as well as one air-con bungalow for 500B; followed by *Harry's* (☎ 077-425447), with bungalows from 350B for fan to 500B for air-con. Also in this area is *Sea Fan* (☎ 077-425204), an upmarket place with rooms starting at 3300B.

The beach in front of Wat Na Phalan is undeveloped and the locals hope it will stay that way – topless bathing is strongly discouraged here.

The next group of places east includes *Anong Villa* (☎ 077-247256), with bungalows from 300B to 700B with fan, and 800B with air-con. *Palm Point Village* (☎ 077-425095) has nice ambience and 350B fan bungalows (air-con is available for 800B). Another choice is *Shady Shack Bungalows* (☎ 077-425392), where prices run from 300B to 600B. *Golden Hut* (☎ 077-425351) has all-fan bungalows for 200B to 300B. *Maenam Resort* (☎ 077-425116) is an upper-budget place with spacious bungalows for 700B to 1000B. *New Sunrise Village* (☎ 077-247219) has a wide assortment of fan accommodation for 150B to 500B, depending on size and proximity to the beach.

Cleopatra's Place (☎ 077-425486), in the middle of Hat Mae Nam, has been recommended for its good seafood and bungalows right on the beach. Fan bungalows cost 200B to 350B, while air-con costs 800B. Discounts are given for long-term stays.

Right on the beach in Hat Mae Nam is *Friendly* (☎ 077-425484), which has clean, well-kept huts for 200B, all with private bathroom. Also good are *New La Paz Villa* (☎ 077-425296), with fan rooms for 300B and air-con from 700B. *Magic View* must be among the cheapest places to stay on the entire island – 80B for a very small hut and 150B for bigger ones with toilet and shower. They're old but quite acceptable. Nearby *Maenam Villa* (☎ 077-425501) has slightly better fan bungalows for 200B to 400B.

Ban Mae Nam's huge *Santiburi Dusit Resort* (☎ 077-425031–8), complete with tennis courts, waterways, ponds, bakery and sports facilities, charges from US$238 in the low season and from US$340 in the high season. Another top-ender is *Paradise Beach Resort* (☎ 077-247227, fax 425290, 18/8 Hat Mae Nam), with deluxe rooms for 3800/4800B in the low/high season, plus Thai-style villas from 4800/5800B low/high season. There's a beachfront restaurant, pool, spa bath and car-rental service as well.

There are at least 10 or 15 other bungalow operations between Laem Na Phra Lan and Laem Sai, where Ao Mae Nam ends.

Hat Bo Phut
หาดบ่อผุด

This beach has a reputation for peace and quiet, and those who regularly come here hope it will stay that way; this is not the place to show up looking for a party. The beach tends to be a little on the muddy side and the water can be too shallow for swimming during the dry season – a curse that can be a blessing because it keeps development rather low-key and has preserved Bo Phut's village atmosphere.

Near Bo Phut village there's a string of bungalows in all price ranges, including the farthest north, budget-friendly *Sunny* (☎ 077-427031), with all fan bungalows for 200B to 400B. Next to it is the new *Starfish & Coffee Bungalows* (☎ 077-425085), which has pleasant glass-fronted bungalows on the beach for 650B, or 1000B if you use the air-con. Fan duplexes a bit inland cost 450B. *Sandy Resort* (☎ 077-425353) offers wood-and-concrete bungalows for 750B with fan and 1000B with air-con. Breakfast is included in these prices.

The upmarket *World Resort* (☎ 077-425355) has a pool and a wide range of bungalows (350B with fan, and up to 2250B with air-con, breakfast included), while at the long-running, well-managed *Peace Bungalow* (☎ 077-425357), rooms go for 600B to 2500B, depending on amenities and proximity to the shore.

More money to spend? Go for semi-luxurious *Samui Palm Beach* (☎ 077-425494) at 3300B to 6500B, or *Samui Euphoria* (☎ 077-425100), a posh spot with rooms and bungalows for 2500B and up (2000B low season), including breakfast.

Proceeding east, a road off the main round-island road runs to the left and along the bay towards the village. One of the golden oldies here is ***Ziggy Stardust*** (☎ *077-425173*), a clean, well-landscaped and popular place with huts for 300B and a couple of nicer family bungalows with air-con, hot water and fridge for 1000B. Next to Ziggy's is the brightly coloured ***Rasta Baby*** (☎ *077-245295*), a small hotel with rooms for 200B to 300B with fan. It's friendly but the rooms are a tad squalid – then again most guests are too stoned to notice. Nearby, on the inland side where there's no sea view, ***Smile House*** (☎ *077-425361*) charges 400B to 500B for fan rooms, and 1400B for air-con. There's also a large swimming pool.

Up the street from Smile and facing the ocean is ***The Lodge*** (☎ *077-425337*), featuring an interesting three-storey design. Rooms with air-con and TV cost 1200B to 1400B. Next door you'll find the original ***Boon Bungalows*** (☎ *077-425362*), still holding on with cheap, closely spaced huts from 100B to 200B a night.

If you continue through the village along the water, you'll find the isolated ***Sand View*** (☎ *077-425438*), with huts for 200B to 400B. This area is sometimes called Hat Bang Rak. ***Summer Night Resort*** (☎ *077-425199*) stretches over a fairly large area and offers fan rooms for 400B and air-con at 600B.

The village has a couple of cheap local-style restaurants as well as French, German, Spanish and Italian restaurants. ***Bird in the Hand*** next door to The Lodge serves good, reasonably priced Thai and Western food in a rustic setting overlooking the water. A little farther east on Bo Phut's main street, a food stall called ***Ubon Wan Som Tam*** serves cheap and tasty Isan food.

Hat Bang Rak
หาดบางรักษ์

Hat Bang Rak (also called Hat Phra Yai, Big Buddha Beach) has nearly 15 bungalow operations. The best is the moderately expensive, very well kept ***Comfort Nara Garden Resort*** (☎ *077-425364, fax 425292*), with air-con rooms starting at 1120B, nicely landscaped grounds, a seaside restaurant and a small swimming pool. It's just a 10-minute, 30B van ride from the airport and is hence a favourite with Bangkok Airways flight crews. This is also one of the cheapest places where you can make reservations.

The ***Pongpetch Servotel*** (☎ *077-245100*) has all air-con bungalows with TV and fridge ranging from 500B to 1300B, depending on the size and location.

The pleasant ***Secret Garden Bungalows*** (☎ *077-425419, fax 245253*) is a good choice, with A-frame bungalows starting at 400B (1200B to 1500B with air-con); all have nice sitting areas in front. There's also a beach pub and restaurant.

The well-run ***Como's Bungalow*** (☎ *077-425210*) has comfortable concrete bungalows for 300B with fan. A better deal is the wooden 600B air-con bungalow that sleeps three.

LA Resort (☎ *077-425330*) is about the cheapest place here, with prices ranging from 200B for a small room close to the road to 400B for a big bungalow on the beach.

Ao Thong Son & Ao Thong Sai
อ่าวท้องสน/อ่าวท้องทราย

The big cape between Hat Bang Rak and Chaweng is actually a series of four capes and coves, the first of which is Ao Thong Son. The road to Thong Son is a bit on the hellish side, but that keeps this area quiet and secluded. ***Samui Thongson Resort*** (☎ *077-230799*) was undergoing renovations at last visit but fan rooms were expected to cost around 800B. ***Thongson Bay Bungalows*** next door has old-style bungalows for 250B to 500B for fan, 1000B for air-con.

The next cove along is as yet undeveloped. The third, Ao Thong Sai, has the heavily guarded ***Tongsai Bay Cottages & Hotel*** (☎ *077-425015, fax 425462*, e *tongsai@ loxinfo.co.th; in Bangkok* ☎ *02-254 0056, fax 254 0054*), with 72 suites (most with private spa bath) and a swimming pool, tennis courts and private beach. Rates start at 11,770B.

Hat Choeng Mon
หาดเชิงมน

The largest cove following Ao Thong Sai has several names, but the beach is generally known as Hat Choeng Mon. It's clean, quiet and recommended for families or for those who don't need nightlife and a variety of restaurants (these can be found at nearby Hat Chaweng anyway).

At Choeng Mon you'll find the well-run, popular *PS Villa* (☎ 077-425160). You'll pay for 400B for fan bungalows, while air-con ones go for 700B to 1500B. *Choeng Mon Bungalow* has small but passable concrete bungalows with fan for 200B. Air-con goes for 600B, or 800B with TV and fridge. *Chat Kaew Resort* has decent wooden bungalows with fan for 350B, and concrete ones with air-con for 500B. *Island View* (250B to 800B) and the well laid-out *Sun Sand Resort* have sturdy thatched-roof bungalows connected by wooden walkways on a breezy hillside. The establishment was undergoing renovations at last visit but was expected to offer fan rooms for 500B to 750B, depending on proximity to the beach. Across from the beach is **Ko Fan Yai**, an island that can be reached on foot in low tide.

Between Choeng Mon Bungalow Village and PS Villa are two top-end places. The 216-room *Imperial Boat House Hotel* (☎ 077-425041, ⓔ imperial@ksc.net.th; in Bangkok fax 02-261 9533) has a three-storey hotel with rooms for 3500B and 34 separate two-storey bungalows made from authentic teak rice-barges for 6500B. Amenities include two restaurants, a beach bar, air-con lobby lounge and a boat-shaped swimming pool. Just north is *The White House* (☎ 077-245315, fax 425233, ⓔ whitehouse@sawadee.com; in Bangkok ☎ 02-237 8734), a collection of deluxe bungalows costing from 3900B to 4500B (700B less in the low season). The hotel motto is 'Where each guest is a president!'.

Next is a smaller bay called Ao Yai Noi, just before North Chaweng. This little bay is quite picturesque, with large boulders framing the white-sand beach. At the secluded *IKK Bay Resort*, unusual stone bungalows cost 350B to 600B, while the long-running, eco-friendly *Coral Bay Resort* (☎ 077-422223, fax 422392, ⓔ info@coralbay.net) has larger, well-spaced two-person bungalows with air-con, set on grassy grounds with a pool, starting from 2500B (2000B in the low season). Coral Bay Resort serves the best Thai food in the area.

Hat Chaweng
หาดเฉวง

Hat Chaweng, Samui's longest beach, has the island's highest concentration of bunga-

lows and tourist hotels. Prices are moving upmarket fast, and there is a commercial 'strip' behind the central beach jam-packed with restaurants, souvenir shops, bars and discos. So many in fact, that once you're on the strip you may have difficulty finding a path back down to the beach. It's perfectly acceptable to cut through any bungalow establishment to make your way to the beach. The beach is beautiful here, and local developers are finally cleaning up some of the trashy areas behind the bungalows that were becoming a problem in the 1980s.

Chaweng has kilometre after kilometre of bungalows – perhaps 70 or more in all – so have a look around before deciding on a place. There are basically three sections: North Chaweng, Hat Chaweng proper and Chaweng Noi. In this section we don't attempt to describe every single place in existence, but do provide a broad sampling of reliable accommodation in several price ranges.

North Chaweng Places here are mostly in the 400B to 800B range; simple bungalows with private bathroom at the northernmost end go for even less. Besides being less expensive than places farther south, North Chaweng is out of earshot of central Chaweng's throbbing discos.

The *Papillon Resort* (☎/fax 077-231169, 01-476 6169) is the northernmost place and offers concrete bungalows starting at 500B, as well as more-expensive air-con units for 800B to 1250B.

Venus Resort (☎ 077-422406) has fan bungalows for 200B to 500B while *Lazy Wave* (☎ 077-413170) charges 800B with fan only. *Marine Bungalows* has fan units for 200B to 400B, plus air-con for 800B. In this same area *Lagoon Cottages* (☎ 01-979 4740) charges 350B for fan and 900B for air-con.

The well-designed and decorated, vaguely Mediterranean-style *Corto Maltese* (☎/fax 077-230041) is a more upmarket place that seems very popular with the French. A single/double with air-con costs 2990B and rooms sleeping up to four are 4490B. All rooms have air-con, fan, minibar, hot water and TV. On the property there's a pool and bar area as well. Prices are a bit lower at *Chaweng Pearl Cabana* (☎ 077-422116), where you'll pay 500B to 800B for a fan room, up to 1200B for air-con.

At the end nearest to central Chaweng is a small group of upmarket places starting at 3000B or more: *Chaweng Blue Lagoon Hotel* (☎ 077-422037, fax 422401), *Muang Kulaypan Hotel* (☎ 077-422305, e kulaypan@ sawadee.com; in Bangkok ☎ 02-713 0668) and *Amari Palm Reef Resort* (☎ 077-422015, fax 422394; in Bangkok ☎ 02-267 9708, fax 267 9707). The Amari is the nicest of the lot, with individual two-storey, Thai-style cottages and two swimming pools; it's also the most environmentally conscious luxury resort on the island, using filtered sea water for most first uses and recycled grey water for landscaping. Rooms and bungalows start at US$136/145 for singles/doubles and go up to US$203 for a terrace room or suite.

There are also a couple of mid-range places in the area, including *The Island* (☎ 077-230752), which has fan rooms for 450B and air-con for 800B to 1200B. The Island also has a very popular open-air restaurant.

Hat Chaweng Central The central area, Hat Chaweng proper, is the longest and has the most bungalows and hotels. This is also where the strip behind the hotels and huts is centred, with restaurants (most with videos), bars (yes, the girlie bar scene is sneaking in), discos, video parlours, pool halls, tourist police, TAT minioffice, post office, minimarts, one-hour photo-developing labs, tailors, souvenir shops and currency exchange booths.

Water sports are big here too, so you can rent sailboards, go diving, sail a catamaran, charter a junk and so on. Parasailing costs around 400B and water-skiing is 300B per hour. This area also has the highest average prices on the island, not only because accommodation is more upmarket but simply because this is the prettiest beach on the island. In general, the places get more expensive as you move from north to south; many are owned by the same families who owned them under different names 10 or 15 years ago, and some have just added the word 'Resort' to the name.

If you're on a strict budget, *Lucky Mother* (☎ 077-230931), much farther down is among the least-expensive places along this strip, with decent fan bungalows from 250B to 400B. A primitive hut (shared bathroom) is only 150B. Discounts for long-term stays are given during the low season.

OP Bungalow (☎ 077-422424) is the first place at the northern end of central Chaweng and has comfortable concrete bungalows with fan for 500B and air-con for 700B. Air-con bungalows on the edge of the beach go for 1000B. *Samui Natien Resort* (☎ 077-422405, fax 422309) is next and has bungalows set among dense palm and other natural vegetation for 1200B to 1500B. *Chaweng Villa* (☎ 077-231123) offers air-con bungalows for 1700B, while *Coconut Grove* and *Ann Coconut* are central Chaweng bargains at 250B to 400B for fan, 700B and up for air-con. A rather large drawback for some is that these sit smack in the middle of Bangkok Airways' flight path. *Montien House* (☎ 077-422169, fax 421221) has a loyal following for its well-equipped cottages on landscaped grounds, costing from 940B for rooms with fan to 1640B for rooms with air-con, breakfast included. *Samui Royal Beach* (☎ 077-422154, fax 422155) is a bit cheaper at 450B fan, 700B to 800B air-con.

If you're getting the idea that this isn't the beach for budget backpackers, you're right; but surprisingly, a couple of popular cheapies have survived between the 3800B *Beachcomber* (☎ 077-422041, fax 422388) and Central Samui Beach Resort (see entry farther on). The most popular and least expensive of these is *Charlie's Hut* (☎ 077-422343), with huts in the 150B to 300B range. In peak season this place fills early, so to save money it may be easier to go to another beach entirely – or try North Chaweng.

Tradewinds (☎/fax 077-230602) is a newer place where 20 bungalows with air-con, hot water, refrigerators and large balconies face a pleasant garden area. The resort offers dive trips, kayaking, snorkelling and even lawn croquet. Rates are 2000B to 2500B, including breakfast.

A bit farther south, the queen of the central Chaweng properties is the *Central Samui Beach Resort* (☎ 077-230500, fax 422385), a huge neocolonial-style place with rooms starting at 6300B, plus two bars, a restaurant, swimming pool, tennis courts and health centre.

Nearby *Poppies Samui* (☎ 077-422419, fax 422420, e poppies@samart.co.th), inspired by the original Poppies on Bali's

Kuta Beach, offers 24 Thai-style cottages containing everything from IDD phones to atrium baths, for 7240B, including breakfast. Check out its Web site at www.kohsamui.net/poppies.

Finishing off central Chaweng are the established *Joy Resort* (☎ 077-422244) with clean air-con bungalows for 1200B, and the more upmarket *Samui Resotel (Munchies Resort;* ☎ *077-422374, fax 422421)*, with rooms for 1500B to 2000B, depending on whether you stay in the hotel wing or in a bungalow on the beach.

Places to Eat Most bungalows and all the hotels on the beach provide food service of some kind. Back on the 'strip' are dozens of restaurants and cafes serving international cuisines, with Italian places outnumbering the rest. Recommended spots include *Juzz'a Pizza* (pasta, pizza, recorded jazz, near the Green Mango), *Ali Baba* (Indian, north central Chaweng), *The Islander* (moderately priced seafood, up from the Green Mango), *Le Boulangerie* (French bakery, on the main access road to the beach), *Ark Bar* (good 99B Western breakfasts, on the beach), *Bongoes Restaurant & Bar* (everything from pseudo-Thai to burgers, on the beach), *Sea Side Restaurant* (barbecued seafood, on the beach) and two branches of *Will Wait* (decent breakfasts and baked goods) in south and central Chaweng.

Entertainment The *Reggae Pub* is part of a huge zoo-like complex off the beach with several bars and a huge open-air dance floor. It hosts a 'rasta full-moon party' and frequent beer-drinking contests. Another popular dance place is the *Green Mango*, which stays open late.

A newer club is *Full Cycle*, a techno dance club with a stark, modern decor. *Santa Fe*, a huge place with an American South-West theme, is popular with young Thais. *Sweet Soul* is another all-night dance place.

A couple of mellower alternatives to the raging clubs are *The Club* and *Frog & Gecko Pub;* the latter has a satellite TV set to the sports channel.

Penny Lane Rock Cafe plays classic rock tracks from the 1960s to the 1990s, and also supplies satellite TV, darts, snooker, backgammon and other pub diversions.

In the evenings *The Mask,* on the beach near Bongoes Restaurant & Bar, sets up grass mats, cushions and low tables on the sand for drinks under the stars. At last visit the management indicated that The Mask was due for a name change.

Chaweng Noi This area is off by itself around a headland at the southern end of central Hat Chaweng. One place that straddles the headland on both bays is the aptly named *First Bungalow Beach Resort* (☎ 077-422327, fax 422243), the first built on this beach in 1970. It's gone way upmarket since then, and a room in the main building costs 3500B and a bungalow on the beach costs 4000B, although discounts of 500B are sometimes given. Rooms at the *Fair House Beach Resort & Hotel* (☎ 077-422256, fax 422373) start at 2500B in the hotel wing, 2900B to 3500B for bungalows. The *New Star* (☎ 077-422407, fax 422346) is cheaper, with comfortable bungalows for 1200B to 1800B, depending on size. The advantage to staying in this area is that it's fairly insulated from the glitz and clatter of central Chaweng.

The plush, multistorey *Imperial Samui Hotel* (☎ 077-422020, fax 422396) is built on a slope in the middle of Chaweng Noi proper and prices start at 5850B for air-con accommodation with telephone and TV – up to 40% less in the low season. The Imperial's 56 cottages and 24-room hotel are built in a pseudo-Mediterranean style with two swimming pools and a terrace restaurant with a view. Finally there's the 120-room, hotel-style *Victorian Resort* (☎ 077-422011, fax 422111), with all air-con rooms starting at 1890B, including breakfast. Amenities include a restaurant, swimming pool and sauna.

Coral Cove (Ao Thong Yang)
อ่าวท้องยาง

Another series of capes and coves starts at the end of Chaweng Noi, beginning with scenic Coral Cove (or Ao Thong Yang, but not to be confused with the bay of the same name on the western side of the island). The only establishment with immediate beach access is *Coral Cove Resort* (☎ 077-422126), where bungalows cost 600B with fan, 1200B with air-con.

Ao Thong Ta Khian, Ko Samui, Surat Thani Province

ANDREW LUBRAN

A sea of masts in a southern-Thai port

CHRIS MELLOR

Ko Nang Yuan, Surat Thani Province

Shady path on Ko Tao, Surat Thani Province

Paradise Bungalows, Ko Samui, Surat Thani

Nearby is the more upmarket *Coral Cove Chalet* (☎ 077-422173, 422496), with nicely furnished air-con rooms with TV for 2200B single/double. A restaurant on the property serves Thai, Chinese and Western dishes. Other amenities include a pub, conference room and swimming pool. Farther south is the friendly *Blue Horizon Bungalows* (☎ 077-422426, fax 230293, ℮ montien@ samart.co.th), with fan rooms for 400B, small air-con rooms for 700B and a larger bungalow for 900B.

Hi Coral Cove (☎ 077-422495), on a lovely, remote spot above the bay, charges 300B for fan, and 700B to 900B for air-con, including breakfast – good value if you don't mind walking to the beach. The bungalows at *Beverly Hills Resort & Restaurant* (☎ 077-422232) sit atop a cliff overlooking Hat Chaweng. High-season rates are 300B for huts with fan and attached bathroom, 600B for larger fan bungalows of concrete, or 800B for air-con. Even if you don't stay here, you should consider having a meal in the restaurant, if only for the incredible view.

On the headlands between Ao Thong Yang and Ao Thong Ta Khian are a few places taking advantage of the seclusion and views, including *Golden Cliffs Resort*, which has primitive huts for as little as 250B. This place also rents by the month (3000B). *Bird's Eye View Bungalow* has wooden bungalows with balconies overlooking Hat Chaweng. Rooms cost 1200B with air-con, and 400B to 500B with fan.

Ao Thong Ta Khian
อ่าวท้องตะเคียน

This is another small, steep-sided cove, similar to Coral Cove and banked by huge boulders. The *Samui Silver Beach Resort* has bungalows overlooking the bay for 400B to 700B with fan and 800B to 1000B with air-con, and a pleasant restaurant with a beach view. Going south, *Thong Ta Kian Villa* (☎ 077-230978) has concrete bungalows for 350B with fan, 600B with air-con, and 900B with TV and fridge. At the southern end of the cove is the *Samui Yacht Club* (☎/fax 077-422400), with luxurious Thai-style bungalows for 2000B to 3000B (500B less in the low season). If you like to fish, this is a good area for shorecasting.

Jubilee Restaurant, an open-air place on the side of the road, has a nice view and serves everything from simple rice and noodle dishes to shark steak and curries. There are also a couple of other good *seafood restaurants* on the bay.

Hat Lamai
หาดละไม

After Chaweng, this is Samui's most popular beach for travellers. Hat Lamai rates are just a bit lower than at Chaweng but it's without the larger places like the Central Samui or the Imperial (yet) and there are fewer 500B-plus places. As with the Chaweng's accommodation listings, the following is just a cross section of some of the many places to stay.

There continue to be reports of burglaries and muggings at Lamai. Take care with valuables – have them locked away in a guesthouse or hotel office if possible. Muggings mostly occur in dark lanes and along unlit parts of the beach at night.

Northern Hat Lamai Accommodation at the north-eastern end of the beach is quieter and moderately priced, although the sand isn't very deep. The semi-secluded *Royal Blue Lagoon Beach Resort* (☎ 077-424086) has rooms with a garden view for 2090B, and rooms with a sea view for 2530B. This is a bit overpriced for the area and the facilities offered, even though the resort has a pool and a good open-air seafood restaurant. Considerably less expensive is the simpler *Lamai Garden* with fan rooms for 200B to 400B (up to 1200B with air-con).

Spa Resort (☎ 077-230855, fax 424126) is a new-agey place that offers herbal sauna, massage, clay facials, natural foods, meditation and yes, even fasting and colon-cleansing. At the moment simple bungalows here cost 250B to 550B, all with fan and private bathroom. The restaurant serves vegetarian and seafood dishes. Other activities include *taijiquan* (t'ai chi), *qi gong* (chi kung; Chinese breathing exercises), yoga and mountain biking. Fees for health services are extra.

Several cheaper, more easy-going places in the 200B to 400B range, including *My Friend* (☎ 077-425187), *Tapee* (☎ 077-424096) and *Sukasem* (☎ 077-424119), follow to the south before the strip of sand is interrupted by an estuary. Rooms at the latter are 300B to 700B.

At the top of the next section of beach is the cheap *New Hut*, with 150B to 200B huts that accommodate two people. The proprietor has been known to eject guests who don't eat in the restaurant, and we continue to get comments about rudeness and behaviour bordering on violence.

Sand Sea Resort (☎ 077-424026) is a more upmarket place with air-con rooms for 1500B and fan rooms for 900B. In the low season its prices are 1000B and 700B.

After another estuary, *Pavilion Resort* (☎ 077-424420, fax 424029) enjoys a bit more thatched-roof Thai-style charm. All rooms, whether in the hotel wing (3400B to 3600B) or cottages (5000B), come with air-con, balconies, personal safe, hair dryer, minibar, TV and telephone. There is also a spa bath and swimming pool on the property. Discounts of up to 40% are sometimes given.

Hat Lamai Central Down into the main section of Lamai is a string of places charging 300B to 800B, including *Mui* (☎ 077-232400), *Utopia* (☎ 077-233113) and *Magic Resort* (☎ 077-424229). The 76-room *Weekender Resort & Hotel* (☎ 077-424429, 424011; in Bangkok ☎ 02-466 2083) has three types of accommodation: Thai-style houses (2100B); rooms in the main building (1470B); and bungalows (1330B). There's a wide variety of activities to choose from, including minigolf, swimming and a bit of nightlife.

Moving into the centre of Hat Lamai, you'll come to *Coconut Beach Bungalow*, with fan rooms for 500B and air-con for 800B. These prices drop to 350B and 700B in the low season. *Lamai Inn 99* (☎ 077-424427, fax 424211) has fan bungalows for 500B and air-con for 800B to 1200B, depending on amenities.

This is the part of the bay closest to Ban Lamai village and the beginning of the Lamai 'scene'. Just about every kind of service is available here, including currency exchange offices, medical service units, supermarkets, one-hour photo labs, clothing shops, bike and jeep rental places, travel agencies with postal and international telephone services, restaurants (many with videos), discos, bars and food stalls.

Next comes a string of slightly upmarket 300B to 600B places, including *Sea Breeze*, with fan rooms for 250B to 500B and air-con rooms for 600B and up. Nearby is *Varinda Resort* with fan rooms for 350B to 500B and air-con for 700B. The *Aloha* (☎ 077-424418, 424419, ✉ aloha@loxinfo.co.th) is a two-storey resort where bungalows start at 1700B single/double and suites go up to 4200B. All of these have fairly elaborate dining areas; the Aloha has a good restaurant with seafood, Thai and European food.

Also in this area is *Galaxy Resort* (☎ 077-424441), with 1500B rooms in a hotel building as well as Thai-style cottages for 2000B. Fully equipped bungalows on the beach go for 2200B. *Golden Sand* (☎ 077-424031/2, fax 424430) is still good at 600B for bungalows with fan and 1100B to 1900B for air-con.

Finishing up central Hat Lamai is a mixture of places charging anywhere from 80B to 600B. *Paradise* (☎ 077-424290) has been here for more than 20 years and is the second-longest running place on the beach, with fan rooms from 300B to 600B and air-con from 800B.

Bill Resort (☎ 077-233054), formerly Bungalow Bill, has bungalows that are close together but spacious inside for 500B with fan and bathroom, and air-con bungalows on the beach with hot shower and fridge for 1000B to 1200B.

The *White Sand* (☎ 077-424298) is another Lamai original and huts are now 200B and up. Nearby are *Amity* and *Wanchai*, both charging from 100B with communal facilities and 200B with private bathroom.

Nice Resort 2 has concrete huts for 450/600B single/double with fan, 1800B with air-con. Finally, there's the *Sun Rise*, where acceptable huts go for 250B, and new bungalows cost 500B with fan or 800B with air-con.

Places to Eat Lamai doesn't have as wide a variety of places to eat as Chaweng. Most visitors seem to dine wherever they're staying. Once again Italian cuisine is well represented. *Il Tempio* does pizza, Italian and Thai, while *Gelateria Rossini* specialises in home-made Italian ice cream and cakes.

A branch of *Will Wait*, behind the Galaxy Resort, does good breakfasts and has a large selection of baked goods.

Entertainment Lamai has one large dance club, the long-running **Bauhaus Pub**, where DJ-ed music is interspersed with short drag shows and muay thai demos. **Y2K Disco** is mostly a Thai scene and can get pretty wild some nights.

There are several lanes lined with Pattaya-style outdoor bars. By and large it's a fàràng-male-dominated scene, but unlike in Pattaya and other similar mainland places where Western males tend to take on Thai females as temporary appendages, you may see more than a few Western women spending their holidays with young Thai men on Lamai.

Ao Bang Nam Cheut At this point a headland interrupts Ao Lamai and the bay beyond is known as Ao Bang Nam Cheut, named after the freshwater stream that runs into it. During the dry months the sea is too shallow for swimming, but in the late rainy season when the surf is too high elsewhere on the island's other beaches this can be a good area for swimming. Look for the well-known phallus-like 'Grandfather' and yoni-like 'Grandmother' rock formations.

Just south-west of the famous outcropping, **Swiss Chalet** (☎ 077-424321) has large bungalows overlooking the sea, but at last visit it was closed while the Swiss owner was in Switzerland, and the staff were unable to disclose prices. Next door, the old-timer **Rocky** has gone semi-upmarket, with concrete bungalows for 500B with fan and 1200B with air-con.

Ao Na Khai & Laem Set
อ่าวหน้าค่าย/แหลมเส็ด

Just beyond the village of Ban Hua Thanon at the southern end of Ao Na Khai is an area sometimes called Hat Na Thian. As at Lanai, the places along the southern end of the island are pretty rocky, which means good snorkelling (there's also a long reef here) – but perhaps not such good swimming.

Maria Resort (☎ 077-233395) has air-con bungalows with TV, phone, hot water and fridge for 1200B, or 1400B including breakfast. The cheaper **Wanna Samui Resort** has bungalows with fan for 200B to 250B and air-con for 600B to 700B.

Turn right here, follow the coast to the foot of Khao Thaleh, and the secluded **Laem Set Inn** (☎ 077-424393, fax 424394, e inn@laemset.com) commands a pretty corner of the sand-and-boulder beach. Rustic but charming three-person bungalows start at US$75 with veranda, hot-water shower, fan and sea view. More contemporary air-con rooms facing the sea cost from US$120 to US$400. On the premises there's a minor art gallery and a good Thai restaurant.

At Laem Set you pay for atmosphere and ecological sensitivity more than for amenities; some people will find this just what they're looking for, while others may feel they can find better value on the more popular beaches.

Central Samui Village (formerly the Samui Butterfly Garden; ☎ 077-424020, fax 424022), beside Laem Set Inn, features stylish, modern wooden cottages linked by wooden walkways over a rocky landscape. Good landscaping, a pool and a mixed Thai-foreign clientele are pluses. Cottages with garden views cost 3250B, while ones with sea views go for 3750B.

Ao Bang Kao
อ่าวบางเก่า

This bay at the very southern end of the island between Laem Set and Laem So has several on-again off-again but inexpensively priced accommodation options. You'll need to get off the round-island road onto winding sand roads for a couple of kilometres to find these places: The best of the lot is the friendly **River Garden**, with coconut wood huts for just 150B.

Ao Thong Krut & Ko Taen
อ่าวท้องกรูด/เกาะแตน

Next to the village of Ban Thong Krut on Ao Thong Krut is, what else, **Thong Krut** (TK Tour), where fan bungalows with private bathroom are 300B to 500B, or 800B for air-con. The beach here is not very private as it's a jumping-off point for boats to nearby islands as well as a mooring for local fishing boats.

From here you can arrange boat trips to four offshore islands: **Ko Taen, Ko Rap, Ko Mot Daeng** (which has the best coral) and

Ko Mat Sum. Three separate trails have been laid out on Ko Taen for trekkers who want to get a look at the local flora and fauna. Pick up a guide book for the trails at the TAT office in Na Thon before you go. Ko Taen has three bungalow operations along the east coast beach at Ao Awk, including *Tan Village* and *Coral Beach Bungalows* (☎ 01-956 3076), both in the range of 250B to 350B a night. In a sharply curving bay on the western side, *Dam Bungalows* and *BS Cove* are similar. Ko Mat Sum has good beaches where travellers sometimes camp. Rubbish can be a problem, though, perhaps because there are fewer bungalow proprietors to organise cleanups.

Regular boats going to Ko Taen (50B, 20 minutes) leave at 10 am and 4 pm. The boats leave from Ko Taen at 8 am and 3 pm. If you want to have a good look at the islands, fishing boats carrying up to 10 people can be chartered in Ban Thong Krut for about 1500B; try at one of the seafood restaurants along the main beach – *Ging Pakarang* is probably the best of the lot. Seagull Coral Tour (☎ 077-423303) offers an 8 am-to-3.30 pm boat tour to Ko Taen and Ko Mat Sum costing 600B, including lunch, nonalcoholic beverages, snorkelling gear, boat transport and pick-up anywhere on Samui.

West Coast

Several bays along Samui's western side have accommodation options, including Thong Yang, where the Don Sak and Khanom vehicle ferries dock. The beaches here turn to mud flats at low tide, however, so they're more or less for people seeking to get away from the east coast scene, not for beach fanatics.

Ao Phangkha Around Laem Hin Khom on the bottom of Samui's western side is little Ao Phangkha, sometimes called Emerald Cove. The secluded *Emerald Cove* offers huts for 80B to 300B, while *Sea Gull* and *Pearl Bay* (☎ 077-423110) charge from 200B to 500B, depending on the time of year. Both enjoy nice settings and are very quiet. During the low season there are so few guests on this cove that the bungalow proprietors tend to let the rubbish pile up.

Ao Taling Ngam Dominating the northern end of this shallow curving bay from its perch atop a steep hill, *Le Royal Meridian Baan Taling Ngam* (☎ 077-423019, fax 423220; in Bangkok ☎ 02-236 0400) remains Samui's most ultra-exclusive resort. The compound boasts tennis courts, two swimming pools, a fitness centre and a full complement of equipment and instructors for kayaking, windsurfing and diving. As it's not right on the beach, a shuttle service transports guests back and forth. Luxuriously appointed accommodation containing custom-made Thai-style furnishings start at US$300 for a deluxe room and cost up to US$550 for a cliff villa or deluxe suite, not including 20% tax and service.

Sharing the same bay just below Le Royal Meridian, *Wiesenthal* (☎/fax 077-235165) offers nine well-spaced bungalows amid a coconut grove for 300B to 400B for a regular bungalow, 700B for a family-size air-con bungalow. The Swiss-managed restaurant serves good Thai and European food.

Ao Taling Ngam is a 15B to 20B săwngthăew ride from Na Thon or the vehicle ferry pier. Le Royal Meridian, of course, provides airport/ferry transfers for all guests.

Ao Thong Yang The vehicle ferry jetty is at the southern end of this bay. Near the pier are *In Foo Palace* (☎ 077-423066), where rooms with fan cost 400B to 500B, and *Ar-An Inn* (400B with fan, 650B to 800B with air-con). The best of the lot is *Coco Cabana Beach Club* (☎ 077-423174), which has only rooms with fan for 500B.

The vehicle ferry jetty may soon be moved to another location or this one may remain in operation and a second built elsewhere along the coast. Either way the local accommodation will be affected by the change, possibly winding down and eventually closing.

Ao Chon Khram On the way north to Na Thon is sweeping Ao Chon Khram, with the *Lipa Lodge* and *International Bungalows & Big John Seafood Restaurant* (☎ 077-423025). The Lipa Lodge is especially nice, with a good site on the bay. Most huts are 350B, with a few as high as 650B. There is a good restaurant and bar here that's not bad for the money. International Bungalows offers bungalows with fan for 500B and air-con rooms for 800B, but these aren't quite up to Lipa Lodge's standards. Between them is the upmarket *Rajapruek Samui Resort* (☎ 077-423115), where rooms are 500B with fan, and 800B and up with air-con and hot water. Farther north, the isolated and slightly more expensive 20-room *Siam Residence Resort* (☎ 077-420008) has rooms for US$132 (garden view) to US$172 (sea view). All four of these places will provide free transport to and from the Thong Yang pier for guests.

Getting There & Away

Air Bangkok Airways flies 12 times daily to Ko Samui from Bangkok. There is an office in Chaweng (☎ 077-420133) and another at the airport (☎ 077-422513). The fare is 3180B one way (3510B in the reverse direction, including Ko Samui's airport tax). Fares for children are half the adult fare. The flight duration is one hour and 20 minutes.

Bangkok Airways also offers twice daily flights between Samui and Phuket as well as daily flights to Krabi, Pattaya and Singapore. During the high season flights may be completely booked out as many as six weeks in advance, so be sure to plan accordingly. If Samui flights are full, you might try flying to Surat Thani from Bangkok aboard THAI (see the Surat Thani Getting There & Away section for details).

The Samui airport departure tax is 400B for domestic and international flights. The attractive Samui airport is all open-air and has a nice bar, restaurant, money exchange and hotel reservations counter.

Bus The government-bus fares from Bangkok's Southern bus terminal don't include the cost of the ferry. These are 605B for VIP and 396B for 1st-class air-con. Most private buses from Bangkok charge around 400B for the same journey and include the ferry fare. From Thanon Khao San in Bangkok it's possible to get bus/ferry combination tickets for as little as 300B, but service is substandard and theft is more frequent than on the more expensive buses. If an agency on Thanon Khao San claims to be able to get you to Samui for less, it is almost certainly a scam as no profit can be made at such low prices. Surat Thani bus companies

Phantip (☎ 077-421221/2) and Songserm (☎ 077-421316) have offices in Na Thon.

From Na Thon, Phantip Travel runs air-con buses to Surat (100B), Krabi (210B), Phuket (230B) and Hat Yai (240B), leaving the waterfront road in Na Thon daily at 7.30 am. These fares include the ferry ride.

To Surat Thani a bus/ferry combination ticket costs 80B ordinary (six times daily), 100B air-con (three times).

Train The SRT sells train/bus/ferry tickets straight through to Samui from Bangkok. These save you only 10B or 20B on 2nd-class tickets; for all other routes a combination ticket costs around 50B more than separate train, bus (from the train station to piers) and boat tickets. It may be worth it to avoid the hassles of separate bookings/connections. See the Surat Thani Getting There & Away section for details on train travel.

Boat To sort out the ferry situation you have to understand that there are four ferry piers on the Surat Thani coast and two on Ko Samui (five if you count the three piers on the north coast that serve Ko Pha-Ngan). Songserm Travel runs express ferry boats from Tha Thong, 6km north-east of central Surat, and slow night boats from the Ban Don pier in town. These take passengers only. The express boats used to leave from the same pier in Ban Don as the night ferry – when the river is unusually high they may use this pier again.

Vehicle ferries run from Don Sak, and from Khanom around 15km south-east at certain times of year. These are the lines that get most of the bus/boat and some of the train/bus/boat combination business.

Which boat you take will depend on what's next available when you arrive at the bus terminal in Surat or the train station in Phun Phin – touts working for the ferry companies will lead you to one or the other.

During the low season (any time except December to February or August), young Thais may throng the piers around departure time for the Ko Samui boats, inviting fàràng to stay at this or that bungalow. This same tactic is employed at Tha Na Thon and Tha Thong Yang upon arrival at Ko Samui. During the high tourist season, this isn't necessary as almost every place is booked out. Some of the out-of-the-way places to stay put touts on the boats to pass around photo albums advertising their establishments.

Two piers – one each in Bo Phut and Bang Rak – have boats to Hat Rin Nai on Ko Pha-Ngan's south coast. There are usually three departures daily for 100B (150B on full-moon nights); these boats take only 30 minutes to reach Hat Rin. See Laem Hat Rin in the Ko Pha-Ngan section later in this chapter for more details.

Express Boat Two express boats go to Samui (Na Thon) daily from Tha Thong and each takes two to 2½ hours to reach the island. During this period the departure times are usually 7.30 am and 2 pm, although these change from time to time.

The express ferry boats have two decks, one with seats below and an upper deck that is really just a big luggage rack – good for sunbathing. Passage is 150B each way, but this fare seesaws from season to season; if any rivals to Songserm appear on the scene (as has happened twice in the last few years), Songserm tends to drop its fares immediately to as little as 50B one way to drive the competition out of business.

From Na Thon back to Surat, there are departures at 7.15 am, noon and 2.30 pm from November to May; and 7.30 am and 2.30 pm from June to October. The 7.15 am boat fare includes a bus ride to the train station in Phun Phin; the afternoon boats include a bus to the train station and to the Talat Kaset bus terminal in Ban Don.

Night Ferry There is also a slow boat for Samui that leaves Tha Ban Don in Surat Thani each night at 11 pm, reaching Na Thon around 5 am. This one costs 100B for the upper deck (including pillows and mattresses), and 80B down below (straw mats only).

The locals use this boat extensively and the craft is in better shape than some of the express boats. It's particularly recommended if you arrive in Surat Thani too late for the fast boat and don't want to stay in Surat Thani overnight.

The night ferry back to Samui leaves Na Thon at 9 pm, arriving at 3 am; you can stay on the boat to catch some more sleep until 8 am. Ignore the touts trying to herd passengers onto buses to Bangkok, as these won't leave till 8 am or later anyway.

Don't leave your bags unattended on the night ferry, as thefts can be a problem. The thefts usually occur when you drop your bags on the ferry well before departure and then go for a walk around the pier area. Most victims don't notice anything's missing until they unpack after arrival on Samui.

Vehicle Ferry Tour buses run directly from Bangkok to Ko Samui, via the vehicle ferry from Don Sak in Surat Thani Province, for around 400B. Check with the big tour-bus companies or any travel agency. A pier at nearby Khanom is also used by Songserm, which is now competing with the Raja company whose pier is at Don Sak.

From Thanon Talat Mai in Surat Thani you can get bus/ferry combination tickets straight through to Na Thon (80B ordinary, 100B air-con). Pedestrians or people in private vehicles can also take the ferry directly from Don Sak; it leaves roughly every two hours between 8 am and 5 pm, and takes one hour to reach Tha Thong Yang on Samui. In the opposite direction, ferries leave Thong Yang between 7 am and 4 pm; in this direction the trip takes around 1½ hours. During the rainy season the number of daily departures may decrease to as few as three, particularly in September.

Without the bus included, the straight fare for pedestrians is 50B, for a motorcycle and driver 80B, and for a car and driver 200B. Passengers in private vehicles pay the pedestrian fare. The ferry trip takes about 1½ hours to reach Don Sak, which is 60km from Surat Thani.

Buses between the Surat Thani bus terminal and Don Sak cost 17B and take 45 minutes to an hour to arrive at the ferry terminal. If you're coming north from Nakhon Si Thammarat, this might be the ferry to take, although from Surat Thani the Tha Thong ferry is definitely more convenient.

From Ko Samui, air-con buses to Bangkok leave from near the old pier in Na Thon at 1.30 and 3.30 pm daily, both arriving in Bangkok around 5 am after a stopover in Surat. Other through bus services from Na Thon include Hat Yai, Krabi and Phuket; all of these buses leave Na Thon around 7.30 am, arriving at their destinations around six hours later (around 250B). Check with the several travel agencies in Na Thon for the latest routes.

Getting Around

It is quite possible to hitch around the island, although anyone on the island with a car is likely to want to boost their income by charging for rides.

To/From the Airport Samui Limousine operates an air-con van service between Samui airport and Hat Bang Rak (30B), Chaweng (120B), Lamai (100B), Na Thon (100B) and Mae Nam (100B). For other beaches you'll have to rely on săwngthăew or taxis. Chartered taxis from the airport cost 250B to anywhere on the island. A chartered taxi to the pier at Hat Bang Rak should be no more than 100B.

Săwngthăew & Bus Săwngthăew fares are 15B from Na Thon to Mae Nam; 20B to Bo Phut, Hat Bang Rak and Lamai; and 30B to Chaweng or Choeng Mon. From the car-ferry landing in Thong Yang, rates are 10B to Na Thon; 30B to Lamai, Mae Nam and Bo Phut/Hat Bang Rak; and 40B to Chaweng and Choeng Mon. A few years ago official fares were posted for these routes, but nowadays săwngthăew drivers insist on overcharging newcomers, so take care. Săwngthăew run regularly during daylight hours only. A regular bus between Thong Yang and Na Thon costs 10B. Note that if you're arriving in Thong Yang on a bus (via the vehicle ferry), your bus/boat fare includes a ride into Na Thon, but not elsewhere.

Car & Motorcycle You can rent motorcycles from several places in Na Thon as well as at various bungalows around the island. The going rate is 150B per day for a 100cc bike, but for longer periods you can get the price down (say 280B for two days, 400B for three days etc). Rates are generally lower in Na Thon and it makes more sense to rent from there if you're going back that way. Take it easy on the bikes; every year several fàràng die or are seriously injured in motorcycle accidents on Samui, and besides, the locals really don't like seeing their roads become race tracks. A helmet law is enforced with some vigour from time to time. Besides avoiding a steep fine, wearing a helmet may save your life.

Suzuki Caribian jeeps can be hired for around 800B per day from various Na Thon agencies as well as at Chaweng and Lamai.

Aside from all the small independents doing rentals, Avis Rent-A-Car has a branch at Hat Mae Nam's Santiburi Dusit Resort (☎ 077-425031).

KO PHA-NGAN

เกาะพะงัน

postcode 84280 • pop 10,300

Ko Pha-Ngan, about a half-hour boat ride north of Ko Samui, has become the island of choice for those who find Samui too crowded or too expensive. It started out as a sort of 'back-door escape' from Samui but is well-established now, with a regular boat service and over 200 places to stay around the 190-sq-km island. It's definitely worth a visit for its remaining deserted beaches (they haven't all been built upon) and, if you like snorkelling, for its live coral formations.

Although hordes of backpackers have discovered Ko Pha-Ngan, the lack of an airport and relative absence of paved roads have so far spared it from tourist-hotel and package-tour development. Compared with Samui, Ko Pha-Ngan has a lower concentration of bungalows, less-crowded beaches and coves, and an overall less 'modern' atmosphere. Pha-Ngan aficionados say the seafood is fresher and cheaper than on Samui's beaches, but really it varies from place to place. As Samui becomes more expensive for both travellers and investors, more and more people will be drawn to Pha-Ngan. But for the time being, overall living costs remain about half what you'd pay on Samui.

Except at the island's party capital, Hat Rin, the island hasn't yet been cursed with video and blaring stereos; unlike on Samui, travellers interact rather than staring over one another's shoulders at a video screen.

Dangers & Annoyances

While many travellers may like to sample some of the local herb, it may be wise to think twice. There are constant reports of travellers being offered and sold marijuana or other drugs by restaurant or bungalow owners, and then being promptly busted by policemen who *somehow* know exactly who, when and where to check.

Police roadblocks along the road between Thong Sala and Hat Rin are becoming increasingly common, especially during the week leading up to the infamous full-moon party on Hat Rin. These aren't cursory checks, either; if you're on a motorcycle the police look in the fuel tank, check the tyres and search all your gear. One traveller reported the cops played 'a sort of pocket billiards' with his testicles looking for dope – not just pot, but ecstasy, acid, amphetamines and anything else an enterprising dealer might be shipping in for the big party. The result is often a steep fine (50,000B seems to be the standard fee) and in some cases deportation. Not exactly the makings of a laid-back vacation.

Those who come specifically seeking an organic buzz should take note: A hallucinogenic plant, newly exploited on the island, has caused a number of travellers to pay an unscheduled visit to the local psychiatric hospital. Called *tôn lamphong* in Thai, the plant is possibly related to datura, a member of the highly toxic nightshade family. Eating any part of the plant causes some people to be completely whacked for a couple of days. Locals say it's becoming a problem because people who are on it act pretty much like wandering zombies – stumbling down streets and clawing at thin air – oblivious to anything but their own hallucinations, which they try to follow and grasp. Some guesthouses/restaurants are reportedly offering the plant to travellers who ask for magic mushrooms, apparently because the tôn lamphong has not yet been made illegal.

Waterfalls

In the interior of the island are four year-round waterfalls and a number of more seasonal ones. Boulders carved with the royal insignia of Rama V, Rama VII and Rama IX, all of whom have visited the falls, can be found at **Nam Tok Than Sadet**, which cascades along Khlong Than Sadet in the eastern part of the island. Rama V so liked this island that he made 18 trips here between 1888 and 1909. A pleasant way to get to the falls is on one of Cactus Club's Reggae Magic Boat Trips, which leave from Hat Rin Nok at 10.30 am and return at 6 pm and include stops at Hat Khuat and Hat Khom. The cruise costs 350B per person and includes food and refreshments. Contact Cactus Club or Outback Bar in Hat Rin for information about when the next cruise will get under way.

Nam Tok Phaeng is off the main road between Thong Sala and Ban Chalok Lam, almost in the centre of the island. A third falls, **Nam Tok Than Prapat**, is situated near the eastern shore in an area that can be reached by road or boat, while **Nam Tok Than Prawet** is in the north-east near Ao Thong Nai Pan.

Wat Khao Tham
วัดเขาถ้ำ

This cave temple is beautifully situated on top of a hill near the little village of Ban Tai. An American monk lived in this temple for over a decade and his ashes are interred on a cliff overlooking a field of palms below the wát.

It's not a true wát since there are only a couple of monks and a nun in residence (among other requirements, a quorum of five monks is necessary for a temple to reach wát status).

Ten-day meditation retreats (2900B) taught by an American-Australian couple are held here during the latter half of most months. Write to Wat Khao Tham, PO Box 8, Ko Pha-Ngan, Surat Thani 84280 for information, or preregister in person.

Anyone under 25 years of age must talk with the teachers before being accepted for the retreat. A bulletin board at the temple also has information.

Thong Sala
ท้องศาลา

About half of Ko Pha-Ngan's total population of 10,000 lives in and around the small port town of Thong Sala. This is where the ferry boats from Surat Thani and Samui (Na Thon) dock, although there are also smaller boats from Mae Nam and Bo Phut on Samui that moor at Hat Rin.

The town sports several restaurants, travel agents, clothing shops and general stores. You can rent motorcycles here for 150B to 250B per day.

Information Bovy Supermarket on the main street leading from the pier sells just about anything you might need – sunglasses, sunscreen, liquor, snorkelling gear, cereal, cosmetics, even Frisbees – for short or long-term stays on the island.

The monthly *Phangan Newsletter* contains information about transport and activities on the island.

Money If you're continuing on to other areas of the island and need to do some banking, this is the place to do it. Krung Thai Bank, Siam City Bank and Siam Commercial Bank buy and sell travellers cheques and can arrange money transfers and credit-card cash advances; Siam Commercial generally has the best service.

Hat Rin also has some foreign exchange services as complete as those available in Thong Sala.

Post & Communications The post office is at the southern end of town, in the direction of Hat Rin; it's open from 8.30 am to noon and 1 to 4.30 pm weekdays and from 9 am to noon on Saturday. Since the arrival of new telephone lines in 1999, the number of places offering long-distance telephone and fax services has grown tremendously. Just look for the signs.

Most businesses offering long-distance telephone and fax services are also hooked into the Internet. They're quite numerous – just look for the many signs advertising 'Email'.

Maps Visid Hongsombud's *Guide Map of Koh Pha-Ngan & Koh Tao* (look for the picture of the bespectacled Mr Visid on the cover) is detailed and up to date, as well as being printed on waterproof stock.

KO PHA-NGAN

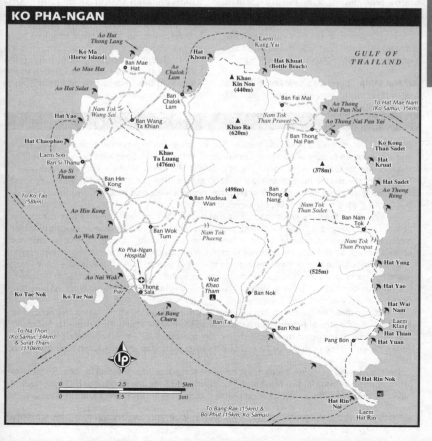

Medical Services The Ko Pha-Ngan Hospital (☎ 077-377034), about 2.5km north of Thong Sala off the road to Chalok Lam, offers 24-hour emergency services. Anything that can wait till Bangkok should wait, where medical facilities are higher quality.

Places to Stay & Eat At the *Pha-Ngan Chai Hotel* (☎ 077-377068, fax 377032), on the bay about 150m south of the pier, all rooms come with air-con, phone and TV and cost 900B and up. *Bua Kao Inn* (☎ 077-377226) offers rooms with private facilities in a guesthouse-like place for 300/400B single/double, 500B with air-con. There's a very popular restaurant downstairs. The similar *Kao Guest House* (☎ 077-238061, 210/9–10 Thanon Thong Sala-Chalok Lam) nearby rents rooms with fan for 250B to 300B and with air-con for 400B. This one also has a coffee shop.

Several cafes near the pier cater to fàràng tastes and also sell boat tickets. There are also a couple of karaoke bars in Thong Sala.

Ao Nai Wok There are a few beach bungalows within about 2km north of the pier. Although the beach here isn't spectacular, it's a fairly nice area to while away a few days – especially if you want to be near Thong Sala. People waiting for an early boat back to Surat or on to Ko Tao may choose to stay here (or south of Thong Sala at Ao Bang Charu) since transport times from other parts of the island can be unpredictable. Swimming at this beach is best from December to April, when water levels are high. A reef offshore offers OK snorkelling.

Turn left at the first main crossing from the pier, then walk straight till the road crosses a concrete bridge, and then turn left again where the road dead-ends at a T-intersection. Soon you'll come to *Phangan* (150B with shared bathroom, up to 300B with bathroom), *Charn* (100B, all with bathroom, high season up to 120B), *Siriphun* (200B to 600B, all with bathroom) and *Tranquil Resort* (80B with shared bathroom, up to 500B with attached bathroom). All are within about 2km of each other. Siriphun seems particularly good value and it still has the best kitchen in the area; Siriphun also has some larger houses for long-term rentals.

Sang's Clinic

It's been a decade since Suriya Sang finished nursing school in the provincial capital of Surat Thani and was assigned to duty at Ko Pha-Ngan's hospital in Thong Sala. Soon after her arrival, Sang, as she is known to her friends, decided to open a clinic in Hat Rin to serve the villagers. But it wasn't long before she treated her first fàràng (Western) patient. 'The Full Moon Parties were very small back then but when a visitor got sick or hurt they would always be directed to my clinic. It's easier than making a trip to Thong Sala', Sang explains.

The sign above the rustic wooden structure that houses the clinic reads 'Nursing Home' and a list of services is displayed in English, including pregnancy testing, wound dressing and vaccinations for rabies and Japanese encephalitis. 'Most of the westerners I see are suffering from simple cuts and scrapes – nearly all of which are sustained in motorcycle accidents. Earaches are also very common. I don't know why but people from Western countries often seem to have what looks like many years' worth of wax in their ears. They go swimming and the water sometimes gets trapped in their ears, causing pain and a loss of hearing. When I wash their ears out, the westerners are always very surprised at all the wax that comes pouring out'.

Predictably, there are complaints of a different sort around full-moon time. 'Lately I've noticed an increase in the number of patients who have ingested too many diet pills. They dance for hours and feel no fatigue or hunger. If they aren't strong they collapse, or else their heart rate goes way up. About the only thing I can do for them is to administer an IV drip and give them some Valium to help them calm down'.

The high number of visitors needing first aid or medical advice has caused a crop of copy-cat 'clinics' to open up around Hat Rin. None of them, according to Sang, are qualified to be giving medical advice or prescribing drugs. 'All the local people come to me because they know I'm a nurse with

Beaches

Most of the beach bungalow operations are still concentrated north and south-east of Thong Sala and especially on the southern end of the island at Hat Rin, but there are many other places to stay around the island as well. Because there are few paved roads on Pha-Ngan, transport can be a bit of a problem, although the situation is constantly improving as enterprising Thais set up taxi and boat services running between beaches.

Many of the huts on Pha-Ngan have been established by entrepreneurs from Ko Samui with several years' experience in the bungalow business. Huts with shared bathing facilities go for 100B to 150B a night on average and as little as 80B between May and October; many of these do not have electricity or running water. Some have generators that are only on for limited hours in the evening, and the lights dim when staff make a fruit shake. For many people, of course, this adds to Pha-Ngan's appeal.

Other places are moving into the 200B to 400B range, which almost always includes a private bathroom, and there are a few scattered spots on the west and south-east coasts with resort-like amenities for 500B and up. As travel to Pha-Ngan seems particularly seasonal, you should be able to talk bungalow rates down 30% to 40% when occupancy is low. During the peak months (December to February and July and August), there can be a shortage of rooms at the most popular beaches and even the boats coming to the island can be dangerously overcrowded.

Since many of the cheaper bungalows make the bulk of their profits from their restaurants rather than from renting huts, bungalow owners have been known to eject guests after a few days if they don't take meals where they're staying. The only way to avoid this, besides forgoing your own choice of restaurants, is to get a clear agreement beforehand on how many days you can stay. This seems to be a problem only at the cheaper (80B to 100B) places.

There are a number of beaches with accommodation on Pha-Ngan; the following are listed moving in an anticlockwise direction from Thong Sala.

Sang's Clinic

many years' experience. Of course visitors don't know this so they go to the first 'clinic' they see'.

Sang, who speaks fluent English, says there's a difference in what Thais and westerners expect from a visit to the clinic. 'Thais want medicine of some kind. If they don't get it they feel they haven't gotten their money's worth. Westerners want explanations: What it is they are suffering from, what they should do to cure it, and why'.

Despite Sang's assurances, she finds some fàràng sceptical at her medical advice. 'Many Europeans are against taking antibiotics. They say that antibiotics are rarely prescribed in Europe. I try to explain to them that the tropical climate here often causes wounds to become infected and that antibiotics are usually the best treatment. If the patient still refuses I tell them to keep the wound clean and come back if it seems to be going septic. They're usually back within a day or two'.

Sang's clinic is located near the Hat Rin pier and is open in the evenings after she returns from work at the hospital in Thong Sala.

STEVEN MARTIN

Ao Bang Charu South of Thong Sala, the shallow beach here is not one of the island's best, but it's close to town and so is popular with people waiting for boats or others with bank business.

Sundance (☎ 077-238103), Ban Puen, Pha-Ngan Villa and *Moonlight* have similar wooden or concrete bungalows in the 150B to 300B range. *Vieng Thai (☎ 077-377247)* nearby has sturdy wooden bungalows for 200B to 300B. Following a coconut grove to the south are the distinctive high-pitched roofs of *Charm Beach Resort (☎ 077-377165)*, a nicely landscaped place with prices starting at 300B and going up to 500B for a triple on the beach. *Chokana Resort (☎ 077-238085)* has big, solidly built hexagonal cottages in addition to more-traditional huts costing from 150B with fan to 1300B with air-con. Charm Beach and Chokana Resort have decent restaurants.

Ban Tai & Ban Khai Between the villages of Ban Tai and Ban Khai there is a series of sandy beaches with well-spaced bungalow operations. Many have replaced their thatched huts with accommodation made of less-perishable materials that typically charge 150B to 300B. Some establishments still have a few cheap huts on hand (80B to 100B) but these are likely to be relegated to a corner of the lot far from the beach. Not all of the bungalows here have signs indicating their positions from the paved road; to really survey the area you must walk along the beach. *Dewshore (☎ 077-238128)* can be reached from a road in the centre of Ban Tai, and offers well-constructed bungalows on nicely landscaped grounds for 350B to 500B with fan, 800B to 1300B with air-con.

Starting around the southern outskirts of Ban Tai you'll find a long string of very similar bungalow operations. These include *King's Bungalows, Mac Bay Resort, Liberty, Silver Moon, Green Peace* and *Golden Beach*. Mac Bay Resort stands out as one of the better choices. King's Bungalows is also a good place to stay and the owner speaks French as well as English.

Long-tail boats to other parts of the island can be chartered from Ban Khai. At one time there was a regular boat service to/from Hat Rin, but with the paving of the road all the way to Hat Rin it has been discontinued.

A săwngthăew from Thong Sala costs 20B per person to Ban Tai, 30B to Ban Khai; a motorbike taxi is 30B to Ban Tai, 40B to Ban Khai.

Laem Hat Rin This long cape juts southeast and has beaches along both its westward and eastward sides. The eastward side has the best beach, Hat Rin Nok, a long sandy strip lined with coconut palms. The snorkelling here is pretty good, but between October and March the surf can be a little hairy. The western side more or less acts as an overflow for people who can't find a place to stay on the eastern side, as the beach is often too shallow for swimming. Together these beaches have become the most popular on the island.

Hat Rin Nok (Outer Rin Beach, often referred to as Sunrise Beach) has gradually become a more or less self-contained town, complete with travel agencies, money-changers, minimarts, restaurants, bars, tattoo shops and outdoor discos. A pier on Hat Rin Nai (Inner Rin Beach, often referred to as Sunset Beach) serves boats from the north-west coast of Ko Samui, a half hour away.

Hat Rin Nok is famous for its monthly 'full-moon parties', featuring all-night beach dancing and the ingestion of various illicit substances – forget about sleeping on these nights unless you get a place off the beach. Even when the moon isn't full, several establishments blast dance music all night long – head for the western side if you prefer a quieter atmosphere.

Suan Saranrom (Garden of Joys) psychiatric hospital in Surat Thani has to take on extra staff during full-moon periods to handle the number of fàràng who freak out on magic mushrooms, acid or other abundantly available hallucinogens. There are plenty of other drugs available from the local drug mafia and drug-dependent visitors, and the police occasionally conduct raids. Travellers, especially women, should be watchful of their personal safety at these parties; assaults have occasionally been reported. See the boxed text 'Full Mooning' for more information on this event.

Full Mooning

Ravers from around the globe have been gathering for the monthly party for at least 10 years now, and the crowd shows no sign of retreat. When I jumped ashore in 1990 for my first Hat Rin mooner it was a relatively small affair of perhaps 800 people, tops. 'Shroom shakes, massive spliffs and glistening capsules of E were sold like sticks of barbecued *lûuk chín plaa* (fish balls) at a *ngaan wát* (temple fair). The heart of the party pulsated in front of Paradise Bungalows, where Thai DJs longtailed over from Samui to do the knob-twisting.

Nowadays around 5000 ravers – as many as 8000 during the December-to-February peak season – turn up for the party, which has split among several beachfront venues: Paradise Bungalows, Bongo Club, Drop In, Vinyl Club, Cactus Club and Tommy's Resort. On a recent FM party the Cactus drew the steadiest crowd with a concoction of techno, house, drum 'n' bass, reggae, ambient and R&B. But Hat Rin's visiting DJs – who may hail from Belgium, the UK, Israel, Singapore and Thailand, among other places – are notoriously fickle, so by the time you reach Hat Rin somewhere else will probably be the 'in' house.

Dancers and groovers spill out of the open-air dance halls onto the beach and right up to the water's edge. Some people do their thing standing in the shallow breakers, but watch out where you plant yourself – by 2 am there's a chorus line of lads – well, mostly lads – releasing excess bodily fluids into the Gulf. In terms of partygoers, the numbers peak at around 5 or 6 am. The last of the DJs don't shut down till around 11 am. Some ravers take catnaps for an hour or three some time between midnight and 5 am, just so they can be up and at it for sunrise.

Drugs are still available but these days the more hardcore partakers have moved on to other beaches due to a pumped-up police presence (both uniformed and undercover) at Hat Rin's now-legendary full-moon raves. Still, sober observers can amuse themselves trying to guess what's energising the folks hip-hopping in Day-Glo paint beneath black-light tubes rigged to overhead nets. Mushrooms? Ecstasy? Diet pills? Red Bull?

Although the Tourism Authority of Thailand (TAT) once announced intentions to turn the Hat Rin FM into a family occasion complete with sporting events and beauty contests, authorities have yet to stop or coopt the party and it's still very much in the original spirit of 'let's paint up and shake it'. The whole event is well organised by Thai residents who run the bungalows and bars along Hat Rin. Public pay-toilets are even available at Anant (Anan) Bungalows. The proprietors also clean the beach of substantial morning-after litter when the party is over.

Full Moon Party Tips

Safety Be watchful of your personal belongings and personal safety. Keep in mind that this is one night when you can expect people who may never otherwise indulge to be acting a little weird. Don't keep valuables in your bungalow – it's a big night for break-ins, especially at the cheaper bungalows. Buy a padlock and take advantage of the many places that offer lockers for rent. Ravers playing with fireworks add to the potential mayhem. If you're staying alone on the western side of the peninsula, think about having friends escort you home after dark.

Local police report that there is a fatality at every other Full-Moon Party. Most are drowning victims who break off their partying for a refreshing swim and are never again seen alive. Others die as a result of accidents that probably wouldn't happened if the victims were in full control of their faculties. In January of 2000 a young Briton somehow managed to fall head-first down a metre-wide well. It was three days before his body was discovered.

Accommodation If you arrive on full-moon day or even the day before, you can forget about finding a vacant room or bungalow on either Hat Rin Nok (called 'Sunrise Beach' by tourists) or Hat Rin Nai (aka 'Sunset Beach'). Your best bet is to head over the rocky hills to the southern end of the cape to places like Hua Laem Resort, Seaview Resort, Sun Cliff Resort, and especially Lighthouse Bungalows and Leela Beach Bungalows, which are the furthest from the action and may have something available.

SOUTHERN GULF

Full Mooning

Many ravers travel to Hat Rin four or five days in advance to nail down a room, meet friends and 'warm up' for the party. Hat Rin and environs can house, at most, around 2000 people, while the rave attracts 5000 or more on a good full moon. Loads of partygoers, especially Thais, boat over from Samui during the afternoon, party all night, then boat back the next morning, thereby sidestepping the accommodation dilemma.

Food Beachfront barbecues offer fresh grilled seafood until around 11 pm, after which the pickings are slim. Several beach bungalows shut down their restaurants the morning after so that staff can get some sleep. If you wake before noon you may have to wander into the village between inner and outer Hat Rin to find something to feed your abused stomach.

Transport If you're coming over from Ko Samui for the party, take one of the thrice-daily ferries from Big Buddha Pier or Bo Phut Pier on Samui (80B), or hop on one of the frequent speedboats in operation the day and night of the full moon for 200B one way, 300B return. The speedboats continue to depart from Big Buddha and Bo Phut until around 1 am, reaching a peak number of trips between 8 pm and midnight.

What to bring If you're just a night-tripper all you'll need is a change of clothes, swimsuit, sarong (for sitting or sleeping on the beach), ID (just in case) and money.

Drugs Thai police often set up inspection points on the road between Thong Sala and Hat Rin on days leading up to the full-moon party. All vehicles, including bicycles and motorcycles, are stopped and the passengers searched thoroughly. People go to jail, or pay through the nose. The going rate – or 'fine' if you wish – for escaping a small pot bust is 50,000B.

Check your lunar calendar for upcoming full moon party dates, or log onto www.googol.com/moon.

Joe Cummings with much inspiration from Nima Chandler

Money Siam City Bank has a foreign exchange kiosk near the Pha-Ngan Bayshore.

Post & Communications There's a licensed post office on the road between the two sides of the peninsula. In 1999 new telephone lines reached the island, resulting in over 200 new telephones in Hat Rin alone. Consequently an explosion of places offering long-distance telephone and fax services has hit the town and travellers need only look for the ubiquitous signs to locate them.

There is no shortage of places to send and receive email in Hat Rin. A large Internet access place near the Pha-Ngan Bayshore has several computer terminals and no waiting.

Diving Phangan Divers (☎ 077-375117, e info@phangandivers.com), near the pier, charges 700B for beach dive trips, 2000B for a dive trip to Sail Rock or Ang Thong National Marine Park and 8000B

for full certification including lunch and two dives. A snorkelling set can be rented for 100B to 150B.

Massage Chakra Traditional Thai Massage (☎ 077-375244), located on Hat Rin Nok between Paradise Bungalows and Drop Inn Bar, offers expert massage for 200B for one hour or 300B for two. Yan, the proprietor, studied massage as a monk and is adept at traditional Thai as well as deep tissue techniques.

At the time of writing a new health spa was in the works. 'Anahata' is slated to have a sauna, Jacuzzis, massage and even a kitchen doing up healthy food and drink, and will be located on the road to Thong Sala, between Ban Khai and Ban Tai.

Gym Jungle Gym, on the road between the two sides of the cape, near the pier on Hat Rin Nai, offers muay thai and other martial arts training, Thai and Western massage, sauna, aerobics, yoga and a full range of weight machines and free weights. Daily and monthly user fees are available, plus separate charges for instruction, massage and sauna.

Places to Stay The bungalows here are stacked rather closely together and are among the most expensive on the island. Starting from the south, *Paradise Bungalows* (☎ 077-375244) is one of the oldest establishments and offers a variety of cottages from near the beach to inland on the rocks, plus rooms in a motel-like structure perpendicular to the beach. Costs range from 350B to 700B. The rather slummy *Beach Blue* continues the trend of renting motel-like rows of rooms extending away from the beach for 150B to 250B a night.

Next are the slightly more upmarket *Anant Bungalows* and *Haadrin Resort* (☎ 077-375259), with rooms in the 200B to 600B range. *Phangan Orchid Resort* (☎ 077-375156) is on the more-expensive side, with small rooms with fan for 400B, and an air-con place on the beach for 1200B.

Sunrise Resort (☎ 077-375145), more or less in the middle of the beach, is another long-runner; fan huts made of local materials are priced from 350B to 550B (1200B for air-con), depending on position relative to the beach and the current occupancy rate.

Pha-Ngan Bayshore Resort (☎ 077-375227) occupies the middle section of the beach and charges 500/700B for one/two-bed fan rooms and up to 1500B for a large air-con bungalow on the beach. On the premises there's an Internet centre and a second-hand bookshop with English and German books.

Next is *Tommy Resort* (☎ 077-375215/6), a popular old-timer. Bungalows here cost from 200B with communal bathroom to 700B with private facilities. The similar *Palita Lodge* (☎ 077-377132) has a group of 35 wooden bungalows next door that cost 250B to 700B.

Towards the northern end of the beach is the relatively quiet *Seaview Haadrin Resort;* well-spaced bungalows with attached bathroom cost 250B to 600B.

Built into the rocky headland at the northern end of Hat Rin, the *Mountain Sea Bungalows* shares a set of concrete stairs (inundated by the surf at high tide) with the *Serenity Hill Bungalows*. Each has huts

with private facilities for 300B to 500B; an advantage of staying here is that it's quieter at night than at places right on the beach.

Behind the main row of beach lodgings a second row of bungalows has mushroomed, including *Bumblebee Huts*, *Haad Rin Hill* and *Bongo*. All of these are in the 100B to 300B range. Nearby *Jonathan* has fan rooms for 400B and air-con for 800B.

Perched on the slopes of the hills in the centre of Hat Rin's southernmost point, overlooking the sea and catching sunset rays amid huge boulders and lots of vegetation, is *Sun Cliff Resort* (☎ 077-375134). It offers 28 nicely appointed bungalows on stilts for 200B (for smaller ones) to 1200B (for quite large ones). All come with fan and attached shower and toilet; most have balconies with hammocks facing the sea. *Sea Breeze* is even farther up the hill – it's quite a climb in the dark – and has a setup similar to Sun Cliff for 200B to 1000B.

In a similar position on the opposite side of the highlands is the less inspiring and less expensive *Hua Laem Resort*. To find Sun Cliff and Hua Laem, follow signs posted along the cross-cape road.

A separate trail forks off the cross-cape road and leads up and over the highlands to *Leela Beach Bungalows*, a set of bamboo-thatch huts with beds and mosquito nets for 80B to 100B. These are spaciously set in a flat coconut-grove and there's a thin strip of sand in front and good breezes. Leela Beach once belonged to the Rajneesh cult and a board bearing a large photo of 'Osho' has been turned into a signboard. It's a 15- or 20-minute walk from Hat Rin.

Continue following the path through Leela till it meets a 100m raised wooden walkway around a rocky headland to find *Lighthouse Bungalow*. At night – or when the surf is high – walking along this walkway could be very tricky. Lighthouse's 18 simple bungalows, perched dramatically on boulders, cost 150B with outside bathroom and 200B with inside facilities. It has its own generator, with power from 6 to 11 pm only. It's a 30-minute walk here without luggage; you can hire a long-tail at Hat Rin to shuttle you to Lighthouse's own pier for 100B. During monsoons the wind can be quite strong at this spot.

Across the ridge on the western side is Hat Rin Nai, which overall is much quieter than Hat Rin Nok. Here you'll find long-runners *Palm Beach* (100B to 150B) and *Sunset Bay Resort* (150B to 300B), plus a string of places in the 200B to 350B range including: *Dolphin, Charung* (☎ 077-375168), *Friendly, Family House* (air-con also available, 600B to 1200B) and *Neptune's Villa*. Family House and Charung are the best of the pack – quiet and well maintained. The *Rin Beach Resort* (☎ 077-375112) has a few larger huts with private bathroom and fan from 400B, as well as concrete air-con bungalows for 800B. Rooms are also available in an unspeakably ugly row building for 500B to 600B.

At the northern end of Hat Rin Nai, around a small headland, are a bunch of cheapies including: *Blue Hill, Sun Beach, Sandy, Coral, Sooksom* and *Grammy*, all in the 100B to 150B range. For 100B, the nicest thatched bungalows (with attached bathroom) are those at Blue Hill, situated on a hill above the beach.

Places to Eat Restaurants here are still less expensive than on Samui, although prices are creeping well beyond 'local'. The seafood is good and fresh, particularly at *Lucky Crab* and *Dew & Dome*, not far from the pier. The *Rin Beach Kitchen & Bakery*, up towards Hat Rin Nok, offers a wide variety of cakes, rolls and other baked goods. Nearby *Chicken Corner* grills Thai-style chicken, then chops it up and makes tasty chicken sandwiches.

The friendly *Outback Bar*, just up the road from the pier, is fast becoming a Hat Rin institution. This is the place to come for a hearty meal of steak and chips – without the high-volume video noise (gunshots, screeching tyres) that blares forth from many of Hat Rin's other eating establishments. Outback Bar is also a great place to have a few drinks before heading down to the late-night clubs on Hat Rin Nok.

The Shell, on the road between the Hat Rin Nok and Hat Rin Nai, is a popular if a bit pricey Italian food place. *Old Lamp*, on the road immediately parallel to Hat Rin Nok, has become very popular for its well-prepared stuffed baked potatoes, Thai food, sandwiches, salads, and fruit shakes, served in a rustic and dimly lit atmosphere. *Oi's Kitchen* and *J Mon Thai Food* on the same road are two of the more traditionally Thai

places in Hat Rin, and are not expensive. *Orchid Restaurant & Bar*, on the cross-cape road towards Hat Rin Nai, is popular for video dining. Near the pier, *Om Ganesh* has good Indian food. Try a combination of chicken malai tikka and garlic nan.

Getting There & Away Săwngthăew taxis go back and forth between Hat Rin and Thong Sala for 50B. This road was paved with concrete in 1996. The steeper, windier passages are more dangerous now than before the paving, since everyone drives faster and the smooth surface doesn't afford much braking traction.

Motorcycles can be rented in Hat Rin Nok. Take extra care when riding motorbikes on this road as lots of people wipe out on the steep downhill slopes; there's no shoulder on the road either, so watch out for passing vehicles.

There are regular ferries at least three times a day from two piers on northern Ko Samui, Bo Phut and Hat Bang Rak. Departures are around 10.30 am and 1 and 4 pm, and the cost is 100B per person. During the monthly Hat Rin full-moon party the number of departures increases (as does the price of passage) and by midnight speedboats are leaving these piers every 15 or 30 minutes until around 3 or 4 am. We recommend you take one of the day boats as they're safer and less crowded.

East Coast Beaches Between Hat Rin and the village of Ban Nam Tok are several little coves, where you'll find the white-sand beaches of **Hat Yuan** (2.5km north of Hat Rin) and **Hat Wai Nam** (3.5km).

There are a handful of places with huts on Hat Yuan, which is connected by an inland trail with Hat Rin. These include *Good Hope* and *Lazy Fish*, and cost 100B to 200B a night. Long-term stays can be arranged for much less.

At the north-eastern end of Hat Yuan, round a headland, there is accommodation at Hat Thian's *The Sanctuary*, a new-age-oriented spot built into boulders overlooking the beach. Bungalows with shared facilities cost 80B to 100B, with attached bathroom up to 1000B; instruction in yoga, taijiquan, meditation and massage is available. The Sanctuary can be reached on foot or by boat (February to November only). Nearby, the

Haad Tien Resort has wood-and-bamboo bungalows with mosquito nets and attached bathroom for 120B to 200B. To get a boat there from Hat Rin contact Yogurt Home 3 in Hat Rin's commercial ghetto.

Over the next headland at Hat Wai Nam is *Wai Nam Hut*, where huts go for 150B to 200B. If the weather is favourable, boats can be hired to reach these beaches by asking around at Hat Rin Nok.

After that there's little else until **Hat Sadet**. A dirt track (traversable on foot but only partially by motorcycle) runs from Hat Rin to Pang Bon, then follows the coast before heading inland to Ban Nam Tok and Nam Tok Than Sadet.

Hat Yao (5km from Hat Rin) and Hat Yang (6km) are virtually deserted. After that, 2.5km north of Ban Nam Tok by dirt track, is the pretty double bay of Ao Thong Reng, where *Thong Reng Resort* bungalows are 100B to 300B. Above the beach on the headland, *Than Sadet Resort* offers huts for 150B to 250B. North of the headland, a pretty cove ringed by Hat Sadet features a string of places in the 100B to 350B range, including, at last pass, *Silver Cliff Bungalows*, *Mai Pen Rai*, *Mai Pen Rai II*, *JS Hut* and *Nid's*.

The rough dirt track from Ban Tai to Hat Sadet is passable, subject to weather.

Ao Thong Nai Pan This bay is really made up of two bays, **Ao Thong Nai Pan Yai** and **Ao Thong Nai Pan Noi**. The latter has the best all-round swimming beach, although Thong Nai Pan Yai is quieter. At the eastern end of Ao Thong Nai Pan Yai there's a good set of rocks for advanced climbers.

On the beach at Thong Nai Pan Yai, south-east of Ban Thong Nai Pan, are the *White Sand*, *AD View*, *Nice Beach* and *Central* (☎ 077-299059), all with huts costing from 150B to 200B with shared bathroom, 300B to 800B for nicer ones with attached bathroom. The other end of the beach features the similarly priced *Pen's*, *Pingjun Resort*, *Candle* (☎ 077-377073) and *Chanchit Dreamland*.

Up on Thong Nai Pan Noi are the very nicely situated *Panviman Resort* (☎/fax 077-377048; in Bangkok ☎ 02-910 8660) and *Thong Ta Pan Resort*. Panviman sits on a cliff between two beaches and offers 40 rooms (all with private bathroom) in

wooden bungalows or in a two-storey building for 1000B with fan, up to 1800B with air-con. Panviman accepts both MasterCard and Visa. Rooms at the much more basic but clean *Thong Ta Pan Resort*, at the northern end of the smaller bay, cost 200B to 450B.

Nearby is *Star Hut II*, with huts for 120B with shared facilities, 180B to 250B with private toilet and shower. Behind Star Hut II, away from the beach, the *Honey Bungalow* charges 150B with outside bathroom and 250B with private bathroom. *Star Hut I* has huts for 180B without bathroom, 250B to 300B with. Just behind it is *Bio's*, with a few huts as well as a laid-back restaurant with several vegie dishes and a bar that's popular at night. The huts are rather rustic affairs with shared facilities and go for 100B to 150B.

Săwngthăew taxis from Thong Sala to Thong Nai Pan cost 100B. During the low season it can be difficult to find enough people to convince a săwngthăew driver to go at that price, so you may have to charter a vehicle. If you're travelling light it's possible to take a motorcycle taxi there for 150B. Panviman runs its own taxi service from the Thong Sala pier. Take care if you're riding a motorcycle here, as this is probably the most dangerous road on the island – very steep in places, and mostly unsealed.

Hat Khuat & Hat Khom These are two pretty bays with beaches on the northern end of Pha-Ngan and are still largely undeveloped because of the distances from major transport points to Samui and the mainland. Some of the island's cheapest accommodation is found on these bays – hence it's popular with long-termers – but that means there's more likelihood of being evicted from your hut if you don't buy meals from the bungalow kitchens. Be sure to establish whether you'll be required to buy meals before taking a hut.

Hat Khuat (Bottle Beach) is the slightly larger of the two and there's a handful of bungalows stretched across the beach, all in the 100B to 350B range – *Bottle Beach I*, *Bottle Beach II*, *Bottle Beach III* and *Smile Bungalow*. Boats to Hat Khuat leave twice a day during the dry season from Ban Chalok Lam (40B).

West of Hat Khuat, 2.5km across Laem Kung Yai, is Hat Khom, where the *Coral Bay* rents standard huts for 100B without bathroom, 200B to 400B with attached bathroom. Next door are the newly opened *Ocean Bay* (☎ 077-377231) and *Had Khom*, the former offering huts without bathroom for 150B, or 300B to 350B with. Had Khom is similar, with huts for 200B to 300B. You can walk to Hat Khuat from Ban Chalok Lam via a steep trail; it can also be done on a dirtbike or a 4WD vehicle. Ocean Bay has a jeep and will pick up guests in Thong Sala if you call in advance.

The fishing village of **Ban Chalok Lam** at the centre of Ao Chalok Lam features several small family-owned grocery stores, laundry services and lots of fish drying at the side of the main street. You can also rent bikes and diving equipment. Of the several restaurants, the best are *Seaside* and *Porn*. There are also a few inexpensive *noodle stands* around.

Chaloklum Diving School here offers scuba courses in English or German. There are also some places to stay along Hat Chalok Lam at the eastern and western edges of the bay. Starting from the north-eastern corner of the village, *Fanta* has several rows of huts starting at 150B per person, and a fair chunk of beach frontage.

Across Khlong Ok via a footbridge, *Try Tong Resort* offers largish wooden cabins facing the bay and canal for 80B to 200B (closed during the rainy season). There's no beach at Try Thong except for a small chunk with boulders at the surf line. Farther on towards Hat Khom is *Thai Life*, with simple huts for 50B, and better bungalows with facilities for up to 200B.

At the other end of Hat Chalok Lam, west of the village, is the slightly nicer *Wattana* with huts for 100B and bungalows with fan for 250B. The beach is better here, too. Still, we've received mixed reports on this place; some people loved it, others didn't.

The road between Thong Sala and Ban Chalok Lam is sealed all the way, and săwngthăew do the route regularly for 40B per person. You can do the same trip by motorcycle for 60B.

Ao Chalok Lam is a good place to hire boats for explorations of the northern coast as many fishermen dock here (particularly from February to September). During this season boats run regularly from here to Hat Khuat twice a day for 40B per person. On some days the service may be cancelled due to high surf, so anyone electing to stay at Hat Khuat should leave a couple of extra days when planning their departure from the island, just in case.

Ao Hat Thong Lang & Ao Mae Hat As you move west on Ko Pha-Ngan, as on Ko Samui, the sand gets browner and coarser. The secluded beach and cove at Ao Hat Thong Lang had no accommodation at the time of writing.

An all-weather road leads west from Chalok Lam to Ban Mae Hat, a small fishing village with a few bungalow resorts. The beach at Ao Mae Hat isn't fantastic, but there is a bit of coral offshore. Close by, a little inland via a well-marked dirt track (200m off the road from Chalok Lam near the 9km marker), is **Nam Tok Wang Sai**, also known as Paradise Falls.

Towards the north-eastern end of the bay, *Maehaad Bungalows* has good, simple thatched huts for 50B plus wood-and-thatch huts with private bathroom for up to 150B, while *Crystal Island Garden* has small wooden huts in the same price range. Nearby *Mae Hat Bay Resort* has larger bungalows for 300B. Crystal Island has the better beach view. Moving south-westward, the *Island View Cabana* offers good clapboard huts from 150B to 250B for nicer ones. The Island View also has a good restaurant.

Wang Sai Resort, at the south-western end of Mae Hat, offers nice-sized bungalows built among boulders on a hillside; all have views of the beach and bay. Rates range from 100B to 200B, depending on the position on the slope. An open-air restaurant is situated well away from the huts, down on the beach. A dive operation here offers instruction and guided trips. On Ko Ma (Horse Island), opposite the beach, *Ko Ma Dive Resort* has a few bungalows for 200B to 300B.

Hat Salat & Hat Yao These coral-fringed beaches are fairly difficult to reach – the road from Ban Si Thanu to the south is very bad in spots, even for experienced dirtbikers – come by boat if possible. Hat Yao is a long, pretty beach with a reasonable drop-off that makes it one of the island's best swimming beaches. It's also good for snorkelling. Equipment can be rented at the Phangan Divers branch at Haad Yao Bungalows.

Hat Salat has *My Way*, with huts for 80B to 150B, and *Salad Hut* with newer bungalows for 200B to 300B. Down at Hat Yao are the basic *Benjawan*, *Dream Hill*, *Graceland*, *Blue Coral Beach*, *Sandy Bay*, *Silver Beach*, *Ibiza*, *Seaboard*, *Bayview* and *Hat Thian*; the latter two are isolated on a beach north of Hat Yao around the headland, and the road is very steep and rocky. Most of these places offer basic huts starting at 60B to 100B, as well as more-luxurious bungalows for up to 800B.

Along the best section of beach is *Haad Yao Bungalows* (☎ 01-228 1947), which sensibly charges extra for basic accommodation if you don't eat there and has 200B to 800B bungalows. At the end of this bay is the two-storey, open-air *Eagle Pub*, a cool spot for a drink at night.

Hat Chaophao & Ao Si Thanu

Hat Chaophao is a rounded beach two headlands south of Hat Yao; around a larger headland at the southern end of Ao Chaophao is Ao Si Thanu. In these areas you begin to see the occasional mangrove along the coast; inland there's a pretty lagoon at the southern end of Hat Chaophao.

There are several places to stay along the beach at Hat Chaophao. The popular *Jungle Huts*, *Sea Flower*, *Sri Thanu* and *Great Bay* all have bungalows with private bathroom for 100B to 300B. The Sea Flower (its card reads 'no telephone numbers, no air condition') is especially well run. At the southern end of the bay, past curving Laem Niat, *Bovy Resort* has standard huts with attached bathroom for 100B – when it's open. Ask at the Bovy Supermarket in Thong Sala to make sure.

On the rounded, pine-studded cape of Laem Son, at the northern end of Ao Si Thanu proper, lies *Laem Son I & II*, with simple, quiet, shaded huts for 100B to 250B, and nicer bungalows for up to 500B, depending on the season. South over a creek comes *Seaview Rainbow*, with bungalows for 200B to 400B. Down towards the southern end of the bay, *Lada* offers 200B to 250B bungalows with fan and bathroom.

Loy Fa and *Chai*, both sitting high on a point at the southern end of the bay on the cape of Laem Si Thanu, offer good views and sturdy huts. Nicely landscaped Loy Fa, the better-run of the two, offers good-sized wooden cottages for 150B and concrete ones for 200B, all with fan, mosquito net, toilet and shower. Loy Fah also has two large, 500B cottages at the bottom of the cliff on a private cove. In the low season you can knock 50% off these rates. Down at the southern base of the cliff is the similarly priced *Nantakarn*, but it's not as good value.

Ao Hin Kong/Ao Wok Tum This long bay – sometimes divided in two by a stream that feeds into the sea – is just a few kilometres north of Thong Sala but so far has hardly any development. At the centre of Hin Kong, not far from the village of Ban Hin Kong, is the basic *Lipstick Cabana* (☎ 077-377294), with rooms for 60B to 250B.

Down around the cape that separates Ao Wok Tum from Ao Nai Wok are *Woktum Bay*, *OK*, *Darin*, *Sea Scene*, *Porn Sawan*, *Cookies* and *Beach 99*, most with simple huts for 60B to 80B. Darin and Sea Scene also have bungalows with private bathroom in the 150B to 250B range. Săwngthăew to this area cost 30B per person but you won't see them outside ferry departure/arrival times.

See the earlier Thong Sala section for accommodation just north of Thong Sala at Ao Nai Wok.

Getting There & Away

Ko Samui Songserm Travel (☎ 077-377046) operates express boats between Tha Na Thon on Ko Samui and Tha Thong Sala on Ko Pha-Ngan two or three times daily, depending on the season. The trip takes 50 minutes and costs 100B each way.

Boats go direct from the pier at Samui's Hat Bang Rak to Hat Rin Nai on Ko Pha-Ngan for 100B (150B on full-moon nights). The boat sometimes leaves from the pier at Bo Phut instead. This boat departs from Bang Rak/Bo Phut just about every day at 10.30 am and 1 and 3.30 pm, depending on the weather and number of prospective passengers, and takes 40 to 45 minutes to reach the bay at Hat Rin. In the reverse direction it usually leaves at 9.30 and 11.30 am and 2.30 pm and takes 30 to 40 minutes.

From January to September there is also one boat a day from Hat Mae Nam on Samui to Ao Thong Nai Pan on Pha-Ngan, with a stop at Hat Rin. The fares are 150B and 100B respectively and the boat usually leaves Mae Nam around 1 pm. In the reverse direction the boat starts from Ao Thong Nai Pan around 8 am.

Faster, more-powerful speedboats carrying 35 passengers go between Hat Mae Nam and Na Thon in Samui and Thong Sala for 200B; this boat only takes about half an hour to reach Thong Sala.

Surat Thani You can also take a slow night ferry direct to Thong Sala from Tha Ban Don in Surat (150B lower deck, 200B upper deck, 6½ hours, 10 pm).

The night ferry can be a rough ride when seas are high – November is the worst month. As on the night ferry to Samui, don't leave your bags unattended on the boat – there have been several reports of theft.

Ko Tao Subject to weather conditions, there are a total of four daily boats between Thong Sala and Ko Tao, 45km north. The trip takes from 1½ hours to 2½ hours, depending on the boat, and costs 150B to 200B one way. Departures are at 7 and 11.30 am and 1 pm.

A speedboat runs between Thong Sala and Ko Tao once a day for 350B per person; it leaves at 12.30 pm and the crossing takes less than an hour.

Train/Bus/Boat Combinations At Bangkok's Hualamphong station you can purchase train tickets that include a bus from the Surat Thani train station (Phun Phin) to Tha Ban Don and then a ferry to Ko Pha-Ngan. These generally cost around 30B to 50B more than if you buy each ticket separately yourself.

Getting Around
A couple of roads branch out from Thong Sala, primarily to the north and the south-east. One road goes north-west from Thong Sala a few kilometres along the shoreline to the villages of Ban Hin Kong and Ban Si Thanu. From Ban Si Thanu the road runs north-east across the island to Ban Chalok Lam. Another road goes straight north from Thong Sala to Chalok Lam. There is also a

very poor dirt track along the west coast from Ban Si Thanu to Ao Hat Yao and Ao Hat Salat.

Hat Khuat can be reached on foot from Ban Fai Mai (2km) or Ban Chalok Lam (4km), but there are also boats.

The road south-east from Thong Sala to Ban Khai passes an intersection where another road goes north to Ban Thong Nang and Ban Thong Nai Pan. The paved road to Hat Rin is now passable year-round, so there's regular transport between Thong Sala and Hat Rin. Even with the paving, only experienced motorbike riders should attempt the section between Ban Khai and Hat Rin. Steep grades, blind turns and a slippery road surface make it the second-most-dangerous piece of road on the island, after the road to Thong Nai Pan (although there are more fatalities along the Hat Rin stretch, due to greater speeds).

Săwngthăew and motorcycle taxis handle all the public transport along island roads. Some places can only be reached by motorcycle; some places only by boat or on foot.

You can rent motorcycles in Thong Sala for 200B to 250B a day.

Săwngthăew & Motorcycle Taxi From Thong Sala, săwngthăew to Hat Chaophao and Hat Yao are 40B and 50B per person respectively, while motorcycle taxis cost 50B and 80B. To Ban Khai it's 30B by săwngthăew, and 40B by motorcycle; if you're only going as far as Wat Khao Tham or Ban Tai the fare is 30B for motorcycles and drops to 20B for a săwngthăew.

A săwngthăew from Thong Sala to Ban Chalok Lam costs 40B, a motorcycle taxi 50B. To get to Hat Rin from Thong Sala, a săwngthăew costs 50B one way while a motorbike is 70B.

Thong Nai Pan can be reached from Thong Sala by săwngthăew (100B) or motorcycle (150B).

Boat There are daily boats from Ao Chalok Lam to Hat Khuat at 8 am and 1 and 5 pm (returning at 9.30 am and 3 and 6 pm) for 40B per person. Boats run between Thong Sala and Hat Yao daily at noon for 40B per person. The service operates from January to September, depending on the weather. Boats can also be chartered from beach to beach; the price is negotiable.

KO TAO
เกาะเต่า

Ko Tao translates as 'turtle island', so-named because of its shape. It's only about 21 sq km and the population of 750 is mostly involved in fishing, growing co-conuts and tourism. Snorkelling and diving are particularly good due to the island's distance from the mouth of Mae Nam Tapi, which affords high visibility and an abundance of coral. Most of the beaches are too shallow for swimming, with the exception of Ao Leuk (Deep Bay).

Since it takes three to five hours to get here from the mainland (from either Chumphon or Surat Thani via Ko Pha-Ngan), Ko Tao doesn't get people coming over for day trips or for quick overnighters. Still, the island can become quite crowded during the high season, when Hat Ao Mae, Hat Sai Ri and Ao Chalok Ban Kao have people sleeping on the beach waiting for huts to vacate.

Ban Mae Hat, on the western side of the island, is where inter-island boats land. The only other villages on the island are **Ban Hat Sai Ri**, about midway up the western coast, and **Ban Chalok Ban Kao** to the south. Just 1km off the north-western shore of the island is **Ko Nang Yuan**, which is really three islands joined by a sand bar.

The granite promontory of **Laem Tato** at the southern tip of Ko Tao makes a nice hike from Ban Chalok Ban Kao. About the only thing of historic interest on the island is a large boulder where King Rama V had his initials carved to commemorate a royal visit in 1900. The boulder, located at the southern end of Hat Sai Ri, has become something of a local shrine and is the focus of a small ceremony every October.

Information
Ban Mae Hat, a one-street town with a busy pier, is the only commercial centre on the island. Here you'll find a police station, post and telephone office, travel agents, dive shops, restaurants and general stores. Boat tickets can be purchased at a booking office by the harbour as well as from travel agents. At Mr J's store near the school between Hat Ao Mae and Hat Sai Ri, you'll find information on accommodation and transportation as well as a decent selection of books. Mr J also offers a Thai visa-extension service.

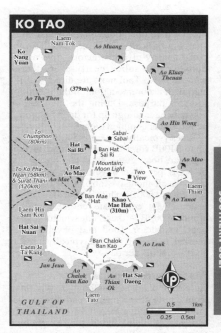

Money Krung Thai Bank has a money-exchange window near the pier, and there are also several moneychangers.

Post & Communications The post office and public phone office in Ban Mae Hat is open from 8.30 am to 4 pm daily. Beware of private phone offices, which charge exorbitant rates.

Maps Map aficionados should pick up a copy of Visid Hongsombud's *Guide Map of Koh Pha-Ngan & Koh Tao*. Besides being very detailed and reasonably up-to-date, it is printed on waterproof stock.

Diving & Snorkelling
Relative to its size, Ko Tao has a large number of dive centres, with some of Thailand's lowest prices for training and/or excursions. Underwater visibility is high and the water is cleaner than around most other inhabited islands in the gulf. Due to the fàràng presence, the best spots have English names such as White Rock, Shark Island, Chumphon Pinnacle, Green Rock and South-West Pinnacles.

SOUTHERN GULF

At the time of writing there were more than 20 dive operations on the island, most charging basically the same rates. To support so many dive instructors, dive operations have to solicit nearly every tourist who visits Ko Tao; most are directly affiliated with accommodation on the island for just this purpose. During the high season you may have to sign up for diving or you'll be refused accommodation.

Rates typically run from 800B per dive, up to 5400B for a 10-dive package (including gear, boat, guide, food and beverages) or 550B per dive if you bring your own gear. An all-inclusive introductory dive lesson costs 1500B, while a four-day, open-water PADI certificate course goes for around 8000B – these rates include gear, boat, instructor, food and beverages. A snorkel, mask and fins are typically hired as a set for 100B per day.

Massage & Taijiquan

Here & Now (e hereandnow_tao@hotmail .com), just off the inland road directly behind Ban's Diving Resort, offers classes in *taijiquan* (t'ai chi) and *qi gong* taught by a German expat. Nine-session early-morning or evening courses cost 1800B. His wife and daughter also offer traditional Thai massage for 550B for 2½ hours.

Places to Stay

With the steady transformation of Ko Tao into a diving resort, accommodation has moved upmarket. Especially along Hat Ao Mae and Hat Sai Ri, the days of the thatched hut are over. Most of the bungalow operations along these beaches are quite eye-catching and set on nicely landscaped grounds. The telling difference between bungalow operations here and those on Ko Pha-Ngan's Hat Rin or Ko Samui's Hat Chaweng is that here the reception desk is usually a dive shop. Walk in prepared to sign up for a dive course and you will find that prices for accommodation are quite reasonable for the amenities provided – as low as 150B to 300B – or sometimes free! Of course, if you're not interested in diving it's likely that you'll be directed to some vague place farther up the beach. Keep in mind that even if you do sign up for a dive course at one of these places, your welcome will wear out soon after the course is finished. If

business is slow you may get away with not taking a diving course, but you'll find the price of accommodation is about three times higher than if you had. Also, be sure to note the check-out time where you're staying. Many places on Ko Tao want you gone by 11 am, but some will have you up and out as early as 10 am!

Some of the cheaper bungalows operations – especially those at the northern end of Hat Sai Ri and at Ao Tha Then – will give you the boot if you don't buy food at their restaurants; we still receive reports of visitors being locked out of their bungalows or being violently ejected.

During the high season from December to March it can be difficult to find accommodation anywhere on the island. On arrival at Ban Mae Hat it may be best to follow a tout who can find vacant bungalows, otherwise your chances of finding a place on your own might be very slim.

Ao Mae Hat Ao Mae, the shallow bay just north of Ban Mae Hat, has plenty of coral but the southern end gets a lot of rubbish from the pier area at Ban Mae Hat. *Crystal* (☎ *077-456106, fax 456105)* is for divers only and offers standard bungalows with fan and bathroom for 500B. If you dive with Crystal the price drops to 200B; if you take a beginners course, the room is free. *Beach Club* (☎ *077-456222)* has fan bungalows for 800B and comfortable air-con duplexes for 1500B.

On the headland overlooking the bay is *Queen Resort* (☎ *077-456002)*, the first non-dive oriented place you'll come to walking north from the pier. Rustic wooden bungalows with fan and bathroom go for 250B to 350B (50B less without bathroom). There's a good restaurant on the premises. *Tommy's Resort* (☎ *077-456039)* is a divers-only place that has fan bungalows for 500B and air-con for 800B. Just beyond Tommy's, the *View Cliff Restaurant & Bungalows* offers basic huts with fan for 250B and larger air-con huts for 1000B to 1900B, depending on the season.

Hat Sai Ri Around the headland to the north is the longest beach, with a string of dive operations and bungalows, starting with *In Touch*, a creatively decorated spot where bungalows with private bathroom cost just 300B to 450B. Next is the larger *AC Resort II* (☎ *077-456195*), which has sturdy bungalows with attached bathroom and nice landscaping in the 250B to 500B range.

AC Resort I (☎ *077-456033*) will only rent rooms to people who agree in advance to sign up for their dives. Rooms are 250B to 500B with attached bathroom and fan, and 800B for air-con.

Bing Bungalow (☎ *077-456172*), on the other side of the road, has cheaper wooden bungalows for 150B with attached bathroom.

Ban's Diving Resort (☎ *077-456061*) offers sturdy bungalows ranging from 300B for fan to 800B for air-con. There's even a swimming pool at this place, one of the two biggest diving schools on the island.

The sign at *Haad Sai Ree Resort* is only that – the bungalows behind it belong to Ban's Diving Resort next door.

Ko Tao Marina Resort (☎ *077-456173*) has fan rooms ranging from 300B to 550B (depending on the location) and air-con for 850B. Next are a couple of cheapies: *SB Cabana* (☎ *077-456005*) has clean wooden bungalows with fan and attached bathroom for 250B to 300B. Nearby *Sai Ree Cottages* (☎ *077-456126*) has much the same arrangement for 250B.

Sea Shell Resort and *Lotus Resort* (☎ *077-456271*) are both run by a friendly English-speaking Thai woman from Ko Samui. Neither place is affiliated with a dive operation. At Sea Shell, fan rooms with bathroom go for 400B to 700B while air-con costs 1500B. Lotus is steeper in price by comparison, 1200B for a fan bungalow on the beach and 1600B for air-con. Both places are clean and very well run, although compared to the others, this area is rather lacking in shade.

Next is *New Way* (☎ *077-456208*), which used to be popular with long-termers but has become more dive-oriented of late. It has standard wooden bungalows with fan and bathroom from 150B.

Big Blue Resort (☎ *077-456179*) has wooden bungalows with fan and bathroom and will give you four nights free if you sign up for a dive course. These rooms would normally go for 200B to 300B but you'll not be welcome here if you don't want to dive.

Simple Life (☎ *077-456142*) offers concrete fan bungalows for 300B and larger wooden affairs for 400B. Just in case you've brought a pool cue along with your mask and fins, Simple Life's bar occasionally holds pool tournaments.

The air-con stucco cottages at *Sunset Buri Resort* (☎ *077-456266*) go for a Mediterranean look. They start at 800B for rooms with fan (500B in the low season) and there's a swimming pool.

Farther north along Hat Sai Ri are four places in the 200B to 400B range: *Sai Ree Hut*; *O-Chai* (seems to attract a loyal following of long-termers); *Blue Wind* (good restaurant attached); and *Pranee's* (☎ *077-456080*). The latter is on a large lot and boasts electric power all night. It's quiet and is a good place for families. A nice bungalow with fan and private bathroom costs 200B to 300B, depending on proximity to the beach.

About half a kilometre up the road behind Ban Hat Sai Ri is *Sabai-Sabai*, which has comfortable and tastefully done bungalows that are used exclusively as accommodation for dive students. If you want to stay here you can sign up for a course at Crystal on Hat Ao Mae and request accommodation at Sabai-Sabai. The attached *Orchid Restaurant* is said to be good.

North of the beach, in an area called Ao Ta Then, there are several operations with inexpensive basic bungalows – most off the beach and built high on the rocks – including *Golden Cape*, *Silver Cliff*, *Sun Sea*, *Sun Lord* and *Eden Resort*, all in the 200B to 300B range. Silver Cliff is the best choice – some huts have great bay views. Farther north, the lone *CFT* has basic huts for 100B and bungalows with attached bathroom for up to 400B.

Ao Muang & Ao Kluay Theuan On the northern and north-eastern tip of the island, accessible only by boat, are two coral-fringed coves without bungalow accommodation. As the pressure for places to stay increases, new operations should start appearing at both.

Ao Hin Wong South of Ao Kluay Theuan by sea, or 2km north-east of Ban Hat Sai Ri by trail, is tranquil Ao Hin Wong. *Hin Wong Bungalows* and *Green Tree* have huts for 80B to 100B with shared bathroom.

Ao Mao, Laem Thian & Ao Tanot Continuing clockwise around the island, Ao Mao, connected by a 2km dirt trail to Ban Hat Sai Ri, is another cove with no beach accommodation so far. On the cape that juts out over the northern end of Ao Tanot, *Laem Thian* has huts built among the rocks for 80B to 150B with shared bathroom. Bungalows with private bathroom go for 600B to 800B.

Ao Tanot proper, to the south, is one of the island's best spots for snorkelling and features a good set of bungalow operations, the proprietors of which so far cooperate to keep the beach clean. The well-landscaped *Tanote Bay Resort* (☎ 01-970 4703) charges 200B to 500B for 24 simple but well-maintained huts, all with private bathroom, while *Poseidon* has very simple huts for 100B and bungalows with attached bathroom for 300B to 400B. *Mountain Reef Resort* has bungalows with attached bathroom for 300B to 400B. The friendly *Diamond Beach* offers huts for 100B to 150B. *Bamboo Hut* has 15 decked bungalows for 150B to 500B; the kitchen specialises in spicy southern Thai–style food.

From May to August it is difficult to get to Ao Tanot by boat as the water is very shallow and the taxi boats may become stranded or even damage the coral. Some years it's possible to make the trip, but this depends on tidal cycles.

Khao Mae Hat On the way to Ao Tanot from Mae Hat, a path forks off the main track and leads up the slopes of 310m-high Khao Mae Hat in the centre of the island to *Two View*, so named because it affords sunrise and sunset views of both sides of the island. It's about an hour's walk up the path from Ao Tanot. There are only six bungalows, which cost 80B/100B for single/double. There is no electricity or generator: Kerosene lamps and candles provide light at night. Organically grown vegetarian food (without MSG!) and herbal teas are available in the restaurant. Two View advertises three-day meditation retreats, as well as courses in massage, chakra-balancing, yoga, rebirthing, natural colon-cleansing and sessions to help you recall past lives. Prices for courses start at 600B and run up to US$220. Two View shuts down in October and November.

A couple of other places are farther along the same trail atop the ridge in the centre of the island. *Mountain* has rooms for 50B to 100B, as does the nearby *Moon Light*. Both places are more easily accessed from a trail that leads from near Tommy's on Hat Ao Mae.

Ao Leuk & Hat Sai Daeng Ao Leuk, connected by a 2.2km dirt track with Ban Mae Hat, has the lone *Ao Leuk Resort,* with eight huts for 200B to 300B with attached bathroom. Nearby *Nice Moon* has only six simple bungalows with bathroom, starting at 250B.

Another kilometre or so south is Hat Sai Daeng, where *Coral View Resort* (☎ 01-970 0378) has 16 well-built bungalows all with private bathroom starting at 350B in the high season (a bit less in the low season). Coral View is run by a friendly Australian-Thai couple and if you call in advance and make a reservation, they will send a taxi boat to pick you up at the pier at Ban Mae Hat.

Ao Thian Ok & Laem Tato Farther west on the side of the impressive Laem Tato is pretty Ao Thian Ok, where the friendly *Rocky* has rooms from 350B to 500B, 100B less during the low season. The food at *New Heaven,* a restaurant atop the cliff overlooking the bay and resort, is quite expensive for the minuscule portions served.

Ao Chalok Ban Kao This nicely situated coral beach, about 1.7km south of Ban Mae Hat by road, has become quite crowded. In the high season it can be very difficult to find a vacant hut and some travellers end up sleeping on the floor of a restaurant for a night or two until something is available.

On the hill overlooking the western part of the bay you'll find *Laem Khlong* (☎ 077-456083) with fan rooms for 500B – but it's not on the beach – and *Sunshine II,* which has bungalows for 350B and up. Next is *Sunshine* (☎ 077-456219), with basic but clean bungalows for 200B to 300B, all with fan and attached bathroom. *Buddha View Dive Resort* (☎ 077-456074/5, ⓔ buddha@samart.co.th) next door has comfortable bungalows for free if you book its open-water dive course for 7800B. There's also a swimming pool on the premises. This is one of the two big dive schools on the island and its getting bigger. The restaurant is one of the better ones outside Hat Sai Ri.

Next is *Tropicana* (☎ *077-456167*), where bungalows with fan and bathroom are 400B to 600B. *Big Fish* (☎ *077-456132*) is another bungalow-cum-dive-centre with free accommodation for dive students. Those uninterested in diving need not apply.

Towards the eastern end of the bay, *Ko Tao Cottage Dive Resort* (☎ *077-456198*, e *ktcdive@samart.co.th*) has some of the island's most luxurious accommodation for 550B to 780B. Naturally there's a dive centre here, and you get 30% off the room rates when you sign up for a course.

Around a couple of small points to the south along Laem Tato is a beach that can only be reached on foot at low tide. Here *Taa Toh Lagoon* offers 25 screened huts with private bathroom for 250B to 500B. Nearby *Freedom Beach* has a few basic bungalows for 100B with attached bathroom, better ones for 150B and a furnished wooden bungalow with a view for 400B. Connected by a network of bridges and walkways, bungalows at the *Pond Resort* perch on rocks overlooking the bay and start at 300B. Also on the hillside is the rather shabby *Aud Bungalow* for 250B to 350B.

South-West of Mae Hat As might be expected, beaches just south of town get better the farther south you go. A few hundred metres south-west of Mae Hat, across a stream and down a footpath, is the upmarket *Sensi Paradise Resort* (☎ *077-456244*), with solid cottages for 850B (fan) to 3200B (air-con), as well as a few larger places with sleeping lofts suitable for families for 3500B. Another semi-upmarket place, *Ko Tao Royal Resort* (☎ *077-456157*), offers bungalows for 800B to 1500B with fan and toilet and 2500B with air-con. *Blue Diamond* (☎ *077-456255*) has decent fan bungalows for 800B, half that in the low season. *Thai Style* next door has a similar arrangement for 100B less.

A couple of kilometres farther south of Ban Mae Hat is a series of small beaches collectively known as **Hat Sai Nuan**, where

you'll find the popular *Siam Cookie* and *Char Bungalows*, both charging 100B to 300B.

At **Laem Je Ta Kang** about 1.2km west of Ao Chalok Ban Kao, on a difficult-to-reach rocky area between two beaches, you'll find *Tao Thong Villa* (100B to 450B). South of Laem Je Ta Kang, on **Ao Jun Jeua**, are *Sunset* (100B to 150B) and *Moon Dance* (250B). The Sunset has a beautiful point that juts out into the sea. The only way to get to these places is to walk along the dirt track from Mae Hat or take a long-tail boat.

Ko Nang Yuan This pretty little tripartite island is occupied by *Ko Nangyuan Dive Resort* (☎ *077-456091/2, fax 456093*) where, as the name suggests, the emphasis is on diving. Accommodation starts at 1200B for fan bungalows and goes up to 1700B for air-con. A package deal is offered in which you can stay three nights and take a four-day dive course for 9000B to 10,000B, depending on the season. Regular daily boats from Tha Ban Mae Hat to Nang Yuan leave at 10.30 am and 5.30 pm. In the opposite direction boats leave at 8.30 am and 4 pm. The round trip costs 60B. You can easily charter a ride for 100B at any time of day. Note that the management does not allow any plastic bottles on the island – these will be confiscated on arrival.

Places to Eat
In Ban Mae Hat there's a string of simple seafood restaurants with dining platforms built over the water's edge. *Baan Yaay* and *Liab Thale* are two of the better ones. The *Swiss Bakery*, next to the post office, sells very good breads and pastries; it's open from 7 am to 6 pm. There are also several *restaurants* on Hat Sai Ri, most associated with bungalows, as well as a few *eateries* in Ban Hat Sai Ri.

Entertainment
If after a day of diving you have any energy left, head to Hat Sai Ri, where the bar at the *AC Resort* throws a party every other night. A hipper scene can be found at *Venus*, a dance club under a canopy of trees along the beach just north of Ban's Diving Resort. To keep things interesting, the house DJ hosts weekly theme nights.

SOUTHERN GULF

Getting There & Away

Bangkok Bus/boat combination tickets from Bangkok cost 750B to 850B and are available from travel agents on Thanon Khao San. Promotional bus/boat combination tickets in the opposite direction are sometimes offered for as little as 500B.

Beware of travel agents on Ko Tao selling boat/train combinations. Usually this involves receiving a 'voucher' that you are supposed to be able to exchange for a train ticket in Surat Thani or Chumphon; more than a few travellers have found the vouchers worthless. If you book train reservations a few days (or more) in advance, any legitimate agency on Ko Tao should be able to deliver the train tickets themselves. It's same-day or day-before reservations that usually have voucher problems.

Chumphon At least three boats from the mainland run daily from Chumphon to Ko Tao. Departures may be fewer if the swells are high. The slow boat leaves Chumphon at midnight (200B, five or six hours). In the opposite direction it departs from Ko Tao at 10 am. See the Chumphon section for more details.

A speedboat departs from Chumphon at 7.30 am (from Ban Mae Hat at 10.30 am) and takes about one hour and 40 minutes, and costs 400B per person.

Surat Thani Every night, depending on the weather, a boat runs between Surat Thani (Tha Thong) and Ko Tao, a seven- to eight-hour trip for 350B one way. From Surat, boats depart at 11 pm. From Ban Mae Hat the departure time is 8.30 pm.

Ko Pha-Ngan Depending on weather conditions, boats run daily between the Thong Sala pier on Ko Pha-Ngan and Ban Mae Hat on Ko Tao. The trip takes anywhere from 2½ to three hours and costs 150B per person. Boats leave Thong Sala at 11.30 am and return from Ko Tao at 9.30 am the next day.

Songserm runs an express boat to Thong Sala daily at 10.30 am and 2.30 pm (250B, 1½ hours). Need faster service? Once a day – again depending on marine conditions – a speed boat does the trip in an hour, leaving at 9.30 am (350B).

Ko Samui A slow boat leaves Ko Tao daily at 9.30 am and arrives at Hat Mae Nam at 1 pm (250B). Speedboats leave at 9.30 am and 3 pm, arriving an hour and 20 minutes later at Na Thon and Hat Mae Nam respectively (450B).

Getting Around

Săwngthăew cost 30B per person from the pier to Hat Sai Ri and Ao Chalok Ban Kao. To bays on the other side of the island, like Ao Tanot, expect to pay about 50B (less if the săwngthăew is full). At night it may take up to 100B to motivate a driver. Long-tail boats can be chartered for up to 2000B a day, depending on the number of passengers carried.

Between 9 and 10 am (weather permitting) a round-island boat leaves from Hat Sai Ri and stops off in four or five places, including Ko Nang Yuan, while people snorkel and swim, returning to Hat Sai Ri around 4 pm. The cost is 250B per person.

Walking is an easy way to get around the island, but some trails aren't clearly marked and can be difficult to follow. You can walk around the whole island in a day, although the undulating, rocky paths make it a challenging proposition.

Nakhon Si Thammarat Province

Much of this large southern province is covered with rugged mountains and forests, which were, until recently, the last refuge of Thailand's communist insurgents. The province's eastern border is formed by the Gulf of Thailand and much of the provincial economy is dependent on fishing and prawn (shrimp) farming. Along the north coast are several nice beaches: **Khanom**, **Nai Phlao**, **Tong Yi**, **Sichon** and **Hin Ngam**.

In the interior are several caves and waterfalls, including **Nam Tok Phrom Lok**, **Tham Thong Phannara** and **Nam Tok Yong**. Besides fishing, Nakhon residents earn a living by growing coffee, rice, rubber and fruit (especially *mangkhút*, or mangosteen).

KHAO LUANG NATIONAL PARK
อุทยานแห่งชาติเขาหลวง

Known for its beautiful mountain and forest walks, cool streams, waterfalls and fruit orchards, this 570-sq-km park in the centre of the province surrounds **Khao Luang**, at 1835m the highest peak in peninsular Thailand. Along with other forested igneous peaks to the west, Khao Luang provides a watershed that feeds Mae Nam Rapi. Local Thais practise a unique form of agriculture called *sŭan rôm* (shade garden, or shade farm). Instead of clear-cutting the forest, they leave many indigenous trees intact, randomly interspersing them with betel, mangosteen, rambutan, langsat, papaya, durian and banana trees. Cleverly placed bamboo and PVC pipes irrigate the mixed orchards without the use of pumps.

Wildlife includes clouded leopard, tiger, elephant, banteng, gaur, tapir, serow, musk deer, macaque, civet, binturong and Javan mongoose, plus over 200 bird species and more than 300 orchid varieties (including several indigenous species).

Park bungalows can be rented for 600B to 1000B per night and sleep six to 12 people. Reservations can be made by calling ☎ 075-309047. *Camping* is permitted along the trail to the summit of Khao Luang (see Hiking Trails later). There are a few private *bungalows* and *cafes* on the road to the park offices that offer accommodation and food. Standard national park admission fees apply (20B for Thais, 200B for foreigners).

Hiking Trails
Although park facilities are so far scant, the park now features several nature trails. You can hike 2.5km through dense tropical forest to the top of **Nam Tok Karom** from the national park headquarters near Lan Saka (25km from Nakhon Si Thammarat), off Rte 4015. Every 500m or so there are shelters and seats. To reach seven-tiered **Nam Tok Krung Ching**, a half-day walk, you'll have to take the Krung Ching nature trail from Nopphitam at the north-eastern border of the park, off Rte 4140. Along the way you'll pass the world's largest tree fern, an old communist insurgent camp, Tham Pratuchai (a cave also used by the communists) and a mangosteen forest. This trail, too, is lined with seats and shelters. The falls are most impressive right after the rainy season has ended, in November and December.

A more challenging trail leads from a car park near Khiriwong to the **summit of Khao Luang**, a 14-hour walk best divided into two or more days. Night-time temperatures at the summit can drop to 5°C, so come prepared with plenty of warm clothing, and sleeping bags if you have them. At 600m, Kratom Suan Sainai offers a simple-roofed shelter and also marks the upper limit of the fruit plantations. In the dry season you can camp next to a riverbed at Lan Sai, about a six-hour walk from the car park. A five-hour walk farther on, along a section of very steep trail, you'll enter a cloud forest full of rattan, orchids, rhododendrons, ferns and stunted oaks. From here it's another three hours to the summit, where, if the weather is clear, you'll be rewarded with stunning views of layer after layer of mountains rolling into the distance.

The best and safest way to appreciate the Khao Luang trek is to go with a guide from the Kiriwong Village Ecotourism Club (☎ 075-309010) in Khiriwong. For about 1300B per person the villagers can arrange a two- or three-night trek along with all meals and guide services. The guides can point out local flora and fauna that you might otherwise miss. The only time to do this hike is January to June, when the trails are dry and leeches not as bad. During heavy rains the trail can be impassable for days.

Getting There & Away
To reach the park, take a sǎwngthǎew (25B) from Nakhon Si Thammarat to the village of Khiriwong at the base of Khao Luang. The entrance to the park and the offices of the Royal Forest Department are 33km from the centre of Nakhon on Rte 4015, an asphalt road that climbs almost 400m in 2.5km to the office and a further 450m to the car park.

NAKHON SI THAMMARAT
อ.เมืองนครศรีธรรมราช

postcode 80000 • pop 73,600
Centuries before the 8th-century Srivijaya empire subjugated the peninsula, there was a city-state here called Ligor or Lagor, capital of the Tambralinga kingdom, which was well known throughout Oceania. Later, when Sri Lankan-ordained Buddhist monks

established a monastery at the city, the name was changed to the Pali-Sanskrit Nagara Sri Dhammaraja (City of the Sacred Dharma-King), rendered in Thai phonetics as Nakhon Si Thammarat. An overland route between the western port of Trang and eastern port of Nakhon Si Thammarat functioned as a major trade link between Thailand and the rest of the world, as well as between the western and eastern hemispheres. Clergy from Hindu, Muslim, Christian and Buddhist denominations established missions here over the centuries, and even in contemporary Nakhon Si Thammarat you'll find active temples, shrines, mosques and churches representing each of these faiths.

During the early development of the various Thai kingdoms, Nakhon Si Thammarat also became a very important centre of religion and culture. Thai shadow theatre (*năng tàlung*) and classical dance-drama (*lákhon* – the Thai pronunciation of Lagor) were developed in Nakhon Si Thammarat; buffalo-hide shadow puppets and dance masks are still made here.

In the past, people from Nakhon Si Thammarat were stereotyped as somewhat rough and prone to criminal activity, but a new civic pride has developed in recent years and the natives are now quite fond of being called *khon khawn* (Nakhon people). Bovorn (Bowon) Bazaar, a cluster of restaurants and handicraft shops off Thanon Ratchadamnoen, serves as a commercial centre for the city's revitalisation process.

Orientation

Nakhon Si Thammarat can be divided into two sections: the historic half south of the clock tower, and the new city centre north of the clock tower and Khlong Na Meuang. The new city has all the hotels and most of the restaurants, as well as more movie theatres per square kilometre than anywhere else in Thailand.

Information

Tourist Offices The TAT office (☎ 075-346515/6, 01-979 1242, ℮ tatnakon@nrt.cscoms.com) is housed in a 1926-vintage building (formerly a club for Thai government officers, restored in 1993) in the north-western corner of the Sanam Na Meuang (City Park) off Thanon Ratchadamnoen, near the police station. It distributes the usual helpful information printed in English, and can also assist with any tourism-related problems.

Post & Communications The main post office is on Thanon Ratchadamnoen, and is open from 8.30 am to 4.30 pm weekdays. An upstairs telephone office with international service is open from 8 am to 11 pm daily.

Nakhon Si Thammarat National Museum
พิพิธภัณฑสถานแห่งชาติ
นครศรีธรรมราช

This is past the principal wát on Thanon Ratchadamnoen heading south, across from Wat Thao Khot and Wat Phet Jarik, on the left heading south. Since the Tambralinga (or Tampaling) kingdom traded with Indian, Arabic, Dvaravati and Champa states, much art from these places found its way to the Nakhon Si Thammarat area, and some is now on display in the national museum here. Notable are Dong-Son bronze drums, Dvaravati Buddha images and Pallava (south Indian) Hindu sculpture. Locally produced art is also on display.

If you've already had your fill of the usual Thai art-history surveys from Ban Chiang to Ayuthaya, go straight to the Art of Southern Thailand exhibit in a room to the left of the foyer. Here you'll find many fine images of Nakhon Si Thammarat provenance, including the Phutthasihing, U Thong and late Ayuthaya styles. The Nakhon Si Thammarat–produced Ayuthaya style seems to be the most common, with distinctive, almost comical, crowned faces. The so-called Phutthasihing-style Buddha looks a little like the Palla-influenced Chiang Saen Buddha, but is shorter and more 'pneumatic'.

Admission to the museum is 30B and its hours are 9 am to 4 pm Wednesday to Sunday. It's a 5B săwngthăew ride from the new town.

Wat Phra Mahathat
วัดพระมหาธาตุ

This is the city's most historic site, reputed to have been founded by Queen Hem Chala over a thousand years ago. Bronze statues representing the queen and her brother

Nakhon Si Thammarat Festivals

Every year in mid-October there is a southern Thai festival called Chak Phra Pak Tai held in Nakhon Si Thammarat (as well as Songkhla and Surat Thani). In Nakhon Si Thammarat the festival is centred on Wat Mahathat and includes performances of *năng tàlung* (shadow-puppet theatre) and *lákhon* as well as the parading of Buddha images around the city to collect donations for local temples.

In the 3rd lunar month (February to March) the city holds the colourful Hae Phaa Khun That, in which a lengthy cloth *jataka* painting is wrapped around the main chedi at Wat Phra Mahathat.

stand in front of the east wall facing Thanon Ratchadamnoen, and her spirit is said to be associated with the large standing Buddha in the south-eastern cloister. Locals make daily offerings of flower garlands to both this Buddha image and the statue of the queen, believing her spirit watches over the city and its residents.

This is the biggest wát in Southern Thailand, comparable to Wat Pho and other large Bangkok wát. If you like wát, this one is well worth a trip. Reconstructed in the mid-13th century, the huge complex features a 78m chedi, crowned by a solid gold spire weighing several hundred kilograms. Numerous smaller grey-black chedi surround the main chedi.

Besides the distinctive *bòt* (central sanctuary) and chedi there are many intricately designed *wíhăan* (halls) surrounding the chedi, several of which contain crowned Nakhon Si Thammarat/Ayuthaya-style Buddhas in glass cabinets. One of the wíhăan houses a funky museum with some carved wooden *khrút* (Garuda, Vishnu's mythical bird-mount); old votive tablets; Buddha figures of every description, including a standing Dvaravati figure; a Buddha styled after the Siwichai *naga* (dragon-headed serpent); pearl-inlaid alms bowls; and other oddities. A 12m whale skeleton lies in the back of the complex under the northern cloister.

A *mondòp*, the fortress-looking structure towards the northern end of the temple grounds, holds a Buddha footprint – one of the better designs in Thailand.

Wat Phra Mahathat's full name, Wat Phra Mahathat Woramahawihan, is sometimes abbreviated as Wat Phra Boromathat. It's about 2km from the new town centre – hop on any *săwngthăew* going down Thanon Ratchadamnoen and it'll cost 5B.

Wat Na Phra Boromathat
วัดหน้าพระบรมธาตุ
Opposite Wat Phra Mahathat, this is the residence for monks serving at Mahathat. There is a nice Gandhara-style fasting Buddha in front of the bòt here.

Phra Phuttha Sihing Chapel
หอพระพุทธสิหิงค์
The Phra Phuttha Sihing Chapel (Haw Phra Phuttha Sihing), next to the provincial offices, contains one of Thailand's three identical Phra Singh Buddhas, one of which is supposed to have been cast in Sri Lanka before being brought to Sukhothai (through Nakhon Si Thammarat), Chiang Mai and later, Ayuthaya. The other images are at Wat Phra Singh in Chiang Mai and the National Museum in Bangkok – each is claimed to be the original.

Other Places of Worship
In addition to the original Sri Lankan monks who arrived in 13th century Nakhon to teach Theravada Buddhism, many other missionaries – Catholics from Portugal, Hindus from India, Muslims from the Middle East and Mahayana Buddhists from Japan – also stationed themselves in the city. A legacy of these visitors is the variety and number of non-Theravadin places of worship surviving today.

Two **Hindu temples**, one a Shiva shrine and one a Vishnu shrine, can be found along Thanon Ratchadamnoen inside the city walls. Brahman priests from these temples take part each year in the Royal Ploughing Ceremony in Bangkok. One temple houses a locally famous Shivalingam (phallic object) that is worshipped by women hoping to bear children.

Farther north, on the eastern side of Thanon Ratchadamnoen towards the town centre, is the green-hued **Matsayit Yamia** (Friday Mosque), and there are at least two other mosques in the area. On the opposite

SOUTHERN GULF

side of the road, a bit farther south, is the quaint **Bethlehem Church**.

Nakhon's most important non-Buddhist shrine, the **Lak Meuang** (City Pillar), is at the northern end of Sanam Na Meuang. The newly constructed shrine housing the phallic-shaped pillar consists of five chedi-like structures of stucco and marble arranged like the dots on a die. The porticoes of the structure bear a depiction of Rahu swallowing the sun. Inside the central structure is the Lak Meuang; looking like an elaborate *mukhalinga* (a phallus with a face, symbol of Shiva in his function as divine creator), the tip of the pillar decorated with eight faces.

Shadow Puppet Workshop

Traditionally, there are two styles of shadow puppets: *năng tàlung* and *năng yài*. The former are similar in size to the Malay- and Indonesian-style puppets, while the latter are nearly life-size and are unique to Thailand. Both are intricately carved from buffalo hide. Performances of Thai shadow theatre are rare nowadays (usually only during festivals), but there are two places in town where you can see the puppets being made.

The acknowledged master of shadow-puppet manufacture and performance is Suchart Subsin, a Nakhon resident with a workshop at 110/18 Soi 3, Thanon Si Thammasok, not far from Wat Phra Mahathat. Khun Suchart has received several awards for his mastery and preservation of the craft and has performed for the king. His workshop is open to the public; if enough people are assembled he may even be talked into providing a performance at his small outdoor studio. Puppets can be purchased here (and here only, as he refuses to sell them through distributors) at reasonable prices. On some puppets the fur is left on the hide for additional effect – these cost a bit more as special care must be taken in tanning them.

Another craftsperson, Mesa Chotiphan, has a workshop in the northern part of town where visitors are welcome. Mesa's house is at 558/4 Soi Rong Jeh, Thanon Ratchadamnoen. Call ☎ 075-343979 if you would like to be picked up from somewhere in the city. To get here on your own, go north from the city centre on Thanon Ratchadamnoen and, 500m north of the sports field, take the soi opposite the Chinese cemetery (before you reach the golf course and military base).

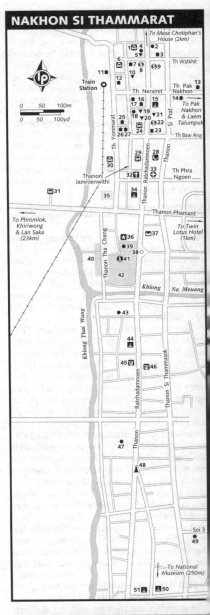

NAKHON SI THAMMARAT

PLACES TO STAY	OTHER		35	Market
3 Taksin Hotel	1 Taxis to Surat Thani,		36	Police Station
7 Thai Fa Hotel	Chumphon & Ranong		37	Main Post Office &
11 Phetpailin Hotel	2 THAI Office			Telephone Office
12 Si Thong Hotel	4 Crystal Palace		38	Circle
13 Nakorn Garden Inn	6 Share Taxis to Sichon &		39	Lak Meuang
14 Grand Park Hotel	Khanom			(City Pillar)
16 Thai Hotel	8 Bangkok Bank		40	Handicraft Shops
17 Siam Hotel	9 Thai Farmers Bank		41	TAT Office
23 Thai Lee Hotel	15 Wat Buranaram		42	Sanam Na Meuang
25 Muang Thong Hotel	18 Muang Thai Tours			(City Park)
26 Nakhon Hotel	22 Siam Commercial Bank		43	Prison
27 Bue Loung (Bua Luang)	24 Minivans to Surat Thani		44	Wat Sema Meuang
Hotel	28 Matsayit Yamia (Friday		45	Shiva Shrine
	Mosque)		46	Vishnu Shrine
PLACES TO EAT	29 Minivans to Phuket		47	Provincial Offices; Phra
5 Dam Kan Aeng	30 Share-Taxi Terminal			Phuttha Sihing Chapel
10 Yong Seng Restaurant	31 Bus Station		48	Clock Tower
19 Sin Ocha Bakery	32 Bethlehem Church		49	Suchart's Workshop
20 Kuang Meng	33 Christian Hospital		50	Wat Na Phra Boromathat
21 Bovorn Bazaar	34 Wat Maheyong		51	Wat Phra Mahathat

SOUTHERN GULF

Places to Stay – Budget

Most of Nakhon Si Thammarat's hotels are near the train and bus stations. The best budget value in town is still the friendly *Thai Lee Hotel* (☎ 075-356948, *1130 Thanon Ratchadamnoen),* where spacious clean rooms with fan, shower and toilet cost 160/240B single/double. The ones at the back are a little quieter. This hotel enforces a midnight curfew, so find another one if you're in town for the nightlife.

On Thanon Yommarat (spelt 'Yammaraj' on some signs), almost opposite the train station, is the *Si Thong Hotel* (☎ 075-356357), with adequate rooms for 140B to 180B with fan and bathroom. Also on Thanon Yommarat is the *Nakhon Hotel* (☎ 075-356318), with similar rates but better-kept facilities than at the Si Thong. An air-con room with two beds here costs 350B.

On Thanon Jamroenwithi is the large *Siam Hotel* (☎ 075-356090), where rooms with fan and bathroom cost from 150B. Farther south on this street is the *Muang Thong Hotel* (☎ 075-356177), where 150/200B will get you a semi-clean single/double room with fan and bathroom, and 350B will get you air-con. A block north of the Siam, on the same side of the street, is the *Thai Fa Hotel* (☎ 075-356727), a small, two-storey place with adequate rooms for 120B to 180B.

Places to Stay – Mid-Range

At one time Nakhon Si Thammarat's flashiest hotel, the 240-room *Thai Hotel* (☎ 075-341509, fax 344858) on Thanon Ratchadamnoen, two blocks from the train station, now seems rather ordinary compared to the competition, with singles/doubles with fan for 200/290B, and well-kept air-con rooms going for 380B to 450B. The more expensive air-con rooms are larger, better furnished and have a refrigerator stocked up with snacks. All rooms come with cable TV. The six-storey *Taksin Hotel* (☎ 075-342790, fax 342793) has no Roman-script sign but is located off Thanon Si Prat, nestled in a string of massage places. The Taksin charges 380B for air-con rooms with TV and 450B for rooms with hot water and fridge.

The *Bue Loung Hotel* (Bua Luang; ☎ 075-341518, fax 343418), on Soi Luang Meuang off Thanon Jamroenwithi, has large, clean singles/doubles with fan and bathroom for 170B (240B with TV) and air-con rooms for 270B (340B with TV and fridge).

The nearby *Phetpailin* (☎ 075-341896, fax 343943), a block north, is similar but charges 160/220B for rooms with fan and 360B with air-con.

The quiet *Nakorn Garden Inn* (☎ 075-344831, fax 342926, 1/4 Thanon Pak Nakhon), east of the centre, has rooms with air-con and TV for 445B.

Places to Stay – Top End

The new *Grand Park Hotel* (☎ 075-317666, fax 317675, 1204/79 Thanon Pak Nakhon) offers nicely furnished, spacious, carpeted rooms with fridge and TV for 750B and suites for 1400B (discounted to 600B and 900B respectively). Parking is available.

Nakhon's top spot is on Thanon Phattanakan Khukhwang, in the extreme southeastern corner of town opposite the Lotus Super Center. The 16-storey, 413-room *Twin Lotus Hotel* (☎ 075-323777, fax 323821, 97/8 Thanon Phattanakan Khukhwang; in Bangkok ☎ 02-711 0360, fax 381 0930) offers all the amenities expected by Bangkok business travellers, such as IDD phones, minibars, satellite TV, restaurants, a cocktail lounge, coffee shop, karaoke, massage, a swimming pool, saunas, and a fully equipped gym. Nonsmoking rooms are available. Rates are 1100B for a superior single/double room, 1400B for a deluxe room and 2500B for a junior suite, and twice that for the 'executive suite'. Discounts are easily obtained.

Places to Eat

There are lots of funky old Chinese restaurants along Thanon Yommarat and Thanon Jamroenwithi. The latter street is the city's main culinary centre. At night the entire block running south from the Siam Hotel is lined with cheap *food vendors* – Muslim stands opposite the hotel sell delicious *rotii klûay* (banana pancakes), *khâo mòk kài* (chicken biryani) and *mátàbà* (murtabak; pancakes stuffed with chicken or vegetables) in the evening and by day there are plenty of rice and noodle shops. *Yong Seng* (no Roman-script sign) is a good, inexpensive Chinese restaurant on Thanon Jamroenwithi.

To try some of Nakhon's excellent Thai coffee, stop by *Hao Coffee* at Bovorn Bazaar. Basically an update of an original Hokkien-style coffee shop once run by the owner's family in Nakhon, Hao Coffee serves international coffees as well as southern-Thai Hokkien-style coffee (listed as 'Hao coffee' on the menu) served with a tea chaser. Ask for fresh milk *(nom sòt)* if you abhor powdered nondairy creamer.

Bovorn Bazaar offers several other culinary delights. Adjacent to Hao Coffee is *Khrua Nakhon*, a large open-air restaurant serving real Nakhon cuisine, including khâo yam (southern-style rice salad), *kaeng tai plaa* (spicy fish curry), *khànǒm jiin* (curry noodles served with a huge tray of vegies) and seafood. The restaurant also has egg-and-toast breakfasts; you can order Hao coffee from next door if you'd like. With a banyan tree in front and a modest display of southern-Thai folk art, the atmosphere is hard to beat. Get there early as it's only open from 7 am to 3 pm. Behind Khrua Nakhon in an old house is *Ban Lakhon*, which is also very good for Thai food and is open for dinner.

On the corner of the alley leading into Bovorn Bazaar, *Ligor Home Bakery* (Likaw Ban Tham Khanom) bakes fresh European-style pastries daily. At night the bakery closes and Nakhon's most famous *rotii vendors* set up along the alley. In Nakhon, rotii klûay is a tradition – the vendors here use only fresh mashed bananas, no banana preserves or the like. Other offerings here include rotii with curry *(rotii kaeng)*, with egg *(rotii khài)*, and rotii served as *mátàbà*. It also does great *khànǒm jiip* (dumplings stuffed with a chicken-shrimp mixture), along with Nakhon coffee and better-than-average milk tea. On the north-western corner of Thanon Watkhit and Thanon Ratchadamnoen, the popular Thai-Chinese *Dam Kan Aeng* is packed with hungry customers every night.

Kuang Meng (no Roman-script sign) at 1343/12 Thanon Ratchadamnoen, opposite the Siam Commercial Bank, is a very small Hokkien coffee shop with marble-top tables and very nice pastries. *Sin Ocha Bakery*, opposite the entrance to the Thai Hotel, is a slightly updated Hokkien coffee shop with *tim cham* (dim sum).

Entertainment

Beyond the cinemas in town, there's not a lot of nightlife. *Rock 99% Bar & Grill*, an American roadhouse-style pub inside Bovorn Bazaar, offers draught beer, cocktails and Western pop music, as well as pizza, baked potatoes, sandwiches and a few Thai dishes; this is where the few expats that live in Nakhon Si Thammarat hang out. It's open from 6 pm to 2 am.

Shopping

Several shops along Thanon Tha Chang just behind the TAT office and Sanam Na Meuang, sell Nakhon's famous line of

Ban Khao Beach, Ko Tao, Surat Thani Province

Ornate decorations bring a fishing boat to life in Nakhon Si Thammarat Province.

CHRIS MELLOR

Phra Phuttha Taksin Mingmongkon, Thailand's tallest seated Buddha, Wat Khao Kong, Narathiwat

RICHARD NEBESKY

Guardian *yaksa* statue at a wát in Songkhla

DENNIS JOHNSON

Results of development on Ko Samui, Surat Thani

thǒm (niello), silver and basketry. Den Nakhon, on the grounds of Wat Phra Mahathat, sells thǒm, silver and other local crafts at good prices.

Getting There & Away

Air THAI (☎ 075-342491), 1612 Thanon Ratchadamnoen, has two flights a week to and from Bangkok (2035B).

Bus & Minivan Air-con buses bound for Nakhon Si Thammarat leave Bangkok's Southern bus terminal daily every 30 minutes or so from 5 to 8 pm (414B, 12 hours). Air-con buses from Nakhon Si Thammarat leave for Bangkok at about the same times. There are also five 2nd-class air-con departures (322B) and one VIP departure (640B) nightly.

Ordinary buses from Surat Thani cost 45B and leave four times a day, while air-con departures are slightly less frequent and cost around 70B. Direct buses run from Songkhla via a bridge over the entrance to Thaleh Noi (the inland sea). There are a couple of private bus companies on Thanon Jamroenwithi near the Siam Hotel.

Hourly buses between Nakhon Si Thammarat and Krabi cost 64B (70B air-con) and take about three hours. Other routes include Trang (36B ordinary, 50B air-con), Phattalung (35B ordinary, 63B air-con), Phuket (115B ordinary, 155B air-con) and Hat Yai (64B ordinary, 90B air-con, 100B minivan). The buses leave from the terminal on Thanon Phaniant.

Minivans to Krabi leave from in front of the municipality office every half-hour from 7 am to 3 pm (100B, 2½ hours). Minivans to Surat Thani cost 80B and leave from the same block as the Thai Lee Hotel.

You can also catch minivans to Phuket (150B, five hours).

To Ko Samui there is one air-con bus a day from the main terminal at 11.30 am (130B, three hours).

Train Most southbound trains stop at Thung Song, about 40km west of Nakhon Si Thammarat, from where you must take a bus or taxi to the coast. However, two trains actually go all the way to Nakhon Si Thammarat (there is a branch line from Khao Chum Thong to Nakhon Si Thammarat): The rapid No 173, which leaves Bangkok's Hualamphong station at 5.35 pm, arriving in Nakhon Si Thammarat at 9.25 am; and the express No 85, which leaves Bangkok at 7.15 pm and arrives in Nakhon Si Thammarat at 10.50 am.

Most travellers will not be booking a train directly to Nakhon Si Thammarat, but if you want to, 1st class costs 652B, 2nd class 308B and 3rd class 133B, not including surcharges for rapid/express service or sleeping berths.

Share Taxi This seems to be the most popular form of intercity travel out of Nakhon. The huge share-taxi terminal on Thanon Yommarat has taxis to Yala (130B), Thung Song (30B), Khanom (50B), Sichon (30B), Krabi (90B), Hat Yai (80B), Trang (70B) and Phattalung (60B). A second, smaller stand on Thanon Thewarat has taxis to Surat Thani (80B), Chumphon (140B) and Ranong (180B).

Getting Around

Blue sǎwngthǎew run north-south along Thanon Ratchadamnoen and Thanon Si Thammasok for 5B (a bit more at night). Motorcycle taxi rides start at 10B and cost up to 50B for longer distances.

Songkhla Province

SONGKHLA

อ.เมืองสงขลา

postcode 90000 • pop 87,600
Songkhla, 950km from Bangkok, is another former Srivijaya satellite on the east coast. Not much is known about the pre-8th-century history of Songkhla, a name derived from the Yawi (a language spoken in the Malay Peninsula; the written form uses the classic Arabic script plus five additional letters) *singora* – a mutilated Sanskrit reference to a lion-shaped mountain (today called Khao Daeng) west of the present-day city on the opposite side of the harbour entrance. The original settlement lay at the foot of Khao Daeng, where two cemeteries and the ruins of a fort are among the oldest structural remains.

About 3km north of Ban Hua Khao village off Rte 4063 (the road to Nakhon Si Thammarat) is the tomb of Suleiman

SOUTHERN GULF

(1592–1668), a Muslim trader who was largely responsible for Songkhla's commercial eminence during the 17th century. Just south of Suleiman's tomb, a Dutch graveyard testifies to a 17th-century Dutch presence, as well (look for large granite slabs in an overgrown area next to a Total warehouse). Suleiman's son Mustapha fell out of favour with Ayuthaya's King Narai, who burned the settlement to the ground in the next century.

Songkhla later moved across the harbour to its present site on a peninsula between Thaleh Sap Songkhla (an inland sea) and the South China Sea (or Gulf of Thailand, depending on how you look at it). Today's population is a colourful mixture of Thais, Chinese and Malays, and the local architecture and cuisine reflect this combination. Older southern Thais still refer to the city as Singora or Singkhon.

The seafood served along the white-sand Hat Samila is excellent, although the beach is not that great for swimming, especially if you've just come from the Ko Samui archipelago. Beaches are not Songkhla's main attraction, but the evergreen casuarina trees along Hat Samila give it a rather nice visual effect. The town has plenty of other curiosities to offer.

Over the last decade Songkhla has become increasingly Westernised due to the influx of multinational oil company employees – particularly British and American. This, along with a strong Thai navy presence, has created a wealthier-than-average Thai city.

Orientation

The town has a split personality; the charming older town is west of Thanon Ramwithi towards the waterfront; and the new town is east of Thanon Ramwithi – a modern mix of business and suburbia.

Information

Money Songkhla is well supplied with banks, and you'll find ATMs at Bangkok Bank (Thanon Nakhon Nai), Thai Farmers Bank (Thanon Nakhon Nai) and Siam Commercial Bank (Thanon Saiburi), all in the old town area.

Post & Communications The post office is opposite the department store on Thanon Wichianchom, and is open from 8.30 am to 3.30 pm weekdays; international calls can be made upstairs from 8 am to 6 pm daily.

Consulates in Songkhla The Malaysian consulate (☎ 074-311062, 311104) is at 4 Thanon Sukhum, near Hat Samila. Other foreign missions include a Chinese consulate (☎ 074-311494) on Thanon Sadao, not far from the Royal Crown Hotel; and an Indonesian consulate (☎ 074-311544) on the western end of Thanon Sadao, near the Thanon Ramwithi intersection.

Songkhla National Museum
พิพิธภัณฑสถานแห่งชาติสงขลา

Housed in a 100-year-old building of southern Sino-Portuguese architecture, between Thanon Rong Meuang and Thanon Jana (off Thanon Wichianchom), this is easily the most picturesque national museum in Thailand. Along with the innate architectural charms of its curved rooflines and thick walls, it's a quiet, breezy building with a tranquil garden in front. The museum contains exhibits from all national art-style periods, particularly the Srivijaya, including a 7th- to 9th-century Shivalingam found in Pattani. Also on display are Thai and Chinese ceramics and sumptuous Chinese furniture owned by the local Chinese aristocracy. The museum is open from 9 am to 4 pm Wednesday to Sunday (closed national holidays); admission is 30B.

Prem Tinsulanonda Museum
พิพิธภัณฑ์พธานะรงค์

Dwarfed by the Queen Hotel next door, the Prem Tinsulanonda Museum is touted as the birthplace of Thailand's 16th prime minister, who served from 1980 to 1988. The 'museum' is a wooden house that was actually built recently upon the site of Prem's birthplace, and contains some of the furniture and personal effects that graced the original home. While something of a shrine to Prem, the museum is worth a visit even if you have little interest in Thai politics – it's a charming example of the combination of breezy verandas and cosy interiors that constitutes the traditional Thai house. The museum is open from 8.30 am to 4 pm daily except Monday. Admission is free.

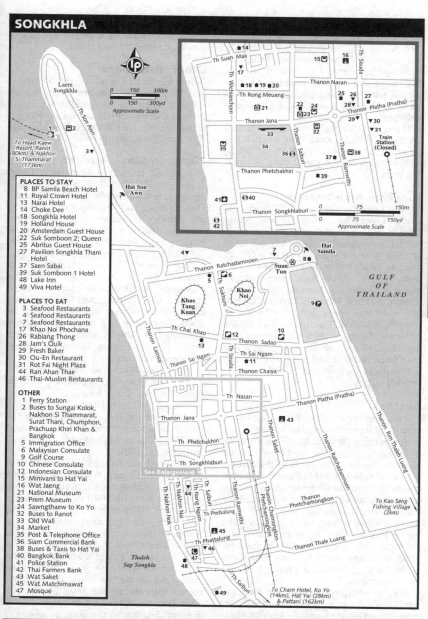

SONGKHLA

To Haad Kaew Resort, Ranot (80km) & Nakhon Si Thammarat (173km)

Laem Songkhla

Hat Son Awn

Train Station (Closed)

Hat Samila

GULF OF THAILAND

Suan Tun

Khao Tang Kuan

Khao Noi

Thaleh Sap Songkhla

See Enlargement

To Kao Seng Fishing Village (2km)

To Charn Hotel, Ko Yo (14km), Hat Yai (28km) & Pattani (162km)

PLACES TO STAY
8   BP Samila Beach Hotel
11   Royal Crown Hotel
13   Narai Hotel
14   Choke Dee
18   Songkhla Hotel
19   Holland House
20   Amsterdam Guest House
22   Suk Somboon 2; Queen
25   Abritus Guest House
27   Pavilion Songkhla Thani Hotel
37   Saen Sabai
39   Suk Somboon 1 Hotel
48   Lake Inn
49   Viva Hotel

PLACES TO EAT
3   Seafood Restaurants
4   Seafood Restaurants
7   Seafood Restaurants
17   Khao Noi Phochana
26   Rabiang Thong
28   Jam's Quik
29   Fresh Baker
30   Ou-En Restaurant
31   Rot Fai Night Plaza
44   Ran Ahan Thae
46   Thai-Muslim Restaurants

OTHER
1   Ferry Station
2   Buses to Sungai Kolok, Nakhon Si Thammarat, Surat Thani, Chumphon, Prachuap Khiri Khan & Bangkok
5   Immigration Office
9   Golf Course
10   Chinese Consulate
12   Indonesian Consulate
15   Minivans to Hat Yai
16   Wat Jaeng
21   National Museum
23   Prem Museum
24   Sawngthaew to Ko Yo
32   Buses to Ranot
33   Old Wall
34   Market
35   Post & Telephone Office
36   Siam Commercial Bank
38   Buses & Taxis to Hat Yai
40   Bangkok Bank
41   Police Station
42   Thai Farmers Bank
43   Wat Saket
45   Wat Matchimawat
47   Mosque

SOUTHERN GULF

Temples & Chedi

On Thanon Saiburi, **Wat Matchimawat** (Wat Klang) typifies the Sino-Thai temple architecture of 17th-century Songkhla. One of the wíhǎan contains an old marble Buddha image and a small museum. Another temple with similar characteristics, **Wat Jaeng** on Thanon Ramwithi, was recently renovated.

There is a Singhalese-style chedi and royal pavilion atop **Khao Tang Kuan**, a hill rising up at the northern end of the peninsula; to reach the top you'll have to climb 305 steps.

Songkhla Architecture

All that remains of the old King Narai–era city is a lengthy section of wall along Thanon Jana near the museum and main market in the centre of town. A few patches of 19th- and early-20th-century architecture can be seen near the inland sea waterfront. Walk along the back streets parallel to the waterfront – Thanon Nang Ngam, Thanon Nakhon Nai and Thanon Nakhon Nok – to find older Songkhla buildings showing Chinese, Portuguese and Malay influence. Many of them disappeared during Thailand's economic boom, but a few have been restored and hopefully the city will support some sort of historical architectural legacy.

Beaches

The city has begun taking better care of the strip of white sand along **Hat Samila**, and it is now quite a pleasant beach for strolling or for an early morning read on one of the benches placed in the shade of the casuarina trees. At one end of the beach, a **bronze mermaid sculpture**, depicted squeezing water from her long hair in a tribute to Mae Thorani (the Hindu-Buddhist earth goddess), sits atop some rocks. Locals treat the figure like a shrine, tying the waist with coloured cloth and rubbing the breasts for good luck. The rustic seafood restaurants at the back of the beach supply food and cold beverages.

The less-frequented **Hat Son Awn** extends along the eastern shore of the slender cape jutting out between the Gulf of Thailand and Thaleh Sap, immediately northwest of Hat Samila. There are also a few restaurants along this stretch but they are on the opposite side of the road from the beach, and tend to be slightly more expensive than those at Hat Samila.

Other Attractions

A few kilometres south of Hat Samila is **Kao Seng**, a quaint Muslim fishing village – this is where the tourist photos of gaily painted fishing vessels are taken. Sǎwngthǎew run regularly between Songkhla and Kao Seng for 8B per person.

Places to Stay – Budget

The popular and clean **Amsterdam Guest House** (☎ 074-314890, 15/3 Thanon Rong Meuang) is a homey place run by a friendly Dutch woman and has plenty of wandering pet dogs and cats as well as a caged macaque that is said to bite the unwary. Basic rooms with shared bathroom cost 200B and there's a restaurant downstairs.

The recently opened **Abritus Guest House** (☎ 074-326047, 28/16 Thanon Ramwithi, ℮ abritus_th@yahoo.com) is run by a friendly Bulgarian family and has clean fan rooms with shared bathroom for 200B. Downstairs is a restaurant in which guests get a 10% discount on food and drinks. Besides English, German and Russian are spoken here.

The friendly **Narai Hotel** (☎ 074-311078, 14 Thanon Chai Khao) is near the foot of Khao Tang Kuan. It's an older wooden hotel with clean, quiet singles/doubles with fan and shared bathroom (although each room comes with a washbasin) for 200/250B. A huge double room with bathroom is 300B.

The refurbished **Songkhla Hotel** (☎ 074-313505), on Thanon Wichianchom across from the fishing cooperative, has wellscrubbed rooms for 160B with shared bathroom, and 190B with private shower and Thai-style toilet. Just up the street from the Songkhla Hotel, the recently renovated **Choke Dee** (formerly Smile Inn; ☎ 074-311258) is a clean place with mediumsized rooms with ceiling fan and private cold-water shower for 280B, and identical rooms with air-con for 380B (400B with TV). The attached restaurant opens at 5 am. Singles/doubles at the **Suk Somboon 1 Hotel** (☎ 074-311049, 40 Thanon Phetchakhiri) are not bad for 180/250B, although they're just wooden rooms off a large central area. Rooms in the air-con wing next door are 300B.

The *Saen Sabai* (☎ 074-441027, 44/746 Thanon Phetchakhiri) is well located and has clean, if small, rooms in an early-Bangkok-style building for 150B with fan and shared bathroom, 220B with private bathroom, and 270B with air-con. Nearby is the *Suk Somboon 2* (☎ 074-311149, 18 Thanon Saiburi), with singles/doubles with fan and private bathroom for 200/400B, and a few rooms with shared bathroom for only 100B. Next door is an all air-con wing with rooms complete with TV, bathtub and fridge for 400B/500B.

The *Queen* (☎ 074-313072, 20 Thanon Saiburi), next door to the Suk Somboon 2, has decent but nothing-special air-con rooms from 300/400B. The similarly priced *Charn* (Chan; ☎ 074-322347) is on the same road but on the outskirts of the central area on the way to Hat Yai. Air-con rooms in this six-storey hotel go for 250B to 300B.

Places to Stay – Mid-Range

The five-storey *Viva Hotel* (☎ 074-321034–7, fax 312608, 547/2 Thanon Nakhon Nok) has modern, clean air-con rooms for 500/600B. The English-speaking staff are friendly and helpful. The attached coffee shop has live music nightly.

Songkhla's best value in this category is the five-storey *Royal Crown Hotel* (☎ 074-312174, fax 321027, 38 Thanon Sai Ngam), which charges 450B for rooms with air-con, TV with in-house video, fridge and carpet.

Popular with Thais, *Lake Inn* (☎ 074-321441) is a rambling multistorey place with great views onto Thaleh Sap. Rooms are 390B with air-con, carpet, hot water, TV and fridge, 490B with the same plus a bathtub, and 590B with a balcony and lake view.

Places to Stay – Top End

The *BP Samila Beach Hotel* (☎ 074-440222, fax 440442) on the beachfront is Songkhla's swankiest accommodation and has all the amenities, including air-con, IDD phones, fridge, satellite TV and sea or mountain views, for 1250B to 7500B.

The nine-storey *Pavilion Songkhla Thani Hotel* (☎ 074-441850, fax 323716, 17 Thanon Platha) is one block east of

Thanon Ramwithi at the intersection of Thanon Platha and Thanon Sisuda. Large, luxurious rooms with wood panelling, air-con, IDD phones, satellite TV, carpeting and so on start at 900B single/double.

The *Haad Kaew Resort* (☎ 074-331059, fax 331220) on the other side of the Thaleh Sap on the road to Ranot has its own beachfront and a pool (available to nonguests for 50B a day). The landscaped grounds are a plus. Nice air-con rooms with all the amenities cost from 771B to 899B, and comfortable bungalows go for 527B.

Places to Eat

There are lots of good restaurants in Songkhla but a few tend to overcharge foreign tourists. The best seafood place according to locals is the *Ran Ahan Thae* (85 Thanon Nang Ngam), off Thanon Songkhlaburi and parallel to Thanon Saiburi. Look for a brightly lit place just south of the cinema. The *seafood restaurants* on Hat Samila are pretty good too – try the curried crab claws or spicy fried squid. Hours are 11.30 am to 2 pm and 5 to 8 pm, and prices are inexpensive to moderate.

Fancier seafood places are found along Thanon Son Awn near the beach, but these tend to have lots of young Thai hostesses to satisfy the Thai male penchant for chatting up *áw-áw* (young girls). Cheaper and better is another string of seafood places on the beach nearest where Thanon Ratchadamnoen and Thanon Son Awm intersect.

Along Thanon Nang Ngam, north of Thanon Phattalung, in the Chinese section, are several cheap *Chinese noodle and jók (congee) shops*. At the end of Thanon Nang Ngam along Thanon Phattalung (near the mosque) are some modest Thai Muslim restaurants, including *Sharif*, *Suda* and *Dawan*; Sharif and Dawan open at 8 am and close at 9 pm. *Khao Noi Phochana*, on Thanon Wichianchom near the Songkhla Hotel, has a very good lunch-time selection of Thai and Chinese rice dishes and is open from 8 am to 10 pm.

There are several fast-food spots at the intersection of Thanon Sisuda and Thanon Platha, including *Jam's Quik* and *Fresh Baker*, both with burgers, ice cream and Western breakfasts. Next door to the latter is a *Pizza Hut*. There are also a few popular

Thai and Chinese restaurants in the vicinity. The *kíaw náam (wonton soup) place* next to Fresh Baker is cheap and quite good.

Farther south along Thanon Sisuda, near the Chalerm Thong cinema and the old train station, is a hawkers centre and night market called *Rot Fai Night Plaza*. In this section *Ou-En Restaurant* is a very popular Chinese restaurant with outdoor tables; the house speciality is Peking duck. It's open from 4 pm to 3 am.

The very clean *Rabiang Thong* on Thanon Sisuda, near the intersection with Thanon Platha, has a good range of Thai food at moderate prices.

The restaurant at *Abritus Guest House* on Thanon Ramwithi has an extensive breakfast menu, including several kinds of omelettes. It is also known for its delicious potato salad.

Entertainment

The string of bars along Thanon Sadao, between the Chinese and Indonesian consulates, is jokingly referred to among local expats as 'The Dark Side'. Not as ominous as it sounds, this mini bar district caters mainly to oil company employees and other westerners living in Songkhla. *Jessie's Rest*, the bar nearest Soi 5, is run by an Englishman and his Thai wife. There's an ice chest full of beer and good hamburgers, and reliable information about Songkhla's sights is readily obtained here.

On nearby Thanon Sisuda are a few other bars worth checking out including *Uncle Sam's*, *The Boozer* and *Corner Bier*. The latter is the hang-out of Songkhla's Canadian community.

Thais tend to congregate at bars with live music on Thanon Sisuda, of which *Lucky Bar* is a current favourite.

Getting There & Away

Air THAI operates several daily flights between Bangkok and nearby Hat Yai; see the Hat Yai section for details.

Bus, Minivan & Share Taxi Three air-con public buses to Songkhla leave Bangkok's Southern bus terminal daily between 5 and 7.30 pm (514B, 13 hours). In the reverse direction the buses leave between 4.45 and 6.20 pm. One ordinary bus leaves from Bangkok at 2 pm (286B).

Air-con buses from Surat Thani to Songkhla and Hat Yai cost 135B one way. Big green buses from Songkhla to Hat Yai leave every 15 minutes (12B) from Thanon Saiburi, around the corner from the Songkhla Hotel, and can be flagged down anywhere along Thanon Wichianchom or Thanon Saiburi towards Hat Yai. Directly opposite the ferry terminal on Laem Songkhla is a small Baw Khaw Saw (government) terminal for buses going to Sungai Kolok, Nakhon Si Thammarat, Surat Thani, Chumphon, Prachuap Khiri Khan and Bangkok.

Air-con minivans to Hat Yai are 20B; these arrive and depart from a parking area in front of Wat Jaeng. Share taxis are 20B to Hat Yai if there are five other passengers, 100B if chartered; after 8 pm the rates go up to 25B and 125B respectively. Share taxis cost 55B to Pattani and 50B to Yala.

See the Hat Yai Getting There & Away section for more options, as Hat Yai is the main transport hub for Songkhla Province.

Train The old railway spur to Songkhla no longer has a passenger service. See Hat Yai's Getting There & Away section for information on trains to/from nearby Hat Yai.

Boat At the head of Laem Songkhla a government-run car ferry plies the short distance across the channel where the Thaleh Sap meets the Gulf of Thailand. The barge-like ferry holds about 15 cars, plus assorted motorcycles and pedestrians. The fare for the seven-minute ride is 12B per car, plus 3B per person; it operates from 6 am to dusk daily. The ferry stop on the other side is a semi-floating village called Ban Hua Khao. Sathing Phra is 36km north from this point via Rte 408, which terminates in Nakhon Si Thammarat.

Getting Around

A taxi from Hat Yai airport to Songkhla costs 340B. In the reverse direction you should be able to find a car or săwngthăew to the airport for 200B.

For getting around in town, small red săwngthăew circulate around Songkhla and take passengers to any point on their route for 7B. Motorcycle taxis to/from anywhere in town cost 10B per kilometre; rates double after 10 pm or so.

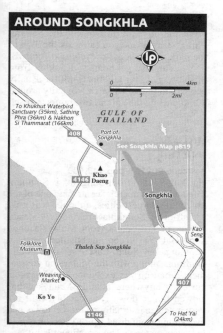

AROUND SONGKHLA

GULF OF THAILAND

To Khukhut Waterbird Sanctuary (35km), Sathing Phra (36km) & Nakhon Si Thammarat (166km)

408

Port of Songkhla

See Songkhla Map p819

▲ Khao Daeng

4146

Songkhla

Kao Seng

Folklore Museum

Thaleh Sap Songkhla

Weaving Market

Ko Yo

4146

To Hat Yai (24km)

407

KO YO
เกาะยอ

An island on the inland sea, Ko Yo (pronounced Kaw Yaw) is worth visiting just to see the **cotton-weaving cottage industry** here. The good-quality, distinctive *phâa kàw yaw* is hand-woven on rustic looms and available on the spot at 'wholesale' prices – meaning you still have to bargain but have a chance of undercutting the usual city price.

Many different households around this thickly forested, sultry island are engaged in cotton-weaving, and there is a central market off the highway so you don't have to go from place to place comparing prices and fabric quality. At the market, prices for cloth and ready-made clothes are excellent if you bargain. If you're more interested in observing the weaving process, take a walk down the road behind the market, where virtually every other house has a loom or two – listen for the clacking sound of the hand-operated wooden looms. As the island gradually gets taken over by condo and vacation-home developments, it's bound to have an impact on the weaving villages.

There are also a couple of semi-interesting wát, Khao Bo and Thai Yaw, to visit. Along the main road through Ko Yo are several large seafood restaurants overlooking Thaleh Sap. *Pornthip* (about half a kilometre before the market) is reportedly the best.

Folklore Museum
สถาบันทักษิณคดีศึกษา

At the northern end of the island at Ban Ao Sai, about 2km past the Ko Yo cloth market, is a large folklore museum run by the Institute of Southern Thai Studies, a division of Si Nakharinwirot University. Opened in 1991, the complex of Thai-style pavilions overlooking the Thaleh Sap Songkhla contains well-curated collections (about 75% with English labels) of folk art as well as a library and souvenir shop. Displays include pottery, beads, shadow puppets, basketry, textiles, musical instruments, boats, religious art, weapons and various household, agricultural and fishing implements. Among these is a superb collection of coconut-grater seats carved into various animal and human shapes.

On the institute grounds is a series of small gardens, including one occasionally used for traditional shadow-theatre performances; a medicinal herb garden; and a bamboo culture garden.

Admission to the museum is 50B for fàràng and 20B for Thais. It's open from 8.30 am to 5 pm daily.

Getting There & Away
From Hat Yai, direct Ko Yo buses – large wooden săwngthăew – leave from near the clock tower on Thanon Jana throughout the day. The fare is 10B. Although the bus terminates farther on, it will stop in front of the cloth market on Ko Yo (ask for *nâa tàlàat*, 'in front of the market'). To get off at the museum, about 2km past the market, ask for *phíphítháphan*. It takes about 30 minutes to reach the museum from Songkhla. Buses to Ranot pass through Ko Yo for the same fare.

Nakhon Si Thammarat– or Ranot-bound buses from Hat Yai also pass through Ko Yo via the new bridge system (part of Rte 4146) and will stop at the market or museum. Another way to get here is to take a Hat Yai–Songkhla bus to the intersection for Ko Yo (7B), then catch the Songkhla-Ranot bus (5B) to the market or museum.

SOUTHERN GULF

KHUKHUT WATERBIRD SANCTUARY
อุทยานนกน้ำคูขุด

On the eastern shore of the Songkhla inland sea, about 30km north of Songkhla near Sathing Phra, is a 520-sq-km sanctuary for waterbirds. Together with the similar Thaleh Noi Wildlife Preserve in Phattalung, the wetlands are habitat for over 200 resident and migrant bird species from the entire Thaleh Sap, including bitterns, egrets and herons (these three are called *nók yaang* in Thai), rare Javanese pond herons, fishing eagles (*nók yìaw plaa),* cormorants *(nók kaa náam),* storks, kites, hawks, falcons, plovers, sandpipers, terns (*nók naang nuan*) and kingfishers.

A book available at the park office has very detailed information on the waterbirds and maps showing habitat. The best months to go bird-watching are November and December, and the worst are from May to August.

You can arrange boat trips through the park service (☎ 074-397042) – it's 200B to 250B for a one-hour bird-watching excursion, and 400B to 500B for two hours to see birds and stop at two islands. Each boat can hold up to seven people.

Places to Stay & Eat
At the time of writing there were no guesthouses or hotels in Sathing Phra, but it's easy to find *rooms* in the village for 100B a night.

About 5km from the turn-off to the park towards Songkhla (opposite the 129km marker), near the gulf side of the peninsula, the friendly *Sathing Phra Resort (☎ 074-455338)* rents clean bungalows with bamboo furniture and tiled floors for 280B to 550B; you can also pitch a tent for 50B. There is a sandy gulf beach nearby and the resort has well-priced seafood. A motorcycle taxi from Sathing Phra to the resort costs 30B.

A rustic *eating area* over the lake near the park office serves good, inexpensive Thai rice dishes and seafood. Its hours are 8 am to 8 pm daily.

Getting There & Away
Buses to Sathing Phra are 13B from Songkhla – take a red Ranot-bound bus. If you're starting from the Folklore Museum on Ko Yo, you can flag a bus or săwngthăew on the road in front of the museum and get to the waterbird sanctuary for 10B. From the bus stop in front of the Sathing Phra district office you can walk the 3km to the park, or get a motorcycle taxi for 10B.

You can also get boats to Khukhut from Phattalung. Long-tail boats (40B) usually leave Lam Pam on Thaleh Noi daily around 12.30 pm and take about two hours to reach Khukhut.

HAT YAI
หาดใหญ่

postcode 90110 • pop 143,600
Hat Yai, 933km from Bangkok, is Southern Thailand's commercial centre and one of the kingdom's largest cities, although it is only a district of Songkhla Province. A steady stream of customers from Malaysia once kept Hat Yai's central business district booming, but South-East Asia's economic doldrums, along with the Malaysian government's ban on the exchange of Malaysian currency anywhere outside Malaysia, has slowed things down considerably. Still it's very much an international market town, and everything from dried fruit to stereos is sold in the shops along Thanon Niphat Uthit Nos 1, 2 and 3, not far from the train station.

Hat Yai is a major transport hub for travel around Southern Thailand and between Thailand and Malaysia. Many travellers stop over in the city on their way to and from Malaysia.

Culturally, Hat Yai is very much a Chinese town at its centre, with loads of gold shops and Chinese restaurants. A substantial Muslim minority is concentrated in certain sections of the city (eg, near the mosque off Thanon Niphat Songkhrao).

Information
Tourist Offices The TAT office (☎ 074-243747, 01-478 8493, e tathatyai@ hatyai.inet.co.th), 1/1 Soi 2, Thanon Niphat Uthit 3, is open daily from 8.30 am to 4.30 pm. The tourist police (☎ 074-246733, 1155) is opposite the Florida Hotel.

Immigration Offices The Hat Yai immigration office (☎ 074-243019, 233760) is on Thanon Phetkasem near the railway bridge, in the same complex as a police station. The nearest Malaysian consulate is in Songkhla (see that section earlier).

HAT YAI

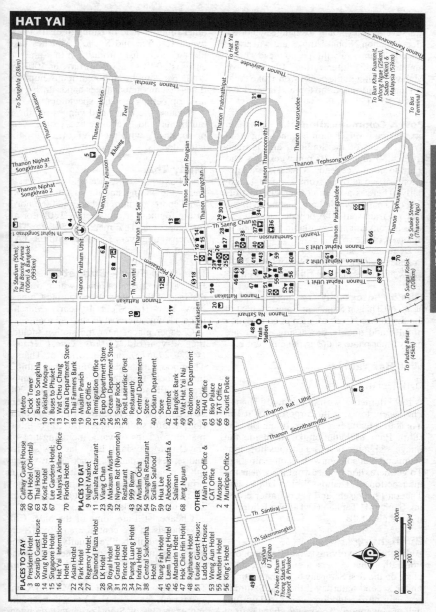

PLACES TO STAY
3 President Hotel
8 Sorasilp Guest House
14 Wang Noi Hotel
15 Singapore Hotel
16 Hat Yai International Hotel
22 Asian Hotel
24 Park Hotel
27 Regency Hotel; Diamond Plaza Hotel
28 LK Hotel
30 Royal Hotel
31 Grand Hotel
33 Prince Hotel
34 Pueng Luang Hotel
37 Indra Hotel
38 Central Sukhontha Hotel
41 Rung Fah Hotel
46 Laem Thong Hotel
47 Mandarin Hotel
48 Hok Chin Hin Hotel
51 Rajthanee Hotel
51 Louise Guest House; Ladda Guest House
53 Weng Aun Hotel
55 Montien Hotel
56 King's Hotel
58 Cathay Guest House
60 OH Hotel (Oriental)
63 Thai Hotel
64 Kosit Hotel
67 Lee Gardens Hotel; Malaysia Airlines Office
70 Florida Hotel

PLACES TO EAT
9 Night Market
11 Sumatra Restaurant
23 Viang Chan
29 Makauan Muslim
32 Niyom Rot (Niyomrosh) Restaurant
43 999 Remy
52 Muslim Ocha
54 Shangria Restaurant
57 Sicilian Seafood
59 Hua Lee
62 Abedeen, Mustafa & Salaiman
68 Jeng Nguan

OTHER
1 Main Post Office & CAT Office
2 Mosque
4 Municipal Office
5 Metro
6 Clock Tower
7 Buses to Songkhla
10 Pakistan Mosque
12 Buses to Phuket
13 Wat Cheu Chang
17 Diana Department Store
18 Thai Farmers Bank
19 Muslim Panich
20 Post Office
21 Immigration Office
25 Expo Department Store
26 Ocean Department Store
35 Sugar Rock
36 Post Laserdisc (Post Restaurant)
39 Central Department Store
40 Odean Department Store
42 Dentnet
44 Bangkok Bank
49 Wat Hat Yai Nai
50 Robinson Department Store
61 THAI Office
65 Biso Palace
66 TAT Office
69 Tourist Police

Money Hat Yai is loaded with banks. There are several after-hours exchange windows along Thanon Niphat Uthit 2 and 3 near the Thanon Thamnoonvithi (pronounced Thammanun Withi) intersection. If you have Malaysian ringgit the banks won't take them but many mid-range and top-end hotels have exchange windows that will.

Post & Communications Hat Yai's main post office is on Thanon Niphat Songkhrao 1, just south of the stadium, and is open from 8.30 am to 4.30 pm weekdays and 9 am to noon weekends. The adjacent telephone office is open from 7 am to 11 pm daily. There is a more convenient post office on Thanon Na Sathani, just north of the Hat Yai train station. A private packing service is conveniently available next door to this post office.

Dentnet, near the corner of Thanon Pratchathipat and Thanon Niphat Uthit 2, has quick terminals and can fill teeth as well.

Film & Photography The Chia Colour Lab at 58–60 Thanon Suphasan Rangsan, next to the Singapore Hotel, offers a good selection of film and quality processing. There are many other photo shops in the city centre.

Wat Hat Yai Nai
วัดหาดใหญ่ใน

A few kilometres west of town, off Thanon Phetkasem towards the airport, is Wat Hat Yai Nai. It features a 35m reclining Buddha (Phra Phut Mahatamongkon). Inside the image's gigantic base is a curious little museum and mausoleum with a souvenir shop. To get here, hop on a sǎwngthǎew near the intersection of Thanon Niphat Uthit 1 and Thanon Phetkasem and get off after crossing Saphan U Taphao (U Taphao Bridge) – it costs about 8B.

Bullfighting

Bullfighting, involving two bulls in opposition rather than a person and a bull, takes place on the first Saturday of each month, or on the second Saturday if the first Saturday is a *wan phrá* (Buddhist worship day; full, half or new moon). The venue changes from time to time, but lately the fights have been held at Noen Khum Thong Stadium on the way to the airport (50B by túk-túk).

On the first Sunday of each month another round is held in Klonggit district (between Hat Yai and Sadao). Matches take place continuously from 9 am to 4 pm and entry is 500B to 800B all day, or 100B to 200B per round – although many hundred times that amount changes hands during the nonstop betting by Thai spectators.

Because the times and venues for these bullfights tend to change every other year or so, check with the TAT office for the latest details.

Muay Thai

Thai boxing matches are held every weekend in the boxing stadium just north of Hat Yai's sports stadium and about 300m north of the fountain. Admission is 180B for all foreigners and Thai men, and 50B for Thai women. Times vary so check with the TAT to confirm the schedule.

Places to Stay – Budget

Hat Yai has dozens of hotels within walking distance of the train station. During Chinese New Year (late February–early March), prices double for most lower-end rooms.

Cheaper places near the station include the 32-year-old *Cathay Guest House* (☎ 074-243815), on the corner of Thanon Thamnoonvithi and Thanon Niphat Uthit 2, three blocks from the station. Rooms range from 160B to 250B; there is also a 90B dorm. The Cathay has become a travellers centre in Hat Yai because of its good location, helpful staff and plentiful travel information for trips onward, including tips on travel in Malaysia. It has a laundry service and serves inexpensive breakfasts as well as other meals (but staff don't mind if you bring in takeaways and eat in the lounge). There is a reliable bus ticket agency downstairs with irregular hours.

Cheaper still are some of the older Chinese hotels in the central area. Rooms are very basic but they're usually secure and service is quite OK – you can get towels and soap on request. The friendly *Weng Aun* (☎ 074-261045), on Thanon Niphat Uthit 1, four doors down from the Muslim Ocha restaurant, is one of Hat Yai's last remaining examples of Sino-Portuguese architecture. Very basic singles in this charmingly decrepit building start at 120B. Another good deal is the *Hok Chin Hin Hotel*

(☎ 074-243258) on Thanon Niphat Uthit 1, a couple of blocks from the train station. Small but very clean rooms with TV, bathroom and fan cost 150/240B single/double; there's a good coffee shop downstairs.

On Thanon Niphat Uthit 1 is the *Mandarin Hotel*, with small, dark double rooms for 220B with fan and bathroom (250B for a triple). The *Grand Hotel* (☎ 074-233669, 257–259 Thanon Thamnoonvithi) is better, with 24 fairly clean rooms with fan and bathroom for 180B and air-con for 350B. At 138/2–3 Thanon Thamnoonvithi, the *Prince Hotel* (☎ 074-243160, fax 232496) offers small, musty rooms with fan and cold water for 150B; air-con rooms are 380B.

Rung Fah Hotel (☎ 074-244808, 117/5–6 Thanon Niphat Uthit 3) was undergoing major renovations at last visit. The *Thai Hotel* (☎ 074-253081, 9 Soi 3, Thanon Rat Uthit), rather out of the way south-west of the train station, features rooms with fan from 150B and air-con rooms for up to 450B.

There's a rash of places in town calling themselves 'guesthouses' that are really small budget hotels. *Louise Guest House* (☎ 074-220966, 21–23 Thanon Thamnoonvithi) is an apartment-style place with clean rooms for 320B with fan, 380B with air-con; all have hot water – not a bad bargain compared with some of the previously described places. At *Ladda Guest House* (☎ 074-220233), next to the Robinson department store complex near the train station, narrow stairs lead to tiny single/double rooms from 200B/240B with fan, and 290B/320B with air-con; it's good value for air-con if the lack of fire exits doesn't frighten you away. Near the Songkhla bus stand off Thanon Phetkasem is *Sorasilp Guest House* (☎ 074-232635), where clean a singles/doubles are 160/200B with fan and cold-water bathroom, 250/350B for air-con. One extra-large room is available for 400B.

Places to Stay – Mid-Range

For some reason hotels in Hat Yai take a disproportionate leap upwards in quality once you move up another 100B to 200B a night.

Very popular with Malaysian visitors as well as other travellers is the *King's Hotel* (☎ 074-234140, fax 236103, 126 Thanon Niphat Uthit 1). Rooms start at 500B with satellite TV, air-con and hot water. Not far

from the train station on Thanon Thamnoonvithi is the *Laem Thong Hotel* (☎ 074-352301, fax 237574), with fairly noisy though comfortable singles/doubles for 250B with fan and cold-water bathroom, and 420B to 600B with air-con. The hotel restaurant serves imported coffee, fàràng breakfasts and Thai dishes.

The *OH Hotel* (Oriental; ☎ 074-230142, fax 354824, 135 Thanon Niphat Uthit 3) has very good singles/doubles with fan in the old wing for 250B. In the new wing, rooms with air-con, TV, phone and hot water cost 450B single/double.

The friendly, security-conscious *Singapore Hotel* (☎ 074-237478, 62–66 Thanon Suphasan Rangsan) has good clean rooms with fan and bathroom for 270/300B single/double, air-con for 380B, and air-con rooms with two beds, satellite TV and hot water for 450B. The friendly *Pueng Luang Hotel* (☎ 074-244548, 241–245 Thanon Saeng Chan) has huge fan rooms with bathroom for 250B, plus a few smaller ones for 200B. Air-con rooms go for 300B. The *Wang Noi Hotel* (☎ 074-231024, 114/1 Thanon Saeng Chan) has better rooms for 220B with fan and 370B with air-con; it's in a relatively quiet location.

The *Indra Hotel* (☎ 074-245886, fax 232464, 94 Thanon Thamnoonvithi) is an older tourist hotel with decent air-con rooms with TV and hot water for 480B. On the premises are a Chinese restaurant, a coffee shop, snooker centre and traditional Thai massage centre. The *Royal Hotel* (☎ 074-351451, 106 Thanon Prachathipat) has rooms starting at 480B with air-con and TV. Catering primarily to Chinese visitors, the older *Kosit Hotel* (☎ 074-234366, fax 232365), on Thanon Niphat Uthit 2, has air-con rooms for 590B, plus a restaurant, karaoke and a massage centre. The *Park Hotel* (☎ 074-233351, fax 232259, 81 Thanon Niphat Uthit 2), connected to a low-rise shopping mall, has similar rooms for 390B.

The *Rajthanee*, at the Hat Yai train station, was padlocked and abandoned at last visit. If it ever reopens, it'll be great for those with an early morning train to catch.

The *Montien Hotel* (☎ 074-234386, fax 230043), on Thanon Niphat Uthit 1, is a large place that caters to Chinese visitors; decent air-con doubles cost 350B to 550B.

Places to Stay – Top End

Top-end accommodation in Hat Yai is mainly geared to Malaysian Chinese weekend visitors, so rates are considerably lower than in Bangkok or Chiang Mai. *Hat Yai International Hotel* (☎ 074-231022, fax 232539, 42–44 Thanon Niphat Uthit 3) offers comfortable rooms with all amenities for 500B to 1400B; the hotel features a coffee house and restaurant with Thai, Chinese and European food, a disco and a traditional massage centre. Also at the lower end of the top-enders is the *Lee Gardens Hotel* (☎ 074-234422, fax 231888) on Thanon Lee Pattana, where 690B buys a room with satellite TV, phone, bathtub and refrigerator.

The modern *President Hotel* (☎ 074-349500, fax 230609, 420 Thanon Phet-kasem) is a white-concrete monolith near the Songkhla share-taxi stand with 110 rooms for 600B. Standing alone at the southern edge of the city centre on Thanon Siphunawat, the *Florida Hotel* (☎ 074-234555, fax 234553) is another tall white hotel with modern but well-worn rooms for 627B, along with the usual Chinese restaurant and massage centre. Also in this category is the *LK Hotel* (☎ 074-230120, fax 238112, 150 Thanon Saeng Chan), where decent doubles with most of the trimmings cost 750B, including breakfast.

Slightly more upmarket are the *Asian Hotel* (☎ 074-053400, fax 234890, 55 Thanon Niphat Uthit 3) and the *Diamond Plaza Hotel* (☎ 074-230130, fax 239824, 62 Thanon Niphat Uthit 3), both of which offer comfortable, modern rooms for 850B to 990B.

The 28-storey *Regency* (☎ 074-353333, fax 234102, 23 Thanon Prachathipat) features rooms and suites stuffed with modern amenities for 1398B double and up. Less-luxurious rooms in the old wing can be had for just 798B. Facilities include a lobby lounge, coffee shop, dim sum restaurant, a gym and a huge swimming pool with a bar.

The nicest hotel in town is the *Central Sukhontha Hotel* (☎ 074-352222, fax 352223, 3 Thanon Sanehanuson), where spacious, fully outfitted rooms cost 1800B and up; facilities include a swimming pool with a snack bar, a sauna, Chinese restaurant, 24-hour cafe, lobby lounge, fitness centre, business centre and shopping mall (with a branch of the Central Department Store).

Places to Eat

Hat Yai is Southern Thailand's gourmet mecca, offering fresh seafood from both the Gulf of Thailand and the Andaman Sea, bird's-nest soup, shark fins, Muslim rotii and curries, Chinese noodles and dim sum. Lots of good, cheap restaurants can be found along the three Niphat Uthit roads, in the markets off side streets between them, and also near the train station. Many Hat Yai restaurants, particularly the Chinese ones, close in the afternoon between 2 and 6 pm – unusual for Thailand.

Thai Although Chinese and Malay food rules in Hat Yai, there are a few Thai places. An old, established Thai restaurant is *Niyom Rot* (Niyomrosh; 219–221 Thanon Thamnoonvithi). The *plaa kràbàwk thâwt* (whole sea mullet fried with eggs intact) is particularly prized here. Its hours are 10.30 am to 2 pm and 5 to 9.30 pm.

The *Viang Chan* (no Roman-script sign) at 12 Thanon Niphat Uthit 2 serves North-Eastern and other Thai dishes along with Chinese cuisine; it opens at 5 pm. *999 Remy*, just around the corner from the Laem Thong Hotel, has a huge selection of curries. It closes around 6 pm.

Chinese Start the day with inexpensive dim sum at *Shangrila* on Thanon Thamnoonvithi near the Cathay Guest House. Specialities include *khànǒm jìip* (dumplings), *saalaapao* (Chinese buns) and *khâo nâa pèt* (roast duck on rice); it's open from 5 am to 3 pm. In the evenings the Chinese-food action moves to *Hua Lee* on the corner of Thanon Niphat Uthit 3 and Thanon Thamnoonvithi; it's open till the wee hours. Another excellent dim sum place is *Aree Dimsum* (116–118 Thanon Saeng Chan), next to the Wang Noi Hotel. Dim sum here costs about 10B to 15B per dish and the restaurant is open from 6 to 11 am and 6.30 to 10 pm daily.

Jeng Nguan is an old feasting stand-by near the end of Thanon Niphat Uthit 1. Try the *tâo hûu thâwt kràwp* (fried bean curd), *hǔu chàlǎam* (shark-fin soup), *bàmìi plaa phàt* (fried noodles with fish), or *kíaw plaa* (fish wonton). It's open from 11 am to 2 pm and 5 to 9 pm.

Several hotels in town have good splurge-style Chinese restaurants, including the JB Hotel's well-regarded *Dynasty*.

Malay & Indian The *Muslim-O-Cha* (Muslim Ocha), across from King's Hotel, is still going strong, with rotii kaeng (*roti chanai* in Malay) in the mornings and curries all day. This is one of the few Muslim cafes in town where women – even non-Muslim – seem welcome. There are a couple of other Muslim restaurants near this one. *Makanan Muslim* at the corner of Thanon Saeng Chan and Thanon Prachathipat is a clean open-air place with rotii and mátàbà.

On Thanon Niyomrat, between Niphat Uthit 1 and 2, are *Abedeen*, *Sulaiman* and *Mustafa*, all specialising in Muslim food. Sulaiman has the best selection, including Indian paratha, dhal, chapati, biryani, and various mutton, chicken, fish and vegie dishes. Abedeen is good for *tôm yam kûng* (spicy prawn and lemon-grass soup), a Thai speciality here rendered in a slightly different way.

Sumatra Restaurant, next to the Pakistan Mosque near the Holiday Plaza Hotel, does Malay dishes like *rojak* (peanut-sauce salad) and *nasi biryani* (spiced rice plate). *Sicilian Seafood*, on Thanon Thamnoonvithi opposite the Laem Thong Hotel, advertises 'Muslim seafood' as well as halal Indian specialities.

Night Markets The extensive night market along Thanon Montri 1 specialises in fresh seafood; you can dine on two seafood dishes and one vegetable dish for less than 200B here if you speak Thai. There are smaller night markets along Thanon Suphasan Rangsan and Thanon Siphunawat.

Other Options Adjacent to the Robinson department store on Thanon Thamnoonvithi are *KFC* and *Mister Donut*. A *McDonald's* restaurant can be found at the Lee Gardens Hotel.

Or for something very different, cruise down *Thanon Ngu* (Snake Street – Soi 1, Thanon Thung Sao), Hat Yai's most popular spot for snake fetishists. After a live snake is slit lengthwise with a scalpel, the blood is drained and drunk with honey, Chinese rice wine or herbal liquor. Besides the blood, the heart, gall bladder and penis are also highly regarded. Skins are sold as wallets, belts and other accessories, while the

meat is boiled for soup. A snake-blood cocktail goes for thousands of baht, but you can sample a bowl of snake soup for just 150B. Snake Street is a 30B túk-túk ride south of the city centre.

Entertainment

Most of the many clubs and coffee shops in town cater to Malaysian clientele. The bigger hotels have discos; among the most popular are the *Disco Palace* (Emperor Hotel), the *Metro* (JB Hotel), the *Diana Club* (Lee Gardens Hotel) and the *Inter* (Hat Yai International Hotel). Cover charges are only 100B to 150B.

The *Post Laserdisc* (Post Restaurant) on Thanon Thamnoonvithi, a block east of the Cathay Guest House, is a music-video and laserdisc restaurant and bar with an excellent sound system and well-placed monitors. It shows mostly Western movies, and programs change nightly – the fairly up-to-date music videos are a filler between the films. The daily schedule starts at noon and goes until midnight – mostly Thais and Western tourists frequent this establishment. There's a 30B charge to view movies upstairs and drink prices are only a little higher than at the average bar. Meals, including breakfast, are served as well.

Opposite the Post Laserdisc, *Sugar Rock* is one of the more durable Hat Yai pubs, with good food, good prices and a low-key atmosphere. It's open from 8 am to midnight.

Shopping

Shopping is Hat Yai's number-one drawcard, with most of the market action taking place along Thanon Niphat Uthit 2 and 3. Here you'll find Thai and Malaysian batik, cheap electronics and inexpensive clothing.

Muslim Panich, at 17 Thanon Niphat Uthit 1, has an excellent selection of south-Indian sarongs, plus Thai, Malay and Indonesian batik. Although you'll find cheaper at the markets, they can't compare with Muslim Panich in terms of quality and selection.

Hat Yai has three major department stores on Thanon Niphat Uthit 3 (Diana, Ocean and Expo) and two on Thanon Thamnoonvithi (Odean and Robinson), plus the newer Central Department Store next to the Central Sukhontha Hotel.

SOUTHERN GULF

DK Book House, about 50m from the train station on Thanon Thamnoonvithi, carries English-language books and maps. On the 4th floor of the Central Department Store is a selection of English books and magazines.

Getting There & Away

Air THAI operates flights between Hat Yai and Bangkok six times daily (2615B, 1½ hours). There is also a daily THAI flight to Hat Yai from Phuket for 910B. THAI's office (☎ 074-233433 for reservations) in Hat Yai is at 166/4 Thanon Niphat Uthit 2.

THAI flies from Hat Yai to Kuala Lumpur and Singapore. Malaysia Airlines flies from Penang, and there are Silk Air flights from Singapore.

Malaysia Airlines (☎ 074-245443) has its office in the Lee Gardens Hotel, with a separate entrance on Thanon Niphat Uthit 1.

Hat Yai International Airport has a post office with an IDD telephone in the arrival area; it's open from 8.30 am to 4.30 pm weekdays, 9 am to noon Saturday, and is closed on Sunday. Other airport facilities include the Sky Lounge Cafe & Restaurant on the ground floor near the domestic check-in, a less expensive coffee shop on the 2nd-floor departure level, and foreign-exchange kiosks.

Bus Green buses to Songkhla leave from outside the small clock tower on Thanon Phetkasem. Share taxis leave from around the corner near the President Hotel.

Air-con buses from Bangkok cost 520B (VIP 760B) and leave the Southern bus terminal at 7 am and 4, 5.30, 6, 6.15, 6.30, 7, 8 and 8.20 pm. The journey takes 14 hours. Private companies sometimes have fares as low as 400B. Ordinary government buses cost 289B and leave Bangkok twice daily, at 5.30 and 9.45 pm.

There are lots of buses running between Phuket and Hat Yai; ordinary buses cost 135B (eight hours) and air-con cost 233B to 243B (six hours). Three daily buses go to Pak Bara (35B, three hours) for Ko Tarutao.

Cathay Tour runs express air-con buses and minivans to Phuket (200B), Krabi (130B), Ko Samui (250B) and Surat Thani (130B). Other buses from Hat Yai include:

destination	fare	duration (hrs)
Ko Samui		
air-con	240B	7
Krabi		
air-con	153B	5
Narathiwat		
ordinary	55B	3
air-con	72B	3
Padang Besar		
ordinary	21B	1½
Pattani		
ordinary	38B	2
air-con	55B	1½
Phattalung		
ordinary	35B	2
Satun		
ordinary	32B	2
air-con	45B	1½
Sungai Kolok		
air-con	148B	4
Surat Thani		
ordinary	103B	6½
air-con	180B	5½
Trang		
ordinary	50B	3
Yala		
ordinary	50B	2½
air-con	60B	2

Agencies that arrange private buses include:

Cathay Tour (☎ 074-235044) Ground floor, Cathay Guest House
Golden Way Travel (☎ 074-233917) 132 Thanon Niphat Uthit 3
Hat Yai Swanthai Tours (☎ 074-239621) 108 Thanon Thamnoonvithi
Pan Siam (☎ 074-237440) 99 Thanon Niphat Uthit 2
Sunny Tour (☎ 074-353060) Thanon Niphat Uthit 2
Universal On-Time Co (☎ 074-231609) 147 Thanon Niphat Uthit 1

Beware of Chaw Wang Tours, about which we have had several reports of bad service and bait-and-switch tactics with buses, particularly between Ko Samui and Hat Yai and between Hat Yai and Malaysia.

Malaysia & Singapore Hat Yai is an important travel junction. From Padang Besar at the Malaysian border, buses cost 21B and take 1½ hours to reach Hat Yai. Buses run every 10 minutes between 6 am and 7.20 pm. Other services include:

destination	fare	duration (hrs)
Butterworth		
(for Penang)	230B	6
Kuala Lumpur	300B–350B	12
Singapore	450B–550B	15

Train Trains from Bangkok to Hat Yai leave Hualamphong station daily at 12.25 pm (rapid No 171), 2.20 pm (special express No 35, 1st and 2nd class only), 2.45 pm (special express No 37), 3.50 pm (rapid No 169) and 10.50 pm (express diesel railcar No 41, 2nd class only), arriving in Hat Yai at 6.30, 7.05, 7.25, 9.45 and 12.17 pm respectively. The basic fare is 734B for 1st class (express only), 345B for 2nd class and 149B for 3rd class.

In the reverse direction, to Bangkok, you can take the 2.45 pm (rapid No 172), 3.15 pm (rapid No 170), 4.20 pm (express diesel railcar No 42), 5.40 pm (special express No 38) or 6.10 pm (special express No 36), which arrive in Bangkok at 8.35, 9.45, 6.35, 10.35 and 11 am respectively.

There are four ordinary 3rd-class trains per day between Hat Yai and Sungai Kolok (31B) and one daily to Padang Besar (10B).

The advance booking office at Hat Yai station is open from 7 am to 5 pm daily. A left-luggage office ('Cloak Room') is open from 6 am to noon and 1 to 5 pm daily.

Car Several travel agencies in town specialise in arranging a private car and driver for a quick trip to the border and back for those who need to cross the border to have their visas renewed automatically. The going rate for this service is 500B to 600B.

Share Taxi Share taxis are a good way of getting from one province to another quickly in the south. There are several share-taxi stands in Hat Yai, each specialising in certain destinations.

In general, share-taxi fares cost about the same as for an air-con bus, but the taxis are about 30% faster. Share taxis also offer door-to-door drop-offs. The downside is that the drivers wait around for enough passengers (usually five) for a departure. If you hit it right the taxi may leave immediately; otherwise you may have to wait for half an hour or more. The drivers also drive at hair-raising speeds – not a pleasant experience for highly strung passengers.

> **Warning**
>
> Care should be taken in selecting travel agencies for bus trips into Malaysia. There are still reports of bus companies demanding 'visa fees' before crossing the border – since visas aren't required for most nationalities, this is a blatant rip-off. The offending company collects your passport on the bus and then asks for the fee – holding your passport hostage. Refuse all requests for visa or border-crossing fees – all services are supposed to be included in the ticket price. Chaw Wang Tours is allegedly one agency of which to be careful.

There is one other small drawback associated with share taxis: The location of the taxi stands tends to change with annoying frequency. According to TAT, share taxis are only semi-legal and therefore the locations of the taxi stands are somewhat fluid. When police inevitably crack down on one queue location, the share taxis move to another one, usually just around the corner. TAT explains that the locals all know where to look when the usual taxi stand has been abandoned. Unfortunately, visitors will be less able to glean this information. Therefore TAT suggests dropping by its office and asking them about the current locations. You may also be able to get this information from Cathay Tours, below the Cathay Guest House.

Malaysia Share taxis are a popular way of travelling between Hat Yai and Penang in Malaysia. They're faster than the tour buses, although less comfortable and more expensive.

Big old Thai-registered Chevys and Mercedes depart from Hat Yai around 9 am every day. You'll find them at the train station or along Thanon Niphat Uthit 1, near King's Hotel.

In Penang you can find them around the cheap travellers hotels in Georgetown. The cost is about 250B or RM24 – this is probably the fastest way of travelling between the two countries and you cross the border with a minimum of fuss.

From Hat Yai the fare to Padang Besar is 100B for the one-hour trip; taxis are on Thanon Duangchan.

Getting Around

To/From the Airport The THAI van costs 50B per person for transport to the city and there's also a private 200B THAI limo service. You can get a THAI limo from the city centre out to the airport by calling ☎ 074-238452.

A regular taxi costs 150B from the airport to the city and about 100B in the reverse direction.

Car Avis Rent-A-Car (☎ 074-352222) maintains an office at the Central Sukhontha Hotel. You may also be able to arrange car rental through travel agencies in town.

Sǎwngthǎew The innumerable sǎwngthǎew around Hat Yai cost 10B per person. Watch out when you cross the street or they'll mow you down.

AROUND HAT YAI
Nam Tok Ton Nga Chang
น้ำตกโตนงาช้าง

Nam Tok Ton Nga Chang (Elephant Tusk Falls), 24km west of Hat Yai via Hwy 4 in Rattaphum district, is a 1200m seven-tier cascade that falls in two streams (thus resembling two tusks). If you're staying in Hat Yai, the falls make a nice break from the hustle and bustle of the city. The waterfall looks its best at the end of the rainy season, (October to December).

To get to the falls take a Rattaphum-bound sǎwngthǎew (25B) from anywhere along Thanon Phetkasem and ask to get off at the *náam tòk* (waterfall).

Khao Nam Khang Tunnels
อุโมงค์ประวัติศาสตร์เขาน้ำค้าง

Located in the Khao Nam Khang National Park, this tunnel complex was used by Communist Party of Malaysia (CPM) guerrillas as a base camp until they finally gave up the struggle in 1989. At least 1km of tunnels on three levels has been preserved and a portion of these have been widened to accommodate visitors. The underground base boasted conference rooms, a radio room, an operating room and, oddly, three long, straight passageways where the tunnel-bound communists could practice riding their motorbikes! The whole complex is said to have taken two years to build.

Park officials say that bungalows to accommodate visitors are planned for the future. In the meantime there is a small restaurant on the premises. The tunnels are open from 9 am to 4 pm daily. To get here it is necessary to have a private vehicle as there are no public buses plying the route. From Hat Yai take Hwy 4 south toward Sadao, turning left at the Sadao district office and driving for another 26km. The tunnels are located about 4km beyond the park headquarters.

Yala Province

Yala is the most prosperous of the four predominantly Muslim provinces in Southern Thailand, mainly due to income derived from rubber production. It is also the number-one business and education centre for the region.

YALA
อ.เมืองยะลา

postcode 95000 ● pop 70,600
The fast-developing capital is sometimes known as 'the cleanest city in Thailand' and has won several awards for this (its main competitor is Trang). Yala is a city of parks, wide boulevards and orderly traffic.

One of the biggest regional **festivals** in Thailand is held in Yala during May or June to pay respect to the city's guardian spirit, Jao Phaw Lak Meuang. Chinese New Year is also celebrated here with some zest, as there are many Chinese living in the capital.

The Muslim population is settled in the rural areas of the province, for the most part, although there is a sizable Muslim quarter near the train station in town – you'll know it by the sheep and goats wandering in the streets and by the modern mosque – one of Yala's tallest buildings and the largest mosque in Thailand.

Information

The post and telephone office on Thanon Siriros (Sirirot) offers international telephone service from 8.30 am to 4.30 pm on weekdays, and from 9 am to noon on weekends.

Things to See & Do

Phrupakoi Park, just west of the round-about, has a big artificial lake where people can fish, boat and eat in floating restaurants. Yala residents seem obsessed with water recreation, possibly as a consequence of living in the only land-locked province in the south.

Places to Stay – Budget & Mid-Range

Yala has quite a few hotels at low to moderate price levels. In the town centre there are lots of old Chinese hotels – so it's like Hat Yai in the old days, but funkier and grittier. A strange cast of characters inhabit these hotels – basically transients from all over South and South-East Asia.

Starting from the bottom, the ***Shanghai Hotel*** (☎ *073-212037, 36–34 Thanon Ratakit)* and ***Saen Suk Hotel*** are nearly identical Chinese hotels with Chinese restaurants on the ground floor. Both are on the same block on Thanon Ratakit, in the business district not far from the train station. They have somewhat dreary rooms from 80B to 100B; the Saen Suk is a bit cleaner, and its restaurant is also better, specialising in generous plates of khâo man kài (chicken rice).

Next to the Shanghai, the ***Muang Thong Hotel*** (☎ *073-212671)* is similar, with rooms for 100B and a restaurant downstairs.

Nearby, on the other side of Thanon Ratakit, the ***Metro Hotel*** (☎ *073-212175)* has better rooms for 100B to 120B and a better restaurant downstairs.

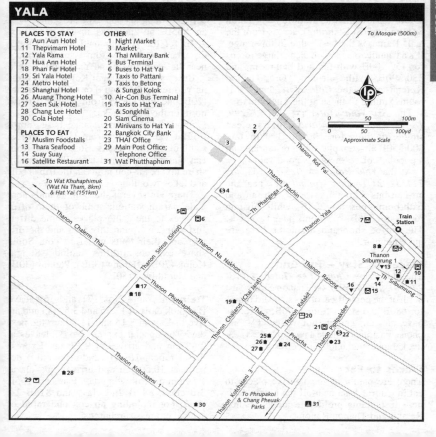

YALA

PLACES TO STAY
8 Aun Aun Hotel
11 Thepvimarn Hotel
12 Yala Rama
17 Hua Ann Hotel
18 Phan Far Hotel
19 Sri Yala Hotel
24 Metro Hotel
25 Shanghai Hotel
26 Muang Thong Hotel
27 Saen Suk Hotel
28 Chang Lee Hotel
30 Cola Hotel

PLACES TO EAT
2 Muslim Foodstalls
13 Thara Seafood
14 Suay Suay
16 Satellite Restaurant

OTHER
1 Night Market
3 Market
4 Thai Military Bank
5 Bus Terminal
6 Buses to Hat Yai
7 Taxis to Pattani
9 Taxis to Betong
    & Sungai Kolok
10 Air-Con Bus Terminal
15 Taxis to Hat Yai
    & Songkhla
20 Siam Cinema
21 Minivans to Hat Yai
22 Bangkok City Bank
23 THAI Office
29 Main Post Office;
    Telephone Office
31 Wat Phutthaphum

SOUTHERN GULF

The **Aun Aun Hotel** (☎ 073-212216), on Thanon Pipitpakdee, is the first hotel you see as you walk into town from the train station. The Aun Aun has none-too-clean rooms for 90B without bathroom, 140B with private bathroom. One asset is that the rooms have screen doors, so you can open your door for ventilation without worrying much about insects. The manager at Aun Aun speaks good English.

Over on Thanon Siriros are two newer side-by-side Chinese hotels that are much cleaner than all the aforementioned. The **Hua Ann Hotel** and **Phan Far Hotel** both offer clean, sizable rooms with fan and private bathroom for 180/250B single/double; the Hua Ann also has air-con rooms for 380B. Both hotels have coffee shops downstairs in the typical layout.

The **Thepvimarn Hotel** (☎ 073-212400), a left turn from the station on Thanon Sribumrung (Si Bamrung), across from the Yala Rama, is the best value in this range. It's a friendly place, with clean, large rooms for 150/200B with fan and bathroom, and 330/390B with air-con. On Thanon Kotchaseni 1, the **Cola Hotel** has 250B rooms similar to those at the Thepvimarn.

The **Sri Yala Hotel** (☎ 073-212299, 18–22 Thanon Chaijarus) offers clean singles/doubles for 190/240B with fan, 300/350B air-con, plus a lift, restaurant and a popular coffee shop; it's good value.

At the **Yala Rama** (☎ 073-212563, fax 214532, 21 Thanon Sribumrung), near the air-con bus terminal, a room with fan and bathroom goes for 265B, while air-con rooms are 396B. All rooms have two beds. The coffee shop and nightclub here are quite popular.

Places to Stay – Top End

The plush new **Chang Lee Hotel** (☎ 073-244340, fax 244599), on Thanon Siriros just north of the post office, offers standard rooms for 680B and suites from 1100B; all rooms have air-con, carpet, hot water, TV and phone. Facilities include a pool, business centre, karaoke, nightclub and coffee shop.

Places to Eat

There are plenty of inexpensive places to eat in central Yala near all the hotels. Chinese restaurants proliferate along Thanon Ratakit and Thanon Ranong.

The popular **Thara Seafood** (no English sign), on the corner of Thanon Pipitpakdee and Thanon Sribumrung, serves excellent seafood at moderate prices. House specialities include *kûng phǎo* (grilled prawns) and *plaa òp bai toei* (fish baked in pandanus leaves). The **Suay Suay** indoor/outdoor restaurant, on Thanon Sribumrung near the Yala Rama hotel, and the big **Satellite** restaurant, on the corner of Thanon Pipitpakdee and Thanon Ranong, specialise in steamed cockles. In the morning Satellite also does good *jók* (rice congee) and Chinese dumplings.

The **day market** on Thanon Siriros has a good selection of fresh fruit. The **Muslim food stalls** nearby serve rotii kaeng in the early morning – a cheap and filling breakfast.

Getting There & Away

Bus & Share Taxi Air-con buses (1st class) between Bangkok and Yala are 558B, VIPs are 865B and 2nd-class air-con buses cost 434B for the 16-hour haul. In Yala long-distance buses leave from a small terminal near the Thepvimarn and Yala Rama hotels.

Buses south to Sungai Kolok (18B ordinary, three to 3½ hours) or north to Pattani (20B, one hour) leave from Thanon Siriros, north of the train tracks.

Short- to medium-distance buses north (to Hat Yai etc) leave from Thanon Siriros, south of the train tracks. Buses to and from Hat Yai cost 50B and take 2½ hours; by share taxi or air-con minivan the trip is 60B and takes two hours.

There are several share-taxi stands near Yala's train station; some of them offer services to the same places, some differ. Just wander around this area and the drivers and their touts will find you. Some share-taxi possibilities include Sungai Kolok (70B), Betong (80B), Pattani (30B) and Narathiwat (50B).

Train The rapid Nos 171 and 169 leave Bangkok daily at 12.25 and 3.50 pm and arrive in Yala at 8.15 and 11.30 am the next day. The special express No 37 leaves at 2.45 pm and arrives at 9.13 am. Express diesel railcar No 41 (2nd-class only) departs at 10.50 pm and arrives in Yala at 1.50 pm the following day. Fares are 165B 3rd class, 382B 2nd class and 815B 1st class, not including air-con and rapid or special express surcharges.

From Hat Yai, ordinary trains to Yala are 16B for 3rd class and take 2½ hours. From Sungai Kolok, at the Malaysian border, trains are 15B for a 2½ hour trip. To/from Surat Thani the 3rd-class fare is 58B.

AROUND YALA
Wat Na Tham
วัดหน้าถ้ำ

Outside town, about 8km west off the Yala–Hat Yai highway, is Wat Khuhaphimuk (also called Wat Na Tham, Cave-Front Temple), a Srivijaya-period cave temple established around AD 750. Inside the cave is Phra Phutthasaiyat, a long, reclining Buddha image sculpted in the Srivijaya style. For Thais, this is one of the three most-venerated Buddhist pilgrimage points in Southern Thailand (the other two are Wat Boromathat in Nakhon Si Thammarat and Wat Phra Boromathat Chaiya in Surat Thani). There is a small museum in front of the cave, with artefacts of local provenance.

To get here, take a sǎwngthǎew going west towards the town of Yaha via Rte 4065, and ask to get off at the road to Wat Na Tham – the fare is 5B. It's about a 1km walk to the wát from the highway.

Two kilometres past Wat Na Tham is **Tham Silpa**, a well-known cave with Buddhist polychrome murals from the Srivijaya era as well as prehistoric monochromatic paintings of primitive hunters. A monk from Wat Na Tham may be able to guide you here. There are several other caves nearby worth exploring for their impressive stalactite and stalagmite formations.

Pattani Province

PATTANI
อ.เมืองงปัตตานี

postcode 94000 • pop 42,200

The provincial capital of Pattani provides a heavy contrast to Yala. In spite of its basic function as a trading post operated by the Chinese for the benefit (or exploitation, depending on your perspective) of the surrounding Muslim villages, the town has a more Muslim character than Yala. In the streets, you are more likely to hear Yawi than any Thai-language dialect.

The markets are visually quite similar to markets in Kota Bharu in Malaysia. The town as a whole is a bit dirtier than Yala, but the riverfront area is interesting.

Pattani was until rather recently the centre of an independent principality that included Yala and Narathiwat. It was also one of the earliest kingdoms in Thailand to host international trade; the Portuguese established a trading post here in 1516, the Japanese in 1605, the Dutch in 1609 and the British in 1612. A cosmopolitan collection of antique cannon unearthed at Pattani and now on display at the national museum in Songkhla attests to the competitive nature of trade in early Pattani. During WWII, Japanese troops landed in Pattani to launch attacks on Malaya and Singapore.

Orientation & Information
The centre of this mostly concrete town is at the intersection of Thanon Naklua Yarang (the north-south road running between Yala and Pattani harbour) and Thanon Ramkomud, which runs east-west between Songkhla and Narathiwat. Intercity buses and taxis stop at this intersection.

Thanon Ramkomud becomes Thanon Rudee after crossing Thanon Naklua Yarang, and it is along Thanon Rudee that you can see what is left of old Pattani architecture, the Sino-Portuguese style that was once so prevalent throughout Southern Thailand.

Pattani's main post office is on Thanon Pipit, near the bridge. The attached CAT office provides overseas telephone service from 7 am to 10 pm daily.

Several banks are found along the south-eastern end of Thanon Pipit, near the intersection with Thanon Naklua Yarang.

As in Yala, Narathiwat, Satun and Trang, all street signs are in tortured English transliterations of Thai (better than no transliterations at all, for those who can't read Thai).

Mosques
Thailand's second-largest mosque is the **Matsayit Klang**, a traditional structure of green hue, probably still the most important mosque in Southern Thailand. It was built in the early 1960s.

The oldest mosque in Pattani is the **Matsayit Kreu-Se**, built in 1578 by an

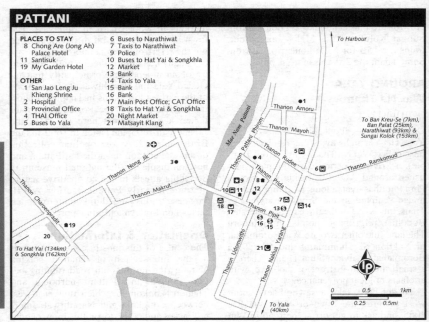

PATTANI

PLACES TO STAY
8 Chong Are (Jong Ah)
  Palace Hotel
11 Santisuk
19 My Garden Hotel

OTHER
1 San Jao Leng Ju
  Khieng Shrine
2 Hospital
3 Provincial Office
4 THAI Office
5 Buses to Yala

6 Buses to Narathiwat
7 Taxis to Narathiwat
9 Police
10 Buses to Hat Yai & Songkhla
12 Market
13 Bank
14 Taxis to Yala
15 Bank
16 Bank
17 Main Post Office; CAT Office
18 Taxis to Hat Yai & Songkhla
20 Night Market
21 Matsayit Klang

immigrant Chinese named Lim To Khieng who had married a Pattani woman and converted to Islam. Actually, neither To Khieng, nor anyone else, ever completed the mosque (see the boxed text 'The Uncompleted Mosque').

The brick, Arab-style building has been left in its original semicompleted, semiruined form, but the faithful keep up the surrounding grounds. The mosque is in the village of Ban Kreu-Se, about 7km east of Pattani next to Hwy 42 at the 10km marker; a gaudy Chinese temple has been built next to it.

The tree from which Lim Ko Niaw hanged herself has been enshrined at the **San Jao Leng Ju Kieng** (or San Jao Lim Ko Niaw), the site of an important Chinese-Muslim festival in late February or early March. During the festival a wooden image of Lim Ko Niaw is carried through the streets; additional rites include fire-walking and seven days of vegetarianism. The shrine is in the northern end of town towards the harbour.

Another festival fervently celebrated in Pattani is **Hari Rayo**, the Muslim month of fasting during the 10th lunar month.

Laem Tachi

The only beach near town is at Laem Tachi, a cape that juts out over the northern end of Ao Pattani. You must take a boat taxi to get here, either from Tha Pattani or from Yaring district at the mouth of Mae Nam Pattani. This white-sand beach is about 11km long, but is sometimes marred by refuse from Ao Pattani, depending on the time of year and the tides.

Places to Stay & Eat

The *Chong Are Palace Hotel* (*Jong Ah;* ☎ 073-349711, 38 Soi Talat Tetiwat), off Thanon Prida, is a decent place with rooms for 160B with fan and cold-water bathroom, and 210B with air-con (plus another 50B if you want TV). The *Santisuk* (☎ 073-349122, 29 Thanon Pipit) has OK rooms for 150B with private bathroom and fan, 200B with TV and 400B with air-con.

A favourite with travelling businesspeople, the four-storey *My Garden Hotel* (☎ 073-331055, fax 348200, 8/28 Thanon Charoenpradit) is about 1km outside town and is good mid-range value – 300B for a large double with fan and bathroom, and

500B for air-con with cable TV, bathtub, good hot-water showers, phone and fridge. The disco is very popular on weekends. Săamláw and săwngthăew drivers may know it by its former name, the Dina.

The *Chong Are* restaurant, next to the hotel of the same name, serves a range of decent Thai and Chinese food.

A *night market* with plenty of food vendors convenes opposite My Garden Hotel each evening.

Shopping
Thai Muslims in Southern Thailand have their own traditional batik methods that are similar but not identical to the batik of north-eastern Malaysia.

The best place to shop for local batik is at the Palat Market (Talat Nat Palat), which is off Hwy 42 between Pattani and Saiburi in Ban Palat. The market is held all day Wednesday and Sunday only.

If you can't make it to the Palat Market, there are several shops along Thanon Rudee in Pattani that sell local and Malaysian batik at slightly higher prices.

Getting There & Away
Air No flights are available from Pattani at this time. However, Pattani's THAI office (☎ 073-335939) at 9 Thanon Prida will check you in and take you to the Hat Yai airport (110km away) as part of the service for no extra charge.

Bus & Share Taxi Pattani is only 40km from Yala. Share taxis cost 30B and take about 30 minutes; buses cost only 20B but take around an hour. From Narathiwat, a share taxi is 50B, a minivan 60B, and a bus 30B. From Hat Yai ordinary buses cost 38B and air-con 55B.

From Bangkok there is only one ordinary bus (285B, 17 hours, 6.30 pm).

A 1st-class air-con bus departs from Bangkok at 10 am and 6 pm (563B). In the reverse direction these buses leave Pattani at 2 and 2.30 pm. VIP buses to Pattani leave Bangkok at 5.30 pm and cost 875B. From Pattani to Bangkok VIP buses leave at 2.30 pm.

Getting Around
Săwngthăew go anywhere in town for 7B per person.

The Uncompleted Mosque
The story goes that To Khieng's sister, Lim Ko Niaw, sailed from China on a sampan to try to persuade her brother to abandon Islam and return to his homeland. To demonstrate the strength of his faith, To Khieng began building the Matsayit Kreu-Se. His sister then put a curse on the mosque, saying it would never be completed. Then, in a final attempt to dissuade To Khieng, she hanged herself from a nearby cashew tree. In his grief, Khieng was unable to complete the mosque, and to this day it remains unfinished; supposedly every time someone tries to work on it, lightning strikes.

Narathiwat Province

NARATHIWAT
อ.เมืองนราธิวาส

postcode 96000 • pop 41,700
Narathiwat is a pleasant, even-tempered town – one of Thailand's smallest provincial capitals – with a character all of its own. Many of the buildings are wooden structures, 100 or more years old. The local businesses seem to be owned by both Muslims and Chinese, and nights are particularly peaceful because of the relative absence of the male drinking sessions typical of most upcountry towns in Thailand.

The town is right on the sea, and some of the prettiest beaches on Southern Thailand's east coast are just outside town.

A promenade has been installed along the waterfront at the southern end of town.

Local radio stations broadcast in a mix of Yawi, Thai and Malay, with musical selections to match – from North-Eastern Thailand's country music, *lûuk thûng*, to Arabic-melodied *dangdut*. Many signs around town appear in Yawi as well as Thai, Chinese and English.

Every year during the third week of September, the **Narathiwat Fair** features *kaw-lae* (fishing boat) racing, a singing dove contest judged by the queen, handicraft displays and *sílá* martial arts exhibitions. Other highlights include performances of the local dance forms, *ram sam pen* and *ram ngeng*.

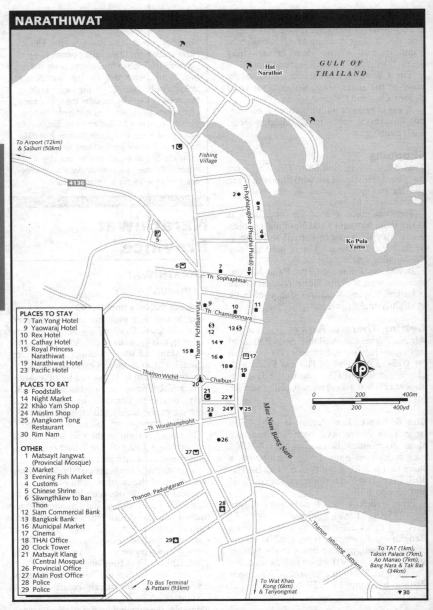

NARATHIWAT

SOUTHERN GULF

GULF OF THAILAND

Hat Narathat

To Airport (12km) & Saiburi (50km)

4136

Fishing Village

Th Puphapugdee (Phupha Phakdi)

Ko Pula Yama

Th Sophaphisai

Th Chamroonnara

Thanon Pichitbamrung

Thanon Wichit

Chaibun

Thanon Padungaram

Mae Nam Bang Nara

Thanon Jaturong Ratsami

Th Worakhamphiphit

To TAT (1km), Taksin Palace (1km), Ao Manao (7km), Bang Nara & Tak Bai (34km)

To Bus Terminal & Pattani (93km)

To Wat Khao Kong (6km) & Tanyongmat

To 30

0   200   400m
0   200   400yd

PLACES TO STAY
7 Tan Yong Hotel
9 Yaowaraj Hotel
10 Rex Hotel
11 Cathay Hotel
15 Royal Princess Narathiwat
19 Narathiwat Hotel
23 Pacific Hotel

PLACES TO EAT
8 Foodstalls
14 Night Market
22 Khâo Yam Shop
24 Muslim Shop
25 Mangkorn Tong Restaurant
30 Rim Nam

OTHER
1 Matsayit Jangwat (Provincial Mosque)
2 Market
3 Evening Fish Market
4 Customs
5 Chinese Shrine
6 Sǎwngthǎew to Ban Thon
12 Siam Commercial Bank
13 Bangkok Bank
16 Municipal Market
17 Cinema
18 THAI Office
20 Clock Tower
21 Matsayit Klang (Central Mosque)
26 Provincial Office
27 Main Post Office
28 Police
29 Police

Information

A new TAT office (☎ 073-516144, 01-957 5647, ⓔ tatnara@cscoms.com) is located a few kilometres south of town on the road to Tak Bai. The friendly staff distribute maps and brochures covering points of interest in the area. It's open from 8.30 am to 4.30 pm daily.

The main post office is on Thanon Pichitbamrung. An attached international phone office is open from 7 am to 10 pm daily.

Hat Narathat
หาดนราทัศน์

Just north of town is a small Thai-Muslim fishing village at the mouth of Mae Nam Bang Nara, lined with the large painted fishing boats (kaw-lae) that are peculiar to Narathiwat and Pattani. Near the fishing village is Hat Narathat, a sandy beach 4km to 5km long that serves as a kind of public park for locals, with outdoor seafood restaurants, tables and umbrellas. The constant sea breeze here is excellent for **windsurfing**, although only the occasional visiting Malaysian seems to take advantage of this. Shade is provided by a mixture of casuarinas and coconut palms.

The beach is only 2km north of the town centre – you can easily walk here or take a săamláw. This beach extends all the way north to Pattani, interrupted only by the occasional stream or river mouth; the farther north you go the cleaner and prettier the beach becomes. Almost the entire coast between Narathiwat and Malaysia, 40km south, is sandy beach.

Matsayit Klang
มัสยิดกลาง

Towards the southern end of Thanon Pichitbamrung stands Matsayit Klang (Central Mosque), an old wooden mosque built in the Sumatran style. It was reportedly built by a prince of the former kingdom of Pattani over 100 years ago. Today it's of secondary importance to the newer Arabian modernist-style provincial mosque (Matsayit Jangwat) at the northern end of town, but is architecturally more interesting.

Wat Khao Kong
วัดเขากง

The tallest seated-Buddha image in Thailand is at Wat Khao Kong, 6km south-west on the way to the train station in Tanyongmat. Called Phra Phuttha Taksin Mingmongkon, the image is 24m high and made of reinforced concrete covered with tiny gold-coloured mosaic tiles that glint magically in the sun. The wát itself isn't much to see. A săwngthăew to Wat Khao Kong costs 5B from the Narathiwat Hotel.

Places to Stay

The cheapest places to stay are all on Thanon Puphapugdee (Phupha Phakdi) along Mae Nam Bang Nara. The best deal is the *Narathiwat Hotel* (☎ 073-511063), a funky wooden building that's quiet, breezy, clean and comfortable. Rooms on the waterfront cost 100B with shared bathroom. The downstairs rooms can sometimes get a bit noisy from the night trade – try to get an upstairs room. Mosquitoes could be a problem, so don't forget your repellent or coils.

Another OK place, a bit farther north on the same side of the street, is the quiet *Cathay Hotel* (☎ 073-511014) – signed in Yawi, English, Thai and Chinese – where spacious, clean if somewhat cheerless rooms with attached bathroom and fan cost 120B. The elderly Chinese owner speaks good English. There's a view of the river from the roof.

The *Rex Hotel* (☎ 073-511134, 6/1–3 Thanon Chamroonnara) is a fair place at 200B for rooms with fan, 300B for air-con. Similar rooms for 160B to 220B with fan and 300B to 360B with air-con are available at the *Yaowaraj Hotel* on the corner of Thanon Chamroonnara and Thanon Pichitbamrung. Because of its busy location, it's not as quiet as the previously mentioned places.

The *Pacific Hotel* (☎ 073-511076) on Thanon Worakhamphiphit has large and clean rooms with fan and bathroom for 350B, plus air-con for 420B.

The *Tan Yong Hotel* (☎ 073-511477), on Thanon Sophaphisai, offers air-con doubles from 495B. Most of the guests are Malaysians and Thai government officials.

SOUTHERN GULF

Narathiwat's top end is a relatively new upmarket place off the western side of Thanon Pichitbamrung, the *Royal Princess Narathiwat* (☎ *073-515041); 126 rooms in an eight-storey building go for 800B all the way up to 18,000B.

Places to Eat
For eating, the *night market* off Thanon Chamroonnara behind the Bang Nara Hotel is good. There are also several inexpensive places along Thanon Chamroonnara, especially the *aahǎan taam sàng (food made to order) place* next to the Yaowaraj Hotel, where you can get just about any Thai-Chinese dish you can think up.

A cluster of *food stalls* on Thanon Sophaphisai at Thanon Puphapugdee serve inexpensive noodle dishes.

On Thanon Puphapugdee at the north-western corner of a soi leading to the back of Matsayit Klang, an elderly couple operates a small *khâo yam shop* (in a wooden building with a tile roof) selling delicious and inexpensive southern-style rice salad. Malay-style fried rice-noodles are served on the side with each order. Curries and rice are also available at this shop. Other places in town have khâo yam in the morning, but this one's is the best so go early before it runs out.

Farther south on the same side of the street is a *Muslim shop* with khâo mòk and duck over rice. Along Thanon Wichit Chaibun west of Thanon Puphapugdee are several inexpensive *Muslim food shops*.

Mangkorn Tong Restaurant is a small seafood place on Thanon Puphapugdee that has a floating dining section out the back. The food's quite good and prices are reasonable.

The outdoor *Rim Nam* restaurant, on Thanon Jaturong Ratsami about 2km south of town, has good mid-priced seafood and curries. About 50m south of Rim Nam is the similar but larger *Bang Nara*; both restaurants are popular with Malaysian tour groups these days.

Shopping
Several batik factories near town will sell batik direct to visitors at decent prices. JK Batik is located at 96/3 Mu 8 Tambon Lamphu (☎ 073-512452), on the way to Wat Khao Kong, and has good prices.

Getting There & Away
Air THAI has one flight daily between Narathiwat and Phuket, connecting with flights to Bangkok. One way to Phuket it's 1155B, 2950B through to Bangkok.

The THAI office in Narathiwat (☎ 073-511161, 513090–2) is located at 322–324 Thanon Puphapugdee; a THAI van between Narathiwat airport (12km north via Rte 4136) and the THAI office costs 30B per person.

Bus & Taxi Share taxis between Yala and Narathiwat cost 50B, buses 40B (with a change in Pattani).

Buses to Narathiwat cost 30B from Pattani. From Sungai Kolok, buses are 25B, share taxis and minivans 40B. To Hat Yai it's 55B by bus (72B air-con), 130B by share taxi or 120B by air-con minivan; the latter leave several times a day from near the Yaowaraj Hotel.

To and from Tak Bai, the other border crossing, it is 15B by sǎwngthǎew (catch one in front of the Narathiwat Hotel), and a taxi costs 25B.

Train The train from Yala costs 13B for 3rd-class seats to Tanyongmat, 20km west of Narathiwat, then it's either a 15B taxi to Narathiwat, or 13B by sǎwngthǎew.

Getting Around
Motorcycle taxis around town cost 10B to 20B, depending on the distance.

Wicker-chair sǎamláw from Malaysia are mainly used for carrying goods back and forth to market; these cost from 10B to 25B depending on distance and amount of cargo.

AROUND NARATHIWAT
Matsayit Wadi Al Husen
มัสยิดวาดีอัลฮูเซ็น

The Matsayit Wadi Al Husen (Wadi Al Husen Mosque) is also known locally as 'Matsayit Song Roi Pi' (200-Year-Old Mosque), and is one of the most interesting mosques in Thailand. Constructed in 1769 of Malabar ironwood, it mixes Thai, Chinese and Malay architectural styles to good effect. It's in the village of Lubosawo in Bajo (Ba-Jaw) district, about 15km northwest of Narathiwat off Hwy 42 (about 10B by sǎwngthǎew).

Wat Chonthara Sing-He
วัดชลธาราสิงเห

During the British colonisation of Malaysia (then called Malaya), the Brits tried to claim Narathiwat as part of their Malayan empire. The Thais constructed Wat Chonthara Sing-He (also known as Wat Phitak Phaendin Thai, 'Protecting Thailand Temple') in Tak Bai district near the Malayan border to prove that Narathiwat was indeed part of Siam, and as a result the British relinquished their claim.

Today it's most notable because of the genuine southern-Thai architecture, rarely seen in a Buddhist temple – the Thai-Buddhist equivalent of the Wadi Al Husen Mosque. A wooden wíhăan here very much resembles a Sumatran-style mosque. An 1873 wíhăan on the grounds contains a reclining Buddha decorated with Chinese ceramics from the Song dynasty. Another wíhăan on the spacious grounds contains murals painted by a famous Songkhla monk during King Mongkut's time (r. 1910–1925). The murals are religious in message but also depict traditional southern-Thai life. There is also a larger, typical Thai wíhăan.

Wat Chon is 34km south-east of Narathiwat in Tak Bai. It's probably not worth a trip from Narathiwat just to see this 100-year-old temple unless you're a real temple freak, but if you're killing time in Tak Bai or Sungai Kolok this is one of the prime local sights. It's next to the river and the quiet, expansive grounds provide a retreat from the busy border atmosphere.

To get here from Narathiwat, take a bus or săwngthăew bound for Ban Taba and get off in Tak Bai. The wát is on the river about 500m from the main Tak Bai intersection.

SUNGAI KOLOK
สุไหงโกลก

The Thai government once planned to move the border crossing from Sungai Kolok to Ban Taba in Tak Bai district, which is on the coast 32km north-east. The Taba crossing is a shorter and quicker route to Kota Bharu, the first Malaysian town of any size, but it looks like Sungai Kolok will remain open as well for a long time. The Thais even maintain a TAT office next to the immigration post.

Still, as a town it's a bit of a mess, with an estimated 1000 or so prostitutes who generate the town's second-most-important source of income. The rest of the economy is given over to Thai-Malaysian shipping; there's an entire district in the north-eastern part of town dedicated to warehouses that store goods moving between countries.

The Thailand-Malaysia border is open from 5 am to 5 pm (6 am to 6 pm Malaysian time). On slow days officials may close the border as early as 4.30 pm.

Information
The TAT office (☎ 073-612126), next to the immigration post, is open from 8.30 am to 5 pm daily.

The post and telephone office is on Thanon Thetpathom, and immigration is near the Merlin Hotel on Thanon Charoenkhet.

Places to Stay & Eat
According to the TAT there are over 45 hotels in Sungai Kolok, most of which accommodate the weekend trips of Malaysian males and bear names like *Marry*, *Come In*, *Honey* and *My Love*. Of the cheaper hotels, only a handful are under 200B and they're mainly for those only crossing for a couple of hours. So if you have to spend the night here it's best to pay a little more and get away from the short-time trade.

Most places in Sungai Kolok will take Malaysian ringgit as well as Thai baht for food or accommodation.

The most inexpensive places are along Thanon Charoenkhet. Here you can find the fairly clean *Thailiang Hotel* (☎ 073-611132) at No 12 for 200B, the *Savoy Hotel* (☎ 073-611093) at No 8/2 for 130B, and the *Asia Hotel* (☎ 073-611101) at No 4–4/1 for 200B (fan and bathroom), or 350B with air-con.

The *Pimarn Hotel* (☎ 073-611464), at No 76–4, is good value at 150B for rooms with fan and bathroom, 200B with TV.

On the corner of Thanon Thetpathom and Thanon Waman Amnoey is the pleasant *Valentine Hotel* (☎ 073-611229), with rooms costing 240B to 300B with air-con. There is also a coffee shop downstairs from the hotel.

Mid-range and top-end hotels in Sungai Kolok include: *Genting Hotel* (☎ 073-613231, Thanon Asia 18), which charges from 450B; the *Grand Garden Hotel*

SOUTHERN GULF

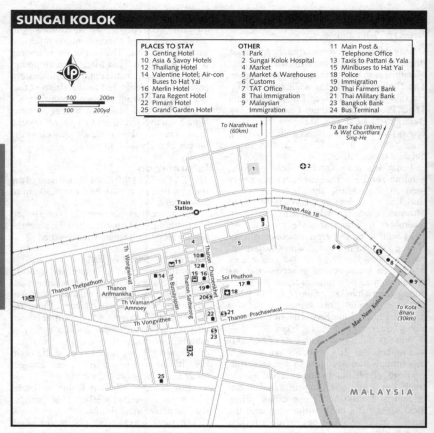

SUNGAI KOLOK

PLACES TO STAY	OTHER	11 Main Post &
3 Genting Hotel	1 Park	Telephone Office
10 Asia & Savoy Hotels	2 Sungai Kolok Hospital	13 Taxis to Pattani & Yala
12 Thailiang Hotel	4 Market	15 Minibuses to Hat Yai
14 Valentine Hotel; Air-con	5 Market & Warehouses	18 Police
Buses to Hat Yai	6 Customs	19 Immigration
16 Merlin Hotel	7 TAT Office	20 Thai Farmers Bank
17 Tara Regent Hotel	8 Thai Immigration	21 Thai Military Bank
22 Pimarn Hotel	9 Malaysian	23 Bangkok Bank
25 Grand Garden Hotel	Immigration	24 Bus Terminal

(☎ 073-613600, 104 Thanon Arifmankha), from 530B; the **Merlin Hotel** (☎ 073-611003, fax 611431, 40 Thanon Charoenkhet), from 350B; and **Tara Regent Hotel** (☎ 073-611401, fax 611801, Soi Phuthon, Thanon Charoenkhet), from 300B.

The town has plenty of food stalls selling Thai, Chinese and Malay food. There's a good Chinese **vegetarian restaurant** between the Asia and Savoy Hotels that's open from 7 am to 6 pm daily.

A cluster of reliable **Malay food vendors** can be found at the market and in front of the train station.

Getting There & Around
Bus & Share Taxi Air-con buses to/from Bangkok (646B, 18 hours) depart from

Bangkok at 6.30 pm (from Sungai Kolok at 1.30 pm). At 9 pm a 2nd-class bus (503B) departs from Bangkok. A VIP bus (1005B) from Bangkok leaves at 5.30 pm. In the reverse direction the bus leaves at 12.30 pm.

To Surat Thani, standard buses cost 155B (taking 10 hours), air-con 285B (nine hours).

Share taxis from Yala to Sungai Kolok cost 70B, from Narathiwat 40B; in Sungai Kolok the taxi stand is at the western end of Thanon Thetpathom. There are also buses from Narathiwat for 25B (35B air-con). Taxis to Narathiwat leave Sungai Kolok from near the train station.

Air-con buses to Hat Yai (148B, about four hours) leave from the Valentine Hotel twice in the morning and twice in the afternoon.

From Hat Yai, departure times are similar. Share taxis to Hat Yai cost 130B and leave from next to the Thailiang Hotel.

The border is about 1km from the centre of Sungai Kolok or the train station. Transport around town is by motorcycle taxi – it's 20B for a ride to the border.

Coming from Malaysia, just follow the old train tracks to your right or, for the town, turn left at the first intersection and head for the high-rises.

From Rantau Panjang (Malaysian side), a share taxi to Kota Bharu will cost about RM5 per person (or RM20 to charter the whole car) and takes around an hour.

The regular yellow-and-orange bus to Kota Bharu costs RM3.50.

Train The rapid No 171 leaves Bangkok at 12.25 pm and arrives at 10 am the next day. The daily special express No 37 to Sungai Kolok departs from Bangkok at 2.45 pm and arrives at 10.55 am the next day. These trains have 1st- (893B), 2nd- (417B) and 3rd- (180B) class fares, which don't include the special express or rapid surcharges of 80B or 40B (and 1st- or 2nd-class sleeping berths if you so choose).

You can also get trains to Sungai Kolok from Yala and Tanyongmat (for Narathiwat), but buses are much faster and more convenient along these routes.

From Sungai Kolok to points farther north (via Yala), however, the train is a reasonable alternative. A train to Hat Yai takes about 4½ hours and costs 31B for a 3rd-class seat, 75B for 2nd class.

Local train Nos 448 and 452 leave Sungai Kolok at 6.30 and 8.55 am, arriving in Hat Yai at 11.30 am and 1.45 pm. You won't find these trains listed on your English train timetable.

Special express No 38 leaves Sungai Kolok at 2.05 pm and arrives in Bangkok at 10.35 am the next day, with stops in Hat Yai (5.40 pm), Surat Thani (10.38 pm) and Hua Hin (6.08 am), among other towns, along the way.

Language

Learning some Thai is indispensable for travelling in the kingdom; naturally, the more language you pick up, the closer you get to Thailand's culture and people. Foreigners who speak Thai are so rare in Thailand that it doesn't take much to impress most Thais with a few words in their own language.

Your first attempts to speak the language will probably meet with mixed success, but keep trying. When learning new words or phrases, listen closely to the way the Thais themselves use the various tones – you'll catch on quickly. Don't let laughter at your linguistic forays discourage you; this apparent amusement is an expression of appreciation. Thais are among the most supportive people in the world when it comes to foreigners learning their language.

Travellers, both young and old, are particularly urged to make the effort to meet Thai college and university students. Thai students are, by and large, eager to meet visitors from other countries. They will often know some English, so communication is not as difficult as it may be with shop owners, civil servants etc, plus they are generally willing to teach you useful Thai words and phrases.

For a handy pocket-size guide to Thai, get a copy of Lonely Planet's excellent *Thai phrasebook*; it contains a section on basic grammar and a broad selection of useful words and phrases for travel in Thailand.

Many people have reported modest success with *Robertson's Practical English-Thai Dictionary* (Charles E Tuttle Co, Tokyo), which has a phonetic guide to pronunciation with tones and is compact in size. If you have difficulty finding it, write to the publisher at 2-6 Suido 1-chome, Bunkyo-ku, Tokyo, Japan.

More serious learners of the language should get Mary Haas' *Thai-English Student's Dictionary* (Stanford University Press, Stanford, California) and George McFarland's *Thai-English Dictionary* (also Stanford University Press) – the cream of the crop. Both of these require that you know the Thai script. The US State Department's *Thai Reference Grammar* by RB

Noss (Foreign Service Institute, Washington, DC, 1964) is good for an in-depth look at Thai syntax.

Other learning texts worth seeking out include:

AUA Language Center Thai Course: Reading & Writing (two volumes) – AUA Language Center (Bangkok), 1979

AUA Language Center Thai Course (three volumes) – AUA Language Center (Bangkok), 1969

Foundations of Thai (two volumes) – by EM Anthony, University of Michigan Press, 1973

A Programmed Course in Reading Thai Syllables – by EM Anthony, University of Hawaii, 1979

Teaching Grammar of Thai – by William Kuo, University of California at Berkeley, 1982

Thai Basic Reader – by Gething & Bilmes, University of Hawaii, 1977

Thai Cultural Reader (two volumes) – by RB Jones, Cornell University, 1969

Thai Reader – by Mary Haas, American Council of Learned Societies, Program in Oriental Languages, 1954

The Thai System of Writing – by Mary Haas, American Council of Learned Societies, Program in Oriental Languages, 1954

A Workbook for Writing Thai – by William Kuo, University of California at Berkeley, 1979

An interactive CD-ROM called *Learning Thai Script* (Allen & Unwin, 1997) is also an excellent resource for teaching yourself to read and write the Thai script.

For information on language courses, see Language under Courses in the Facts for the Visitor chapter.

Dialects

Thailand's official language is Thai as spoken and written in central Thailand. This dialect has successfully become the lingua franca of all Thai and non-Thai ethnic groups in the kingdom. Of course, native Thai is spoken with differing tonal accents and with slightly differing vocabularies as you move from one part of the country to the next, especially in a north to south direction. But it is the central Thai dialect that is most widely understood.

All Thai dialects are members of the Thai half of the Thai-Kadai family of languages and are closely related to languages spoken in Laos (Lao, northern Thai, Thai Lü), northern Myanmar (Shan, northern Thai), north-western Vietnam (Nung, Tho), Assam (Ahom) and pockets of south China (Zhuang, Thai Lü). Modern Thai linguists recognise four basic dialects within Thailand: central Thai (spoken as a first dialect through central Thailand and throughout the country as a second dialect); northern-Thai (spoken from Tak Province north to the Myanmar border); north-eastern Thai (north-eastern provinces towards the Lao and Cambodian borders); and southern Thai (from Chumphon Province south to the Malaysian border). Each of these can be further divided into subdialects; north-eastern Thai, for example, has nine regional variations easily distinguished by those who know Thai well. There are also a number of Thai minority dialects such as those spoken by the Phu Thai, Thai Dam, Thai Daeng, Phu Noi, Phuan and other tribal Thai groups, most of whom reside in the north and north-east.

Vocabulary Differences

Like most languages, Thai distinguishes between 'vulgar' and 'polite' vocabulary, so that *thaan*, for example, is a more polite everyday word for 'eat' than *kin*, and *sǐi-sà* for 'head' is more polite than *hǔa*. When given a choice, foreigners are better off learning and using the polite terms since these are less likely to lead to unconscious offence.

A special set of words, collectively called *kham raachaasàp* (royal vocabulary), is set aside for use with Thai royalty within the semantic fields of kinship, body parts, physical and mental actions, clothing and housing. For example, in everyday language Thais use the word *kin* or *thaan* for 'eat', while with reference to the royal family they say *sà wǒey*. For the most part these terms are used only when speaking to or referring to the king, queen and their children, hence as a foreigner you will have little need to learn them.

Script

The Thai script, a fairly recent development in comparison with the spoken language, consists of 44 consonants (but only 21 separate sounds) and 48 vowel and diphthong possibilities (32 separate signs). Experts disagree as to the exact origins of the script, but it was apparently developed around 800 years ago using Mon and possibly Khmer models, both of which were in turn inspired by south Indian scripts. Like these languages, written Thai proceeds from left to right, though vowel signs may be written before, after, above, below, *or* 'around' (before, after *and* above) consonants, depending on the sign.

Though learning the alphabet is not difficult, the writing system itself is fairly complex, so unless you are planning a lengthy stay in Thailand it should perhaps be foregone in favour of actually learning to speak the language. The names of major places included in this book are given in both Thai and roman script, so that you can at least 'read' the names of destinations at a pinch, or point to them if necessary.

Tones & Pronunciation

In Thai the meaning of a single syllable may be altered by means of different tones – in standard Central Thai there are five: low tone, level or mid tone, falling tone, high tone and rising tone. For example, depending on the tone, the syllable *mai* can mean 'new', 'burn', 'wood', 'not?' or 'not'; ponder the phrase *mái mài mâi mâi mǎi* (New wood doesn't burn, does it?) and you begin to appreciate the importance of tones in spoken Thai. This makes it a rather tricky language to learn at first, especially for those of us unaccustomed to the concept of tones. Even when we 'know' what the correct tone in Thai should be, our tendency to denote emotion, verbal stress, the interrogative etc, through tone modulation often interferes with producing the correct tone. Therefore the first rule in learning to speak Thai is to divorce emotions from your speech, at least until you have learned the Thai way to express them without changing essential tone value.

The following is visual representation in chart form to show relative tone values:

Thai Tones

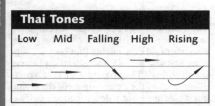

Low	Mid	Falling	High	Rising

The following is a brief attempt to explain the tones. The only way to really understand the differences is by listening to a native or fluent non-native speaker. The range of all five tones is relative to each speaker's vocal range so there is no fixed 'pitch' intrinsic to the language.

1 The low tone is 'flat' like the mid tone, but pronounced at the relative *bottom* of one's vocal range. It is low, level and with no inflection, eg, *bàat* (baht – the Thai currency).

2 The level or mid tone is pronounced 'flat', at the relative middle of the speaker's vocal range, eg, *dii* (good); no tone mark used.

3 The falling tone is pronounced as if you were emphasising a word, or calling someone's name from afar, eg, *mâi* (no/not).

4 The high tone is usually the most difficult for westerners. It is pronounced near the relative top of the vocal range, as level as possible, eg, *máa* (horse).

5 The rising tone sounds like the inflection used by English speakers to imply a question – 'Yes?', eg, *săam* (three).

Words in Thai that appear to have more than one syllable are usually compounds made up of two or more word units, each with its own tone. They may be words taken directly from Sanskrit, Pali or English, in which case each syllable must still have its own tone.

The following is a guide to the phonetic system that has been used for the words and phrases included in this chapter (and throughout the rest of the book when transcribing directly from Thai). It's based on the Royal Thai General System (RTGS), except that it distinguishes: between short and long vowels (eg, 'i' and 'ii'; 'a' and 'aa'; 'e' and 'eh'; 'o' and 'oh'); between 'o' and 'aw' (both would be 'o' in the RTGS); between 'u' and 'eu' (both would be 'u' in the RTGS); and between 'ch' and 'j' (both would be 'ch' in the RTGS).

Consonants

The majority of consonants correspond closely to their English counterparts. Here are a few exceptions:

k	as the 'k' in 'skin'; similar to 'g' in 'good', but unaspirated (no accompanying puff of air) and unvoiced
p	as the 'p' in 'stopper', unvoiced and unaspirated (not like the 'p' in 'put'); actually sounds closer to an English 'b', its voiced equivalent
t	as the 't' in 'forty', unaspirated; similar to 'd' but unvoiced
kh	as the 'k' in 'kite'
ph	as the 'p' in 'put' (never as the 'ph' in 'phone')
th	as the 't' in 'tea'
ng	as the 'nging' in 'singing'; can occur as an initial consonant in (practise by saying 'singing' without the 'si')
r	similar to the 'r' in 'run' but flapped (tongue touches palate); in everyday speech often pronounced like 'l'

Vowels

i	as the 'i' in 'it'
ii	as the 'ee' in 'feet'
ai	as the 'i' in 'pipe'
aa	as the 'a' in 'father'
a	half as long as **aa**, as the 'a' in 'about'
ae	as the 'a' in 'bat' or 'tab'
e	as the 'e' in 'hen'
eh	as the 'a' in 'hate'
oe	as the 'er' in 'fern' (without the 'r' sound)
u	as the 'u' in 'flute'
uu	as the 'oo' in 'food', longer than **u**
eu	as the 'u' in 'fur'
ao	as the 'ow' in 'now'
aw	as the 'aw' in 'jaw' or 'prawn'
o	as the 'o' in 'bone'
oh	as the 'o' in 'toe'
eua	a combination of **eu** and **a**
ia	as 'ee-ya', or as the 'ie' in French *rien*
ua	as the 'ou' in 'tour'
uay	sounds like 'oo-way'
iu	as the 'ew' in 'yew'

iaw	as the 'io' in 'Rio' or Italian *mio*
aew	like a Cockney pronunciation of the 'ow' in 'now'
ehw	as 'air-ooh'
awy	as the 'oi' in 'coin'

Here are a few extra hints to help you with the alphabetic tangle:

- **ph** is never pronounced as the 'ph' in phone but like the 'p' in 'pound' (the 'h' is added to distinguish this consonant sound from the Thai 'p' which is closer to the English 'b'). This can be seen written as **p**, **ph**, and even **bh**.

- to some people, the Thai **k** sounds closer to the English 'g' than the English 'k'. The standard RTGS chooses to use 'k' to represent this sound to emphasise that it is not a 'voiced' sound, but more a glottal stop.

- there is no 'v' sound in Thai; *Sukhumvit* is pronounced Sukhumwit and *Viang* is really Wiang

- **l** and **r** are always pronounced as an 'n' when word-final, eg, *Satul* is pronounced as Satun, *Wihar* as Wihan. The exception to this is when 'er' or 'ur' are used to indicate the sound 'oe', as in 'ampher' *(amphoe)*. In the same way 'or' is sometimes used for the sound 'aw', as in 'Porn' *(phawn)*.

- **l** and **r** are often interchanged in speech and this shows up in some transliterations. For example, *naliga* (clock) may appear as 'nariga' and *râat nâa* (a type of noodle dish) might be rendered 'laat naa' or 'lat na'.

- **u** is often used to represent the short 'a' sound, as in *tam* or *nam*, which may appear as 'tum' and 'num'. It is also used to represent the 'eu' sound, as when *beung* (swamp) is spelt 'bung'.

- phonetically, all Thai words end in a vowel (**a**, **e**, **i**, **o**, **u**), semi-vowel (**w**, **y**), nasal (**m**, **n**, **ng**) or one of three stops (**p**, **t**, **k**). That's it. Words transcribed with 'ch', 'j', 's' or 'd' endings – like Panich, Raj, Chuanpis and Had – should be pronounced as if they end in 't', as in Panit, Rat, Chuanpit and Hat. Likewise 'g' becomes 'k' (Ralug is actually Raluk) and 'b' becomes 'p' (Thab becomes Thap).

- the 'r' in *sri* is always silent, so the word should be pronounced 'sii' (extended 'i' sound, too). Hence 'Sri Racha' really comes out 'Si Racha'.

Transliteration

Writing Thai in roman script is a perennial problem – no wholly satisfactory system has yet been devised to assure both consistency and readability. The Thai government uses the Royal Thai General System of transcription for official government documents in English and for most highway signs. However, local variations crop up on hotel signs, city street signs, menus and so on in such a way that visitors often become confused. Add to this the fact that even the government system has its flaws. For example, 'o' is used for two very different sounds ('o' and the 'aw' in the Vowels section above), as is 'u' (for 'u' and 'eu' above). Likewise for 'ch', which is used to represent two different consonant sounds ('ch' and 'j'). The government transcription system also does not distinguish between short and long vowel sounds, which affect the tonal value of every word.

To top it off, many Thai words (especially names of people and place) have Sanskrit and Pali spellings but their actual pronunciation bears little relation to that spelling if Romanised strictly according to the original Sanskrit/Pali. Thus Nakhon Si Thammarat, if transliterated literally, becomes 'Nagara Sri Dhammaraja'. If you tried to pronounce it using this Pali transcription, very few Thais would be able to understand you.

Generally, names in this book follow the most common practice or, in the case of hotels for example, simply copy their roman script name, no matter what devious process was used in its transliteration! When this transliteration is markedly different from actual pronunciation, the pronunciation is included (according to the system outlined in this section) in parentheses after the transliteration. Where no Roman model was available, names have been transliterated phonetically, directly from Thai. Of course, this will only be helpful to readers who bother to acquaint themselves with the language – and it's surprising how many people manage to stay for great lengths of time in Thailand without learning a word of Thai.

Problems often arise when a name is transliterated differently, even at the same location. 'Thawi', for example, can be seen as Tavi, Thawee, Thavi, Tavee or various other versions. Outside the International Phonetic Alphabet, there is no 'proper' way to transliterate Thai – only wrong ways. The Thais themselves are incredibly inconsistent in this matter, often using English letters that have no equivalent sound in Thai: Faisal for Phaisan, Bhumibol for Phumiphon, Vanich for Wanit, Vibhavadi for Wiphawadi. Sometimes they even mix literal Sanskrit transcription with Thai pronunciation, as in King Bhumibol (which is pronounced Phumiphon and if transliterated according to the Sanskrit would be Bhumibala).

Here are a few words that are often spelt in a way that encourages native English speakers to mispronounce them:

Common Spelling	Pronunciation	Meaning
bung	beung	pond or swamp
ko or *koh*	kàw	island
muang	meuang	city
nakhon or *nakorn*	nákhawn	large city
raja	usually râatchá if at the beginning of a word, râat at the end of a word	royal

Greetings & Civilities

When being polite, the speaker ends his or her sentence with *khráp* (for men) or *khâ* (for women). It is the gender of the speaker that is being expressed here; it is also the common way to answer 'yes' to a question or show agreement.

Greetings/Hello.
  sàwàt-dii   สวัสดี
   (khráp/khâ)   (ครับ/ค่ะ)
How are you?
  sàbai dii rĕu?   สบายดีหรือ?
I'm fine.
  sàbai dii   สบายดี
Thank you.
  khàwp khun   ขอบคุณ

Excuse me.
  khăw thôht   ขอโทษ

I/me
  phŏm   ผม
  (for men)
  dì-chăn   ดิฉัน
  (for women)
you
  khun   คุณ
  (for peers)
  thâan   ท่าน
  (for elders and people in authority)

What's your name?
  khun chêu àrai?   คุณชื่ออะไร?
My name is ...
  phŏm chêu ...   ผมชื่อ...
  (men)
  dì-chăn chêu ...   ดิฉันชื่อ...
  (women)
Do you have ...?
  mii ... măi?/   มี...ไหม/
  ... mii măi?   ...มีไหม?
No.
  mâi châi   ไม่ใช่
No?
  măi?/châi măi?   ไหม?/ใช่ไหม?
(I) like ...
  châwp ...   ชอบ...
(I) don't like ...
  mâi châwp ...   ไม่ชอบ...
(I) would like ...
(+ verb)
  yàak jà ...   อยากจะ...
(I) would like ...
(+ noun)
  yàak dâi ...   อยากได้...

When?
mêua-rai? เมื่อไร?

It doesn't matter.
mâi pen rai ไม่เป็นไร

What is this?
nîi àrai? นี่อะไร?

go
pai ไป

come
maa มา

Language Difficulties

I understand.
khâo jai เข้าใจ

I don't understand.
mâi khâo jai ไม่เข้าใจ

Do you understand?
khâo jai măi? เข้าใจไหม?

A little.
nít nàwy นิดหน่อย

What do you call
this in Thai?
nîi phaasăa thai นี่ภาษาไทย
rîak wâa àrai? เรียกว่าอะไร?

Getting Around

I'd like to go ...
yàak jà pai ... อยากจะไป...

Where is (the) ...?
... yùu thîi năi? ...อยู่ที่ไหน?

airport
sànăam bin สนามบิน

bus station
sàthăanii khŏn sòng สถานีขนส่ง

bus stop
thîi jàwt rót ที่จอดรถ
pràjam thaang ประจำทาง

train station
sàthăanii rót fai สถานีรถไฟ

taxi stand
thîi jàwt rót ที่จอดรถแท็กซี่
tháek-sîi

I'd like a ticket.
yàak dâi tŭa อยากได้ตั๋ว

What time will the ...
leave?
... jà àwk kìi ...จะออกกี่
mohng ? โมง?

bus
rót meh/rót bát รถเมล์/รถบัส

car
rót yon รถยนต์

motorcycle
rót maw-toe-sai รถมอเตอร์ไซค์

train
rót fai รถไฟ

straight ahead
trong pai ตรงไป

left
sái ซ้าย

right
khwăa ขวา

far/not far/near
klai/mâi klai/ ไกล/ไม่ไกล/
klâi ใกล้

Accommodation

hotel
rohng raem โรงแรม

guesthouse
bâan phák บ้านพัก
(kèt háo) (เกสต์เฮาส์)

Do you have a
room available?
mii hâwng wâang มีห้องว่าง
măi? ไหม?

How much is it
per night?
kheun-lá thâo rai? คืนละเท่าไร?

bathroom
hâwng náam ห้องน้ำ
toilet
hâwng sûam ห้องส้วม
room
hâwng ห้อง
hot
ráwn ร้อน
cold
yen เย็น
bath/shower
àap náam อาบน้ำ
towel
phâa chét tua ผ้าเช็ดตัว

Around Town

Can (I/we) change money here?
lâek ngoen thîi níi dâi măi?
แลกเงินที่นี้ได้ไหม?
What time does it open?
ráan pòet mêua rai?
ร้านเปิดเมื่อไร?
What time does it close?
ráan pìt mêua rai?
ร้านปิดเมื่อไร?

bank
thánaakhaan ธนาคาร
beach
hàat หาด
market
tàlàat ตลาด
museum
phíphítháphan พิพิธภัณฑ์
post office
praisànii ไปรษณีย์
restaurant
ráan aahăan ร้านอาหาร
tourist office
sămnák ngaan สำนักงาน
thâwng thîaw ท่องเที่ยว

Shopping

How much?
thâo raí? เท่าไร?
too expensive
phaeng pai แพงไป
How much is this?
nîi thâo rai?/ นี่เท่าไร?/
kìi bàat? กี่บาท?
cheap, inexpensive
thùuk ถูก

Geographical features

beach
hàat sai หาดทราย
countryside
chonnábòt ชนบท
island
kàw เกาะ
lake
tháleh sàap ทะเลสาบ
map
phăen thîi แผนที่
mountain/hill
phuu khăo/khăo ภูเขา/เขา
paddy (field)
(thûng) naa (ทุ่ง) นา
pond
năwng/beung หนอง/บึง
river
mâe náam แม่น้ำ
sea
tháleh ทะเล
town
meuang เมือง
track
thaang ทาง
village
(mùu) bâan (หมู่) บ้าน
waterfall
náam tòk น้ำตก

Health

chemist/pharmacy
  ráan khǎi yaa   ร้านขายยา
dentist
  mǎw fan   หมอฟัน
doctor
  mǎw   หมอ
hospital
  rohng pháyaabaan   โรงพยาบาล
aspirin (pain killer)
  yaa kâe pùat   ยาแก้ปวด
mosquito repellent
  yaa kan yung   ยากันยุง

Please call a doctor.
  kàrúnaa rîak mǎw nòi
  กรุณาเรียกหมอหน่อย
I'm allergic to penicillin.
  pháe yaa phenísinlin
  แพ้ยาเพนิซิลลิน
I'm pregnant.
  tâng khan láew/mee tháwng
  ตั้งครรภ์แล้ว/มีท้อง
It hurts here.
  jèp trong née
  เจ็บตรงนี้
I feel nauseous.
  róosèuk khlêun sâi
  รู้สึกคลื่นไส้
I keep vomiting.
  aajian bòi bòi
  อาเจียนบ่อยๆ
I feel faint.
  róosèuk jà pen lom
  รู้สึกจะเป็นลม
I have diarrhoea.
  tháwng rûang
  ท้องร่วง

Emergencies

I need a doctor.
  tâwng-kaan mǎw   ต้องการหมอ
Help!
  chûay dûay!   ช่วยด้วย
Stop!
  yùt!   หยุด
Go away!
  pai sí!   ไปซิ
I'm lost.
  chǎn lǒng thaang   ฉันหลงทาง

I have a fever.
  pen khâi
  เป็นไข้
I have a stomachache.
  pùat tháwng
  ปวดท้อง
I have a headache.
  pùat hǔa
  ปวดหัว
I have a toothache.
  pùat fan
  ปวดฟัน

Time, Days & Numbers

What's the time?
  kìi mohng láew?   กี่โมงแล้ว?
today
  wan níi   วันนี้
tomorrow
  phrûng níi   พรุ่งนี้
yesterday
  mêua waan   เมื่อวาน

Sunday
  wan aathít   วันอาทิตย์
Monday
  wan jan   วันจันทร์

Tuesday		
wan angkhaan	วันอังคาร	
Wednesday		
wan phút	วันพุธ	
Thursday		
wan phréuhàt	วันพฤหัสฯ	
Friday		
wan sùk	วันศุกร์	
Saturday		
wan săo	วันเสาร์	

0	*sŭun*	ศูนย์
1	*nèung*	หนึ่ง
2	*săwng*	สอง
3	*săam*	สาม
4	*sìi*	สี่
5	*hâa*	ห้า
6	*hòk*	หก
7	*jèt*	เจ็ด
8	*pàet*	แปด
9	*kâo*	เก้า

10	*sìp*	สิบ
11	*sìp-èt*	สิบเอ็ด
12	*sìp-săwng*	สิบสอง
13	*sìp-săam*	สิบสาม
20	*yîi-sìp*	ยี่สิบ
21	*yîi-sìp-èt*	ยี่สิบเอ็ด
22	*yîi-sìp-săwng*	ยี่สิบสอง
30	*săam-sìp*	สามสิบ
40	*sìi-sìp*	สี่สิบ
50	*hâa-sìp*	ห้าสิบ
100	*ráwy*	ร้อย
200	*săwng ráwy*	สองร้อย
300	*săam ráwy*	สามร้อย
1000	*phan*	พัน
10,000	*mèun*	หมื่น
100,000	*săen*	แสน
one million	*láan*	ล้าน
one billion	*phan láan*	พันล้าน

Glossary

aahăan – food

aahăan pàa – 'jungle food', usually referring to dishes made with wild game

ajahn – (*aajaan*) respectful title for teacher; from Sanskrit term *acarya*

amphoe – district, the next subdivision down from province; also written *amphur*

amphoe meuang – provincial capital

ao – bay or gulf

baarámii – charisma or personal power; from Pali-Sanskrit term *parami*, meaning 'perfections'

bàat – a unit of weight equal to 15 grams

baht – (*bàat*) the Thai unit of currency

bai sĭi – sacred thread used by monks or shamans in certain religious ceremonies

bai toey – pandanus leaf; used in cooking and mat making

ban – (*bâan*) house or village

bàw náam ráwn – hot springs

benjarong – traditional five-coloured Thai ceramics

Bodhisattva – in Theravada Buddhism, the term used to refer to the Buddha during the period before he became the Buddha, including his previous lives

bòt – central sanctuary in a Thai temple used for official business of the Order (*sangha*) of monks, such as ordinations; from Pali term *uposatha*

Brahman – pertaining to Brahmanism, an ancient religious tradition in India and the predecessor of both Hinduism and Buddhism; not to be confused with 'Brahmin', the priestly class in India's caste system

chaa – tea

chaihàat – beach; also *hàat* or *hat*

chao bâan – villager

chao leh – sea gypsies; also *chao náam*

chao naa – farmer

chedi – (from the Pali *cetiya*) stupa; monument erected to house a Buddha relic

doi – (in the northern regions) mountain

fàràng – Western, a westerner

ganja – (*kanchaa*) marijuana leaves, sometimes used as a condiment in dishes of *kŭaytĭaw*

gopura – entrance pavilion in traditional Hindu temple architecture, often seen in Angkor-period temple complexes

hàw mòk – fish or seafood steamed in banana leaves

hăw phĭi – spirit shrine in a Buddhist monastery compound

hăw rákhang – bell tower

hăw trai – a Tripitaka (Buddhist scripture) hall

hâwng thăew – two- or three-storey shophouses arranged side by side along a city street

hèt khĭi khwai – psilocybin mushrooms; literally 'buffalo-shit mushrooms'; also called *hèt mao*

hĭn – stone

hong – (*hâwng*) room; in Southern Thailand this word may refer to the island caves semi-submerged in the sea

Isan – (*ìsăn*) general term for North-Eastern Thailand; from the Sanskrit name for the medieval kingdom Isana, which encompassed parts of Cambodia and North-Eastern Thailand

jangwàt – province

jâo meuang – political office in traditional Thai societies throughout South-East Asia; literally, principality chief

jataka – (Thai *chaadòk*) stories of the Buddha's previous lives

jiin – Chinese

jík-kŏh – hoodlum

jók – broken-rice congee

kaafae – coffee

kaafae thŭng – filtered coffee; sometimes called *ko-pĭi* in Southern Thailand

kâew – crystal, jewel, glass, or gem

kài yâang – grilled spiced chicken

kamnan – precinct officer, the next higher official after a *phuu yài bâan* (village chief)

kàp klâem – (literally, with the bottle) drinking food

kàthoey – transvestites and transsexuals; often translated 'lady-boy' in Thai English

kaw-lae – traditional fishing boats of Southern Thailand

khaen – reed instrument common in North-Eastern Thailand

khǎo – hill or mountain

khâo – rice

khâo lǎam – sticky rice soaked in coconut milk and baked in a length of bamboo

khâo mòk – spiced rice steamed with chicken, beef or mutton; a Muslim Thai speciality

khâo tôm – boiled rice soup

khlong – *(khlawng)* canal

khǒhn – masked dance-drama based on stories from the *Ramakian*

khon isǎan – the people of North-Eastern Thailand

king-amphoe – subdistrict

klawng – Thai drums

ko – *(kàw)* island; also *koh*

ko-píi – term for filtered coffee in Southern Thailand; also *kaafae thǔng*

kràbìi-kràbawng – a traditional Thai martial art employing short swords and staves

ku – small *chedi* that is partially hollow and open

kúay hâeng – Chinese-style work shirt

kǔaytǐaw – a noodle soup with fish or pork balls, herbs and spices

kun siang – a kind of sweetened sausage

kùtì – a monk's hut or living quarters

lâap – spicy meat or fish salad with mint leaves

lǎem – cape (in the geographical sense)

lákhon – classical Thai dance-drama

làk meuang – city pillar/phallus

láksànà – characteristic, feature

langsat – *(laangsàat)* small, round fruit grown in Thailand

lâo khǎo – 'white spirit', an often homemade brew

lâo thèuan – home-made (ie, illegal) liquor

lék – little, small (in size)

lí-keh – Thai folk dance-drama

loi kràthong – the ceremony celebrated on the full moon of the end of the rainy season

longyi – Burmese sarong

mâe chii – Thai Buddhist nun

mâe náam – river; literally, water mother

Mahanikai – the larger of the two sects of Theravada Buddhism in Thailand

maha that – common name for temples containing Buddha relics; from the Sanskrit-Pali term *mahadhatu;* literally, great element

mâi sànùk – not fun

málaeng tháp – type of beetle, the wings of which are used in certain handicrafts

mánohraa – Southern Thailand's most popular traditional dance drama

masjid – *(mátsàyít)* mosque

mát-mìi – technique of tie-dying silk or cotton threads and then weaving them into complex patterns, similar to Indonesian *ikat*; also refers to the patterns themselves

mátàbà – Indian pancake stuffed with savouries

mâw hâwm – Thai work shirt

mǎwn khwǎan – wedge-shaped pillow popular in Northern and North-Eastern Thailand; literally, axe pillow

metta – *(mêt-taa)* Buddhist practice of loving kindness

meuang – city or principality

mondòp – small square, spired building in a *wát;* from Sanskrit *mandapa*

muay thai – Thai boxing

mùu-bâan – village

mǔu yaw – white pork sausage

náam – water

náam ngíaw – sweet, spicy sauce used in northern-Thai dishes

náam phrík – chilli sauce

náam plaa – fish sauce

náam tòk – waterfall

nǎem – pickled pork sausage

naga – *(nâak)* a mythical serpent-like being with magical powers

nákhon – city; from the Sanskrit-Pali *nagara;* also spelt *nakhorn*

nǎng – Thai shadow play; movies

něua – north

ngaan sòp – funeral ceremony

ngaan wát – temple fair

ngâwp – traditional Khmer rice farmer's hat

nirvana – (Pali, *nibbana,* Thai *níp-phaan*) in Buddhist teachings, the state of enlightenment; escape from the realm of rebirth

noen – hill

noi – *(náwy)* little, small (amount); also *noy*

nok – *(nâwk)* outside; outer

pàak náam – estuary

paa-té – batik

paa-thâwng-kǒh – Chinese 'doughnut', a common breakfast food

pàk tâi – Southern Thailand

phâakhamáa – piece of cotton cloth worn as a wraparound by men

phâa mát-mìi – thick cotton or silk fabric woven from tie-dyed threads

phâasîn – wraparound for women

phansǎa – 'rains retreat' or Buddhist Lent; a period of three months during the rainy season that is traditionally a time of stricter moral observance for monks and Buddhist lay followers

phǐi – ghost, spirit

phík-sù – a Buddhist monk; from the Sanskrit *bhikshu*, Pali *bhikkhu*

phin – small, three-stringed lute played with a large plectrum

phleng khorâat – Khorat folk song

phleng phêua chii-wít – 'songs for life', modern Thai folk music

phrá – an honourific term used for monks, nobility and Buddha images; from the Pali *vara*, meaning 'excellent'

phrá khrêuang – amulets of monks, Buddhas or deities worn around the neck for spiritual protection; also called *phrá phim*

phrá phuum – earth spirits

phrá sàksìt – monk or amulet believed to have spiritual power

phuu khǎo – mountain

pìi-phâat – classical Thai orchestra

plaa thuu – popular type of mackerel

ponglang – *(pong-laang)* North-Eastern Thai marimba (percussion instrument) made of short logs

prang – *(praang)* Khmer-style tower on temples

prasada – blessed food offered to Hindu or Sikh temple attendees

prasat – *(praasaat)* any of a number of different kinds of halls or residences with religious or royal significance; from the Sanskrit term *prasada*

râi – an area of land measurement equal to 1600 sq metres

reua hǎang yao – long-tailed boat

reuan thǎew – longhouse

reusǐi – an ascetic, hermit or sage (Hindi *rishi*)

rót kàsèt – farm truck

rót pràp aakàat – air-con vehicle

rót thammádaa – ordinary bus (non aircon) or ordinary train (not rapid or express)

rót tûu – a minivan

roti – *(rotii)* round flat bread, common street food often found in Muslim restaurants

sǎalaa – open-sided, covered meeting hall or resting place; from Portuguese term *sala*, literally 'room'; also written *sala*

saalaapao – Chinese dough dumplings

sǎamláw – three-wheeled pedicab; also written *samlor*

sǎmnák sǒng – monastic centre

sǎmnák wípàtsànaa – meditation centre

samsara – in Buddhist teachings, the realm of rebirth and delusion

sàtàang – Thai unit of currency; 100 sàtàang equals 1 baht; usually written *satang*

sǎwngthǎew – (literally, two rows) common name for small pick-up trucks with two benches in the back, used as buses/taxis; also written *songthaew*

sěmaa – boundary stones used to consecrate ground used for monastic ordinations; from Sanskrit-Pali term *sima*

serow – Asian mountain goat

sêua mâw hâwm – blue cotton farmer's shirt

soi – lane or small street

sôm-tam – spicy green papaya salad

Songkran – *(sǒngkraan)* Thai New Year, held in mid-April

sǔan aahǎan – outdoor restaurant with any bit of foliage nearby; literally, food garden

sùkhǎaphíbaan – sanitation district, a political division lower than *thêtsàbaan*

sù-sǎan – cemetery

tâi – south

tàlàat náam – floating market

tambon – precinct, next subdivision below *amphoe;* also written *tambol*

tha – *(thâa)* pier, landing

thâat – four-sided, curvilinear Buddhist reliquary, common in North-Eastern Thailand; also *that*

thâat kràdùuk – bone reliquary, a small stupa containing remains of a Buddhist devotee

tháleh sàap – inland sea or large lake

thâm – cave

tham bun – to make merit

thammájàk – Buddhist wheel of law; from the Pali *dhammacakka*

Thammayutika – one of the two sects of Theravada Buddhism in Thailand; founded by King Rama IV while he was still a monk

thâm reusǐi – hermit cave

thànǒn – street

thêp – angel or divine being; from Sanskrit term deva; also *thewádaa*

thêtsàbaan – a division in towns or cities much like 'municipality'

thúdong – a series of 13 ascetic practices, eg, eating one meal a day, living at the foot of a tree, undertaken by Buddhist monks; a monk who undertakes such practices; a period of wandering on foot from place to place undertaken by monks

thŭng yaang ànaamai – condom

tràwk – alley; also trok

trimurti – collocation of the three principal Hindu deities, Brahma, Shiva and Vishnu

Tripitaka – Theravada Buddhist scriptures

túk-túk – motorised *săamláw*

vipassana – *(wípàtsànaa)* Buddhist insight meditation

wâi – palms-together Thai greeting

wan phrá – Buddhist holy days, falling on the days of the main phases of the moon (full, new and half) each month

wang – palace

wát – temple-monastery; from Pali term *avasa* meaning monk's dwelling

wát pàa – forest monastery

wáthánátham – culture

wíhăan – any large hall in a Thai temple, but not the *bòt;* from Sanskrit term *vihara,* meaning 'dwelling'; also *wihan* or *viharn*

yaa dawng – herbal liquor; also the herbs inserted in *lâo khăo*

yâam – shoulder bag

yài – big

yam – spicy Thai-style salad; usually made with meat or seafood

Yawi – the traditional language of Java, Sumatra and the Malay Peninsula, widely spoken in the most southern provinces of Thailand; the written form uses the classic Arabic script plus five additional letters

ACRONYMS

AUA – American University Alumni

BMA – Bangkok Metropolitan Authority

CAT – Communications Authority of Thailand

CPT – Communist Party of Thailand

KMT – Kuomintang

KNU – Karen National Union

NGO – Nongovernmental Organisation

PLAT – People's Liberation Army of Thailand

SRT – State Railway of Thailand

TAT – Tourism Authority of Thailand

THAI – Thai Airways International

Thanks

Many thanks to the travellers who used the last edition and wrote to us with helpful hints, useful advice and interesting anecdotes. Your names follow:

Becky Abman, Inger Abrahamsen, Tony Abram, Donna Accord, Jan Achten, Philippe Adam, Alisia Adams, Peter Adams, Vic Adams, Benedict Addis, AN Addison, John Aelbrecht, Manuel Affonso, April Aguren, Poranee Ahl, Anna Akerdahl, Alfons Akutowicz, Jose Alcantara, Traca Alger, Natasha Pang Allard, Jean Allemand, Scott Alsop, JA Aluey, Martin Alvheim, Polly Amies, Frode Andersen, Kate Anderson, Kay Anderson, Paula Anderson, Sarah Anderson, Patrick Andnvaux, Davide Andrea, Heather Andres, DG Andrews, Mark Andrews, NI Andrews, Raymond Ang, MY&MV Angell, CR Angus, Montvazski Anita, Judy Anker, Gillian Annett, Mick Anstis, Dr Kodet Antonin, Kenny Archibald, Hania Arentsen, Luke Arnold, Edward Arnoldi, Darunee Asawaprecha, Kiersten Aschauer, Tony Ash, Ian Ashbridge, Kate Ashe, M Asher, Brian Ashton, Graham Askew, Sven Assarsson, Emily Atkinson, Davor Atles, Paul Atroshenko, Kris Attard, Jo Attwood, John & Esther Atwell, Magdalena Aurell, David Aus, Jorg Ausfelt, Todd Austin, Malcolm Ayres, Lara Azria, Hirokazu Azuma.

Koos Baars, Michael Babcock, Mats Backlund, Anne Badger, Eric Baer, Chris Bagley, Andrea Baglioni, Jennifer Ballagh, Beth & Dick Balsamo, Antoon van Balveren, Chris Bannister, Natalie Bannister, Jeremy Barazetti, Matthew Barclay, Michael Barkey, Audre Barnaid, David Barnett, Andre Barneveld Binkhuysen, Craig Barrack, Marg Barr-Brown, Kelsey Barrett, JC Barrett, Jill Barshay, Andrew Barsoom, Jessica Bartlett, Bonnie Baskin, Caroline Bass, Tony Bass, Lynne Bateman, Nataly Bauer, George Bauguess, Jason Baxter, Charles Bazaar, Roger Beattie, Rosemary Beattie, Gareth Beaver, Maggi & Dave Bebb, Martina Beckers, Gill Beddows, Lori Beever, Glenn Behrman, Karin Bekker, Mara Benedict, Christopher Benjamin, Janey Bennett, Jean Bennett, Michele Bennett, Rodney Berg, Robert Berger, Conrad Bergo, Lennart Bergqvist, Kim Bergstrom, Lynn Berk, Joy & Michael Berkowitz, Olivier Berlage, Ron Bernardi, David Bernardini, Brad Bernthal, Anne Best, Ewan Best, Tracey Best, FW Betts, Christopher Betz, Kees Beukelman, Tim Bewer, Brande BH Wulff, Kittikarn Bhumisawasdi, Laurent Biais, Tobias Bickel, Han Biemans, Joe Bigalow, Matt Bigham, Mikin Bilina, Georgina Binder, Matt Birg, Carol Birney, Charlotte Bishop, Mike & Liz Bissett, Eric Bjorkman, Dara Bkk, Adam Black, Avi Black, A Blackburn, Rudi Blacker, Barbara Blackford, Charlie Blackham, Ann Blair, U Blaser, Susan Blick, Howard Blitzer, Henri Blomgvise, John Bloomfield, William Bloomhuff, John D Blyth, Gkanya Boasakul, JD de Boer, G Boer, J Boer, S Boerke, Andy Bolas, Laco Boldessorelli, Claude Bollag, Claudia Bond, Jan Bond, Andrea Bonini, Jon Bonnin, Elas Bonwin, Olaf van den Boom, Bill Booth, Frances Booth, Graham Booth, A Booth, Jang Boran, Dorthe & Thomas Borchmann, Olivier Borgognon, Ellen Bosman, Marethe & Bob Botker, Marco Bottacini, Peter Bottcher, Jean-Pierre Boudrias, Anastasia Bouhoutsos, Anne Boulton, Paul Boundy, Luc Bouwens, F van den Bouwhuijsen, Coleen & Simon Bower, Jean & John Bowler, David Bownes, Rebecca Boyce, Tracey Boyd, MP Boyle, Joel Bradley, Dave Bradshaw, Rodney Braithwaite, B&J Brand, Barbara & John Brand, Mike Braun, Peter Brazier, Jim Brazil, Vanessa Breakwell, Lorenzo Brega, Lisa Breger, Davina Brennan, Peter Brennan, Bill Brentlinger, Henriette Breum, Sandie Breum, Carmen Breznikar, Sjoulije Broer, Susan Bronkhorst, Raymond Brooks, Kevin Broome, Michael Brorsen, Eric Brouwer, Belinda Brown, Colin Brown, Ged Brown, Justin Brown, Lynette Brown, Max Brown, Nigel Brown, Roxanna Brown, Henrik Brun, Michaela Buchholz, Benjamin Buikema, Alexander Bulach, Carol Bullen, Wesley Bullock, Sally Burbage, Anka & Adrean Burgess, Andrew Burnett, Wendy & Lenny Burnett, Andy Burton, George Burton, Anny Bussieres, Michael Bussmann, Brandon Butler, Karen Butts, Laurence Buytaert, Dan Byrne.

Keith Cable, Stuart Cadden, Frank Caglioti, Gwen Cahill, Raffaella Caiconti, Simon Calder, Roger & Sally Callanan, Mario Camiller, Christina Campbell, David Campbell, Helen Campbell, Mark Canavan, Michael Cannon, Eduardo Cardellini Martino, Peter Carison, Danica Carmody, N Carper, Matthew Carr, Tanya Carrey, Maria Carrion, David Carson, R Carter, Rusty Cartmill, Lyle Cassard, Donald Casson, Dianne Caulkett, A Chakraborty, Patra Chakshuvej, Hannah Chambers, Marie-France

Champagne-Thouard, Maxine & Keith Channon, DN & Mr Chapman, Polly Chapman, Helen Chard, Joel & Dorit Chasnoff, Stacy Chatfield, Didier Chaumet, Denise Chavez, Fritzie Chavez, Khattirat Cherdsatirakul, Susan Cherry, Adam Chester, Ted Chi, Pauline Chia, Joelynn Chin, Rocco Chin, Eitan D Chitayat, N Chivers, Wei Choong, Woodrow Chow, Jacky Chrisp, Anne Christianes, Scott Christiansen, Marie Chrysander, Felix Chui, Chukit Chulitkoon, Kylie Cirak, Bernard Citroen, Greg Clackson, Isabelle Claeys, Ann Clancy, Steve Clark, Tim Clark, David Clarke, Michael Clarke, Richard Clarke, Sherril Clarke, KC Clausen, Gavin Clayton, David Clennett, Linda Clevberger, Kate Clifford, H Clyde Wray, Chris Cocks, David Cocksedge, Emiliano Cocucci, Sandie Codron, Pip Coe, Paolo Coen, Jennifer Coffin, AJ Cogan, Brian Cogswell, Rob Cohen, Daniel Colby, David Cole, Peter Coleman, Robert Collins, Vince Colyer, MD Comber, Basil Condos, Alec Connah, Sarah Conning, Alex Connolly, Leeane Cook, Simon A Cook, Tim Cook, Andrew Coop, Earl Cooper, Martin Cooper, Sandra Corbacioglu, Jeff Cornish, Richard Coughlin, Flore Coumau, BF Cox, Raymond F Cragg, B Craig, Sarah Craig-Leyland, Keith Crandall, Anjela Crawley, Katie Crawshaw, S Creaser, Margy Crisp, Mike Crisp, Stephen Croarkin, Matthew Cromack, Susannah Crook, Sally Cross, Terry Crossley, Zsolt Csok, Emily Culbert, Patrick Cullen, Connell Cunningham, Darryl Curtis, Don Curtis, Colin Cuthbert.

Sandy D, Connie Dahlin, Ake Dahllof, Jurgen Dahm, Phillip Dale, Marilyn Daley, Michel J van Dam, Jeff Dane, Greg Darch, Cynthia Dargan, Pip Darvall, Nichola Davenport, Cecilia Davidson, Susan Davidson, John Davis, Peter Davis, Kelly Davison, Peter Davison, Trevor Davison, Alex Dawson, Jason Day, Wilco de Brouwer, Rik de Buyserie, Jeroen de Graaf, Johan De Haes, N De Jong, Marie-Aline de Lavau, Lucien De Prycker, Jeanette de Raaf, Brigitte de Vries, Jan de Weerd, Florens de Wit, Krist Decanniere, Catherine Declercq Bezencon, Frits Dekker, Evert Delanghe, Jessica Dempsey, Van den Berghe, Franz Dennenmoser, Rene Derksen, Julian Derry, Whit Deschner, Julie Desjardins, Nora Devai, John Devitt, Caroline Diamond, Arancha Diaz-Llado, Deborah Dickley, Helmfried Dietsch, Joseph Distlan, Fredrik Divall, Tina Diver, Katie Dobson, Rupert Dodds, Ginni Dofflemyer, Sheila & Paul Doherty, Soren & Rebecca Dohn, Terje Dokland, Jeroen Dolman, Jan Doms, Andy Dong, Annick Donkers, Suzanne Donnelly, Bjorn Donnis, Gunter Doppler, Mike Doria, Thomas Doring, Robyn Dormer, Joseph A Doucet, Michael Doud, Eoin Doyle, Kerry E Doyle, Mike Doyle, Jan Drent, Mary Drever, Martin Drew, Kev & Dot Drinnen, Emma Drysdale, D Dubbin, Fabrice Duchene, GE Duffy, Jerry & Joe Duffy, Vincent Duggan, Wouter Duinker, Tolla Duke, Dr RA Duncan, Iain Dunlop, Sheila Dunning, Jacob Dupont, Hans Durrer, T Duym, Mark Dwyer.

Donna Eade, Rob Earney, Michael Eckert, Peter Edan, Jim Eddis, Darren Eddy, Richard Eden, Jason Edens, Bo Edvinsson, Georgina Edwards, Paul Edwardson, Gordon Eekman, Peter Eichmann, Michael Eisenberg, Roger Eitel, David Eklund, Stanage Elling, M&S Elliott-Herault, Gabrielle Ellis, Joanne Ellis, R Ellison, Dana Elmendorf, Naomi Elmore, Hugh Elsol, David Emes, Deborah Emmett, Don En Shaula, Henrik Enevoldsen, Chris E La Sha P Eng, E Engskar, Bob Ennis, Jim Enright, Birgit Ensslin, Doreen Entwistle, Achara & Don Entz, Roger & Annelie Ericson, Stein Erik Jonasson, H Koster M van Erp, Marjie Essink, Caroline Evans, Chris Evans, Gaynor-M Evans, Helen & Jonathan Evans, Don Evans Jr, Andrew Ewart, Dave Eyland, Thomas Eyre.

Salvati Fabio, Guido Faes, Sybil Faigin, Robert Falk, Suzanne Falkner, Honor Fallon, Sandra Faoro, Marc Faris, James Farley, L Farr, Andreas Faul, Janet Fenton, Magalie Feuillet, Pam & Alan Fey, Gregor Fiedler, Ray Field, AJ Filbee, Dr David Findlon, Gudruu Fink, Maggie Finnicum Reider, Adi Fisher, Leah & Chuck Fisher, Bruce Fitz-Earle, Hans & Anne Fix, Graham Fletcher, Ed Fogden, Anna Fogelmarck, Leonora Foley, Mark Foley, Cathy Forbes, Jeremy Ford, Alan Foster, Megan Foster, Susan Fouche, Trula Fountaine, Beth Fouser, Jack Foxall, Lisa Fragala, John Frampton, Brooke Francis, David Francis, Ray Frank, Christian Frankenfeld, Iain Franklin, Tom Fransen, Vesa Frantsila, Sally Fraser, Edward Freed, Penny & Paul Freel, AM & P Frendesen, Jem Friar, Bill Fridl, Regina Fritsche, Pauline Frizelle, Helmut Frohnwieser, Dave Fuller, Julianne Fuller, Claudia Furrer.

Stacey Gall, Sue Gallagher, Monique Gallwey, Dean Gardiner, John Gardner, Michael Gardner, Christopher Garrenger, Kelley Gary, Vanessa Gatfield, John Gauthier, Bruce Gaylord, Paul H Geissler, Randy Gerber, Peter Germann, Kestrel Gerrard, Dianne Gerrits, Evelyn Gerson, Daryle Gessnen, Yutan Getzler, Stephen Gibb, Joanna Gidney, Boaz Gilboa, Tania Gilchrist, Mary Gillespie, Richard Gillman

Adelheid Gimmler, Stephen Ginn, Roy Gissop, Michele Giuletti, Katie Glynn, Marc Goddard, Cindy & Brian Goke, Maurice Goldberg, Ann & Peter Goldstein, Graham Gollan, Jesus Gonzalez, Josh Gonze, Hilary Goodkind, Anna Goodman, Michael Goodstadt, Alwin Goodwin, Traci Goodwin, Rob Gordon, Rusty Gore, Steven & Lisa Gosling, Harold E Gosse, Mrs & Mr D Gosnold, Hannah & SW Gough Gough, Gita Gould, Louise Gourley, Eli Graham, Phil Graham, Rob Graham, Sally Graham, Ted Graham, Iris Grassl, Moses Graubard, Rick Graves, Kirsty Gray, LN Gray, Alan Green, Bari Green, Barry & Julie Green, Lisa & Chris Green, Malcolm Green, Margaret Greenwood, Eugene Gregg, Haydn Gregory, Marti Griera, Nigel Griffiths, M Grillenberger, Guido Groenen, Ian Grogan, Chloe Groom, Richard Groom, Mrs De & Mr Groot, Ralph Grosse, Michael Grossmann, Joseph G Gschwendtner, Marlane Guelden, Marjolein Guesebroek, Jamie Guillikson, Adam Gumsley, Catherine Gunning, Tamar Gutnick, Bart Gypen.

Michael Hadani, A Haddon, Claire Haddon, Mike Hahn, Sarah-Jane Hair, Amanda Haley, Anthony Halfhide, Jeannie Hall, Jenny Hall, Judy Hall, K Hall, Nigel Hall, Riki Hall, Simon & Nigel Hall, Tom Hallam, Tony Hallam, Tanja Haller, Jonathan Halperin, Leta Hals, Leta Hamilton, David Hammond, AA Hampton, Eric Hananel, Steven Hankey, Timmo Hannay, Sheila Hannon, Danny Hanrahan, Henry Hanrahan, RJ Harbinson, Robert Harker, Catherine Harper, Phil Harper, Philip Harris, Kevin Bryah Harrison, R Harrop, Leslie-Jane Harrower, Jessica Hart, Susan Hart, T Hartall, Tye Hartall, Debbie Hartland, Jackie Hartnell, Dirk Hartwig, Kurt Harwood, Mikkel Hass, Shyla Hassan, Donald Hatch, AC Hatfield, Dr Dick Haugland, Till-Karsten Hauser, Deborah Havens, Ayana Haviv, Tanya Hawkey, Jeremiah Hayes, Jonathan Haynes, Glen Heath, Graham Heath, Claus Hedegaard, Ray Hegarty, Samantha Hegeman, Jennifer Hegle, Klaus Heibing, Sabine Heijman, Helen & Martin Heimering, Hans Heintze, Karen Helman, Shaula Hemmer, Johanna Hemstra, S Henderson, Anne Hendricks, Nathalie Hendrick, W Hendriks, S Hendrix, Allebosch Henk, Aotienne Heon, Jason & Michelle Heppenstall, Peter Herman MD, Armin Hermann, Ofir Hermesh, Richard Hersk, Carsten Herzog, Yossi Herzog, Chris Hetcalf, Gordon Hiebert, Klaus Hiebing, Noriko Higashide, Karsten Hilbert, Christopher Hilborn, Melanie Hill, Klaus Hille, Ted Hillestad, Susanna

Hilmer, Lucy Hilts, Birgit Himmelsbach, J Hinings, Jamie Hinks, Linda Hitchcock, Kareela Hodgson, Geertje Hoekstra, Margriet Hoekstra, Joost Hogeland, Steve Holford, Joergen Holk, Jason Hollis, Paul Holt, Simon Honeybone, Liesbeth Hoogland, Sarah Hopkins, Damien Horigan, Eva Horn Moeller, Ingolf Hosub, Gary N Houston, Sue Houston, J van Hout, Vicki Howarth, Kathleen Howell, Marion Hruger, Suzanne Huggins, Rhidian Hughes, Sue Hughes, Tony Hughes, OE Huiberts, DC Huizinga, Stephanie Hull, Cliff Hunter, Jeff Hurwitz, Paula Hutt, Lars Hylander, Jeffrey Hynds.

Panos Ilias, Steinar Ims, Tineke Indradjaya, George Ionita, Erik Ireland, Martin Ireland, Chris Irwin, Dominick Isaac, Masahiro Ishizeki, Mohammed Ismael, Rita, Gerard, Peter & Elysha Iversen.

Christian Jacobsen, Delacreta Jacques, John Jaeger, Lena Jakobse, Gwen James, R James, Robert James Wood, Peter Jamvold, Gerda Jansen, Mette Jansen, Laskia L Janssen, Alain Janssens, Stuart Jarvis, Ashley Jefferies, Sally & Stewart Jeffrey, Fern Jeffries, Juliette Jeffries, Helena Jenkins, Tina Jensen, Christina Johansson, G Johnson, Katherine Johnson, Marcus E Johnson, Sophy Johnston, Stewart Johnston, Jill Jolliffe, Jan Jonasson, Jacky & Gwyn Jones, Rachael Jones, Rhiannon Jones, Sid Jones, Yolante Jones, Daniel Jordan, EJ Jorissen, David Joy, I Judd, Karen Judge, Adam Jug, Bob Juniel, Tony Jurica, Atte Jussi.

Wolf Kadavanich, Khatijah Abdul Kadir, Samai Kaewudorn, Franz-Josef Kaiser, A Kalaydijian, Per Rui & Unni Karlsen, Renko Karruppannan, Sherman Kassof, Martijn Katan, J Kay Aplin, Finn W Kaysfeld, Dennis Keating, KM Keiler, A Keister, Jalan Kelantan, J Keller, Chris Kelly, Vincent Kelly, Alan Kendall, Maria Kendro, Helen Kent, A Kent, Lucy Kenyon, James Keosaksith, Margo Kerkvliet, Oula Keva, Shirley A Khamlheang, Melanie Kilmarx, Julian King, Martyn King, Rachel Kinnison, Jenny Kirby, Penelope Kirk, Peter Kirsch, Christine Kirschuer, Johar Kitabi, Thomas Kjerstein, Jennifer Klane, Nic Klar, Nicholas Klar, Jochen Klaschka, Rolf Klein, Bjoren Kleppestoe, Malte Klesen, Jose Kliksberg, K Klippert, Soren Klippfjell, Henny & Martin Knight, Henny Knijnenburg, John Knodel, Steve Knowles, Rosalind Knowlson, Angela Knox, Mirja Koch, Cynthia Koens, Malousch Kohler, Jarmo Koivula, Peter J Kok, M Koning, Jhon Koppa, Ben Koppenens, Wendy Korsten, GF Kortschak, Peter Kosin, S Kovalchuk, Frank Kressmann, Manuela Kries,

Peter Krijnen, Lucian Krille, Synnove Krokstad, Jens Kromann, Mike Krosin, Mr Krumme, Erwin Kruse, Peter Kruysifix, David Kulka, Mrs & Mr Kuna, Antti & Helena Kuulasmaa, Pniuoz Kuzmau.

Francine La Fortune, Tom Lahaie, Trung Lai, Tom Lally, Sandy Lam, Doug Lamb, Nick Lambert, John Lam-Po-Tang, Juergen Landauer, Jane Lander, Jean-Marc Lange, Verena Langsdorf, Wake Lankard, Tim Lansham, SK Lanter, Richard Lapin, John Larner, Laura & Robert Larson, Cecilia Larsson, Hanna Lasson, David Latchford, Katy Laurich, Anthony Lavigne, Ian Lavigne, Alex Lawernce, Stephen Lawes, Paul Lawlor, Alan Lawrence, P Lawrence, Kay Lawson, Steve Layton, Christian Le Corre, Clotilde Le Grand, Lynda Leal, Steve Leather, Kathrin Leaver, Cynthia LeCount, Martin Leduc, Colin Lee, Stuart Lee, Philip Leese, Sascha & Fiona Leese, E de Leeuw, Alida Lehnort, Kristy Leissle, Carsten Lekre, Carol & Dave Leligdon, CM Lennie, Nancy L Leonard, Kah Leong, Philippe Leryen, Marie Lesaicherre, AM Lescure, Simon Leslie, Rosenny Lester, Daniel Levi, Jonathan Levine, Cindy Lewis, V Light-Hart, Keith Liker, Calvin Lim, Areerat Limwongsuwan, Henrik & Dorthe Lindberg Olsen, Phil Lindlau, David & Nicky Lingard, Michelle & Matthew Linhardt, Bruce Linker, Marsha Lipets-Maser, Geoff Lipscomb, Annie Liu, Isabel Liu, Vanessa Lloyd, Richard M Loane, Sarina Locke, Shay Lockhart, Rainer Lodes, Bette Logan, Casey Loh, Sharon London, Bill Lonergan, Deborah Long, Jodi Longyear, M Loo, Cheenang Looi, Gabriel Loos, Joris Loos, Lieuwke Loth, A Louth, Michael Low, Johanna Lowe, Roger Loxley, Eric Lucas, K&J Lumley-Jones, Loraine Lundquist, Joe Lunghitano, Caroline Lurie, Rollon Lurker, Tony Luttrell, Bruce Lymm, Anthony Lynch, Petrina Lynch, Jessie Lyons, Sophie Lyttelton.

Allison M, RS Maas, Billy Mac, Ian Macandrew, Stephanie Macco, Padraig MacDonnchadha, John Macey, Laurie MacKay, Bruce Mackie, BE Mackin, Sarah Macleod, John Macuen, Mario Maddalozzo, James Madil, Kathy Madson, Sheldon Madson, Evelynn Maes, Renee Magendans, John Maidment, Marc Ulrich Maier, Justin Maiorana, Hebel Malsam, Aaron W Maness, Jim Manheimer, Steve Maniaci, Ian Mann, Nick Mann, Sabrina Manzocchi, Christophe Marchina, Yvonne van der & Paul Marck, Amy & Dan Marcus, Steve Marcus, S Margherita, E&S Maria, Dave Marini, Paul Markham, Jemma Marks, R Marom, Nikki Marriott, Edward Marshall, Jayne Marshall, Trevor Marshall, Bernhard Marti, David Martin, Lucy Martin, Peter Martin, T Martin, Carla Martins, Nalli Massimo, Roland Massing, Harold Masterson, Steven Mathers, Jane Mathison, Brett Mattews, Curt Matthew, Ken Matthews, Christine Maxwell, Claire May, Emily May, Kevin May, Mabel Mayer, John Mayne, Sue Mayne, Philip Mayo, Sean McCallion, Eoin McCarney, Brian McCarthy, Kelly McCarthy, Pat & Lisa McCarthy, Steve McCormack, Anto McCrory, David McDougal, Rachel McEleney, D McFadden, Kimberley McGrandle, Brends McIntyre, Sarah McKinnon, Kathy McLeish, Carolyn McLeod, Tony McMills, David McNeil, Eleanor Meechaam, Henry Meester, Sander Meijsen, Jane Meiklejohn, Lori Meisner, Martin Mella, Rob Mellett, Liza Meneades, Ana Meneses, Richard Mercer, Angelo Mercure, S Meredith, Clive Metson, Anton MJ Meurs, Matt Mewosiang, Dorthe Meyer, Scott Mickelson, Ulf Mikaelsson, Ulv Mikaelsson, Lynn Mikami, R Mikhail, Forgacs Miklos, Josie Miller, Mark Miller, GE Miller, N Miller, Phil Miller, Rob Miller, Ron Miller, Sally Miller, Tom Miller, Adrian Mills, K Mills, Sumalee Milne, Claire Mitchell, Tom Mockler, Dennis Mogerman, Kurt Moller, Zsolt Molnar, RF Monch, Vicki Moncrief, Kai Monkkonen, Ellen Monsma, C&R Monson, Michael Montague, Simona Montella, Ana Moore, Ann Moore, Dean Moore, Des Moore, Gary Moore, Rebecca Moore, A Moores, Mr Moose, Stephen Morey, Marjorie Morkham, Andrew Morolla, Sarah Morrison, Michael Mortensen, Dave Mountain, Ross Moxley, Patrick Mueller, Peter Muhlhan, Andreas Muhlheim, Anna Muir, Rory Mulholland, Ralph Muller, Andrea Munch, Natalie & Shane Mundy, Imtiaz Muqbil, Cristin Murphy, Patrick Murphy, David Murray, Don Murray, Rainer Mussig, Maarten Muths, Shelley Muzzy, Per A Myhre.

Clare Naden, Moo Naraporn, John Nash, Robert Natarelli, Erik Nauta, Jocelyn Neal, Jeff Nease, Jessy Needham, Thomas Neihsen, Vic & Dana Neirkirk, Tony Nelson, Mark Newell, Anne Newey, Mark Nicholls, Mari Nicholson, Tony Nicol, Maj Nielsen, Christoph Niemann, Mirko Nierhaus, Styrbjorn & Kersti Nilsson, Michal Nis, Kala Nobbs, Jan Dick van der Nol, Ellen Noonan, Elizabeth Norden, Andy Nordin, Dave North, Perri Northage, Steve Northam, Brahma Noyes, MP Nunan.

Sharon O'Toole, Susan Oakden, James O'Connell, Mike Ogden, Anna Oldman, Inal & Justine Olmez, Jan Helge Olsen, Jodi Olstead, Jan O'Neill, Charlie Ong, Teresa Ong

Jackie Origne, Barbara Orlandini, Reg Ormond, Marc Orts, Dan Orzech, Andrew Osborne, Rebecca Osborne, Declan O'Sullivan, Surush Oswal, Sabine Otto, Jan Oudebrunink, Cecilia Ouvares, Bert Jan & Christy Ouwens, Anthea Owen, Linda Owen, Oren & Orly Oz.

Peter Paal, Marco Pace, Tina Pacheco, Tiwa Pacheco, Lucy Packer, Mary Page, Ruth Page, Chris Paine, Rolf Palmberg, Brian Panhuyzen, Arnupap Panichpol, Coslovich Paolo, Andreas Papathakis, Nick Park, Henry A Parker, Tina Parker, Tracey Parker, Joanne Parkinson, Deepa Parry-Gupta, James Parsons, Katherine Pascua, John Pasden, Helen Pastoriza, Bob Patchett, Carolyn Patchett, James Pate, Rachel Paterson, Joyce van der Patten, Mary Patterson, Stephen Pattinson, Claudia Paulick, John Paulsen, Luka Pavlovcic, Sharon Peake, CH Pearce, Caroline Pears, Andrea Pearson, Michael Pearson, Donald John Peck, Garry Peck, Erik Juul Pedersen, AE Peel, Warner Pel, Renate Pelzl, Colin Pendry, Richard Pendry, Edward Pennington, Wendy Pennington, Brad Pentelow, Susan Peoples, Andrea Peracca, Carole Perin, Greg Perrin, Bjorn Persson, Jodi Peter, Andy Peters, Mark Peters, David & A Peterson, Jim Peterson, Steve Petri, Sid Phelan, Tim Phelps, Phillip Phillpou, Jenny Pickard, Tilman Pickartz, Jon Pierce, Dirk-Jan Pinkster, Janet & Guy Pinneo, Pedro Pinto, Anna Piotrowski, Michelle Pirkl, JA Plampin, Taron Plaza, J Plenty, Per Plougmann Poulsen, Johan Pol, Lori Polizzi, Lisa & Ilias Pollard, Marga Pool, Samantha Pooley, ARA Pope, Simon & Alison Porges, Neil Porter, Tom Porter, Kyle Portman, Katherine Potter, René Potvin, Dr Owen Powell, Eveline Powell, James Power, Anna Pragnell Toal, Ged Prescott, Julie Pressley, Anne Price, Carol Price, Trevor & Liz Price, Sylvie Prieur, Carole Pritchard, Mat Probasco, Duncan Proffitt, Suthep Prommoon, Noelene Proud, Wilco Pruysers, Bertil Pslsson, Katrin Puchner, Franca Pugnaghi, Edith J Puny, Dion Puru, Suzy & Neil Purues, Malcolm Purvis.

Anthony M Quest, Dave Quinn, Lesley Quinn.

Rebecca Rabinovitch, Andreas Radtke, Ann Raghava, Seonaid Rait, David Ramm, Jose Ramon Abad, Philippe Raoul, Danielle Rashid, J Rasmussen, Terje Rasmussen, Uffe Rasmussen, Tom Ratcliffe, Paul Rathburn, Heather-Dawn Rau, Melanie Rayski, Clem Read, Dick Real, Keith Ream, Henry Rearden, Christine Reardon, J Rebecca, Guy Redden, Micheal Reddington, Nicholas Redfearn,

Andrew Redman, Brian Reed, Linda Reed, N Rees, R Rees, John Reesby, Chris Reetz, Leni Reeves, Sofia Rehn, Rene Reinert, Gisela Reinhard, Eduard Reitsema, Dominique Renucci, Hunter Reynolds, Kevin Reynolds, Steve Rhodes, Pete Ribbans, Harry Rice, Valerie Rice, E Gail Richardson, Stephen Richardson, H Richrath, Peter Ridgway, Barrie Ridout, Ilja Rijnen, I Rikkers, E Risch, Andrew Ritchie, Rami Rivlin, Alan & Sue Roberts, John Roberts, Louise Roberts, Philip Roberts, Mark Robinson, Paul Robinson, Richard Robinson, Adam Robson, Dr Heinz Dieter Rödder, David Roderick Smith, Low Puay Hwa Roger, Andrew FR Rogers, Bob Rogers, Carol Rogers, John Rogers, Karen Rogers, Pete Rogers, Linda Romolo, Francesca Ronca, Ron Rook, Ann Rooney, Paul Rooney, Richard Rose, Ewen Ross, John Ross, Karen Ross, Simon Ross, Donald Ross Moxley, Dr Volker Rossbach, Julia Rosser, Isabel L Rothery, Jim Rowe, Carolyn Rueben, T&T Ruecha, Martin Ruecker, Martin & Claudia Ruecker, Hannah Rumble, Annette Rups-Eyeland, John Russell, Alan Rutlidge, Kevin Ryan.

Lesley Sabatini, Isabel Sabugueiro, Danny Saddler, Haavard Saksvikronning, M Samantha Saublet, Mimi Samuel, Louise Samuels, Martijn Sandbrink, Stephen Sandiford Hinds, Gabriele Santambrogio, Peng Sarnkam, G Saunders, H Saunders, Carmel Savege, Jim Savidge, H Saxer, Andrew Say, Peter Saynt, Marie & Ed Scarpari, Kimberleigh Schartz, John Schattorie, Janis Schaus, Elke & Bernd Scheffer, Magmar Schellhaas, Astrid Schinharl, Hartmut Schittko, Margo Schlanger, Edward Schlenk, HJ Schmid, Sylvia Schmid, Veronique Schmid, Kerstin Schmidt, Martin Schmidt, Norbert Schmiedeberg, Bernd Schmirler, Martin Schmitt, Stephan Schneider, Jochen J Schnell, Kristian Scholte, Ralf Schramm, Marcel Schrijvers, Fritz Schroeder, Ken Schubauer, Frauke Schuett, Esther Schuhmacher, Marilena Schuite, Emma Schwarcz, Barry Scott, Marie Scott, Peter Scott, Sophia Scott, Martin Searle, Mark & Carol Sechler, Michelle Segal, Caterin Selen, Christina & Martin Semler, Wiyada Sereewichyaswat, Josef Seufzenecker, Geert Job Sevink, Margaret Shallcross, Diana & David Shamash, Rachael Shannon, Kenneth Shapiro, Naomi Sharp, PA&G Sharp, Maddie Shaw, Julie Sheard, Mark & Marion Sheffield, Glen T Shen, P Shenton, Chris Sherman, Deedra Sherron, Tamara Shie, Bill Shipp, Erik F Shores, Roni Shrager, Roni Shragger, David Shu, Nakohn Si

Thammarat, Jonathon Sibtain, E Siebert, Mark Siemelink, Bruce Silvers, C Simons, B Simpson, Nicola Simpson, Ron Simpson, Victoria Sims, Emma Sinton, Jared Sischo, Paul Sivertsen, Desmond Skene-Catling, Richard Skilton, Vicki & Brad Skinner, Jo Sladen, Tony Slark, Robert Slater, Glenn Slayden, Tom Sleigh, Nathalie van der Slikke, Jeroen Slikker, Lionie Sliz, Jayeli & Philip Smale, TW Smallwood, Alex Smith, Doug Smith, Garry Smith, George Smith, Gill Smith, Jon Smith, Kevin Smith, L Smith, Margot Smith, Natasha Smith, Phil & Lisa Smith, Rebecca Smith, Robert Smith, Rodney Smith, Sue Smith, Tara & Alasdair Smith, Alison Smithies, Max Smolka, Karla Snook, Dick Snyder, Lorraine Snyder, Kevin Soerensen, Marianne Soldavini, Henrietta Somers, Lorenzo Sonelli, John Soos, James Sorrell, Peter Sosnowski, Julian Sotnick, Sammy Southall, Fiona Southwell, Chad Sowards, Eduardo Spaccasassi, Debbie Spears, Ruud Spek, Rachel Speth, C&J Spolnik, Elizabeth Stabenow, Loren Stack, Deborah Stafford, Shelley Stansfield, Leo & Lee Stauber-Ferris, Michelle Staude, Rachael Stead, Elliot Steel, Caroline L Steele, Lani Steele, Mike Steele, Lucy Steinert, Sandra Steinmann, Michael Stenmark, Andria Stephanidou, Vanessa Sterling, Tommy Steven, Ted Stirzaker, Carol Stock, Thea Straathof, John Strasburger, Ruth Streicher, Henri Stroband, Marianne Strusinski, Maurizio Sturlesi, Susanna M Suh, Yulgene Suh, Brian Sullivan, Sally Supplee, F Sutten, Peter Suttherg, Prof Poonsak Suvannuparat, Suda Suwanwongkij, Anders Svensson, Jeff Swadling, Rob Swaigen, Helena Swan, Patricia Sweeney, May & John Sweetman, Cheryl Swisher, Cheryl Swisher, Phil Sylvester, Margaret Symons.

Julie & Phillippe Tacon, Alex Lai Hong Tan, Shawn Tan, Sumonwan Tangnuntachai, Christine Tanhueco, Jason Tanner, Richard Tanner, Stephane Taulaigo, Sonia Tavasci, Anna Taylor, Jeff Taylor, Margorie Taylor, Nigel Taylor, Stephen Taylor, Sven Taylor, Vicky Taylor, WC Taylor, Chris & Gwen Teasdale, Mikeal & Anna Teljstedt, A C Tennant, James Terry, Joanne Terry, Lilian Teunissen, Anne-Marie Thepaut, Joanne Thirlwall, I Thomas, Sally Thomas, Andrew Thompson, Basil Thompson, Dave Thompson, James Thompson, Jennifer Thompson, Guy Thonard, David & Teresa Thoreson, Jeanette Thrane, Lisette Thresh, James Tiernan, Andrew Tillett, Dean Tilt, Sue & Ian Timbrell, Michael Tobinsky, Chris Toland, Stephanie

Toohey, Carol Topalian, Eirik Torp, Corinne Toumi, Sarah Treadwell, Connie Tsang, Peter Tse, Ken Tsunoda, Marty Tunney, Melisa Tupou, Marilyn Turner, Melinda Tursky, M Tynan, Graham & Kate Tyson.

Hisae Ubl, Elisabeth Ugel, Maja Ulbrich, Matthew Underwood, David Unkovich, Hafeez ur Rahman, Jaga Urbach, Richard Uren, Helena Urgell, Malin Utterstrom.

B&E Vajda, Martine Vallieres, Melissa Vallillo, Sheryn Valter, C&AP Van Breugel, Rob van den Boorn, JWJ Van Dorp, Jan van Gendt, Johanna van Hal, Mario van Hecke, Jeffery van Hont, Alie van Loon, Aritha van Mourik, Vincent van Rijn, Robert van Weperen, Machteld van Zijp, Pim Vanden Broek, Roger & Maureen Vanstone, Ilona Veen, Jerry van Veenendaal, Peter Veenstra, Liz Venzin, Carl Verhoevem, Mariken Verhoeven, MC Verinue, Rudi Vermeirssen, Laurent Vermeulen, Martin Versteegen, Paul Verwoerd, L L Vestergaard, Sabine Vetler, Kaori & David Vickery, Taulikki Viitaniemi, Claus Vilhelmsen, Jane Vincent, Rachel Vine, Angie Vines, Dick Vis, Frank Visakay, Hanneke Visser, Valerija Vlasov, E Vlierman, Angie Vogel, Roland Vos, Iris Vrabec, Zoran Vrancic, Chris VSR.

Uli Waas, Jason Wadley, Udo Wagler, Reto Wagner, Steve Wagner, Ali Wale, Carol Walker, Shaun Waller, Brian Wallis, Kerremans Walter, Tony & Leanne Walter, Mal Walters, James Waltner, Olivia Wang, Lerdchai Wangtrakoondee, Caroline Ward, Joseph Ward, Lorenzo Ward, Robert Ward, Vronni & Nick Ward, Sachiko Washimi, Susan Waszak, Melanie Wathen, Alex Watson, Wendy Watts, Guy Waysman, David Wayte, David J Weatherby, Penny Webb, Maurice Webber, Gabi Weber, Karin Weber, Peter Webster, Maximilian Weh, Konrad Weichmann, Wolfram Weidemann, Roland Weinmesser, BE Weir, Viktor Weisshaeupl, U Wenteke, SG Wesley, Eric West, Jonas Westberg, Helen Westhead, Anders Westlund, Jen Wheeler, V Whilton, Chris White, Donee White, Peter White, Stephen White, Theresa White, Paul Whitehead, Katharine Whittle, Brendan Whitty, Charlie Wicke Jr, RD Wicks, Roger Wicks, Marie-Claire van de Wiel, Mat Wild, Sam Wilkinson, Gary & Madaline Wilks, M Willemse, Alex Williams, Charlotte Williams, Dave Williams, John Williams, Karen Williams, Kathe Williams, Kieran Williams, M&N Williams, Matthew Williams, Narelle Williams, Reg Williams, Robert Williams, Terry Williams,

VV Williams, Wendy Williams, Don Willliams, Don Wills, David Wilson, Garath Wilson, Josh Wilson, Karen Wilson, Sue Wilson, Zae Wilson, Jan Winning, Stephen Winterstein, Torsten Winzer, Joanna Wiseman, Rob Wisnlowski, Wolfgang Wizsner, Thorsten Wohland, Arne Wolfart, David Wolff, Michael Wolff, Koos Wolthuis, Grace Wong, Suyin Wong, Terry Wong, Warren Wong, Leung-hee Woo, John Wood, Paul Wood, SD Woodhouse, Nick Woodman, Joe Woodruff, Evelyn Woods, Helen Woodward, Simon Woodward, Ken Workman, Martin Worswick, Linda & Phil

Wotherspoon, Chris Wright, S Wright, Theo Wright, Bronwyn Wyatt, Paul Wyatt, Robin Gloster Wyatt, Becky Wyland, Mike Wysocki.

Donald WM Yap, Stephen Yarnold, Jackie & Michael Yates, Michael Yelon, Jason Yelowitz, Dora Yip, Sybren Ykema, B Young, Carol Young, J Young, Patricia Young, Jim Yupangco, Paul Yurewicz.

Billy Zaenglein, Nithaar Zain, RA Zambardino, Rainer & Evelyn Zawadzki, G Zeegers, Carola Zentner, Maike Ziesemer, Marco Zoli, Myriem Zouaq, Zoe Zumbach, S van der Zwart, Rob Zwerink, Suzanne Zyla.

LONELY PLANET

ON THE ROAD

Travel Guides explore cities, regions and countries, and supply information on transport, restaurants and accommodation, covering all budgets. They come with reliable, easy-to-use maps, practical advice, cultural and historical facts and a rundown on attractions both on and off the beaten track. There are over 200 titles in this classic series, covering nearly every country in the world.

 Lonely Planet Upgrades extend the shelf life of existing travel guides by detailing any changes that may affect travel in a region since a book has been published. Upgrades can be downloaded for free from **www.lonelyplanet.com/upgrades**

For travellers with more time than money, **Shoestring** guides offer dependable, first-hand information with hundreds of detailed maps, plus insider tips for stretching money as far as possible. Covering entire continents in most cases, the six-volume shoestring guides are known around the world as 'backpackers bibles'.

For the discerning short-term visitor, **Condensed** guides highlight the best a destination has to offer in a full-colour, pocket-sized format designed for quick access. They include everything from top sights and walking tours to opinionated reviews of where to eat, stay, shop and have fun.

CitySync lets travellers use their Palm™ or Visor™ hand-held computers to guide them through a city with handy tips on transport, history, cultural life, major sights, and shopping and entertainment options. It can also quickly search and sort hundreds of reviews of hotels, restaurants and attractions, and pinpoint their location on scrollable street maps. CitySync can be downloaded from **www.citysync.com**

MAPS & ATLASES

Lonely Planet's **City Maps** feature downtown and metropolitan maps, as well as transit routes and walking tours. The maps come complete with an index of streets, a listing of sights and a plastic coat for extra durability.

Road Atlases are an essential navigation tool for serious travellers. Cross-referenced with the guidebooks, they also feature distance and climate charts and a complete site index.

ESSENTIALS

Read This First books help new travellers to hit the road with confidence. These invaluable predeparture guides give step-by-step advice on preparing for a trip, budgeting, arranging a visa, planning an itinerary and staying safe while still getting off the beaten track.

Healthy Travel pocket guides offer a regional rundown on disease hot spots and practical advice on predeparture health measures, staying well on the road and what to do in emergencies. The guides come with a user-friendly design and helpful diagrams and tables.

Lonely Planet's **Phrasebooks** cover the essential words and phrases travellers need when they're strangers in a strange land. They come in a pocket-sized format with colour tabs for quick reference, extensive vocabulary lists, easy-to-follow pronunciation keys and two-way dictionaries.

Miffed by blurry photos of the Taj Mahal? Tired of the classic 'top of the head cut off' shot? **Travel Photography: A Guide to Taking Better Pictures** will help you turn ordinary holiday snaps into striking images and give you the know-how to capture every scene, from frenetic festivals to peaceful beach sunrises.

Lonely Planet's **Travel Journal** is a lightweight but sturdy travel diary for jotting down all those on-the-road observations and significant travel moments. It comes with a handy time-zone wheel, a world map and useful travel information.

Lonely Planet's eKno is an all-in-one communication service developed especially for travellers. It offers low-cost international calls and free email and voicemail so that you can keep in touch while on the road. Check it out on **www.ekno.lonelyplanet.com**

FOOD & RESTAURANT GUIDES

Lonely Planet's **Out to Eat** guides recommend the brightest and best places to eat and drink in top international cities. These gourmet companions are arranged by neighbourhood, packed with dependable maps, garnished with scene-setting photos and served with quirky features.

For people who live to eat, drink and travel, **World Food** guides explore the culinary culture of each country. Entertaining and adventurous, each guide is packed with detail on staples and specialities, regional cuisine and local markets, as well as sumptuous recipes, comprehensive culinary dictionaries and lavish photos good enough to eat.

OUTDOOR GUIDES

For those who believe the best way to see the world is on foot, Lonely Planet's **Walking Guides** detail everything from family strolls to difficult treks, with 'when to go and how to do it' advice supplemented by reliable maps and essential travel information.

Cycling Guides map a destination's best bike tours, long and short, in day-by-day detail. They contain all the information a cyclist needs, including advice on bike maintenance, places to eat and stay, innovative maps with detailed cues to the rides, and elevation charts.

The **Watching Wildlife** series is perfect for travellers who want authoritative information but don't want to tote a heavy field guide. Packed with advice on where, when and how to view a region's wildlife, each title features photos of over 300 species and contains engaging comments on the local flora and fauna.

With underwater colour photos throughout, **Pisces Books** explore the world's best diving and snorkelling areas. Each book contains listings of diving services and dive resorts, detailed information on depth, visibility and difficulty of dives, and a roundup of the marine life you're likely to see through your mask.

LONELY PLANET

OFF THE ROAD

Journeys, the travel literature series written by renowned travel authors, capture the spirit of a place or illuminate a culture with a journalist's attention to detail and a novelist's flair for words. These are tales to soak up while you're actually on the road or dip into as an at-home armchair indulgence.

The range of lavishly illustrated **Pictorial** books is just the ticket for both travellers and dreamers. Off-beat tales and vivid photographs bring the adventure of travel to your doorstep long before the journey begins and long after it is over.

Lonely Planet **Videos** encourage the same independent, tough-minded approach as the guidebooks. Currently airing throughout the world, this award-winning series features innovative footage and an original soundtrack.

Yes, we know, work is tough, so do a little bit of deskside dreaming with the spiral-bound Lonely Planet **Diary** or a Lonely Planet **Wall Calendar**, filled with great photos from around the world.

TRAVELLERS NETWORK

Lonely Planet Online. Lonely Planet's award-winning Web site has insider information on hundreds of destinations, from Amsterdam to Zimbabwe, complete with interactive maps and relevant links. The site also offers the latest travel news, recent reports from travellers on the road, guidebook upgrades, a travel links site, an online book-buying option and a lively traveller's bulletin board. It can be viewed at **www.lonelyplanet.com** or AOL keyword: lp.

Planet Talk is a quarterly print newsletter, full of gossip, advice, anecdotes and author articles. It provides an antidote to the being-at-home blues and lets you plan and dream for the next trip. Contact the nearest Lonely Planet office for your free copy.

Comet, the free Lonely Planet newsletter, comes via email once a month. It's loaded with travel news, advice, dispatches from authors, travel competitions and letters from readers. To subscribe, click on the Comet subscription link on the front page of the Web site.

LONELY PLANET

Guides by Region

Lonely Planet is known worldwide for publishing practical, reliable and no-nonsense travel information in our guides and on our Web site. The Lonely Planet list covers just about every accessible part of the world. Currently there are 16 series: Travel guides, Shoestring guides, Condensed guides, Phrasebooks, Read This First, Healthy Travel, Walking guides, Cycling guides, Watching Wildlife guides, Pisces Diving & Snorkeling guides, City Maps, Road Atlases, Out to Eat, World Food, Journeys travel literature and Pictorials.

AFRICA Africa on a shoestring • Cairo • Cairo City Map • Cape Town • Cape Town City Map • East Africa • Egypt • Egyptian Arabic phrasebook • Ethiopia, Eritrea & Djibouti • Ethiopian Amharic phrasebook • The Gambia & Senegal • Healthy Travel Africa • Kenya • Malawi • Morocco • Moroccan Arabic phrasebook • Mozambique • Read This First: Africa • South Africa, Lesotho & Swaziland • Southern Africa • Southern Africa Road Atlas • Swahili phrasebook • Tanzania, Zanzibar & Pemba • Trekking in East Africa • Tunisia • Watching Wildlife East Africa • Watching Wildlife Southern Africa • West Africa • World Food Morocco • Zimbabwe, Botswana & Namibia
Travel Literature: Mali Blues: Traveling to an African Beat • The Rainbird: A Central African Journey • Songs to an African Sunset: A Zimbabwean Story

AUSTRALIA & THE PACIFIC Auckland • Australia • Australian phrasebook • Australia Road Atlas • Cycling Australia • Cycling New Zealand • Fiji • Fijian phrasebook • Healthy Travel Australia, NZ & the Pacific • Islands of Australia's Great Barrier Reef • Melbourne • Melbourne City Map • Micronesia • New Caledonia • New South Wales • New Zealand • Northern Territory • Outback Australia • Out to Eat – Melbourne • Out to Eat – Sydney • Papua New Guinea • Pidgin phrasebook • Queensland • Rarotonga & the Cook Islands • Samoa • Solomon Islands • South Australia • South Pacific • South Pacific phrasebook • Sydney • Sydney City Map • Sydney Condensed • Tahiti & French Polynesia • Tasmania • Tonga • Tramping in New Zealand • Vanuatu • Victoria • Walking in Australia • Watching Wildlife Australia • Western Australia
Travel Literature: Islands in the Clouds: Travels in the Highlands of New Guinea • Kiwi Tracks: A New Zealand Journey • Sean & David's Long Drive

CENTRAL AMERICA & THE CARIBBEAN Bahamas, Turks & Caicos • Baja California • Belize, Guatemala & Yucatán • Bermuda • Central America on a shoestring • Costa Rica • Costa Rica Spanish phrasebook • Cuba • Dominican Republic & Haiti • Eastern Caribbean • Guatemala • Havana • Healthy Travel Central & South America • Jamaica • Mexico • Mexico City • Panama • Puerto Rico • Read This First: Central & South America • World Food Mexico • Yucatán
Travel Literature: Green Dreams: Travels in Central America

EUROPE Amsterdam • Amsterdam City Map • Amsterdam Condensed • Andalucía • Austria • Baltic States phrasebook • Barcelona • Barcelona City Map • Belgium & Luxembourg • Berlin • Berlin City Map • Britain • British phrasebook • Brussels, Bruges & Antwerp • Brussels City Map • Budapest • Budapest City Map • Canary Islands • Central Europe • Central Europe phrasebook • Copenhagen • Corfu & the Ionians • Corsica • Crete • Crete Condensed • Croatia • Cycling Britain • Cycling France • Cyprus • Czech & Slovak Republics • Denmark • Dublin • Dublin City Map • Eastern Europe • Eastern Europe phrasebook • Edinburgh • England • Estonia, Latvia & Lithuania • Europe on a shoestring • Europe phrasebook • Finland • Florence • France • Frankfurt Condensed • French phrasebook • Georgia, Armenia & Azerbaijan • Germany • German phrasebook • Greece • Greek Islands • Greek phrasebook • Hungary • Iceland, Greenland & the Faroe Islands • Ireland • Italian phrasebook • Italy • Krakow • Lisbon • The Loire • London • London City Map • London Condensed • Madrid • Malta • Mediterranean Europe • Mediterranean Europe phrasebook • Moscow • Munich • Netherlands • Normandy • Norway • Out to Eat – London • Out to Eat – Paris • Paris • Paris City Map • Paris Condensed • Poland • Polish phrasebook • Portugal • Portuguese phrasebook • Prague • Prague City Map • Provence & the Côte d'Azur • Read This First: Europe • Rhodes & the Dodecanese • Romania & Moldova • Rome • Rome City Map • Russia, Ukraine & Belarus • Russian phrasebook • Scandinavian & Baltic Europe • Scandinavian phrasebook • Scotland • Sicily • Slovenia • South-West France • Spain • Spanish phrasebook • St Petersburg • St Petersburg City Map • Sweden • Switzerland • Tuscany • Ukrainian phrasebook • Venice • Vienna • Walking in Britain • Walking in France • Walking in Ireland • Walking in Italy • Walking in Spain • Walking in Switzerland • Western Europe • World Food France • World Food Ireland • World Food Italy • World Food Spain
Travel Literature: After Yugoslavia • Love and War in the Apennines • The Olive Grove: Travels in Greece • On the Shores of the Mediterranean • Round Ireland in Low Gear • A Small Place in Italy

LONELY PLANET

Mail Order

Lonely Planet products are distributed worldwide. They are also available by mail order from Lonely Planet, so if you have difficulty finding a title please write to us. North and South American residents should write to 150 Linden St, Oakland, CA 94607, USA; European and African residents should write to 10a Spring Place, London NW5 3BH, UK; and residents of other countries to Locked Bag 1, Footscray, Victoria 3011, Australia.

INDIAN SUBCONTINENT & THE INDIAN OCEAN Bangladesh • Bengali phrasebook • Bhutan • Delhi • Goa • Healthy Travel Asia & India • Hindi & Urdu phrasebook • India • Indian Himalaya • Karakoram Highway • Kerala • Madagascar • Maldives • Mauritius, Réunion & Seychelles • Mumbai (Bombay) • Nepal • Nepali phrasebook • Pakistan • Rajasthan • Read This First: Asia & India • South India • Sri Lanka • Sri Lanka phrasebook • Tibet • Tibetan phrasebook • Trekking in the Indian Himalaya • Trekking in the Karakoram & Hindukush • Trekking in the Nepal Himalaya
Travel Literature: The Age of Kali: Indian Travels and Encounters • Hello Goodnight: A Life of Goa • In Rajasthan • Maverick in Madagascar • A Season in Heaven: True Tales from the Road to Kathmandu • Shopping for Buddhas • A Short Walk in the Hindu Kush • Slowly Down the Ganges

MIDDLE EAST & CENTRAL ASIA Bahrain, Kuwait & Qatar • Central Asia • Central Asia phrasebook • Dubai • Farsi (Persian) phrasebook • Hebrew phrasebook • Iran • Israel & the Palestinian Territories • Istanbul • Istanbul City Map • Istanbul to Cairo • Istanbul to Kathmandu • Jerusalem • Jerusalem City Map • Jordan • Lebanon • Middle East • Oman & the United Arab Emirates • Syria • Turkey • Turkish phrasebook • World Food Turkey • Yemen
Travel Literature: Black on Black: Iran Revisited • The Gates of Damascus • Kingdom of the Film Stars: Journey into Jordan

NORTH AMERICA Alaska • Boston • Boston City Map • Boston Condensed • British Columbia • California & Nevada • California Condensed • Canada • Chicago • Chicago City Map • Florida • Great Lakes • Hawaii • Hiking in Alaska • Hiking in the USA • Las Vegas • Los Angeles • Los Angeles City Map • Louisiana & the Deep South • Miami • Miami City Map • Montreal • New England • New Orleans • New York City • New York City City Map • New York City Condensed • New York, New Jersey & Pennsylvania • Oahu • Out to Eat – San Francisco • Pacific Northwest • Rocky Mountains • San Francisco • San Francisco City Map • Seattle • Southwest • Texas • Toronto • USA • USA phrasebook • Vancouver • Virginia & the Capital Region • Washington, DC • Washington, DC City Map • World Food New Orleans
Travel Literature: Caught Inside: A Surfer's Year on the California Coast • Drive Thru America

NORTH-EAST ASIA Beijing • Beijing City Map • Cantonese phrasebook • China • Hiking in Japan • Hong Kong • Hong Kong City Map • Hong Kong Condensed • Hong Kong, Macau & Guangzhou • Japan • Japanese phrasebook • Korea • Korean phrasebook • Kyoto • Mandarin phrasebook • Mongolia • Mongolian phrasebook • Seoul • Shanghai • South-West China • Taiwan • Tokyo • World Food Hong Kong
Travel Literature: In Xanadu: A Quest • Lost Japan

SOUTH AMERICA Argentina, Uruguay & Paraguay • Bolivia • Brazil • Brazilian phrasebook • Buenos Aires • Chile & Easter Island • Colombia • Ecuador & the Galapagos Islands • Healthy Travel Central & South America • Latin American Spanish phrasebook • Peru • Quechua phrasebook • Read This First: Central & South America • Rio de Janeiro • Rio de Janeiro City Map • Santiago de Chile • South America on a shoestring • Trekking in the Patagonian Andes • Venezuela
Travel Literature: Full Circle: A South American Journey

SOUTH-EAST ASIA Bali & Lombok • Bangkok • Bangkok City Map • Burmese phrasebook • Cambodia • Hanoi • Healthy Travel Asia & India • Hill Tribes phrasebook • Ho Chi Minh City • Indonesia • Indonesian phrasebook • Indonesia's Eastern Islands • Java • Lao phrasebook • Laos • Malay phrasebook • Malaysia, Singapore & Brunei • Myanmar (Burma) • Philippines • Pilipino (Tagalog) phrasebook • Read This First: Asia & India • Singapore • Singapore City Map • South-East Asia on a shoestring • South-East Asia phrasebook • Thailand • Thailand's Islands & Beaches • Thailand, Vietnam, Laos & Cambodia Road Atlas • Thai phrasebook • Vietnam • Vietnamese phrasebook • World Food Thailand • World Food Vietnam

ALSO AVAILABLE: Antarctica • The Arctic • The Blue Man: Tales of Travel, Love and Coffee • Brief Encounters: Stories of Love, Sex & Travel • Chasing Rickshaws • The Last Grain Race • Lonely Planet ... On the Edge: Adventurous Escapades from Around the World • Lonely Planet Unpacked • Not the Only Planet: Science Fiction Travel Stories • Sacred India • Travel Photography: A Guide to Taking Better Pictures • Travel with Children

LONELY PLANET

You already know that Lonely Planet produces more than this one guidebook, but you might not be aware of the other products we have on this region. Here is a selection of titles that you may want to check out as well:

Thai phrasebook
ISBN 0 86442 658 5
US$6.95 • UK£4.50

Hill Tribes phrasebook
ISBN 0 86442 635 6
US$5.95 • UK£3.99

South-East Asia phrasebook
ISBN 0 86442 435 3
US$6.95 • UK£3.99

South-East Asia on a shoestring
ISBN 1 86450 158 8
US$21.99 • UK£12.99

Bangkok
ISBN 1 86450 285 1
US$15.99 • UK£9.99

CitySync
ISBN 1 86450 228 2
US$49.99 • UK£29.99

Diving & Snorkeling Thailand
ISBN 1 86450 201 0
US$16.99 • UK£10.99

Thailand's Islands & Beaches
ISBN 0 86442 728 X
US$15.95 • UK£9.99

World Food Thailand
ISBN 1 86450 026 3
US$12.95 • UK£7.99

Available wherever books are sold

Index

Abbreviations

Text

Bold indicates maps.

Bold indicates maps.

Bold indicates maps.

Boxed Text

MAP LEGEND

CITY ROUTES

Freeway .... Freeway
Highway .... Primary Road
Road .... Secondary Road
Street .... Street
Lane .... Lane
.... On/Off Ramp

--- --- --- Unsealed Road
--- →--- One Way Street
.... Pedestrian Street
ⅢⅢⅢⅢ Stepped Street
)--- === Tunnel
)--- === Footbridge

REGIONAL ROUTES

.... Freeway
.... Primary Road
.... Secondary Road
.... Minor Road

BOUNDARIES

--- ··· --- International
--- ··· --- Provincial
--- --- Disputed
.... Wall

HYDROGRAPHY

River, Creek
.... Canal

.... Lake
⊙ ⑤ ⥊ Spring; Waterfalls

TRANSPORT ROUTES & STATIONS

·--o--· .... Train
+ + +--· Underground Train
--⊠-- Skytrain
---⊡-- Ferry

----★ Walking Trail
·········· Walking Tour
.... Path
.... Pier or Jetty

AREA FEATURES

.... Building
❀ .... Park, Gardens

.... Market
.... Sports Ground

⋗ .... Beach
+ + + Cemetery

.... Campus
.... Plaza

POPULATION SYMBOLS

✪ **CAPITAL** .... National Capital
◉ **CAPITAL** .... Provincial Capital

● **CITY** .... City
● **Town** .... Town

◉ Village .... Village
.... Urban Area

MAP SYMBOLS

📍 .... Place to Stay
▼ .... Place to Eat
● .... Point of Interest

⊠ .... Airport	🎦 🎭 .....Cinema, Theatre	🏛 .... Museum	⚲ .... Stupa or Chedi
🔲 .. Archaeological Site	🔲 ◉ .... Dive Site, Snorkelling	🔲 .... National Park	🔲 .... Swimming Pool
⊛ .... Bank	⚓ ❂ Fountain, Golf Course	🔲 🔲 .. Parking, Picnic Area	🔲 .... Taxi or Tuk-Tuk
🔲 🔲 .. Bird Sanctuary, Zoo	⊕ .... Elephant Kraal	🔲 🔲 .. Police, Post Office	☎ .... Telephone
🔲 🔲 .. Bus Terminal, Stop	🔲 ⊕ ..... Embassy, Hospital	🔲 .... Pub or Bar	🔲 .. Temple (Buddhist)
🔲 .... Cafe	⊡ .... Internet Cafe	🔲 .... Sawngthaew	🔲 .... Temple (Hindu)
⌂ .... Cave	❄ ▲ .... Lookout, Mountain	🔲 .... Shopping Centre	🔲 .... Temple (Sikh)
🔲 🔲 .. Cathedral, Church	🔲 🔲 .. Monument, Mosque	🔲 .... Shrine (Chinese)	❶ .... Tourist Information

Note: not all symbols displayed above appear in this book

LONELY PLANET OFFICES

Australia
Locked Bag 1, Footscray, Victoria 3011
☎ 03 8379 8000 fax 03 8379 8111
email: talk2us@lonelyplanet.com.au

UK
10a Spring Place, London NW5 3BH
☎ 020 7428 4800 fax 020 7428 4828
email: go@lonelyplanet.co.uk

USA
150 Linden St, Oakland, CA 94607
☎ 510 893 8555 TOLL FREE: 800 275 8555
fax 510 893 8572
email: info@lonelyplanet.com

France
1 rue du Dahomey, 75011 Paris
☎ 01 55 25 33 00 fax 01 55 25 33 01
email: bip@lonelyplanet.fr
www.lonelyplanet.fr

World Wide Web: www.lonelyplanet.com *or* AOL keyword: lp
Lonely Planet Images: lpi@lonelyplanet.com.au